Fundamentals of Pascal:
Understanding Programming and Problem Solving

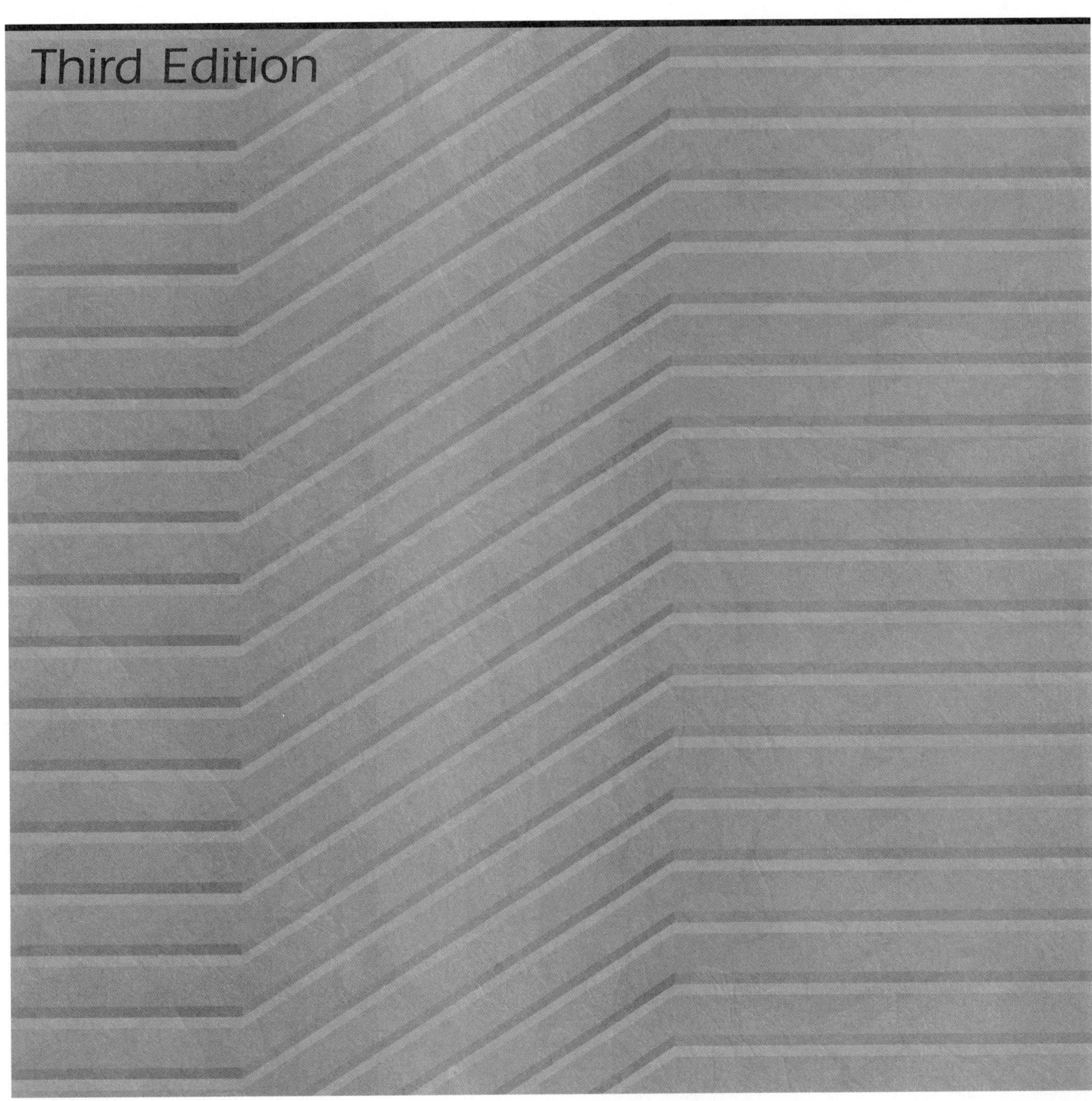

Fundamentals of Pascal:
Understanding Programming and Problem Solving

Third Edition

Douglas W. Nance

Central Michigan University

JOIN US ON THE INTERNET

WWW: http://www.thomson.com

EMAIL: findit@kiosk.thomson.com A service of I(T)P®

South-Western Educational Publishing

an International Thomson Publishing company I(T)P®

Cincinnati • Albany, NY • Belmont, CA • Bonn • Boston • Detroit • Johannesburg • London • Madrid
Melbourne • Mexico City • New York • Paris • Singapore • Tokyo • Toronto • Washington

To my family.
They have borne the brunt of my commitment,
involvement, and preoccupation with writing for the last fifteen years.
I have been blessed with their support, understanding, and love.

Copyeditor: Lorretta Palagi
Index: Margaret Jarpey
Composition: Carlisle Communications, Ltd.
Cover and Text Design: Matt Thiessen/Vickie Grandchamp
Illustration: Miyake Illustration and Design

Photo credits follow the Index.

ISBN 0-314-20554-3

2 3 4 5 BN 01 00 99 98

Printed in the United States of America

I(T)P®

International Thomson Publishing

South-Western Educational Publishing is a division of International Thomson Publishing, Inc. The ITP trademark is used under license.

Contents

Chapter 6 Repetition Statements 237

Chapter 14 Sorting and Merging 713

Chapter 15 Sets 735

Chapter 16 Graphics 763

Chapter 17 Dynamic Variables and Data Structures 865

Preface

Those who teach entry-level courses in computer science are familiar with the problems that beginning students encounter. Initially, students can get so involved in learning a language that they may fail to grasp the significance of using the language to solve problems. Conversely, it is possible to emphasize problem solving to the extent that using a particular language to solve problems becomes almost incidental. The intent of this text is to fall somewhere in between these two extremes. The broader goals are for students to understand language concepts and subsequently be able to use them to solve problems.

Overview and Organization

The third edition of this text was intended to be a fine-tuning of a well-accepted second edition. This goal has been accomplished. Without actually counting, an average of more than 10 changes per page appears to have been made throughout the text. Given the length of the text, this means that approximately 9,000 changes have probably been made in the process of revising the previous edition.

However, as always happens during a revision, more has been done than was originally intended when the process began. In addition to the fine-tuning, I have increased the technical level of presentation, the emphasis on communication as part of computer science, the documentation for loops and selection, the use of descriptive identifiers, and the emphasis on ethics in computer science. All of these changes will be discussed in more detail later in this preface.

As with the second edition, the material in Chapters 1 through 4 is presented at a deliberate pace. If students in the class have already had some programming experience, these chapters may be covered rapidly. However, students must be able to solve problems using top-down design with stepwise refinement. If this is overlooked, they will have difficulty designing solutions to more complex problems later.

Throughout the text, I have attempted to explain and develop concepts carefully. These are illustrated by frequent examples and diagrams. New concepts are then used in complete programs and case studies to show how they aid in solving problems. An early and consistent emphasis has been placed on good writing habits and on producing neat, attractive output. I firmly believe program documentation and readability are important. Thus, I frequently discuss them in the text, and I offer style tips where appropriate.

This text provides a complete one-year course in Pascal. However, there are at least three general scenarios for which this text would be appropriate.

1. A deliberately paced, thorough presentation of concepts would allow you to get through records and/or files in an 18-week semester.
2. An accelerated pace with students who have previous computing experience would allow you to get into Chapter 17 in an 18-week semester.
3. A deliberate pace with a thorough presentation would allow you to present the material in Chapters 1 through 17 in a full-year course.

Subprograms (procedures and functions) are presented in Chapters 7 and 8, after students have become familiar with the concepts of selection and repetition. Many students find working with procedures more difficult than working with selection or repetition statements. Thus, it is to their advantage to become comfortable with some basic concepts in Pascal before encountering the slightly more difficult concepts associated with writing subprograms. At this stage, students are better able to understand the use of parameters. All subsequent work utilizes subprograms in problem solving and program design.

In this edition, Chapter 9 presents text files as well as user-defined data types. Since larger data sets are typically used with arrays and files, it is assumed that most data will be read from data files (rather than entered interactively) after this chapter.

Chapters 10 and 11 develop arrays. Due to the significance of this concept, these chapters contain numerous examples, illustrations, and applications. A selection sort has been used to sort array elements. However, a bubble sort, an insertion sort, and a quick sort have been developed in Chapter 14. Either the bubble sort or the insertion sort could be used in place of the sorting algorithm presented in Section 10.3. Records and files are discussed in Chapters 12 and 13, respectively. Their placement there is traditional. These chapters, combined with Chapters 10 and 11, present a detailed treatment of static data structures.

Chapter 14 is an optional chapter that discusses sorting and merging. For advanced classes, material in this chapter could be used to motivate additional work with data structures. It is possible to use this material with preceding chapters. For example, sorting may be discussed in conjunction with Chapter 10, and merging with Chapter 13.

Chapter 15, Sets, can be presented any time after Chapter 9. Although a full chapter has been devoted to this topic, a working knowledge can be given to students in one or two days. Chapter 16, Graphics, is new to this edition. Material from this chapter can be introduced very early in the course. It has been placed late in the text only because it is not part of standard Pascal. Dynamic variables and data structures are introduced in Chapter 17. A reasonable discussion and development of pointers, linked lists, and binary trees is included. A full development of these concepts would have to come from a second course, with a different text.

T

Pascal statements in this text conform to standard Pascal. Due to the increasing use of Turbo Pascal with personal computers, Turbo Pascal references are included in the margins to indicate where Turbo differs from standard Pascal. These differences are explained in Appendix 6.

Features

This text has a number of noteworthy pedagogical features.

- *Objectives*: A concise list of topics and learning objectives is provided in each section.
- *Communication and Style Tips*: These suggestions for programming style are intended to enhance readability. A conscious attempt to emphasize the need for solid communication skills is developed in this text.
- *Exercises*: Short-answer questions are given at the end of each section.
- *Chapter Review Exercises*: These provide a comprehensive review of the concepts and material presented in the chapter.
- *Programming Problems*: Starting with Chapter 2, lengthy lists of suggestions for complete programs and projects are given at the end of each chapter.
- *Communication in Practice*: Beginning with Chapter 2, suggestions and problems at the end of each chapter give students a variety of ways to improve their communication skills. Suggestions include program documentation, talking with software users, preparing reports, and giving reports.

- *Module specifications*: Specifications are provided for all program modules.
- *Structure charts*: Structure charts reflect modular development and include the use of data flow arrows to emphasize transmission of data to and/or from each module. These charts set the stage for understanding the use of value and variable parameters when procedures are introduced.
- *Notes of Interest*: These tidbits of information are intended to create awareness of and interest in various aspects of computer science.
- *Suggestions for test programs*: Ideas included in exercises encourage students to use the computer to determine answers to questions and to see how to implement concepts in short programs.
- *Focus on Program Design: Case Study:* When appropriate, a complete program is given that illustrates utilization of the concepts developed within the chapter.
- *Running and Debugging Hints*: These ideas precede the summary at the end of the chapters.
- New terms are highlighted when first introduced.
- Margin definitions are provided for new terms.

In the back of the book there is a complete glossary, as well as appendixes on reserved words, standard identifiers, syntax diagrams, character sets, compiler error messages, Turbo Pascal references, the **GOTO** statement, and packing and unpacking. The final section of back matter provides answers to selected exercises.

Changes for the Third Edition

As the discipline of computer science evolves, there are two issues that its textbook authors must address. First, students of Pascal have an increasing level of experience and sophistication with computers. Second, the nature of an entry-level course should reflect current trends and meet current needs. These issues shaped the changes made in the third edition.

Three dominant themes have shaped the changes for this edition. First is the emphasis on communication as an integral part of learning about computer science. Changes made to reflect this emphasis include increased documentation for loops and selection statements and increased attention to descriptive identifiers. **Communication in Practice** problems at the end of Chapters 2 through 17 contain suggestions that allow students to interact with users outside the classroom and then report their results to the class.

The second theme is to increase the technical level of the material presented. Changes made consistent with this theme include:

- New material on numeric representation, including a discussion of representational and cancellation errors
- A discussion of the differences between type compatibility and assignment compatibility
- An emphasis on the difference between an expression and a statement
- Use of the phrase "field selector" when working with records
- Additional material on testing values for programs

Finally, programming in the large received additional emphasis. As previous users know, this has always been a feature of my textbooks. The **Focus on Program Design: Case Study** programs are spread throughout the text. Each case study includes a structure chart, pseudocode development, a complete program, and output from sample runs of the program. This edition contains more material and examples that contain reusable code. Also, several programming problems feature enhancements and subsequent development from previous chapters. These problems are denoted by a special symbol (■) when they appear in the problem set.

Another significant change is the inclusion of a chapter on graphics. Previous work with students has shown that this is a very popular topic. It was not included in earlier versions because it is not part of standard Pascal. However, reviewer comments have convinced me that it is time to include such material in this edition.

This edition maintains the philosophy that computer science is a dynamic discipline. Many concepts are presented in a language-independent manner. Thus, learning a language for the sake of learning the language is frequently deemphasized in favor of emphasizing concepts and problem-solving skills. Further, there is an increasing need for students to see both interactive and batch mode programs. These environments, coupled with popular nonstandard versions of Pascal (Turbo, for example), dictate greater flexibility in text preparation.

Consistent with the philosophy that Pascal is evolving as an introductory course in computer science, this third edition features the following:

- Continuing emphasis on the design of solutions to problems.
- Definitions in the margin that lead to increased emphasis and easier reference.
- Increased emphasis on using the **TYPE** definition section.
- Two sections on using assertions.
- A section on software engineering and subsections throughout the text indicating how new concepts relate to software engineering.
- A section on the software system life cycle.
- Material on abstraction, including subsections on procedural abstraction, data abstraction, and abstract data types.
- A high level of rigor in the development and use of the current terminology associated with subprograms, including discussions of cohesion, encapsulation, and interface.
- Significantly greater emphasis on ethics in computer science.
- Material emphasizing communication in computer science, including text references and exercises in every chapter designed to allow students to interview people, write reports, give oral reports, and write program specifications without writing code.
- Graphic documentation of some algorithms to enable students to understand code more easily by using visual illustrations.
- Continuing use of interactive and batch mode examples in Chapters 1 through 9.
- Occasional use of photographs to clarify and enhance presentations.
- Comments about Turbo Pascal in the text and in Appendix 6 that are appropriate for all versions of Turbo.
- A significant number of mathematical examples and programming problems.
- Of the 41 **Notes of Interest**, 26 are new and 8 have been updated since the last edition.

All of these changes have been made with two thoughts foremost in my mind. It is essential that this edition reflect the current trends and future directions of computer science. It is also essential that concepts continue to be presented in such a manner that beginning students can understand a concept and how it is used to design a solution to some problem. In this regard, every attempt has been made to retain the pedagogical features that have proven to be trademarks of the first two editions, including frequent use of examples, clear exposition of new concepts, use of test programs, and varied exercises in every section.

Ancillaries

A broad-based teaching support package is essential for an introductory course in Pascal. The following ancillary materials are available from South-Western Educational Publishing Company:

1. A Teacher's Guide, which contains chapter objectives and key terms, chapter outlines, and teaching suggestions for each chapter, along with an answer key with answers to all exercises, chapter review questions, and solutions to selected programming problems at the end of each chapter. This guide also has sections containing suggested lesson plans, course outlines, and many helpful insights for teachers. There are also comments on differences between standard and Turbo Pascal, correlations between chapter objectives and exercises, programming problems, and test questions. There is some guidance about the degree of difficulty for the programming problems for which programming solutions are not provided.
2. A complete black line Test Bank, with answers to all questions and programming problems, will be provided to all adopters of the text.
3. A set of transparency masters with key figures from the text will be provided, along with black line masters, for suggested chapter programs.
4. Westest, which is a computerized test-generation system for chapter exams in formats such as multiple choice, short answer, and program listings will also be provided to adopters of this text.

Each program and program segment in the text and all ancillaries have been compiled and run. Hence, original versions were all working. Unfortunately, the publication process does allow errors in code to occur after a program has been run. Every effort has been made to produce an error-free text, although this is virtually impossible. I assume full responsibility for all errors and omissions. If you detect any, please be tolerant and notify me or South-Western Educational Publishing Company so they can be corrected in subsequent printings and editions.

Acknowledgments

I would like to take this opportunity to thank those who in some way contributed to the completion of this text. Several reviewers contributed significant constructive comments during various phases of manuscript development for the second and third editions. They include:

Angela Annis
Grapevine High School
Grapevine, TX

Doug Aylor
Midland High School
Midland, TX

Robert L. Barton
Lawrence Central High School
Indianapolis, IN

Michael L. Coe
Plano Senior High School
Plano, TX

Linda A. Coyne
Edison High School
Edison, NJ

Harry R. (Rick) Culp
Bay High School
Panama City, FL

Bob Densmore
J.J. Pearce High School
Richardson, TX

Brenda Dotson
Millington High School
Millington, TN

Richard Euler
Fort Lauderdale, FL

Sherry Kay Hall
Jayton High School
Jayton, TX

Jim Hertwig
Lincoln High School
Dallas, TX

Sydney King
Madison High School
San Antonio, TX

R. J. Latshaw
Jesuit High School
Tampa, FL

Roy E. Marquez
Garfield Computer Magnet School
Los Angeles, CA

Mercedes A. McGowen
Elgin High School
Elgin, IL

Linda Menn
McCullough High School
The Woodlands, TX

Pam Merkel
Central Merry High School
Jackson, TN

Peggy Mica
Round Rock High School
Round Rock, TX

Shirley Morris
Churchill High School
San Antonio, TX

Joseph C. Pescatrice
Cape Coral High School
Cape Coral, FL

Debby Proctor
Martin County High School
Stuart, FL

Charlotte A. Shepperd
Seguin High School
Seguin, TX

Harry F. Shinn
Huntsville High School
Huntsville, AR

Phyllis Simon
Conway Public Schools
Conway, AR

Douglas Spillers
Callisburg High School
Gainesville, TX

Francis Trees
Westfield High School
Westfield, NJ

RoseAnn Yearick
American High School
Miami Lakes, FL

Producing a textbook requires the coordination, cooperation, patience, and hard work of several people. They provide balance, order, and sensibility that would not be possible without their efforts. The number of people involved with this project is larger than usual due to the acquisition of West Publishing Company by International Thomson Publishing as this text was being prepared. Changes in staff and responsibilities of those who remained after the acquisition meant that many people worked on some part of this project, but very few were there for the entire process. It has been my great good fortune to have worked with an outstanding support staff. They include:

Phyllis Jelinek, Project Manager. She has been the rock that anchored the ship of preparation as it passed through turbulent seas of production. She coordinated ancillaries, worked with reviewers, and helped keep me on schedule in the early stages of preparation. She subsequently became the lead person in coordinating the production and making critical decisions. I am extremely thankful for her devotion to getting a high-quality text produced on schedule.

Dr. James Cowles. He has done yeoman's work in preparing ancillary material. The Teacher's Guide that accompanies this text is unparalleled in its thoroughness and completeness.

Elliot Simon, editorial assistance on galleys. His amazing attention to detail has resulted in a cleaner, more accurate textbook.

Lorretta Palagi, copyeditor. Her excellent skills and eagle-eyed management of heavily revised manuscript have led to something presentable. To the extent that this textbook is readable, she deserves a lion's share of the credit.

Denis Ralling, Editor. We have worked closely since the inception of this project. He has been involved in several aspects of development, including acquiring reviewers, working on design elements, and helping coordinate production. He is exceptionally thorough, competent and friendly. It is a pleasure to work with such a person.

Mary Garvey Verrill, Production Editor. During the initial stages of production, she coordinated the work of all involved with the textbook.

Regan Stilo, Production Editor. Regan took over for Mary Verrill early in the production process, not only ensuring the quality of the text through all remaining steps, but making certain it came out on time and in excellent order. This text could not have come into being without her efforts.

Andrea Bednar, Project Editor. She was friendly, thorough, and easy to work with.

Lori Harvey, Project Editor. She assumed production responsibilities from Andrea Bednar and saw the textbook completed. She did an excellent job of keeping everyone on a tight schedule in order to meet our publishing deadline. I appreciate her supportive, no-nonsense approach to getting the job done. Her continual cooperation contributed to the ease of production.

Jerry Westby, Executive Editor. This is the twenty-first book on which we have worked together. It has been my blessing to have signed that first contract with Jerry and West Publishing 13 years ago. He is one of the most amazing individuals with whom I have ever worked. His sense of what makes a text look good is uncanny. He recognizes what needs to be done and is able to get people to do the work in a timely manner. Thank you, Jerry.

My family and friends deserve special mention for their support and patience. For 15 years, most of my spare time and energy have been devoted to textbook writing. This would not have been possible without their encouragement and understanding.

Finally, there is one person without whose help this project would not have been possible. Helen, who was a student in my first Pascal class, has been of tremendous assistance since we started writing. She worked during every phase of the textbook-preparation process. She prepared tearsheets, read copyedited material, proofread galleys and pages, and made many helpful suggestions. This is the fifteenth text for which Helen has done all of the above. Her unfailing patience and support have been remarkable. Fortunately for me, she has been my wife and best friend for 40 years.

Douglas W. Nance

Chapter 1

Computer Science, Computer Architecture, and Computer Languages

Chapter Outline

A jet airplane crash-lands near a large American city. Though the plane catches fire on impact, all of the passengers and crew members miraculously survive. Investigators find no clues from the crew or the flight recorders that point to the cause of the crash. However, using reports of observers on the ground about the behavior of the plane, they construct a computer simulation of the plane's behavior in the air. From this simulation, they hypothesize that a flaw in the plane's rudder might have caused it to go into a tailspin. They examine the parts of the rudder found at the crash site and confirm their hypothesis. The results of their investigation will be used to correct the flaw in the rudders of several hundred airplanes.

The investigators who constructed this simulation solved a problem by designing a program and running it on a computer. They may not have been trained as computer scientists, but they used techniques that have come to be associated with this exciting field.

This chapter provides a quick introduction to computer science, computer architecture, and computer languages. Section 1.1 provides a preview of the study of computer science. Section 1.2 examines the structure and parts of a computer. Section 1.3 analyzes how computer languages are used to make a computer run.

As you read this chapter, do not be overly concerned about the introduction and early use of terminology. All terms will be subsequently developed. A good approach to an introductory chapter like this is to reread it periodically. This will help you maintain a good perspective about how new concepts and techniques fit in the broader picture of using computers. Finally, remember that learning a language that will make a computer work can be exciting; being able to control such a machine can lead to quite a sense of power.

1.1 Computer Science: A Preview

Computer science is a very young discipline. Electronic computers were initially developed in the 1940s. Those who worked with computers in the 1940s and 1950s often did so by teaching themselves about computers; most schools did not then offer any instruction in computer science. However, as these early pioneers in computers learned more about the machines they were using, a collection of principles began to

Objectives

- to understand that computer science is not computer literacy
- to understand that computer science is:
  a. mathematics and logic
  b. science
  c. engineering
  d. communication
  e. interdisciplinary

evolve into the discipline we now call computer science. Because it emerged from the efforts of people using computers in a variety of disciplines, the influence of these disciplines can often be seen in computer science. With that in mind, in the next sections I briefly define what computer science is (and what it is not).

Computer Science as Computer Literacy

In the 1990s, computer-literate people know how to use various types of computer software to make their professional and domestic lives more productive and easier. This software includes, for instance, word processors for writing and data management systems for storing every conceivable form of information (from address lists to recipes).

The computer-literate person who wants to acquire an understanding of computer science is in much the same position as the driver of a car who wants to learn how to change its spark plugs. For the driver, this curiosity can lead to a study of how automobile engines function generally. For the literate user of computer software, this curiosity can lead from reading the software's instruction manual to designing and writing a program with that software, and then to a deep understanding of a computer as a general-purpose problem-solving tool. The computer-literate person will come to understand that the collection of problems that computer science encompasses and the techniques used to solve those problems are the real substance of this rapidly expanding discipline.

Computer Science as Mathematics and Logic

An **algorithm** is a finite sequence of effective statements that, when applied to a problem, will solve it.

A **programming language** is a formal language that computer scientists use to give instructions to the computer.

The problem-solving emphasis of computer science borrows heavily from the areas of mathematics and logic. Faced with a problem, computer scientists must first formulate a solution. This method of solution, or **algorithm** as it is often called in computer science, must be thoroughly understood before computer scientists make any attempt to implement a solution on the computer. Thus, at the early stages of problem solution, computer scientists work solely with their minds and do not rely on the machine in any way.

Once the solution is understood, computer scientists must then state the solution to this problem in a formal language called a **programming language.** This parallels the fashion in which mathematicians or logicians must develop a proof or argument in the formal language of mathematics. This formal solution as stated in a programming language must then be evaluated in terms of its correctness, style, and efficiency. Part of this evaluation process involves entering the formally stated algorithm as a programmed series of steps for the computer to follow.

Another part of the evaluation process is distinctly separate from a consideration of whether or not the computer produces the "right answer" when the program is executed. Indeed, two of the main areas of emphasis throughout this book are the development of well-designed solutions to problems and the recognition of the difference between such solutions and ones that work, but do so inelegantly. True computer scientists seek not just solutions to problems, but the best possible solutions.

Computer Science as Science

Perhaps nothing is as intrinsic to the scientific method as the formulation of hypotheses to explain phenomena and the careful testing of these hypotheses to prove them right or wrong. This same process plays an integral role in the way computer scientists work.

When confronted with a problem, such as a long list of names that needs to be arranged in alphabetical order, computer scientists formulate a hypothesis in the form of an algorithm that they believe will effectively solve the problem. Using mathematical techniques, they can make predictions about how such a proposed algorithm will solve the problem. But because the problems facing computer scientists arise from the world of real applications, predictive techniques that rely solely on mathematical theory are not sufficient to prove an algorithm correct. Ultimately, computer scientists must implement their solutions on computers and test them in the complex situations that originally gave rise to the problems. Only after such thorough testing can the hypothetical solutions be declared right or wrong.

Moreover, just as many scientific principles are not 100 percent right or wrong, the hypothetical solutions posed by computer scientists are often subject to limitations. An understanding of those limitations—of when the method is appropriate and when it is not—is a crucial part of the knowledge that computer scientists must have. This is analogous to the way in which any scientist must be aware of the particular limitations of a scientific theory in explaining a given set of phenomena.

Do not forget the experimental nature of computer science as you study this book. You must participate in computer science to truly learn it. Although a good book can help, *you* must solve the problems, implement those solutions on the computer, and then test the results. View each of the problems you are assigned as an experiment for which you are to propose a solution and then verify the correctness of your solution by testing it on the computer. If the solution does not work exactly as you hypothesized, do not become discouraged. Instead, ask yourself why it did not work; by doing so you will acquire a deeper understanding of the problem and your solution. In this sense, the computer represents the experimental tool of the computer scientist. Do not be afraid to use it for exploration.

Computer Science as Engineering

Whatever the area of specialization, an engineer must neatly combine a firm grasp of scientific principles with implementation techniques. Without knowledge of the principles, the engineer's ability to design creative models for a problem's solution is severely limited. Such model-building is crucial to the engineering design process. The ultimate design of a bridge, for instance, is the result of an engineer having considered many possible models of the bridge and then selecting the best one. The transformation of abstract ideas into models of a problem's solution is thus central to the engineering design process. The ability to generate a variety of models that can be explored is the hallmark of creative engineering.

Similarly, the computer scientist is a model-builder. Faced with a problem, the computer scientist must construct models for its solution. Such models take the form of an information structure to hold the data pertinent to the problem and the algorithmic method to manipulate that information structure to actually solve the problem. Just as an engineer must have an in-depth understanding of scientific principles to build a model, so must a computer scientist. With these principles, the computer scientist may conceive of models that are elegant, efficient, and appropriate to the problem at hand.

An understanding of principles alone is not sufficient for either the engineer or the computer scientist. Experience in the actual implementation of hypothetical models is also necessary. Without such experience, you can have only very limited intuition about what is feasible and how a large-scale project should be organized to reach a successful conclusion. Ultimately, computers are used to solve problems in the real world. In the real world, you will need to design programs that are completed on time, are within (if not under) the budget, and solve all aspects of the original problem. The experience you acquire in designing problem solutions and then implementing them is vital to your being a complete computer scientist. Hence, remember that you cannot actually study computer science without actively doing it. Merely reading about computer science techniques will leave you with an unrealistic perspective of what is possible.

Computer Science as Communication

As the discipline of computer science continues to evolve, communication is assuming a more significant role. The Association for Computing Machinery, Inc., curriculum guidelines for 1991 state, ". . . undergraduate programs should prepare students to . . . define a problem clearly; . . . document that solution; . . . and to communicate that solution to colleagues, professionals in other fields, and the general public" (p. 7).

It is no longer sufficient to be content with a program that runs correctly. Extra attention should be devoted to the communication aspects associated with such a program. For instance, you might be asked to submit a written proposal prior to designing a solution, or to document a program carefully and completely as it is being designed, or to write a follow-up report after a program has been completed. These are some ways in which communication can be emphasized as an integral part of computer science. Several opportunities are provided in the exercises and problems provided with this text for you to focus on the communication aspects associated with computer science.

Computer Science as an Interdisciplinary Field

The problems solved by computer scientists come from a variety of disciplines—mathematics, physics, chemistry, biology, geology, economics, business, engineering, linguistics, and psychology, to name a few. As a computer scientist working on a problem in one of these areas, you must be a quasi-expert in that discipline as well as in computer science. For instance, you cannot write a program to manage the checking account system of a bank unless you thoroughly understand how banks work and how that bank runs its checking accounts. At minimum, you must be literate enough in other disciplines to converse with the people for whom you are writing programs and to learn precisely what it is they want the computer to do for them. Since such people are often very naive about the computer and its capabilities, you will have to possess considerable communication skills as well as a knowledge of that other discipline.

Are you beginning to think that a computer scientist must be knowledgeable about much more than just the computer? If so, you are correct. Too often, computer scientists are viewed as technicians, tucked away in their own little worlds and not thinking or caring about anything other than computers. Nothing could be further from the truth. The successful computer scientist must be able to communicate, to learn new ideas quickly, and to adapt to ever-changing conditions. Computer science is emerging from its early dark ages into a mature process, one that I hope you will find rewarding and exciting. In studying computer science, you will be developing many talents; this text can get you started on the road to that development process.

1.2 Computer Architecture

Objectives

- to understand the historical development of computers
- to know what constitutes computer hardware
- to know what constitutes computer software
- to understand the various levels of computer languages

This section is intended to provide you with a brief overview of what computers are and how they are used. Although there are various sizes, makes, and models of computers, you will see that they all operate in basically the same straightforward manner. Whether you work on a personal computer that costs a few hundred dollars or on a mainframe that costs in the millions of dollars, the principles of making the machine work are essentially the same.

Data are the particular characters that are used to represent information in a form suitable for storage, processing, and communication.

A **mainframe** computer is typically used by major companies, government agencies, and universities.

A **supercomputer** is a mainframe computer that is capable of amazing speed, often 50,000 times as fast as most microcomputers.

A **minicomputer** is a small version of a mainframe computer. It can be used by several people at once.

A **microcomputer** is a personal computer with relatively limited memory. Generally used by one person at a time.

A **personal computer (PC)** is a self-contained computer with relatively limited memory; often called a microcomputer, it is generally used by one person at a time.

A **workstation** sits on a desktop but has larger storage capacity and faster processing speeds than microcomputers.

A **network** allows users of different computers to communicate and share resources.

Modern Computers

The search for aids to perform calculations is almost as old as number systems. Early devices include the abacus, Napier's bones, the slide rule, and mechanical adding machines. More recently, calculators have changed the nature of personal computing as a result of their availability, low cost, and high speed.

The last few decades have seen the most significant change in computing machines in the world's history as a result of improvements that have led to modern computers. As recently as the 1960s, a computer required several rooms because of its size. However, the advent of silicon chips has reduced the size and increased the availability of computers so that parents are able to purchase personal computers as presents for their children. These computers are more powerful than the early behemoths. A developmental time line is given in Figure 1.1. For a more complete development, see People and Computers, Partners in Problem Solving, by John F. Vinsonhaler, Christian C. Wagner, and Castelle G. Gentry, West Publishing Company, 1989.

What is a computer? According to Webster's New World Dictionary of the American Language (2nd College Edition), a computer is "an electronic machine which, by means of stored instructions and information, performs rapid, often complex calculations or compiles, correlates, and selects data." Basically, a computer can be thought of as a machine that manipulates information in the form of numbers and characters. This information is referred to as **data.** What makes computers remarkable is the extreme speed and precision with which they can store, retrieve, and manipulate data.

Several types of computers currently are available. An oversimplification is to categorize computers as mainframes, supercomputers, minicomputers, or microcomputers. In this grouping, **mainframe** computers are the large machines used by major companies, government agencies, and universities. They have the capability of being used by as many as 100 or more people at the same time and can cost millions of dollars. **Supercomputers** are mainframe computers capable of amazing speed. Some of them can process as many as one billion instructions per second. This is 50,000 times as fast as most microcomputers. **Minicomputers,** in a sense, are smaller versions of large computers. They can be used by several people at once but have less storage capacity and cost far less. **Microcomputers** are frequently referred to as **personal computers** (or **PCs**). They have limited storage capacity (in a relative sense), are generally used by one person at a time, and can be purchased for as little as a few hundred dollars.

Workstations have a larger storage capacity and faster processing speeds than microcomputers, but can still sit on a desktop and rely on similar microprocessing technology.

Most modern computers in organizations such as companies and universities are linked in a network. A **network** allows users of different computers to communicate and share resources. For example, the user of a microcomputer might receive electronic mail from a colleague in another office, send a file to a departmental laser printer, or connect to a cluster of workstations to perform tasks that require intensive processing.

Networked computers make use of a client/server relationship. You can think of clients as users requiring services, and servers as agents that perform services. For

◆ Figure 1.1

Development of computers

Era	Early Computing Devices		Mechanical Computers	Electro-mechanical Computers
Year	1000 B.C.	A.D. 1614	1650	1900 1945
Development	Abacus	Napier's bones	Adding machine Slide rule Difference engine Analytic engine	Cogged wheels Instruction register Operation code Address Plug board Harvard Mark I Tabulating machine

example, a single workstation might be an electronic mail server for 100 personal computers (the clients) in an organization.

Hardware is the actual computing machine and its support devices.

Software consists of programs that make the machine (the hardware) do something, such as word processing, database management, or game playing.

A program is a set of instructions that tells the machine (the hardware) what to do.

As you begin your work with computers, you will hear people talking about **hardware** and **software.** Hardware refers to the actual machine and its support devices. Software refers to programs that make the machine do something. Many software packages exist for today's computers. They include word processing, database programs, spreadsheets, games, operating systems, and compilers. You can (and will!) learn to create your own software. In fact, that is what this book is all about.

A **program** can be thought of as a set of instructions that tells the machine what to do. When you have written a program, the computer will behave exactly as you have instructed it. It will do no more or no less than what is contained in your specific instructions. For example,

```
PROGRAM ComputeAverage (input, output);

VAR
  Num1, Num2, Num3 : integer;
  Average : real;

BEGIN
  writeln ('Enter 3 integers separated by spaces.');
  writeln ('Press <Enter> when finished.');
  readln (Num1, Num2, Num3);
  Average := (Num1 + Num2 + Num3) / 3;
  writeln;
  writeln ('The average is', Average:10:3)
END.
```

Figure 1.1

Development of computers (continued)

Noncommercial Electronic Computers	Batch Processing	Time-Sharing Systems	Personal Computers
1945 1950	1965	1975	Present
First-generation computers Vacuum tubes Machine language programming ENIAC	Second-generation computers Transistors Magnetic core memory Assemblers Compilers UNIVAC I IBM 704	Third-generation computers Integrated circuit technology Operating system software Teleprocessing	Fourth-generation computers Fifth-generation computers (supercomputers) Microprocessors Workstations

is a program that causes a computer to get three integers as input, compute their average, and then print the result. Do not be concerned about specific parts of this program. It is intended only to illustrate the idea of a set of instructions. Very soon, you will be able to write significantly more sophisticated programs.

Learning to write programs requires two skills:

1. You need to be able to use specific terminology and punctuation that can be understood by the machine; you need to learn a programming language.
2. You need to be able to develop a plan for solving a particular problem. As mentioned earlier, such a plan is often referred to as an algorithm, the sequence of steps that, when followed, will lead to a solution of the problem.

Initially, you may think that learning a language is the more difficult task because your problems will have relatively easy solutions. Nothing could be further from the truth! **The single most important thing you can do as a student of computer science is to develop the skill to solve problems.** Once you have this skill, you can learn to write programs in several different languages.

Computer Hardware

Let's take another look at the question: What is a computer? Our previous answer indicated it is a machine. Although there are several forms, names, and brands of computers, each consists of a **main unit** that is subsequently connected to peripheral devices. The main unit of a computer consists of a **central processing unit (CPU)** and **main (primary) memory.** The CPU is the "brain" of the computer. It contains an **arithmetic/logic unit (ALU),** which is capable of performing arithmetic operations and evaluating expressions to see if they are true or false, and the **control unit,**

The **main unit** consists of a central processing unit and main memory.

The **central processing unit (CPU)** is a major hardware component that consists of the arithmetic/logic unit (ALU) and the control unit.

Main (primary) memory is memory contained in the computer.

The **arithmetic/logic unit (ALU)** is the part of the central processing unit that performs arithmetic operations and evaluates expressions.

The **control unit** is the part of the central processing unit that controls the operation of the rest of the computer.

The term **execute** means to perform a program step by step.

A **binary digit** is a digit, either 0 or 1, in the binary number system. Program instructions are stored in memory using a sequence of binary digits. Binary digits are called *bits*.

Bit is an abbreviation for binary digit.

An **input device** is a device that provides information to the computer. Typical devices are keyboards, disk drives, card readers, and tape drives.

An **output device** is a device that allows you to see the results of a program. Typically it is a monitor or printer.

Secondary (auxiliary) memory devices contain memory in a peripheral device, usually a disk or magnetic tape.

which controls the action of remaining components so your program can be followed step by step, or **executed.**

Main memory can be thought of as mailboxes in a post office. It is a sequence of locations where information representing instructions, numbers, characters, and so on can be stored. Main memory is usable while the computer is turned on. It is where the program being executed is stored along with data it is manipulating.

As you develop a greater appreciation of how the computer works, you might wonder: How are data stored in memory? Each memory location has an address and is capable of holding a sequence of **binary digits** (0 or 1), which are commonly referred to as **bits.** Instructions, symbols, letters, numbers, and so on are translated into an appropriate pattern of binary digits and then stored in various memory locations. These are retrieved, used, and changed according to instructions in your program. In fact, the program itself is similarly translated and stored in part of main memory. Main memory can be envisioned as shown in Figure 1.2, and the main unit can be envisioned as in Figure 1.3.

Peripherals can be divided into three categories: **input devices, output devices,** and **secondary (auxiliary) memory devices.** Input devices are necessary to give information to a computer. Programs are entered through an input device and then program statements are translated and stored as previously indicated. One input device (a typical keyboard) is shown in Figure 1.4.

Output devices are necessary to show the results of a program. These are usually your monitor screen, line printer, impact printer, or laser printer (Figure 1.5). Input and output devices are frequently referred to as **I/O devices.**

Secondary (auxiliary) memory devices are used if additional memory is needed. On small computers, these secondary memory devices could be floppy disks or hard disks (Figure 1.6), CD-ROM disks, or magnetic tapes. Programs and data waiting to be executed are kept "waiting in the wings" in secondary memory.

Communication between components of a computer is frequently organized around a group of wires called a **bus.** The relationship between a bus and various computer components is shown in Figure 1.7. A photograph of a bus is shown in Figure 1.8. What appear to be lines between the slots are actually wires imprinted on the underlying board. Boards with wires connected to peripheral devices can be inserted into the slots.

◆ Figure 1.2

Main memory

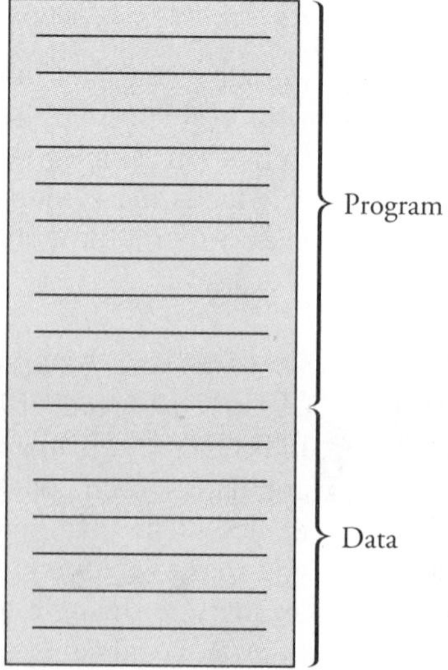

Figure 1.3
Main unit

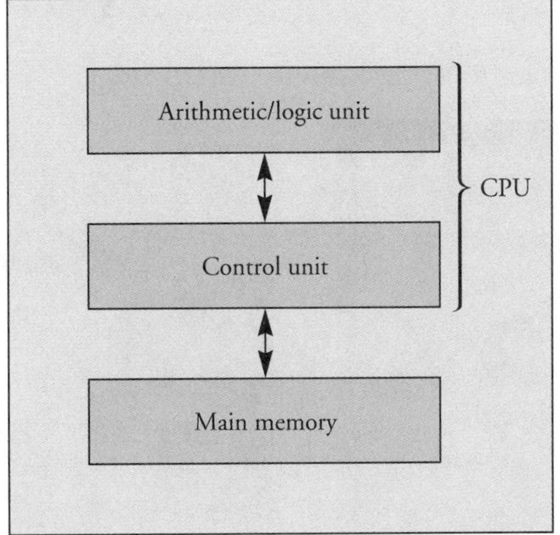

Figure 1.4
Keyboard

An **I/O device** is any device that allows information to be transmitted to or from a computer.

A **bus** is a group of wires that enables communication between components of a computer.

A **modem** is a device used to connect a computer to a telephone line.

Communication among different computers on a network is usually handled in two ways. A personal computer in the home might use a device called a **modem** to connect to a telephone line. The user connects to a remote computer by dialing a telephone number. Computers in organizations are usually connected by cables that run between offices or buildings. These connections allow much faster transmission of information than modems and telephone lines.

Computer Software

As previously stated, software refers to programs that make the machine do something. Software consists of two kinds of programs: system software and applications software.

System software includes what is often called the **operating system.** (You may have heard reference to DOS, which is an acronym for Disk Operating System.) The operating system for a computer is a large program and is usually supplied with a

◆ Figure 1.5

(a) Monitor, (b) line printer (mainframe), (c) impact printer (microcomputer), and (d) laser printer

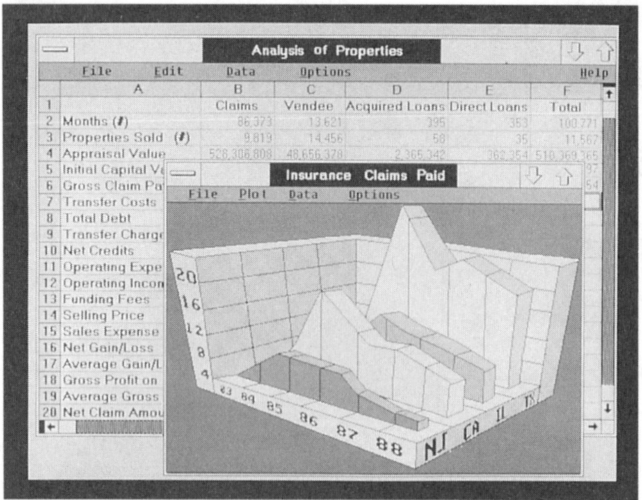

(a)

(b)

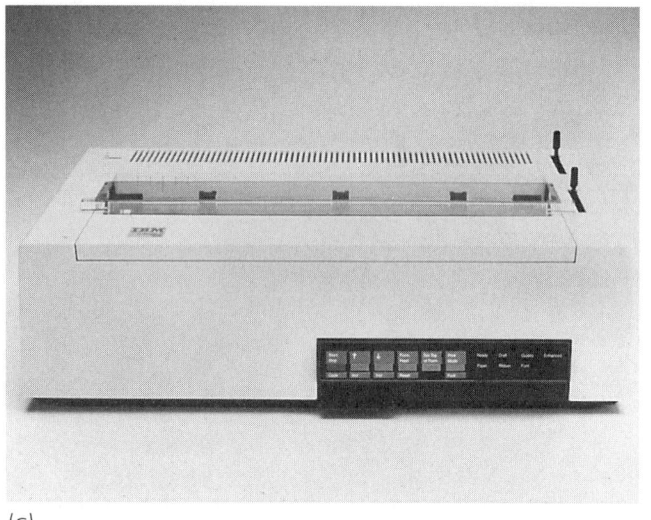

(c)

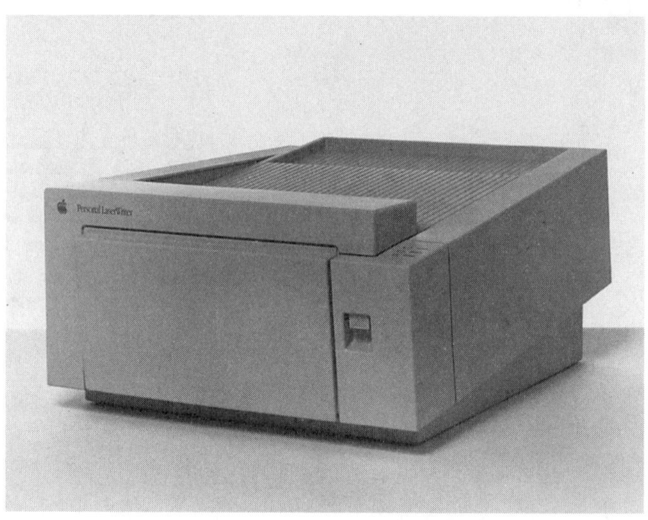

(d)

System software consists of programs that allow users to write and execute other programs, including operating systems such as DOS.

The **operating system** is a large program that allows the user to communicate with the hardware.

computer. This program allows the user to communicate with the hardware. More specifically, an operating system might control computer access (via passwords), allocate peripheral resources (perhaps with a printer queue), schedule shared resources (for CPU use), or control execution of other programs.

Application software consists of programs designed for a specific use. Examples of applications software include programs for word processing, text editing, simulating spreadsheets, playing games, designing machinery, and figuring payrolls. Most computer users work with applications software and have little need for learning a computer language; the programs they require have already been written to accomplish their tasks.

◆ Figure 1.6

(a) Disk drive and (b) microcomputer with hard disk

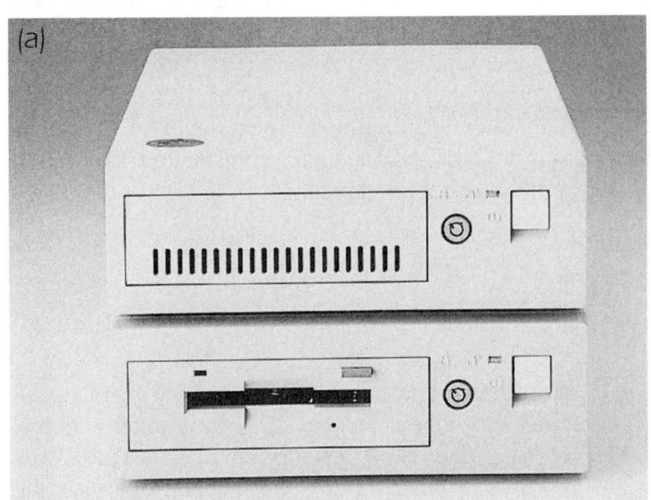

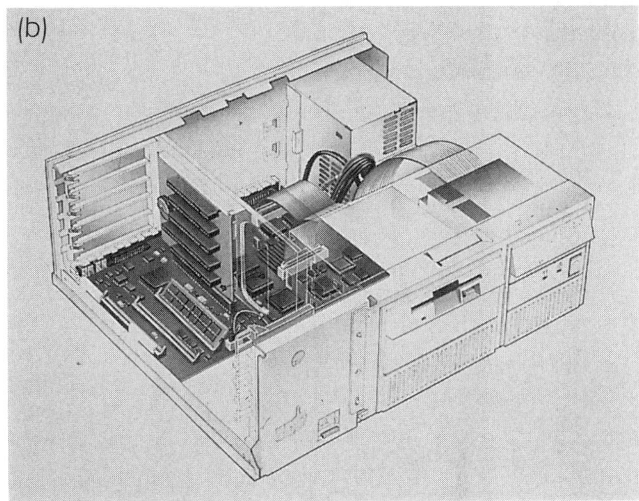

◆ Figure 1.7

An illustration of a bus

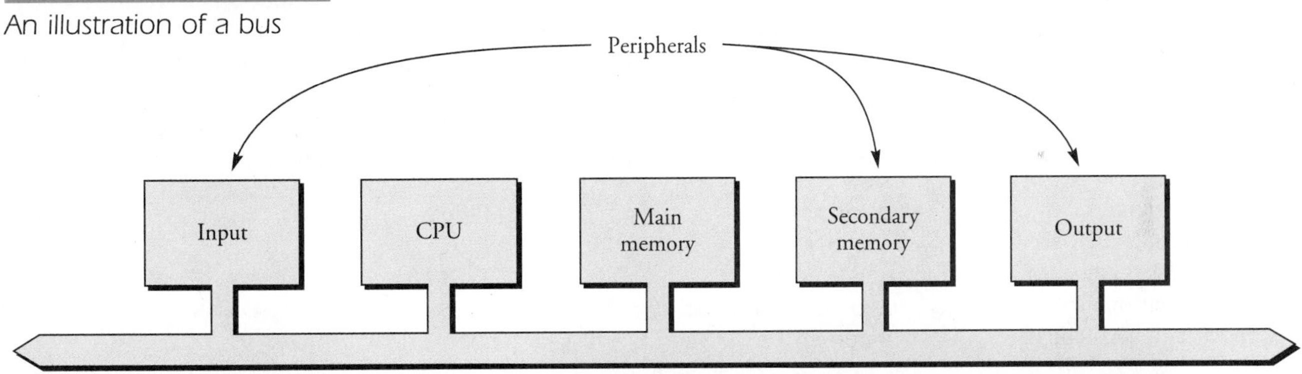

◆ Figure 1.8

Bus

1.3 Computer Languages

Objectives

- to understand what a computer language is
- to understand the difference between a low-level language and a high-level language
- to understand the difference between a source program and an object program

Application software consists of programs designed for specific uses.

Machine language is the language used directly by the computer in all its calculations and processing.

Assembly language is a computer language that allows words and symbols to be used in an unsophisticated manner to accomplish simple tasks.

A **low-level language** is what programmers call an assembly language.

A **high-level language** is any programming language that uses words and symbols to make it relatively easy to read and write a program.

A **compiler** is a computer program that automatically converts instructions in a high-level language to machine language.

What is a computer language? All data transmission, manipulation, storage, and retrieval are actually done by the machine using electrical pulses generated by sequences of binary digits. If eight-digit binary codes are used, there are 256 numbered instructions from 00000000 to 11111111. Instructions for adding two numbers would consist of a sequence of these eight-digit codes.

Instructions written in this form are referred to as **machine language.** It is possible to write an entire program in machine language. However, this is very time consuming and difficult to read and understand. But the next level of computer language allows words and symbols to be used in an unsophisticated manner to accomplish simple tasks. For example, machine language code for adding two integers could be replaced by

```
LOAD A
ADD B
STORE C
```

This causes the number in A to be added to the number in B and the result to be stored for later use in C. This computer language is an **assembly language,** which is generally referred to as a **low-level language.** What actually happens is that words and symbols are translated into appropriate binary digits and the machine uses the translated form. One statement in assembly language typically translates into one statement in machine language.

Although assembly language is an improvement over machine language for readability and program development, it is still a bit cumbersome. Consequently, many **high-level languages** have been developed; these include Pascal, C++, PL/I, FORTRAN, BASIC, COBOL, C, Ada, Modula-2, and Logo. These languages simplify even further the terminology and symbolism necessary for directing the machine to perform various manipulations of data. For example, in these languages, the task of adding two integers would be written as follows:

```
C := A + B;            (Pascal, Modula-2, Ada)
C = A + B;             (C, C++, PL/I)
C = A + B              FORTRAN, BASIC
ADD A, B GIVING C      (COBOL)
MAKE "C :A + :B        (Logo)
```

A high-level language makes it easier to read, write, and understand a program. This book develops the concepts, symbolism, and terminology necessary for using Pascal as a programming language for solving problems. After you have become proficient in using Pascal, you should find it relatively easy to learn the nuances of other high-level languages.

For a moment, let's consider how an instruction such as

```
C := A + B;
```

gets translated into machine code. The actual bit pattern for this code varies according to the machine and software version, but it could be as follows:

0100001100111010001111010100000100101011101000010

To do the translation, a special program called a **compiler** "reads" the high-level instructions and translates them into machine code. One statement in a high-level language typically translates into many statements in machine language. This

A Note of Interest

Advances in Computing Technology

(This information was supplied by Dale Jarman, Manager, Computer Center, Central Michigan University.)

Computing technology has changed at an astounding rate during the last 20 years. One illustration of such change is the amount of main memory available in a typical personal computer (PC). In 1975, less than 1K of memory was available; by 1985, available memory had increased to 512K. Eight years later, in 1993, PCs typically had 16 megabytes (16,000K) of memory, and industry projections indicate 64 megabytes of memory will be common on PCs in 1997. This growth is shown in the upper graph at right.

A second method of considering advances in computing technology is to compare cost to power. The lower graph shows that the cost (in actual dollars) of a personal computer has decreased steadily since 1975. However, the power of the PC has grown tremendously. In this comparison, the Norton power rating, which assigns a power rating of 1 to the 64K machine of 1981 with an 8088 chip, has been used.

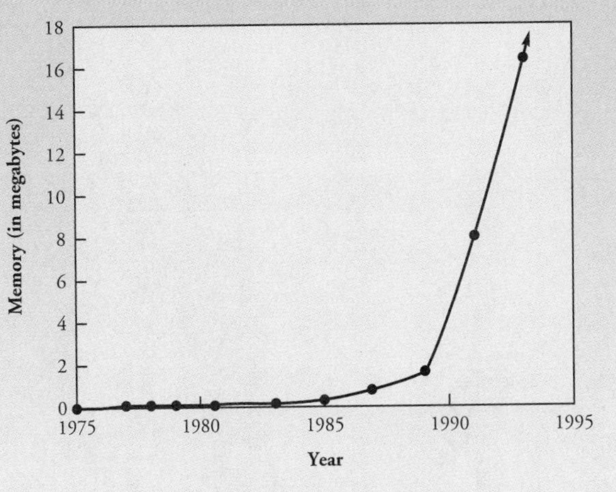

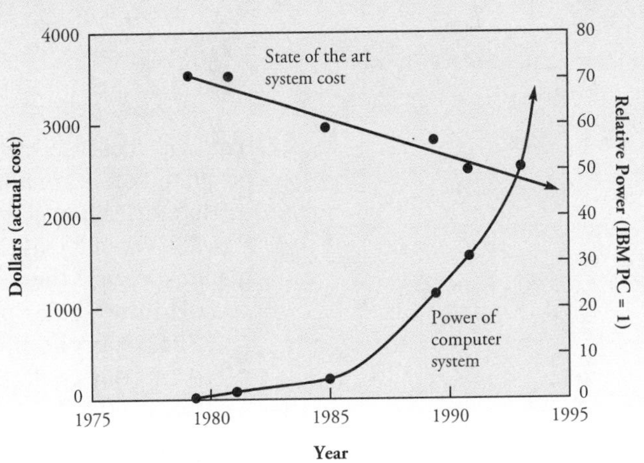

A **system program** is a special program used by the computer to activate the compiler, run the machine code version, and cause output to be generated.

A **source program** is a program written by a programmer.

An **object program** is the machine code version of the source program. This is also called **object code.**

compiled version is then run using some appropriate data. The results are then presented through some form of output device. The special programs that activate the compiler, run the machine-code version, and cause output to be printed are **system programs.** The program you write is a **source program,** and the machine-code version is an **object program** (also referred to as **object code**). This relationship is illustrated in Figure 1.9.

As you will soon see, the compiler does more than just translate instructions into machine code. It also detects certain errors in your source program and prints appropriate messages. For example, if you write the instruction

```
C := (A + B;
```

where a parenthesis is missing, when the compiler attempts to translate this line into machine code, it will detect that ")" is needed to close the parenthetical expression. It will then give you an error message such as

```
ERROR IN VARIABLE
```

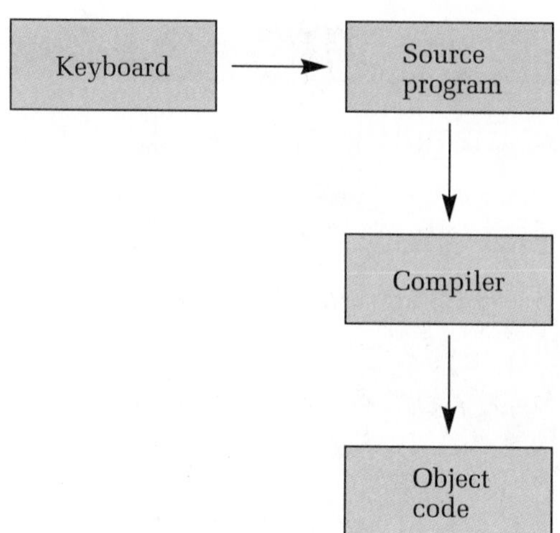

◆ Figure 1.9

Relationship of source program, compiler, and object code

You will then need to correct the error (and any others) and recompile your source program before running it with the data.

Before leaving this introductory chapter, let's consider the question: Why study Pascal? Various languages have differing strengths and weaknesses. Pascal's strong features include the following:

1. It incorporates program structure in a reasonable approximation of English. For example, if a certain process is to be repeated until some condition is met, this could be written in the program as

```
REPEAT
    } (process here)
UNTIL (condition here)
```

2. It allows the use of descriptive words for variables and data types. Thus, programs for computing payrolls could use words like HoursWorked, StateTax, FICA, TotalDeductions, and GrossPay.
3. It facilitates good problem-solving habits; in fact, many people consider this to be Pascal's main strength. As previously noted, developing the skill to solve a problem using a computer program is the most important trait to develop as a beginning programmer. Pascal is structured in such a manner that it encourages—indeed almost requires—good problem-solving skills.

You are now ready to begin a detailed study of Pascal. I hope you find that the time spent and frustrations encountered will result in an exciting and rewarding learning experience. Good luck.

A Note of Interest

Why Learn Pascal?

From the point of view of many potential users, Pascal's major drawback is that it is a compiled rather than an interpreted language. This means that developing and testing a small Pascal program can take a lot longer and involve many more steps than would be necessary with an interpreted language like BASIC. The effect of this drawback has been lessened recently with the development of interpreter programs for Pascal. Even so, most programs written by users of personal computers are small ones designed for quick solutions to particular problems, and the use of Pascal for such programs may be a form of overkill.

Ironically, the characteristics of Pascal that make it relatively unsuited for small programs are a direct consequence of its strengths as a programming language. The discipline imposed by the language makes it easier to understand large programs, but it may be more than a small program demands. For serious development of large programs or for the creation of tools that will be used over and over again (and require modifications from time to time), Pascal is clearly superior.

Experts generally consider Pascal an important language for people who are planning to study computer science or to learn programming. Indeed, the College Entrance Examination Board has recently designated Pascal as the required language for advanced-placement courses in computer science for high school students. While it is true that an experienced programmer can write clearly structured programs in any language, learning the principles of structured programming is much easier in Pascal.

Is Pascal difficult to learn? We don't think so, but the question is relative and may depend on which language you learn first. Programmers become accustomed to the first language they learn, making it the standard by which all others are judged. Even the poor features of the familiar language come to be seen as necessities, and a new language seems inferior. Don't let such subjective evaluations bar your way to learning Pascal, a powerful and elegant programming language.

Summary

Key Terms

algorithm
application software
arithmetic/logic unit (ALU)
assembly language
binary digit
bit
bus
central processing unit (CPU)
compiler
control unit
data
execute
hardware
high-level language
input device
I/O device
low-level language
machine language
mainframe
main (primary) memory
main unit
microcomputer
minicomputer
modem
network
object code
object program
operating system
output device
personal computer (PC)
program
programming language
secondary (auxiliary) memory devices
software
source program
supercomputer
system program
system software
workstation

Chapter Review Exercises

1. State and discuss the characteristics of each of the four classifications of computers.
2. Discuss the skills needed by students of computer science.
3. What are the three major components of any computer?
4. Name five high-level languages.
5. Name three input devices.
6. Name two output devices.
7. Give three reasons for studying Pascal.
8. What are the two parts of the main unit?

Answer each of the following fill-in-the-blank exercises with a single word or phrase.

9. The advent of ______________________ has reduced the size and increased the availability of computers.
10. The information (in the form of characters and numbers) manipulated by a computer is known as ______________________.
11. The actual machine and its support devices are known as ______________________.
12. The programs run by a machine are called ______________________.
13. A set of instructions telling the computer what to do is called a(n) ______________________.
14. A sequence of steps used to solve a problem is a(n) ______________________.
15. CPU stands for ______________________.
16. The two parts of a CPU are the ______________________ and the ______________________.
17. Auxiliary memory exists on ______________________, ______________________, or ______________________.
18. I/O devices are also known as ______________________.
19. All work inside the computer is done by sequences of ______________________. This lowest level language is referred to as ______________________.
20. The next lowest level of language is ______________________.
21. The program you write in a high-level language is called ______________________; its compiled version is called ______________________.

Chapter 2

Writing Your First Programs

Chapter Outline

Chapter 1 presented an overview of computers and computer languages. We are now ready to examine problems that computers can solve. First we need to know how to solve a problem and then we need to learn how to use a programming language to implement our solution on the computer.

Before looking at problem solving and writing programs for the computer, we should consider some psychological aspects of working in computer science. Studying computer science can cause a significant amount of frustration for these reasons:

1. Planning is a critical issue. First, you must plan to develop instructions to solve your problem and then you should plan to translate these instructions into code before you sit down at the keyboard. You should not attempt to type in code "off the top of your head."
2. Time is a major problem. Writing programs is not like completing other assignments. You cannot expect to complete a programming assignment by staying up late the night before it is due. You must begin early and expect to make several revisions before your final version will be ready.
3. Successful problem solving and programming require extreme precision. Generally, concepts in computer science are not difficult; however, implementation of these concepts allows no room for error. For example, one misplaced semicolon in a 1,000-line program could prevent the program from working.

In other words, you must be prepared to plan well, start early, be patient, handle frustration, and work hard to succeed in computer science. If you cannot do this, you may not enjoy computer science or be successful at it.

2.1 Program Development: Top-Down Design

The key to writing a successful program is planning. Good programs do not just happen; they are the result of careful design and patience. Just as an artist commissioned to paint a portrait would not start by shading in the lips and eyes, a good computer programmer would not attack a problem by immediately trying to

Objectives

- to understand what an algorithm is
- to understand what top-down design is
- to understand stepwise refinement
- to understand modularity
- to be able to develop algorithms
- to understand the process of software engineering
- to be aware of the software system life cycle

An **effective statement** is a clear, unambiguous instruction that can be carried out.

write code for a program to solve the problem. Writing a program is like writing an essay: An overall theme is envisioned, an outline of major ideas is developed, each major idea is subdivided into several parts, and each part is developed using individual sentences.

Six Steps to Good Programming Habits

In developing a program to solve a problem, six steps should be followed: Analyze the problem, develop an algorithm, write code for the program, run the program, test the results, and document the program. These steps will help you develop good problem-solving habits and, in turn, solve programming problems correctly. A brief discussion of each of these steps follows:

Step 1. **Analyze the Problem.** This is not a trivial task. Before you can do anything, you must know exactly what it is you are to do. You must be able to formulate a clear and precise statement of what is to be done. You should understand completely what data are available and what may be assumed. You should also know exactly what output is desired and the form it should take.

Step 2. **Develop an Algorithm.** An algorithm is a finite sequence of effective statements that, when applied to the problem, will solve it. An **effective statement** is a clear, unambiguous instruction that can be carried out. Each algorithm you develop should have a specific beginning; at the completion of one step, the next step should be uniquely determined; and the ending should be reached in a reasonable amount of time.

Step 3. **Write Code for the Program.** When the algorithm correctly solves the problem, you can think about translating your algorithm into a high-level language. An effective algorithm will significantly reduce the time you need to complete this step.

Step 4. **Run the Program.** After writing the code, you are ready to run the program. This means that, using an editor, you type the program code into the computer, compile the program, and run the program. At this point, you may discover errors that can be as simple as typing errors or ones that may require a reevaluation of all or parts of your algorithm. The probability of having to make some corrections or changes is quite high.

Step 5. **Test the Results.** After your program has run, you need to be sure that the results are correct, that they are in a form you like, and that your program produces the correct solution in all cases. To be sure the results are correct, you must look at them and compare them with what you expect. For a program that uses arithmetic operations, this means checking some results with pencil and paper. Often you will need to make revisions and return to a previous step.

Step 6. **Document the Program.** It is very important to completely document a working program. The writer knows how the program works; if others are to modify it, they must know the logic used. As you develop the ability to write programs to solve more complex problems, you will find it helpful to include documentation in Step 3 as you write the code.

Top-down design is a design methodology for solving a problem whereby you first state the problem and then proceed to subdivide the main task into major subtasks. Each subtask is then subdivided into smaller subtasks. This process is repeated until each remaining subtask is easily solved.

Stepwise refinement is the process of repeatedly subdividing tasks into subtasks until each subtask is easily accomplished.

Developing Algorithms

Algorithms for solving a problem can be developed by stating the problem and then subdividing the problem into major subtasks. Each subtask can then be subdivided into smaller tasks. This process is repeated until each remaining task is one that is easily solved. This process is known as **top-down design,** and each successive subdivision is referred to as a **stepwise refinement.** Tasks identified at each stage of this process are called **modules.** The relationship between modules can be shown graphically in a **structure chart** as shown in Figure 2.1.

To illustrate how an algorithm is developed, we will use the problem of updating a checkbook after a transaction has been made. A first-level refinement is shown in Figure 2.2. An arrow pointing into a module means information is needed before the task can be performed. An arrow pointing out of a module means the module task has been completed and information required for subsequent work is available. Each of these modules could be further developed as shown in Figure 2.3. Finally, one of the last modules could be developed as shown in Figure 2.4. The complete top-down design could then be envisioned as illustrated in Figure 2.5. Notice that each remaining task can be accomplished in a very direct manner.

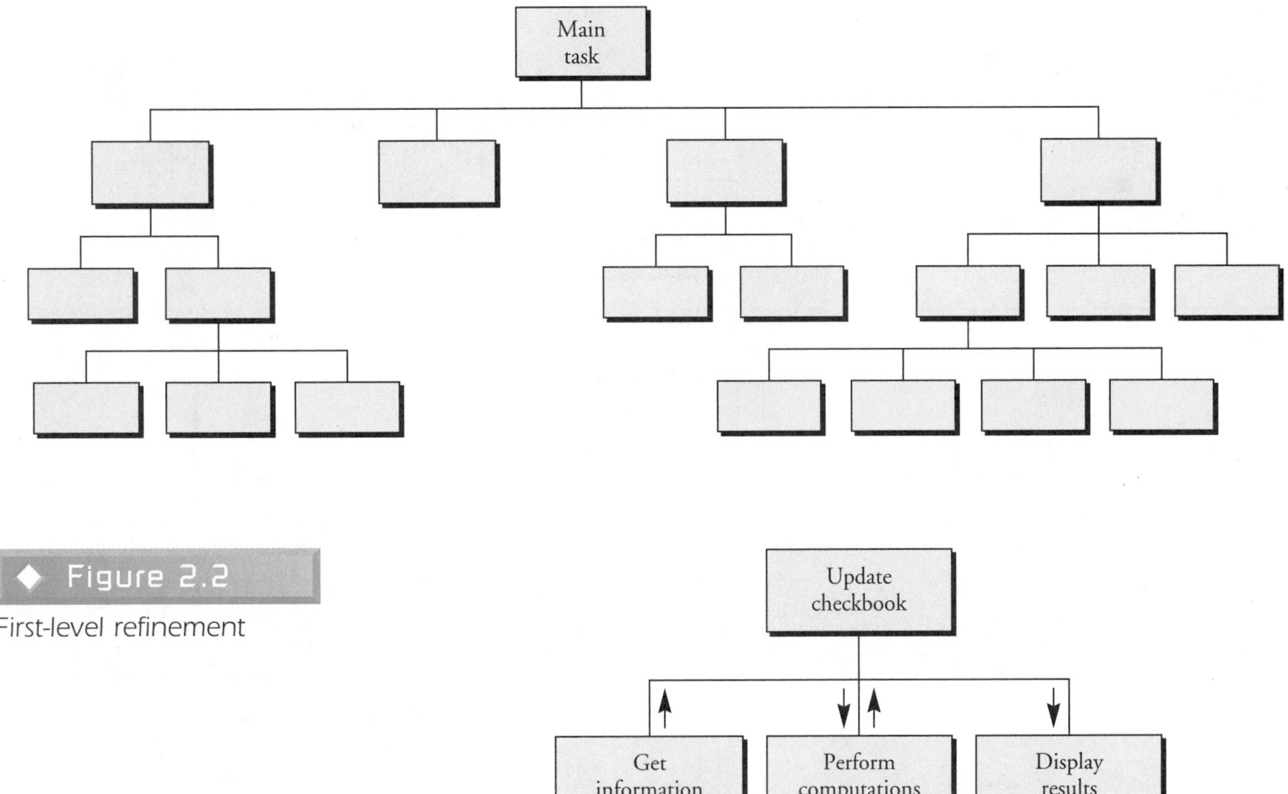

Figure 2.1
Structure chart illustrating top-down design

Figure 2.2
First-level refinement

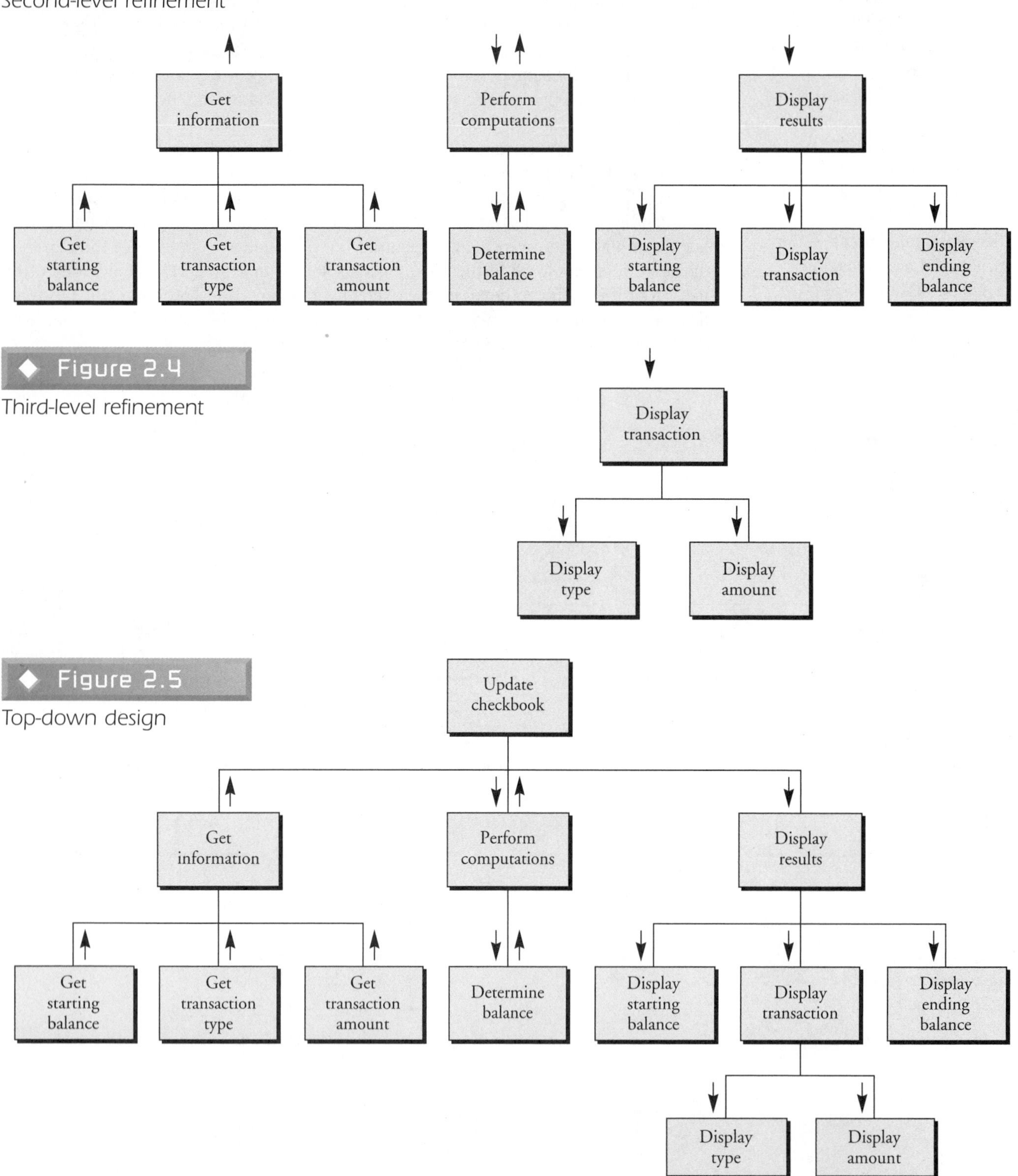

◆ Figure 2.3
Second-level refinement

◆ Figure 2.4
Third-level refinement

◆ Figure 2.5
Top-down design

A **module** is an independent unit that is part of a larger development. Usually a procedure or function.

A **structure chart** is a graphical representation of the relationship between modules.

Module specifications are a description of data received, information returned, and logic used in the module.

As a further aid to understanding how data are transmitted, **module specifications** will be listed for each main (first-level) module. Each module specification includes a description of data received, information returned, and logic used in the module. The module specification for the previous module is

Get Information Module
Data received: None
Information returned: Starting balance
Transaction type
Transaction amount
Logic: Have the user enter information from the keyboard.

For the checkbook problem, complete module specifications are

1. Get Information Module
   Data received: None
   Information returned: Starting balance
   Transaction type
   Transaction amount
   Logic: Have the user enter information from the keyboard.
2. Perform Computations Module
   Data received: Starting balance
   Transaction type
   Transaction amount
   Information returned: Ending balance
   Logic: If transaction is a deposit, add it to the starting balance; otherwise, subtract it from the starting balance.
3. Print Results Module
   Data received: Starting balance
   Transaction type
   Transaction amount
   Ending balance
   Information returned: None
   Logic: Display results in a readable form.

Pseudocode is a stylized half-English, half-code development written in English but suggesting Pascal code.

At least two comments should be made about top-down design. First, different people can (and probably will) have different designs for the solution of a problem. However, each good design will have well-defined modules with functional subtasks. Second, the graphic method just used helps to formulate general logic for solving a problem but is somewhat awkward for translating to code. Thus, we will use a stylized, half-English, half-code method called **pseudocode** to illustrate stepwise refinement in such a design. This will be written in English, but the sentence structure and indentations will suggest Pascal code. Major tasks will be numbered with whole numbers and subtasks with decimal numbers. First-level pseudocode for the checkbook-balancing problem is

1. Get information
2. Perform computations
3. Display results

A second-level pseudocode development produces

1. Get information
   1.1 Get starting balance

A Note of Interest

Object-Oriented Programming (OOP)—Part 1

The concepts of top-down design and modular development are two essential ingredients for a rapidly growing method of developing programs called object-oriented programming (OOP). Several OOP languages, such as Eiffel, Smalltalk, Object Pascal, and C++, have built-in special features that facilitate modular development.

Two significant ramifications of the movement toward object-oriented programming are:

1. The commercial aspect of using large systems developed by OOP. The "objects" in OOP can be used in more than one system; thus, they become more valuable. The use of objects also simplifies problems of maintenance and replacement as systems evolve.
2. The introduction of OOP languages earlier in the computer science curricula of many colleges and universities. Object-oriented programming is currently the introductory programming course at several institutions.

For more information on object-oriented programming, see the **Note of Interest** entitled "Object-Oriented Programming—Part 2" in Chapter 15, Section 15.3.

```
    1.2 Get transaction type
    1.3 Get transaction amount
2. Perform computations
    2.1 IF deposit THEN
            add to balance
        ELSE
            subtract from balance
3. Display results
    3.1 Display starting balance
    3.2 Display transaction
    3.3 Display ending balance
```

Finally, Step 3.2 of the pseudocode is subdivided as previously indicated into

```
3.2 Display transaction
    3.2.1 Display transaction type
    3.2.2 Display transaction amount
```

Two final comments are in order. First, each module developed should be tested with data for that module. Once you are sure each module does what you want, the whole program should work when the modules are used together. Second, the process of dividing a task into subtasks is especially suitable for writing programs in Pascal.

A Pascal program for the checkbook-balancing problem follows:

```
PROGRAM Checkbook (input, output);

VAR
  StartingBalance,
  EndingBalance,
  TransAmount : real;
  TransType : char;
```

```
BEGIN  {  Main program  }

{  Module for getting the data  }

  writeln;
  writeln ('Enter the starting balance and press <Enter>.');
  readln (StartingBalance);                                           1*
  writeln ('Enter the transaction type (D) deposit');
  writeln ('or (W) withdrawal and press <Enter>.');
  readln (TransType);
  writeln ('Enter the transaction amount and press <Enter>.');
  readln (TransAmount);

{  Module for performing computations  }

  IF TransType = 'D' THEN
    EndingBalance := StartingBalance + TransAmount                    2*
  ELSE
    EndingBalance := StartingBalance - TransAmount;

{  Module for printing results  }

  writeln;
  writeln ('Starting Balance       $', StartingBalance:8:2);
  writeln ('Transaction            $', TransAmount:8:2, TransType:2);  3*
  writeln ('---------':33);
  writeln ('Ending Balance         $', EndingBalance:8:2);
  writeln
END.  {  of main program  }
```

Notice how sections of the program correspond to module specifications. Two sample runs of the program produce the following output. Input from the keyboard is shown in color.

```
Enter the starting balance and press <Enter>.
235.16
Enter the transaction type (D) deposit
or (W) withdrawal and press <Enter>.
D
Enter the transaction amount and press <Enter>.
75.00

Starting Balance       $  235.16
Transaction            $   75.00 D
                       ---------
Ending Balance         $  310.16

Enter the starting balance and press <Enter>.
310.16
```

*These numbers refer to the modules previously developed with module specifications.

```
Enter the transaction type (D) deposit
or (W) withdrawal and press <Enter>.
W
Enter the transaction amount and press <Enter>.
65.75

Starting Balance        $  310.16
Transaction             $   65.75 W
                        ---------
Ending Balance          $  244.41
```

You probably would not use the power of a computer for something as simple as this program. You could just press a few calculator keys instead. However, as you will see, the language supports development of subprograms for specific subtasks. You will, for example, soon be able to enhance this program to check for overdrafts, save the new balance for later use, and repeat the process for several transactions. Learning to think in terms of modular development now will aid you not just in creating algorithms to solve problems, but it will aid you in writing programs to solve problems.

Software Engineering

Software engineering is the process of developing and maintaining very large software systems.

The phrase **software engineering** is used to refer to the process of developing and maintaining very large software systems. Before becoming engrossed in the specifics of solving problems and writing relatively small programs, it is instructive to consider the broader picture faced by those who develop software for "real-world" use.

It is not unusual for software systems to be programs that, if written in this size type, would require between 100 and 150 pages of text. These systems must be reliable, economical, and subject to use by a diverse audience. Consequently, software developers must be aware of and practice certain techniques.

As you might imagine, such large programs are not the work of a single individual but are developed by teams of programmers. Issues such as communication, writing style, and technique become as important as developing algorithms to solve particular parts of the problem. Management, coordination, and design are major considerations that need resolution very early in the process. Although you will not face these larger organizational issues in this course, you will see how some of what you learn has implications for larger design issues.

Software engineering has been so titled because techniques and principles from the more established engineering disciplines are used to guide the large-scale development required in major software. To illustrate, consider the problems faced by an engineer who is to design and supervise construction of a bridge. This analysis was presented by Alfred Spector and David Gifford in an article entitled "A Computer Science Perspective on Bridge Design" published in Communications of the ACM (April 1986).

Engineers designing a bridge view it first as a hierarchy of substructures. This decomposition process continues on the substructures themselves until a level of very fundamental objects (such as beams and plates) ultimately is reached. This decomposition technique is similar to the stepwise refinement technique used by software designers, who break a complex problem down into a hierarchy of subproblems, each of which ultimately can be solved by a relatively simple algorithm.

Engineers build conceptual models before actually constructing a bridge. This model-building allows them to evaluate various design alternatives in a way which eventually leads to the best possible design for the application being considered. This process is analogous to the way in which a skilled software designer builds models of a software system using structure charts and first-level pseudocode descriptions of modules. The designer then studies these conceptual models and eventually chooses the most elegant and efficient model for the application.

By the fashion in which engineers initially break down the bridge design, they insure that different aspects of the design can be addressed by different subordinate groups of design engineers working in a relatively independent fashion. This is similar to the goal of a software designer who oversees a program development team. The design of the software system must insure that individual components may be developed simultaneously by separate groups whose work will not have harmful side effects when the components are finally pulled together.

This overview is presented to give you a better perspective on how developments in this text are part of a greater whole. As you progress through your study of Pascal, you will see specific illustrations of how concepts and techniques can be viewed as part of the software engineering process.

Software System Life Cycle

Software engineering is the process by which large software systems are produced. As you might imagine, these systems need to be maintained and modified; ultimately, they are replaced with other systems. This entire process parallels that of an organism: development, maintenance, and subsequent demise. Thus, this process is referred to as the **software system life cycle.** Specifically, a system life cycle can be viewed in the following phases:

The **software system life cycle** is the process of development, maintenance, and demise of a software system.

1. Analysis
2. Design
3. Coding
4. Testing/verification
5. Maintenance
6. Obsolescence

It probably comes as a surprise that computer scientists view this process as having a phase that precedes the design phase. However, it is extremely critical that a problem be completely understood before any attempt is made to design a solution. The analysis phase is complicated by the fact that potential users may not supply enough information when describing their intended use of a system. Analysis requires careful attention to items such as exact form of input, exact form of output, how data entry errors (there will be some) should be handled, how large the databases will become, how much training in using the system will be provided, and what possible modifications might be required as the intended audience increases/decreases. Clearly, the analysis phase requires an experienced communicator.

The design phase is what much of this book is about. This is where the solution is developed using a modular approach. Attention must be paid to such techniques as communication, algorithm development, writing style, and teamwork.

Coding closely follows design. Unfortunately, many beginning students want to write code too quickly. This can be a painful lesson if you have to scrap several days of work because your original design was not sufficient. You are encouraged to make sure your designs are complete before writing any code. In the real world, teams of designers work many hours before programmers ever get a chance to start writing code.

The testing phase of a large system is a significant undertaking. Early testing is done on individual modules to get them running properly. Larger data sets must then be run on the entire program to make sure the modules interact properly with the main program. When the system appears ready to the designers, it is usually field tested by selected users. Each of these testing levels is likely to require changes in the design and coding of the system. The consequences of testing and verification can be much more significant than simply revealing whether or not the software performs correctly. In radiation oncology, for example, computers control the machine that applies radiation therapy. An error in dosage or in the position of the machine can have fatal consequences; in such cases, the level of program verification can become a moral issue.

Finally, the system is released to the public and the maintenance phase begins. This phase lasts throughout the remainder of the program's useful life. During this phase, we are concerned with repairing problems that arise with the system after it has been put into use. These problems are not necessarily bugs introduced during the coding phases. More often they are the result of user needs that change over time. For instance, annual changes in the tax laws necessitate changes in even the best payroll programs. Or problems may be due to misinterpretation of user needs during the early analysis phase. Whatever the reason, we must expect that a program will have to undergo numerous changes during its lifetime. During the maintenance phase, the time spent documenting the original program will be repaid many times over. One of the worst tasks imaginable in software development is to be asked to maintain an undocumented program. Undocumented code can quickly become virtually unintelligible, even to the program's original author. Indeed, one measure of a good program is how well it stands up to the maintenance phase.

Of course, no matter how good a program is, it will eventually become obsolete. At that time, the system life cycle starts all over again with the development of a new system to replace the obsolete one. Hence, the system life cycle is never ending, being itself part of a larger repetitive pattern that continues to evolve with changing user needs and more powerful technology.

Communication and Style Tips

Effective communication is an important part of learning computer science. In recognition of this fact, this text contains two threads that consistently emphasize communication. First, several **Communication and Style Tips** contain notes about communication and suggestions for improving communication as it relates to developing programs.

The second thread is contained in the **Programming Problems** section, which appears at the end of each chapter. Each chapter contains some **Communication in Practice** problems, which emphasize communication rather than program development. This is consistent with the Association for Computing Machinery, Inc., Curriculum Guidelines for 1991, which state, "Students should be encouraged to develop strong communication skills, both oral and written."

You are encouraged to discuss these ideas with your instructor and to incorporate them as part of your program development when appropriate.

A Note of Interest

Software Verification

Sitting 70 kilometers east of Toronto on the shore of Lake Ontario, the Darlington Nuclear Generating Station looks much like any other large nuclear power plant of the Canadian variety. But behind its ordinary exterior lies an unusual design feature.

Darlington is the first Canadian nuclear station to use computers to operate the two emergency shutdown systems that safeguard each of its four reactors. In both shutdown systems, a computer program replaces an array of electrically operated mechanical devices—switches and relays—designed to respond to sensors monitoring conditions critical to a reactor's safe operations, such as water levels in boilers.

Darlington's four reactors supply enough electricity to serve a city of two million people. Its Toronto-based builder, Ontario Hydro, opted for sophisticated software rather than old-fashioned hardware in the belief that a computer-operated shutdown system would be more economical, flexible, reliable, and safe than one under mechanical control.

But that approach carried unanticipated costs. To satisfy regulators that the shutdown software would function as advertised, Ontario Hydro engineers had to go through a frustrating but essential checking process that required nearly three years of extra effort.

"There are lots of examples where software has gone wrong, with serious consequences," says engineer Glenn H. Archinoff of Ontario Hydro. "If you want a shutdown system to work when you need it, you have to have a high level of assurance."

The Darlington experience demonstrates the tremendous effort involved in establishing the correctness of even relatively short and straightforward computer programs. The 10,000 "lines" of instructions, or code, required for each shutdown system pale in comparison with the 100,000 lines that constitute a typical word processing program or the millions of lines needed to operate a long-distance telephone network or a space shuttle.

Note: In the exercises, an asterisk preceding an exercise number indicates that the solution is in the section entitled Answers to Selected Exercises at the back of the text.

Exercises 2.1

Which of the statements in Exercises 1–5 are effective? Why or why not?

*1. Pay the cashier $9.15.

2. Water the plants a day before they die.

*3. Determine all positive prime numbers less than 1,000,000.

4. Choose X to be the smallest positive fraction.

*5. Invest your money in a stock that will increase in value.

What assumptions need to be made in Exercises 6–8 to understand the problem as stated?

6. Find the largest number of a set of numbers.

*7. Alphabetize a list of names.
8. Compute charges for a telephone bill.

Outline the main tasks for solving Exercises 9–13. Then refine each of these main tasks into a sufficient number of levels so that each exercise can be solved in a well-defined manner.

*9. Write a good term paper.
10. Take a vacation.
*11. Choose a college.
12. Get a summer job.
*13. Compute the semester average for a student in a computer science course and display all pertinent data.

In Exercises 14 and 15, use pseudocode to write a solution for each problem. Indicate each stage of your development.

14. Compute the average test score for five students in a class. Input for this problem consists of five scores. Output should include each score and the average of these scores.
*15. Compute the wages for two employees of a company. The input information consists of the hourly wage and the number of hours worked in one week. The output should contain a list of all deductions, gross pay, and net pay. For this problem, assume deductions are made for federal withholding taxes, state withholding taxes, social security, and union dues.
16. Develop an algorithm to find the total, average, and largest number in a given list of 25 numbers.
17. Draw a structure chart and write module specifications for Exercise 14.
18. Draw a structure chart and write module specifications for Exercise 15.
19. Draw a structure chart and write module specifications for Exercise 16.

2.2 Writing Programs

Objectives

- to recognize reserved words and predefined standard identifiers
- to recognize and declare valid identifiers
- to know the three basic components of a program
- to understand the basic structure of a Pascal program

Words in Pascal

Consider the following complete Pascal program:

```
PROGRAM Example (input, output);

CONST
  Skip = ' ';
  LoopLimit = 10;

VAR
  Index, Number, Sum : integer;
  Average : real;

BEGIN
  Sum := 0;
  FOR Index := 1 TO LoopLimit DO
    BEGIN
      writeln ('Please enter a number and press <Enter>.');
      readln (Number);
      Sum := Sum + Number
    END;
  Average := Sum / LoopLimit;
```

```
  writeln;
  writeln (Skip:15, 'The average is', Average:8:2);
  writeln;
  writeln (Skip:15, 'The number of scores is', LoopLimit:3)
END.
```

Reserved words are words that have predefined meanings that cannot be changed.

Standard identifiers are predefined words whose meanings can be changed if needed.

Programmer-supplied identifiers are identifiers provided by the person writing a program.

This program—and most programming languages—requires the use of words when writing code. In Pascal, words that have predefined meanings that cannot be changed are called **reserved words.** Some other predefined words, **standard identifiers,** can have their meanings changed if the programmer has strong reasons for doing so. Other words, **programmer-supplied identifiers,** must be created according to a well-defined set of rules but can have any meaning, subject to those rules.

In the body of this text, reserved words are capitalized and in bold type; standard identifiers are lowercase and in bold type. Reserved words used in the example programs are capitalized and standard identifiers are lowercase. This convention is not required by the language.

Reserved Words

In Pascal, reserved words are predefined and cannot be used in a program for anything other than the purpose for which they are reserved. Some examples are **AND, OR, NOT, BEGIN, END, IF,** and **FOR.** As you continue in Pascal, you will learn where and how these words are used. At this time, however, you need only become familiar with the reserved words in Table 2.1; they are also listed in Appendix 1. (*Note:* In this text, the symbol **T** appears in the margin to alert you to cases in which Turbo Pascal differs from standard Pascal. These differences are explained in Appendix 6.)

Table 2.1

Reserved words

T

AND	**ELSE**	**IF**	**OR**	**THEN**
ARRAY	**END**	**IN**	**PACKED**	**TO**
BEGIN	**FILE**	**LABEL**	**PROCEDURE**	**TYPE**
CASE	**FOR**	**MOD**	**PROGRAM**	**UNTIL**
CONST	**FORWARD**	**NIL**	**RECORD**	**VAR**
DIV	**FUNCTION**	**NOT**	**REPEAT**	**WHILE**
DO	**GOTO**	**OF**	**SET**	**WITH**
DOWNTO				

Standard Identifiers

Keywords are either reserved words or predefined identifiers.

A second set of predefined words, standard identifiers, can have their meanings changed by the programmer. For example, if you could develop a better algorithm for the trigonometric function **sin,** you could then substitute it in the program. However, a standard identifier should not be used for anything other than its intended use. Some standard identifiers are listed in Table 2.2 and in Appendix 2. The term **keywords** is used to refer to both reserved words and standard identifiers in subsequent discussions.

Syntax and Syntax Diagrams

Syntax is the formal rules governing construction of valid statements.

Syntax refers to the rules governing construction of valid statements. Syntax includes the order in which statements occur, together with appropriate punctuation.

Table 2.2

Standard identifiers

Data Types	Constants	Functions	Procedures	Files
boolean	**false**	**abs**	**dispose**	**input**
char	**maxint**	**arctan**	**get**	**output**
integer	**true**	**chr**	**new**	
real		**cos**	**pack**	
text		**eof**	**page**	
		eoln	**put**	
		exp	**read**	
		ln	**readln**	
		odd	**reset**	
		ord	**rewrite**	
		pred	**unpack**	
		round	**write**	
		sin	**writeln**	
		sqr		
		sqrt		
		succ		
		trunc		

Syntax diagramming is a method to formally describe the legal syntax of language structures.

Syntax diagramming is a method that formally describes the legal syntax of language structures. **Syntax diagrams** show the permissible alternatives for each part of each kind of sentence and where the parts may appear. The symbolism we use is shown in Figure 2.6. A combined listing of syntax diagrams is contained in Appendix 3.

Figure 2.6

Symbols used in syntax diagrams

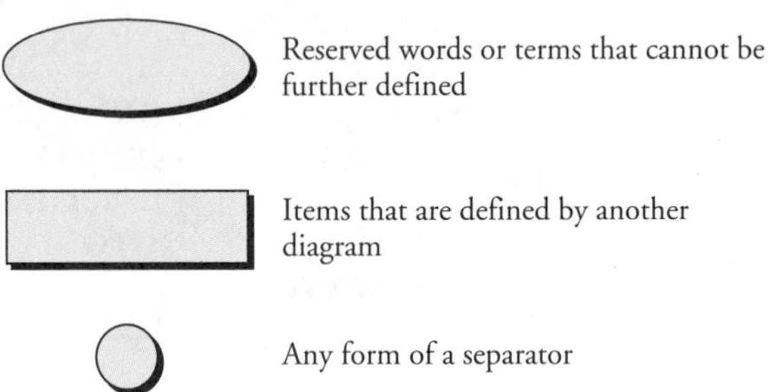

Syntax diagrams are diagrams that show the permissible alternatives for each part of each kind of sentence and where the parts may appear.

Arrows are used to indicate possible alternatives. To illustrate, a syntax diagram for forming words in the English language is

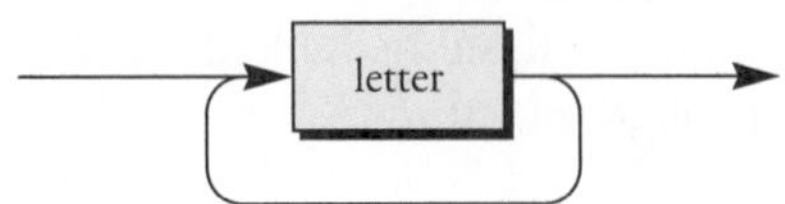

If the word must start with a vowel, the diagram is

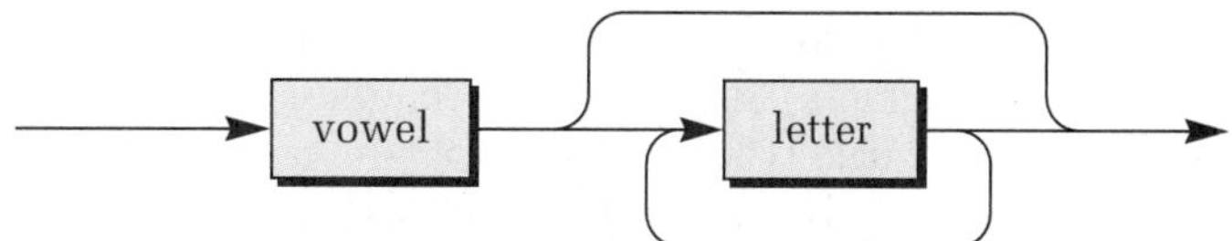

where vowel and letter are defined in a manner consistent with the English alphabet. Syntax diagrams are used throughout the text to illustrate formal constructs. You are encouraged to become familiar with them.

Identifiers

T

Reserved words and standard identifiers are restricted in their use. Most Pascal programs require other programmer-supplied identifiers; the more complicated the program, the more identifiers needed. **A valid identifier must start with a letter of the alphabet and must consist only of letters and digits.** A syntax diagram for forming identifiers is

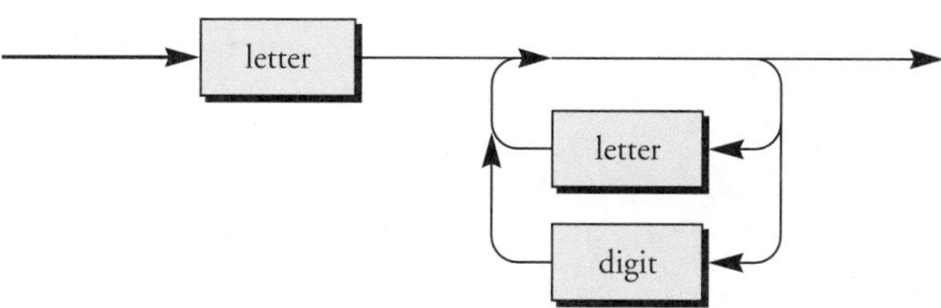

Table 2.3 gives some valid and invalid identifiers along with the reasons for those that are invalid. A valid identifier can be of any length. However, some versions of Pascal recognize only the first part of a long identifier (for example, the first 8 or the first 10 characters). Therefore, identifiers such as MathTestScore1 and MathTestScore2 might be the same identifier to a computer and could not be used as different identifiers in a program. Thus, you should learn what restrictions are imposed by your compiler.

Table 2.3

Valid and invalid identifiers

Identifier	Valid	If Invalid, Reason
`Sum`	Yes	
`X + Y`	No	"+" is not allowed
`Average`	Yes	
`Text1`	Yes	
`1stNum`	No	Must start with a letter
`X`	Yes	
`K mart`	No	Spaces are not allowed
`ThisIsaLongOne`	Yes	

The most common use of identifiers is to name the variables to be used in a program. Other uses for identifiers include the program name, symbolic constants, new data types, and subprogram names, all of which are discussed later. Always use descriptive names for identifiers, even though single-letter identifiers are permitted. As you will soon discover, descriptive names make programs easier to follow.

Basic Program Components

A program in Pascal consists of three components: a program heading, an optional declaration section, and an executable section. These three components are illustrated in the program shown in Figure 2.7.

◆ Figure 2.7

Components of a program

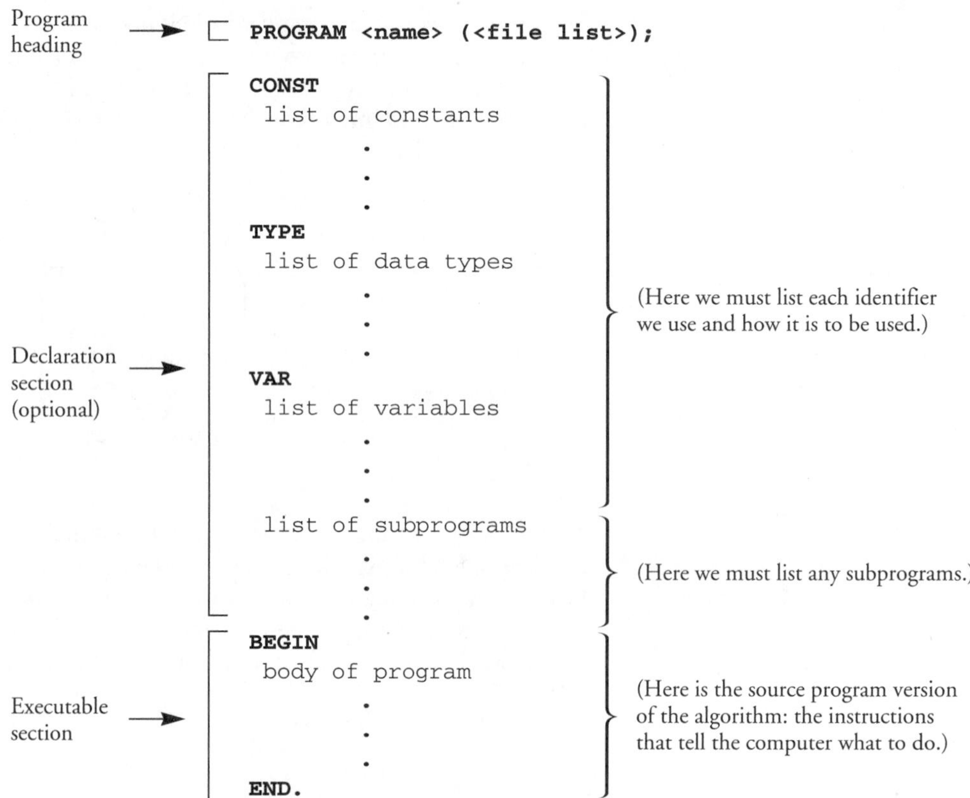

The syntax diagram for a program is

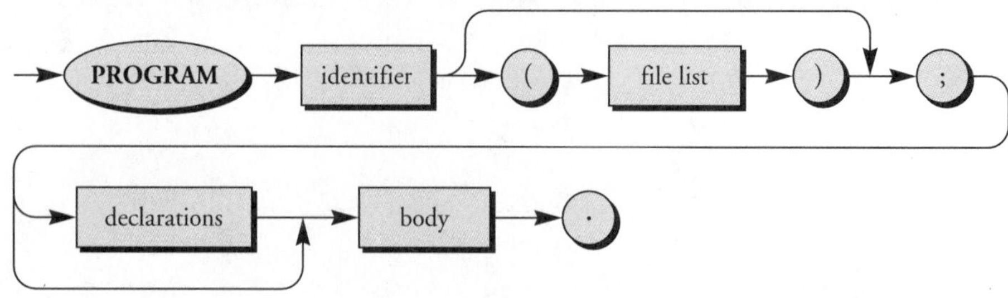

Figure 2.8 illustrates the program components of the sample program (**PROGRAM** Example) that started this section.

◆ Figure 2.8

Components of **PROGRAM** Example

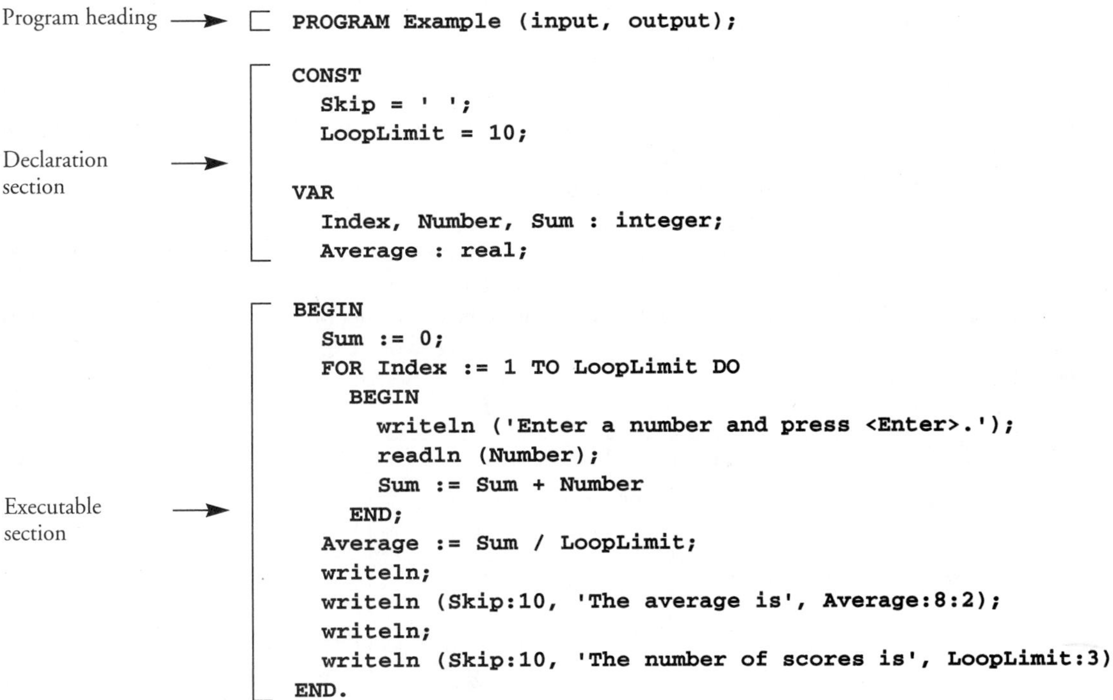

Program heading
Declaration section
Executable section
PROGRAM Example (input, output);
CONST
  Skip = ' ';
  LoopLimit = 10;
VAR
  Index, Number, Sum : integer;
  Average : real;
BEGIN
  Sum := 0;
  FOR Index := 1 TO LoopLimit DO
    BEGIN
      writeln ('Enter a number and press <Enter>.');
      readln (Number);
      Sum := Sum + Number
    END;
  Average := Sum / LoopLimit;
  writeln;
  writeln (Skip:10, 'The average is', Average:8:2);
  writeln;
  writeln (Skip:10, 'The number of scores is', LoopLimit:3)
END.

The **program heading** is the first statement of any Pascal program; it must contain the reserved word **PROGRAM.**

The **program heading** is the first statement of any Pascal program. It is usually one line and must contain the reserved word **PROGRAM;** the program name, which must be a valid identifier; and a list of files used. The semicolon at the end of the program heading is not considered part of the heading; it is used to separate the heading from the rest of the program. If the program receives input or produces output, the list of files must include the files **input** and/or **output.** Some other versions (for example, Turbo Pascal) do not have this requirement. The respective parts of a program heading are

PROGRAM <name> (<file list>)

The template or fill-in-the-blanks form just presented is used throughout this book. Reserved words and standard identifiers are shown. You must use identifiers to replace the words in lowercase letters and enclosed in arrowheads "< >". Thus

PROGRAM <name> (<file list>)

could become

```
PROGRAM Rookie (input, output);
```

A syntax diagram for a program heading follows:

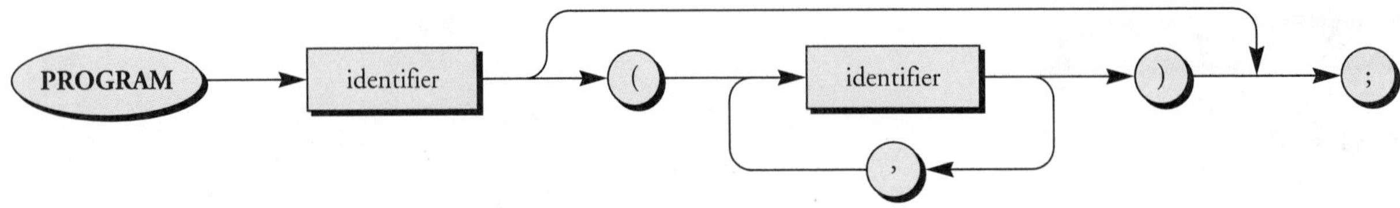

The **main block** is the executable portion of a program. It often calls other parts of a program.

The **declaration section** is the section used to declare (name) all symbolic constants, data types, variables, and subprograms that are necessary to the program.

The **constant definition section** is the section where program constants are defined for subsequent use.

The remainder of the program is sometimes referred to as the **main block;** major divisions are the declaration section and the executable section. The **declaration section** is used to declare (name) all symbolic constants, data types, variables, and subprograms that are necessary to the program. All constants named in the declaration section are normally referred to as being defined. Thus, we generally say variables are declared and constants are defined.

When constants are defined, they appear in the **constant definition section** of the declaration section after the reserved word **CONST.** The form for defining a constant is

```
CONST
  <identifier1> = <value 1>;
  <identifier2> = <value 2>;
        .
        .
        .
  <identifiern> = <value n>;
```

Values of constant identifiers cannot be changed during program execution. The syntax diagram for the **CONST** part is

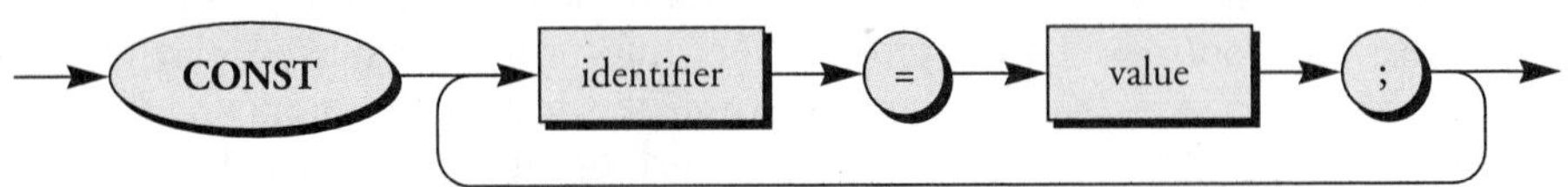

If "value" is one character or a string of characters, it must be enclosed in single quotation marks (apostrophes); for example,

```
CONST
  Date = 'July 4, 1776';
```

Any number of constants may be defined in this section. Maximum readability is achieved when the constants are listed consecutively and aligned down the page. A typical constant definition portion of the declaration section could be

```
CONST
  Skip = ' ';
  Name = 'George Washington';
  Date = 'July 4, 1776';
  Splats = '*****************************';
```

```
Line = '-----------------------------';
ClassSize = 35;
SpeedLimit = 65;
CmToInches = 0.3937;
Found = true;
```

A **standard simple type** is any one of the predefined data types **integer, real, char,** or **boolean.**

The **variable declaration section** is the section of the declaration section where program variables are declared for subsequent use.

The **TYPE** portion of the declaration section is explained in Section 8.1. For now, we assume data used in a Pascal program are one of the four **standard simple types: integer, real, char,** or **boolean.** Discussion of types **integer, real,** and **char** is in Section 2.3; discussion of **boolean** is in Section 5.1.

The **variable declaration section** of the declaration section must be listed after the **TYPE** portion, if present, and must begin with the reserved word **VAR.** This section must contain all identifiers for variables to be used in the program; if a variable is used that has not been declared, an error will occur when the program is compiled.

The form required for declaring variables is somewhat different from that used for defining constants: it requires a colon instead of an equal sign and specific data types. The simplest correct form is

```
VAR
  <identifier1> : <data type 1>;
  <identifier2> : <data type 2>;
       .
       .
       .
  <identifiern> : <data type n>;
```

The syntax diagram is

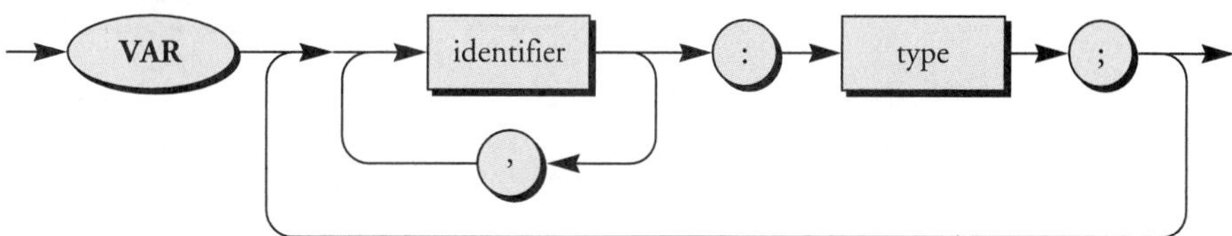

The reserved word **VAR** may appear only once in a program (exceptions will be noted when subprograms are developed). If no variables are to be used, a variable declaration section is not needed; however, this seldom happens. A typical variable declaration section could look like this:

```
VAR
  Sum : integer;
  Average : real;
  Num1, Num2, Num3 : integer;
  Ch : char;
```

Four other examples of permissible methods of writing this declaration section are

```
VAR
  Num1 : integer;
  Num2 : integer;
```

```
    Num3 : integer;
    Sum : integer;
    Ch : char;
    Average : real;

  VAR
    Num1, Num2, Num3, Sum : integer;
    Ch : char;
    Average : real;

  VAR
    Num1,
    Num2,
    Num3,
    Sum : integer;
    Ch : char;
    Average : real;

  VAR
    Num1, Num2,
    Num3, Sum : integer;
    Ch : char;
    Average : real;
```

The **executable section** contains the statements that cause the computer to do something.

The third basic program component is the **executable section.** This section contains the statements that cause the computer to do something. It must start with the reserved word **BEGIN** and conclude with the reserved word **END.** Also, a period must follow the last **END** in the executable section. The syntax diagram is

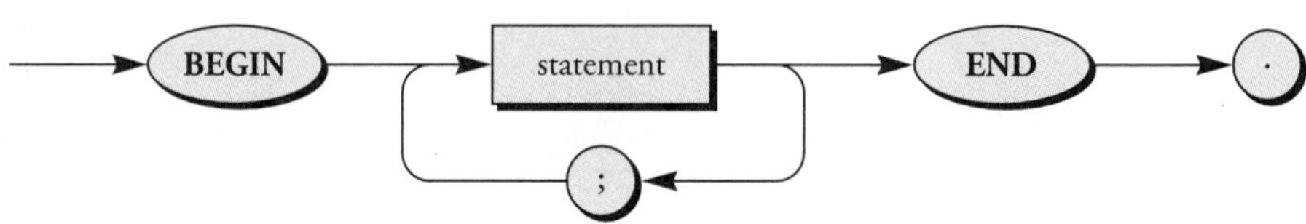

Statements in Pascal

A **statement** is the basic unit of expression in Pascal.

The **statement** in Pascal is the basic unit of expression. A program consists of a sequence of statements separated by semicolons. Statements perform two functions in a program: declarations and processing.

A **declaration statement** defines constants and types in the **CONST** and **TYPE** sections, declares variables in the **VAR** section, and is used as the program heading.

Declaration statements are used for the program heading and to define constants in the **CONST** section, define types in the **TYPE** section, and declare variables in the **VAR** section. Each of the following is an example of a declaration statement:

```
PROGRAM Rookie (input, output)
Date = 'July 4, 1776'
J, Number, Sum : integer
```

A **processing statement** causes the computer to take action when a program is run.

Processing statements cause the computer to take action when a program is run. The compiler creates machine-language instructions from processing statements. These instructions are executed according to the sequence dictated by the program.

Processing statements are often referred to as executable statements. In the sample program in Figure 2.8, the following are processing statements:

```
Sum := 0
Average := Sum / LoopLimit
writeln
writeln (Skip:10, 'The average is ', Average:8:2)

FOR Index := 1 TO LoopLimit DO
  BEGIN
    writeln ('Enter a number and press <Enter>.');
    readln (Number);
    Sum := Sum + Number
  END
```

A **simple statement** is a single-action, executable statement.

A **compound statement** uses the reserved words **BEGIN** and **END** to make several simple statements into a single compound statement.

An **executable statement** is the basic unit of grammar in Pascal, consisting of valid identifiers, standard identifiers, reserved words, numbers, and/or characters, together with appropriate punctuation.

The first four statements are **simple statements.** The last statement is a **compound statement.** Compound statements are developed further in Section 5.2.

Writing Code in Pascal

We are now ready to examine the use of the executable section of a program. In Pascal, the basic unit of grammar is an **executable statement,** which consists of valid identifiers, standard identifiers, reserved words, numbers, and/or characters together with appropriate punctuation.

One of the main rules for writing code in Pascal is that a semicolon is used to separate executable statements. For example, if the statement

```
writeln ('The results are':20, Sum:8, ' and', Aver:6:2)
```

were to be used in a program, it would (almost always) require a semicolon between it and the next executable statement. Thus, it should be

```
writeln ('The results are':20, Sum:8, ' and', Aver:6:2);
```

In one instance, an executable statement does not need a following semicolon. When a statement is followed by the reserved word **END,** a semicolon is not required. This is because **END** is not a statement by itself, but part of a **BEGIN . . . END** pair. However, if a semicolon is included, it will not affect the program. You can visualize the executable section as shown in Figure 2.9.

◆ Figure 2.9

Executable section

```
                  BEGIN
                    <statement 1>;
                    <statement 2>;
                        .
Executable  -->         .
section                 .
                    <statement n - 1>;
                    <statement n>
                  END.
```

Pascal does not require that each statement be on a separate line. Actually, you could write a program as one long line (which would wrap around to fit the screen) if you wish; however, it would be very difficult to read. Compare, for example, the readability of

A Note of Interest

Blaise Pascal

Blaise Pascal (1623–1662) began a spectacular, if short, mathematical career at a very early age. He was a brilliant child. As a youngster of 14, he attended meetings of senior French mathematicians. At age 16, he had so impressed the famous mathematician Descartes with his writings that Descartes refused to believe the author could be so young.

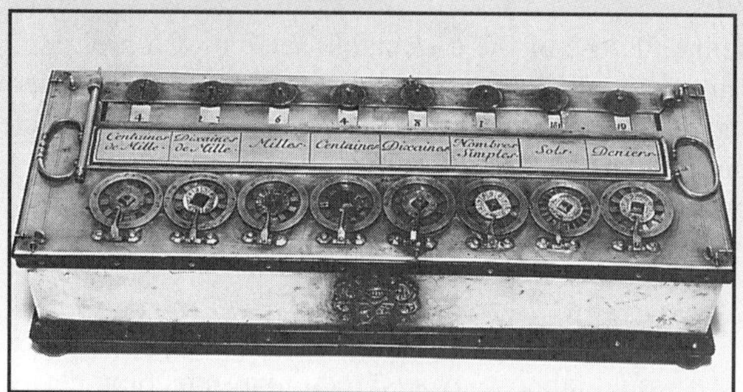

Two years later, Pascal invented a calculating machine, the Pascaline (shown at right), which stands as the very remote predecessor of the modern computer. The Pascaline could add and subtract; it functioned by a series of eight rotating gears, similar to an automobile's odometer. Pascal's machine was opposed by tax clerks of the era, who viewed it as a threat to their jobs. Pascal presented his machine to Queen Christina of Sweden in 1650; it is not known what she did with it.

In spite of his obvious talent for mathematics, Pascal devoted most of his adult life to questions of theology; his work in this area is still regularly studied. A man who often perceived omens in events around him, Pascal concluded that God's plan for him did not include mathematics and dropped the subject entirely. However, while experiencing a particularly nagging toothache when he was 35, Pascal let his thoughts wander to mathematics and the pain disappeared.

He took this as a heavenly sign and made a quick but intensive return to mathematical research. In barely a week, he managed to discover the fundamental properties of the cycloid curve. With that, Pascal again abandoned mathematics. In 1662, at the age of 39, he died.

```
PROGRAM ReadCheck (output); CONST Name = 'George';
Age = 17; VAR Index, Sum : integer; BEGIN Sum := 0;
FOR Index := 1 TO 10 DO Sum := Sum + Index; writeln
('My name is ':28, Name); writeln ('My age is ':27, Age);
writeln; writeln ('The sum is ':28, Sum) END.
```

to that of this program:

```
PROGRAM ReadCheck (output);

CONST
  Name = 'George';
  Age = 17;

VAR
  Index, Sum : integer;

BEGIN
  Sum := 0;
  FOR Index := 1 TO 10 DO
    Sum := Sum + Index;
  writeln ('My name is ':28, Name);
```

```
  writeln ('My age is ':27, Age);
  writeln;
  writeln ('The sum is ':28, Sum)
END.
```

You are not expected to know what the statements mean at this point, but it should be obvious that the second program is much more readable than the first. In addition, it is easier to change if corrections are necessary. However, these programs are executed identically because Pascal ignores extra spaces and line boundaries.

A good principle to follow is to use spacing to enhance readability. Decide on a style you like (and your teacher can tolerate) and use it consistently. Most programmers, however, include a space before a left parenthesis and after a right parenthesis when appropriate but no spaces immediately inside parentheses; for example:

```
PROGRAM LooksNice (input, output);
```

Exercises 2.2

1. List the rules for forming valid identifiers.

In Exercises 2–13, which are valid identifiers? Give an explanation for those that are invalid.

2. `7Up`
*3. `Payroll`
4. `Room222`
*5. `Name List`
6. `A`
*7. `A1`
8. `1A`
*9. `Time&Place`
10. `CONST`
*11. `X*Y`
12. `ListOfEmployees`
*13. `Lima,Ohio`

In Exercises 14–20, which are valid program headings? Give an explanation for those that are invalid.

14. `PROGRAM Rookie (output)`
*15. `PROGRAM Pro (input, output);`
16. `TestProgram (input, output);`
*17. `PROGRAM (output);`
18. `PROGRAM GettingBetter (output);`
*19. `PROGRAM Have Fun (input, output);`
20. `PROGRAM 2ndOne (output);`
21. Name the three main sections of a Pascal program.

Write constant definition statements for the information requested in Exercises 22–25.

*22. Your name.
*23. Your age.
*24. Your birth date.
*25. Your birthplace.

In Exercises 26–31, find all errors in the definitions and declarations.

26.
```
CONST
  Company : 'General Motors';
VAR
  Salary : real;
```

*27.
```
VAR
  Age = 18;
```
28.
```
VAR
  Days : integer;
  Ch : char;
CONST
  Name = 'John Smith';
```
*29.
```
CONST
  Car : 'Cadillac';
```
30.
```
CONST
  Score : integer;
```
*31.
```
VAR
  Num1, Num2, Num3 : real;
  Score,
  Num : integer;
```
32. Discuss the significance of a semicolon when writing Pascal statements.

2.3 Data Types and Output

Objectives

- to understand and be able to use the data types **integer, real,** and **char**
- to understand the difference between the floating-point form and fixed-point form of decimal numbers
- to understand the syntax for and use of **write** and **writeln** for output
- to be able to format output

A **data type** is a formal description of the set of values that a variable can have.

Data Type integer

Pascal requires that all data used in a program be given a **data type.** Since numbers in some form will be used in computer programs, we will first look at numbers of type **integer,** which are integers that are positive, negative, or zero.

Some rules that must be observed when using integers are

1. Plus (+) signs do not have to be written before a positive integer. For example, +283 and 283 have the same value and both are allowed.
2. Minus (–) signs must be written when using a negative number.
3. Leading zeros are ignored. For example, 00073, +073, 0073, and 73 all have the same value.
4. Decimal points cannot be used when writing integers. Although 14 and 14.0 have the same value, 14.0 is not of type **integer.**
5. Commas cannot be used when writing integers. 271,362 is not allowed; it must be written as 271362.

The syntax diagram for an integer is

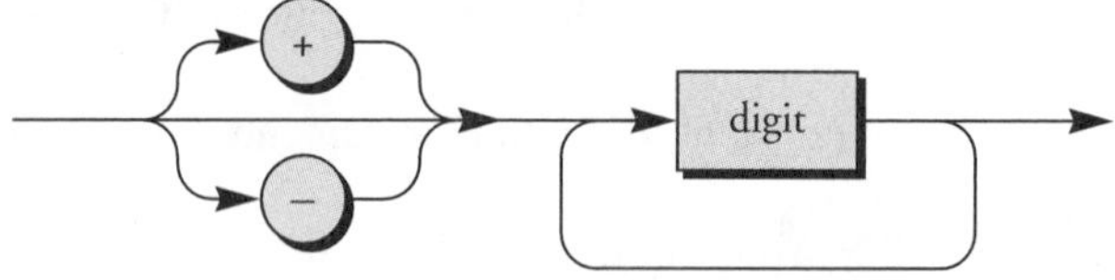

T

There is a limit on the largest and the smallest integer constant. The largest such constant is **maxint** and the smallest is usually **–maxint** or (**–maxint**–1). The constants **maxint** and **–maxint** are recognized by every version of Pascal; however, different machines have different values for them. This section ends with a program that enables you to discover the value of **maxint** on your computer. Operations with integers are examined in Section 3.1 and integer variables are discussed in Chapter 3.

Data Type real

Fixed point is a method of writing decimal numbers in which the decimal is placed where it belongs in the number.

Floating point is a method for writing numbers in scientific notation to accommodate numbers that have very large or very small values. Exactly one nonzero digit must appear to the left of the decimal.

Working with real numbers requires using the appropriate form for expressing the number. When using decimal notation, numbers of type **real** must be written with a decimal point, with at least one digit on each side of the decimal. Thus, .2 is not a valid **real** but 0.2 is.

Plus (+) and minus (−) signs for data of type **real** are treated exactly as they are for data of type **integer.** When working with reals, however, both leading and trailing zeros are ignored. Thus, +23.45, 23.45, 023.45, 23.450, and 0023.45000 have the same value.

All reals seen thus far have been in **fixed-point** form. The computer will also accept reals in **floating-point** (or exponential) form. Floating-point form is an equivalent method for writing numbers in scientific notation to accommodate numbers that have very large or very small values. The difference is that instead of writing the base decimal times some power of 10, the base decimal is followed by E and the appropriate power of 10. For example, 231.6 in scientific notation would be 2.316×10^2 and in floating-point form would be 2.316E2. Table 2.4 sets forth several fixed-point decimal numbers with the equivalent scientific notation and floating-point form.

▼ Table 2.4

Forms for equivalent numbers

Fixed-Point Form	Scientific Notation	Floating-Point Form
46.345	4.6345×10	4.6345E1
59214.3	5.92143×10^4	5.92143E4
0.00042	4.2×10^{-4}	4.2E−4
36000000000.0	3.6×10^{10}	3.6E10
0.000000005	5.0×10^{-9}	5.0E−9
−341000.0	-3.41×10^5	−3.41E5

Floating-point form for real numbers does not require exactly one digit on the left of the decimal point. In fact, it can be used with no decimal points written. To illustrate, 4.16E1, 41.6, 416.0E-1, and 416E-1 have the same value and all are permissible. However, it is not a good habit to use floating-point form for decimal numbers unless exactly one digit appears to the left of the decimal. In most other cases, fixed-point form is preferable.

The syntax diagram for a floating-point number is

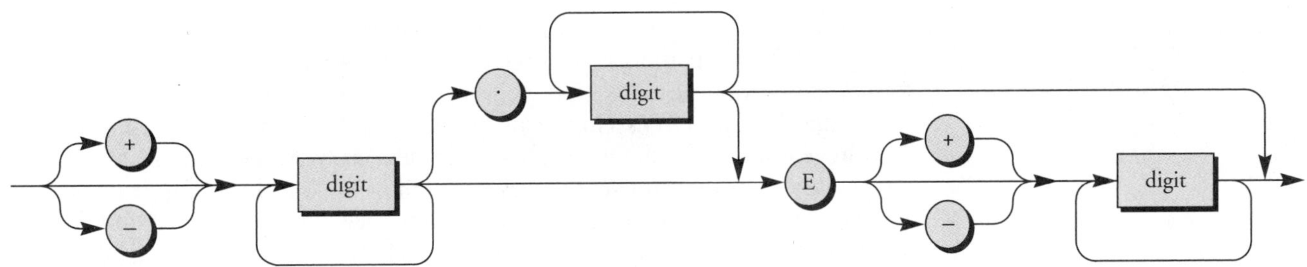

When using reals in a program, you may use either fixed-point or floating-point form. But the computer prints out reals in floating-point form unless you specify otherwise. Formatting output is discussed later in this section.

Data Type char

Another data type available in Pascal is **char**, which is used to represent character data. Data of type **char** can be only a single character (which could be a blank space). These characters come from an available character set that differs somewhat from computer to computer, but always includes the letters of the alphabet; the digits 0, 1, 2, 3, 4, 5, 6, 7, 8, and 9; and special symbols such as #, &, !, +, –, *, /, and so on. Two common character sets are given in Appendix 4.

Character constants of type **char** must be enclosed in single quotation marks when used in a program. Otherwise, they will be treated as variables and subsequent use will cause a compilation error. Thus, to use the letter A as a constant, you would type 'A'. The use of digits and standard operation symbols as characters is also permitted; for example, '7' would be considered a character, but 7 is an integer.

A **string constant** is one or more characters used as a constant in a program.

A **string** is an abbreviated name for a string constant.

If a word of one or more characters is used as a constant in a program, it is referred to as a **string constant.** String constants, generally called **strings,** may be defined in the **CONST** portion of the declaration section. The entire string must be enclosed in single quotation marks. Some sample definitions are

```
CONST
  Name = 'John Q. Public';
  Date = 'July 4, 1776';
  Splats = '************************';
```

Students with experience using BASIC usually expect the equivalent of a string variable for storing names and other information. A string is not a standard Pascal data type; standard Pascal does not have such a feature. However, an analogous feature, packed arrays of characters, is presented in Section 10.5.

When a single quotation mark is needed within a string, it is represented by two single quotation marks. For example, if the name desired was O'Malley, it would be represented by

```
'O''MALLEY'
```

When a single quotation mark is needed as a single character, it can be represented by placing two single quotation marks within single quotation marks. When typed, this appears as ''''. Note that these are all single quotation marks; use of the double quotation mark character here will not produce the desired result.

Data Type string (Optional: Nonstandard)

Standard Pascal does not provide for a **string** data type. However, since many versions of Pascal (particularly Turbo) do contain a **string** data type, we have decided to include mention of this data type in this edition of the book.

Having the data type **string** available allows a programmer to design programs that are capable of using strings of characters as well as numeric data. This is particularly useful when using names of people and companies, for example. Later, we will see how such strings can be incorporated into a program; for now, it is sufficient for you to be aware that several versions of nonstandard Pascal provide a **string** data type.

Output

T

One goal of most programs is to print something. What gets displayed (either on a screen or on paper) is referred to as **output.** The two program statements that produce output are **write** and **writeln** (pronounced "write line"). They are usually followed by character strings, numbers, numeric expressions, or variable names enclosed in parentheses. The general form is

Output is information that is produced by a program.

> **write** (<expression 1>, <expression 2>, . . . , <expression *n*>)
>
> or
>
> **writeln** (<expression 1>, <expression 2>, . . . , <expression *n*>)

A syntax diagram for **write** (applicable also for **writeln**) is

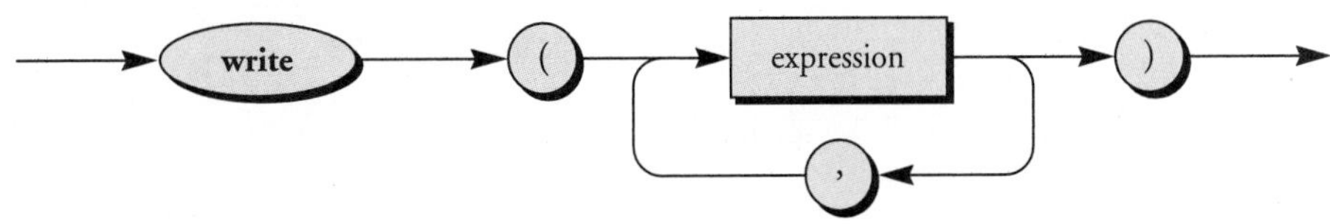

A **writeln** can also be used as a complete statement; for example,

```
writeln;
```

causes a blank line to be displayed. This technique is frequently used to produce more readable output.

The **write** statement causes subsequent output to be on the same line, whereas **writeln** causes the subsequent output to be on the next line. This is because **writeln** is actually a **write** statement followed by a line feed. When output is to a monitor, **writeln** causes the cursor to move to the next line for the next I/O operation. To illustrate,

```
write ('This is a test.');
writeln ('How many lines are printed?');
```

causes the output

```
This is a test.How many lines are printed?
```

whereas

```
writeln ('This is a test.');
writeln ('How many lines are printed?');
```

causes the output

```
This is a test.
How many lines are printed?
```

Note the following:

1. Some printers reserve the first column for carriage control. Thus, the first character in a string on the left side of a page would not be printed.
2. Some implementations use a buffer to gather output from **write** statements and then print the gathered line when a **writeln** is encountered.
3. Some implementations require a **writeln** for the last output statement. Without this **writeln,** output gathered in a buffer does not get printed.

When an output statement is executed, character strings can be printed by enclosing the string in single quotation marks within the parentheses. Numeric data can be printed by including the desired number or numbers within the parentheses. Thus

```
writeln (100)
```

produces

```
       100
```

and

```
writeln (100, 87, 95)
```

produces

```
       100       87        95
```

T

The spaces at the beginning of the lines and between the numbers are caused by a default field width. Many implementations of Pascal use a predetermined field width for output. This predetermined default width will be used unless output is controlled by the programmer. Methods for controlling field width of output are examined shortly.

Example 2.1

Let's write a complete Pascal program to print the address

1403 South Drive
Apartment 3B
Pittsburgh, PA 15238

A complete program to print this is

```
PROGRAM Address (output);

BEGIN
  writeln ('1403 South Drive');
  writeln ('Apartment 3B');
  writeln ('Pittsburgh, PA', 15238)
END.
```

When this program is run on a computer that uses a default field width of 10 positions, we get

T

```
1403 South Drive
Apartment 3B
Pittsburgh, PA     15238
```

Communication and Style Tips

Using **writeln** at the beginning and end of the executable section will separate desired output from other messages or directions. Thus, the previous program for printing an address could have been

```
PROGRAM Address (output);

BEGIN
  writeln;
  writeln ('1403 South Drive');
  writeln ('Apartment 3B');
  writeln ('Pittsburgh, PA', 15238);
  writeln
END.
```

Example 2.2

Now let's combine various methods of using **writeln** to write a complete Pascal program that produces the following output:

```
COMPUTER SCIENCE 150
--------------------

TEST SCORES:
       100        98        93
        89        82        76
        73        64
```

The program would be

```
PROGRAM PrintScores (output);

BEGIN
  writeln;
  writeln ('COMPUTER SCIENCE 150');
  writeln ('--------------------');
  writeln;
  writeln ('TEST SCORES:');
  writeln (100, 98, 93);
  writeln (89, 82, 76);
  writeln (73, 64);
  writeln
END.
```

When designing a program to solve a problem, you should constantly be aware of how the output should appear. The spacing of output on a line can be controlled by formatting expressions in **write** and **writeln** statements.

Formatting Integers

If the programmer does not control the output, each integer will be printed in a predetermined field width (unless the integer exceeds the field width). This default field width depends on the machine and version of Pascal being used. In this text, we assume a width of 10 spaces. Negative signs occupy one position in the field and plus signs are not printed. Spacing of output on a page will frequently be denoted by an underscore for each blank space. Some **writeln** statements and their output with a default field width of 10 follow:

Program Statement	Output
`writeln (123);`	`_______123`
`writeln (+5062);`	`______5062`
`writeln (-12);`	`_______-12`
`writeln (0);`	`_________0`

A complete Pascal program to illustrate the field width for these integers is

```
PROGRAM PrintInteger (output);

BEGIN
  writeln;
  writeln (123);
  writeln (+5062);
  writeln (-12);
  writeln (0);
  writeln
END.
```

Formatting is designating the desired field width when printing integers, reals, Boolean values, and character strings.

Controlling output is referred to as **formatting.** It is relatively easy to format output for integers. Using a **writeln** statement, the desired field width is designated by placing a colon (:) after the integer (or identifier) and then an integer specifying the field width. The integer printed will be right justified in the specified field. The general form for formatting integers is

> **write** (<integer>:<*n*>)
>
> or
>
> **writeln** (<integer>:<*n*>)

Some examples for formatting integer output are

Program Statement	Output
`writeln (123:6);`	`___123`
`writeln (15, 10:5);`	`________15___10`
`writeln (-263:7, 21:3);`	`___-263_21`
`writeln (+5062:6);`	`__5062`
`writeln (65221:3);`	`65221`

Note that in the preceding illustration, an attempt is made to specify a field width smaller than the number of digits contained in the integer. Most versions of Pascal will automatically print the entire integer; however, some versions will print only in the specified width. The following program will enable you to find out exactly what your machine will do:

```
PROGRAM FieldWidth (output);

BEGIN
  writeln;
  writeln ('This program will check field width.');
  writeln ('         1         2         3');
  writeln ('123456789012345678901234567890');
  writeln;
  writeln (123:5);
  writeln (12345:3);
  writeln (1);
  writeln (-12345:4)
END.
```

When this program is run on a VAX 8530 with a VMS operating system, the output is

```
This program will check field width.
         1         2         3
123456789012345678901234567890

  123
12345
         1
-12345
```

When this program is run on an IBM PC using Turbo Pascal, the output is

```
This program will check field width.
         1         2         3
123456789012345678901234567890

  123
12345
1
-12345
```

Formatting Reals

As with data of type **integer,** data of type **real** can be used in **writeln** statements. If no formatting is used, the output will be in floating-point form. Different machines and different versions of Pascal produce a variety of default field widths. As examples, some use a standard field width of 16 and some use a standard width of 22. Assuming a field width of 22, the program

```
PROGRAM UnformattedReals (output);

BEGIN
  writeln;
  writeln (231.45);
```

```
    writeln (0.00456);
    writeln (4.0);
    writeln (-526.1E5);
    writeln (0.91E-8);
    writeln
  END.
```

produces

```
__2.3145000000000E+002
__4.5600000000000E-003
__4.0000000000000E+000
_-5.2610000000000E+007
__9.1000000000000E-009
```

Most programs using data of type **real** require a neater method of expressing the output. This can be accomplished by formatting. To format reals you must specify both the field width and the number of decimal places to the right of the decimal. This is done by writing the real, followed by a colon (:), followed by an integer, followed by a colon and another integer. For example, if you are writing a program that prints wages of workers, you could get a field width of eight with two places to the right of the decimal as follows:

```
writeln (231.45:8:2);
```

where 231.45 is the computed wage, 8 specifies the field width, and 2 specifies how many digits appear to the right of the decimal. The output for this statement is

```
__231.45
```

The general form for formatting reals is

> **write** (<real>:<*n*1>:<*n*2>)
>
> or
>
> **writeln** (<real>:<*n*1>:<*n*2>)

Use of this formatting procedure causes the following to happen:

1. The decimal point uses one position in the specified field width.
2. Leading zeros are not printed.
3. Trailing zeros are printed to the specified number of positions to the right of the decimal.
4. Leading plus (+) signs are omitted.
5. Leading minus (–) signs are printed and use one position of the specified field.
6. Digits appearing to the right of the decimal have been rounded rather than truncated.

As with integers, if a specified field width is too small, most versions of Pascal will default to the minimum width required to present all digits to the left of the decimal as well as the specified digits to the right of the decimal. The following table illustrates how output using data of type **real** can be formatted:

Program Statement	Output
writeln (765.432:10:3)	___765.432
writeln (023.14:10:2)	_____23.14
writeln (65.50:10:2)	_____65.50
writeln (+341.2:10:2)	____341.20
writeln (-341.2:10:2)	___-341.20
writeln (16.458:10:2)	_____16.46
writeln (0.00456:10:4)	____0.0046

Reals in floating-point form can also be used in a formatted **writeln** statement. Output from the following complete program

```
PROGRAM FormatReals (output);

BEGIN
  writeln;
  writeln (1.234E2:10:2);
  writeln (-723.4E-3:10:5);
  writeln (-723.4E-3:10:3);
  writeln (6.435E2:10:2, 2.3145E2:10:2);
  writeln
END.
```

is

```
____123.40
__-0.72340
____-0.723
____643.50____231.45
```

Formatting Strings

Strings and string constants can be formatted using a single colon (:) followed by a positive integer "*n*" to specify field width. The general form for formatting strings is

> **write** ('<string>':<*n*>)
> or
> **writeln** ('<string>':<*n*>)

The string will be right justified in the field. Unlike reals, strings are truncated when necessary. The following program illustrates such formatting:

```
PROGRAM StringFormat (output);

CONST
  Indent = ' ';

BEGIN
  writeln;
```

A Note of Interest

Computer Ethics: The ACM Code of Ethics

The Association for Computing Machinery (ACM) is the flagship organization for computing professionals. The ACM supports the publication of research and new trends in computer science, sponsors conferences and professional meetings, and sets professional standards for computer scientists. Standards concerning the conduct and professional responsibility of computer scientists are published in the ACM Code of Ethics. The Code is a basis for ethical decision making and for judging complaints involving violations of professional and ethical standards.

The Code lists general moral imperatives for computer professionals:

1. Contribute to society and human well-being.
2. Avoid harm to others.
3. Be honest and trustworthy.
4. Be fair and take action not to discriminate.
5. Honor property rights, including copyrights and patents.
6. Give proper credit for intellectual property.
7. Respect the privacy of others.
8. Honor confidentiality.

The Code also lists several more specific professional responsibilities:

1. Strive to achieve the highest quality, effectiveness, and dignity in both the process and products of professional work.
2. Acquire and maintain professional competence.
3. Know and respect existing laws pertaining to professional work.
4. Accept and provide appropriate professional review.
5. Give comprehensive and thorough evaluations of computer systems and their impact, including analysis of possible risks.
6. Honor contracts, agreements, and assigned responsibilities.
7. Improve public understanding of computing and its consequences.
8. Access computing and communication resources only when authorized to do so.

In addition to these principles, the Code offers a set of guidelines to provide professionals an explanation of various issues related to the principles. The complete text of the ACM Code of Ethics is available at the ACM's World Wide Web site, http://www.acm.org.

```
    writeln (Indent:4, 'Note the strings below.');
    writeln (Indent:4, '-----------------------');
    writeln;
    writeln ('This is a sample string.':35);
    writeln ('This is a sample string.':30);
    writeln ('This is a sample string.':25);
    writeln ('This is a sample string.':20);
    writeln
  END.
```

The output from this program is

```
    Note the strings below.
    ----------------------

           This is a sample string.
      This is a sample string.
 This is a sample string.
This is a sample string.
```

Communication and Style Tips

The constant "Indent" in the last program is used to control indented output. Since Pascal does not have a tabbing or spacing command, you might want to also define something like

```
Skip = ' ';
```

in the **CONST** section. Thus, you would have

```
CONST
  Indent = ' ';
  Skip = ' ';
```

You could then use

```
Indent:n
```

for indenting and

```
Skip:n
```

for spacing on a line.

Test Programs

A **test program** is a short program written to provide an answer to a specific question.

Programmers should develop the habit of using **test programs** to improve their knowledge and programming skills. Test programs should be relatively short and written to provide an answer to a specific question. For example, **maxint** was discussed earlier in this section. It was mentioned that the value of **maxint** depended on the machine being used. You could use a test program to discover what your computer uses for **maxint.** A complete program that accomplishes this is

```
PROGRAM TextMax (output);

BEGIN
  writeln ('Maxint is ', maxint)
END.
```

Notice that a brief message, 'Maxint is', is included to explain the output. Such a message (or output label) is almost always desirable.

Test programs allow you to play with the computer. You can answer "What if" questions by adopting a "try it and see" attitude. This is an excellent way to become comfortable with your computer and the programming language you are using. For example, you might change the previous test program to

```
PROGRAM TextMax (output);

BEGIN
  writeln ('Maxint is ', maxint);
  writeln ('TooMuch is ', maxint + 1)
END.
```

Exercises 2.3

In Exercises 1–7, which are valid **integers**? Explain why the others are invalid.

*1. 521
2. −32.0
*3. 5,621
4. +00784
*5. +65
6. 6521492183
*7. −0

In Exercises 8–17, which are valid **reals**? Explain why the others are invalid.

8. 26.3
*9. +181.0
10. −.14
*11. 492.
12. +017.400
*13. 43E2
14. −0.2E−3
*15. 43,162.3E5
16. −176.52E+1
*17. 1.43000E+2

In Exercises 18–22, change the fixed-point decimals to floating-point decimals with exactly one nonzero digit to the left of the decimal.

18. 173.0
*19. 743927000000.0
20. −0.000000023
*21. +014.768
22. −5.2

In Exercises 23–27, change the floating-point decimals to fixed-point decimals.

*23. −1.0046E+3
24. 4.2E−8
*25. 9.020E10
26. −4.615230E3
*27. −8.02E−3

In Exercises 28–34, indicate the data type.

28. −720
*29. −720.0
30. 150E3
*31. 150
32. '150'
*33. '23.4E2'
34. 23.4E−2

Write and run test programs for Exercises 35 and 36.

35. Examine the output for a decimal number without field width specified; for example,

```
writeln (2.31);
```

36. Try to print a message without using quotation marks for the following character string:

```
writeln (Hello);
```

In Exercises 37 and 38, write a program that produces the indicated output.

*37.
```
Score
-----
  86
  82
  79
```
where "S" is in column 10.

38.
```
  Price
-------
$ 19.94
$100.00
$ 58.95
```
where "P" is in column 50.

39. Assume the hourly wages of five student employees are

$ 5.00
$ 5.25

$ 4.75
$ 6.00
$ 5.50

Write a program that produces the following output, where "E" of Employee is in column 20.

```
------------------------

Employee      Hourly Wage

------------------------

    1            $ 5.00

    2            $ 5.25

    3            $ 4.75

    4            $ 6.00

    5            $ 5.50

------------------------
```

40. What is the output from the following segment of code?

```
writeln ('My test average is', 87.5);
writeln ('My test average is':20, 87.5:10);
writeln ('My test average is':25, 87.5:10:2);
writeln ('My test average is':25, 87.5:6:2);
```

*41. Write a program that produces the following output. Start "Student Name" in column 20 and "Test Score" in column 40.

```
Student Name           Test Score

Adams, Mike                 73
Conley, Theresa             86
Samson, Ron                 92
O'Malley, Colleen           81
```

42. The Great Lakes Shipping Company is going to use a computer program to generate billing statements for their customers. Write a complete Pascal program that will produce the following heading.

```
                  GREAT LAKES SHIPPING COMPANY
                   SAULT STE. MARIE, MICHIGAN
  ----------------------------------------------------
     Thank you for doing business with our company.
     The information listed below was used to
     determine your total cargo fee. We hope you
     were satisfied with our service.
  ----------------------------------------------------
  CARGO       TONNAGE        RATE/TON        TOTAL DUE
```

In Exercises 43–45, what output is produced by the statements or sequence of statements when executed by the computer?

43. `writeln (1234, 1234:8, 1234:6);`

44. `writeln (12:4, -21:4, 120:4);`

45.
```
writeln ('FIGURE  AREA  PERIMETER');
writeln ('-----------------------');
writeln;
writeln ('SQUARE', 16:5, 16:12);
writeln;
writeln ('RECT ', 24:5, 20:12);
```

46. Write a complete program to produce the following table:

```
WIDTH        LENGTH        AREA
  4             2             8
 21             5           105
```

What output is produced when each segment of code shown in Exercises 47–52 is executed?

*47. `writeln (2.134:15:2);`

48. `writeln (423.73:5:2);`

*49. `writeln (-42.1:8:3);`

50. `writeln (-4.21E3:6:2);`

*51. `writeln (10.25);`

52. `writeln (1.25, 1.25:6:2, 1.25:6:1);`

*53. Write a complete program that produces the following output:

```
Hourly Wage     Hours Worked     Total
    5.00            20.0         100.00
    7.50            15.25        114.375
```

Summary

Key Terms

compound statement
constant definition section
data type
declaration section
declaration statement
effective statement
executable section
executable statement
fixed point
floating point
formatting
keywords
main block
module
module specifications
output
processing statement
program heading
programmer-supplied identifiers
pseudocode
reserved words
simple statement
software engineering
software system life cycle
standard identifiers
standard simple type
statement
stepwise refinement
string
string constant
structure chart
syntax
syntax diagrams
syntax diagramming
test program
top-down design
variable declaration section

Keywords

BEGIN
char
CONST
END
input
integer

maxint **output** **PROGRAM** **real** **VAR** **write** **writeln**

Key Concepts

- Six steps in problem solving include analyze the problem, develop an algorithm, write code for the program, run the program, test the results against answers manually computed with paper and pencil, and document the program.
- Top-down design is a process of dividing tasks into subtasks until each subtask can be readily accomplished.
- Stepwise refinement refers to refinements of tasks into subtasks.
- A structure chart is a graphic representation of the relationship between modules.
- Software engineering is the process of developing and maintaining large software systems.
- The software system life cycle consists of the following phases: analysis, design, coding, testing/verification, maintenance, and obsolescence.
- Valid identifiers must begin with a letter and can contain only letters and digits.
- The three components of a Pascal program are program heading, declaration section, and executable section.
- Statements are the basic units of expression.
- The two basic kinds of statements are declaration and executable (processing) statements.
- Semicolons are used to separate statements.
- Extra spaces and blank lines are ignored in Pascal.
- Output is generated by using **write** or **writeln.**
- Strings are formatted using a single colon followed by a positive integer that specifies the total field width; for example,

```
writeln ('This is a string':30);
```

- The following table summarizes the use of the data types **integer, real,** and **char.**

Data Type	Permissible Data	Formatting
integer	numeric	one colon; for example, `writeln (25:6);`
real	numeric	two colons; for example, `writeln (123.45:8:2);`
char	character	one colon; for example, `writeln ('A':6);`

Chapter Review Exercises

1. List the six steps in developing a program.

For Exercises 2–6, write pseudocode showing the tasks needed for solving each problem.

2. Determine the weekly salary of a worker.
3. Find the batting average of a baseball player.
4. Find the slope of a line. (Remember that the slopes can be undefined.)
5. Determine the letter grade earned on a test.
6. Find the smallest number from a set of 50 numbers.

For Exercises 7–12, state whether or not the identifiers are valid. If not, explain why.

7. C
8. Chapter2
9. For
10. Alpha
11. 6weeks
12. Here-and-there

For Exercises 13–16, explain why the program headings are invalid.

13. `PROGRAM Test.`
14. `PROGRAM (input, output):`
15. `PROGRAM 1test (input, output);`
16. `PROGRAM-One (output);`

For Exercises 17–20, write constant definition statements for the information requested.

17. Your city
18. The year
19. Your school name
20. Your grade number

Programming Problems

Write and run a short program for each of the following:

1. A program to print your initials in block letters. Your output could look like

```
 JJJJJ          A           CC
   J           A A         C  C
   J          A   A       C
   J          AAAAA       C
J  J          A   A        C  C
 JJ           A   A         CC
```

2. Design a simple picture and print it using **writeln** statements. If you plan the picture using a sheet of graph paper, keeping track of spacing will be easier.
3. A program to print out your mailing address.
4. Our Lady of Mercy Hospital prints billing statements for patients when they are ready to leave the hospital. Write a program that displays a heading for each statement as follows:

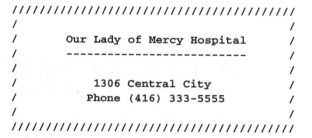

```
/////////////////////////////////////////
/                                       /
/        Our Lady of Mercy Hospital     /
/        --------------------------     /
/                                       /
/            1306 Central City          /
/          Phone (416) 333-5555         /
/                                       /
/////////////////////////////////////////
```

5. Your computer science instructor wants course and program information included as part of every assignment. Write a program that can be used to display this information. Sample output is

```
*************************************
*                                   *
*   Author:          Mary Smith     *
*   Course:          CPS-150        *
*   Assignment:      Program #3     *
*   Due Date:        September 18   *
*   Instructor:      Mr. Samson     *
*                                   *
*************************************
```

6. As part of a programming project that will compute and print grades for each student in your class, you have been asked to write a program that produces aheading for each student report. The columns in which the various headings should be are

- The border for the class name starts in column 30.
- Student Name starts in column 22.
- Test Average starts in column 42.
- Grade starts in column 57.

Write a program to print the heading as follows:

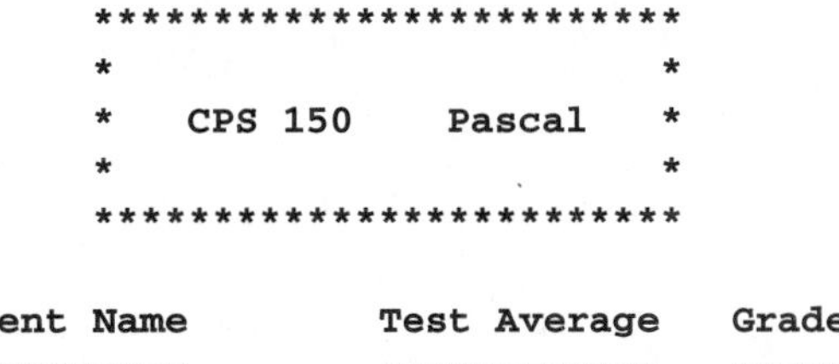

```
        ************************
        *                      *
        *   CPS 150    Pascal  *
        *                      *
        ************************

Student Name        Test Average   Grade
------------        ------------   -----
```

Communication in Practice

1. Exchange complete programs with a classmate and critique the use of descriptive identifiers. Offer positive suggestions as to what would help others read and understand the program.
2. Discuss the issue of using descriptive identifiers with each of the following:
   a. Another student in your class
   b. A college student in computer science
   c. A computer science instructor (not your own)
   d. A professional programmer

   Prepare a written report of your conversations with these people, and present the results to your class.
3. Obtain a copy of the complete ACM Code of Ethics (see the **Note of Interest** in this chapter entitled "Computer Ethics: The ACM Code of Ethics"). Read the guideline pertaining to the principle "Respect the privacy of others," and prepare a written report on this topic to present to your class.

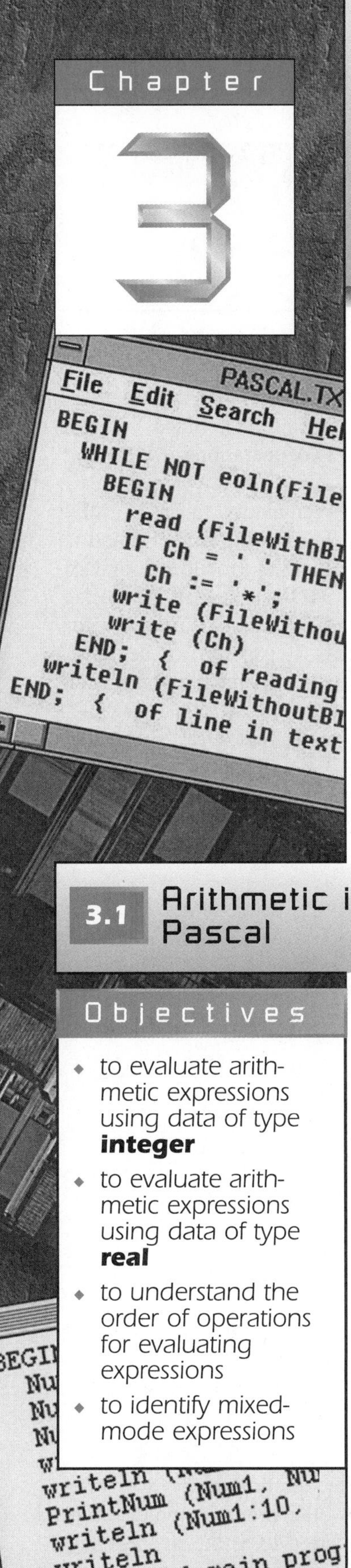
PASCAL.TX
File Edit Search Hel
BEGIN
WHILE NOT eoln(File
BEGIN
read (FileWithBl
IF Ch = ' ' THEN
Ch := '*';
write (FileWithou
write (Ch)
END; { of reading
writeln (FileWithoutBl
END; { of line in text
writeln
PrintNum (Num1, Nu
writeln (Num1:10,
writeln
END. { of main prog
line 10

Chapter 3

Arithmetic, Variables, Input, Constants, and Standard Functions

Chapter Outline

In this chapter we discuss arithmetic operations, using data in a program, obtaining input, and using constants and variables. We also discuss the use of functions to perform standard operations such as finding the square root or absolute value of a number.

3.1 Arithmetic in Pascal

Objectives

- to evaluate arithmetic expressions using data of type **integer**
- to evaluate arithmetic expressions using data of type **real**
- to understand the order of operations for evaluating expressions
- to identify mixed-mode expressions

Expressions

An **expression** in Pascal occurs when two or more values are combined to produce a single value. Expressions can include constants, variables, and functions, and can be as elaborate as you choose to make them. Each of the following is an example of an expression:

```
2 + 3
TotalPoints / 5
sqrt(B * B - 4 * A * C)
```

Expressions can be used to form program statements. For example,

```
Sum := 2 + 3
Average := TotalPoints / 5
Discriminant := sqrt(B * B - 4 * A * C)
```

are three executable statements that contain arithmetic expressions. In this chapter, we examine expressions to see how they can be used in statements.

Basic Operations for Integers

Integer arithmetic in Pascal allows the operations of addition, subtraction, and multiplication to be performed. The notation for these operations is as follows:

Objectives

(continued)

- to distinguish between valid and invalid mixed-mode expressions
- to evaluate mixed-mode expressions

Symbol	Operation	Example	Value
+	Addition	`3 + 5`	8
−	Subtraction	`43 - 25`	18
*	Multiplication	`4 * 7`	28

Noticeably absent from this list is a division operation. This is because **integer arithmetic operations** are expected to produce integer answers. Since division problems might not produce integers, Pascal provides two operations, **MOD** and **DIV,** to produce integer answers.

An **expression** is the combination of two or more values to produce a single value.

Integer arithmetic operations are those operations allowed on data of type **integer.** This includes the operations of addition, subtraction, multiplication, **MOD,** and **DIV** to produce integer answers.

In a standard division problem, there is a quotient and remainder. In Pascal, **DIV** produces the quotient and **MOD** produces the remainder when the first operand is positive. For example, in the problem 17 divided by 3, 17 **DIV** 3 produces 5, and 17 **MOD** 3 produces 2. Avoid using **DIV** 0 (zero) and **MOD** 0 (zero). A precise description of how **MOD** works is given in the *Second Draft ANSI Standard for Pascal* as "A term of the form i mod j shall be an error if j is zero or negative, otherwise the value of i mod j shall be that value of $(i - (k * j))$ for integral k such that $0 \leq i \bmod j < j$."

Several integer expressions and their values are shown in Table 3.1. Notice that when 3 is multiplied by −2, the expression is written as 3 ∗ (−2) rather than 3 ∗ −2. This is because consecutive operators cannot appear in an arithmetic expression. However, this expression could be written as −2 ∗ 3.

Table 3.1

Values of integer expressions

Expression	Value
`-3 + 2`	−1
`2 - 3`	−1
`-3 * 2`	−6
`3 * (-2)`	−6
`-3 * (-2)`	6
`17 DIV 3`	5
`17 MOD 3`	2
`17 DIV (-3)`	−5
`-17 DIV 3`	−5
`-17 MOD 3`	−2
`-17 DIV (-3)`	5

Order of Operations for Integers

The **precedence rule** is the order of priority in which numeric operations are performed.

Expressions involving more than one operation are frequently used when writing programs. When this happens, it is important to know the order in which these operations are performed. The order of operations is referred to as the **precedence rule.** These are the priorities for the precedence rule:

1. All expressions within a set of parentheses are evaluated first. If there are parentheses within parentheses (the parentheses are nested), the innermost expressions are evaluated first.
2. The operations $*$, **MOD,** and **DIV** are evaluated next in order from left to right.
3. The operations + and – are evaluated last from left to right.

These are similar to algebraic operations; they are summarized in Table 3.2. To illustrate how expressions are evaluated, consider the values of the expressions listed in Table 3.3.

Table 3.2

Integer arithmetic priority

Expression or Operation	Priority
`(    )`	1. Evaluate from inside out
`*, MOD, DIV`	2. Evaluate from left to right
`+, -`	3. Evaluate from left to right

Table 3.3

Evaluating integer expressions

Expression	Value
`3 - 4 * 5`	−17
`3 - (4 * 5)`	−17
`(3 - 4) * 5`	−5
`3 * 4 - 5`	7
`3 * (4 - 5)`	−3
`17 - 10 - 3`	4
`17 - (10 - 3)`	10
`(17 - 10) - 3`	4
`-42 + 50 MOD 17`	−26

As expressions get more elaborate, it is helpful to list partial evaluations in a manner similar to the order in which the computer performs the evaluations. For example, suppose the expression

```
(3 - 4) + 18 DIV 5 + 2
```

is to be evaluated. If we consider the order in which subexpressions are evaluated, we get

```
(3 - 4) + 18 DIV 5 + 2
   ↓
  -1    + 18 DIV 5 + 2
               ↓
  -1    +     3    + 2
        ↓
        2          + 2
              ↓
              4
```

Using MOD and DIV

MOD and **DIV** can be used when it is necessary to perform conversions within arithmetic operations. For example, consider the problem of adding two weights given in units of pounds and ounces. This problem can be solved by converting both weights to ounces, adding the ounces, and then converting the total ounces to pounds and ounces. The conversion from ounces to pounds can be accomplished by using **MOD** and **DIV.** If the total number of ounces is 243, then

```
243 DIV 16
```

yields the number of pounds (15), and

```
243 MOD 16
```

yields the number of ounces (3).

Representation of Integers

Binary notation is a method of representing integers using only 0's and 1's.

A **word** is a unit of memory consisting of one or more bytes.

Computer representation of integers is different from what we see when we work with integers. Integers are stored and integer operations are performed in **binary notation.** Thus, the integer 19, which can be written as

$$\begin{aligned} 19 &= 16 + 0 + 0 + 2 + 1 \\ &= 1 \cdot 2^4 + 0 \cdot 2^3 + 0 \cdot 2^2 + 1 \cdot 2^1 + 1 \cdot 2^0 \end{aligned}$$

is stored as 1 0 0 1 1. This binary number is actually stored in a **word** in memory, which consists of several individual locations called bits, as mentioned in Chapter 1. The number of bits used to store an integer is machine dependent. If you use a 16-bit machine, then 19 is represented as

0	0	0	0	0	0	0	0	0	0	0	1	0	0	1	1

19

In this representation, the leftmost bit is reserved for the sign of the integer.

We can now make two observations regarding the storage and mechanics of the operation of integers. First, integer operations produce exact answers; numbers are stored exactly (up to the limits of the machine). Second, a maximum and a minimum number (**maxint** and **–maxint**–1, respectively) can be represented. In a 16-bit machine, **maxint** is

0	1	1	1	1	1	1	1	1	1	1	1	1	1	1	1

where the 0 represents a positive number. This number is

$$2^{14} + 2^{13} + 2^{12} + \cdots + 2^2 + 2^1 + 2^0$$

which equals 32,767. The lower bound for negative numbers is

1	0	0	0	0	0	0	0	0	0	0	0	0	0	0	0

Integer overflow occurs when an attempt is made within a program to use an integer outside the range (**–maxint**–1, **maxint**).

which represents $-2^{15} = -32{,}768$. This is **–maxint**–1.

T

If a program contains an integer operation that produces a number outside the range (**–maxint**–1, **maxint**), this is referred to as **integer overflow,** which means the number is too large or too small to be stored. Ideally, an error message is printed when such a situation arises. Some systems print a message such as **ARITHMETIC OVERFLOW** when this occurs; other systems merely assign a meaningless value and continue with the program. In Section 5.3, we discuss how to protect a program against this problem.

Basic Operations for Reals

Real arithmetic operations are those operations allowed on data of type **real.** This includes addition, subtraction, multiplication, and division.

The operations of addition, subtraction, and multiplication are the same for data of type **real** as for integers. Additionally, division is now permitted. Since **MOD** and **DIV** are restricted to data of type **integer,** the symbol for division of data of type **real** is "/". The **real arithmetic operations** are as follows:

Symbol	Operation	Example	Value
+	Addition	`4.2 + 19.36`	23.56
−	Subtraction	`19.36 - 4.2`	15.16
*	Multiplication	`3.1 * 2.0`	6.2
/	Division	`54.6 / 2.0`	27.3

Division is given the same priority as multiplication when arithmetic expressions are evaluated by the computer. The rules for order of operation are the same as those for evaluating integer arithmetic expressions. A summary of these operations is shown in Table 3.4.

▼ Table 3.4

Real arithmetic priority

Expression or Operation	Priority
`(   )`	1. Evaluate from inside out.
`*, /`	2. Evaluate from left to right.
`+, -`	3. Evaluate from left to right.

Here are some sample calculations using data of type **real:**

Expression	Value
`3.5 * 2.0 - 1.0`	6.0
`2.0 * (1.2 - 4.3)`	−6.2
`2.0 * 1.2 - 4.3`	−1.9
`-12.6 / 3.0 + 3.0`	−1.2
`-12.6 / (3.0 + 3.0)`	−2.1

As with integers, consecutive operation signs are not allowed. Thus, if you want to multiply 4.3 by −2.0, you can use −2.0 ∗ 4.3 or 4.3 ∗ (−2.0), but you cannot use 4.3 ∗ − 2.0. As expressions get a bit more complicated, it is again helpful to write out the expression and evaluate it step by step. For example,

```
-4.3 * (10.1 + (72.3 / 3.0 - 4.5)) + 18.2
                      ↓
-4.3 * (10.1 +   (24.1    - 4.5)) + 18.2
                            ↓
-4.3 * (10.1 +          19.6)     + 18.2
                 ↓
-4.3 *            29.7            + 18.2
         ↓
      -127.71                     + 18.2
                          ↓
                       -109.51
```

Representation of Reals

As with integers, real numbers are stored and operations are performed using binary digits. Unlike integers, however, the storage and representation of real numbers frequently produce answers that are not exact. For example, an operation such as

```
1 / 3
```

produces the repeating decimal 0.3333. . . . At some point, this decimal must be truncated or rounded so that it can be stored. Such conversions produce **round-off errors.**

A **round-off error** occurs when a decimal is either truncated or rounded off.

Now let's consider some errors that occur when working with real numbers. A value very close to zero may be stored as zero. Thus, you may think you are working with

$$1.23 \times 10^{-20} = 0.0000000000000000000123$$

but, in fact, this value may have been stored as 0. This condition is referred to as **underflow.** Generally, this would not be a problem because replacing numbers very close to zero with 0 does not affect the accuracy of most answers. However, sometimes this replacement can make a difference; therefore, you should be aware of the limitations of the system on which you are working.

Underflow occurs if a value is too small to be represented by a computer. The value is automatically replaced by zero.

Since operations with real numbers are not stored exactly, errors referred to as **representational errors** can be introduced. To illustrate, suppose we are using a machine that only yields three digits of accuracy (most machines exhibit much greater accuracy) and we want to add the three numbers 45.6, −45.5, and .215. The order in which we add these numbers makes a difference in the result we obtain. For example, −45.5 + 45.6 yields .1. Then, .1 + .215 yields .315. Thus, we have

Representational errors are caused by rounding and subsequent grouping of operands in arithmetic operations.

$$(-45.5 + 45.6) + .215 = .315$$

However, if we consider 45.6 + .215 first, then the arithmetic result is 45.815. Since our hypothetical computer only yields three digits of accuracy, this result will be stored as 45.8. Then, −45.5 + 45.8 yields .3. Thus, we have

$$-45.5 + (45.6 + .215) = .3$$

This illustration produces a representational error.

Another form of representational error occurs when numbers of substantially different size are used in an operation. For example, consider the problem

2 + 0.0005

We would expect this total to be 2.0005, but stored to only three digits of accuracy, the result would be 2.00. In effect, the smaller of two numbers of substantially different size is canceled. Thus, this form of representational error is referred to as a **cancellation error.**

A **cancellation error** occurs when numbers of significantly different size are added or subtracted.

Although representational and cancellation errors cannot be avoided, their effects can be minimized. Operations should be grouped in such a way that numbers of approximately the same magnitude are used together before their resultant operand is used with another number. For example, all very small numbers should be summed before adding them to larger numbers.

One problem associated with how real numbers are stored and manipulated is that they should not be tested for equality. We will soon see how numbers can be compared and used to terminate certain conditions. In general, you should avoid using reals when strict checking for equality is required.

Real overflow occurs when an attempt is made to store very large real numbers.

Attempting to store very large real numbers can result in **real overflow.** In principle, real numbers are stored with locations reserved for the exponents. An oversimplified illustration using base 10 digits is

	1	2	3	+	0	8

for the number 123×10^8. Different computers place different limits on the size of the exponent that can be stored. An attempt to use numbers outside the defined range causes overflow in much the same way that integer overflow occurs. When real overflow occurs, some machines halt execution and print an error message, such as `FLOATING POINT OVERFLOW.` Others assign a meaningless value and continue operations.

T

Mixed Expressions

Mixed-mode expressions are those containing data of both **integer** and **real** types; the value will be given as a real and not as an integer.

Arithmetic expressions that use data of two or more types are called **mixed-mode expressions.** When a mixed-mode expression involving both **integer** and **real** data types is evaluated, the result will be of type **real.** A **real** also results if division (/) is used with integers. When formatting the output of mixed expressions, always format for reals. (*Note:* Avoid using **MOD** and **DIV** with mixed-mode expressions.)

Exercises 3.1

In Exercises 1–10, find the value of each expression.

*1. `17 - 3 * 2`
2. `-15 * 3 + 4`
*3. `123 MOD 5`
4. `123 DIV 5`
*5. `5 * 123 DIV 5 + 123 MOD 5`
6. `-21 * 3 * (-1)`
*7. `14 * (3 + 18 DIV 4) - 50`
8. `100 - (4 * (3 + 2)) * (-2)`
*9. `-56 MOD 3`
10. `14 * 8 MOD 5 - 23 DIV (-4)`

In Exercises 11–17, find the value of each expression.

*11. `3.21 + 5.02 - 6.1`
12. `6.0 / 2.0 * 3.0`
*13. `6.0 / (2.0 + 3.0)`
14. `-20.5 * (2.1 + 2.0)`
*15. `-2.0 * ((56.8 / 4.0 + 0.8) + 5.0)`
16. `1.04E2 * 0.02E3`
*17. `800.0E-2 / 4.0 + 15.3`

In Exercises 18–27, which are valid expressions? For those that are, indicate whether they are of type **integer** or **real.** Evaluate each of the valid expressions.

18. `18 - (5 * 2)`
*19. `(18 - 5) * 2`
20. `18 - 5 * 2.0`
*21. `25 * (14 MOD 7.0)`
22. `1.4E3 * 5`
*23. `28 / 7`
24. `28.0 / 4`
*25. `-5.21 + 16`
26. `24 DIV 6 / 3`
*27. `24 DIV (6 / 3)`
28. What output is produced by the following program?

```
PROGRAM MixedMode (output);

BEGIN
  writeln;
  writeln ('   Expression    Value');
  writeln ('   ----------    -----');
  writeln;
  writeln ('   10 / 5', 10 / 5:13:3);
  writeln ('   2.0+7*(-1)', 2.0 + 7 * (-1));
  writeln
END.
```

In Exercises 29–34, indicate which are executable Pascal statements. Explain why the others are not executable.

*29. `writeln (-20 DIV 4.0:8:3);`
30. `writeln (-20 DIV 4:8:3);`
*31. `writeln (-20 DIV 4:8);`
32. `writeln (8 - 3.0 * 5:6);`
*33. `writeln (7 * 6 DIV 3 / 2:6:2);`
34. `writeln (-17.1 + 5 * 20.0:8:3);`
35. Find out how your system handles integer overflow by running the following program:

```
PROGRAM IntegerOverflow (output);
BEGIN
  writeln;
  writeln ('Maxint is ', maxint);
  writeln ('Maxint + 1 is ', maxint + 1);
  writeln ('-Maxint - 2 is ', -maxint - 2)
END.
```

3.2 Using Variables

Objectives

- to understand utilization of storage area
- to distinguish between the name of a memory location and the value in a memory location
- to be able to use variables in assignment statements, expressions, and output statements

Memory Locations

It is frequently necessary to store values for later use. This is done by putting the value into a **memory location** by using a symbolic name to refer to this location. If

A **memory location** is a storage cell that can be accessed by address.

A **variable** is a memory location, referenced by an identifier, whose value can be changed during a program.

A **constant** is a memory location whose contents cannot be changed.

the contents of the location are to be changed during a program, the symbolic name is referred to as a **variable;** if the contents are not to be changed, it is referred to as a **constant.**

A graphic way to think about memory locations is to envision them as boxes; each box is named and a value is stored inside. For example, suppose a program is written to add a sequence of numbers. If we name the memory location to be used Sum, initially we have

Sum

which depicts a memory location that has been reserved and can be accessed by a reference to Sum. If we then add the integers 10, 20, and 30 and store them in Sum, we have

60
Sum

It is important to distinguish between the name of a memory location (Sum) and the value or contents of a memory location (60). The name does not change during a program, but the contents can be changed as often as necessary. (Note that contents of memory locations that are referred to by constants cannot be changed.) If 30 were added to the contents in the previous example, the new value stored in Sum could be depicted as

90
Sum

Symbolic names representing memory locations containing values that will be changing must be declared in the **VAR** section of the program (as indicated in Section 2.2); for example,

```
VAR
  Sum : integer;
```

Those that represent memory locations whose values will not be changing must be declared in the **CONST** section.

Assignment Statements

An **assignment statement** is a method of putting values into memory locations.

Now let's examine how the contents of variables are manipulated. A value may be put into a memory location with an **assignment statement** in the form of

<variable name> := <value>

or

<variable name> := <expression>

where "variable name" is the name of the memory location. For example, if Sum were initially zero, then

```
Sum := 30;
```

changes

0	to	30
Sum		Sum

The syntax diagram for this is

Some important rules concerning assignment statements follow:

1. The assignment is always made from right to left (←).
2. The syntax for assigning requires a colon followed immediately by an equal sign (:=).
3. Only one variable can be on the left side of the assignment symbol.
4. Constants cannot be on the left side of the assignment symbol.
5. The expression may be a constant, a constant expression, a variable, or a combination of variables and constants.
6. Values on the right side of the assignment symbol are not changed by the assignment.
7. The variable and expression must match in data type. An exception is that an integer expression can be assigned to a real variable, in which case the result of the expression evaluation gets converted to a real value.

Two common errors that beginners make are (1) trying to assign from left to right and (2) forgetting the colon when using an assignment statement.

Repeated assignments can be made. For example, if Sum is an integer variable, the statements

```
Sum := 50;
Sum := 70;
Sum := 100;
```

produce first 50, then 70, and finally 100, as shown.

~~50~~ ~~70~~ 100
Sum

In this sense, memory is destructive in that it retains only the last value assigned.

Pascal variables are symbolic addresses that can hold values. When a variable is declared, the type of values it can store must be specified (declared). Storing a value of the wrong type in a variable leads to a program error. This means that data types must match when using assignment statements: reals must be assigned to **real** variables, integers to **integer** variables, and characters to **char** variables. The only exception is that an integer can be assigned to a **real** variable; however, the integer is then converted to a real. If, for example, Average is a **real** variable and the assignment statement

```
Average := 21;
```

is made, the value is stored as the real 21.0.

The assignment of a constant to a character variable requires that the constant be enclosed in single quotation marks. For example, if Letter is of type **char** and you want to store the letter C in Letter, use the assignment statement

```
Letter := 'C';
```

This could be pictured as

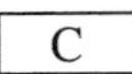
Letter

Only one character can be assigned or stored in a character variable.

To illustrate working with assignment statements, assume that the variable declaration portion of the program is

```
VAR
  Sum : integer;
  Average : real;
  Letter : char;
```

Examples of valid and invalid assignment statements using the variable declarations just declared are shown in Table 3.5.

Table 3.5

Assignment statements

Statement	Valid	If Invalid, Reason
`Sum := 50;`	Yes	
`Sum := 10.5;`	No	Data types do not match
`Average := 15.6;`	Yes	
`Average := 33;`	Yes	
`Letter := 'A';`	Yes	
`Letter := 'HI';`	No	Not a single character
`Letter := 20;`	No	Data types do not match
`Letter := 'Z';`	Yes	
`Letter := A;`	?	Valid if A is a variable or constant of type **char**
`Sum := 7;`	Yes	
`Letter := '7';`	Yes	
`Letter := 7;`	No	Data types do not match
`Sum := '7';`	No	Data types do not match

Using Expressions

The actual use of variables in a program is usually more elaborate than what we have just seen. Variables may be used in any manner that does not violate their type declarations. This includes both arithmetic operations and assignment statements. For example, if Score1, Score2, Score3, and Average are **real** variables,

```
Score1 := 72.3;
Score2 := 89.4;
Score3 := 95.6;
Average := (Score1 + Score2 + Score3) / 3.0;
```

is a valid fragment of code.

Now let's consider the problem of accumulating a total. Assuming NewScore and Total are integer variables, the following code is valid:

```
Total := 0;
NewScore := 5;
Total := Total + NewScore;
NewScore := 7;
Total := Total + NewScore;
```

As this code is executed, the values of memory locations for Total and NewScore could be depicted as

	Total	NewScore
`Total := 0;`	0	
`NewScore := 5;`	0	5
`Total := Total + NewScore;`	5	5
`NewScore := 7;`	5	7
`Total := Total + NewScore;`	12	7

Output

Variables and variable expressions can be used when creating output. When used in a **writeln** statement, they perform the same function as a constant. For example, if the assignment statement

```
Age := 5;
```

has been made, these two statements,

```
writeln (5);
writeln (Age);
```

produce the same output. If Age1, Age2, Age3, and Sum are integer variables and the assignments

```
Age1 := 21;
Age2 := 30;
Age3 := 12;
Sum := Age1 + Age2 + Age3;
```

are made, then

```
writeln ('The sum is ', 21 + 30 + 12);
writeln ('The sum is ', Age1 + Age2 + Age3);
writeln ('The sum is ', Sum);
```

all produce the same output.

A Note of Interest

Ethics and Computer Science

Ethical issues in computer science are rapidly gaining public attention. As evidence, consider the following article from the Washington Post.

> Should law-enforcement agencies be allowed to use computers to help them determine whether a person ought to be jailed or allowed out on bond? Should the military let computers decide when and on whom nuclear weapons should be used?
>
> While theft and computer viruses have not gone away as industry problems, a group of 30 computer engineers and ethicists who gathered in Washington recently agreed that questions about the proper use of computers is taking center stage. At issue is to what degree computers should be allowed to make significant decisions that human beings normally make.
>
> Already, judges are consulting computers, which have been programmed to predict how certain personality types will behave. Judges are basing their decisions more on what the computer tells them than on their own analysis of the arrested person's history. Computers are helping doctors decide treatments for patients. They played a major role in the July 1988 shooting of the Iranian jetliner by the USS Vincennes, and they are the backbone of this country's Strategic Defense Initiative ("Star Wars").
>
> Representatives from universities, IBM Corp., the Brookings Institution, and several Washington theological seminaries [recently discussed] what they could do to build a conscience in the computer field.
>
> The computer industry has been marked by "creativity and drive for improvement and advancement," not by ethical concerns, said Robert Melford, chairman of the computing-ethics subcommittee of the Institute of Electrical and Electronics Engineers.
>
> Computer professionals, Melford said, often spend much of their time in solitude, separated from the people affected by their programs who could provide valuable feedback.
>
> Unlike hospitals, computer companies and most organized computer users have no staff ethicists or ethics committees to ponder the consequences of what they do. Few businesses have written policies about the proper way to govern computers. But there is evidence that technical schools, at least, are beginning to work an ethical component into their curricula. For example, in recent years, all computer engineering majors at Polytechnic University in Brooklyn have been required to take a course in ethics. The Massachusetts Institute of Technology is considering mandating five years of study instead of the current four to include work in ethics.
>
> Affirmation that such questions should be addressed by computer scientists is contained in the 1991 curriculum guidelines of the Association for Computing Machinery, Inc. These guidelines state that Undergraduates should also develop an understanding of the historical, social, and ethical context of the discipline and the profession.

You will see further **Notes of Interest** on this area of critical concern later in this book.

Formatting variables and variable expressions in **writeln** statements follows the same rules that were presented in Chapter 2 for formatting constants. The statements needed to write the sum of the problem we just saw in a field width of four are

```
writeln ('The sum is ', (21 + 30 + 12):4);
writeln ('The sum is ', (Age1 + Age2 + Age3):4);
writeln ('The sum is ', Sum:4);
```

The next two examples illustrate the use of variables, assignment statements, and formatting.

Example 3.1

Suppose you want a program to print data about the cost of three pairs of pants and the average price of the pants. The variable declaration section might include:

```
VAR
  JeansPrice, CordsPrice,
  SlacksPrice,
  Total, Average : real;
```

A portion of the program can be

```
JeansPrice := 27.95;
CordsPrice := 25.95;
SlacksPrice := 30.95;
Total := JeansPrice + CordsPrice + SlacksPrice;
Average := Total / 3;
```

The output can be created by

```
writeln;
writeln ('Pants          Price');
writeln ('-----          -----');
writeln;
writeln ('Jeans', JeansPrice:13:2);
writeln ('Cords', CordsPrice:13:2);
writeln ('Slacks', SlacksPrice:12:2);
writeln;
writeln ('Total', Total:13:2);
writeln;
writeln ('The average price is', Average:8:2);
```

and the output is

```
Pants          Price
-----          -----

Jeans          27.95
Cords          25.95
Slacks         30.95

Total          84.85

The average price is   28.28
```

Example 3.2

Now let's see how we can use a variable of type **integer** to examine the problem of integer overflow. If we try to store an integer larger than **maxint** in a variable of type **integer,** we cause integer overflow. A test program to see what occurs is

```
PROGRAM IntOverFlow;

VAR
  Num : integer;
```

```
BEGIN
  Num := maxint + 1;
  writeln (Num)
END.
```

When this program is typed exactly as it appears here and then compiled, an error message such as

```
Error 76: Constant out of range.
```

may be given.

Software Engineering Implications

Self-documenting code is code written with descriptive identifiers so that the purpose of the code is evident to those other than the original programmer.

The communication aspect of software engineering can be simplified by judicious choices of meaningful identifiers. Systems programmers must be aware that others will need to read and analyze the code over time. Some extra time spent thinking about and using descriptive identifiers provides great time savings during the testing and maintenance phases. Using descriptive identifiers is part of the process referred to as writing **self-documenting code,** which is discussed in Chapter 4.

Exercises 3.2

For Exercises 1–8, assume the variable declaration section of a program is

```
VAR
  Age, IQ : integer;
  Income : real;
```

Indicate which are valid assignment statements. For those that are invalid, give the reason.

*1. `Age := 18;`

2. `IQ := Age + 100;`

*3. `IQ := 120.5;`

4. `Age + IQ := 150;`

*5. `Income := 22000;`

6. `Income := 100 * (Age + IQ);`

*7. `Age := IQ / 3;`

8. `IQ := 3 * Age;`

9. Write and run a test program to illustrate what happens when values of one data type are assigned to variables of another type.

For Exercises 10–13, suppose A, B, and Temp are declared as **integer** variables. Indicate the contents of A and B at the end of each sequence of statements.

10.
```
A := 5;
B := -2;
A := A + B;
B := B - A;
```

*11.
```
A := 31;
B := 26;
Temp := A;
A := B;
B := Temp;
```

12.
```
A := 0;
B := 7;
A := A + B MOD 2 * (-3);
B := B + 4 * A;
```

*13.
```
A := -8;
B := 3;
Temp := A + B;
A := 3 * B;
B := A;
Temp := Temp + A + B;
```

14. Suppose X and Y are real variables and the assignments

```
X := 121.3;
Y := 98.6;
```

have been made. What **writeln** statements would cause the following output?

a. `The value of X is  121.3`

b. `The sum of X and Y is  219.9`

c.
```
X =      121.3
Y =       98.6
         -----
Total =  219.9
```

For Exercises 15–18, write a single assignment statement for each formula.

*15. $d = rt$

16. $I = prt$

*17. $S = n(n - 1) / 2$

18. $C = 5 / 9 (F - 32)$

For Exercises 19–22, if A and B are integer variables with values of 3 and 5, respectively, what are the values of the following expressions?

*19. `A DIV B + A MOD B`

20. `B - A * A + B`

*21. `B + A * B DIV 3 - A MOD 3`

22. `A + (A - B) / B + 4`

*23. Assume the variable declaration section of a program is

```
VAR
  Age, Height : integer;
  Weight : real;
  Gender : char;
```

What output is created by the following program fragment?

```
Age := 18;
Height := 73;
Weight := 186.5;
Gender := 'M';
writeln ('Gender', Gender:13);
writeln ('Age', Age:14);
writeln ('Height', Height:11, ' inches');
writeln ('Weight', Weight:14:1, ' lbs');
```

24. Write a complete program that allows you to add five integers and then print

a. the integers.

b. their sum.

c. their average.

*25. Assume Ch and Age have been appropriately declared. What output is produced by the following program fragment?

```
Ch := 'M';
Age := 21;
writeln ('********************************':40);
writeln ('*':11, '*':29);
write ('*':11, 'Name':7, 'Age':9);
writeln ('Gender':9, '*':4);
writeln ('*':11, '----':7, '---':9, '------':9, '*':4);
writeln;
write ('*':11, 'Jones':8, Age:8, Ch:9, '*':4);
writeln;
```

```
writeln ('*':11, '*':29);
writeln ('******************************':40);
```

For Exercises 26 and 27, assume the variable declaration section of a program is

```
VAR
  Weight1, Weight2 : integer;
  AverageWeight : real;
```

and the following assignment statements are made:

```
Weight1 := 165;
Weight2 := 174;
AverageWeight := (Weight1 + Weight2) / 2;
```

26. What output is produced by the following section of code?

```
writeln ('Weight');
writeln ('------');
writeln;
writeln (Weight1);
writeln (Weight2);
writeln;
writeln ('The average weight is', (Weight1 + Weight2) / 2);
```

27. Write a segment of code to produce the following output without using any calculations in the **writeln** statements.

```
             Weight
             ------

                165
                174
                ---
Total           339

The average weight is 169.5 pounds.
```

28. Modify Example 3.2 as follows:

```
PROGRAM IntOverFlow;

VAR
  Num : integer;

BEGIN
  Num := maxint;
  writeln (Num);
  writeln (Num + 1)
END.
```

Run this program, and discuss the results.

29. Assume the variable declaration section of a program is

```
VAR
  Letter : char;
```

and the following assignment is made:

```
Letter := 'A';
```

What output is produced from the following segment of code?

```
writeln ('This reviews string formatting.':40);
writeln ('When a letter', Letter, 'is used,');
writeln ('Oops!':14, 'I forgot to format.':20);
writeln ('When a letter':22, Letter:2, 'is used,':9);
writeln ('it is a string of length one.':38);
```

3.3 Input

Objectives

- to be able to use **read** and **readln** to get data for a program
- to understand the difference between interactive input and batch input
- to understand the concept of end-of-line markers
- to understand the concept of end-of-file markers

Input is data obtained by a program during its execution.

An **input statement** is an executable statement used to obtain input for a program.

Earlier, "running a program" was subdivided into the three general categories of getting the data, manipulating it appropriately, and displaying the results. Our work thus far has centered on creating output and manipulating data. We are now going to focus on how to get data for a program.

Input Statements

Data for a program are usually obtained from an input device, which can be a keyboard, terminal, card reader, disk, or tape. When such data **(input)** are obtained, the standard file **input** must be included in the file list of the program heading. (Some interactive systems use a different method. Check with your teacher.) Your program heading will (probably) have the form

T

PROGRAM <program name> **(input, output)**

The Pascal statements used to get data are **read** and **readln.** These statements are analogous to **write** and **writeln** for output. General forms for these **input statements** are

read (<variable name>)
read (<variable 1>, <variable 2>, . . . , <variable *n*>)
readln (<variable name>)
readln (<variable 1>, <variable 2>, . . . , <variable *n*>)
readln

A simplified syntax diagram for **read** and **readln** statements is

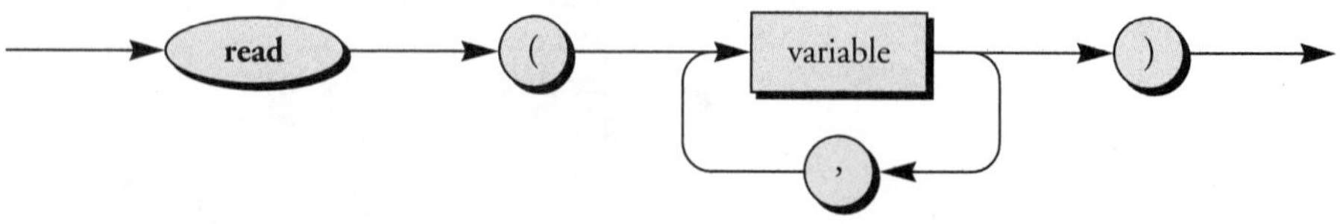

See Appendix 3 for a more detailed diagram.

When **read** or **readln** is used to get data, the value of the data item is stored in the indicated memory location. Data read into a program must match the type of variable in the variable list. To illustrate, if a variable declaration section includes

```
VAR
  Age : integer;
  Wage : real;
```

and the data items are

```
21        5.25
```

then

```
readln (Age, Wage);
```

results in

21	5.25
Age	Wage

T

An **end-of-line marker (eoln)** is a special marker inserted by the machine to indicate the end of a line in the data. In this text it is represented by a black column (█).

To illustrate the difference between **read** and **readln,** we must first learn about a line of data. Either from the terminal or from a text file, numeric data items are entered on a line, with blanks separating items. When you have finished creating a data line, you press <Enter> on the keyboard. This causes the computer to create a special symbol it recognizes as an **end-of-line marker (eoln).** If we use the symbol █ to represent this marker, two lines of integer data could be shown by

89 93 78█

95 84 100 68█

When either **read** or **readln** is first used, a data pointer (represented by a vertical arrow) is positioned at the beginning of the first (and perhaps the only) line.

89 93 78█ line 1
↑
pointer

95 84 100 68█ line 2

As data items are read using **read,** the pointer moves to the first position past the last data item read. Thus, if Score1 and Score2 are declared as integer variables, the statement

```
read (Score1, Score2);
```

results in

89 93 78█ line 1
↑

95 84 100 68█ line 2

89	93
Score1	Score2

The **readln** statement works in the same manner, with one exception. After it has read a value for each variable in its list, it causes the pointer to skip over the data items remaining on that line and go to the beginning of the next line. Thus, if the pointer is at the beginning of line 1,

```
readln (Score1, Score2);
```

results in

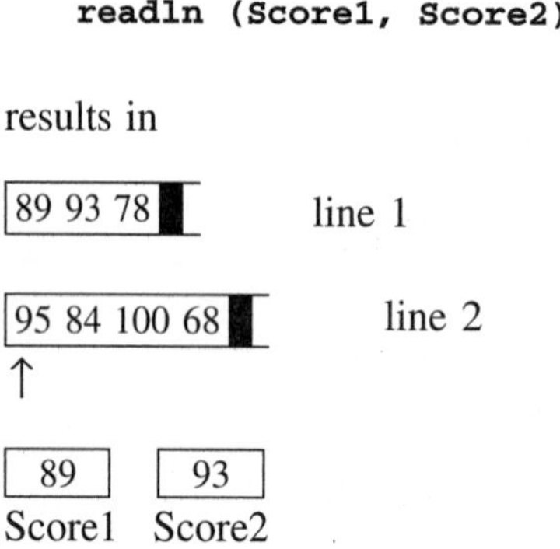

Variables in the variable list of a **read** or **readln** statement can be listed singly or in any combination that does not result in a type conflict when data are read. For example, for the data line

89 93 78
↑

```
read (Score1, Score2);
```

could be replaced by

```
read (Score1);
read (Score2);
```

Interactive Input

Interactive input is a method of getting data into a program from the keyboard. User interaction is required during execution.

If you are working on a system in which input is expected from a keyboard—called **interactive input**—**read** or **readln** causes the program to halt and wait for data items to be typed. After you enter the data and press <Enter>, an end-of-line marker is placed after the last data item entered. In this text, we use **readln** when getting input interactively. The difference between **read** and **readln** is that **readln** causes a line feed, which produces two effects. First, all remaining (unread) data items on a line are skipped. Second, output from **write** or **writeln** statements will start on the next line rather than on the same line. For example, when working interactively, consider the statements

```
read (A);
write (A);
```

and

```
readln (A);
write (A);
```

When these statements are executed and you enter the number 45 and press <Enter>, the first statements cause

```
4545
```

to appear on the screen, and the second statements cause

```
45
45
```

to appear if pressing <Enter> causes a line feed.

Consider the following program that finds the average of three integers:

```
PROGRAM ComputeAverage (input, output);

CONST
  Skip = ' ';

VAR
  Score1, Score2, Score3 : integer;
  Average : real;

BEGIN
  readln (Score1, Score2, Score3);
  Average := (Score1 + Score2 + Score3) / 3;
  writeln;
  writeln (Skip:10, 'The numbers are', Score1:4, Score2:4, Score3:4);
  writeln;
  writeln (Skip:10, 'Their average is', Average:8:2);
  writeln
END.
```

When this program is run, execution will halt at the line

```
readln (Score1, Score2, Score3);
```

A **prompt** is a marker on the terminal screen that requests input data.

and a **prompt** will appear on the screen. At this point, you must enter at least three integers and press <Enter> (or some sequence of integers and <Enter> until at least three numbers are read in as data items). The remaining part of the program will then be executed, and the output (using 20, –14, and 81 as input)

```
The numbers are  20 -14  81
Their average is   29.00
```

will be displayed.

Interactive programs should display a prompting message so the user knows what to do when a prompt appears. For example, the problem in the previous example can be modified by the lines

```
writeln ('Please enter 3 scores separated by spaces');
writeln ('and then press <Enter>.');
```

before the line

```
readln (Score1, Score2, Score3);
```

The screen will display the message

```
Please enter 3 scores separated by spaces
and then press <Enter>.
```

when the program is run.

User-friendly is a term used to describe an interactive program with clear, easy-to-follow messages for the user.

Clearly stated screen messages to the person running a program are what make a program **user-friendly.** For long messages or several lines of output, you can use **readln** as a complete statement to halt execution. When you press <Enter>, the program will continue. When **readln** is used for input, <Enter> must be pressed before program execution will continue.

Note: Some users of this textbook will be working in an interactive environment; others will not be. Consequently, both interactive and noninteractive examples are included.

Communication and Style Tips

A variable or expression may be used as a field-width specifier for formatting. When running interactive programs, this idea can be used to control desired accuracy as follows:

```
writeln ('How many places of accuracy?');
readln (Places):
   .
   .
   .
writeln ('Result is ', Result:Places+2: Places);
```

Example 3.3

Pythagorean triples are sets of three integers that satisfy the Pythagorean theorem; that is, integers *a, b,* and *c* such that $a^2 + b^2 = c^2$. The numbers 3, 4, 5 are such a triple because $3^2 + 4^2 = 5^2$. Formulas for generating Pythagorean triples are $a = m^2 - n^2$, $b = 2mn$, and $c = m^2 + n^2$, where *m* and *n* are positive integers such that $m > n$. This program allows the user to enter values for *m* and *n* and then have the Pythagorean triple printed.

```
PROGRAM PythagoreanTriple (input, output);

VAR
  M, N, A, B, C : integer;

BEGIN
  writeln ('Enter a positive integer and press <Enter>.');
  readln (N);
  writeln ('Enter a positive integer greater than ', N);
  writeln ('and press <Enter>.');
  readln (M);
  A := (M * M) - (N * N);
  B := 2 * M * N;
  C := (M * M) + (N * N);
```

```
  writeln;
  writeln ('For M = ', M, ' and N = ', N);
  writeln ('the Pythagorean triple is ', A:5, B:5, C:5)
END.
```

Sample runs of this program (using data 1,2 and 2,5) produce the following:

```
Enter a positive integer and press <Enter>.
1
Enter a positive integer greater than 1
and press <Enter>.
2

For M = 2 and N = 1
the Pythagorean triple is    3    4    5

Enter a positive integer and press <Enter>.
2
Enter a positive integer greater than 2
and press <Enter>.
5

For M = 5 and N = 2
the Pythagorean triple is   21   20   29
```

Batch Input

Batch processing is a technique of executing the program and data from a file that has been created. User interaction with the computer is not required during execution.

Batch input is input for a program being run in batch mode. Also referred to as **stream input.**

An **end-of-file marker (eof)** is a special marker inserted by the machine to indicate the end of the data file. In this text it is represented by a black box (■).

Batch processing is a technique for executing programs and data without user interaction with the computer. If you are working on a system that uses batch processing, input data will have been previously entered in a file created by you or the teacher. Input in this form is referred to as **batch input** or **stream input** and can be envisioned as lines listed consecutively and separated by end-of-line markers. For example,

| 93 84 95 ▮ 87 80 73 91 ▮ |

represents two lines of data with three integers on the first line and four integers on the second line. When data are read from such an input file, a pointer is moved as previously indicated.

One additional feature should be noted when using batch input. Since all data lines will have been previously entered, a special marker is inserted by the machine to indicate the end of the input file. This is referred to as an **end-of-file marker (eof)** and is represented in this text by the symbol ■ placed immediately after the last end-of-line marker. Thus, the previous input file would be illustrated by

| 93 84 95 ▮ 87 80 73 91 ▮ ■ |

Reading Numeric Data

Reading numeric data into a program is reasonably straightforward. At least one blank must be used to separate items on each data line. Since leading blanks are ignored, the statement

```
read (<variable name>);
```

will cause the next numeric value to be stored in the appropriate memory location. An end-of-line marker will be read as a blank, so even if the next item is on another line, it will be located and stored as desired. In each case, the pointer will be advanced as before.

Some caution should be exercised when both reals and integers are in the input file. As long as the variable data type matches the numeric data type, there will be no problem. Thus, if the variable declaration section is

```
VAR
  A : integer;
  X : real;
```

and a data line is

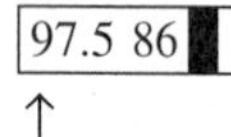
97.5 86
↑

read (X, A) causes

97.5	86
X	A

However, **read** (A, X) will result in an error because A is of type **integer** and 97 is read into A. The pointer is then positioned at the decimal:

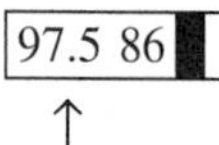
97.5 86
↑

An attempt to read a value into X may then result in a type mismatch error.

One exception to type mismatch errors is that an integer value can be read into a variable of type **real.** However, it is then stored as a real and must be used accordingly.

Character Sets

Before we look at reading character data, we need to examine the way in which character data are stored. In the **char** data type, each character in the set of allowable characters is associated with an integer. Thus, the sequence of characters is associated with a sequence of integers. The particular sequence used by a machine for this purpose is referred to as the **collating sequence** for that **character set.** The following two sequences are currently in use:

A **collating sequence** is the particular order sequence for a character set used by a machine.

A **character set** is the list of characters available for data and program statements.

1. American Standard Code for Information Interchange (ASCII)
2. Extended Binary Coded Decimal Interchange Code (EBCDIC)

Each collating sequence contains an ordering of the characters in a character set and is listed in Appendix 4. For programs in this text, we use the ASCII code. Fifty-two of the characters are letters, 10 are digits, and the rest are special characters, as shown here:

b̸ ! " # $ % & ' ( ) * + , – . / 0 1 2 3 4 5 6 7 8 9 : ; < = > ? @
A B C D E F G H I J K L M N O P Q R S T U V W X Y Z [\ ] ^ — '
a b c d e f g h i j k l m n o p q r s t u v w x y z { | } ~

Note: Of the special characters, b̸ is the symbol to denote a blank.

Reading Character Data

Reading characters is much different from reading numeric data. The following features apply to reading character data from an input file:

1. Only one character can be read at a time.
2. Each blank is a separate character.
3. Each end-of-line marker is read as a blank.
4. If the pointer is positioned at a numeric data item and you read a character variable, the digit indicated by the pointer will be read as a character.
5. After the character has been read, the pointer is advanced one position.

To illustrate the features of reading character data, we assume a variable declaration of

```
VAR
  Ch1, Ch2, Ch3 : char;
```

and a stream input of

WDN 89 ▮ MJS 94 ▮ ■

↑

Further, we assume Ch1, Ch2, and Ch3 have not been assigned values and have not had values read into them. They can be visualized as

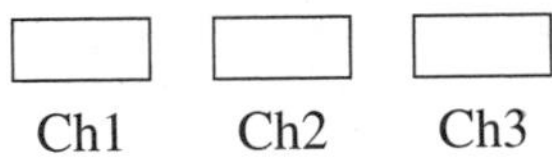

If

```
read (Ch1);
```

is executed, we have

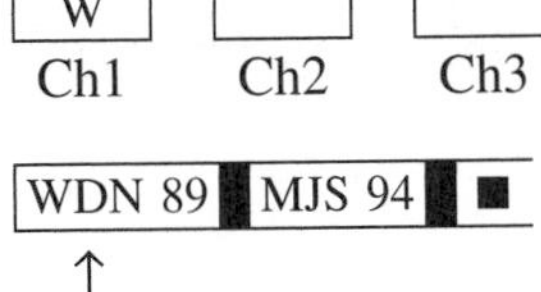

If the line of code

```
read (Ch2, Ch3);
```

is then executed, we have

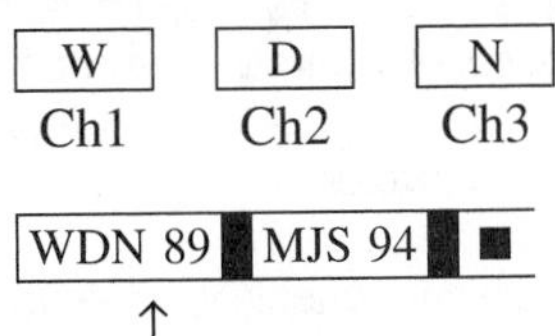

If the next **read** command in the program is

```
read (Ch1, Ch2, Ch3);
```

we obtain

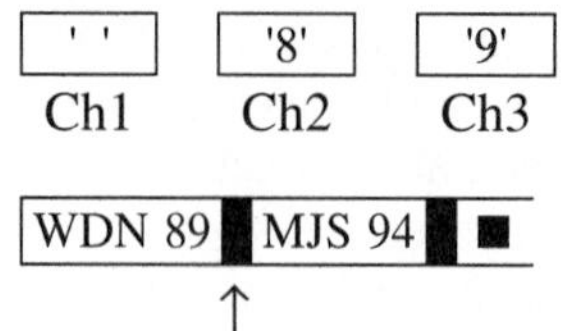

Since we are reading character variables, the blank is read as a character and the number 89 is read as two characters, '8' and '9', so we cannot perform arithmetic operations with them.

The pointer is now positioned at an end-of-line marker, and it may seem that the three characters (MJS) can now be read by

```
read (Ch1, Ch2, Ch3);
```

However, this is incorrect; the end-of-line marker is read as a blank, and we actually obtain

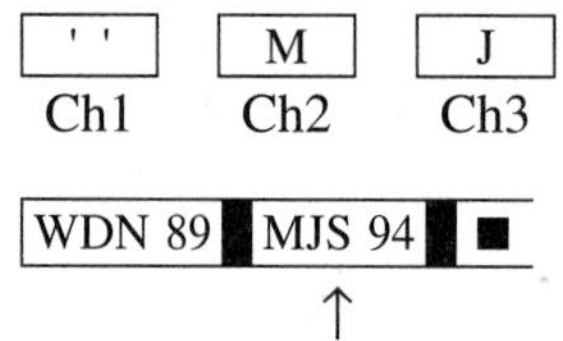

Some computers add a blank at the end of a data line in order to have an even number of character positions. Thus, you may want a data line to be

WN 89

but when you enter the line, it could be stored as

WN 89

Check with your teacher regarding this feature of your machine.

When reading data from a stream input, you eventually get the pointer positioned at the end-of-file marker. If you attempt to read more data, you may get an error message, such as

```
PROGRAM TERMINATED AT LINE 5 IN PROGRAM PRAC.
TRIED TO READ DATA641 PAST EOS/EOF.
                                    ---   PRAC   ---
              A =       UNDEF
```

When you see such a message, check your **read** statements to see if you are trying to read past the end-of-file marker.

The material in Table 3.6 indicates what happens when an attempt is made to read data into a variable location where the data type is different from the data in the file.

Table 3.6

Results of reading data of varying types

Variable Type	Attempt to Read	Result
integer	integer	Will read as expected
	real	Will read integer portion of real
	character	Error message (unless the character is a blank)
real	integer	Will read the integer and convert it to a real
	real	Will read as expected
	character	Error message (unless the character is a blank)
char	integer	Will read one position as a character and advance the pointer one position
	real	Will read one position as a character and advance the pointer one position
	character	Will read as expected

Exercises 3.3

1. Discuss the difference between using **read** and **readln** to get data for a program.
2. What is the difference between an end-of-line marker and an end-of-file marker?

For Exercises 3–13, assume a variable declaration section is

```
VAR
  Num1, Num2 : integer;
  Num3 : real;
  Ch : char;
```

and you wish to enter the data

```
15 65.3 -20
```

Explain what results from each statement. Also indicate what values are assigned to appropriate variables.

*3. `readln (Num1, Num2, Num3);`
4. `readln (Num1, Num2, Ch, Num3);`
*5. `readln (Num2, Num3, Ch, Num2);`
6. `readln (Num2, Num3, Ch, Ch, Num2);`
*7. `readln (Num3, Num2);`
8. `readln (Num1, Num3);`
*9. `readln (Num1, Ch, Num3);`
10. `read (Num1, Num3, Num2);`
*11. `read (Num1, Num3, Ch, Num2);`
12. `read (Num1, Num3, Ch, Ch, Num2);`
*13. `read (Num2, Num1, Ch, Num2);`
14. Write a program statement to be used to print a message to the screen directing the user to enter data in the form used for Exercises 3–13.

For Exercises 15–18, assume a stream input is illustrated as

18	▮	19M	▮	–14.3	▮	JO	▮	142.1F	▮	■

and the variable declaration section of the program is

```
VAR
  A, B : integer;
  X, Y : real;
  Ch : char;
```

What output is produced from each of the following segments of code? Assume the pointer is positioned at the beginning for each problem.

*15.
```
read (A);
read (B, Ch);
writeln (A:5, B:5, Ch:5);
```

16.
```
read (Ch);
write (Ch:10);
readln (Ch);
writeln (Ch);
read (Ch);
writeln (Ch:10);
```

*17.
```
read (A, B, Ch, X);
writeln (A, B, Ch, X);
writeln (A:5, B:5, Ch:5, X:10:2);
read (Ch);
writeln (Ch:5);
```

18.
```
readln;
read (Ch, Ch);
readln (Y);
writeln (Ch:5, Y:10:2);
```

For Exercises 19–26, use the stream input and variable declaration section in Exercises 15–18 to indicate the contents of each variable location and the position of the pointer after each segment of code is executed. Assume the pointer is positioned at the beginning for each problem.

*19. `read (Ch, A);`

20. `readln (Ch, A);`

*21. `readln;`

22.
```
readln;
readln;
```

*23. `readln (A, B, Ch, X);`

24. `read (A, B, Ch, Y);`

*25.
```
readln (A, Ch);
readln (Ch, Ch, B);
```

26. `read (A, B, Ch, X, Ch);`

For Exercises 27–31, use the stream input and variable declaration section in Exercises 15–18 to indicate which of the following segments of code produces an error. Explain why each error occurs.

*27. `read (X, Y);`

28.
```
readln (A);
read (B);
```

*29. **readln** (Ch);
readln (Ch);
readln (Ch);

30. **read** (X, A, Ch, B, Ch);

*31. **readln**;
read (Ch, Ch, A, Ch, B);

For Exercises 32–36, write an appropriate prompting message and an appropriate input statement.

32. Desired input is three positive integers followed by –999.
*33. Desired input is number of hours worked and hourly pay rate.
34. Desired input is the game statistics for one basketball player (check with a coach to see what must be entered).
*35. Desired input is price of an automobile and the state sales tax rate.
36. Desired input is a student's initials, age, height, weight, and gender.

*For Exercises 37–44, assume variables are declared as in Exercises 3–13. If an input statement is

```
readln (Num1, Num2, Ch, Num3);
```

indicate which lines of data do not result in an error message. For those that do not, indicate the values of the variables. For those that produce an error, explain what the error is.

37. 83 95 100■
38. 83 95.0 100■
39. 83-72 93.5■
40. 83-72   93.5■
41. 83.5■
42. 70 73-80.5■
43. 91 92 93 94■
44. -76-81-16.5■
45. Why is it a good idea to print out values of variables that have been read into a program?
46. Suppose Price is a variable of type **real** and you have a program statement

    ```
    read (Price);
    ```

    What happens if you enter 17.95? How does this input statement compare to **readln** (Price)?
47. Discuss the advantages and disadvantages of using separate prompting messages for individual data entries.

3.4 Using Constants

Objectives

- to be aware of appropriate use of constants
- to be able to use constants in programs
- to be able to format constants

The word *constant* has several interpretations. In this section, it will refer to values defined in the **CONST** definition subsection of a program. Recall that a Pascal program consists of a program heading, a declaration section, and an executable section. The declaration section contains a variable declaration subsection, discussed in Section 3.2, and possibly a constant definition subsection. When both are used, the **CONST** subsection must precede the **VAR** subsection. We now examine uses for constants defined in the **CONST** subsection.

Rationale for Uses

There are many reasons to use constants in a program. If a number is to be used frequently, the programmer may wish to give it a descriptive name in the **CONST** definition subsection and then use the descriptive name in the executable section, thus making the program easier to read. For example, if a program included a segment that computed a person's state income tax, and the state tax rate was 6.25 percent of taxable income, the **CONST** section might include

```
CONST
  StateTaxRate = 0.0625;
```

This defines both the value and type for StateTaxRate. In the executable portion of the program, the statement

```
StateTax := Income * StateTaxRate;
```

computes the state tax owed. Or suppose you wanted a program to compute areas of circles. Depending on the accuracy you desire, you could define pi "π" as

```
CONST
  Pi = 3.14159;
```

You could then have a statement in the executable section such as

```
Area := Pi * Radius * Radius;
```

where Area and Radius are appropriately declared variables.

Perhaps the most important use of constants is for values that are currently fixed but subject to change for subsequent runs of the program. If these are defined in the **CONST** section, they can be used throughout the program. If the value changes later, only one change need be made to keep the program current. All uses of the constant in the program need not be located. Some examples might be

```
CONST
  MinimumWage = 5.15;
  SpeedLimit = 65;
  Price = 0.75;
  StateTaxRate = 0.0625;
```

Constants can also be used to name character strings that occur frequently in program output. Suppose a program needs to print two different company names. Instead of typing the names each time they are needed, the following definition could be used:

```
CONST
  Company1 = 'First National Bank of America';
  Company2 = 'Metropolitan Bank of New York';
```

Company1 and Company2 could then be used in **writeln** statements.

Constants can also be defined for later repeated use in making output more attractive. Included could be constants for underlining and for separating sections of output. Some definitions could be

```
CONST
  Underline = '---------------------------------';
  Splats = '**********************************';
```

To separate the output with asterisks, the statement

```
writeln (Splats, Splats);
```

A Note of Interest

Defined Constants and Space Shuttle Computing

An excellent illustration of the utilization of defined constants in a program was given by J. F. ("Jack") Clemons, manager of avionics flight software development and verification for the space shuttle on-board computers. In an interview with David Gifford, editor for Communications of the ACM, Clemons was asked: "Have you tried to restructure the software so that it can be changed easily?"

His response was "By changing certain data constants, we can change relatively large portions of the software on a mission-to-mission basis. For example, we've designed the software so that characteristics like atmospheric conditions on launch day or different lift-off weights can be loaded as initial constants into the code. This is important when there are postponements or last-minute payload changes that invalidate the original inputs."

could be used. In a similar fashion

```
writeln (Underline);
```

could be used for underlining.

Software Engineering Implications

The appropriate use of constants is consistent with principles of software engineering. Communication between teams of programmers is enhanced when program constants have been agreed on. Each team should have a list of these constants for use as members work on their part of the system.

The maintenance phase of the software system life cycle is also aided by use of defined constants. Clearly, a large payroll system is dependent on being able to perform computations that include deductions for federal tax, state tax, FICA, Medicare, health insurance, retirement options, and so on. If appropriate constants are defined for these deductions, system changes are easily made as necessary. For example, the 1996 salary limit for deducting FICA taxes is $62,700. Since this amount changes regularly, we could define

```
CONST
  FICALimit = 62700.00;
```

Program maintenance is then simplified by changing the value of this constant as the law changes.

Formatting Constants

Formatting numeric constants is identical to formatting reals and integers as discussed in Section 2.3. If the constant definition section contains

```
CONST
  Pi = 3.14159;
  SpeedLimit = 55;
```

then

```
writeln ('Pi is used as', Pi:10:5);
writeln ('Speed limit is', SpeedLimit:4);
```

produces

```
Pi is used as   3.14159
Speed limit is  55
```

When character strings are defined as constants, a single positive integer can be used for formatting. This integer establishes the field width for the character string and right justifies the character string in the output field. For example, suppose the constant definition section includes

```
CONST
  Company1 = 'First National Bank of America';
  Company2 = 'Metropolitan Bank of New York';
  Underline = '-----------------------------';
  Splats = '****************************************';
```

If the program contains the program fragment

```
writeln;
writeln (Splats:50);
writeln;
writeln (Company1:45);
writeln (Underline:45);
writeln;
writeln (Company2:44);
writeln (Underline:45);
writeln;
writeln (Splats:50);
```

these statements produce the output

```
****************************************

     First National Bank of America
     ------------------------------

     Metropolitan Bank of New York
     ------------------------------

****************************************
```

Exercises 3.4

1. One use of constants is for values that are used throughout a program but are subject to change over time (minimum wage, speed limit, and so on). List at least five items in this category that were not mentioned in this section.
2. Assume the **CONST** definition section of a program is

```
CONST
  CourseName = 'Computer Science';
  TotalPts = 100;
  Underline = '----------------------------------';
```

and we want output as follows:

```
Course:  Computer Science  Test #1
----------------------------------

Total Points   100
```

Fill in the appropriate formatting positions in the following **writeln** statements to produce the indicated output.

```
writeln ('Course:':17, CourseName:    , 'Test #1':9);
writeln (Underline:    );
writeln;
writeln ('Total Points':22, TotalPts:    );
```

*3. Using the same **CONST** definition section as in Exercise 2, what output is produced by the following segment of code?

```
writeln;
writeln (CourseName:20, 'Test #2':18);
writeln (Underline:38);
writeln;
writeln ('Total points':16, TotalPts:20);
writeln ('My score':12, 93:24);
writeln ('Class average':17, 82.3:19:1);
```

Use the constant definition section to define appropriate constants for the information in Exercises 4–12.

4. Your name.
5. Today's date.
6. Your social security number.
7. Your age.
8. The name of your school.
9. The number of students in your class.
10. The average age of students in your class.
11. The average hourly wage of steelworkers.
12. The price of a new car.

3.5 Standard Functions

Objectives

- to understand reasons for having standard functions
- to be able to use standard functions in a program
- to be able to use appropriate data types for arguments of standard functions

Some standard operations required by programmers are squaring numbers, finding square roots of numbers, rounding numbers, and truncating numbers. Because these operations are so basic, Pascal provides **standard (built-in) functions** for them. Various versions of Pascal and other programming languages have differing standard functions available, so you should always check which functions can be used. Appendix 2 lists the standard functions available in most versions.

A function can be used in a program if it appears in the form

<function name> (<argument>)

where **argument** is a value or a variable with an assigned value. When a function is listed in this manner, it is said to be **invoked** or **called.** A function is invoked by using its name and argument in an expression or statement. If, for example, you want to square the integer 5,

A **standard function** is a built-in function available in most versions of Pascal.

An **argument** is a value or expression passed in a function or procedure call.

To **invoke (call)** a function means to refer to the function in an executable statement.

```
sqr(5)
```

produces the desired result.

The syntax diagram for this is

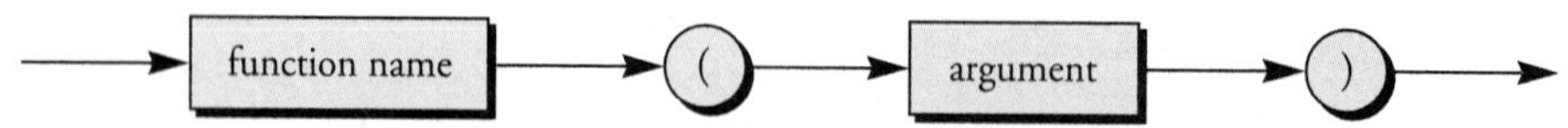

Many functions operate on numbers, starting with a given number and returning some associated value. Table 3.7 shows five standard functions, each with its argument type, data type produced, and an explanation of the value returned.

Table 3.7

Numeric function calls and return types

Function Call	Argument Type	Type of Return	Function Value
sqr(argument)	**real** or **integer**	Same as argument	Returns the square of the argument
sqrt(argument)	**real** or **integer** (nonnegative)	**real**	Returns the square root of the argument
abs(argument)	**real** or **integer**	Same as argument	Returns absolute value of the argument
round(argument)	**real**	**integer**	Returns value rounded to the nearest integer
trunc(argument)	**real**	**integer**	Returns value truncated to an integer

Several examples of specific function expressions together with the value returned by each expression are depicted in Table 3.8.

Using Functions

When a function is invoked, it produces a value in much the same way that 3 + 3 produces 6. Thus, use of a function is similar to the use of constants or values of an expression. Since function calls are not complete Pascal statements, they must be used within some statement. Typical uses are in assignment statements,

```
X := sqrt(16.0);
```

output statements,

```
writeln (abs(-8):20);
```

Table 3.8

Values of function expressions

Expression	Value
`sqr(2)`	4
`sqr(2.0)`	4.0
`sqr(-3)`	9
`sqrt(25.0)`	5.0
`sqrt(25)`	5.0
`sqrt(0.0)`	0.0
`sqrt(-2.0)`	Not permissible
`abs(5.2)`	5.2
`abs(-3.4)`	3.4
`abs(-5)`	5
`round(3.78)`	4
`round(8.50)`	9
`round(-4.2)`	−4
`round(-4.7)`	−5
`trunc(3.78)`	3
`trunc(8.5)`	8
`trunc(-4.2)`	−4
`trunc(-4.7)`	−4

or arithmetic expressions

```
X := round(3.78) + trunc(-4.1);
```

Arguments of functions can be expressions, variables, or constants. However, be sure the argument is always appropriate. For example,

```
A := 3.2;
X := sqrt(trunc(A));
```

is appropriate, but

```
A := -3.2;
X := sqrt(trunc(A));
```

produces an error since **trunc**(−3.2) has the value −3 and **sqrt**(−3) is not a valid expression.

The following example illustrates how functions can be used in expressions.

Example 3.4

Find the value of the following expression:

```
4.2 + round(trunc(2.0 * 3.1) + 5.3) - sqrt(sqr(-4.1));
```

The solution is

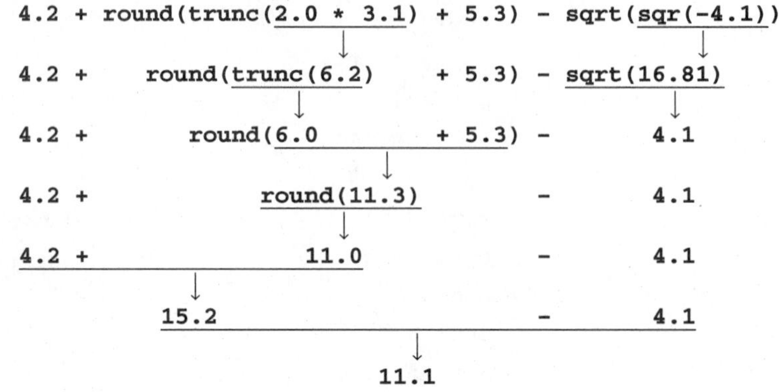

Character Functions

An **ordinal data type** is a data type ordered in some association with the integers; each integer is the ordinal of its associated character.

Ordering a character set requires associating an integer with each character. Data types ordered in some association with the integers are known as **ordinal data types.** Each integer is the ordinal of its associated character. Integers are therefore considered to be an ordinal data type. Character sets are also considered to be an ordinal data type, as shown in Table 3.9. In each case, the ordinal of the character appears to the left of the character. Real numbers are not an ordinal data type.

Using ASCII, as shown in Table 3.9, the ordinal of a capital A is 65, the ordinal of the character representing the arabic number 1 is 49, the ordinal of a blank (ƀ) is 32, and the ordinal of a lowercase a is 97.

Pascal provides several standard functions that have arguments of ordinal type. These are listed in Table 3.10 together with a related function **chr** that returns a character when called.

Again using the ASCII collating sequence shown in Table 3.9, we can determine the value of these functions as shown in Table 3.11.

Variables and variable expressions can be used as arguments for functions. For example, if Ch is a **char** variable and the assignment statement

```
Ch := 'D';
```

is made, then **ord**(Ch) has the value 68.

Now let's consider a short program that allows the use of standard functions **ord, pred, succ,** and **chr.**

```
PROGRAM FunctionTest (output);

VAR
  Num : integer;
  Ch : char;

BEGIN
  Ch := 'C';
  writeln ('Ord of C is', ord(Ch):5);
  writeln ('Succ of C is', succ(Ch):4);
  writeln ('Pred of C is', pred(Ch):4);
  writeln ('Chr of 67 is', chr(67):4);
```

```
  Num := 0;
  writeln ('The ordinal of Num is' ord(Num):4)
END.
```

When this program is run, the output is

```
Ord of C is    67
Succ of C is    D
```

▼ Table 3.9

ASCII ordering of a tcharacter set

Ordinal	Character	Ordinal	Character	Ordinal	Character
32	ƀ	64	@	96	‘
33	!	65	A	97	a
34	”	66	B	98	b
35	#	67	C	99	c
36	$	68	D	100	d
37	%	69	E	101	e
38	&	70	F	102	f
39	’	71	G	103	g
40	(	72	H	104	h
41	)	73	I	105	i
42	*	74	J	106	j
43	+	75	K	107	k
44	,	76	L	108	l
45	-	77	M	109	m
46	.	78	N	110	n
47	/	79	O	111	o
48	0	80	P	112	p
49	1	81	Q	113	q
50	2	82	R	114	r
51	3	83	S	115	s
52	4	84	T	116	t
53	5	85	U	117	u
54	6	86	V	118	v
55	7	87	W	119	w
56	8	88	X	120	x
57	9	89	Y	121	y
58	:	90	Z	122	z
59	;	91	[	123	{
60	<	92	\	124	|
61	=	93	]	125	}
62	>	94	↑	126	~
63	?	95	—		

Note: Codes 00–31 and 127 are nonprintable control characters.

```
Pred of C is   B
Chr of 67 is   C
The ordinal of Num is  0
```

You should obtain a complete list of characters available and their respective ordinals for your local system. Note particular features, such as **succ**('R') is not 'S' when using EBCDIC; and **chr**(n) is nonprintable for $n < 32$ or $n > 126$ when using ASCII.

One of the uses for functions **chr** and **ord** is to convert between uppercase and lowercase letters. Closely related is the conversion of a digit (entered as a **char** value) to its integer value. The next example shows how to convert an uppercase letter to lowercase. Other conversions are deferred to the exercises.

Table 3.10

Function calls with ordinal arguments or character values

Function Call	Argument Type	Type of Result	Function Value
ord(argument)	Any ordinal type	**integer**	Ordinal corresponding to argument
pred(argument)	Any ordinal type	Same as argument	Predecessor of the argument
succ(argument)	Any ordinal type	Same as argument	Successor of the argument
chr(argument)	**integer**	**char**	Character associated with the ordinal of the argument

Table 3.11

Values of character functions

Expression	Value
`ord('E')`	69
`ord('9')`	57
`ord(9)`	9
`ord('>')`	62
`pred('N')`	'M'
`pred('A')`	'@'
`succ('(')`	')'
`succ('!')`	'"'
`chr(74)`	'J'
`chr(32)`	'b̸'
`chr(57)`	'9'
`chr(59)`	';'
`chr(114)`	'r'

A Note of Interest

Herman Hollerith

Herman Hollerith (1860–1929) was hired by the United States Census Bureau in 1879 at the age of 19. Since the 1880 census was predicted to take a long time to complete (it actually took until 1887), Hollerith was assigned the task of developing a mechanical method of tabulating census data. He introduced his census machine in 1887. It consisted of four parts:

1. A punched paper card that represented data using a special code (Hollerith code)
2. A card punch apparatus
3. A tabulator that read the punched cards
4. A sorting machine with 24 compartments

Using Hollerith's techniques and equipment, the 1890 census tabulation was completed in one-third the time required for the previous census tabulation. This included working with data for 12 million additional people.

Hollerith proceeded to form the Tabulating Machine Company (1896), which supplied equipment to census bureaus in the United States, Canada, and Western Europe. After a disagreement with the census director, Hollerith began marketing his equipment in other commercial areas. Hollerith sold his company in 1911. It was later combined with 12 others to form the Computing-Tabulating-Recording Company, a direct ancestor of International Business Machines Corp.

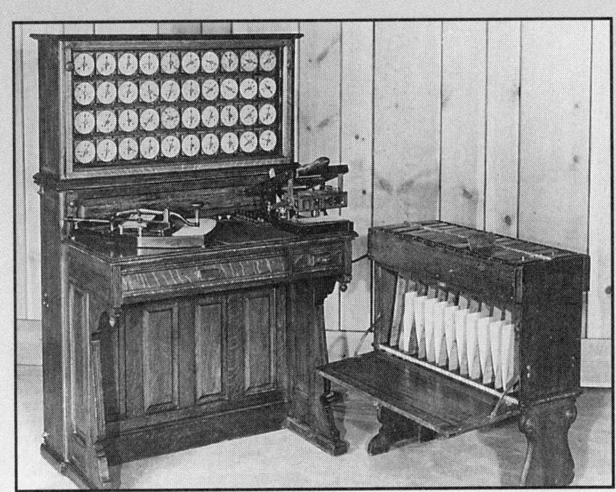

In the meantime, Hollerith's successor at the census bureau, James Powers, redesigned the census machines. He then formed his own company, which subsequently became Remington Rand and Sperry Univac.

Example 3.5

To show how functions **chr** and **ord** can be used to convert an uppercase letter to lowercase, let's assume our task is to convert the letter 'H' into the letter 'h'. Using the ASCII chart shown in Table 3.9, we first note that the ordinal of 'H' is 72. We subtract the ordinal of 'A' from this to obtain

```
ord('H') - ord('A')
```

which is

```
72 - 65 = 7
```

We now add the ordinal of 'a' to get

```
ord('H') - ord('A') + ord('a')
```

which yields

```
72 - 65 + 97 = 104
```

This is the ordinal of 'h'. It can be converted to the letter by using **chr.** Thus

```
chr(ord('H') - ord('A') + ord('a'))
```

produces the letter 'h'. In general, the following is sufficient for converting from uppercase to lowercase:

```
Lowercase := chr(ord(Uppercase) - ord('A') + ord('a'));
```

Note that if you always use the same ASCII ordering, −**ord**('A') + **ord**('a') could be replaced by the constant 32. If you choose to do this, it should be done in the **CONST** section. A typical definition is

```
CONST
  UpperToLowerShift = 32;
```

You would then write the lowercase conversion as

```
Lowercase := chr(ord(Uppercase) + UpperToLowerShift);
```

Exercises 3.5

In Exercises 1–6, find the value of each expression.

*1. `abs(-11.2) + sqrt(round(15.51))`

2. `trunc(abs(-14.2))`

*3. `4 * 11 MOD (trunc(trunc(8.9) / sqrt(16)))`

4. `sqr(17 DIV 5 * 2)`

*5. `-5.0 + sqrt(5 * 5 - 4 * 6) / 2.0`

6. `3.1 * 0.2 - abs(-4.2 * 9.0 / 3.0)`

*7. Write a test program that illustrates what happens when an inappropriate argument is used with a function. Be sure to include something like **ord**(15.3).

8. Two standard algebraic problems come from the Pythagorean theorem and the quadratic formula. Assume variables *a, b,* and *c* have been declared in a program. Write Pascal expressions that allow you to evaluate

   a. the length of the hypotenuse of a right triangle

   $$(\sqrt{a^2 + b^2})$$

   b. both solutions to the quadratic formula

   $$\frac{-b \pm \sqrt{b^2 - 4ac}}{2a}$$

In Exercises 9–15, indicate whether the expression is valid or invalid. Find the value of those that are valid; explain why the others are invalid.

*9. `-6 MOD (sqrt(16))`

10. `8 DIV (trunc(sqrt(65)))`

*11. `sqrt(63 MOD 2)`

12. `abs(-sqrt(sqr(3) + 7))`

*13. `sqrt(16 DIV (-3))`

14. `sqrt(sqr(-4))`

*15. `round(14.38 * 10) / 10`

16. The standard function **round** permits you to round to the nearest integer. Write an expression that permits you to round the real number X to the nearest tenth.

In Exercises 17–23, find the value of the expression (using ASCII).

17. `ord(13 + 4 MOD 3)`
18. `pred(succ('E'))`
19. `succ(pred('E'))`
20. `ord(5)`
21. `ord('5')`
22. `chr(ord('+'))`
23. `ord(chr(40))`

For Exercises 24–26, assume the variable declaration section of a program is

```
VAR
  X : real;
  A : integer;
  Ch : char;
```

What output is produced by each program fragment?

24.
```
X := -4.3;
writeln (X:6:2, abs(X):6:2, trunc(X):6, round(X):6);
```
*25.
```
X := -4.3;
A := abs(round(X));
writeln (ord(A));
writeln (ord('A'));
```
26.
```
Ch := chr(26);
writeln (Ch:5, pred(Ch):5, succ(Ch):5);
```
27. Write a complete program to print each uppercase letter of the alphabet and its ordinal in the collating sequence used by your machine's version of Pascal.

For Exercises 28 and 29, use ASCII to show how each of the following conversions can be made.

28. A lowercase letter converted to its uppercase equivalent

*29. A digit entered as a **char** value converted to its indicated numeric value

For Exercises 30 and 31, use the following formulas to write the Pascal statement or statements necessary to produce the desired result.

30. volume = $\frac{1}{3}\pi r^2 h$ (volume of a cone)

*31. volume = $\frac{4}{3}\pi r^3$ (volume of a sphere)

The **Communication and Style Tips** that follow provide a quick reference to writing styles and suggestions. Such tips are intended to stimulate rather than terminate your imagination. (See page 100.)

The **Focus on Program Design: Case Study** sections contain complete programs to illustrate concepts developed in the chapter. In each case, a typical problem is stated, a solution is developed in pseudocode and illustrated with a structure chart, and module specifications are written for appropriate modules.

Focus on Program Design: Case Study

The Unit Price of Pizza

Let's write a complete program to find the unit price for a pizza. Input for the program consists of the price and size of the pizza. Size is the diameter of the pizza ordered. Output consists of the price per square inch. A first-level pseudocode development is

1. Get the data
2. Perform the computations
3. Print the results

Communication and Style Tips

1. Use descriptive identifiers. Words (Sum, Score, Average) are easier to understand than letters (A, B, C or X, Y, Z).
2. Constants can be used to create neat, attractive output. For example,

```
CONST
  Splats = '********************************';
  Underline = '-----------------------';
  Border = '*                              *';
```

3. Use the constant definition section to define an appropriately named blank and use it to control line spacing for output. Thus, you could have

```
CONST
  Skip = ' ';
  Indent = ' ';
```

and then output statements could be

```
writeln (Skip:20, message, Skip:10, message);
```

or

```
writeln (Indent:20, message, Skip:10, message);
```

4. As you write Pascal statements, use blanks for line spacing within the program. Spacing between words and expressions should resemble typical English usage. Thus,

```
PROGRAM EarlyBird (input, output);
```

is preferable to

```
PROGRAM   EarlyBird    (      input, output );
```

5. Output of a column of reals should have decimal points in a line.

```
 14.32
181.50
 93.63
```

6. Output can be made more attractive by using columns, left and right margins, underlining, and blank lines.
7. Extra **writeln**s at the beginning and end of the executable section will separate desired output from other messages.

```
BEGIN
  writeln;
      .
      . (program body here)
      .
  writeln
END.
```

A structure chart for this problem is given in Figure 3.1.

Figure 3.1

Structure chart for the pizza problem

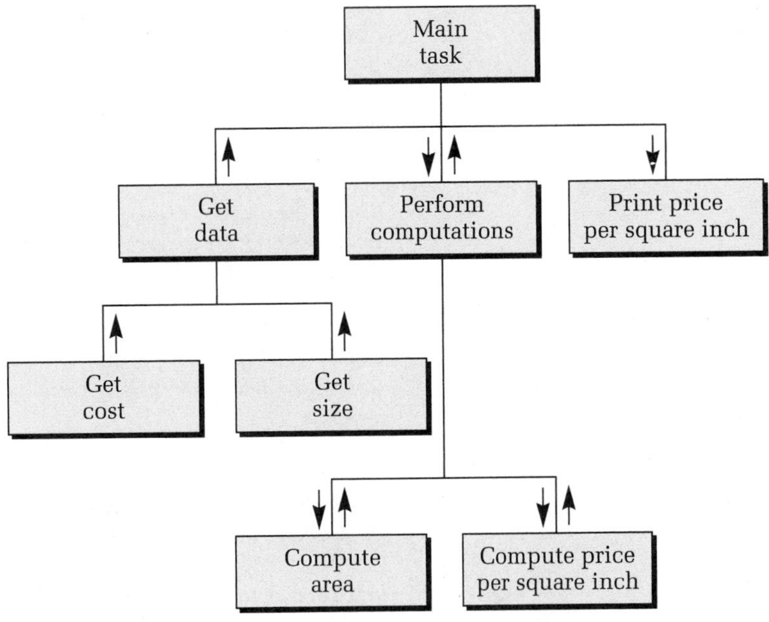

Module specifications for the main modules are

1. Get Data Module
   Data received: None
   Information returned: Price
   Size
   Logic: Have the user enter price and size.
2. Perform Computation Module
   Data received: Price
   Size
   Information returned: Price per square inch
   Logic: Given the diameter, find the radius.
   Compute the area using Area = Pi * Radius * Radius.
   Price per square inch is found by dividing Price by Area.
3. Print Results Module
   Data received: PricePerSquareInch
   Information returned: None
   Logic: Print the price per square inch.

A further refinement of the pseudocode produces

1. Get the data
   1.1 Get price
   1.2 Get size
2. Perform the computations
   2.1 Compute area
   2.2 Calculate unit price

Step 3 of the pseudocode, "Print the results" merely requires the price per square inch to be printed, so no further development is required.

A complete program for this is

```
PROGRAM PizzaCost (input, output);

CONST
  Pi = 3.14;

VAR
  Size, Radius, Cost, Area,
  PricePerSquareInch : real;

BEGIN
  writeln ('Enter the pizza price and press <Enter>.');
  readln (Cost);                                              } 1
  writeln ('Enter the pizza size and press <Enter>.');
  readln (Size);

  Radius := Size / 2;
  Area := Pi * sqr(Radius);                                   } 2
  PricePerSquareInch := Cost / Area;

  writeln ('The price per square inch is $',
            PricePerSquareInch:4:2)                           } 3
END.
```

A sample run of this program yields

```
Enter the pizza price and press <Enter>.
10.50
Enter the pizza size and press <Enter>.
16
The price per square inch is $0.05
```

Summary

Key Terms

argument
assignment statement
batch processing
batch (stream) input
binary notation
cancellation error
character set
collating sequence: ASCII, EBCDIC
constant
end-of-file marker (**eof**)
end-of-line marker (**eoln**)
expression
input
input statement
integer arithmetic operations: +, −, *, **MOD, DIV**
integer overflow
interactive input
invoke (call)
memory location
mixed-mode expressions
ordinal data type
precedence rule
prompt
real arithmetic operations: +, −, *, /
real overflow
representational errors
round-off error
self-documenting code
standard (built-in) function
underflow
user-friendly
variable
word

Keywords

abs	**MOD**	**round**
chr	**ord**	**sqr**
DIV	**pred**	**sqrt**
eof	**read**	**succ**
eoln	**readln**	**trunc**

Key Concepts

- Operations and priorities for data of type **integer** and **real** are summarized as follows:

Data Type	Operations	Priority
integer	∗, **MOD, DIV**	1. Evaluate in order from left to right.
	+, −,	2. Evaluate in order from left to right.
real	∗, /	1. Evaluate in order from left to right.
	+, −	2. Evaluate in order from left to right.

- Mixed-mode expressions return values of type **real.**
- Priority for order of operations on mixed-mode expressions is

  1. ∗, /, **MOD, DIV** in order from left to right
  2. +, − in order from left to right

- Real overflow is caused by a value too large for computing on a particular machine.
- Underflow is caused by a value too small (close to zero) for computing. These numbers are automatically replaced by zero.
- Round–off errors, representational errors, and cancellation errors are possible when working with data of type **real.**
- A memory location can have a name that can be used to refer to the contents of the location.
- The name of a memory location is different from the contents of the memory location.
- Self-documenting code includes the use of descriptive identifiers.
- Assignment statements are used to assign values to memory locations, for example,

```
Sum := 30 + 60;
```

- Variables and variable expressions can be used in output statements.
- The **read(ln)** statement is used to get data from an input file. Correct form is
  read(ln) (<variable name>);
  read(ln) (<variable 1>, <variable 2>, . . . , <variable *n*>);
- The **read** (<variable name>) statement causes a value to be transferred to the variable location and the input file pointer to be advanced to the first position following the data item.
- The use of **readln** is similar to the use of **read** except that **readln** causes the input file pointer to advance to the beginning of the next line of data after data have been read.

- End-of-line markers are inserted at the end of each line of data (when <Enter> is pressed).
- An end-of-file marker is inserted after the end-of-line marker for the last line of data.
- Interactive input expects data items to be entered from the keyboard at appropriate times during execution of the program.
- Batch input expects data to be read from a file previously created.
- Data types for variables in a **read** or **readln** statement should match data items entered as input.
- Appropriate uses for constants in the **CONST** definition section include frequently used numbers; current values subject to change over time, for example, (MinimumWage = 5.15); and character strings for output.
- Character strings are formatted using a single colon.
- Five standard numeric functions available in Pascal are **sqr, sqrt, abs, round,** and **trunc.**
- Functions can be used in assignment statements, for example,

```
X := sqrt(16.0);
```

  in output statements

```
writeln (abs(-8):20);
```

  and in arithmetic expressions

```
X := round(3.78) + trunc(-4.1);
```

- Four standard character functions available in Pascal are **ord, pred, succ,** and **chr.**

Chapter Review Exercises

For Exercises 1–3, write variable declarations.

1. An integer called A
2. Real numbers named Numberl, Number2, and Number3
3. A character variable called First and a real number called Second

For Exercises 4–9, indicate whether the number is an **integer** or a **real.**

4. 7
5. 0.0
6. 403.0
7. 4.8
8. 2E8
9. –3954

For Exercises 10–19, if A is an **integer,** B is a **real,** and C is a **char,** which assignment statements are valid? If they are invalid, explain why.

10. `A ;= round(A);`
11. `B := sqr(abs(B);`
12. `B := ord(c);`
13. `C := A + B;`
14. `A := A + B;`
15. `B :+ A + 1;`
16. `A + 1 := B;`
17. `C := 'Chapter 3';`
18. `A := 8 / 3;`
19. `B = 3.0 * 3.2;`

Write constant definitions for Exercises 20–24.

20. The name of your favorite football team
21. The number of miles you live from your school

22. The number of ounces in a pound
23. The capital of your state
24. The room number of your computer class
25. Explain the difference between reading numeric and character data.

For Exercises 26–29, suppose the data line

```
AB 5 6.7 C■
```

is entered into a program that uses the variables

```
X, Y : integer;
J, K : real;
M, N, P : char;
```

Explain what happens when each statement is executed.

26. `readln (M,N,X,J,P);`
27. `readln (M,N,A,B);`
28. `readln (M,N,J,P);`
29. `read (M,N,P,J,K);`

For Exercises 30–33, find the value of the expression.

30. **sqr**(4) – **abs**(–12) * **round**(0.6)
31. **sqrt**(**abs**(–25)) – **sqr**(5.2)
32. **pred**(34) **MOD** **succ**(10)
33. **succ**(**chr**(**ord**(**pred**('J'))))

Programming Problems

Write a complete Pascal program for each of the following problems. Each program should use one or more **read** or **readln** statements to obtain necessary values. For interactive programs, each **read** or **readln** should be preceded by an appropriate prompting message.

1. Susan purchases a computer for $985. The sales tax on the purchase is 5.5 percent. Compute and print the total purchase price.
2. Find and print the area and perimeter of a rectangle that is 4.5 feet long and 2.3 feet wide. Print both rounded to the nearest tenth of a foot.
3. Compute and print the number of minutes in a year.
4. Light travels at $3 * 10^8$ meters per second. Compute and print the distance that a light beam would travel in one year. (This is called a light year.)
5. The 1927 New York Yankees won 110 games and lost 44. Compute their winning percentage and print it rounded to three decimal places.
6. A 10-kilogram object is traveling at 12 meters per second. Compute and print its momentum (momentum is mass times velocity).
7. Convert 98.0 degrees Fahrenheit to degrees Celsius.
8. Given a positive number, print its square and square root.
9. The Golden Sales Company pays its salespeople $.27 for each item they sell. Given the number of items sold by a salesperson, print the amount of pay due.
10. Given the length and width of a rectangle, print its area and perimeter.

11. The kinetic energy of a moving object is given by the formula:

    $KE = (1/2)mv^2$

    Given the mass (m) and the speed (v) of an object, find its kinetic energy.
12. Aretha wants a program that will enable her to balance her checkbook. She wishes to enter a beginning balance, five letters for an abbreviation for the recipient of the check, and the amount of the check. Given this information, write a program that will find the new balance in her checkbook.
13. A supermarket wants to install a computerized weighing system in its produce department. Input to this system will consist of a three-letter identifier for the type of produce, the weight of the produce purchase (in pounds), and the cost per pound of the produce. A typical input screen would be

```
Enter each of the following:

Description <Enter>
ABC
Weight <Enter>
2.0
Cost/lb. <Enter>
1.98
```

Print a label showing the input information along with the cost of the purchase. The label should appear as follows:

```
%%%%%%%%%%%%%%%%%%%%%%%%%%%%%%%%%%%%%%%%%%%%%
        Penny Spender Supermarket
            Produce Department

  ITEM      WEIGHT       COST/lb      COST
   ABC      2.0 lb        $1.98      $3.96

               Thank you!

%%%%%%%%%%%%%%%%%%%%%%%%%%%%%%%%%%%%%%%%%%%%%
```

14. The New-Wave Computer Company sells its product, the NW-PC, for $675. In addition, they sell memory expansion cards for $69.95, disk drives for $198.50, and software for $34.98 each. Given the number of memory cards, disk drives, and software packages desired by a customer purchasing an NW-PC, print a bill of sale that appears as follows:

```
***************************
    New Wave Computers

  ITEM                COST
1  NW-PC            $675.00
2  Memory card       139.90
1  Disk Drive        198.50
4  Software          139.92
                    -------
      TOTAL        $1153.32
```

15. Write a test program that allows you to see the characters contained within the character set of your computer. Given a positive integer, you can use the **chr**

function to determine the corresponding character. On most computers, only integers less than 255 are valid for this. Also, remember that most character sets contain some unprintable characters such as ASCII values less than 32. Print your output in the form:

```
Character number nn is x.
```

16. Mr. Vigneault, a coach at Shepherd High School, is working on a program that can be used to assist cross-country runners in analyzing their times. As part of the program, a coach enters elapsed times for each runner, given in units of minutes, seconds, and hundredths. In a 5,000-meter (5K) race, elapsed times are entered at the one-mile and two-mile marks. These elapsed times are then used to compute "splits" for each part of the race (that is, how long it takes a runner to run each of the three race segments).

    Write a complete program that will accept as input three times, given in units of minutes, seconds, and hundredths, and then produce output that includes the split for each segment. Typical input would be

```
Runner number                  234
Mile times:                1   5:34.22
                           2  11:21.67
Finish time:                  17:46.85
```

    Typical output would be

```
Runner number                  234
Split one                      5:34.22
Split two                      5:47.45
Split three                    6:25.18
Finish time                   17:46.85
```

17. The Swim-More Pool Installation Company installs rectangular swimming pools surrounded by a cement edge that extends three feet from each side of the pool. The cement is poured to a uniform depth of four inches. Write a program that accepts as input the dimensions of the pool and then provides as output the number of cubic yards of cement needed along with the total cost of the cement. Use the constant definition section to define the price per yard. Contact a local cement company to obtain the current price.

Communication in Practice

1. Modify one of the programs you have written for this chapter by changing all constant and variable identifiers to single-letter identifiers. Exchange your modified program with another student who has done the same thing. After reading the exchanged program, discuss the use of meaningful identifiers with the other student. Suggest identifiers for the program you are reading.
2. Many (but not all) instructors in beginning computer science courses encourage their students to use meaningful identifiers when writing code. It is natural to wonder to what extent this practice is followed outside the educational world. Investigate this issue by contacting several programmers who work for nearby companies. Prepare a complete written report of your conversations for distribution to class members. Include charts that summarize your findings.

Chapter 4

Designing and Writing Complete Programs

Chapter Outline

We can now begin to take a thorough look at writing more elaborate programs. Chapter 2 gave us the three basic components of a program: program heading, declaration section, and executable section. Chapter 3 provided some additional tools for use in constructing programs, specifically, the use of variables, input, constants, and standard functions. Before using these ideas to write programs that solve problems, however, we need to look at the way in which programs should be constructed. The idea is to first design the program and then write code for the program. You should never start writing code to solve a problem until you have an adequately designed solution. In this chapter, we look at how the writing of code follows in a natural fashion from a carefully designed algorithm. We then examine typical errors, which include both mechanical errors (syntax, declaration, assignment, and so on) and logic errors (why your program doesn't solve the problem).

4.1 Writing Code

Objectives

- to be able to write code from pseudocode
- to be able to use program comments
- to be able to use indenting and blank lines to enhance readability

Writing Code from Pseudocode

The process of writing statements that are part of a program to solve a problem is referred to as "writing code." This expression is commonly used and we will use it throughout the text. To illustrate the idea of writing actual code to solve a problem from an algorithm developed using pseudocode, consider the problem of computing your bowling score for an evening. Assume you are to read in three integer scores, compute their average, and print the scores together with the average. A design for this problem is shown in Figure 4.1.

Corresponding pseudocode is

1. Read in Score1, Score2, and Score3
2. Compute
   2.1 Let Sum = Score1 + Score2 + Score3
   2.2 Let Average = Sum divided by 3
3. Display results
   3.1 Display scores
   3.2 Display average

Assuming Score1, Score2, and Score3 have been declared as **integer** variables, then

1. Read in Score1, Score2, Score3

is coded as

```
read (Score1, Score2, Score3);
```

Assuming Sum and Average have been declared as **integer** and **real** variables, respectively, then

2.1 Let Sum = Score1 + Score2 + Score3
2.2 Let Average = Sum divided by 3

is coded as

```
Sum := Score1 + Score2 + Score3;
Average := Sum / 3.0;
```

The third line of pseudocode,

3. Display results

◆ Figure 4.1
Top-down design

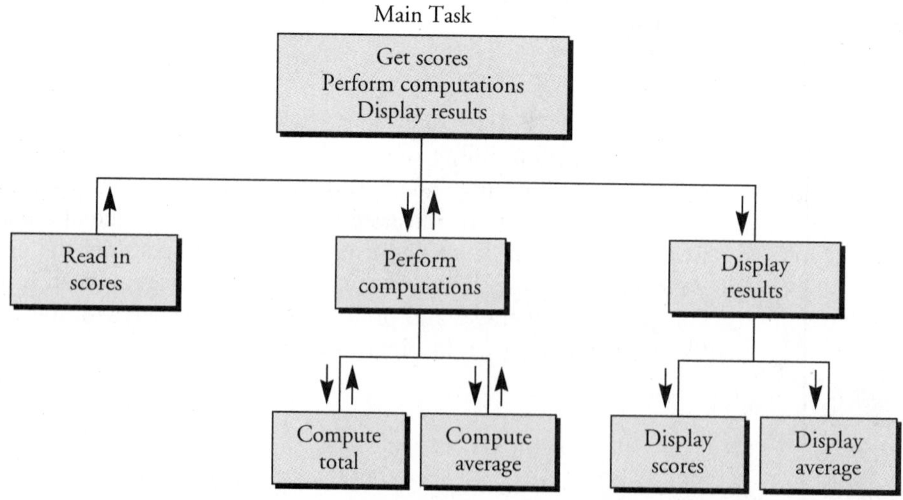

requires us to know the desired form for the output. For example, assume we would like the following output produced:

```
Game        Score
----        -----

  1           150
  2           178
  3           162

Your series total is     490
The average score is  163.33
```

Before writing code for this you need to be aware of the significance of being able to produce attractive output. Many students feel that just getting the desired information printed is a sufficient accomplishment. This is not true! It is extremely important that you develop good habits with respect to producing clear, attractive output. Consider the following ideas:

1. Use **writeln** to produce blank lines where appropriate.
2. Use **writeln** ('--------') with the appropriate number of hyphens for underlining.
3. Move the output in from the left margin of the page.
4. Use appropriate left margins and columns for various sections of the output.
5. Use descriptive headings and messages.

Consider the problem of writing code for the bowling problem just described. If the constant definition section includes

```
CONST
  Skip = ' ';
```

the output can be accomplished by using **writeln** statements as follows:

```
writeln (Skip:19, 'Game', Skip:6, 'Score');
writeln (Skip:19, '----', Skip:6, '-----');
writeln;
writeln (1:22, Score1:11);
writeln (2:22, Score2:11);
writeln (3:22, Score3:11);
writeln;
writeln (Skip:19, 'Your series total is', Sum:8);
writeln (Skip:19, 'The average score is', Average:8:2);
writeln;
```

Each line of pseudocode has now been translated into Pascal statements, so we can write a complete program using five variables (Sum, Score1, Score2, Score3, and Average) to solve the problem. The program follows:

```
PROGRAM Bowling (input, output);
CONST
  Skip = ' ';
VAR
  Score1, Score2, Score3 : integer;
  Sum : integer;
  Average : real;
```

```
BEGIN
  writeln ('Please enter 3 scores and press <Enter>.');
  readln (Score1, Score2, Score3);
  Sum := Score1 + Score2 + Score3;
  Average := Sum / 3.0;
  writeln;
  writeln (Skip:19, 'Game', Skip:6, 'Score');
  writeln (Skip:19, '----', Skip:6, '-----');
  writeln;
  writeln (1:22, Score1:11);
  writeln (2:22, Score2:11);
  writeln (3:22, Score3:11);
  writeln;
  writeln (Skip:19, 'Your series total is', Sum:8);
  writeln (Skip:19, 'The average score is', Average:8:2);
  writeln
END.
```

When this program is run on the computer, we obtain the following output:

```
Please enter 3 scores and press <Enter>.
150 178 162

                   Game      Score
                   ----      -----

                      1        150
                      2        178
                      3        162

                   Your series total is     490
                   The average score is  163.33
```

Program Comments

A **comment** is a nonexecutable statement used to make a program more readable.

Programming languages typically include some provision for putting **comments** in a program. These comments are nonexecutable and are used to document and explain various parts of the program. In Pascal, the form for including comments in a program is

```
{ ... comment ... }
or
(* ... comment ... *)
```

You should check with your teacher to see which form is preferred.

As you write more sophisticated and complex programs, you will see the need for documentation and comments. Let's now go back to **PROGRAM** Bowling and see how comments could be used to enhance the readability of the program.

The line of code

```
writeln;
```

causes the printer to skip one line; a line comment could be used to explain this. Thus, the line of code could be

```
writeln;  {  Skip one line   }
```

Since comments are nonexecutable, the output is not affected but the program is now more readable.

A second major use of comments is for program documentation. Suppose your teacher would like you to include the following as part of a program but not as part of the output:

Course number
Assignment number
Due date
Author
Teacher

This documentation is frequently included immediately after (or before) the program heading and could be written as either a single comment or a series of comments. A sample documentation section is

```
{     Course Number                       CPS 150        }
{     Assignment                          One            }
{     Due Date                            Sept. 20       }
{     Author                              Mary Smith     }
{     Teacher                             Mr. Jones      }
```

These comments do not affect the output; they merely enhance readability. You should try several ways to include comments within a program. You are limited only by your imagination and your teacher's wishes. Let's now rewrite **PROGRAM** Bowling using a documentation section and other comments within the program.

```
PROGRAM Bowling (input, output);
{           Course Number          CPS 150                        }
{           Assignment             One                            }
{           Due Date               Sept. 20                       }
{           Author                 Mary Smith                     }
{           Teacher                Mr. Jones                      }
CONST
  Skip = ' ';
VAR
  Score1, Score2, Score3 : integer;
  Sum : integer;
  Average : real;
BEGIN
  writeln ('Please enter 3 scores and press <Enter>.');
  readln (Score1, Score2, Score3);             {  Get the scores  }
  Sum := Score1 + Score2 + Score3;
  Average := Sum / 3.0;
  writeln;
  writeln (Skip:19, 'Game', Skip:6, 'Score'); {  Print heading   }
  writeln (Skip:19, '----', Skip:6, '-----');
  writeln;
  writeln (1:22, Score1:11);                {  Print the results  }
  writeln (2:22, Score2:11);
  writeln (3:22, Score3:11);
  writeln;
  writeln (Skip:19, 'Your series total is', Sum:8);
```

```
  writeln (Skip:19, 'The average score is', Average:8:2);
  writeln
END.
```

Program Style

A major point to remember when writing a program is to make it easy to read. Three commonly used methods for improving readability are indenting sections of code, using blank lines, and using program comments.

First, indenting is used to identify sections of code and should roughly correspond to the indenting implied by pseudocode. No standard exists regarding the number of spaces to use for indenting. However, we find that one space makes programs difficult to read, and four or more spaces sometimes does not leave sufficient space for complicated programs. Therefore, all sample programs in this text will use two spaces for indenting.

Many programmers use the leftmost column for the reserved words **PROGRAM, CONST, VAR, BEGIN,** and **END,** where **BEGIN** and **END** denote the start and finish, respectively, of the executable portion of the program. Other statements are indented at least two spaces. This does not affect the program; it simply makes it easier to read.

A second stylistic technique is to use blank lines to separate sections of code. The use of blank lines is not standardized; it depends on your preference for readability. A note of caution, however: Too many blank lines can be distracting. To illustrate how blank lines may be used, consider the following version of the previous program to compute bowling scores:

```
PROGRAM Bowling (input, output);

{          Course Number          CPS 150                        }
{          Assignment             One                            }
{          Due Date               Sept. 20                       }
{          Author                 Mary Smith                     }
{          Teacher                Mr. Jones                      }

CONST
  Skip = ' ';

VAR
  Score1, Score2, Score3 : integer;
  Sum : integer;
  Average : real;

BEGIN
  writeln ('Please enter 3 scores and press <Enter>.');
  readln (Score1, Score2, Score3);            {  Get the scores  }

  Sum := Score1 + Score2 + Score3;
  Average := Sum / 3.0;

  writeln;
  writeln (Skip:19, 'Game', Skip:6, 'Score'); {  Print heading  }
  writeln (Skip:19, '----', Skip:6, '-----');
  writeln;
```

```
  writeln (1:22, Score1:11);                { Print the results  }
  writeln (2:22, Score2:11);
  writeln (3:22, Score3:11);
  writeln;
  writeln (Skip:19, 'Your series total is', Sum:8);
  writeln (Skip:19, 'The average score is', Average:8:2);
  writeln
END.
```

Since this is such a short program, you may not notice much difference in readability between the two versions, but blank lines have been used to separate all sections of the program and parts within the executable section.

A third method for enhancing readability is the use of program comments for program description, a variable dictionary, and section comments. Let's first consider the problem of describing the program. Each program should contain some description of what the program does. The program description generally follows the program heading. You will realize the necessity for such descriptions as you accumulate a group of programs. A program description for our bowling problem could read as follows:

```
{  This is one of our early complete Pascal    }
{  programs. It solves the problem of          }
{  listing bowling scores and computing the    }
{  total and average. In addition to this,     }
{  the final version will contain an initial   }
{  effort to develop a programming style       }
{  using                                       }
{          1.  Indenting                       }
{          2.  Blank lines                     }
{          3.  Program comments                }
```

A **variable dictionary** is a listing of the meaning of variables used in a program.

Another relatively standard use of program comments is to establish a **variable dictionary.** In short programs, the need for this is not obvious; however, it is essential for longer programs.

Several styles can be used to describe variables. One method is to place comments on the same line as the variables in the variable declaration section. For example, for the bowling problem, you might use

```
VAR
  Score1, Score2, Score3 : integer;   {  Scores for games  }
  Sum : integer;                       {  Sum of the scores  }
  Average : real;                 {  Average of game scores  }
```

A second method is to use a separate comment section preceding the variable declaration section, such as

```
{            Variable Dictionary              }
{                                             }
{      Average      Average game score        }
{      Score1       Score for game one        }
{      Score2       Score for game two        }
{      Score3       Score for game three      }
{      Sum          Sum of the scores         }
```

You are encouraged to try both styles of describing variables as well as other variations you might like.

Another use of program comments is to describe what a section of code does. In **PROGRAM** Bowling, the executable section consists of three sections: get data, perform computations, and produce output. A comment block could be used to describe what happens in each portion of the program:

```
{  Get the scores  }
        .
        .
        .
{  Perform the computations  }
        .
        .
        .
{  Print the heading  }
        .
        .
        .
{  Print the results  }
        .
        .
        .
```

At this stage, you may be thinking that developing a style for writing programs was the subject of Shakespeare's play *Much Ado About Nothing,* since none of these suggestions has anything to do with whether or not a program runs. Not true. It is fairly easy to learn to write short programs. As you continue your study of computer science, you will accumulate programs that are progressively longer and more complex. You should begin now to develop a concise, consistent style for writing programs.

Now we will incorporate all the previous suggestions for writing style into **PROGRAM** Bowling.

```
PROGRAM Bowling (input, output);

{          Course Number          CPS 150                    }
{          Assignment             One                        }
{          Due Date               Sept. 20                   }
{          Author                 Mary Smith                 }
{          Teacher                Mr. Jones                  }

{                      Program Comments                      }
{                                                            }
{    This is one of our early complete Pascal programs.  It  }
{    solves  the  problem  of  listing  bowling  scores  and }
{    computing  the  total  and  average.  In addition, the  }
{    final version contains an initial effort to  develop a  }
{    programming style using                                 }
{                                                            }
{                        1.  Indenting                       }
{                        2.  Blank lines                     }
{                        3.  Program comments                }
```

```
CONST
  Skip = ' ';

VAR                                      {    Variable Dictionary     }
  Score1, Score2, Score3 : integer;      {  Scores for three games    }
  Sum : integer;                         {  Sum of the three scores   }
  Average : real;                        {  Average game score        }

BEGIN
  writeln ('Please enter 3 scores and press <Enter>.');
  readln (Score1, Score2, Score3);                {  Get the scores  }

  Sum := Score1 + Score2 + Score3;
  Average := Sum / 3.0;

  writeln;
  writeln (Skip:19, 'Game', Skip:6, 'Score'); {  Print a heading  }
  writeln (Skip:19, '----', Skip:6, '-----');
  writeln;

  writeln (1:22, Score1:11);                   {  Print the results  }
  writeln (2:22, Score2:11);
  writeln (3:22, Score3:11);
  writeln;
  writeln (Skip:19, 'Your series total is', Sum:8);
  writeln (Skip:19, 'The average score is', Average:8:2);
  writeln
END.
```

When this program is run, the output is

```
Please enter 3 scores and press <Enter>.
150 178 162

                   Game      Score
                   ----      -----

                      1        150
                      2        178
                      3        162

                   Your series total is     490
                   The average score is  163.33
```

Software Engineering Implications

Perhaps the greatest difference between beginning students in computer science and "real-world" programmers is how they perceive the need for documentation. Typically, beginning students want to make a program run; they view anything that delays this process as an impediment. Thus, some students consider using descriptive identifiers, writing variable dictionaries, describing a problem as part of program documentation, and using appropriate comments throughout a program as bothersome.

A Note of Interest

Program Documentation—EDS Style

The following information was provided by Patrick J. Goss, Manager for EDS (Electronic Data Systems). His primary function is to supervise the Sales Range System for EDS customer, Xerox, in Rochester, New York.

Program documentation plays a significant part in the training and subsequent work efforts of the systems engineering group at EDS, as it does in any software development group. To illustrate the importance of documentation in software systems developed and maintained by EDS, consider the emphasis at EDS on documentation standards, reasons for stressing documentation, training for and enforcement of coding standards, and specific examples of using documentation.

Documentation Standards

Standards for documentation by systems engineers include

- The use of "flower boxes" (enclosure by asterisks) to physically separate and identify elements
- Strict naming conventions for variables, data sets, and programs
- Emphasis on structured, modularized code
- Complete documentation of the purpose of each routine within the program
- Complete documentation of the overall function of the total program, with particular emphasis on the business function it serves
- Complete documentation of the subsystem interfaces
- The use of descriptive and standard variable names that are consistent throughout the program, system, and related subsystems
- The consistent use of indentation and alignment to improve program readability

Reasons for Stressing Documentation

EDS has several reasons for placing a heavy emphasis on program documentation. First, well-documented systems are easier to maintain; the work can be streamlined when changes need to be made. Second, the use of personnel is more flexible, so staff members can be moved in and out of assignments with little or no decline in productivity. Third, the learning curve on systems support is reduced. Fourth, stress on production support/abend resolutions (system stop) is also reduced. Finally, on-call responsibilities can be rotated because it is easier to solve problems with well-documented systems.

Training and Enforcement

Systems engineers at EDS receive uniform and intensive training in program development and the use of documentation. Initial training occurs during a 10-week course in Plano, Texas. It is not unusual for program participants to work 12 to 15 hours per day, seven days a week. Approximately 20 percent of their time is spent on documentation-related issues. The successful completion rate by participants is sometimes less than 50 percent.

After the training session, maintenance of documentation skills and in-service training is provided by "walk-throughs" on every system change. These inspections involve a team of at least three peers and a secretary to record comments. During these sessions, developers are told to "check your ego at the door." Graduates from recent technical training sessions are often used as peers in order to guarantee adherence to current standards.

Some Current Examples

The result of EDS's emphasis on program documentation is perhaps best illustrated by examining some current programs.

A recent capstone project from the technical training session is a program that contains 1,934 lines, of which 670 (35 percent) are comment lines. When the systems engineers return to their jobs, they put their practice to work. Three programs in use in 1993 consist of length and documentation as follows:

Program Length	Comment Lines	Percent Documentation
1,213	397	33
1,236	247	20
3,234	854	26

In contrast, system designers and programmers who write code for a living often spend up to 50 percent of their time and effort on documentation. There are at least three reasons for this difference in perspective.

First, real programmers work on large, complex systems with highly developed logical paths. Without proper documentation, even the person who actually developed an algorithm will have difficulty following the logic six months later. Second, communication between and among teams is required as systems are developed. Complete, clear statements about what the problems are and how they are being solved are essential. Third, programmers know they can develop algorithms and write subsequent code. They are trained, so problems of searching, sorting, and file manipulation are routine to them. Knowing they can solve a problem allows them to devote more time and energy to documenting how the solution is to be achieved.

Focus on Program Design: Case Study 4.1

Preparing Monthly Statements

Let's conclude this section by writing a program to assist the treasurer of the local chapter of Lions International, a civic organization dedicated to assisting those who have vision deficiencies. The treasurer would like help in computing and printing a monthly statement for each member. To write the program, we need to know the following:

1. What regular charges should be included each month?
2. Will there be any miscellaneous charges?
3. How do members decrease the amount due?
4. What information needs to be included as part of the output?

We assume these questions are answered as follows:

1. Regular monthly charges are meals and dues. These will be defined in the **CONST** section.
2. There may be miscellaneous charges for club pins, guests for dinner meetings, and so on.
3. Members may decrease the amount due in two ways: They may pay all or part of the balance due, or they may earn credit toward their account if they purchase some supplies needed for a club activity.
4. The output should include the previous balance, all new charges, payments and credits toward the balance, and the new balance. Typical output for one club member could be

```
Please enter member identification number.
Press <Enter> when finished.
134
Previous balance?  Press <Enter> when finished.
50
Amount of miscellaneous charges?
3.00
Payments made during month?
30
Amount of other credits toward account?
2
```

```
              Local Lions Club
               September 1997

Member number:  134

Previous balance due:                 $ 50.00

Meal charges:                 11.00
Dues:                          2.50
Miscellaneous:                 3.00
                            -------
Total new charges:                    + 16.50

Payments made:                30.00
Other credits:                 2.00
                            -------
Total paid                            - 32.00
                                      -------

New Balance due:                      $ 34.50
```

Algorithm Development

Now that the problem is sufficiently defined, we can develop an algorithm for its solution. We will continue using pseudocode with stepwise refinement as we develop our algorithm. Here is the initial pseudocode for this problem:

1. Get information for one member
2. Compute total charges
3. Compute total payments and credits
4. Compute new balance
5. Display the monthly statement

Module specifications for the five main modules are as follows:

1. Get Data Module
   Data received: None
   Information returned: Member number
   Previous balance
   Miscellaneous charges
   Payments made
   Other credits
   Logic: Use **readln** statements to get data.
2. Compute Total Charges Module
   Data received: Meal charges
   Dues
   Miscellaneous charges
   Information returned: Total charges
   Logic: Sum all new charges.
3. Compute Total Payments Module
   Data received: Payments made
   Credits
   Information returned: Total of payments and credits
   Logic: Sum payments made and credits.

4. Compute New Balance Module
   Data received: Previous balance
   Total charges
   Total payments
   Information returned: New balance
   Logic: Subtract total payments from the sum of the previous balance and total charges.
5. Display Statement Module
   Data received: Member number
   Previous balance
   All new charges
   Total new charges
   All payments and credits
   Total payments/credits
   New balance
   Information returned: None
   Logic: Use **writeln** statements to produce the desired output.

A structure chart for this problem is given in Figure 4.2.
A second-level pseudocode solution is

1. Get information for one member
   1.1 Previous balance
   1.2 Miscellaneous charges
   1.3 Payments/credits
2. Compute total charges
3. Compute total payments and credits
4. Compute new balance
5. Display the monthly statement
   5.1 Display the heading
   5.2 Display previous balance

◆ Figure 4.2

Structure chart for Local Lions Club program

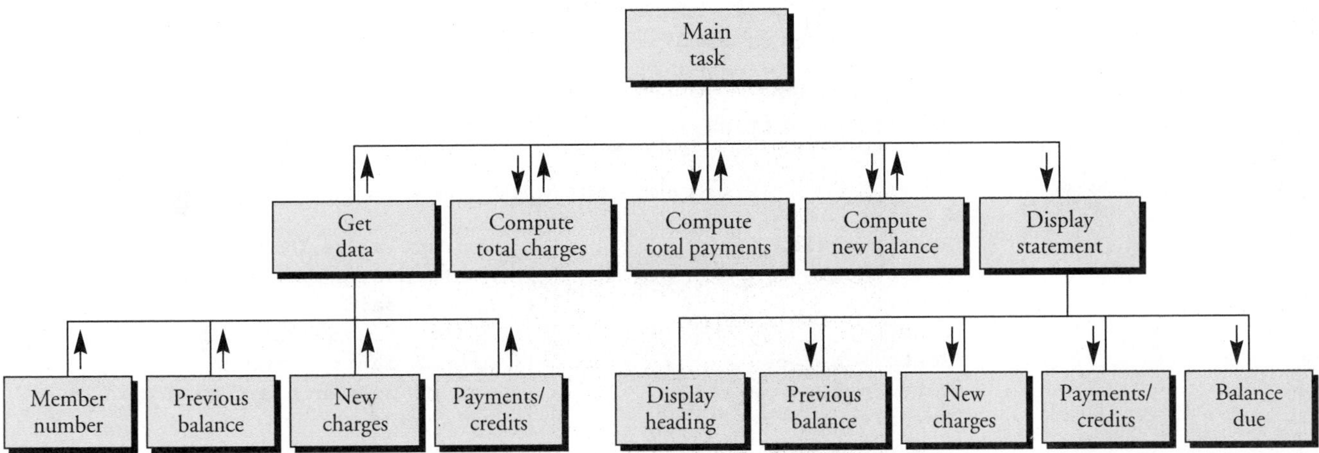

5.3 List new charges
5.4 List payment/credits
5.5 Display new balance

We now need to decide if further refinement is needed. Since each pseudocode line can be implemented in a relatively direct fashion, some programmers might choose to make no further refinements. However, we will further refine Step 5.3 to obtain

5.3 List new charges
  5.3.1 Meal costs
  5.3.2 Dues
  5.3.3 Miscellaneous

Assume data for one member are

```
Previous balance due     =    $50.00
Meal charges             =    $11.00
Dues                     =    $ 2.50
Miscellaneous            =    $ 3.00
Payments made            =    $30.00
Other credits            =    $ 2.00
```

A program to solve this problem can now be written that incorporates previous suggestions of writing style.

```
PROGRAM MonthlyStatement (input, output);

  {  This program is designed to print a monthly statement for  }
  {  members of Local Lions Club.  Information for a member is  }
  {  obtained, subtotals are computed, the new balance is       }
  {  computed, and all information is printed in a reasonable   }
  {  manner.  Note the use of the CONST section to define       }
  {  values that are currently stable but subject to change    }
  {  over time.                                                 }

CONST
  ClubName = 'Local Lions Club';
  Month = 'September 1997';
  Underline = '-------';
  Indent = ' ';
  MealCharge = 11.00;
  Dues = 2.50;

VAR
  PreviousBalance,              {  Balance at end of last month  }
  Miscellaneous,                {  Nonstandard charges           }
  Payments,                     {  Amount paid                   }
  Credits,                      {  Credit toward account         }
  MonthlyCharges,               {  Amount due for month          }
  TotalPaid,                    {  Sum of payments and credits   }
  NewBalance : real;            {  Balance due                   }
  MemberNumber : integer;       {  Member identification number  }
```

```
BEGIN  {  Program  }

  {  Get data  }
  writeln ('Please enter member identification number.');
  writeln ('Press <Enter> when finished.');
  readln (MemberNumber);
  writeln ('Previous balance?  Press <Enter> when finished.');
  readln (PreviousBalance);                                              1
  writeln ('Amount of miscellaneous charges?');
  readln (Miscellaneous);
  writeln ('Payments made during month?');
  readln (Payments);
  writeln ('Amount of other credits toward account?');
  readln (Credits);

  {  Compute total charges  }                                            2
  MonthlyCharges := MealCharge + Dues + Miscellaneous;

  {  Compute payments and credits  }                                     3
  TotalPaid := Payments + Credits;

  {  Compute new balance  }                                              4
  NewBalance := PreviousBalance + MonthlyCharges - TotalPaid;

  {  Now print all information  }
  writeln;
  writeln (Indent:9, ClubName);
  writeln (Indent:10, Month);
  writeln;
  writeln ('Member number:   ', MemberNumber);
  writeln;
  writeln ('Previous balance due:', '$':11, PreviousBalance:6:2);
  writeln;
  writeln ('Meal charges:', MealCharge:17:2);
  writeln ('Dues:', Dues:25:2);
  writeln ('Miscellaneous:', Miscellaneous:16:2);
  writeln (Underline:30);                                                5
  writeln ('Total new charges:', '+':14, MonthlyCharges:6:2);
  writeln;
  writeln ('Payments made:', Payments:16:2);
  writeln ('Other credits:', Credits:16:2);
  writeln (Underline:30);
  writeln ('Total paid', '-':22, TotalPaid:6:2);
  writeln (Underline:38);
  writeln;
  writeln ('New balance due:', '$':16, NewBalance:6:2);
  writeln
END.  {  of program  }
```

Output from this program follows:

```
Please enter member identification number.
Press <Enter> when finished.
134
```

```
Previous balance?  Press <Enter> when finished.
50
Amount of miscellaneous charges?
3.00
Payments made during month?
30
Amount of other credits toward account?
2

                  Local Lions Club
                   September 1997

Member number:   134

Previous balance due:                 $ 50.00

Meal charges:                 11.00
Dues:                          2.50
Miscellaneous:                 3.00
                            -------
Total new charges:                    + 16.50

Payments made:                30.00
Other credits:                 2.00
                            -------
Total paid                            - 32.00
                                      -------

New Balance due:                      $ 34.50
```

Exercises 4.1

Write Pascal statements for each of the lines of pseudocode shown in Exercises 1–7.

*1. Add the scores from Test1, Test2, Test3, and Test4

2. Let Average = Total divided by 4

*3. Let TotalIncome = Salary plus Tips

4. Let Time = Distance divided by Rate

*5. Let Grade = TotalPoints divided by 6

6. Write out your name, TotalPoints, and Grade

*7. Write out NumberAttending, TicketPrice, and TotalReceipts

8. Assume the output for a program to compute parking lot fees is to contain
   a. Vehicle type (car or truck)
   b. Time in
   c. Time out
   d. Total time
   e. Parking fee

   Use **writeln** statements to produce a suitable heading for this output.

*9. Given the following algorithm in pseudocode form, write a complete program that will compute the volume of a box.

   1. Assign dimensions
   2. Compute volume
   3. Display results
      3.1 Dimensions
      3.2 Volume

10. List four uses for program comments.

A Note of Interest

Communication Skills Needed

Emphasis on communication has been increasing in almost every area of higher education. Evidence of this is the current trend toward "writing across the curriculum" programs implemented in many colleges and universities in the 1980s. Indications that this emphasis is shared among computer scientists was given by Paul M. Jackowitz, Richard M. Plishka, and James R. Sidbury, University of Scranton, when they stated, "Make it possible to write programs in English, and you will discover that programmers cannot write in English."

All computer science educators are painfully aware of the truth of this old joke. We want our students to be literate. We want them to have well-developed writing skills and the capacity to read technical journals in our area. But too often we produce skilled programmers whose communication skills are poor and who have almost no research skills. We must alleviate this problem. Since the organizational techniques used to write software are the same ones that should be used to write papers, computing science students should have excellent writing skills. We should exploit this similarity in skills to develop better writers.

Further, Janet Hartman of Illinois State University and Curt M. White of Indiana-Purdue University at Fort Wayne noted, "Students need to practice written and oral communication skills, both in communications classes and computer classes. Students should write system specifications, project specifications, memos, users' guides, or anything else that requires them to communicate on both nontechnical and technical levels. They should do presentations in class and learn to augment their presentations with audiovisual aids."

On a more general note, the need for effective communication skills in computer science has been acknowledged in the 1991 curriculum guidelines of the Association for Computing Machinery, Inc. These guidelines state that

> "undergraduate programs should prepare students to apply their knowledge to specific, constrained problems and produce solutions. This includes the ability to . . . communicate that solution to colleagues, professionals in other fields, and the general public."

11. Discuss variations in program writing styles for each of the following:
    a. Using blank lines.
    b. Using program comments.
    c. Writing variable dictionaries.
12. Use program comments to create a program description section that might be used to solve the problem of computing semester grades for a class.

In Exercises 13–20, which program comments are written in valid form.

*13.
```
{          message here          }
```

14.
```
(*                               *)
(*         message here          *)
(*                               *)
```

*15.
```
(*
           message here
                                 *)
```

16.
```
 *         message here          *)
```

*17.
```
{*****************************
 *                           *
 *         message here      *
 *                           *
 *****************************}
```

18.
```
(*                          *
(*      message here        *
(*                          *)
```

*19.
```
(*                          *)
 *                          *)
 *      message here        *)
 *                          *)
 *                          *)
```

20.
```
{****************************}
{*                          *}
{*      message here        *}
{*                          *}
{****************************}
```

4.2 Beginners' Errors

Objectives

- to be aware of typical errors caused by incorrect syntax
- to be aware of typical errors made in the declaration section of a program
- to be aware of typical errors made when using assignment statements
- to be aware of typical errors made when using **writeln** to produce output

A **compilation error** is an error detected when the program is being compiled.

A **syntax error** is an error in spelling, punctuation, or placement of certain key symbols in a program.

What you learn in this chapter will help you avoid problems when you first work with Pascal. You are now aware of the significance of carefully designing an algorithm to solve a problem before you attempt to write a program. Also, you are now able to write code to implement a simple algorithm via a Pascal program. Therefore, to help you avoid frustration, we examine some typical errors made when writing code.

In an ideal situation, you would submit your program to the computer and it would run with no errors and produce exactly what you desire for output on the first attempt. Since this probably will not happen, you need to be aware of the kinds of errors that can occur. These fall into three general categories: compilation errors, run-time errors, and design errors.

Compilation errors are errors detected when the program is being compiled. These include **syntax errors,** which are errors in spelling, punctuation, or the placement of certain key symbols in a program. **Run-time errors** are errors that are detected during execution of the program. **Design errors** are errors that occur in the design of the algorithm or in coding the program that implements the algorithm. These are also referred to as **logic errors.**

Syntax

Syntax refers to the rules that govern the construction of valid statements, which include errors in spelling, punctuation, and the placement of certain key symbols. Errors made by improper use of syntax are usually easy to identify and correct.

First, let's examine uses of the semicolon. This is the fundamental punctuation mark in Pascal; it is used to separate statements. It first appears after the program heading statement and then *between* complete statements throughout the program. Semicolons may appear to be used at the end of each line. This is not true. In particular, certain keywords appear on a line but are not complete statements. Also, semicolons are not required between a statement and **END.**

To see how semicolons are needed, consider the example given in Table 4.1. The program to the left in this table has no semicolons; the one on the right has the minimum number of semicolons required to make the program run: four. Two comments are in order. First, since Pascal ignores extra blanks and line boundaries, the semicolons do not have to be written directly after the statements. Second, as

Table 4.1

An illustration of the use of semicolons in a program

Incorrect Program		Correct Program
`PROGRAM CheckSemi (output)`	(1)	`PROGRAM CheckSemi (output);`
`VAR`		`VAR`
`  Num1, Num2 : real`	(2)	`  Num1, Num2 : real;`
`BEGIN`		`BEGIN`
`  Num1 := 3.0`	(3)	`  Num1 := 3.0;`
`  Num2 := 2 * Num1`	(4)	`  Num2 := 2 * Num1;`
`  writeln (Num1:5:2, Num2:5:2)`		`  writeln (Num1:5:2, Num2:5:2)`
`END.`		`END.`

(1) A semicolon must appear after the program heading.
(2) A semicolon must appear after each declaration list in the variable declaration section.
(3) and (4) A semicolon must appear between complete statements in the executable portion of the program.

A **run-time error** is an error detected when, after compilation is completed, an error message results instead of the correct output.

A **design error** is an error such that a program runs, but unexpected results are produced. Also referred to as a **logic error.**

A **logic error** is an error in the design of a program.

we've seen before, a semicolon is not required at the end of the last statement preceding the reserved word **END.**

A second syntax error results from using the symbol for equality "=" instead of the symbol for an assignment statement ":=". This problem is compounded because several programming languages use the equal sign to assign values to variables, and the equal sign is used to define values in the **CONST** section.

A third type of syntax error occurs when writing program comments. Many of these occur when a comment begins with "(*" and ends with "*)". As comments get longer and you attempt to produce attractive readable programs, you may produce some of the following errors:

1. Improper beginning:
   (instead of (* or {
2. Improper ending:
) instead of *) or }
   * instead of *)
   $) instead of *)
3. Extra blanks:
   (*   comment   *   ) instead of (*   comment   *)
4. No close for a long comment (no ending parenthesis or brace):

```
{************************************
 *                                  *
 *   This is a long comment with    *
 *   improper closing punctuation.  *
 *                                  *
 ************************************
```

A fourth type of syntax error is the omission of the period after **END** at the end of the executable portion of the program. This error will be detected by the compiler.

A fifth type of error that some computer programmers consider a syntax error is the misspelling of keywords. Table 4.2 sets forth a program with seven misspelled keywords. You may think the identifiers Inital and Scre are also misspelled keywords. But remember: They are not keywords and can be used as spelled in the declaration section. It is not good practice to use identifiers like this, however, since you could easily spell them differently throughout the program and they would not be recognized as variables by the compiler.

▼ Table 4.2

Spelling keywords and identifiers

Incorrect Spelling	Correct Spelling
`PROGRM Spelling (output);`	`PROGRAM`
`VR`	`VAR`
`  Wage : reale;`	`real`
`  Inital : chr;`	`char`
`  Scre : interger;`	`integer`
`BEGN`	`BEGIN`
`  Wage := 5.0;`	
`  Inital := 'D';`	
`  Scre := 75;`	
`  writln (Wage:10:2, Inital:3, Scre:5)`	
`END.`	`writeln`

Declarations

Errors sometimes made when defining constants in the **CONST** section include these:

1. Using an assignment statement rather than an equal sign:

Incorrect	*Correct*
`CONST`	`CONST`
`  MaxScore := 100;`	`  MaxScore = 100;`

2. Omitting single quotation marks from string constants:

Incorrect	*Correct*
`CONST`	`CONST`
`  Name = Mary Smith;`	`  Name = 'Mary Smith';`
`  Letter = Z;`	`  Letter = 'Z';`

3. Using single quotation marks around numerical constants:

Incorrect	*Correct*
`CONST`	`CONST`
`  MaxScore = '100';`	`  MaxScore = 100;`

The declaration

```
MaxScore = '100';
```

will not result in an error during compilation. Technically, it is not an error. However, this declaration makes MaxScore a string rather than the integer constant 100. Consequently, you could not assign MaxScore to an integer variable or use it in arithmetic computations.

More errors are usually made in the variable declaration section than in the constant definition section. Several illustrations of incorrect variable declarations and the corrected versions are shown in Table 4.3.

Table 4.3

Errors in declaration sections

Incorrect	Correct

VAR
  Num1; Num2 : real
	VAR
	  Num1, Num2 : real;

VAR
  Age ; integer;
	VAR
	  Age : integer;

VAR
  Initial = char;
	VAR
	  Initial : char;

VAR
  Wage : real;
  Score
  Hours : integer;
	VAR
	  Wage : real;
	  Score,
	  Hours : integer;

Assignment Statements

In Section 3.2 you assigned a value to a variable with a statement such as

```
Score := 87;
```

Some common mistakes in assignment statements are

1. Trying to put more than one variable on the left of an assignment statement:

Incorrect	*Correct*
`X + Y := Z;`	`Z := X + Y;`
`A + 3 := B;`	`B := A + 3;`

2. Trying to make an assignment from left to right:

Incorrect	*Correct*
`87 := Score;`	`Score := 87;`

3. Trying to assign the value of one identifier (A) to another identifier (B) from left to right:

Incorrect	*Correct*
`A := B;`	`B := A;`

(This statement will not be detected as an error during compilation; thus, your program will run, but you will probably get incorrect results.)

4. Attempting to assign a value of one data type to a variable of another data type. If, for example, Score had been declared as an **integer** variable, each of the following would produce an error:

a. `Score := 77.3;`

b. `Score := 150 / 3;`

c.
```
A := 18.6;
Score := A;
```

There is an exception to this rule. The value of an **integer** data type can be assigned to a variable of type **real.** For example, if Average is a **real,** then

```
Average := 43;
```

is a valid assignment statement. However, 43 is then stored as the **real** 43.0 rather than the **integer** 43.

5. Attempting to use undeclared variables and constants. This error often results from listing the variables used in the program in the variable declaration section after the program has been written, and inadvertently omitting some variable from the list. During the compilation, you will get an error message something like "Identifier not declared" when the variable first appears in a line of code. This is easily corrected by adding the variable to the **VAR** section.

   This same error results from misspelling identifiers. For example, if the **VAR** section has

```
VAR
  Initial : char;
```

and you use the statement

```
Inital := 'D';
```

in the executable section, you will get an error message. The error message will be the same as that for an undeclared identifier because the compiler did not find Inital in its list of previously declared identifiers. Misspellings are not obvious and are difficult to detect. This is another reason for using descriptive identifiers; they are common words and you are less likely to misspell them.

   One advantage of Pascal as a programming language is that since you cannot use variables unless you declare them, misspelled variables are detected at compilation time. In some other languages (BASIC, for example), if you misspell a variable or create one unintentionally, the problem may not be discovered until after a sample run has been made.

Using `writeln`

The last general category of errors concerns statements used to create output. Section 2.3 discussed the use of **writeln** for creating a line of output. We have subsequently used this as part of executable statements in several examples. In an attempt to help you avoid making certain errors, we will examine common incorrect uses of **writeln.**

1. Format errors. When using format control with **writeln** statements, three errors are typical.
   a. Attempting to format an integer as a real:

Incorrect	*Correct*
`writeln (Score:20:2);`	`writeln (Score:20);`

b. Attempting to use a noninteger as a format control number:

Incorrect	*Correct*
`writeln (Average:20:2.0);`	`writeln (Average:20:2);`

where Average is a **real** variable.

c. Attempting to format a real as an integer. This will not cause a compilation error; your program will run, but you will get unexpected output. For example, suppose Average is a **real** variable whose value is 83.42 and you want a line of output to be

```
The average score is:     83.42
```

If you use the statement

```
writeln ('The average score is:':30, Average:10);
```

the output is

```
The average score is:  8.3E+001
```

Floating-point form is used for the real but the total field width is controlled by the use of ":10". This statement should be written

```
writeln ('The average score is:':30, Average:10:2);
```

2. Using quotation marks inappropriately. Errors of this type result from omitting needed single quotation marks or putting quotation marks where they are not needed. Remember that character strings must be enclosed in single quotation marks. For example, assume you want the output Hello.

Incorrect	*Correct*
`writeln (Hello:20);`	`writeln ('Hello':20);`

A more subtle problem arises when constants and variables have been declared in the **CONST** and **VAR** declaration sections. To illustrate, assume these sections are as follows:

```
CONST
  Name = 'Mary Smith';
  Age = 18;
VAR
  A : integer;
```

and consider the following program fragments:

a. `writeln ('My name is':20, Name:15);`

This is correct and produces

```
My name is     Mary Smith
```

b. `writeln ('My name is':20, 'Name':15);`

This format is also correct but produces

```
My name is          Name
```

This program runs, but you get incorrect output.

c. `writeln ('My age is':20, Age:4);`

This is correct and produces

```
My age is  18
```

d. Assume the assignment A := 10 has been made in the program and consider

```
writeln ('A':5, A:5);
```

This produces

```
    A   10
```

Note that using 'A' creates a character string of one character, but using A causes the contents of A to be printed. This suggests a method of obtaining descriptive output. If you want both the name of a variable and the value of a variable, you could use

```
writeln ('A =':5, A:5);
```

to obtain

```
  A =   10
```

3. Attempting to have an executable statement within the parentheses.

Incorrect	*Correct*

`writeln (A := B + C);`	`A := B + C;`
	`writeln (A);`
	or
	`writeln (B + C);`

Attempts to do this probably result from the fact that expressions can be used in **writeln** statements. Assuming suitable declarations of variables, each of the following is correct:

```
writeln (A + B:15);
writeln ('Her IQ is':10, Age + 100:5);
writeln ('The total is':20, Average * 12:6:2);
```

Although each of the previous statements is correct, many instructors prefer all operations to be performed outside **writeln** statements. Thus, instead of using the statement

```
writeln (A + B:15);
```

the statements

```
C := A + B;
writeln (C:15);
```

could be used.

In summary, you should now be aware of some errors you may make at some time during your programming career. They are easily corrected, and you will make fewer of them as you write more programs.

A Note of Interest

Computer Ethics: Copyright, Intellectual Property, and Digital Information

For hundreds of years, copyright law has existed to regulate the use of intellectual property and enforce the rights of its owners. At stake are the rights of authors and publishers to make a return on their investment in works of the intellect, which include printed matter (books, articles, etc.), art, photography, music, film, and video.

More recently, copyright law has been extended to include software and other forms of digital information. This prohibits the purchaser from reproducing the copyrighted software for sale or free distribution to others. If the software is stolen, or "pirated," the perpetrator can be prosecuted and punished by law. However, copyright law also allows for "fair use." Fair use is, for example, where the software purchaser may make backup copies for personal use. When the purchaser sells the copyrighted software to another user, the seller thereby relinquishes the right to use it and the new purchaser acquires this right (sometimes known as a "site-specific" right to use the software).

When attorneys or legislators draft copyright legislation, governments try to balance the rights of authors and publishers to a return on their work against the rights of the public to fair use. In the case of printed matter and other works that have a physical embodiment, the meaning of fair use is relatively clear. Without fair use, borrowing a book from a library or playing a CD at a high school event would be illegal.

With the rapid rise of digital information and its easy transmission on networks, different interest groups, such as authors, publishers, users, and computer professionals, are beginning to question the traditional balance of ownership rights and fair use. For example, is browsing a copyrighted manuscript on a network service an instance of fair use? Or does it involve a reproduction of the manuscript that violates the rights of the author or publisher? Is the manuscript a physical piece of intellectual property when browsed, or just a temporary pattern of bits in a computer's memory? Users and technical experts tend to favor free access to any information placed on a network. Publishers and, to a lesser extent, authors tend to worry that their work, when placed on a network, will be resold for profit, sometimes without their consent or knowledge.

Legislators who are struggling with the adjustment of copyright law to a digital environment face many of these same questions and concerns. Providers and users of digital information should also be aware of copyright issues. For a detailed discussion, see Pamela Samuelson, "Regulation of Technologies to Protect Copyrighted Works," Communications of the ACM, Volume 39, Number 7 (July, 1996), pp. 17–22.

Exercises 4.2

*1. Find two syntax errors in the following program fragment:

```
X := 3 * Y
Y = 4 - 2 * Z;
writeln (X, Y);
```

2. Write a test program to illustrate what happens when extra semicolons are used in a program.

*3. Add the minimum number of semicolons required to make the following program syntactically correct:

```
PROGRAM ExerciseThree (output)

CONST
  Name = 'Jim Jones'
  Age = 18
```

```
VAR
  Score : integer

BEGIN
  Score := 93
  writeln ('Name':13, Name:15)
  writeln ('Age':12, Age:16)
  writeln ('Score':14, Score:14)
END.
```

4. Find all incorrect uses of "=" and ":=" in the following program:

```
PROGRAM ExerciseFour (output);

CONST
  Name := 'Jim Jones';
  Age := 18;

VAR
  Score = integer;

BEGIN
  Score = 93;
  writeln (Name:10, Age:10, Score:10)
END.
```

*5. Find and correct all misspelled keywords in the following program:

```
PROGRRAM ExercseFiv (output);

VAR
  X, Y : reals;
  Nam : chr;
  Scor : interger;

BEGIN
  X := 3.0;
  Y := X * 4.2;
  Nam := 'S';
  Scor := X + Y;
  writln (X:4:2, Y:4:2, Nam:3, Scor:4)
END.
```

For Exercises 6–15, assume the variable declaration section of a program is

```
VAR
  A, Score : integer;
  X : real;
  Init : char;
```

Indicate which assignment statements are valid and which are invalid. Explain those that are invalid.

6. `A := 4 * (-3);`
*7. `Score := 1 * 2.0;`
8. `A := Score MOD 8;`
*9. `X := Score / 6;`
10. `X := X + A;`
*11. `A := X + A;`
12. `Init := 'M';`
*13. `Init := A;`
14. `Init := 'A';`
*15. `X := Init;`

For Exercises 16–24, assume the declaration section of a program is

```
CONST
  Name = 'John Harris';

VAR
  A, B : integer;
  Wages : real;
  CourseName : char;
```

Indicate which of the following statements are valid and which are invalid. Explain those that are invalid.

16. `A := A + B;`
*17. `A + B := A;`
18. `C := A - 2;`
*19. `Wage := 5.75;`
20. `CourseName := 'C';`
*21. `Wages := Hours * 6.0;`
22. `CourseName := Name;`
*23. `Name := 'John Harris';`
24. `A := 2 * Wages;`

For Exercises 25–34 assume the declaration section of a program is the same as in Exercises 16–24. Label each as valid or invalid. Correct those that are invalid.

*25. `writeln (Name);`
26. `writeln (Name:20);`
*27. `writeln ('Name':20);`
28. `writeln (A, B);`
*29. `writeln ('A', 'B');`
30. `writeln ('A = ', A);`
*31. `writeln ('A = ':10, A:3, B = :10, B:3);`
32. `writeln ('A = ':10, 'A':3);`
*33. `writeln (Wages, ' are wages');`
34. `writeln (' Wages are', Wages);`
*35. Find all errors in the following program:

```
PROGRAM Errors (output(;

(*****************************************)
(*                                       *)
(*  There are thirteen errors.           $)
(*                                       *)
(****************************************

VAR
  Day : char;
  Percent : real
  A, B ; int;

BEGIN    (  Program  )
  Day = 'M';
  Percentage := 72 / 10;
  A := 5;
  B := A * 3.2;
  writln (A, B:20);
  writeln (Day:10:2);
  writeln (A + B:8, Percent:8)
END
```

4.3 Making a Program Run

Objectives

- to be able to understand the difference between compilation errors, run-time errors, and design errors
- to be able to use the following error-correcting techniques: debugging, program walk-throughs, echo checking, short programs, and design error checking

Now that we have examined some typical errors, you may think all programs will run on the first try. Unfortunately, this is not true. All programmers eventually encounter problems when trying to make a program run. Although some short programs may run the first time and produce the desired output, you should always plan time for correcting your program. This is a normal part of a programmer's life, and you should not get discouraged when you have to rework a program.

Compilation Errors

Recall from the previous section that compilation errors are errors detected when the program is being compiled; the printed error messages are usually sufficient to enable you to correct your program. As you gain experience, you will make fewer errors of this type. Your program will not run until all compilation errors are removed, so you must develop the ability to correct these errors.

Run-Time Errors

Run-time errors occur after you have corrected all compilation errors in your program but you run your program and get partial output or error messages instead of output. A run-time error occurs in the following incorrect program:

```
PROGRAM RunError (output);

VAR
  Num1, Num2 : integer;

BEGIN
  Num1 := 3;
  Num2 := 0;
  Num1 := Num1 DIV Num2;
  writeln (Num1, Num2)
END.
```

The compiler will not detect any errors, but when this is run, you will get a message something like the following (depending on your computer and version of Pascal):

T

```
Program terminated  at line 9 in program RunError.
Division by zero.
                          ---  RunError  ---
          Num1 =      3                              Num2 =     0
```

Another example of a run-time error is trying to read the value of a variable that has been declared as an **integer,** but is entered as the value of a different type (for example, **real** or **char**). As you develop more programming skills, you may encounter run-time errors involving the logical flow of your program that are generally more difficult to locate and correct.

Design or Logic Errors

Design (logic) errors occur after you have eliminated both compilation errors and run-time errors. At this stage, your program runs and produces output; however, when you examine the output, it is not what you want. The problems can include having columns incorrectly lined up, having incorrect values for the output, or not getting all of the output. For example, the program

```
PROGRAM DesignError (output);

VAR
  Score : integer;

BEGIN
  writeln;
  writeln ('Scores':20);
  writeln ('------':25);
  Score := 87;
  writeln (Score);
  Score := 92;
  writeln (Score);
  writeln
END.
```

produces the output

```
            Scores
                 ------
   87
   92
```

instead of

```
            Scores
            ------

              87
              92
```

Therefore, the program should be modified as follows:

```
PROGRAM DesignError (output);

CONST
  LabelWidth = 20;

VAR
  Score : integer;

BEGIN
  writeln;
  writeln ('Scores':LabelWidth);
  writeln ('------':LabelWidth);
  writeln;
  Score := 87;
  writeln (Score:18);
  Score := 92;
  writeln (Score:18);
  writeln
END.
```

Programmers use many different techniques to detect errors. We now examine some of the more common of these helpful practices, which include program walk-throughs (traces), echo checking, and writing short programs.

Communication and Style Tips

We have been using constants Skip and Indent to control spacing of output. If some strings are to be right justified (abutting the right-hand margin), we can define a constant as in **PROGRAM** DesignError as

```
CONST
  LabelWidth = 20;
```

and use it to format strings. For example,

```
writeln ('Scores':LabelWidth);
writeln ('-----':LabelWidth);
```

Debugging Techniques

Debugging is the process of eliminating errors, or "bugs," from a program.

Debugging is a term used to refer to the process of eliminating errors. (This term dates back to 1945. Computer scientists were working on the Mark II and suddenly something went wrong. During a check of the machine, someone found that a moth was caught in one of the relays. It was removed, and the first computer had been "debugged." The term is now used in a somewhat broader sense.) When trying to debug a program, you can do several things. First, carefully reading the code will help you identify and eliminate many of the errors mentioned in the previous section, such as syntax errors, invalid identifiers, incorrect spelling, and incorrect use of **writeln** statements. This technique requires patience and thoroughness, but will save you time in the long run.

T

A second debugging technique is to use compiler error messages to help you correct errors you missed during your careful reading of code. Since these messages vary from machine to machine (they are implementation dependent), you will have to learn to interpret the messages printed by your machine.

Errors causing compiler error messages are not always easy to find. Sometimes an error message on one line is the result of a previous error several lines earlier. For example, the program

```
PROGRAM CompileError (output);

{  This will detect a compilation error  $

CONST
  Name = 'Mary Smith';
  Indent = ' ';

VAR
  Age : integer;

BEGIN
  Age := 18;
  writeln (Indent:10, 'My name is', Name:15);
  writeln (Indent:10, 'My age is', Age:3)
END.
```

when compiled, may produce

```
*** Incomplete program.
Compiler error message(s).
```

This can be corrected by changing the comment line

```
{  This will detect a compilation error  $
```

to

```
{  This will detect a compilation error  }
```

Once you remove the syntax error ($), you should have an error-free compilation and be ready to run the program.

A third debugging technique can be utilized after you get an error-free compilation. Run the program and get a list of run-time error messages. (If you have been very careful, you may not have any run-time errors.) Consider this program:

```
PROGRAM RunTimeError (output);

VAR
  Num1, Num2 : integer;
  Average : real;

BEGIN
  Num1 := 10;
  Average := (Num1 + Num2) / 2.0;
  writeln ('The average is':20, Average:10:2)
END.
```

There are no compilation errors in the program, but the output is something equivalent to

T

```
Program terminated at line 9 in program RunTimeErr.
Integer larger than maxint.
                              --- RunTimeErr ---
  Average =   Undef                                    Num1 =     10
     Num2 =   Undef
```

and not the desired output because Num2 has not been assigned a value.

Use these messages to analyze and correct your program. Remember, these messages are implementation dependent and it will take time before you can understand them.

Program Walk-Through

Program walk-through is the process of carefully following (with pencil and paper) the steps the computer uses to solve the problem given in a program. Also referred to as **trace.**

A **program walk-through**, sometimes referred to as a **trace,** is used to describe the process of using paper and pencil to carefully follow the steps the computer uses to solve the problem given in your program. Two types of walk-throughs are used by programmers. First, you follow the logical flow of your program. During this check, you are not looking for syntax errors; you are merely making sure that the order in which things are done is correct. This type of checking will be more efficient after you have written more programs. A second type of program walk-through keeps track of the values of the variables on paper. The next example illustrates this idea.

A Note of Interest

A Software Glitch

The software glitch that disrupted AT&T's long-distance telephone service for nine hours in January 1990 dramatically demonstrates what can go wrong even in the most reliable and scrupulously tested systems. Of the roughly 100 million telephone calls placed with AT&T during that period, only about one-half got through. The breakdown cost the company more than $60 million in lost revenues, and considerably inconvenienced and irritated telephone-dependent customers.

The trouble began at a "switch"—one of 114 interconnected, computer-operated electronic switching systems scattered across the United States. These sophisticated systems, each a maze of electronic equipment housed in a large room, form the backbone of the AT&T long-distance telephone network.

When a local exchange delivers a telephone call to the network, it arrives at one of these switching centers, which can handle up to 700,000 calls an hour. The switch immediately springs into action. It scans a list of 14 different routes it can use to complete the call and, at the same time, hands off the telephone number to a parallel signaling network, invisible to any caller. This private data network allows computers to scout the possible routes and to determine whether the switch at the other end can deliver the call to the local company it serves.

If the answer is no, the call is stopped at the original switch to keep it from tying up a line and the caller gets a busy signal. If the answer is yes, a signaling-network computer makes a reservation at the destination switch and orders the original switch to pass along the waiting call—after that switch makes a final check to ensure that the chosen line is functioning properly. The whole process of passing a call down the network takes 4 to 6 seconds. Because the switches must keep in constant touch with the signaling network and its computers, each switch has a computer program that handles all the necessary communications between the switch and the signaling network.

AT&T's first indication that something might be amiss appeared on a giant video display at the company's network control center in Bedminster, New Jersey. At 2:25 P.M. on Monday, January 15, 1990, network managers saw an alarming increase in the number of red warning signals appearing on many of the 75 video screens showing the status of various parts of AT&T's worldwide network. The warnings signaled a serious collapse in the network's ability to complete calls within the United States.

To bring the network back up to speed, AT&T engineers first tried a number of standard procedures that had worked in the past. This time, the methods failed. The engineers realized they had a problem never seen before. Nonetheless, within a few hours, they managed to stabilize the network by temporarily cutting back on the number of messages moving through the signaling network. They cleared the last defective link at 11:30 P.M. that night.

Meanwhile, a team of more than 100 telephone technicians tried frantically to track down the fault. Because the problem involved the signaling network and seemed to bounce from one switch to another, they zeroed in on the software that permitted each switch to communicate with the signaling-network computers.

The day after the slowdown, AT&T personnel removed the apparently faulty software from each switch, temporarily replacing it with an earlier version of the communications program. A close examination of the flawed software turned up a single error in one line of the program. Just one month earlier, network technicians had changed the software to speed the processing of certain messages, and the change had inadvertently introduced a flaw into the system.

From that finding, AT&T could reconstruct what had happened.

Example 4.1

Let's walk through the following program.

```
PROGRAM WalkThru (output);

VAR
  Num1, Num2 : integer;

BEGIN
  Num1 := 5;
  Num2 := Num1 + 4;
  Num1 := Num2 - 2;
  Num2 := Num1 * 5;
  Num2 := Num2 DIV 3;
  writeln (Num1:5, Num2:5)
END.
```

To walk through this program, we will list the variables and then proceed through the program one line at a time.

Statement	Value of Num1	Value of Num2
`Num1 := 5;`	5	Undefined
`Num2 := Num1 + 4;`	5	9
`Num1 := Num2 - 2;`	7	9
`Num2 := Num1 * 5;`	7	35
`Num2 := Num2 DIV 3;`	7	11

At the end of the program, Num1 has the value 7 and Num2 has the value 11.

Echo checking is a technique whereby the computer prints values of variables and data used in a program.

Echo Checking

Echo checking is a technique whereby you let the computer check the values of your variables and the data used in your program. When reading values or changing the value of a variable, you could use a **writeln** statement to immediately print out the new value with a short, descriptive message. To illustrate, consider the short **PROGRAM** WalkThru in Example 4.1. An echo check could be implemented by inserting **writeln** statements as follows:

```
PROGRAM WalkThru (output);

VAR
  Num1, Num2 : integer;

BEGIN
  Num1 := 5;
  writeln ('Num1 =', Num1:3);
  Num2 := Num1 + 4;
  writeln ('Num2 =', Num2:3);
  Num1 := Num2 - 2;
  writeln ('Num1 =', Num1:3);
```

```
      Num2 := Num1 * 5;
      writeln ('Num2 =', Num2:3);
      Num2 := Num2 DIV 3;
    writeln ('Num2 =', Num2:3);
    writeln (Num1:5, Num2:5)
  END.
```

The output for this program is

```
Num1 =  5
Num2 =  9
Num1 =  7
Num2 = 35
Num2 = 11
    7   11
```

You can echo check input data similarly. For example, if an input statement is

```
readln (Num1, Num2);
```

the values can be checked by inserting an output statement such as

```
writeln ('Num1 =', Num1, ' Num2 =', Num2);
```

You probably will not want to print each variable value in the final program. Therefore, once your program produces the desired output, remove the **writeln** statements used for checking and you have a working program.

Short Programs

Using short test programs is another technique for error checking. It is particularly effective on longer, more complex programs, but to illustrate, consider the following short example.

Example 4.2

Suppose you are writing a program and you want to exchange the values of variables Num1 and Num2. You think this could be accomplished by

```
Num1 := Num2;
Num2 := Num1;
```

You could write a short program to check this as follows:

```
PROGRAM ExchangeCheck (output);

VAR
  Num1, Num2 : integer;

BEGIN
  Num1 := 5;
  Num2 := 10;
  writeln ('Num1 =', Num1:3, ' Num2 =', Num2:3);

{  Now exchange  }
```

```
    Num1 := Num2;
    Num2 := Num1;
    writeln ('Num1 =', Num1:3, ' Num2 =', Num2:3)
  END.
```

When you run this short program, the output

```
Num1 =  5 Num2 = 10
Num1 = 10 Num2 = 10
```

indicates your method of exchanging values did not work and you have to redesign your program. The exchange could be accomplished by declaring a third variable Temp and then using the code

```
Temp := Num1;
Num1 := Num2;
Num2 := Temp;
```

Example 4.2 is quite simple, but as you start writing programs to solve complex problems, you will find that using short programs is a very effective technique.

Exercises 4.3

*1. Perform a program walk-through for the following program segment to determine the values of Num1, Num2, and Num3 at the end of the segment.

```
Num1 := 33;
Num2 := -2;
Num1 := Num1 - 5;
Num2 := Num1;
Num3 := Num2 + 2;
Num1 := Num2;
Num3 := Num1 - Num2 + 1;
Num1 := Num1 + 1;
```

2. Write a separate test program to illustrate what error message appears for each of the following:
   a. dividing by zero.
   b. printing a variable that has not been assigned a value.
   c. using a variable that has not been assigned a value.

For Exercises 3 and 4, correct all compilation errors. Check your results by running each program exactly as it is written here and examining the compilation error messages.

*3.
```
PROGRAM CompileErrors (output);

CONST
  Max = 100.0 : real;

VAR
  Score, Sum : integer
```

```
BEGIN
  Score := 86.0;
  Sum := Score + 0;
  Score + Sum := Sum
  writeln (Sum:15:2)
END.
```

4. **PROGRAM Compile Errors (output);**

```
VAR
  Num1 : integer;
  Ch : char;

BEGIN
  Ch := 'M';
  Num1 := 83;
  Num2 := Num1 - 10;
  writeln (' The value of Num1 is:20, Num1:6);
  writeln (Ch:20)
END.
```

*5. Suppose the output from a program is as follows:

```
NameJohn   JohnsAge   18
  Test Scores
-----
73                  82                  96
```

Indicate a more desirable form for the output and describe what changes could be made in the program to achieve those desired results.

6. Consider this program:

```
PROGRAM Donations (output);

VAR
  Amount1, Amount2,
  Amount3, Amount4,
  Sum : real;

BEGIN
  Amount1 := 100.0;
  Amount2 := 150.0;
  Amount3 := 75.0;
  Amount4 := 200.50;
  Sum := Amount1 + Amount2 + Amount3 + Amount4;
  writeln ('Donations':29);
  writeln (Amount1:28:2);
  writeln (Amount2:28:2);
  writeln (Amount3:28:2);
  writeln (Amount4:28:2);
  writeln ('------':28);
  writeln (Sum:28:2)
END.
```

The output for this program is

```
Donations
  100.00
  150.00
   75.00
  200.50
  ------
  525.50
```

Change the program so the output would be

```
          Donations
          ---------

          $ 100.00
          $ 150.00
          $  75.00
          $ 200.50
          ---------

Total     $ 525.50
```

*7. The following program has no compilation errors, but it does contain some run-time errors. Find them and indicate what could be done to correct them.

```
PROGRAM RunErrors (output);

VAR
  A : integer;
  X : real;
  Ch : char;

BEGIN
  A := 4;
  X := 100.0;
  Ch := 'F';
  X := X / (4 MOD 2);
  X := 3 * X;
  writeln (Ch:5, X:8:2, A:5)
END.
```

8. List three types of errors made by computer programmers. Discuss their differences and what methods can be used to correct them.
9. Use **writeln** statements in the following program to echo check the values of each of the variables. Indicate what the output would be when you run the echo-check version.

```
PROGRAM EchoCheck (output);

VAR
  Sum, Score, Count : integer;
  Average : real;

BEGIN
  Count := 0;
```

```
    Sum := 0;
    Score := 86;
    Sum := Sum + Score;
    Count := Count + 1;
    Score := 89;
    Sum := Sum + Score;
    Count := Count + 1;
    Average := Sum / Count;
    writeln;
    writeln ('There were':20, Count:3, ' scores.');
    writeln;
    writeln ('The average is':24, Average:6:2)
  END.
```

Focus on Program Design: Case Study 4.2

Student Progress Report

By now you should be able to implement the six steps in problem solving. You should also be able to write complete programs that include the following features:

- Clear program documentation and writing style
- The ability to get data from a keyboard
- Neat, attractive output

By way of example, we end this chapter with a case study of a complete program in which problem solving and design features are demonstrated. Once you feel comfortable that you can use these skills as illustrated, you can easily add new programming skills to your repertoire.

Mr. Lae Z. Programmer, teacher of computer science, wants a program that will allow him to give an individual progress report to each student in his computer science class. The report for each student should include the student's initials, three test scores, test average, five quiz scores, weighted quiz total, and final percentage. We will develop a program for this problem and test it by running it for two students. In Chapter 6, we will see how this program could be conveniently used for the entire class.

The first step in problem solving is to understand the problem. For this particular problem, we need to know what the input will look like, how quizzes are to be weighted, how final percentage is to be computed, and what form is desired for the output. Let's assume these questions have been asked and answered as follows:

1. The data for a student consist of the student's initials followed by three test scores and then five quiz scores. Scores will be integers and will be separated by blanks. The test scores are based on 100 points each and the quiz scores are based on 10 points each. Thus, the data could be

   three initials (MJS)
   three test scores (91 87 79)
   five quiz scores (8 10 10 9 7)

2. The quizzes are to be counted as the equivalent of one 100-point test. Thus, their total should be multiplied by two when computing the weighted total.
3. Final percentage is to be computed based on a total of 400 points: 100 for each test and 100 for the quiz total.

4. The interim report should look like

```
                    **********************
                    *                    *
                    *   Interim Report   *
                    *                    *
                    **********************

Class:          Computer Science
Date:           October 15
Teacher:        Mr. Lae Z. Programmer

                Test        Test          Quiz            Quiz
Initials       Scores      Average       Scores           Total
------------------------------------------------------------
  MJS         91 87 79     85.67      8 10 10  9  7        88

Final percentage =   86.25
--------------------------
```

The second step in problem solving is to develop an algorithm. This will be done using stepwise refinement. As a first level of pseudocode, we have

1. Get data for student
2. Perform computations
3. Display student report

Module specifications for the modules corresponding to Steps 1, 2, and 3 are

1. Get Data Module
   Data received: None
   Information returned: Three initials
   Five quiz scores
   Three test scores
   Logic: Use **read** statements to get data.
2. Perform Computations Module
   Data received: Five quiz scores
   Three test scores
   Information returned: Test average
   Weighted quiz total
   Final percentage
   Logic: Divide total of test scores by three.
   Multiply quiz total by two for weighting.
   Sum totals and divide by four for final average.
3. Display Student Report Module
   Data received: All input data
   Test average
   Quiz total
   Final percentage
   Information returned: None
   Logic: Use **writeln** statements to display information in desired format.

Let's now refine the pseudocode for Steps 1, 2, and 3.

1. Get data for student
   1.1 Get initials

1.2 Get test scores
1.3 Get quiz scores

Each of these lines could be refined further. For example, Step 1.1 could be subdivided into

1.1 Get initials
    1.1.1 Get first initial
    1.1.2 Get second initial
    1.1.3 Get third initial

At some stage, you have to decide what is a sufficient refinement when developing an algorithm. This will vary according to students and teachers. In general, when you have a clearly defined statement that can be accomplished by a single line of code, there is no need for subsequent refinement. In fact, a single line of pseudocode may require several lines of written code in a program. The important thing to remember is that algorithm development via pseudocode is only a step in helping solve a problem; it is not the solution itself.

Refining Step 2, we could have

2. Perform computations
    2.1 Compute test average
    2.2 Compute quiz total
    2.3 Compute final percentage

This can be further refined to

2. Perform computations
    2.1 Compute test average
        2.1.1 Add test scores
        2.1.2 Divide by three
    2.2 Compute quiz total
        2.2.1 Add quiz scores
        2.2.2 Multiply by two
    2.3 Compute final percentage
        2.3.1 Add test totals to quiz total
        2.3.2 Divide by four

A structure chart for the student with the second module developed through three levels is given in Figure 4.3. Refining Step 3 might result in

3. Display student report
    3.1 Display report heading
    3.2 Display student information

This can be further refined to

3. Display student report
    3.1 Display report heading
        3.1.1 Display title
        3.1.2 Display class information
        3.1.3 Display column headings
    3.2 Display student information
        3.2.1 Display initials

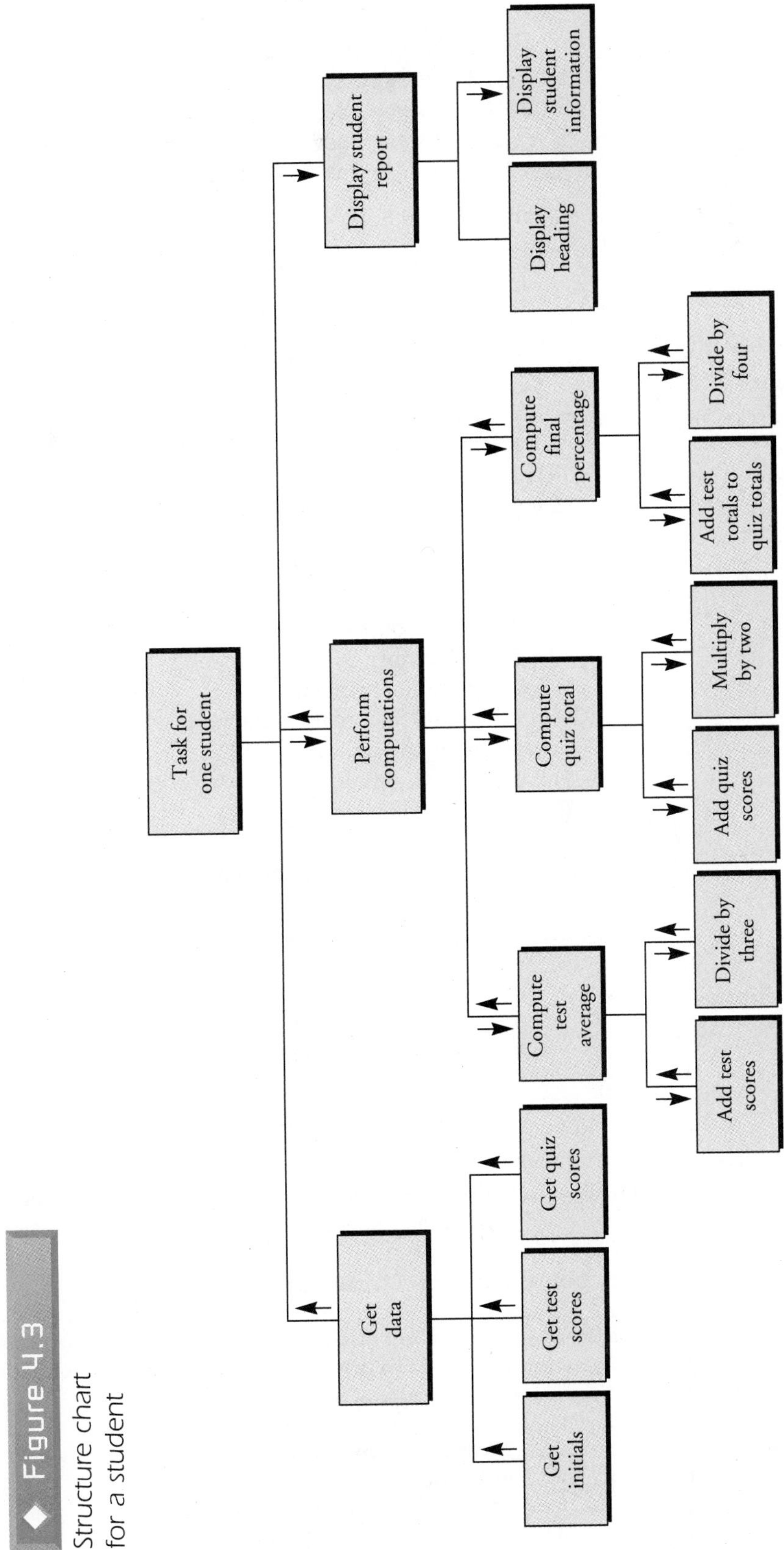

◆ Figure 4.3

Structure chart for a student

3.2.2 Display test scores
3.2.3 Display test average
3.2.4 Display quiz scores
3.2.5 Display quiz total
3.2.6 Display final percentage

The complete algorithm is

1. Get data for student
    1.1 Get initials
        1.1.1 Get first initial
        1.1.2 Get second initial
        1.1.3 Get third initial
    1.2 Get test scores
    1.3 Get quiz scores
2. Perform computations
    2.1 Compute test average
        2.1.1 Add test scores
        2.1.2 Divide by three
    2.2 Compute quiz total
        2.2.1 Add quiz scores
        2.2.2 Multiply by two
    2.3 Compute final percentage
        2.3.1 Add test totals to quiz total
        2.3.2 Divide by four
3. Display student report
    3.1 Display report heading
        3.1.1 Display title
        3.1.2 Display class information
        3.1.3 Display column headings
    3.2 Display student information
        3.2.1 Display initials
        3.2.2 Display test scores
        3.2.3 Display test average
        3.2.4 Display quiz scores
        3.2.5 Display quiz total
        3.2.6 Display final percentage

You may now write code for the algorithm. In the following version, an attempt to create presentable output has included boxed descriptions of headings, centering on the page when appropriate, underlining, skipping lines, and carefully created columns.

```
PROGRAM StudentReport (input, output);

{    This program is written for Mr. Lae Z. Programmer.  It      }
{    produces an interim progress report for a student. The      }
{    following features have been included.                      }
{                                                                }
{         1.  Program documentation                              }
{         2.  Writing style                                      }
{         3.  Use of interactive input                           }
{         4.  Descriptive variables                              }
{         5.  Neat, attractive output                            }
```

```
CONST
  Splats = '**********************';
  Edge =   '*                    *';
  Line = '--------------------------------------------------------';
  Skip = ' ';

VAR
  FinalPercent : real;            {    Final class percentage    }
  Init1, Init2, Init3 : char;     {      Initials for student    }
  Quiz1, Quiz2, Quiz3,
  Quiz4, Quiz5 : integer;         {   Quiz scores for student    }
  QuizTotal : integer;            {       Sum of five quizzes    }
  Test1, Test2, Test3 : integer;  {   Test scores for student    }
  TestAverage : real;             {    Average of three tests    }
  TestTotal : integer;            {  Sum of three test scores    }

BEGIN  {  Program  }

{  Get data for student  }
  writeln ('Please enter student''s initials and press <Enter>.');
  readln (Init1, Init2, Init3);
  writeln ('Now enter 3 test scores and press <Enter>.');                1
  readln (Test1, Test2, Test3);
  writeln ('Enter 5 quiz scores and press <Enter>.');
  readln (Quiz1, Quiz2, Quiz3, Quiz4, Quiz5);

{  Perform necessary computations  }
  TestTotal := Test1 + Test2 + Test3;
  TestAverage := TestTotal / 3.0;                                         2
  QuizTotal := (Quiz1 + Quiz2 + Quiz3 + Quiz4 + Quiz5) * 2;
  FinalPercent := (TestTotal + QuizTotal) / 4.0;

{  Print the title  }
  writeln;
  writeln (Skip:30, Splats);
  writeln (Skip:30, Edge);
  writeln (Skip:30, '*   Interim Report   *');
  writeln (Skip:30, Edge);
  writeln (Skip:30, Splats);

{  Print the class information  }
  writeln;
  writeln (Skip:15, 'Class:        Computer Science');
  writeln (Skip:15, 'Date:         October 15');
  writeln (Skip:15, 'Teacher:      Mr. Lae Z. Programmer');                 3
  writeln;

{  Print the column headings  }
  writeln (Skip:27, 'Test', 'Test':10, 'Quiz':13, 'Quiz':14);
  writeln (Skip:15, 'Initials', 'Scores':9, 'Average':11,
          'Scores':12, 'Total':13);
  writeln (Skip:15, Line);

{  Print the student information  }
  write (Init1:18, Init2, Init3);
```

```
   write (Test1:7, Test2:3, Test3:3);
   write (TestAverage:9:2);
   write (Quiz1:6, Quiz2:3, Quiz3:3, Quiz4:3, Quiz5:3);
   writeln (QuizTotal:7);
   writeln;
   writeln (Skip:15, 'Final percentage = ', FinalPercent:7:2);
   writeln (Skip:15, '--------------------------');
   writeln
END.
```

A Note of Interest

Debugging or Sleuthing?

Investigating why programs don't work as expected requires ingenuity. The reason can be quite bizarre. To illustrate, consider two situations reported by Jon Bentley in Communications of the ACM.

1. When a programmer used his new computer terminal, all was fine when he was sitting down, but he couldn't log in to the system when he was standing up. That behavior was 100 percent repeatable: He could always log in when sitting and never when standing.
2. A banking system had worked for quite some time, but halted the first time it was used on international data. Programmers spent days scouring the code, but they couldn't find any stray command that would return control to the operating system.

What do you think are possible solutions? The answers are set forth just before the **Programming Problems** for this chapter.

Summary

Key Terms

comment
compilation error
debugging
design (logic) error
echo checking
program walk-through (trace)
run-time error
syntax error
variable dictionary

Key Concepts

- It is not sufficient to produce correct output; your output should also be clear, neat, and attractive.
- Attractive output is produced by using blank lines as appropriate, underlining, right- and left-hand margins, columns, and descriptive headings and messages.
- Comments are nonexecutable statements that can be included in a program using the form

```
{  ...comment...  }
```

or

```
(*  ...comment...  *)
```

- Program readability is enhanced by indenting, using blank lines, and using program comments.

- Programs should be documented by using a variable dictionary and a comment section to describe the program.
- Common syntax errors result from inappropriate use of the semicolon, using "=" for assigning rather than ":=", incorrectly starting or ending comments, forgetting the period at the end of the program, or misspelling keywords.
- Other sources of errors for beginners include errors made in declarations, or assignment statements, or in using **writeln.**
- Program errors can be detected and eliminated (debugged) by program walk-throughs, echo checking, use of short programs, and design error checking.
- When writing a complete program, make sure you have answered all questions concerning input, processing, and output before you attempt to design the solution.
- After all questions are answered, design a solution to the problem; refine steps in the solution until you can easily write code for the program.
- When writing the program, use a neat, consistent, readable writing style. Your documentation should include a program description section, a variable dictionary, and, when appropriate, comment sections and line comments. You should use consistent indenting and blank lines to separate code.
- The output for your program should be neat and readable; features should include use of the middle of the output page, appropriate titles and headings, columns where appropriate, blank lines, and underlining.

Chapter Review Exercises

1. Explain the importance of the use of frequent comments and the use of writing styles such as blank lines and variable dictionaries in Pascal programming.

In Exercises 2–17, correct any errors in the Pascal statements.

2. `X := 3Y + 4;`
3. `Z = 2 + T;`
4. `writeln ("The answer is ":5, A:3);`
5. `readln (sqrt(G));`
6. `D := 'This is a list of characters.';`
7. ```
   VAR
     Var1 = real;
     Var2; Var3 = integer;
   ```
8. `A := abst(-5.2);`
9. `X := ord(7.2);`
10. `writeln ('Question 10':12:5);`
11. `PROGRAM 4Chapter (input; output)`
12. ```
    CONST
      A := 15;
    ```
13. `T := 5.3 MOD 1.8;`
14. `readln (A:5);`
15. `writeln (Pascal Programming:18);`
16. ```
    VAR
      a : real,
      b ; integer,
      c ; char.
    ```
17. `(&  This is a comment.  &)`
    ```

18. Explain the difference between a compilation error, a run-time error, and a design error.
19. What output is produced from the following program?

```
PROGRAM Exercise (output);

CONST
  A = 5;

VAR
  B : real;
  C, D : integer;

BEGIN
  B := 4.5;
  C := sqr(A);
  D := C + 5;
  B := abs(B);
  C := succ(C);
  B := B + C * A;
  writeln (B:5:2, A:6, C:4)
END.
```

20. Correct all errors in the following program:

```
PROG Test (output)

VAR
  A, B : integer
  C : real;

BEGIN
  writeln (Enter an integer and a real number);
  readln (A, C);
  B := A + B
  C := pred(C) + 4;
  D := sqr(C);
  A := 0;
  B := B DIV A;
  writeln (A:5, B:5:2, C:5)
END
```

A Note of Interest

Debugging or Sleuthing: Answers

1. The problem was in the terminal's keyboard: the tops of two keys were switched. When the programmer was seated, he was a touch-typist and the problem went unnoticed; when he stood, he was led astray by hunting and pecking.
2. When the programmers observed the behavior more closely, they found that the problem occurred as they entered data for the country of Ecuador. When the user typed the name of the capital city (Quito), the program interpreted that as a request to quit the run.

Programming Problems

Before going on, you should test your knowledge of the material by writing a complete program for some of the following problems. For each problem you solve, include an algorithm development with an accompanying structure chart. Write module specifications for each main module. Problems marked by a color box to the left of the number will be referred to in later chapters.

1. The Roll-Em Lanes bowling team would like to have a computer program to print the team results for one series of games. The team consists of four members whose names are Weber, Fazio, Martin, and Patterson. Each person on the team bowls three games during the series; thus, the input will be three lines, each with four integer scores. Your output should include all input data, individual series totals, game average for each member, team series, and team average.

   Sample output is

```
Name            Game 1    Game 2    Game 3    Total    Average
----            ---- -    ---- -    ---- -    -----    -------
Weber             212       220       190
Fazio             195       235       210
Martin            178       190       206
Patterson         195       215       210

        Team Total:

        Team Average:
```

■ 2. The Natural Pine Furniture Company has recently hired you to help them convert their antiquated payroll system to a computer-based model. They know you are still learning, so all they want right now is a program that will print a one-week pay report for three employees. You should use the constant definition section for the following:

   a. Federal withholding tax rate 18%
   b. State withholding tax rate 4.5%
   c. Hospitalization $25.65
   d. Union dues $7.85

   Input for each employee is
   a. Employee's initials
   b. Number of hours worked
   c. Hourly rate

   Your output should include a report for each employee and a summary report for the company files. A sample employee form follows:

```
Employee:       JTM
Hours Worked:   40.00
Hourly Rate:     9.75

     Total Wages:

     Deductions:
          Federal Withholding
          State Withholding
```

```
          Hospitalization
          Union Dues
               Total Deductions

     Net Pay
```

Output for a summary report could be:

```
          Natural Pine Furniture Company
                  Weekly Summary

    Gross Wages:

    Deductions:
         Federal Withholding
         State Withholding
         Hospitalization
         Union Dues
             Total Deductions

    Net Wages:
```

3. The Child-Growth Encyclopedia Company wants a computer program that will print a monthly sales chart. Products produced by the company, prices, and sales commissions for each are

a. Basic encyclopedia	$325.00	22%
b. Child educational supplement	$127.50	15%
c. Annual update book	$ 18.95	20%

Write a program that will get the monthly sales data for two sales regions and produce the desired company chart. Data are a two-letter code for the region followed by three integers representing number of products a, b, and c sold, respectively. The prices may vary from month to month and should be defined in the constant definition section. The commissions are not subject to change.

Sample data are

MI 150 120 105
FL 225 200 150

Typical output could be:

```
REGION                               SALES
------                               -----
               (Encyclopedia)  (Supplement)  (Update)

MI                  150             120          105
FL                  225             200          150

Total Sales:

Total Commission:
```

4. The Village Variety Store is having its annual Christmas sale. They would like you to write a program to produce a daily report for the store. Each item sold is identified by a code consisting of one letter followed by one digit. Your

report should include data for three items. Input for each item consists of item code, number of items sold, original item price, and reduction percentage. Your report should include a chart with the input data, sale price per item, and total amount of sales per item. You should also print a daily summary.
Sample data are

A1 13 5.95 15
A2 24 7.95 20
A3 80 3.95 50

Typical output form could be:

```
Item Code  # Sold  Original Price  Reductions  Sale Price  Income
---------  ------  --------------  ----------  ----------  ------

   A1         13        $5.95          15%         $5.06   $65.78

Daily Summary
----- -------

   Gross Income:
```

5. The Holiday-Out Motel Company, Inc., wants a program that will print a statement for each overnight customer. Input for each customer is room number (integer), number of nights (integer), room rate (real), telephone charges (real), and restaurant charges (real). You should use the constant definition section for the date and current tax rate. Each customer statement should include all input data, the date, tax rate and amount, total due, appropriate heading, and appropriate closing message. Test your program by running it for two customers. The tax rate applies only to the room cost. Typical data are

135 3 39.95 3.75 57.50

A customer statement form is

```
       Holiday-Out Motel Company, Inc.
       ----------- ----- -------- ----

Date: XX-XX-XX
Room #                         135
Room Rate:                   $39.95
Number of Nights:              3

Room Cost:                  $119.85
Tax: XXX%                      4.79
     Subtotal:                           $124.64

Telephone:                                  3.75
Meals:                                     57.50

     TOTAL DUE                           $185.89

      Thank you for staying at Holiday-Out
                 Drive safely
                Please come again
```

6. As a part-time job this semester, you are working for the Family Budget Assistance Center. Your boss has asked you to write and execute a program that will analyze data for a family. Input for each family will consist of

Family ID number	(**integer**)
Number in family	(**integer**)
Income	(**real**)
Total debts	(**real**)

Your program should output the following:

a. An appropriate header.
b. The family's identification number, number in family, income, and total debts.
c. Predicted family living expenses ($3,000 times the size of the family).
d. The monthly payment necessary to pay off the debt in one year (Debt / 12).
e. The amount the family should save [the family size times 2 percent of the income minus debt—FamSize * 0.02 * (income – debt)].
f. Your service fee (0.5 percent of the income).

Run your program for the following two families:

Identification Number	Size	Income	Debt
51	4	18000.00	2000.00
72	7	26000.00	4800.00

Output for the first family could be:

```
        Family Budget Assistance Center
                  March 1997
           Telephone: (800)555-1234

Identification number                 51
Family size                            4
Annual income                 $ 18000.00
Total debt                    $  2000.00
Expected living expenses      $ 12000.00
Monthly payment               $   166.67
Savings                       $  1280.00
Service fee                   $    90.00
```

7. The Caswell Catering and Convention Service has asked you to write a computer program to produce customers' bills. The program should read in the following data:

a. The number of children to be served.
b. The number of adults to be served.
c. The cost per adult meal.
d. The cost per child's meal (60 percent of the cost of the adult's meal).
e. The cost for dessert (same for adults and children).
f. The room fee (no room fee if catered at the person's home).

g. A percentage for tip and tax (not applied to the room fee).
h. Any deposit should be deducted from the bill.

The following are sample data for this problem:

Data	Child Count	Adult Count	Adult Cost	Dessert Cost	Room Rate	Tip/ Tax	Deposit
1	7	23	12.75	1.00	45.00	18%	50.00
2	3	54	13.50	1.25	65.00	19%	40.00
3	15	24	12.00	0.00	45.00	18%	75.00
4	2	71	11.15	1.50	0.00	6%	0.00

Data set 1 was used to produce the following sample output:

```
Caswell Catering and Convention Service
              Final Bill

             Number of adults:           23
           Number of children:            7
Cost per adult without dessert:    $  12.75
Cost per child without dessert:    $   7.65
             Cost per dessert:     $   1.00
                     Room fee:     $  45.00
            Tip and tax rate:          0.18

    Total cost for adult meals:    $ 293.25
    Total cost for child meals:    $  53.55
        Total cost for dessert:    $  30.00
              Total food cost:     $ 376.80
             Plus tip and tax:     $  67.82
                Plus room fee:     $  45.00
                                   $ 489.62
                                   ---------
                                   $ 489.62

                 Less deposit:     $  50.00
                                   ---------
                  Balance due:     $ 439.62
```

Write a program and test it using data sets 2, 3, and 4.

8. The Maripot Carpet Store has asked you to write a computer program to calculate the amount a customer should be charged. The president of the company has given you the following information to help in writing the program:
   a. The carpet charge is equal to the number of square yards purchased times the carpet cost per square yard.
   b. The labor cost is equal to the number of square yards purchased times the labor cost per square yard. A fixed fee for floor preparation is added to some customers' bills.
   c. Large-volume customers are given a percentage discount but the discount applies only to the carpet charge, not to the labor costs.
   d. All customers are charged 4 percent sales tax on the carpet; there is no sales tax on the labor cost.

The following are sample data for this problem:

Customer	Sq. yds.	Cost per sq. yd.	Labor per sq. yd.	Prep. Cost	Discount
1	17	18.50	3.50	38.50	0.02
2	40	24.95	2.95	0.00	0.14
3	23	16.80	3.25	57.95	0.00
4	26	21.25	0.00	80.00	0.00

The data for customer 1 were used to produce the following sample output.

```
Square yards purchased:          17
  Cost per square yard:  $    18.50
 Labor per square yard:  $     3.50
Floor preparation cost:  $    38.50
       Cost for carpet:  $   314.50
        Cost for labor:  $    98.00
    Discount on carpet:  $     6.29
         Tax on carpet:  $    12.33
    Charge to customer:  $   418.54
```

Write a program and test it for customers 2, 3, and 4.

9. The manager of the Croswell Carpet Store has asked you to write a program to print customers' bills. The manager has given you the following information:
   a. The store expresses the length and width of a room in terms of feet and tenths of a foot. For example, the length might be reported as 16.7 feet.
   b. The amount of carpet purchased is expressed as square yards. It is found by dividing the area of the room (in square feet) by nine.
   c. The store does not sell a fraction of a square yard. Thus, square yards must always be rounded up.
   d. The carpet charge is equal to the number of square yards purchased times the carpet cost per square yard. Sales tax equal to 4 percent of the carpet cost must be added to the bill.
   e. All customers are sold a carpet pad at $2.25 per square yard. Sales tax equal to 4 percent of the pad cost must be added to the bill.
   f. The labor cost is equal to the number of square yards purchased times $2.40, which is the labor cost per square yard. No tax is charged on labor.
   g. Each customer is identified by a five-digit number and that number should appear on the bill.

   The sample output follows:

```
         Croswell Carpet Store
                Invoice

     Customer number:    26817
             Carpet :   574.20
                Pad :    81.00
              Labor :    86.40
```

```
Subtotal :   741.60

Plus tax :    26.21

   Total :   767.81
```

Write the program and test it for the following three customers.

i. Mr. Wilson (customer 81429) ordered carpet for his family room, which measures 25 feet long and 18 feet wide. The carpet sells for $12.95 per square yard.

ii. Mr. and Mrs. Adams (customer 04246) ordered carpet for their bedroom, which measures 16.5 feet by 15.4 feet. The carpet sells for $18.90 per square yard.

iii. Ms. Logan (customer 39050) ordered carpet that cost $8.95 per square yard for her daughter's bedroom. The room measures 13.1 by 12.5 feet.

10. Each week Abduhl's Flying Carpets pays its salespeople a base salary plus a bonus for each carpet they sell. In addition, they pay a commission of 10 percent of the total sales by each salesperson.

Write a program to compute a salesperson's salary for the month by inputting Base, Bonus, Quantity, and Sales, and making the necessary calculations. Use the following test data:

Salesperson	Base	Bonus	Quantity	Commission	Sales
1	250.00	15.00	20	10%	1543.69
2	280.00	19.50	36	10%	2375.90

The commission figure is 10 percent. Be sure you can change this easily if necessary. Sample output follows:

```
     Salesperson :    1
            Base :  250.00
           Bonus :   15.00
        Quantity :   20
     Total Bonus :  300.00
      Commission :   10%
           Sales : 1543.69
Total Commission :  154.37
             Pay :  704.37
```

11. Write a complete program to calculate and print the pay for a babysitter who gets $1.50 per hour between 6:00 P.M. and 10:00 P.M. and $2.50 per hour for each subsequent hour. Sample output is

```
Number of hours from 6:00 - 10:00 P.M.   3 @ 3.00 =  9.00
Number of hours after 10:00 P.M.         2 @ 5.00 = 10.00
                                                   ------
Total due                                          $19.00
```

Use the **CONST** section to define the hourly rates.

■ 12. Cramer's rule is a method for solving a system of linear equations. If you have two equations with variables x and y, written as

$$ax + by = c$$
$$dx + ey = f$$

then the solution for x and y can be given as

$$x = \frac{\begin{vmatrix} c & b \\ f & e \end{vmatrix}}{\begin{vmatrix} a & b \\ d & e \end{vmatrix}}, \quad y = \frac{\begin{vmatrix} a & c \\ d & f \end{vmatrix}}{\begin{vmatrix} a & b \\ d & e \end{vmatrix}}$$

Using this notation

$$\begin{vmatrix} a & b \\ d & e \end{vmatrix}$$

is the determinant of the matrix

$$\begin{bmatrix} a & b \\ d & e \end{bmatrix}$$

and is equal to $ae - bd$.

Write a complete program that will solve a system of two equations using Cramer's rule. Input will be all coefficients and constants in the system. Output will be the solution to the system. Typical output is

```
For the system of equations

  x + 2y = 5
 2x -  y = 0

we have the solution

  x = 1
  y = 2
```

Note: Do not allow the expression ($ae - bd$) to equal zero. In the next chapter, we will see how to have the program guard against this possibility.

Communication in Practice

1. Exchange complete programs with a classmate, and critique the use of comments for program documentation. Offer positive suggestions as to where and what kind of comments would be helpful for others who wish to read and understand the program.
2. Remove all documentation from a program you have written for this chapter. Exchange this version with another student who has done the same thing. Write documentation for the exchanged program. Compare your documentation with that originally written for the program. Discuss the differences and similarities with the other student.

3. Contact a professional programmer, and discuss the issue of program documentation. Find out what portion of that programmer's time is spent on documenting large programs. In general, how many lines of code does the programmer write compared to the number of lines of documentation? Are there certain documentation standards to which the programmer must adhere? Prepare a written report of your findings. Deliver an oral report to your class.
4. Contact instructors of computer science, and discuss documentation issues with them. Prepare a written report describing both the similarities and differences in their philosophies about documentation. Deliver a five-minute report to your class. Include descriptive charts prepared for an overhead projector as part of your presentation.
5. Prepare to debate the issue of whether or not documentation standards should be adopted by an influential national group of computer scientists. What would be the advantages and disadvantages of having such standards? As part of the preparation for your debate, prepare your own set of documentation standards.
6. Read at least two articles on the issue of copyright and digital information (see the **Note of Interest** entitled "Computer Ethics: Copyright, Intellectual Property, and Digital Information" in this chapter), and prepare a report on this topic to present to your class.

Chapter 5

Selection Statements

Chapter Outline

The previous chapters set the stage for using computers to solve problems. You have seen how programs in Pascal can be used to get data, perform computations, and print results. You should be able to write complete, short programs, so it is now time to examine other aspects of programming.

A major feature of a computer is its ability to make decisions. For example, a condition is examined and a decision is made as to which program statement is next executed. Statements that permit a computer to make decisions are called **selection statements.** Selection statements are examples of **control structures** because they allow the programmer to control the flow of execution of program statements.

5.1 Boolean Expressions

Objectives

- to be able to use the data type **boolean**
- to be able to use **eoln** and **eof** as functions
- to be able to use relational operators

Before looking at decision making, we need to examine the logical constructs in Pascal, which include a new data type called **boolean.** This data type allows you to represent something as true or false. Although this sounds relatively simple (and it is), this is a very significant feature of computers.

The boolean Data Type

Thus far, we have used only the three data types **integer, real,** and **char;** a fourth data type is **boolean.** A typical declaration of a Boolean variable is

```
VAR
  Flag : boolean;
```

Objectives

(continued)

- to understand the hierarchy for and use simple and compound Boolean expressions
- to be able to use the logical connectives **AND, OR,** and **NOT**

A **selection statement** is one that allows the process of executing possible alternate segments of code. Pascal selection statements are **IF . . . THEN, IF . . . THEN . . . ELSE,** and **CASE.**

A **control structure** is a structure that controls the flow of execution of program statements.

In general, Boolean variables are declared by

VAR
<variable 1>,
<variable 2>,
.
.
.
<variable *n*> : **boolean;**

There are only two values for variables of the **boolean** data type: **true** and **false.** These are both constant standard identifiers and can only be used as Boolean values. When these assignments are made, the contents of the designated memory locations will be the assigned values. For example, if the declaration

```
VAR
  Flag1, Flag2 : boolean;
```

is made,

```
Flag1 := true;
Flag2 := false;
```

produces

true	false
Flag1	Flag2

As with other data types, if two variables are of type **boolean,** the value of one variable can be assigned to another variable as

```
Flag1 := true;
Flag2 := Flag1;
```

and can be envisioned as

true	true
Flag1	Flag2

Note that quotation marks are not used when assigning the values **true** or **false** since these are Boolean constants, not strings.

The **boolean** data type is an ordinal type. Thus, there is an order relationship between **true** and **false**: **false** < **true.** Furthermore, the **ord** function can be applied to the **boolean** values: **ord(false)** = 0, and **ord(true)** = 1.

Output of boolean

Boolean variables can be used as arguments for **write** and **writeln.** Thus,

```
Flag := true;
writeln (Flag);
```

produces

```
TRUE
```

However, some versions will not support output of Boolean variables.

The field width for Boolean output varies with the machine being used. It can be controlled by formatting with a colon followed by a positive integer to designate the field width. The Boolean value will appear right justified in the field. To illustrate, if Flag is a Boolean variable with the value **false,** the segment of code

```
writeln (Flag:6);
writeln (Flag:8);
```

produces the output

```
_FALSE
___FALSE
```

Boolean constants **true** and **false** can also be used in **write** and **writeln** statements. For example,

```
write (true);
writeln (false);
writeln (true:6, false:6);
```

executed on a machine using a default field width of 10 columns produces

```
______TRUE_____FALSE
__TRUE_FALSE
```

Although Boolean variables and constants can be assigned and used in output statements, they cannot be used in input statements. Thus, if Flag is a Boolean variable, a statement such as

```
read (Flag);
```

produces an error. Instead, the user typically reads some value and then uses this value to assign an appropriate Boolean value to a Boolean variable. This technique will be illustrated later.

The Standard Identifiers eoln and eof as Functions

T

In Section 3.3, the concepts end of line (**eoln**) and end of file (**eof**) were presented as markers placed in a stream input to separate lines and to designate the end of a data file. Both **eoln** and **eof** are built-in Boolean functions that indicate when the pointer is positioned at one of these markers. If the data pointer is positioned at an end-of-line marker, then **eoln** is **true;** otherwise, **eoln** is **false.** Similarly, if the pointer is positioned at the end-of-file marker, **eof** is **true;** otherwise, **eof** is **false.** An exception to the **eoln** value being **false** when the pointer is not at end-of-line marker occurs when the pointer is at an end-of-file marker. In this case, **eoln** may have the value **true** or may not be defined.

Since **eoln** and **eof** are built-in functions, they can be used in assignment statements. To illustrate, assume we have the data file

↑

with the pointer positioned at the beginning of the file. Furthermore, assume the variable declaration section of a program includes

```
VAR
  A, B : integer;
  Ch1, Ch2 : char;
  EolnFlag, EofFlag : boolean;
```

If no previous assignments have been made, we have

A	B	Ch1	Ch2	EolnFlag	EofFlag

The assignments

```
EolnFlag := eoln;
EofFlag := eof;
```

might be envisioned as

A	B	Ch1	Ch2	EolnFlag	EofFlag
				false	**false**

If the line of code

```
read (Ch1, Ch2);
```

is executed, the data pointer is

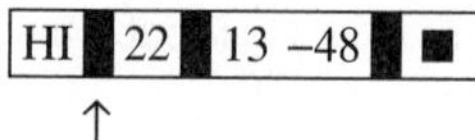

and the assignment statements

```
EolnFlag := eoln;
EofFlag := eof;
```

result in

A	B	Ch1	Ch2	EolnFlag	EofFlag
		H	I	**true**	**false**

If the next three lines of code are

```
readln (A);
EolnFlag := eoln;
EofFlag := eof;
```

this produces

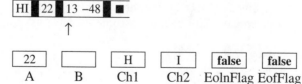

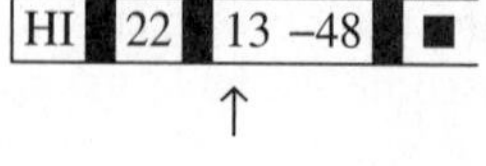

A	B	Ch1	Ch2	EolnFlag	EofFlag
22		H	I	**false**	**false**

Then

```
read (A, B);
EolnFlag := eoln;
EofFlag := eof;
```

produces

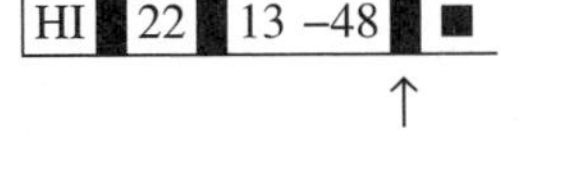

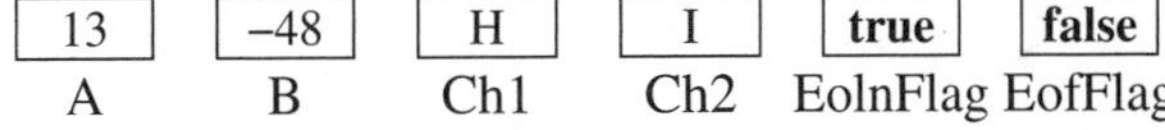

And finally

```
read (Ch1);
EolnFlag := eoln;
EofFlag := eof;
```

produces

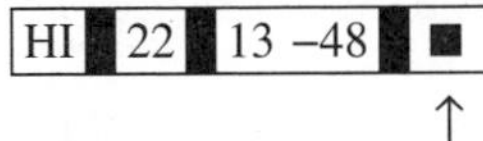

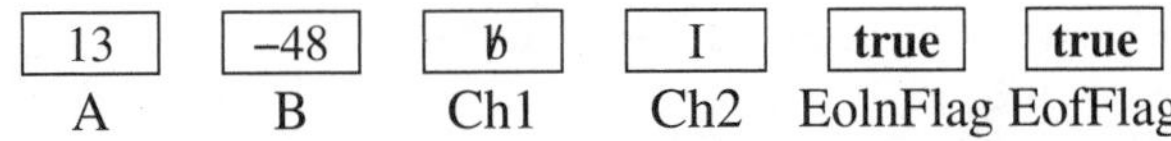

Both **eoln** and **eof** can also be used in output statements. For example

```
writeln (eoln, eof);
write (eoln:6, eof:6);
```

are appropriate statements.

The following example illustrates the use of **eoln** and **eof** in output statements and how their values change according to the data pointer for a stream input. (This example assumes input from a data file.)

Example 5.1

Let's write a short program that allows us to examine a line of data and the respective values of **eoln** and **eof.** Suppose the data file is

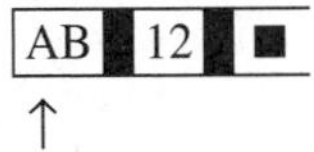

and we want to produce a chart that indicates the values after each character is read. The chart heading should include the character read, **eoln** value, and **eof** value. The code needed to produce one line of the chart is

```
read (Ch);
writeln (Ch:15, eoln:20, eof:20);
```

Since we can read four characters and two end-of-line markers from this data file, this segment of code needs to be executed six times. An attempt to **read** (Ch) seven times would produce an error because we would be trying to read past the end-of-file marker. The complete program for this example follows:

```
PROGRAM ReadCheck (input, output);

CONST
  Indent = ' ';

VAR
  Ch : char;

BEGIN  {  Program  }

  {  Print a heading for the output  }
  writeln;
  writeln (Indent:10, 'Character read', 'eoln value':17, 'eof value':19);
  writeln (Indent:10, '--------------', '----------':17, '---------':19);
  writeln;

  {  Now read the data file  }
  read (Ch);
  writeln (Indent:15, Ch, eoln:22, eof:20);
  read (Ch);
  writeln (Indent:15, Ch, eoln:22, eof:20);
  read (Ch);
  writeln (Indent:15, Ch, eoln:22, eof:20);
  read (Ch);
  writeln (Indent:15, Ch, eoln:22, eof:20);
  read (Ch);
  writeln (Indent:15, Ch, eoln:22, eof:20);
  read (Ch);
  writeln (Indent:15, Ch, eoln:22, eof:20);
  writeln
END.  {  of program  }
```

The output from this program is

```
Character read          eoln value          eof value
--------------          ----------          ---------
     A                    false               false
     B                     true               false
                          false               false
     1                    false               false
     2                     true               false
                           true                true
```

Relational Operators and Simple Boolean Expressions

A **relational operator** is an operator used for comparison of data items of the same type.

In arithmetic, integers and reals can be compared using equalities (=) and inequalities (<, >, ≠, and so on). Pascal also provides for the comparison of numbers or values of variables. The operators used for comparison are called **relational operators** and there are six of them. Their arithmetic notation, Pascal notation, and meaning are given in Table 5.1.

Table 5.1

Relational operators

Arithmetic Operation	Relational Operator	Meaning
$=$	`=`	Is equal to
$<$	`<`	Is less than
$>$	`>`	Is greater than
$\leq$	`<=`	Is less than or equal to
$\geq$	`>=`	Is greater than or equal to
$\neq$	`<>`	Is not equal to

Earlier in this section, we saw how Boolean values can be generated using the built-in functions **eoln** and **eof** when reading data. Now let's examine some methods of generating Boolean values. This is necessary so we can control selection in a program.

A **simple Boolean expression** is an expression where two numbers or variable values are compared using a single relational operator.

When two numbers or variable values are compared using a single relational operator, the expression is referred to as a **simple Boolean expression.** Each simple Boolean expression has the Boolean value **true** or **false,** according to the arithmetic validity of the expression. In general, only data of the same type can be compared; thus, integers must be compared to integers, reals must be compared to reals, and characters must be compared to characters. The usual exception can be applied here; that is, reals can be compared to integers. When comparing reals, however, the computer representation of a real number might not be the exact real number intended. Therefore, the equality (=) comparison should be avoided. Instead, the absolute value of the difference should be checked to see if it is smaller than a given value.

Table 5.2 sets forth several Boolean expressions and their respective Boolean values, assuming the assignment statements A := 3 and B := 4 have been made.

Arithmetic expressions can also be used in simple Boolean expressions. Thus,

```
4 < (3 + 2)
```

Table 5.2

Values of simple Boolean expressions

Simple Boolean Expression	Boolean Value
$7 = 7$	**true**
$-3.0 = 0.0$	**false**
$4.2 > 3.7$	**true**
$-18 < -15$	**true**
$13 < 100$	**true**
$13 <= 100$	**true**
$13 <= 13$	**true**
$0.012 > 0.013$	**false**
$-17.32 <> -17.32$	**false**
$A <= B$	**true**
$B > A$	**true**

has the value **true.** When the computer evaluates this expression, the parentheses dictate that (3 + 2) be evaluated first and then the relational operator. Sequentially, this becomes

```
4 < (3 + 2)
4 <    5
true
```

What if the parentheses had not been used? Could the expression be evaluated? This type of expression necessitates a priority level for the relational operators and the arithmetic operators. A summary for the priority of these operations is

Expression	Priority
*, /, **MOD, DIV**	1
+, −	2
=, <, >, <=, >=, <>	3

Thus, we see that the relational operators are evaluated last. As with arithmetic operators, these are evaluated in order from left to right. Thus, the expression

```
4 < 3 + 2
```

could be evaluated without parentheses and would have the same Boolean value.

The following example illustrates the evaluation of a somewhat more complex Boolean expression.

Example 5.2

Indicate the successive steps in the evaluation of the Boolean expression

```
10 MOD 4 * 3 - 8 <= 18 + 30 DIV 4 - 20
```

The steps in this evaluation are

```
10 MOD 4 * 3 - 8 <= 18 + 30 DIV 4 - 20
   ↓
   2     * 3 - 8 <= 18 + 30 DIV 4 - 20        first pass
           ↓
           6 - 8 <= 18 + 30 DIV 4 - 20
                             ↓
           6 - 8 <= 18 +      7     - 20
             ↓         ↓                      second pass
            - 2 <=     25           - 20
                             ↓
            - 2 <=           5
                     ↓                        third pass
                    true
```

As shown in Example 5.2, parentheses are not required when using arithmetic expressions with relational operators. However, it is usually a good idea to use them to enhance the readability of the expression and to avoid using an incorrect expression.

Logical operators are the logical connectives (**AND, OR**) and negation (**NOT**).

Negation is the use of the logical operator **NOT** to negate the Boolean value of an expression.

Compound Boolean expression refers to the complete expression when logical connectives and negation are used to generate Boolean values.

Logical Operators and Compound Boolean Expressions

Boolean values may also be generated by using **logical operators** with simple Boolean expressions. The logical operators used by Pascal are **AND, OR,** and **NOT. AND** and **OR** are used to connect two Boolean expressions. **NOT** is used to negate the Boolean value of an expression; hence, it is sometimes referred to as **negation.** When these connectives or negation are used to generate Boolean values, the complete expression is referred to as a **compound Boolean expression.**

If **AND** is used to join two simple Boolean expressions, the resulting compound expression is **true** only when both simple expressions are **true.** If **OR** is used, the result is **true** if either or both of the expressions are **true.** These rules are summarized as follows:

Expression 1 (E1)	Expression 2 (E2)	E1 AND E2	E1 OR E2
true	**true**	**true**	**true**
true	**false**	**false**	**true**
false	**true**	**false**	**true**
false	**false**	**false**	**false**

As previously indicated, **NOT** merely produces the logical complement of an expression as follows:

Expression (E)	NOT E
true	**false**
false	**true**

When these operators are used with relational expressions, parentheses are required because logical operators are evaluated before relational operators. Illustrations of the Boolean values generated using logical operators are given in Table 5.3.

Table 5.3

Values of compound Boolean expressions

Expression	Boolean Value
(4.2 >= 5.0) **AND** (8 = (3 + 5))	**false**
(4.2 >= 5.0) **OR** (8 = (3 + 5))	**true**
(−2 < 0) **AND** (18 >= 10)	**true**
(−2 < 0) **OR** (18 >= 10)	**true**
(3 > 5) **AND** (14.1 = 0.0)	**false**
(3 > 5) **OR** (14.1 = 0.0)	**false**
NOT (18 = (10 + 8))	**false**
NOT (− 4 > 0)	**true**

A Note of Interest

George Boole

George Boole was born in 1815 in Lincoln, England. Boole was the son of a small shopkeeper and his family belonged to the lowest social class. In an attempt to rise above his station, Boole spent his early years teaching himself Latin and Greek. During this period, he also received elementary instruction in mathematics from his father.

At the age of 16, Boole worked as a teacher in an elementary school. He used most of his wages to help support his parents. At the age of 20 (after a brief, unsuccessful attempt to study for the clergy), he opened his own school. As part of his preparation for running his school, he had to learn more mathematics. This activity led to the development of some of the most significant mathematics of the nineteenth century.

Boole's major contributions were in the field of logic. An indication of his genius is given by the fact that his early work included the discovery of invariants. The mathematical significance of this is perhaps best explained by noting that the theory of relativity developed by Albert Einstein would not have been possible without the previous work on invariants.

Boole's first published contribution was "The Mathematical Analysis of Logic," which appeared in 1848 while he was still working as an elementary teacher and the sole support of his parents. In 1849, he was appointed Professor of Mathematics at Queen's College in Cork, Ireland. The relative freedom from financial worry and time constraints that the college appointment provided allowed him to pursue his work in mathematics. His masterpiece, "An Investigation of the Laws of Thought, on which Are Founded the Mathematical Theories of Logic and Probabilities," was published in 1854. Boole was then 39, relatively old for such original work. According to Bertrand Russell, pure mathematics was discovered by Boole in this work.

The brilliance of Boole's work laid the foundation for what is currently studied as formal logic. The data type, Boolean, is named in honor of Boole because of his contribution to the development of logic as part of mathematics. Boole died in 1864. His early death resulted from pneumonia contracted by keeping a lecture engagement when he was soaked to the skin.

Complex Boolean expressions can be generated by using several logical operators in an expression. The priority for evaluating these operators follows:

Operator	Priority
NOT	1
AND	2
OR	3

When complex expressions are being evaluated, the logical operators, arithmetic expressions, and relational operators are evaluated during successive passes through the expression. The priority list is now as follows:

Expression or Operation	Priority
( )	1. Evaluate from inside out.
NOT	2. Evaluate from left to right.
*, /, **MOD, DIV, AND**	3. Evaluate from left to right.
+, −, **OR**	4. Evaluate from left to right.
<, <=, >, >=, =, <>	5. Evaluate from left to right.

Thus, an expression like

```
0 < X AND X < 2
```

produces an error. It must be written as

```
(0 < X) AND (X < 2)
```

The following examples illustrate evaluation of some complex Boolean expressions.

Example 5.3

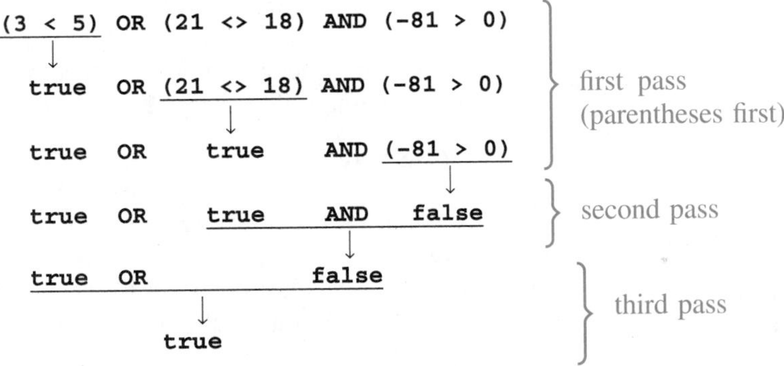

Example 5.4

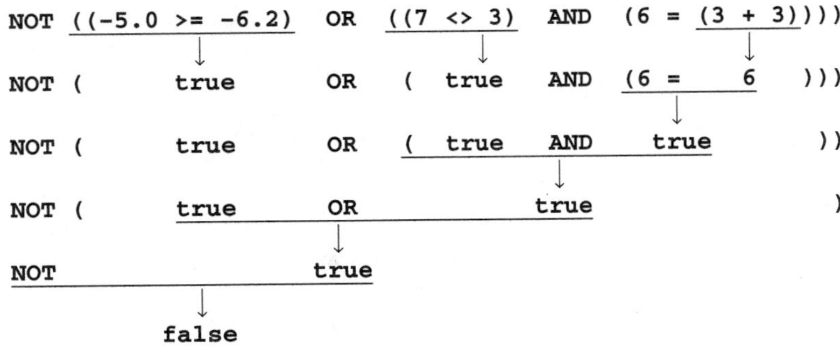

NOT ((-5.0 >= -6.2) OR ((7 <> 3) AND (6 = (3 + 3))))
NOT (true OR (true AND (6 = 6)))
NOT (true OR (true AND true))
NOT (true OR true)
NOT true
false

Example 5.5

Let's assume X and Y are real variables, Flag is a Boolean variable, and the assignment statements

```
X := 12.5;
Y := -100;
Flag := true;
```

have been made. Then (X <> 7/3) **OR NOT** ((X >= 4) **AND** (**NOT** Flag)) can be evaluated as:

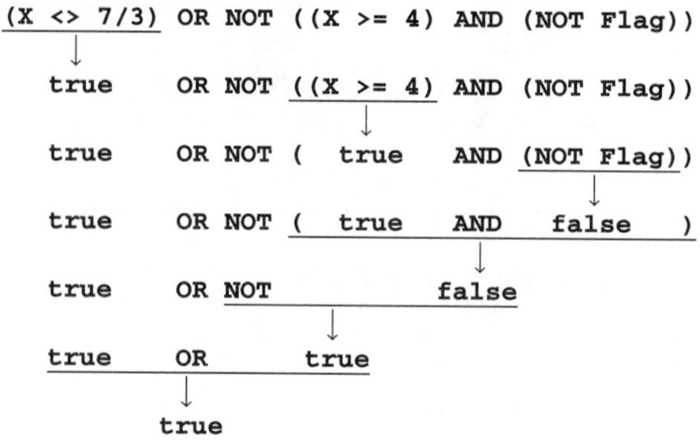

Extra care should be taken with the syntax of Boolean expressions. For example, the expression

```
3 < 4 AND 100 > 80
```

in a program produces an error. Since relational expressions are evaluated last, the first pass through this expression would attempt to evaluate

```
4 AND 100
```

This is not valid because logical operators can only operate on Boolean values **true** and **false.**

If an expression produces a Boolean value and is evaluated before a connective, then that expression would not have to be in parentheses. For example,

```
(3 < 5) AND NOT (0 >= -2)
```

is a valid expression, evaluated as follows:

```
(3 < 5)  AND  NOT (0 >= -2)
   ↓
true     AND  NOT (0 >= -2)
                    ↓
true     AND  NOT   true
                ↓
true     AND     false
          ↓
        false
```

No additional parentheses are needed because **NOT** is evaluated before **AND.**

Exercises 5.1

*1. Assume the variable declaration section of a program is

```
VAR
  Flag1, Flag2 : boolean;
```

What output is produced by the following segments of code?

```
Flag1 := true;
Flag2 := false;
writeln (Flag1, true:6, Flag2:8);
Flag1 := Flag2;
writeln (Flag2:20);
```

2. Write a test program that illustrates what happens when Boolean expressions are not enclosed in parentheses. For example,

```
3 < 5 AND 8.0 <> 4 * 3
```

For Exercises 3–8, assume the variable declaration section of a program is

```
VAR
  Ch : char;
  Flag : boolean;
```

Indicate if the assignment statement is valid or invalid.

*3. `Flag := 'true';`

4. `Flag := T;`

*5. `Flag := true;`

6. `Ch := Flag;`

*7. `Ch := true;`

8. `Ch := 'T';`

In Exercises 9–15, indicate whether the expression is valid or invalid. Evaluate those that are valid.

*9. `3 < 4 OR 5 <> 6`

10. `NOT 3.0 = 6 / 2`

*11. `NOT (true OR false)`

12. `NOT true OR false`

*13. `NOT true OR NOT false`

14. `NOT (18 < 25) AND OR (-3 < 0)`

*15. `8 * 3 < 20 + 10`

For Exercises 16–22, indicate if the simple Boolean expression is **true, false,** or invalid.

16. `-3.01 <= -3.001`

*17. `-3.0 = -3`

18. `25 - 10 <> 3 * 5`

*19. `42 MOD 5 < 42 DIV 5`

20. `-5 * (3 + 2) > 2 * (-10)`

*21. `10 / 5 < 1 + 1`

22. `3 + 8 MOD 5 >= 6 - 12 MOD 2`

In Exercises 23–27, evaluate the expression.

*23. `(3 > 7) AND (2 < 0) OR (6 = 3 + 3)`

24. `((3 > 7) AND (2 < 0)) OR (6 = 3 + 3)`

*25. `(3 > 7) AND ((2 < 0) OR (6 = 3 + 3))`

26. `NOT ((-4.2 <> 3.0) AND (10 < 20))`

*27. `(NOT (-4.2 <> 3.0)) OR (NOT (10 < 20))`

For Exercises 28–32, assume the variable declaration section of a program is

```
VAR
  Int1, Int2 : integer;
```

```
Real1, Real2 : real;
Flag1, Flag2 : boolean;
```

and the values of the variables are

0	8	−15.2	−20.0	**false**	**true**
Int1	Int2	Real1	Real2	Flag1	Flag2

Evaluate each expression.

28. `(Int1 <= Int2) OR NOT (Real2 = Real1)`
*29. `NOT (Flag1) OR NOT (Flag2)`
30. `NOT (Flag1 AND Flag2)`
*31. `((Real1 - Real2) < 100/Int2) AND ((Int1 < 1) AND NOT (Flag2))`
32. `NOT ((Int2 - 16 DIV 2) = Int1) AND Flag1`
33. DeMorgan's Laws state the following.
    a. **NOT** (A **OR** B) is equivalent to (**NOT** A) **AND** (**NOT** B).
    b. **NOT** (A **AND** B) is equivalent to (**NOT** A) **OR** (**NOT** B).

    Write a test program that demonstrates the validity of each of these equivalency statements.

5.2 IF . . . THEN Statements

Objectives

- to learn the form and syntax required for using an **IF . . . THEN** statement
- to understand the flow of control when using an **IF . . . THEN** statement
- to be able to use an **IF . . . THEN** statement in a program
- to understand why compound statements are needed
- to understand how **BEGIN . . . END** are used to write compound statements

The first decision-making statement we will examine is the **IF . . . THEN** statement. **IF . . . THEN** is used to make a program do something only when certain conditions are met. The form and syntax for an **IF . . . THEN** statement are

> **IF** <Boolean expression> **THEN**
>   <statement>

where <statement> represents any Pascal statement.

The Boolean expression can be any valid expression that is either **true** or **false** at the time of evaluation. If it is **true,** the statement following the reserved word **THEN** is executed. If it is **false,** control is transferred to the first program statement following the complete **IF . . . THEN** statement. In general, code has the form

> <statement 1>;
> **IF** <Boolean expression> **THEN**
>   <statement 2>;
> <statement 3>

as illustrated in Figure 5.1.

As a further illustration of how an **IF . . . THEN** statement works, consider the following program fragment:

```
Sum := 0.0;
read (Num);
IF Num > 0.0 THEN
  Sum := Sum + Num;
writeln (Sum:10:2);
```

◆ Figure 5.1

IF . . . THEN flow diagram

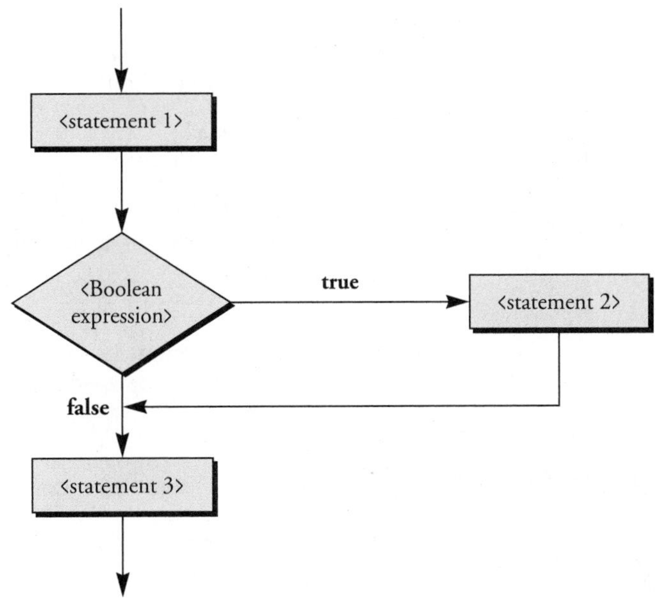

Objectives

(continued)

- to be able to use correct syntax in writing a compound statement
- to be able to design programs using **IF . . . THEN** statements

If the value read is 75.85, prior to execution of the **IF . . . THEN** statement, the contents of Num and Sum are

75.85	0.0
Num	Sum

The Boolean expression Num > 0.0 is now evaluated and, since it is **true,** the statement

```
Sum := Sum + Num;
```

is executed and we have

75.85	75.85
Num	Sum

The next program statement is executed and produces the output

```
75.85
```

However, if the value read is –25.5, the variable values are

–25.5	0.0
Num	Sum

The Boolean expression Num > 0.0 is **false** and control is transferred to the line

```
writeln (Sum);
```

Thus, the output is

```
0.00
```

Now, let's suppose we want one objective of a program to be to count the number of zeros in the input. Assuming suitable initialization and declaration, a program fragment for this task could be

```
readln (Num);
IF Num = 0 THEN
  ZeroCount := ZeroCount + 1;
```

One writing style for using an **IF . . . THEN** statement calls for indenting the program statement to be executed if the Boolean expression is **true.** This, of course, is not required.

```
IF Num = 0 THEN
  ZeroCount := ZeroCount + 1;
```

could be written

```
IF Num = 0 THEN ZeroCount := Zerocount + 1;
```

However, the indenting style for simple **IF . . . THEN** statements is consistent with the style used with more elaborate conditional statements.

Compound Statements

The last concept we need to consider before looking further at selection in Pascal is a compound statement. Simple statements conform to the syntax diagram for statements shown in Appendix 3. In a Pascal program, simple statements are separated by semicolons. Thus,

```
readln (A, B);
A := 3 * B;
writeln (A);
```

are three simple statements.

In some instances, it is necessary to perform several simple statements when a condition or some conditions are true. For example, you may want the program to do certain things if a condition is true. In this situation, several simple statements that can be written as a single compound statement would be helpful. In general, several Pascal constructs require compound statements. A **compound statement** is created by using the reserved words **BEGIN** and **END** at the beginning and end of a sequence of simple statements. Correct syntax for a compound statement is

A **compound statement** uses the reserved words **BEGIN** and **END** to make several simple statements into a single compound statement.

BEGIN
    <statement 1>;
    <statement 2>;
        .
        .
        .
    <statement *n*>
END;

Statements within a compound statement are separated by semicolons. The last statement before **END** does not require a semicolon; however, if a semicolon is used here, it will not affect the program.

A **BEGIN . . . END block** is the segment of code between **BEGIN** and **END** that, when a compound statement is executed within a program, is treated as a single statement.

When a compound statement is executed within a program, the entire segment of code between **BEGIN** and **END** is treated as a single statement. This is referred to as a **BEGIN . . . END block.** It is important that you develop a consistent, acceptable style for writing compound statements. What you use will vary according to your teacher's wishes and your personal preferences. Examples in this text will indent each simple statement within a compound statement two spaces. Thus,

```
BEGIN
  read (Num1, Num2);
  Num1 := 3 * Num2;
  writeln (Num1)
END;
```

is a compound statement in a program; what it does is easily identified.

Some examples of compound statements follow. Although the concept, syntax, and writing style do not appear to be difficult at this point, one of the most frequent errors for beginning programmers is incorrect use of compound statements.

Example 5.6

Let's write a compound statement that allows the user to read a real, print the real, and add it to a total. Assuming variables have been suitably declared and initialized, a compound statement to do this is

```
BEGIN
  writeln ('Enter a real number and press <Enter>.');
  readln (Num);
  writeln (Num:8:2);
  Total := Total + Num
END;
```

Example 5.7

Suppose you are writing a program to enable your teacher to compute grades for your class. For each student, the program must read three scores, add the scores, compute the average score, print the scores, and print the test average. Again, assuming variables have been suitably declared, a compound statement for this could be

```
BEGIN
  writeln ('Enter three scores and press <Enter>.');
  readln (Score1, Score2, Score3);
  Total := Score1 + Score2 + Score3;
  Average := Total / 3.0;
  write (Score1:6, Score2:6, Score3:6);
  writeln (Average:12:2)
END;
```

Using Compound Statements

As you might expect, compound statements can be (and frequently are) used as part of an **IF . . . THEN** statement. The form and syntax for this are

IF <Boolean expression> **THEN**
  BEGIN
    <statement 1>;
    <statement 2>;
    .
    .
    .
    <statement *n*>
  END;

Program control is exactly as before depending on the value of the Boolean expression. For example, suppose you want to determine how many positive numbers are entered as data and also compute their sum. This can be partially accomplished by the program fragment

```
Sum := 0.0;
Count := 0;
read (Num);
IF Num > 0.0 THEN
  BEGIN
    Sum := Sum + Num;
    Count := Count + 1
  END;  {  of IF...THEN  }
```

The following example designs a program to solve a problem using an **IF . . . THEN** statement.

Example 5.8

Let's write a program that reads two integers and prints them in the following order: larger first, smaller second. The first-level pseudocode solution is

1. Read numbers
2. Determine larger
3. Print a heading
4. Print results

Step 1 is a single line of code, and Steps 3 and 4 will be some **writeln** statements. However, Step 2 requires some refinement. A second-level solution could be

1. Read numbers
2. Determine larger
   2.1 **IF** Num 1 < Num 2 **THEN** exchange numbers
3. Print a heading
4. Print results
   4.1 Print a heading
   4.2 print Num1 (larger)
   4.3 print Num2 (smaller)

Step 2.1 is further refined to produce

2.1 **IF** Num1 < Num2 **THEN** exchange numbers
   2.1.1 Temp gets Num1

2.1.2 Num1 gets Num2
2.1.3 Num2 gets Temp

We can now write code for the program to solve this problem.

```
writeln ('Enter two integers and press <Enter>.');
readln (Num1, Num2);
IF Num1 < Num2 THEN
  BEGIN
    Temp := Num1;
    Num1 := Num2;
    Num2 := Temp
  END;  {  of IF...THEN  }
writeln (Num1:15, Num2:15);
```

A complete program for this example follows.

```
PROGRAM UseIFTHEN (input, output);

{    This program illustrates using an IF . . . THEN statement.   }
{    Two numbers are read and then printed in order, larger       }
{    first.                                                       }

CONST
  Skip = ' ';

VAR
  Num1,                                     {  First number        }
  Num2,                                     {  Second number       }
  Temp : integer;                           {  Temporary variable  }

BEGIN  {  Program  }

  writeln ('Enter two integers and press <Enter>.');
  readln (Num1, Num2);

  {  Print a heading  }
  writeln;
  writeln ('Larger number', Skip:10, 'Smaller number');
  writeln ('-------------', Skip:10, '--------------');
  writeln;

  {  Exchange numbers if necessary  }
  IF Num1 < Num2 THEN
    BEGIN
      Temp := Num1;
      Num1 := Num2;
      Num2 := Temp
    END;  {  of IF...THEN  }
  writeln (Num1:7, Num2:23);
  writeln
END.  {  of program }
```

A sample run of this program produces

```
Enter two integers and press <Enter>.
18 30
```

```
Larger number        Smaller number
-------------        --------------

     30                   18
```

Exercises 5.2

In Exercises 1–6, what output is produced from the program fragment? Assume the following assignment statements precede each fragment.

```
A := 10;
B := 5;
```

*1.
```
IF A <= B THEN
  B := A;
writeln (A, B);
```

2.
```
IF A <= B THEN
  BEGIN
    B := A;
    writeln (A, B)
  END;
```

*3.
```
IF A < B THEN
  Temp := A;
A := B;
B := Temp;
writeln (A, B);
```

4.
```
IF A < B THEN
  BEGIN
    Temp := A;
    A := B;
    B := Temp
  END;
writeln (A, B);
```

*5.
```
IF (A < B) OR (B - A < 0) THEN
  BEGIN
    A := A + B;
    B := B - 1;
    writeln (A, B)
  END;
writeln (A, B);
```

6.
```
IF (A < B) AND (B - A < 0) THEN
  BEGIN
    A := A + B;
    B := B - 1;
    writeln (A, B)
  END;
writeln (A, B);
```

7. Write a test program to illustrate what happens when a semicolon is inadvertently inserted after **THEN** in an **IF . . . THEN** statement. For example,

```
IF A > 0 THEN;
  Sum := Sum + A;
```

In Exercises 8–11, find and explain the errors in the program fragment. You may assume all variables have been suitably declared.

8.
```
IF A := 10 THEN
  writeln (A);
```

*9.
```
X := 7;
IF 3 < X < 10 THEN
  BEGIN
    X := X + 1;
    writeln (X)
  END;
```

10.
```
Count := 0;
Sum := 0;
A := 50;
IF A > 0 THEN
  Count := Count + 1;
  Sum := Sum + A;
```

*11.
```
read (Ch);
IF Ch = 'A' OR 'B' THEN
  writeln (Ch:10);
```

A Note of Interest

New Legal Research Uses Plain English

In October 1992, West Publishing introduced WIN® (WESTLAW is Natural™), a Natural Language search method that allows legal researchers to describe their issue in plain English when using WESTLAW®, West's computer-assisted legal research service. This Natural Language search method offers researchers an alternative to the traditional Boolean language format, which uses terms and connectors query formulation. For example, suppose an attorney wanted to submit DNA profiling as significant evidence in a criminal case. The attorney would need to research whether the results of such testing would be admissible in court. WIN allows the WESTLAW user to simply pose the question in plain English; for example:

Is DNA profiling evidence admissible in a criminal trial?

Using Boolean methods, the attorney would have to enter the query in the following format:

D.N.A. /p profil! /p evidence /p admiss! admit! inadmiss! /p criminal /s trial

WIN works by identifying the key concepts within a question and then comparing the concepts with documents in its databases. Through sophisticated statistical methods, WIN retrieves documents based on how frequently a concept occurs in a document and how infrequently it occurs in a database. The results retrieved most closely match the search description.

In Exercises 12 and 13, what output is produced from the following program fragment? Assume variables have been suitably declared.

12.
```
J := 18;
IF J MOD 5 = 0 THEN
  writeln (J);
```

*13.
```
A := 5;
B := 90;
B := B DIV A - 5;
IF B > A THEN
  B := A * 30;
writeln (A, B);
```

14. Can a simple statement be written as a compound statement using a **BEGIN . . . END** block? Write a short program that allows you to verify your answer.

*15. Discuss the differences in the following programs. Predict the output for each program using sample values for Num.

a.
```
PROGRAM Exercise15a (input, output);

VAR
  Num : integer;

BEGIN
  writeln ('Enter an integer and press <Enter>.');
  readln (Num);
  IF Num > 0 THEN
    writeln;
    writeln ('The number is':22, Num:6);
    writeln;
    writeln ('The number squared is':30, Num * Num:6);
    writeln ('The number cubed is':28, Num * Num * Num:6);
    writeln
END.
```

b.
```
PROGRAM Exercise15b (input, output);

VAR
  Num : integer;

BEGIN
  writeln ('Enter an integer and press <Enter>.');
  readln (Num);
  IF Num > 0 THEN
    BEGIN  {  Start output  }
      writeln;
      writeln ('The number is':22, Num:6);
      writeln;
      writeln ('The number squared is':30, Num * Num:6);
      writeln ('The number cubed is':28, Num * Num * Num:6);
      writeln
    END  {  of IF...THEN  }
END.
```

16. Discuss writing style and readability of compound statements.

In Exercises 17–20, find all errors in each compound statement.

*17.
```
BEGIN
  read (A)
  writeln (A)
END;
```

18.
```
BEGIN
  Sum := Sum + Num
END;
```

*19.
```
BEGIN
  read (Size1, Size2);
  writeln (Size1:8, Size2:8)
END.
```

20.
```
BEGIN
  readln (Age, Weight);
  TotalAge := TotalAge + Age;
  TotalWeight := TotalWeight + Weight;
  writeln (Age:8, Weight:8)
```

*21. Write a single compound statement that will:
   a. Read three integers as input.
   b. Add them to a previous total.
   c. Print the numbers on one line.
   d. Skip a line (output).
   e. Print the new total.

22. Write a program fragment that reads three reals as input, counts the number of positive reals, and accumulates the sum of positive reals.

*23. Write a program fragment that reads three characters as input and then prints them only if they have been read in alphabetical order (for example, it prints “boy” but does not print “dog”).

24. Given two integers, A and B, A is a divisor of B if B **MOD** A = 0. Write a complete program that reads two positive integers A and B and then, if A is a divisor of B,
   a. Print A.
   b. Print B.
   c. Print the result of B divided by A.

For example, the output could be

```
A is 14
B is 42
B divided by A is 3
```

5.3 IF . . . THEN . . . ELSE Statements

Objectives

- to learn the form and syntax required for using an **IF . . . THEN . . . ELSE** statement
- to understand the flow of control when using an **IF . . . THEN . . . ELSE** statement
- to be able to use an **IF . . . THEN . . . ELSE** statement in a program

Form and Syntax

In Section 5.2 we discussed the one-way selection statement **IF . . . THEN.** The second selection statement we will examine is the two-way selection statement **IF . . . THEN . . . ELSE.** The correct form and syntax for **IF . . . THEN . . . ELSE** are

```
IF <Boolean expression> THEN
    <statement>
ELSE
    <statement>
```

Flow of control when using an **IF . . . THEN . . . ELSE** statement is as follows:

1. The Boolean expression is evaluated.
2. If the Boolean expression is **true,** the statement following **THEN** is executed and control is transferred to the first program statement following the complete **IF . . . THEN . . . ELSE** statement.
3. If the Boolean expression is **false,** the statement following **ELSE** is executed and control is transferred to the first program statement following the **IF . . . THEN . . . ELSE** statement.

A flow diagram is given in Figure 5.2.

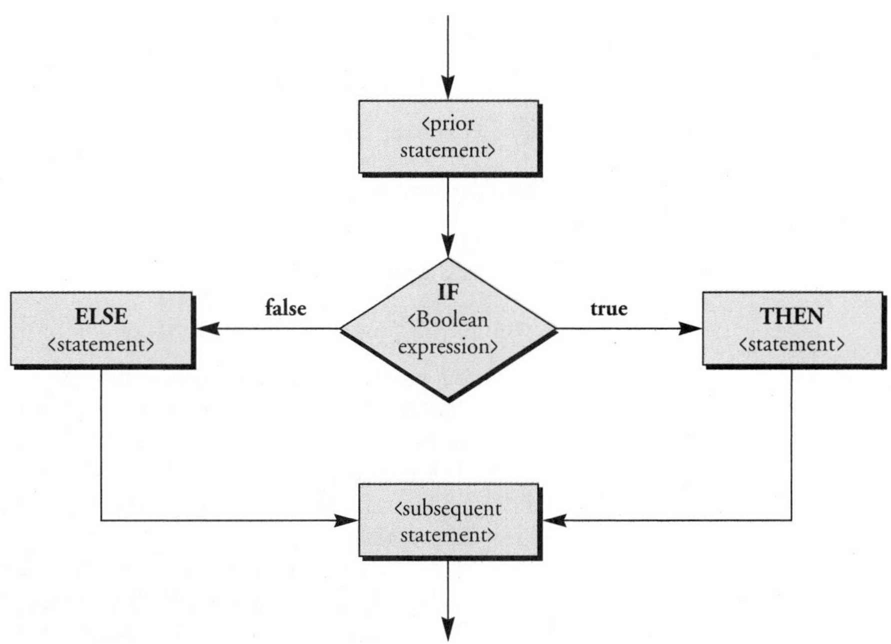

Figure 5.2
IF . . . THEN . . . ELSE flow diagram

Objectives

(continued)

- to be able to design programs using **IF . . . THEN . . . ELSE** statements

To illustrate this flow of control, let's consider the problem of printing the larger of two numbers by using an **IF . . . THEN . . . ELSE** statement in the following code:

```
readln (Num1, Num2);
IF Num1 > Num2 THEN
  writeln (Num1)
ELSE
  writeln (Num2);
writeln ('All done');
```

If the values read are

80	15
Num1	Num2

the Boolean expression Num1 > Num2 is **true** and the statement

```
writeln (Num1)
```

is executed to produce

```
80
```

Control is then transferred to the next program statement,

```
writeln ('All done');
```

and the output is

```
80
All done
```

However, if the values read are

10	75
Num1	Num2

the Boolean expression Num1 > Num2 is **false,** control is transferred to

```
writeln (Num2);
```

and the output is

```
75
All done
```

with the 75 printed from the **ELSE** option of the **IF . . . THEN . . . ELSE** statement.

A few points to remember concerning **IF . . . THEN . . . ELSE** statements follow:

1. The Boolean expression can be any valid expression having a value of **true** or **false** at the time it is evaluated.
2. The complete **IF . . . THEN . . . ELSE** statement is one program statement and is separated from other complete statements by a semicolon whenever appropriate.
3. There is no semicolon preceding the reserved word **ELSE.** A semicolon preceding the reserved word **ELSE** causes the compiler to treat the **IF . . . THEN** portion as a complete program statement and the **ELSE** portion as a

separate statement. This produces an error message indicating that **ELSE** is being used without an **IF . . . THEN.**

4. Writing style should include indenting within the **ELSE** option in a manner consistent with indenting in the **IF . . . THEN** option.

Example 5.9

Let's write a program fragment that keeps separate counts of the negative and nonnegative numbers entered as data. Assuming all variables have been suitably declared, an **IF . . . THEN . . . ELSE** statement could be used as follows:

```
writeln ('Please enter a number and press <Enter>.');
readln (Num);
IF Num < 0 THEN
  NegCount := NegCount + 1
ELSE
  NonNegCount := NonNegCount + 1;
```

Using Compound Statements

Program statements in both the **IF . . . THEN** option and the **ELSE** option can be compound statements. When using compound statements in these options, you should use a consistent, readable indenting style. Remember to use **BEGIN . . . END** for each compound statement, and do not put a semicolon before **ELSE.** We next consider some examples that require the use of compound statements within **IF . . . THEN . . . ELSE** statements.

Example 5.10

Suppose you want a program to read a number, count it as negative or nonnegative, and print it in either a column of nonnegative numbers or a column of negative numbers. Assuming all variables have been suitably declared and initialized, the fragment might be

```
writeln ('Please enter a number and press <Enter>.');
readln (Num);
IF Num < 0 THEN
  BEGIN
    NegCount := NegCount + 1;
    writeln (Num:15)
  END  {  of IF...THEN option  }
ELSE
  BEGIN
    NonNegCount := NonNegCount + 1;
    writeln (Num:30)
  END;  {  of ELSE option   }
```

Example 5.11

Let's write a program fragment that computes gross wages for an employee of the Florida OJ Canning Company. A data line consists of three initials, the total hours worked, and the hourly rate. Thus a typical data line is

```
JHA 44.5 12.75
```

Overtime (more than 40 hours) is computed as time-and-a-half. The output should include all input data and the gross wages. A first-level pseudocode for this problem could be

1. Get the data
2. Perform computation
3. Print results

Step 1 can be accomplished by **readln** statements. Step 2 can be refined to

2. Perform computation
   2.1 **IF** Hours <= 40.0 **THEN**
   compute regular time
   ELSE
   compute time-and-a-half

Step 2.1 can be written as

```
IF Hours <= 40.0 THEN
  TotalWage := Hours * PayRate
ELSE
  BEGIN
    Overtime := 1.5 * (Hours - 40.0) * PayRate;
    TotalWage := 40 * PayRate + Overtime
  END;
```

Step 3 could be refined to

3. Print results
   3.1 Print initials
   3.2 Print Hours and PayRate
   3.3 Print TotalWage

The program fragment for this problem is

```
writeln ('Please enter three initials and press <Enter>.');
readln (Init1, Init2, Init3);
writeln ('Now enter hours worked and pay rate.');
writeln ('Press <Enter> when finished.');
readln (Hours, PayRate);
IF Hours <= 40.0 THEN
  TotalWage := Hours * PayRate
ELSE
  BEGIN
    Overtime := 1.5 * (Hours - 40.0) * PayRate;
    TotalWage := 40 * PayRate + Overtime
  END;
writeln;
write (Init1:5, Init2, Init3);
write (Hours:10:2, PayRate:10:2);
writeln ('$':10, TotalWage:7:2);
```

If this fragment is run on the data line given at the beginning of this example, we get

```
Please enter three initials and press <Enter>.
JHA
Now enter hours worked and pay rate.
Press <Enter> when finished.
44.50 12.75

    JHA      44.50      12.75         $ 596.06
```

Robust refers to the state in which a program is completely protected against all possible crashes from bad data and unexpected values.

Robust Programs

If a program is completely protected against all possible crashes from bad data and unexpected values, it is said to be **robust.** The preceding examples have all assumed that desired data would be accurately entered from the keyboard. In actual practice, this is seldom the case. **IF ... THEN ... ELSE** statements can be used to guard against bad data entries. For example, if a program is designed to use positive numbers, you could guard against negatives and zero by

```
writeln ('Enter a positive number and press <Enter>.')
readln (Number);
IF Number <= 0 THEN
  writeln ('You entered a nonpositive number.');
ELSE
  .
  .  (code for expected action here)
  .
```

This program protection can be used anywhere in a program. For example, if you are finding square roots of numbers, you could avoid a program crash by

```
IF Num < 0 THEN
  writeln ('The number ', Num, ' is negative.')
ELSE
  .
  .  (rest of action here)
  .
```

To further illustrate the idea of writing robust programs, you might use an **IF ... THEN ... ELSE** statement to guard against integer overflow by using something like

```
IF Num > maxint THEN
   .
   .  (error message)
   .
ELSE
   .
   .  (code for action here)
   .
```

However, if Num is greater than **maxint,** you already have an overflow problem. We can solve this problem and also guard against negative integer overflow by using

```
IF abs(Num) / OverflowGuard > maxint / OverflowGuard THEN
   .
   .  (error)
   .
ELSE
   .
   .  (code for action here)
   .
```

where OverflowGuard is a defined constant (100, for example).

In actual practice, students need to balance robustness against length and efficiency of code. Overemphasis on making a program robust can detract from time spent learning new programming concepts. You should discuss this with your teacher and determine the best course of action. Generally, there should be an agreement between the programmer and the customer regarding the level of robustness required. For most programs and examples in this text, it is assumed that valid data are entered when requested.

Exercises 5.3

In Exercises 1–3, what output is produced from the program fragment? Assume all variables are suitably declared.

*1.
```
A := -14;
B := 0;
IF A < B THEN
  writeln (A, abs(A))
ELSE
  writeln (A * B);
```

2.
```
A := 50;
B := 25;
Count := 0;
Sum := 0;
IF A = B THEN
  writeln (A, B)
ELSE
  BEGIN
    Count := Count + 1;
    Sum := Sum + A + B;
    writeln (A, B)
  END;
writeln (Count, Sum);
```

*3.
```
Temp := 0;
A := 10;
B := 5;
IF A > B THEN
  writeln (A, B)
ELSE
  Temp := A;
  A := B;
  B := Temp;
writeln (A, B);
```

4. Write a test program that illustrates what error message occurs when a semicolon precedes **ELSE** in an **IF . . . THEN . . . ELSE** statement. For example,

```
PROGRAM SyntaxError (output);

VAR
  A, B : integer;

BEGIN
  A := 10;
```

```
    B := 5;
    IF A < B THEN
      writeln (A);
    ELSE
      writeln (B)
  END.
```

In Exercises 5–7, find all errors in the program fragment.

*5.
```
IF Ch <> '.' THEN
  CharCount := CharCount + 1;
  writeln (Ch)
ELSE
  PeriodCount := Period Count + 1;
```

6.
```
IF Age < 20 THEN
  BEGIN
    YoungCount := YoungCount + 1;
    YoungAge := YoungAge + Age
  END;
ELSE
  BEGIN
    OldCount := OldCount + 1;
    OldAge := OldAge + Age
  END;  {  of ELSE option  }
```

*7.
```
IF Age < 20 THEN
  BEGIN
    YoungCount := YoungCount + 1;
    YoungAge := YoungAge + Age
  END
ELSE
  OldCount := OldCount + 1;
  OldAge := OldAge + Age;
```

8. Assume the declaration section

```
VAR
  MaxValue,
  X, Y, Z : real;
```

is part of a program and X, Y, and Z have values assigned to them.

a. Write a segment of code that uses **IF . . . THEN** statements to assign the largest value to MaxValue.

b. Write a segment of code that uses **IF . . . THEN . . . ELSE** statements to assign the largest value to MaxValue.

9. Write a program to help balance your checkbook. Your program should read an entry from the data, keep track of the number of deposits and checks, and keep a running balance. Each line of input consists of a character, D (deposit) or C (check), followed by an amount.

10. Write an interactive program that determines the slopes of two lines. Input consists of two points (X1, Y1) and (X2, Y2) on each line. The slope of each nonvertical line is to be computed. A special message should be printed if the line is vertical (X1 = X2). For other lines, output should indicate if they are parallel ($m_1 = m_2$), perpendicular ($m_1 = -1/m_2$), or neither.

5.4 Nested and Extended IF Statements

Objectives

- to learn the form and syntax required for using nested **IF** statements
- to know when to use nested **IF** statements
- to be able to use extended **IF** statements
- to be able to trace the logic when using nested **IF** statements
- to develop a consistent writing style when using nested **IF** statements

A **nested IF statement** is a selection statement used within another selection statement.

An **extended IF statement** occurs when an **IF . . . THEN . . . ELSE** statement is used in the **ELSE** option of a selection statement.

Multiway Selection

In Sections 5.2 and 5.3, we examined one-way (**IF . . . THEN**) and two-way (**IF . . . THEN . . . ELSE**) selection. Since each of these is a single Pascal statement, either can be used as part of a selection statement to achieve multiple selection. In this case, the multiple selection statement is referred to as a **nested IF statement.** Nested statements can be any combination of **IF . . . THEN** or **IF . . . THEN . . . ELSE** statements.

To illustrate, let's write a program fragment to issue interim progress reports for students in a class. If a student's score is below 50, the student is failing. If the score is between 50 and 69 inclusive, the progress is unsatisfactory. If the score is 70 or above, the progress is satisfactory. The first decision to be made is based on whether the score is below 50 or not; the design is

```
IF Score >= 50 THEN
  .
  .   (progress report here)
  .
ELSE
  writeln ('You are currently failing.':34);
```

We now use a nested **IF . . . THEN . . . ELSE** statement for the progress report for students who are not failing. The complete fragment is

```
IF Score >= 50 THEN
  IF Score > 69 THEN
    writeln ('Your progress is satisfactory.':38)
  ELSE
    writeln ('Your progress is unsatisfactory.':40)
ELSE
  writeln ('You are currently failing.':34);
```

One particular instance of nesting selection statements requires special development. When additional **IF . . . THEN . . . ELSE** statements are used in the **ELSE** option, we call this an **extended IF statement** and use the following form:

IF <condition 1> **THEN**
.
.   (action 1 here)
.
ELSE IF <condition 2> **THEN**
.
.   (action 2 here)
.
ELSE IF <condition 3> **THEN**
.
.   (action 3 here)
.
ELSE
.
.   (action 4 here)
.

Using this form, we can redesign the previous fragment that printed progress reports as follows:

```
IF Score > 69 THEN
  writeln ('Your progress is satisfactory.':38)
ELSE IF Score > 50 THEN
  writeln ('Your progress is unsatisfactory.':40)
ELSE
  writeln ('You are currently failing.':34);
```

Another method of writing the nested fragment is to use sequential conditional statements as follows:

```
IF Score > 69 THEN
  writeln ('Your progress is satisfactory.':38);
IF (Score <= 69) AND (Score >= 50) THEN
  writeln ('Your progress is unsatisfactory.':40);
IF Score < 50 THEN
  writeln ('You are currently failing.':34);
```

However, this is less efficient because each **IF . . . THEN** statement is executed each time through the program. You should generally avoid using sequential **IF . . . THEN** statements if a nested statement can be used; this reduces execution time for a program.

Tracing the flow of logic through nested **IF** statements can be tedious. However, it is essential that you develop this ability. For practice, let's trace through the following example.

Example 5.12

Let's consider the nested statement

```
IF A > 0 THEN
  IF A MOD 2 = 0 THEN
    Sum1 := Sum1 + A
  ELSE
    Sum2 := Sum2 + A
ELSE
  IF A = 0 THEN
    writeln ('A is zero':18)
  ELSE
    NegSum := NegSum + A;
writeln ('All done':17);
```

We will trace through this statement and discover what action is taken when A is assigned 20, 15, 0, and –30, respectively. For A := 20, the statement A $>$ 0 is **true,** hence

```
A MOD 2 = 0
```

is evaluated. This is **true,** so

```
Sum1 := Sum1 + A
```

is executed and control is transferred to

```
writeln ('All done':17);
```

For A := 15, A > 0 is **true** and

```
A MOD 2 = 0
```

is evaluated. This is **false,** so

```
Sum2 := Sum2 + A
```

is executed and control is again transferred out of the nested statement to

```
writeln ('All done':17);
```

For A := 0, A > 0 is **false,** thus

```
A = 0
```

is evaluated. Since this is **true,** the statement

```
writeln ('A is zero':18)
```

is executed and control is transferred to

```
writeln ('All done':17);
```

Finally, for A := –30, A > 0 is **false,** thus

```
A = 0
```

is evaluated. This is **false,** so

```
NegSum := NegSum + A
```

is executed and then control is transferred to

```
writeln ('All done':17);
```

Note that this example traces through all possibilities involved in the nested statement. It is essential to do this to guarantee that your statement is properly constructed.

Designing solutions to problems that require multiway selection can be difficult. A few guidelines can help. If a decision has two courses of action and if one is complex and the other is fairly simple, nest the complex part in the **IF . . . THEN** option and the simple part in the **ELSE** option. This method is frequently used to check for bad data. An example of the program design for this is

```
        .
        .  (get the data)
        .
IF DataOK THEN
        .
        .  (complex action here)
        .
ELSE
    (message about bad data)
```

This method can also be used to guard against dividing by zero in computation. For instance, we can have

```
Divisor := <value>;
IF Divisor <> 0 THEN
      .
      .  (proceed with action)
      .
ELSE
  writeln ('Division by zero');
```

When several courses of action can be considered sequentially, an extended **IF . . . THEN . . . ELSE** statement should be used. To illustrate, consider the program fragment in the following example.

Example 5.13

Let's write a program fragment that allows you to assign letter grades based on students' semester averages. Grades are to be assigned according to the scale

```
100 >= X >= 90      A
90 > X >= 80        B
80 > X >= 70        C
70 > X >= 55        D
55 > X              E
```

Extended **IF**s can be used to accomplish this as follows:

```
IF Average >= 90 THEN
  Grade := 'A'
ELSE IF Average >= 80 THEN
  Grade := 'B'
ELSE IF Average >= 70 THEN
  Grade := 'C'
ELSE IF Average >= 55 THEN
  Grade := 'D'
ELSE
  Grade := 'E';
```

Since any Average over 100 or less than zero would be a sign of some data or program error, this example could be protected with a statement as follows:

```
IF (Average <= 100) AND (Average >= 0) THEN
  .
  .  (compute letter grade)
  .
ELSE
  writeln ('There is an error. Average is ':38, Average:8:2);
```

Protecting parts of a program in this manner will help you avoid unexpected results or program crashes. It also allows you to identify the source of an error.

Form and Syntax

The rule for matching **ELSE** statements in nested selection statements is:

When an **ELSE** *is encountered, it is matched with the most recent* **THEN** *that has not yet been matched.*

Matching **IF . . . THEN** statements with **ELSE** statements is a common source of errors. When designing programs, you should be very careful to match them correctly. A situation that can lead to an error is an **IF . . . THEN . . . ELSE** statement such as

```
IF <condition 1> THEN
        .
        .  (action 1)
        .
ELSE
        .
        .  (action 2)
        .
```

where action 1 consists of an **IF . . . THEN** statement. Specifically, suppose we want a fragment of code to read a list of positive integers and print those that are perfect squares. A method of protecting against negative integers and zero could be

```
readln (Num);
IF Num > 0 THEN
        .
        .  (action 1 here)
        .
ELSE
  writeln (Num, ' is not positive.');
```

If we now develop action 1 so that it prints only those positive integers that are perfect squares, it is

```
IF abs(sqrt(Num) - trunc(sqrt(Num))) < 0.0001 THEN
  writeln (Num)
```

Nesting this selection statement in our design, we have

```
readln (Num);
IF Num > 0 THEN
  IF abs(sqrt(Num) - trunc(sqrt(Num))) < 0.0001 THEN
    writeln (Num)
ELSE
  writeln (Num, ' is not positive.');
```

If we now use this segment with input of 20 for Num, the output is

```
20 is not positive.
```

Thus, this fragment is not correct. The indenting is consistent with our intent, but the actual execution of the fragment treated the code as

```
readln (Num);
IF Num > 0 THEN
  IF abs(sqrt(Num) - trunc(sqrt(Num))) < 0.0001 THEN
    writeln (Num)
  ELSE
    writeln (Num, ' is not positive.');
```

An **empty statement** makes use of a semicolon to indicate that no action is to be taken. Also referred to as a **null statement.**

because the **ELSE** is matched with the most recent **THEN.** This problem can be resolved in several ways. We could use an **ELSE** option with an **empty (null) statement.** Thus, we would have

```
readln (Num);
IF Num > 0 THEN
  IF abs(sqrt(Num) - trunc(sqrt(Num))) < 0.0001 THEN
    writeln (Num)
  ELSE  {  Do nothing  }
ELSE
  writeln (Num, ' is not positive.');
```

The second **IF . . . THEN** statement can be isolated by enclosing it in a **BEGIN . . . END** block. Thus, we would have

```
readln (Num);
IF Num > 0 THEN
  BEGIN
    IF abs(sqrt(Num) - trunc(sqrt(Num))) < 0.0001 THEN
      writeln (Num)
  END
ELSE
  writeln (Num, ' is not positive.');
```

Or we could redesign the fragment as follows:

```
readln (Num);
IF Num <= 0 THEN
  writeln (Num, ' is not positive.');
ELSE IF abs(sqrt(Num) - trunc(sqrt(Num))) < 0.0001 THEN
  writeln (Num);
```

The following example reviews the importance of proper indenting.

Example 5.14

What output will be produced when the following fragment of code is executed?

```
A := 15;
IF A > 0 THEN
  IF A MOD 2 = 0 THEN
    writeln (A + 100)
ELSE
  writeln (A - 100);
```

This fragment results in the output

```
-85
```

The indenting of this fragment is misleading. Since an **ELSE** is matched with the last **IF . . . THEN,** it should be written as

```
A := 15;
IF A > 0 THEN
  IF A MOD 2 = 0 THEN
    writeln (A + 100)
  ELSE
    writeln (A - 100);
```

Communication and Style Tips

It is very important to use a consistent, readable writing style when using nested or extended **IF** statements. The style used here for nested **IF** statements is to indent each nested statement two spaces. Also, each **ELSE** of an **IF . . . THEN . . . ELSE** statement is in the same column as the **IF** of that statement. This allows you to see at a glance where the **ELSE** statements match with the **IF . . . THEN** statements; for example,

```
IF...THEN
  IF...THEN
  ELSE
ELSE
```

In an extended **IF** statement, all the **ELSE** statements are aligned on the same indenting level as the first **IF**. This reinforces the concept of extended **IF**; for example,

```
IF...THEN
ELSE IF...THEN
ELSE IF...THEN
ELSE
```

If you want the design to be consistent with the originally written form, you could rewrite the fragment as

```
A := 15;
IF A <= 0 THEN
  writeln (A - 100)
ELSE
  IF A MOD 2 = 0 THEN
    writeln (A + 100);
```

Using semicolons before **ELSE** statements becomes more of a problem as you nest to several layers and use compound statements within the nesting. In some cases, it may be wise to redesign a complex, deeply nested fragment to enhance readability.

We conclude this section with a complete program that uses nested **IF** statements.

Focus on Program Design: Case Study 5.1

Employee Payroll

Let's write a program that computes the gross pay for an employee of the Clean Products Corporation of America. The corporation produces three products: A, B, and C. Supervisors earn a commission of 7 percent of sales and representatives earn 5 percent. Bonuses of $100 are paid to supervisors whose commission exceeds $300 and to representatives whose commission exceeds $200.

Typical input consists of an S for supervisor or an R for representative. This is followed by three integers, which represent the number of units of each of the products sold. A sample input screen is

```
Enter S or R for classification.
S
Enter ASales, BSales, CSales
1100 990 510
```

Since product prices may vary over time, the constant definition section will be used to indicate the current prices. The section for this problem will be

```
CONST
  SuperRate = 0.07;
  RepRate = 0.05;
  APrice = 13.95;
  BPrice = 17.95;
  CPrice = 29.95;
```

A first-level pseudocode development for this problem might be

1. Get the data
2. Compute commission and bonus
3. Print a heading
4. Print a summary

The structure chart for this is shown in Figure 5.3. Step 1 will be a single **readln** statement. Step 2 is further developed as

2. Compute commission and bonus
   2.1 **IF** employee is a supervisor **THEN**
         compute supervisor's earnings
       ELSE
         compute representative's earnings

where "compute supervisor's earnings" is refined to

    2.1.1 Compute commission from sales of A
    2.1.2 Compute commission from sales of B
    2.1.3 Compute commission from sales of C
    2.1.4 Compute total commission
    2.1.5 Compute supervisor's bonus

Structure chart for the Clean Products Corporation of America problem

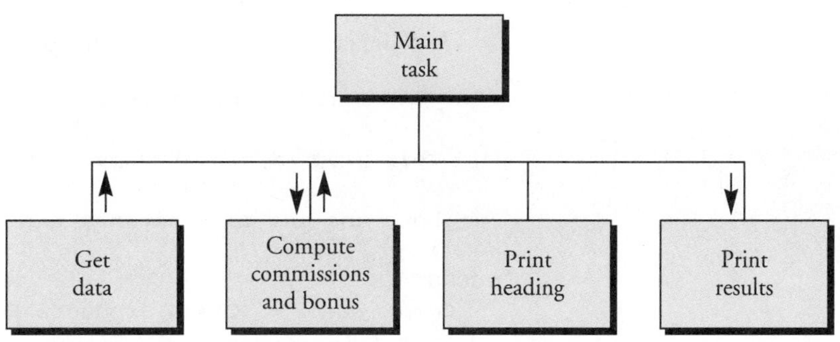

```
2.1.5.1 IF total commission > 300 THEN
            bonus is 100.00
        ELSE
            bonus is 0.00
```

A similar development follows for computing a representative's earnings. Step 3 will be an appropriate heading. Step 4 will contain whatever you feel is appropriate for output. It should include at least the number of sales, amount of sales, commissions, bonuses, and total compensation.

A complete pseudocode solution to this problem is

```
1. Get the data
2. Compute commission and bonus
   2.1 IF employee is a supervisor THEN
       2.1.1  Compute commission from sales of A
       2.1.2  Compute commission from sales of B
       2.1.3  Compute commission from sales of C
       2.1.4  Compute total commission
       2.1.5  Compute supervisor's bonus
              2.1.5.1 IF total commission > 300 THEN
                          bonus is 100.00
                      ELSE
                          bonus is 0.00
       ELSE
       2.1.6  Compute commission from sales of A
       2.1.7  Compute commission from sales of B
       2.1.8  Compute commission from sales of C
       2.1.9  Compute total commission
       2.1.10 Compute representative's bonus
              2.1.10.1 IF total commission > 200 THEN
                           bonus is 100.00
                       ELSE
                           bonus is 0.00
3. Print a heading
4. Print a summary
   4.1 Print input data
   4.2 Print sales data
   4.3 Print commission
   4.4 Print bonus
   4.5 Print total earnings
```

A complete program to solve this problem follows:

```
PROGRAM ComputeWage (input, output):

{  This program computes gross pay for an employee.   }

{  Note the use of constants and selection.            }

CONST
  CompanyName = 'Clean Products Corporation of America';
  Line = '-------------------------------------';
```

```
  SuperRate = 0.07;
  RepRate = 0.05;
  APrice = 13.95;
  BPrice = 17.95;
  CPrice = 29.95;
  Month = 'June';
  Skip = ' ';

VAR
  ASales, BSales,
  CSales : integer;         {  Sales of products A, B, C          }
  AComm, BComm, CComm,      {  Commission on sales of A, B, C     }
  Bonus,                    {  Bonus, if earned                   }
  TotalCommission : real;   {  Commission on all products         }
  Classification : char;    {  S-Supervisor or R-Representative   }

BEGIN  {  Program  }

  {  Get the data  }
  writeln ('Enter S or R for classification.');
  readln (Classification);
  writeln ('Enter ASales, BSales, CSales');
  readln (ASales, BSales, CSales);

  {  Now compute compensation due  }
  IF Classification = 'S' THEN                        {  Supervisor }
    BEGIN
      AComm := ASales * APrice * SuperRate;
      BComm := BSales * BPrice * SuperRate;
      CComm := CSales * CPrice * SuperRate;
      TotalCommission := AComm + BComm + CComm;
      IF TotalCommission > 300.0 THEN
        Bonus := 100.0
      ELSE
        Bonus := 0.0
    END  {  of IF...THEN option  }
  ELSE
    BEGIN                                         {  Representative }
      AComm := ASales * APrice * RepRate;
      BComm := BSales * BPrice * RepRate;
      CComm := CSales * CPrice * RepRate;
      TotalCommission := AComm + BComm + CComm;
      IF TotalCommission > 200.0 THEN
        Bonus := 100.0
      ELSE
        Bonus := 0.0
    END;  {  of ELSE option  }

  {  Print a heading;  }
  writeln;
  writeln (Skip:10, CompanyName);
  writeln (Skip:10, Line);
  writeln;
  writeln (Skip:10, 'Sales Report for:', Skip:3, Month);
  writeln;
```

```
  {  Now print the results  }
  write (Skip:10, 'Classification:');
  IF Classification = 'S' THEN
    writeln (Skip:5, 'Supervisor')
  ELSE
    writeln (Skip:5, 'Representative');
  writeln;
  writeln (Skip:12, 'Product     Sales     Commission');
  writeln (Skip:12, '-------     -----     ----------');
  writeln;
  writeln (Skip:15, 'A', ASales:13, AComm:14:2);
  writeln (Skip:15, 'B', BSales:13, BComm:14:2);
  writeln (Skip:15, 'C', CSales:13, CComm:14:2);
  writeln;
  writeln ('Subtotal':31, '$':3, TotalCommission:9:2);
  writeln;
  writeln ('Your bonus is:':31, '$':3, Bonus:9:2);
  writeln ('-------':43);
  writeln;
  writeln ('Total Due':31, '$':3, (TotalCommission + Bonus):9:2);
  writeln
END.  {  of program  }
```

A sample run of this program produces

```
Enter S or R for classification.
S
Enter ASales, BSales, CSales
1100 990 510

          Clean Products Corporation of America
          -------------------------------------

          Sales Report for:   June

          Classification:     Supervisor

            Product     Sales     Commission
            -------     -----     ----------

               A         1100       1074.15
               B          990       1243.93
               C          510       1069.21

                         Subtotal  $  3387.30

                    Your bonus is:  $   100.00
                                       -------

                        Total Due  $  3487.30
```

Program Testing

In actual practice, a great deal of time is spent testing programs in an attempt to make them run properly when they are installed for some specific purpose. Formal program verification is discussed in Section 5.6 and is developed more fully in subsequent course work. However, examining the issue of which data are minimally necessary for program testing is appropriate when working with selection statements.

As you might expect, test data should include information that tests every logical branch in a program. Whenever a program contains an **IF . . . THEN . . . ELSE** statement of the form

```
IF  <condition> THEN
        .
        .   (action 1 here)
        .
ELSE
        .
        .   (action 2 here)
        .
```

the test data should guarantee that both the **IF . . . THEN** and the **ELSE** options are executed.

A bit more care is required when selecting test data for nested and extended **IF** statements. In general, a single **IF . . . THEN . . . ELSE** statement requires at least two data items for testing. If an **IF . . . THEN . . . ELSE** statement is nested within the **IF . . . THEN** option, at least two more data items are required to test the nested selection statement.

For purposes of illustration, let's reexamine the program in **Focus on Program Design: Case Study 5.1:** Employee Payroll. This program contains the logic

```
IF Classification = 'S' THEN
   .
   .
   .
  IF TotalCommission > 300.00 THEN
     .
     .
     .
  ELSE
     .
     .
     .
ELSE
   .
   .
   .
  IF TotalCommission > 200.00 THEN
     .
     .
     .
  ELSE
     .
     .
     .
```

To see what data should minimally be used to test all logic paths, consider the following table:

Classification	Total Commission
S	400.00
S	250.00
R	250.00
R	150.00

It is a good idea to also include boundary conditions in the test data. Thus, the table could also have listed 300.00 as the total commission for S and 200.00 as the total commission for R.

In summary, you should always make sure every logical branch is executed when running the program with test data.

Exercises 5.4

For Exercises 1–4, consider the program fragment

```
IF X >= 0.0 THEN
  IF X < 1000.00 THEN
    BEGIN
      Y := 2 * X;
      IF X <= 500 THEN
        X := X / 10
    END
  ELSE
    Y := 3 * X
ELSE
  Y := abs(X);
```

Indicate the values of X and Y after this fragment is executed for the initial values of X.

*1. `X := 381.5;`

2. `X := -21.0;`

*3. `X := 600.0;`

4. `X := 3000.0;`

5. Write a nested **IF . . . THEN . . . ELSE** statement that has separate branches for positive integers, zero, and negative integers. The branch for positive integers should distinguish between even and odd integers. Write and run a test program that checks each of these branches.

For Exercises 6–9, rewrite the fragment using nested **IF**s without compound conditions. (You may assume the values for Ch will be M or F.)

6.
```
IF (Ch = 'M') AND (Sum > 1000) THEN
  X := X + 1;
IF (Ch = 'M') AND (Sum <= 1000) THEN
  X := X + 2;
IF (Ch = 'F') AND (Sum > 1000) THEN
  X := X + 3;
IF (Ch = 'F') AND (Sum <= 1000) THEN
  X := X + 4;
```

*7.
```
read (Num);
IF (Num > 0) AND (Num <= 10000) THEN
  BEGIN
    Count := Count + 1;
    Sum := Sum + Num
  END
ELSE
  writeln ('Value out of range':27);
```

8.
```
IF (A > 0) AND (B > 0) THEN
  writeln ('Both positive':22)
ELSE
  writeln ('Some negative':22);
```

*9.
```
IF ((A > 0) AND (B > 0)) OR (C > 0) THEN
  writeln ('Option one':19)
ELSE
  writeln ('Option two':19);
```

For each of the fragments given in Exercises 10–13, indicate the output using the following assignment statements.

a.
```
A := -5;
B := 5;
```

b.
```
A := -5;
B := -3;
```

c.
```
A := 10;
B := 8;
```

d.
```
A := 10;
B := -4;
```

10.
```
IF A < 0 THEN
  IF B < 0 THEN
    A := B
ELSE
  A := B + 10;
writeln (A, B);
```

*11.
```
IF A < 0 THEN
  BEGIN
    IF B < 0 THEN
      A := B
  END
ELSE
  A := B + 10;
writeln (A, B);
```

12.
```
IF A >= 0 THEN
  A := B + 10
ELSE
  IF B < 0 THEN
    A := B;
writeln (A, B);
```

*13.
```
IF A >= 0 THEN
  A := B + 10;
IF B < 0 THEN
  A := B;
writeln (A, B);
```

14. In Example 5.13, we assigned grades to students. Rewrite the grade assignment fragment using a different nesting. Could you rewrite it without using any nesting? Should you?

*15. Many nationally based tests report scores and indicate in which quartile the score lies. Assuming the following quartile designation,

Score	Quartile
100–75	1
74–50	2
49–25	3
24–0	4

write a program fragment to read a score as input and report in which quartile the score lies.

16. What are the values of A, B, and C after the following program fragment is executed?

```
A := -8;
B := 21;
C := A + B;
IF A > B THEN
  BEGIN
    A := B;
    C := A * B
  END
ELSE
  IF A < 0 THEN
    BEGIN
      A := abs(A);
      B := B - A;
      C := A * B
    END
  ELSE
    C := 0;
```

17. Create minimal sets of test data for each part of Exercises 10–13 and for Exercise 16. Explain why each data item has been included.
18. Discuss a technique that could be used as a debugging aid to guarantee that all possible logical paths of a program have been used.

5.5 CASE Statements

Objectives

- to know the form and syntax required for using **CASE** statements
- to understand how **CASE** statements can be used as an alternate method for multiway selection
- to be able to use **CASE** statements in designing programs to solve problems

Thus far, this chapter has examined one-way selection, two-way selection, and multiway selection. Section 5.4 illustrated how multiple selection can be achieved using nested and extended **IF** statements. Since multiple selection can sometimes be difficult to follow, Pascal provides an alternative method of handling this concept, the **CASE** statement.

Form and Syntax

CASE statements can often be used when there are several options that depend on the value of a variable or expression. The general structure for a **CASE** statement is

```
CASE selector OF
    <label list 1> : <statement 1>;
    <label list 2> : <statement 2>;
         .              .
         .              .
         .              .
    <label list n> : <statement n>
END
```

and is shown graphically in Figure 5.4.

◆ Figure 5.4

CASE flow diagram

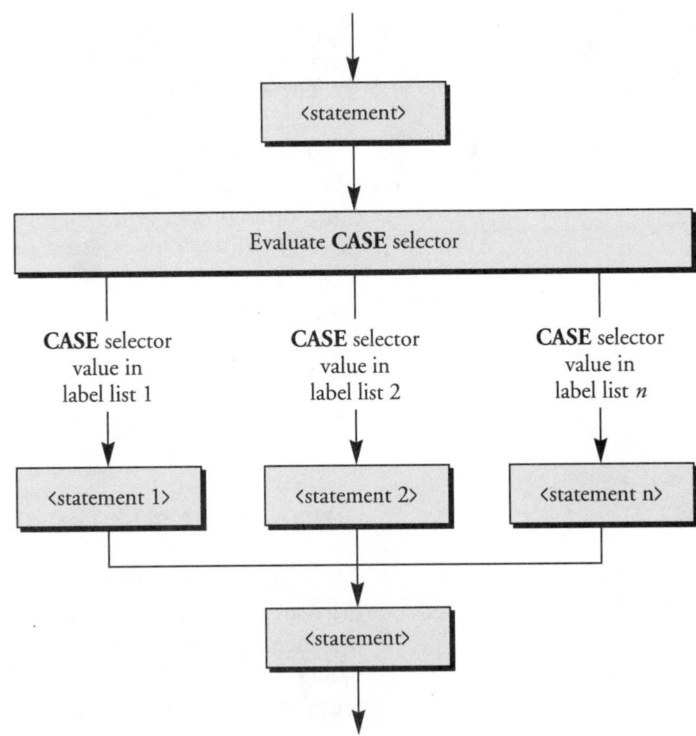

The selector can be any variable or expression whose value is any data type we have studied previously except for **real** (only ordinal data types can be used). Values of the selector constitute the label list. Thus, if Age is a variable whose values are restricted to 16, 17, and 18, we could have

```
CASE Age OF
  16 : <statement 1>;
  17 : <statement 2>;
  18 : <statement 3>
END;  {  of CASE Age  }
```

When this program statement is executed, the value of Age will determine to which statement control is transferred. More specifically, the program fragment

```
Age := 17;
CASE Age OF
  16 : writeln ('Soon I''ll get my driver''s permit.');
  17 : writeln ('I just got my driver''s license.');
  18: writeln ('This is my second year of driving.')
END;
```

produces the output

```
I just got my driver's license.
```

Before considering more examples, several comments are in order.

1. The flow of logic within a **CASE** statement is as follows:

   a. The value of the selector is determined.
   b. The value is found in the label list.
   c. The statement following the value in the list is executed.
   d. Control is transferred to the first program statement following the **CASE** statement **END.**
2. The selector can have a value of any type previously studied except **real.** Only ordinal data types may be used.
3. Several values, separated by commas, may appear on one line. For example, if Age could have any integer value from 15 to 25 inclusive, the **CASE** statement could appear as

```
CASE Age OF
  15, 16, 17     : <statement 1>;
  18, 19, 20, 21 : <statement 2>;
  22, 23, 24     : <statement 3>;
  25             : <statement 4>
END;  {  of CASE Age  }
```

4. All possible values of the **CASE** selector do not have to be listed. However, if a value that is not listed is used, most versions of Pascal produce an error message and execution is terminated. Consequently, it is preferable to list all values of the **CASE** selector. If certain values require no action, list them on the same option with a null statement; for example,

```
CASE Age OF
  16 : <statement 1>;
  17 : ;  {  Do nothing  }
  18 : <statement 2>
END;  {  of CASE Age  }
```

5. Values for the selector can appear only once in the list. Thus,

```
CASE Age OF
  16     : <statement 1>;
  16, 17 : <statement 2>;      (error)
  18     : <statement 3>
END;  {  of CASE Age  }
```

   produces an error since it is not clear which statement should be executed when the value of Age is 16.
6. Proper syntax for using **CASE** statements includes
   a. a colon that separates each label from its respective statement;
   b. a semicolon that follows each statement option except the statement preceding **END;**
   c. commas that are placed between labels on the same option.
7. For the first time, **END** is used without a **BEGIN.** An appropriate program comment should indicate the end of a **CASE** statement. Therefore, our examples will include

```
END;  {  of CASE  }
```

8. Statements for each option can be compound; if they are, they must be in a **BEGIN . . . END** block.

Communication and Style Tips

Writing style for a **CASE** statement should be consistent with your previously developed style. The lines containing options should be indented, the colons should be lined up, and **END** should start in the same column as **CASE**. Thus, a typical **CASE** statement is

```
CASE Score OF
  10, 9, 8        : writeln ('Excellent');
  7, 6, 5         : writeln ('Fair');
  4, 3, 2, 1, 0   : writeln ('Failing')
END;  {  of CASE Score  }
```

At this stage, let's consider several examples that illustrate various uses of **CASE** statements. Since these examples are for the purpose of illustration, the examples will be somewhat contrived. Later examples will serve to illustrate how these statements are used in solving problems.

Example 5.15

The selector can have a value of type **char,** and the ordinal of the character determines the option. Thus, the label list must contain the appropriate characters in single quotation marks. If Grade has values 'A', 'B', 'C', 'D', or 'E', a **CASE** statement could be

```
CASE Grade OF
  'A' : Points := 4.0;
  'B' : Points := 3.0;
  'C' : Points := 2.0;
  'D' : Points := 1.0;
  'E' : Points := 0.0
END;  {  of CASE Grade  }
```

Example 5.16

To avoid inappropriate values for the **CASE** selector, the entire **CASE** statement may be protected by using an **IF . . . THEN . . . ELSE** statement. For example, suppose you are using a **CASE** statement for number of days worked. You expect the values to be 1, 2, 3, 4, or 5, so you could protect the statement by

```
IF (NumDays > 0) AND (NumDays < 6) THEN
  CASE NumDays OF
    1 : <statement 1>;
    2 : <statement 2>;
    3 : <statement 3>;
    4 : <statement 4>;
    5 : <statement 5>
  END  {  of CASE NumDays  }
ELSE
  writeln ('Value of NumDays', NumDays, 'is out of range.');
```

A good debugging technique is to print the value of the selector in your **ELSE** option.

Example 5.17

Compound statements are required if there is a need to execute more than one simple statement as part of a selector option. The following general form is appropriate:

```
CASE Age OF
  16 : BEGIN
         .
         .
         .
       END;
  17 : BEGIN
         .
         .
         .
       END;
  18 : BEGIN
         .
         .
         .
       END
END;  {  of CASE Age  }
```

T

OTHERWISE Option

Some versions of Pascal provide an additional reserved word and option, **OTHERWISE,** which can be used with **CASE** statements. The general structure for this option is

```
CASE <selector> OF
    <label 1> : <statement 1>;
        .
        .
        .
    <label n> : <statement n>
OTHERWISE
    <statement 1>;
    <statement 2>;
        .
        .
        .
    <statement n>
END  {  of CASE  }
```

This option can be used if the same action is to be taken for several values of the **CASE** selector. It can also be used to protect against a **CASE** selector that is out of range. Note that the statements following **OTHERWISE** are executed sequentially and do not have to be in a **BEGIN . . . END** block. You should check your version of Pascal to see if this option is available to you.

Equivalent of Extended IFs

As previously indicated, **CASE** statements can sometimes be used instead of extended **IF**s when multiple selection is required to solve a problem. The following example illustrates this use.

Example 5.18

Let's rewrite the following program fragment using a **CASE** statement.

```
IF (Score = 10) OR (Score = 9) THEN
  Grade := 'A'
ELSE IF (Score = 8) OR (Score = 7) THEN
  Grade := 'B'
ELSE IF (Score = 6) OR (Score = 5) THEN
  Grade := 'C'
ELSE
  Grade := 'E';
```

If we assume Score is an integer variable with values 0, 1, 2, . . . , 10, we can use the **CASE** statement as follows:

```
CASE Score OF
  10, 9          : Grade := 'A';
  8, 7           : Grade := 'B';
  6, 5           : Grade := 'C';
  4, 3, 2, 1, 0 : Grade := 'E'
END;  {  of CASE Score  }
```

Use in Problems

CASE statements should not be used for relational tests involving large ranges of values. For example, if one wanted to examine a range from 0 to 100 to determine test scores, nested selection would be better than a **CASE** statement. We close this section with some examples that illustrate how **CASE** statements can be used in solving problems.

Example 5.19

Let's write a program for a gasoline station owner who sells four grades of gasoline: regular, premium, unleaded, and super unleaded. The program reads a character (R, P, U, S) that designates which kind of gasoline was purchased and then takes subsequent action. The outline for this fragment is

```
readln (GasType);
CASE GasType OF
  'R' : <action for regular unleaded>;
  'M' : <action for mid-grade>;
  'S' : <action for super unleaded>
END;  {  of CASE GasType  }
```

Example 5.20

An alternative method of assigning letter grades based on integer scores between 0 and 100 inclusive is to divide the score by 10 and assign grades according to some scale. This idea could be used in conjunction with a **CASE** statement as follows:

```
NewScore := Score DIV 10;
CASE NewScore OF
  10, 9          : Grade := 'A';
  8              : Grade := 'B';
  7              : Grade := 'C';
  6, 5           : Grade := 'D';
  4, 3, 2, 1, 0  : Grade := 'E'
END;  {  of CASE NewScore  }
```

Exercises 5.5

1. Discuss the need for program protection when using a **CASE** statement.
2. Write a test program to see whether or not the **OTHERWISE** option is available on your system.

*3. Show how the following **CASE** statement could be protected against unexpected values:

```
CASE Age DIV 10 OF
  10, 9, 8, 7 : writeln ('These are retirement years.');
  6, 5, 4     : writeln ('These are middle age years.');
  3, 2        : writeln ('These are mobile years.');
  1           : writeln ('These are school years.')
END;  {  of CASE Age  }
```

In Exercises 4–9, find all the errors.

4.
```
CASE A OF
  1          :  ;
  2          : A := 2 * A
  3          ; A := 3 * A;
  4; 5; 6 : A := 4 * A
END;  {  of Case A  }
```

*5.
```
CASE Num OF
  5              : Num := Num + 5;
  6, 7           ; Num := Num + 6;
  7, 8, 9, 10 : Num := Num + 10
END;  {  of CASE Num  }
```

6.
```
CASE Age OF
  15, 16, 17 : YCount := YCount + 1;
               writeln (Age, YCount);
  18, 19, 20 : MCount := MCount + 1;
  21         : writeln (Age)
END;  {  of CASE Age  }
```

*7.
```
CASE Ch OF
  A : Points := 4.0;
  B : Points := 3.0;
  C : Points := 2.0;
  D : Points := 1.0;
  E : Points := 0.0
END;  {  of CASE Ch  }
```

8.
```
CASE Score OF
  5        : Grade := 'A';
  4        : Grade := 'B';
  3        : Grade := 'C';
  2, 1, 0 : Grade := 'E';
```

*9.
```
CASE Num / 10 OF
  1 : Num := Num + 1;
  2 : Num := Num + 2;
  3 : Num := Num + 3
END;  {  of CASE Num  }
```

In Exercises 10–13, what output is produced from the program fragment?

10.
```
A := 5;
Power := 3;
CASE Power OF
  0 : B := 1;
  1 : B := A;
  2 : B := A * A;
  3 : B := A * A * A
END;  {  of CASE Power  }
writeln (A, Power, B);
```

*11.
```
GasType := 'S';
write ('You have purchased   ');
CASE GasType OF
  'R' : write ('Unleaded Regular');
  'P' : write ('Unleaded Plus');
  'S' : write ('Super Unleaded')
END;  {  of CASE GasType  }
writeln (' gasoline');
```

12.
```
A := 6;
B := -3;
CASE A OF
  10, 9, 8 : CASE B OF
               -3, -4, -5 : A := A * B;
                0, -1, -2 : A := A + B
             END;
   7, 6, 5 : CASE B OF
               -5, -4 : A := A * B;
               -3, -2 : A := A + B;
               -1,  0 : A := A - B
             END
END;  {  of CASE A  }
writeln (A, B);
```

*13.
```
Symbol := '-';
A := 5;
B := 10;
CASE Symbol OF
  '+' : Num := A + B;
  '-' : Num := A - B;
  '*' : Num := A * B
END;  {  of CASE Symbol  }
writeln (A, B, Num);
```

For Exercises 14–16, rewrite the program fragment using a **CASE** statement.

14.
```
IF Power = 1 THEN
  Num := A;
IF Power = 2 THEN
```

```
  Num := A * A;
IF Power = 3 THEN
  Num := A * A * A;
```

*15. Assume Score is an integer between 0 and 10.

```
IF Score < 9 THEN
  IF Score < 8 THEN
    IF Score < 7 THEN
      IF Score < 5 THEN
        Grade := 'E'
      ELSE
        Grade := 'D'
    ELSE
      Grade := 'C'
  ELSE
    Grade := 'B'
ELSE
  Grade := 'A';
```

16. Assume Measurement is either M or N.

```
IF Measurement = 'M' THEN
  BEGIN
    writeln ('This is a metric measurement.');
    writeln ('It will be converted to nonmetric.');
    Length := Num * CMToInches
  END
ELSE
  BEGIN
    writeln ('This is a nonmetric measurement.');
    writeln ('It will be converted to metric.');
    Length := Num * InchesToCM
  END;
```

*17. Show how a **CASE** statement could be used in a program to compute college tuition fees. Assume there are different fee rates for undergraduates (U), graduates (G), foreign students (F), and special students (S).

18. Use nested **CASE** statements to design a program fragment to compute postage for domestic (nonforeign) mail. The design should provide for minimal weights only for both letters and packages. Each can be sent first, second, third, or fourth class.

19. Write an interactive program that allows the user to convert between Celsius and Fahrenheit temperatures. The program should present the user with a menu, such as

```
MENU CHOICES

F - Celsius to Fahrenheit
C - Fahrenheit to Celsius
Q - Quit

Type your choice and press <Enter>.
```

A **CASE** statement should be used to provide the options listed.

5.6 Assertions (Optional)

Objectives

- to know how to use assertions as preconditions
- to know how to use assertions as post-conditions

Assertions are special comments used with selection and repetition that state what you expect to happen and when certain conditions will hold.

A **precondition** is an assertion written before a particular statement.

A **postcondition** is an assertion written after a segment of code.

An **assertion** is a program comment in the form of a statement about what you expect to be true at the point in the program where the assertion is placed. For example, if you wish to compute a test average by dividing the SumOfScores by NumberOfStudents, you could use an assertion in the following manner:

```
{ Assertion: NumberofStudents <> 0 }
ClassAverage := SumOfScores / NumberOfStudents;
```

Assertions are usually Boolean-valued expressions and typically concern program action. Assertions frequently come in pairs: one preceding program action, and one following the action. In this format, the first assertion is a **precondition** and the second is a **postcondition.**

```
IF Num1 < Num2 THEN
  BEGIN
    Temp := Num1;
    Num1 := Num2;
    Num2 := Temp
  END;
```

The intent of this code is to have the value of Num1 be greater than or equal to Num2. We can make an assertion as follows:

```
IF Num1 < Num2 THEN
  BEGIN
    Temp := Num1;
    Num1 := Num2;
    Num2 := Temp
  END;

{  Assertion: Num1 >= Num2  }
```

Assertions written before particular statements are preconditions; those written after are postconditions. For example, in the previous statement, if Num1 and Num2 are both intended to be positive, we can write

```
{  Assertion: Num1 >= 0 AND Num2 >= 0  }        ← Precondition

IF NUM1 < Num2 THEN
  BEGIN
    Temp := Num1;
    Num1 := Num2;
    Num2 := Temp
  END;

{  Assertion: Num1 >= Num2  }                    ← Postcondition
```

In practice, you may choose to label preconditions and postconditions, as the following comments illustrate:

```
{  Precondition: Num1 >= 0 and Num2 >= 0  }

IF Num1 < Num2 THEN
  BEGIN
    Temp := Num1;
```

```
      Num1 := Num2;
      Num2 := Temp
    END;

  { Postcondition: Num1 >= Num2 }
```

As a second example, consider a **CASE** statement used to assign grades based on quiz scores.

```
CASE Score OF
  10          : Grade := 'A';
  9, 8        : Grade := 'B';
  7, 6        : Grade := 'C';
  5, 4        : Grade := 'D';
  3, 2, 1, 0  : Grade := 'E'
END;  { of CASE Score }
```

Assertions can be used as preconditions and postconditions in the following manner:

```
{ Precondition:  Score is an integer between 0 and 10
                 inclusively }

CASE Score OF
  10          : Grade := 'A';
  9, 8        : Grade := 'B';
  7, 6        : Grade := 'C';
  5, 4        : Grade := 'D';
  3, 2, 1, 0  : Grade := 'E'
END;  { of CASE Score }

{ Postcondition:  Grade has been assigned a letter grade
                  according to the scale
            10          -> A
            8, 9        -> B
            6, 7        -> C
            4, 5        -> D
            0, 1, 2, 3  -> E  }
```

Program proof is an analysis of a program that attempts to verify the correctness of program results.

Assertions can be used in program proofs. Simply put, a **program proof** is an analysis of a program that attempts to verify the correctness of program results. A detailed study of program proofs is beyond the scope of this text. If, however, you use assertions as preconditions and postconditions now, you will better understand them in subsequent courses. If you do choose to use assertions in this manner, be aware that the postcondition of one action is the precondition of the next action.

Focus on Program Design: Case Study 5.2

Gas-N-Clean Service Station

The Gas-N-Clean Service Station sells gasoline and has a car wash. Fees for the car wash are $1.25 with a gasoline purchase of $10.00 or more and $3.00 otherwise. Three kinds of gasoline are available: regular unleaded at $1.199, mid-grade at $1.299, and super unleaded at $1.379 per gallon. Let's write a program that prints a

statement for a customer. Input consists of number of gallons purchased, kind of gasoline purchased (R, M, S, or, for no purchase, N), and car wash desired (Y or N). We use the constant definition section for gasoline prices. Our output should include appropriate messages. Sample output for these data is shown on p. 222.

A first-level pseudocode development is

1. Get data
2. Compute charges
3. Print results

A structure chart for this problem is given in Figure 5.5. Module specifications for the main modules are

1. Get Data Module
   Data received: None
   Information returned: Number of gallons purchased
                         Type of gasoline
                         Whether or not a car wash is desired
   Logic: Get information interactively from the keyboard.
2. Compute Charges Module
   Data received: NumGallons
                  GasType
                  WashOption
   Information returned: GasCost
                         WashCost
                         TotalCost
   Logic: Use a **CASE** statement to compute the GasCost.
          Use nested selection to determine the WashCost.
          Sum GasCost and WashCost to get TotalCost.
3. Print Results Module
   Data received: NumGallons
                  GasType
                  WashOption

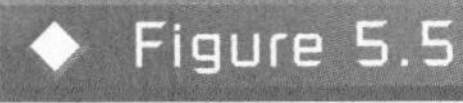

◆ Figure 5.5

Structure chart for the Gas-N-Clean Service Station problem

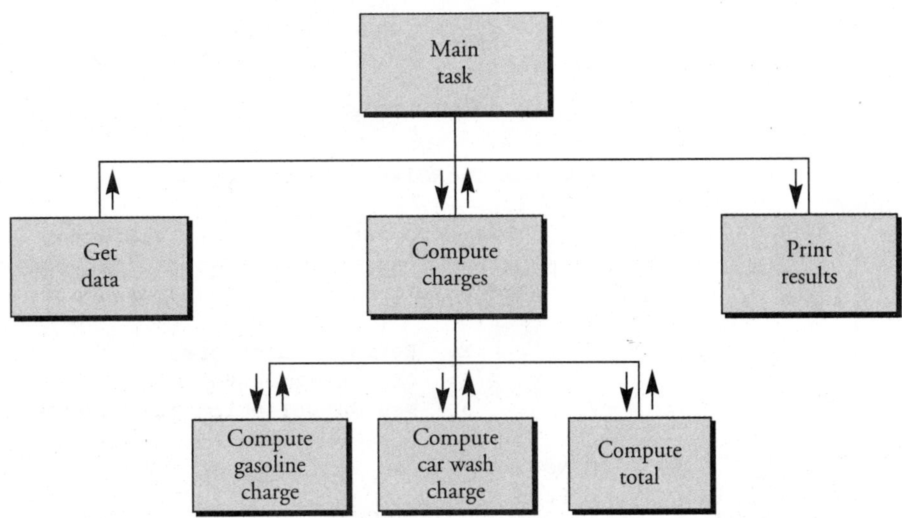

GasCost
WashCost
TotalCost
Information returned: None
Logic: Use several **writeln** statements.

Refinement of the pseudocode for these modules produces

1. Get data
   1.1 Read number of gallons
   1.2 Read kind of gas purchased
   1.3 Read car wash option
2. Compute charges
   2.1 Compute gasoline charge
   2.2 Compute car wash charge
   2.3 Compute total
3. Print results
   3.1 Print heading
   3.2 Print information in transaction
   3.3 Print closing message

Module 2, Compute Charges, consists of three subtasks. A refined pseudocode development of this module is

```
2. Compute charges
   2.1 Compute gasoline charge
       2.1.1 CASE GasType OF
                'R'
                'M'
                'S'
                'N'
   2.2 Compute car wash charge
       2.2.1 IF WashOption is yes THEN
                compute charge
             ELSE
                charge is 0.0
   2.3 Compute total
       2.3.1 Total is GasCost plus WashCost
```

A Pascal program for this problem follows.

```
PROGRAM GasNClean (input, output);

{    This program prints a statement for customers of     }
{    Gas-N-Clean Service Station.  It computes the amount due }
{    for gasoline and car wash.  Features used include:   }
{                                                          }
{        1.  Defined constants                             }
{        2.  CASE statements                               }
{        3.  Nested selection (IF...THEN...ELSE)           }

CONST
  Skip = ' ';
  Date = 'July 25, 1997';
```

```
  RegularPrice = 1.199;
  MidGradePrice = 1.299;
  SuperUnleadedPrice = 1.379;

VAR
  GasType,             { Type of gasoline purchased (R-M-S-N)     }
  WashOption : char;   { Character designating wash option (Y-N) }
  NumGallons,          { Number of gallons purchased              }
  GasCost,             { Computed cost for gasoline               }
  WashCost,            { Cost of car wash                         }
  Total : real;        { Total amount due                         }

BEGIN  {  Program  }

  {  Get the data  }
  writeln ('Enter number of gallons and press <Enter>.');
  readln (NumGallons);
  writeln ('Enter gas type (R, M, S, or N) and press <Enter>.');      1
  readln (GasType);
  writeln ('Enter Y or N for car wash and press <Enter>.');
  readln (WashOption);
  writeln;

  {  Compute gas cost  }
  CASE GasType OF
    'R'  :  GasCost := NumGallons * RegularPrice;
    'M'  :  GasCost := NumGallons * MidGradePrice;
    'S'  :  GasCost := NumGallons * SuperUnleadedPrice;
    'N'  :  GasCost := 0.0
  END;  {  of CASE GasType  }

  {  Compute car wash cost  }
  IF WashOption = 'Y' THEN                                            2
    IF GasCost >= 10.0 THEN
      WashCost := 1.25
    ELSE
      WashCost := 3.0
  ELSE
    WashCost := 0.0;

  Total := GasCost + WashCost;

  {  Print a heading for the customer ticket  }
  writeln (Skip:13, '*****************************************');
  writeln (Skip:13, '*                                       *');
  writeln (Skip:13, '*     Gas-N-Clean Service Station       *');
  writeln (Skip:13, '*                                       *');
  writeln (Skip:13, '*', Skip:12, Date, Skip:13, '*');
  writeln (Skip:13, '*                                       *');
  writeln (Skip:13, '*****************************************');
  writeln;

  {  Now print the results  }
  writeln (Skip:10, 'Amount of gasoline purchased:', Skip:3,
           NumGallons:6:3, ' gallons');
```

```
    write (Skip:10, 'Price per gallon:', Skip:13, '$');
    CASE GasType OF
      'R' : writeln (RegularPrice:7:3);
      'M' : writeln (MidGradePrice:7:3);
      'S' : writeln (SuperUnleadedPrice:7:3);
      'N' : writeln (0.0:7:3)
    END;  {  of CASE GasType  }
    writeln;
    writeln(Skip:10, 'Total gasoline cost', Skip:19, '$',
            GasCost:6:2);
    IF WashCost > 0 THEN
      writeln (Skip:10, 'Car wash cost', Skip:25, '$',
               WashCost:6:2);                                    3
    writeln (Skip:48, '-------');
    writeln (Skip:25, 'Total due', Skip:14, '$', TotalCost:6:2);

    {  Print a closing message  }
    writeln;
    writeln (Skip:21, 'Thank you for stopping');
    writeln (Skip:23, 'Please come again');
    writeln;
    writeln (Skip:13, 'Remember to buckle up and drive safely');
    writeln
  END.  {  of program  }
```

Output for a customer who purchased 11.3 gallons of super unleaded gasoline and did not want a car wash is

```
Enter number of gallons and press <Enter>.
11.3
Enter gas type (R, M, S, or N) and press <Enter>.
S
Enter Y or N for car wash and press <Enter>.
N

             ***************************************
             *                                     *
             *     Gas-N-Clean Service Station     *
             *                                     *
             *            July 25, 1997            *
             *                                     *
             ***************************************

          Amount of gasoline purchased:   11.300 gallons
          Price per gallon:              $  1.379

          Total gasoline cost                    $ 15.58
                                                 -------
                         Total due               $ 15.58

                     Thank you for stopping
                       Please come again

             Remember to buckle up and drive safely
```

Running and Debugging Hints

1. **IF . . . THEN . . . ELSE** is a single statement in Pascal. Thus, a semicolon before the **ELSE** creates an **IF . . . THEN** statement and **ELSE** appears incorrectly as a reserved word.
2. A misplaced semicolon used with an **IF . . . THEN** statement can also be a problem. For example,

   Incorrect
   ```
   IF A > 0 THEN;
     writeln (A);
   ```
   Correct
   ```
   IF A > 0 THEN
     writeln (A);
   ```
3. Be careful with compound statements as options in an **IF . . . THEN . . . ELSE** statement. They must be in a **BEGIN . . . END** block.

Incorrect
```
IF A >= 0 THEN
  writeln (A);
  A := A + 10
ELSE
  writeln ('A is negative');
```
Correct
```
IF A >= 0 THEN
  BEGIN
    writeln (A);
    A := A + 10
  END
ELSE
  writeln ('A is negative');
```

4. Your test data should include values that will check both options of an **IF . . . THEN . . . ELSE** statement.
5. **IF . . . THEN . . . ELSE** can be used to check for other program errors. In particular,
   a. Check for bad data by
   ```
   read (<data>);
   IF (<good data>) THEN
     .
     .  (proceed with program)
     .
   ELSE
     .  (error message here)
     .
     .
   ```
   b. Check for reasonable computed values by
   ```
   IF (<unreasonable values>) THEN
     .
     .  (proceed with program)
     .
   ELSE
     .
     .  (error message here)
     .
   ```

(continued)

For example, if you were computing a student's test average, you could have

```
IF (TestAverage <= 100) AND (TestAverage >= 0) THEN
   .
   .  (proceed with program)
   .
ELSE
   .
   .  (error message here)
   .
```

6. Be careful with Boolean expressions. You should always keep expressions reasonably simple, use parentheses, and minimize use of **NOT.**
7. Be careful to properly match **ELSE**s with **IF**s in nested **IF . . . THEN . . . ELSE** statements. Indenting levels for writing code are very helpful.

```
IF <condition 1> THEN
  IF <condition 2> THEN
     .
     .  (action here)
     .
  ELSE
     .
     .  (action here)
     .
ELSE
     .
     .  (action here)
     .
```

8. The form for using extended **IF** statements is

```
IF <condition 1> THEN
   .
   .  (action 1 here)
   .

ELSE IF <condition 2> THEN
   .
   .  (action 2 here)
   .
ELSE
   .
   .  (final option here)
   .
```

9. Be sure to include the **END** of a **CASE** statement.

Summary

Key Terms

BEGIN . . . END block
compound Boolean expression
compound statement
control structure
empty (null) statement
extended **IF** statement
logical operators: **AND, OR, NOT**
negation
nested **IF** statement
relational operator
robust
selection statement
simple Boolean expression

Key Terms (optional)

assertion
postcondition
precondition
program proof

Keywords

AND
boolean
CASE
ELSE
false
IF
NOT
OF
OR
OTHERWISE (nonstandard)
THEN
true

Key Concepts

- Relational operators are =, >, <, >=, <=, <>.
- Priority for evaluating relational operators is last.
- Logical operators **AND, OR,** and **NOT** are used as operators on Boolean expressions.
- Variables of type **boolean** may only have values **true** or **false.**
- A complete priority listing of arithmetic operators, relational operators, and logical operators is

Expression or Operation	Priority
( )	1. Evaluate from inside out.
NOT	2. Evaluate from left to right.
*, /, **MOD, DIV, AND**	3. Evaluate from left to right.
+, −, **OR**	4. Evaluate from left to right.
<, <=, >, >=, =, <>	5. Evaluate from left to right.

- A selection statement is a program statement that transfers control to various branches of the program.
- A compound statement is sometimes referred to as a **BEGIN . . . END** block; when it is executed, the entire segment of code between the **BEGIN** and **END** is treated like a single statement.
- **IF . . . THEN . . . ELSE** is a two-way selection statement.
- A semicolon should not precede the **ELSE** portion of an **IF . . . THEN . . . ELSE** statement.

- If the Boolean expression in an **IF . . . THEN . . . ELSE** statement is **true,** the command following **THEN** is executed; if the expression is **false,** the command following **ELSE** is executed.
- Multiple selections can be achieved by using decision statements within decision statements; this is termed multiway selection.
- An extended **IF** statement is a statement of the form

```
IF <condition 1> THEN
      .
      . (action 1 here)
      .
ELSE IF <condition 2> THEN
      .
      . (action 2 here)
      .
ELSE IF <condition 3> THEN
      .
      . (action 3 here)
      .
ELSE
      .
      . (action 4 here)
      .
```

- Program protection can be achieved by using selection statements to guard against unexpected results.
- **CASE** statements sometimes can be used as alternatives to multiple selection.
- **CASE** statements use an **END** without any **BEGIN.**
- **OTHERWISE,** a reserved word in some versions of Pascal, can be used to handle values not listed in the **CASE** statement.

Chapter Review Exercises

In Exercises 1–8, indicate if the **boolean** expressions are **true, false,** or invalid.

1. `5 < (7 - 2)`
2. `((8 + 7) < 12) OR ((12 + 6) > 10)`
3. `((8 + 7) < 12) AND ((12 + 6) > 10)`
4. `8 + 7 > 4 OR 6 + 3 > 5`
5. `NOT (12 > (5 + 9))`
6. `(18 <> (4 + 5 * 2)) AND (NOT (16 = (5 * 4)))`
7. `15 MOD 8 > 6 MOD 3`
8. `NOT (8.3 < 5.4) OR (4.5 > -3.5)`

In Exercises 9–13, assume that C is of **char** type and B is of **boolean** type. State if the assignment statements are valid or invalid and, if invalid, explain why.

9. `B := 'false';`
10. `C := 'false';`
11. `B := C;`
12. `B := 'T';`
13. `C := 'T';`

For Exercises 14–20, write a valid Pascal statement.

14. Add 4 to the value of the integer variable A if C is greater than 5.4.

15. Print the value of H if the **boolean** G is **true.**
16. Print either the word "Zero" or "Non-Zero" based on the value of the real variable D.
17. Add 5 to the value of A and print out this new value if the integer H is negative.
18. Print the letter "A" if G > 90, "B" if G is between 80 and 90, or "C" if G is less than 80.
19. Read new values for A or B if either of them is less than 0.0.
20. Skip three lines if the value of the integer variable LineCnt is greater than 64.

Write Exercises 21 and 22 with nested **IF** statements.

21. If the value of the integer variable A is 2, square it. If it is 3, read in a new value for A. If it is 4 or 5, multiply it by 3 and print out the new value.
22. G is a character variable. If it contains either "A" or "D", print the letter. If it contains "B", print the value of the **real** variable H using a ten-character field with three places after the decimal. If it is "C", print the value of G.
23. Rewrite Exercise 21 using a **CASE** statement.
24. Rewrite Exercise 22 using a **CASE** statement.
25. Rewrite the program fragment in Example 5.13 using a **CASE** statement.

Programming Problems

The first 13 problems listed here are relatively short, but to complete them you must use concepts presented in this chapter.

Some of the remaining programming problems are used as the basis for writing programs for Chapters 6 and 7 as well as for this chapter. In this chapter, each program is run on a very limited set of data. Material in Chapter 6 permits us to run the programs on larger data bases. In Chapter 7 we develop the programs using subprograms for various parts. Since the problems marked by a box are referred to and used repeatedly, carefully choose which ones you work on and then develop them completely.

1. A three-minute telephone call to Scio, New York, costs $1.15. Each additional minute costs $0.26. Given the total length of a call in minutes, print the cost.
2. When you first learned to divide, you expressed answers using a quotient and a remainder rather than a fraction or decimal quotient. For example, if you divided 7 by 2, your answers would have been given as 3 r. 1. Given two integers, divide the larger by the smaller and print the answer in this form. Do not assume that the numbers are entered in any order.
3. Revise Problem 2 so that, if there is no remainder, you print only the quotient without a remainder or the letter r.
4. Given the coordinates of two points on a graph, find and print the slope of a line passing through them. Remember that the slope of a line can be undefined.
5. ■ Remember Mr. Lae Z. Programmer (Case Study 4.2, Chapter 4)? He now wishes to change his grading system. He gives five tests, then averages only the four highest scores. An average of 90 or better earns a grade of A, 80–89 a grade of B, and so on. Write a program that accepts five test scores and prints the average and grade according to this method.
6. Given the lengths of three sides of a triangle, print whether the triangle is scalene, isosceles, or equilateral.

7. Given the lengths of three sides of a triangle, determine whether or not the triangle is a right triangle using the Pythagorean theorem. Do not assume that the sides are entered in any order.
8. Given three integers, print only the largest.
9. The island nation of Babbage charges its citizens an income tax each year. The tax rate is based upon the following table:

Income	Tax Rate
$ 0–5,000	0
5,001–10,000	3%
10,001–20,000	5.5%
20,001–40,000	10.8%
over $40,000	23.7%

   Write a program that, given a person's income, prints the tax owed rounded to the nearest dollar.
10. Many states base the cost of car registration on the weight of the vehicle. Suppose the fees are as follows:

Weight	Cost
0–1,500 pounds	$23.75
1501–2,500 pounds	27.95
2501–3,000 pounds	30.25
Over 3000 pounds	37.00

   Given the weight of a car, find and print the cost of registration.
11. The Mapes Railroad Corporation pays an annual bonus as a part of its profit sharing plan. This year all employees who have been with the company for 10 years or more receive a bonus of 12 percent of their annual salary, and those who have worked at Mapes from 5 through 9 years receive a bonus of 5.75 percent. Those who have been with the company less than 5 years receive no bonus.

   Given the initials of an employee, the employee's annual salary, and the number of years employed with the company, find and print the bonus. All bonuses are rounded to the nearest dollar. Output should be in the following form:

```
            MAPES RAILROAD CORP.

Employee xxx           Years of service nn
     Bonus earned: $ yyyy
```

12. A substance floats in water if its density (mass/volume) is less than 1 g/cm^3. It sinks if it is 1 or more. Given the mass and volume of an object, print whether it will sink or float.

13. Mr. Arthur Einstein, your school's physics teacher, wants a program for English-to-metric conversions. You are given a letter indicating whether the measurement is in pounds (P), feet (F), or miles (M). Such measures are to be converted to newtons, meters, and kilometers, respectively. (There are 4.9 newtons in a pound, 3.28 feet in a meter, and 1.61 kilometers in a mile.) Given an appropriate identifying letter and the size of the measurement, convert it to metric units. Print the answer in the following form:

```
3.0 miles = 4.83 kilometers.
```

■ 14. The Caswell Catering and Convention Service (Problem 7, Chapter 4) has decided to revise its billing practices and is in need of a new program to prepare bills. The changes Caswell wishes to make follow.

a. For adults, the deluxe meals will cost $15.80 per person and the standard meals will cost $11.75 per person, dessert included. Children's meals will cost 60 percent of adult meals. Everyone within a given party must be served the same meal type.
b. There are five banquet halls. Room A rents for $55.00, room B rents for $75.00, room C rents for $85.00, room D rents for $100.00, and room E rents for $130.00. The Caswells are considering increasing the room fees in about six months and this should be taken into account.
c. A surcharge, currently 7 percent, is added to the total bill if the catering is to be done on the weekend (Friday, Saturday, or Sunday).
d. All customers will be charged the same rate for tip and tax, currently 18 percent. It is applied only to the cost of food.
e. To induce customers to pay promptly, a discount is offered if payment is made within ten days. This discount depends on the amount of the total bill. If the bill is less than $100.00, the discount is .5 percent; if the bill is at least $100.00 but less than $200.00, the discount is 1.5 percent; if the bill is at least $200.00 but less than $400.00, the discount is 3 percent; if the bill is at least $400.00 but less than $800.00, the discount is 4 percent; and, if the bill is at least $800.00, the discount is 5 percent.

Test your program on each of the following three customers.

Customer A: This customer is using room C on Tuesday night. The party includes 80 adults and 6 children. The standard meal is being served. The customer paid a $60.00 deposit.

Customer B: This customer is using room A on Saturday night. Deluxe meals are being served to 15 adults. A deposit of $50.00 was paid.

Customer C: This customer is using room D on Sunday afternoon. The party includes 30 children and 2 adults, all of whom are served the standard meal.

Output should be in the same form as that for Problem 7 in Chapter 4.

■ 15. State University charges $90.00 for each semester hour of credit, $200.00 per semester for a regular room, $250.00 per semester for an air-conditioned room, and $400.00 per semester for food. All students are charged a $30.00 matriculation fee. Graduating students must also pay a $35.00 diploma fee. Write a program to compute the fees that must be paid by a student. Your program should include an appropriate warning message if a student is taking more than 21 credit hours or fewer than 12 credit hours. A typical line of data for one student would include room type (R or A), student number (in four digits), credit hours, and graduating (T or F).

16. Write a program to determine the day of the week a person was born given his or her birth date. Following are the steps you should use to find the day of the week corresponding to any date in this century.
    a. Divide the last two digits of the birth year by 4. Put the quotient (ignoring the remainder) in Total. For example, if the person was born in 1983, divide 83 by 4 and store 20 in Total.
    b. Add the last two digits of the birth year to Total.
    c. Add the day portion of the birth date to Total.
    d. Using the following table, find the "month number" and add it to Total.

January = 1	May = 2	September = 6
February = 4	June = 5	October = 1
March = 4	July = 0	November = 4
April = 0	August = 3	December = 6

    e. If the year is a leap year and, if the month you are working with is either January or February, then subtract 1 from the Total.
    f. Find the remainder when Total is divided by 7. Look up the remainder in the following table to determine the day of the week the person was born. Note that you should not use this procedure if the person's year of birth is earlier than 1900.

1 = Sunday	5 = Thursday
2 = Monday	6 = Friday
3 = Tuesday	0 = Saturday
4 = Wednesday	

    A typical line of data is

```
5 – 15 78
```

    where the first entry (5 – 15) represents the month and day (May 15) and the second entry (78) represents the birth year. An appropriate error message should be printed if a person's year of birth is before 1900.

17. Community Hospital needs a program to compute and print a statement for each patient. Charges for each day are as follows:
    a. room charges
        i. private room—$341.00
        ii. semiprivate room—$330.00
        iii. ward—$285.00
    b. telephone charge—$3.00
    c. television charge—$5.00

    Write a program to get a line of data, compute the patient's bill, and print an appropriate statement. A typical line of data is

```
3PYY
```

    where "3" indicates the number of days spent in the hospital, "P" represents the room type (P, S, or W), "N" represents the telephone option (Y or N), and "Y" represents the television option (Y or N). A statement for the data given follows.

```
            Community Hospital

          Patient Billing Statement

      Number of days in hospital:      3
      Type of room:                  Private

      Room charge                $1023.00
      Telephone charge           $    9.00
      Television charge          $   15.00
                                 --------

           TOTAL DUE             $1047.00
```

18. Write a program that converts degrees Fahrenheit to degrees Celsius and degrees Celsius to degrees Fahrenheit. (Use the formula CelsTemp = 5/9 * (FarenTemp − 32).) In a typical data line, the temperature is followed by a designator (F or C) indicating whether the given temperature is Fahrenheit or Celsius.

■ 19. The city of Mt. Pleasant bills its residents for sewage, water, and sanitation every three months. The sewer and water charge is figured according to how much water is used by the resident. The scale is

Amount (gallons)	Rate (per gallon)
Less than 1,000	$0.03
1,000 to 2,000	$30 + $0.02 for each gallon over 1,000
2,000 or more	$50 + $0.015 for each gallon over 2,000

The sanitation charge is $7.50 per month.

Write a program to read the number of months for which a resident is being billed (1, 2, or 3), how much water was used, and print out a statement with appropriate charges and messages. Use the constant definition section for all rates and include an error check for incorrect number of months. A typical line of data is

```
3 2175
```

■ 20. Al Derrick, owner of the Lucky Wildcat Well Corporation, wants a program to help him decide whether or not a well is making money. Data for a well are on one or two lines. The first line contains a single character (D for a dry well, O for oil found, and G for gas found) followed by a real number for the cost of the well. If an "O" or "G" is detected, the cost will be followed by an integer indicating the volume of oil or gas found. In this case, there will also be a second line containing an "N" or "S" indicating whether or not sulfur is present. If there is sulfur, the "S" will be followed by the percentage of sulfur present in the oil or gas.

Unit prices are $5.50 for oil and $2.20 for gas. These should be defined as constants. Your program should compute the total revenue for a well (reduce output for sulfur present) and print out all pertinent information with an appropriate message to Mr. Derrick. A gusher is defined as a well with profit in excess of $50,000. Typical data are

```
G 8000.00 20000
```

```
S 0.15
```

21. The Mathematical Association of America hosts an annual summer meeting. Each state sends one official delegate to the section officer's meeting at this summer session. The national organization reimburses the official state delegates according to the following scale:

Round-trip Mileage	Rate
0–500 miles	15 cents per mile
501–1,000 miles	$75.00 plus 12 cents for each mile over 500
1,001–1,500 miles	$135.00 plus 10 cents for each mile over 1,000
1,501–2,000 miles	$185.00 plus 8 cents for each mile over 1,500
2,001–3,000 miles	$225.00 plus 6 cents for each mile over 2,000
Over 3,000 miles	$285.00 plus 5 cents for each mile over 3,000

Write a program that will accept as input the number of round-trip miles for a delegate and compute the amount of reimbursement.

22. Mr. Lae Z. Programmer (Problem 5) now wants you to write a program to compute and print out the grade for a student in his class. The grade is based on three examinations (worth a possible 100 points each), five quizzes (10 points each), and a 200-point final examination. Your output should include all scores, the percentage grade, and the letter grade. The grading scale is

$$
\begin{array}{rcll}
90 \le \text{average} & \le & 100 & \text{A} \\
80 \le \text{average} & < & 90 & \text{B} \\
70 \le \text{average} & < & 80 & \text{C} \\
60 \le \text{average} & < & 70 & \text{D} \\
0 \le \text{average} & < & 60 & \text{E}
\end{array}
$$

Typical input is

```
80 93 85
```
(examination scores)

```
9 10 8 7 10
```
(quiz scores)

```
175
```
(final examination)

23. Mr. Lae Z. Programmer now wants you to modify Problem 22 by adding a check for bad data. Any time an unexpected score occurs, you are to print an appropriate error message and terminate the program.

24. A quadratic equation is one of the form

$$ax^2 + bx + c = 0$$

where $a \neq 0$. Solutions to this equation are given by

$$x = \frac{-b \pm \sqrt{b^2 - 4ac}}{2a}$$

where the quantity $(b^2 - 4ac)$ is referred to as the discriminant of the equation. Write a program to read three integers as the respective coefficients (a, b, and c), compute the discriminant, and print out the solutions. Use the following rules:
   a. discriminant = 0 → single root.
   b. discriminant < 0 → no real number solution.
   c. discriminant > 0 → two distinct real solutions.

25. Write an interactive program that receives as input the lengths of three sides of a triangle. Output should first identify the triangle as scalene, isosceles, or equilateral. The program should use the Pythagorean theorem to determine whether or not scalene or isosceles triangles are right triangles. An appropriate message should be part of the output.

26. The sign on the attendant's booth at the Pentagon parking lot is

PENTAGON VISITOR PARKING	
Cars:	
First 2 hours	Free
Next 3 hours	0.50/hour
Next 10 hours	0.25/hour
Trucks:	
First 1 hour	Free
Next 2 hours	1.00/hour
Next 12 hours	0.75/hour
Senior Citizens:	no charge

Write a program that will accept as input a one-character designator (C, T, or S) followed by the number of minutes a vehicle has been in the lot. The program should then compute the appropriate charge and print a ticket for the customer. Any part of an hour is to be counted as a full hour.

27. Some businesses use attention-getting telephone numbers with an 800 prefix (for example, 1-800-STARTUP) so more customers will become familiar with the business telephone numbers. Write an interactive program that allows the user to enter a seven-letter telephone message and then have the corresponding telephone number printed. Typical input will consist of seven letters. Typical output will consist of the message and the associated telephone number.

28. Write a program that will add, subtract, multiply, and divide fractions. Input will consist of a single line representing a fraction arithmetic problem as follows:

integer/integer operation integer/integer

For example, a line of input might be

```
2/3 + 1/2
```

Your program should

a. Check for division by zero.
b. Check for proper operation symbols.
c. Print the problem in its original form.
d. Print the answer.
e. Print all fractions in horizontal form.

Your answer need not be in lowest terms. For the sample input

```
2/3 + 1/2
```

sample output is

$$\frac{2}{3} + \frac{1}{2} = \frac{7}{6}$$

29. The force of gravity is different for each of the nine planets in our solar system. For example, on Mercury it is only 0.38 times as strong as on Earth. Thus, if you weigh 100 pounds (on Earth), you would weigh only 38 pounds on Mercury. Write a program that allows you to enter your (Earth) weight and your choice of planet to which you would like your weight converted. Output should be your weight on the desired planet together with the planet name. The screen message for input should include a menu for planet choice. Use a **CASE** statement in the program for computation and output. The relative forces of gravity are

Earth	1.00
Jupiter	2.65
Mars	0.39
Mercury	0.38
Neptune	1.23
Pluto	0.05
Saturn	1.17
Uranus	1.05
Venus	0.78

■ 30. In Problem 12, Chapter 4, you were asked to write a program to solve a system of equations using Cramer's rule. Rewrite that program using an **IF . . . THEN . . . ELSE** statement to protect against division by zero when you divide by the determinant of the coefficient matrix.

Communication in Practice

1. Using a completed program you wrote from this chapter, remove all documentation pertaining to selection statements. Exchange this version with another student who has prepared a similar version. Write documentation for all selection statements in the other student's program. Compare your results with the program author's original version. Discuss the differences and similarities between programs with your class.
2. Contact a programmer and discuss the concept of robustness in a program. Prepare a report of your conversation for class. Your report should include a list of specific instances illustrating how programmers make programs robust.

3. Conduct an unscientific survey of at least two people from each of the following groups: students in upper-level computer science courses, instructors of computer science, and programmers working in industry. Your survey should attempt to ascertain the importance of and use of robustness at each level. Discuss the similarities and differences of your findings with those of other class members.
4. Selecting appropriate test data for a program that uses nested selection is not a trivial task. Create diagrams that allow you to trace the flow of logic when nested selection is used. Use your diagrams to draw conclusions about the minimal test data required to test all the branches of a program that uses nested selection to various levels.

Chapter 6

Repetition Statements

Chapter Outline

The previous chapter on selection introduced you to a programming concept that takes advantage of a computer's ability to select. A second major concept utilizing the speed of a computer is repetition. Many problems require a process to be repeated. When this is the case, some form of controlled repetition is needed.

This chapter examines the different methods Pascal permits for performing some process repeatedly. For example, as yet we cannot conveniently write a program that solves the simple problem of adding the integers from 1 to 100 or processing the grades of 30 students in a class. By the end of this chapter, you will be able to solve these problems three different ways. The three forms of repetition (loops) are

1. **FOR . . . TO . . . DO**
2. **WHILE . . . DO**
3. **REPEAT . . . UNTIL**

Each of these three loops contains the basic constructs necessary for repetition: A variable is assigned some value, the variable value changes at some point in the loop, and repetition continues until the value reaches some predetermined value. When the predetermined value (or Boolean condition) is reached, repetition is terminated and program control moves to the next executable statement.

6.1 Classifying Loops

Objectives

- to understand the difference between a pretest loop and a posttest loop
- to understand what a fixed repetition loop is
- to understand when to use a fixed repetition loop
- to understand what a variable control loop is

Pretest and Posttest Loops

A loop that uses a condition to control whether or not the body of the loop is executed before going through the loop is a **pretest (entrance-controlled) loop.** The testing condition is the **pretest condition.** If the condition is **true,** the body of the loop is executed. If the condition is **false,** the program skips to the first line of code following the loop. The **FOR** loops and the **WHILE . . . DO** loop are pretest loops.

A loop that examines a Boolean expression after the loop body is executed is a **posttest (exit-controlled) loop.** This is the **REPEAT . . . UNTIL** loop.

A **pretest loop** is a loop in which the control condition is tested before the loop is executed. **WHILE . . . DO** and **FOR** are pretest loops. Also referred to as an **entrance-controlled loop.**

A **pretest condition** is a condition that controls whether the body of the loop is executed before going through the loop.

Fixed Repetition versus Variable Condition Loops

Fixed repetition (iterated) loops are used when it can be determined in advance how often a segment of code needs to be repeated. For instance, you might have a predetermined number of repetitions of a segment of code for (1) a program that adds the integers from 1 to 100 or (2) a program that uses a fixed number of data lines (for example, game statistics for a team of 12 basketball players). The number of repetitions need not be constant. For example, a user might enter information during execution of an interactive program that would determine how often a segment is to be repeated. **FOR** loops are fixed repetition loops.

Variable condition loops are needed to solve problems in which conditions change within the body of the loop. These conditions involve end-of-line markers, end-of-file markers, sentinel values, Boolean flags, or arithmetic expressions. A variable condition loop uses a control feature that provides more power than is available in many early languages such as BASIC and FORTRAN. **WHILE . . . DO** and **REPEAT . . . UNTIL** loops are variable condition loops.

6.2 FOR Loops

Objectives

- to understand how the loop control variable is used in a loop
- to understand the flow of control when using a fixed repetition loop in a program
- to be able to use a **FOR . . . TO . . . DO** loop in a program
- to be able to use a **FOR . . . DOWNTO . . . DO** loop in a program

There are two kinds of **FOR** loops: the **FOR . . . TO . . . DO** loop and the **FOR . . . DOWNTO . . . DO** loop. These loops are pretest and fixed repetition loops.

FOR...TO...DO Loops

The form necessary for using a **FOR . . . TO . . . DO** loop is

```
    FOR <index> := <initial value> TO <final value> DO
      <statement>
or
    FOR <index> := <initial value> TO <final value> DO
      BEGIN
        <statement 1>;
        <statement 2>;
             .
             .
             .
        <statement n>
      END
```

A **FOR . . . TO . . . DO** loop is considered to be a single executable statement. The actions performed in the loop are referred to as the "body" of the loop. The **index** is an identifier that is assigned values for each repetition of the loop. The internal logic of a **FOR . . . TO . . . DO** loop is as follows:

1. The index is assigned the initial value.
2. The index value is compared to the final value.
3. If the index value is less than or equal to the final value
   a. The body of the loop is executed.
   b. The index value is incremented by 1.
   c. Another check with the final value is made.
4. If the index value exceeds the final value
   a. The index may revert to an unassigned status.

A **posttest loop** is a loop where the control condition is tested after the loop is executed. **REPEAT . . . UNTIL** is a posttest loop. Also referred to as an **exit-controlled loop.**

A **fixed repetition loop** is a loop used if the number of times a segment of code needs to be repeated is known in advance. **FOR . . . TO . . . DO** is a fixed repetition loop. Also referred to as an **iterated loop.**

A **variable condition loop** is a loop in which conditions change within the body of the loop.

An **index** is a variable used for control values in a **FOR** loop.

An **accumulator** is a variable that sums values.

b. Control of the program is transferred to the first statement following the loop.

A flow diagram of the **FOR . . . TO . . . DO** loop is given in Figure 6.1.

Accumulators

The problem of adding the integers from 1 to 100 needs only one statement in the body of the loop. This problem can be solved by code that constructs an **accumulator,** which merely sums values of some variable. In the following code, the index variable Number successively assumes the values 1, 2, 3, . . ., 100.

```
Sum := 0;
FOR Number := 1 TO 100 DO
  Sum := Sum + Number;
```

Number	Sum	
1	0	← Initial value
2	1	← Values on successive passes through loop
3	3	
4	6	
5	10	
.	.	
.	.	
.	.	

This program segment contains an example of graphic documentation. Throughout the text, these insets will be used to help illustrate what the code is actually doing. The insets are not part of the program; they merely show what some specific code is trying to accomplish.

To see how Sum accumulates these values, let's trace through the code for several values of Number. Initially, Sum is set to zero by

```
Sum := 0;
```

◆ Figure 6.1

FOR . . . TO . . . DO flow diagram

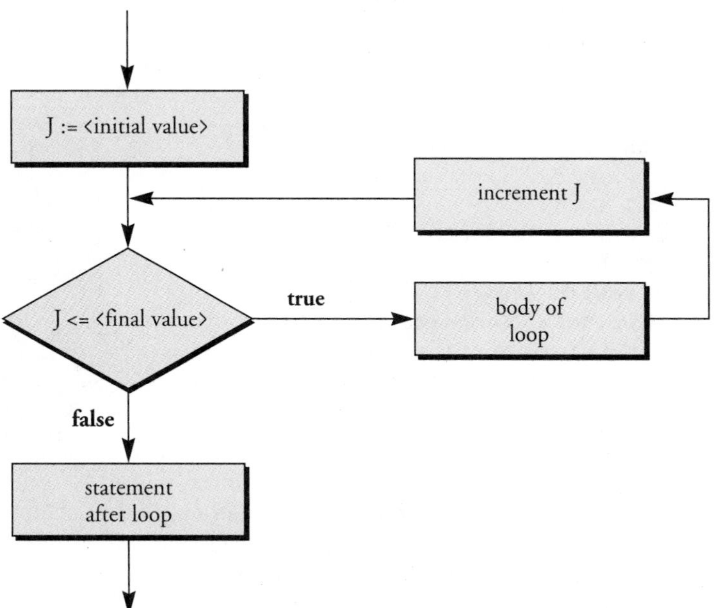

When Number is assigned the value 1,

```
Sum := Sum + Number;
```

produces

1	~~0~~1
Number	Sum

When Number = 2, we get

2	~~1~~3
Number	Sum

Number = 3 yields

3	~~3~~6
Number	Sum

Note that Sum has been assigned a value equal to 1 + 2 + 3. The final value of Number is 100. Once this value has been assigned to Sum, the value of Sum will be 5050, which is the sum 1 + 2 + 3 + . . . + 100.

Accumulators are frequently used in loops. The general form for this use is

```
Accumulator := 0;          {  Before loop  }
FOR Number := <initial value> TO <final value> DO
  BEGIN
    .
    .        (loop body here)
    .
    Accumulator := Accumulator + <new value>
  END;  {  of FOR loop  }
```

For another example using this type of loop, assume you are writing a program that requires 30 test scores to be read from an input file where each score is on a separate line. Furthermore, each score is to be printed and added to Total. The code for this is

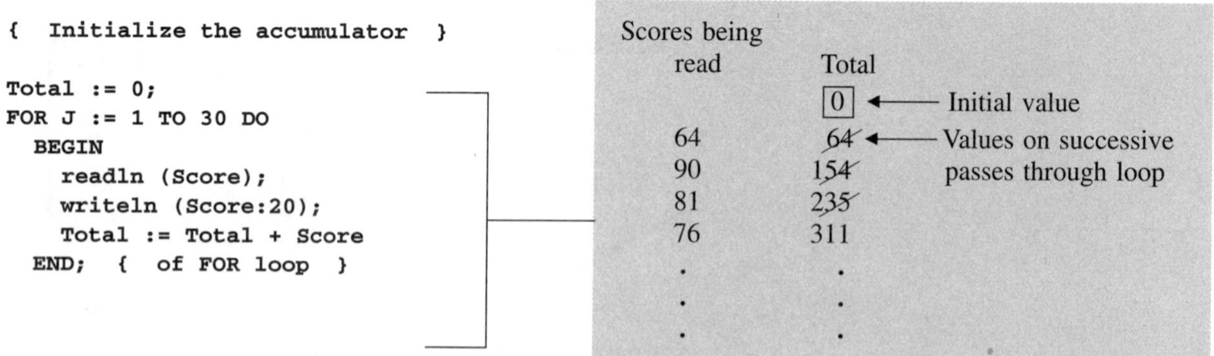
{ Initialize the accumulator }
Total := 0;
FOR J := 1 TO 30 DO
BEGIN
readln (Score);
writeln (Score:20);
Total := Total + Score
END; { of FOR loop }
Scores being read
Total
0
Initial value
64
64
Values on successive passes through loop
90
154
81
235
76
311

In this fragment, Total is the accumulator.

Some comments concerning the syntax and form of **FOR . . . TO . . . DO** loops are now necessary.

1. The words **FOR, TO,** and **DO** are reserved and must be used only in the order **FOR . . . TO . . . DO.**
2. The index must be declared as a variable. Although it can be any ordinal data type, we will use mostly integer examples.
3. The index variable can be any valid identifier.
4. The index can be used within the loop just as any other variable except that the value of the index variable cannot be changed by the statements in the body of the loop.
5. The initial and final values may be constants or variable expressions with appropriate values.
6. If either the initial value or the final value is a variable expression, it should not be changed by the statements in the body of the loop. If either value is changed, unexpected results will be produced.
7. The loop will be repeated for each value of the index in the range indicated by the initial and final values.
8. T The last value assigned to the index during the last pass through the loop might not be retained in the index. When the loop is finished, the index variable may revert to a state of having no assigned value.

At this point you might try writing some test programs to see what happens if you don't follow these rules. Then consider the following examples, which illustrate the features of **FOR . . . TO . . . DO** loops.

Example 6.1

Let's write a segment of code to list the integers from 1 to 10 together with their squares and cubes. This can be done by

```
FOR Index := 1 TO 10 DO
  writeln (Index, Index * Index, Index * Index * Index);
```

This segment produces

```
 1      1      1
 2      4      8
 3      9     27
 4     16     64
 5     25    125
 6     36    216
 7     49    343
 8     64    512
 9     81    729
10    100   1000
```

Example 6.2

Let's write a segment of code that allows us to examine the value of the index variable before a loop, during each execution of the loop, and after the loop. Assume the index variable is Index and that no value has been previously assigned to it. The following segment of code

T

```
writeln ('Before the loop, Index =  ', Index);
writeln;
FOR Index := 5 TO 10 DO
```

```
    writeln ('The value of Index is', Index:4);
  writeln;
  writeln ('After the loop, Index =  ', Index);
```

will, on certain machines, produce the output

```
Before the loop, Index =  -288230376118026063

The value of Index is   5
The value of Index is   6
The value of Index is   7
The value of Index is   8
The value of Index is   9
The value of Index is  10

After the loop, Index =  -576460752303423487
```

Example 6.3

Let's construct a **FOR . . . TO . . . DO** loop that shows what happens when the initial value is greater than the final value.

```
writeln ('This is before the loop.');
writeln;
FOR Index := 10 TO 1 DO
  writeln (Index);
writeln ('This is after the loop.');
```

This segment of code produces the output

```
This is before the loop.

This is after the loop.
```

Because the initial value of the index exceeded the ending value originally, control of the program was transferred to the first executable statement following the loop.

Example 6.4

Let's use **FOR . . . TO . . . DO** loops to produce the following design:

```
******************************
*                            *
*                            *
*                            *
*                            *
*                            *
******************************
```

This problem requires a bit of development. A first-level pseudocode development could be

1. Produce the top line
2. Produce the center lines
3. Produce the bottom line

and second-level development

2. Produce the center lines
   2.1 **FOR** Line := 2 **TO** 6 **DO**
   produce a middle line

We could now code the algorithm as follows:

```
PROGRAM DesignBox (output);

CONST
  Splats = '******************************';
  Edge =   '*                            *';
  Skip = ' ';

VAR
  Line : integer;

BEGIN
  writeln (Skip:10, Splats);
  FOR Line := 2 TO 6 DO
    writeln (Skip:10, Edge);
  writeln (Skip:10, Splats)
END.
```

The index of a loop can also be used for formatting. This is particularly useful when the output is in the form of a design. The next example illustrates this.

Example 6.5

The index of a **FOR . . . TO . . . DO** loop can be of type **char.** To illustrate this, consider the loop

```
FOR Ch := 'a' TO 'e' DO
  write (Ch:2);
writeln;
```

The output from this segment of code is

```
 a b c d e
```

Example 6.6

Let's use a **FOR . . . TO . . . DO** loop to print the letters of the alphabet on a diagonal. Since **char** is an ordinal data type, this can be accomplished by

```
Indent := 1;
FOR Ch := 'A' to 'Z' DO
  BEGIN
    writeln (Ch:Indent);
    Indent := Indent + 1
  END;
```

which produces

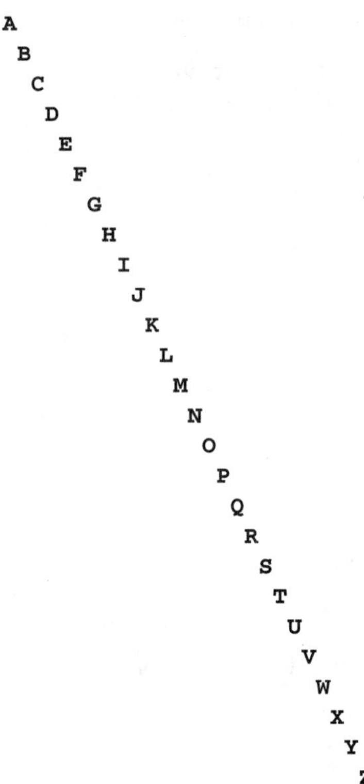

Example 6.7

When computing compound interest, it is necessary to evaluate the quantity $(1 + R)^N$ where R is the interest rate for one time period and N is the number of time periods. A **FOR . . . TO . . . DO** loop can be used to perform this computation. If we declare a variable Base, this can be solved by

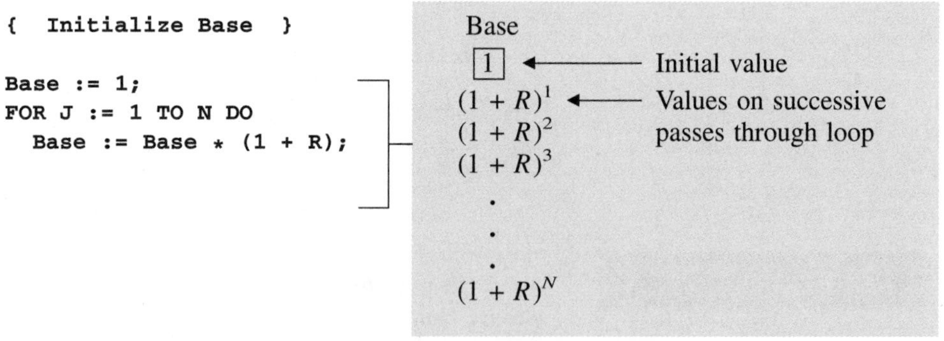

```
{  Initialize Base  }

Base := 1;
FOR J := 1 TO N DO
  Base := Base * (1 + R);
```


FOR . . . DOWNTO . . . DO Loops

A second pretest, fixed repetition loop is the **FOR . . . DOWNTO . . . DO** loop. This loop does exactly what you expect; it is identical to a **FOR . . . TO . . . DO** loop except the index variable is decreased by 1 instead of increased by 1 each time it passes through the loop. This is referred to as a **decrement.** The test is index value >= final value. The loop terminates when the index value is less than the final value. Proper form and syntax for a loop of this type are

A **decrement** is a decrease by 1 in a variable used as a loop index.

> **FOR** <index> := <initial value> **DOWNTO** <final value> **DO**
> <statement>
>
> or
>
> **FOR** <index> := <initial value> **DOWNTO** <final value> **DO**
> **BEGIN**
> <statement 1>;
> <statement 2>;
> .
> .
> .
> <statement *n*>
> **END**

The conditions for **FOR . . . DOWNTO . . . DO** loops are the same as those for **FOR . . . TO . . . DO** loops. We will now consider some examples of **FOR . . . DOWNTO . . . DO** loops.

Example 6.8

Let's illustrate the index values of a **FOR . . . DOWNTO . . . DO** loop by writing the index value during each pass through the loop. The segment of code for this could be

```
FOR Index := 20 DOWNTO 15 DO
  writeln ('Index =', Index:4);
```

and the output is

```
Index =  20
Index =  19
Index =  18
Index =  17
Index =  16
Index =  15
```

The index of a loop can also be used for formatting, as illustrated in the next two examples.

Example 6.9

Let's use a **FOR . . . DOWNTO . . . DO** loop to produce the design

```
    ***
   ***
  ***
 ***
***
```

If we assume the first line of output ends in column 20, the code for this is

```
FOR Index := 20 DOWNTO 16 DO
  writeln ('***': Index);
```

Example 6.10

Let's determine the output from the following fragment of code:

```
Sum := 0;
FOR Index := 3 DOWNTO -2 DO
  BEGIN
    Sum := Sum + Index;
    writeln ('*':10 + abs(Index))
  END;  {  of FOR loop  }
writeln (Sum:15);
```

Before printing the output, let's trace through the variable values:

Index	Sum	10 + abs(Index)
Unassigned	0	Undefined
3	3	13
2	5	12
1	6	11
0	6	10
−1	5	11
−2	3	12

The output is

```
            * ←—— column 13
           *
          *
         *
          *
           *
              3
```

From this point on, both **FOR . . . TO . . . DO** and **FOR . . . DOWNTO . . . DO** loops will be referred to as **FOR** loops. The form intended should be clear from the context.

Writing Style

As you can see, writing style is an important consideration when writing code using loops. There are three features to consider. First, the body of the loop should be indented. Compare the following:

```
FOR Index := 1 TO 10 DO
  BEGIN
    readln (Num, Amt);
    Total1 := Total1 + Amt;
    Total2 := Total2 + Num;
    writeln ('The number is', Num:6)
  END;  {  of FOR loop  }
writeln ('The total amount is', Total1:8:2);
Average := Total2 / 10;
```

and

```
FOR Index := 1 TO 10 DO
BEGIN
readln (Num, Amt);
Total1 := Total1 + Amt;
Total2 := Total2 + Num;
writeln ('The number is', Num:6)
END;  {  of FOR loop  }
writeln ('The total amount is', Total1:8:2);
Average := Total2 / 10;
```

The indenting in the first segment makes it easier to determine what is contained in the body of the loop. In the second segment, without any indenting, the beginning and the end of the body of the loop are not as easy to see.

It is not sufficient merely to indent code that is included in a loop. If a compound statement is the body of a loop, **BEGIN** and **END** must be included as part of the statement. Thus

```
FOR Index := 1 TO 5 DO
  readln (Number);
  Sum := Sum + Number;
```

does not accomplish the desired task. The code should be

```
FOR Index := 1 TO 5 DO
  BEGIN
    readln (Number);
    Sum := Sum + Number
  END;  {  of FOR loop  }
```

Second, blank lines can be used before and after a loop for better readability. Compare the following:

```
readln (X, Y);
writeln (X:6:2, Y:6:2);
writeln;

FOR Index := -3 TO 5 DO
  writeln (Index:3, '*':5);

Sum := Sum + X;
writeln (Sum:10:2);
```

and

```
readln (X, Y);
writeln (X:6:2, Y:6:2);
writeln;
FOR Index := -3 TO 5 DO
  writeln (Index:3, '*':5);
Sum := Sum + X;
writeln (Sum:10:2);
```

Again, the first segment is clearer because it emphasizes that the entire loop is a single executable statement and makes it easy to locate the loop.

Third, appropriate comments make loops more readable. Comments that state the purpose of a loop and the condition for entering the loop should be given prior to entering the loop. A comment should always accompany the **END** of a compound statement that is the body of a loop. The general form for this is

```
{  Get a test score.  There are 50 scores.  }
FOR Index := 1 TO 50 DO
  BEGIN
    .
    . (body of the loop)
    .
  END;  {  of FOR loop  }
```

Example 6.11 uses a **FOR** loop to solve a problem.

Communication and Style Tips

There are three features you may wish to incorporate as you work with **FOR** loops. First, loop limits can be defined as constants or declared as variables and then have assigned values. Thus, you could have

```
CONST
  LoopLimit = 50;
```

Second, the loop control variable could be declared as

```
VAR
  LCV : integer;
```

The loop could then be written as

```
FOR LCV := 1 TO LoopLimit DO
      .
      .   (body of the loop here)
      .
```

Third, a loop limit could be declared as a variable and then have the user enter a value during execution.

```
VAR
  LoopLimit : integer;
    .
    .
    .
  writeln ('How many entries?');
  readln (LoopLimit);
  FOR LCV := 1 TO LoopLimit DO
    .
    .
    .
```

Example 6.11

Let's write a segment of code to compute the test average for each of 30 students in a class and the overall class average. Data for each student consist of the student's initials and four test scores. Sample data for one student are

THS
87 94 85 93

A first-level pseudocode development is

1. Print a heading
2. Initialize Total
3. Process data for each of 30 students
4. Compute class average
5. Print a summary

A **FOR** loop could be used to implement Step 3. The step could first be refined to

3. Process data for each of 30 students
   3.1 Get data for a student
   3.2 Compute average
   3.3 Add to Total
   3.4 Print student data

The code for this step is

```
FOR Student := 1 TO ClassSize DO
  BEGIN
    writeln ('Enter three initials and press <Enter>.');
    readln (Init1, Init2, Init3);
    writeln ('Enter four test scores and press <Enter>.');
    readln (Score1, Score2, Score3, Score4);
    Average := (Score1 + Score2 + Score3 + Score4) / 4;
    Total := Total + Average;
    writeln;
    write (Init1:4; Init2, Init3);
    write (Score1:6, Score2:6, Score3:6, Score4:6);
    writeln (Average:10:2)
  END;  {  of FOR loop  }
```

Exercises 6.2

In Exercises 1–4, what output is produced from each segment of code?

*1.
```
FOR LCV := 3 TO 8 DO
  writeln ('*':LCV);
```

2.
```
FOR LCV := 1 TO 10 DO
  writeln (LCV:4, ' :', (10 - LCV):5);
```

*3.
```
A := 2;
FOR LCV := (3 * 2 - 4) TO 10 * A DO
  writeln ('**', LCV:4);
```

4.
```
FOR LCV := 50 DOWNTO 30 DO
  writeln (51 - LCV:5);
```

A Note of Interest

Charles Babbage

The first person to propose the concept of the modern computer was Charles Babbage (1791–1871), a man truly ahead of his time. Babbage was a professor of mathematics at Cambridge University, as well as an inventor. As a mathematician, he realized the time-consuming and boring nature of constructing mathematical tables (squares, logarithms, sines, cosines, and so on). Since the calculators developed by Pascal and [Gottfried Wilhelm] Leibniz (1646–1716) could not provide the calculations required for these more complex tables, Babbage proposed the idea of building a machine that could compute the various properties of numbers, accurate to 20 digits.

With a grant from the British government, he designed and partially built a simple model of the difference engine. However, the lack of technology in the 1800s prevented him from making a working model. Discouraged by his inability to materialize his ideas, Babbage imagined a better version, the analytical engine, which would be a general-purpose, problem-solving machine.

The similarities between the analytical engine and the modern computer are amazing. Babbage's analytical engine, which was intended to be a steam-powered device, had four components:

1. A "mill" that manipulated and computed the data
2. A "store" that held the data
3. An "operator" of the system that carried out instructions
4. A separate device that entered data and received processed information via punched cards

After spending many years sketching variations and improvements for this new model, Babbage received some assistance in 1842 from Ada Augusta Byron (see the next **Note of Interest**).

For Exercises 5 and 6, write test programs.

*5. Illustrate what happens when the loop control variable is assigned a value inside the loop.

6. Demonstrate how an accumulator works. For this test program, sum the integers from 1 to 10. Your output should show each partial sum as it is assigned to the accumulator.

In Exercises 7–10, write segments of code using **FOR . . . TO . . . DO** or **FOR . . . DOWNTO . . . DO** loops to produce the designs indicated.

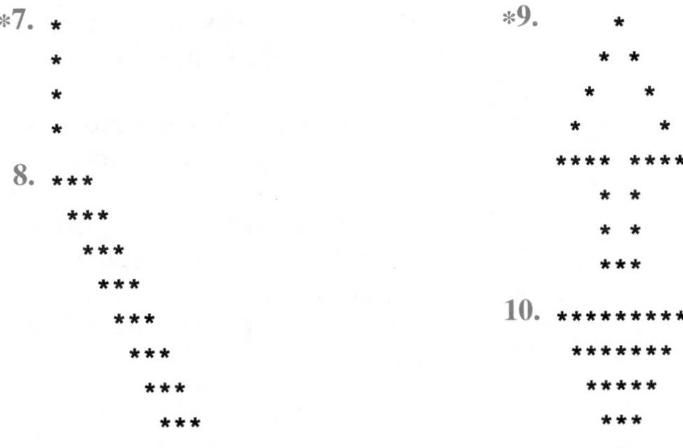

*7.
```
*
*
*
*
```

8.
```
***
 ***
  ***
   ***
    ***
     ***
      ***
       ***
```

*9.
```
    *
   * *
  *   *
 *     *
**** ****
   * *
   * *
   ***
```

10.
```
*********
 *******
  *****
   ***
    *
```

In Exercises 11–14, which segments of code do you think accomplish their intended tasks? For those that do not, what changes would you suggest?

*11.
```
FOR K := 1 TO 5 DO;
  writeln (K);
```

12.
```
Sum := 0;
FOR J := 1 TO 10 DO
  readln (A);
  Sum := Sum + A;
writeln (Sum:15);
```

*13.
```
Sum := 0;
FOR Index = -3 TO 3 DO
  Sum := Sum + Index;
```

14.
```
A := 0;
FOR Index := 1 TO 10 DO
  BEGIN
    A := A + Index;
    writeln (Index:5, A:5, A + Index:5)
  END;
writeln (Index:5, A:5, A + Index:5);
```

In Exercises 15 and 16, produce the output using both a **FOR . . . TO . . . DO** loop and a **FOR . . . DOWNTO . . . DO** loop.

*15.
```
1  2  3  4  5
```

16.
```
*
 *
  *
   *
    *
```

*17. Rewrite the following segment of code using a **FOR . . . DOWNTO . . . DO** loop to produce the same result.

```
Sum := 0;
FOR Index := 1 TO 4 DO
  BEGIN
    writeln ('*':21 + Index);
    Sum := Sum + Index
  END;
```

18. Rewrite the following segment of code using a **FOR . . . TO . . . DO** loop to produce the same result.

```
FOR Index := 10 DOWNTO 2 DO
  writeln (Index:Index);
```

*19. Write a complete program that produces a table showing the temperature equivalents in degrees Fahrenheit and degrees Celsius. If you write this as an interactive program, let the user enter the starting and ending values. Otherwise, list values between 0° C and 100° C. (In either case, use the formula

CelsTemp = 5/9 * (FarenTemp − 32)

20. Write a complete program that produces a chart consisting of the multiples of 5 from −50 to 50 together with the squares and cubes of these numbers.
21. The formula $A = P(1 + R)^N$ can be used to compute the total amount due A when a principal P has been borrowed at a monthly rate R for a period of N months. Write a complete program that will read in the principal, annual interest rate (divide by 12 for monthly rate), and number of months, and then produce a chart that shows how much will be due at the end of each month.

6.3 WHILE . . . DO Loops

Objectives

- to understand when variable repetition should be used in a program
- to understand why **WHILE . . . DO** is a variable repetition loop
- to understand the flow of control when using a **WHILE . . . DO** loop
- to be able to use a counter in a **WHILE . . . DO** loop
- to be able to use a **WHILE . . . DO** loop in a program

FOR loops (loops in which the body of the loop is repeated a fixed number of times) were presented in Section 6.2. However, the **FOR** loop is inappropriate for some problems, since a segment of code may need to be repeated an unknown number of times. The condition controlling the loop must be an expression rather than a constant. Recall that Pascal provides two repetition statements with variable control conditions: one with a pretest condition, and one with a posttest condition.

The pretest loop with variable conditions in Pascal is the **WHILE . . . DO** loop. The condition controlling the loop is a Boolean expression written between the reserved words **WHILE** and **DO.** The correct form and syntax of such a loop are

```
WHILE <Boolean expression> DO
  <statement>;
or
WHILE <Boolean expression> DO
  BEGIN
    <statement 1>;
    <statement 2>;
        .
        .
        .
    <statement n>
  END
```

The flow diagram for a **WHILE . . . DO** loop is given in Figure 6.2.

◆ Figure 6.2

WHILE . . . DO flow diagram

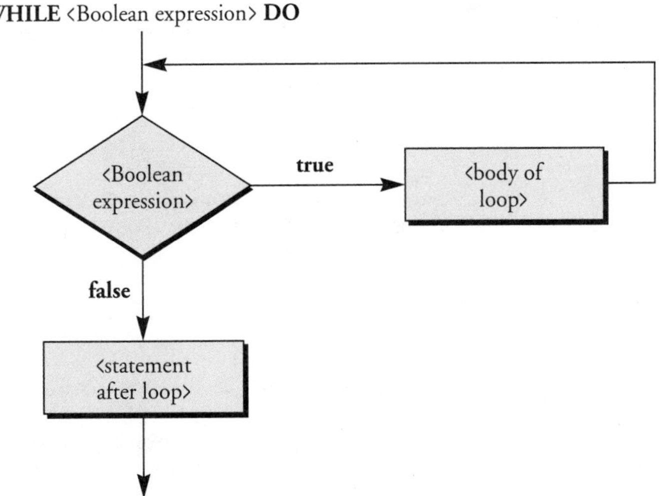

Program control when using a **WHILE . . . DO** loop is in the following order:

1. The loop condition is examined.
2. If the loop condition is **true,** the entire body of the loop is executed before another check is made.
3. If the loop condition is **false,** control is transferred to the first line following the loop. For example,

```
A := 1;
WHILE A < 0 DO
  BEGIN
    Num := 5;
    writeln (Num);
    A := A + 10
  END;
writeln (A);
```

produces the single line of output

```
1
```

Before analyzing the components of the **WHILE . . . DO** statement, let's consider two short examples.

Example 6.12

This example allows us to print values from an input file as long as the values are positive (assuming there is a nonpositive value in the file).

```
readln (A);
WHILE A > 0 DO
  BEGIN
    writeln (A);
    readln (A)
  END;  {  of WHILE loop  }
```

Example 6.13

This example prints some powers of 2.

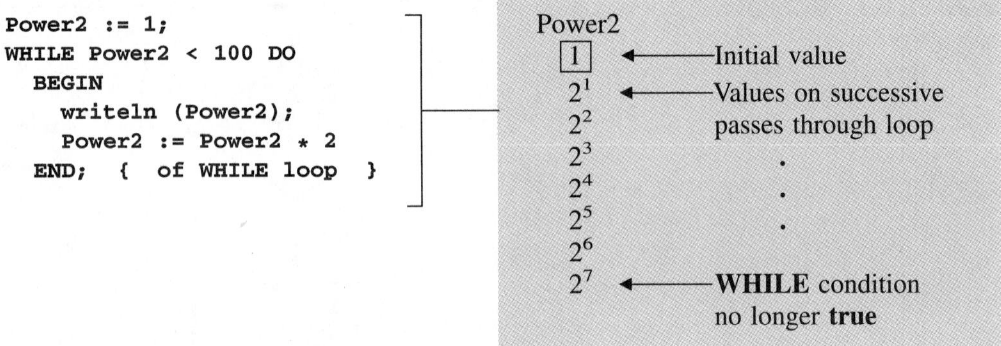

Power2 := 1;
WHILE Power2 < 100 DO
BEGIN
writeln (Power2);
Power2 := Power2 * 2
END; { of WHILE loop }
Power2
1
Initial value
Values on successive passes through loop
WHILE condition no longer true

The output from this segment of code is

```
1
2
4
8
16
32
64
```

Keeping these examples in mind, let's examine the general form for using a **WHILE . . . DO** loop.

1. The Boolean expression can be any expression that has Boolean values. Standard examples include relational operators and Boolean variables; thus, each of the following would be appropriate:

```
WHILE J < 10 DO
WHILE A <> B DO
WHILE Done = false DO
WHILE Continue DO
WHILE NOT eoln DO
WHILE NOT eof DO
```

2. The Boolean expression must have a value prior to entering the loop.
3. The body of the loop can be a single statement or a compound statement.
4. Provision must be made for appropriately changing the loop control condition in the body of the loop. If no such changes are made, the following could happen:
   a. If the loop condition is **true** and no changes are made, a condition called an **infinite loop** is caused. For example,

An **infinite loop** is a loop in which the controlling condition is not changed in such a manner as to allow the loop to terminate.

```
A := 1;
WHILE A > 0 DO
  BEGIN
    Num := 5;
    writeln (Num)
  END;
writeln (A);
```

The condition A > 0 is **true,** the body is executed, and the condition is retested. However, since the condition is not changed within the loop body, A > 0 will always be **true.** This causes the loop to be repeated with no provision for termination, resulting in an infinite loop. It will not produce a compilation error, but when you run the program, the output will be a list of 5's.

b. If the loop condition is **true** and changes are made, but the condition never becomes **false,** you again have an infinite loop. An example of this is

```
PowerOf3 := 1;
WHILE PowerOf3 <> 100 DO
  BEGIN
    writeln (PowerOf3);
    PowerOf3 := PowerOf3 * 3
  END;
```

Since the variable Power3 is never assigned the value 100, the condition Power3 <> 100 is always **true** and you never get out of the loop.

The best way to avoid an infinite loop is to be sure the loop control variable eventually reaches the terminating condition. This causes loop execution to cease. An alternative but less efficient method is to put a counter inside the loop and add a Boolean condition to the loop control statement. Thus, if the loop is to terminate after at most 100 repetitions, the general form could be

```
Counter := 0;
WHILE <condition> AND (Counter < 100) DO
  BEGIN
    .
    .
    .
    Counter := Counter + 1  {  Guard against infinite loop  }
  END;  {  of WHILE loop  }
```

Sentinel Values

A **sentinel value** is a special value that indicates the end of a set of data or of a process.

The Boolean expression of a variable control loop is frequently controlled by a **sentinel value.** For example, an interactive program may require the user to enter numeric data. When there are no more data, the user will be instructed to enter a special (sentinel) value, which signifies the end of the process. The following example illustrates the use of such a sentinel.

Example 6.14

Let's write a segment of code that allows the user to enter a set of test scores interactively and then prints the average score.

```
NumScores := 0;
Sum := 0;
writeln ('Enter a score and press <Enter>, -999 to quit.');
readln (Score);
WHILE Score <> -999 DO
```

```
  BEGIN
    NumScores := NumScores + 1;
    Sum := Sum + Score;
    writeln ('Enter a score and press <Enter>, -999 to quit.');
    readln (Score)
  END;
IF NumScores > 0 THEN
  BEGIN
    Average := Sum / NumScores;
    writeln;
    writeln ('The average of', NumScores:4, ' scores is',
             Average:6:2)
  END  {  of IF...THEN option  }
ELSE
  writeln ('Division by zero!');
```

Note that in Example 6.14, one value is read outside the loop so that the Boolean expression

```
Score <> -999
```

is valid the first time it is read. This is a specific example of the general form

```
readln (<value>);
WHILE <value condition> DO
  BEGIN
    .
    .  (process value)
    .
    readln (<value>)
  END;
```

A **priming read** is a **read** performed before a loop is referenced.

The **read** performed before the loop is referred to as a **priming read.**

Writing Style

Writing style for **WHILE . . . DO** loops should be similar to that adopted for **FOR** loops. Indenting, skipping lines, and comments should all be used to enhance readability.

Using Counters

Since **WHILE . . . DO** loops may be repeated a variable number of times, it is a common practice to count the number of times the loop body is executed. This is accomplished by declaring an appropriately named integer variable, initializing it to zero before the loop, and then incrementing it by one each time through the loop. For example, if you use Count for your variable name, Example 6.13 (in which we printed some powers of two) could be modified to

```
Count := 0;
PowerOf2 := 1;

{  Display powers less than 100  }
WHILE PowerOf2 < 100 DO
```

```
  BEGIN
    writeln (PowerOf2);
    PowerOf2 := PowerOf2 * 2;
    Count := Count + 1
  END;  {  of WHILE...DO  }

writeln ('There are', Count:4, ' powers of 2 less than 100.');
```

The output from this segment of code is

```
1
2
4
8
16
32
64
There are   7 powers of 2 less than 100.
```

A **counter** is a variable used to count the number of times some process is completed.

Although the process is tedious, it is instructive to trace the values of variables through a loop where a **counter** is used. Therefore, let's consider the segment of code we have just seen. Before the loop is entered, we have

0	1
Count	Power2

The loop control is Power2 $<$ 100 (1 $<$ 100). Since this is **true,** the loop body is executed and the new values become

1	2
Count	Power2

Prior to each successive time through the loop, the condition Power2 $<$ 100 is checked. Thus, the loop produces the sequence of values

Count	Power2
1	2
2	4
3	8
4	16
5	32
6	64
7	128

Although Power2 is 128, the remainder of the loop is executed before checking the loop condition. Once a loop is entered, it is executed completely before the loop control condition is reexamined. Since 128 $<$ 100 is **false,** control is transferred to the statement following the loop.

WHILE NOT eoln

A standard problem encountered when getting data from an input file is reading the data until an end-of-line marker is encountered. Since **eoln** is a Boolean function that returns the value **true** only when the data pointer is positioned at the end-of-line marker (or end-of-file marker on some systems), a **WHILE . . . DO** loop can be used with **eoln** to solve this problem. To illustrate this use of **eoln** with **WHILE** loops, consider the problem of reading and printing a line of data, character by character.

A first-level pseudocode development for solving this problem is

1. Set left margin
2. Get a line of data

A second-level development is

1. Start in column 10
2. Get a line of data
   WHILE NOT eoln DO
   2.1 Get a character
   2.2 Print a character

This is sufficient development from which to write code. (Some implementations require a file name as an argument when using **eoln** and **eof.** In such instances, you would have to write **eoln (input)** or some equivalent statement.)

A segment of code to solve this problem is

```
write (' ':9);

{  Now get a data line  }
WHILE NOT eoln DO
  BEGIN
    read (Ch);
    write (Ch)
  END;  {  of WHILE loop  }
```

If this segment is executed for the following data file and the pointer is as indicated

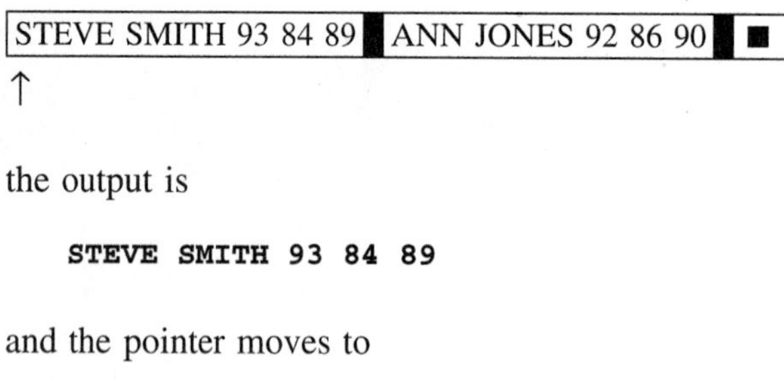

the output is

```
STEVE SMITH 93 84 89
```

and the pointer moves to

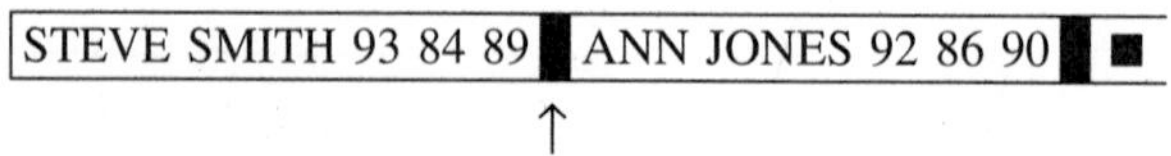

Now **eoln** is **true;** thus, **NOT eoln** is **false** and the loop is finished. As our next example, let's use a version of the same problem but count the number of characters (including blanks) in the line.

Example 6.15

Let's write a segment of code that allows us to examine a data line. Output should include the data line and the number of positions in the line. A first-level pseudocode development is

1. Initialize counter
2. Set left margin
3. Get a line of data
4. Print the message

A second-level development is

1. Initialize counter
2. Set left margin
3. Get a line of data
   WHILE NOT eoln DO
   3.1 Get a character
   3.2 Print the character
   3.3 Increment counter
4. Print the message

We can now write the code as

```
Count := 0;  {  Initialize counter  }
write (' ':9);  {  Set margin  }

{  Now get a data line  }
WHILE NOT eoln DO
  BEGIN
    read (Ch);
    write (Ch);
    Count := Count + 1
  END;  {  of WHILE loop  }

{  Now print a message  }
writeln;
writeln('There are', Count:4, ' positions in the line.');
```

Example 6.16

Let's write a program to find the average of some numbers that are on one line of data. A first-level pseudocode is

1. Initialize variables
2. Get numbers from the data line
3. Compute average
4. Print the results

A refinement of this is

1. Initialize variables
   1.1 Count
   1.2 Sum
2. Get numbers from the data line
   WHILE NOT eoln DO

   2.1 Get a number
   2.2 Add to Sum
   2.3 Increment counter
3. Compute average
4. Print the results
   4.1 Print how many numbers
   4.2 Print the average

We can now write the following code:

```
{  Initialize  }
Count := 0;
Sum := 0;

{  Get one line of data  }
WHILE NOT eoln DO
  BEGIN
    read (Num);
    Sum := Sum + Num;    {  Accumulator  }
    Count := Count + 1   {  Counter  }
  END;  {  of WHILE loop  }

{  Now compute average  }
Average := Sum / Count;

{  Now print results  }
writeln;
writeln ('There were':19, Count:4, ' numbers in the line.');
writeln;
writeln ('Their average is':25, Average:8:2);
```

Note that this example does not work for implementations that add blanks to the end of data lines because the data pointer may not be at the end-of-line marker after the last number is read.

WHILE NOT eof

Another problem encountered when getting information from an input file is how to recognize when the end-of-file marker has been encountered. Since **eof** is a Boolean function, it can be used with a **WHILE . . . DO** loop in a manner similar to the use of **eoln.** For example, suppose a data file has one real number per line and you want to examine the file. The segment of code is then

```
WHILE NOT eof DO
  BEGIN
    readln (X);
    writeln (X:10:2)
  END;  {  of WHILE loop  }
```

Some implementations require a file variable for **eof.** In such a case, the form would be

```
WHILE NOT eof(<file variable>) DO
```

If the data file is

A Note of Interest

Ada Augusta Byron

Ada Augusta Byron, Countess of Lovelace (1815–1852), became interested in Charles Babbage's efforts when she was translating a paper on the analytical engine from French to English. Upon meeting Babbage, she began the task of writing an original paper. Through the process, she documented Babbage's ideas and made it possible to understand Babbage's original intentions. Over time, she became a full collaborator on the project, correcting some errors and suggesting the use of the binary system of storage rather than the decimal.

Lady Lovelace's most important contribution was her concept of a loop. She observed that a repetition of a sequence of instructions often was necessary to perform a single calculation. Thus, she discovered that by using a single set of cards and a conditional jump facility, the calculation could be performed with a fraction of the effort. This idea has earned her the distinction of being the first programmer.

In honor of her role as the first computer programmer, the United States Department of Defense named a programming language Ada.

14.73	▮	121.45	▮	0.02	▮	−141.1	▮	■

↑

the output from this segment is

```
  14.73
 121.45
   0.02
-141.10
```

Many programming problems require the same manipulations and output for each line of data. In these situations, a programmer develops code for operating on one line of data and then uses that code until the end-of-file marker is encountered. Problems of this type require careful attention, especially with respect to two items.

1. The data lines must be correctly formatted.
2. A **readln** statement should be used to advance the pointer. There are ways to avoid using **readln** for this purpose, but this is the easiest way to advance the pointer to the beginning of the next data line. If the pointer is not advanced, the **eof** condition will not be recognized appropriately.

The next example illustrates the use of the **WHILE . . . DO** loop with the **eof** condition.

Example 6.17

Let's write a segment of code to compute the wages for several employees. Assume each line of data consists of the following information about one employee: three initials, the hourly rate (real), and the number of hours worked (integer). There are blanks before each number; thus, the data file could be

MTM 14.60 40	▮	BRL 13.95 42	▮	HMN 10.50 20	▮	MJB 21.0 35	▮	■

↑

To get the data from one line of the file, the code could be

```
read (Init1, Init2, Init3);
read (HourRate);
readln (Hours);
```

or

```
readln (Init1, Init2, Init3, HourRate, Hours);
```

or other equivalent forms. Gross wages would be computed by

```
GrossWage := HourRate * Hours;
```

If output is to be in the form of a chart, a line of output could be generated by

```
writeln (Init1:5, Init2, Init3, HourRate:15:2,
         Hours:15, GrossWage:15:2);
```

The segment of code that produces the information desired for each employee is

```
WHILE NOT eof DO
  BEGIN
    readln (Init1, Init2, Init3, HourRate, Hours);
    GrossWage := HourRate * Hours;
    writeln (Init1:5, Init2, Init3, HourRate:16:2,
             Hours:15, GrossWage:14:2)
  END;  {  of WHILE loop  }
```

Now let's consider the design and implementation of a complete program to solve the problem of computing wages for employees. We will assume the input file has the same format and the output consists of a reasonably formatted chart. A first-level pseudocode development for the problem is

1. Print a chart heading
2. Process each data line

A second-level development is

1. Print a chart heading
2. Process each data line
   WHILE NOT eof DO
   2.1 Get a line of data
   2.2 Compute the wage
   2.3 Print the information

We are now ready to write code for this problem. The complete program follows:

```
PROGRAM ComputeWages (input, output);

{  This program computes wages for several employees of a company.   }
{  The significant new feature is the use of a WHILE...DO loop with  }
{  eof as a Boolean loop control.                                    }
```

```
CONST
  Marks = '//////////////////////////////';
  Edge =  '/                            /';
  Skip = ' ';

VAR
  GrossWage,                        { Wages before deductions }
  HourRate : real;                  { Hourly rate of pay      }
  Hours : integer;                  { Number of hours worked  }
  Init1, Init2, Init3 : char;       { Initials for employee   }

BEGIN { Program }

  { Print a heading }
  writeln;
  writeln (Skip:7, Marks);
  writeln (Skip:7, Edge);
  writeln (Skip:7, '/ Hi-Speed Bicycle Company /');
  writeln (Skip:7, Edge);
  writeln (Skip:7, '/      Payroll Report      /');
  writeln (Skip:7, Edge);
  writeln (Skip:7, Marks);
  writeln;
  writeln ('Employee', 'Pay Rate':14, 'Hours Worked':20, 'Gross':8);
  writeln ('----------------------------------------------------');
  writeln;

  { Now start the loop to process a line of data }
  WHILE NOT eof DO
    BEGIN
      readln (Init1, Init2, Init3, HourRate, Hours);
      GrossWage := HourRate * Hours;
      write (Skip:2, Init1, Init2, Init3);
      writeln (HourRate:16:2, Hours:15, GrossWage:14:2)
    END; { of WHILE loop }

  writeln
END. { of program }
```

If the data file is as indicated in Example 6.17, the output is

```
       //////////////////////////////
       /                            /
       / Hi-Speed Bicycle Company /
       /                            /
       /      Payroll Report      /
       /                            /
       //////////////////////////////

Employee     Pay Rate        Hours Worked   Gross
----------------------------------------------------

  MTM          14.60              40       584.00
  BRL          13.95              42       585.90
  HMN          10.50              20       210.00
  MJB          21.00              35       735.00
```

Compound Conditions

All previous examples and illustrations of **WHILE . . . DO** loops have used simple Boolean expressions. However, since any Boolean expression can be used as a loop control condition, compound Boolean expressions can also be used. For example,

```
readln (A, B);
WHILE (A > 0) AND (B > 0) DO
  BEGIN
    writeln (A, B);
    A := A - 5;
    B := B - 3
  END;
```

will go through the body of the loop only when the Boolean expression (A > 0) **AND** (B > 0) is **true.** Thus, if the values of A and B are obtained from the data file

17 8 ▮

the output from this segment of code is

```
17        8
12        5
 7        2
```

Compound Boolean expressions can be as complex as you wish to make them. However, if several conditions are involved, the program can become difficult to read and debug. Therefore, you may wish to redesign your solution to avoid this problem.

Exercises 6.3

1. Compare and contrast **FOR** loops with **WHILE . . . DO** loops.
2. Write a test program that illustrates what happens when you have an infinite loop.

In Exercises 3–7, what output is produced from the segment of code?

*3.
```
K := 1;
WHILE K <= 10 DO
  BEGIN
    writeln (K);
    K := K + 1
  END;
```

4.
```
A := 1;
WHILE 17 MOD A <> 5 DO
  BEGIN
    writeln (A, 17 MOD A);
    A := A + 1
  END;
```

*5.
```
A := 2;
B := 50;
WHILE A < B DO
  A := A * 3;
writeln (A, B);
```

6.
```
Count := 0;
Sum := 0;
WHILE Count < 5 DO
  BEGIN
    Count := Count + 1;
    Sum := Sum + Count;
    writeln ('The partial sum is', Sum:4)
  END;
writeln ('The count is', Count:4);
```

*7.
```
X := 3.0;
Y := 2.0;
WHILE X * Y < 100 DO
  X := X * Y;
writeln (X:10:2, Y:10:2);
```

In Exercises 8–11, indicate which are infinite loops and explain why they are infinite.

8.
```
J := 1;
WHILE J < 10 DO
  writeln (J);
  J := J + 1;
```

*9.
```
A := 2;
WHILE A < 20 DO
  BEGIN
    writeln (A);
    A := A * 2
  END;
```

10.
```
A := 2;
WHILE A <> 20 DO
  BEGIN
    writeln (A);
    A := A * 2
  END;
```

*11.
```
B := 15;
WHILE B DIV 3 = 5 DO
  BEGIN
    writeln (B, B DIV 5);
    B := B - 1
  END;
```

For Exercises 12–16, assume the variable declaration section of a program is

```
VAR
  Ch1, Ch2 : char;
  Age : integer;
  Num : real;
```

the data file is

A 18 – 14.3B ■ C 21 10.0D ■ E 19 – 11.5F ■ ■

↑

and the pointer is positioned at the beginning of the file for each segment. What output is produced by each segment of code?

12.
```
WHILE NOT eoln DO
  BEGIN
    read (Ch1);
    write (Ch1)
  END;  {  of WHILE loop  }
writeln;
```

*13.
```
WHILE NOT eof DO
  BEGIN
    read (Ch1);
    write (Ch1)
  END;  {  of WHILE loop  }
writeln;
```

14.
```
WHILE NOT eoln AND NOT eof DO
  BEGIN
    read (Ch1);
    write (Ch1)
  END;  {  of WHILE loop  }
writeln;
```

*15.
```
WHILE NOT eoln OR NOT eof DO
  BEGIN
    read (Ch1);
    write (Ch1)
  END;  {  of WHILE loop  }
writeln;
```

16.
```
WHILE NOT eof DO
  BEGIN
    readln (Ch1, Age, Num, Ch2);
    writeln (Ch1:3, Age:3, Num:6:2, Ch2:3)
  END;  {  of WHILE loop  }
```

*17. If the data file and variables are as stated for Exercises 12–16, is there anything wrong with the following **WHILE . . . DO** loop?

```
WHILE NOT eoln DO
  BEGIN
    readln (Ch1, Age, Num, Ch2);
    writeln (Ch1:3, Age:3, Num:6:2, Ch2:3)
  END;  {  of WHILE loop  }
```

18. Assume Ch is a character variable and a data file is

XYZ 13	▮	ABC 21	▮	MNO 25	▮	■

↑

What output is produced by the following **WHILE . . . DO** loop?

```
WHILE NOT eof DO
  BEGIN
    read (Ch);
    write ('Ch is':10, Ch:3);
    write ('eoln is':10, eoln:7);
    writeln ('eof is':10, eof:7)
  END;  {  of WHILE loop  }
```

19. Write a segment of code that allows you to find the number of lines in a data file.

In Exercises 20–27, write a segment of code that uses a **WHILE . . . DO** loop.

20. Read three values and print their sum as long as they are all positive.
*21. Read three values and print their sum as long as one of them is positive.
22. Print a table of cubes of integers from 1 to *N*, where the value of *N* is entered from the keyboard.
*23. Print a table of squares of integers starting with 1 and continuing until the difference of consecutive squares exceeds 25.
24. Write a complete program that will find the smallest positive integer *N* such that the sum 1 + 2 + . . . + *N* exceeds some value entered from the keyboard.
*25. Write a segment of code that reads a positive integer and prints a list of powers of that integer that are less than 10,000.
26. Print a positive real number (Num); then print successive values, where each value is 0.5 less than the previous value. The list should continue as long as values to be printed are positive.
27. Modify the program in Section 6.3 to compute employee wages (**PROGRAM** ComputeWages) by incorporating the following:
    a. A counter to count the number of employees
    b. A computation for the total hours worked by all employees
    c. A computation for the total wages paid to all employees
    d. A computation for the average wage of all employees
    e. A printed summary of the extra information

6.4 REPEAT . . . UNTIL Loops

Objectives

- to understand that a **REPEAT . . . UNTIL** loop is a posttest loop
- to understand the flow of control using a **REPEAT . . . UNTIL** loop
- to be able to use a **REPEAT . . . UNTIL** loop in a program
- to be able to use **REPEAT . . . UNTIL** loops with multiple conditions

In the previous two sections, we discussed two kinds of repetition. We looked at fixed repetition using **FOR** loops and variable repetition using **WHILE . . . DO** loops. Pascal provides a second form of variable repetition, a **REPEAT . . . UNTIL** loop, which is a posttest (exit-controlled) loop.

The basic form and syntax of a **REPEAT . . . UNTIL** loop is

```
REPEAT
   <statement 1>;
   <statement 2>;
        .
        .
        .
   <statement n>
UNTIL <Boolean expression>
```

A flow diagram for a **REPEAT . . . UNTIL** loop is given in Figure 6.3.

Prior to examining this form, let's consider the following fragment of code:

```
Count := 0;
REPEAT
  Count := Count + 1;
  writeln (Count)
UNTIL Count = 5;
writeln ('All done':10);
```

◆ Figure 6.3

REPEAT . . . UNTIL flow diagram

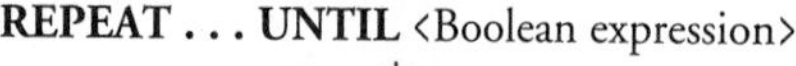

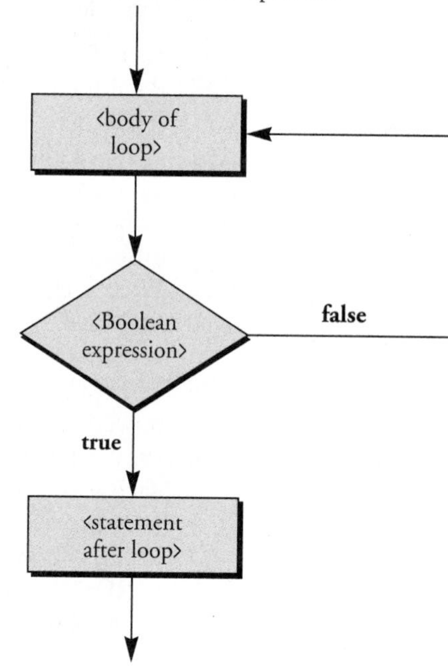

The output for this fragment is

```
        1
        2
        3
        4
        5
All done
```

Keeping this example in mind, the following comments concerning the use of a **REPEAT . . . UNTIL** loop are in order:

1. All simple statements in the body of a **REPEAT . . . UNTIL** statement are executed in the order in which they appear. Thus, a compound statement is not needed when multiple actions are desired within the loop.
2. A semicolon is not required between the last statement in the body of the loop and the reserved word **UNTIL.**
3. The Boolean expression must have a value before it is used at the end of the loop.
4. The loop must be entered at least once because the Boolean expression is not evaluated until after the loop body has been executed.
5. When the Boolean expression is evaluated, if it is **false,** control is transferred back to the top of the loop; if it is **true,** control is transferred to the next program statement.
6. Provision must be made for changing values inside the loop so that the Boolean expression used to control the loop will eventually be **true.** If this is not done, an infinite loop will result, as in the following code:

```
J := 0;
REPEAT
  J := J + 2;
  writeln (J)
UNTIL J = 5;
```

7. Your writing style for using **REPEAT . . . UNTIL** loops should be consistent with your style for using other loop structures.

There are two important differences between **WHILE . . . DO** and **REPEAT . . . UNTIL** loops. First, a **REPEAT . . . UNTIL** loop must be executed at least once, but a **WHILE . . . DO** loop can be skipped if the initial value of the Boolean expression is **false.** For this reason, **REPEAT . . . UNTIL** loops are generally used less frequently than **WHILE . . . DO** loops. The second difference is that a **REPEAT . . . UNTIL** loop is repeated until the Boolean expression becomes **true.** In a **WHILE . . . DO** loop, repetition continues until the Boolean expression becomes **false.**

Example 6.18

Let's use a **REPEAT . . . UNTIL** loop to print the powers of two that are less than 100. This can be done by

```
PowerOf2 := 1;
REPEAT
  writeln (PowerOf2);
  PowerOf2 := PowerOf2 * 2
UNTIL PowerOf2 > 100;
```

When run, this segment produces

```
1
2
4
8
16
32
64
```

As was the case with **WHILE . . . DO** loops, sentinel values can be used to determine when a process should terminate. These can be in the form of some predetermined data value (for example, –999) or the result of a response to a question on the screen asking whether or not the person running the program wishes to continue. This is illustrated in Example 6.19.

Example 6.19

Let's write a segment of code to allow a positive integer to be entered from the keyboard and then print a table of squares less than or equal to the indicated value. Code for this is

```
N := 0;
writeln ('Enter a positive integer and press <Enter>.');
readln (UpperLimit);
writeln ('The squares less than or equal to ',
         UpperLimit,' are:');
writeln;
REPEAT
  writeln (N * N);
  N := N + 1
UNTIL N * N > UpperLimit;
```

A sample run for this segment is

```
Enter a positive integer and press <Enter>.
200
The squares less than or equal to 200 are:
0
1
4
9
16
25
36
49
64
81
100
121
144
169
196
```

Another method of controlling the termination of a loop is to use a value defined in the constant definition section. For example, if you were using some approximation technique where a certain degree of accuracy was required, you could define

```
DesiredAccuracy = <value here>;
```

and then terminate a loop with something like

```
.
.
.
UNTIL abs(NewGuess - OldGuess) < DesiredAccuracy;
```

This method is illustrated in the following example.

Example 6.20

An early method of approximating square roots was the Newton-Raphson method. This method consisted of starting with an approximation and then getting successively better approximations until the desired degree of accuracy was achieved. Writing code for this method, each NewGuess is defined to be

```
NewGuess := 1/2 * (OldGuess + Number / OldGuess)
```

Thus, if the number entered was 34 and the first approximation was 5, the second approximation would be

```
1/2 * (5 + 34 / 5)       (5.9)
```

and the third approximation would be

```
1/2 * (5.9 + 34 / 5.9)       (5.83135593)
```

Let's see how a **REPEAT ... UNTIL** loop can be used to obtain successively better approximations until a desired degree of accuracy is reached. Assume we wish to approximate the square root of the value contained in Number. Also, assume OldGuess contains a first approximation, and DesiredAccuracy is a defined constant. A loop used in the solution of this problem is

```
writeln (NewGuess:12:8);

{  Compute and list approximation   }
REPEAT
  OldGuess := NewGuess;
  NewGuess := 1/2 * (OldGuess + Number / OldGuess);
  writeln (NewGuess:12:8)
UNTIL abs(NewGuess - OldGuess) < DesiredAccuracy;
```

If DesiredAccuracy is 0.0001, Number is 34, and NewGuess is originally 5, the output from this segment is

```
5.00000000
5.90000000
5.83135593
5.83095191
5.83095189
```

Compound Conditions

The Boolean expression used with a **REPEAT . . . UNTIL** loop can be as complex as you choose to make it. However, as with **WHILE . . . DO** loops, if the expression gets too complicated, you might enhance program readability and design by redesigning the algorithm to use simpler expressions.

Suppose a data file consists of one real number per line and you want to print the numbers until either a negative number is encountered or the end-of-file condition is **true.** A loop for this is

```
REPEAT  {  Start loop  }
  readln (Num);
  writeln (Num:20:2)
UNTIL (Num < 0) OR eof;
```

The data file

14.3	■	87.2	■	56.9	■	−999	■	46.8	■	97.3	■	■

↑

produces

```
  14.30
  87.20
  56.90
-999.00
```

Data Validation

Variable condition loops can be used to make programs more robust. In particular, suppose you are writing an interactive program that expects positive integers to be entered from the keyboard, with a sentinel value of –999 to be entered when you wish to quit. You can guard against bad data by using the following:

```
REPEAT
  writeln ('Enter a positive integer, <-999> to quit.');
  readln (Num)
UNTIL (Num > 0) OR (Num = -999);
```

Data validation is the process of examining data prior to its use in a program.

This process of examining data prior to its use in a program is referred to as **data validation,** and loops are useful for such validation. A second example of using a loop for this purpose follows.

Example 6.21

One problem associated with interactive programs is guarding against keyboard errors. This example illustrates how a **REPEAT . . . UNTIL** loop can be used to prevent the user from entering something other than the anticipated responses. Specifically, suppose users of an interactive program are asked to indicate whether or not they wish to continue by entering either a Y or N. The screen message could be

```
Do you wish to continue?  <Y or N>
```

We wish to allow Y, y, N, or n to be used as an appropriate response. Any other entry is considered an error. This can be accomplished by the following:

```
{  Read one of Y, y, N, or n  }
REPEAT
  writeln ('Do you wish to continue?  <Y or N>');
  readln (Response);
  GoodResponse := (Response = 'Y') OR (Response = 'y') OR
                  (Response = 'N') OR (Response = 'n')
UNTIL GoodResponse;
{  A valid response has been read  }
```

Any response other than the ones permitted as good data (Y, y, N, n) results in GoodResponse being **false** and the loop being executed again.

Exercises 6.4

*1. Discuss the differences between using a **REPEAT . . . UNTIL** loop and a **WHILE . . . DO** loop to read data. Be sure to consider the possibility of trying to read from an empty file.

2. Write a test program that illustrates what happens when the initial condition for a **REPEAT . . . UNTIL** loop is **false.** Compare this with a similar condition for a **WHILE . . . DO** loop.

In Exercises 3–6, indicate what output is produced.

*3.
```
A := 0;
B := 10;
REPEAT
  A := A + 1;
  B := B - 1;
  writeln (A, B)
UNTIL A > B;
```

4.
```
Power := 1;
REPEAT
  Power := Power * 2;
  writeln (Power)
UNTIL Power > 100;
```

*5.
```
J := 1;
REPEAT
  writeln (J);
  J := J + 1
UNTIL J > 10;
```

6.
```
A := 1;
REPEAT
  writeln (A, 17 MOD A);
  A := A + 1
UNTIL 17 MOD A = 5;
```

In Exercises 7–10, indicate which are infinite loops and explain why.

*7.
```
J := 1;
REPEAT
  writeln (J)
UNTIL J > 10;
J := J + 1;
```

8.
```
A := 2;
REPEAT
  writeln (A);
  A := A * 2
UNTIL A > 20;
```

*9.
```
A := 2;
REPEAT
  writeln (A);
  A := A * 2
UNTIL A = 20;
```

10.
```
B := 15;
REPEAT
  writeln (B, B DIV 5);
  B := B - 1
UNTIL B DIV 3 <> 5;
```

For Exercises 11–15, assume the variable declaration section of a program is

```
VAR
  Ch1, Ch2 : char;
  Age : integer;
  Num : real;
```

the data file is

A 18 −1.3B ▮ C 21 10.0D ▮ 3 19 −11.5F ▮ ■

↑

and the pointer is positioned at the beginning of the file. What output is produced by each of the following segments of code?

*11.
```
REPEAT
  read (Ch1);
  write (Ch1)
UNTIL eoln;
writeln;
```

12.
```
REPEAT
  read (Ch1);
  write (Ch1)
UNTIL eof;
writeln;
```

*13.
```
REPEAT
  read (Ch1);
  write (Ch1)
UNTIL eoln OR eof;
writeln;
```

14.
```
REPEAT
  read (Ch1);
  write (Ch1)
UNTIL eoln AND eof;
writeln;
```

*15.
```
REPEAT
  readln (Ch1, Age, Num, Ch2);
  writeln (Ch1:3, Age:3,
                Num:6:2, Ch2:3)
UNTIL eof;
```

In Exercises 16–21, write a segment of code that uses a **REPEAT . . . UNTIL** loop.

16. Print a table of cubes of integers from 1 to *N*, where the value of *N* is entered from the keyboard.

*17. Print a table of squares of integers starting with 1 and continuing until the difference of consecutive squares exceeds 25.

18. Read three values and print their sum as long as they are all positive.
*19. Read three values and print their sum as long as one of them is positive.
20. Print a positive real number (Num), and then print successive values where each value is 0.5 less than the previous value. The list should continue as long as values to be printed are positive.
*21. Find the smallest positive integer *N* such that the sum 1 + 2 + . . . + *N* exceeds some value entered from the keyboard.
22. Give an example of a situation that would require a predetermined number of repetitions.
*23. Write a segment of code that uses a **REPEAT . . . UNTIL** loop to read a positive integer and then print a list of powers of the integer that are less than 10,000.
24. In mathematics and science, many applications require a certain level or degree of accuracy obtained by successive approximations. Explain how the process of reaching the desired level of accuracy would relate to loops in Pascal.
25. Write a program that utilizes the algorithm for approximating a square root as shown in Example 6.20. Let the defined accuracy be 0.0001. Input should consist of a number whose square root is desired. Your program should guard against bad data entries (negatives and zero). Output should include a list of approximations and a check of your final approximation.

6.5 Comparison of Loops

Objectives

- to understand the similarities and differences between any two types of loops
- to understand why variable loops cannot, in general, be converted to fixed loops
- to be able to convert (when possible) from one type of loop to another

The last three sections have presented three loops used in Pascal: one fixed loop (**FOR . . . TO . . . DO**), and two variable loops (**WHILE . . . DO** and **REPEAT . . . UNTIL**). It is natural to wonder if any of these can replace any other. As you will see in this section, we could get by with only one type of loop. However, program design and personal preference make it convenient to have all three loops available. This section will examine the similarities and differences among loops and show how some of the loops can be rewritten as another type of loop.

Similarities and Differences

You probably have noticed by now that the three loops have some similarities and differences; for easy reference, these are summarized in Table 6.1.

Conversion of Loops

It is an interesting exercise to rewrite a loop using a different loop. In some cases, this can always be done; in others, it can only be accomplished when certain conditions are present. There are six possibilities for such rewriting; we will examine four and leave two for the exercises at the end of this section.

First, let's rewrite a **FOR** loop as a **WHILE . . . DO** loop. Both are pretest loops, but the **WHILE . . . DO** structure is a form of variable repetition. To accomplish our objective, we must use a counter in the **WHILE . . . DO** loop in a manner similar to the index in a **FOR** loop. Thus, we will initialize the counter outside the loop and change it accordingly inside the loop. The Boolean expression in the **WHILE . . . DO** loop will be written so that the last index value produces the final time through the loop.

Table 6.1

Comparing and contrasting loops

Traits of Loops	FOR . . . TO . . . DO Loop	WHILE . . . DO Loop	REPEAT . . . UNTIL Loop
Pretest loop	Yes	Yes	No
Posttest loop	No	No	Yes
BEGIN . . . END for compound statements	Required	Required	Not required
Repetition	Fixed	Not fixed	Not fixed
Loop index	Yes	No	No
Index automatically incremented	Yes	No	No
Boolean expression used	No	Yes	Yes

Example 6.22

Let's rewrite the following **FOR** loop using a **WHILE . . . DO** loop:

```
Sum := 0;
FOR K := 5 TO 10 DO
  BEGIN
    Sum := Sum + K;
    writeln (K)
  END;  {  of FOR loop  }
writeln (Sum);
```

The initialization must correspond to K := 5 and the Boolean expression that causes the loop to be exited must correspond to K > 10. With these requirements in mind, the revision becomes

```
K := 5;
Sum := 0;
WHILE K < 11 DO
  BEGIN
    Sum := Sum + K;
    writeln (K);
    K := K + 1
  END;  {  of WHILE loop  }
writeln (Sum);
```

The changes illustrated in Example 6.22 can always be made; any **FOR** loop can be rewritten as a **WHILE . . . DO** loop. The only other loop that can always be rewritten as another loop is a **REPEAT . . . UNTIL** loop; it can always be converted to a **WHILE . . . DO** loop. In this revision, the Boolean expression of the **WHILE . . . DO** loop will be the logical complement (opposite) of that used in the **REPEAT . . . UNTIL** loop. A revision of this type is illustrated in the following example.

Example 6.23

Let's rewrite the **REPEAT . . . UNTIL** loop using a **WHILE . . . DO** loop.

```
readln (A);
REPEAT
  writeln (A);
  A := A * A
UNTIL A > 100;
```

The Boolean expression A > 100 will be replaced by A <= 100 in the new loop.

```
readln (A);
writeln (A);
A := A * A;
WHILE A <= 100 DO
  BEGIN
    writeln (A);
    A := A * A
  END;  {  of WHILE loop  }
```

As demonstrated by the last two examples, Pascal programmers could use only the **WHILE . . . DO** loop structure. However, since there are cases in which one of the other two may be preferred, beginning courses in Pascal typically present and use all three loops.

Some conversions require special circumstances to be true before the conversions can be made. Let's consider the problem of rewriting a **WHILE . . . DO** loop as a **FOR** loop. Since a **WHILE . . . DO** loop is a variable repetition loop and uses a Boolean expression for loop control, both of these must be suitable for conversion before the loop can be rewritten as an index loop. For example,

```
K := 1;
WHILE K < 10 DO
  BEGIN
    writeln (K);
    K := K + 1
  END;  {  of WHILE loop  }
```

can be rewritten as

```
FOR K := 1 TO 9 DO
  writeln (K);
```

This form requires less code and is certainly preferable. On the other hand, consider the loop

```
WHILE NOT eoln DO
  BEGIN
    read (Ch);
    write (Ch)
  END;  {  of WHILE loop  }
```

Since the number of characters in the data line is unknown, this cannot be conveniently rewritten as a **FOR** loop.

Now let's consider the problem of rewriting a **WHILE . . . DO** loop as a **REPEAT . . . UNTIL** loop. Since both loops use Boolean expressions for loop control, logical complements can be used for the transition. However, **WHILE . . . DO** is a pretest loop and **REPEAT . . . UNTIL** is a posttest loop. Since a posttest loop must be executed at least once before the exit condition is checked, a pretest loop that is not entered cannot be written as a posttest loop. Thus,

```
A := 10;
WHILE A < 5 DO
  BEGIN
    writeln (A);
    A := A * 2
  END;  {  of WHILE loop  }
```

cannot be rewritten as a **REPEAT . . . UNTIL** loop. However, if the **WHILE . . . DO** loop is executed at least once, it can be revised into a **REPEAT . . . UNTIL** loop. The next example illustrates this.

Example 6.24

Let's rewrite the following using a **REPEAT . . . UNTIL** loop:

```
A := 1;
Power := 3;
WHILE A < 100 DO
  BEGIN
    writeln (A);
    A := A * Power
  END;  {  of WHILE loop  }
```

The Boolean expression for a **REPEAT . . . UNTIL** loop becomes A >= 100 and the revision is

```
A := 1;
Power := 3;
REPEAT
  writeln (A);
  A := A * Power
UNTIL A >= 100;
```

When considering the loop conversions in the exercises, carefully note fixed repetition versus variable repetition and pretest versus posttest conditions.

Which Loop to Use

Which loop should you choose when repetition is needed in a program? There is no quick, easy answer to this question. We can offer some general guidelines, but even they leave the question fairly open.

First, if a process is to be repeated a predetermined number of times, a **FOR** loop is appropriate. The key to choosing this loop statement is that a variable condition would not be needed to determine how often the loop is repeated.

A second, more difficult question is whether to use a **REPEAT . . . UNTIL** loop or a **WHILE . . . DO** loop when a variable control is necessary. As just discussed, **REPEAT** loops can always be written as **WHILE** loops and often **WHILE** loops can be written as **REPEAT** loops. How then do you decide which to use?

If you know the statements within a loop will always be executed at least once, you can use a **REPEAT . . . UNTIL** loop. When designing a solution to a problem, if you decide to repeat some process until a condition changes, using a **REPEAT . . . UNTIL** loop with an appropriate **boolean** variable allows the code to be written in a manner consistent with how you think about the solution. For example, suppose you wish to have test scores entered interactively for the purpose of computing an average. You know there will always be scores to enter, so your loop design could be

```
REPEAT
  .
  .     (action here)
  .
UNTIL NoMoreScores;
```

Not all loops will be entered automatically. For example, loops that include reading data from a data file may need to check the Boolean functions **eoln** or **eof** before attempting to read data. Otherwise, a program crash may occur if the loop attempts to read past the end-of-file marker (or to read from an empty file). This can be prevented by using a **WHILE . . . DO** loop such as

```
WHILE NOT eof DO
  BEGIN
    .
    .     (action here)
    .
  END;
```

The **WHILE . . . DO** loop is considered to be the most general loop because it includes the possibility of not being entered at all.

Occasionally, the logical conditions used to decide whether or not the loop should be repeated will read in a more natural fashion in one of the repetition statements. To illustrate, suppose two Boolean conditions need to be **true** for a loop to be repeated. A **REPEAT . . . UNTIL** loop such as

```
REPEAT
  .
  .
  .
UNTIL NOT <condition 1> OR NOT <condition 2>;
```

might be rewritten as the **WHILE . . . DO** loop

```
WHILE <condition 1> AND <condition 2> DO
  BEGIN
    .
    .    (action here)
    .
  END;
```

This version appears easier to read and would be preferred by many programmers.

In summary, the issue of which loop to use is still open. You should discuss this with your teacher and be able to use any of the three loops when designing your solution to a problem.

Exercises 6.5

1. Compare and contrast the three looping structures discussed in this section.

In Exercises 2–4, determine whether or not the conversions indicated can be made.

2.
```
Sum: = 0;
FOR K := 1 TO 100 DO
  Sum := Sum + K;
```
   a. Convert to **REPEAT . . . UNTIL?**
   b. Convert to **WHILE . . . DO?**

*3.
```
Count := 0;
Sum := 0;
readln (A);
WHILE A <> 0 DO
```

```
  BEGIN
    Sum := Sum + A;
    Count := Count + 1;
    readln (A)
  END;
```

a. Convert to **REPEAT . . . UNTIL?**
b. Convert to **FOR . . . TO . . . DO?**
c. Convert to **FOR . . . DOWNTO . . . DO?**

4.
```
X := 0.0;
REPEAT
  writeln (X:20:2);
  X := X + 0.5
UNTIL X = 4.0;
```

a. Convert to **WHILE . . . DO?**
b. Convert to **FOR . . . TO . . . DO?**
c. Convert to **FOR . . . DOWNTO . . . DO?**

*5. For each of the conversions you indicated were possible in Exercises 2–4, write the revised loop.

6. Explain completely the problems encountered when trying to make the following loop conversions.
a. **FOR . . . TO . . . DO** to **REPEAT . . . UNTIL**
b. **REPEAT . . . UNTIL** to **FOR . . . TO . . . DO**

*7. Explain why the following cannot be rewritten as a **REPEAT . . . UNTIL** loop:

```
WHILE 6 < 5 DO
  BEGIN
    .
    .  (loop body)
    .
  END;
```

6.6 Loop Verification (Optional)

Objectives

- to understand how input assertions and output assertions can be used to verify loops
- to understand how loop invariants and loop variants can be used to verify loops

Loop verification is the process of guaranteeing that a loop performs its intended task. Such verification is part of program testing and correctness, which we discussed in Chapter 4.

Some work has been done on constructing formal proofs that loops are "correct." We now examine a modified version of loop verification; a complete treatment of the issue will be the topic of subsequent course work.

Preconditions and Postconditions with Loops

Preconditions and postconditions can be used with loops. Loop preconditions are referred to as **input assertions;** they are comments that indicate what can be expected to be true before the loop is entered. Loop postconditions are referred to as **output assertions;** they are comments that indicate what can be expected to be true when the loop is exited.

To illustrate input and output assertions, let's consider the mathematical problem of summing the proper divisors of a positive integer. For example, we have

Loop verification is the process of documenting a loop to guarantee the loop performs its intended task.

An **input assertion** is a loop precondition.

An **output assertion** is a loop postcondition.

Integer	Proper Divisors	Sum
6	1, 2, 3	6
9	1, 3	4
12	1, 2, 3, 4, 6	16

Consider a program with a positive integer as input and the following as output: a determination of whether the integer is perfect (Sum = integer), abundant (Sum > integer), or deficient (Sum < integer). As part of the program, it is necessary to sum the divisors. A loop to perform this task is

```
DivisorSum := 0;
FOR TrialDivisor := 1 TO Num DIV 2 DO
  IF Num MOD TrialDivisor = 0 THEN
    DivisorSum := DivisorSum + TrialDivisor;
```

An input assertion for this loop is

```
{  Precondition: 1. Num is a positive integer.           }
{                2. DivisorSum = 0.                        }
```

An output assertion is

```
{  Postcondition: DivisorSum is the sum of all proper    }
{                 divisors of Num.                         }
```

When these assertions are placed in the previous code, we have

```
DivisorSum := 0;

{  Precondition: 1. Num is a positive integer.           }
{                2. DivisorSum = 0.                        }

FOR TrialDivisor := 1 TO Num DIV 2 DO
  IF Num MOD TrialDivisor = 0 THEN
    DivisorSum := DivisorSum + TrialDivisor;

{  Postcondition: DivisorSum is the sum of all proper    }
{                 divisors of Num.                         }
```

A **loop invariant** is an assertion that expresses a relationship between variables that remains constant throughout all iterations of the loop.

A **loop variant** is an assertion that changes in terms of its truth between the first and final executions of the loop.

Invariant and Variant Assertions

A **loop invariant** is an assertion that expresses a relationship between variables that remains constant throughout all iterations of the loop. In other words, it is a statement that is true both before the loop is entered and after each pass through the loop. A loop invariant assertion for the preceding code segment would be

```
{  DivisorSum is the sum of proper divisors of Num that  }
{  are less than or equal to TrialDivisor.                }
```

A **loop variant** is an assertion that changes in terms of its truth between the first and final executions of the loop. The loop variant expression should be stated in such a way that it guarantees the loop is exited. Thus, it contains some statement about the loop variable being incremented (or decremented) during execution of the loop. A loop variant assertion in the preceding code could be

```
{  TrialDivisor is incremented by 1 each time through   }
{  the loop.  It eventually exceeds the value Num DIV 2,}
{  at which point the loop is exited.                   }
```

Loop variant and loop invariant assertions usually occur in pairs.

We now use four kinds of assertions—input, output, variant, and invariant—to produce the formally verified loop that follows:

```
DivisorSum := 0;

{  Precondition:  1.  Num is a positive integer.   }     (input
{                 2.  DivisorSum = 0.              }      assertion)

FOR TrialDivisor := 1 TO Num DIV 2 DO

{  TrialDivisor is incremented by 1 each time      }     (variant
{  through the loop. It eventually exceeds the     }      assertion)
{  value Num DIV 2, at which point the loop is     }
{  exited.                                         }

  IF Num MOD TrialDivisor = 0 THEN
    DivisorSum := DivisorSum + TrialDivisor;

{  DivisorSum is the sum of proper divisors of     }     (invariant
{  Num that are less than or equal to              }      assertion)
{  TrialDivisor.                                   }

{  Postcondition: DivisorSum is the sum of         }     (output
{  all proper divisors of Num.                     }      assertion)
```

In general, code that is presented in this text does not include formal verification of the loops. This issue is similar to robustness. In an introductory course, a decision must be made regarding the trade-off between learning new concepts and writing robust programs with formal verification of loops. We encourage the practice, but space and time considerations make it inconvenient to include such documentation at this level. We close this discussion with another example illustrating loop verification.

Example 6.25

Let's consider the problem of finding the greatest common divisor (GCD) of two positive integers. To illustrate, we have

Num1	Num2	GCD (Num1, Num2)
8	12	4
20	10	10
15	32	1
70	40	10

The following segment of code produces the GCD of two positive integers after they have been ordered as Small, Large.

```
TrialGCD := Small;
GCDFound := false;
WHILE NOT GCDFound DO
  IF (Large MOD TrialGCD = 0) AND
     (Small MOD TrialGCD = 0) THEN
    BEGIN
      GCD := TrialGCD;
      GCDFound := true
    END  {  of IF...THEN option  }
  ELSE
    TrialGCD := TrialGCD - 1;
```

Using assertions as previously indicated, this code would appear as

```
TrialGCD := Small;
GCDFound := false;

{  Precondition:  1.  Small <= Large.                 }
{                 2.  TrialGCD (Small) is the first   }
{                     candidate for GCD.              }
{                 3.  GCDFound is false.              }

WHILE NOT GCDFound DO

{  TrialGCD assumes integer values ranging from Small  }
{  to 1. It is decremented by 1 each time through the  }
{  loop. When TrialGCD divides both Small and Large,   }
{  the loop is exited. Exit is guaranteed since 1      }
{  divides both Small and Large.                       }

  IF (Large MOD TrialGCD = 0) AND
     (Small MOD TrialGCD = 0) THEN
    BEGIN

    {  When TrialGCD divides both Large and Small,     }
    {  then GCD is assigned that value.                }

      GCD := TrialGCD;
      GCDFound := true
    END  {  of IF...THEN option  }
  ELSE
    TrialGCD := TrialGCD - 1;

{  Postcondition:  GCD is the greatest common divisor  }
{                  of Small and Large.                 }
```

Exercises 6.6

1. Write appropriate input and output assertions for each of the following loops:
   a. `readln (Score);`

```
WHILE Score <> -999 DO
  BEGIN
    NumScores := NumScores + 1;
    Sum := Sum + Score;
    writeln ('Enter a score; -999 to quit.');
    readln (Score)
  END;  {  of WHILE loop  }
```

b.
```
Count := 0;
Power2 := 1;
WHILE Power2 < 100 DO
  BEGIN
    writeln (Power2);
    Power2 := Power2 * 2;
    Count := Count + 1
  END;  {  of WHILE loop  }
```

c. (From Example 6.20)

```
REPEAT
  OldGuess := NewGuess;
  NewGuess := 1/2 * (OldGuess + Number / OldGuess);
  writeln (NewGuess:12:8)
UNTIL abs(NewGuess - OldGuess) < DesiredAccuracy;
```

2. Write appropriate loop invariant and loop variant assertions for each of the loops in Exercise 1.
3. The following loop comes from a program called HiLo. The first player enters a target number, and the second player enters a number (Guess). The computer then displays a message indicating whether the guess is correct, too high, or too low. Add appropriate input, output, loop invariant, and loop variant assertions to the following code.

```
Correct := false;
Count := 0;
WHILE (Count < MaxTries) AND (NOT Correct) DO
  BEGIN
    Count := Count + 1;
    writeln ('Enter choice number ', Count);
    readln (Guess);
    IF Guess = TargetNumber THEN
      BEGIN
        Correct := true;
        writeln ('Congratulations!')
      END  {  of IF...THEN option  }
    ELSE IF Guess < TargetNumber THEN
      writeln ('Your guess is too low')
    ELSE
      writeln ('Your guess is too high')
  END;  {  of WHILE loop  }
```

6.7 Nested Loops

Objectives

- to be able to use nested loops
- to understand the flow of control when using nested loops
- to be able to use a consistent writing style when using nested loops

In this chapter, we examined three loop structures. Each of them has been discussed with respect to syntax, semantics, form, writing style, and use in programs. But remember that each loop is treated as a single Pascal statement. In this sense, it is possible to have a loop as one of the statements in the body of another loop. When this happens, the loops are said to be **nested loops.**

Loops can be nested to any depth: that is, a loop can be within a loop within a loop, and so on. Also, any of the three loops can be nested within any other loop. However, a programmer should be careful not to design a program with nesting that is too complex. If program logic becomes too difficult to follow, you might be better served by redesigning the program.

A **nested loop** occurs when a loop is one of the statements in the body of another loop.

Flow of Control

As a first example of using a loop within a loop, consider

```
FOR K := 1 TO 5 DO
  FOR J := 1 TO 3 DO
    writeln (K + J);
```

When this fragment is executed, the following happens:

1. K is assigned a value.
2. For each value of K, the following loop is executed:

```
FOR J := 1 TO 3 DO
  writeln (K + J);
```

Thus, for K := 1, the "inside," or nested, loop produces the output

```
2
3
4
```

At this point, K := 2 and the next portion of the output produced by the nested loop is

```
3
4
5
```

The complete output from these nested loops is

```
2 }
3 } from K := 1
4 }
3 }
4 } from K := 2
5 }
4 }
5 } from K := 3
6 }
5 }
6 } from K := 4
7 }
6 }
7 } from K := 5
8 }
```

As you can see, for each value assigned to the index of the outside loop, the inside loop is executed completely. Suppose you want the output to be printed in the form of a chart as follows:

```
2    3    4
3    4    5
4    5    6
5    6    7
6    7    8
```

The pseudocode design to produce this output is

1. **FOR** K := 1 **TO** 5 **DO**
   produce a line

A refinement of this is

1. **FOR** K := 1 **TO** 5 **DO**
   1.1 Print on one line
   1.2 Advance the printer

The Pascal code for this development becomes

```
FOR K := 1 TO 5 DO
  BEGIN
    FOR J := 1 TO 3 DO
      write ((K + J):4);
    writeln
  END;  {  of FOR loop  }
```

Our next example shows how nested loops can be used to produce a design.

Example 6.26

Use nested **FOR** loops to produce the output

```
*
**
***
****
*****
```

where the left asterisks are in column 10. The first-level pseudocode to solve this problem could be

1. **FOR** K := 1 **TO** 5 **DO**
   produce a line

A refinement of this could be

1. **FOR** K := 1 **TO** 5 **DO**
   1.1 Print on one line
   1.2 Advance the printer

Step 1.1 is not yet sufficiently refined, so our next level could be

1. **FOR** K := 1 **TO** 5 **DO**
   1.1 Print on one line

1.1.1 Put a blank in column 9
1.1.2 Print K asterisks
1.2 Advance the printer

We can now write a program fragment to produce the desired output as follows:

```
FOR Line := 1 TO 5 DO
  BEGIN
    write (' ':9);
    FOR J := 1 TO Line DO
      write ('*');
    writeln
  END;  {  of outer loop  }
```

A significant feature has been added to this program fragment. Note that the loop control for the inner loop is the index of the outer loop.

Communication and Style Tips

When working with nested loops, use line comments to indicate the effect of each loop control variable. For example,

```
FOR Line := 1 TO 5 DO   {  Each value produces a line  }
  BEGIN
    write (' ':9);
    FOR J := 1 TO Line DO   {  This moves across one line  }
      write ('*');
    writeln
  END;  {  of outer loop  }
```

Thus far, nested loops have been used only with **FOR** loops, but any of the loop structures may be used in nesting. Our next example illustrates a **REPEAT . . . UNTIL** loop nested within a **WHILE . . . DO** loop.

Example 6.27

Let's trace the flow of control and indicate the output for the following program fragment:

```
A := 10;
B := 0;
WHILE A > B DO
  BEGIN
    writeln (A:5);
    REPEAT
      writeln (A:5, B:5, (A + B):5);
      A := A - 2
    UNTIL A <= 6;
    B := B + 2
  END;  {  of WHILE loop  }
writeln;
writeln ('All done':20);
```

The assignment statements produce

10	0
A	B

and A > B is **true;** thus, the **WHILE . . . DO** loop is entered. The first time through this loop the **REPEAT . . . UNTIL** loop is used. Output for the first pass is

```
10
10    0   10
```

and the values for A and B are

8	0
A	B

The Boolean expression A <= 6 is **false** and the **REPEAT . . . UNTIL** loop is executed again to produce the next line of output

```
 8    0    8
```

and the values for A and B become

6	0
A	B

At this point, A <= 6 is **true** and control transfers to the line of code

```
B := B + 2;
```

Thus, the variable values are

6	2
A	B

and the Boolean expression A > B is **true.** This means the **WHILE . . . DO** loop will be repeated. The output for the second time through this loop is

```
 6
 6    2    8
```

The inner loop is exited and the values for the variables become

4	4
A	B

Now A > B is **false** and control is transferred to the line following the **WHILE . . . DO** loop. Output for the complete fragment is

```
10
10    0   10
 8    0    8
 6
 6    2    8

           All done
```

Example 6.27 is a bit contrived, and tracing the flow of control somewhat tedious. However, it is important for you to be able to follow the logic involved in using nested loops.

Our next example is much more standard. Be sure you understand it thoroughly, because you will need to be able to use it as part of subsequent programs.

Example 6.28

Let's use nested loops to reproduce an unknown data file. The first-level pseudocode for the solution to this problem could be

1. **WHILE NOT eof DO**
   reproduce a line of data

A refinement of this could be

1. **WHILE NOT eof DO**
   1.1 Set a left margin
   1.2 Reproduce a data line
   1.3 Advance the input data pointer
   1.4 Advance the output pointer

Step 1.2 could then be refined to

1.2 Reproduce a data line
  1.2.1 **WHILE NOT eoln DO**
    1.2.1.1 Read a character
    1.2.1.2 Write a character

The complete algorithm for this fragment is now

1. **WHILE NOT eof DO**
   1.1 Set a left margin
   1.2 Reproduce a data line
     1.2.1 **WHILE NOT eoln DO**
       1.2.1.1 Read a character
       1.2.1.2 Write a character
   1.3 Advance the input data pointer
   1.4 Advance the output pointer

The code for this algorithm can now be written as follows:

```
WHILE NOT eof DO  {  Process one line  }
  BEGIN
    write (' ':10);
    WHILE NOT eoln DO  {  Process one character  }
      BEGIN
        read (Ch);
        write (Ch)
      END;  {  of inner WHILE loop  }
    readln;
    writeln
  END;  {  of outer WHILE loop  }
```

If this program fragment is run using the data file

BRL 268–36–0729 M 38 ■	HBT 231–48–2136 F 18 ■	LMN 133–24–0966 F 21 ■	■

↑

the output is

```
BRL 268-36-0729 M 38
HBT 231-48-2136 F 18
LMN 133-24-0966 F 21
```

Being able to examine a data file is essential for beginning programmers. Consequently, in the exercises for this section, you will be asked to write a complete program to examine a data file. You should use Example 6.28 as the basis of your program; then keep your program and run it to examine data files for subsequent programs.

Writing Style

As usual, you should be aware of the significance of using a consistent, readable style of writing when using nested loops. There are at least three features you should consider.

1. **Indenting.** Each loop should have its own level of indenting. This makes it easier to identify the body of the loop. If the loop body consists of a compound statement, the **BEGIN** and **END** should start in the same column. Using our previous indenting style, a typical nesting might be

```
FOR K := 1 TO 10 DO
  BEGIN
    WHILE A > 0 DO  {  Start WHILE loop  }
      BEGIN
        REPEAT      {  Start REPEAT loop  }
          .
          .
          .
        UNTIL <condition>;  {  End of REPEAT loop  }
        <statement>
      END;  {  of WHILE loop  }
    <statement>
  END;  {  of FOR loop  }
```

   If the body of a loop becomes very long, it is sometimes difficult to match the **BEGIN**s with the proper **END**s. In this case, you should either redesign the program or be especially careful.

2. **Using comments.** Comments can precede a loop and explain what the loop will do, or they can be used with statements inside the loop to explain what the statement does. Comments should be used to indicate the end of a loop where the loop body is a compound statement.
3. **Skipping lines.** This is an effective way of isolating loops within a program and making nested loops easier to identify.

A note of caution is in order with respect to writing style. Program documentation is important; however, excessive use of comments and skipped lines can detract from readability. You should develop a happy medium.

Statement Execution in Nested Loops

Using nested loops can significantly increase the number of times statements are executed in a program. Suppose a program contains a **REPEAT . . . UNTIL** loop that is to be executed six times before it is exited. This is illustrated by

```
         ┌ REPEAT
         │    .
6 times  │    .            (action here)
         │    .
         └ UNTIL  <condition 1>;
```

If one of the statements inside this loop is another loop, the inner loop will also be executed six times. Suppose this inner loop is repeated five times whenever it is entered. This means each statement within the inner loop will be executed 6 × 5 = 30 times when the program is run. This is illustrated by

```
         ┌ REPEAT
         │   .
         │   .           (action here)
         │   .
6 times  │   WHILE <condition 2> DO                             ┐
         │      BEGIN                                           │
         │        <statement>                  ┐ 30 times       │ 5 times
         │      END;  {  of WHILE loop  }                       ┘
         │   .
         │   .
         │   .
         └ UNTIL <condition 1>;
```

When a third level of nesting is used, the number of times a statement is executed can be determined by the product of three factors, $n_1 * n_2 * n_3$, where n_1 represents the number of repetitions of the outside loop, n_2 represents the number of repetitions for the first level of nesting, and n_3 represents the number of repetitions for the innermost loop.

We close this section with two more examples of nested loops. The first one analyzes a program fragment with nested loops; the second asks you to write a program to produce a certain output.

Example 6.29

Let's find the output produced by the following program fragment of nested loops. Assume A and B have been declared as integer variables and the data file is

4 7	▮	■

↑

The fragment

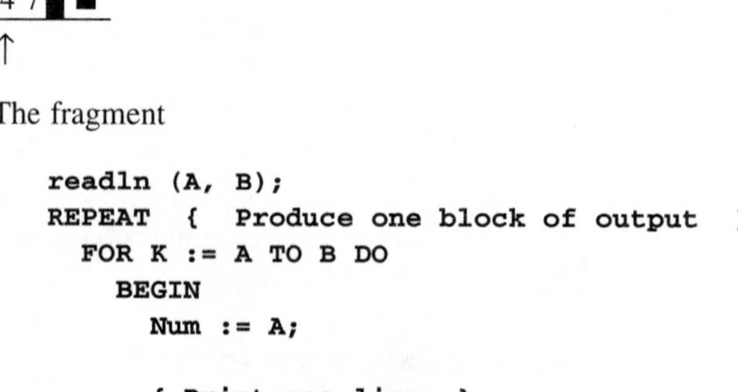

```
readln (A, B);
REPEAT  {  Produce one block of output  }
  FOR K := A TO B DO
    BEGIN
      Num := A;

      { Print one line  }
      WHILE Num <= B DO
```

```
            BEGIN
              write (Num:4);
              Num := Num + 1
            END;  {  of WHILE loop  }
          writeln
        END;  {  of FOR loop  }
      A := A + 1;
      writeln
    UNTIL A = B;  {  end of REPEAT loop  }
```

produces the output

```
    4   5   6   7
    4   5   6   7
    4   5   6   7
    4   5   6   7

    5   6   7
    5   6   7
    5   6   7

    6   7
    6   7
```

Example 6.30

This example presents a complete program that outputs the multiplication table from 1×1 to 10×10. A suitable heading should be part of the output.

```
PROGRAM MultTable;

CONST
  Indent = ' ';

VAR
  Row, Column : integer;

BEGIN  {  Program  }

  writeln;
  writeln (Indent:22, 'Multiplication Table');
  writeln (Indent:22, '--------------------');
  writeln (Indent:15, '( Generated by nested FOR loops )');
  writeln;

  {  Print the column heads  }
  writeln (Indent:11, '    1   2   3   4   5   6   7   8   9  10');
  writeln (Indent:8, '---!----------------------------------------');

  {  Now start the loop for printing rows  }
  FOR Row := 1 TO 10 DO
    BEGIN  {  Print one row  }
      write (Row:10, ' !');
      FOR Column := 1 TO 10 DO
```

```
        write (Row * Column:4);
      writeln;
      writeln (Indent:11, '!')
    END;  {  of each row  }
  writeln
END.  {  of program  }
```

The output from this program is

```
                 Multiplication Table
                 --------------------
           ( Generated by nested FOR loops )

           1   2   3   4   5   6   7   8   9  10
 ---!----------------------------------------
   1 !     1   2   3   4   5   6   7   8   9  10
     !
   2 !     2   4   6   8  10  12  14  16  18  20
     !
   3 !     3   6   9  12  15  18  21  24  27  30
     !
   4 !     4   8  12  16  20  24  28  32  36  40
     !
   5 !     5  10  15  20  25  30  35  40  45  50
     !
   6 !     6  12  18  24  30  36  42  48  54  60
     !
   7 !     7  14  21  28  35  42  49  56  63  70
     !
   8 !     8  16  24  32  40  48  56  64  72  80
     !
   9 !     9  18  27  36  45  54  63  72  81  90
     !
  10 !    10  20  30  40  50  60  70  80  90 100
     !
```

Exercises 6.7

*1. Write a program that allows the size of a multiplication table to be entered from the keyboard. The requested table should then be printed as output. For example, if you enter 2 3, output is

```
1 * 1 = 1
1 * 2 = 2
1 * 3 = 3
2 * 1 = 2
2 * 2 = 4
2 * 3 = 6
```

For Exercises 2–5, write a complete program that allows you to examine a data file (see Example 6.28). Run your program using the indicated data files.

2. | This is a one liner.▮ ■ |

3. | b̸ b̸ | ▮ | ■ |

4. | * | ▮ | ** | ▮ | *** | ▮ | **** | ▮ | ***** | ▮ | ■ |

5. | 87 | ▮ | 93 | ▮ | 76 | ▮ | 92 | ▮ | 80 | ▮ | −999 | ▮ | ■ |

In Exercises 6–10, what output is produced from the program fragment?

6.
```
FOR K := 2 TO 6 DO
  BEGIN
    FOR J := 5 TO 10 DO
      write (K + J);
    writeln
  END;
```

*7.
```
FOR K := 2 TO 6 DO
  BEGIN
    FOR J := 5 TO 10 DO
      write (K * J);
    writeln
  END;
```

8.
```
Sum := 0;
A := 7;
WHILE A < 10 DO
  BEGIN
    FOR K := A TO 10 DO
      Sum := Sum + K;
    A := A + 1
  END;
writeln (Sum);
```

*9.
```
Sum := 0;
FOR K := 1 TO 10 DO
  FOR J := (10 * K - 9) TO (10 * K) DO
    Sum := Sum + J;
writeln (Sum);
```

10. Assume the data file is

| 12 3 | ▮ | 10 3 | ▮ | 8 3 | ▮ | ■ |
↑

```
WHILE NOT eof DO
  BEGIN
    readln (Length, Width);
    LineCount := 1;
    REPEAT
      write (' ':9, Length);
      FOR K := 1 TO Length DO
        write ('*');
      writeln;
      LineCount := LineCount + 1
    UNTIL LineCount = Width;
    writeln
  END;  {  of WHILE NOT eof  }
```

In Exercises 11–14, write a program fragment that uses nested loops to produce each design.

*11.
```
*****
 ****
  ***
   **
    *
```

*13.
```
***
***
***
***
******
******
******
```

12.
```
   *
  ***
 *****
*******
 *****
  ***
   *
```

14.
```
   *
  ***
 *****
*******
  ***
  ***
  ***
```

*15. Write a program fragment that uses nested loops to produce the following output:

```
2     4     6     8    10
3     6     9    12    15
4     8    12    16    20
5    10    15    20    25
```

16. What output is produced from the following segment of code?

```
A := 4;
B := 7;
REPEAT  {  Produce one block of output  }
  FOR K := A TO B DO
    BEGIN
      Num := A;

      {  Print one line  }
      WHILE Num <= B DO
        BEGIN
          write (Num:4);
          Num := Num + 1
        END;  {  of WHILE loop  }
      writeln
    END;  {  of FOR loop  }

  A := A + 1;
  writeln
UNTIL A = B;  {  end of REPEAT loop  }
```

17. Write an interactive program that generates a pyramid of asterisks. Input will consist of a positive integer N from 1 to 20. Output will consist of a pyramid of asterisks with N layers. For example, for $N = 3$, the output would be

```
  *
 * *
* * *
```

6.8 Repetition and Selection

Selection within Repetition (Loops)

In Chapter 5, we discussed the use of selection statements. In this chapter, we have discussed the use of three different loops. It is now time to see how these elements are used together. We first examine selection statements contained within the body of a loop.

Example 6.31

Let's write a program fragment that counts all the blanks in a line of data. The loop control for this problem will be the end-of-line function. A first-level pseudocode is

1. Initialize variables
2. **WHILE NOT eoln DO**
   2.1 Process a character

This can be refined to

1. Initialize variables
2. **WHILE NOT eoln DO**
   2.1 Process a character
      2.1.1 Read a character
      2.1.2 **IF** character is a blank **THEN**
         2.1.2.1 Add 1 to BlankCount

Objectives

- to be able to use a selection statement within the body of a loop
- to be able to use a loop within an option of a selection statement

The code for this fragment is

```
BlankCount := 0;
WHILE NOT eoln DO
  BEGIN
    read (Ch);
    IF Ch = ' ' THEN
      BlankCount := BlankCount + 1
  END;  {  of WHILE loop  }
```

Just as **IF . . . THEN** statements can be used with loops, **IF . . . THEN . . . ELSE** statements can be similarly used, as the next example illustrates.

Example 6.32

Let's write a program fragment that computes gross wages for employees of the Florida OJ Canning Company. A data line consists of three initials, the total hours worked, and the hourly rate; for example,

JHA 44.5 12.75 ■ ■

Overtime (more than 40 hours) is computed at time-and-a-half. The output should include all input data and a column of gross wages. A first-level pseudocode development for this program is

1. **WHILE NOT eof DO**
   1.1 Process a line of data
   1.2 Print results

This can be refined to

1. **WHILE NOT eof DO**

1.1 Process a line of data
  1.1.1 Get data
  1.1.2 Compute wage
1.2 Print results

Step 1.1.2 can be refined to

1.1.2 Compute wage
  1.1.2.1 **IF** Hours <= 40.0 **THEN**
        compute regular timer
      ELSE
        compute time-and-a-half

and the final algorithm for the fragment is

1. **WHILE NOT eof DO**
   1.1 Process a line of data
     1.1.1 Get data
     1.1.2 Compute wage
       1.1.2.1 **IF** Hours <= 40.0 **THEN**
             compute regular time
           ELSE
             compute time-and-a-half
   1.2 Print results

The code for this fragment is

```
WHILE NOT eof DO
  BEGIN
    read (Init1, Init2, Init3);
    readln (Hours, PayRate);
    IF Hours <= 40.0 THEN
      TotalWage := Hours * PayRate
    ELSE
      BEGIN
        Overtime := 1.5 * (Hours - 40.0) * PayRate;
        TotalWage := 40 * Payrate + Overtime
      END;  {  of ELSE option  }
    write (Init1:5, Init2, Init3);
    write (Hours:10:2, PayRate:10:2);
    writeln ('$':10, TotalWage:7:2)
  END;  {  of WHILE loop  }
```

If the data file is

JHA 44.5 12.75	▮	RBT 40.0 9.8	▮	SML 37.5 11.50	▮	■

↑

the output from this fragment is

```
JHA      44.50     12.75          $ 596.06
RBT      40.00      9.80          $ 392.00
SML      37.50     11.50          $ 431.25
```

Repetition (Loops) within Selection

The next example illustrates the use of a loop within an **IF . . . THEN** statement.

Example 6.33

Let's write a fragment of code to find the smallest and/or largest value in a list of numbers. The numbers will be in a data file, with one number on each line. We will assign the first number to both Small and Large and then identify the smallest and largest numbers from the list.

```
{  Assign the first number in the list  }
{  to both Small and Large              }
readln (Num);
Small := Num;
Large := Num;

{  Now read the rest of the list and identify  }
{  the smallest and largest numbers            }
REPEAT
  readln (Num);
  IF Num > Large THEN
    Large := Num;
  IF Num < Small THEN
    Small := Num
UNTIL eof;
```

To close this section, let's consider the design of a slightly more complex problem.

Example 6.34

Let's design a solution and write a program fragment that will do the following:

1. Check the first character of each line of a data file.
2. If the character read is a Y, process the line. (Processing a line consists of counting the number of occurrences of the letter A contained in the line.)
3. If the character read is not a Y, skip the line.
4. Count the total number of lines.
5. Count the number of lines processed.
6. Assume there is an unknown number of data lines.
7. Print the total number of lines, the number of lines processed, and the number of occurrences of the letter A in the lines processed.

A first-level pseudocode for this problem is

1. Initialize counter
2. **WHILE NOT eof DO**
   check each line of data
3. Print results

A second-level development is

1. Initialize counter
   1.1 Initialize TotalLines
   1.2 Initialize ProcessedLines
   1.3 Initialize ACount

2. **WHILE NOT eof DO**
    2.1 **read** Ch
    2.2 **IF** Ch = 'Y' **THEN**
        process the line
    2.3 Increment TotalLines
3. Print results
    3.1 Print TotalLines
    3.2 Print ProcessedLines
    3.3 Print ACount

Step 2.2 could be refined to

2.2 **IF** Ch = 'Y' **THEN**
    2.2.1 Increment ProcessedLines
    2.2.2 **WHILE NOT eoln DO**
        count the As
    2.2.3 Advance pointer

and finally, Step 2.2.2 becomes

2.2.2 **WHILE NOT eoln DO**
    2.2.2.1 read Ch
    2.2.2.2 **IF** Ch = 'A' **THEN**
        increment ACount

A complete development of Step 2 is

2. **WHILE NOT eof DO**
    2.1 **read** Ch
    2.2 **IF** Ch = 'Y' **THEN**
        2.2.1 Increment ProcessedLines
        2.2.2 **WHILE NOT eoln DO**
            2.2.2.1 **read** Ch
            2.2.2.2 **IF** Ch = 'A' **THEN**
                increment ACount
        2.2.3 Advance pointer
    2.3 Increment TotalLines

The code for this part of the program is

```
WHILE NOT eof DO
  BEGIN
    read (Ch);
    IF Ch = 'Y' THEN
      BEGIN
        ProcessedLines := ProcessedLines + 1;
        WHILE NOT eoln DO
          BEGIN
            read (Ch);
            IF Ch = 'A' THEN
              ACount := ACount + 1
          END;  {  of WHILE NOT eoln  }
        readln  {  Advance pointer  }
      END;  {  of processing one line  }
    TotalLines := TotalLines + 1
  END;  {  of WHILE NOT eof  }
```

Exercises 6.8

For Exercises 1 and 2, find and explain the errors in each program fragment. Assume all variables have been suitably declared.

*1.
```
A := 25;
Flag := true;
WHILE Flag = true DO
  IF A >= 100 THEN
    BEGIN
      writeln (A);
      Flag := false
    END;
```

2.
```
FOR K := 1 TO 10 DO
  writeln (K, K * K);
IF K MOD 3 = 0 THEN
  BEGIN
    write (K);
    writeln (' is a multiple of three')
  END;  {  of IF...THEN  }
```

For Exercises 3–8, what output is produced from each program fragment? Assume variables have been suitably declared.

*3.
```
FOR K := 1 TO 100 DO
  IF K MOD 5 = 0 THEN
    writeln (K);
```

4.
```
J := 20;
IF J MOD 5 = 0 THEN
  FOR K := 1 TO 100 DO
    writeln (K);
```

*5.
```
A := 5;
B := 90;
REPEAT
  B := B DIV A - 5;
  IF B > A THEN
    B := A + 30
UNTIL B < 0;
writeln (A, B);
```

6.
```
Count := 0;
FOR K := -5 to 5 DO
  IF K MOD 3 = 0 THEN
    BEGIN
      write ('K =  ', K:4, '  output  ');
      WHILE Count < 10 DO
        BEGIN
          Count := Count + 1;
          writeln (Count:4)
        END;  {  of WHILE loop  }
      Count := 0;
      writeln
    END;  {  of IF...THEN  }
```

*7.
```
A := 5;
B := 2;
```

```
IF A < B THEN
  FOR K := A TO B DO
    writeln (K)
ELSE
  FOR K := A DOWNTO B DO
    writeln (K);
```

8.
```
FOR K := -5 TO 5 DO
  BEGIN
    write ('K =   ', K:4, '  output  ');
    A := K;
    IF K < 0 THEN          {  K = -5, -4, -3, -2, -1  }
      REPEAT
        writeln (-2 * A:5);
        A := A + 1
      UNTIL A > 0
    ELSE                   {  K = 0, 1, 2, 3, 4, 5  }
      WHILE (A MOD 2 = 0) DO
        BEGIN
          writeln (A);
          A := A + 1
        END;  {  of WHILE loop  }
    writeln
  END;  {  of FOR loop  }
```

*9. Write a program fragment that reads reals from a data file, counts the number of positive reals, and accumulates their sum.

10. Write a program that counts all the periods in a data file.

*11. Write a program that reproduces a data file but omits all blanks.

12. Given two integers, A and B, A is a divisor of B if B **MOD** $A = 0$. Write a complete program that reads a positive integer B from a data file and then prints all the positive divisors of B.

Focus on Program Design: Case Study

Printing Prime Numbers

This problem on printing prime numbers was chosen because it illustrates several concepts studied in this chapter. Specifically, the problem is to write a program that accepts a positive integer as input and then prints all primes less than or equal to the integer read. Thus, if the number read is 17, typical output would be

```
------------------------------------------------

          The number is 17.  The prime numbers
          less than or equal to 17 are:

                          2
                          3
                          5
                          7
                         11
                         13
                         17
```

The solution to this problem requires the combined use of repetition and selection. Nested repetition with different kinds of loops is also used. The algorithmic development utilizes several mathematical properties of divisors of integers. This particular problem is very appropriate for discussing algorithm efficiency. Input is from a data file, so a **WHILE NOT eof DO** loop is used as the main loop for the body of the program.

Note the mathematical property that a number K is prime if it has no divisors (other than 1) less than its square root. Thus, when we check for divisors, it is only necessary to check up to **sqrt**(K). Also note that, by definition, 1 is not prime.

A first-level pseudocode for this problem is

WHILE NOT eof DO
1. Get a number
2. **IF** Number is 1 **THEN**
   2.1 Print message for 1
   ELSE
   2.2 Process the number

A structure chart for this problem is given in Figure 6.4. Module specifications for the main modules are

1. Get Data Module
   Data received: None
   Information returned: A positive integer
   Logic: Read an integer from the data file.

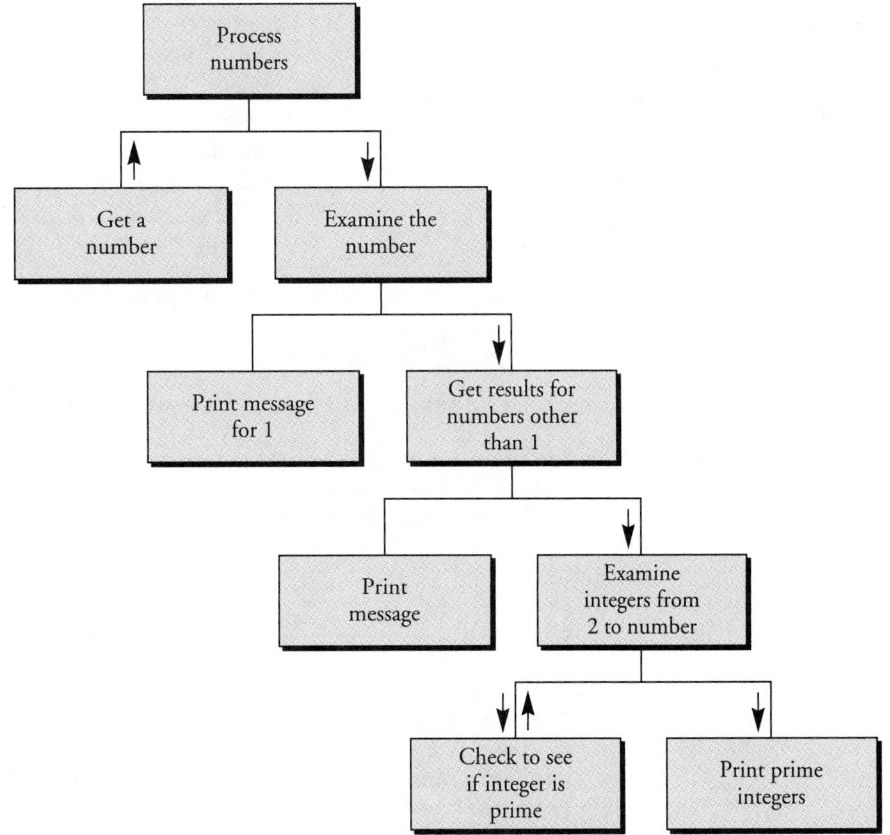

◆ Figure 6.4

Structure chart for **PROGRAM** ListPrimes

2. Examine the Number Module
   Data received: The integer read
   Information returned: None
   Logic: **IF** the number is 1 **THEN** print a message.
   ELSE
   Print a message
   FOR Candidate := 2 **TO** Number **DO**
   Check Candidate for a prime number.
   IF Candidate is prime **THEN** print it.

Step 2.2 of the pseudocode can be refined to

2.2 Process the number
  2.2.1 Print message
  2.2.2 Check for primes less than or equal to number

Step 2.2.2 can then be refined to

2.2.2 **FOR** Candidate := 2 **TO** Number **DO**
  2.2.2.1 Check to see if Candidate is prime
  2.2.2.2 **IF** Candidate is prime **THEN**
  print Candidate in list of primes

A complete pseudocode solution for this problem is

WHILE NOT eof DO
1. Get a number
2. **IF** Number is 1 **THEN**
   2.1 Print a message for 1
   ELSE
   2.2 Process the number
     2.2.1 Print message
     2.2.2 **FOR** Candidate := 2 **TO** Number **DO**
       2.2.2.1 Check to see if Candidate is prime
       2.2.2.2 **IF** Candidate is prime **THEN**
       print Candidate in list of primes

A complete program for this problem follows. This has been run using the input file

10 ■	17 ■	1 ■	25 ■	2 ■	■

```
PROGRAM ListPrimes (input, output);

{  This program reads positive integers from an input file and then   }
{  lists prime numbers less than or equal to each number read.         }
{  Note how loops are featured.                                        }

CONST
  Skip = ' ';
  Dashes = '----------------------------------------------';

VAR
  Candidate,                 {  Loop index variable                 }
  Divisor,                   {  Possible divisor of a number        }
  Number : integer;          {  Integer read from input             }
  Prime : boolean;           {  Boolean variable used in prime check }
  LimitForCheck : real;      {  Holds final value in FOR loop       }
```

```
BEGIN  { Program }
  WHILE NOT eof DO
    BEGIN
      readln (Number);
      IF Number = 1 THEN

        { Print a message for #1 }
        BEGIN
          writeln;
          writeln (Skip:10, Dashes);
          writeln;
          writeln (Skip:20, '1 is not prime by definition.')
        END  { of IF...THEN option }

      ELSE
        BEGIN
          writeln;
          writeln (Skip:10, Dashes);
          writeln;
          writeln (Skip:20, 'The number is ', Number,
                   '.  The prime numbers');
          writeln (Skip:20, 'less than or equal to ', Number, ' are:');
          writeln;

          { Check all integers from 2 to Number }
          FOR Candidate := 2 TO Number DO
            BEGIN
              Prime := true;
              Divisor := 2;
              LimitForCheck := sqrt(Candidate);

              { See if Candidate is prime }
              WHILE (Divisor <= LimitForCheck) AND Prime DO
                IF Candidate MOD Divisor = 0 THEN
                  Prime := false          { Candidate has a divisor }
                ELSE
                  Divisor := Divisor + 1;
              IF Prime THEN               { Print in list of primes }
                writeln (Candidate:35)
            END  { of FOR loop }
        END  { of ELSE option }
    END  { of WHILE loop }
END.  { of program }
```

The output for this program is as follows:

```
          ----------------------------------------------------

                    The number is 10.  The prime numbers
                    less than or equal to 10 are:

                                  2
                                  3
                                  5
                                  7

          ----------------------------------------------------
```

```
          The number is 17.  The prime numbers
          less than or equal to 17 are:

                         2
                         3
                         5
                         7
                        11
                        13
                        17
----------------------------------------------------

          1 is not prime by definition.

----------------------------------------------------

          The number is 25.  The prime numbers
          less than or equal to 25 are:

                         2
                         3
                         5
                         7
                        11
                        13
                        17
                        19
                        23
----------------------------------------------------

          The number is 2.  The prime numbers
          less than or equal to 2 are:

                         2
```

More efficient algorithms do exist. However, the purpose of this program is to see how loops can be used to solve a problem.

Running and Debugging Hints

1. Most errors involving loops are not compilation errors. Thus, not until you try to run the program will you be able to detect most errors.
2. Remember to include **BEGIN** and **END** as part of a compound statement in the body of **FOR . . . TO . . . DO** and **WHILE . . . DO** loops.
3. A syntax error that will not be detected by the compiler is a semicolon after a **WHILE . . . DO.** The fragment

(continued)

```
WHILE NOT eof DO;
  BEGIN
    readln (A);
    writeln (A)
  END;
```

is incorrect and will not get past

```
WHILE NOT eof DO;
```

The misplaced semicolon causes repetition of the null statement. Note that this is an infinite loop.

4. Carefully check your data file when using loops to input data. Be sure your lines are carefully formatted, you have been careful with blank spaces at the end of a line, and you have used **eof** and **readln** whenever possible.
5. Carefully check entry conditions for each loop.
6. Carefully check exit conditions for each loop. Make sure the loop is exited (not infinite) and that you have the correct number of repetitions.
7. Loop entry, execution, and exit can be checked by:
   a. Pencil-and-paper check on initial and final values
   b. Count of the number of repetitions
   c. Use of debugging **writeln**s
      i. Boolean condition prior to loop
      ii. Variables inside loop
      iii. Values of the counter in loop
      iv. Boolean values inside the loop
      v. Values after loop is exited
8. Infinite loops may cause a system-level error. Such an error may cause the loss of source code unless it has been saved before execution of the program.

Summary

Key Terms

accumulator
counter
data validation
decrement
fixed repetition (iterated) loop
index
infinite loop
nested loop
posttest (exit-controlled) loop
pretest condition
pretest (entrance-controlled) loop
priming read
sentinel value
variable condition loop

Key Terms (optional)

input assertion
loop invariant
loop variant
loop verification
output assertion

Keywords

DO
DOWNTO
FOR
REPEAT
TO
UNTIL
WHILE

Key Concepts

- The following table provides a comparison summary of the three repetition structures discussed in this chapter.

Traits of Loops	FOR . . . TO . . . DO Loop	WHILE . . . DO Loop	REPEAT . . . UNTIL Loop
Pretest loop	Yes	Yes	No
Posttest loop	No	No	Yes
BEGIN . . . END for compound statements	Required	Required	Not required
Repetition	Fixed	Not fixed	Not fixed
Loop index	Yes	No	No
Index automatically incremented	Yes	No	No
Boolean expression used	No	Yes	Yes

- A fixed repetition loop (**FOR . . . TO . . . DO**) is to be used when you know exactly how many times something is to be repeated. The basic form for a **FOR . . . TO . . . DO** loop is

```
FOR <index> := <initial value> TO <final value> DO
  <statement>
```

or

```
FOR <index> := <initial value> TO <final value> DO
  BEGIN
    <statement 1>;
    <statement 2>;
        .
        .
        .
    <statement n>
  END
```

After the loop is finished, the value of the index variable may become unassigned. Program control is transferred to the first executable statement following the loop.

- A sentinel value is a special value that signifies the end of a set of data. These are typically used for variable repetition loops.
- A **WHILE . . . DO** loop is a pretest loop that can have a variable loop control; a typical loop is

```
WHILE NOT <sentinel value> DO
  BEGIN
    readln (Score);
    Sum := Sum + Score;
    Count := Count + 1
  END;  {  of WHILE loop  }
```

- A counter is a variable whose purpose is to indicate how often the body of a loop is executed.
- An accumulator is a variable that sums values.
- An infinite **WHILE . . . DO** loop results when a **true** loop control condition is never changed to **false.**
- **WHILE NOT eoln DO** is a typical Boolean condition used to detect when the end of a data line is encountered.
- **WHILE NOT eof DO** is a typical Boolean condition used to detect when the end of a data file is encountered.
- A posttest loop has a Boolean condition checked after the loop body has been completed.
- A **REPEAT . . . UNTIL** loop is a posttest loop; a typical loop is

```
REPEAT
  readln (Num);
  Sum := Sum + Num;
  Count := Count + 1
UNTIL eof;
```

- **FOR** loops can always be rewritten as equivalent **REPEAT . . . UNTIL** or **WHILE . . . DO** loops.
- **REPEAT . . . UNTIL** loops can always be rewritten as **WHILE . . . DO** loops.
- **REPEAT . . . UNTIL** and **WHILE . . . DO** are variable control loops; **FOR** is a fixed control loop.
- **WHILE . . . DO** and **FOR** are pretest loops; **REPEAT . . . UNTIL** is a posttest loop.
- Any one of these loops can be nested within any other of the loops.
- Indenting each loop is important for program readability.
- Several levels of nesting make the logic of a program difficult to follow.
- Loops and conditionals are frequently used together. Careful program design will facilitate writing code in which these concepts are integrated; typical forms are

```
WHILE <condition 1> DO
  BEGIN
    .
    .
    .
    IF <condition 2> THEN
      .
      .
      .
    ELSE
      .
      .
      .
    .
    .
    .
  END;  {  of WHILE loop  }
```

and

```
IF <condition> THEN
  BEGIN
    .
    .
    .
    FOR <index> := <initial value> TO <final value> DO
      BEGIN
        .
        .
        .
      END;  {  of FOR loop  }
    .
    .
    .
  END  {  of IF...THEN option  }
ELSE
  .
  .
  .
```

Chapter Review Exercises

In Exercises 1–12, indicate if the statement is valid or invalid. If invalid, explain why.

1. `FOR K := 1 TO 10 DO`
2. `FOR J = 1 TO 5 STEP 2 DO`
3. `FOR J := 10 TO 1 DO`
4. `FOR X := 1.0 TO 3.0 DO`
5. `FOR C := 'A' TO 'Z' DO`
6. `FOR K := A DOWNTO B DO`
7. `J := 1 TO 10 DO`
8. `WHILE J := 1 DO`
9. `WHILE M = 1.5 DO`
10. `WHILE X <> 'A' DO`
11. `WHILE K := 1 TO 10 DO`
12. `WHILE BooleanVariable DO`

For Exercises 13–16, write a program to print a table of integers, their squares, and their square roots using integers running from 1 to 25.

13. Use a **FOR . . . TO . . . DO** loop.
14. Use a **FOR . . . DOWNTO . . . DO** loop.
15. Use a **WHILE . . . DO** loop.
16. Use a **REPEAT . . . UNTIL** loop.

17. Write a program that uses **FOR** loops to produce the following pattern.

18. Use nested loops to produce the following numbering.

```
1

1
2

1
2
3

1
2
3
4
```

19. Is it possible to execute a **FOR** loop without ever continuing into the statements that are inside the loop? Is this also true of **WHILE . . . DO** loops? **REPEAT . . . UNTIL** loops?
20. Brian wants the following program segment to print a list of numbers and their cubes. What happens when it is executed? Can you correct it for him (if necessary)?

```
FOR K := 1 TO 10 DO;
  Z := K * K * K;
  writeln (K:10, Z:10);
```

For Exercises 21 and 22, rewrite Example 6.1 from Section 6.2. Allow the chart length to be entered interactively.

21. Using a **WHILE . . . DO** loop.
22. Using a **REPEAT . . . UNTIL** loop.
23. Explain why it is important to use proper indentation, blank lines, and comments when writing programs that involve loops.

Programming Problems

■ 1. The Caswell Catering and Convention Service (Problem 7, Chapter 4 and Problem 14, Chapter 5) wants you to upgrade their program so they can use it for all of their customers. Modify it to run with an unknown number of customers.

2. Modify your program for a service station owner **(Focus on Program Design: Case Study 5.2)** so that it can be used for an unknown number of customers. Your output should include the number of customers and all other pertinent items in a daily summary.

■ 3. Modify the Community Hospital program (Problem 17, Chapter 5) so that it can be run with data containing information for all patients leaving the hospital in one day. Include appropriate bad data checks and daily summary items.

4. The greatest common divisor (GCD) of two integers *a* and *b* is a positive integer *c* such that *c* divides *a*, *c* divides *b*, and for any other common divisor *d* of *a* and *b*, *d* is less than or equal to *c*. (For example, the GCD of 18 and 45 is 9.)

   One method of finding the GCD of two positive integers (*a*, *b*) is to begin with the smaller (*a*) and see if it is a divisor of the larger (*b*). If it is, then the smaller is the GCD. If it is not, find the next largest divisor of *a* and see if it is a divisor of *b*. Continue this process until you find a divisor of both *a* and *b*. This is the GCD of *a* and *b*.

   Write an interactive program that will accept two positive integers as input and then print out their GCD. Enhance your output by printing all divisors of *a* that do not divide *b*. A sample run could produce

```
Enter two positive integers.
42 72

The divisors of 42 that do not divide 72 are:

    42
    21
    14
     7

The GCD of 42 and 72 is 6.
```

5. The least common multiple (LCM) of two positive integers *a* and *b* is a positive integer *c* such that *c* is a multiple of both *a* and *b* and for any other multiple *m* of *a* and *b*, *c* is a divisor of *m*. (For example, the LCM of 12 and 8 is 24.)

   Write an interactive program that allows the user to enter two positive integers and then print the LCM. The program should guard against bad data and should allow the user the option of "trying another pair" or quitting.

6. A perfect number is a positive integer such that the sum of the proper divisors equals the number. Thus, 28 = 1 + 2 + 4 + 7 + 14 is a perfect number. If the sum of the divisors is less than the number, it is deficient. If the sum exceeds the number, it is abundant.
   a. Write an interactive program that allows the user to enter a positive integer and then displays the result indicating whether the number entered is perfect, deficient, or abundant.
   b. Write another interactive program that allows the user to enter a positive integer *N* and then displays all perfect numbers less than or equal to *N*.

   Your programs should guard against bad data and should allow the user the option of entering another integer or quitting.

7. In these days of increased awareness of automobile mileage, more motorists are computing their miles per gallon (mpg) than ever before. Write a program that will perform these computations for a traveler. Data for the program will be entered on lines indicated by the following table:

Odometer Reading	Gallons of Fuel Purchased
18828(start)	—
19240	9.7
19616	10.2
19944	8.8
20329	10.1
20769(finish)	10.3

The program should compute the mpg for each tank and the cumulative mpg each time the tank is filled up. Your output should produce a chart with the following headings:

```
Odometer  Odometer  Fuel    Miles   Fuel    Miles   Mpg     Mpg
(begin)   (end)     (tank)  (tank)  (trip)  (trip)  (tank)  (trip)
```

8. Parkside's Other Triangle is generated from two positive integers, one for the size and one for the seed. For example,

Size 6, Seed 1

```
1 2 4 7 2 7
  3 5 8 3 8
    6 9 4 9
      1 5 1
        6 2
          3
```

Size 5, Seed 3

```
3 4 6 9 4
  5 7 1 5
    8 2 6
      3 7
        8
```

Size gives the number of columns. Seed specifies the starting value for column 1. Column n contains n values. The successive values are obtained by adding 1 to the previous value. When 9 is reached, the next value becomes 1.

Write a program that reads pairs of positive integers and produces Parkside's Other Triangle for each pair. The check for bad data should include checking for seeds between 1 and 9 inclusive.

9. Modify the sewage, water, and sanitation problem (Problem 19, Chapter 5) so that it can be used with data containing appropriate information for all residents of the community.

10. Modify the program for the Lucky Wildcat Well Corporation (Problem 20, Chapter 5) so that it can be run on data containing information about all of Al Derrick's wells. The first line of data consists of a positive integer that represents the total number of wells drilled.

11. Modify the program concerning the Mathematical Association of America (Problem 21, Chapter 5). There will be 50 official state delegates attending the next summer national meeting. The new data will contain the two-letter

state abbreviation for each delegate. Output should include one column with the state abbreviation and another with the amount reimbursed.

12. In Fibonacci's sequence, 0, 1, 1, 2, 3, 5, 8, 13, . . . , the first two terms are 0 and 1 and each successive term is formed by adding the previous two terms. Write a program that will read positive integers and then print the number of terms indicated by each integer read. Be sure to test your program with data that include the integers 1 and 2.

■ 13. Mr. Lae Z. Programmer is at it again. Now that you have written a program to compute the grade for one student in his class (Problems 5, 22, and 23, Chapter 5), he wants you to modify this program so it can be used for the entire class. He will help you by making the first line of data be a positive integer representing the number of students in the class. Your new version should compute an overall class average and the number of students receiving each letter grade.

■ 14. Modify the Pentagon visitor parking lot problem (Problem 26, Chapter 5) so that it can be used for all customers in one day. Time should be entered in military style as a four-digit integer. The lot opens at 0600 (6:00 A.M.) and closes at 2200 (10:00 P.M.). Your program should include appropriate summary information.

■ 15. The Natural Pine Furniture Company (Problem 2, Chapter 4) now wants you to refine your program so that it will print a one-week pay report for each employee. You do not know how many employees there are, but you do know that all information for each employee is on a separate line. Each line of input will contain the employee's initials, the number of hours worked, and the hourly rate. You are to use the constant definition section for the following:

Federal withholding tax rate	18%
State withholding tax rate	4.5%
Hospitalization	$25.65
Union dues	$ 7.85

Your output should include a report for each employee and a summary report for the company files.

16. Orlando Tree Service, Incorporated, offers the following services and rates to its customers:

a. tree removal	$500 per tree
b. tree trimming	$80 per hour
c. stump grinding	$25 plus $2 per inch for each stump whose diameter exceeds ten inches. The $2 charge is only for the diameter inches in excess of ten.

Write a complete program to allow the manager, Mr. Sorwind, to provide an estimate when he bids on a job. Your output should include a listing of each separate charge and a total. A 10 percent discount is given for any job whose total exceeds $1,000. A typical input file is

```
R 7 T 6.5 G 8■8 10 12 14 15 15 20 25■
```

where "R," "T," and "G" are codes for removal, trimming, and grinding, respectively. The integer following "G" represents the number of stumps to be ground. The next line of integers represents the diameters of stumps to be ground.

17. A standard science experiment is to drop a ball and see how high it bounces. Once the "bounciness" of the ball has been determined, the ratio gives a bounciness index. For example, if a ball dropped from a height of 10 feet bounces 6 feet high, the index is 0.6 and the total distance traveled by the ball is 16 feet after one bounce. If the ball continues to bounce, the distance after two bounces will be 10 ft + 6 ft + 6 ft + 3.6 ft = 25.6 ft. Note the distance traveled for each successive bounce is the distance to the floor plus 0.6 of that distance as the ball comes back up.

    Write an interactive program that lets the user enter the initial height of the ball and the number of times the ball is allowed to continue bouncing. Output should be the total distance traveled by the ball. At some point in this process, the distance traveled by the ball becomes negligible. Use the **CONST** section to define a "negligible" distance (for example, 0.00001 inches). Terminate the computing when the distance becomes negligible. When this stage is reached, include the number of bounces as part of the output.

18. Write a program that prints a calendar for one month. Input consists of an integer specifying the first day of the month (1 = Sunday) and an integer specifying how many days are in a month.

■ 19. An amortization table shows the rate at which a loan is paid off. It contains monthly entries showing the interest paid that month, the principal paid, and the remaining balance. Given the amount of money borrowed (the principal), the annual interest rate, and the amount the person wishes to repay each month, print an amortization table. (Be certain that the payment desired is larger than the first month's interest.) Your table should stop when the loan is paid off, and should be printed with the following heads.

```
MONTH NUMBER   INTEREST PAID   PRINCIPAL PAID   BALANCE
```

20. Computers use the binary system, which is based on powers of 2. Write a program that prints out the first 15 powers of 2 beginning with 2 to the zero power (2^0). Print your output in headed columns.

21. Print a list of the positive integers less than 500 that are divisible by either 5 or 7. When the list is complete, print a count of the number of integers that were found.

22. Write a program that reads in 20 real numbers, then prints the average of the positive numbers and the average of the negative numbers.

■ 23. In 1626, the Dutch settlers purchased Manhattan Island from the Indians. According to legend, the purchase price was $24. Suppose that the Indians had invested this amount at 3 percent annual interest compounded quarterly. If the money had earned interest from the start of 1626 to the end of last year, how much money would the Indians have in the bank today? (*Hint:* Use nested loops for the compounding.)

24. Write a program to print the sum of the odd integers from 1 to 99.

25. The theory of relativity holds that as an object moves, it gets smaller. The new length of the object can be determined from the formula:

$$\text{New length} = \text{Original length} * \sqrt{1 - B^2}$$

where B^2 is the percentage of the speed of light at which the object is moving, entered in decimal form. Given the length of an object, print its new length for speeds ranging from 0 to 99 percent of the speed of light. Print the output in the following columns:

```
Percent of Light Speed     Length
----------------------     ------
```

26. Mr. Christian uses a 90 percent, 80 percent, 70 percent, 60 percent grading scale. Given a list of test scores, print out the number of As, Bs, Cs, Ds, and Fs on the test. Terminate the list of scores with a sentinel value.

27. The mathematician Gottfried Leibniz determined a formula for estimating the value of π.

```
pi          1   1   1   1   1
-- = 1 - - + - - - + - - - + . . .
4           3   5   7   9  11
```

Evaluate the first 200 terms of this formula and print its approximation of π.

28. In a biology experiment, Carey finds that a sample of an organism doubles in population every 12 hours. If she starts with 1,000 organisms, in how many hours will she have one million?

29. Pascal does not have a mathematical operator that permits raising a number to a power. It is easy to write a program to perform this function, however. Given an integer to represent the base number and a positive integer to represent the power desired, write a program that prints the number raised to that power.

30. Mr. Thomas has negotiated a salary schedule for his new job. He will be paid one cent the first day, with the daily rate doubling each day. Write a program that will find his total earnings for 30 days. Print your results in a table set up as follows:

```
Day Number     Daily Salary     Total Salary
     1             .01              .01
     2             .02              .03
     3
     .
     .
     .
    30
```

31. Write a program to print the perimeter and area of rectangles using all combinations of lengths and widths running from 1 foot to 10 feet in increments of 1 foot. Print the output in headed columns.

32. Teachers in most school districts are paid on a salary schedule that provides a salary based on their number of years of teaching experience. Suppose that a beginning teacher in the Babbage School District is paid $21,000 the first year. For each year of experience after this up to 12 years, a 4 percent increase over the preceding value is received. Write a program that prints a salary schedule for teachers in this district. The output should appear as follows:

```
Years Experience            Salary
----------------            ------
       0                   $21,000
       1                   $21,840
       2                   $22,714
       3                   $23,622
       .
       .
       .
      12
```

(Actually, most teachers' salary schedules are more complex than this. As an additional problem, you might like to find out how the salary schedule is determined in your school district and write a program to print the salary schedule.)

33. The Euclidean algorithm can be used to find the greatest common divisor (GCD) of two positive integers (n_1, n_2). For example, if $n_1 = 72$ and $n_2 = 42$, you can use this algorithm in the following manner.

(1) Divide the larger (72) by the smaller (42):

$$72 = 42 * 1 + 30$$

(2) Divide the divisor (42) by the remainder (30):

$$42 = 30 * 1 + 12$$

(3) Repeat this process until you get a remainder of zero:

$$30 = 12 * 2 + 6$$
$$12 = 6 * 2 + 0$$

The last nonzero remainder is the GCD of n_1 and n_2.

Write an interactive program that lets the user enter two integers and then prints out each step in the process of using the Euclidean algorithm to find their GCD.

34. Cramer's rule for solving a system of equations was given in Problem 12, Chapter 4 and was enhanced in Problem 30, Chapter 5 by guarding against division by zero. Add a further enhancement to your program by using a loop to guarantee that the coefficients and constants entered by the user are precisely the ones intended.

35. Gaussian elimination is another method used to solve systems of equations. To illustrate, if the system is

$$x - 2y = 1$$
$$2x + y = 7$$

Gaussian elimination starts with the augmented matrix

$$\left[\begin{array}{cc|c} 1 & -2 & 1 \\ 2 & 1 & 7 \end{array}\right]$$

and produces the identity matrix on the left side

$$\left[\begin{array}{cc|c} 1 & 0 & 3 \\ 0 & 1 & 1 \end{array}\right]$$

At this stage, the solution to the system is seen to be $x = 3$ and $y = 1$.

Write an interactive program in which the user enters coefficients for a system of two equations containing two variables. The program should then solve the system and display the answer. Your program should include the following:

(1) A check for bad data

(2) A solvable system check .

(3) A display of partial results as the matrix operations are performed

36. Reexamine the output for the **Focus on Program Design: Case Study** in this chapter. In particular, note that the prime numbers less than 10 are 2, 3, 5, and 7. Using this list, 10 can be written as 3 + 7, the sum of primes 3 and 7. It is conjectured that this is possible for all positive, even integers greater than 2. (For example, 24 = 17 + 7.)

   a. Write an interactive program that accepts a positive, even integer as input and then displays that number as the sum of two primes. Your program should validate input and supply an appropriate message for invalid data. The program should also give the user the option of repeating the process if desired.

   b. Enhance the program in (a) by displaying a list of consecutive, positive, even integers written as the sum of primes. Input should consist of the number of lines desired. Thus, for input of Num = 5, output would be

```
 4 = 2 + 2
 6 = 3 + 3
 8 = 3 + 5
10 = 3 + 7
12 = 5 + 7
```

37. A Pythagorean triple consists of three integers A, B, and C such that $A^2 + B^2 = C^2$. For example, 3, 4, 5 is such a triple because $3^2 + 4^2 = 5^2$. These triples can be generated by positive integers m and n ($m > n$), where $a = m^2 - n^2$, $b = 2mn$, and $c = m^2 + n^2$. These triples will be primitive (with no common factors) if m and n have no common factors and are not both odd. Write a program that allows the user to enter a value for m and then prints out all possible primitive Pythagorean triples such that $m > n$. For the input value of $m = 5$, typical output is

```
m     n     a     b     c      a*a      b*b      c*c
------------------------------------------------------
2     1     3     4     5        9       16       25
3     2     5    12    13       25      144      169
4     1    15     8    17      225       64      289
4     3     7    24    25       49      576      625
5     2    21    20    29      441      400      841
5     4     9    40    41       81     1600     1681
```

38. The **Focus on Program Design: Case Study** problem in this chapter determines whether or not an integer is prime by checking for divisors less than or equal to the square root of the number. The check starts with 2 and increments trial divisors by 1 each time, as seen by the code

```
Prime := true;
Divisor := 2;
LimitForCheck := sqrt(Candidate);
WHILE (Divisor <= LimitForCheck) AND Prime DO
  IF Candidate MOD Divisor = 0 THEN
    Prime := false
  ELSE
    Divisor := Divisor + 1;
```

Other methods can be used to determine whether or not an integer N is prime. For example, you may

a. Check divisors from 2 to $N - 1$, incrementing by 1.
b. Check divisors from 2 to $(N - 1) / 2$, incrementing by 1.
c. Check divisor 2, 3, 5, . . ., $(N - 1) / 2$, incrementing by 2.
d. Check divisor 2, 3, 5, . . ., sqrt(N), incrementing by 2.

Write a program that allows the user to choose between these options in order to compare the relative efficiency of different algorithms.

39. The prime factorization of a positive integer is the positive integer written as the product of primes. For example, the prime factorization of 72 is

$$72 = 2 * 3 * 3 * 4$$

Write a program that allows the user to enter a positive integer and then displays the prime factorization of the integer. Enhancements to this program could include an error trap for bad data and a loop for repeated trials.

40. Several interesting mathematical properties can be determined by looking at multiplication tables in modular number systems with bases of less than 10. The product of two numbers in a system is said to be the remainder when the normal product (base 10) is divided by the new base. To illustrate, the multiplication table in base 4 is

	0	1	2	3
0	0	0	0	0
1	0	1	2	3
2	0	2	0	2
3	0	3	2	1

Write an interactive program that allows the user to choose a base between 2 and 9, inclusive, and then displays the multiplication table for that base. Have the program guard against bases being entered that are less than 2 or greater than 9.

Communication in Practice

1. Using a completed program from this chapter, remove all documentation and replace all identifiers with one- or two-letter identifiers. Exchange this version with another student who has prepared a similar version of a different program. Add documentation and change identifiers to meaningful identifiers. Compare your results with the text version of the program. Discuss the similarities and differences with your class.
2. As you might expect, teachers of computer science do not agree as to whether a **REPEAT . . . UNTIL** loop or a **WHILE . . . DO** loop is the preferred variable control loop in Pascal. Interview several computer science teachers at your school to determine what preference (if any) they have regarding these two forms of repetition. Prepare a class report based on your interviews. Include the advantages and disadvantages of each form of repetition.
3. Examine the repetition constructs of at least five other programming languages. Prepare a report that compares and contrasts repetition in each of the languages. Be sure to include information such as which languages provide for both fixed and variable repetition and which languages have more than one kind of variable repetition. Which language appears to have the most desirable form of repetition? Include your rationale for this decision in your report.
4. Examine some old computer science texts and talk to some computer science teachers who worked with the early languages to see how repetition was achieved in the "early days." Prepare a brief chronological chart for class display that depicts the various stages in the development of repetition in computer programming.

Chapter 7

Subprograms: Writing Procedures and Functions

Chapter Outline

Recall the process of solving a problem by the stepwise refinement of tasks into subtasks, which was discussed in Section 2.1. This top-down design method is especially suitable when writing Pascal programs to solve problems using subprograms.

This concept is not difficult to understand. A **subprogram** is a program within a program and is provided by most programming languages. Each subprogram should complete some task, the nature of which can range from simple to complex.

7.1 Program Design

Objectives

- to understand the concepts of modularity and bottom-up testing
- to be aware of the use of structured programming

Modularity

We have previously discussed and illustrated the process of solving a problem by top-down design. Using this method, we divide the main task into major subtasks, and then continue to divide the subtasks (stepwise refinement) into smaller subtasks until all subtasks can be easily performed. Once an algorithm for solving a problem has been developed using top-down design, the programmer then writes code to translate the general solution into a Pascal program.

As you have seen, code written to perform one well-defined subtask is referred to as a module. One should be able to design, code, and test each module in a program independently from the rest of the program. In this sense, a module is a subprogram containing all definitions and declarations needed to perform the indicated subtask. Everything required for the subtask (but not needed in other parts of the program) can be created in the subprogram. Consequently, the definitions and declarations have meaning only when the module is being used.

A program that has been created using modules to perform various tasks is said to possess **modularity.** In general, modular programs are easier to test, debug, and correct than programs that are not modular because each independent module can be tested by running it from a test driver. Then, once the modules are running correctly, they can become part of a longer program. This independent testing of modules is referred to as **bottom-up testing.**

A **subprogram** is a program within a program. Procedures and functions are subprograms.

Modularity is the property possessed by a program that is written using modules.

Bottom-up testing is the method of independent testing of modules.

Structured Programming

Structured programming is the process of developing a program where emphasis is placed on the correspondence between independent modules. Connections between these modules are specified in parameter lists and are usually controlled by the main driver or program. Structured programming is especially suitable to large programs being worked on by teams. By carefully designing the modules and specifying what information is to be received by and returned from the module, a team of programmers can independently develop its module and then have it connect to the complete program.

This chapter is devoted to seeing how subprograms can be written to accomplish specific tasks. There are two types of subprograms in standard Pascal: procedures and functions. First, we examine the writing of procedures; then we learn how to write user-defined functions (we discussed built-in functions in Section 3.5).

7.2 Procedures without Parameters

Objectives

- to be aware of some uses for procedures
- to be aware of differences in procedures
- to understand the form of a procedure
- to be able to use a procedure in a program

Structured programming is programming that parallels a solution to a problem achieved by top-down design.

A **procedure** is a subprogram designed to perform a specific task as part of a larger program. Procedures are not limited to returning a single value to the main program.

A **procedure** is a subprogram designed to perform a specific task as part of a larger program. Two significant uses of procedures are to enhance the top-down design philosophy of problem solving and to avoid having to write repeated segments of code.

Procedures facilitate problem solving. For instance, if the pseudocode design for the solution to a problem is

1. Get the data
2. Process the data
3. Print the results

a procedure can be written for each of these tasks and the program can then call each procedure as needed. The idea of using a procedure to implement a line of pseudocode is very important and, as you develop more programming skills, procedures will become an integral part of how you write a program.

Another use of procedures is for the repetition of several lines of code throughout a program. A procedure can be written using several lines of code; then whenever that task is needed, a single call to the procedure is sufficient.

Form and Syntax

Now let's see how a procedure is written. Basically, a procedure is a program and, as such, it has the same divisions as a complete program.

Procedure heading →

Declaration section (optional) →

Executable section →

The procedure heading must contain the reserved word **PROCEDURE** followed by the procedure name, which can be any valid identifier. Since no parameters are used at this point, the form for a procedure heading is

PROCEDURE <procedure name>

A Note of Interest

Structured Programming

From 1950 to the early 1970s, programs were designed and written on a linear basis. A program written and designed on such a basis can be called an unstructured program. Structured programming, on the other hand, organizes a program around separate, semi-independent modules that are linked together by a single sequence of simple commands.

In 1964, mathematicians Corrado Bohm and Guiseppe Jacopini proved that any program logic, regardless of complexity, can be expressed by using sequence, selection, and iteration. This result is termed the structure theorem. Combined with the efforts of Edger W. Dijkstra, applications of the structure theorem have led to a significant move toward structured programming and away from the use of **GOTO** statements. In fact, in a letter to the editor of Communications of the ACM, Volume 11, March 1968, Dijkstra states that the **GOTO** statement "should be abolished from all 'higher level' programming languages. . . . [The **GOTO** statement] is just too primitive; it is too much an invitation to make a mess of one's program."

Structured programming concepts were first applied to a large-scale data processing application in the IBM Corporation's "New York Times Project" from 1969 to 1971. Using these techniques, programmers posted productivity figures from four to six times higher than those of the average programmer. In addition, the error rate was a phenomenally low 0.0004 per line of coding.

It is important to develop the habit of using descriptive names for procedures. For example, if you are going to write a procedure to print a heading for the output, PrintHeader might be a good choice. This allows you to recognize the task the procedure is supposed to accomplish and makes the program more readable. Each of the following would be a reasonable, descriptive procedure heading:

```
PROCEDURE PrintHeader;          PROCEDURE ComputeTotalPoints;
PROCEDURE GetData;              PROCEDURE PrintScores;
PROCEDURE ComputeTax;           PROCEDURE PrintCourseInfo;
```

The declaration section of a procedure is identical to the declaration section of a program containing **CONST** and **VAR** subsections.

The executable section of a procedure resembles the executable section of a program in that it must start with the reserved word **BEGIN,** but it differs in a significant way: The **END** of a procedure is followed by a semicolon instead of a period. Thus, a procedure will have the following basic form:

```
PROCEDURE <procedure name>;

  CONST
    (list of constants)

  VAR
    (list of variables)

  BEGIN
    .
    .     (body of procedure)
    .
  END;
```

The syntax diagram for this is

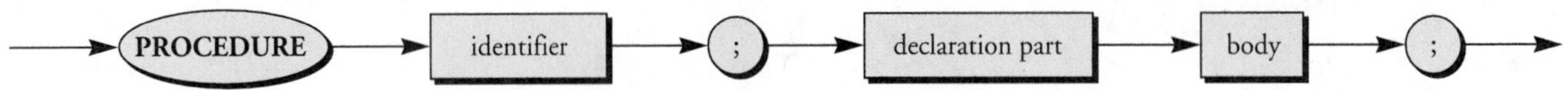

Constants and variables declared in a procedure can only be used within that procedure and are said to be local to that procedure.

Example 7.1

Let's write a program for Our Lady of Mercy Hospital. The program is to print a billing statement for each patient as the patient leaves the hospital. The following heading should appear on each statement:

```
/////////////////////////////////////////
/                                       /
/       Our Lady of Mercy Hospital      /
/       --------------------------      /
/                                       /
/           1306 Central City           /
/          Phone (416) 555-3333         /
/                                       /
/////////////////////////////////////////
```

The procedure that prints this heading is

```
PROCEDURE DisplayHeading;
  CONST
    Marks = '/////////////////////////////////////////';
    Edge = '/                                       /';
    Skip = ' ';
  BEGIN
    writeln;
    writeln (Skip:10, Marks);
    writeln (Skip:10, Edge);
    writeln (Skip:10, '/', Skip:7, 'Our Lady of Mercy Hospital', Skip:6, '/');
    writeln (Skip:10, '/', Skip:7, '--------------------------', Skip:6, '/');
    writeln (Skip:10, Edge);
    writeln (Skip:10, '/', Skip:11, '1306 Central City', Skip:11, '/');
    writeln (Skip:10, '/', Skip:10, 'Phone (416) 555-3333', Skip:9, '/');
    writeln (Skip:10, Edge);
    writeln (Skip:10, Marks);
    writeln
  END;  {  of PROCEDURE DisplayHeading  }
```

Placement in a Program

Procedures are an extension of the declaration section of the program. They are placed in the declaration section after the variable declaration subsection. Thus, a full program with a procedure has the following form:

```
PROGRAM <program name> (output);

CONST

VAR

PROCEDURE <procedure name>;

   CONST

   VAR

   BEGIN  {  PROCEDURE  }
     .
     .   (body of procedure)
     .
   END;  {  of PROCEDURE  }

BEGIN    {  Main program  }
  .
  .        (body of program)
  .
END.     {  of main program  }
```

Using procedures in a program can make a program harder to read unless you enhance the readability by using comments, blank lines, and indenting. You should develop a style with which you are comfortable. Most examples in this text will use the following style:

1. Procedures will be preceded and followed by a row of asterisks.
2. A comment section separated by blank lines will follow the procedure heading.
3. Except for the procedure heading, the procedure code will be indented.

Therefore, our general form for putting a procedure in a program will be

```
PROGRAM <program name> (output);

CONST

VAR

{*********************************************}

PROCEDURE <procedure name>;

   {  A brief description of the procedure  }

   CONST
                                   (continued)
```

```
    VAR

    BEGIN
       .
       .     (body of procedure)
       .
    END;  {  of PROCEDURE <procedure name>  }

  {********************************************}

  BEGIN  {  Main program  }
     .
     .     (body of main program)
     .
  END.  {  of main program  }
```

Calling a Procedure

Now that you know how to write a procedure and where it belongs in a program, you need to know how to call the procedure from the main program. Since no parameters will be used in procedures at this point, a procedure name as a statement in the main program will cause the procedure to be executed by the computer. For example, if PrintHeader is the name of a procedure,

```
BEGIN  {  Main program  }
  PrintHeader;
     .
     .  (remainder of program)
     .
END.  {  of main program  }
```

will cause the procedure PrintHeader to be executed first in the main program.

When a procedure name is encountered as a program statement, control of execution is transferred to the procedure. At that time, the procedure is run as a separate program and when the procedure is complete, control returns to the next statement in the main program following the call to the procedure. The following short program to call a procedure illustrates this control.

```
PROGRAM FirstProcedure (output);

{*************************************************************}

PROCEDURE PrintMessage;
  BEGIN
    writeln ('This is written from the procedure.':)
  END;  {  of PROCEDURE PrintMessage  }

{*************************************************************}

BEGIN  {  Main program  }
  writeln;
  writeln ('This is written from the main program.');
  writeln;
```

```
   PrintMessage;
   writeln
 END.  {  of main program  }
```

The output from this program is

```
   This is written from the main program.

   This is written from the procedure.
```

Example 7.2

As another example, let's construct a short program that calls a procedure several times. The procedure will print the message

```
   This is written by a procedure.
   Now return to the main program.
```

Furthermore, let's have the main program print a message that includes a count of how often the procedure is called. A pseudocode design could be

1. Initialize counter
2. Print message
3. Call procedure
4. Increment counter
5. Print message
6. Call procedure
7. Increment counter
8. Print message
9. Call procedure

The program for this design is

```
PROGRAM ProcedurePractice (output);

{  This program illustrates multiple calls to a procedure for       }
{  printing a message.                                              }

CONST
  Indent = ' ';
  LoopLimit = 3;

VAR
  Index : integer;

{*******************************************************************}

PROCEDURE PrintMessage;

  {  This procedure displays a two-line message every time it is   }
  {  called.                                                       }

  BEGIN
    writeln;
    writeln (Indent:20, 'This is written by a procedure.');
    writeln (Indent:20, 'Now return to the main program.');
```

```
    writeln
  END;  {  of PROCEDURE PrintMessage  }

{*******************************************************************}

BEGIN  {  Main program  }

  FOR Index := 1 TO LoopLimit DO
    BEGIN
      writeln (Indent:10, 'This is written from the main program.');
      writeln (Indent:10, 'It is call #', Index:3,
               ' to the procedure.');
      PrintMessage
    END  {  of FOR loop  }
END.  {  of main program  }
```

The output from this program is

```
This is written from the main program.
It is call #  1 to the procedure.

          This is written by a procedure.
          Now return to the main program.

This is written from the main program.
It is call #  2 to the procedure.

          This is written by a procedure.
          Now return to the main program.

This is written from the main program.
It is call #  3 to the procedure.

          This is written by a procedure.
          Now return to the main program.
```

Communication and Style Tips

If a constant is going to be used in several procedures, it could be declared in the constant definition section of the main program and then used by each subprogram. For example,

```
CONST
  Indent = ' ';
```

Multiple Procedures

You should now be able to write a procedure with no parameters, know where it belongs in a program, and be able to call it from the main body of the program. The next step is to use more than one procedure in a program. Each procedure is developed separately and listed sequentially after the variable declaration subsection of the main program. Thus, the basic program with multiple procedures appears as follows:

PROGRAM <program name> (**output**);

CONST

VAR

PROCEDURE <procedure name 1>;

PROCEDURE <procedure name 2>;

.
.
.

PROCEDURE <procedure name *n*>;

BEGIN { Main program }

.
.
.

END. { of main program }

These procedures can be called in any order and as often as needed. Just remember that when a procedure is called from the main program, control is transferred to the procedure, the procedure is executed, and control then returns to the next program statement. The following program illustrates the use of multiple procedures:

```
PROGRAM MultipleProcedures (output);

CONST
  Indent = ' ';

{*****************************************************}

PROCEDURE Message1;

  { This is procedure one }

  BEGIN
    writeln;
    writeln (Indent:10, 'This is from Procedure #1')
  END; { of PROCEDURE Message1 }

{*****************************************************}

PROCEDURE Message2;

  { This is procedure two }

  BEGIN
    writeln;
    writeln (Indent:10, 'This is from Procedure #2')
  END; { of PROCEDURE Message2 }
```

```
{*****************************************************}

PROCEDURE Message3;

  {  This is procedure three  }

  BEGIN
    writeln;
    writeln (Indent:10, 'This is from Procedure #3')
  END;  {  of PROCEDURE Message3  }

{*****************************************************}

BEGIN  {  Main program  }
  Message1;
  Message2;
  Message3;
  Message2;
  Message1;
  writeln
END.  {  of main program  }
```

The output from this program is

```
This is from Procedure #1

This is from Procedure #2

This is from Procedure #3

This is from Procedure #2

This is from Procedure #1
```

Using Procedures to Produce Output

We close this section with some examples using procedures to produce output. By learning how to write and use procedures in this very limited fashion, you should be better able to work with them when they become more complicated.

Example 7.3

Your computer science teacher wants course and program information to be included as part of the output of a program. Let's write a procedure that can be used to print this information. Sample output is

```
**************************************
*                                    *
*   Author:          Mary Smith      *
*   Course:          CPS-150         *
*   Assignment:      Program #3      *
*   Due Date:        September 18    *
*   Teacher:         Mr. Samson      *
*                                    *
**************************************
```

The procedure to do this is

```
PROCEDURE PrintInfo;
  CONST
    Indent = ' ';
  BEGIN
    writeln (Indent:30, '**************************************');
    writeln (Indent:30, '*                                    *');
    writeln (Indent:30, '*   Author:            Mary Smith    *');
    writeln (Indent:30, '*   Course:            CPS-150       *');
    writeln (Indent:30, '*   Assignment:        Program #3    *');
    writeln (Indent:30, '*   Due Date:          September 18  *');
    writeln (Indent:30, '*   Teacher:           Mr. Samson    *');
    writeln (Indent:30, '*                                    *');
    writeln (Indent:30, '**************************************')
  END;  {  of PROCEDURE PrintInfo  }
```

Example 7.4

As part of a program that computes and prints grades for each student in your class, you have been asked to write a procedure that produces a heading for each student report. Assume the following:

- The border for the class name starts in column 30
- Student Name starts in column 20
- Test Average starts in column 40
- Grade starts in column 55

The heading should appear as

```
                         *************************
                         *                       *
                         *   CPS 150     Pascal  *
                         *                       *
                         *************************

     Student Name          Test Average   Grade
     ------------          ------------   -----
```

A descriptive name for this procedure could be PrintHeader. With this information, the procedure could be written as follows:

```
PROCEDURE PrintHeader;

  {  This procedure prints a heading for each student as  }
  {  part of a class report.                              }

  CONST
    Skip = ' ';
  BEGIN
    writeln;
    writeln (Skip:29, '*************************');
    writeln (Skip:29, '*                       *');
    writeln (Skip:29, '*   CPS 150     Pascal  *');
    writeln (Skip:29, '*                       *');
    writeln (Skip:29, '*************************');
    writeln;
```

```
    write (Skip:19, 'Student Name');
    writeln (Skip:8, 'Test Average', Skip:3, 'Grade');
    write (Skip:19, '------------');
    writeln (Skip:8, '------------', Skip:3, '-----');
    writeln
  END;  {  of PROCEDURE PrintHeader  }
```

Focus on Program Design: Case Study 7.1

Airport Parking Lot Receipts

The Greater Metro Airport has hired you to write a program that will print a ticket for each parking lot customer. The parking lot authorities want each ticket to contain a suitable message and the amount to be paid on leaving the parking lot. A pseudocode design for this problem is

1. For each customer
   - 1.1 Assign amount due
   - 1.2 Print heading
   - 1.3 Print amount due
   - 1.4 Print closing message

We will write procedures for Steps 1.2 and 1.4 of this design. Each ticket will have the following heading:

```
Greater Metro Airport
     Parking Lot

       April 15
```

Each ticket will contain the following message concerning the charge for parking:

```
Your charge is $XX.XX
```

Each ticket will contain the following closing message:

```
     Thank you for using the
      Greater Metro Airport

     Please drive carefully
-----------------------------------
```

A procedure to print the heading is

```
PROCEDURE PrintHeader;

  {  This procedure prints a ticket heading  }

  CONST
    Date = 'April 15';
  BEGIN
    writeln;
    writeln (Indent:20, 'Greater Metro Airport');
    writeln (Indent:25, 'Parking Lot');
    writeln;
    writeln (Indent:27, Date);
    writeln
  END;  {  of PROCEDURE PrintHeader  }
```

A procedure to print the closing message is

```
PROCEDURE PrintMessage;

  {  This procedure prints a closing message  }

  BEGIN
    writeln;
    writeln (Indent:20, 'Thank you for using the');
    writeln (Indent:21, 'Greater Metro Airport');
    writeln;
    writeln (Indent:20, 'Please drive carefully');
    writeln (Indent:15, '----------------------------------');
    writeln
  END;  {  of PROCEDURE PrintMessage  }
```

A complete program for two customers follows. This can be modified later to accommodate several customers.

```
PROGRAM ParkingLot (input, output);

CONST
  Indent = ' ';

VAR
  Fee : real;

{*************************************************************************}

PROCEDURE PrintHeader;

  {  This procedure prints a ticket heading  }

  CONST
    Date = 'April 15';
  BEGIN
    writeln;
    writeln (Indent:20, 'Greater Metro Airport');
    writeln (Indent:25, 'Parking Lot');
    writeln;
    writeln (Indent:27, Date);
    writeln
  END;  {  of PROCEDURE PrintHeader  }

{*************************************************************************}

PROCEDURE PrintMessage;

  {  This procedure prints a closing message  }

  BEGIN
    writeln;
    writeln (Indent:20, 'Thank you for using the');
    writeln (Indent:21, 'Greater Metro Airport');
    writeln;
    writeln (Indent:20, 'Please drive carefully');
```

```
    writeln (Indent:15, '-----------------------------------');
    writeln
  END;  {  of PROCEDURE PrintMessage  }

{***************************************************************************}

BEGIN  {  Main program  }

  {  Process customer one  }
  writeln ('Enter amount due and press <Enter>.');
  readln (Fee);
  PrintHeader;
  writeln (Indent:20, 'Your charge is $', Fee:6:2);
  PrintMessage;

  {  Process customer two  }
  writeln ('Enter amount due and press <Enter>.');
  readln (Fee);
  PrintHeader;
  writeln (Indent:20, 'Your charge is $', Fee:6:2);
  PrintMessage
END.  {  of main program  }
```

The output from this program for each of two customers is

```
Enter amount due and press <Enter>.
5.75

                    Greater Metro Airport
                         Parking Lot

                           April 15

                    Your charge is $  5.75

                    Thank you for using the
                     Greater Metro Airport

                    Please drive carefully
               -----------------------------------

Enter amount due and press <Enter>.
8.00

                    Greater Metro Airport
                         Parking Lot

                           April 15

                    Your charge is $  8.00

                    Thank you for using the
                     Greater Metro Airport

                    Please drive carefully
               -----------------------------------
```

We can use procedures without parameters to do more than just print headings and closing messages. To illustrate, consider the following example.

Example 7.5

Interactive programming frequently requires the use of a menu to give the user a choice of options. For example, suppose you want a menu to be

```
Which of the following recipes do you wish to see?

  (T)acos
  (J)ambalaya
  (G)umbo
  (Q)uit

Enter the first letter and press <Enter>.
```

This screen message could then be written as a procedure menu, and the main program could use the **REPEAT . . . UNTIL** loop

```
REPEAT
  Menu;
  readln (Selection);
  CASE Selection OF
    'T' : Tacos;
    'J' : Jambalaya;
    'G' : Gumbo;
    'Q' : GoodbyeMessage
  END  {  of CASE Selection  }
UNTIL Selection = 'Q';
```

where Tacos, Jambalaya, Gumbo, and GoodbyeMessage are each separate procedures with appropriate messages.

Exercises 7.2

*1. Explain the difference between a procedure and a program.

2. What output will be produced when the following procedure is called from the main program?

```
PROCEDURE ExerciseTwo;
  CONST
    Splats = '******************************';
    Line = '-------------';
    Skip = ' ';
  BEGIN
    writeln (Skip:24, Splats);
    writeln (Skip:9, '*', Skip:19' '*');
    write (Skip:9, '*', '  Sample Output');
    writeln ('*':5);
    writeln (Skip:9, '*', Line:15, '*':5);
    writeln (Skip:9, '*', Skip:19, '*');
    writeln (Skip:24, Splats)
  END;
```

*3. Write a procedure that will produce the following:

```
******************************
*                            *
*       <your name here>     *
*     <today's date here>    *
*                            *
******************************
```

4. Write a program that calls the procedure in Exercise 3 five times.

In Exercises 5–8, create a suitable message for the heading of the billing statements and write a procedure for each that will print the heading when called from the main program.

*5. R & R Produce Company
6. Atlas Athletic Equipment
*7. Sleep E-Z-E Motel
8. Pump-Your-Own Service Station
*9. Consider the following output:

```
///////////////////////////////
/                             /
/       Special Olympics      /
/       ------- --------      /
///////////////////////////////

///////////////////////////////
/                             /
/       Special Olympics      /
/       ------- --------      /
///////////////////////////////

///////////////////////////////
/                             /
/       Special Olympics      /
/       ------- --------      /
///////////////////////////////
```

a. Write a program that produces this output without using procedures.
b. Write a program that produces this output using a procedure.

10. Consider the following program:

```
PROGRAM ExerciseTen (output);

CONST
  Splats = '*************************';
  Edge = '*                       *';
  Skip = ' ';

VAR
  Interest : real;

BEGIN  {  Main program  }
  writeln;
  writeln (Skip:5, Splats);
  writeln (Skip:5, Edge);
  writeln (Skip:5, '*    Federal Savings    *');
```

```
  writeln (Skip:5, '*    Monthly Report        *');
  writeln (Skip:5, Edge);
  writeln (Skip:5, Splats);
  writeln;
  Interest := 114.53;
  writeln ('Thank you for banking with Federal Savings.');
  writeln ('Your current interest payment is below.');
  writeln ('$':10, Interest:8:2);
  writeln;
  Interest := 87.93;
  writeln ('Thank you for banking with Federal Savings.');
  writeln ('Your current interest payment is below.');
  writeln ('$':10, Interest:8:2);
  writeln
END.  {  of main program  }
```

The output of this program is

```
     *************************
     *                       *
     *    Federal Savings    *
     *    Monthly Report     *
     *                       *
     *************************

Thank you for banking with Federal Savings.
Your current interest payment is below.
         $  114.53

Thank you for banking with Federal Savings.
Your current interest payment is below.
         $   87.93
```

Rewrite this program using

a. a procedure for the heading.

b. a procedure for the customer message.

*11. What output is produced by the following program?

```
PROGRAM ExerciseEleven (output);

CONST
  Skip = ' ';

PROCEDURE Number1;
  BEGIN
    writeln (Skip:10, 'She loves me.')
  END;  {  of PROCEDURE Number1  }

PROCEDURE Number2;
  BEGIN
    writeln (Skip:10, 'She loves me not.')
  END;  {  of PROCEDURE Number2  }

BEGIN  {  Main program  }
  Number1;
  Number2;
```

```
  Number1;
  Number2;
  Number1
END.  {  of main program  }
```

12. Rewrite the following program using indenting, blank lines, comments, and comment sections to enhance readability.

```
PROGRAM Plain (output);
VAR
Score1, Score2 : integer;
Average : real;
PROCEDURE PrintHeader;
BEGIN
writeln;
writeln ('Your test results are below.':36);
writeln;
writeln ('Keep up the good work!':30);
writeln
END;
BEGIN
PrintHeader;
Score1 := 89;
Score2 := 95;
Average := (Score1 + Score2) / 2.0;
writeln ('Score1':20, Score1:6);
writeln ('Score2':20, Score2:6);
writeln;
writeln ('Your average is':23, Average:8:2)
END.
```

13. Write a complete Pascal program that will display any of the numbers 9, 8, 7, 6, 5, 4, 3, 2, 1, or 0 on the screen in the following manner:

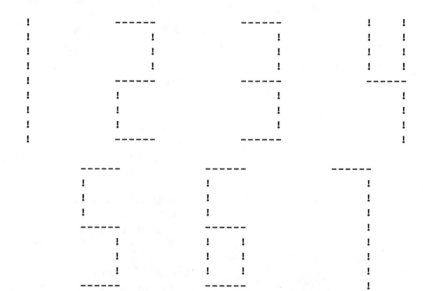

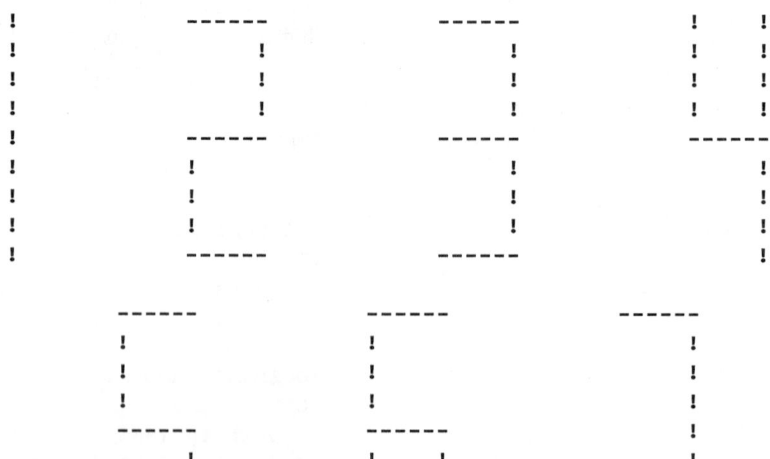

```
------        ------        ------
!    !        !    !        !    !
!    !        !    !        !    !
!    !        !    !        !    !
------        ------        !    !
!    !             !        !    !
!    !             !        !    !
!    !             !        !    !
------             !        ------
```

Use a procedure for each number. Allow the user the option of repeating the program.

7.3 Procedures with Parameters

Objectives

- to be able to use correct form and syntax when writing a procedure
- to understand the difference between variable parameters and value parameters
- to understand the difference between formal parameters and actual parameters
- to be able to use a procedure in a program

Form and Syntax

Procedures for headings without parameters are written in the following form:

```
PROCEDURE PrintHeading;
  BEGIN
    .
    .  (statements for desired output)
    .
  END;
```

Procedures of this type are very limited in that there is no data transmission or change of values of variables between the procedure and the main program. The general form of a procedure with parameters is

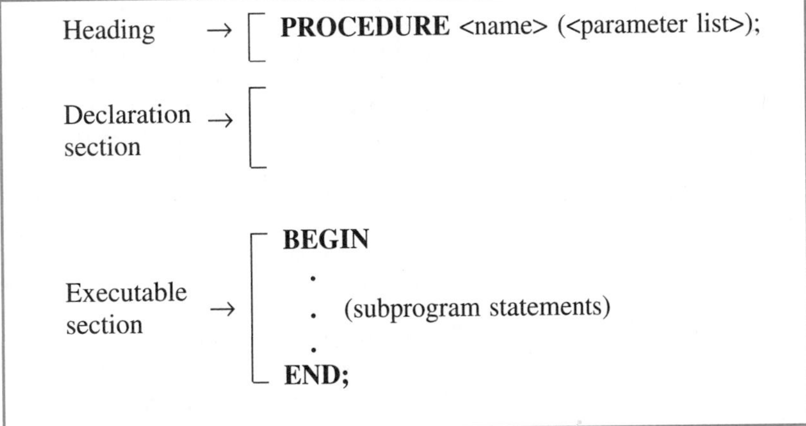

The significant change between this form and the form of procedures for headings is the use of parameters.

Parameters

Parameters are used so that values of variables may be transmitted (or passed) from the main program to the procedure and from the procedure to the main program. If values are to be passed only from the main program to the procedure, the parameters are called **value parameters.** If values are to be returned to the main program, the parameters are called **variable parameters.**

A **value parameter** is a formal parameter that is local to a subprogram. Values of these parameters are not returned to the calling program.

A **variable parameter** is a formal parameter that is not local to a subprogram. Values of these parameters are returned to the calling program.

When using parameters with procedures, the following should be noted:

1. The number and order of parameters in the parameter list must match the number and order of variables or values used when calling the procedure from the main program.
2. The type of parameters must match the corresponding type of variables or values used when calling the procedure.
3. The parameter types are declared in the procedure heading.

Parameters contained in a procedure are **formal parameters.** Formal parameters can be thought of as blanks in the heading of the procedure waiting to receive values from the parameters in a calling program. Parameters contained in the procedure call from the main program are **actual parameters.** Actual parameters are also referred to as arguments.

A **formal parameter** is a variable, declared and used in a procedure or function declaration, that is replaced by an actual parameter when the procedure or function is called.

An **actual parameter** is a variable or expression contained in a procedure or function call and passed to that procedure or function.

To illustrate formal and actual parameters used with procedures, consider the following complete program:

```
PROGRAM ProcDemo (output);

VAR
  Num1, Num2 : integer;
  Num3 : real;

{***********************************************}

PROCEDURE PrintNum (N1, N2 : integer;
                    N3 : real);
  BEGIN
    writeln;
    writeln ('Number1 = ', N1:3);
    writeln ('Number2 = ', N2:3);
    writeln ('Number3 = ', N3:6:2)
  END;  {  of PROCEDURE PrintNum  }

{***********************************************}

BEGIN  {  Main program  }
  Num1 := 5;
  Num2 := 8;
  Num3 := Num2 / Num1;
  PrintNum (Num1, Num2, Num3)
END.  {  of main program  }
```

When this program is run, the output is

```
Number1 =    5
Number2 =    8
Number3 =    1.60
```

In this program, N1, N2, and N3 are formal parameters; Num1, Num2, and Num3 are actual parameters. Now let's examine the relationship between the parameter list in the procedure

```
PROCEDURE PrintNum (N1, N2 : integer; N3 : real);
```

and the procedure call in the main program,

```
PrintNum (Num1, Num2, Num3)
```

In this case, Num1 corresponds to N1, Num2 corresponds to N2, and Num3 corresponds to N3. Notice that both the number and type of variables in the parameter list correspond with the number and type of variables listed in the procedure call.

Value Parameters

The preceding procedure demonstrates the use of value parameters or of one-way transmission of values. Different memory areas have been set aside for the variables Num1, Num2, and Num3 and for N1, N2, and N3. Thus, initially we have

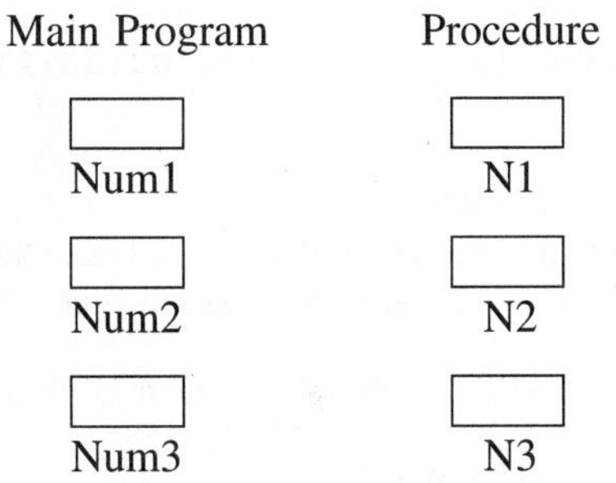

Main Program	Procedure
[ ] Num1	[ ] N1
[ ] Num2	[ ] N2
[ ] Num3	[ ] N3

This memory allocation occurs whenever the procedure PrintNum is called. The assignment statements

```
Num1 := 5;
Num2 := 8;
Num3 := Num2 / Num1;
```

produce

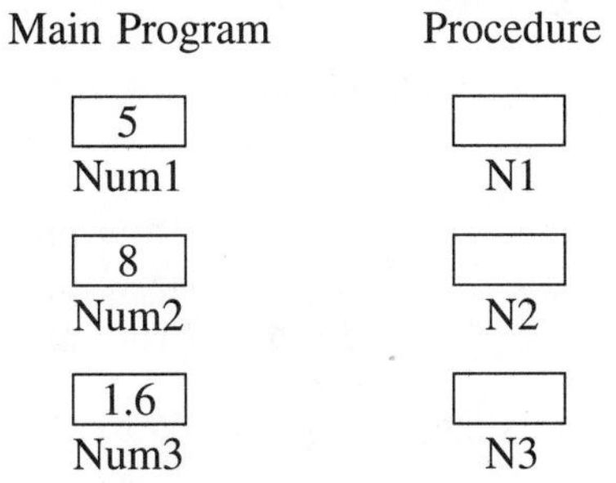

Main Program	Procedure
[5] Num1	[ ] N1
[8] Num2	[ ] N2
[1.6] Num3	[ ] N3

When the procedure PrintNum is called from the main program by

```
PrintNum (Num1, Num2, Num3)
```

the values are transmitted to N1, N2, and N3, respectively, as follows:

Main Program	Procedure
5	5
Num1	N1
8	8
Num2	N2
1.6	1.6
Num3	N3

At this stage, **PROCEDURE** PrintNum can use N1, N2, and N3 in any appropriate manner.

These are value parameters because values are passed from the main program to the procedure only. If the procedure changes the value of N1, N2, or N3, the corresponding values of Num1, Num2, and Num3 will not be changed. For example, suppose the procedure is changed to

```
PROCEDURE PrintNum (N1, N2 : integer;
                    N3 : real);
  BEGIN
    writeln (N1:10, N2:10, N3:10:2);
    N1 := 2 * N1;
    N2 := 2 * N2;
    N3 := 2 * N3;
    writeln (N1:10, N2:10, N3:10:2)
  END;  {  of PROCEDURE PrintNum  }
```

Furthermore, suppose the main program is changed to

```
BEGIN  {  Main program  }
  Num1 := 5;
  Num2 := 8;
  Num3 := Num2 / Num1;
  writeln;
  writeln (Num1:10, Num2:10, Num3:10:2);
  PrintNum (Num1, Num2, Num3);
  writeln (Num1:10, Num2:10, Num3:10:2);
  writeln
END.  {  of main program  }
```

When this program is run, the output is

```
 5         8        1.60   (from main program)
 5         8        1.60   (from procedure)
10        16        3.20   (from procedure)
 5         8        1.60   (from main program)
```

The first line of this output is produced by the first

```
writeln (Num1:10, Num2:10, Num3:10:2);
```

of the main program. The next two lines of output come from the procedure. The last line of output is produced by the second

```
writeln (Num1:10, Num2:10, Num3:10:2);
```

of the main program. You should carefully note that after the procedure changes the values of N1, N2, and N3, the values of Num1, Num2, and Num3 have not been changed. Thus, we have

Main Program	Procedure
5	10
Num1	N1
8	16
Num2	N2
1.6	3.2
Num3	N3

Variable Parameters

You will frequently want a procedure to change values in the main program. This can be accomplished by using variable parameters in the parameter list. Placing the reserved word **VAR** before the appropriate formal parameters in the procedure heading causes all formal parameters listed between **VAR** and the subsequent data type to become variable parameters. If value parameters of the same type are needed, they must be listed elsewhere. A separate **VAR** declaration is needed for each data type used when listing variable parameters. The use of **VAR** in a parameter list is slightly different from the use of **VAR** in the declaration of variables, yet it is the same reserved word.

When variable parameters are declared, transmission of values appears to be two-way rather than one-way: that is, values are sent from the main program to the procedure and from the procedure to the main program. Actually, when variable parameters are used, values are not transmitted at all. Variable parameters in the procedure heading are merely aliases for actual variables used in the main program. Thus, variables are said to be **passed by reference** rather than by value. When variable parameters are used, any change of values in the procedure produces a corresponding change of values in the main program.

Passed by reference refers to the use of variable parameters in subprograms.

To illustrate the declaration of variable parameters, consider the procedure heading

```
PROCEDURE PrintNum (VAR N1, N2 : integer; N3 : real);
```

In this case, N1 and N2 are variable parameters corresponding to integer variables in the main program and N3 is a value parameter corresponding to a real variable. This procedure can be called from the main program by

```
PrintNum (Num1, Num2, Num3);
```

To illustrate the passing of values, assume the procedure is

```
PROCEDURE PrintNum (VAR N1, N2 : integer; N3 : real);

  BEGIN
    writeln (N1:5, N2:5, N3:10:2);
    N1 := 2 * N1;
    N2 := 2 * N2;
    N3 := 2 * N3;
    writeln (N1:5, N2:5, N3:10:2)
  END;  { of PROCEDURE PrintNum  }
```

If the corresponding variables in the main program are Num1, Num2, and Num3, respectively, initially we have

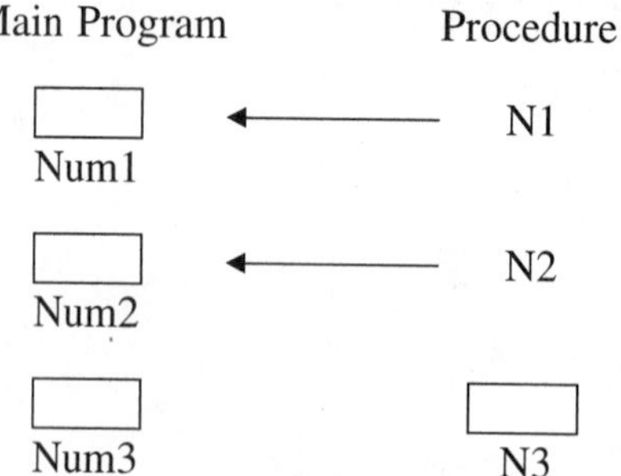

Technically, N1 and N2 do not exist as variables. They contain pointers to the same memory locations as Num1 and Num2, respectively. Thus, a statement in the procedure such as

```
N1 := 5;
```

causes the memory location reserved for Num1 to receive the value 5; that is, it causes the net action

```
Num1 := 5;
```

For this reason, constants cannot be used when calling a procedure with variable parameters.

```
PrintNum (3, 4, 5);
```

produces an error because 3 and 4 correspond to variable parameters.

If the main program makes the assignment statements

```
Num1 := 5;
Num2 := 8;
Num3 := Num2 / Num1;
```

we have

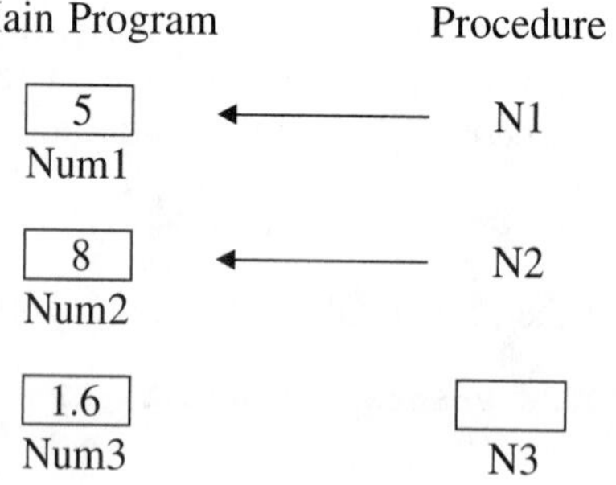

When the procedure is called and the following statements from the procedure

```
N1 := 2 * N1;
N2 := 2 * N2;
N3 := 2 * N3;
```

are executed, we have

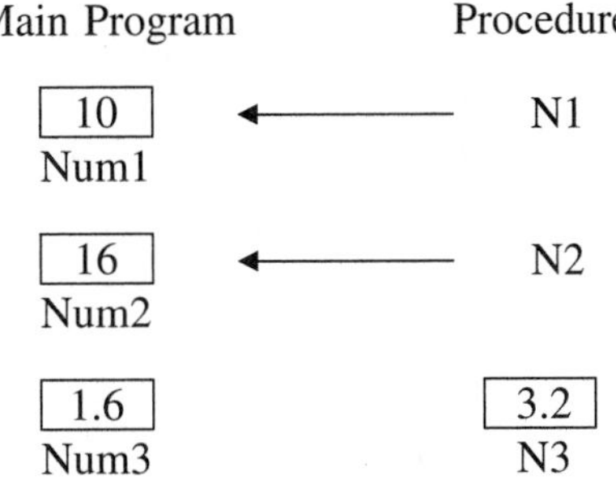

Notice that the variable parameters N1 and N2 produce changes in the corresponding variables in the main program, but the value parameter N3 does not.

Now let's consider a short, complete program that illustrates the difference between variable and value parameters. In this program (and throughout the text), the graphic documentation that accompanies the program highlights the way in which parameters are passed between the main program and the procedure.

```
PROGRAM ProcDemo2 (output);

VAR
  X, Y : real;
  Ch : char;

{*****************************************************}

PROCEDURE DemonstrateVar (VAR X1 : real;
                          Y1 : real;
                          VAR Ch1 : char);
  BEGIN
    writeln (X1:10:2, Y1:10:2, Ch1:5);
    X1 := 2 * X1;
    Y1 := 2 * Y1;
    Ch1 := '*';
    writeln (X1:10:2, Y1:10:2, Ch1:5)
  END;  {  of PROCEDURE DemonstrateVar  }

{*****************************************************}

BEGIN  {  Main program  }
  X := 3.6;
  Y := 5.2;
  Ch := 'A';
  writeln (X:10:2, Y:10:2, Ch:5);
  DemonstrateVar (X, Y, Ch);
  writeln (X:10:2, Y:10:2, Ch:5)
END.  {  of main program  }
```

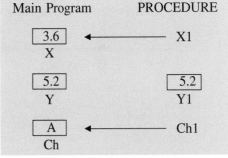

Main Program	PROCEDURE
3.6 X ←	X1
5.2 Y	5.2 Y1
A Ch ←	Ch1

The output from the program is

```
3.60     5.20    A    (from main program)
3.60     5.20    A    (from procedure)
7.20    10.40    *    (from procedure)
7.20     5.20    *    (from main program)
```

The variables can be depicted as

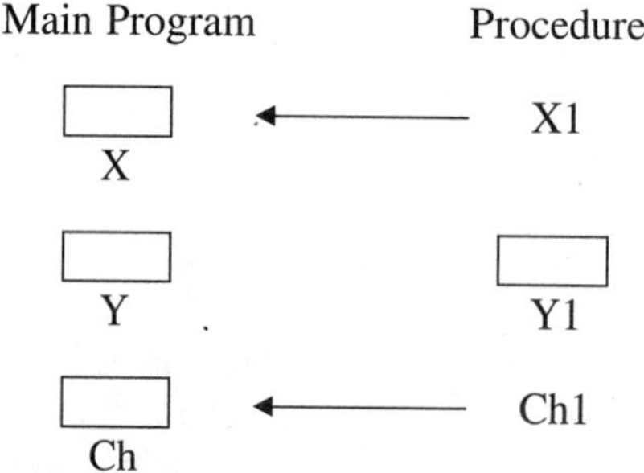

The assignment statements

```
X := 3.6;
Y := 5.2;
Ch := 'A';
```

produce

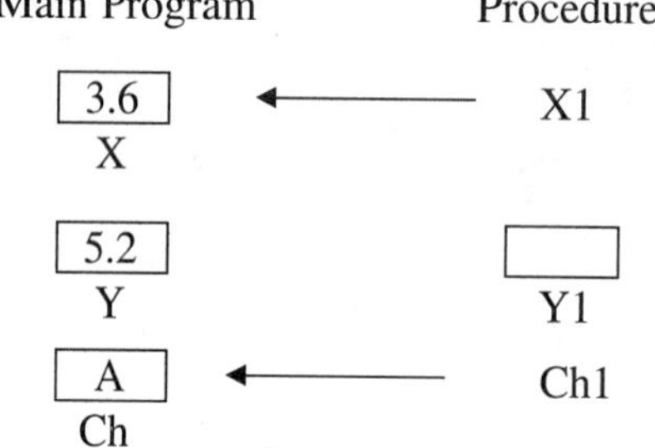

When the procedure is called by

```
DemonstrateVar (X, Y, Ch);
```

the contents can be envisioned as

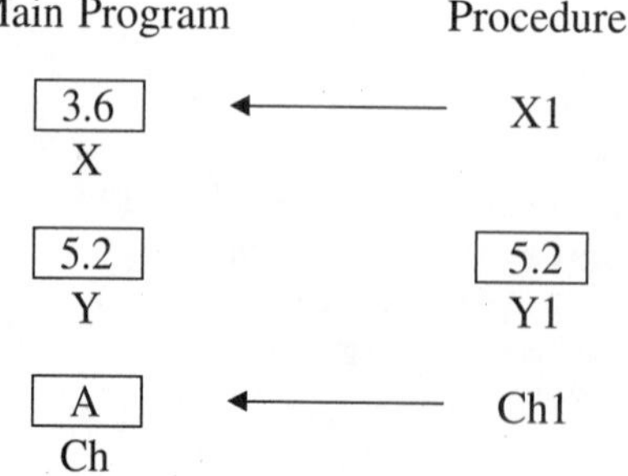

When the procedure assignment statements

```
X1 := 2 * X1;
Y1 := 2 * Y1;
Ch1 := '*';
```

are executed, the variables become

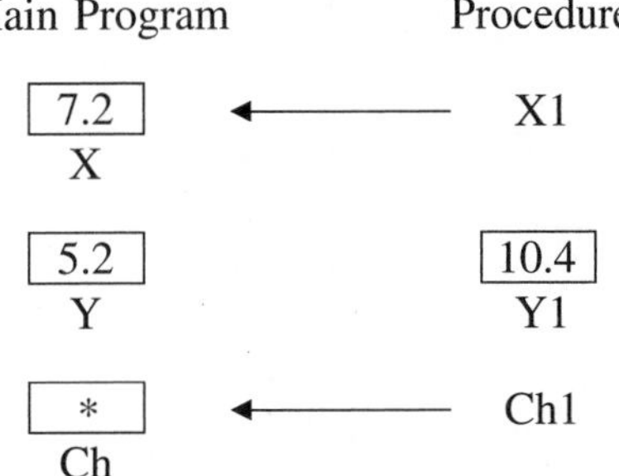

Notice that changes in the variable parameters X1 and Ch1 produce corresponding changes in X and Ch, but a change in the value parameter Y1 does not produce a change in Y.

Side Effects

A **side effect** is an unintentional change in a variable that is the result of some action taken in a program.

A **side effect** is an unintentional change in a variable that results from some action taken in a program. Side effects are frequently caused by the misuse of variable parameters. Since any change in a variable parameter causes a change in the corresponding actual parameter in the calling program or procedure, you should use variable parameters only when your intent is to produce such changes. In all other cases, use value parameters.

To illustrate how a side effect can occur, suppose you are working with a program that computes the midterm and final grades for students in a class. For the midterm grade, Quiz1 and Quiz2 are doubled and then added to Test1. Using variable parameters in a procedure for this yields

```
PROCEDURE ComputeMidTerm (VAR Q1, Q2, T1 : integer);
  BEGIN
    Q1 := 2 * Q1;
    Q2 := 2 * Q2;
       .
       .  (rest of procedure)
       .
```

When this is called from the main program by

```
ComputeMidTerm (Quiz1, Quiz2, Test1);
```

the values in Quiz1 and Quiz2 will be changed. This was probably not the intent when ComputeMidTerm was called. This unwanted side effect can be avoided by making Q1 and Q2 value parameters. Thus, the procedure heading becomes

```
PROCEDURE ComputeMidTerm (Q1, Q2, T1 : integer);
```

Writing Style

As previously discussed, procedures are located in the declaration section of a program.

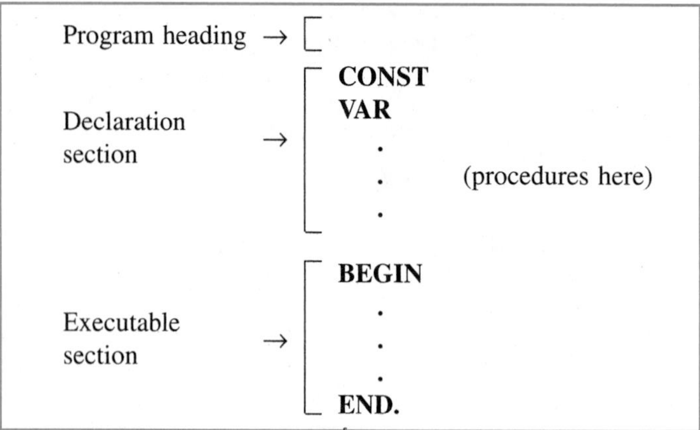

There is no limit to the number of procedures that can be used in a program. Within the procedure, consistent use of comments, blank lines, and indents should be maintained. A program containing three procedures might be organized as follows:

```
PROGRAM ThreeProcs (input, output);

CONST

VAR

PROCEDURE <one here>

PROCEDURE <two here>

PROCEDURE <three here>

BEGIN  {  Main program  }
    .
    .  (Main program here)
    .
END.  {  of main program  }
```

When a program contains several procedures, they can be called from the main part of the program in any order.

Documenting Subprograms

Each subprogram should contain documentation sufficient to allow the reader to understand what information is given to the subprogram, what task is to be performed, and what information is to be returned to the calling program. This information aids in debugging programs. In this text, the headings of subprograms in complete programs will be followed by documentation in the form

```
{  Given:   Statement of information sent from program     }
{  Task:    Statement of task(s) to be performed            }
{  Return:  Statement of value(s) to be returned            }
```

A Note of Interest

Computer Ethics: Hacking and Other Intrusions

A famous sequence of computer intrusions was originally detailed by Clifford Stoll. The prime intruder came to Stoll's attention in August 1986, when he attempted to penetrate a computer at Lawrence Berkeley Laboratory (LBL). Management at LBL went along with Stoll's recommendation that they attempt to unmask the intruder, even though the risk was substantial because the intruder had gained system-manager privileges.

Markus H., a member of a small group of West Germans, was an unusually persistent intruder, but no computer wizard. He made use of known deficiencies in the half-dozen or so operating systems with which he was familiar, but he did not invent any new modes of entry. He penetrated 30 of the 450 computers then on the network system at LBL.

After Markus H. was successfully traced, efforts were instituted to make LBL's computers less vulnerable. To insure security, it would have been necessary, for instance, to change all passwords overnight and recertify each user. This and other demanding measures were deemed impractical. Instead, deletion of all expired passwords was instituted; shared accounts were eliminated; monitoring of incoming traffic was extended, with alarms set in key places; and education of users was attempted.

The episode was summed up by Stoll as a powerful learning experience for all those concerned about computer security. That the intruder was caught at all is a testimony to the ability of a large number of concerned professionals to keep the tracing effort secret.

In a later incident, an intruder left the following embarrassing message in the computer file assigned to Clifford Stoll: "The cuckoo has egg on his face." The reference is to Stoll's book, The Cuckoo's Egg, which tracks the intrusions of the West German hacker just described. The embarrassment was heightened by the fact that the computer, owned by Harvard University, with which astronomer Stoll is now associated, is on the Internet network. The intruder, or intruders, who goes by the name of Dave, also attempted to break into dozens of other computers on the same network—and succeeded.

The name Dave was used by one or more of three Australians arrested by the federal police down under. The three, who at the time of their arrest were 18, 20, and 21 years of age, successfully penetrated computers in both Australia and the United States.

The three Australians went beyond browsing to damage data in computers in their own nation and the United States. At the time they began their intrusions in 1988 (when the youngest was only 16), there was no law in Australia under which they could be prosecuted. It was not until legislation making such intrusions prosecutable was passed that the police began to take action.

When subprograms are separately developed and illustrated, this documentation will not be included; instead, text development immediately preceding the subprogram will serve the same purpose.

We close this section with a sample program using four procedures. The program reads data that consist of three reals, computes their average, and then prints the results. A first-level pseudocode development for this program is

1. Get data
2. Process data
3. Print header
4. Print results

We can write a procedure for each of the pseudocode steps.

1. Get data

becomes

```
PROCEDURE GetData (VAR S1, S2, S3 : real);
  BEGIN
    writeln ('Enter three reals and press <Enter>.');
    readln (S1, S2, S3)
  END;  {  of PROCEDURE GetData  }
```

Note that this procedure uses variable parameters so that values from the procedure are transmitted back to the program.

2. Process data

becomes

```
PROCEDURE FindAverage (S1, S2, S3 : real;
                       VAR Aver : real);
  BEGIN
    Aver := (S1 + S2 + S3) / 3
  END;  {  of PROCEDURE FindAverage  }
```

Note that S1, S2, and S3 are value parameters and Aver is a variable parameter. When this procedure is called from the main program, it returns the computed average.

3. Print header

becomes

```
PROCEDURE PrintHeader;
  CONST
    Indent = ' ';
  BEGIN
    writeln;
    writeln (Indent:30, 'Scores');
    writeln (Indent:30, '------');
    writeln
  END;  {  of PROCEDURE PrintHeader  }
```

4. Print results

becomes

```
PROCEDURE PrintResults (S1, S2, S3, Av : real);
  BEGIN
    writeln (S1:36:2);
    writeln (S2:36:2);
    writeln (S3:36:2);
    writeln ('------':36);
    writeln;
    writeln (Av:36:2)
  END;  {  of PROCEDURE PrintResults  }
```

The main part of the program is

```
BEGIN  {  Main program  }
  GetData (Score1, Score2, Score3);
  FindAverage (Score1, Score2, Score3, Average);
  PrintHeader;
  PrintResults (Score1, Score2, Score3, Average)
END.  {  of main program  }
```

The complete program is

```
PROGRAM ProcDemo3 (input, output);

{   This program demonstrates  the use of procedures.  Both      }
{   value and variable parameters are featured.  Notice how      }
{   the main program  consists only of calling  appropriate      }
{   procedures.                                                   }

VAR
  Average : real;                 {  The average of three reals  }
  Score1, Score2,
  Score3 : real;                  {  Three scores to be read     }

{*************************************************************}

PROCEDURE GetData (VAR S1, S2, S3 : real);

  {  Given:   Nothing                                          }
  {  Task:    Read three scores                                }
  {  Return:  Scores read                                      }

  BEGIN
    writeln ('Enter three reals and press <Enter>.');
    readln (S1, S2, S3)
  END;  {  of PROCEDURE GetData  }

{*************************************************************}

PROCEDURE FindAverage (S1, S2, S3 : real;
                       VAR Aver : real);

  {  Given:   Three scores                                     }
  {  Task:    Find their average                               }
  {  Return:  The average score                                }

  BEGIN
    Aver := (S1 + S2 + S3) / 3
  END;  {  of PROCEDURE FindAverage  }

{*************************************************************}

PROCEDURE PrintHeader;

  {  Given:   Nothing                                          }
  {  Task:    Print a heading                                  }
  {  Return:  Nothing                                          }

  CONST
    Indent = ' ';
  BEGIN
    writeln (Indent:30, 'Scores');
    writeln (Indent:30, '------');
    writeln
  END;  {  of PROCEDURE PrintHeader  }

{*************************************************************}
```

```
PROCEDURE PrintResults (S1, S2, S3, Av : real);

  {  Given:    Three scores and their average                    }
  {  Task:     Print the scores and their average                }
  {  Return:   Nothing                                           }

  BEGIN
    writeln (S1:36:2);
    writeln (S2:36:2);
    writeln (S3:36:2);
    writeln ('------':36);
    writeln (Av:36:2)
  END;  {  of PROCEDURE PrintResults  }

{****************************************************************}


BEGIN  {  Main program  }
  GetData (Score1, Score2, Score3);
  FindAverage (Score1, Score2, Score3, Average);
  PrintHeader;
  PrintResults (Score1, Score2, Score3, Average)
END.  {  of main program  }
```

Main Program		PROCEDURE GetData
89.3 Score1	←	S1
92.4 Score2	←	S2
84.6 Score3	←	S3

Main Program	PROCEDURE PrintResults
89.3 Score1	89.3 S1
92.4 Score2	92.4 S2
84.6 Score3	84.6 S3
88.77 Average	88.77 Av

Main Program		PROCEDURE FindAverage
89.3 Score1		89.3 S1
92.4 Score2		92.4 S2
84.6 Score3		84.6 S3
88.77 Average	←	Aver

If the data entered are

```
89.3 92.4 84.6
```

a sample run of this program is

```
Enter three reals and press <Enter>.
89.3 92.4 84.6
```

```
Scores
------

 89.30
 92.40
 84.60
------
 88.77
```

Exercises 7.3

1. Explain the difference between value parameters and variable parameters and the difference between actual parameters and formal parameters.
2. Write a test program to find what happens if the parameter lists do not match when a procedure is called from the main program. Investigate each of the following:
   a. correct number of parameters, wrong order
   b. incorrect number of parameters

In Exercises 3–5, indicate which parameters are value parameters and which are variable parameters.

*3.
```
PROCEDURE Demo1 (VAR A, B : integer;
                 X : real);
```
4.
```
PROCEDURE Demo2 (VAR A : integer;
                 B : integer;
                 VAR X : real;
                 Ch : char);
```
*5.
```
PROCEDURE Demo3 (A, B : integer;
                 VAR X, Y, Z : real;
                 Ch : char);
```

In Exercises 6–10, indicate which are appropriate procedure headings. Explain the problem with those that are inappropriate.

6.
```
PROCEDURE Prac1 (A : integer : Y : real);
```
*7.
```
PROCEDURE Error? (Ch1, Ch2 : char);
```
8.
```
PROCEDURE Prac2 (A, VAR B : integer);
```
*9.
```
PROCEDURE Prac3 (A, B, C : integer
                 VAR X, Y, : real
                 Ch : char
                 Flag : boolean);
```
10.
```
PROCEDURE Prac4 (VAR A : integer,
                 X : real);
```

In Exercises 11–15, indicate how the procedures would be called from the main program.

*11.
```
PROCEDURE Prob11 (A, B : integer;
                  Ch : char);
```
12.
```
PROCEDURE PrintHeader;
```
*13.
```
PROCEDURE FindMax (N1, N2 : integer;
                   VAR NewMax : integer);
```
14.
```
PROCEDURE Switch (VAR X, Y : real);
```
*15.
```
PROCEDURE SwitchAndTest (VAR X, Y : real;
                         VAR F1 : boolean);
```

In Exercises 16–19, using the following procedure,

```
PROCEDURE Switch (VAR A, B : integer);
  VAR
    Temp : integer;
  BEGIN
    Temp := A;
    A := B;
    B := Temp
  END;  {  of PROCEDURE Switch  }
```

indicate the output produced by the fragment of code in the main program.

16.
```
Num1 := 5;
Num2 := 10;
writeln (Num1, Num2);
Switch (Num1, Num2);
writeln (Num1, Num2);
Switch (Num1, Num2);
writeln (Num1, Num2);
```

*17.
```
Num1 := -3;
Num2 := 2;
IF Num1 > Num2 THEN
  Switch (Num1, Num2)
ELSE
  Switch (Num2, Num1);
writeln (Num2, Num1);
```

18.
```
N := 3;
M := 20;
Switch (M, N);
writeln (M, N);
Switch (N, M);
writeln (N, M);
```

*19.
```
Count := 0;
Max := 10;
WHILE Count < Max DO
  BEGIN
    Switch (Count, Max);
    writeln (Count, Max);
    Count := Count + 1
  END;  {  of WHILE...DO  }
```

In Exercises 20–24, write a procedure and indicate how it would be called from the main program.

20. Print the heading for the output

```
   Acme National Electronics
      Board of Directors
        Annual Meeting
```

*21. Find the maximum and average of three reals. Both values are to be returned to the main program.

22. Count the number of occurrences of the letter A in a line of character data. The count should be returned to the main program and the line of data should be printed.

*23. Convert Fahrenheit temperature to Celsius.

24. Find and print all divisors of a positive integer.

In Exercises 25–32, assume a program contains the variable declaration section

```
VAR
  Num1, Num2 : integer;
  X, Y : real;
  Ch1, Ch2 : char;
```

Furthermore, suppose the same program contains a procedure whose heading is

```
PROCEDURE Demo (VAR N1, N2 : integer;
                X1 : real;
                Ch : char);
```

Indicate which are appropriate calls to the procedure Demo. Explain those that are inappropriate.

*25. `Demo (Num1, Num2);`
26. `Demo (Num1, Num2, X);`
*27. `Demo (Num1, Num2, X, Ch1);`
28. `Demo (X, Y, Num1, Ch2);`
*29. `Demo (Num2, X, Y, Ch1);`
30. `Demo (Num1, Num2, Ch2);`
*31. `Demo;`
32. `Demo (Num2, Num1, Y, Ch1);`

7.4 User-Defined Functions

Objectives

- to be able to use the correct form and syntax for writing a function
- to be able to call a function from the main program
- to be able to write a function to perform a specific task

A **function** is a subprogram whose purpose is to return a single value to the calling program.

A **function** is a subprogram whose purpose is to return a single value to the calling program.

A **user-defined function** is a subprogram (function) written by the programmer to perform a specific task. Functions return one value when called.

A **function** is a subprogram whose purpose is to return a single value to the calling program. Two kinds of functions are available: standard functions and user-defined functions. The standard functions **sqr, sqrt, abs, round,** and **trunc** were introduced in Section 3.5. To review briefly, some concepts to note when using these functions follow.

1. An argument is required thus, **sqrt**(Y) and **abs**(−21) are appropriate.
2. Standard functions can be used in expressions; for example,

```
X := sqrt(Y) + sqrt(Z);
```

3. Standard functions can be used in output statements; for example,

```
writeln (sqr(3):8);
```

The Need for User-Defined Functions

It is relatively easy to envision the need for functions that are not on the list of standard functions available in Pascal. For example, if you must frequently cube numbers, it would be convenient to have a function Cube so you could make an assignment such as

```
X := Cube(Y);
```

Other examples from mathematics include an exponential function (x^Y), computing a factorial ($n!$), computing a discriminant ($b^2 - 4ac$), and finding roots of a quadratic equation

$$\left(\frac{-b \pm \sqrt{b^2 - 4ac}}{2a}\right)$$

In business, a motel might like to have available a function to determine a customer's bill given the number in the party, the length of stay, and any telephone charges. Similarly, a hospital might like a function to compute the room charge for a patient given the type of room (private, ward, and so on) and various other options, including telephone (yes or no) and television (yes or no). Functions such as these are not standard functions. However, in Pascal, we can create **user-defined functions** to perform these tasks.

Form and Syntax

A user-defined function is a subprogram; as such, it is part of the declaration section of the main (or calling) program. A user-defined function has the components

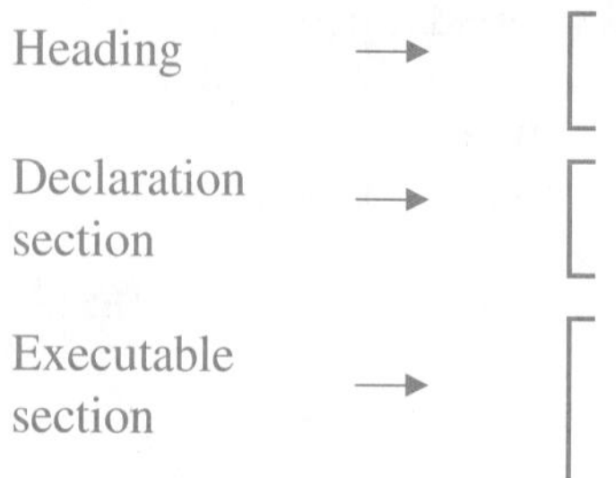

The general form for a function heading is

FUNCTION <function name> (<parameter list>) : <return type>

A syntax diagram for this is

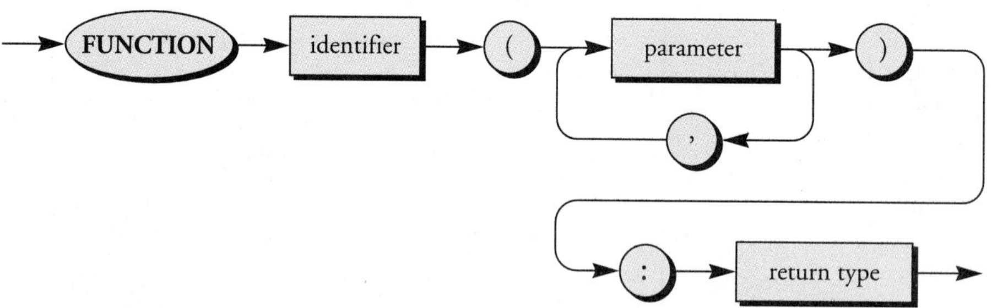

A function to compute the cube of an integer could have the heading

```
FUNCTION Cube (X : integer) : integer;
```

As with procedures, the formal parameter list (variables in the function heading) must match the number and corresponding types of actual parameters (variables in the function call) used when the function is called from the main program. Thus, if you are writing a function to compute the area of a rectangle and you want to call the function from the main program by using

```
RectArea := Area(Width, Length);
```

the function Area could have the heading

```
FUNCTION Area (W, L : integer) : integer;
```

The two formal parameters W and L correspond to the actual parameters Width and Length, assuming Width and Length are of type **integer.** In general, you should make sure the formal parameter list and the actual parameter list match up as indicated:

```
(W, L : integer)
(Width, Length)
```

An exception to this rule is that an actual parameter of type **integer** may be associated with a formal parameter of type **real.**

Several additional comments on the general form of a function are now in order:

1. **FUNCTION** is a reserved word and must be used only as indicated.
2. The term "function name" is any valid identifier.
   a. The function name should be descriptive.
   b. Some value must be assigned to the function name in the executable section of the function. The last assigned value will be the value returned to the main program; for example, in the function Cube, we have

      ```
      Cube := X * X * X;
      ```

   c. The function name can only be used on the left side of an assignment statement within the function. For example,

      ```
      Cube := Cube + 1;
      ```

      and

      ```
      writeln (Cube);
      ```

      produce errors. (An exception to this rule involves recursion and will be discussed in Chapter 8.)
3. The term "return type" declares the data type for the function name. This indicates what type will be returned to the main program.
4. A function can return a single value of any of the data types **integer, real, char,** or **boolean.**

As in the main program, there does not have to be a declaration section for a function. When there is one, only variables needed in the function are declared. Further, the section is usually not very elaborate because the purpose of a function is normally a small, single task.

Finally, the executable section for a function must perform the desired task, assign a value to the function name, terminate with a semicolon rather than a period, and have the general form

```
BEGIN
  .
  .  (work of function here)
  .
END;
```

We now illustrate user-defined functions with several examples.

Example 7.6

Let's write a function to compute the cube of an integer. Since the actual parameter from the main program will be of **integer** type, we could have

```
FUNCTION Cube (X : integer) : integer;
  BEGIN
    Cube := X * X * X
  END;
```

A typical call to this function from the main program is

```
A := Cube(5);
```

Example 7.7

Let's write a function to compute the average of three reals. We know the actual parameters will be three reals, so our function could be written as

```
FUNCTION Average (N1, N2, N3 : real) : real;
  BEGIN
    Average := (N1 + N2 + N3) / 3
  END;
```

and called from the main program by

```
X := Average(Num1, Num2, Num3):
```

Example 7.8

Given two positive integers, *m* and *n,* write a function to compute m^n (*m* to the power of *n*). Since there will be two actual parameters, the formal parameter list will require two variables of type **integer.** The function will return an integer, so the return type will be **integer.** The desired function is

```
FUNCTION Power (Base, Exponent : integer) : integer;
  VAR
    Temp, K : integer;
  BEGIN
    Temp := Base;
    For K := 2 TO Exponent DO
      Temp := Temp * Base;
    Power := Temp
  END;  {  of FUNCTION Power  }
```

This could be called from the main program by

```
A := Power(3, 5);
```

Since the function given in Example 7.8 is more elaborate than those we have seen previously, we should examine it more closely. First, notice that we need additional variables, Temp and K. Now let's trace what happens to the various values and variables.

When Power (3, 5) is encountered in the main program, control is transferred to **FUNCTION** Power, and Base and Exponent receive their respective values. At this stage, the variables could be depicted as

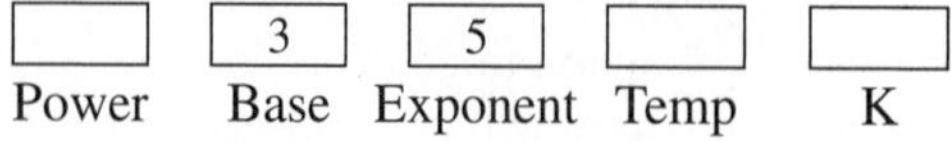

The first executable statement in the function causes

Power	Base	Exponent	Temp	K
	3	5	3	

The first pass through the loop produces

	3	5	9	2
Power	Base	Exponent	Temp	K

At the completion of the loop, K becomes unassigned and Power is assigned the final value of Temp to produce

243	3	5	243	
Power	Base	Exponent	Temp	K

Each iteration multiplies Temp by an additional factor of Base. After the final iteration, control is transferred back to the main program and the value in Power is assigned accordingly. Thus,

```
A := Power(3, 5)
```

yields

243
A

Example 7.9

Now let's write a function to compute the total charge for a hospital room. Actual parameters will be the number of days (**integer**) and room type (**char**). We may assume rates for private (P), semiprivate (S), and ward (W) have been defined in the **CONST** definition section of the main program. A typical function is

```
FUNCTION RoomCharge (NDays : integer;
                     RmType : char) : real;
  BEGIN
    CASE RmType OF
      'P' : RoomCharge := NDays * PrivateRate;
      'S' : RoomCharge := NDays * SemiprivateRate;
      'W' : RoomCharge := NDays * WardRate
    END  {  of CASE RmType  }
  END;  {  of FUNCTION RoomCharge  }
```

This function could be called from the main program by

```
RoomAmount := RoomCharge(NumDays, RoomType);
```

Use in a Program

Now that you have seen several examples of user-defined functions, let's consider their use in a program. Once they are written, they can be used in the same manner as standard functions, usually in one of the following forms:

1. Assignment statements

```
A := 5;
B := Cube(A);
```

2. Arithmetic expressions

```
A := 5;
B := 3 * Cube(A) + 2;
```

3. Output statements

```
A := 5;
writeln (Cube(A):17);
```

4. Boolean expressions

```
IF Cube(A) < B THEN
          .
          .
          .
```

In general, a function (rather than a procedure) should be used when a single value is to be returned from a subprogram.

Position in a Program

All procedures and functions (subprograms) are placed after the variable declaration section for the main program. Program execution begins with the first statement of the main program. Execution of the function occurs only when it is called from the main program or from some other subprogram. The writing style for functions is consistent with that used for procedures. We now illustrate this with a complete program that prints a chart of the integers 1 to 10 together with their squares and cubes. The function Cube will be used as previously written.

```
PROGRAM Table (output);

VAR
  Index : integer;

{*****************************************************************}

PROCEDURE PrintHeading;

  {  Given:   Nothing                                              }
  {  Task:    Print a heading for the table                        }
  {  Return:  Nothing                                              }

  BEGIN
    writeln;
    writeln ('Number':28, 'Number Squared':18, 'Number Cubed':16);
    writeln ('------':28, '--------------':18, '------------':16)
  END;  {  of PROCEDURE PrintHeading  }

{*****************************************************************}

FUNCTION Cube (X : integer) : integer;

  {  Given:   An integer                                           }
  {  Task:    Cube the integer                                     }
  {  Return:  The cube of the integer                              }
```

```
  BEGIN
    Cube := X * X * X
  END;  {  of FUNCTION Cube  }

{*****************************************************************}

BEGIN  {  Main program  }
  PrintHeading;
  FOR Index := 1 TO 10 DO
    writeln (J:25, sqr(J):14, Cube(J):17);
  writeln
END.  {  of main program  }
```

The output from this program is

```
  Number     Number Squared     Number Cubed
  ------     --------------     ------------
     1              1                 1
     2              4                 8
     3              9                27
     4             16                64
     5             25               125
     6             36               216
     7             49               343
     8             64               512
     9             81               729
    10            100              1000
```

A Power Function

Example 7.8 illustrates how an integer can be raised to a positive integer power, but it would not allow you to compute $3^{2.5}$. Now that you know how to write a function, you can use the built-in functions **ln** and **exp** to write a power function. Before we do this, however, let's consider how these functions can be used to produce the desired result.

First, **exp** and **ln** are inverse functions in the sense that **exp** (**ln**(X)) = X for all positive X. Thus, we have $3^{2.5}$ = **exp**(**ln**($3^{2.5}$)). Using properties of logarithms,

$$\mathbf{ln}(a^b) = b * \mathbf{ln}(\mathrm{a})$$

Hence, **exp**(**ln**($3^{2.5}$)) = **exp**(2.5 ∗ **ln**(3)). Since each of these operations can be performed in standard Pascal, we can compute $3^{2.5}$ by

$$3^{2.5} = \mathbf{exp}(2.5 * \mathbf{ln}(3))$$

or more generally,

$$A^X = \mathbf{exp}(X * \mathbf{ln}(A))$$

If we let Base denote the base A and Exponent denote the exponent X, we can now write a function Power as

```
FUNCTION Power (Base, Exponent : real) : real;
  BEGIN
    Power := exp(Exponent * ln(Base))
  END;  {  of FUNCTION Power  }
```

This can be called from the main program by

```
Base := 3;
Exponent := 2.5;
Num := Power(Base, Exponent);
```

Guarding against Overflow

As we discussed in Chapter 3, integer overflow occurs when the absolute value of an integer exceeds **maxint** and real overflow occurs when a value is obtained that is too large to be stored in a memory location. Both of these values vary according to the compiler being used. The maximum value of an integer is stored in **maxint.** Unfortunately, there is no convenient analogue for reals. You will need to check your system manual to determine how large a real can be. Typically, this limit will be given in the form $9999 * 10^x$. Both the number of nines and the integer x will vary.

One method that is used to guard against integer overflow is based on the principle of checking a number against some function of **maxint.** Thus, if you want to multiply a number by 10, you would first compare it to **maxint DIV** 10. A typical segment of code could be

```
IF Num > maxint DIV 10 THEN
  .
  .  (overflow message)
  .
ELSE
  BEGIN
    Num := Num * 10;
      .
      .  (rest of action)
      .
  END;
```

We can now use this same idea with a **boolean** valued function. For example, consider the function

```
FUNCTION NearOverflow (Num : integer) : boolean;
  BEGIN
    NearOverflow := (Num > maxint DIV 10)
  END;
```

This could be used in the following manner:

```
IF NearOverflow(Num) THEN
  .
  .  (overflow message)
  .
ELSE
  BEGIN
    Num := Num * 10;
      .
      .  (rest of action)
      .
  END;
```

This same idea could be incorporated into a variable control loop. A typical **WHILE** loop could be

```
WHILE <condition> AND NOT NearOverflow(Num) DO
  BEGIN
    .
    .  (action here)
    .
  END;
```

In this case, as soon as Num gets relatively close to **maxint,** the loop would be terminated.

Multiple Functions

Programs can contain more than one function. When several user-defined functions are needed in a program, each one should be developed and positioned in the program as previously indicated. For readability, be sure to use blank lines and comment sections to separate each function.

When a program contains several functions, they can be called from the main part of the program in any order. However, if one function contains a call to another function, the function being called must appear before the function from which it is called. (We will examine an exception to this when we consider forward reference in Section 8.3.)

Exercises 7.4

1. Explain the difference between procedures and functions.
2. Write a test program to see what happens when the function name is used on the right side of an assignment statement. For example,

```
FUNCTION Total (OldSum, NewNum : integer) : integer;
  BEGIN
    Total := OldSum;
    Total := Total + NewNum
  END;
```

In Exercises 3–7, indicate which are valid function headings. Explain what is wrong with those that are invalid.

*3. `FUNCTION RoundTenth (X : real);`

4. `FUNCTION MakeChange (X, Y) : real;`

*5. `FUNCTION Max (M1, M2, M3 : integer) : integer;`

6. `FUNCTION Sign (Num : real) : char;`

*7. `FUNCTION Truth (Ch : char, Num : real) : boolean;`

In Exercises 8–10, find all errors in the function.

8.
```
FUNCTION MaxOf2 (N1, N2 : integer) : integer;
  BEGIN
    IF N1 > N2 THEN
      MaxOf2 := N1
  END;
```

*9.
```
FUNCTION AvOf2 (N1, N2 : integer) : integer;
  BEGIN
    AvOf2 := (N1 + N2) / 2
  END;
```

10.
```
FUNCTION Total (L : integer) : integer;
  VAR
    J : integer;
  BEGIN
    Total := 0;
    FOR J := 1 TO L DO
      Total := Total + J
  END;
```

Write a separate function to perform each of the actions requested in Exercises 11–17.

*11. Find the maximum of two reals.

12. Find the maximum of three reals.

*13. Round a real to the nearest tenth.

14. Convert degrees Fahrenheit to degrees Celsius.

*15. Determine the sign of a real number.

16. Examine an integer to see if it is a multiple of five; if so, return the **boolean** value **true;** if not, return the **boolean** value **false.**

*17. Compute the charge for cars at a parking lot; the rate is 75 cents per hour or fraction thereof.

18. Write a program that uses the function you wrote for Exercise 17 to print a ticket for a customer who parks in the parking lot. Assume the input is in minutes.

*19. The factorial of a positive integer n is

$$n! = n * (n - 1) * \ldots * 2 * 1$$

Write a function (Factorial) that will compute and return $n!$.

20. Write a complete program using Cube and Factorial that will produce a table of the integers 1 to 10 together with their squares, cubes, and factorials.

*21. Write a function (Arithmetic) that will receive a sign (+ or $*$) and two integers (N1, N2) and then compute and return either N1 + N2 or N1 $*$ N2, depending on the sign received.

22. Write a program that allows the user to enter a Base (a) and Exponent (x) and then have the program print the value of a^x.

23. Algebra teachers often have students play "guess the rule." The first person writes down a rule (function), such as $y = x^2 + 1$. A second person then gives a value for x. The first person indicates the function value associated with the input. Thus, for $x = 3$, y would be 10 if $y = x^2 + 1$. The game continues until the second person "guesses the rule." Write a program that allows you to play this game with another student. Write it in such a way that it can be easily modified to use different functions.

24. Write a program that reads integers from a data file. The program should identify the largest and smallest integers read. Include a user-defined function to find the average of the largest and smallest values. Output should consist of the values read, the number of values read, the largest value, the smallest value, the average of all values, and the average of the largest and smallest values.

Focus on Program Design: Case Study 7.2

Finding the Least Common Multiple

The summary program for this chapter illustrates the use of procedures as part of a modular development. Consider the problem of finding the least common multiple (LCM) of integers *A* and *B*. The LCM of two positive integers *A* and *B* is the smallest positive integer that is a multiple of both *A* and *B*. For example, the LCM of 12 and 15 is 60.

Our program is an interactive program that receives two positive integers as input. Output consists of the numbers given as input and their least common multiple. A sample run of this program produces

```
This program allows you to find the
LEAST COMMON MULTIPLE of two positive integers.

Please enter the first integer.
12
Please enter the second integer.
15

The LCM of 12 and 15 is 60

In this case we have              12 *     5 = 60
                                  15 *     4 = 60
```

Features of this program include a check for bad data and a special message if the numbers entered are relatively prime. A reasonable first-level pseudocode development for this program is

1. Get the data
2. Put the numbers in order Small, Large
3. Find the least common multiple (LCM)
4. Print the results

A structure chart for this pseudocode is given in Figure 7.1. Module specifications for this problem are

1. GetNumbers Module
   Data received: None
   Information returned: Two positive integers
   Logic: Have the user enter two positive integers.
2. Order Module
   Data received: Two positive integers
   Information returned: The integers in order Small, Large
   Logic: **IF** Num2 is less than Num1 **THEN** switch them.
3. FindLCM Module
   Data received: Two positive integers in order Small, Large
   Information returned: The LCM of Num1, Num2
   Logic: Increase multiples of the larger number until a multiple of the smaller number is found.
4. PrintResults Module
   Data received: Num1, Num2, and the LCM
   Information returned: None

Structure chart for **PROGRAM** LeastCommonMultiple

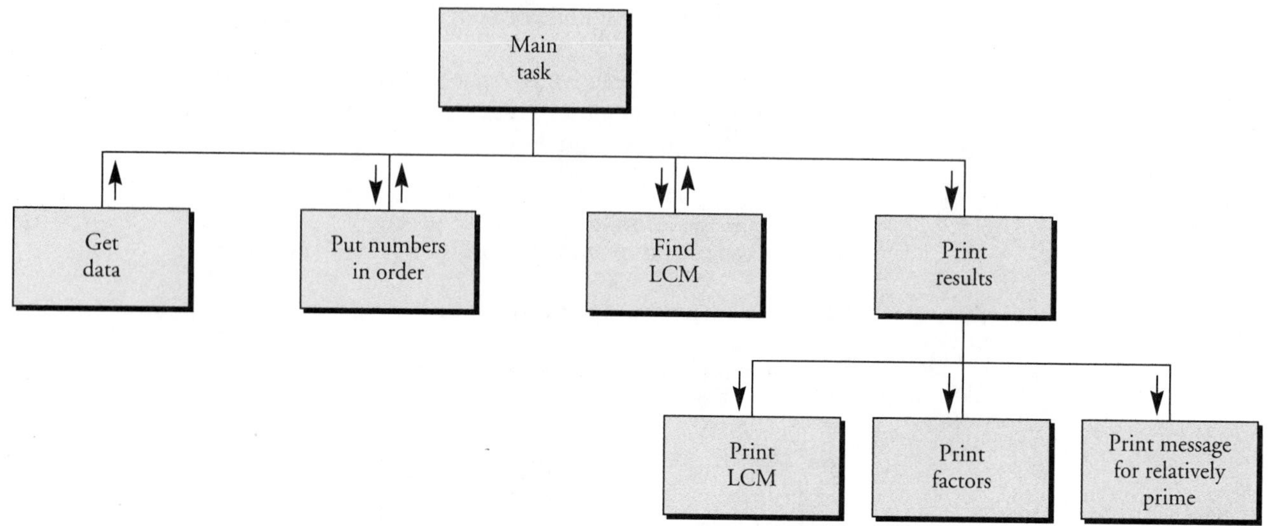

Logic: Print the LCM.
Print the products that show how Num1, Num2 are factors of LCM.
Print a special message if the LCM is Num1 * Num2.

The GetNumbers module has the user enter two positive integers as input. There is a bad data check to assure that each integer is positive. The Order module guarantees that Num1 <= Num2.

The FindLCM module can be further developed as

3. Find the least common multiple (LCM)
   3.1 Initialize Factor to 1
   3.2 Initialize LCMFound to **false**
   WHILE NOT LCMFound **DO**
   3.3 **IF** Num1 divides Num2 * Factor **THEN**
      3.3.1 LCM is Num2 * Factor
      3.3.2 LCMFound is **true**
      ELSE
      3.3.3 Increment Factor by 1

The PrintResults module can be as simple as printing the LCM, but we will display slightly more descriptive information here. Thus, the PrintResults module is developed as

4. Print the results
   4.1 Display the LCM
   4.2 Display how Num1 divides LCM
   4.3 Display how Num2 divides LCM
   4.4 Display a special message if Num1 * Num2 equals LCM

A complete program to solve this problem follows:

```
PROGRAM LeastCommonMultiple (input, output);

{  This program finds and displays the least common multiple (LCM)  }
{  of two positive integers.  The procedure for input illustrates    }
{  the robust property of guaranteeing that each integer is          }
{  positive.  After the numbers are put in order Num1 <= Num2, the   }
{  algorithm for finding the LCM is to consider multiples of Num2    }
{  until Num1 divides some multiple.  At that point, the multiple    }
{  of Num2 is the LCM.  Note that a special message is displayed     }
{  when Num1 and Num2 are relatively prime (no factors in common).   }

CONST
  Skip = ' ';

VAR
  Small, Large, LCM : integer;

{*******************************************************************}

PROCEDURE GetNumbers (VAR Num1, Num2 : integer);

  {  Given:   Nothing                                                }
  {  Task:    Get two positive integers as input                    }
  {  Return:  Two positive integers:  Num1, Num2                    }

  BEGIN
    writeln ('This program allows you to find the');
    writeln ('LEAST COMMON MULTIPLE of two positive integers.');
    writeln;                                                              1
    REPEAT
      writeln ('Please enter the first integer.');
      readln (Num1)
    UNTIL Num1 > 0;

    REPEAT
      writeln ('Please enter the second integer.');
      readln (Num2)
    UNTIL Num2 > 0
  END;  {  of PROCEDURE GetNumbers  }

{*******************************************************************}

PROCEDURE Order (VAR Num1, Num2 : integer);

  {  Given:   Two positive integers                                  }
  {  Task:    Put them in order so that Num1 <= Num2                 }
  {  Return:  Two positive integers: Num1 <= Num2                    }     2

  VAR
    Temp : integer;
  BEGIN
    IF Num2 < Num1 THEN
```

```
        BEGIN
          Temp := Num1;
          Num1 := Num2;
          Num2 := Temp
        END  {  of IF...THEN  }
    END;  {  of PROCEDURE Order  }

{*******************************************************************}

PROCEDURE FindLCM (Small, Large : integer;
                   VAR LCM : integer);

  {  Given:   Two positive integers (Num1, Num2) with Num1 <= Num2    }
  {  Task:    Find their LCM by considering multiples of Num2         }
  {  Return:  The LCM of Num1, Num2                                   }

  VAR
    Factor : integer;
    LCMFound : boolean;
  BEGIN
    Factor := 1;
    LCMFound := false;
    WHILE NOT LCMFound DO                                                    3

      {  Find the first time Small is a divisor of Large * Factor  }
      IF (Large * Factor MOD Small = 0) THEN
        BEGIN
          LCM := Large * Factor;
          LCMFound := true
        END  {  of IF...THEN option  }
      ELSE
        Factor := Factor + 1
  END;  {  of PROCEDURE FindLCM  }

{*******************************************************************}

PROCEDURE PrintResults (Num1, Num2, LCM : integer);

  {  Given:   Num1, Num2, LCM of Num1 and Num2                        }
  {  Task:    Display the LCM, products that show that Num1 and       }
  {                Num2 divide LCM, and a special message if          }
  {                Num1 * Num2 = LCM                                  }
  {  Return:  Nothing                                                 }

  VAR
    OtherFactor : integer;
  BEGIN
    writeln;                                                                 4
    writeln ('The LCM of ', Num1, ' and ', Num2, ' is ', LCM);
    writeln;
    write ('In this case we have ');
    OtherFactor := LCM DIV Num1;
    writeln (Skip:9, Num1:4, ' * ', OtherFactor:4, ' = ', LCM);
    OtherFactor := LCM DIV Num2;
    writeln (Skip:30, Num2:4, ' * ', OtherFactor:4, ' = ', LCM);
```

```
    IF LCM = Num1 * Num2 THEN
      BEGIN
        writeln;
        writeln ('Notice that these numbers are relatively prime.')
      END  {  of IF...THEN  }
  END;  {  of PROCEDURE PrintResults  }

{*******************************************************************}

BEGIN  {  Main program  }
  GetNumbers (Small, Large);
  Order (Small, Large);
  FindLCM (Small, Large, LCM);
  PrintResults (Small, Large, LCM)
END.  {  of main program  }
```

Sample runs of this program produce the following:

```
This program allows you to find the
LEAST COMMON MULTIPLE of two positive integers.

Please enter the first integer.
12
Please enter the second integer.
15

The LCM of 12 and 15 is 60

In this case we have            12 *    5 = 60
                                15 *    4 = 60

This program allows you to find the
LEAST COMMON MULTIPLE of two positive integers.

Please enter the first integer.
18
Please enter the second integer.
25

The LCM of 18 and 25 is 450

In this case we have            18 *   25 = 450
                                25 *   18 = 450

Notice that these numbers are relatively prime.

This program allows you to find the
LEAST COMMON MULTIPLE of two positive integers.

Please enter the first integer.
10
Please enter the second integer.
20

The LCM of 10 and 20 is 20
```

```
In this case we have              10 *    2 = 20
                                  20 *    1 = 20

This program allows you to find the
LEAST COMMON MULTIPLE of two positive integers.

Please enter the first integer.
-4
Please enter the first integer.
4
Please enter the second integer.
6

The LCM of 4 and 6 is 12

In this case we have               4 *    3 = 12
                                   6 *    2 = 12
```

Running and Debugging Hints

1. Each subprogram can be tested separately to see if it is producing the desired result. This is accomplished by a main program that calls and tests only the subprogram in question.
2. Be sure the type and order of actual parameters and formal parameters agree. For example,

```
PROCEDURE GetData (VAR Init1, Init2 : char; Sc : integer);
          GetData (Initial1, Initial2, Score);
```

3. Carefully distinguish between value parameters and variable parameters. If a value is to be returned to the main program, it must be passed by reference using a variable parameter. This means it must be declared with **VAR** in the procedure heading.

Summary

Key Terms

actual parameter (argument)	modularity	subprogram
bottom-up testing	passed by reference	user-defined function
formal parameter	procedure	value parameter
function	side effect	variable parameter
	structured programming	

Keywords

exp	**ln**	**PROCEDURE**
FUNCTION		

Key Concepts

- A subprogram is a program within a program; procedures and functions are subprograms.
- Subprograms can be utilized to perform specific tasks in a program. Procedures are often used to initialize variables (variable parameters), get data (variable parameters), print headings (no variables needed), perform computations (value and/or variable parameters), and print data (value parameters).
- The general form of a procedure heading is

PROCEDURE <name> (<parameter list>)

- A typical procedure heading that could be used when writing a procedure to produce the heading for the output is

```
PROCEDURE PrintHeader;
```

- A procedure is called, or invoked, from the main program by a reference to the procedure name.

```
BEGIN  {  Main program  }
  PrintHeader
END.  {  of main program  }
```

  PrintHeader is the procedure call statement.
- Procedures are placed in a program after the variable declaration section and before the start of the executable section for the main program.

```
PROGRAM Practice (input, output);

VAR

PROCEDURE PrintTitle;                        ┐
  BEGIN                                      │
    .                                        │
    .                                        ├ placement of procedure
    .                                        │
  END;  {  of PROCEDURE PrintTitle  }        ┘

BEGIN  {  Main program  }
  .
  .
  .
END.  {  of main program  }
```

- Value parameters are used when values are passed only from the main program to the procedure; a typical parameter list is

```
PROCEDURE PrintData (N1, N2 : integer;
                     X, Y : real);
```

- Variable parameters are used when values are to be returned to the main program; a typical parameter list is

```
PROCEDURE GetData (VAR Init1, Init2 : char;
                   VAR N1 : integer);
```

- A formal parameter is listed in a subprogram heading; it is like a blank waiting to receive a value from the calling program.

formal parameters

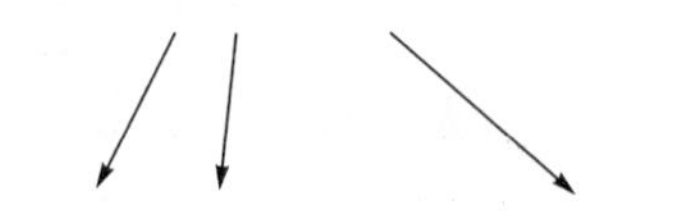

```
PROCEDURE PrintNum (N1, N2 : integer; N3 : real);
```

- An actual parameter is a variable listed in a subprogram call in the calling program.

actual parameters

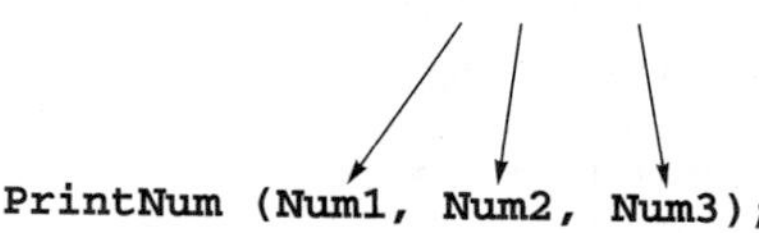

```
PrintNum (Num1, Num2, Num3);
```

- The formal parameter list in the subprogram heading must match the number and types of actual parameters used in the main program when the subprogram is called.

```
PROCEDURE PrintNum (N1, N2 : integer; N3 : real);
PrintNum (Num1, Num2, Num3);
```

- A user-defined function is a subprogram that performs a specific task.
- The form of a user-defined function is

```
FUNCTION <function name> (<parameter list>) : <return type>;
  VAR
  BEGIN
      .
      .  (work of function here)
      .
  END;
```

- An assignment must be made to the function name in the body of the function.
- Within the function, the function name can only be used on the left of an assignment statement.
- A function returns exactly one value; a procedure may return none or several.

Chapter Review Exercises

1. Explain the difference between a value parameter and a variable parameter. Give an example of how each is used.
2. Explain the difference between an actual parameter and a formal parameter.

3. A procedure is defined as

```
PROCEDURE SampleProc (A : integer;
                      VAR B : real;
                      C : char);
```

Which parameters in this definition are variable parameters and which are value parameters?

In Exercises 4–12, which procedure calls are valid? (Int1 represents an integer variable. Real1 represents a real, and Ch1 represents a character.) If the call is invalid, explain why.

4. `SampleProc (Int1, Real1, Ch1);`
5. `SampleProc;`
6. `SampleProc (Int1; VAR Real1, Ch1);`
7. `SampleProc (Int1; Real1; Ch1);`
8. `SampleProc (Int1, Ch1);`
9. `SampleProc (3, 5.0, 'X');`
10. `SampleProc (Real1, Int1, Ch1);`
11. `SampleProc (Int1, Int2, Int3);`
12. `SampleProc (Real1, Int1, Ch1);`
13. Write a procedure to print the following:

```
<<<<<<<<<<<<<<<<<<<<<<<<<<>>>>>>>>>>>>>>>>>>>>>>>>>>

               Programming in Pascal

                    is GREAT!!

<<<<<<<<<<<<<<<<<<<<<<<<<<>>>>>>>>>>>>>>>>>>>>>>>>>>
```

14. Write a main program to print the message from Exercise 13 five times.

In Exercises 15–21, indicate whether the statement is a valid procedure declaration. Explain the problem for those that are invalid.

15. `PROCEDURE Exercise15 (A : integer, Y : real);`
16. `PROCEDURE Exercise16 (VAR A; X : integer);`
17. `PROCEDURE Exercise17 (VAR A : integer; VAR B : integer);`
18. `PROCEDURE (VAR A : integer; B : char);`
19. `PROCEDURE Exercise19 (VAR A : integer: VAR B : integer);`
20. `PROCEDURE Exercise20 (A : integer; VAR B : char);`
21. `PROCEDURE Exercise21 (VAR A : integer; VAR C : char);`

For Exercises 22–26, write a statement that can be used to call the procedure or function.

22. `PROCEDURE Exercise22 (VAR A, B : integer; C : real);`
23. `PROCEDURE Exercise23 (VAR A : integer; B : real);`
24. `FUNCTION Exercise24 (A : integer; B : real) : real;`
25. `PROCEDURE Exercise25;`
26. `FUNCTION Exercise26 (A : real) : char;`

For Exercises 27–33, indicate which are valid function headings. Explain the problem with those that are invalid.

27. `FUNCTION Exercise27 (X : real);`
28. `FUNCTION Exercise28;`
29. `FUNCTION Exercise29 (VAR A : integer) : integer;`

30. `FUNCTION Exercise30 (X : real) : char;`
31. `FUNCTION Exercise31 (A : integer; B : real) : boolean;`
32. `FUNCTION Exercise32 (A : integer; B : real) : integer;`
33. `FUNCTION Exercise33 (A, B : real; C : integer) ; integer;`
34. Write statements that can be used to call the valid functions in Exercises 27–33.
35. Why are variable parameters used in a procedure designed to initialize variables?

Programming Problems

To facilitate the use of subprograms in writing programs to solve problems, some programming problems for this chapter consist of redesigning previous programs.

■ 1. In Chapter 6 (Problem 1), you modified the program for the Caswell Catering and Convention Service (Problem 7, Chapter 4, and Problem 14, Chapter 5) so that they could use it for all of their customers. Now, revise the program so that you use a separate procedure for each of the following:
   a. Compute meal cost.
   b. Compute room rate.
   c. Compute surcharge.
   d. Compute discount.
   e. Print a statement.

   Use functions to compute the tax and tip.

2. A prime number is a positive integer that can be divided evenly only by 1 and the number itself (for example, 17). Write a program that will determine whether or not a given positive integer is prime. (*Hint:* you only have to check for divisors less than or equal to the square root of the number being tested. Thus, if 79 is the positive integer being examined, the check of divisors would be 2, 3, . . ., 9.) Write a function that returns a **boolean** value of **true** for a prime number or **false** otherwise (a composite number). Make use of the fact that if 2 is not a divisor, then no other even integer will be a divisor.
3. The Fairfield College faculty recently signed a three-year contract that included salary increments of 7 percent, 6 percent, and 5 percent, respectively, for the next three years. Write a program that allows a user to enter the current salary and then prints the compounded salary for each of the next three years.
4. In Chapter 5 (Problem 17) and Chapter 6 (Problem 3), you wrote and revised a program for the Community Hospital. Now, write functions to
   a. Compute room charge.
   b. Compute telephone charge.
   c. Compute television charge.
5. In Chapter 6 (Problem 7) you wrote a program to compute the miles per gallon for each tank of gas used by a traveler and the cumulative miles per gallon each time the tank was filled. Revise that program by writing procedures to get a line of data and print a line of output. Write functions to compute the mileage per tank and the total mileage.
6. In Chapter 6 (Problem 8), you wrote a program that read pairs of positive integers and produced Parkside's Other Triangle for each pair. Write procedures to
   a. Get the data.
   b. Check for bad data.
   c. Print the triangle.

7. In Chapter 5, you wrote a program for Mr. Lae Z. Programmer (Problems 5, 22, and 23). You revised that program in Chapter 6 (Problem 13). Now it's time to revise it again. Write procedures to get the data Mr. Lae Z. Programmer has requested (the overall class average and the number of students receiving each letter grade) and to print the results. Use a function to compute the grade.

8. Problem 14 in Chapter 6 asked that you revise the Pentagon visitor parking lot problem you worked on in Chapter 5 (Problem 26). Using that program, write procedures to get the data and print results. Develop one function to compute the number of hours in the parking lot and another to compute the parking fee.

9. Write a program to get the coefficients of the quadratic equation $ax^2 + bx + c = 0$ from the keyboard and then print the value of the discriminant $b^2 - 4ac$. A sample display for getting input is

```
Enter coefficients a, b, and c for the quadratic
     equation ax² + bx + c = 0
a = ?
b = ?
c = ?
```

Run this program at least three times using test data that result in $b^2 - 4ac = 0$, $b^2 - 4ac > 0$, and $b^2 - 4ac < 0$.

10. The program written in the **Focus on Program Design: Case Study 7.2** segment of this chapter allows the user to enter two positive integers and then displays the least common multiple. Enhance this program by including a procedure that allows the user to decide whether or not to continue. The new main program should be

```
BEGIN  {  Main program  }
  MoreTrials := true;
  WHILE MoreTrials DO
    BEGIN
      GetNumbers (Num1, Num2);
      Order (Num1, Num2);        {  Num1 <= Num2  }
      FindLCM (Num1, Num2, LCM);
      PrintResults (Num1, Num2, LCM);
      CheckForRepetition (MoreTrials)
    END  {  of WHILE loop  }
END.  {  of main program  }
```

11. Reconsider Problem 9, in which you were asked to write a program to display the value of the discriminant of a quadratic equation. Solutions to the quadratic equation depend on the value of the discriminant, as follows:
a. $b^2 - 4ac = 0$ (exactly one solution)
b. $b^2 - 4ac > 0$ (two distinct solutions)
c. $b^2 - 4ac < 0$ (no real solutions)
Create a modular development for a program that evaluates the discriminant, indicates the number of real solutions, and displays any real solutions that exist. Write module specifications for each module in your design. Assuming a subprogram is used for each module, give a complete description of all parameters used in your design.

12. The irrational number e can be written as the infinite series

$$e = \frac{1}{0!} + \frac{1}{1!} + \frac{1}{2!} + \frac{1}{3!} + \ldots$$

Using a specified number of terms from the series, write a function Eapprox that approximates e. Thus, Eapprox(1) = 1, Eapprox(2) = 2, Eapprox(3) = 2.5, and so on. Use the function Eapprox in a program that lists the first 10 approximations to e. Use the function Factorial developed in the exercises for Section 7.4. Make your program interactive by allowing the user to choose (a) the number of terms used or (b) the degree of accuracy desired before approximations terminate. Use the standard function **exp**(1) as a comparison for approximated values.

13. Write an interactive program that displays a monthly calendar for any given year. Input will be the desired year and the day of the week for January 1 of the given year. Use a separate procedure for each month. Note that the last day of one month (Thursday, for example) precedes the first day of the next month (Friday, for example). The heading for each month should consist of the name of the month and column headings for the days of the week. A typical heading would be

```
                    OCTOBER

     S    M     Tu    W    Th    F    S

-----------------------------------------
```

Every year that is evenly divisible by 4 is a leap year (February has 29 days), except that years that mark centuries must be evenly divisible by 400 to be leap years (2000 is a leap year, but 2100 is not).

14. An amount of money P is invested at a rate of interest R that is compounded n times per year. The amount A due the investor after t years is given by

$$A = P\left(1 + \frac{Rt}{n}\right)^{nt}$$

Write an interactive program that allows the user to investigate different investment options. For example, using your program, the user should be able to decide if it is better to invest a certain amount at 6 percent compounded annually or at $5\frac{1}{2}$ percent compounded monthly. Input will consist of the amount to be invested, the rate of interest, the number of times the interest is compounded per year, and the number of years the money will be invested.

Communication in Practice

1. Discuss the issue of documenting subprograms with teachers of computer science, students who have completed courses in computer science, and some of your classmates. Prepare a report for the class on this issue. Your report should contain information about different forms of documentation, the perceived need for documentation by various groups, the significance of documenting data transmission, and so forth. If possible, use specific examples to illustrate good documentation of subprograms versus poor documentation of subprograms.

Chapter 8

Subprograms: Using Procedures and Functions

Chapter Outline

Being able to write procedures and functions represents a major step in learning to use Pascal to solve problems. Now that you have some familiarity with subprograms, we look at some aspects of their use in the design of solutions to programming problems.

8.1 Scope of Identifiers

Objectives

- to understand what is meant by local identifiers
- to understand what is meant by global identifiers
- to understand the scope of an identifier
- to recognize appropriate and inappropriate uses for global identifiers
- to be able to use appropriate names for local and global identifiers

Global and Local Identifiers

Identifiers used to declare variables in the declaration section of a program can be used throughout the entire program. For purposes of discussion here, we will think of the program as a **block** and each subprogram as a **subblock** or block for the subprogram. Each block may contain a parameter list, a local declaration section, and the body of the block. A program block for **PROGRAM** ShowScope can be envisioned as shown in Figure 8.1. Furthermore, if X1 is a variable in ShowScope, we will indicate this as shown in Figure 8.2, where an area in memory has been set aside for X1. When a program contains a subprogram, a separate memory area within the memory area for the program is set aside for the subprogram to use during execution. Thus, if ShowScope contains a procedure named Subprog1, we can envision this as shown in Figure 8.3. If Subprog1 contains the variable X2, we have the program shown in Figure 8.4, which could be indicated in the program by

```
PROGRAM ShowScope (input, output);

VAR
  X1 : real;

PROCEDURE Subprog1 (X2 : real);
```

The **scope of an identifier** refers to the block in which it is declared or defined. When subprograms are used, each identifier is available only to the block in which it is declared; this includes all subprograms contained within the subprogram block. Identifiers are not available outside their blocks.

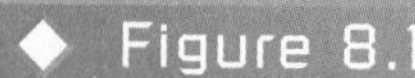

◆ Figure 8.1

Program heading and main block

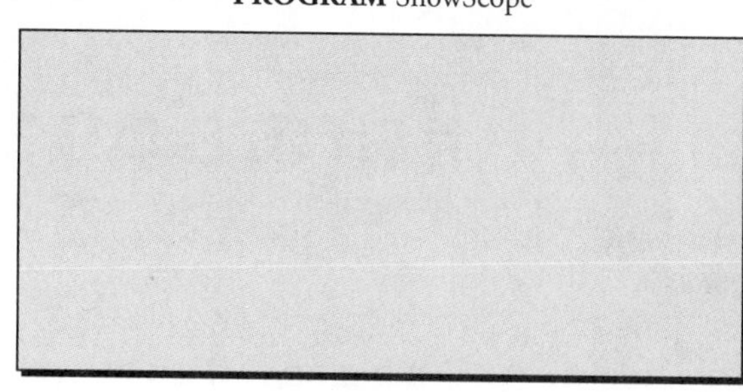

◆ Figure 8.2

Variable location in main block

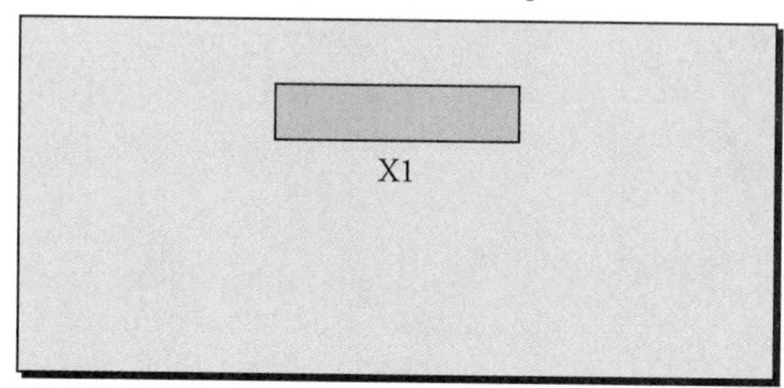

◆ Figure 8.3

An illustration of a subblock

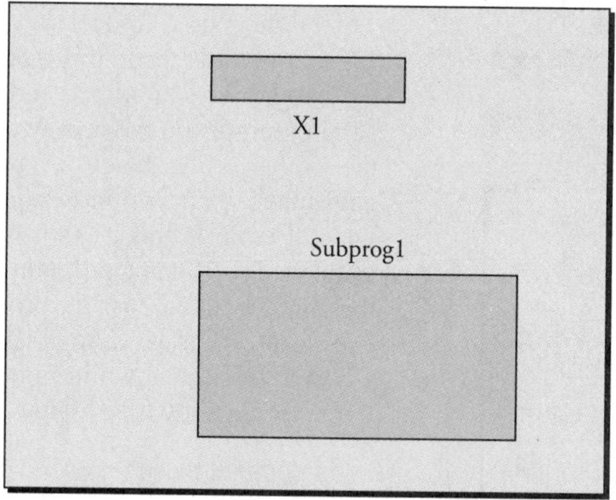

A **block** is part of a program in Pascal, which can be thought of as having a heading and a block. The block contains an optional declaration part and a compound statement. The block structure for a subprogram is a subblock.

Identifiers that are declared in the main block are called **global identifiers** (or **global variables**); identifiers that are restricted to use within a subblock are called **local identifiers** (or **local variables**). Variable X1 in the previous illustration can be used in the main program and in **PROCEDURE** Subprog1; therefore, it is a global identifier. On the other hand, variable X2 can be used only within the procedure where it is declared; therefore, it is a local identifier. Any attempt to reference X2 outside the procedure will result in an error. Identifiers used in a block in which they are not declared are said to be **nonlocal identifiers** to that block.

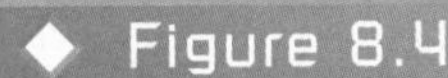

Figure 8.4

Variable location within a subblock

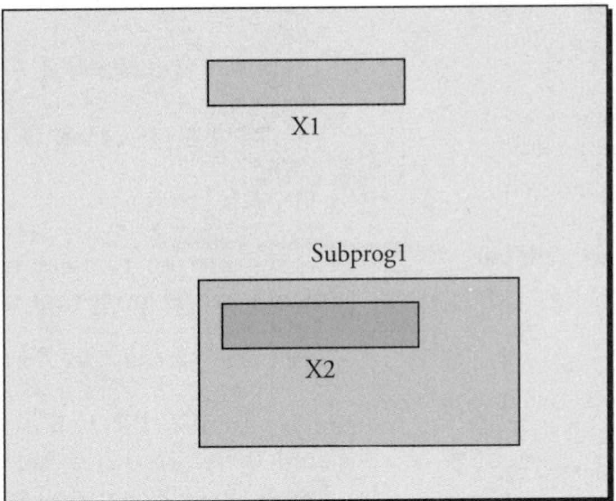

Figure 8.5

Local and global identifiers

PROGRAM ShowScope

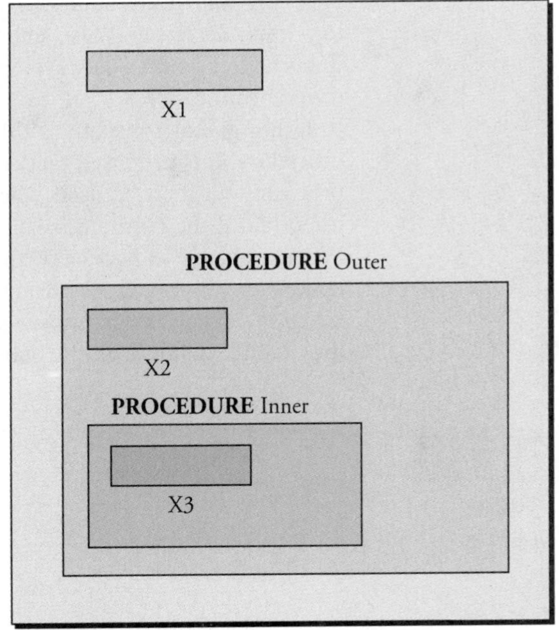

A **subblock** is a block structure for a subprogram.

Figure 8.5 illustrates the scope of identifiers. In this figure, the scope of X3 is **PROCEDURE** Inner, the scope of X2 is **PROCEDURE** Outer, and the scope of X1 is **PROGRAM** ShowScope. When procedures are nested like this, the scope of an identifier is the largest block in which it is declared.

Now let's examine an illustration of local and global identifiers. Consider the following program and procedure declaration:

The **scope of an identifier** is the largest block in which the identifier is available.

A **global identifier** is an identifier that can be used by the main program and all subprograms in a program. Also referred to as a **global variable.**

A **local identifier** is an identifier that is restricted to use within a subblock of a program. Also referred to as a **local variable.**

Nonlocal identifiers are identifiers that are used in a block in which they are not defined.

```
PROGRAM ScopePrac (output);

VAR
  A, B : integer;

PROCEDURE Subprog (A1 : integer);
  VAR
    X : real;
```

Blocks for this program can be envisioned as shown in Figure 8.6.

Since A and B are global identifiers, the statement

```
writeln (A, B, A1, X:10:2);
```

could be used in **PROCEDURE** Subprog, although A and B are not specifically declared there. However, this statement could not be used in the main program because A1 and X are local to **PROCEDURE** Subprog.

Using Global Identifiers and Constants

In general, it is not good practice to refer to global identifiers within procedures. Using locally defined identifiers helps to avoid unexpected side effects and protects your programs. In addition, locally defined identifiers facilitate debugging and top-down design and also enhance the portability of procedures. This is especially important if a team is developing a program by having different people work on different procedures.

Using global constants is different. Since constant values cannot be changed by a procedure, it is preferred that constants be defined in the **CONST** section of the main program and then be used whenever needed by any subprogram. This is especially important if the constant is subject to change over time (for example, StateTaxRate). When a change is necessary, one change in the main program is all that is needed to make all subprograms current. If a constant is used in only one procedure (or function), some programmers prefer to have it defined near the point of use. Thus, they would define it in the subprogram in which it is used.

◆ Figure 8.6

Relation of variables for **PROGRAM** ScopePrac

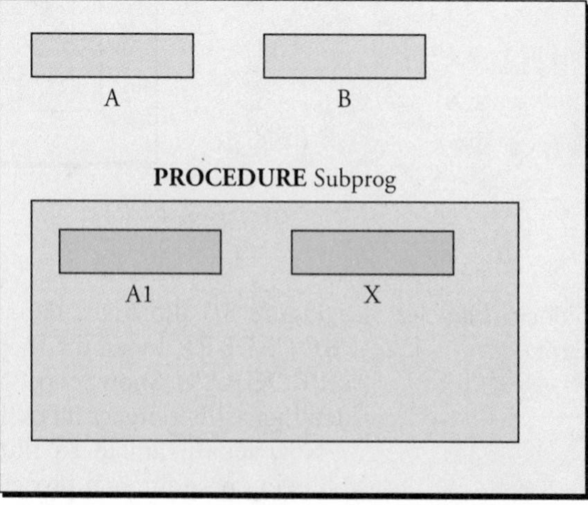

Name of Identifiers

Because separate areas in memory are set aside when subprograms are used, it is possible to have identifiers with the same name in both the main program and a subprogram. Thus

```
PROGRAM Demo (input, output);

VAR
  Age : integer;

PROCEDURE Subprog (Age : integer);
```

can be envisioned as shown in Figure 8.7.

When the same name is used in this manner, any reference to this name will result in action being taken as locally as possible. Thus, the assignment statement

```
Age := 20;
```

made in **PROCEDURE** Subprog assigns 20 to Age in the procedure but not to Age in the main program (see Figure 8.8).

Now that you know you can use the same name for an identifier in a subprogram and the main program, the question is "Should you?" There are two schools of thought regarding this issue. If you use the same name in the procedures as you do in the main program, it facilitates matching parameter lists and independent development of procedures. However, this practice can be confusing when you first start working with subprograms. Thus, some teachers prefer using different, but related, identifiers. For example,

```
GetData (Score1, Score2);
```

in the main program could have a procedure heading of

```
PROCEDURE GetData (VAR PScore1, PScore2 : integer);
```

◆ Figure 8.7

Using identifiers in subprograms

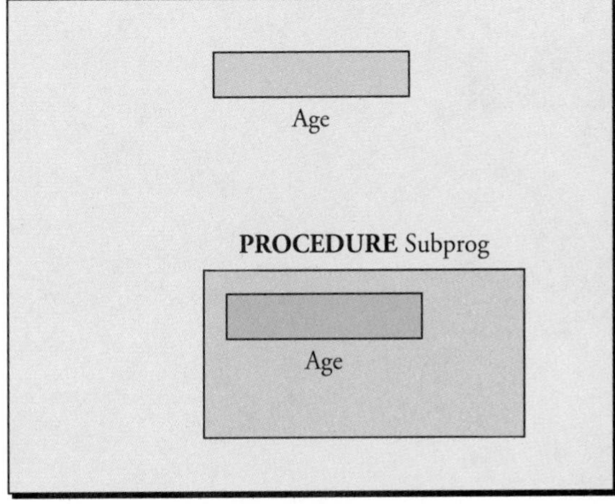

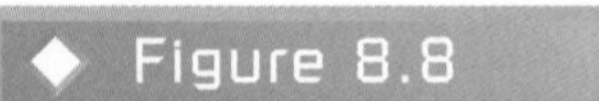

Assigning values in subprograms

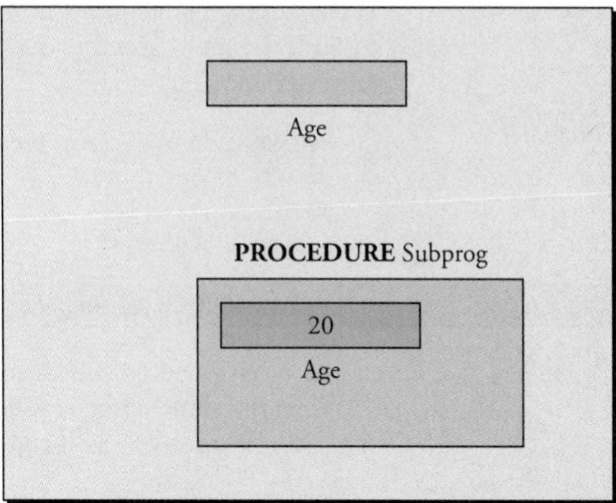

where the letter P denotes an identifier in the procedure. Although this may facilitate better understanding in early work with subprograms, it is less conducive to portability and independent development of procedures. Both styles are used in this text.

Multiple Procedures

More than one procedure can be used in a program. When this occurs, all the previous uses and restrictions of identifiers apply to each procedure. Blocks for multiple procedures can be depicted as shown in Figure 8.9. Identifiers in the main program can be accessed by each procedure. However, local identifiers in the procedures cannot be accessed outside their blocks.

When a program contains several procedures, they can be called from the main program in any order, but only if they are not contained in another procedure (see Nesting in Section 8.3). If one procedure contains a call to another procedure (or function), the subprogram being called must appear before the procedure from which it is called. (An exception is available if the **FORWARD** statement is used; see Section 8.3.)

◆ Figure 8.9

Blocks for multiple subprograms

PROCEDURE A

PROCEDURE B

PROCEDURE C

The same names for identifiers can be used in different procedures. Thus, if the main program uses variables Wage and Hours and both of these are used as arguments in calls to different procedures, you have the situation shown in Figure 8.10. Using the same names for identifiers in different procedures makes it easier to keep track of the relationship among variables in the main program and their associated parameters in each subprogram.

◆ Figure 8.10

Identifiers in multiple subprograms

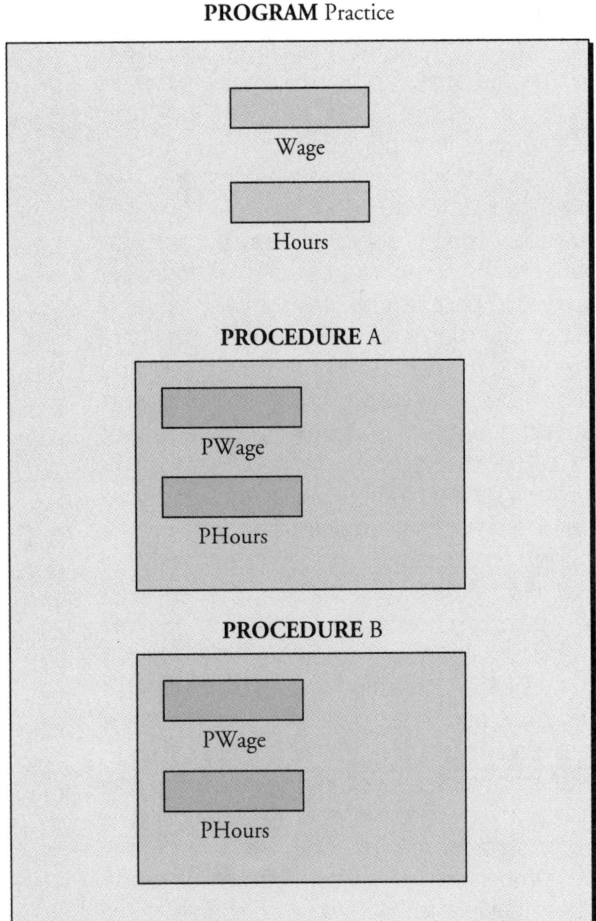

Exercises 8.1

1. Explain the difference between local and global identifiers.
2. State the advantages of using local identifiers.
3. Discuss some appropriate uses for global identifiers. List several constants that would be appropriate global definitions.
4. What is meant by the scope of an identifier?
5. Write a test program that will enable you to see
   a. what happens when an attempt is made to access an identifier outside of its scope; and

A Note of Interest

Inspections: Debugging in the 1990s

(The following information was provided at the author's request by Franco E. Mau, Development Engineer at Tandem Computers Incorporated, Cupertino, California.)

The process of debugging software has become multifaceted. One form of finding code defects currently used by Tandem Computers Incorporated is the use of "inspections." This inspection process was pioneered by Bill Fagan at IBM in the late 1970s and was introduced at Tandem Computers Incorporated in 1989.

Simply stated, an inspection is a team process of finding defects, particularly in software packages and smaller segments of computer code. An inspection team consists of at least five members: the author (code writer), a moderator, a reader, and two inspectors, one of whom also serves as a recorder. A typical session is about two hours long; many sessions are required to inspect a single software package.

Prior to an inspection session, the reader and both inspectors spend about two hours examining the package or code to be reviewed. At the beginning of the inspection process for a document, initial rules are established concerning what kinds of defects (logical, syntactic, and so on) are being sought. Subsequently, all defects are related to these initial rules.

During a session, authors are available only to make clarifications and otherwise are not involved in the discussion. All members of the inspection team are active participants in the inspection. The moderator sets the pace, makes sure all participants are prepared, inspects code, and generally coordinates the session. The reader provides an oral description of what the code is attempting to accomplish. The recorder records code defects on forms. The code line numbers are listed with respective references to how the lines relate to the defects being sought.

All participants in an inspection are encouraged to stress professionalism. They must be willing to communicate and share their technical expertise. When discussing defects in the code or algorithms, they are expected to make technical comments and to avoid personal references. Inspections focus on the work—not on the author. The style of the code or algorithms is not criticized; the sole purpose of an inspection is to find defects. Consistent with this philosophy, managers are not present at inspections and inspection results may not be used to evaluate employee performance.

Inspections are typically conducted before the code is run. Particular importance is paid to the boundary conditions associated with the software package. This helps to identify defects that may not be apparent because "the program runs." A defect can be something that is incorrect or something that is missing. All defects identified in the inspection become part of a database. If no defects are found, it is assumed the inspection is not sufficient.

The primary positive result of an inspection is that it does identify defects. In a typical two-hour session, while inspecting 200 to 300 lines of code, four to six defects may be identified. However, a second, but important, by-product of inspections is the training of personnel. Authors of code learn more about how to avoid defects in the future; readers and inspectors learn how to improve their own work. Finally, all involved learn from the shared expertise of the inspection team. This is especially helpful when the team consists of members with diverse backgrounds.

In summary, inspections have proved to be very valuable. They result in improved communication, higher morale, in-service training, and better software packages.

---

b. how the values change as a result of assignments in the subprogram and the main program when the same identifier is used in the main program and a procedure.

6. Review the following program fragment:

```
PROGRAM Practice (input, output);

VAR
  A, B : integer;
  X : real;
  Ch : char;
```

```
PROCEDURE Sub1 (A1 : integer);
  VAR
    B1 : integer;
  BEGIN
    .
    .
    .
  END;  {  of PROCEDURE Sub1  }

PROCEDURE Sub2 (A1 : integer;
              VAR B1 : integer);
  VAR
    X1 : real;
    Ch1 : char;
  BEGIN
    .
    .
    .
  END;  {  of PROCEDURE Sub2  }
```

a. List all global identifiers.
b. List all local identifiers.
c. Indicate the scope of each identifier.

*7. Provide a schematic representation of the program fragment and all subprograms and identifiers in Exercise 6.

8. Using the program fragment with identifiers and subprograms as depicted in Figure 8.11, state the scope of each identifier.

◆ Figure 8.11

Schematic for **PROGRAM** ExerciseEight

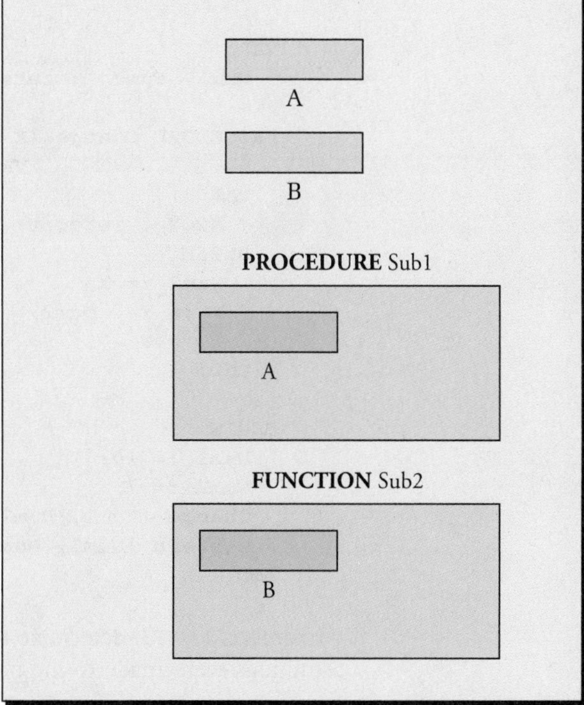

* 9. What is the output from the following program?

```
PROGRAM ExerciseNine (output);

VAR
  A : integer;

PROCEDURE Sub1 (A : integer);
  BEGIN
    A := 20;
    writeln (A)
  END;  {  of PROCEDURE Sub1  }

PROCEDURE Sub2 (VAR A : integer);
  BEGIN
    A := 30;
    writeln (A)
  END;  {  of PROCEDURE Sub2  }

BEGIN  {  Main program  }
  A := 10;
  writeln (A);
  Sub1 (A);
  writeln (A);
  Sub2 (A);
  writeln (A)
END.  {  of main program  }
```

10. What is the output from the following program?

```
PROGRAM ExerciseTen (output);

VAR
  Num1, Num2, : integer;

PROCEDURE Change (X : integer;
                  VAR Y : integer);
  VAR
    Num2 : integer;
  BEGIN
    Num2 := X;
    Y := Y + Num2;
    X := Y
  END;

BEGIN
  Num1 := 10;
  Num2 := 7;
  Change (Num1, Num2);
  writeln (Num1, Num2)
END.
```

For Exercises 11–13, determine the output of the program set forth in Exercise 10 if substitutions were made to the procedure headings as follows:

*11. `PROCEDURE Change (VAR X : integer; Y : integer);`

12. `PROCEDURE Change (X, Y : integer);`

*13. `PROCEDURE Change (VAR X, Y : integer);`

In Exercises 14–16, assume that the variable declaration section of a program is

```
VAR
  Age, Hours : integer;
  Average : real;
  Initial : char;
```

Furthermore, assume that procedure headings and declaration sections for procedures in this program are as presented in Exercises 14–16. Find all errors.

14.
```
PROCEDURE Average (Age1, Hrs : integer;
                   VAR Aver : real);
```

*15.
```
PROCEDURE Sub1 (Hours : integer;
                VAR Average : real);
  VAR
    Age : integer;
    Init : char;
```

16.
```
PROCEDURE Compute (Hrs : integer;
                   VAR Aver : real);
  VAR
    Age : real;
```

*17. Discuss the advantages and disadvantages of using the same names for identifiers in a subprogram and the main program.

18. Write appropriate headings and declaration sections for the program and subprograms illustrated in Figure 8.12.

*19. Find all errors in the following program.

```
PROGRAM ExerciseNineteen (output);

VAR
  X, Y : real;

PROCEDURE Sub1 (VAR X1 : real);
  BEGIN
    writeln (X1:20:2);
    writeln (X:20:2);
    writeln (Y:20:2)
  END;  {  of PROCEDURE Sub1  }

BEGIN  {  Main program  }
  X := 10.0;
  Y := 2 * X;
  writeln (X:20:2, Y:20:2);
  Sub1 (X);
  writeln (X1:20:2);
  writeln (X:20:2);
  writeln (Y:20:2)
END.  {  of main program  }
```

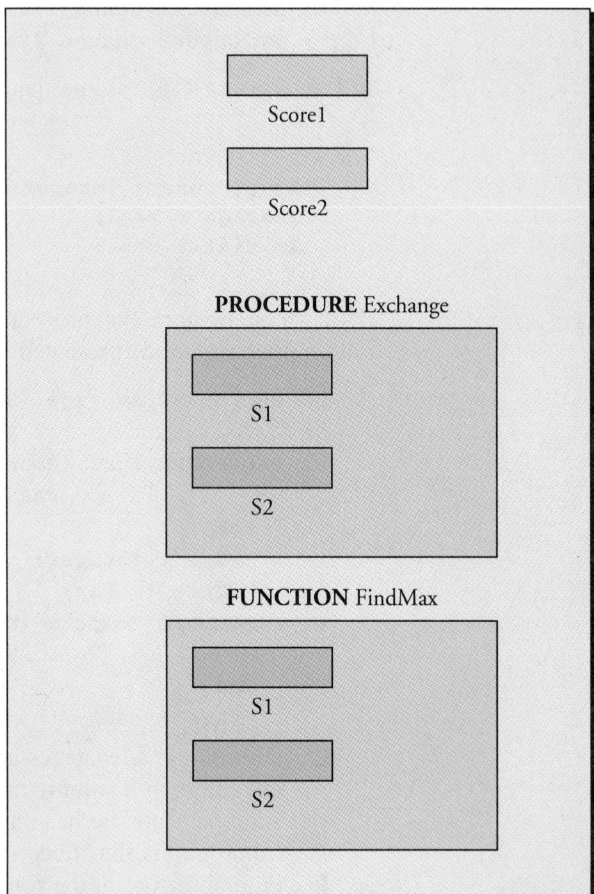

◆ Figure 8.12

Schematic for **PROGRAM** ExerciseEighteen

8.2 Using Subprograms

Objectives

- to understand how subprograms can be used to design programs
- to be able to use procedures to get data for programs
- to be able to use subprograms to perform tasks required in programs
- to be able to use procedures for output

Program Design

Throughout this text you have seen examples of problems solved by the development of a sequence of tasks. Tasks are stated in the order in which they are to be performed and then each task is refined according to its level of complexity. Now that you are capable of using procedures and functions in a program, you should see how they can be used to design a program for solving a problem. After the algorithm for solving the problem has been developed in pseudocode, subprograms can be written for the various tasks and then called from the main program as needed.

To illustrate, let's consider how a program could be designed using subprograms. We will not write the subprograms at this point; we will only indicate how they would be used in designing the program. Our problem is to compute grades for a class. A first-level pseudocode development could be

1. Initialize variables
2. Print a heading
3. Process grades for each student
4. Print a summary

This could be refined to

1. Initialize variables
2. Print a heading
3. Process grades for each student
   WHILE more students **DO**
   3.1 Get data
   3.2 Compute average
   3.3 Compute letter grade
   3.4 Print data
   3.5 Compute totals
4. Print a summary
   4.1 Print class average
   4.2 Print number receiving each grade

Subprograms can be used to design a program consistent with this algorithm as illustrated in Table 8.1. Note that this particular choice of procedures and functions is not the only solution available to us; there are many other ways to use subprograms in a program to solve our problem.

Table 8.1

Subprograms from pseudocode

Pseudocode Statement	Subprogram
1. Initialize variables	**PROCEDURE** Initialize
2. Print a heading	**PROCEDURE** PrintHeader
3. Process grades for each student	
WHILE more students **DO**	
3.1 Get data	**PROCEDURE** GetData
3.2 Compute average	**FUNCTION** Average
3.3 Compute letter grade	**FUNCTION** LetterGrade
3.4 Print data	**PROCEDURE** PrintData
3.5 Compute totals	**PROCEDURE** ComputeTotals
4. Print a summary	
4.1 Print class average	**PROCEDURE** PrintAverage
4.2 Print number receiving each grade	**PROCEDURE** PrintNumGrades

Now that we have identified procedures and functions for various tasks in this problem, we can write the program design. Since we are relatively early in the design stage, we will not include parameters for the subprograms. However, as we develop each subprogram, we will indicate appropriate value and variable parameters.

The main program could be

```
BEGIN  { Main program }
  Initialize (          );
  PrintHeader;
  WHILE MoreStudents DO
    BEGIN
      GetData (         );
```

```
        Aver := Average(              );
        LetGrade := LetterGrade(              );
        PrintData (            );
        ComputeTotals (              )
      END;
    PrintAverage (              );
    PrintNumGrades (              )
  END.  {  of main program  }
```

Procedures for Initializing Variables

It may be required that variables be initialized at the beginning of the program. This initialization can be done in the main program or in a procedure; it is generally the first step in developing an algorithm. Thus,

1. Initialize variables

will frequently be listed as a line of pseudocode and, when a procedure is written to implement this task, the program design becomes

```
BEGIN  {  Main program  }
  Initialize (          );
```

Procedures for initializing require variable parameters because variables in the main program will subsequently be used with the initial values assigned in **PROCEDURE** Initialize.

The program for our grading problem will require initialization of variables Count, ClassTotal, NumA, NumB, NumC, NumD, and NumE. Appropriate initialization can be accomplished by the following procedure:

```
PROCEDURE Initialize (VAR Count : integer;
                      VAR ClassTotal : real;
                      VAR NumA, NumB, NumC, NumD, NumE : integer);
  BEGIN
    Count := 0;
    ClassTotal := 0.0;
    NumA := 0;
    NumB := 0;
    NumC := 0;
    NumD := 0;
    NumE := 0
  END;  {  of PROCEDURE Initialize  }
```

This procedure can be called from the main program by

```
Initialize (Count, ClassTotal, NumA, NumB,
            NumC, NumD, NumE);
```

Procedures for Headers

Procedures for headers facilitate program design. Unless you are using page numbers, inputting dates, or making some other heading change, no parameters are needed for this kind of procedure. You should include such a procedure in all programs you write.

Procedures for Input

As noted earlier, a simplified pseudocode version of most programs is

1. Get the data
2. Process the data
3. Print results

Now let's take a closer look at procedures for input. Because the data obtained will be used in the program, you will need to declare variable parameters in the procedure heading. Thus, if each line of data contains three integer test scores, a reasonable procedure heading is

```
PROCEDURE GetData (VAR Score1, Score2, Score3 : integer);
```

The actual procedure would be

```
PROCEDURE GetData (VAR Score1, Score2, Score3 : integer);
  BEGIN
    readln (Score1, Score2, Score3)
  END;  {  of PROCEDURE GetData  }
```

The procedure can be called from the main program by

```
GetData (Score1, Score2, Score3);
```

Note that the identifiers are selected so the program will be easier to read and debug.

Subprograms for Tasks

The second step in the problem solution

2. Process the data

can be quite complex. When an algorithm is developed to solve a problem, this step usually requires several levels of refinement. Once each level has been sufficiently refined, subprograms can be developed to implement it. Then the main program can call a major subprogram; this subprogram in turn calls the appropriate subprograms as needed.

When writing procedures for various tasks, you need to be careful with the use of value and variable parameters. If the main program needs a different value of the variable for later use in the program, you must then use a variable parameter. For instance, you would need a variable parameter if a count is being made in a procedure or if a running total is being kept. However, if the procedure merely performs some computation with the values received, then the values may be passed with value parameters.

To illustrate, let's consider some of the tasks from our earlier problem of computing grades for a class. One task was to print the data for one student. The initials, three test scores, test average, and letter grade are available for each student. Since the procedure only prints the data, all values can be passed by value parameters. If typical output for one student is the line

```
BRL          89   93   95     92.33    A
```

the procedure could be

A Note of Interest

Niklaus Wirth

Niklaus Wirth began his work in the computing field by taking a course in numerical analysis at Laval University in Quebec, Canada. However, the computer (Alvac III E) was frequently out of order and the hexadecimal code programming exercises went untested. He received his doctorate from the University of California, Berkeley, in 1963.

After other early experiences in programming, it became apparent to Wirth that computers of the future had to be more effectively programmable. Consequently, he joined a research group that worked on developing a compiler for an IBM 704. This language was NELIAC, a dialect of ALGOL 58. In rapid succession, he developed or contributed to the development of Euler, ALGOL W, and PL360. In 1967, he returned to Switzerland and established a team of three assistants with whom he developed and implemented the language Pascal.

Pascal was the first major programming language to implement the ideas and methodology of structured programming and was initially developed to teach programming concepts. It is particularly successful as a teaching language because it allows the teacher to focus on structures and concepts rather than on features and peculiarities. However, Pascal has rapidly expanded beyond its initial purpose and has found increasing acceptance in business and scientific applications.

```
PROCEDURE PrintData (Initial1, Initial2, Initial3 : char;
                     Score1, Score2, Score3 : integer;
                     Aver : real;
                     LetGrade : char);
  BEGIN
    write (Initial1:20, Initial2, Initial3);
    write (Score1:10, Score2:5, Score3:5);
    writeln (Aver:10:2, LetGrade:5)
  END;  {  of PROCEDURE PrintData  }
```

Another task from the same problem was to compute running totals for the class. To do this, we need to count the number of students, accumulate averages so we can compute a class average, and count the number of students receiving each letter grade. In this case, both value and variable parameters will be needed. Formal variable parameters will be used for the actual parameters

```
Count
ClassTotal
NumA, NumB, NumC, NumD, NumE
```

and formal value parameters will be used for the actual parameters

```
Aver
LetGrade
```

With the variables thus identified, the procedure could be

```
PROCEDURE ComputeTotals (Aver : real;
                         LetGrade : char;
                         VAR Count : integer;
                         VAR ClassTotal : real;
                         VAR NumA, NumB, NumC, NumD, NumE : integer);
```

```
BEGIN
  Count := Count + 1;
  ClassTotal := ClassTotal + Aver;
  CASE LetGrade OF
    'A' : NumA := NumA + 1;
    'B' : NumB := NumB + 1;
    'C' : NumC := NumC + 1;
    'D' : NumD := NumD + 1;
    'E' : NumE := NumE + 1
  END  {  of CASE LetGrade  }
END;  {  of PROCEDURE ComputeTotals  }
```

This procedure could be called from the main program by

```
ComputeTotals (Aver, LetGrade, Count, ClassTotal,
               NumA, NumB, NumC, NumD, NumE);
```

Finally, let's consider **FUNCTION** Average. This function receives three integer test scores, computes their average, and returns a real to the main program. The function could be

```
FUNCTION Average (Score1, Score2, Score3 : integer) : real;
  BEGIN
    Average := (Score1 + Score2 + Score3) / 3
  END;  {  of FUNCTION Average  }
```

This could be called from the main program by

```
Aver := Average(Score1, Score2, Score3);
```

Use of subprograms facilitates the writing of programs for problems with solutions that have been developed using top-down design. A procedure or function can be written for each main task. Each subprogram can contain its own subprograms if needed.

How complex should a procedure or function be? In general, functions should be relatively short and perform a specific task. Procedures can be longer but probably should be no more than one page of printout. Some programmers prefer to limit procedures to no more than one full screen. If a procedure is longer than a page or screen, you might consider subdividing the task into smaller procedures.

Procedures for Output

A standard part of every program is to generate some output. Thus, when designing a program, the general task

3. Print results

can either have a single procedure written for it or it can be refined into subtasks and have a procedure written for each subtask. When writing procedures for output, only value parameters are needed. Since you are only printing results, it is not necessary to pass values back to the main program.

Writing procedures for output can be tedious because of the need for neat, attractive output. Be careful to use columns when appropriate, the center of the page, underlining, blank lines, spacing within a line (formatting), and appropriate messages.

Reusable Code

A significant use of subprograms is to develop procedures and functions that can be used in subsequent programs. To illustrate, let's develop a procedure called Swap that interchanges the values in two variables. We will then use this procedure in the text whenever it is necessary to interchange values of variables. This technique is often used with sorting algorithms.

```
PROCEDURE Swap (VAR Num1, Num2 : integer);
  VAR
    Temp : integer;
  BEGIN
    Temp := Num1;
    Num1 := Num2;
    Num2 := Temp
  END;  {  of PROCEDURE Swap  }
```

Using this procedure, we can now exchange the values of two variables by a call to Swap, such as

```
Swap (Number1, Number2);
```

Functions versus Procedures

When should you use a function instead of a procedure in a program? A general rule is to think of a function as a construct that returns only one value. Thus, a function would be used when a single value is required in the main program. Variable parameters can be used with functions, but this is discouraged in good programming practices.

What Kind of Parameters Should Be Used?

One should use variable parameters when information is going to be returned to the main program; otherwise, use value parameters. The choices will be apparent if data flow arrows or module specifications are used when designing the solution to the problem.

Using Stubs

Stub programming is a no-frills, simple version of a final program.

As programs get longer and incorporate more subprograms, a technique frequently used to get the program running is **stub programming.** A stub program is a no-frills, simple version of what will be a final program. It does not contain details of output and full algorithm development. It does contain a rough version of each subprogram and all parameter lists. When the stub version runs, you know your logic is correct and values are appropriately being passed to and from subprograms. Then you can fill in necessary details to get a complete program.

Using Drivers

The main program is sometimes referred to as the main driver. When subprograms are used in a program, this driver can be modified to check subprograms in a sequential fashion. For example, suppose a main driver is

```
BEGIN  {  Main driver  }
  Initialize (Count, Sum);
```

```
    MoreData := true;
    WHILE MoreData DO
      GetData (Sum, Count, MoreData);
    PrintResults (Sum, Count)
  END.
```

The first procedure could be checked by putting comment indicators around the rest of the program and temporarily adding a statement to print values of variables. Thus, you could run the following version:

```
BEGIN  {  Main driver  }
  Initialize (Count, Sum);
  writeln ('Count is', Count; ' Sum is', Sum);
{  MoreData := true;
    WHILE MoreData DO
    GetData (Sum, Count, MoreData);
  PrintResults (Sum, Count)  }
END.
```

Once you are sure the first subprogram is running, you can remove the comment indicators, delete the **writeln** statement, and continue through the main driver to check successive subprograms.

Cohesive Subprograms

A **cohesive subprogram** is one that has been developed to perform a single task.

The cohesion of a subprogram is the degree to which the subprogram performs a single task. A subprogram that is developed in such a way is called a **cohesive subprogram.** As you use subprograms to implement a design based on modular development, you should always try to write cohesive subprograms.

The property of cohesion is not well defined. Subtask complexity varies in the minds of different programmers. In general, if the task is unclear, the corresponding subprogram will not be cohesive. When this happens, you should subdivide the task until a subsequent development allows cohesive subprograms.

To illustrate briefly the concept of cohesion, reconsider the first-level design of a problem to compute grades for a class. Step 3 of this design could be

3. Process grades for each student.

Clearly, this is not a well-defined task. Thus, if you were to write a subprogram for this task, the subprogram would not be cohesive. When we look at the subsequent development

3. Process grades for each student
   WHILE NOT eof DO
   3.1 Get a line of data
   3.2 Compute average
   3.3 Compute letter grade
   3.4 Print data
   3.5 Compute totals

we see that procedures to accomplish subtasks 3.1, 3.2, 3.3, and 3.4 will be cohesive because each subtask consists of a single task. The final subtask, compute totals, may or may not result in a cohesive subprogram. More information is needed before you can decide what is to be done at this step.

Procedural Abstraction

Procedural abstraction is the process of considering only what a procedure is to do rather than the details of the procedure.

The purpose of using procedures is to simplify reasoning. During the design stage, as a problem is subdivided into tasks, the problem solver (you) should have to consider only "what" a procedure is to do and not be concerned about "how" the procedure accomplishes the task. Instead, the procedure name and comments at the beginning of the procedure should be sufficient to inform the user as to what the procedure does. Developing procedures in this manner is referred to as **procedural abstraction.**

Procedural abstraction is the first step in designing and writing a procedure. A list of parameters and comments about the action of the procedure should be written before you write the procedure body. This forces clarity of thought and aids design. Using this method might perhaps cause you to discover that your design is not sufficient to solve the task and that redesign is necessary. Therefore, you could reduce design errors and save time when writing code.

Procedural abstraction becomes especially important when teams work on a project. Each member of the writing team should be able to understand the purpose and use of procedures written by other team members without having to analyze the body of each procedure. This is analogous to the situation in which you use a predefined function without really understanding how the function works.

Procedural abstraction is perhaps best formalized in terms of preconditions and postconditions. Recall from Sections 5.6 and 6.6 that a precondition is a comment that states precisely what is true before a certain action is taken. A postcondition states what is true after the action has been taken. Carefully written preconditions and postconditions used with procedures enhance the concept of procedural abstraction.

In summary, procedural abstraction means that when writing or using procedures, you should think of them as single, clearly understood units, each of which accomplishes a specific task.

Encapsulation

Encapsulation is the process of placing all implementation details in a distinct physical package.

Encapsulation is the process of placing all implementation details in a distinct physical package. This is closely related to the process of using procedural abstraction to design a problem solution. Procedural abstraction separates what a procedure does from how it is done. Developing the implementation details of a procedure—including everything necessary to accomplish the task of the procedure as part of the procedure—is referred to as encapsulation.

Encapsulation is a key concept in object-oriented programming (OOP). Programming languages that support object-oriented programming enforce encapsulation to differing degrees. Standard Pascal does not support object-oriented programming.

Interface and Documentation

The **interface** of a subprogram is a formal statement of how communication occurs between the subprogram and the main program and between the subprogram and other subprograms.

Independent subprograms (whether procedures or functions) need to communicate with the main program and with other subprograms. A formal statement of how such communications occur is called the **interface** of the subprogram. An interface usually consists of comments at the beginning of a subprogram and includes all the documentation the reader will need to use the subprogram. This information typically consists of

1. What is received by the subprogram when called
2. What task the subprogram performs
3. What is returned after the subprogram performs its task
4. How the subprogram is called

This information aids in debugging the program. In this text, as explained in Section 7.3, our interface consists of the three-part documentation section

```
{  Given:    <Statement of information sent from the program>  }
{  Task:     <Statement of task(s) to be performed>             }
{  Return:   <Statement of value(s) returned to the program>    }
```

The headings of subprograms in complete programs are given in this manner. When subprograms are separately developed and illustrated, this documentation is not included; instead, text development immediately preceding the subprogram serves the same purpose. How a subprogram is called is usually apparent from the identifiers listed in the subprogram heading.

We conclude this section with the following case study.

Focus on Program Design: Case Study 8.1

Perfect Numbers

Positive integers are considered to be perfect if the sum of the proper divisors equals the number. For example, 6, with proper divisors of 1, 2, and 3 is a perfect number. If the sum is greater than the number, the positive integer is abundant. If the sum is less than the number, the integer is deficient. Given these descriptions, let's consider the development of a program that will get a positive integer as input, determine whether it is deficient, perfect, or abundant, and print an appropriate message. A first-level pseudocode development for this is

1. Get the number
2. Sum the divisors
3. Print the results

A structure chart for this problem is given in Figure 8.13.

Module specifications for the main modules follow. Here, and in the remainder of the text, the module names are written as they would be in procedures and functions in code.

◆ Figure 8.13

Structure chart for **PROGRAM** PerfectNumbers

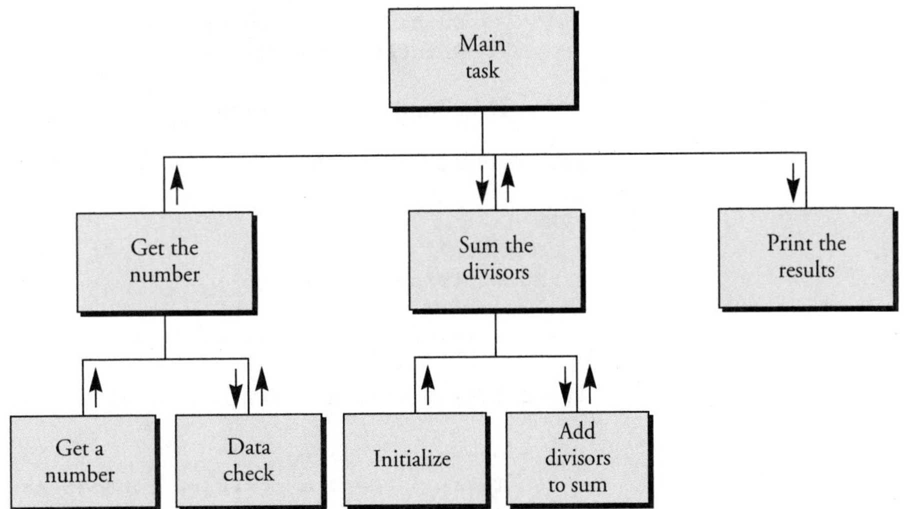

1. GetNumber Module
   Data received: None
   Information returned: Positive integer
   Logic: Get a number interactively.
   Use a **REPEAT** loop to guarantee good data.
2. SumDivisors Module
   Data received: Number
   Information returned: SumOfDivisors
   Logic: Initialize SumOfDivisors to zero.
   Use a **FOR** loop to check for divisors.
   In each case, add each divisor to SumOfDivisors.
3. PrintResults Module
   Data received: Number
   SumOfDivisors
   Information returned: None
   Logic: Use nested **IF . . . THEN . . . ELSE** to print appropriate message.

A second-level pseudocode development is

1. Get the number
   1.1 Get a number
   1.2 Check for good data
2. Sum the divisors
   2.1 Initialize sum of divisors to zero
   2.2 **FOR** each divisor less than the number, add divisor to sum of divisor
3. Print the results
   3.1 **IF** SumOfDivisors is less than Number **THEN**
   deficient message
   ELSE IF SumOfDivisor equals Number **THEN**
   perfect message
   ELSE
   abundant message

The main program for this would be

```
GetNumber (Number);
SumDivisors (Number, SumOfDivisors);
PrintResults (Number, SumOfDivisors);
```

The complete program follows:

```
PROGRAM PerfectNumbers (input, output);

VAR
  Number,                         {  Number to be examined      }
  SumOfDivisors : integer;        {  Sum of divisors of number  }

{***************************************************************}

PROCEDURE GetNumber (VAR Number : integer);

  {  Given:   Nothing                                            }
  {  Task:    Read a positive integer entered from the keyboard  }    1
  {  Return:  The number read                                    }
```

```
 BEGIN
   REPEAT
     writeln ('Enter a positive integer and press <Enter>.');
     readln (Number)
   UNTIL Number > 0
 END;  {  of PROCEDURE GetNumber  }

{***************************************************************}

PROCEDURE SumDivisors (Number : integer;
                       VAR SumOfDivisors : integer);

  {  Given:   A positive integer, Number                          }
  {  Task:    Sum the divisors of Number                          }
  {  Return:  SumOfDivisors of Number                             }
                                                                      2
  VAR
    TrialDivisor : integer;
  BEGIN
    SumOfDivisors := 0;
    FOR TrialDivisor := 1 TO Number DIV 2 DO
      IF Number MOD TrialDivisor = 0 THEN
        SumOfDivisors := SumOfDivisors + TrialDivisor
  END;  {  of PROCEDURE SumDivisors  }

{***************************************************************}

PROCEDURE PrintResults (Number, SumOfDivisors : integer);

  {  Given:   Number and SumOfDivisors                            }
  {  Task:    Print a message that indicates whether              }
  {                the integer read was deficient,                }
  {                perfect, or abundant                           }
  {  Return:  Nothing                                             }

  BEGIN                                                               3
    writeln;
    write ('The number ', Number, ' is ');
    IF SumOfDivisors < Number THEN
      writeln ('deficient.')
    ELSE IF SumOfDivisors = Number THEN
      writeln ('perfect.')
    ELSE
      writeln ('abundant.');
    writeln
  END;  {  of PROCEDURE PrintResults  }

{***************************************************************}

BEGIN  {  Main program  }
  GetNumber (Number);
  SumDivisors (Number, SumOfDivisors);
  PrintResults (Number, SumOfDivisors)
END.  {  of main program  }
```

Sample runs of this program produce the following results:

```
Enter a positive integer and press <Enter>.
-9
Enter a positive integer and press <Enter>.
6

The number 6 is perfect.

Enter a positive integer and press <Enter>.
100

The number 100 is abundant.

Enter a positive integer and press <Enter>.
28

The number 28 is perfect.

Enter a positive integer and press <Enter>.
50

The number 50 is deficient.

Enter a positive integer and press <Enter>.
35

The number 35 is deficient.
```

Exercises 8.2

*1. Discuss whether value parameters or variable parameters should be used in a procedure to
   a. initialize variables.
   b. get data.
   c. print results.

2. Write a test program that utilizes subprograms for solving the problem of reading integers, computing their sum and average, and printing results. The main program should be along the lines of

```
BEGIN
  Initialize (Count, Total);
  MoreData := true;
  WHILE MoreData DO
    GetData (Count, Total, MoreData);
  Average := FindAverage(Count, Total);
  PrintHeading;
  PrintResults (Count, Total, Average)
END.
```

*3. Suppose the pseudocode for solving a problem is

   1. Initialize variables
   2. Print a heading
   3. **WHILE** Flag = **true DO**

3.1 Get new data
3.2 Perform computations
3.3 Increment counter
3.4 Check Flag condition
4. Print results

Show how subprograms could be used to design a program to implement this algorithm.

4. You have been asked to write a program for the Sleep Cheap motel chain. Each line of data contains information for one customer. This information consists of number of nights occupancy (integer), room rate (real), and telephone charges (real). Your program should print a statement for each customer and keep totals for the number of customers served, total room charges, and total telephone charges. Assume the pseudocode for solving this problem is

   1. Initialize variables
   2. **WHILE MoreCustomers DO**
      2.1 Get customer data
      2.2 Perform computations
      2.3 Print statement
      2.4 Add totals
   3. Print summary

   a. Design a program to implement this algorithm.
   b. Write a procedure or function for each statement of the algorithm.

*5. Given real numbers *a, b,* and *c,* write a function to compute the discriminant ($b^2 - 4ac$).

6. Given a positive integer *a* and any integer *b* (positive, negative, or zero), write a function that computes a^b.

7. Write a complete program to solve the grading problem posed at the beginning of this section.

8. Modify the program of the **Focus on Program Design: Case Study 8.1** to allow the user to check several numbers without having to rerun the program each time.

8.3 Forward Reference and Nesting

Objectives

- to be able to use forward reference for multiple subprograms
- to be able to use multiple subprograms in a program
- to be able to use nested subprograms in a program
- to understand the scope of identifiers when using multiple and nested subprograms

By now you should be familiar with the important concepts of procedures and functions and relatively comfortable with using them for the modular design of a program. As you examined material in Chapter 7 and the first two sections of this chapter, you may have noticed that use of subprograms was restricted to the main program calling procedures or functions and procedures or functions calling previously declared subprograms. In this section we will examine more sophisticated uses of subprograms—specifically, forward reference and nesting.

Subprograms That Call Other Subprograms

Sections 7.2, 7.3, and 7.4 included brief discussions concerning the use of multiple functions and procedures. Thus far, a subprogram has been able to call only subprograms that have been previously declared. For example, suppose a program has two functions (**FUNCTION** A and **FUNCTION** B) and a procedure

(**PROCEDURE** C). As shown in Figure 8.14, **FUNCTION** B could call **FUNCTION** A and **PROCEDURE** C could call either **FUNCTION** A or **FUNCTION** B. Any other calls would result in errors.

◆ Figure 8.14

Multiple subprograms

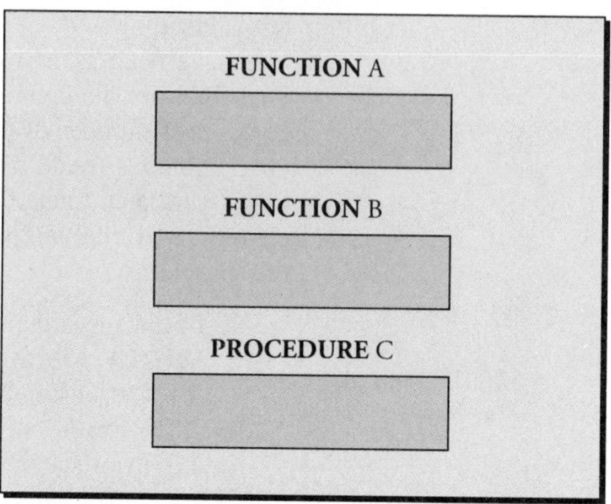

Forward Reference

These restrictions on function and procedure calls impose limitations on program development. There may be times when it is either desirable or necessary for a subprogram to call another subprogram that appears later in the declaration section. This can be accomplished by a **forward reference.**

Forward reference is a method that allows a subprogram to call another subprogram that appears later in the declaration section.

A forward reference is achieved by listing the function or procedure heading with all parameters followed by the reserved word **FORWARD.** If a function is to be forward referenced, the function type should be included as part of the heading listed; for example,

```
FUNCTION B (X : real) : real; FORWARD;
```

When the function or procedure is declared later in the program, the parameter list and function type are omitted. To illustrate, consider

```
FUNCTION B (X : real) : real; FORWARD;

FUNCTION A (Ch : char) : char;
  BEGIN
      .
      .
      .
  END;  {  of FUNCTION A  }

FUNCTION B;
  BEGIN
      .
      .
      .
  END;  {  of FUNCTION B  }
```

In this case, **FUNCTION** A can call **FUNCTION** B because **FUNCTION** B has been forward referenced. **FUNCTION** B can call **FUNCTION** A because **FUNCTION** A is declared before **FUNCTION** B.

Forward reference may be necessary so that subprograms can be listed in a particular order to make a program more readable. A programmer may, for instance, choose to list functions in order of complexity from least complex to most complex or from most complex to least complex. Either listing might necessitate a forward reference. Also, a program design may require a forward reference for some subprograms. If **FUNCTION** A has an option that calls **FUNCTION** B and **FUNCTION** B has an option that calls **FUNCTION** A, one of them must have a forward reference.

In summary, when using forward reference, you should

1. List all parameters and function types when the forward reference is made.
2. Use the reserved word **FORWARD** as a statement when the forward reference is made.
3. Omit the parameter list when the forward-referenced subprogram is written.
4. Use a comment to indicate the parameter list for the forward-referenced subprogram as shown in the **Communication and Style Tips**.

Nesting

Because a subprogram can contain the same sections as the main program, the declaration section of a function or procedure can contain functions or procedures. When this occurs, the subprograms are **nested subprograms.** Subprograms can be nested to any level desired by the programmer. However, as we have seen, several levels of nesting tend to make programs difficult to follow and debug. If the nesting is too complicated, you should redesign the program.

Nested subprograms are functions or procedures within functions or procedures.

Communication and Style Tips

When using a forward reference, add a line comment to indicate parameters when the subprogram is developed.

```
FUNCTION First (S1, S2, S3 : integer) : integer; FORWARD;
      .
      .
      .

FUNCTION Second (<parameter list>) : <return type>;
  BEGIN
      .
      .
      .
  END;  {  of FUNCTION Second  }

FUNCTION First;  {  (S1, S2, S3 : integer) : integer  }
```

comment here

Figure 8.15

Nested subprograms

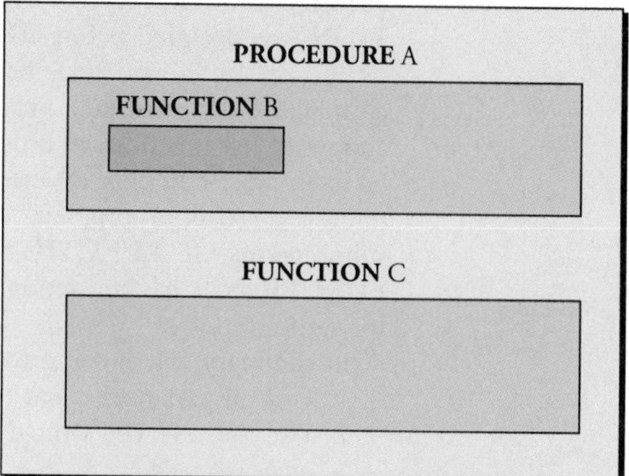

Nested subprograms can be represented as shown in Figure 8.15. This schematic representation of nesting assists us in understanding the scope of various identifiers. Remember, identifiers are restricted to the block and all subblocks in which they are declared. To illustrate, suppose variables are declared in a program as shown in Figure 8.16. There, X, which is declared in the main program, can be accessed by any subprogram in this program. In particular, even the nested function, **FUNCTION** B, could use values in X from the main program. However, X1 can only be used by

Figure 8.16

Variables in nested subprograms

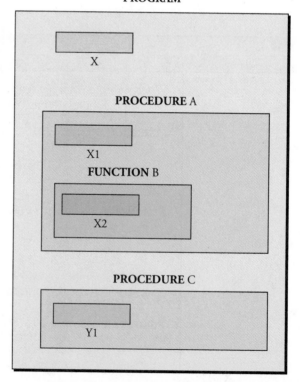

PROGRAM

X

PROCEDURE A

X1

FUNCTION B

X2

PROCEDURE C

Y1

PROCEDURE A and **FUNCTION** B. The variables used in Figure 8.16 and their scope are shown in Table 8.2.

Table 8.2

Scope of variables for nested subprograms

Variable	Scope (can be accessed by)
X	Main program **PROCEDURE** A **FUNCTION** B **PROCEDURE** C
X1	**PROCEDURE** A **FUNCTION** B
X2	**FUNCTION** B
Y1	**PROCEDURE** C

We conclude the discussion on nesting subprograms with an example that illustrates nested functions. The principles behind it apply to any combination of nested subprograms and to any level of nesting.

Example 8.1

Let's write a function TotalCharge to compute the total charge for guests of a motel chain. You may assume that RoomRate and TaxRate have been defined in a **CONST** section of the main program and that NumNights has been assigned an appropriate value. The function will be called by

```
AmountDue := TotalCharge(NumNights);
```

For purposes of this example, the tax will be computed by a nested function Tax. Thus, we have

```
FUNCTION TotalCharge (NumNights : integer) : real;
  VAR
    RoomCharge, RoomTax : real;

  FUNCTION Tax (RoomCharge : real) : real;
    BEGIN
      Tax := RoomCharge * TaxRate
    END;  {  of FUNCTION Tax  }

  BEGIN  {  TotalCharge  }
    RoomCharge := NumNights * RoomRate;
    RoomTax := Tax(RoomCharge);
    TotalCharge := RoomCharge + RoomTax
  END;  {  of FUNCTION TotalCharge  }
```

Figure 8.17 is a schematic representation of the constants, variables, and functions used in Example 8.1.

◆ Figure 8.17

Schematic for Example 8.1

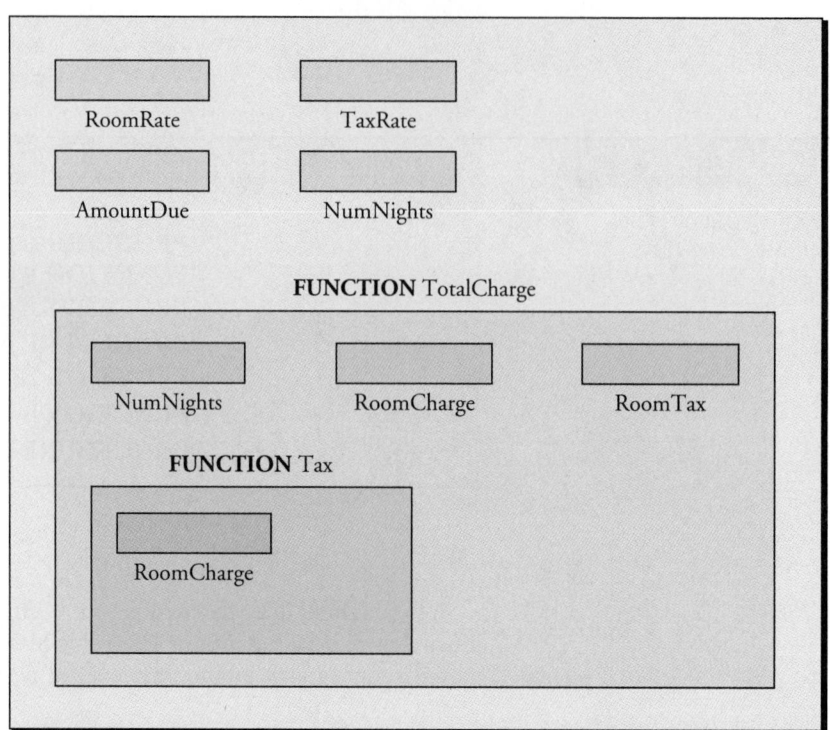

Exercises 8.3

*1. Discuss the scope of identifiers in nested subprograms.

2. Explain why forward reference could be necessary in a program.

In Exercises 3–7, find and correct all errors.

*3.
```
PROCEDURE AddTwo (VAR B : integer);
  BEGIN
    B := AddOne(B);
    B := AddOne(B)
  END;  {  of PROCEDURE AddTwo  }
FUNCTION AddOne (A : integer) : integer;
  BEGIN
    AddOne := A + 1
  END;  {  of FUNCTION AddOne  }
```

4.
```
FUNCTION AddOne (A : integer) : integer;
  BEGIN
    AddOne := A + 1
  END;  {  of FUNCTION AddOne  }
PROCEDURE AddTwo (VAR B : integer);
  BEGIN
    B := AddOne(B);
    B := AddOne(B)
  END;  {  of PROCEDURE AddTwo  }
```

*5.
```
FUNCTION AddOne (A : integer) : integer; FORWARD;
PROCEDURE AddTwo (VAR B : integer);
  BEGIN
```

```
    B := AddOne(B);
    B := AddOne(B)
  END;  {  of PROCEDURE AddTwo  }
FUNCTION AddOne (A : integer) : integer;
  BEGIN
    AddOne := A + 1
  END;  {  of FUNCTION AddOne  }
```

6.
```
FUNCTION AddOne (A : integer) : integer; FORWARD;
PROCEDURE AddTwo (VAR B : integer);
  BEGIN
    B := AddOne(B);
    B := AddOne(B)
  END;  {  of PROCEDURE AddTwo  }
FUNCTION AddOne;
  BEGIN
    AddOne := A + 1
  END;  {  of FUNCTION AddOne  }
```

*7.
```
FUNCTION AddOne (A : integer) : integer; FORWARD;
PROCEDURE AddTwo (VAR B : integer);
  BEGIN
    B := AddOne(B);
    B := AddOne(B)
  END;   {  of PROCEDURE AddTwo  }
FUNCTION AddOne;  {  (A : integer) : integer  }
  BEGIN
    AddOne := A + 1
  END;  {  of FUNCTION AddOne  }
```

8. Consider the block structure shown in Figure 8.18 for **PROGRAM** ExerciseEight.
   a. Indicate which subprograms can be called from the main program.
   b. Indicate all appropriate calls from one subprogram to another subprogram.
   c. List three inappropriate calls and explain why they cannot be made.

*9. Give a schematic representation and indicate the scope of identifiers for the following subprograms contained in **PROGRAM** ExerciseNine.

```
PROGRAM ExerciseNine (input, output);

VAR
  X, Y : real;
  Ch : char;

PROCEDURE A (VAR X1 : real;
                 Ch1 : char);
  VAR
    J : integer;
  FUNCTION Inner (M : integer;
                  Y1 : real) : real;
    BEGIN
        .
        .
    END;  {  of FUNCTION Inner  }
```

◆ Figure 8.18

Schematic for **PROGRAM** ExerciseEight

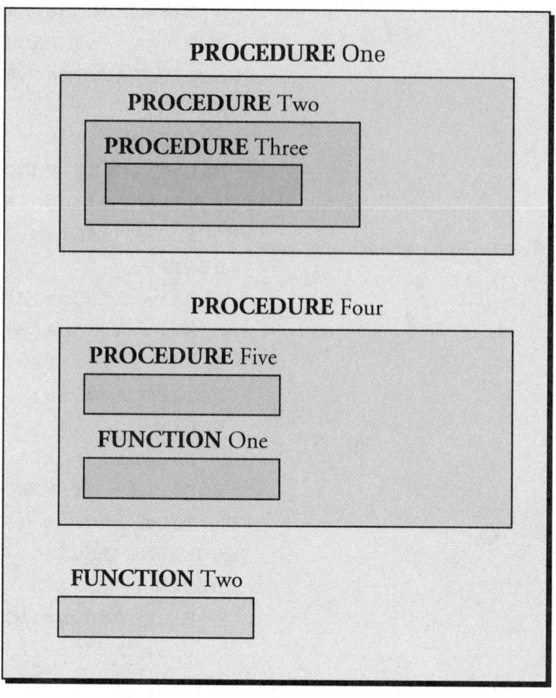


```
  BEGIN  { PROCEDURE A  }
     .
     .
  END;  { of PROCEDURE A  }

PROCEDURE B (X1 : real;
             VAR Ch2 : char);
  BEGIN  { PROCEDURE B  }
     .
     .
  END;  { of PROCEDURE B  }
```

10. Write a test program to illustrate what happens when one subprogram calls another subprogram that is listed later.
11. Consider the following program:

```
PROGRAM ExerciseEleven (input, output);

VAR
  A, B, Num : integer;

FUNCTION MaxPower (A1, B1 : integer) : integer;
  VAR
    Prod, K : integer;

  PROCEDURE Sort (VAR A2, B2 : integer);
    VAR
      Temp : integer;
```

```
    BEGIN  {  PROCEDURE Sort  }
      IF B2 < A2 THEN
        BEGIN
          Temp := A2;
          A2 := B2;
          B2 := Temp
        END  {  of IF...THEN  }
    END;  {  of PROCEDURE Sort  }

  BEGIN  {  FUNCTION MaxPower  }
    Sort (A1, B1);
    Prod := A1;
    FOR K := 1 to B1 - 1 DO
      Prod := Prod * A1;
    MaxPower := Prod
  END;  {  of FUNCTION MaxPower  }

BEGIN  {  Main program  }
  writeln ('Enter two numbers and press <Enter>.');
  readln (A, B);
  Num := MaxPower (A, B);
  writeln (Num)
END.  {  of main program  }
```

a. Give a schematic representation and indicate the scope of identifiers.
b. What is the output if the numbers read for A and B are 5 and 3, respectively?
c. Explain what this program does for positive integers A and B.

8.4 Recursion

Objectives

- to understand how recursion can be used to solve a problem
- to be able to use recursion to solve a problem
- to understand what happens in memory when recursion is used

In our previous work with subprograms, we have seen instances in which one subprogram calls another subprogram. In Chapter 6 on repetition, we learned how to use the **FOR, WHILE,** and **REPEAT** statements to control iterative processes. Now let's see how a subprogram that calls itself can be used to control an iterative process.

Recursive Processes

Many problems can be solved by having a subtask call itself as part of the solution. This process is called **recursion;** subprograms that call themselves are **recursive subprograms.** Recursion is frequently used in mathematics. Consider, for example, the definition of $n!$ (n factorial) for a non-negative integer n. This is defined by

$0! = 1$

$1! = 1$

for $n > 1$, $n! = n * (n - 1)!$

Thus, $6! = 6 * 5!$
$= 6 * 5 * 4!$
$= 6 * 5 * 4 * 3!$
$= 6 * 5 * 4 * 3 * 2!$
$= 6 * 5 * 4 * 3 * 2 * 1$

Recursion is the process of a subprogram calling itself.

A **recursive subprogram** is a subprogram that calls itself.

Another well-known mathematical example is the Fibonacci sequence. In this sequence, the first term is 1, the second term is 1, and each successive term is defined to be the sum of the previous two. More precisely, the Fibonacci sequence

$$a_1, a_2, a_3 \ldots, a_n$$

is defined by

$$a_1 = 1$$
$$a_2 = 1$$
$$a_n = a_{n-1} + a_{n-2} \text{ for } n > 2$$

This generates the sequence

1, 1, 2, 3, 5, 8, 13, 21, . . .

In both examples, note that the general term was defined by using the previous term or terms.

What applications does recursion have for computing? In many instances, a procedure or function can be written to accomplish a recursive task. If the language allows a subprogram to call itself (Pascal does, FORTRAN does not), it is sometimes easier to solve a problem by this process.

Example 8.2

As an example of a recursive function, consider the sigma function—denoted by $\sum_{i=1}^{n} i$—which is used to compute the sum of integers from 1 to n.

```
FUNCTION Sigma (N : integer) : integer;
  BEGIN
    IF N <= 1 THEN
      Sigma := N
    ELSE
      Sigma := N + Sigma(N - 1)
  END;  { of FUNCTION Sigma  }
```

To illustrate how this recursive function works, suppose it is called from the main program by a statement such as

```
Sum := Sigma(5);
```

In the **ELSE** portion of the function, we first have

```
Sigma := 5 + Sigma(4)
```

At this stage, note that Sigma(4) must be computed. This call produces

```
Sigma := 4 + Sigma(3)
```

If we envision these recursive calls as occurring on levels, we have

```
1. Sigma := 5 + Sigma(4)
  2. Sigma := 4 + Sigma(3)
    3. Sigma := 3 + Sigma(2)
      4. Sigma := 2 + Sigma(1)
        5. Sigma := 1
```

The end of the recursion has been reached. The steps for assigning values are reversed. Thus, we have

```
        5. Sigma := 1
      4. Sigma := 2 + 1
    3. Sigma := 3 + 3
  2. Sigma := 4 + 6
1. Sigma := 5 + 10
```

Before we analyze what happens in memory when recursive subprograms are used, some comments about recursion are in order.

The **stopping state** is the well-defined termination of a recursive process. This is also called a **degenerate case.**

A **recursive step** is a well-defined step that leads to the stopping state in the recursive process.

1. The recursive process must have a well-defined termination. This termination is referred to as a **stopping state** (or **degenerate case**). In Example 8.2, the stopping state was

```
IF N <= 1 THEN
  Sigma := N
```

2. The recursive process must have well-defined steps that lead to the stopping state. These steps are called **recursive steps.** In Example 8.2, these steps were

```
Sigma := N + Sigma(N - 1)
```

What Really Happens?

A **stack** is a dynamic data structure where access can be made from only one end. Referred to as a LIFO (last-in, first-out) structure.

What really happens when a subprogram calls itself? First, we need to examine the idea of a **stack.** Imagine a stack as a pile of cafeteria trays: the last one put on the stack is the first one taken off the stack. This is what occurs in memory when a recursive subprogram is used. Each call to the subprogram can be thought of as adding a tray to the stack. In the previous function, the first call creates a level of recursion that contains the partially complete assignment statement

```
Sigma := 5 + Sigma(4)
```

This corresponds to the first tray in the stack. In reality, this is an area in memory waiting to receive a value for 5 + Sigma(4). At this level, operation is temporarily suspended until a value is returned for Sigma(4). However, the call Sigma(4) produces

```
Sigma := 4 + Sigma(3)
```

This corresponds to the second tray on the stack. As before, operation is temporarily suspended until Sigma(3) is computed. This process is repeated until finally the last call, Sigma(1), returns a value.

At this stage, the stack may be envisioned as illustrated in Figure 8.19. Since different areas of memory are used for each successive call to Sigma, each variable Sigma represents a different memory location.

The levels of recursion that have been temporarily suspended can now be completed in reverse order. Thus, since the assignment

```
Sigma(1) := 1
```

has been made, then

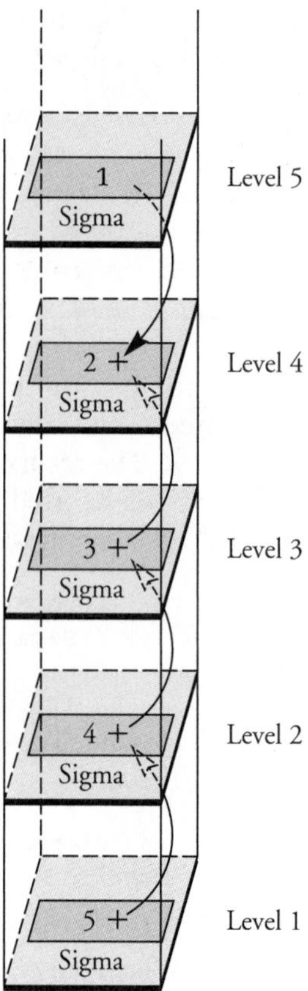

◆ Figure 8.19

Stack for **FUNCTION** Sigma

```
Sigma(2) := 2 + Sigma(1)
```

becomes

```
Sigma(2) := 2 + 1
```

This then permits

```
Sigma(3) := 3 + Sigma(2)
```

to become

```
Sigma(3) := 3 + 3
```

Continuing until the first level of recursion has been reached, we obtain

```
Sigma := 5 + 10
```

This "unstacking" is illustrated in Figure 8.20.

Notice that the recursive function illustrated in Example 8.2 uses a value parameter. In general, any formal parameter that relates to the size of the problem must be a value parameter. If the formal parameter (*N*, for example) were variable, it would not be possible to use the expression $N - 1$ as an actual parameter in a recursive call.

"Unstacking"
FUNCTION Sigma

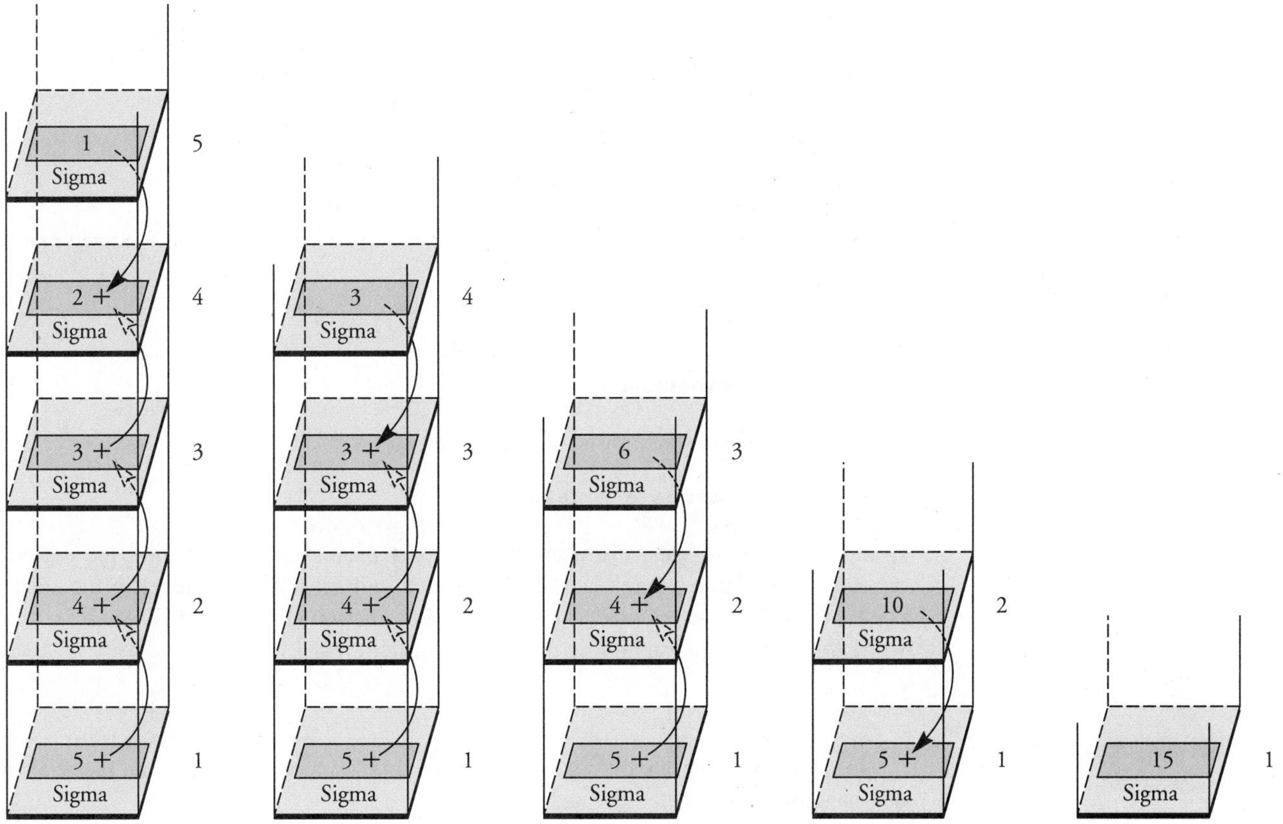

Example 8.3

Now let's consider a second example of recursion in which a procedure is used recursively to print a line of text in reverse order. Assume the line of text has only one period and this is at the end of the line. The stopping state occurs when the character read is a period. Using the data line

This is a short sentence.■

a complete program follows:

```
PROGRAM LineInReverse (input, output);

{   This program uses a procedure recursively to print a line        }
{   of text in reverse.                                               }

{*****************************************************************}

PROCEDURE StackItUp;

  {  Given:   Nothing                                                 }
```

```
  {  Task:     Read one character; print if a period; if not, call }
  {                 this same procedure                              }
  {  Return:  Nothing                                                }

  VAR
    OneChar : char;
  BEGIN
    read (OneChar);
    IF OneChar <> '.' THEN
      StackItUp;
    write (OneChar)
  END;  {  of PROCEDURE StackItUp  }

{******************************************************************}

BEGIN  {  Main program  }
  StackItUp;
  writeln
END.  {  of main program  }
```

Output from this program is

```
.ecnetnes trohs a si sihT
```

In this program, as each character is read, it is placed on a stack until the period is encountered. At that time, the period is printed and then, as each level in the stack is passed through in reverse order, the character on that level is printed. The stack created while this program is running is illustrated in Figure 8.21.

Example 8.4

Now let's consider another example of a recursive function. Recall, the factorial of a non-negative integer, *n*, is defined to be

$$1 * 2 * 3 * \ldots * (n - 1) * n$$

and is denoted by $n!$. Thus,

$$4! = 1 * 2 * 3 * 4$$

For the sake of completing this definition, $1! = 1$ and $0! = 1$. A recursive function to compute $n!$ is

```
FUNCTION Factorial (N : integer) : integer;
  BEGIN
    IF N = 0 THEN
      Factorial := 1
    ELSE
      Factorial := N * Factorial(N - 1)
  END;  {  of FUNCTION Factorial  }
```

If this function is called from the main program by a statement such as

```
Product := Factorial(4);
```

we envision the levels of recursion as

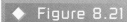

◆ Figure 8.21

Stack created by **PROCEDURE** StackItUp

.
e
c
n
e
t
n
e
s
t
r
o
h
s
a
s
i
s
i
h
T

```
1. Factorial := 4 * Factorial(3)
   2. Factorial := 3 * Factorial(2)
      3. Factorial := 2 * Factorial(1)
         4. Factorial := 1 * Factorial(0)
            5. Factorial(0) := 1
```

Successive values would then be assigned in reverse order to produce

```
            5. Factorial(0) := 1
         4. Factorial := 1 * 1
      3. Factorial := 2 * 1
   2. Factorial := 3 * 2
1. Factorial := 4 * 6
```

Why Use Recursion?

You may have noticed that the previous recursive functions Sigma and Factorial could have been written using iteration rather than recursion. For example, we could write

```
FUNCTION IterSigma (N : integer) : integer;
  VAR
    Index, Sum : integer;
```

```
BEGIN
  Sum := 0;
  FOR Index := 1 TO N DO
    Sum := Sum + Index;
  IterSigma := Sum
END;  {  of FUNCTION IterSigma  }
```

It is not coincidental that the recursive function Sigma can be rewritten using the iterative function IterSigma. In principle, any recursive subprogram can be rewritten in a nonrecursive manner. Furthermore, recursion generally requires more memory than equivalent iteration and is usually difficult for beginning programmers to comprehend. Why then do we use recursion? There are several reasons. First, a recursive thought process may be the best way to think about solving the problem. If so, it naturally leads to using recursion in a program. A classical example of this is the Towers of Hanoi problem, which requires a sequence of moving disks on pegs. This problem is fully developed in Example 8.5.

Second, some recursive solutions can be very short compared to iterative solutions. Some nonrecursive versions may require an explicit stack and unusual coding. In some instances, use of a recursive algorithm can be very simple, and some programmers consider recursive solutions elegant because of this simplicity. The Towers of Hanoi problem provides an example of such elegance.

Third and finally, subsequent work in Pascal can be aided by recursion. For example, one of the fastest sorting algorithms available, the quick sort, uses recursion (see Section 14.1). Also, recursion is a valuable tool when working with dynamic data structures (Chapter 14).

Having now seen several reasons why recursion should be used, let's consider when recursion should not be used. If a solution to a problem is easier to obtain by using nonrecursive methods, it is usually preferable to use them. A nonrecursive solution may require less execution time and use memory more efficiently. Referring to the previous examples, the recursive function Factorial should probably be written using iteration, but reversing a line of text would typically be done by using recursion because a nonrecursive solution is difficult to write.

In summary, recursion is a powerful and necessary programming technique. You should therefore become familiar with using recursive subprograms, be able to recognize when a recursive algorithm is appropriate, and be able to implement a recursive subprogram.

Example 8.5

A classic problem called the Towers of Hanoi problem involves three pegs and disks as depicted in Figure 8.22. The object is to move the disks from peg A to peg C. The rules are that only one disk may be moved at a time and a larger disk can never be placed on a smaller disk. (Legend has it that this problem—but with 64 disks—was given to monks

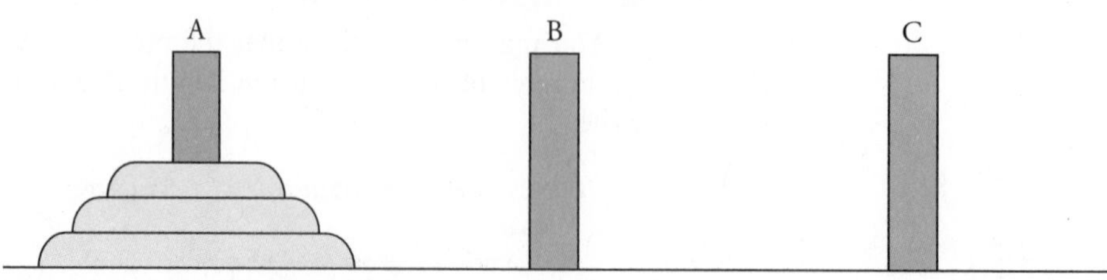

◆ Figure 8.22
Towers of Hanoi problem

in an ancient monastery. The world was to come to an end when all 64 disks were in order on peg C.)

To see how this problem can be solved, let's start with a one-disk problem. In this case, merely move the disk from peg A to peg C. The two-disk problem is almost as easy. Move disk 1 to peg B, disk 2 to peg C, and use the solution to the one-disk problem to move disk 1 to peg C. (Note the reference to the previous solution.)

Things get a little more interesting with a three-disk problem. First, use the two-disk solution to get the top two disks in order on peg B. Then move disk 3 to peg C. Finally, use a two-disk solution to move the two disks from peg B to peg C. Again, notice how a reference was made to the previous solution. By now you should begin to see the pattern for solving the problem. However, before generalizing, let's first look at the four-disk problem. As expected, the solution is as follows:

1. Use the three-disk solution to move three disks to peg B.
2. Move disk 4 to peg C.
3. Use the three-disk solution to move the three disks from peg B to peg C.

This process can be generalized as a solution to the problem for n disks:

1. Use the $(n - 1)$-disk solution to move $(n - 1)$ disks to peg B.
2. Move disk n to peg C.
3. Use the $(n - 1)$-disk solution to move $(n - 1)$ disks from peg B to peg C.

This general solution is recursive in nature because each particular solution depends on a solution for the previous number of disks. This process continues until there is only one disk to move. This corresponds to the stopping state when a recursive program is written to solve the problem. A complete interactive program follows that prints each step in the solution to this problem:

```
PROGRAM TowersOfHanoi (input, output);

{   This program uses recursion to solve the classic  Towers     }
{   of Hanoi problem.                                            }

VAR
  NumDisks : integer;

{*************************************************************}

PROCEDURE ListTheMove (NumDisks : integer;
                       StartPeg, LastPeg, SparePeg : char);

  { Given:   The number of disks to move, the initial peg       }
  {               FirstPeg, the working peg SparePeg, and       }
  {               the destination peg LastPeg                   }
  { Task:    Move NumDisks from FirstPeg to LastPeg using       }
  {               SparePeg; involves recursive calls            }
  { Return:  Nothing                                            }

  BEGIN
    IF NumDisks = 1 THEN
      writeln ('Move a disk from ', StartPeg, ' to ', LastPeg)
    ELSE
      BEGIN
        ListTheMove (NumDisks-1, StartPeg, SparePeg, LastPeg);
        writeln ('Move a disk from ', StartPeg, ' to ', LastPeg);
        ListTheMove (NumDisks-1, SparePeg, LastPeg, StartPeg)
```

```
    END  { of ELSE option  }
  END;  {  of PROCEDURE ListTheMove  }

{***************************************************************}

BEGIN  {  Main program  }
  writeln ('How many disks in this game?');
  readln (NumDisks);
  writeln;
  writeln ('Start with ', NumDisks, ' disks on Peg A');
  writeln;
  writeln ('Then proceed as follows:');
  writeln;
  ListTheMove (NumDisks, 'A', 'C', 'B')
END.  {  of main program  }
```

Sample runs for three-disk and four-disk problems produce the following:

```
How many disks in this game?
3

Start with 3 disks on Peg A

Then proceed as follows:

Move a disk from A to C
Move a disk from A to B
Move a disk from C to B
Move a disk from A to C
Move a disk from B to A
Move a disk from B to C
Move a disk from A to C

How many disks in this game?
4

Start with 4 disks on Peg A

Then proceed as follows:

Move a disk from A to B
Move a disk from A to C
Move a disk from B to C
Move a disk from A to B
Move a disk from C to A
Move a disk from C to B
Move a disk from A to B
Move a disk from A to C
Move a disk from B to C
Move a disk from B to A
Move a disk from C to A
Move a disk from B to C
Move a disk from A to B
Move a disk from A to C
Move a disk from B to C
```

Exercises 8.4

*1. Explain what is wrong with the following recursive function:

```
FUNCTION Recur (X : real) : real;
  BEGIN
    Recur := Recur(X / 2)
  END;
```

2. Write a recursive function that reverses the digits of a positive integer. If the integer input is 1234, output should be 4321.

For Exercises 3–5, consider the following recursive function:

```
FUNCTION A (X : real;
            N : integer) : real;
  BEGIN
    IF N = 0 THEN
      A := 1.0
    ELSE
      A := X * A(X, N - 1)
  END;  {  of FUNCTION A  }
```

*3. What would the value of Y be for each of the following?
   a. `Y := A(3.0, 2);`
   b. `Y := A(2.0, 3);`
   c. `Y := A(4.0, 4);`
   d. `Y := A(1.0, 6);`

4. Explain what standard computation is performed by **FUNCTION** A.

*5. Rewrite **FUNCTION** A using iteration rather than recursion.

6. Recall the Fibonacci sequence, 1, 1, 2, 3, 5, 8, 13, 21, . . . , where for $n > 2$ the nth term is the sum of the previous two. Write a recursive function to compute the nth term in the Fibonacci sequence.

*7. Write a function that uses iteration to compute $n!$.

Focus on Program Design: Case Study 8.2

Finding Prime Numbers

This is an updated version of the program in Chapter 6 in which you were asked to write a program that accepts a positive integer as input and then prints all primes less than or equal to the integer read. The version in this chapter is interactive and includes

- a bad data check
- a sentinel value for input
- procedures to accomplish subtasks

Typical output for the integer 17 is

```
Enter a positive integer, <-999> to quit.
17
```

```
-----------------------------------------------

              The number is 17.  The prime numbers
              less than or equal to 17 are:

                           2
                           3
                           5
                           7
                          11
                          13
                          17

Enter a positive integer, <-999> to quit.
-999
```

A first-level pseudocode development for this problem is

1. Get a number
WHILE MoreData **DO**
2. Examine the number
3. Get a number

A second-level development is

1. Get a number
   1.1 Get entry from the keyboard
   1.2 Check for valid entry
WHILE MoreData **DO**
2. Examine the number
   IF Number is 1 **THEN**
   2.1 Print a message for 1
   ELSE
   2.2 Print primes less than Number
3. Get a number
   3.1 Get entry from keyboard
   3.2 Check for valid entry

Step 2.2 can be refined to

2.2 Print primes less than Number
    2.2.1 Print a message
    2.2.2 Check for primes less than or equal to Number

Step 2.2.2 can be further developed to

2.2.2 Check for primes less than or equal to Number
      FOR Candidate := 2 **TO** Number **DO**
      2.2.2.1 Check to see if Candidate is prime
      2.2.2.2 If Candidate is prime **THEN** print Candidate in list of primes

Thus, the complete pseudocode development is

1. Get a number
   1.1 Get entry from the keyboard
   1.2 Check for valid entry

WHILE MoreData **DO**
2. Examine the number
   IF Number is 1 **THEN**
   2.1 Print a message for 1
   ELSE
   2.2 Print primes less than Number
      2.2.1 Print a message
      2.2.2 Check for primes less than or equal to Number
         FOR Candidate := 2 **TO** Number **DO**
         2.2.2.1 Check to see if Candidate is prime
         2.2.2.2 **IF** Candidate is prime **THEN** print Candidate in list of primes
3. Get a number
   3.1 Get entry from the keyboard
   3.2 Check for valid entry

With this pseudocode development, the main program would be

```
BEGIN  {  Main program  }
  GetANumber (Num, MoreData);
  WHILE MoreData DO
    BEGIN
      IF Num = 1 THEN
        PrintOneMessage
      ELSE
        BEGIN
          PrintMessage (Num);
          ListAllPrimes (Num)
        END;  {  of ELSE option  }
      GetANumber (Num, MoreData)
    END  {  of WHILE loop  }
END.  {  of main program  }
```

Procedures would be written for each of the following modules:

GetANumber
PrintOneMessage
PrintMessage
ListAllPrimes

Module specifications for these modules are

1. GetANumber Module
   Data received: None
   Information returned: Number
   Boolean flag MoreData
   Logic: Get an entry from the keyboard.
   Make sure the entry is valid or the sentinel value for terminating the process.
   If the entry is the sentinel value, set the **boolean** variable MoreData to false.
2. PrintOneMessage Module
   Data received: None

Information returned: None
Logic: Print a message about one.

3. PrintMessage Module

   Data received: Number
   Information returned: None
   Logic: Print a heading for the list of primes.

4. ListAllPrimes Module

   Data received: Number
   Information returned: None
   Logic: For each integer less than or equal to Number, check to see if it is prime.
   If it is prime, print it in a list of primes.

A complete program for this problem follows:

```
PROGRAM ListPrimes (input, output);

{  This program is an enhancement of the program in Chapter 6.      }
{  This version features:                                            }
{       a.  a bad data check                                         }
{       b.  a sentinel value for input                               }
{       c.  procedures and functions to accomplish tasks             }

CONST
  Skip = ' ';
  Dashes = '-----------------------------------------------------';

VAR
  Number : integer;
  MoreData : boolean;

{*******************************************************************}

PROCEDURE GetANumber (VAR Number : integer;
                      VAR MoreData : boolean);

  {  Given:   Nothing                                               }
  {  Task:    Read an integer entered from the keyboard             }
  {  Return:  The integer read                                      }

  BEGIN                                                                   1

    {  Get valid input from the keyboard  }
    REPEAT
      writeln ('Enter a positive integer, <-999> to quit.');
      readln (Number);
      MoreData := Number <> -999
    UNTIL (Number > 0) OR (Number = -999)
  END;  {  of PROCEDURE GetANumber  }

{*******************************************************************}
```

```
PROCEDURE PrintOneMessage;

  {  Given:   Nothing                                                }
  {  Task:    Print a message for 1                                  }
  {  Return:  Nothing                                                }

  BEGIN                                                                  2
    writeln;
    writeln (Skip:10, Dashes);
    writeln;
    writeln (Skip:20, '1 is not prime by definition.');
    writeln
  END;  {  of PROCEDURE PrintOneMessage  }

{*******************************************************************}

PROCEDURE PrintMessage (Number : integer);

  {  Given:   The integer read                                       }
  {  Task:    Print a heading for the output                         }
  {  Return:  Nothing                                                }

  BEGIN                                                                  3
    writeln;
    writeln (Skip:10, Dashes);
    writeln;
    writeln (Skip:20, 'The number is ', Number,'.  The prime numbers');
    writeln (Skip:20, 'less than or equal to ', Number, ' are:');
    writeln
  END;  {  of PROCEDURE PrintMessage  }

{*******************************************************************}

FUNCTION StillChecking (Candidate, Divisor : integer) : boolean;

  {  Given:   Candidate, Divisor                                     }
  {  Task:    See if divisor needs to be checked                     }
  {  Return:  A boolean flag to terminate divisor checks             }

  BEGIN
    StillChecking := Divisor <= sqrt(Candidate)
  END;  {  of FUNCTION StillChecking  }

{*******************************************************************}    4

PROCEDURE ListAllPrimes (Number : integer);

  {  Given:   The integer read                                       }
  {  Task:    List all primes less than or equal to the integer      }
  {                read                                              }
  {  Return:  Nothing                                                }

  VAR
    Prime:  boolean;
    Candidate, Divisor : integer;
```

```
  BEGIN

    {  Check all integers from 2 to Number  }
    FOR Candidate := 2 TO Number DO
      BEGIN
        Prime := true;
        Divisor := 2;

        {  See if Candidate is prime  }
        WHILE StillChecking(Candidate, Divisor) AND Prime DO
         IF Candidate MOD Divisor = 0 THEN
           Prime := false;           {  Candidate has a divisor   }
         ELSE
           Divisor := Divisor + 1;
        IF Prime THEN                 {  Print in list of primes  }
          writeln (Candidate:35)
       END  {  of FOR loop  }
  END;  {  of PROCEDURE ListAllPrimes  }

{*******************************************************************}

BEGIN  {  Main program  }
  GetANumber (Number, MoreData);
  WHILE MoreData DO
    BEGIN
      IF Number = 1 THEN
        PrintOneMessage
      ELSE
        BEGIN
          PrintMessage (Number);
          ListAllPrimes (Number)
        END;  {  of ELSE option  }
      GetANumber (Number, MoreData)
    END  {  of WHILE loop  }
END.  {  of main program  }
```

Sample output for this program follows:

```
Enter a positive integer, <-999> to quit.
10

          --------------------------------------------------

                    The number is 10.  The prime numbers
                    less than or equal to 10 are:

                                  2
                                  3
                                  5
                                  7

Enter a positive integer, <-999> to quit.
17
```

```
          --------------------------------------------------

                    The number is 17.  The prime numbers
                    less than or equal to 17 are:

                                 2
                                 3
                                 5
                                 7
                                11
                                13
                                17

Enter a positive integer, <-999> to quit.
1

          --------------------------------------------------

                    1 is not prime by definition.

Enter a positive integer, <-999> to quit.
25

          --------------------------------------------------

                    The number is 25.  The prime numbers
                    less than or equal to 25 are:

                                 2
                                 3
                                 5
                                 7
                                11
                                13
                                17
                                19
                                23

Enter a positive integer, <-999> to quit.
-3
Enter a positive integer, <-999> to quit.
2

          --------------------------------------------------

                    The number is 2.  The prime numbers
                    less than or equal to 2 are:

                                 2

Enter a positive integer, <-999> to quit.
-999
```

Running and Debugging Hints

1. You can use related or identical variable names in the parameter lists. For example, either

```
PROCEDURE Compute (N1, N2 : integer;
                   VAR Av : real);
```

or

```
PROCEDURE Compute (Number1, Number2 : integer;
                   VAR Average : real);
```

can be called by

```
Compute (Number1, Number2, Average);
```

2. When using recursion, make sure the recursive process will reach the stopping state.

Summary

Key Terms

block
cohesive subprogram
degenerate case
encapsulation
forward reference
global identifier (variable)
interface
local identifier (local variable)
nested subprograms
nonlocal identifier
procedural abstraction
recursion
recursive step
recursive subprogram
scope of an identifier
stack
stopping state
stub programming
subblock

Keyword

FORWARD

Key Concepts

- Global identifiers can be used by the main program and all subprograms.
- Local identifiers are available only to the subprogram in which they are declared.
- Each identifier is available to the block in which it is declared; this includes all subprograms contained within the block.
- Identifiers are not available outside their blocks.
- The scope of an identifier refers to the blocks in which the identifier is available.
- Understanding scope of identifiers is aided by graphic illustration of blocks in a program; thus,

```
PROGRAM Practice (input, output);

VAR
  X, Y, Z : real;
```

```
PROCEDURE Sub1 (X1 : real);
  VAR
    X2 : real;
  BEGIN
    .
    .
    .
  END;  {  of PROCEDURE Sub1  }

PROCEDURE Sub2 (X1 : real);
  VAR
    Z2 : real;
```

can be visualized as shown in Figure 8.23.

- Forward reference of a subprogram can be achieved by listing the function or procedure heading with all parameters, followed by the reserved word **FORWARD** as:

```
FUNCTION B (X : real) : real; FORWARD;
```

- Recursion is a process whereby a subprogram calls itself.
- A recursive subprogram must have a well-defined stopping state.
- Recursive solutions are usually elegant and short but generally require more memory than iterative solutions.

◆ Figure 8.23

Schematic of blocks in a program

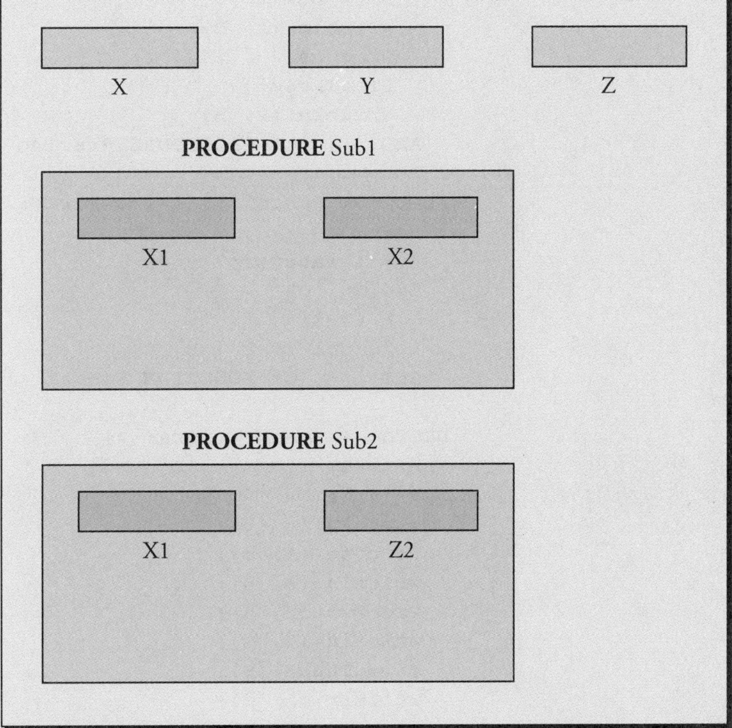

Chapter Review Exercises

For Exercises 1–4, examine the following program:

```
PROGRAM Exercise1To4 (output);

VAR
A, B : integer;

PROCEDURE ProcOne (A : integer; VAR B : integer);
  BEGIN
    A := 2;
    B := B + 1;
    writeln (A, B)
  END; {  of PROCEDURE ProcOne  }

PROCEDURE ProcTwo (VAR A : integer; B : integer);

  PROCEDURE ProcThree (A, B : integer);
    BEGIN
      A := 10;
      B := 11;
      writeln (A, B)
    END;  {  of PROCEDURE ProcThree  }

  BEGIN  {  PROCEDURE ProcTwo  }
    ProcOne;
    A := A + 1;
    B := B * 2;
    writeln (A, B);
    ProcOne;
    ProcThree;
    writeln (A, B)
  END;  {  of PROCEDURE ProcTwo  }

FUNCTION Funct1 (A : integer) : integer;
  VAR
    B : integer;
  BEGIN
    B := 3;
    Funct1 := A + B
  END;  {  of FUNCTION Funct1  }

BEGIN  {  Main program  }
  A := 4;
  B := 5;
  writeln (A, B);
  ProcOne (A, B);
  writeln (A, B);
  ProcTwo (A, B);
  writeln (A, B);
  B := Funct1(B);
  writeln (A, B);
  ProcOne (B, A);
```

```
  writeln (A, B)
END.  {  of main program  }
```

1. What output is produced by the program?
2. Draw a diagram showing the block structure of the program.
3. What is the scope of each variable?
4. Make a table showing the permissible procedure and function calls in the program.
5. Explain what is wrong with the following recursive function:

```
FUNCTION Recur (Num : integer) : integer;
  BEGIN
    Recur := 1 + Recur(Num)
  END;
```

6. Write a program containing a recursive routine that prints the integers from 1 to a value input by the program user. All values should be printed in the recursive routine.

Programming Problems

1. Many teachers use various weights (percentage of the final grade) for test scores. Write a program that allows the user to enter three test scores. Output should consist of the input data, the weighted score for each test, and the total score (sum of the weighted scores).
2. The Natural Pine Furniture Company (Problem 2, Chapter 4 and Problem 15, Chapter 6) has recently hired you to help them convert their antiquated payroll system to a computer-based model. They know you are still learning, so all they want right now is a program that will print a one-week pay report for three employees. You should use the constant definition section for the following:
   a. Federal withholding tax rate 18%
   b. State withholding tax rate 4.5%
   c. Hospitalization $25.65
   d. Union dues $7.85

   The input will contain each employee's initials, the number of hours worked, and the employee's hourly rate. Your output should include a report for each employee and a summary report for the company files. A sample employee form follows:

```
Employee:      JTM
Hours Worked:  40.00
Hourly Rate:    9.75

     Gross Wages:

     Deductions:
          Federal Withholding
          State Withholding
          Hospitalization
          Union Dues
               Total Deductions

     Net Wages
```

Output for a summary report could be

```
              Natural Pine Furniture Company
                      Weekly Summary

Gross Wages:

Deductions:
     Federal Withholding
     State Withholding
     Hospitalization
     Union Dues
          Total Deductions

Net Wages
```

3. The Child-Growth Encyclopedia Company (Problem 3, Chapter 4) wants a computer program that will print a monthly sales chart. Products produced by the company, prices, and sales commissions for each are
   a. Basic encyclopedia $325.00 22%
   b. Child educational supplement $127.50 15%
   c. Annual update book $ 18.95 20%

   Write a program that will get the monthly sales data for two sales regions and produce the desired company chart. Monthly sales data for one region consist of a two-letter region identifier (such as MI) and three integers representing the number of units sold for each product listed above. A typical input screen would be

```
What is your sales region?
MI

How many Basic Encyclopedias were sold?
150

How many Child Supplements were sold?
120

How many Annual Updates were sold?
105
```

The prices may vary from month to month and should be defined in the constant definition section. The commissions are not subject to change. Sample input is

```
MI  150  120  105
TX  225  200  150
```

Typical output could be

```
                         Monthly Sales Chart

                            Basic              Child          Annual
                Region   Encyclopedia       Supplement        Update

Units sold      MI           150               120              105
```

```
(by region)     TX            225              200              150
                              ---              ---              ---
Total units sold:             375              320              255

      Price/unit          $325.00          $127.50           $18.95
Gross Sales:          $121,875.00       $40,800.00        $4,832.25

      Commission rate         22%              15%              20%

Commissions paid:      $26,812.50        $6,120.00          $966.45
```

4. As a part-time job this semester, you are working for the Family Budget Assistance Center (Problem 6, Chapter 4). Your boss has asked you to write and execute a program that will analyze data for a family. Input for each family will consist of

   Family ID number (**integer**)
   Number in family (**integer**)
   Income (**real**)
   Total debts (**real**)

   Your program should output the following:

   a. An appropriate header.
   b. The family's identification number, number in family, income, and total debts.
   c. Predicted family living expenses ($3000 × the size of the family).
   d. The monthly payment necessary to pay off the debt in one year.
   e. The amount the family should save (the family size × 2 percent of the income − debt, FamilySize $*$ 0.02 (income − debt)).
   f. Your service fee (.5 percent of the income).

   Run your program for the following two families:

Identification Number	Size	Income	Debt
51	4	18000.00	2000.00
72	7	26000.00	4800.00

   Output for the first family could be

```
        Family Budget Assistance Center
                  March 1997
          Telephone: (800) 555-1234

Identification number                   51
Family size                              4
Annual income                   $ 18000.00
Total debt                      $  2000.00
Expected living expenses        $ 12000.00
Monthly payment                 $   166.67
Savings                         $  1280.00
Service fee                     $    90.00
```

5. A Pythagorean triple consists of three integers *A, B,* and *C* such that $A^2 + B^2 = C^2$. For example, 3, 4, 5 is such a triple because $3^2 + 4^2 = 5^2$. These triples can be generated by positive integers *m, n,* $(m > n)$, where $a = m^2 - n^2$, $b = 2mn$, and $c = m^2 + n^2$. These triples will be primitive (no common factors) if *m* and *n* have no common factors and are not both odd. Write a program that allows the user to enter a value for *m* and then prints out all possible primitive Pythagorean triples such that $m > n$. Use one function to find the greatest common factor of *m* and *n,* another to see if *m* and *n* are both odd, and another to guard against overflow. For the input value of $m = 5$, typical output would be

```
m    n    a    b    c  a^2  b^2  c^2
--------------------------------------
2    1    3    4    5    9   16   25
3    2    5   12   13   25  144  169
4    1   15    8   17  225   64  289
4    3    7   24   25   49  576  625
5    2   21   20   29  441  400  841
5    4    9   40   41   81 1600 1681
```

6. The **Focus on Program Design: Case Study 8.2** determines whether or not an integer is prime by checking for divisors less than or equal to the square root of the number. The check starts with 2 and increments trial divisors by 1 each time, as seen by the code

```
Prime := true;
Divisor := 2;
WHILE (Divisor <= sqrt(Candidate)) AND Prime DO
  IF Candidate MOD Divisor = 0 THEN
    Prime := false
  ELSE
    Divisor := Divisor + 1;
```

Other methods can be used to determine whether or not an integer *N* is prime. For example, you can
(1) Check divisors from 2 to $N - 1$, incrementing by 1.
(2) Check divisors from 2 to $(N - 1) / 2$, incrementing by 1.
(3) Check divisor 2, 3, 5, . . . $(N - 1) / 2$, incrementing by 2.
(4) Check divisor 2, 3, 5, . . . sqrt(*N*), incrementing by 2.
Write an interactive program that allows the user to choose between these options to compare the relative efficiency of different algorithms. Use a function for each option.

7. The prime factorization of a positive integer is the positive integer written as the product of primes. For example, the prime factorization of 72 is

$$72 = 2 * 3 * 3 * 4$$

Write an interactive program that allows the user to enter a positive integer and then displays the prime factorization of the integer. A minimal main program could be

```
BEGIN  { Main program }
  GetANumber (Num);
```

```
    NumberIsPrime := PrimeCheck(Num);
    IF NumberIsPrime THEN
      writeln (Num, ' is prime.')
    ELSE
      PrintFactorization (Num)
  END.  {  of main program  }
```

Enhancements to this program could include an error trap for bad data and a loop for repeated trials.

8. The greatest common divisor of two positive integers a and b, GCD (a,b), is the largest positive integer that divides both a and b. Thus, GCD(102, 30) = 6. This can be found by using the division algorithm as follows:

$$102 = 30 * 3 + 12$$
$$30 = 12 * 2 + 6$$
$$12 = 6 * 2 + 0$$

Note that

$$\begin{aligned} GCD(102, 30) &= GCD(30, 12) \\ &= GCD(12, 6) \\ &= 6 \end{aligned}$$

In each case, the remainder is used in the next step. The process terminates when a remainder of zero is obtained. Write a recursive function that returns the GCD of two positive integers.

9. A palindrome is a number or word that is the same when read forward or backward. For example, *12321* and *mom* are palindromes. Write a recursive function that can be used to determine whether or not an integer is a palindrome. Use this function in a complete program that reads a list of integers and then displays the list with an asterisk following each palindrome.

10. Recall the Fibonacci sequence discussed at the beginning of this chapter. Write a recursive function that returns the nth Fibonacci number. Input for a call to the function will be a positive integer.

11. Probability courses often contain problems that require students to compute the number of ways r items can be chosen from a set of n objects. It is shown that there are

$$C(n, r) = \frac{n!}{r!\,(n - r)!}$$

such choices. This is sometimes referred to as "n choose r." To illustrate, if you wish to select three items from a total of five possible objects, there are

$$C(5, 3) = \frac{5!}{3!\,(5 - 3)!} = \frac{5 * 4 * 3 * 2 * 1}{(3 * 2 * 1)\,(2 * 1)} = 10$$

such possibilities. In mathematics, the number of $C(n, r)$ is a binomial coefficient because, for appropriate values of n and r, it produces coefficients in the expansion of $(x + y)^n$. Thus

$$(x + y)^4 = C(4, 0)x^4 + C(4, 1)x^3y + C(4, 2)x^2y^2 + C(4, 3)xy^3 + C(4, 4)y^4$$

a. Write a function that returns the value $C(n, r)$. Arguments for a function call will be integers n, r such that $n > r \geq 0$. [*Hint:* Simplify the expression $n! / r! (n - r)!$ before computing.]

b. Write an interactive program that receives as input the power to which a binomial is to be raised. Output should be the expanded binomial.

12. You have been asked to write a program to compute and print statements for customers of a telephone company. The company has three basic rates, depending on the day and the time of day the call occurs. The legend for basic rates is

Daytime rate	D	\$0.22/minute
Evening rate	E	\$0.15/minute
Night/weekend rate	N	\$0.12/minute

Time periods for these rates are

D—8:00 A.M. until 5:00 P.M., Monday through Friday
E—5:00 P.M. until 10:00 P.M., Sunday through Friday
N—10:00 P.M. until 8:00 A.M., Sunday through Friday and
10:00 P.M. Friday until 5:00 P.M., Sunday

Charges for calls are based on minutes used during a time period. Thus, to compute the total charge of a call made during one time period and completed in a different time period, two different rates must be used. Time will be entered in military style: 0100 is 1:00 A.M., 1200 is noon, and 2400 is midnight. To be competitive, the company has implemented a Calling Friends option; any call made to someone on the Calling Friends list will be discounted 20 percent.

Each data line will consist of a single-letter designator for the beginning rate, the day the call was initiated (M, T, W, R, F, S, U), the starting time of the call, and the ending time of the call. Calling Friends calls will be identified by an F, positioned as the first letter on the data line. (This F is optional.) Typical data lines are

```
EM 2055 2101
```

```
FER 2104 2127
```

```
DW 1100 1108
```

```
NF 2300 2350
```

Your program should read a data file and print a statement for a customer. The statement should include columns for the day, starting time (nonmilitary), code for rate (D, E, or N), number of minutes, and total charge for the call. The total charge for the billing period should be included as part of the output.

Communication in Practice

1. Modify one of your programs from this section by saving only the documentation, constant definitions, variable declaration section, subprogram headings, and main driver. Exchange your modified version with a student who has prepared a

similar version. Using the modified version, reconstruct the tasks of the program. Discuss your results with the student who wrote the program.

2. Modify one of your programs from this section by deleting all documentation. Exchange your modified version with a student who has prepared a similar version. Using the modified version, write documentation for the program. Compare your results with the other student's original version.
3. Reread the material in Section 8.2 concerning procedural abstraction. Then, from **Programming Problems** 1, 2, 3, and 4, select one that you have not yet worked. Develop a structure chart and write module specifications for each module required for the problem you have chosen. Also, write a main driver for your program and write complete documentation for each subprogram, including comments about all parameters.
4. Return to **Programming Problem** 7 and solve it as a team project for a four-member team and one project director. The project director is responsible for the final design of the main program and must ensure that adequate communication exists among team members. Each of the four team members should develop complete documentation for one of the following four tasks:
   a. a loop for repeated trials
   b. data input with a bad data check
   c. a function to determine whether or not the number is prime
   d. a procedure that lists the prime factors of the composite numbers

   The final team project should be a report that includes a complete main driver, a description of the tasks for each team member, complete documentation for each subtask, and a summary of the communication required for the team to work together.

Chapter 9

Text Files and Enumerated Data Types

Chapter Outline

Now that you have completed eight chapters, you have made a significant step in the process of learning to use a programming language for the purpose of solving problems. We have covered the essential elements of arithmetic, variables, input/output, selection, repetition, and subprograms, and are now ready to look at a somewhat different area of Pascal.

Thus far, you have been unable to work with large amounts of data. To write programs that solve problems using large databases, it is necessary to be able to store, retrieve, and manage the data. In this chapter, we first look at the storage and retrieval of data (text files) and then study a feature of Pascal (enumerated data types) that facilitates handling of the data.

These topics are not closely related, but because both are useful when working with data structures, which are examined in Chapter 10, we present them together. As you study this material, remember that we are "setting the stage" for working with large amounts of data.

9.1 Text Files

Objectives

- to understand how data can be stored in text files
- to be able to **read** from a text file

The implementation of concepts presented in this section depends on the computer you are using; it is very system dependent. Your teacher will probably supplement this material with examples and explanations suitable for your particular environment. At the very least, you should be able to use the manual for your system for reference.

Consider the relatively simple problem of using a computer to compute and print water bills for a community of 30,000 customers. If the data needed consist of a customer name, address, and amount of water used, you can imagine that entering this information interactively every billing period would involve an enormous amount of time and expense and would probably result in errors in the data. Furthermore, it is often desirable to save information between runs of a program for later use.

Objectives

(continued)

- to be able to **write** to a text file
- to understand the difference between internal and external files

To serve these needs, we can store data in some secondary storage device, usually magnetic tapes or disks. Data can be created separately from a program, stored on these devices, and then accessed by programs when necessary. It is also possible to update and save information for other runs of the same program or for running another program using these same data. For now we will store all data in **text files** (other kinds of files are examined in Chapter 13).

Creating a Text File

Text files can be created by a text editor or by a program. Often the editor you use to create your program can be used to create a text file. The use of text editors varies significantly and you should consult your teacher and/or manual to use this method. This, however, is how your teacher may create data files for you to use with subsequent programming problems.

A **text file** is a file of characters that is divided into lines.

Data in a text file can be thought of as a sequence of characters stored in a sequence of lines. As we have already seen, each line has an end-of-line (**eoln**) marker (▌) after it and each file has an end-of-file (**eof**) marker (■) after the last end-of-line marker. For example, suppose a text file is used to store data for students in a class. If each line consists of an identification number for each student followed by three scores, a typical file might look like this:

```
00723 85 93 100▌

00131 78 91 85▌

00458 82 75 86▌ ■
```

Technically these lines are stored as one continuous stream with end-of-line markers used to differentiate between lines and the end-of-file marker to signify the end of one file.

```
00723 85 93 100▌00131 78 91 85▌00458 82 75 86▌ ■
```

However, we frequently use separate lines to illustrate lines in a text file. Both end-of-line and end-of-file markers are appropriately placed by the computer at the time a file is created. When characters are read, **eoln** markers are read as blanks.

When a text file in secondary storage is to be used by a program, a file variable (or symbolic file name) must be included in the file list, along with the standard files **input** and **output** as part of the program heading. If the file variable is not specified, the standard file **input** is assumed. Thus, if ClassList is the file variable, a heading might be

```
PROGRAM ClassRecordBook (input, output, ClassList);
```

This file variable must be declared in the variable declaration section and is of type **text.** Thus, the declaration section would include

```
VAR
  ClassList : text;
```

The file variable ClassList must be associated with the text file, which is stored externally. This may be done by creating a procedure file prior to compiling and running the program. It may also be accomplished within the program; for example, in Turbo Pascal, an **assign** statement is used for this purpose. Thus, if the data needed in a program are stored on a disk under the name Data1, the statement

```
assign (ClassList, 'Data1');
```

establishes the desired relationship between the file variable ClassList and the data stored externally in the text file Data1.

Reading from a Text File

Opened for reading refers to the positioning of a pointer at the beginning of a file for the purpose of reading from the file.

Before data can be read from a file, the file must be **opened for reading** using the form

> **reset** (<file variable>)

This statement moves a data pointer to the first position of the first line of the data file to be read. Thus,

```
reset (ClassList);
```

positions the pointer as follows:

00723 85 93 100 ▮ 00131 78 91 85 ▮ 00458 82 75 86 ▮ ■

↑
pointer here

Reading from a text file is very similar to getting input interactively or reading from a standard input file. Standard procedures **read** and **readln** are used with appropriate variables as arguments in either format as shown:

> **read** (<file variable>, <input list>)
>
> or
>
> **readln** (<file variable>, <input list>)

If the file variable is not specified, the standard file **input** is assumed. Thus, data from one line of the file of student test scores, ClassList, can be obtained by

```
readln (ClassList, IDNumber, Score1, Score2, Score3);
```

As data items are read using **readln,** values are stored in the designated variables and the pointer is moved to the first position past the end-of-line marker. Thus,

```
reset (ClassList);
readln (ClassList, IDNumber, Score1, Score2, Score3);
```

results in

00723	85	93	100
IDNumber	Score1	Score2	Score3

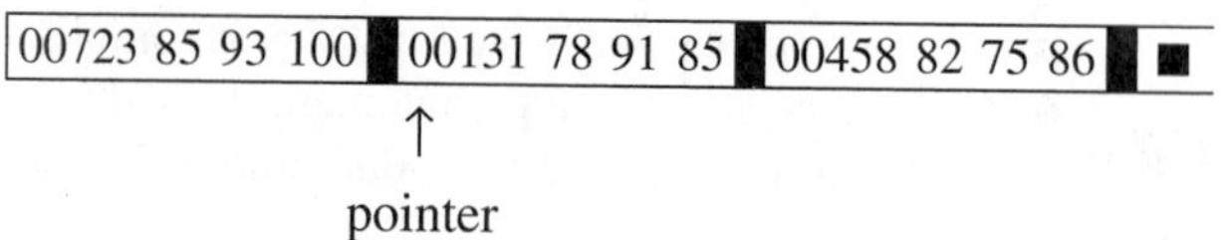

It is not necessary to read all values in a line of data. If only some values are read, a **readln** statement still causes the pointer to move to the first position past the end-of-line marker. Thus,

```
reset (ClassList);
readln (ClassList, IDNumber, Score1);
```

results in

00723	85	?	?
IDNumber	Score1	Score2	Score3

00723 85 93 100 ▮ 00131 78 91 85 ▮ 00458 82 75 86 ▮ ■

↑ pointer

However, when data items are read using **read,** the pointer moves to the first position past the last data item read. Thus, the statement

```
read (ClassList, IDNumber, Score1);
```

results in the following:

00723	85
IDNumber	Score1

00723 85 93 100 ▮ 00131 78 91 85 ▮ 00458 82 75 86 ▮ ■

↑ pointer

Variables in the variable list of **read** and **readln** can be listed one at a time or in any combination that does not result in a type conflict. For example,

```
readln (ClassList, IDNumber, Score1);
```

can be replaced by

```
read (ClassList, IDNumber);
readln (ClassList, Score1);
```

However, unnecessary procedure calls are inefficient.

Pascal has two Boolean-valued functions that may be used when working with text files: **eoln** (for end-of-line) and **eof** (for end-of-file). Only if the data pointer is at an end-of-line or end-of-file marker is the **boolean** function **eoln**(<file variable>) **true.** Similarly, **eof**(<file variable>) is **true** only when the data pointer is positioned at the end-of-file marker. This allows both **eoln**(<file variable>) and **eof**(<file variable>) to be used as **boolean** conditions when designing problem solutions. Thus, part of a solution might be

```
WHILE NOT eof(<file variable>) DO
  <process a line of data>
```

In this loop, data from one line of the text file would typically be read by a **readln** statement. This allows the end-of-file condition to become true after the last data line has been read.

Text files can contain any character available in the character set being used. When numeric data are stored, the system converts a number to an appropriate character representation. When this number is retrieved from the file, another conversion takes place to change the character representation to a number.

Example 9.1

Now let's write a short program that uses the text file ClassList and the end-of-file (**eof**) condition. If the problem is to print a listing of student identification numbers, test scores, and test averages, a first-level pseudocode development is

1. Print a heading
2. Print a heading
3. **WHILE NOT eof**(<file variable>) **DO**
   3.1 Process a line of data

Step 3.1 can be refined to

3.1 Process a line of data
  3.1.1 Get the data
  3.1.2 Compute test average
  3.1.3 Print the data

A short program to accomplish this task follows:

```
PROGRAM ClassRecordBook (input, output, ClassList);

{   This program uses data from a text file.  Data for each     }
{   student are on a separate line in the file.  Lines  are     }
{   processed until there are no more lines.                    }

VAR
  Score1, Score2, Score3,              {  Test scores            }
  IDNumber : integer;                  {  Student number         }
  TestAverage : real;                  {  Average of three tests }
  ClassList : text;                    {  Text file              }

{*****************************************************************}

FUNCTION Average (Score1, Score2, Score3 : integer) : real;

  {  Given:   Three integers                                      }
  {  Task:    Compute their average                               }
  {  Return:  The average of three integers                       }

  BEGIN
    Average := (Score1 + Score2 + Score3) / 3
  END;  {  of FUNCTION Average  }

{*****************************************************************}
```

```
PROCEDURE PrintHeading;

  {  Given:   Nothing                                              }
  {  Task:    Print the heading                                    }
  {  Return:  Nothing                                              }

  CONST
    Skip = ' ';

  BEGIN
    writeln ('Identification Number', Skip:5, 'Test Scores',
             Skip:5, 'Average');
    writeln ('---------------------', Skip:5, '-----------',
             Skip:5, '-------');
    writeln
  END;   {  of PROCEDURE PrintHeading  }

{*****************************************************************}

BEGIN  {  Main program  }
  reset (ClassList);
  PrintHeading;
  WHILE NOT eof(ClassList) DO
    BEGIN
      readln (ClassList, IDNumber, Score1, Score2, Score3);
      TestAverage := Average(Score1, Score2, Score3);
      writeln (IDNumber:10, Score1:19, Score2:4, Score3:4,
               TestAverage:11:2)
    END  {  of WHILE NOT eof DO loop  }
END.  {  of main program  }
```

When this program is run using the text file ClassList with values

00123 85 93 100	■	00131 78 91 85	■	00458 82 75 86	■	■

the following output is produced:

```
Identification Number     Test Scores     Average
---------------------     -----------     -------

       123                 85  93 100      92.67
       131                 78  91  85      84.67
       458                 82  75  86      81.00
```

A note of caution is in order. Any attempt to **read** beyond the end of a file results in an error. To illustrate, if

```
read (ClassList, IDNumber, Score1, Score2, Score3);
```

had been used in the previous example instead of

```
readln (ClassList, IDNumber, Score1, Score2, Score3);
```

an error would have occurred because, when **read** is used with the last line of data, the data pointer is positioned as

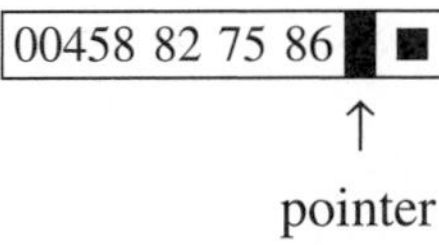

At this point, even though **eoln**(ClassList) is **true, eof**(ClassList) is still **false** and the loop for processing a line of data would be entered one more time. Using **readln,** however, positions the data pointer as

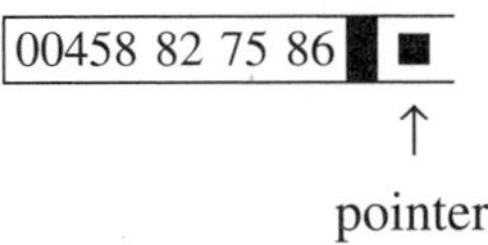

and this causes the end-of-file condition to be **true** when expected.

Writing to a Text File

It is also possible to write to a text file. If you want the file saved for later use, a file variable must be included in the file list as part of the program heading just as is done when reading from files. The file variable must also be declared to be of type **text.** Before writing to a file, it must be **opened for writing** using the form

Opened for writing refers to the positioning of a pointer at the beginning of a file for the purpose of writing to the file.

rewrite (<file variable>)

This standard procedure creates an empty file with the specified name. Any values previously in the file are erased by this statement. Data are then written to the file using standard procedures **write** and **writeln.** The general form is

write (<file variable>, <list of values>)
or
writeln (<file variable>, <list of values>)

Either statement causes the list of values to be written on one line in the file. The difference is that **writeln** causes an end-of-line marker to be placed after the last data item. Using **write** allows the user to continue entering data items on the same line with subsequent **write** or **writeln** statements. If desired,

```
writeln (<file variable>);
```

can be used to place an end-of-line marker at the end of a data line.

Formatting can be used to control spacing of data items in a line of text. For example, since numeric items must be separated, the user might choose to put test scores in a file using the following code:

```
writeln (ClassList, Score1:4, Score2:4, Score3:4);
```

If the scores are 85, 72, and 95, the line of data created is

85 72 95 ■

and each integer is allotted four columns. Let's now illustrate writing to a file with an example.

Example 9.2

Let's write a program that allows you to create a text file containing data for students in a class. Each line in the file is to contain a student identification number followed by three test scores. A first-level pseudocode development is

1. Open the file
2. **WHILE** more data **DO**
   2.1 Process a line

Step 2.1 can be refined to

2.1 Process a line
   2.1.1 Get data from keyboard
   2.1.2 Write data to text file

A complete program for this pseudocode follows:

```
PROGRAM CreateFile (input, output, ClassList);

{   This program creates a text file.  Each line of the file     }
{   contains data for one student.  Data are entered  inter-     }
{   actively from the keyboard and then written to the file.     }

VAR
  Score1, Score2, Score3,          {  Scores for three tests       }
  IDNumber : integer;              {  Student number               }
  Response : char;                 {  Indicator for continuation   }
  MoreData : boolean;              {  Loop control variable        }
  ClassList : text;                {  Text file                    }

{*************************************************************}

PROCEDURE GetStudentData (VAR IDNumber, Score1, Score2,
                          Score3 : integer);

  {  Given:   Nothing                                          }
  {  Task:    Get IDNumber and three test scores from the      }
  {                keyboard                                    }
  {  Return:  IDNumber, Score1, Score2, and Score3             }

  BEGIN
    write ('Please enter a student ID number');
    writeln (' and three test scores.');
    writeln ('Separate entries by a space.');
    writeln;
    readln (IDNumber, Score1, Score2, Score3)
  END;  {  of PROCEDURE GetStudentData  }

{**************************************************************}

BEGIN  {  Main program  }
  rewrite (ClassList);                        {  Open for writing  }
  MoreData := true;
```

```
  WHILE MoreData DO
    BEGIN
      GetStudentData (IDNumber, Score1, Score2, Score3);
      writeln (ClassList, IDNumber, Score1:4, Score2:4, Score3:4);

      {  Check for more data  }
      writeln;
      writeln ('Any more students?  Y or N');
      readln (Response);
      IF (Response = 'N') OR (Response = 'n') THEN
        MoreData := false
    END  {  of WHILE...DO loop  }
END.  {  of main program  }
```

External and Internal Files

An **external file** is a file used to store data in secondary storage between runs of a program.

All files used thus far have been **external files,** which are files that are stored in secondary memory and are external to main memory. If a program is to use an external file, a file variable must be included in the file list portion of the program heading. The file variable must then be declared in the variable declaration section as type **text.**

T

An **internal file** [or **scratch (temporary) file**] is a file that is used for processing only and is not saved in secondary storage.

On some occasions, it is desirable to use a file only while the program is running and it is not necessary to save the contents for later use. In such a case, an **internal file** [also called a **scratch (temporary) file**] can be created by declaring a file variable of type **text** in the variable declaration section but not including it in the file list of the program heading. Internal files are normally used during file processing when it is desirable to save temporarily the contents of a file that is being altered. Our next example illustrates use of an internal file.

Example 9.3

Let's write a program that allows you to update the text file ClassList from Example 9.2 by adding one more test score to each line of data. We need two text files in this program: ClassList (external) and TempFile (internal). With these two files, we can create new lines in TempFile by reading a line from ClassList and getting a score from the keyboard. When all lines have been updated, we copy TempFile to ClassList. A first-level pseudocode solution for this problem is

1. Open the files (**reset** ClassList, **rewrite** TempFile)
2. **WHILE NOT eof**(ClassList) **DO**
   2.1 Read one line
   2.2 Get new score
   2.3 Write one line to TempFile
3. Open files (**reset** TempFile, **rewrite** ClassList)
4. Update file
   WHILE NOT eof (TempFile) **DO**
   4.1 Read one line from TempFile
   4.2 Write one line to ClassList

A complete program for this problem is

```
PROGRAM UpdateClassList (input, output, ClassList);

{   This program updates an existing text  file.  The process   }
```

```
{   requires a second file.  Contents of the external file are  }
{   copied to a temporary internal file and the external  file  }
{   is then updated one line at a time.                         }

VAR
  Score1, Score2,                     {  Scores for four tests  }
  Score3, Score 4,
  IDNumber : integer;                 {  Student number         }
  ClassList, TempFile : text;         {  Text files             )

BEGIN  {  Program  }
  reset (ClassList);                              {  Open files  }
  rewrite (TempFile);

  WHILE NOT eof(ClassList) DO              {  Copy to TempFile  }
    BEGIN
      readln (ClassList, IDNumber, Score1, Score2, Score3);
      writeln ('Enter a new test score for student ', IDNumber);
      readln (Score4);
      writeln (TempFile, IDNumber, Score1:4, Score2:4,
               Score3:4, Score4:4)
    END;  {  of lines in ClassList  }

  reset (TempFile);                               {  Open files  }
  rewrite (ClassList); { Note: contents of old ClassList erased }

  WHILE NOT eof(TempFile) DO              {  Copy to ClassList  }
    BEGIN
      readln (TempFile, IDNumber, Score1, Score2, Score3, Score4);
      writeln (ClassList, IDNumber, Score1:4, Score2:4, Score3:4,
               Score4:4)
    END  {  of copying TempFile to ClassList  }
END.  {  of program  }
```

Example 9.4

As an illustration of how to use **eoln,** let's write a program that replaces all blanks in a text file with asterisks. Output is directed to the monitor and a new text file is created for the purpose of saving the altered form of the original text file. Note that reading a character advances the data pointer only one character position unless **readln** is used. A first-level pseudocode development is

1. Open the files

WHILE NOT eof(FileWithBlanks) **DO**

2. Process one line
3. Prepare for the next line

A second-level pseudocode development is

1. Open the files
   1.1 Open FileWithBlanks
   1.2 Open FileWithoutBlanks

WHILE NOT eof(FileWithBlanks) **DO**

2. Process one line
   2.1 Read a character

2.2 **IF** character is a blank **THEN**
   2.2.1 Replace with an asterisk
2.3 Write character to FileWithoutBlanks
2.4 Write character to the screen
3. Prepare for the next line
   3.1 Insert end-of-line marker in FileWithoutBlanks
   3.2 End-of-line marker to screen
   3.3 Advance pointer in FileWithBlanks

A complete program for this problem follows:

```
PROGRAM DeleteBlanks (input, output, FileWithBlanks,
                      FileWithoutBlanks);

{  This  program illustrates  using eof  and eoln  with a text  }
{  file.  It replaces blanks with asterisks.                    }

VAR
  FileWithBlanks,               {  Existing text file           }
  FileWithoutBlanks : text;     {  Altered text file            }
  Ch : char;                    {  Used for reading characters  }

BEGIN
  reset (FileWithBlanks);                    {  Open the files  }
  rewrite (FileWithoutBlanks);
  WHILE NOT eof(FileWithBlanks) DO
    BEGIN                                  {  Process one line  }
      WHILE NOT eoln(FileWithBlanks) DO
        BEGIN
          read (FileWithBlanks, Ch);
          IF Ch = ' ' THEN
            Ch := '*';
          write (FileWithoutBlanks, Ch);
          write (Ch)                    {  Write to the screen  }
        END;    {  of reading one line  }
      writeln (FileWithoutBlanks);       {  Insert end-of-line  }
      writeln;
      readln (FileWithBlanks)           {  Advance the pointer  }
    END  {  of lines in text file  }
END.  {  of program  }
```

On the final time through the loop, **readln** changes the pointer from

last line ▌■
↑
pointer

to

last line ▌■
↑
pointer

Hence, **eof**(FileWithBlanks) becomes **true.**

When this program is run using the text file

```
This is a text file with normal blanks.
After it has been processed by
PROGRAM DeleteBlanks, every blank will
be replaced with an asterisk "*".
```

the output to the screen is

```
This*is*a*text*file*with*normal*blanks.
After*it*has*been*processed*by
PROGRAM*DeleteBlanks,*every*blank*will
be*replaced*with*an*asterisk*"*".
```

The external text file FileWithoutBlanks also contains the version shown as output.

Reading Mixed Data

It is often necessary to include data of more than one type in a text file. For example, each line of a data file might contain a person's age and gender:

18M	■	21F	■	20F	■	18M	■	20M	■	20F	■	■

When reading data from such a file, you must guard against reading data into a variable that is not consistent with the type of data being read. The data from the data file here can be read by

```
WHILE NOT eof(Data) DO
  BEGIN
    readln (Data, Age, Gender);
      .
      .  (process data here)
      .
  END;
```

The material in this section allows us to make a substantial change in our approach to writing programs. We now proceed by assuming data files exist for a program. This somewhat simplifies program design and also allows us to design programs for large sets of data. Consequently, most programs developed in the remainder of this text use text files for input. In some cases, the standard file **input** is assumed. If you wish to continue with interactive programs, you should be able to make appropriate modifications.

■ Exercises 9.1

1. Explain the difference between an external file and an internal file. Give appropriate uses for each.
2. Write a test program that allows you to print a line of text from a file to the output file.
*3. Explain what is wrong with using

   ```
   writeln (ClassList, Score1, Score2, Score3);
   ```

   if you want to write three scores to the text file ClassList.
4. Write a program that allows the user to display a text file line by line.

For Exercises 5–8, assume that a text file, InFile, is as illustrated:

18 ▮ 19M ▮ –14.3 ▮ JO ▮ 142.1F ▮ ■

The pointer is positioned at the beginning of the file and the variable declaration section of a program is

```
VAR
  A, B : integer:
  X, Y : real;
  CH : char;
  InFile : text;
```

What output is produced from each segment of code?

*5. `read (InFile, A);`
`read (Infile, B, Ch);`
`writeln (A:5, B:5, Ch:5);`

6. `read (Infile, Ch);`
`write (Ch:10);`
`readln (InFile, Ch);`
`writeln (Ch);`
`read (InFile, Ch);`
`writeln (Ch:10);`

*7. `read (InFile, A, B, Ch, X);`
`writeln (A, B, Ch, X);`
`writeln (A:5, B:5, Ch:5, X:10:2);`
`read (InFile, Ch);`
`writeln (Ch:5);`

8. `readln (InFile);`
`read (InFile, Ch, Ch);`
`readln (InFile, Y);`
`writeln (Ch:5, Y:10:2);`

For Exercises 9–16, using the same input and variable declaration section in Exercises 5–8, indicate the contents of each variable location and the position of the pointer after the segment of code is executed. Assume the pointer is positioned at the beginning for each problem.

*9. `read (InFile, Ch, A);`

10. `readln (InFile, Ch, A);`

*11. `readln (InFile);`

12. `readln (InFile);`
`readln (InFile);`

*13. `readln (InFile, A, B, Ch, X);`

14. `read (InFile, A, B, Ch, Y);`

*15. `readln (InFile, A, Ch);`
`readln (Infile, Ch, Ch, B);`

16. `read (InFile, A, B, Ch, X, Ch);`

For Exercises 17–21, again use the same input and variable declaration section as in Exercises 5–8. Indicate if the exercise produces an error and, if so, explain why an error occurs.

*17. `read (InFile, X, Y);`

18. `readln (InFile, A);`
    `read (InFile, B);`

*19. `readln (InFile, Ch);`
    `readln (InFile, Ch);`
    `readln (InFile, Ch);`

20. `read (InFile, X, A, Ch, B, Ch);`

*21. `readln (InFile);`
    `read (InFile, Ch, Ch, A, Ch, B);`

22. Write a complete Pascal program that reads your (three) initials and five test scores from a text file. Your program should then compute your test average and print all information in a reasonable form with suitable messages.

23. Write a program that allows you to create a text file that contains your name, address, social security number, and age. **reset** the file and have the information printed as output. Save the file in secondary storage for later use.

24. Show what output is produced from the following program. Also indicate the contents of each file after the program is run.

```
PROGRAM ExerciseTwentyFour (input, output, F2);

VAR
  Ch : char;
  F1, F2 : text;

BEGIN
  rewrite (F1);
  rewrite (F2);
  writeln (F1, 'This is a test.');
  writeln (F1, 'This is another line.');
  reset (F1);
  WHILE NOT eof(F1) DO
    BEGIN
      WHILE NOT eoln(F1) DO
        BEGIN
          read (F1, Ch);
          IF Ch = ' ' THEN
            writeln ('*')
          ELSE
            write (F2, Ch)
        END
      readln (F1)
    END
END.
```

*25. Write a program that deletes all blanks from a text file. Your program should save the revised file for later use.

26. Write a program using a **CASE** statement to scramble a text file by replacing all blanks with an asterisk (*), and replacing all A's with U's and E's with I's. Your program should print the scrambled file and save it for subsequent use.

27. Write a program to update a text file by numbering the lines consecutively as 1, 2, 3, ...

28. Write a program to count the number of words in a text file. Assume that each word is followed by a blank or a period.
29. Write a program to find the longest word in a text file. Output should include the word and its length.
30. Write a program to compute the average length of words in a text file.

9.2 TYPE Definitions in Pascal

Objectives

- to understand what is meant by ordinal data type
- to be able to declare enumerated data types
- to be able to use enumerated data types in a program
- to understand why enumerated data types are of value in writing programs

Ordinal Data Types

Of the data types we have previously used, **integer, char,** and **boolean** are called ordinal data types. Recall that a data type is ordinal if values of that type have an immediate predecessor and an immediate successor. The exceptions are that the first listed element has only a successor and the last listed element has only a predecessor. For example, data of type **integer** are ordinal and can be listed as **–maxint –1,** . . . , –1, 0, 1, 2, . . . , **+maxint.** The Boolean values **false** and **true** and data of type **char** are listed according to the collating sequence shown in Appendix 4. Data of type **real** are not ordinal because a given real has neither an immediate predecessor nor an immediate successor. Permissible values for data of the three ordinal data types are summarized as follows:

Data Type	Values
integer	**–maxint –1** to **maxint**
char	Character set in a collating sequence
boolean	**true, false**

The four data types **integer, char, boolean,** and **real** used thus far are standard data types. We are now ready to see how Pascal allows us to define other data types, called enumerated data types.

Simple Enumerated Data Types

An **enumerated data type** is a user-defined data type.

The declaration section of a program may contain a **TYPE** definition section that can be used to define a data type. In this section, an **enumerated data type** is defined by the programmer and allows a discrete number of values for that data type, for example,

```
TYPE
  Weekday = (Mon, Tues, Wed, Thur, Fri);
```

After such a definition has been made, the variable declaration section can contain identifiers of the type Weekday. Thus, we could have

```
VAR
  Day : Weekday;
```

Values in an enumerated data type can be any legal identifier. Several comments are now in order concerning the **TYPE** definition.

A **user-defined data type** is a data type that is defined in the **TYPE** definition section by the programmer. Also referred to as enumerated data type.

1. Simple enumerated data types are frequently referred to as **user-defined data types.** (Other structured enumerated data types are discussed later.)
2. This defined type will be an ordinal data type with the first defined constant having ordinal zero. Ordinal values increase by 1 in order from left to right. Every constant except the first has a predecessor, and every constant except the last has a successor. Using the previously defined **TYPE** Weekday, we have

```
Mon     Tues    Wed     Thur    Fri
 ↕       ↕       ↕       ↕       ↕
 0       1       2       3       4
```

3. Variables can be declared to be of the new type.
4. The values defined in the **TYPE** definition section are constants that can be used in the program. These values must be valid identifiers.
5. No identifier can belong to more than one enumerated data type.
6. Identifiers that are defined values cannot be used as operands in arithmetic expressions.
7. Enumerated data types are for internal use only; you cannot **read** or **write** values of these variables.

Thus, given the previous **TYPE** definition of Weekday and the variable declaration of Day, each of the following would be an appropriate program statement:

1. `Day := Tues;`
2. `Day := pred(Day);`
3.
```
IF Day = Mon THEN
  .
  .
  .
ELSE
  .
  .
  .
```
4.
```
FOR Day := Mon TO Fri DO
  BEGIN
    .
    .
    .
  END;
```

Now that we have seen an example of an enumerated data type and some typical related program statements, let's look at a more formal method of definition. In general, we have

> **TYPE**
> <type identifier> = (<constant1>, <constant2>, . . . , <constant*n*>);
> **VAR**
> <identifier> : <type identifier>;

The **TYPE** definition section is part of the declaration section of a program. It follows the constant definition section (**CONST**) and precedes the variable declaration section (**VAR**), as shown in Figure 9.1.

◆ Figure 9.1

Placement of **TYPE** definition section

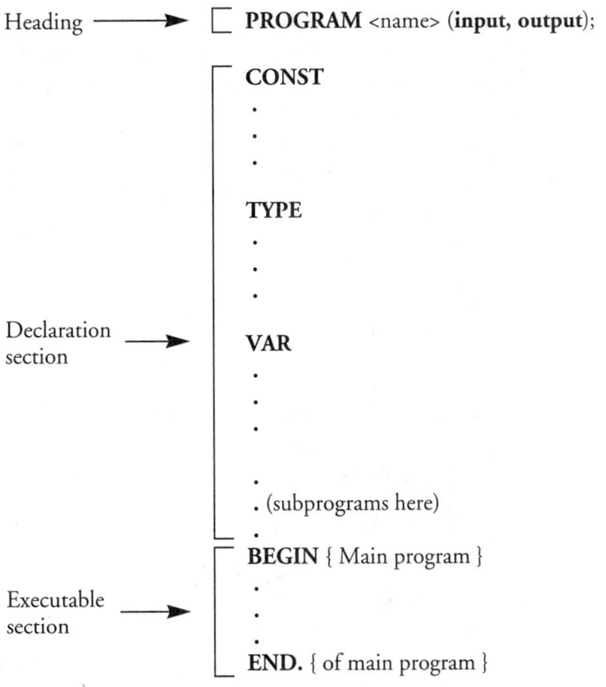
Heading
PROGRAM <name> (input, output);
CONST
TYPE
Declaration section
VAR
(subprograms here)
BEGIN { Main program }
Executable section
END. { of main program }

The following short program illustrates the placement and use of enumerated data types.

```
PROGRAM TypePrac (output);

CONST
  Skip = ' ';

TYPE
  Weekday = (Mon, Tues, Wed, Thur, Fri);

VAR
  Day : Weekday;

BEGIN
  Day := Wed;
  IF Day < Fri THEN
    writeln (Skip:20, 'Not near the weekend.')
  ELSE
    writeln (Skip:20, 'The weekend starts tomorrow.')
END.
```

The output from this program is

```
Not near the weekend.
```

Reasons for Using Enumerated Data Types

At first it may seem like a lot of trouble to define new types for use in a Pascal program, but there are several reasons for using them. In fact, being able to create enumerated data types is one of the advantages of using Pascal as a programming language. Why? With enumerated data types, you can express clearly the logical structure of data, enhance the readability of your program, provide program protection against bad data values, and declare parameters in subprograms.

Suppose you are working on a program to count the number of days in the month of a certain year. Enumerated data types allow you to use the following definition and subsequent declaration:

```
TYPE
  AllMonths = (Jan, Feb, March, April, May, June, July,
               Aug, Sept, Oct, Nov, Dec);
VAR
  Month : AllMonths;
```

With this definition it is easier to understand what the code does. It could contain a statement such as

```
IF (Month = Feb) AND (Year MOD 4 = 0) THEN
  NumDays := 29;
```

This clearly indicates that you are counting the extra day in February for a leap year. (This is an oversimplification of checking for a leap year. See Exercise 16 at the end of this section.)

Enumerated data types can be used in **CASE** statements. For example, movie ticket prices are frequently broken into three categories: youth, adult, and senior citizen. If the following definition and declaration

```
TYPE
  Categories = (Youth, Adult, Senior);
VAR
  Patron : Categories;
```

were made, a program statement could be something like

```
CASE Patron OF
  Youth  : Price := YouthPrice;
  Adult  : Price := AdultPrice;
  Senior : Price := SeniorPrice
END;  {  of CASE Patron  }
```

Once an enumerated data type has been defined at the global level, it is available to all subprograms. Thus, if you have a function for counting the days, a typical function heading might be

```
FUNCTION NumDays (Month : AllMonths;
                  Year : integer) : integer;
```

This aspect of enumerated data types will become more significant when we examine structured data types, including arrays and records.

A Note of Interest

Career Opportunities in Computer Science

The list "Fastest Growing Occupations, 1990–2005," published by the Bureau of Labor Statistics, includes computer programmers and computer systems analysts. During this time period, the number of these jobs is expected to increase by 78.9 percent. Computer scientists and systems analysts held about 828,000 jobs in 1994. Although they are found in most industries, the greatest concentration is in the computer and data processing services industry. In addition, tens of thousands of job openings will result annually from the need to replace workers who move into managerial positions or other occupations, or who leave the labor force. Employment of computer professionals is expected to grow much faster than the average of all occupations through the year 2005 (Occupational Outlook Handbook-1996-1997).

A recent survey of employers was conducted to determine which academic disciplines were of greatest interest to employers. Of these, 60 percent mentioned computer science.

The relative ranking of the disciplines has remained very stable since 1980 when they were first compiled. The same three disciplines—computer science, electrical engineering, and mechanical engineering—have been on the top of the list, sought after by about two-thirds of the responding companies. (Peterson, Job Opportunities).

Unemployment among computer specialists is traditionally exceptionally low, and almost all who enter the workforce find jobs. In 1994, the median annual income was about $44,000 for a systems analyst. Computer scientists with advanced degrees generally earn more than systems analysts. (Occupational Outlook Handbook-1996-1997).

All able students—particularly women and minorities, who have been traditionally underrepresented in the sciences—are encouraged to consider computer science as a career.

Recall the limitation imposed on variables that are of an enumerated type: They are for internal use only; you cannot **read** or **write** values of these variables. Thus, in the earlier example using months of the year, you could have the following statement:

```
Month := June;
```

but not

```
writeln (Month);
```

However, as we saw in Section 5.5, use of a **CASE** statement allows translation procedures to be written with relative ease.

We close this section with some typical definitions for enumerated data types. These are intended to improve program readability. You are encouraged to incorporate enumerated data types into your subsequent programs. In general, you are limited only by your imagination.

```
TYPE
  SoftDrinks = (Pepsi, Coke, SevenUp, Orange, RootBeer);
  Seasons = (Winter, Spring, Summer, Fall);
  Colors = (Red, Orange, Yellow, Green, Blue, Indigo, Violet);
  ClassStanding = (Freshman, Sophomore, Junior, Senior);
  Ranks = (Sarg, Lieut, Cptn, Major, Corp);
  Fruits = (Apple, Orange, Banana);
  Vegetables = (Corn, Peas, Broccoli, Spinach);
```

Given these type definitions, each of the following would be a reasonable variable declaration:

```
VAR
  Pop, Soda : SoftDrinks;
  Season : Seasons;
  Hue : Colors;
  Class : ClassStanding;
  Rank : Ranks;
  Appetizer : Fruits;
  SideDish : Vegetables;
```

Exercises 9.2

1. Explain what is meant by ordinal data type.
2. Write a test program to see what happens in each of the following instances:
   a. Try to **write** the value of a variable that is an enumerated data type.
   b. Try to find the predecessor (**pred**) of a defined constant that has zero as its ordinal in an enumerated type.

In Exercises 3–5, find all errors in the definitions.

*3.
```
TYPE
  Names = (John, Joe, Mary, Jane);
  People = (Henry, Sue, Jane, Bill);
```
4.
```
TYPE
  Colors = (Red, Blue, Red, Orange);
```
*5.
```
TYPE
  Letters = A, C, E;
```
6. Assume the **TYPE** definition

```
TYPE
  Colors = (Red, Orange, Yellow, Blue, Green);
```

   has been given. Indicate whether each of the following is **true** or **false:**
   a. `Orange < Blue`
   b. `(Green <> Red) AND (Blue > Green)`
   c. `(Yellow < Orange) OR (Blue >= Red)`

For Exercises 7–14, assume the **TYPE** definition and variable declaration

```
TYPE
  AllDays = (Sun, Mon, Tues, Wed, Thur, Fri, Sat);
VAR
  Day, Weekday, Weekend : AllDays;
```

have been given. Indicate which are valid program statements and, for those that are invalid, explain why.

*7. `Day := Tues;`
8. `Day := Tues + Wed;`
*9. `Weekday := Sun;`
10.
```
IF Day = Sat THEN
  writeln ('Clean the garage.':30);
```
*11.
```
IF (Day < Sat) AND (Day > Sun) THEN
  writeln ('It is a workday.':30)
```

```
ELSE
  writeln ('It is the weekend.':30);
```

12.
```
FOR Day := Mon TO Fri DO
  writeln (Day);
```

*13.
```
read (Day);
IF Day < Sat THEN
  Weekday := Day;
```

14.
```
Wed := Tues + 1;
```

15. Assume the following definitions and declarations have been made in a program:

```
TYPE
  Cloth = (Flannel, Cotton, Rayon, Orlon);
VAR
  Material : Cloth;
  NumberOfYards, Price : real;
```

What output is produced by the following segment of code?

```
Material := Cotton;
NumberOfYards := 3.5;
IF (Material = Rayon) OR (Material = Orlon) THEN
  Price := NumberOfYards * 4.5
ELSE IF Material = Cotton THEN
  Price := NumberOfYards * 2.75
ELSE
  Price := NumberOfYards * 2.5;
writeln (Price:30:2);
```

16. Find the complete definition of a leap year in the Gregorian calendar. Define appropriate data types and write a segment of code that would indicate whether or not a given year was a leap year.

9.3 Subrange as a Data Type

Objectives

- to be able to define a subrange as a data type
- to be able to use subrange data types in a program
- to understand compatibility of data types
- to understand why subrange data types are used in a program

Defining Subranges

In Section 9.2, we learned how to define new data types using the **TYPE** definition section. Now we will investigate yet another way to define new data types.

A **subrange** of an existing ordinal data type may be defined as a data type by

> **TYPE**
> <identifier> = <initial value> . . <final value>

where the initial value and final value are separated by two periods. For example, a subrange of the integers could be defined by

```
TYPE
  USYears = 1776..1997;
```

When defining a subrange, the following items should be noted:

1. The original data type must be an ordinal type.

A **subrange** is the defined subset of values of an existing ordinal data type.

2. Any valid identifier may be used for the name of the type.
3. The initial and final values must be of the original data type.
4. The underlying data type is ordered. In this ordering, the initial value of a defined subrange must occur before the final value.
5. Only values in the indicated subrange (endpoints included) may be assigned to a variable of the type defined by the subrange.
6. The same value may appear in different subranges.

Some of these points are illustrated in the following example.

Example 9.5

Consider the subranges Weekdays and Midweek of the enumerated ordinal Days.

```
TYPE
  Days = (Sun, Mon, Tues, Wed, Thur, Fri, Sat);      {  Enumerated  }
  Weekdays = Mon..Fri;                                {  Subrange    }
  Midweek = Tues..Thur;                               {  Subrange    }
VAR
  SchoolDay : Weekdays;
  Workday : Midweek;
```

In this case, Days is defined first and we can then define appropriate subranges. Because the variable SchoolDay is declared as of type Weekdays, we can use any of the values Mon, Tues, Wed, Thur, or Fri with SchoolDay. However, we cannot assign either Sat or Sun to SchoolDay.

Notice that Tues, Wed, and Thur are values that appear in different type definitions. However, since they appear in subranges, this will not produce an error. Furthermore,

```
Workday := Tues;
```

and

```
SchoolDay := Workday;
```

are both acceptable statements.

Some other subrange definitions are

```
TYPE
  Grades = 'A'..'E';
  Alphabet = 'A'..'Z';
  ScoreRange = 0..100;
  Months = (Jan, Feb, Mar, Apr, May, June, July, Aug, Sept,
            Oct, Nov, Dec);
  Year = Jan..Dec;
  Summer = June..Aug;
```

Months is not a subrange here. However, once defined, an appropriate subrange such as Summer can be defined. With these subranges defined, each of the following declarations would be appropriate:

```
VAR
  FinalGrade : Grades;
  Letter : Alphabet;
```

```
TestScore : ScoreRange;
SumMonth : Summer;
```

Subrange limits may be ignored by some compilers. Thus, the assignment of a value outside the specified range may not cause a compilation error. Since the value that will be stored cannot be predicted, subranges should not be used as a form of program protection because program crashes can be caused by inappropriate values.

Compatibility of Variables

Type compatible variables have the same base type. A value parameter and its argument must be type compatible.

Now that we know how to define subranges of existing ordinal data types, we need to look carefully at compatibility of variables. Variables are **type compatible** if they have the same base type. Thus, in

```
TYPE
  AgeRange = 0..110;
VAR
  Age : AgeRange;
  Year : integer;
```

the variables Age and Year are type compatible because they both have **integer** as the base type (AgeRange is a subrange of integers). If variables are type compatible, assignments can be made between them or they can be manipulated in any manner that variables of that base type can be manipulated.

Even when variables are type compatible, caution should be exercised when making assignment statements. To illustrate, using Age and Year as previously declared, consider the following statements:

```
Age := Year;
Year := Age;
```

Since Age is of type AgeRange and AgeRange is a subrange of **integer,** any value in Age is acceptable as a value that can be assigned to Year. Thus,

```
Year := Age;
```

is permissible. However, since values for Age are restricted to the defined subrange, it is possible that

```
Age := Year;
```

will produce an error. Since Age and Year are type compatible, there will not be a compilation error, but consider

```
Year := 150;
Age := Year;
```

Since 150 is not in the subrange for Age, execution could be halted; an error message would then be printed.

Type identical variables are declared with the same type identifier. A variable parameter and its argument must be of identical type.

Two variables are said to be **type identical** if—and only if—they are declared with the same type identifier. It is important to distinguish between variables of compatible and identical type when using subprograms. A value parameter and its argument must be type compatible; a variable parameter and its argument must be type identical. A type-compatibility error will be generated if these rules are not followed. To illustrate, consider

```
TYPE
  GoodScore = 60..100;
VAR
  Score1, Score2 : GoodScore;
PROCEDURE Compute (HS1 : integer;
                   VAR HS2 : GoodScore);
```

This procedure may be called by

```
Compute (Score1, Score2);
```

Note that HS1 is a value parameter and must only be compatible with Score1, whereas HS2 is a variable parameter and must be identical in type to Score2. However, if the procedure heading is

```
PROCEDURE Compute (VAR HS1 : integer;
                   HS2 : GoodScore);
```

then an attempt to call the procedure by

```
Compute (Score1, Score2);
```

will result in an error because Score1 and HS1 are not type identical.

Assignment compatible means an expression can be assigned to a variable.

An expression is considered to be **assignment compatible** with a variable if at least one of the following is true:

1. The variable and the expression are type identical.
2. They are compatible ordinal types such that the value of the expression is contained in the range of the variable.
3. The variable is of type **real,** and the expression is of type **integer.**

When used as data types for parameters, **TYPE** definitions must be defined in the main program because they cannot be defined in a subprogram heading. However, **TYPE** definitions can be defined internally for subprograms.

Communication and Style Tips

The **CONST** and **TYPE** definition sections can be used together to enhance readability and facilitate program design. For example, rather than use the subrange

```
TYPE
  USYears = 1776..1997;
```

you could define an ending constant and then use it as indicated.

```
CONST
  CurrentYear = 1997;
TYPE
  USYears = 1776..CurrentYear;
```

A Note of Interest

Keeping Pace with Changing Technology

Technology is changing so rapidly that it is almost futile to comment on the "current" state of events. However, we will do so for two reasons. The first reason is to make you aware of rapidly changing technology; and the second reason is because it is always interesting to mark a point in time from an historical perspective. Thus, we offer observations about the status of the memory game and microchip processor speeds in mid-1996.

External Memory

It is predicted that the memory game is about to undergo a tremendous revolution. Digital video disks (DVDs) are the latest disks in the ever-changing world of data storage. They will be marketed as 4.75-inch disks (the same as current CDs). When recorded on two sides, they will hold up to 18 gigabytes. The basic entry-level DVD with only one side recorded will hold 4.7 gigabytes. That is as much as 7.5 ordinary CDs or 3450 3.5-inch high-density floppy disks. Potential computer applications are enormous. Current projections indicate the DVD will come to market first as a read-only drive, like current CD-ROMs. By the end of 1997, rewritable DVDs should be marketed. By the year 2000, industry analysts project that 120 million DVDs will be marketed, a business expected to be worth more than $20 billion a year.

In its read-only format, a DVD will create memories large enough to hold not just encyclopedias, but entire libraries. In rewritable configurations, DVDs will allow PCs to map the heavens or project accurate star maps from any perspective in the sky. They will reduce mainframe computer storage systems from rooms of drives to a few DVD players on a bookshelf.

The potential for entertainment is immense. A single disk will be able to hold one movie of over two hours on a side with three audio tracks. Current projections claim that interactive players will allow the viewer to choose camera angles such as pan, scan, widescreen, and close-up for as many as nine camera angles. These disks combined with high-definition television and high-end audio equipment could create multiple-track playback equipment for home users that today is confined to professional recording studios.

Processing Speed

Microchip processor speeds are also changing rapidly. Processor speeds used to double about every 18 months. That was true in the relatively early days, when we went from the 286 chip to the 386 and 486 chips. Now, doubling seems to occur in 9 to 12 months. In 1981, chips ran with a clock speed of 4.7 megahertz, about 1/40 of the current rate for off-the-shelf PC processors.

Industry analysts predict that new technology will be required in order for the processing speeds to continue to grow as they have. Current leading-edge developments include the use of gallium arsenide (which is potentially toxic) as a conductor, elaborate parallel processing designs, and searches for new ways to open and shut transistors within semiconductors.

Research is also being done to see if it is possible to use photons rather than electrons for tripping switches. Photons are both swifter and sleeker than electrons, but they are more difficult to control. Other schemes use beryllium atoms chilled to near absolute zero and photon streams colliding with streams of cesium atoms. Both of these efforts result in a switch that can be on and off at the same time, a result that makes it possible to do what is almost impossible! For example, with such technology, it is conjectured that a task that currently would require 1600 linked computers 800,000 years to accomplish could be reduced to a time span of 30 years.

Software Engineering Implications

Enumerated types and subranges are features of Pascal that are consistent with principles of software engineering. As previously stated, communication, readability, and maintenance are essential when developing large systems. The use of enumerated types and subranges is important in all of these areas. To illustrate, suppose a program includes working with a chemical reaction that normally occurs at approximately 180° Fahrenheit. If the definition section includes

```
TYPE
  ReactionRange = 150..210;
```

subsequent modules could use a variable such as

```
VAR
  ReactionTemp : ReactionRange;
```

In Chapter 10, you will see how the use of enumerated or user-defined data types is even more essential to maintaining principles of software engineering. Specifically, defining data structures becomes an important design consideration.

Exercises 9.3

In Exercises 1–5, indicate whether the **TYPE** definitions, subsequent declarations, and uses are valid or invalid. Explain what is wrong with those that are invalid.

*1.
```
TYPE
  Reverse = 10..1;
```

2.
```
TYPE
  Bases = (Home, First, Second, Third);
  Double = Home..Second;
  Score = Second..Home;
```

*3.
```
TYPE
  Colors = (Red, White, Blue);
  Stripes = Red..White;
VAR
  Hue : Stripes;
BEGIN
  Hue := Blue;
```

4.
```
TYPE
  Weekdays = Mon..Fri;
  Days = (Sun, Mon, Tues, Wed, Thur, Fri, Sat);
```

*5.
```
TYPE
  ScoreRange = 0..100;
  HighScores = 70..100;
  Midscores = 50..70;
  LowScores = 20..60;
VAR
  Score1 : Midscores;
  Score2 : HighScores;
BEGIN
  Score1 : = 60;
  Score2 := Score1 + 70;
```

6. Write a test program to see what happens when you try to use (assign, read, and so on) a value for a variable that is not in the defined subrange.

In Exercises 7–10, explain why each subrange definition might be used in a program.

*7. `Dependents = 0..20;`

8. `HoursWorked = 0..60;`

*9. `QuizScores = 0..10;`

10. `TotalPoints = 0..700;`

In Exercises 11–15, indicate a reasonable subrange and explain your answer.

*11. `TwentiethCentury =`

12. `Digits =`

*13. `JuneTemp =`

14. `WinterRange =`

*15.
```
Colors = (Black, Brown, Red, Pink, Yellow, White);
  LightColors =
```

For Exercises 16–21, assume the declaration section of a program contains the following:

```
TYPE
  ChessPieces = (Pawn, Knight, Bishop, Rook, King, Queen);
  Expendable = Pawn..Rook;
  Valuable = King..Queen;
  LowRange = 0..20;
  Midrange = 40..80;
VAR
  Piece1 : Valuable;
  Piece2 : Expendable;
  Piece3 : ChessPieces;
  Score1 : LowRange;
  Score2 : Midrange;
  Score3 : integer;
```

Indicate which pairs of variables are type compatible.

16. `Piece1 and Piece2`
*17. `Piece2 and Piece3`
18. `Piece3 and Score1`
*19. `Score1 and Score2`
20. `Score1 and Score3`
*21. `Piece2 and Score3`

For Exercises 22–26, assume the declaration section of a program contains the following:

```
TYPE
  PointRange = 400..700;
  FlowerList = (Rose, Iris, Tulip, Begonia);
  Sublist = Rose..Tulip;
VAR
  TotalPts : PointRange;
  Total : integer;
  Flower : Sublist;
  OldFlower : FlowerList;
```

The procedure heading is

```
PROCEDURE TypePrac (A : PointRange;
                    VAR B : integer;
                    F1 : Sublist);
```

Indicate which are valid calls to this procedure.

22. `TypePrac (TotalPts, Total, Flower);`
*23. `TypePrac (Total, TotalPts, Flower);`
24. `TypePrac (TotalPts, Total, OldFlower);`
*25. `TypePrac (Total, Total, Flower);`
26. `TypePrac (Total, Total, OldFlower);`

9.4 Operations on Ordinal Data Types

Objectives

- to be able to use functions **ord, pred,** and **succ** with enumerated data types
- to be able to use ordinal data types in Boolean expressions
- to be able to use ordinal data types in **CASE** statements
- to be able to use ordinal data types as loop indices

Functions for Ordinal Data Types

Earlier, we characterized ordinal data types as types in which there is a first and last listed element and each element other than the first and last has an immediate predecessor and an immediate successor. Of the standard data types, only **real** is not ordinal. The enumerated data types defined thus far are all ordinal. Because the enumerated data types are all ordinal, the functions **ord, pred,** and **succ** can be used on them. Thus, if we have the definition

```
TYPE
  Days = (Sun, Mon, Tues, Wed, Thur, Fri, Sat);
  Weekdays = Mon..Fri;
```

the following function calls have the values shown:

Function Call	Value
ord(Sun)	0
ord(Wed)	3
pred(Thur)	Wed
succ (Fri)	Sat
ord(**pred**(Fri))	4

When using functions on enumerated data types, the following should be noted:

1. The first-listed identifier has ordinal zero.
2. Successive ordinals are determined by the order in which identifiers are listed.
3. The function call **pred** should not be used on the first identifier; **succ** should not be used on the final identifier.
4. If a subrange data type is defined, the functions return values consistent with the underlying base type; for example, **ord**(Wed) = 3.

Using Ordinal Values of Enumerated Data Types

Now that we are somewhat familiar with ordinal data types and functions that use them as arguments, let's consider some ways in which they can be incorporated into programs. One typical use is in Boolean expressions. Suppose you are writing a program to compute the payroll for a company that pays time-and-a-half for working on Saturday. Assume the definition and declaration

```
TYPE
  Workdays = (Mon, Tues, Wed, Thur, Fri, Sat);
VAR
  Day : Workdays;
```

have been made. A typical segment of code is

```
Day := <some value>;
IF Day = Sat THEN
  ComputeOvertime (<calculation>)
ELSE
  ComputeRegularPay (<calculation>)
```

A second use is with **CASE** statements. As previously explained, one limitation of enumerated data types is that they have no external representation (you cannot **read** or **write** their values). However, this limitation can be circumvented by appropriate use of a **CASE** statement. For example, suppose we have the following definition and declaration:

```
TYPE
  Colors = (Red, White, Blue);
VAR
  Hue : Colors;
```

If you wish to print the value of Hue, you could do so in the following way:

```
CASE Hue OF
  Red   : writeln ('Red':20);
  White : writeln ('White':20);
  Blue  : writeln ('Blue':20)
END;  {  of CASE Hue  }
```

A third use is as a loop index. For example, consider

```
TYPE
  AllDays = (Sun, Mon, Tues, Wed, Thur, Fri, Sat);
VAR
  Day : AllDays;
```

Each of the following would be an appropriate loop:

1.
```
FOR Day := Mon TO Fri DO
  BEGIN
    .
    .
    .
  END;
```
2.
```
Day := Mon;
WHILE Day < Sat DO
  BEGIN
    Day := succ(Day);
        .
        .
        .
  END;
```
3.
```
Day := Sun;
REPEAT
  Day := succ(Day);
    .
    .
    .
UNTIL Day = Fri;
```

The loop control in a **FOR** loop is based on the ordinals of the values of the loop index. Thus, the statement

```
FOR Day := Mon TO Fri DO
```

A Note of Interest

Computer Ethics: Viruses

Tiny programs that deliberately cause mischief are epidemic among computers and cause nervousness among those who monitor them. Written by malicious programmers, computer viruses are sneaked into computer systems by piggybacking them on legitimate programs and messages. There, they may be passed along or instructed to wait until a prearranged moment to burst forth and destroy data.

At NASA headquarters in Washington, several hundred computers had to be resuscitated after being infected. NASA officials have taken extra precautions and reminded their machines' users to follow routine computer hygiene: Don't trust foreign data or strange machines.

Viruses have the eerie ability to perch disguised among legitimate data, just as biological viruses hide among genes in human cells, and then spring out unexpectedly, multiplying and causing damage. Experts say that even when they try to study viruses under controlled conditions, the programs can get out of control and erase everything in a computer. The viruses can be virtually impossible to stop if their creators are determined enough.

"The only way to protect everybody against them is to do something much worse than the viruses: stop talking to one another with computers," says William H. Murray, an information-security specialist at Ernst and Whinney, financial consultants in Hartford, Connecticut.

Hundreds of programs and files have been destroyed by the viruses, and thousands of hours of repair or prevention time have been logged. Programmers have quickly produced antidote programs with such titles as "Vaccine," "Flu Shot," "Data Physician," and "Syringe."

Experts say known damage is minimal compared to the huge, destructive potential. They express the hope that the attacks will persuade computer users to minimize access to programming and data.

Viruses are the newest of evolving methods of computer mayhem. One type of virus is the "Trojan horse": It looks and acts like a normal program but contains hidden commands that eventually take effect, ordering mischief. The "time bomb" explodes at a set time; the "logic bomb" goes off when the computer arrives at a certain result during normal computation. The "salami attack" executes barely noticeable acts, such as shaving a penny from thousands of accounts.

A virus typically is written as perhaps only a few hundred characters in a program containing tens of thousands of characters. When the computer reads legitimate instructions, it encounters the virus, which instructs the computer to suspend normal operations for a fraction of a second.

During that time, the virus instructs the computer to check for other copies of itself and, if none are found, to make and hide copies. Instruction to commit damage may be included.

Is Your Machine at Risk?

1. Computer viruses are actually miniature computer programs. Most were written by malicious programmers intent on destroying information in computers for fun.
2. Those who write virus programs often conceal them on floppy disks that are inserted in the computer.
3. A malicious programmer makes the disk available to others, saying it contains a useful program or game. These programs can be lent to others or put onto computerized "bulletin boards," where anyone can copy them for personal use.
4. A computer receiving the programs will "read" the disk and the tiny virus program at the same time. The virus may then order the computer
   - To read the virus and follow instructions.
   - To make a copy of the virus and place it on any disk inserted in the machine today.
   - To check the computer's clock and, on a certain date, to destroy all information that tells where data is stored on any disk: if an operator has no way of retrieving information, it is destroyed.
   - Not to list the virus programs when the computer is asked for an index of programs.
5. In this way, the computer will copy the virus onto many disks—perhaps all or nearly all the disks used in the infected machine. The virus may also be passed over the telephone, when one computer sends or receives data from another.
6. Ultimately, hundreds or thousands of people may have infected disks and potential time bombs in their systems.

is treated like the statement

```
FOR Index := 1 TO 5 DO
```

because **ord**(Mon) is 1 and **ord**(Fri) is 5.

In the **WHILE . . . DO** and **REPEAT . . . UNTIL** loops, the user must be sure to increment (increase the ordinal of) the variable. One method of doing this is to use the function **succ.**

Exercises 9.4

For Exercises 1–7, suppose the following **TYPE** definition is given:

```
TYPE
  Trees = (Oak, Ash, Maple, Pine);
  SlackType = (Denim, Cotton, Polyester);
```

Give the value of the expression. Indicate any expression that is invalid.

*1. **pred**(Ash)
2. **succ**(Denim)
*3. **ord**(Polyester)
4. **ord**(**pred**(Oak))
*5. **ord**(**succ**(Maple))
6. **succ**(Polyester)
*7. **ord**(**pred**(**succ**(Oak)))

8. Write a test program that lists the ordinals of values in a subrange of an enumerated data type.

The character set for some computers is such that **ord**('A') = 65 and **ord**('Z') = 90. For Exercises 9–14, assuming such a sequence, what is the value of the expression? Indicate any expressions that are invalid.

*9. **chr** (**ord** ('D'))
10. **ord** (**chr** (75))
*11. **chr** (3 + **ord** ('E'))
12. **ord** (**chr** (20 **DIV** 3) + **chr** (70))
*13. **ord**(**pred**('K') + 3)
14. **succ**(**chr**(**ord**('Z') – 1))

*15. Write a program that will list the letters of the alphabet and their respective ordinals for the character set used with your machine.

For Exercises 16–19, assume the **TYPE** definition and variable declaration

```
TYPE
  AllDays = (Sun, Mon, Tues, Wed, Thur, Fri, Sat);
VAR
  Day : AllDays;
```

are made.

16. What would be the output from the following **REPEAT . . . UNTIL** loop?

```
Day := Sun;
REPEAT
  CASE Day OF
    Sat, Sun                     : writeln ('Weekend':20);
    Mon, Tues, Wed, Thur, Fri : writeln ('Weekday':20)
  END;  { of CASE Day }
  Day := succ(Day)
UNTIL Day = Sat;
```

*17. Rewrite the previous loop as both a **WHILE . . . DO** loop and a **FOR** loop.

18. Find another method to control the loop variable (for example, replace

```
Day := succ(Day)
```

and make any other necessary changes).

*19. Revise the loop so that all seven days are considered.

For Exercises 20 and 21, convert an integer character to its corresponding numerical value, for example, the character '2' to the number 2. Since the digits are listed sequentially in every character set, this could be accomplished by

```
ord('2') - ord('0');
```

20. Write a function to convert a single character digit ('0', '1', . . ., '9') to its corresponding numerical value.

*21. Write a function to convert a two-digit number read as consecutive characters into the corresponding numerical value.

22. Suppose you are working with a program that reads an integer representing a month of the year (Jan = 1). Write a function to convert the integer into the appropriate month.

Focus on Program Design: Case Study

Using Enumerated Data Types

The summary program for this chapter computes the number of days in your birth year from your birthday to the end of the year. Sample input (if you were born on March 16, 1979) would be

```
3 16 79
```

We want the output to be

```
During your birth year,  1979,
you were alive  291 days.
```

Features of this program include enumerated data types and subranges. In particular, note the data type

```
AllMonths = (Jan, Feb, March, April, May, June,
             July, Aug, Sept, Oct, Nov, Dec);
```

A reasonable first-level pseudocode design for this program is

1. Get data
2. Assign month
3. Compute days
4. Print results

A structure chart for this is given in Figure 9.2. Module specifications for this problem are

1. GetData Module
   Data received: None

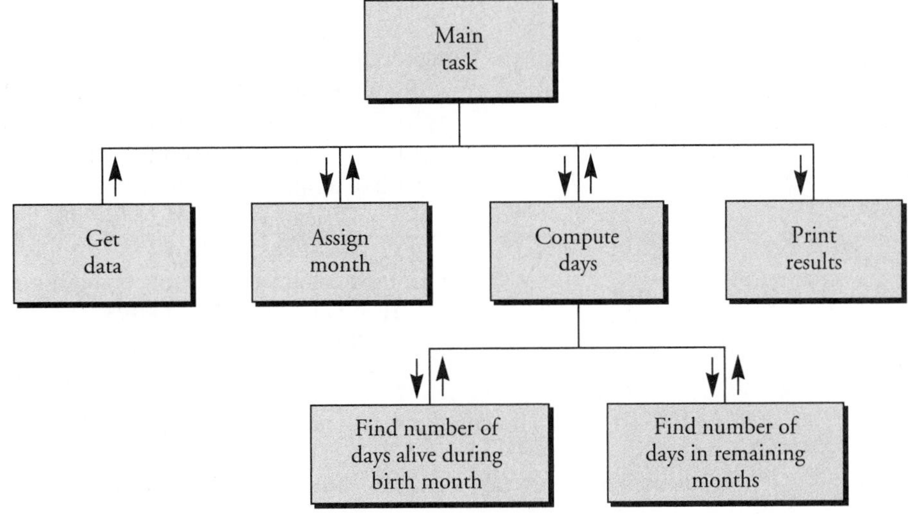

◆ Figure 9.2
Structure chart for **PROGRAM** Birthday

Information returned: Day
Month
Year of birth
Logic: Have the user enter his/her birth date.

2. AssignMonth Module
Data received: A numerical equivalent of the birth month
Information returned: The name of the birth month
Logic: A **CASE** statement assigns the name of the birth month to BirthMonth, which is an enumerated data type.
3. ComputeDays Module
Data received: Month
Day
Year of birth
Information returned: The number of days alive during the year of birth
Logic: Compute the number of days alive during the month of birth.
Compute the number of days in the remaining months.
4. PrintResults Module
Data received: Number of days alive during the year of birth
Year of birth
Information returned: None
Logic: Use **write(ln)** statements to print the results in a readable form.

GetData merely consists of a **readln** statement; AssignMonth is a procedure using a **CASE** statement (a function could be used here instead); and PrintResults prints the information in a readable form. A function for computing the number of days is further developed as

3. Compute days
   3.1 Compute days alive during birth month
   3.2 Compute total of days in remaining months

This could be refined to

3. Compute days
   3.1 Compute days alive during birth month
      3.1.1 Compute for months with 31 days
      3.1.2 Compute for months with 30 days
      3.1.3 Compute for February
         IF leap year **THEN** use 29 days
         ELSE use 28 days
   3.2 Compute total of days in remaining months
      IF NOT December **THEN**
         FOR rest of months **DO**
            Add number of days in month

The complete program to solve this problem follows:

```
PROGRAM Birthday (input, output);

{  This program determines how many days you were alive during  }
{  your  birth year.  Input is your  birth  date.  Later,  you  }
{  can use this  program as the basis for a biorhythm program.  }
{  Note the use of enumerated data types and subranges.         }

TYPE
  AllMonths = (Jan, Feb, March, April, May, June,
               July, Aug, Sept, Oct, Nov, Dec);
  DayRange = 1..31;
  MonthRange = 1..12;
  YearRange = 0..99;

VAR
  BirthMonth : AllMonths;        {  Literal form of birth month    }
  DayNum : DayRange;             {  The day you were born          }
  Month : MonthRange;            {  Birth month                    }
  TotalDays : integer;           {  Days alive in birth year       }
  Year : YearRange;              {  Representation of birth year   }

{*****************************************************************}

PROCEDURE GetData (VAR Month : MonthRange;
                   VAR Day : DayRange;
                   VAR Year : YearRange);

  {  Given:   Nothing                                              }
  {  Task:    Enter your birthdate in the form 3 16 79             }
  {  Return:  Month, day, and year of birth                        }      1

  BEGIN
    writeln ('Please enter your birth date in the form 3 16 79.');
    writeln ('Press <Enter> when finished.');
    readln (Month, Day, Year)
  END;  {  of PROCEDURE GetData  }

{*****************************************************************}
```

```
PROCEDURE AssignMonth (Month : MonthRange;
                       VAR BirthMonth : AllMonths);

  {  Given:   A numerical equivalent of the birth month          }
  {  Task:    Convert to literal BirthMonth                      }
  {  Return:  Literal BirthMonth                                 }

  BEGIN
    CASE Month OF
       1 : BirthMonth := Jan;
       2 : BirthMonth := Feb;
       3 : BirthMonth := March;                                        2
       4 : BirthMonth := April;
       5 : BirthMonth := May;
       6 : BirthMonth := June;
       7 : BirthMonth := July;
       8 : BirthMonth := Aug;
       9 : BirthMonth := Sept;
      10 : BirthMonth := Oct;
      11 : BirthMonth := Nov;
      12 : BirthMonth := Dec
    END  {  of CASE Month  }
  END;  {  of PROCEDURE AssignMonth  }

{***************************************************************}


FUNCTION ComputeDays (BirthMonth : AllMonths;
                      DayNum : DayRange;
                      Year : YearRange) : integer;

  {  Given:   The month, day, and year of birth                  }
  {  Task:    Compute the days alive during the year of birth    }
  {  Return:  Number of days alive during the year of birth      }

  VAR
    Days : integer;
    Mon : AllMonths;

  BEGIN                                                                3

    {  Compute days alive in birth month  }
    CASE BirthMonth OF
      Jan, March, May, July, Aug, Oct, Dec : Days := 31 - DayNum + 1;
      April, June, Sept, Nov               : Days := 30 - DayNum + 1;
      Feb                                  : IF Year MOD 4 = 0 THEN
                                               Days := 29 - DayNum + 1
                                             ELSE
                                               Days := 28 - DayNum + 1

    END;  {  of CASE BirthMonth  }
```

```
    {  Now compute days in remaining months  }
    IF BirthMonth <> Dec THEN
      FOR Mon := succ(BirthMonth) TO Dec DO
        CASE Mon OF
          Jan, March, May, July, Aug, Oct, Dec : Days := Days + 31;
          April, June, Sept, Nov               : Days := Days + 30;
          Feb                                  : IF Year MOD 4 = 0 THEN
                                                   Days := Days + 29
                                                 ELSE
                                                   Days := Days + 28
        END;  {  of CASE Mon  }

    {  Assign total days to function name  }
    ComputeDays := Days
  END;  {  of FUNCTION ComputeDays  }

{*************************************************************}

PROCEDURE PrintResults (TotalDays : integer;
                        Year : YearRange);

  {  Given:   Birth year and total days alive during that year  }
  {  Task:    Print a message indicating the year of birth and  }
  {                number of days alive during that year        }
  {  Return:  Nothing                                           }
```

4

```
  BEGIN
    writeln ('During your birth year,', (Year + 1900):5, ',');
    writeln ('you were alive', TotalDays:5, ' days.');
    writeln
  END;  {  of PROCEDURE PrintResults  }

{*************************************************************}

BEGIN  {  Main program  }
  GetData (Month, DayNum, Year);
  AssignMonth (Month, BirthMonth);
  TotalDays := ComputeDays(BirthMonth, DayNum, Year);
  PrintResults (TotalDays, Year)
END.  {  of main program  }
```

A sample run of this program produces the following output:

```
Please enter your birth date in the form 3 16 79.
Press <Enter> when finished.
3 16 79
During your birth year, 1979,
you were alive  291 days.
```

Running and Debugging Hints

1. An end-of-line marker is read as a blank. Thus, when reading data of type **char,** you must remember to read past the end-of-line marker so that the end-of-file marker will be recognized.
2. External text files must be listed in the program heading file list as well as in the variable declaration section.
3. Be aware of the possibility of extra blanks at the beginning or end of lines in a text file. Some implementations cause these to be inserted when creating a text file.
4. The end-of-line marker is read as a blank. Thus, when working with character data in a text file, it may appear that extra blanks are in the file. However, the **eoln** function still returns **true** when the pointer is positioned at an end-of-line marker.
5. Subranges should be used if the bounds of a variable are known.
6. Enumerated data types should be used to enhance readability.
7. Be careful not to use **pred** with the first element in a list or **succ** on the last element.
8. Make sure variable parameters passed to subprograms are type identical. For example, using the declaration

   ```
   TYPE
     Weekdays = (Mon, Tues, Wed, Thur, Fri);
   VAR
     Day : Weekdays;
   ```

   if a procedure call is

   ```
   PrintChart (Day);
   ```

   a procedure heading could be

   ```
   PROCEDURE PrintChart (VAR Wkday : Weekdays);
   ```

9. A value parameter and its argument must be type compatible.

Summary

Key Terms

assignment compatible	opened for reading	text file
enumerated data type	opened for writing	type compatible
external file	scratch (temporary) file	type identical
internal file	subrange	user-defined data type

Keywords

reset	**text**	**TYPE**
rewrite		

Key Concepts

- Text files can be used to store data between runs of a program.
- A text file can be declared by

```
VAR
  <file name> : text;
```

- An external file exists outside the program block in secondary storage. When used, it must be included in the file list as part of the program heading.
- An internal file exists within the program block. Values stored there will be lost when the program is no longer running.
- Text files must be opened before they can be written to or read from. Before reading from a file, it can be opened by

```
reset (<file variable>);
```

  Before writing to a file, it can be opened by

```
rewrite (<file variable>);
```

- Reading from a text file can be accomplished by

```
read (<file variable>, <list of variables>);
```

  or

```
readln (<file variable>, <list of variables>);
```

- Writing to a text file can be accomplished by

```
write (<file variable>, <list of values>);
```

  or

```
writeln (<file variable>, <list of values>);
```

  If no file variable is given, the procedures apply to the standard file **input.**
- A data type is ordinal if data of that type have a first and last listed element and each element other than the first and last has an immediate predecessor and an immediate successor.
- Enumerated data types can be defined by using the **TYPE** definition section. Typical syntax and form are

```
TYPE
  Weekdays = (Mon, Tue, Wed, Thur, Fri);
```

- When an enumerated data type has been defined,
  1. The newly defined type will be an ordinal data type.
  2. Variables can be declared to be of the new type.
  3. The identifiers declared in the **TYPE** definition section are constants that can be used in the program.
  4. No identifier can belong to more than one data type.
  5. Identifiers that are defined values cannot be used as operands in expressions.
- You cannot **read** or **write** values of an enumerated data type.

- A subrange of an existing ordinal data type can be defined by

> **TYPE**
> <identifier> = <initial value> . . <final value>

Examples are

```
TYPE
  ScoreRange = 0..100;
  Alphabet = 'A'..'Z';
```

- Type-compatible variables have the same base type.
- Type-identical variables must have the same type identifier.
- An expression can be assigned to a variable only if the expression is assignment compatible with the variable.
- Two significant reasons for using subranges are program protection and program readability.
- The functions **pred, succ,** and **ord** can be used with enumerated data types and subranges of existing ordinal data types.
- When one of the functions **pred, succ,** or **ord** is used with an argument whose value is in a subrange, reference is to the base data type, not the subrange; thus, in

```
TYPE
  Letters = 'J'..'O';
```

ord('J') does not have the value 0. Rather, it yields the appropriate ordinal for the collating sequence being used. In the ASCII collating sequence, **ord**('J') yields 74.

Chapter Review Exercises

1. Show all definitions and declarations necessary to create a text file named Exercise1Text. Show how to put values into the file so that it looks like

For Exercises 2–7, use the text file from Exercise 1. Assume the variables are declared as follows:

```
A, B : integer;
C, D : char;
E : real;
```

Indicate if the statements are valid. If so, indicate what values are read and where the pointer is after the statement is executed. Assume the pointer is at the beginning for each exercise.

2. `read (Exercise1Text, A, C, B);`
3. `readln (Exercise1Text, A, C, B);`
4. `read (Exercise1Text, A, B, C);`
5. `read (Exercise1Text, A, C, D);`
6. `read (Exercise1Text, A, C, E);`
7. `readln (Exercise1Text);`

8. Write a segment of code to write the integers 1 through 10 to a text file.
9. Explain the difference between **read** and **readln** statements used with a text file.
10. What is the purpose of a **reset** statement?
11. Write a segment of code to count the number of lines in a text file.

For Exercises 12–19, find all the errors in the type declarations.

12. `Exercise12 = (Red; Blue; Yellow);`
13. `Exercise13 = 10..1;`
14. `Exercise14 = 'A', 'B', 'C', 'D';`
15. `Exercise15 = 'A'..'E';`
16. `Exercise16 = 'E'..'A';`
17. `Exercise17 = (Red, Orange, Yellow);`
18. `Exercise18 = ('Red', 'Orange', 'Yellow');`
19. `Exercise19 = 1.0..2.5;`

For Exercises 20–29, assume the following type and variable declarations are made:

```
TYPE
  Month = (Jan, Feb, Mar, Apr, May, Jun,
           Jul, Aug, Sep, Oct, Nov, Dec);
  Summer = Jun..Sep;
  LastCentury = 1801..1900;
VAR
  Date, Start : Month;
  Season : Summer;
  Year : LastCentury;
  J : integer;
```

Indicate if the statement is valid or invalid. If invalid, explain why.

20. `J := Date;`
21. `read (Year);`
22. `Year := 1986;`
23. `J := Year + 2;`
24. `Summer := Aug;`
25. `Summer := succ(May);`
26. `Start := pred(Jan);`
27. `J := ord(pred(Jun);`
28. `read (Season);`
29. `Start := Start + 1;`

For Exercises 30–36, using the same declarations as in Exercises 20–29, indicate if the statement is valid or invalid. If invalid, explain why.

30. `writeln (Date, J);`
31. `writeln (Year);`
32. `writeln (ord(succ(Aug)));`
33. `writeln (Summer);`
34. `writeln (succ(Year));`
35. `writeln (pred(ord(Jan)));`
36. `writeln (Start);`

Using the same declarations as in Exercises 20–29, indicate if Exercises 37–42 are **true**, **false**, or invalid.

37. `Jan < Feb`
38. `ord(Mar) = 3`
39. `ord(Jan) = 0`
40. `pred(Mar) > succ(Jan)`
41. `Apr = Mar + 1`
42. `2000 = Year`

For Exercises 43 and 44, consider the following type and variable declarations:

```
TYPE
  Hours = 1..40;
  Letters = 'A'..'Z';
  Scores = 0..100;
  Passing = 60..100;
VAR
  HoursWorked, Overtime : Hours;
  Grades : Letters;
  Test1, Test2 : Scores;
  GoodGrade : Passing;
  J, K : integer;
  Average : real;
  Names : char;
```

43. Which of the variables are type identical?
44. Which of the variables are type compatible?

For Exercises 45–49, use the declarations from Exercises 43 and 44 and the procedure heading:

```
PROCEDURE Demo (VAR A : Hours;
                B : Scores;
                VAR C : Letters);
```

Which of the following procedure calls are valid? If invalid, explain why.

45. `Demo (Overtime, J, Names);`
46. `Demo (J, K, Grades);`
47. `Demo (HoursWorked, Test1, Grades);`
48. `Demo (GoodGrade, GoodGrade, Grades);`
49. `Demo (Overtime, Average, Grades);`

Programming Problems

1. Write a program to compute the payroll for a company. Data for each employee will be on two lines. Line 1 contains an employee number followed by the hourly wage rate. Line 2 contains seven integer entries indicating the hours worked each day. Wages are to be computed at time-and-a-half for anything over eight hours on a weekday and double time for any weekend work. Deductions should be withheld as follows:
   a. State income tax 4.6%
   b. Federal income tax 21.0%
   c. Social Security (FICA) 6.2%
   d. Medicare tax 1.45%

   Employee numbers are the subrange 0001 . . 9999. You should define and use a data type for the days of the week.
2. The Caswell Catering and Convention Service (Problem 7, Chapter 4; Problem 14, Chapter 5; Problem 1, Chapter 6; and Problem 1, Chapter 7) wants to up-

grade their existing computer program. Use the **TYPE** definition section for each of the following and revise the program you developed previously as appropriate.

a. The room names have been changed to a color-coded scheme as follows:

Room A	RedRoom
Room B	BlueRoom
Room C	YellowRoom
Room D	GreenRoom
Room E	BrownRoom

b. Use a subrange for the room rents.

c. Use defined constants for the low value and high value of the room rents.

3. State University (Problem 15, Chapter 5) wants you to upgrade its computer program by using the **TYPE** definition section for each of the following:
   a. The room types will be Regular or AirConditioned.
   b. Students' numbers will be between 0001 and 9999 (use **CONST** for end values).
   c. Credit hours taken must be between 1 and 25.
   d. The GoodRange for credit hours is 12 to 21.

   Your new version should be able to be used on a data file with several students' information.

4. Al Derrick (Problem 20, Chapter 5, and Problem 10, Chapter 6) wants you to revise his program by using the **TYPE** definition section to enhance readability and ensure protection against bad data. Your new version should run for several wells and include: types of wells (Dry, Oil, and Gas), volume for gas (between 10,000 and 100,000), and volume for oil (between 2,000 and 50,000).

■ 5. Mr. Lae Z. Programmer is relentless. He wants you to modify your latest version of the grading program (Problems 5, 22, and 23, Chapter 5; Problem 13, Chapter 6; or Problem 7, Chapter 7) by using the **TYPE** definition section. Your new version should include a range for test scores (from 0 to 100), a range for quiz scores (from 0 to 10), and a range for the final examination (from 0 to 200).

6. Upgrade your most recent version of the Pentagon visitor parking lot program (Problem 26, Chapter 5; Problem 14, Chapter 6; or Problem 8, Chapter 7) by using the **TYPE** definition section. Time in and time out will be between 0600 and 2200 (6:00 A.M. and 10:00 P.M.). Vehicle type should be denoted by Car, Truck, or Senior.

7. Read a text file containing a paragraph of text. Count the number of words in the paragraph. Assume that consecutive words are separated by at least one blank.

8. Write a program to print the contents of a text file omitting any occurrences of the letter "e" from the output.

9. A text file contains a list of integers in order from lowest to highest. Write a program to read and print the text file with all duplications eliminated.

10. Mr. John Napier, professor at Lancaster Community College, wants a program to compute grade point averages. Each line of a text file contains three initials followed by an unknown number of letter grades. These grades are A, B, C, D, or F. Write a program that reads the file and prints a list of the students' initials

and their grade point averages. (Assume an A is 4 points, a B is 3 points, and so on.) Print an asterisk next to any grade point average that is greater than 3.75.

11. An amortization table (Problem 19, Chapter 6) shows the rate at which a loan is paid off. It contains monthly entries showing the interest paid that month, the principal paid, and the remaining balance. Given the amount of money borrowed (the principal), the annual interest rate, and the amount the person wishes to repay each month, print an amortization table. (The payment desired must be larger than the first month's interest.) Your table should stop when the loan is paid off, and should be printed with the following heads:

    ```
    MONTH NUMBER   INTEREST PAID   PRINCIPAL PAID   BALANCE
    ```

    Create an enumerated data type for the month number. Limit the program to require that the loan be paid back within 60 months.

12. In 1626, the Dutch settlers purchased Manhattan Island from the Indians (Problem 23, Chapter 6). According to legend, the purchase price was $24. Suppose the Indians had invested this amount at 3 percent annual interest compounded quarterly. If the money had earned interest from the start of 1626 to the end of last year, how much money would the Indians have in the bank today? (*Hint:* Use nested loops for the compounding.) Create an enumerated data type for the range of years (1626 to last year) that will be used.

13. Mr. Christian (Problem 26, Chapter 6) uses a 90 percent, 80 percent, 70 percent, 60 percent grading scale on his tests. Given a list of test scores, print the number of A's, B's, C's, D's, and F's on the test. Terminate the list of scores with a sentinel value. Use a subrange of the integers for the input grades.

14. Write a program to print the perimeter and area of rectangles using all combinations of lengths and widths running from 1 foot to 10 feet in increments of 1 foot. Print the output in headed columns. Use a subrange to restrict the lengths and widths from 1 to 10.

15. Write a program that can serve as a "triangle analyzer" (Problem 25, Chapter 5). Each line of input should consist of three positive integers representing the lengths of the sides of a triangle. Initially, your program should determine whether or not a triangle with the indicated side lengths is possible. (The length of the longest side cannot exceed the sum of the lengths of the other two sides.) Permissible triangles should then be identified as scalene, isosceles, or equilateral, according to the number of sides of equal length. Finally, all right triangles should be identified. Your program should utilize a user-defined data type for the triangle types Scalene, Isosceles, and Equilateral.

Communication in Practice

1. Select a problem that you have not done from the **Programming Problems** section in this chapter. For that problem, write documentation that includes a complete description of
   a. required input
   b. required output
   c. required processing and computation

Exchange your documentation with another student who has been given the same assignment. Compare your results.

2. Remove all documentation from a program you have written for this chapter. Exchange this version with another student who has done the same thing. Write documentation for the exchanged program. Compare your documentation with that originally written for the program. Discuss the differences and similarities in documentation with the other student.
3. Contact a programmer or college student majoring in computer science, and discuss the issue of using enumerated and other user-defined data types. Among other things, find out how often (or even if) that person uses such data types, how important he or she considers such data types to be as part of a programming language, and some specific examples of how he or she uses enumerated data types. Give an oral report of your findings to your class.
4. Enumerated and other user-defined data types are one advantage of using Pascal as a programming language. Examine several other programming languages to see if they include a comparable feature. Prepare a chart that summarizes your findings.
5. Select a team of three or four students, and contact businesspeople who use computers for data storage. Find out exactly how they enter, store, and retrieve data. Discuss how they use their databases and how large the databases are. Ask them what they like and dislike about data entry and retrieval and if they have suggestions for modifying any aspect of working with their databases. Prepare a report for class that summarizes your team's findings.

Chapter 10

One-Dimensional Arrays

Chapter Outline

This chapter begins a significant new stage of programming. Until now, we have been unable to manipulate and store large amounts of data in a convenient way. For example, if we wanted to work with a long list of numbers or names, we had to declare a separate variable for each number or name. Fortunately, Pascal and all other programming languages provide several structured variables to facilitate solving problems that require working with large amounts of data. Simply put, a structured variable uses one identifier to reserve a large amount of memory. This memory is capable of holding several individual values. The structured variables discussed in this text are arrays, records, files, and sets.

Arrays (the topic of this chapter) are designed to handle large amounts of data of the same type in an organized manner. Arrays are used whenever data need to be stored for subsequent use in a program. The use of arrays permits us to set aside a group of memory locations that we can then manipulate as a single entity or as separate components. Some very standard applications for array variables include creating tabular output (tables), alphabetizing a list of names, analyzing a list of test scores, manipulating character data, and keeping an inventory.

10.1 Basic Idea and Notation

Objectives

- to understand the basic concept of an array
- to use correct notation for arrays

In many instances, several variables of the same data type are required. At this point, let's work with a list of five integers: 18, 17, 21, 18, and 19. Prior to this chapter, we would have declared five variables (A, B, C, D, and E) and assigned them appropriate values or read them from an input file. This would have produced five values in memory, each accessed by a separate identifier:

18	17	21	18	19
A	B	C	D	E

Objectives

(continued)

- to be able to declare arrays with variable declarations and with type definitions
- to be able to use array components with appropriate arithmetic operations
- to be able to use array components with appropriate **read** and **write** statements

An **array** is a structured variable designed to handle data of the same type.

A **component of an array** is one element of the array data type. Also called an **element of the array.**

An **index** of an array component is the relative position of the component in the array. Also called the **subscript** of the component.

If the list is very long, this would be an inefficient way to work with these data. An alternative is to use an array. In Pascal, we declare a variable as an array variable using either of the following methods:

1.
```
VAR
  List : ARRAY [1..5] OF integer;
```
2.
```
TYPE
  Numbers = ARRAY [1..5] OF integer;
VAR
  List : Numbers;
```

Given either of these declarations, we now have five integer variables with which to work. They are denoted by

List[1]	List[2]	List[3]	List[4]	List[5]

and each is referred to as a **component,** or **element, of the array.** A good way to visualize these variables is to assume that memory locations are aligned in a column on top of each other and the name of the column is List. If we then assign the five values of our list to these five variables, we have in memory

List

18	List[1]
17	List[2]
21	List[3]
18	List[4]
19	List[5]

The components of an array are referred to by their relative position in the array. This relative position is called the **index,** or **subscript,** of the component. In the array of our five values, the component List[3] has an index of 3 and value of 21. For the sake of convenience, you may choose to depict an array by listing only the index beside its appropriate component. Thus, List could be shown as

List

	1
	2
	3
	4
	5

If you choose this method, remember that the array elements are referenced by the array name and the index (for example, List[3] for the third component). Whichever method you use, it is important to remember that each array component is a variable and can be treated exactly like any other declared variable of that base type in the program.

Declaring an Array

An array type can be defined as a user-defined type, and then an appropriate variable can be declared to be of this type. An earlier declaration was

```
TYPE
  Numbers = ARRAY [1..5] OF integer;
VAR
  List : Numbers;
```

Now let's examine this declaration more closely. Several comments are in order.

1. The data type Numbers is a user-defined data type.
2. **ARRAY** is a reserved word and is used to indicate that an array type is being defined.
3. "[1 . . 5]" is the syntax that indicates the array consists of five memory locations accessed by specifying each of the numbers, 1, 2, 3, 4, and 5. We frequently say the array is "of length five." The information inside the brackets is the **index type** and is used to refer to components of an array. This index type can be any ordinal data type that specifies a beginning value and an ending value. However, subranges of data type **integer** are the most easily read and frequently used index types.
4. The reserved word **OF** refers to the data type for the components of the array.
5. The keyword **integer** indicates the data type for the components. This can, of course, be any valid data type.
6. The identifier List can be any valid identifier. As always, it is good practice to use descriptive names to enhance readability.

The **index type** is the data type used for specifying the range for the index of an array. The index type can be any ordinal data type that specifies an initial and final value.

The general form for defining an array type is

> **TYPE**
> <name> = **ARRAY** [<index type>] **OF** <component type>

where <name> is any valid identifier, <index type> is any ordinal data type that specifies both an initial value and a final value, and <component type> is any predefined or user-defined data type (except files). The syntax diagram for defining an array is

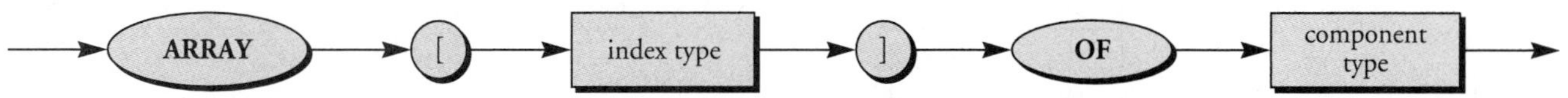

The following example illustrates another declaration of an array variable.

Example 10.1

Suppose you want to create a list of 10 integer variables for the hours worked by 10 employees as follows:

Employee Number	Hours Worked
1	35
2	40
3	20
4	38
5	25
6	40
7	25
8	40
9	20
10	45

Let's declare an array that has 10 components of type **integer,** and show how it can be visualized. A descriptive name could be Hours. There are 10 items, so we will use **ARRAY** [1 . . 10] in the definition. Since the data consist of integers, the component type will be **integer.** An appropriate definition and subsequent declaration could be

```
TYPE
  HourList = ARRAY [1..10] OF integer;
VAR
  Hours : HourList;
```

At this stage, the components can be visualized as

Hours

	Hours[1]
	Hours[2]
	Hours[3]
	Hours[4]
	Hours[5]
	Hours[6]
	Hours[7]
	Hours[8]
	Hours[9]
	Hours[10]

After making appropriate assignment statements, Hours can be visualized as

Hours

35	Hours[1]
40	Hours[2]
20	Hours[3]
38	Hours[4]
25	Hours[5]
40	Hours[6]
25	Hours[7]
40	Hours[8]
20	Hours[9]
45	Hours[10]

Other Indices and Data Types

The previous two arrays used index types that were subranges of the **integer** data type. Although this is a common way to specify the index to an array, we can use subranges of any ordinal type for this definition. The following examples illustrate some array definitions with other indices and data types.

Example 10.2

Suppose you want to declare an array to allow you to store the hourly price for a share of IBM stock. A descriptive name could be StockPrice. A price is quoted at each hour from 9:00 A.M. to 3:00 P.M., so we will use **ARRAY** [9 . . 15] in the definition section. Since the data consist of reals, the component type must be **real.** A possible declaration could be

```
TYPE
  StockPriceList = ARRAY [9..15] OF real;
VAR
  StockPrice : StockPriceList;
```

This will allow you to store the 9:00 A.M. price in StockPrice[9], the 1:00 P.M. price in StockPrice[13], and so on.

Example 10.3

The declaration

```
TYPE
  AlphaList = ARRAY [-2..3] OF char;
VAR
  Alpha : AlphaList;
```

will reserve components that can be depicted as

Alpha

	Alpha[−2]
	Alpha[−1]
	Alpha[0]
	Alpha[1]
	Alpha[2]
	Alpha[3]

Each component is a character variable.

Example 10.4

The declaration

```
TYPE
  TotalHoursList = ARRAY ['A'..'E'] OF integer;
VAR
  TotalHours : TotalHoursList;
```

will reserve components that can be depicted as

Total Hours

	'A'
	'B'
	'C'
	'D'
	'E'

Components of this array are integer variables.

Example 10.5

The declaration

```
TYPE
  FlagValues = ARRAY [1..4] OF boolean;
VAR
  Flag : FlagValues;
```

will produce an array with components that are **boolean** variables.

It is important to note that in each example, the array components have no assigned values until the program specifically makes some kind of assignment. Declaring an array does not assign values to any of the components.

Two additional array definitions and subsequent declarations follow:

1.
```
TYPE
  Days = (Mon, Tues, Wed, Thur, Fri, Sat, Sun);
  Workdays = ARRAY [Mon..Fri] OF real;
VAR
  HoursWorked : Workdays;
```
2.
```
TYPE
  List50 = ARRAY [1..50] OF real;
  List25 = ARRAY [1..25] OF integer;
  String20 = ARRAY [1..20] OF char;
VAR
  PhoneCharge : List50;
  Score : List25;
  Word : String20;
  A, B, C, D : List50;
```

Note that a more efficient method of manipulating character data than the strings just used is presented in Section 10.5, where we discuss packed arrays.

Assignment Statements

Suppose we have declared an array

```
A : ARRAY [1..5] OF integer;
```

and we want to put the values 1, 4, 9, 16, and 25 into the respective components. We can accomplish this with the assignment statements

Communication and Style Tips

Descriptive constants and type identifiers should be utilized when working with arrays. For example, if you are working with an array of test scores for a class of 35 students, you could have

```
CONST
  ClassSize = 35;
TYPE
  TestScores = 0..100;
  ScoreList = ARRAY [1..ClassSize] OF TestScores;
VAR
  Score : ScoreList;
```

```
A[1] := 1;
A[2] := 4;
A[3] := 9;
A[4] := 16;
A[5] := 25;
```

If variables B and C of type **integer** are declared in the program, then the following are also appropriate assignment statements:

```
A[3] := B;
C := A[2];
A[2] := A[5];
```

If we want to interchange the values of two components (for example, exchange A[2] with A[3]), we could use a third integer variable:

```
B := A[2];
A[2] := A[3];
A[3] := B;
```

This exchange is frequently used in sorting algorithms, so let's examine it more closely. Assume B contains no previously assigned value, and A[2] and A[3] contain 4 and 9, respectively, as follows:

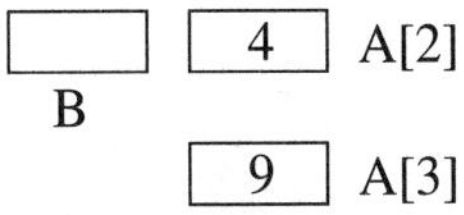

```
[   ]  [ 4 ] A[2]
  B
       [ 9 ] A[3]
```

The assignment statement

```
B := A[2];
```

produces

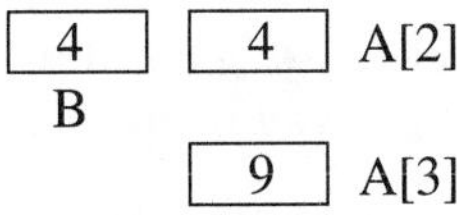

```
[ 4 ]  [ 4 ] A[2]
  B
       [ 9 ] A[3]
```

The assignment statement

```
A[2] := A[3];
```

produces

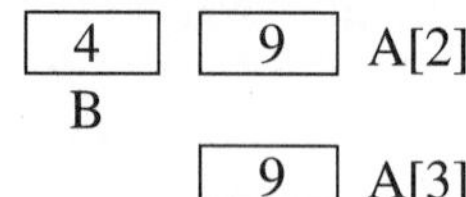

and finally the assignment statement

```
A[3] := B;
```

produces

4 9 A[2]
B
4 A[3]

in which the original values of A[2] and A[3] are interchanged.

The next example illustrates the use of a **TYPE** definition and a subsequent assignment statement.

Example 10.6

Given the following segment of code,

```
TYPE
  Seasons = (Fall, Winter, Spring, Summer);
  TemperatureList = ARRAY [Seasons] OF real;
VAR
  AvTemp : TemperatureList;
```

an assignment statement such as

```
AvTemp[Fall] := 53.2;
```

would be appropriate. The array would then be

AvTemp

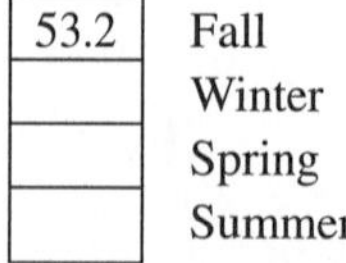

Arithmetic

Components of an array can also be used in any appropriate arithmetic operation. For example, suppose A is the array of integers

A

1	A[1]
4	A[2]
9	A[3]
16	A[4]
25	A[5]

and the values of the components of the array are to be added. This can be accomplished by the statement

```
Sum := A[1] + A[2] + A[3] + A[4] + A[5];
```

Each of the following would also be a valid use of an array component:

```
B := 3 * A[2];
C := A[4] MOD 3;
D := A[2] * A[5];
```

For the array A given, these assignment statements produce

55	12	1	100
Sum	B	C	D

Some invalid assignment statements and the reasons they are invalid follow.

`A[0] := 7;`	(0 is not a valid subscript for this array.)
`A[2] := 3.5;`	(Component A[2] is not of type **real.**)
`A[2.0] := 3;`	(A subscript of type **real** is not allowed.)

Reading and Writing

Since array components are names for variables, they can be used with **read, readln, write,** and **writeln.** For example, if Score is an array of five integers and you want to input the scores 65, 43, 98, 75, and 83 from a data file, you could use the code

```
readln (Data, Score[1], Score[2], Score[3], Score[4], Score[5]);
```

which produces the array

Score

65	Score[1]
43	Score[2]
98	Score[3]
75	Score[4]
83	Score[5]

If we want to print the scores above 80, we could use the code

```
writeln (Score[3]:10, Score[5]:10);
```

to produce

```
        98        83
```

A Note of Interest

Monolithic Idea—Invention of the Integrated Circuit

One of the most significant breakthroughs in the history of technology occurred in the late 1950s. Prior to 1958, computer circuitry was limited because transistors, diodes, resistors, and capacitors were separate units that had to be wired together and soldered by hand. Although designers could design intricate computer supercircuits using 500,000 transistors, they were almost impossible to build because of the extensive handwork involved. For example, a circuit with 100,000 components could require more than 1,000,000 soldered connections. It was virtually impossible to assemble that many components without human error. Thus, the electronics industry was faced with an apparently insurmountable limit.

About this time, Jack St. Clair Kilby developed what has come to be known as the "monolithic idea." He decided you could put the components of an entire circuit in a monolithic block of silicon. The idea, together with Robert Noyce's work on interconnecting circuits, allowed electronics engineers to overcome the obstacle presented by separate components. Kilby and Noyce's work resulted in the integrated circuit, the most important new product in the history of electronics. For their efforts, both men were awarded the National Medal of Science.

It is important to note that we cannot **read** or **write** values into or from an entire array by a reference to the array name. (An exception is explained in Section 10.5.) Statements such as

```
read (Data, A),
writeln (A)
```

are invalid if A is an array.

Out-of-range array references should be avoided. For example, if the array A has index values 1. .5, a reference to A[6] or A[0] will produce an error. This will become more of a problem when we start to process arrays with loops in the next section.

Exercises 10.1

In Exercises 1–4, define an array type and declare subsequent variables.

*1. A list of 35 test scores

2. The prices of 20 automobiles

*3. The answers to 50 true or false questions

4. A list of letter grades for the classes you are taking this semester

*5. Write a test program in which you declare an array of three components, read values into each component, sum the components, and print the sum and value of each component.

For Exercises 6–11, find all errors in the definitions of array types.

6.
```
TYPE
  Time = ARRAY [1..12] OF Hours;
```

*7.
```
TYPE
  Scores = ARRAY [1..30] OF integer;
```

8.
```
TYPE
  Alphabet = ARRAY OF char;
```

*9.
```
TYPE
  List = ARRAY [1 TO 10] OF real;
```

10.
```
TYPE
  Answers = ARRAY [OF boolean];
```
*11.
```
TYPE
  X = ARRAY [1...5] OF real;
```

For Exercises 12–23, assume the array List is declared as

```
TYPE
  Scores = ARRAY [1..100] OF integer;
VAR
  List : Scores;
```

and all other variables have been appropriately declared. Label each code fragment as valid or invalid. Include an explanation for any that are invalid.

12. `read (Data, List[3]);`

*13. `A := List[3] + List[4];`

14. `writeln (List);`

*15. `List[10] := 3.2;`

16. `Max := List[50];`

*17. `Average := (List[1] + List[8]) / 2;`

18. `write (List[25, 50, 75, 100]);`

*19. `write ((List[10] + List[90]):25);`

20.
```
FOR J := 1 TO 100 DO
  read (Data, List);
```
*21. `List[36] := List[102];`

22. `Scores[47] := 92;`

*23. `List[40] := List[41] / 2;`

In Exercises 24–26, change the code fragment so that the **TYPE** definition section is used to define the array type.

24.
```
VAR
  LetterList : ARRAY [1..100] OF 'A'..'Z';
```
*25.
```
VAR
  CompanyName : ARRAY [1..30] OF char;
```
26.
```
VAR
  ScoreList : ARRAY [30..59] OF real;
```
*27. Consider the array declared by

```
TYPE
  ListOfSizes = ARRAY [1..5] OF integer;
VAR
  WaistSize : ListOfSizes;
```

a. Sketch how the array should be envisioned in memory.

b. After assignments

```
WaistSize[1] := 34;
WaistSize[3] := 36;
WaistSize[5] := 32;
WaistSize[2] := 2 * 15;
WaistSize[4] := (WaistSize[1] + WaistSize[3]) DIV 2;
```

are made, sketch the array and indicate the contents of each component.

For Exercises 28–30, let the array Money be declared by

```
TYPE
  List3 = ARRAY [1..3] OF real;
VAR
  Money : List3;
```

Let Temp, X, and Y be **real** variables and assume Money has the indicated values:

Money	
19.26	Money[1]
10.04	Money[2]
17.32	Money[3]

If Money contains these initial values before each segment is executed, what does the array contain after each section of code?

28.
```
Temp := 173.21;
X := Temp + Money[2];
Money[1] := X;
```

*29.
```
IF Money[2] < Money[1] THEN
  BEGIN
    Temp := Money[2];
    Money[2] := Money[1];
    Money[1] := Temp
  END;
```

30.
```
Money[3] := 20 - Money[3];
```

31. Let the array List be declared by

```
TYPE
  Scores = ARRAY [1..5] OF real;
VAR
  List : Scores;
```

Write a program segment to initialize all components of List to 0.0.

10.2 Using Arrays

Objectives

- to be able to use loops to read data into an array from a text file
- to be able to use loops to write data from an array
- to be able to assign array values by aggregate assignment and by component assignment
- to be able to use loops with arrays to solve programming problems

Loops for Input and Output

One advantage of using arrays is the small amount of code needed when loops are used to manipulate array components. For example, suppose a list of 100 scores stored in a data file is to be used in a program. If an array is declared by

```
TYPE
  List100 = ARRAY [1..100] OF integer;
VAR
  Score : List100;
  Data : text;
```

the data file can be read into the array using a **FOR** loop as follows:

```
FOR J := 1 TO 100 DO
  read (Data, Score[J]);
```

Remember, a statement such as **read** (Score) is invalid. Data can only be read into individual components of the array.

Loops can be similarly used to produce output of array components. For example, if the array of test scores just given is to be printed in a column, then

```
FOR J := 1 TO 100 DO
  writeln (Score[J]);
```

will accomplish this. If the components of Score contain the values

Score

78	Score[1]
93	Score[2]
.	.
.	.
.	.
82	Score[100]

the loop for writing produces

```
78
93
.
.
.
82
```

Note that we cannot cause the array components to be printed by a statement such as **write** (Score) or **writeln** (Score). These statements are invalid. We must refer to the individual components.

Loops for output are seldom this simple. Usually we are required to format the output in some manner. For example, suppose the array Score is as declared and we wish to print these scores 10 to a line, each with a field width of five spaces. The following segment of code would accomplish this:

```
FOR J := 1 TO 100 DO
  BEGIN
    write (Score[J]:5);
    IF J MOD 10 = 0 THEN
      writeln
  END;
```

Loops for Assigning

Loops can also be used to assign values to array components. At certain times, we might want an array to contain values that are not read from an input file. The following examples show how loops can be used to handle such instances.

Example 10.7

Recall array A in Section 10.1 in which we made the following assignments:

```
A[1] := 1;
A[2] := 4;
A[3] := 9;
A[4] := 16;
A[5] := 25;
```

These assignments could have been made with the loop

```
FOR  J := 1 TO 5 DO
  A[J] := J * J;
```

Example 10.8

Suppose the components of an array must contain the letters of the alphabet in order from A to Z. Using the ASCII character set, the desired array could be declared by

```
TYPE
  Letters = ARRAY [1..26] OF char;
VAR
  Alphabet : Letters;
```

The array Alphabet could then be assigned the desired characters by the statement

```
FOR J := 1 TO 26 DO
  Alphabet[J] := chr(J - 1 + ord('A'));
```

If

```
J := 1;
```

we have

```
Alphabet[1] := chr(ord('A'));
```

Thus,

```
Alphabet[1] := 'A';
```

Similarly, for

```
J := 2;
```

we have

```
Alphabet[2] := chr(1 + ord('A'));
```

Eventually we obtain

Alphabet

'A'	Alphabet[1]
'B'	Alphabet[2]
'C'	Alphabet[3]
.	.
.	.
.	.
'Z'	Alphabet[26]

Assignment of values from components of one array to corresponding components of another array is a frequently encountered problem. For example, suppose the arrays A and B are declared as

```
TYPE
  List50 = ARRAY [1..50] OF real;
VAR
  A, B : List50;
```

If B has been assigned values and you want to put the contents of B into A component by component, you could use the loop

```
FOR J := 1 TO 50 DO
  A[J] := B[J];
```

However, for problems of this type, Pascal allows the entire array to be assigned by

```
A := B;
```

This aggregate assignment actually causes 50 assignments to be made at the component level. The arrays must be type identical to do this.

Processing with Loops

Loops are especially suitable for reading, writing, and assigning array components and can be used in conjunction with arrays to process data. For example, suppose A and B are declared as

```
TYPE
  List100 = ARRAY [1..100] OF real;
VAR
  A, B : List100;
```

If we want to add the values of components of B to the respective values of components of A, we could use the loop

```
FOR J := 1 TO 100 DO
  A[J] := A[J] + B[J];
```

It would appear that since

```
A := B;
```

is valid, this could be accomplished by

```
A := A + B;
```

Not true. Pascal does not allow the aggregate addition of A + B, where A and B are arrays.

The following examples illustrate additional uses of loops for processing data contained in array variables.

Example 10.9

Earlier in this section, we read 100 test scores into an array. Assume the scores have been read and we now wish to find the average score and the largest score. Assume variables Sum, Max, and Average have been appropriately declared. The following segment will compute the average:

```
Sum := 0;
FOR J := 1 TO 100 DO
  Sum := Sum + Score[J];
Average := Sum / 100;
```

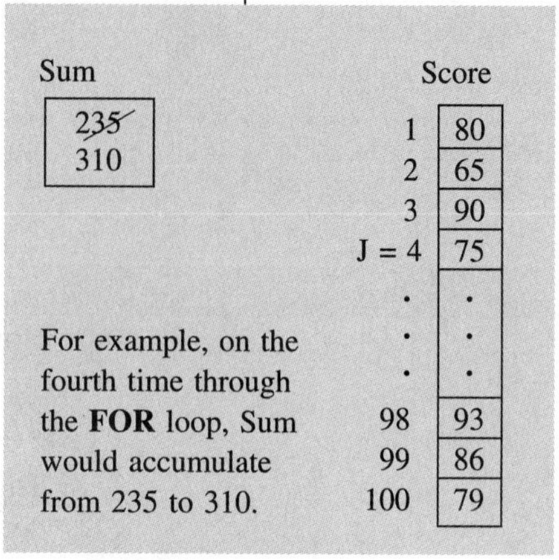

Sum

235 (crossed out)
310

Score

	Score
1	80
2	65
3	90
J = 4	75
.	.
.	.
.	.
98	93
99	86
100	79

For example, on the fourth time through the **FOR** loop, Sum would accumulate from 235 to 310.

The maximum score can be found by using the following segment of code:

```
Max := Score[1];
FOR J := 2 TO 100 DO
  IF Score[J] > Max THEN
    Max := Score[J];
```

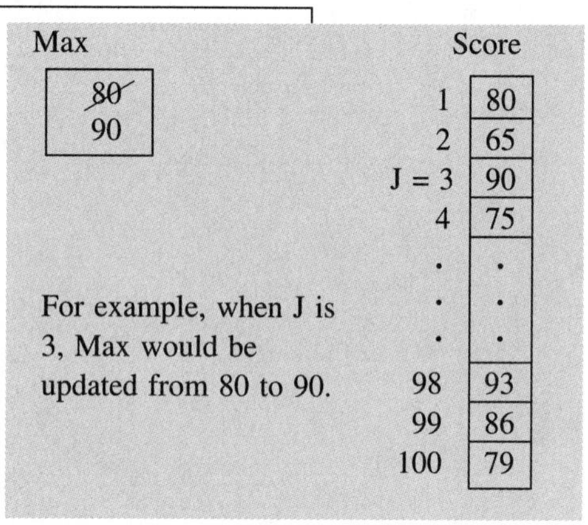

Max

80 (crossed out)
90

	Score
1	80
2	65
J = 3	90
4	75
.	.
.	.
.	.
98	93
99	86
100	79

For example, when J is 3, Max would be updated from 80 to 90.

Example 10.10

Let's write a segment of code to find the smallest value of array A and the index of the smallest value. Assume the variables have been declared as

```
TYPE
  Column100 = ARRAY [1..100] OF real;
VAR
  A : Column100;
  Min : real;
  Index : integer;
```

and the values have been read into components of A. The following algorithm will solve the problem:

1. Assign 1 to Index

2. **FOR** J := 2 **TO** 100 **DO**
   IF A[J] < A[Index] **THEN** assign J to Index
3. Assign A[Index] to Min

The segment of code is

```
Index := 1;
FOR J := 2 TO 100 DO
  IF A[J] < A[Index] THEN
    Index := J;
Min := A[Index];
```

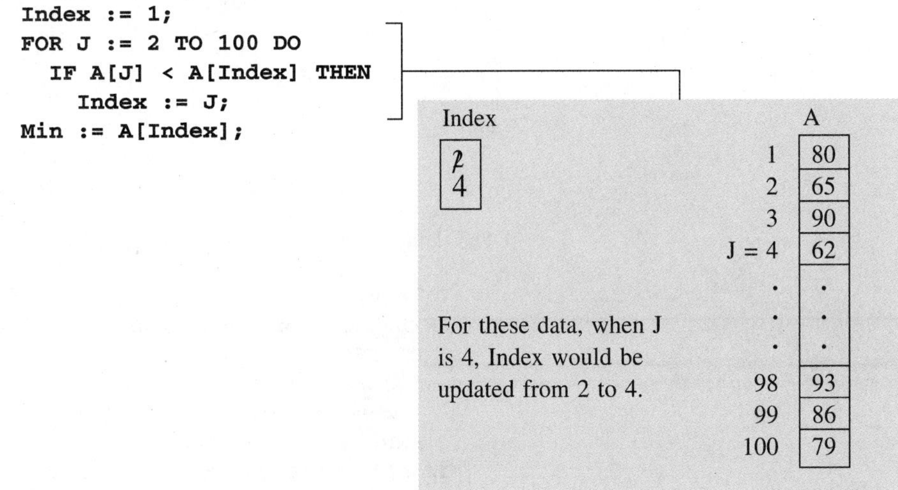

A very standard problem encountered when working with arrays is what to do when we don't know exactly how many components of an array will be needed. In such instances, we must select some upper limit for the length of the array. A standard procedure is to declare a reasonable limit, keeping these two points in mind:

1. The length must be sufficient to store all the data.
2. The amount of storage space must not be excessive; do not set aside excessive amounts of space that will not be used.

To guard against the possibility of not reading all the data into array elements, an **IF . . . THEN** statement, such as

```
IF NOT eof(Data) THEN
  writeln ('There are more data.');
```

could be included in the procedure used to get data from the data file. These points are illustrated in the following example. The array will be partially filled when the number of checks is less than the array length. This information can be retained by including a program statement such as

```
NumberOfChecks := J;
```

after the loop is exited.

Example 10.11

Suppose an input file contains an unknown number of dollar amounts from personal checks. We want to write a segment of code to read them into an array and output the number of checks. Since the data are in dollars, we use real components and the identifier Check as follows:

```
TYPE
  List = ARRAY [1..?] OF real;
VAR
  Check : List;
```

If we think there are fewer than 50 checks, we can define a constant by

```
CONST
  MaxChecks = 50;
```

and then define List by

```
List = ARRAY [1..MaxChecks] OF real;
```

The data are then accessed using a **WHILE . . . DO** loop:

```
J := 0;
WHILE NOT eof(Data) AND (J < MaxChecks) DO
  BEGIN
    J := J + 1;
    readln (Data, Check[J])
  END;
IF NOT eof(Data) THEN
  writeln ('There are more data');
NumberOfChecks := J;
```

Communication and Style Tips

Indices with semantic meaning can be useful when working with arrays. For example, suppose you are writing a program that includes the inventory for shoe styles in a shoe store. If the styles are loafer, wing tip, docksider, high pump, low pump, and plain tie, you would define

```
TYPE
  Style = (Docksider, HighPump, Loafer, LowPump,
           PlainTie, WingTip);
  ShoeInventory = ARRAY [Docksider..WingTip] OF integer;
VAR
  Stock : ShoeInventory;
  ShoeType : Style;
```

Typical program statements could be

```
Stock[WingTip] := 25;
Stock[Loafer] := Stock[Loafer] - 3;
FOR ShoeType := Docksider..WingTip DO
  writeln (Stock[ShoeType]);
```

Now we have the data in the array, we know the number of data items, and NumberOfChecks can be used as a loop limit. Then the loop

```
FOR J := 1 TO NumberOfChecks DO
  BEGIN
    writeln;
    writeln ('Check number':20, J:4, '$':5, Checks[J]:7:2)
  END;
```

will print the checks on every other line.

Exercises 10.2

For Exercises 1–4, assume the following array declarations:

```
TYPE
  NumList = ARRAY [1..5] OF integer;
  AnswerList = ARRAY [1..10] OF boolean;
  NameList = ARRAY [1..20] OF char;
VAR
  List, Score : NumList;
  Answer : AnswerList;
  Name : NameList;
```

Indicate the contents of the arrays after each segment of code.

*1.
```
FOR J := 1 TO 5 DO
  List[J] := J DIV 3;
```

2.
```
FOR J := 2 TO 6 DO
  BEGIN
    List[J-1] := J + 3;
    Score[J-1] := List[J-1] DIV 3
  END;
```

*3.
```
FOR J := 1 TO 10 DO
  IF J MOD 2 = 0 THEN
    Answer[J] := true
  ELSE
    Answer[J] := false;
```

4.
```
FOR J := 1 TO 20 DO
  Name[J] := chr(J + 64);
```

5. Write a test program to illustrate what happens when you try to use an index that is not in the defined subrange for an array. For example, try to use the loop

```
FOR J := 1 TO 10 DO
  read (Data, A[J]);
```

when A has been declared as

```
TYPE
  NumList = ARRAY [1..5] OF integer;
VAR
  A : NumList;
```

6. Let the array Best be declared by

```
TYPE
  List30 = ARRAY [1..30] OF integer;
VAR
  Best : List30;
```

and assume that test scores have been read into Best. What does the following section of code do?

```
Count := 0;
FOR J := 1 TO 30 DO
  IF Best[J] > 90 THEN
    Count := Count + 1;
```

*7. Declare an array and write a segment of code to
   a. Read 20 integer test scores into the array.
   b. Count the number of scores ≥ 55.

8. Declare an array using the **TYPE** definition section and write a section of code to read a name of 20 characters from a line of input.

*9. Let the array List be declared by

```
TYPE
  Numbers = ARRAY [11..17] OF integer;
VAR
  List : Numbers;
```

and assume the components have values of

List	
−2	List[11]
3	List[12]
0	List[13]
−8	List[14]
20	List[15]
14	List[16]
−121	List[17]

Show what the array components would be after the following program segment is executed:

```
FOR J := 11 TO 17 DO
  IF List[J] < 0 THEN
    List[J] := 0;
```

10. Assume the array A is declared as

```
TYPE
  List100 = ARRAY [1..100] OF real;
VAR
  A : List100;
```

Write a segment of code that uses a loop to initialize all components to zero.

For Exercises 11–13, let the array N be declared as

```
TYPE
  String10 = ARRAY [1..10] OF char;
VAR
  N : String10;
```

and assume the array components have been assigned the following values:

J	O	H	N		S	M	I	T	H
N[1]	N[2]	N[3]	N[4]	N[5]	N[6]	N[7]	N[8]	N[9]	N[10]

What output is produced by each exercise?

*11. `FOR J := 1 TO 10 DO`
```
      write (N[J]);
    writeln;
```
12. `FOR J := 1 TO 5 DO`
```
      write (N[J+5]);
    write (', ');
    FOR J := 1 TO 4 DO
      write (N[J]);
    writeln;
```
*13. `FOR J := 10 DOWNTO 1 DO`
```
      writeln (N[J]);
```

For Exercises 14–18, let arrays A, B, and C be declared as follows:

```
TYPE
  FirstList = ARRAY [21..40] OF real;
  SecondList = ARRAY [-4..15] OF real;
VAR
  A, B : FirstList;
  C : SecondList;
```

Indicate if the following are valid or invalid. Include an explanation for those that are invalid.

14. `FOR J := 21 TO 40 DO`
```
      A[J] := C[J-25];
```
*15. `A := B;`

16. `A := C;`

*17. `FOR J := 1 TO 10 DO`
```
      B[J+20] := C[J-5];
```
18. `FOR J := 11 TO 20 DO`
```
      B[J+20] := A[J+20];
```
*19. Assume an array has been declared as

```
TYPE
  List50 = ARRAY [1..50] OF integer;
VAR
  TestScore : List50;
```

Write a segment of code to print a suitable heading (assume this is a list of test scores) and then output a numbered list of the array components.

20. Write a program segment to read 100 real numbers from a text file, compute the average, and find both the largest and smallest values.
21. The following can be used to input the values in Example 10.11. Discuss how it differs from the method used in that example.

```
FOR J := 1 TO 50 DO
  IF NOT eof(Data) THEN
    readln (Data, Check[J]);
```

10.3 Selection Sort

Objective

- to be able to sort an array using the selection sort

A common use for arrays is sorting their components in either ascending or descending order. Several sorting algorithms are given in Chapter 14, but here we consider one of the easier methods, the selection sort.

Suppose we have an array A of five integers that we wish to sort from smallest to largest. The values currently in A are as depicted in the array on the left below; we wish to end up with values as shown in the array on the right:

A			A	
6	A[1]		1	A[1]
4	A[2]		4	A[2]
8	A[3]		6	A[3]
10	A[4]		8	A[4]
1	A[5]		10	A[5]

A **selection sort** is a sorting algorithm that sorts the components of an array in either ascending or descending order. This process puts the smallest or largest element in the top position and repeats the process on the remaining array components.

The basic idea of a **selection sort** is

1. Find the smallest number in the array and exchange it with A[1].
2. Find the smallest number among A[2] through A[5] and exchange it with A[2].
3. Continue this process until the array is sorted.

The first step produces

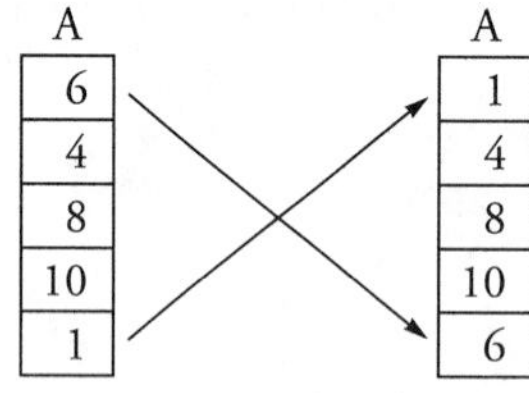

The second step produces

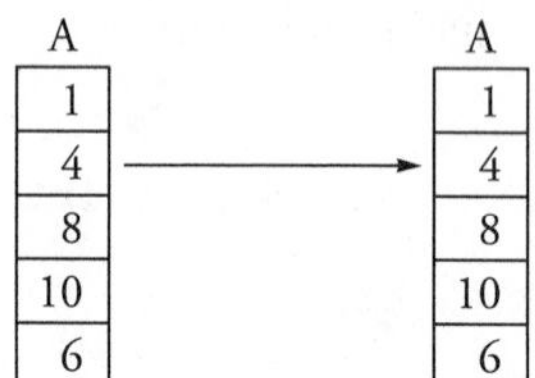

A Note of Interest

Computer Science and Women in Business

Among the rapid growth companies not to be overlooked are women-owned businesses. According to Peterson's Job Opportunities in Engineering and Technology, 1997, "There are six and one-half million women-owned businesses in the United States today. Virtually all of them have fewer than 250 employees. In each of the last five years, more than half of the three million businesses formed in the United States were started by a woman. Moreover, the gender profile of the personnel in a woman-owned company is typically two-thirds female."

Although women entrepreneurs are starting new businesses at a faster rate than their male counterparts, they have more difficulty attracting capital for new ventures. Thus, they tend to create businesses which substitute labor for capital.

Peterson continues by stating, "Women entrepreneurs have proven themselves heroines in the current United States economic recovery with the best and most expansive of [their businesses] growing from an average initial capital of $38,000 to an average valuation of $90 million in 15 years. They also are providing training grounds for their employees to leave and launch their own businesses, which creates an ever-widening circle of women hiring mostly women."

The Association for Computing Machinery (ACM) has taken an active role in promoting computer science as a career for women. The ACM Committee on the Status of Women has made the following recommendations:

- Ensure equal access to computers for young girls and boys and develop educational software appealing to both.
- Establish programs (such as science fairs, scouting programs, and conferences in which women speak about their careers in science and engineering) to encourage high school girls to continue with math and science.
- Develop programs to pair undergraduate women with women graduate students or faculty members who serve as role models and provide encouragement and advice.
- Provide women with opportunities for successful professional experiences (such as involvement in research projects), beginning as early as the undergraduate years.
- Establish programs that make women computer scientists visible to undergraduates and graduate students. Women can be invited to campuses to give talks or to serve as visiting faculty members (as, for example, in the National Science Foundation's Visiting Professorships for Women).
- Encourage men and women to serve as mentors for young women in the field.
- Maintain lists of qualified women computer scientists to increase the participation of women in influential positions, such as program committees, editorial boards, and policy boards.
- Establish more reentry programs that enable women who have stopped their scientific training prematurely to retrain as computer scientists.
- Increase awareness of and sensitivity to subtle discrimination and its effects.
- Develop and enforce safety procedures on campus. Provide safe access at all hours to public terminal areas, well-lit routes from offices to parking lots, and services to escort those walking on campus after dark.
- Provide affordable, quality childcare.

To provide support for women computer professionals, several organizations have been established that focus on networking, including Systers, the Association for Women in Computing (AWC), and the International Network of Women in Technology (WITI).

Notice that since the second smallest number is already in place, we do not need to make an exchange. The third step produces

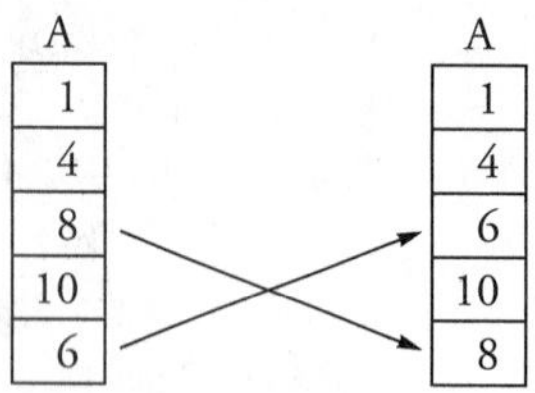

The fourth and final step yields the sorted list.

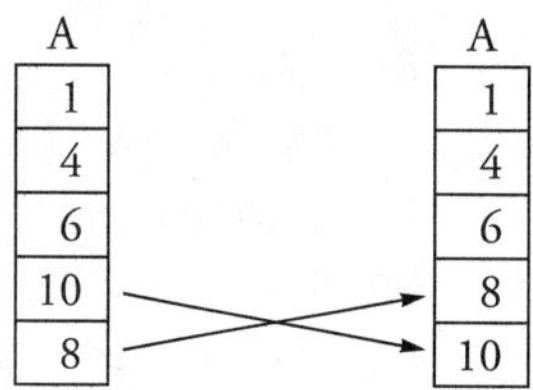

Before writing the algorithm for this sorting procedure, note the following:

1. If the array is of length n, we need $n - 1$ steps.
2. We must be able to find one of the smallest remaining numbers.
3. We need to exchange appropriate array components.

When searching for one of the smallest remaining numbers, it is not necessary to exchange values. Thus, note that strict inequality (<) rather than weak inequality (<=) is used when looking for the smallest remaining value. The algorithm to sort by selection is

1. **FOR** J := 1 **TO** N – 1
   - 1.1 Find the smallest value among A[J], A[J+1], . . . , A[N], and store the index of the smallest value in Index
   - 1.2 Exchange the values of A[J] and A[Index] if necessary

In Example 10.10, we wrote a segment of code to find the smallest value of array A. With suitable changes, we can incorporate this in the segment of code for a selection sort:

```
Index := 1;
FOR J := 2 TO ArrayLength DO
  IF A[J] < A[Index] THEN
    Index := J;
```

Let A be an array of length n and assume all variables have been appropriately declared. Then the following segment of code will sort A from low to high:

```
FOR J := 1 TO N - 1 DO      {  Find the minimum N - 1 times  }
  BEGIN
    Index := J;
    FOR K := J + 1 TO N DO
      IF A[K] < A[Index] THEN
        Index := K;          {  Find index of smallest number  }
    IF Index <> J THEN
      BEGIN
        Temp := A[Index];
        A[Index] := A[J];
        A[J] := Temp
      END  {  of exchange  }
  END;  {  of FOR J loop  }
```

1
2
3
.
.
.
J – 1
J
For a given value of J, these values are already positioned correctly.
.
.
.
N – 1
N
The inner loop finds and stores the position of smallest among these values in Index. Positions Index and J then are exchanged.

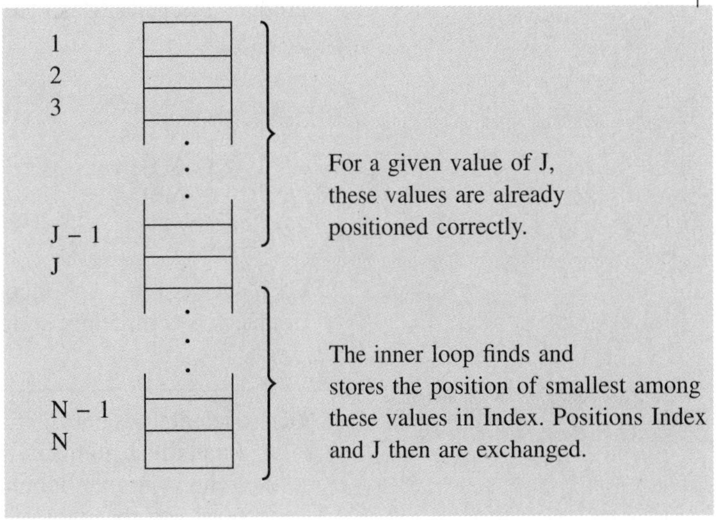

Now let's trace this sort for the five integers in the array we sorted at the beginning of this section.

A	
6	A[1]
4	A[2]
8	A[3]
10	A[4]
1	A[5]

For J := 1, Index := 1, and this produces

1
Index

For the loop **FOR** K := 2 **TO** 5, we get successive assignments

K	Index
2	2
3	2
4	2
5	5

The statements

```
Temp := A[Index];
A[Index] := A[J];
A[J] := Temp;
```

produce the partially sorted array

A	
1	A[1]
4	A[2]
8	A[3]
10	A[4]
6	A[5]

Each successive J value continues to partially sort the array until J := 4. This pass produces a completely sorted array.

Example 10.12

Our concluding example

1. Inputs real numbers from a data file.
2. Echo prints the numbers in a column with a width of six spaces, with two places to the right of the decimal (:6:2).
3. Sorts the array from low to high.
4. Prints the sorted array using the same output format.

An expanded development for this is

1. Print header—prints a suitable explanation of the program and includes a heading for the unsorted list
2. Get data (echo print)—uses a **WHILE** loop to read the data and print them in the same order in which they are read
3. Sort list—uses the selection sort to sort the array from low to high
4. Display sorted list—uses a **FOR** loop to display the sorted list

```
PROGRAM ArraySample (input, output, DataFile);

{   This program illustrates the use of a sorting algorithm      }
{   with an array of reals.  Output includes data in both an     }
{   unsorted and a sorted list.  The data are formatted  and     }
{   numbered to enhance readability.                             }

CONST
  Skip = ' ';
  ListMax = 20;
```

```
TYPE
  NumList = ARRAY [1..ListMax] OF real;

VAR
  Index : integer;       {  Stores position of an element          }
  J, K : integer;        {  Indices                                }
  NumReals : integer;    {  Length of the list                     }
  Temp : real;           {  Temporary storage for array elements   }
  List : NumList;        {  Array of reals                         }
  DataFile : text;       {  File of data                           }

{*****************************************************************}

PROCEDURE PrintHeading;

  {  Given:   Nothing                                              }
  {  Task:    Print a heading for the output                       }
  {  Return:  Nothing                                              }

  BEGIN
    writeln;
    writeln ('This sample program does the following:');
    writeln;
    writeln (Skip:2, '<1> Gets reals from a data file.');
    writeln (Skip:2, '<2> Echo prints the data.');
    writeln (Skip:2, '<3> Sorts the data from low to high.');
    writeln (Skip:2, '<4> Prints a sorted list of the data.');
    writeln
  END;  {  of PROCEDURE PrintHeading  }

{*****************************************************************}

BEGIN  {  Main program  }

  {  Print the heading  }
  PrintHeading;

  {  Get the data and echo print it  }
  writeln ('The original data are as follows:');
  writeln;
  NumReals := 0;
  reset (DataFile);
  WHILE NOT eof(DataFile) AND (NumReals < ListMax) DO
    BEGIN
      NumReals := NumReals + 1;
      readln (DataFile, List[NumReals]);
      writeln (Skip:2, '<', NumReals:2, '>', List[NumReals]:6:2)
    END;  {  of WHILE NOT loop  }
  IF NOT eof(DataFile) THEN
    writeln ('There are more data.');

  {  Now sort the list  }
  FOR J := 1 TO NumReals - 1 DO
    BEGIN
      Index := J;
```

```
      FOR K := J + 1 TO NumReals DO
        IF List[K] < List[Index] THEN
          Index := K;
      IF Index <> J THEN
        BEGIN
          Temp := List[Index];
          List[Index] := List[J];
          List[J] := Temp
        END { of exchange }
    END; { of FOR loop (selection sort) }

  { Now print the sorted list }
  writeln;
  writeln ('The sorted list is as follows:');
  writeln;
  FOR J := 1 TO NumReals DO
    writeln (Skip:2, '<' J:2, '>', List[J]:6:2)
END. { of main program }
```

The output for this program is

```
This sample program does the following:

  <1> Gets reals from a data file.
  <2> Echo prints the data.
  <3> Sorts the data from low to high.
  <4> Prints a sorted list of the data.

The original data are as follows:

  < 1> 34.56
  < 2> 78.21
  < 3> 23.30
  < 4> 89.90
  < 5> 45.00
  < 6> 56.80
  < 7> 39.01
  < 8> 45.56
  < 9> 34.40
  <10> 45.10
  <11> 98.20
  <12>  5.60
  <13>  8.00
  <14> 45.00
  <15> 99.00
  <16> 56.78
  <17> 56.78
  <18> 45.00
  <19> 89.80
  <20> 95.60

The sorted list is as follows:

  < 1>  5.60
  < 2>  8.00
```

```
< 3> 23.30
< 4> 34.40
< 5> 34.56
< 6> 39.01
< 7> 45.00
< 8> 45.00
< 9> 45.00
<10> 45.10
<11> 45.56
<12> 56.78
<13> 56.78
<14> 56.80
<15> 78.21
<16> 89.80
<17> 89.90
<18> 95.60
<19> 98.20
<20> 99.00
```

Exercises 10.3

*1. Assume the following array Column is to be sorted from low to high using the selection sort:

Column

–20
10
0
10
8
30
–2

a. Sketch the contents of the array after each of the first two passes.
b. How many exchanges are made during the sort?

2. Write a test program that prints the partially sorted arrays after each pass during a selection sort.

*3. Change the code for the selection sort so it sorts an array from high to low.

4. Write a complete program to
   a. Read 10 reals into an array from an input file.
   b. Sort the array from high to low if the first real is positive; sort the array from low to high if the first real is negative.
   c. Print a numbered column containing the sorted reals with the format :10:2.

5. Modify the selection sort by including a counter that counts the number of assignments of array elements made during a sort.

6. Using the modification in Exercise 5, sort lists of differing lengths that contain randomly generated numbers. On a graph similar to the one shown here, display the number of assignments made for each sort. Use lists with lengths of multiples of 10.

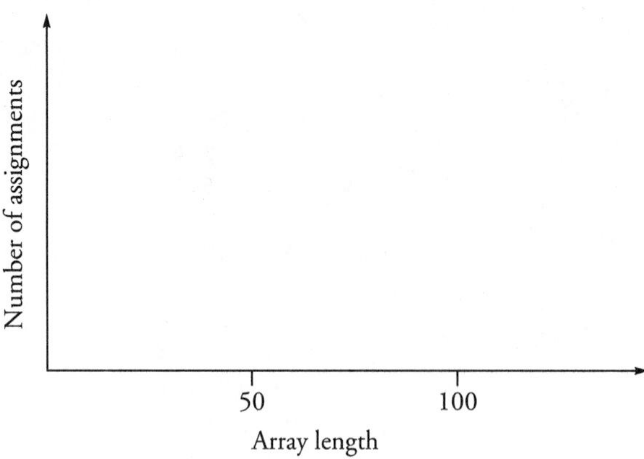

10.4 Arrays and Subprograms

Objective

- to be able to use arrays correctly with subprograms

Basic Idea and Notation

Procedures and functions should be used with arrays to maintain the structured design philosophy. Before we look at specific examples, let's examine the method and syntax necessary for passing an array to a procedure. Remember, to pass either a value parameter or a variable parameter to a procedure, we must declare an actual parameter of exactly the same type as the formal parameter in the procedure heading. In addition, if more than one parameter is passed, there must be a one-for-one ordered matching of the actual parameters with the formal parameters in the heading of the procedure.

First, let's consider how a procedure can be used to read data into an array. Suppose the definitions and declarations include

```
CONST
  ListMax = 20;
TYPE
  NumList = ARRAY [1..ListMax] OF real;
```

We use two variable parameters in the procedure heading, List and ListLength. Thus, the heading is

```
PROCEDURE GetData (VAR List : Numlist;
                   VAR ListLength : integer);
```

Within **PROCEDURE** GetData, we can now read values into the array List by the code

```
ListLength := 0;          {  Initialize  }
WHILE NOT eof AND ListLength < ListMax DO
  BEGIN
    ListLength := ListLength + 1;
    readln (List[ListLength])
  END;  {  of WHILE loop  }
IF NOT eof THEN
  writeln ('There are more data.');
```

The complete procedure is

```
PROCEDURE GetData (VAR List : NumList;
                   VAR ListLength : integer);

  {  Given:   Nothing                              }
  {  Task:    Read integers into the array List    }
  {  Return:  The array of integers List and the   }
  {                length of the list ListLength   }

  BEGIN
    ListLength := 0;          {  Initialize  }
    WHILE NOT eof AND ListLength < ListMax DO
      BEGIN
        ListLength := ListLength + 1;
        readln (List[ListLength])
      END;  {  of WHILE loop  }
    IF NOT eof THEN
      writeln ('There are more data.')
  END;  {  of PROCEDURE GetData  }
```

This procedure is called by

```
GetData (List, ListLength);
```

Notice that the procedure call and the procedure heading

```
PROCEDURE GetData (VAR List : NumList;
                   VAR ListLength : integer);
```

exhibit the desired matching of variables. Since variable parameters are used, both List and ListLength are passed by reference and are available to the rest of the program.

Let's briefly consider the heading for **PROCEDURE** GetData. Note that we use the data type NumList when declaring the variable parameter List. A common mistake is to attempt to build a data type inside the procedure heading. This does not work. The heading

```
PROCEDURE GetData (VAR List : ARRAY [1..ListMax] OF real;
                   VAR ListLength : integer);
```

produces an error message because Pascal compilers check for name equivalence rather than structure equivalence. To illustrate, you could have two arrays

```
Position : ARRAY [1..3] OF real;
Nutrition : ARRAY [1..3] OF real;
```

where Position is used to represent coordinates of a point in space and Nutrition is used to represent the volume, weight, and caloric content of a serving of food. Although Position and Nutrition have the same structure, they have significantly different meanings. Thus, requiring name equivalence decreases the chance of inadvertent or meaningless uses of structured variables. Also, compiler implementation of name equivalence is easier than compiler implementation of structure equivalence.

Next, we consider passing an array to a function. Suppose we want to find the average of an array of integers. Using the previous definitions and declarations, the data are obtained by

```
GetData (List, ListLength);
```

where the array List contains ListLength integers. A function to find the average of the numbers in the array List is

```
FUNCTION CalculateAverage (Scores : NumList;
                           NumScores : integer) : real;
  VAR
    Index, Sum : integer;
  BEGIN
    Sum := 0;
    FOR Index := 1 TO NumScores DO
      Sum := Sum + Scores[Index];
    CalculateAverage := Sum / NumScores
  END;  {  of FUNCTION CalculateAverage  }
```

This function can be called by

```
Average := CalculateAverage(List, ListLength);
```

The next example is a complete program that features the use of an array with subprograms.

Example 10.13

Let's develop a program that reads data from a data file into an array, computes the average of the array elements, and uses two procedures to display the results.

```
PROGRAM TestScores (input, output, ScoreFile);

{  This program illustrates the use of arrays and sub-          }
{  programs.  Specifically, subprograms are used to             }
{     1.  read data into an array                               }
{     2.  compute the average of array elements                 }
{     3.  print contents of the array                           }

CONST
  MaxLength = 100;

TYPE
  List = ARRAY [1..MaxLength] OF integer;

VAR
  Scores : List;                    {  Array of scores          }
  Average : real;                   {  Average score            }
  Length : integer;                 {  Length of the array      }
  ScoreFile : text;                 {  Data file                }

{*****************************************************************}

PROCEDURE GetData (VAR Scores : List;
                   VAR Length : integer);

  {  Given:   Nothing                                          }
  {  Task:    Read integers into the array Scores              }
  {  Return:  The array of integers Scores and the             }
  {                 length of the list Length                  }
```

```
  BEGIN
    Length := 0;
    reset (ScoreFile);
    WHILE NOT eof(ScoreFile) AND (Length < MaxLength) DO
      BEGIN
        Length := Length + 1;
        readln (ScoreFile, Scores[Length])
      END;  {  of WHILE loop  }
    IF NOT eof(ScoreFile) THEN
      writeln ('There are more data.')
  END;  {  of PROCEDURE GetData  }

{***************************************************************}

FUNCTION ComputeAverage (Scores : List;
                         Length : integer) : real;

  {  Given:   A list of scores                                  }
  {  Task:    Compute the average score                         }
  {  Return:  The average score                                 }

  VAR
    Index, Sum : integer;
  BEGIN
    Sum := 0;
    FOR Index := 1 TO Length DO
      Sum := Sum + Scores[Index];
    ComputeAverage := Sum / Length
  END;  {  of FUNCTION ComputeAverage  }

{***************************************************************}

PROCEDURE PrintHeader;

  {  Given:   Nothing                                           }
  {  Task:    Print a heading for the output                    }
  {  Return:  Nothing                                           }

  BEGIN
    writeln;
    writeln ('Test Scores');
    writeln ('---- ------');
    writeln
  END;  {  of PROCEDURE PrintHeader  }

{***************************************************************}

PROCEDURE PrintResults    (Scores : List;
                           Average : real;
                           Length : integer);

  {  Given:   Array of scores and average score                 }
  {  Task:    Print the scores in a list and print the average  }
  {                score                                        }
  {  Return:  Nothing                                           }
```

```
VAR
  J : integer;
BEGIN
  FOR J := 1 TO Length DO
    writeln (Scores[J]:5);
  writeln;
  writeln ('The average score on this test was',
           Average:6:2, '.')
END;  {  of PROCEDURE PrintResults  }

{******************************************************************}

BEGIN  {  Main program  }
  GetData (Scores, Length);
  Average := ComputeAverage(Scores, Length);
  PrintHeader;
  PrintResults (Scores, Average, Length)
END.  {  of main program  }
```

Sorting arrays is a standard problem for programmers. Now that we can pass arrays to procedures and functions, let's consider a problem in which an unknown number of reals are to be read from an input file and a sorted list (high to low) is to be printed as output. A first-level pseudocode design is

1. Get data (**PROCEDURE** GetData)
2. Sort list (**PROCEDURE** Sort)
3. Print header (**PROCEDURE** PrintHeader)
4. Print sorted list (**PROCEDURE** PrintData)

Since the number of data items is unknown, we will have to declare an array that is of sufficient length to store all the data but that does not use an unreasonable amount of memory. The nature of the problem will provide sufficient information for this declaration. For now, assume we know there are at most 50 data items. Then the following declaration will be sufficient:

```
CONST
  MaxLength = 50;
TYPE
  NumList = ARRAY [1..MaxLength] OF real;
VAR
  List : NumList;
  Length : integer;
```

The procedure to sort the array uses a version of the selection sort in Section 10.3. Both the array and the number of data items need to be passed to the procedure. An appropriate procedure is

```
PROCEDURE Sort (VAR List : NumList;
                Length : integer);
  VAR
    J, K, Index : integer;
    Temp : real;
  BEGIN
    FOR J := 1 TO Length - 1 DO
```

```
      BEGIN
        Index := J;
        FOR K := J + 1 TO Length DO
          IF List[K] > List[Index] THEN
            Index := K;
        IF Index <> J THEN
          Swap (List[Index], List[J])
      END  {  of FOR J loop  }
  END;  {  of PROCEDURE Sort  }
```

Swap is a procedure that interchanges values of the variables. **PROCEDURE** Sort can be called by the statement

```
Sort (List, Length);
```

After suitable procedures are written for getting the data, printing a header, and printing the data, the main body of the program could be

```
BEGIN  {  Main program  }
  GetData (List, Length);
  Sort (List, Length);
  PrintHeader;
  PrintData (List, Length)
END.  {  of main program  }
```

Arrays and Variable Parameters

Now let's reconsider the issue of value parameters and variable parameters used with arrays. Because value parameters require separate memory of approximately the same size as that used by actual parameters in the main program, value parameters that are array types can require a great deal of memory. Thus, many programmers use only variable parameters when they work with arrays. This saves memory and speeds execution. Since most of your programs are relatively short and process small data files, this will not be a major problem. However, as databases become larger and you use more elaborate structures, you may wish to consider using variable parameters for arrays even when changes are not made in the variables.

Software Engineering Implications

Passing arrays is a software engineering concern. Passing arrays by reference results in a significant saving of memory. The problem this creates when several modules (teams) use the same array is that inadvertent changes made in an array within a specific module now become changes in the array used by other modules. These side effects do not occur if the array is passed as a value parameter.

How do designers solve this problem? There is no clear solution. If the arrays are fairly small and memory allocation is not a problem, arrays should be passed as value parameters when possible. When conditions require arrays to be passed by reference, it is extremely important to guarantee that no unwanted changes are made. This requirement increases the need for careful and thorough documentation.

Data Abstraction

Now that you are somewhat comfortable with the concept of an array as a data structure, it is time to take a broader look at how data relate to structures used to store and manipulate data. When designing the solution to a problem, it is not important to be initially concerned about the specifics of how data will be manipulated. These implementation details can (and should) be dealt with at a fairly low level in a modular development. The properties of a data structure will, however, be part of the design at a fairly high level.

Data abstraction is the separation between the conceptual definition of a data structure and its eventual implementation.

The separation between the conceptual definition of a data structure and its eventual implementation is called **data abstraction.** This process of deferring details to the lowest possible level parallels the method of designing algorithms: design first and do implementation details last.

Data abstraction is not a well-defined process, but we will attempt to illustrate it here. Suppose you are designing a program that will be required to work with a list of names and an associated list of numbers (student names and test scores). Reasonable tasks would be to

1. Get the data
2. Sort the lists by name or number
3. Print the lists

In your design, you might have procedures such as

```
GetNames (<procedure here>);
GetScores (<procedure here>);
SortByName (<procedure here>);
SortByScore (<procedure here>);
PrintNamesAndScores (<procedure here>);
```

Even though you have not yet worked with the implementation details required to write the procedures, you could use data structure properties in a design. For example, at this point, you probably could design a problem solution using some of the previously mentioned procedures that work with an array of names and/or an array of associated test scores.

Abstract Data Types

An **abstract data type (ADT)** consists of a class of objects, a defined set of properties of these objects, and a set of operations for processing the objects.

Two abstraction concepts have been previously discussed: procedural abstraction and data abstraction. A third form of abstraction arises from the use of defined types. Specifically, an **abstract data type (ADT)** consists of a class of objects, a defined set of properties of these objects, and a set of operations for processing the objects.

Our work thus far has been fairly limited in terms of what can be considered an abstract data type. However, it is possible to think of an array as a list. The class of objects is then lists. Some properties of these lists include identical element type, order, varying lengths, and direct access to individual components. Operations for processing the lists include searching for an element, sorting in ascending or descending order, inserting an element, and deleting an element.

As before, it is not necessary to be overly concerned about specific implementation details at this point. But your growth as a computer scientist will be enhanced if you develop a perspective of abstract data types and use this perspective in the design of problem solutions.

Much of the remainder of this book is devoted to developing properties of data structures and operations for processing these structures. As you progress through the material on higher dimensional arrays, records, files, and sets, try to analyze each structure with related properties and operations as an abstract data type.

Abstraction and Sorting

Now that we have seen how a sort can be coded, let's consider how we can make the sort more reusable. First, consider the exchange of elements

```
Temp := A[Index];
A[Index] := A[J];
A[J] := Temp
```

We can now write a procedure to perform this task:

```
PROCEDURE Swap (VAR Element1, Element2 : ItemType);
  VAR
    Temp : ItemType;
  BEGIN
    Temp := Element1;
    Element1 := Element2;
    Element2 := Temp
  END;  {  of PROCEDURE Swap  }
```

This procedure can be called by

```
Swap (Element1, Element2);
```

whenever it is needed. Note that the defined type ItemType has been used as a data type.

We can further abstract the selection sort by placing greater emphasis on enumerated data types. To illustrate, consider the definition section

```
CONST
  MaxLength = 50;

TYPE
  ItemType = integer;
  ListType = ARRAY [1..MaxLength] OF ItemType;

VAR
  List : ListType;
  ListLength : integer;
```

Given these definitions, we can rewrite the selection sort as

```
PROCEDURE SelectionSort (VAR List : ListType;
                             Length : integer);
  VAR
    J, K, Index : integer;
  BEGIN
    FOR J := 1 TO Length - 1 DO
      BEGIN
        Index := J;
        FOR K := J + 1 TO Length DO
          IF List[K] > List[Index] THEN
            Index := K;
        IF Index <> J THEN
          Swap (List[Index], List[J])
      END  {  of FOR J loop  }
  END;  {  of PROCEDURE SelectionSort  }
```

This procedure can be called by

```
SelectionSort (List, Length)
```

PROCEDURE SelectionSort can now be used to sort arrays with different item types by redefining ItemType in the **TYPE** definition section.

Exercises 10.4

For Exercises 1–10, assume the following declarations have been made in a program:

```
TYPE
  Row = ARRAY [1..10] OF integer;
  Column = ARRAY [1..30] OF real;
  String20 = ARRAY [1..20] OF char;
  Week = (Sun, Mon, Tues, Wed, Thur, Fri, Sat);
VAR
  List1, List2 : Row;
  Aray : Column;
  Name1, Name2 : String20;
  Day : Week;
  A, B : ARRAY [1..10] OF integer;
```

Indicate which are valid **PROCEDURE** declarations. Write an appropriate line of code that will call each procedure that is valid. Include an explanation for declarations that are invalid.

*1. `PROCEDURE NewList (X : Row; Y : Column);`
2. `PROCEDURE NewList (VAR X : Row : VAR Y : Column);`
*3. `PROCEDURE NewList (X : ARRAY [1..10] OF integer);`
4. `PROCEDURE NewList (VAR X, Y : Row);`
*5. `PROCEDURE NewList (VAR Column : Column);`
6. `PROCEDURE WorkWeek (Days : ARRAY [Mon..Fri] OF Week);`
*7. `PROCEDURE Surname (X : Name);`
8. `PROCEDURE Surnames (X, Y : String20);`
*9. `PROCEDURE GetData (X : Week; VAR Y : Name);`
10. `PROCEDURE Table (VAR X : Row; VAR Y : Row);`
11. Write a test program that illustrates what happens when you define an array structure in a procedure heading. For example,

```
PROCEDURE Sort (List : ARRAY [1..20] OF real);
```

For Exercises 12–15, when possible, use the **TYPE** and **VAR** declaration sections of Exercises 1–10 to write **PROCEDURE** declarations so that the statement in the main program is an appropriate call to a procedure. Explain any inappropriate calls.

12. `OldList (List1, Aray);`
*13. `ChangeList (List1, Name1, Day);`
14. `Scores (A, B);`
*15. `Surname (String20);`

For Exercises 16–19, write an appropriate **PROCEDURE** declaration and a line of code to call each procedure.

16. A procedure to read 20 test scores into an array and save them for later use.

*17. A procedure to count the number of occurrences of the letter A in an array of 50 characters.

18. A procedure to take two arrays of 10 integers each and produce a sorted array of 20 integers for later use.

*19. A procedure to read integer test scores from a data file, count the number of scores, count the number of scores greater than or equal to 90, and save this information for later use.

For Exercises 20–22, assume the following declarations have been made:

```
TYPE
  Column10 : ARRAY [1..10] OF integer;
VAR
  List1, List2 : Column10;
  K : integer;
```

Indicate the contents of the array after the call to the corresponding procedure.

20.
```
PROCEDURE Sample (VAR List1 : Column10;
                      List2 : Column10);
  VAR
    J : integer;
  BEGIN
    FOR J := 1 TO 10 DO
      BEGIN
        List1[J] := J * J;
        List2[J] := List[J] MOD 2
      END
  END;  {  of PROCEDURE Sample  }
BEGIN  {  Main program  }
  .
  .
  .
  FOR K := 1 TO 10 DO
    BEGIN
      List1[K] := 0;
      List2[K] := 0
    END;
  Sample (List1, List2);
```

*21. Replace the procedure call with

```
Sample (List2, List1);
```

22. Replace the procedure call with consecutive calls

```
Sample (List1, List2);
Sample (List2, List1);
```

For Exercises 23–25, declare appropriate variables, write the indicated procedures, and call the procedures from the main program.

23. Read a line of text from a data file that contains 30 characters.
24. Count the number of blanks in the line of text.
25. Print the line of text of Exercise 23 in reverse order and print the number of blanks.

26. Write a procedure to examine an array of integers and then return the maximum value, minimum value, and number of negative values to the main program.
27. Discuss some details of how you would implement reading a list of names into an array.
28. Suppose you have an array of student names and an array of these students' test scores. How would the array of names be affected if you sorted the test scores from high to low?

10.5 Packed Arrays

Objectives

- to be able to use correct notation for packed arrays
- to understand the advantages and disadvantages of packed arrays
- to be able to use string variables

One weakness of standard Pascal is the absence of a **string data type.** Since this text is written assuming standard Pascal is being used, this section shows how arrays can be used to simulate a string data type. Most nonstandard versions of Pascal do, however, have such a type. If your version of Pascal has the string data type available, you may wish to skip this section.

A **string data type** is a data type that permits a sequence of characters.

T

Basic Idea and Notation

Arrays are useful for handling large amounts of data. One of the disadvantages of using arrays, however, is that they require large amounts of memory. In particular, arrays of character data use much more memory than is necessary. To illustrate, let's take a closer look at an array declared by

```
VAR
  Examine : ARRAY [1..5] OF char;
```

When this structured variable is declared, the following variables are reserved.

Examine

Examine[1]
Examine[2]
Examine[3]
Examine[4]
Examine[5]

Each component of the array Examine is one word in memory and each word consists of several **bytes.** Let's consider the array Examine, in which each word consists of four bytes. The array would be pictured as

A **byte** is a sequence of bits used to encode a character in memory.

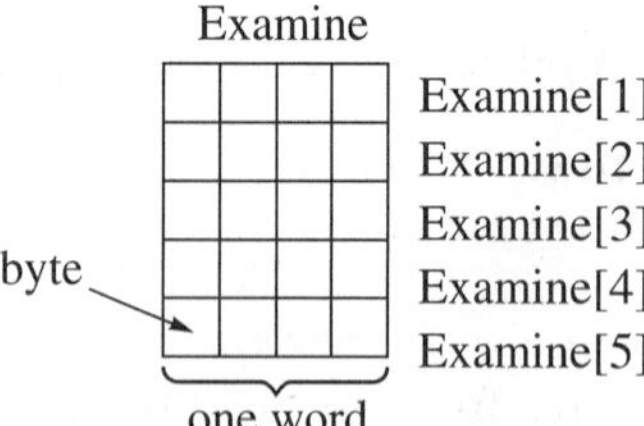

We could assign the word "HELLO" to the array Examine by either

```
Examine[1] := 'H';
Examine[2] := 'E';
```

```
Examine[3] := 'L';
Examine[4] := 'L';
Examine[5] := 'O';
```

or

```
Examine := 'HELLO'
```

depending on which version of Pascal is being used. In either case, after the assignment, the array would look like

Examine

H				Examine[1]
E				Examine[2]
L				Examine[3]
L				Examine[4]
O				Examine[5]

because a byte is the unit of storage necessary for storing a character variable.

As you can see, 20 bytes of storage have been reserved, but only 5 have been used. Pascal provides a more efficient way of defining arrays that does not use unnecessary amounts of storage space. Instead of declaring a variable as an array, we can declare a variable as a **packed array.** Given this declaration, the computer then packs the data in consecutive bytes.

A **packed array** is an array that has had data placed in consecutive bytes.

Packed arrays can be used with any data type. However, it is not always wise to do so because it takes longer to access individual components of a packed array than it does to access individual components of an array that has not been declared as packed. Storage space is saved, but time may be lost. For more information on using arrays that are packed and arrays that are not packed **(unpacked arrays),** see Appendix 8.

An **unpacked array** is an array in which data are not in consecutive bytes.

Now let's consider the declaration

```
TYPE
  String5 = PACKED ARRAY [1..5] OF char;
VAR
  Examine : String5;
```

and the assignment of the word "HELLO" as before. Using a packed array, we then have the following in memory.

Examine

H	E	L	L	O			

Notice that less than two words (5 bytes) are used to store what previously required five words (20 bytes). We can still access the individual components as before. For example,

```
writeln (Examine[2]);
```

produces

```
E
```

as a line of output.

Character Strings

Every programming language needs to be able to handle character data. Names, words, phrases, and sentences are frequently used as part of some information that must be analyzed. In standard Pascal, character strings are formed by declaring packed arrays of character variables. For example, if the first 20 spaces of an input line are reserved for a customer's name, an appropriate character string could be declared by

```
TYPE
  String20 = PACKED ARRAY [1..20] OF char;
VAR
  Name : String20;
```

If the line of input is

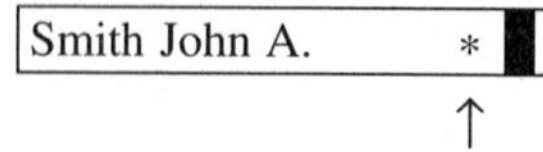

position 21

we could read the name into the packed array by the code

```
FOR J := 1 TO 20 DO
  read (DataFile, Name[J]);
```

Now when we refer to the array Name, we can envision the string

```
'Smith John A.'
```

But since we declared a fixed-length string, the actual string is

```
'Smith John A.       '
```

There are at least three important uses for string variables.

1. String variables of the same length can be compared (Boolean values); this permits alphabetizing.
2. String variables can be written using a single **write** or **writeln** statement; they cannot be read using a single **read** statement.
3. A single assignment statement can assign text to a string variable.

Let's examine each use individually.

Comparing String Variables

Strings of the same length can be compared using the standard relational operators: "=, <, >, <>, <=, and >=." For example, if 'Smith' and 'Jones' are strings, then 'Smith' < 'Jones', 'Smith' <> 'Jones', and so on are all valid Boolean expressions. The Boolean value is determined by the collating sequence. Using the collating sequence for the ASCII character set, the following comparisons yield the indicated values.

Comparison	Boolean Value
'Smith' < 'Jones'	**false**
'Jake' < 'John'	**true**
'ABC' = 'ABA'	**false**
'Smith Doug' < 'Smith John'	**true**

But what happens if we want to evaluate 'William Joe' < 'Williams Bo'? Since a character-by-character comparison is implemented by the computer, no decision is made until the blank following the *m* of William is compared to the *s* of Williams. Using the full ASCII character code, this Boolean expression is **true,** which is how these strings are alphabetized.

Writing String Variables

Recall the declaration

```
TYPE
  String20 = PACKED ARRAY [1..20] OF char;
VAR
  Name : String20;
```

When data are read from an input file, a loop is used to get the data one character at a time.

```
FOR J := 1 TO 20 DO
  read (DataFile, Name[J]);
```

If we now want to write the string Name, we can use a single **write** or **writeln** statement, such as

```
writeln (Name);
```

It is not necessary to print a string that contains a separate reference to each character.

Assigning Text to a String

The third feature of string variables is that a single assignment can be used to assign text to a string. If Name is a string of length 20, then

```
Name := 'Smith John A.       ';
```

is a valid statement. Note that there must be exactly 20 characters in the text string in order for this assignment to be valid. The statements

```
Name := 'Smith John A.';
Name := 'Theodore Allen Washington';
```

are both invalid because the text strings are not exactly 20 characters long.

Some standard problems will be encountered when trying to read data into a packed array. First, assume we have to read a line of data that consists of a company name. Further, assume we do not know the length of the name. The input line could be

```
Prudent Investors Company
```

or

```
Com Mfg. Co.
```

If we know the company name will be no more than 30 characters long, we can declare a fixed-length array in the following manner:

```
CONST
  MaxLength = 30;
TYPE
  String30 = PACKED ARRAY [1..MaxLength] OF char;
VAR
  CompanyName : String30;
```

The name can then be read by the following segment of code:

```
FOR J := 1 TO MaxLength DO
  IF NOT eoln(CompanyFile) THEN
    read (CompanyFile, CompanyName[J])
  ELSE
    CompanyName[J] := ' ';
readln (CompanyFile);  {  Advance the pointer  }
```

This will read the name and then fill the array with blanks to the desired length. Applied to the two data lines just mentioned, this segment of code would produce the following character strings:

```
'Prudent Investors Company     '
'Com Mfg. Co.                  '
```

Second, we may want to read data from an input file in which a field of fixed length is used for some character data. For example, suppose the first 30 spaces of an input line are reserved for the company name and that some other information is also to appear on the same line. We could have

```
Prudent Investors Company     1905 South Drive
                              ↑
                           column 31
```

These data could be accessed by the loop

```
FOR J := 1 TO 30 DO
  read (CompanyFile, CompanyName[J]);
```

Although the second format for an input file is easier to use, it is sometimes difficult to obtain data in such a precise manner. Hence, we must be able to read data both ways.

Strings in a Program

We are now ready to write a short program using packed arrays. Suppose we want to get two names from a data file, arrange them alphabetically, and then print the alphabetized list. Assume the names are in a field of fixed length 25 on two adjacent lines. A first-level pseudocode development is

1. Get the data (**PROCEDURE** GetData)
2. Arrange alphabetically (**PROCEDURE** Alphabetize)
3. Print the data (**PROCEDURE** PrintData)

A procedure to get one line of data is

```
PROCEDURE GetData (VAR Name : NameString);
  VAR
    J : integer;
```

```
    BEGIN
      FOR J := 1 to MaxLength DO
        read (DataFile, Name[J]);
      readln (DataFile)  {  Advance the pointer  }
    END;  {  of PROCEDURE GetData  }
```

After the two names have been read from the input file, they can be arranged alphabetically by

```
  PROCEDURE Alphabetize (VAR Name1, Name2 : NameString);
    VAR
      Temp : NameString;
    BEGIN
      IF Name2 < Name1 THEN
        BEGIN  {  Exchange when necessary  }
          Temp := Name1;
          Name1 := Name2;
          Name2 := Temp
        END  {  of IF...THEN  }
    END;  {  of PROCEDURE Alphabetize  }
```

The procedure for printing the name should include some header and some formatting of the names. For example, suppose you want to say

```
  The alphabetized list is below.
  --- ------------ ---- -- -----
```

and then print the list indented 10 spaces after skipping a line. A procedure to do this is

```
  PROCEDURE PrintData (Name1, Name2 : NameString);
    BEGIN
      writeln;
      writeln (Skip:10, 'The alphabetized list is below.');
      writeln (Skip:10, '--- ------------ ---- -- -----');
      writeln;
      writeln (Skip:20, Name1);
      writeln (Skip:20, Name2)
    END;  {  of PROCEDURE PrintData  }
```

We can now write the complete program.

```
PROGRAM SampleNames (input, output, DataFile);

CONST
  Skip = ' ';
  MaxLength = 25;

TYPE
  NameString = PACKED ARRAY [1..MaxLength] OF char;

VAR
  Name1, Name2 : NameString;
  DataFile : text;

{*****************************************************************}
```

```
PROCEDURE GetData (VAR Name : NameString);

  {  Given:   Nothing                                          }
  {  Task:    Read a name from the data file                   }
  {  Return:  One name (string of MaxLength characters)        }

  VAR
    J : integer;
  BEGIN
    FOR J := 1 TO MaxLength DO
      read (DataFile, Name[J]);
    readln (DataFile)  {  Advance the pointer  }
  END;  {  of PROCEDURE GetData  }

{*************************************************************}

PROCEDURE Alphabetize  (VAR Name1, Name2 : NameString);

  {  Given:   Two names                                        }
  {  Task:    Sort the names alphabetically                    }
  {  Return:  The names in sorted order                        }

  VAR
    Temp : NameString;
  BEGIN
    IF Name2 < Name1 THEN
      BEGIN                         {  Exchange when necessary  }
        Temp := Name1;
        Name1 := Name2;
        Name2 := Temp
      END  {  of IF...THEN  }
  END;  {  of PROCEDURE Alphabetize  }

{*************************************************************}

PROCEDURE PrintData (Name1, Name2 : NameString);

  {  Given:   Names in alphabetical order                      }
  {  Task:    Print the names                                  }
  {  Return:  Nothing                                          }

  BEGIN
    writeln;
    writeln (Skip:10, 'The alphabetized list is below.');
    writeln (Skip:10, '--- ------------ ---- -- ------');
    writeln;
    writeln (Skip:20, Name1);
    writeln (Skip:20, Name2)
  END;  {  of PROCEDURE PrintData  }

{*************************************************************}

BEGIN  {  Main program  }
  reset (DataFile);
  GetData (Name1);
```

```
  GetData (Name2);
  Alphabetize (Name1, Name2);
  PrintData (Name1, Name2)
END.  {  of main program  }
```

Exercises 10.5

For Exercises 1–6, indicate which string comparisons are valid. For those that are, indicate whether they are **true** or **false** using the full ASCII character set.

*1. `'Mathematics' <> 'CompScience'`

2. `'Jefferson' < 'Jeffersonian'`

*3. `'Smith Karen' < 'Smithsonian'`

4. `'#45' <= '$45'`

*5. `'Hoof in mouth' = 'Foot in door'`

6. `'453012' > '200000'`

*7. Write a test program that allows you to examine the Boolean expression

```
'William Joe' < 'Williams Bo'
```

For Exercises 8–11, suppose Message is declared as

```
TYPE
  String50 = PACKED ARRAY [1..50] OF char;
VAR
  Message : String50;
```

and the input file consists of the line

```
To err is human. Computers do not forgive.
```

What output is produced by each segment?

8.
```
FOR J := 1 TO 50 DO
  IF NOT eoln(Data) THEN
    read (Data, Message[J])
  ELSE
    Message[J] := ' ';
writeln (Message);
```

*9.
```
FOR J := 1 TO 50 DO
  IF NOT eoln(Data) THEN
    read (Data, Message[J])
  ELSE
    Message[J] := ' ';
Count := 0;
FOR J := 1 TO 50 DO
  IF Message[J] = ' ' THEN
    Count := Count + 1;
writeln (Message);
writeln ('There are', Count:3, 'blanks,':8);
```

10.
```
FOR J := 1 TO 20 DO
  read (Data, Message[2+J]);
FOR J := 21 TO 40 DO
  Message[J] := ' ';
```

```
FOR J := 41 TO 50 DO
  Message[J] := '*';
writeln (Message);
```

*11.
```
FOR J := 1 TO 50 DO
  IF NOT eoln(Data) THEN
    read (Data, Message[J])
  ELSE
    Message[J] := ' ';
writeln (Message);
FOR J := 50 DOWNTO 1 DO
  write (Message[J]);
```

For Exercises 12–15, assume the following declarations:

```
TYPE
  String10 = PACKED ARRAY [1..10] OF char;
  String20 = PACKED ARRAY [1..20] OF char;
VAR
  A, B : String10;
  C : String20;
```

Indicate if the expression is valid or invalid.

12. `A := B;`

*13. `C := A + B;`

14.
```
FOR J := 1 TO 20 DO
  C[J] := A[J] + B[J];
```

*15.
```
FOR J := 1 TO 20 DO
  IF J <= 10 THEN
    A[J] := C[J]
  ELSE
    B[J-10] := C[J];
```

16. Using the declarations given for Exercises 12–15, write a segment of code that will make the string C consist of the strings A and B where the lesser (alphabetically) of A and B is the first half of C.

*17. Assume a packed array Message of length 100 has been declared and data have been read into it from an input file. Write a segment of code to count the number of occurrences of the letter *M* in the string Message.

18. Write a test program to see what happens if you try to read in an entire packed array with one **read** or **readln** statement.

10.6 Searching Algorithms

Objectives

- to be able to use a sequential search to find the first occurrence of a value

The need to search an array for a value is a common problem. For example, you might wish to replace a test score for a student, delete a name from a directory or mailing list, or upgrade the pay scale for certain employees. These and other problems require you to be able to examine elements in some list until the desired value is located. When it is found, some action is taken. In this section, we assume all lists are nonempty.

Sequential Search

The first searching algorithm we examine is the most common method, a **sequential (linear) search.** This process is accomplished by examining the first

Objectives

(continued)

- to be able to use a sequential search to find all occurrences of a value
- to be able to use a binary search to find a value
- to understand the relative efficiency of a binary search compared to a sequential search

A **sequential (linear) search** is the process of examining the first element in a list and proceeding to examine the elements in order until a match is found.

element in some list and then proceeding to examine the elements in the order in which they appear until a match is found. Variations of this basic process include searching a sorted list for the first occurrence of a value, searching a sorted list for all occurrences of a value, and searching an unsorted list for the first occurrence of a value.

To illustrate a sequential search, suppose we have an array A of integers and we want to find the first occurrence of some particular value (Num). If the desired value is located as we search the array, its position is printed. If the value is not in the array, an appropriate message should be printed. The code for such a search is

```
Index := 1;
WHILE (Num <> A[Index]) AND (Index < Length) DO
  Index := Index + 1;
```

This can be written as a procedure. For example, **PROCEDURE** Search, which searches for the desired number, follows:

```
PROCEDURE Search  (VAR A : NumList;
                   Num, Length : integer;
                   VAR Index : integer;
                   VAR Found : boolean);

  {  Given :   An array A; a number Num to search for;  }
  {                the array length Length; and a        }
  {                boolean flag Found                    }
  {  Task:     Search the array for the first            }
  {                occurrence of Num; Found should       }
  {                indicate whether or not a match       }
  {                is found                              }
  {  Return:   The index of the number being searched    }
  {                for; a boolean value indicating       }
  {                whether or not the number has         }
  {                been located                          }

  VAR
    Index : integer;
  BEGIN
    Found := false;
    Index := 1;
    WHILE (Num <> A[Index]) AND (Index < Length) DO
      Index := Index + 1;
    IF Num = A[Index] THEN
      Found := true
  END;  {  of PROCEDURE Search  }
```

This procedure can be called by

```
Search (List, Num, Length, Index, Found);
```

Code for a reasonable message is

```
IF Found THEN
  writeln (Num, ' is in position', Index:5)
ELSE
  writeln (Num, ' is not in the list.')
```

Now let's consider some variations of this problem. Our code works for both a sorted and an unsorted list. However, if we are searching a sorted list, the algorithm can be improved. For example, if the array components are sorted from low to high, we need to continue the search only until the value in an array component exceeds the value of Num. At that point, there is no need to examine the remaining components. The only change required in the loop for searching is to replace

```
Num <> A[Index]
```

with

```
Num > A[Index]
```

Thus, we have

```
Index := 1;
WHILE (Num > A[Index]) AND (Index < Length) DO
  Index := Index + 1;
```

A relatively easy modification of the sequential search is to examine a list for all occurrences of some value. If searching an array, you would generally print the positions and values when a match is found. To illustrate, if A is an array of integers and Num has an integer value, we can search A for the number of occurrences of Num by

```
Count := 0;
FOR Index := 1 TO Length DO
  IF Num = A[Index] THEN
    BEGIN
      Count := Count + 1;
      writeln (Num, ' is in position', Index:5)
    END;
```

This code works for an unsorted list. A modification of the code for working with a sorted list is included as an exercise.

Binary Search

Searching relatively small lists sequentially does not require much computer time. However, when the lists get longer (as, for example, telephone directories and lists of credit card customers), sequential searches are inefficient. In a sense, they correspond to looking up a word in the dictionary by starting at the first word and proceeding word by word until the desired word is found. Since extra computer time means considerably extra expense for most companies where large amounts of data must be frequently searched, a more efficient way of searching is needed.

A **binary search** is the process of examining a middle value of a sorted array to see which half contains the value in question and halving until the value is located.

If the list has been sorted, it can be searched for a particular value by a method referred to as a binary search. Essentially, a **binary search** consists of examining a middle value of an array to see which half contains the desired value. The middle value of this half is then examined to see which half of the half contains the value in question. This halving process is continued until the value is located or it is determined that the value is not in the list. (Remember, in order to use a binary search, the list must be sorted. This sorting process has its own costs, which should be evaluated, but this subject is outside the scope of this text.)

The code for this process is relatively short. If A is the array to be searched for Num, and First, Mid, and Last are integer variables such that First contains the index of the first possible position to be searched and Last contains the index of the last possible position, the code for a list in ascending order is

```
Found := false;
WHILE NOT Found AND (First <= Last) DO
  BEGIN
    Mid := (First + Last) DIV 2;
    IF Num < A[Mid] THEN
      Last := Mid - 1
```

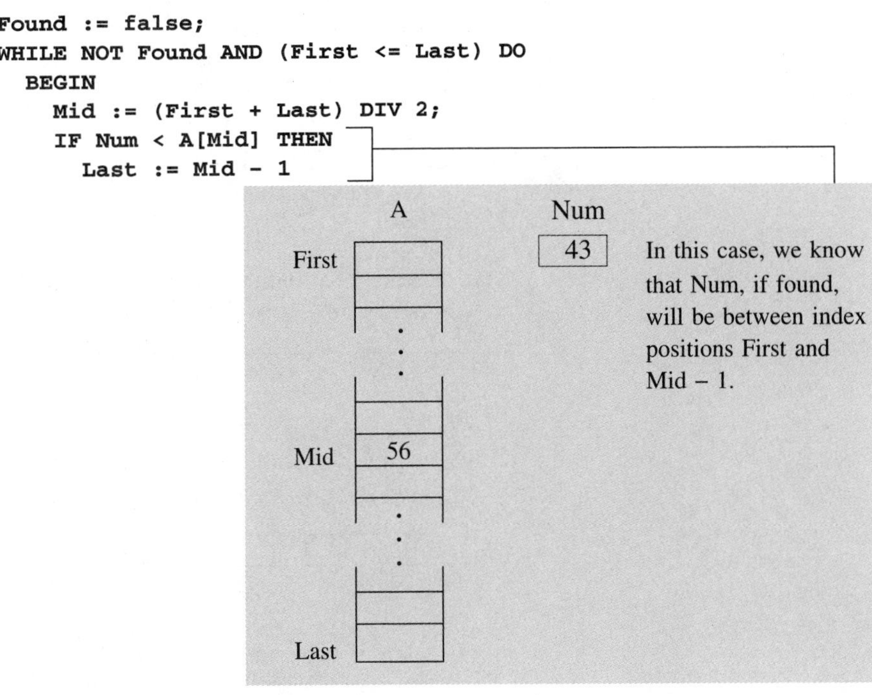
A
Num
First
43
In this case, we know that Num, if found, will be between index positions First and Mid – 1.
Mid
56
Last

```
    ELSE IF Num > A[Mid] THEN
      First := Mid + 1
    ELSE
      Found := true
  END;
```

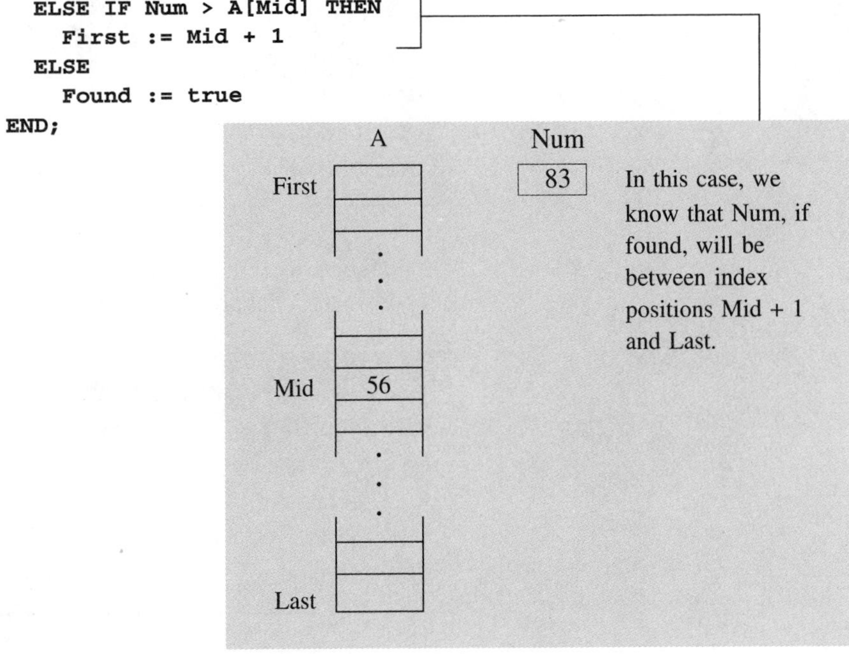
A
Num
First
83
In this case, we know that Num, if found, will be between index positions Mid + 1 and Last.
Mid
56
Last

When this loop is executed, it is exited when the value is located or it is determined that the value is not in the list. Depending on what is to be done with the value being searched for, we can modify action at the bottom of the loop or use the values in Found and Mid outside the loop. For example, if we just want to know where the value is, we can change

```
Found := true
```

to

```
BEGIN
  Found := true;
  writeln (Num, ' is in position', Mid:5)
END;
```

Before continuing, let's walk through this search to better understand how it works. Assume A is the array

4	7	19	25	36	37	50	100	101	205	220	271	306	321

A[1] A[14]

with values as indicated. Furthermore, assume Num contains the value 25. Then initially, First, Last, and Num have the values

First	Last	Num
1	14	25

A listing of values by each pass through the loop produces

	First	Last	Mid	A[Mid]	Found
Before loop	1	14	Undefined	Undefined	**false**
After first pass	1	6	7	50	**false**
After second pass	4	6	3	19	**false**
After third pass	4	4	5	36	**false**
After fourth pass	4	4	4	25	**true**

To illustrate what happens when the value being looked for is not in the array, suppose Num contains 210. The listing of values then produces

	First	Last	Mid	A[Mid]	Found
Before loop	1	14	Undefined	Undefined	**false**
After first pass	8	14	7	50	**false**
After second pass	8	10	11	220	**false**
After third pass	10	10	9	101	**false**
After fourth pass	11	10	10	205	**false**

At this stage, First > Last and the loop is exited.

Inserting and Deleting in a Sorted Array

Arrays are typically searched because we want to either insert an element into the array or delete an element from the array. To illustrate, let's consider array A

2	5	8	10	10	12	15	18	21	30
A[1]	A[2]								A[10]

If we remove element 12 from the array, we end up with

2	5	8	10	10	15	18	21	30
A[1]	A[2]							A[9]

Note that 12 has been deleted from the array and each element listed "after" 12 in the array has been "advanced" one position.

To illustrate what happens when an element is to be inserted into an array, again consider array A

2	5	8	10	10	12	15	18	21	30
A[1]	A[2]								A[10]

If we want to insert 17 into the sorted array, we first determine that it belongs between 15 and 18. We then reassign elements 18, 21, and 30 to produce

2	5	8	10	10	12	15		18	21	30
A[1]	A[2]						↑ 17 goes here			A[11]

The number 17 is then assigned to the appropriate array component to produce the array

2	5	8	10	10	12	15	17	18	21	30
A[1]	A[2]									A[11]

Writing the code for inserting and deleting elements in a sorted array is deferred to the exercises at the end of this section.

Relative Efficiency of Searches

Now let's examine briefly the efficiency of a binary search compared to a sequential search. For purposes of this discussion, assume that a sequential search on a list of 15 items requires at most 15 microseconds. The nature of a sequential search is such that every time the list length is doubled, the maximum searching time is also doubled. Figure 10.1 illustrates this increase.

Next, assume that a list of 15 items requires a maximum of 60 microseconds when searched by a binary search. Since this process consists of successively halving the list, at most four passes will be required to locate the value. This means each pass uses 15 microseconds. When the list length is doubled, it requires only one more pass. Thus, a list of 30 items requires 75 microseconds and a list of 60 items requires 90 microseconds. This is shown graphically in Figure 10.2. The comparison of these sequential and binary searches is shown on the same graph in Figure 10.3.

◆ Figure 10.1

Sequential search

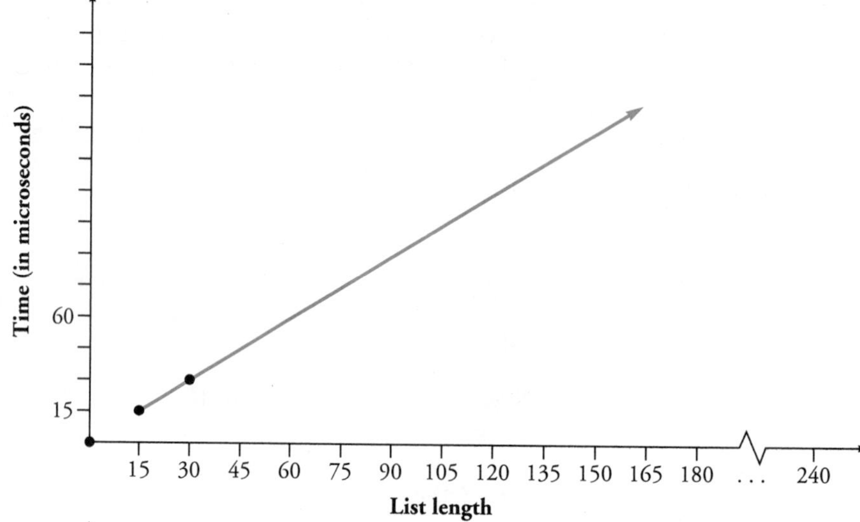

◆ Figure 10.2

Binary search

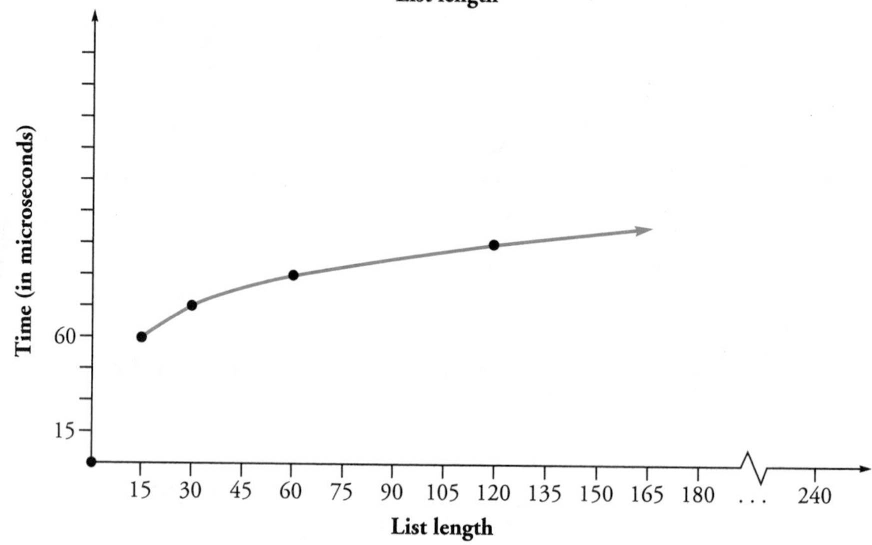

◆ Figure 10.3

Sequential search versus binary search

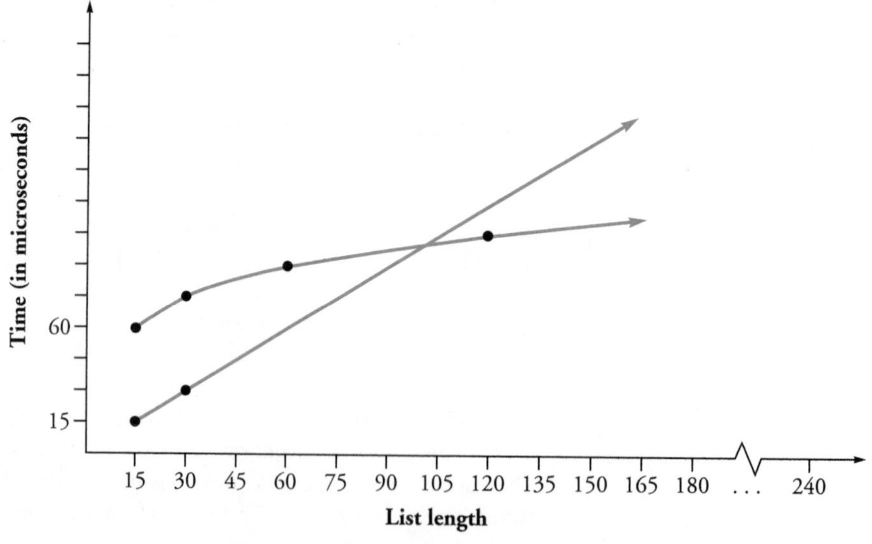

Exercises 10.6

*1. Write a sequential search using a **FOR** loop to locate and print all occurrences of the same value.

2. Discuss whether or not **PROCEDURE** Search can be rewritten as a function.

*3. Modify the sequential search by putting a counter in the loop to count how many passes are made when searching a sorted array for a value. Write and run a program that uses this version on lists of length 15, 30, 60, 120, and 240. In each case, search for a value that is
   a. In the first half.
   b. In the second half.
   c. Not there.

   Plot your results on a graph.

4. Repeat Exercise 3 for a binary search.

5. Suppose the array A is

18	25	37	92	104

A[1] A[5]

   Trace the values using a binary search to look for
   *a. 18
   b. 92
   *c. 76

For Exercises 6–9, suppose a sorted list of social security numbers is in secondary storage in a file named StudentNum.

6. Show how this file can be searched for a certain number using a sequential search.

7. Show how this file can be searched for a certain number using a binary search.

8. Show how a binary search can be used to indicate where a new number can be inserted in proper order.

*9. Show how a number can be deleted from the file.

10. Write a procedure to read text from a data file and determine the number of occurrences of each vowel.

11. Using a binary search on an array of length 35, what is the maximum number of passes through the loop that can be made when searching for a value?

12. Using worst-case possibilities of 3 microseconds for a sequential search of a list of 10 items and 25 microseconds for a binary search of the same list, construct a graph illustrating relative efficiency for these two methods applied to lists of longer lengths.

13. Modify the sequential search that you developed in Exercise 1 to list all occurrences of a value so that it can be used on a sorted list; that is, have it stop after the desired value has been passed in the list.

14. Discuss methods that can be used to design programs to guard against searching empty lists.

15. Write a procedure to
   a. Insert an element into a sorted array.
   b. Delete an element from a sorted array.

16. The length of a string is the number of positions from the first nonblank character to the last nonblank character. Thus, the packed array

T	h	i	s		i	s		a		s	t	r	i	n	g	.													

would have a length of 17. Write a function that receives a packed array of type [1 . . 30] of **char** and returns the length of the string.

17. Write a procedure to search a sorted list and remove all duplicates.

Focus on Program Design: Case Study

Sorting an Array

The sample program for this chapter features the use of arrays and subprograms. Since sorting an array is a common practice, it has been included as part of the program. Specifically, suppose the Home Sales Realty Company, Inc., wants to print a list containing the amount of all sales for a month. Each sale amount is recorded on a separate line of input and the number of homes sold is less than 20. Write a program to do the following:

1. Read the data from the input file.
2. Print the data in the order in which it is read with a suitable header and format.
3. Print a sorted list (high to low) of sales with a suitable header and formatting.
4. Print the total number of sales for the month, the total amount of sales, the average sale price, and the company commission (7 percent).

Sample data would be

```
 85000
 76234
115100
 98200
121750
 76700
```

where each line represents the sale price of a home. Typical output would include an unsorted list of sales, a sorted list of sales, and appropriate summary data.

A first-level pseudocode development is

1. Get data (**PROCEDURE** GetData)
2. Print header (**PROCEDURE** PrintHeading1)
3. Print unsorted list (**PROCEDURE** PrintList)
4. Sort list (**PROCEDURE** Sort)
5. Print header (**PROCEDURE** PrintHeading2)
6. Print sorted list (**PROCEDURE** PrintList)
7. Compute data (**FUNCTION** Total and **PROCEDURE** Compute)
8. Print results (**PROCEDURE** PrintResults)

Notice that **PROCEDURE** PrintList is called twice and **PROCEDURE** PrintResults includes output for total number of sales, total amount of sales, average sale price, and company commission, all printed with suitable headings.

A structure chart for the program is given in Figure 10.4.

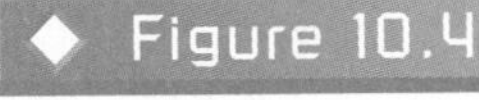

Structure chart for Home Sales Realty Company, Inc., program

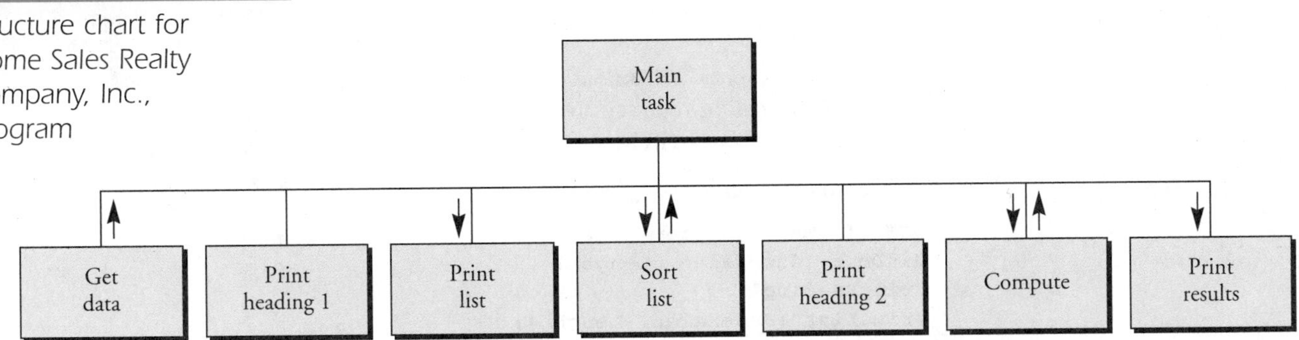

Module specifications for the main modules are

1. GetData Module
   Data received: None
   Information returned: Sales for a month
   Number of sales
   Logic: Use a **WHILE** loop to read entries into an array.
2. PrintHeading1 Module
   Data received: None
   Information returned: None
   Logic: Use **writeln** statements to print a suitable heading for an unsorted list.
3. PrintList Module
   Data received: Array of sales with number of sales
   Information returned: None
   Logic: Use a **FOR** loop with the array length as a loop control variable to print the list of sales for a month.
4. Sort Module
   Data received: Unsorted array of sales
   Number of sales
   Information returned: Sorted array of sales
   Logic: Use a selection sort to sort the array.
5. PrintHeading2 Module
   Data received: None
   Information returned: None
   Logic: Use **writeln** statements to print a suitable heading for the sorted list.
6. Compute Module
   Data received: Array of sales with number of sales
   Information returned: Total sales
   Average sale
   Company commission
   Logic: Use a function to compute the total sales.
   Use a procedure to compute the average sale.
   Compute company commission by using a defined constant, CommissionRate.

7. <u>PrintResults Module</u>
   Data received: Number of sales
   Total sales
   Average sales
   Company commission
   Information returned: None
   Logic: Use **writeln** statements to print a summary report.

The main program is

```
BEGIN  {  Main program  }
  GetData (JuneSales, Length);
  PrintHeading1;
  PrintList (JuneSales, Length);
  Sort (JuneSales, Length);
  PrintHeading2;
  PrintList (JuneSales, Length);
  Compute (TotalSales, AverageSale, CompanyCom, JuneSales, Length);
  PrintResults (TotalSales, AverageSale, CompanyCom, Length)
END.  {  of main program  }
```

The complete program for this problem is

```
PROGRAM MonthlyList (input, output, SalesData);

{  This program illustrates the use of arrays with procedures    }
{  and  functions.  Note the  use of both  value and variable    }
{  parameters.  Also note  that a procedure  is  used to sort    }
{  the array.                                                    }

CONST
  Skip = ' ';
  CommissionRate = 0.07;
  MaxLength = 20;

TYPE
  List = ARRAY [1..MaxLength] OF real;

VAR
  JuneSales : List;              {  Number of June sales          }
  TotalSales,                    {  Total of June sales           }
  AverageSale,                   {  Amount of average sale        }
  CompanyCom : real;             {  Commission for the company    }
  Length : integer;              {  Array length of values        }
  SalesData : text;              {  Data in text file             }

{*************************************************************}

PROCEDURE GetData (VAR JuneSales : List;
                   VAR Length : integer);

  {  Given:   Nothing                                       }
  {  Task:    Read selling prices into array JuneSales      }
  {  Return:  Array of JuneSales and array length           }   1

  BEGIN
    Length := 0;
```

```
    reset (SalesData);
    WHILE NOT eof(SalesData) AND (Length < MaxLength) DO
      BEGIN
        Length := Length + 1;
        readln (SalesData, JuneSales[Length])
      END  {  of WHILE NOT eof  }
  END;  {  of PROCEDURE GetData  }

{*****************************************************************}

PROCEDURE PrintHeading1;

  {  Given:   Nothing                                              }
  {  Task:    Print a heading for the unsorted list of sales       }
  {  Return:  Nothing                                              }
                                                                      2
  BEGIN
    writeln ('An unsorted list of sales for the');
    writeln ('month of June is as follows:');
    writeln ('---------------------------------');
    writeln
  END;  {  of PROCEDURE PrintHeading1  }

{*****************************************************************}

PROCEDURE PrintList (JuneSales : List;
                     Length : integer);

  {  Given:   An unsorted array (with length) of Sales for June  }
  {  Task:    Print the list                                     }
  {  Return:  Nothing                                            }
                                                                      3
  VAR
    J : integer;
  BEGIN
    FOR J := 1 TO Length DO
      writeln (Skip:4, '<', J:2, '>', '$':2, JuneSales[J]:11:2)
  END;  {  of PROCEDURE PrintList  }

{*****************************************************************}

PROCEDURE Swap (VAR Num1, Num2 : real);

  {  Given:   Two reals in Num1 and Num2                         }
  {  Task:    Interchange their values                           }
  {  Return:  Interchanged values                                }

  VAR
    Temp : real;
  BEGIN
    Temp := Num1;
    Num1 := Num2;
    Num2 := Temp
  END;  {  of PROCEDURE Swap  }

{*****************************************************************}
```

```
PROCEDURE Sort (VAR JuneSales : List;
                Length : integer);

  {  Given:   An unsorted array (with length) of sales for June  }
  {  Task:    Use a selection sort to sort the list              }
  {  Return:  A sorted list of sales for June                    }

  VAR
    J, K, Index : integer;
    Temp : real;
  BEGIN                                                              4
    FOR J := 1 TO Length - 1 DO
      BEGIN
        Index := J;
        FOR K := J + 1 TO Length DO
          IF JuneSales[K] > JuneSales[Index] THEN
            Index := K;
        IF Index <> J THEN
          Swap (JuneSales[Index], JuneSales[J])
      END  {  of FOR J loop  }
  END;  {  of PROCEDURE Sort  }

{***************************************************************}

PROCEDURE PrintHeading2;

  {  Given:   Nothing                                            }
  {  Task:    Print a heading for the sorted list of sales       }
  {  Return:  Nothing                                            }

  BEGIN                                                              5
    writeln;
    writeln ('Sales for the month of June');
    writeln ('sorted from high to low are:');
    writeln ('----------------------------');
    writeln
  END;  {  of PROCEDURE PrintHeading2  }

{***************************************************************}

FUNCTION Total (JuneSales : List;
                Length : integer) : real;

  {  Given:   An array (with length) of June sales               }
  {  Task:    Sum the array components                           }
  {  Return:  Total of sales for June                            }

  VAR   J : integer;
    Sum : real;                                                      6
  BEGIN
    Sum := 0;
    FOR J := 1 TO Length DO
      Sum := Sum + JuneSales[J];
    Total := Sum
  END;  {  of FUNCTION Total  }

{***************************************************************}
```

```
PROCEDURE Compute (VAR TotalSales, AverageSale, CompanyCom : real;
                   VAR JuneSales : List;
                   Length : integer);

  {  Given:   An array (with length) of June sales                }
  {  Task:    Compute TotalSales, AverageSale, and CompanyCom     }
  {                for the month of June                          }
  {  Return:  TotalSales, AverageSale, and CompanyCom             }

  BEGIN
    TotalSales := Total(JuneSales, Length);
    AverageSale := TotalSales / Length;
    CompanyCom := TotalSales * CommissionRate
  END;  {  of PROCEDURE Compute  }

{*****************************************************************}

PROCEDURE PrintResults (TotalSales, AverageSale, CompanyCom : real;
                        Length : integer);

  {  Given:   TotalSales, AverageSale, CompanyCom, and number     }
  {               of sales (Length) for June                      }
  {  Task:    Print summary information for the month             }
  {  Return:  Nothing                                             }

  BEGIN
    writeln;                                                          7
    writeln ('There were', Length:2, ' sales during June.');
    writeln;
    writeln ('The total sales were', '$':2, TotalSales:12:2);
    writeln;
    writeln ('The average sale was', '$':2, AverageSale:12:2);
    writeln;
    writeln ('The company commission was', '$':2,
             CompanyCom:12:2);
    writeln
  END;  {  of PROCEDURE PrintResults  }

{*****************************************************************}

BEGIN  {  Main program  }
  GetData (JuneSales, Length);
  PrintHeading1;
  PrintList (JuneSales, Length);
  Sort (JuneSales, Length);
  PrintHeading2;
  PrintList (JuneSales, Length);
  Compute (TotalSales, AverageSale, CompanyCom, JuneSales, Length);
  PrintResults (TotalSales, AverageSale, CompanyCom, Length)
END.  {  of main program  }
```

The output for this program is

```
An unsorted list of sales for the
month of June is as follows:
```

```
--------------------------------

    < 1> $   85000.00
    < 2> $   76234.00
    < 3> $  115100.00
    < 4> $   98200.00
    < 5> $  121750.00
    < 6> $   76700.00

Sales for the month of June
sorted from high to low are:
----------------------------

    < 1> $  121750.00
    < 2> $  115100.00
    < 3> $   98200.00
    < 4> $   85000.00
    < 5> $   76700.00
    < 6> $   76234.00

There were 6 sales during June.

The total sales were $   572984.00

The average sale was $    95497.33

The company commission was $    40108.88
```

Running and Debugging Hints

1. Be careful not to misuse type identifiers. For example, in

```
TYPE
  String = PACKED ARRAY [1..10] OF char;
VAR
  Word : String;
```

String is a data type; hence, a reference such as String := 'First name' is incorrect.

2. Do not attempt to use a subscript that is out of range. Suppose we have

```
VAR
  List : ARRAY [1..6] OF integer;
```

An inadvertent reference such as

```
FOR J := 1 TO 10 DO
  writeln (List[J]);
```

(continued)

may produce an error message indicating that the subscript is out of range.

3. Counters are frequently used with loops and arrays. Be careful to make the final value the correct value. For example,

```
Count := 1;
WHILE NOT eof(<file name>) DO
  BEGIN
    readln (<file name>, A[Count]);
    Count := Count + 1
  END;
```

used on the data file

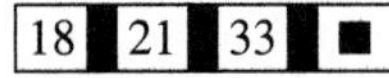

will have a value of 4 in Count when this loop is exited. This could be corrected by rewriting the segment as

```
Count := 0;
WHILE NOT eof(<file name>) DO
  BEGIN
    Count := Count + 1;
    readln (<file name>, A[Count])
  END;
```

4. Comparing array components can lead to errors in using subscripts. Two common misuses are
   a. Attempting to compare A[J] to A[J + 1]. If this does not stop at array length – 1, then J + 1 will be out of range.
   b. Attempting to compare A[J – 1] to A[J]. This presents the same problem at the beginning of an array. Remember, J – 1 cannot have a value less than the initial index value.

5. Make sure the array index is correctly initialized. For example,

```
J := 0;
WHILE NOT eof(<file name>) DO
  BEGIN
    J := J + 1;
    readln (<file name>, A[J])
  END;
```

Note that the first value is then read into A[1].

(continued)

6. After using a sequential search, make sure you check to see if the value has been found. For example, if Num contains the value 3 and A is the array

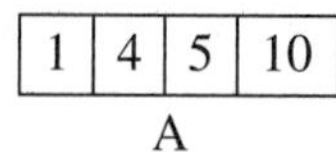

the search

```
Index := 1;
WHILE (Num <> A[Index]) AND (Index < Length) DO
  Index := Index + 1;
```

yields values

Depending on program use, you should check for Num = A [Index] or use a Boolean flag to indicate if a match has been found.

Summary

Key Terms

abstract data type (ADT)
array
binary search
byte
component (element) of an array
data abstraction
index (subscript)
index type
packed array
selection sort
sequential (linear) search
string data tape
unpacked array

Keywords

ARRAY
PACKED
string

Key Concepts

- An array is a structured variable; a single declaration can reserve several variables.
- It is good practice to define array types in the **TYPE** declaration section and then declare a variable of that type; for example,

```
CONST
  ListMax = 30;
TYPE
  NumList = ARRAY [1..ListMax] OF real;
VAR
  List : NumList
```

◆ Arrays can be visualized as lists; thus, the previous array could be envisioned as

```
List
+------+
|      |  1
+------+
|      |  2
+------+
|      |  3
+------+
|  .   |  .
|  .   |  .
|  .   |  .
+------+
|      |  30
+------+
```

◆ Each component of an array is a variable of the declared type and can be used the same as any other variable of that type.

◆ Loops can be used to read data into arrays; for example,

```
J := 0;
WHILE NOT eof(<file name>) AND (J < MaxLength) DO
  BEGIN
    J := J + 1;
    readln (<file name>, List[J])
  END;
```

◆ Loops can be used to print data from arrays; for example, if Score is an array of 20 test scores, they can be printed by

```
FOR J := 1 TO 20 DO
  writeln (Score[J]);
```

◆ Manipulating components of an array is generally accomplished by using the index as a loop variable; for example, assuming the previous Score, to find the smallest value in the array we can use

```
Small := Score[1];
FOR J := 2 TO 20 DO
  IF Score[J] < Small THEN
    Small := Score[J];
```

◆ A selection sort is one method of sorting elements in an array from high to low or low to high; for example, if A is an array of length *n,* a low-to-high sort is

```
FOR J := 1 TO N - 1 DO
  BEGIN
    Index := J;
    FOR K := J + 1 TO N DO
      IF A[K] < A[Index] THEN
        Index := K;
    IF Index <> J THEN
      BEGIN
        Temp := A[Index];
        A[Index]:= A[J];
        A[J]:= Temp
      END  {  of exchange  }
  END;  {  of selection sort  }
```

◆ When arrays are to be passed to subprograms, the type should be defined in the **TYPE** section; thus, we could have

```
TYPE
  List200 = ARRAY [1..200] OF real;

PROCEDURE Practice (X : List200);
```

- If the array being passed is a variable parameter, it should be declared accordingly; for example,

```
PROCEDURE GetData (VAR X : List200);
```

- Sorting arrays is conveniently done using procedures; such procedures facilitate program design.
- Data abstraction is the process of separating a conceptual definition of a data structure from its implementation details.
- An abstract data type (ADT) consists of a class of objects, a defined set of properties for these objects, and a set of operations for processing the objects.
- Character strings can be formed by declaring packed arrays of character variables to reduce the memory required for string storage and manipulation; a typical packed array declaration is

```
TYPE
  String20 = PACKED ARRAY [1..20] OF char;
VAR
  Name : String20;
```

- Character strings (packed arrays of characters) can be compared; this facilitates alphabetizing a list of names.
- Character strings can be printed using a single **write** or **writeln** statement; thus, if Name is a packed array of characters, it can be printed by

```
writeln (Name:30);
```

- Packed arrays of characters must still be read one character at a time.
- A single assignment statement can be used to assign a string to a packed array of the same length; for example,

```
Name := 'Smith John';
```

- A sequential search of a list consists of examining the first item in a list and then proceeding through the list in sequence until the desired value is found or the end of the list is reached; code for this search is

```
Index := 1;
WHILE (Num <> A[Index]) AND (Index < Length) DO
  Index := Index + 1;
```

- A binary search of a list consists of deciding which half of the list might contain the value in question and then which half of that half, and so on; code for this search is

```
Found := false;
WHILE NOT Found AND (First <= Last) DO
  BEGIN
    Mid := (First + Last) DIV 2;
    IF Num < A[Mid] THEN
      Last := Mid - 1
```

```
    ELSE IF Num > A[Mid] THEN
      First := Mid + 1
    ELSE
      Found := true
  END;
```

Chapter Review Exercises

Assume the following declarations are made:

```
VAR
  A : ARRAY [1..10] OF integer;
  B : ARRAY ['A'..'F'] OF char;
  C : ARRAY [1..5] OF real;
  X, Y : integer;
  Z : real;
```

Of Exercises 1–15, which are valid subscripted variables? Rewrite the variable declarations using type declarations.

1. `A[1]`
2. `B[1]`
3. `C[1]`
4. `C[1.0]`
5. `B['A']`
6. `B[A]`
7. `A[X+Y]`
8. `A[X MOD Y]`
9. `B[X+Y]`
10. `A[10]`
11. `C[10]`
12. `A(5)`
13. `A[X/Z]`
14. `C[0]`
15. `A[A[4]]`

For Exercises 16–21, assume the array A defined as in Exercises 1–15 contains the following values:

1	4	6	8	9	3	7	10	2	9

Indicate if the following are valid subscripts of A and, if so, find the value of the subscript. If invalid, explain why.

16. `A[2]`
17. `A[5]`
18. `A[A[2]]`
19. `A[4+7]`
20. `A[A[5] + A[2]]`
21. `A[pred(A[3])]`

For Exercises 22–26, write array declarations. Define the arrays as data types.

22. X, an array of **integer** with subscripts from 0 to 5.
23. Z, an array of **char** with subscripts from 1 to 10.
24. M, an array of **real** with subscripts from 5 to 10.
25. T, an array of **boolean** with subscripts from –5 to 5.
26. D, an array of **char** with subscripts from 'A' to 'Z'.

For Exercises 27–33, list the errors in the array declarations.

27. `C : ARRAY [1..10];`
28. `D : ARRAY [-5..5] OF boolean;`
29. `E = ARRAY [1..3] OF integer;`

30. `F : ARRAY [1.0..5.0] OF real;`
31. `G : ARRAY 1..10 [OF integer];`
32. `ARRAY [0..100] OF char;`
33. `H : ARRAY [10..1] OF integer;`
34. Write a segment of code to store the first 10 even positive numbers into subscripts 1 through 10 of the array Even.
35. Write a segment of code that reads 20 integers and then prints the numbers in reverse order from the way in which they were read.
36. Write a segment of code to perform a selection sort to put an array of 20 real numbers into ascending order.
37. Write a procedure that reads 20 characters from a data file called CharFile and returns these characters to the main program.
38. Write an appropriate call to the procedure in Exercise 37.
39. Rewrite the procedure in Exercise 37 to count the number of blanks read.
40. Declare a packed array to hold 20 characters. Write a procedure to read the characters and print the array contents.
41. What condition must be true before a binary search can be used on a list?
42. Write a function that counts the number of occurrences of the letter *A* in an array of 100 characters.
43. Write a sequential search that returns the position of the number 5 in an array of 20 integers.
44. Rewrite Exercise 43 using a binary search. Assume the list is sorted from low to high.

Programming Problems

1. Write a program to read an unknown number of integer test scores from an input file (assume at most 150 scores). Print the original list of scores, the scores sorted from low to high, the scores sorted from high to low, the highest score, the lowest score, and the average score.
2. Write a program to help you balance your checkbook. The input consists of the beginning balance and then a sequence of transactions, each followed by a transaction code. Deposits are followed by a D and withdrawals are followed by a W. The output should consist of a list of transactions, a running balance, an ending balance, the number of withdrawals, and the number of deposits. Include an appropriate message for overdrawn accounts.
3. Write a program to read a line of text as input. Print the original line of text, the line of text in reverse order, and the number of vowels contained in the line.
4. Write a program that sorts data of type **real** as they are read from the text file. Do this by putting the first data item in the first component of an array and then inserting each subsequent number in the array in order from high to low. Print the sorted array. Assume there are at most 25 numbers.
5. A palindrome is a word (or number) that is the same forward and backward. Write a program to read several lines of text as input. Inspect each word to see if it is a palindrome. The output should list all palindromes and a count of the number of palindromes in the message.
6. One of the problems faced by designers of word processors is that of printing text without separating a word at the end of a line. Write a program to read

several lines of text as input. Then print the message with each line starting in column 10 and no line exceeding column 70. No word should be separated at the end of a line.

7. Your local state university has to raise funds for an art center. As a first step, they are going to approach 20 previously identified donors and ask for additional donations. Because the donors wish to remain anonymous, only the respective totals of their previous donations are listed in a data file. After the donors are contacted, the additional donations are listed at the end of the data file in the same order as the first 20 entries. Write a computer program to read the first 20 entries into one array and the second 20 entries into a second array. Compute the previous total donations and the new donations for the art center. Print the following:
   a. The list of previous donations
   b. The list of new donations
   c. An unsorted list of total donations
   d. A sorted list of total donations
   e. Total donations before the fund drive
   f. Total donations for the art center
   g. The maximum donation for the art center

■ 8. Write a program that can be used as a text analyzer. Your program should be capable of reading a text file and keeping track of the frequency of occurrence of each letter of the alphabet. There should also be a count of all characters (including blanks) encountered that are not in the alphabet. Your output should be the data file printed line by line followed by a histogram reflecting the frequency of occurrence of each letter in the alphabet. For example, the following histogram indicates five occurrences of *a,* two of *b,* and three of *c.*

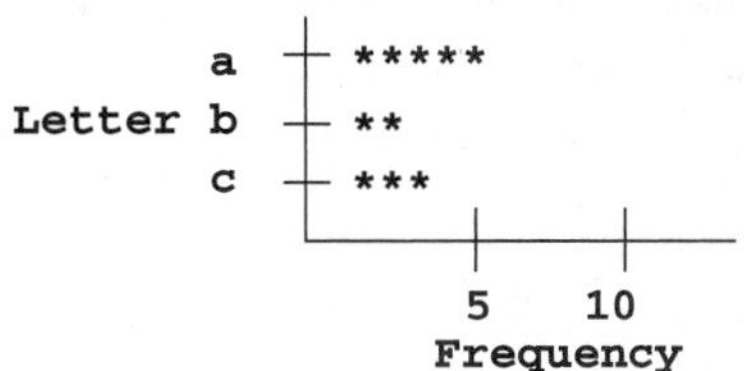

9. The Third Interdenominational Church has on file a list of all of its benefactors (a maximum of 20 names, each up to 30 characters) along with an unknown number of amounts that each has donated to the church. You have been asked to write a program that does the following:
   a. Print the name of each donor and the amount (in descending order) of any donations given by each.
   b. Print the total amounts in ascending order.
   c. Print the grand total of all donations.
   d. Print the largest single amount donated and the name of the benefactor who made this donation.

10. Read in a list of 50 integers from the data file NumberList. Place the even numbers into an array called Even, the odd numbers into an array called Odd, and the negatives into an array called Negative. Print all three arrays after all numbers have been read.

11. Read in 300 real numbers. Print the average of the numbers followed by all the numbers that are greater than the average.

12. Read in the names of five candidates in a class election and the number of votes received by each. Print the list of candidates, the number of votes they

received, and the percentage of the total vote they received sorted into order from the winner to the person with the fewest votes. Assume that all names are 20 characters in length.

13. In many sports events, contestants are rated by judges with an average score being determined by discarding the highest and lowest scores and averaging the remaining scores. Write a program in which eight scores are entered, computing the average score for the contestant.

14. Given a list of 20 test scores (integers), print the score that is nearest to the average.

15. The Game of Nim is played with three piles of stones. There are three stones in the first pile, five stones in the second, and eight stones in the third. Two players alternate taking as many stones as they like from any one pile. Play continues until someone is forced to take the last stone. The person taking the last stone loses. Write a program that permits two people to play the game of Nim using an array to keep track of the number of stones in each pile.

16. There is an effective strategy that can virtually guarantee victory in the game of Nim. Devise a strategy and modify the program in Problem 15 so that the computer plays against a person. Your program should be virtually unbeatable if the proper strategy is developed.

17. The median of a set of numbers is the value in the middle of the set if the set is arranged in order. The mode is the number listed most often. Given a list of 21 numbers, print the median and mode of the list.

18. Rewrite Problem 17 to permit the use of any length list of numbers.

19. The standard deviation is a statistic frequently used in education measurement. Write a program that, given a list of test scores, will find and print the standard deviation of the numbers. If the N scores are represented by $X_1, X_2, \ldots, X_N$ and the average score is denoted by $\overline{X}$, then the standard deviation is

$$\sqrt{\frac{\sum_{i=1}^{N} (X_i - \overline{X})^2}{N - 1}}$$

20. Revise Problem 19 so that after the standard deviation is printed, you can print a list of test scores that are more than one standard deviation below the average and a list of the scores more than one standard deviation above the average.

21. The z-score is defined as the score earned on a test divided by the standard deviation. Given a data file containing an unknown number of test scores (maximum of 100), print a list showing each test score (from highest to lowest) and the corresponding z-score.

■ 22. Salespeople for the Wellsville Wholesale Company earn a commission based on their sales. The commission rates are as follows:

Sales	Commission3
$0–1,000	3%
1,001–5,000	4.5%
5,001–10,000	5.25%
Over 10,000	6%

In addition, any salesperson who sells above the average of all salespeople receives a $50 bonus, and the top salesperson receives an additional $75 bonus. Given the names and amounts sold by each of 20 salespeople, write a program that prints a table showing the salesperson's name, the amount sold, the commission rate, and the total amount earned. The average sales should also be printed.

23. Ms. Alicia Citizen, your school's Student Government advisor, has come to you for help. She wants a program to total votes for the next Student Government election. Fifteen candidates will be in the election with five positions to be filled. Each person can vote for up to five candidates. The five highest vote getters will be the winners.

    A data file called VoteList contains a list of candidates (by candidate number) voted for by each student. Any line of the file may contain up to five numbers, but if it contains more than five numbers, it is discarded as a void ballot. Write a program to read the file and print a list of the total votes received by each candidate. Also, print the five highest vote getters in order from highest to lowest vote totals.

24. The data file TeacherList contains a list of the teachers in your school along with the room number to which each is assigned. Write a program that, given the name of the teacher, performs a linear search to find and print the room to which the teacher is assigned.

25. Rewrite your program in Problem 24 so that, given a room number, the name of the teacher assigned to that room is found using a binary search. Assume the file is arranged in order of room numbers.

26. Write a language translation program that permits the entry of a word in English, with the corresponding word of another language being printed. The dictionary words can be stored in separate arrays. The English array should be sorted in alphabetical order prior to the first entry of a word to be translated.

27. Elementary and middle school students are often given the task of converting numbers from one base to another. For example, 19 in base 10 is 103 in base 4 ($1 \times 4^2 + 0 \times 4^1 + 3 \times 4^0$). Conversely, 123 in base 4 is 27 in base 10. Write an interactive program that allows the user to choose from the following menu:

```
<1>  Convert from base 10 to base A.
<2>  Convert from base A to base 10.
<3>  Quit
```

    If option 1 or 2 is chosen, the user should then enter the intended base and the number to be converted. A sample run of the program would produce the following output:

```
This program allows you to convert between bases.
Which of the following would you like?

   <1>  Convert from base 10 to base A
   <2>  Convert from base A to base 10
   <3>  Quit

Enter your choice and press <Enter>.
1

Enter the number in base 10 and press <Enter>.
237
```

```
Enter the new base and press <Enter>.
4

The number 237 in base 4 is:  3231

Press <Enter> to continue

This program allows you to convert between bases.
Which of the following would you like?

     <1>  Convert from base 10 to base A
     <2>  Convert from base A to base 10
     <3>  Quit

Enter your choice and press <Enter>.
2

What number would you like to have converted?
2332

Converting to base 10, we get:

     2 *    1 =          2
     3 *    4 =         12
     3 *   16 =         48
     2 *   64 =        128
                    ------
The base 10 value is   190

Press <Enter> to continue

This program allows you to convert between bases.
Which of the following would you like?

     <1>  Convert from base 10 to base A
     <2>  Convert from base A to base 10
     <3>  Quit

Enter your choice and press <Enter>.
3
```

28. A popular children's game is Hangman. The first player selects a word, and the second player guesses letters that may be in that word. Whenever a correct choice is made by the second player, he or she is shown the partially completed word. The game terminates when the correct word is guessed by the second player (the second player wins) or when a predetermined number of incorrect choices of letters have been made by the second player (the first player wins).

    Write an interactive version of this game that can be played by two players. Output should include a display of all letters previously selected by the second player. Allow the players to choose from different levels of difficulty, using the following scale:

Number of Misses	Level of Difficulty
0–3	Expert
4–6	Very Good
7–10	Average
11–16	Beginner
17–25	Needs Practice

Communication in Practice

1. Write a short paper describing the selection sort.
2. One of the principles underlying the concept of data abstraction is that the implementation details of data structures should be deferred to the lowest possible level. To illustrate, consider the high-level design to which we referred in our previous discussion of data abstraction. Our program required you to work with a list of names and an associated list of student test scores. The following procedures were suggested.

   GetNames (<procedure here>);
   GetScores (<procedure here>);
   SortByName (<procedure here>);
   SortByScore (<procedure here>);
   PrintNamesAndScores (<procedure here>);

   Write complete documentation for each of these modules, including a description of all parameters and data structures required. Present your documentation to the class. Ask if your classmates have questions about the number or type of parameters, the data structures required, and/or the main tasks to be performed by each module.
3. Contact a computer programmer at a local business and discuss with him/her the use of lists as a data type. Ask what kinds of programming problems require the use of a list, how the programmers handle data entry (list length), and what operations they perform on the list (search, sort, and so on). Give an oral report of your findings to the class.
4. Select a programming problem from this chapter that you have not yet worked. Construct a structure chart and write all documentary information necessary for the problem you have chosen. Do not write code. When you are finished, have a classmate read your documentation to see if it makes clear precisely what is to be done.

Chapter 11

Arrays of More Than One Dimension

Chapter Outline

Chapter 10 illustrated the significance and uses of one-dimensional arrays. There are, however, several kinds of problems that require arrays of more than one dimension. For example, if you want to work with a table that has both rows and columns, a one-dimensional array will not suffice. Such problems can be solved using arrays of more than one dimension.

11.1 Two-Dimensional Arrays

Objectives

- to be able to declare two-dimensional arrays
- to be able to use correct notation for two-dimensional arrays
- to be able to create tabular output using two-dimensional arrays
- to be able to **read** and **write** with two-dimensional arrays

Basic Idea and Notation

One-dimensional arrays are very useful when working with a row or column of numbers. However, suppose we want to work with data that are best represented in tabular form. For example, box scores in baseball are reported with one player name listed for each row and one statistic listed for each column. Another example is a teacher's grade book, in which a student name is listed for each row and his or her test and/or quiz scores are listed for each column. In both cases, a multiple reference is needed for a single data item.

In Pascal, multiple reference is accomplished by the use of **two-dimensional arrays.** In these arrays, the row subrange always precedes the column subrange and the two subranges are separated by commas. To illustrate, suppose we want to print the table

```
1   2   3   4
2   4   6   8
3   6   9  12
```

where we need to access both the row and column for a single data entry. This table could be produced by either of the following declarations:

1.
```
VAR
  Table : ARRAY [1..3, 1..4] OF integer;
```
2.
```
TYPE
  Matrix = ARRAY [1..3, 1..4] OF integer;
VAR
  Table : Matrix;
```

Objectives

(continued)

- to be able to manipulate components of two-dimensional arrays
- to be able to use two-dimensional arrays with procedures

The index [1 . . 3, 1 . . 4] of each of these declarations differs from one-dimensional arrays. These declarations reserve memory that can be visualized as three rows, each of which holds four variables. Thus, 12 variable locations have been reserved as shown.

Table

As a second illustration of the use of two-dimensional arrays, suppose we want to print the batting statistics for a softball team of 15 players. If the statistics consist of at bats (AB), hits (H), runs (R), and runs batted in (RBI) for each player, we naturally choose to work with a 15 × 4 table. Hence, a reasonable variable declaration is

A **two-dimensional array** is an array in which each element is accessed by a reference to a pair of indices.

```
TYPE
  Table15X4 = ARRAY [1..15, 1..4] OF integer;
VAR
  Stats : Table15X4;
```

The reserved memory area can be visualized as

Stats

with 60 variable locations reserved.

Before proceeding further, let's examine another method of declaring two-dimensional arrays. Our 3 × 4 table could be thought of as three arrays, each of length four, as follows:

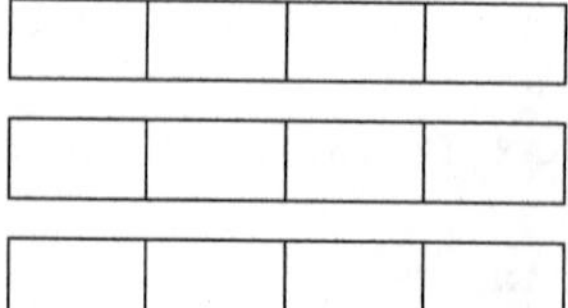

Hence, we have a list of arrays and we can declare the table by

```
TYPE
  Row = ARRAY [1..4] OF integer;
  Matrix = ARRAY [1..3] OF Row;
VAR
  Table : Matrix;
```

The softball statistics could be declared by

```
CONST
  NumberOfStats = 4;
  RosterSize = 15;
TYPE
  PlayerStats = ARRAY [1..NumberOfStats] OF integer;
  TeamTable = ARRAY [1..RosterSize] OF PlayerStats;
VAR
  Stats : TeamTable;
```

Semantic indices such as enumerated types could be utilized by

```
TYPE
  Stat = (AtBat, Hits, Runs, RBI);
  StatChart = ARRAY [1..15, Stat] OF integer;
VAR
  Player : StatChart;
```

Communication and Style Tips

When working with charts or tables of a fixed grid size (say 15 × 4), descriptive identifiers could be

```
Chart15X4
```

or

```
Table15X4
```

If the number of rows and columns varies for different runs of the program (for example, the number of players on a team could vary from year to year), you could define a type by

```
CONST
  NumRows = 15;
  NumColumns = 4;
TYPE
  RowRange = 1..NumRows;
  ColumnRange = 1..NumColumns;
  TableMXN = ARRAY [RowRange, ColumnRange] OF integer;
VAR
  Stats : TableMXN;
```

In this case, a typical entry is

```
Player[5, Hits] := 2;
```

In general, a two-dimensional array can be defined by

> **ARRAY** [<row index>, <column index>] **OF** <element type>;
>
> or
>
> **TYPE**
> RowType = **ARRAY** [<column index>] **OF** <element type>;
> Table = **ARRAY** [<row index>] **OF** RowType;

Whichever method of declaration is used, the problem now becomes one of accessing individual components of the two-dimensional array. For example, in the table

1	2	3	4
2	4	6	8
3	6	9	12

the 8 is in row 2 and column 4. Note that both the row and column position of an element must be indicated. Therefore, in order to put an 8 in this position, we can use assignment statements such as

```
Row := 2;
Column := 4;
Table[Row, Column] := 8;
```

These assignment statements could be used with either of the declaration forms mentioned earlier.

Next, let's assign the values just given to the appropriate variables in Table by 12 assignment statements as follows:

```
Table[1,1] := 1;
Table[1,2] := 2;
Table[1,3] := 3;
Table[1,4] := 4;
Table[2,1] := 2;
Table[2,2] := 4;
Table[2,3] := 6;
Table[2,4] := 8;
Table[3,1] := 3;
Table[3,2] := 6;
Table[3,3] := 9;
Table[3,4] := 12;
```

As you can see, this is extremely tedious. Instead, we can note the relationship between the indices and the assigned values and make the row index Row and the column index Column. The values to be assigned are then Row $*$ Column and we can use nested loops to perform these assignments as follows:

```
FOR Row := 1 TO 3 DO
  FOR Column := 1 TO 4 DO
    Table[Row, Column] := Row * Column;
```

Since two-dimensional arrays frequently require working with nested loops, let's examine what this segment of code does more closely. When Row := 1, the loop

```
FOR Column := 1 TO 4 DO
  Table[1, Column] := 1 * Column;
```

is executed. This performs the four assignments

```
Table[1,1] := 1 * 1;
Table[1,2] := 1 * 2;
Table[1,3] := 1 * 3;
Table[1,4] := 1 * 4;
```

and we have the memory area

Table

1	2	3	4

Similar results hold for Row := 2 and Row := 3 and we produce a two-dimensional array that can be visualized as

Table

1	2	3	4
2	4	6	8
3	6	9	12

The following examples will help you learn to work with and understand the notation for two-dimensional arrays.

Example 11.1

Let's assume the declaration

```
TYPE
  Table5X4 = ARRAY [1..5, 1..4] OF integer;
VAR
  Table : Table5X4;
```

has been made and consider the segment of code

```
FOR Row := 1 TO 5 DO
  FOR Column := 1 TO 4 DO
    Table[Row, Column] := Row DIV Column;
```

When Row := 1, the loop

```
FOR Column := 1 TO 4 DO
  Table[1, Column] := 1 DIV Column;
```

is executed. This causes the following assignment statements:

```
Table[1,1] := 1 DIV 1;
Table[1,2] := 1 DIV 2;
Table[1,3] := 1 DIV 3;
Table[1,4] := 1 DIV 4;
```

The contents of the memory area after that first pass through the loop are

Table

1	0	0	0

When Row := 2, the assignments are

```
Table[2,1] := 2 DIV 1;
Table[2,2] := 2 DIV 2;
Table[2,3] := 2 DIV 3;
Table[2,4] := 2 DIV 4;
```

Table now has values as follows:

Table

1	0	0	0
2	1	0	0

The contents of Table after the entire outside loop has been executed are

Table

1	0	0	0
2	1	0	0
3	1	1	0
4	2	1	1
5	2	1	1

Example 11.2

Let's declare a two-dimensional array and write a segment of code to produce the memory area and contents depicted as follows:

2	3	4	5	6	7	8
3	4	5	6	7	8	9
4	5	6	7	8	9	10
5	6	7	8	9	10	11

An appropriate definition is

```
TYPE
  Table4X7 : ARRAY [1..4, 1..7] OF integer;
```

or

```
TYPE
  Table4X7 : ARRAY [1..4] OF
                 ARRAY [1..7] OF integer;
```

```
VAR
  Table : Table4X7;
```

A segment of code to produce the desired contents is

```
FOR Row := 1 TO 4 DO
  FOR Column := 1 TO 7 DO
    Table[Row, Column] := Row + Column;
```

Reading and Writing

Most problems that involve the use of two-dimensional arrays require data to be read from an input file into the array and values to be written from the array to create some tabular form of output. For example, consider the two-dimensional array for softball statistics.

```
TYPE
  Table15X4 = ARRAY [1..15, 1..4] OF integer;
VAR
  Stats : Table15X4;
```

If the data file consists of 15 lines and each line contains statistics for one player as follows,

```
AB H R RBI
4  2 1 1   (player #1)
3  1 0 1   (player #2)
   .          .
   .          .
   .          .
0  0 0 0   (player #15)
```

we can get the data from the file by reading it one line at a time for 15 lines. This is done using nested loops as follows:

```
FOR Row := 1 TO 15 DO
  BEGIN
    FOR Column := 1 TO 4 DO
      read (DataFile, Stats[Row, Column]);
    readln (DataFile)
  END;
```

When Row := 1, the loop

```
FOR Column := 1 TO 4 DO
  read (DataFile, Stats[Row, Column]);
```

reads the first line of data. In a similar manner, as Row assumes the values 2 through 15, the lines 2 through 15 are read. If the data are to be entered from the keyboard, this code can be modified to include

```
writeln ('Enter player stats on one line.');
writeln ('Press <Enter> after each line.');
writeln;
writeln ('AB   H   R   RBI');
```

before the loop. The loop is then modified to

```
FOR J := 1 TO 15 DO
  BEGIN
    FOR K := 1 TO 4 DO
      read (Stats[J, K]);
    readln
  END;  {  of FOR loop  }
```

After the data are read into an array, some operations and/or updating will be performed and we will display the data in tabular form. For example, suppose we want to print the softball statistics in the 15 × 4 table using only three spaces for each column. We note the following:

1. Three spaces per column can be controlled by formatting the output.
2. One line of output can be generated by a **FOR** loop containing a **write** statement; for example,

```
FOR Column := 1 TO 4 DO
  write (Stats[Row, Column]:3);
```

3. The output buffer will be dumped to the printer after each **write** loop by using **writeln.**
4. We do this for 15 lines by employing another loop,

```
FOR Row := 1 TO 15 DO
  BEGIN
    FOR Column := 1 TO 4 DO
      write (Stats[Row, Column]:3);
    writeln
  END;
```

This last segment of code produces the desired output.

In actual practice, we will also be concerned with headings for our tables and with how the data are positioned on the page. For example, suppose we want to identify the columns of softball statistics as AB, H, R, and RBI; underline the headings; and start the output (AB) in column 25. The following segment of code accomplishes our objectives:

```
writeln (Skip:24, 'AB H  R RBI');
writeln (Skip:24, '-----------');
writeln;
FOR Row := 1 TO 15 DO
  BEGIN
    write (Skip:22);  {  Set the left margin  }
    FOR Column := 1 TO 4 DO
      write (Stats[Row, Column]:3);
    writeln  {  Advance to next line  }
  END;
```

The data file used earlier for our ballplayers causes an output of

```
AB H  R RBI
-----------

4  2  1  1
3  1  0  0
   .
   .
   .
0  0  0  0
```

Manipulating Two-Dimensional Array Components

Often we want to work with some but not all of the components of an array. For example, suppose we have a two-dimensional array of test scores for students in a class. If there are 20 students with five scores each, an appropriate two-dimensional array can be declared as

```
TYPE
  Table20X5 = ARRAY [1..20, 1..5] OF integer;
VAR
  Score : Table20X5;
```

After scores have been read into the array Score, we can envision the memory area as follows:

Score

98	86	100	76	95	(student #1)
72	68	65	74	81	(student #2)
85	81	91	84	83	(student #3)
					.
					.
					.
					.
					.
					.
					.
					.
					.
					.
					.
					.
					.
					.
					.
					.
76	81	72	87	80	(student #20)

When printing a table with test scores, we usually compute several items, including total points for each student, percentage grade for each student, and average score for each test. Thus, we need to declare three additional data structures:

1. An array of length 20 for the total points

2. An array of length 20 for the percentage grades
3. An array of length 5 for the test averages

Let's examine what is required for each of these computations. First, to get the total points for each student, we declare a one-dimensional array to store these values, so we can assume the declaration

```
TYPE
  List20 = ARRAY [1..20] OF integer;
VAR
  TotalPoints : List20;
```

Since the first student's test scores are in the first row, we can write

```
TotalPoints[1] := Score[1,1] + Score[1,2] +
                  Score[1,3] + Score[1,4] +
                  Score[1,5];
```

To compute this total for each student, we can use the loop

```
FOR Student := 1 TO 20 DO
  TotalPoints[Student] := Score[Student, 1] +
                          Score[Student, 2] +
                          Score[Student, 3] +
                          Score[Student, 4] +
                          Score[Student, 5];
```

which produces the following array of totals:

TotalPoints

455	TotalPoints[1]
360	TotalPoints[2]
424	TotalPoints[3]
.	.
.	.
.	.
396	TotalPoints[20]

If the two-dimensional array has several columns, we can use a loop to sum an array of numbers. We can, for instance, write a loop to sum the five test scores for the first student in our table.

```
TotalPoints[1] := 0;
FOR Test := 1 TO 5 DO
  TotalPoints[1] := TotalPoints[1] + Score[1, Test];
```

To do this for each student, we use a second loop:

```
FOR Student := 1 TO 20 DO
  BEGIN
    TotalPoints[Student] := 0;
    FOR Test := 1 TO 5 DO
      TotalPoints[Student] := TotalPoints[Student] +
                              Score[Student, Test]
  END;
```

The second task in our problem is to compute the percentage grade for each student. If we want to save these percentages, we can declare an array by

```
TYPE
  Column20 = ARRAY [1..20] OF real;
VAR
  Percent : Column20;
```

and include a segment of code

```
FOR Student := 1 TO 20 DO
  Percent[Student] := TotalPoints[Student] / 5;
```

The third task is to determine the average score for each of the five tests. To find each of these numbers, we need to add all 20 scores for each test and divide the respective total by 20. First we need to find the sum of each column and to declare an array in which to store the averages. The declaration could be

```
TYPE
  List5 = ARRAY [1..5] OF real;
VAR
  TestAv : List5;
```

We now need a loop to find the total of each column. Assuming that an integer variable Sum is declared, we can sum the first column by

```
Sum := 0;
FOR Student := 1 TO 20 DO
  Sum := Sum + Score[Student, 1];
```

We can now find the average score by

```
TestAv[1] := Sum / 20;
```

To do this for each column, we use a second loop:

```
FOR Test := 1 TO 5 DO              {  Test is the column subscript  }
  BEGIN
    Sum := 0;
    FOR Student := 1 TO 20 DO    {  Student is the row subscript  }
      Sum := Sum + Score[Student, Test];
    TestAv[Test] := Sum / 20
  END;
```

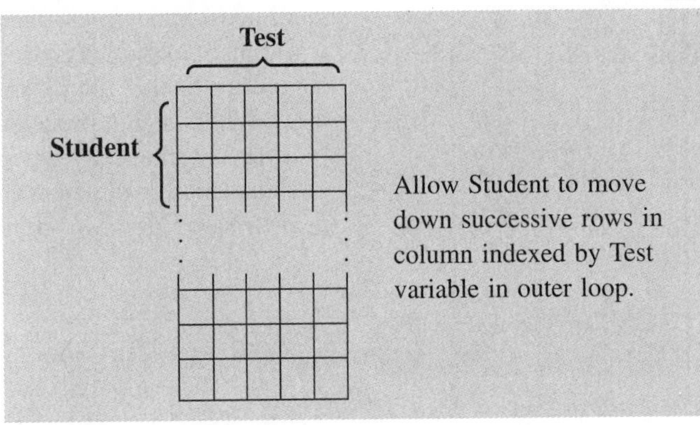
Test
Student
Allow Student to move down successive rows in column indexed by Test variable in outer loop.

A concluding example of manipulating elements of two-dimensional arrays follows.

Example 11.3

Let's assume we have the declarations

```
CONST
  NumRows = 20;
  NumColumns = 50;
TYPE
  Table = ARRAY [1..NumRows,
                 1..NumColumns] OF integer;
  List = ARRAY [1..NumRows] OF integer;
VAR
  Chart : Table;
  Max : List;
```

and values have been read into the two-dimensional array from an input file. Let's write a segment of code to find the maximum value in each row and then store this value in the array Max. To find the maximum of row one, we can write

```
Max[1] := Chart[1,1];
FOR Column := 2 TO NumColumns DO
  IF Chart[1, Column] > Max[1] THEN
    Max[1] := Chart[1, Column];
```

To do this for each of the rows, we use a second loop as follows:

```
FOR Row := 1 TO NumRows DO
  BEGIN
    Max[Row] := Chart[Row, 1];
    FOR Column := 2 TO NumColumns DO
      IF Chart[Row, Column] > Max[Row] THEN
        Max[Row] := Chart[Row, Column]
  END;
```

Procedures and Two-Dimensional Arrays

When we start writing programs with two-dimensional arrays, we will use procedures as before to maintain the top-down design philosophy. As with one-dimensional arrays, there are three relatively standard uses of procedures in most problems involving two-dimensional arrays: to get the data, to manipulate the data, and to display the data.

When using procedures with data that require the use of an array as a data structure, the array type must be defined in the **TYPE** section. The actual parameters and formal parameters can then be of the defined array type. As with one-dimensional arrays, we pass two-dimensional arrays by reference to conserve memory allocation.

Example 11.4

Western Jeans, Inc., wants a program to help them keep track of their inventory of jeans. The jeans are coded by waist size and inseam. The waist sizes are the integer values from 24 to 46 and the inseams are the integer values from 26 to 40. Thus, there are 23 waist sizes and 15 inseams for each waist size. The first 23 lines of the data file contain the starting inventory. Each line corresponds to a waist size and contains 15 integers, one for each inseam. The next 23 lines of the data file contain the sales information for a day. Let's write a program to find and print the closing inventory. A first-level pseudocode development for this program is

1. Get starting inventory
2. Get new sales
3. Update inventory
4. Print heading
5. Print closing inventory

Each of these steps uses a procedure. Since there are 23 waist sizes and 15 inseams, we use definitions as follows:

```
CONST
  FirstWaist = 24;
  LastWaist = 46;
  FirstInseam = 26;
  LastInseam = 40;
TYPE
  WaistSizes = FirstWaist..LastWaist;
  InseamSizes = FirstInseam..LastInseam;
  Table = ARRAY [WaistSizes, InseamSizes] OF integer;
```

and declare the variables

```
VAR
  Inventory : Table;
  Sales : Table;
  Data : text;
```

Assuming variables have been declared and constants have been defined as needed, we write the following procedure to get the starting inventory:

```
PROCEDURE GetData (VAR Matrix : Table);
  VAR
    Row, Column : integer;
  BEGIN
    FOR Row := FirstWaist TO LastWaist DO
      BEGIN
        FOR Column := FirstInseam TO LastInseam DO
          read (Data, Matrix[Row, Column]);
        readln (Data)
      END
  END;
```

This procedure can be called from the main program by

```
GetData (Inventory);
```

The next task is to get the sales for a day. Since this merely requires the next 23 lines from the data file to be read, we do not need to write a new procedure. We call GetData again by

```
GetData (Sales);
```

We now need a procedure to update the starting inventory. This updating can be accomplished by sending both two-dimensional arrays to a procedure and then finding the respective differences of components.

```
PROCEDURE Update (VAR Inventory : Table;
                  VAR Sales : Table);
  VAR
    Row, Column : integer;
  BEGIN
    FOR Row := FirstWaist TO LastWaist DO
      FOR Column := FirstInseam TO LastInseam DO
        Inventory[Row, Column] := Inventory[Row, Column]-
                                  Sales[Row, Column]
  END;
```

This procedure is called by the statement

```
Update (Inventory, Sales);
```

The procedure for the heading is as before, so we do not need to write it here. Let's assume the arrays have been assigned the necessary values. The output procedure then will be

```
PROCEDURE PrintData (VAR Inventory : Table);
  CONST
    Mark = ' !';
  VAR
    Row, Column : integer;
  BEGIN
    FOR J := FirstWaist TO LastWaist DO
      BEGIN
        write (Row:6, Mark);
        FOR Column := FirstInseam TO LastInseam DO
          write (Inventory[Row, Column]:4);
        writeln;
        writeln (Mark:6)
      END  {  of printing one row  }
  END;
```

This procedure can be called from the main program by

```
PrintData (Inventory);
```

Once these procedures are written, the main program becomes

```
BEGIN  {  Main program  }
  reset (Data);
  GetData (Inventory);
  GetData (Sales);
  Update (Inventory, Sales);
  PrintHeading;
  PrintData (Inventory)
END.  {  of main program  }
```

Exercises 11.1

For Exercises 1–3, declare a two-dimensional array for the tables described; use both the **ARRAY** [. . , . .] and **ARRAY** [. .] **OF ARRAY** [. .] forms.

*1. A table with real number entries that shows the prices for four different drugs charged by five drug stores.

2. A table with character entries that shows the grades earned by 20 students in six courses.

*3. A table with integer entries that shows the 12 quiz scores earned by 30 students in a class.

4. Write a test program to read integers into a 3 × 5 array and then print the array components together with each row sum and each column sum.

For Exercises 5–8, sketch what is reserved in memory. In each case, state how many variables are available to the programmer.

*5.
```
TYPE
  ShippingCostTable = ARRAY [1..10] OF
                      ARRAY [1..4] OF real;
  GradeBookTable = ARRAY [1..35, 1..6] OF integer;
VAR
  ShippingCost : ShippingCostTable;
  GradeBook : GradeBookTable;
```

6.
```
TYPE
  Matrix = ARRAY [1..3, 2..6] OF integer;
VAR
  A : Matrix;
```

*7.
```
TYPE
  Weekdays = (Mon, Tues, Wed, Thur, Fri);
  Chores = (Wash, Iron, Clean, Mow, Sweep);
  ScheduleTable = ARRAY [Weekdays, Chores] OF boolean;
VAR
  Schedule : ScheduleTable;
```

8.
```
TYPE
  Questions = 1..50;
  Answers = 1..5;
  Table = ARRAY [Questions, Answers] OF char;
VAR
  AnswerSheet : Table;
```

For Exercises 9–12, assume the array A has been declared as

```
TYPE
  Table3X5 = ARRAY [1..3, 1..5] OF integer;
VAR
  A : Table3X5;
```

Indicate the array contents produced by each of the following:

*9.
```
FOR J := 1 TO 3 DO
  FOR K := 1 TO 5 DO
    A[J,K] := J - K;
```

10.
```
FOR J := 1 TO 3 DO
  FOR K := 1 TO 5 DO
    A[J,K] := J;
```

*11.
```
FOR K := 1 TO 5 DO
  FOR J := 1 TO 3 DO
    A[J,K] := J;
```
12.
```
FOR J := 3 DOWNTO 1 DO
  FOR K := 1 TO 5 DO
    A[J,K] := J MOD K;
```

For Exercises 13–15, let the two-dimensional array A be declared by

```
TYPE
  Table3X6 = ARRAY [1..3, 1..6] OF integer;
VAR
  A : Table3X6;
```

Write nested loops that cause the following values to be stored in A:

*13. **A**

3	4	5	6	7	8
5	6	7	8	9	10
7	8	9	10	11	12

14. **A**

0	0	0	0	0	0
0	0	0	0	0	0
0	0	0	0	0	0

*15. **A**

2	2	2	2	2	2
4	4	4	4	4	4
6	6	6	6	6	6

16. Declare a two-dimensional array and write a segment of code that reads the following input file into the array.

```
13.2 15.1 10.3 8.2 43.6
37.2 25.6 34.1 17.0 15.2
```

*17. Suppose an input file contains 50 lines of data and the first 20 spaces of each line are reserved for a customer's name. The rest of the line contains other information. Declare a two-dimensional array to hold the names and write a segment of code to read the names into the array. A sample line of input is

```
Smith John O        268-14-1801
                    ↑
                    position 21
```

For Exercises 18–20, assume the declaration

```
TYPE
  Table4X5 = ARRAY [1..4, 1..5] OF real;
```

```
VAR
  Table : Table4X5;
```

has been made and values have been read into Table as follows:

Table

-2.0	3.0	0.0	8.0	10.0
0.0	-4.0	3.0	1.0	2.0
1.0	2.0	3.0	8.0	-6.0
-4.0	1.0	4.0	6.0	82.0

Indicate what the components of Table will be after each of the following segments of code is executed:

18.
```
FOR J := 1 TO 4 DO
  FOR K := 1 TO 5 DO
    IF J MOD K = 0 THEN
      A[J,K] := 0
    ELSE
      A[J,K] := -1;
```

*19.
```
FOR J := 1 TO 4 DO
  IF A[J,1] <> 0 THEN
    FOR K := 2 TO 5 DO
      A[J,K] := A[J,K] / A[J,1];
```

20.
```
FOR K := 1 TO 5 DO
  IF A[1,K] = 0 THEN
    FOR J := 2 TO 4 DO
      A[J,K] := 0;
```

*21. Let the two-dimensional array Table be declared as in Exercises 18–20. Declare additional arrays as needed and write segments of code for the following:
   a. Find and save the minimum of each row.
   b. Find and save the maximum of each column.
   c. Find the total of all the components.

22. Example 11.4 illustrates the use of procedures with two-dimensional arrays. For actual use, Western Jeans would also need a list indicating what to order to maintain the inventory. Write a procedure (assuming all declarations have been made) to print a table indicating which sizes of jeans have a supply fewer than four. Do this by putting an asterisk (*) in the cell if the supply is low or a blank if the supply is adequate.

*23. Suppose you want to work with a table that has three rows and eight columns of integers.
   a. Declare an appropriate two-dimensional array that can be used with procedures.
   b. Write a procedure to replace all negative numbers with zero.
   c. Show what is needed to call this procedure from the main program.

24. If A and B are matrices of size $m \times n$, their sum $A + B$ is defined by $A + B = [a + b]_{ij,}$ where a and b are corresponding components in A and B. Write a program to
   a. Read values into two matrices of size $m \times n$.
   b. Compute the sum.
   c. Print the matrices together with the sum.

25. If A and B are matrices of sizes $m \times n$ and $n \times p$, their product is defined to be the $m \times p$ matrix AB, where

$$AB = [c_{ik}],\ c_{ik} = \sum_{j=1}^{n} a_{ij}b_{jk}$$

Write a program to do the following:
*a. Read values into two matrices that have a defined product.
*b. Compute their product.
c. Print the matrices and their product.

11.2 Arrays of String Variables

Objectives

- to understand that an array of string variables is a two-dimensional array
- to be able to declare an array of string variables
- to be able to read data into an array of string variables
- to be able to alphabetize a list of names

Basic Idea and Notation

Recall from Section 10.5 that we define string variables as packed arrays of characters. A typical declaration for a name 20 characters in length is

```
TYPE
  NameString = PACKED ARRAY [1..20] OF char;
VAR
  Name : NameString;
```

Thus, Name could be envisioned as

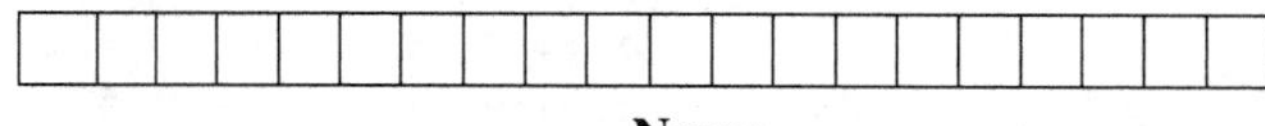

Name

It is a natural extension to next consider the problem of working with an array of strings. For example, if we need a data structure for 50 names, this can be declared by

```
TYPE
  NameString = PACKED ARRAY [1..20] OF char;
  NameList = ARRAY [1..50] OF NameString;
VAR
  Name : NameList;
```

Name can then be envisioned as

Name	
	Name[1]
	Name[2]
	Name[3]
⋮	⋮
	Name[50]

where each component of Name is a packed array of 20 characters. (Many compilers have a string type that behaves differently.)

Alphabetizing a List of Names

One standard problem that programmers face is that of alphabetizing a list of names. For example, programs that work with class lists, bank statements, magazine subscriptions, names in a telephone book, credit card customers, and so on require alphabetizing. As indicated, Pascal provides the facility for using an array of packed arrays as a data structure for such lists.

Problems that require alphabetizing names contain at least three main tasks: get the data, alphabetize the list, and print the list. Before writing procedures for each of these tasks, let's consider some associated problems. When getting the data, the programmer will usually encounter one of two formats. First, data may be entered with a constant field width for each name. Each name is then typically followed by some additional data item. Thus, if each name uses 20 character positions and position 21 contains the start of numeric data, the input file might be

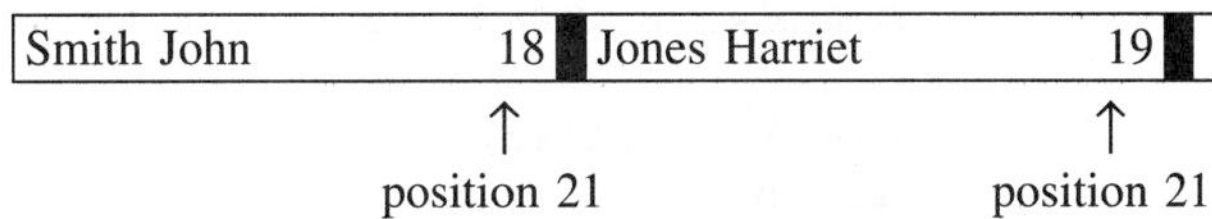

In this case, the name can be read into the appropriate component by a fixed loop. The first name can be accessed by

```
FOR K := 1 TO 20 DO
  read (Data, Name[1,K]);
```

and the second name by

```
FOR K := 1 TO 20 DO
  read (Data, Name[2,K]);
```

A second form for entering data is to use some symbol to indicate the end of a name. When the data are in this form, the user must be able to recognize the symbol and fill the remaining positions with blanks. Thus, the data file can be

Smith John*18	Jones Harriet*19

In this case, the first name can be obtained by

```
K := 0;
read (Data, Ch);
WHILE (Ch <> '*') AND (K < 20) DO
  BEGIN
    K := K + 1;
    Name[1,K] := Ch;
    read (Data, Ch)
  END;
FOR J := K + 1 TO 20 DO
  Name[1,J] := ' ';
```

This process will fill the remaining positions in the name with blanks. Thus, Name[1] would be

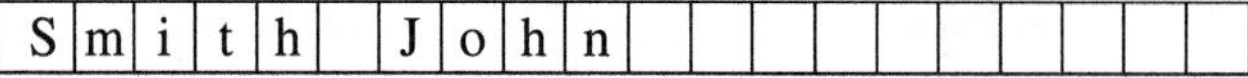

Name [1]

The second name in the data file would be similarly read. The only change is from Name[1,K] to Name[2,K].

The next problem in getting data is determining how many lines are available. If the number of lines is known, a **FOR** loop can be used. More realistically, however, there will be an unknown number of lines and the user will need the **eof** condition in a variable control loop and a counter to determine the number of names. To illustrate, assume there are an unknown number of data lines, where each line contains a name in the first 20 positions. If the declaration section of a program is

```
TYPE
  NameString = PACKED ARRAY [1..20] OF char;
  NameList = ARRAY [1..50] OF NameString;
VAR
  Name : NameList;
  Length : integer;
```

then a procedure to get the data is

```
PROCEDURE GetData (VAR Name : NameList;
                   VAR Length : integer);
  VAR
    K : integer;
  BEGIN
    Length := 0;
    reset (Data);
    WHILE NOT eof(Data) AND (Length < 50) DO
      BEGIN
        Length := Length + 1;            {  Increment counter  }
        FOR K := 1 TO 20 DO
          read (Data, Name[Length, K]);  {  Get a name  }
        readln  (Data)                   {  Advance the pointer  }
      END;
    IF NOT eof(Data) THEN
      writeln ('There are more data.')
  END;  {  of PROCEDURE GetData  }
```

This procedure is called from the main program by

```
GetData (Name, Length);
```

Now let's consider the problem of alphabetizing a list of names. If we assume the same data structure we've just seen and let Length represent the number of names, a procedure to sort the list alphabetically (using the selection sort discussed in Section 10.3) is

```
PROCEDURE SelectionSort (VAR Name : NameList;
                         Length : integer);
  VAR
    J, K, Index : integer;
    Temp : NameString;
```

```
BEGIN
  FOR J := 1 TO Length - 1 DO
    BEGIN
      Index := J;
      FOR K := J + 1 TO Length DO
        IF Name[K] < Name[Index] THEN
          Index := K;
      IF Index <> J THEN
        BEGIN
          Temp := Name[Index];
          Name[Index] := Name[J];
          Name[J] := Temp
        END  {  of exchange  }
    END  {  of sort  }
END;  {  of PROCEDURE SelectionSort  }
```

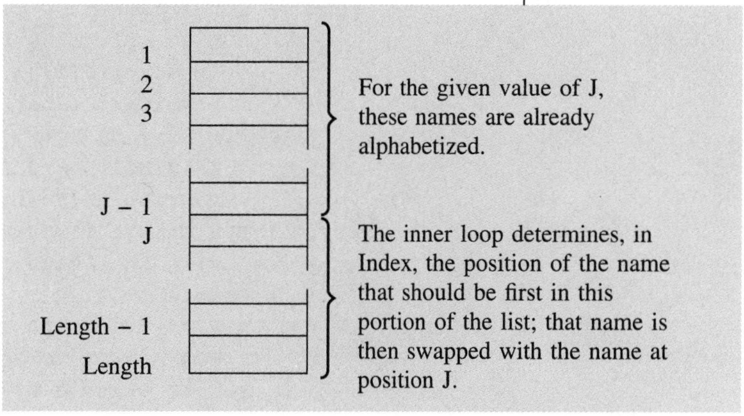

1
2
3
J – 1
J
Length – 1
Length
For the given value of J, these names are already alphabetized.
The inner loop determines, in Index, the position of the name that should be first in this portion of the list; that name is then swapped with the name at position J.

This procedure is called from the main program by

```
SelectionSort (Name, Length);
```

Once the list of names has been sorted, the user often wants to print the sorted list. A procedure to do this is

```
PROCEDURE PrintData (VAR Name : NameList;
                         Length : integer);
  VAR
    J : integer;
  BEGIN
    FOR J := 1 TO Length DO
      writeln (Name[J]:50)
  END;  {  of PROCEDURE PrintData  }
```

This procedure is called from the main program by

```
PrintData (Name, Length);
```

We can now use these procedures in a simple program that gets the names, sorts them, and prints them as follows:

```
BEGIN  {  Main program  }
  GetData (Name, Length);
```

```
  Sort (Name, Length);
  PrintData (Name, Length)
END.  {  of main program  }
```

Exercises 11.2

Assume the following declarations and definitions

```
TYPE
  String20 = PACKED ARRAY [1..20] OF char;
  StateList = ARRAY [1..50] OF String20;
VAR
  State : StateList;
```

have been made and an alphabetical listing of the 50 states of the United States of America is contained in the data structure State. Furthermore, assume that each state name begins in position 1 of each component. Indicate the output for Exercises 1–4.

*1.
```
FOR J := 1 TO 50 DO
  IF State[J,1] = 'O' THEN
    writeln (State[J]:35);
```
2.
```
FOR J := 50 DOWNTO 1 DO
  IF J MOD 5 = 0 THEN
    writeln (State[J]:35);
```
*3.
```
FOR J := 1 TO 50 DO
  writeln (State[J,1]:10, State[J,2]);
```
4.
```
CountA := 0;
FOR J := 1 TO 50 DO
  FOR K := 1 TO 20 DO
    IF State[J,K] = 'A' THEN
      CountA := CountA + 1;
writeln (CountA:20);
```
*5. Assume you have a sorted list of names in the form last name, first name. Write a fragment of code to inspect the list of names and print the full name of each Smith on the list.

The procedure in this section to get names from an input file assumes the names in the file are of fixed length and that there is an unknown number of data lines. Modify the procedure for each situation given in Exercises 6–9.

6. Variable-length names followed by an asterisk (*) and a known number of data lines
*7. Variable-length names followed by an asterisk (*) and an unknown number of data lines
8. Fixed-length names (20 characters) and a known number of data lines
9. Names entered in the form first name, space, last name are to be sorted by last name
10. Write a complete program to read 10 names from a data file (where each line contains one name of 20 characters), sort the names in reverse alphabetical order, and print the sorted list.
11. If each line of a data file contains a name followed by an age, for example,

Smith John	18	■

↑

position 21

the data will be put into two arrays, one for the names and one for the ages. Show how the sorting procedure can be modified so that the array of ages will keep the same order as the array of names.

11.3 Parallel Arrays (Optional)

Objectives

- to understand when parallel arrays should be used to solve a problem
- to be able to use parallel arrays to solve a problem

Parallel arrays are arrays of the same length but with different component data types.

In many practical situations, more than one type of array is required to handle the data. For example, we may wish to keep a record of names of people and their donations to a charitable organization. We can accomplish this by using a packed array of names and an equal-length array of donations. Programs for such situations can use **parallel arrays**—arrays of the same length with elements in the same relative positions in each array. These arrays have the same index type. However, most uses of parallel arrays have the added condition of different data types for the array components; otherwise, a two-dimensional array would suffice. Generally, in situations that call for two or more arrays of the same length but of different data types, parallel arrays can be used. Later we will see that this situation can also be handled as a single array of records.

Using Parallel Arrays

Let's look at a typical problem that requires working with both a list of names and a list of numbers. Suppose the input file consists of 30 lines, each of which contains a name in the first 20 spaces and an integer starting in space 21 that is the amount of a donation. We are to read all data into appropriate arrays, alphabetize the names, print the alphabetized list with the amount of each donation, and find the total of all donations.

This problem can be solved using parallel arrays for the list of names and the list of donations. Appropriate declarations are

```
CONST
  NumberOfDonors = 30;
TYPE
  NameString = PACKED ARRAY [1..20] OF char;
  IndexType = 1..NumberOfDonors;
  NameList = ARRAY [IndexType] OF NameString;
  AmountList = ARRAY [IndexType] OF integer;
```

Communication and Style Tips

Since parallel arrays use the same index type, definitions could have the form

```
CONST
  NumberOfDonors = 30;
TYPE
  String20 = PACKED ARRAY [1..20] OF char;
  IndexType = 1..NumberOfDonors;
  NameList = ARRAY [IndexType] OF String20;
  AmountList = ARRAY [IndexType] OF integer;
```

```
VAR
  Donor : NameList;
  Amount : AmountList;
  Data : text;
```

A procedure to read the data from an input file is

```
PROCEDURE GetData (VAR Donor : NameList;
                   VAR Amount : AmountList);
  VAR
    J, K : integer;
  BEGIN
    reset (Data);
    FOR J := 1 TO NumberOfDonors DO
      BEGIN
        FOR K := 1 TO 20 DO
          read (Data, Donor[J,K]);
        readln (Data, Amount[J])
      END
  END;  {  of PROCEDURE GetData  }
```

This procedure could be called by

```
GetData (Donor, Amount);
```

After this procedure has been called from the main program, the parallel arrays can be envisioned as

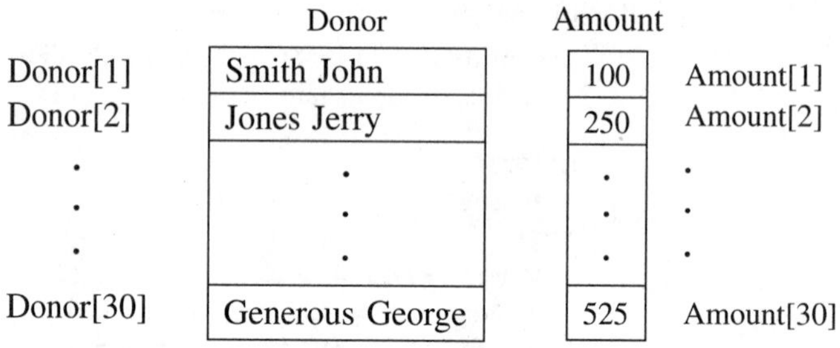

	Donor	Amount	
Donor[1]	Smith John	100	Amount[1]
Donor[2]	Jones Jerry	250	Amount[2]
.	.	.	.
.	.	.	.
.	.	.	.
Donor[30]	Generous George	525	Amount[30]

The next task is to alphabetize the names. However, we must be careful to keep the amount donated with the name of the donor. This can be accomplished by passing both the list of names and the list of donations to the sorting procedure and modifying the code to include exchanging the amount of donation whenever the names are exchanged. Since NumberOfDonors is defined in the constant section, a Length argument is not needed. Using the procedure heading

```
PROCEDURE Sort (VAR Donor : NameList;
                VAR Amount : AmountList);
```

the code for sorting is changed in order to interchange both a name and an amount. Thus,

```
TempDonor := Donor[Index];
Donor[Index] := Donor[J];
Donor[J] := TempDonor;
```

becomes

```
TempDonor := Donor[Index];
TempAmount := Amount[Index];
Donor[Index] := Donor[J];
Amount[Index] := Amount[J];
Donor[J] := TempDonor;
Amount[J] := TempAmount;
```

The procedure for sorting the list of names and rearranging the list of donations accordingly is called by

```
Sort (Donor, Amount);
```

The next task this program requires is to find the total of all donations. The following function can perform this task:

```
FUNCTION Total (Amount : AmountList) : integer;
  VAR
    Sum, J : integer;
  BEGIN
    Sum := 0;
    FOR J := 1 TO NumberOfDonors DO
      Sum := Sum + Amount[J];
    Total := Sum
  END;  {  of FUNCTION Total  }
```

This function is called by

```
TotalDonations := Total(Amount);
```

where TotalDonations has been declared as an **integer** variable.

Our last task is to print the alphabetized list together with the respective donations and the total of all donations. If Donor and Amount have been sorted appropriately, we can use the following procedure to produce the desired output:

```
PROCEDURE PrintData (VAR Donor : NameList;
                     VAR Amount : AmountList;
                     TotalDonations : integer);
  VAR
    J : integer;
  BEGIN
    FOR J := 1 TO NumberOfDonors DO
      BEGIN
        write (Donor[J]:40);
        writeln ('$':2, Amount[J]:5)
      END;  {  of FOR J loop  }
    writeln ('------':47);
    writeln ('Total':40, '$':2, TotalDonations:5);
    writeln
  END;  {  of PROCEDURE PrintData  }
```

This is called by

```
PrintData (Donor, Amount);
```

A complete program for this problem follows:

```
PROGRAM Donations (input, output, Data);

{   This program reads data from a file where each line        }
{   consists of a donor name followed by the  amount  donated.  }
{   Output consists of an alphabetically sorted list  together  }
{   with the amount of each donation.  This is accomplished by  }
{   using parallel arrays.  The  total amount  donated is also  }
{   listed.                                                     }

CONST
  NumberOfDonors = 30;
  MaxLength = 20;

TYPE
  NameString = PACKED ARRAY [1..20] OF char;
  IndexType = 1..NumberOfDonors;
  NameList = ARRAY [IndexType] OF NameString;
  AmountList = ARRAY [IndexType] OF integer;

VAR
  Amount : AmountList;          {  An array for amounts donated  }
  Donor : NameList;             {  An array for donor names      }
  TotalDonations : integer;     {  Total amount donated          }
  Data : text;                  {  Data in text file             }

{*************************************************************}

PROCEDURE GetData (VAR Donor : NameList;
                   VAR Amount : AmountList);

  {  Given:   Nothing                                            }
  {  Task:    Read names and donations into respective arrays    }
  {  Return:  Parallel arrays of names and donations             }

  VAR
    J, K : integer;
  BEGIN
    reset (Data);
    FOR J := 1 TO NumberOfDonors DO
      BEGIN
        FOR K := 1 TO MaxLength DO
          read (Data, Donor[J,K]);
        readln (Data, Amount[J])
      END
  END;  {  of PROCEDURE GetData  }

{*************************************************************}

PROCEDURE SelectionSort (VAR Donor : NameList;
                         VAR Amount : AmountList);

  {  Given:   Unsorted parallel arrays of names and donations   }
  {  Task:    Sort alphabetically                                }
```

```
  {  Return:  An alphabetically sorted list of names with        }
  {                respective donations                          }

  VAR
    TempDonor : NameString;
    TempAmount : integer;
    J, K, Index : integer;
  BEGIN
    FOR J := 1 TO NumberOfDonors - 1 DO
      BEGIN
        Index := J;
        FOR K := J + 1 TO NumberOfDonors DO
          IF Donor[K] < Donor[Index] THEN
            Index := K;
        IF Index <> J THEN            {  Exchange if necessary  }
          BEGIN
            TempDonor := Donor[Index];
            TempAmount := Amount[Index];
            Donor[Index] := Donor[J];
            Amount[Index] := Amount[J];
            Donor[J] := TempDonor;
            Amount[J] := TempAmount
          END  {  of exchange  }
      END  {  of one pass  }
  END;  {  of PROCEDURE SelectionSort  }

{***************************************************************}

FUNCTION Total (Amount : AmountList) : integer;

  {  Given:   An array of amounts                                }
  {  Task:    Sum the components of the array                    }
  {  Return:  The total of array components                      }

  VAR
    Sum, J : integer;
  BEGIN
    SUM := 0;
    FOR J := 1 TO NumberOfDonors DO
      Sum := Sum + Amount[J];
    Total := Sum
  END;  {  of FUNCTION Total  }

{***************************************************************}

PROCEDURE PrintHeading;

  {  Given:   Nothing                                            }
  {  Task:    Print a heading for the output                     }
  {  Return:  Nothing                                            }

  BEGIN
    writeln ('Donor Name':33, 'Donation':15);
    writeln ('----------':33, '--------':15);
    writeln
  END;  {  of PROCEDURE PrintHeading  }

{***************************************************************}
```

```
PROCEDURE PrintData  (VAR Donor : NameList;
                      VAR Amount : AmountList;
                      TotalDonations : integer);

  {  Given:   Parallel arrays of names and donations and total  }
  {               donations                                      }
  {  Task:    Print a list of names and amounts donated; end     }
  {               with the total of all donations                }
  {  Return:  Nothing                                            }

  VAR
    J : integer;
  BEGIN
    FOR J := 1 TO NumberOfDonors DO
      writeln (Donor[J]:40, '$':2, Amount[J]:5);
    writeln ('------':47);
    writeln ('Total':40, '$':2, TotalDonations:5);
    writeln
  END;  {  of PROCEDURE PrintData  }

{*************************************************************}

BEGIN  {  Main program  }
  GetData (Donor, Amount);
  SelectionSort (Donor, Amount);
  TotalDonations := Total(Amount);
  PrintHeading;
  PrintData (Donor, Amount, TotalDonations)
END.  {  of main program  }
```

Output created from an input file of 30 lines is

```
      Donor Name          Donation
      ----------          --------

   Alexander Candy         $  300
   Anderson Tony           $  375
   Banks Marj              $  375
   Born Patty              $  100
   Brown Ron               $  200
   Darnell Linda           $  275
   Erickson Thomas         $  100
   Fox William             $  300
   Francis Denise          $  350
   Generous George         $  525
   Gillette Mike           $  350
   Hancock Kirk            $  500
   Higgins Sam             $  300
   Janson Kevin            $  200
   Johnson Ed              $  350
   Johnson Martha          $  400
   Jones Jerry             $  250
   Kelly Marvin            $  475
   Kneff Susan             $  300
```

```
Lasher John              $  175
Lyon Elizabeth           $  425
Moore Robert             $  100
Muller Marjorie          $  250
Smith John               $  100
Trost Frostie            $   50
Trudo Rosemary           $  200
Weber Sharon             $  150
Williams Art             $  350
Williams Jane            $  175
Wilson Mary              $  275
                         ------
                   Total $ 8275
```

Exercises 11.3

*1. Which of the following are appropriate declarations for parallel arrays? Explain.

a.
```
TYPE
  String15 = PACKED ARRAY [1..15] OF char;
  List15 = ARRAY [1..15] OF real;
VAR
  Names : ARRAY [1..10] OF String15;
  Amounts : List15;
```

b.
```
TYPE
  Chart = ARRAY [1..12, 1..10] OF integer;
  String10 = PACKED ARRAY [1..10] OF char;
  List = ARRAY [1..12] OF String10;
VAR
  Table : Chart;
  Names : List;
```

2. Write a test program to read names and amounts from an input file. Your program should print both lists and the total of the amounts. Assume each line of data is similar to

```
Jones Mary          7.35
                       ↑
                 position 21
```

3. Declare appropriate arrays and write a procedure to read data from a data file where there are an unknown number of lines (but less than 100) and each line contains a name (20 spaces), an age (**integer**), a marital status (**char**), and an income (**real**). A typical data line is

```
Smith John          35M 28502.16
```

4. Write a procedure to sort the arrays of Exercise 3 according to income.

*5. Modify the code of Exercise 3 to accommodate data entered in the data file in the following format:

20 positions

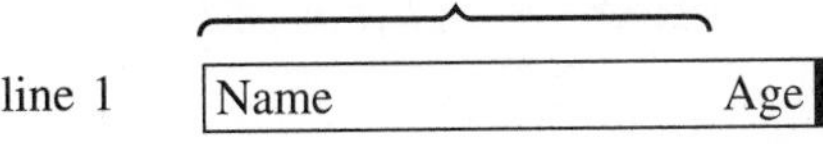

line 1 | Name Age

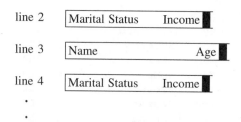

line 2 | Marital Status Income |

line 3 | Name Age |

line 4 | Marital Status Income |

.
.
.

6. Parallel arrays can be used when working with a list of student names and the grades the students receive in a class.
   a. Define array types, and declare subsequent arrays that could be used in such a program.
   b. Write a function that counts the number of occurrences of each letter grade A, B, C, D, and E.

11.4 Higher-Dimensional Arrays

Objectives

- to understand when arrays of dimensions greater than two are needed
- to be able to define and declare data structures for higher-dimensional arrays
- to be able to use higher-dimensional arrays in a program

A **higher-dimensional array** is an array of more than two dimensions.

Thus far we have worked with arrays of one and two dimensions. Arrays of three, four, or higher dimensions can also be declared and used. Pascal places no limitation on the number of dimensions an array can have.

Declarations of Higher-Dimensional Arrays

Declarations of **higher-dimensional arrays** usually assume one of two basic forms. First, a three-dimensional array can be declared using the form

ARRAY [1 . . 3, 1 . . 4, 1 . . 5] **OF** <data type>

Each dimension can vary in any of the ways used for arrays of one or two dimensions and the data type can be any standard or user-defined ordinal data type. Second, a three-dimensional array can be declared as an array of two-dimensional arrays using the form

ARRAY [1 . . 3] **OF ARRAY** [1 . . 4, 1 . . 5] **OF** <data type>

Each of these declarations will reserve 60 locations in memory. This can be visualized as shown in Figure 11.1.

An array of dimension n can be defined by

ARRAY [1 . . a_1, 1 . . a_2, . . . , 1 . . a_n] **OF** <data type>

which would reserve $a_1 * a_2 * \cdots * a_n$ locations in memory. A general definition is

ARRAY [a_1 . . b_1, a_2 . . b_2, . . . , a_n . . b_n] **OF** <data type>

where $a_i \leq b_i$ for $1 \leq i \leq n$.

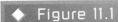

◆ Figure 11.1

Three-dimensional array with components A[I,J,K]

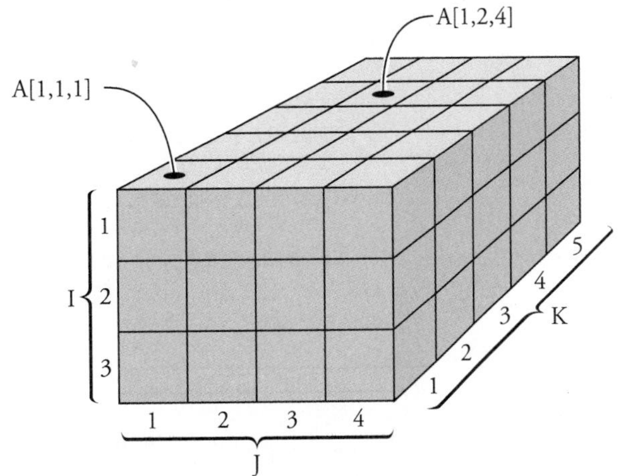

It is possible to visualize multidimensional arrays in an inductive manner. As examples, a four-dimensional array can be visualized as a one-dimensional array with each component being a three-dimensional array; a five-dimensional array can be visualized as a one-dimensional array with each component being a four-dimensional array; and so on.

Declarations and uses of higher-dimensional arrays are usually facilitated by descriptive names and user-defined data types. For example, suppose we want to declare a three-dimensional array to hold the contents of a book of tables. If there are 50 pages and each page contains a table of 15 rows and 10 columns, a reasonable declaration is

```
TYPE
  Page = 1..50;
  Row = 1..15;
  Column = 1..10;
  Book = ARRAY [Page, Row, Column] OF integer;
VAR
  Item : Book;
```

When this declaration is compared to

```
TYPE
  Book = ARRAY [1..50, 1..15, 1..10] OF integer;
VAR
  Item : Book;
```

we realize that both arrays are identical in structure. However, in the first declaration, it is easier to see what the dimensions represent.

Accessing Components

Elements in higher-dimensional arrays are accessed and used in a manner similar to two-dimensional arrays. The difference is that in a three-dimensional array, each element needs three indices for reference. A similar result holds for other dimensions. To illustrate using this notation, recall the declaration

```
TYPE
  Page = 1..50;
```

```
  Row = 1..15;
  Column = 1..10;
  Book = ARRAY [Page, Row, Column] OF integer;
VAR
  Item : Book;
```

If we want to assign a 10 to the item on page 3, row 5, column 7, the statement

```
Item[3,5,7] := 10;
```

accomplishes this. Similarly, this item can be printed by

```
write (Item[3,5,7]);
```

Using this same declaration, we can do the following:

1. Print the fourth row of page 21 with the following segment of code:

```
FOR K := 1 TO 10 DO
  write (Item[21,4,K]:5);
writeln;
```

2. Print the top row of every page by using

```
FOR I := 1 TO 50 DO
  BEGIN
    FOR K := 1 TO 10 DO
      write (Item[I,1,K]:5);
    writeln
  END;
```

3. Print page 35 by using

```
FOR J := 1 TO 15 DO
  BEGIN
    FOR K := 1 TO 10 DO
      write (Item[35,J,K]:5);
    writeln
  END;
```

4. Print every page that does not have a zero in the first row and the first column by using

```
FOR I := 1 TO 50 DO
  IF Item[I,1,1] <> 0 THEN
    FOR J := 1 TO 15 DO
      BEGIN
        FOR K := 1 To 10 DO
          write (Item[I,J,K]:5);
        writeln
      END;
```

As another illustration of the use of higher-dimensional arrays, consider the situation where the manager of a high-rise office complex wants a program to assist in keeping track of the tenants in each office. Suppose there are 20 floors, each with the floor plan shown in Figure 11.2. Each wing contains five rooms.

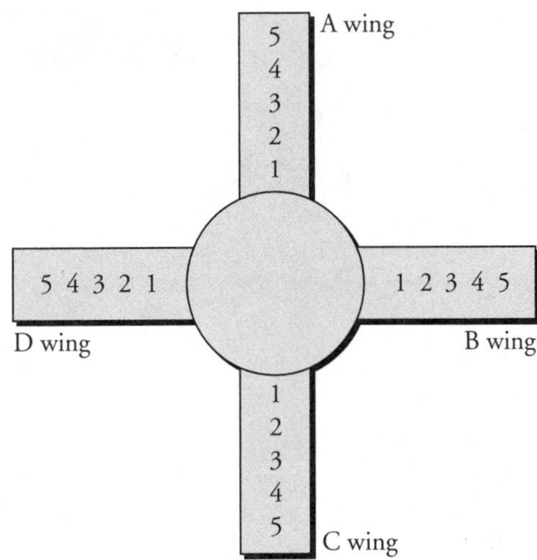

◆ Figure 11.2
High-rise floor plan

First, let's declare an appropriate array where the tenant's name can be stored. (Assume each name consists of 20 characters.) This can be accomplished by

```
TYPE
  Floors = 1..20;
  Wings = 'A'..'D';
  Offices = 1..5;
  Name = PACKED ARRAY [1..20] OF char;
  Occupant = ARRAY [Floors, Wings, Offices] OF Name;
VAR
  Tenant : Occupant;
  Floor : Floors;
  Wing : Wings;
  Office : Offices;
```

Note that this is really a four-dimensional array, since the data type Name is **PACKED ARRAY.**

Now let's write a segment of code to print a list of names of all tenants on the top floor. To get the names of all tenants of the twentieth floor, we need to print the names for each office in each wing. Assuming a field width of 30 columns, the following code completes the desired task:

```
FOR Wing := 'A' TO 'D' DO
  FOR Office := 1 TO 5 DO
    writeln (Tenant[20, Wing, Office]:30);
```

How would we write a segment of code to read the name of the new tenant on the third floor, B wing, room 5 from the data file? Recall that character strings must be read one character at a time. Tenant [3,'B',5] is the variable name. Since this is a packed array, the code for reading is

```
FOR L := 1 TO 20 DO
  read (Data, Tenant[3,'B',5,L]);
```

Assume the string 'Unoccupied   ' has been entered for each vacant office and we are to write a segment of code to list all vacant offices. This problem

A Note of Interest

Computer Ethics: Worms

In The Shockwave Rider (1975), J. Brunner developed the notion of an omnipotent "tapeworm" program running loose through a network of computers—an idea that seemed rather disturbing but was then well beyond current capabilities. The basic model, however, was a very provocative one: a program or a computation that can move from machine to machine, harnessing resources as needed and replicating itself when necessary.

On November 2, 1988, Cornell computer science graduate student Robert Morris released a worm program into the ARPANET. Over an eight-hour period, it invaded between 2500 and 3000 VAX and Sun computers running the Berkeley UNIX operating system. The worm program disabled virtually all of the computers by replicating rampantly and clogging them with many copies. Many of the computers had to be disconnected from the network until all copies of the worm could be expurgated and until the security loopholes that the worm used to gain entry could be plugged. Most computers were fully operational within two or three days. No files were damaged on any of the computers invaded by the worm.

This incident gained much public attention and produced a widespread outcry in the computer community, perhaps because so many people saw that they had been within a hair's breadth of losing valuable files. After an investigation, Cornell suspended Morris and decried his action as irresponsible. In July 1989, a grand jury brought an indictment against Morris for violation of the Federal Computer Privacy Act of 1986. He was tried and convicted in January 1990.

requires us to examine every name and print the location of the unoccupied offices. Hence, when we encounter the name 'Unoccupied   ', we want to print the respective indices. This is accomplished by

```
FOR Floor := 1 TO 20 DO
  FOR Wing := 'A' TO 'D' DO
    FOR Office := 1 TO 5 DO
      IF Tenant[Floor, Wing, Office] = 'Unoccupied          '
        THEN writeln (Floor:5, Wing:5, Office:5);
```

As you can see, working with higher-dimensional arrays requires very careful handling of the indices. Nested loops are frequently used for processing array elements and proper formatting of output is critical.

Exercises 11.4

In Exercises 1–4, how many memory locations are reserved in each declaration?

*1.
```
TYPE
  Block = ARRAY [1..2, 1..3, 1..10] OF char;
VAR
  A : Block;
```

2.
```
TYPE
  Block = ARRAY [-2..3] OF ARRAY [2..4, 3..6] OF real;
VAR
  A : Block;
```

*3.
```
TYPE
  Color = (Red, Black, White);
  Size = (Small, Large);
  Year = 1950..1960;
  Specifications = ARRAY [Color, Size, Year];
VAR
  A : Specifications;
```

4.
```
TYPE
  String15 = PACKED ARRAY [1..15] OF char;
  List10 = ARRAY [1..10] OF String15;
  NameTable = ARRAY [1..4] OF List10;
VAR
  A : NameTable;
```

*5. Write a test program to read values into an array of size 3 × 4 × 5. Assuming this represents three pages, each of which contains a 4 × 5 table, print the table for each page together with a page number.

6. Declare a three-dimensional array that a hospital could use to keep track of the types of rooms available: private (P), semiprivate (S), and ward (W). The hospital has four floors, five wings, and 20 rooms in each wing.

For Exercises 7 and 8, consider the declaration

```
TYPE
  Pages = 1..50;
  Rows = 1..15;
  Columns = 1..10;
  Book = ARRAY [Pages, Rows, Columns] OF integer;
VAR
  Page : Pages;
  Row : Rows;
  Column : Columns;
  Item : Book;
```

7. Write a segment of code to do each of the following:
   a. Print the fourth column of page 3.
   b. Print the top seven rows of page 46.
   c. Create a new page 30 by adding the corresponding elements of page 31 to page 30.

8. What is a general description of the output produced by the following segments of code?

   a.
```
FOR Page := 1 TO 15 DO
  BEGIN
    FOR Column := 1 TO 10 DO
      write (Item[Page, Page, Column]:4);
    writeln
  END;
```

   b.
```
For Page := 1 TO 50 DO
  FOR Column := 1 TO 10 DO
    writeln (Item[Page, Column, Column]:(Column+4));
```

Use the following problem statement, definitions, and declarations for Exercises 9–12. An athletic conference consisting of 10 universities wishes to have a program to keep track of the number of athletic grants-in-aid for each team at each institution. The conference programmer has defined the following structure:

```
CONST
  MaxGrants = 90;
TYPE
  Schools = 'A'..'J';
  Sports = (Baseball, Basketball, CrossCountry,
            FieldHockey, Football, Golf, Gymnastics,
            Swimming, Tennis, Track, Volleyball, Wrestling);
  Sex = (Male, Female);
  NumberOfGrants = 0..MaxGrants;
  GrantChart = ARRAY [Schools, Sports, Sex] OF NumberOfGrants;
VAR
  NumGrants : integer;
  Grants : GrantChart;
  School : Schools;
  Sport : Sports;
  Gender : Sex;
```

9. How many memory locations are reserved in the array Grants?
10. Explain what tasks are performed by each of the following segments of code:
    a.
    ```
    NumGrants := 0;
    FOR School := 'A' TO 'J' DO
      FOR Sport := Baseball TO Wrestling DO
        NumGrants := NumGrants +
                     Grants[School, Sport, Female];
    ```
    b.
    ```
    Sum := 0;
    FOR School := 'A' TO 'J' DO
      FOR Sport := Baseball TO Wrestling DO
        FOR Gender := Male TO Female DO
          IF Grants[School, Sport, Gender] = 0 THEN
            Sum := Sum + 1;
    ```
11. Write a segment of code for each of the following tasks:
    a. Find the total number of grants for each school.
    b. Find the total number of grants for each sport.
    c. List all schools that have 10 or more grants in field hockey.
12. Explain how a **CASE** statement can be used to help display all sports (indicate gender) and the number of grants in each sport for school D.

Focus on Program Design: Case Study

Airline Seating

This program simulates the solution to a problem that could be posed by a small airline. Mountain-Air Commuters, Inc., is a small airline commuter service. Each of its planes is a 30-passenger plane with a floor plan as follows:

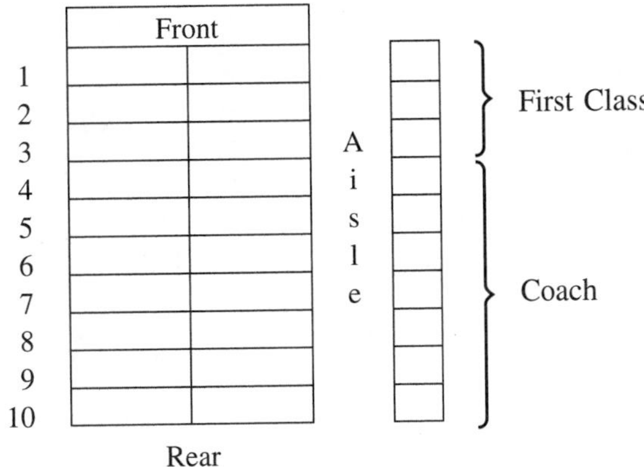

The first three rows are designated as first class because the seats are wider and there is more leg room. (In reality, most commuter planes do not have a first class section. However, rather than include the large database needed for larger planes, we simulate the problem using a seating plan with only 10 rows.)

Write a program that assigns seats to passengers on a first-come, first-served basis according to the following rules:

1. First class and coach requests must be honored; if seats in the requested sections are all full, the customer's name should go on a waiting list for the next flight.
2. Specific seat requests should be honored next; if a requested seat is occupied, the person should be placed in the same row, if possible.
3. If a requested row is filled, the passenger should be seated as far forward as possible.
4. If all seats are filled, the passenger's name is put on a waiting list for the next flight.

Output should include a seating chart with passenger names appropriately printed and a waiting list for the next flight. Each data line (input) contains the passenger's name, first class (F) or coach (C) designation, and seat request indicating the row and column desired.

A typical line of data would be

```
Smith John                    C 5 2
```

where C represents a coach choice, 5 is a request for row five, and 2 is the preferred seat.

A first-level pseudocode development for this problem is

1. Initialize variables
2. **WHILE NOT eof DO** process a name
3. Print a seating chart
4. **IF** there is a waiting list **THEN** print the list

A complete structure chart for this problem is given in Figure 11.3. Module specifications for the main modules are

1. Initialize Module

   Data received: None

◆ Figure 11.3

Structure chart for Mountain-Air Commuters, Inc., problem

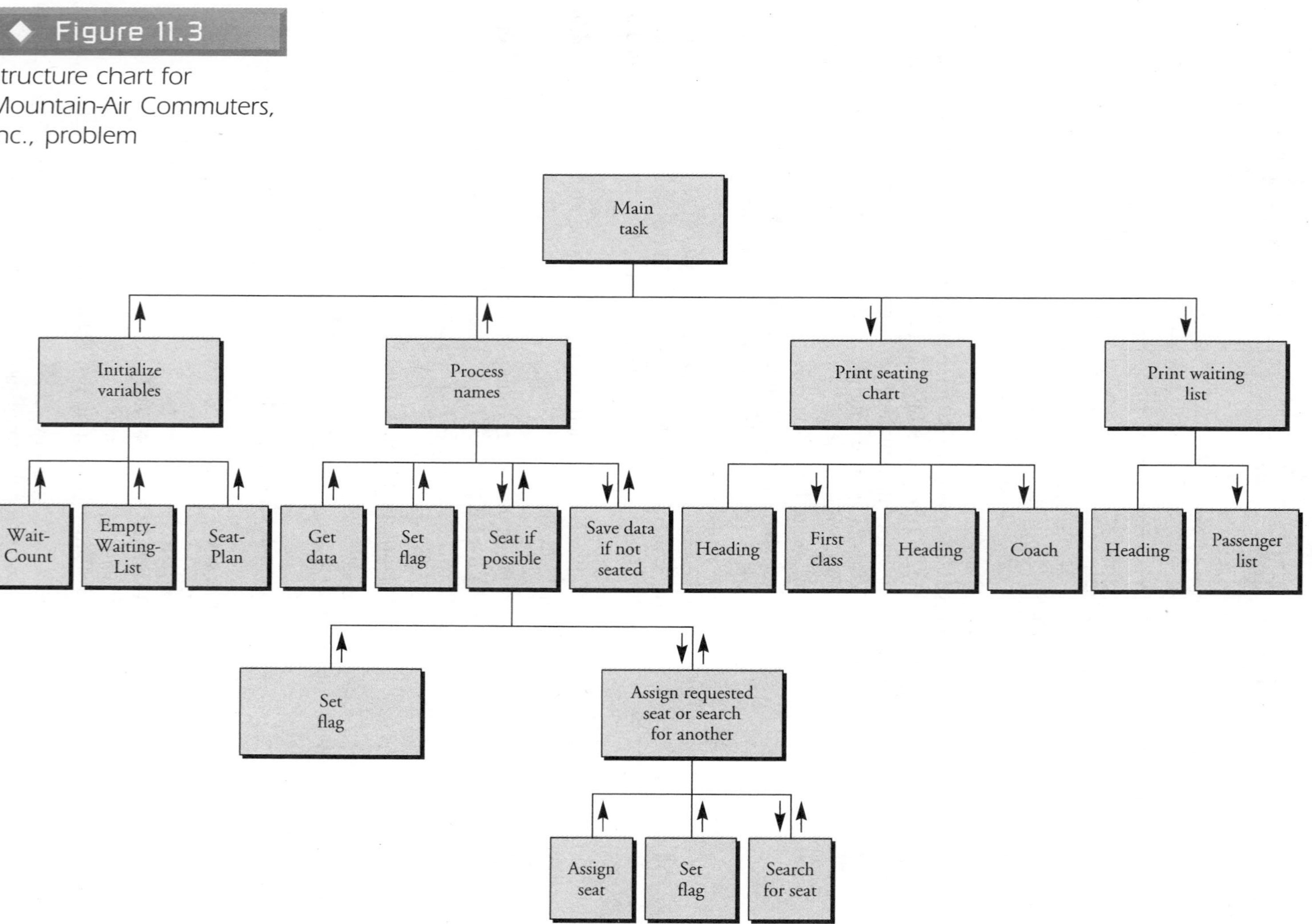

Information returned: Value for WaitCount
Value for EmptyWaitingList
Value for SeatPlan

Logic: Assign beginning values to the parameters.
Use nested loops to initialize the array SeatPlan.

2. ProcessAName Module

   Data received: None
   Information returned: A seating chart
   A Boolean value for extra passengers
   A waiting list for the next flight

   Logic: Get a name, section preference, and seat choice.
   Search to see if a seat can be found.
   If yes, then ticket.
   If no, then save relevant information.

3. PrintSeatingChart Module

   Data received: A two-dimensional array of names of ticketed passengers.
   Information returned: None
   Logic: Print the seating plan indicating row, seat, and section choice for each passenger.

4. PrintWaitingList Module

   Data received: Parallel arrays for the passenger's name, section choice, and seat preference
   Information returned: None
   Logic: Use a loop to print an appropriately titled list of passengers for the next flight.

A further development of the pseudocode is

1. Initialize variables
   1.1 Initialize WaitCount
   1.2 Initialize EmptyWaitingList
   1.3 Initialize SeatPlan
2. **WHILE NOT eof DO** process a name
   2.1 Get passenger information
   2.2 Set Boolean flag Seated for **false**
   2.3 Seat if possible
   2.4 **IF NOT** seated **THEN** save relevant information
3. Print a seating chart
   3.1 Print a heading
   3.2 Print the first class section
   3.3 Print a heading
   3.4 Print the coach section
4. **IF** there is a waiting list **THEN** print the list
   4.1 Print a heading
   4.2 Print passenger list with four columns

Step 2.3 needs some additional refinement. Further development yields

2.3 Seat if possible
   2.3.1 Set Seated to **false**
   2.3.2 **IF** requested seat is available **THEN**

2.3.2.1 Assign seat
2.3.2.2 Set Seated to **true**
ELSE
2.3.2.3 Search for another seat

A complete program for this is

```
PROGRAM SeatingPlan (input, output, Data);

{   This  program  prints  a  seating  plan  for  an   airline.  }
{   Passengers  are  assigned  seats  on  a  first-come, first-  }
{   served basis.  Seating requests  must be honored.  If  all   }
{   seats  are  filled  in  a  section,  the  passenger's name   }
{   and seat preference are placed on a waiting list for the     }
{   next flight.  Features of this program include               }
{                                                                }
{        a.  defined constants                                   }
{        b.  user-defined data types                             }
{        c.  multidimensional arrays                             }
{        d.  subprograms for modular development                 }

CONST
  NumRows = 10;
  NumColumns = 3;
  MaxLength = 25;
  FirstClassBegin = 1;
  FirstClassEnd = 3;
  CoachBegin = 4;
  CoachEnd = 10;
  EmptyString = '                    ';
  Skip = ' ';
  MaxNameLength = 20;

TYPE
  NameString = PACKED ARRAY [1..MaxNameLength] OF char;
  SeatingPlan = ARRAY [1..NumRows, 1..NumColumns] OF NameString;
  NotSeatedList = ARRAY [1..MaxLength] OF NameString;
  SectionOptionList = ARRAY [1..MaxLength] OF char;
  SeatChoiceList = ARRAY [1..MaxLength, 1..2] OF integer;

VAR
  Seated : boolean;                   { Indicator for seat found  }
  WaitingList : NotSeatedList;        { Name list for next flight }
  WaitCount : integer;                { Counter for waiting list  }
  EmptyWaitingList : boolean;         { Indicator for empty list  }
  Seat : SeatingPlan;                 { 2-dim array of seats      }
  Name : NameString;                  { String for names          }
  SectionChoice : char;               { First class or coach      }
  RowChoice, ColumnChoice : integer;  { Seat preference           }
  SectionOption : SectionOptionList;  { Array of section options  }
  SeatChoice : SeatChoiceList;        { Array of seat choices     }
  Data : text;                        { Data file                 }

{****************************************************************}
```

```
PROCEDURE Initialize (VAR Seat : SeatingPlan);

  {  Given:   A two-dimensional array of strings                   }
  {  Task:    Initialize all cells to an empty string              }
  {  Return:  An initialized two-dimensional array                 }

  VAR                                                                   1
    J, K : integer;
  BEGIN
    FOR J := 1 TO NumRows DO
      FOR K := 1 TO NumColumns DO
        Seat[J,K] := EmptyString
  END;  {  of PROCEDURE Initialize  }

{*****************************************************************}

PROCEDURE GetAName (VAR Name : NameString;
                    VAR SectionChoice : char;
                    VAR RowChoice,
                    ColumnChoice : integer);

  {  Given:   Nothing                                                }
  {  Task:    Read a name and section and seat preferences           }
  {                from the input file                               }
  {  Return:  Passenger name and section and seat preferences        }

  VAR
    J : integer;
  BEGIN
    FOR J := 1 TO MaxNameLength DO
      read (Data, Name[J]);
    readln (Data, SectionChoice, RowChoice, ColumnChoice)
  END;  {  of PROCEDURE GetAName  }

{*****************************************************************}

PROCEDURE SeatIfPossible (Name : NameString;                            2
                          VAR Seat : SeatingPlan;
                          RowChoice,
                          ColumnChoice : integer;
                          SectionChoice : char;
                          VAR Seated : boolean);

  {  Given:   Passenger name and section and seat preferences     }
  {  Task:    If requested seat is available, assign to seat;     }
  {                if seat is not available, use Search to        }
  {                check for an alternate seat                    }
  {  Return:  Seat assignment if one has been made;               }
  {           Boolean flag to indicate if seat was found          }

  PROCEDURE Search (Name : NameString;
                    VAR Seat : SeatingPlan;
                    VAR Seated : boolean;
                    FirstRow,
                    LastRow : integer);
```

```
      {  Given:    Passenger name, current seating chart, row        }
      {                 designators for first class and coach        }
      {                 sections                                     }
      {  Task:     Search indicated rows to see if an alternate seat}
      {                 is available; if yes, assign passenger to it}
      {  Return:   Updated seating plan and Boolean flag indicating }
      {                 whether or not a seat was found              }

      VAR
        Row, Column : integer;
      BEGIN  {  PROCEDURE Search  }
        Seated := false;
        Row := FirstRow;
        REPEAT
          Column := 1;                          {  Start searching rows  }
          REPEAT                                {  Search one row        }
            IF Seat[Row, Column] = EmptyString THEN
              BEGIN
                Seat[Row, Column] := Name;                                      2
                Seated := true
              END
            ELSE
              Column := Column + 1
          UNTIL Seated OR (Column > NumColumns);
          Row := Row + 1                      {  Search next row       }
        UNTIL Seated OR (Row > LastRow)
      END;  {  of PROCEDURE Search  }

    BEGIN  {  PROCEDURE SeatIfPossible  }
      Seated := false;
      IF Seat[RowChoice, ColumnChoice] = EmptyString THEN
        BEGIN
          Seat[RowChoice, ColumnChoice] := Name;
          Seated := true
        END
      ELSE
        CASE SectionChoice OF
          'F'  :  Search (Name, Seat, Seated,
                          FirstClassBegin, FirstClassEnd);
          'C'  :  Search (Name, Seat, Seated,
                          CoachBegin, CoachEnd)
        END  {  of CASE SectionChoice  }
    END;  {  of PROCEDURE SeatIfPossible  }

  {*****************************************************************}

  PROCEDURE PrintSeatingChart (VAR Seat : SeatingPlan);

    {  Given:   The seating chart and a two-dimensional array of   }
    {                names                                          }
    {  Task:    Print the passenger names in rows and columns       }
    {                according to their assigned seats              }
    {  Return:  Nothing                                             }

    VAR
      J, K : integer;
```

```
BEGIN
  writeln;
  writeln (Skip:10, 'MOUNTAIN-AIR COMMUTERS');
  writeln (Skip:15, 'Seating Chart');
  writeln;
  writeln ('First class section');
  writeln ('-------------------');
  writeln;
  FOR J := 1 TO FirstClassEnd DO
    BEGIN
      FOR K := 1 TO NumColumns DO
        write (Seat[J,K]:22);
      writeln                                                    3
    END;  {  of FOR J loop  }
  writeln;
  writeln ('Coach section');
  writeln ('-------------');
  writeln;
  FOR J := CoachBegin TO CoachEnd DO
    BEGIN
      FOR K := 1 TO NumColumns DO
        write (Seat[J,K]:22);
      writeln
    END;  {  of FOR J loop  }
  writeln
END;  {  of PROCEDURE PrintSeatingChart  }

{*****************************************************************}

PROCEDURE PrintWaitingList  (VAR WaitingList : NotSeatedList;
                             VAR SectionOption : SectionOptionList;
                             VAR SeatChoice : SeatChoiceList;
                                 WaitCount : integer);

  {  Given:   An array of names of passengers not seated, and    }
  {                the section and seat preferences for each     }
  {  Task:    Print a waiting list for the next flight           }
  {  Return:  Nothing                                            }

  VAR
    J : integer;
  BEGIN                                                          4
    writeln;
    writeln (Skip:10, 'Waiting list for next flight');
    writeln;
    writeln ('NAME':10, 'SECTION CHOICE':27,
             'ROW NUMBER':15, 'COLUMN NUMBER':15);
    write ('-----------------------------------');
    writeln ('-----------------------------------');
    writeln;
    FOR J := 1 TO WaitCount DO
      writeln ('<', J:2, '>', WaitingList[J]:22, SectionOption[J]:4,
               SeatChoice[J,1]:18, SeatChoice[J,2]:13)
  END;  {  of PROCEDURE PrintWaitingList  }

{*****************************************************************}
```

```
BEGIN  {  Main program  }
  WaitCount := 0;
  EmptyWaitingList := true;
  Initialize (Seat);
  reset (Data);
  WHILE NOT eof(Data) DO
    BEGIN
      GetAName (Name, SectionChoice, RowChoice, ColumnChoice);
      Seated := false;
      SeatIfPossible (Name, Seat, RowChoice, ColumnChoice,
                      SectionChoice, Seated);
      IF NOT Seated THEN   {  Save information for waiting list  }
        BEGIN
          WaitCount := WaitCount + 1;
          WaitingList[WaitCount] := Name;
          SectionOption[WaitCount] := SectionChoice;
          SeatChoice[WaitCount, 1] := RowChoice;
          SeatChoice[WaitCount, 2] := ColumnChoice;
          EmptyWaitingList := false
        END  {  of IF NOT Seated  }
    END;  {  of WHILE NOT eof  }
  PrintSeatingChart (Seat);
  IF NOT EmptyWaitingList THEN
    PrintWaitingList (WaitingList, SectionOption, SeatChoice,
                      WaitCount)
END.  {  of main program  }
```

Using the data file

```
Smith John          F 3 2
Alexander Joe       C 9 3
Allen Darcy         F 3 2
Jones Mary          C 8 1
Humphrey H          C 8 2
Johnson M           F 3 1
Eastman Ken         F 1 1
Winston Sam         C 8 3
Smythe Susan        C 9 1
Hendricks J B       C 9 2
Hanson Cynthia      C 9 3
Zoranson Steve      C 10 1
Radamacher Joe      C 10 3
Borack Bill         C 10 2
Seracki Don         C 9 2
Henry John          F 1 2
Steveson Enghart    F 1 3
Johansen Mary       F 2 1
Smith Martha        F 2 2
Jones Martha        F 2 3
Rinehart Jim        F 3 3
Rinehart Jane       F 3 2
Swenson Cecil       C 4 1
Swenson Carol       C 4 2
Byes Nikoline       C 4 3
Byes Jennifer       C 5 3
```

```
Harris John          C 5 2
Harris Judy          C 5 1
Hartman F G          C 6 1
Hartman D T          C 6 2
Lakes William        C 6 3
Lampton George       C 7 1
Hayes Woodrow        C 7 2
Champion M G         C 7 3
Thomas Lynda         C 8 1
Sisler Susan         C 8 2
Stowers Steve        C 8 3
Banks M J            C 5 3
Banks H W            C 5 2
Brown Susan          C 3 1
Wince Ann            C 8 2
Wince Joanne         C 8 1
```

sample output is

```
                 MOUNTAIN-AIR COMMUTERS
                      Seating Chart

First class section
-------------------

  Allen Darcy           Eastman Ken           Henry John
  Steveson Enghart      Johansen Mary         Smith Martha
  Johnson M             Smith John            Jones Martha

Coach section
-------------

  Hanson Cynthia        Seracki Don           Swenson Cecil
  Swenson Carol         Byes Nikoline         Byes Jennifer
  Harris John           Harris Judy           Hartman F G
  Hartman D T           Lakes William         Lampton George
  Jones Mary            Humphrey H            Winston Sam
  Smythe Susan          Hendricks J B         Alexander Joe
  Zoranson Steve        Borack Bill           Radamacher Joe

    Waiting list for next flight

      NAME              SECTION CHOICE     ROW NUMBER  COLUMN NUMBER
----------------------------------------------------------------------
< 1>  Rinehart Jim            F                3             3
< 2>  Rinehart Jane           F                3             2
< 3>  Hayes Woodrow           C                7             2
< 4>  Champion M G            C                7             3
< 5>  Thomas Lynda            C                8             1
< 6>  Sisler Susan            C                8             2
< 7>  Stowers Steve           C                8             3
< 8>  Banks M J               C                5             3
< 9>  Banks H W               C                5             2
<10>  Brown Susan             C                3             1
<11>  Wince Ann               C                8             2
<12>  Wince Joanne            C                8             1
```

Running and Debugging Hints

1. Use subrange types with descriptive identifiers for specifying index ranges. For example,

```
TYPE
  Page = 1..50;
  Row = 1..15;
  Column = 1..10;
  Book = ARRAY [Page, Row, Column] OF real;
```

2. Develop and maintain a systematic method of processing nested loops. For example, students with mathematical backgrounds will often use I, J, and K as index variables for three-dimensional arrays.
3. Be careful to properly subscript multidimensional array components.
4. When using an array of packed arrays as a list of strings, remember that in standard Pascal, strings must be read in one character at a time. However, strings can be written by a single **writeln** command.
5. When sorting one array in a program that uses parallel arrays, remember to make similar component exchanges in all arrays.
6. Define all data structures in the **TYPE** definition section.

Summary

Key Terms

higher-dimensional array   two-dimensional array

Key Term (Optional)

parallel arrays

Key Concepts

- Two-dimensional arrays can be declared in several ways; one descriptive method is

```
TYPE
  Chart4X6 = ARRAY [1..4, 1..6] OF real;
VAR
  Table : Chart4X6;
```

- Nested loops are frequently used to **read** and **write** values in two-dimensional arrays; for example, data can be read by

```
FOR Row := 1 TO 4 DO
  FOR Column := 1 TO 6 DO
    read (Data, Table[Row, Column]);
```

- When processing the components of a single row or single column, leave the appropriate row or column index fixed and let the other index vary as a loop index; for example, to sum row 3, use

```
Sum := 0;
FOR Column := 1 TO NumOfColumns DO
  Sum := Sum + A[3, Column];
```

To sum column 3, use

```
Sum := 0;
FOR Row := 1 TO NumOfRows DO
  Sum := Sum + A[Row, 3];
```

- An array of strings in Pascal is a special case of a two-dimensional array; the data structure is an array of packed arrays and can be declared by

```
TYPE
  NameString = PACKED ARRAY [1..20] OF char;
  NameList = ARRAY [1..50] OF NameString;
VAR
  Name : NameList;
```

- Arrays of strings (packed arrays of characters) can be alphabetized by using the selection sort.
- Three standard procedures used in programs that work with arrays of strings are (1) get the data, (2) alphabetize the array, and (3) print the alphabetized list.
- Parallel arrays can be used to solve problems that require arrays of the same index type but of different data types.
- A typical problem in which one would use parallel arrays involves working with a list of names and an associated list of numbers (for example, test scores). In Chapter 12 we will see that this can also be done with a single array of records.
- A typical data structure declaration for using names and scores is

```
TYPE
  NameString = PACKED ARRAY [1..20] OF char;
  NameList = ARRAY [1..30] OF NameString;
  ScoreList = ARRAY [1..30] OF integer;
VAR
  Name : NameList;
  Score : ScoreList;
```

- Data structures for solving problems can require arrays of three or more dimensions.
- A typical declaration for an array of three dimensions is

```
TYPE
  Dim1 = 1..10;
  Dim2 = 1..20;
  Dim3 = 1..30;
  Block = ARRAY [Dim1, Dim2, Dim3] OF real;
VAR
  Item : Block;
```

In this array, a typical component is accessed by

```
Item[I,J,K]
```

- Nested loops are frequently used when working with higher-dimensional arrays; for example, all values on the first level of array Item as just declared can be printed by

```
FOR J := 1 TO 20 DO
  BEGIN
    FOR K := 1 TO 30 DO
      BEGIN
        write (Item[1,J,K]:5:2);
        writeln
      END;  {  of 1 line  }
    writeln
  END;  {  of 20 lines  }
```

- When working with subprograms, array variables are usually passed by reference.

Chapter Review Exercises

For Exercises 1–6, using the following table,

Table

5	8	12	9
4	6	1	10
11	2	7	3

indicate the value of the statement.

1. `Table[3,2]`
2. `Table[1,3]`
3. `Table[3,4]`
4. `Table[2,1]`
5. `Table[3,3]`
6. `Table[1,4]`
7. Write the necessary declarations for the table in Exercises 1–6.
8. Write a declaration for SampleTable using a **TYPE** definition in the declaration.

Sample Table

3	4	6	2	7
1	12	9	6	8

For Exercises 9–13, using SampleTable from Exercise 8, write the proper notation for the table position that contains the value listed.

9. 6
10. 2
11. 1
12. 12
13. 8
14. Suppose the contents of SampleTable (Exercise 8) are read from the following data lines:

    3 4 6 2 7 ▮ 1 12 9 6 8 ▮ ■

    Write a fragment of code to read these data into the proper positions in the table.
15. Write a fragment of code to print SampleTable (Exercise 8) in tabular form.
16. Write a fragment of code to add the values in columns two through five in each row of SampleTable (Exercise 8) to the value in the column preceding it.
17. Write an appropriate procedure declaration and call from the main program to permit passing SampleTable (Exercise 8) to a procedure as a variable parameter.
18. Write an appropriate declaration for an array containing 50 names of up to 25 characters each.
19. Write an array declaration for a table that holds the responses to 50 multiple choice test items (letters *A* through *E*) for 100 students.

20. Write a procedure that permits input of data into the array declared in Exercise 19.
21. An array of names is stored in a table in the form

    Smith John

    Each name is 20 characters long. Write a procedure to get the names and print them in the form

    John Smith
22. Write array declarations for a list of 20 people (up to 25 characters per name) and their grade point averages (real numbers).
23. Write a fragment of code to read data into the arrays in Exercise 22. Assume each line of data consists of a name and a grade point average in the form

    Smith John* 3.89
24. Write a fragment of code to sort the arrays in Exercise 22 in order from highest GPA to lowest.

For Exercises 25–30, find any errors in the array declarations.

25.
```
TYPE
  Exercise25 : ARRAY [1..20, 1..30] OF integer;
```
26.
```
TYPE
  Exercise26 = ARRAY [1..5, 1..30] OF ArrayType;
```
27.
```
VAR
  Exercise27 : ARRAY [1..5, 10..20] OF integer;
```
28.
```
TYPE
  Exercise28 = PACKED ARRAY [10,20] OF char;
```
29.
```
TYPE
  Exercise29 = [1..30, 1..10] OF char;
```
30.
```
VAR
  Exercise30 : ARRAY [1..10; -5..5] OF integer;
```
31. Write **TYPE** and **ARRAY** declarations suitable for an array to hold records for a high school football team. Data consist of an opponent's name for each of 10 games and a **boolean** variable; **true** indicates win, **false** indicates a loss. Data are stored in the table for each of the last 10 years.

Programming Problems

■ 1. The local high school sports boosters are conducting a fund drive to help raise money for the athletic program. As each donation is received, the person's name and amount of donation are entered on one line in a data file. Write a program to do the following:
   a. Print an alphabetized list of all donors together with their corresponding donations.
   b. Print a list of donations from high to low together with the donors' names.
   c. Compute and print the average and total of all donations.

■ 2. Because they did not meet their original goal, your local high school sports boosters (Problem 1) are at it again. For their second effort, each donor's name and donation are added as a separate line at the end of the previously sorted list. Write a program to produce lists, sum, and average as in Problem 1. No donor's name should appear more than once in a list.

■ 3. Mr. Lae Z. Programmer (Problems 5, 22, and 23, Chapter 5; Problem 13, Chapter 6; Problem 7, Chapter 7; and Problem 5, Chapter 9) now expects you to write a program to perform all record keeping for the class. For each student, consecutive lines of the data file contain the student's name, 10 quiz scores, six program scores, and three examination scores. Your output should include the following:
   a. An alphabetized list together with
      i. quiz total
      ii. program total
      iii. examination total
      iv. total points
      v. percentage grade
      vi. letter grade
   b. The overall class average
   c. A histogram depicting the grade distribution

4. The All Metro Basketball Conference consists of 10 teams. The conference commissioner has created a data file in which each line contains one school's name, location, and nickname for the school team. You are to write a program to read these data and then produce three lists, each of which contains all information about the school. All lists are to be sorted alphabetically, the first by school name, the second by school location, and the third by nickname.

5. Upgrade the program for Mountain-Air Commuters, Inc., in this chapter's **Case Study** so it can be used for each of five daily flights. Passengers on a waiting list must be processed first. Print a seating chart for each flight.

6. Add yet another upgrade to the Mountain-Air Commuters, Inc., program (Problem 5). Write an interactive version to consider the possibility of seating passengers who wish to be seated together in the same row. If no such seating is possible, they should then be given a choice of alternate seating (if possible) or taking a later flight.

7. Salespersons at McHenry Tool Corporation are given a monthly commission check. The commission is computed by multiplying the salesperson's gross monthly sales by the person's commission rate.

   Write a program to compute a salesperson's monthly commission computed to the nearest penny. The program should prepare a list of all salespersons in descending order based on monthly commission earned, with the person earning the highest commission on top. Each salesperson's commission should be printed next to his or her name. At the bottom of the list, indicate the total monthly commission (summed across all salespersons) and the average commission per salesperson. McHenry never employs more than 60 salespersons.

   Any names of persons who have invalid data should be printed separately. Data are invalid if the commission rate is not between 0.01 and 0.50, or if the gross monthly sales figure is negative.

8. To reduce their costs, the McHenry Tool Corporation (Problem 7) is switching from monthly to biannual commission checks. The commission is now computed by multiplying a person's commission rate by the sum of his or her gross monthly sales for a six-month period. McHenry has asked you to develop the necessary computer program. The program should differ from that of Problem 7 in the following ways:

a. Each name on the output should be followed by the six figures for gross monthly sales. The columns should be labeled "January" through "June." Total six-month gross sales should be given next, followed by rate of commission, and amount of six-month commission check to the nearest cent.
b. Commission rates are based on gross six-month sales.

Sales	Commission Rate (%)
0–$19,999	3.0
$20,000–$39,999	5.0
$40,000–$59,999	5.5
$60,000–$79,999	6.0
$80,000–$89,999	6.5
$90,000 or more	8.0

c. At the bottom of each column, the program should provide the total and the mean for that column. (The column for commission rates does not require a total, only a mean.)

9. The Registrar of a community college (enrollment less than 2000) has asked you to write a program to figure grade point averages for an unknown number of students.

   The output should be an alphabetized roster showing the gender, identification number (social security number), grade point average (rounded to three decimal places), and class status (freshman, sophomore, junior, or senior) for each student.

   The data provide the name, gender (M or F), social security number (ID), and number of semesters completed. Also provided are the number of courses taken and the letter grade and number of credits for each course. The possible letter grades are A (4 points), B (3 points), C (2 points), D (1 point), and E (0 points). Class status is determined by the number of credits as follows:

1–25 credits	Freshman
26–55 credits	Sophomore
56–85 credits	Junior
86 or more credits	Senior

10. You have just started work for the Michigan Association of Automobile Manufacturers and have been asked to analyze sales data on five subcompact cars for the last six months. Your analysis should be in table form and should include the name of each make and model, a model's sales volume for each month, a model's total and average sales volume for six months, a model's total sales revenue for six months, and the total and average sales volume for each month. In addition, your output should include the total and average sales volume of all models for the entire six months and the make and model name of the car with the largest total sales revenue and the amount of that revenue.

11. You have been asked to write a program to assist with the inventory and ordering for Tite-Jeans, Inc. They manufacture three styles: straight, flair, and peg. In

each style, waist sizes vary by integer values from 24 to 46 and inseams vary by integer values from 26 to 40. Write a program to do the following:

a. Read the starting inventory.
b. Read daily sales.
c. Print the ending inventory for each style.
d. Print order charts for each style that is low in stock (fewer than three).
e. Print an emergency order list for those that are out of stock.

12. You have been asked to write a program that will grade the results of a true–false quiz and display the results in tabular form. The quiz consists of 10 questions. The data file for this problem consists of (1) correct responses (answer key) on line one, and (2) a four-digit student identification number followed by that student's 10 responses on each successive line. Thus, the data file would be

```
TFFTFTTFTT
0461 TTFTTFTFTT
3218 TFFTTTTFTT
    .
    .
    .
```

Your program should read the key and store it in an array. It should then read the remaining lines, storing the student identification numbers in one array and the number of correct responses in a parallel array. Output should consist of a table with three columns: one for the student identification number, one for the number of correct responses, and one for the quiz grade. Grade assignments are A (10 correct), B (9), C (8–7), D (6–5), E (4–0). Your output should also include the quiz average for the entire class.

13. A few members (total unknown, but no more than 25) at Oakland Mountain Country Club want to computerize their golf scores. Each member plays 20 games, some 18 holes and some 9 holes. Each member's name (no more than 20 characters) is written on a data card, followed on a second card by the 20 scores. Each score is immediately followed by an E or an N, indicating 18 or 9 holes, respectively.

Write a program to read all the names and scores into two parallel two-dimensional arrays. Calculate everyone's 18-hole average. (Double the 9-hole scores before you store them in the array and treat as 18-hole scores.) Calculate how much each average is over or under par (par is 72 and should be declared as a constant). Output should be each name, average, difference from par, and scores.

14. Write a program to keep statistics for a basketball team consisting of 15 players. Statistics for each player should include shots attempted, shots made, and shooting percentage; free throws attempted, free throws made, and free throw percentage; offensive rebounds and defensive rebounds; assists; turnovers; and total points. Appropriate team totals should be listed as part of the output.

15. A magic square is a square array of positive integers such that the sum of each row, column, and diagonal is the same constant. For example,

16	3	2	13
5	10	11	8
9	6	7	12
4	15	14	1

is a magic square whose constant is 34. Write a program to input four lines of four positive integers. The program should then determine whether or not the square is a magic square. Program efficiency should be such that computation ends as soon as two different sums have been computed.

16. Pascal's triangle can be used to recognize coefficients of a quantity raised to a power. The rules for forming this triangle of integers are such that each row must start and end with a 1, and each entry in a row is the sum of the two values diagonally above the new entry. Thus, four rows of Pascal's triangle are

```
      1
    1   1
  1   2   1
1   3   3   1
```

This triangle can be used as a convenient way to get the coefficients of a quantity of two terms raised to a power (binomial coefficients). For example,

$$(a + b)^3 = 1 \times a^3 + 3a^2b + 3ab^2 + 1 \times b^3$$

where the coefficients 1, 3, 3, and 1 come from the fourth row of Pascal's triangle. Write a complete program to print Pascal's triangle for 10 rows.

17. Your high school principal has come to you for help. She wants you to develop a program to maintain a list of the 20 students in the school with the highest scores on the SAT test. Input is from a text file containing the name (20 characters), and the total SAT score (verbal plus mathematical). Write a program that, when all data have been read, prints a list of the 20 highest scores from highest to lowest, and the students' names. Assume that no two students have the same score.

18. The transpose of a matrix (table) is a new matrix with the row and column positions reversed. That is, the transpose of matrix A, an M by N matrix is an N by M matrix, with each element, $A[m, n]$ stored in $B[n, m]$. Given a 3×5 matrix of integers, create a matrix that is its transpose. Print both the original matrix and the new matrix.

■ 19. Mr. Laven, a mathematics teacher at your school, wants you to write a program to help him keep his students' grades. He wants to keep track of up to 30 grades for each of up to 35 students. Your program should read grades and names from a text file, and then print the following:
   a. A table showing the names in alphabetical order and grades received by each student
   b. An alphabetical list of students with their corresponding total points and average score
   c. A list of averages from high to low with corresponding students' names

20. Write a program in which a person can enter data into a 5×7 matrix. Print the original matrix along with the average of each row and column.

21. Matrix M is symmetric if it has the same number of rows as columns, and if each element $M[x,y]$ is equal to $M[y, x]$. Write a program to check a matrix entered by the user to see if it is symmetric or not.

22. The determinant of a 2×2 matrix

$$A = \begin{bmatrix} a\,b \\ c\,d \end{bmatrix}$$

is det A = $\begin{vmatrix} a\,b \\ c\,d \end{vmatrix}$ = $ad - bc$. The determinant of a 3 × 3 matrix

$$A = \begin{bmatrix} a\,b\,c \\ d\,e\,f \\ g\,h\,i \end{bmatrix}$$

is det $A = a\begin{vmatrix} e\,f \\ h\,i \end{vmatrix} - b\begin{vmatrix} d\,f \\ g\,i \end{vmatrix} + c\begin{vmatrix} d\,e \\ g\,h \end{vmatrix}$.

Write an interactive program that computes the determinant of a 3 × 3 matrix. Input consists of reals forming the 3 × 3 matrix. Output should be a display that includes the input matrix, a developmental step using 2 × 2 submatrices, and the value of the determinant. The program should contain a function for computing the determinant of a 2 × 2 matrix.

23. The following table shows the total sales for salespeople of the Falcon Manufacturing Company:

Salesperson	Week 1	Week 2	Week 3	Week 4
Anna, Michael	30	25	45	18
Henderson, Marge	22	30	32	35
Johnson, Fred	12	17	19	15
Yamagata, Tye	32	30	33	31
Ryan, Renee	22	17	28	16

The price of the product being sold is $1,985.95. Write a program that permits the input of the previous data, and prints both a replica of the original table and a table showing the dollar value of sales for each individual during each week along with their total sales. Also, print the total sales for each week and the total sales for the company.

24. Your high school office wants a computerized system for finding telephone numbers of students. The program should read a list of up to 20 students and their telephone numbers from a text file. It should permit the entry of a student's name, and then print the name and telephone number. (A binary search could be used for this.) If the name is not found, an appropriate message should be printed.

25. A graph in the field of graph theory consists of a collection of vertices and edges. For example, graph G

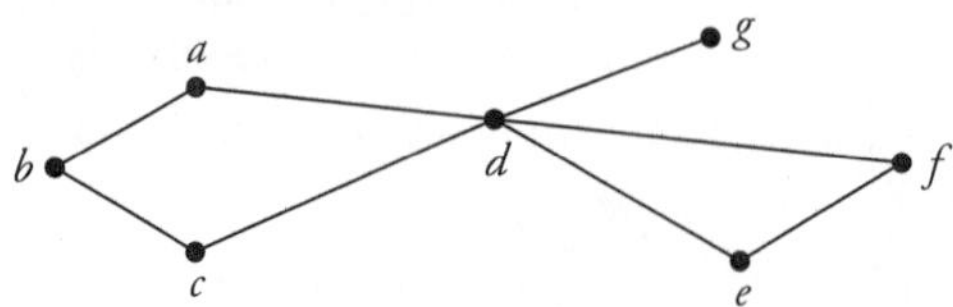

contains seven vertices and eight edges. Two vertices are adjacent if they are joined by an edge. In graph G, therefore, *a* is adjacent to *b* but *a* is not adjacent to *g*.

The adjacency matrix of a graph is a square matrix consisting of 1's and 0's, which indicate whether or not two vertices are adjacent. If the two vertices are adjacent, the corresponding entry is a 1; if they are not adjacent, the entry is a 0. For graph G, the adjacency matrix is as follows:

	a	*b*	*c*	*d*	*e*	*f*	*g*
a	0	1	0	1	0	0	0
b	1	0	1	0	0	0	0
c	0	1	0	1	0	0	0
d	1	0	1	0	1	1	1
e	0	0	0	1	0	1	0
f	0	0	0	1	1	0	0
g	0	0	0	1	0	0	0

Write a program that accepts as input the adjacency matrix of graph G. Each input line represents one row of the graph. Output should consist of the adjacency matrix with vertices indicated for the rows and columns and a list of all edges in the graph.

26. Write a program to permit two people to play the game of Battleship. Your program should record the ship positions, hits, misses, and ship sinkings for each player.
27. Rewrite the Battleship program (Problem 26) to have a person play against the computer.

Communication in Practice

1. Select a problem from the **Programming Problems** in this chapter that you have not done. Write documentation for that problem that includes a complete description of the following:
   a. Required input
   b. Required output
   c. Required processing and computation
2. Assume you are directing the development of a spelling checker to be used in conjunction with a text editor. Work up a complete set of specifications that can be used by the team that will do the actual development. Your specifications should include a description of the main tasks to be performed by the team, a statement of the expected form of input and output for the finished product, and documentation standards to be included in the development of each component.
3. Arrange a visit with a travel agent or an airline reservation agent, and discuss the information the agent requests from prospective passengers. If possible, have the agent set up a mock booking using the computerized reservation system. Examine the screen displays.

   Prepare a report of your visit for the class. Be sure to discuss how the designers of the reservation system may have used multidimensional arrays.

4. Contact someone who uses a spreadsheet as part of his or her daily work. Have the person show you several routine operations with the spreadsheet. In particular, find out how to adjust the size of the spreadsheet, sum rows, sum columns, and use functions to define entries for specific locations.

   Give an oral report of your discussion to your class. Explain how the various spreadsheet operations relate to what you have studied about two-dimensional arrays.
5. Select a problem from the **Programming Problems** in this chapter that you have not done. Construct a structure chart and write all documentary information necessary for the problem you have chosen. Do not write code. When you are finished, have a classmate read your documentation to see if it is clear precisely what is to be done.
6. Delete all documentation from one of the programs you prepared for this chapter. Exchange your modified version with a student who has prepared a similar version. Write documentation for the exchanged program. Compare your results with your classmate's original version.

Chapter 12

Records

Chapter Outline

Chapters 10 and 11 dealt extensively with the concept of the structured data type **ARRAY.** When we declare an array, we reserve a predetermined number of memory locations. The variables representing these memory locations are of the same base type and can be accessed by reference to the index of an array element.

All components of an array must be of the same data type—a serious limitation since in many situations this is not possible. For example, a bank may wish to keep a record of the name, address, telephone number, marital status, social security number, annual salary, total assets, and total liabilities of each customer. As we saw in Chapter 11, parallel arrays can be used to solve some of these problems. Fortunately, Pascal provides another structured data type, **RECORD,** which allows heterogeneous information to be stored, accessed, and manipulated. A record contains fields, which can be of different data types. In this chapter you learn how to declare records, how to access the various fields within a record, and how to work with arrays of records.

12.1 Record Definitions

Objectives

- to understand the basic idea of **RECORD** as a structured data type
- to be able to declare a record
- to be able to use fields of a record

Records as a Structured Data Type

A **record** is a collection of fields that may be treated as a whole or individually. To illustrate, a record that contains fields for a customer's name, age, and annual income could be visualized as shown in Figure 12.1. This schematic representation may help you understand why a record is considered a structured data type and may help familiarize you with the idea of using fields in a record.

RECORD Definition and Declaration

Now let's consider our first example of a formally declared record. Assume we want a record to contain a customer's name, age, and annual income. The following definition and subsequent declaration can be made:

◆ Figure 12.1

Fields in a record

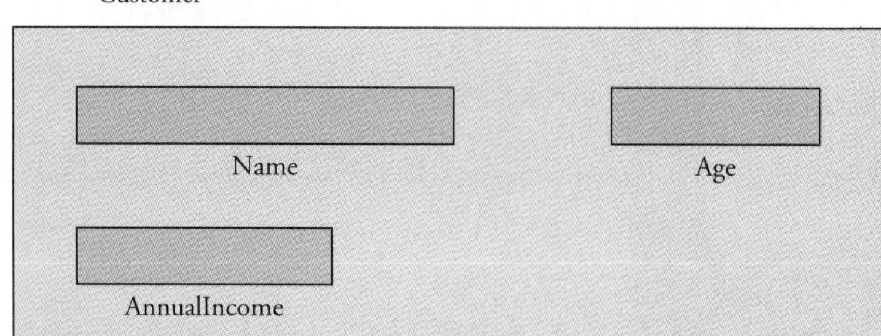

A **record** is a data structure that is a collection of fields that can be treated as a whole or that will allow you to work with individual fields.

A **field** is a component of a record.

```
TYPE
  CustomerInfo = RECORD
                   Name : PACKED ARRAY [1..30] OF char;
                   Age : integer;
                   AnnualIncome : real
                 END;  {  of RECORD CustomerInfo  }
VAR
  Customer : CustomerInfo;
```

Components of a record are called **fields** and each field has an associated data type. The general form for defining a record data type using the **TYPE** definition section is

> **TYPE**
> <type identifier> = **RECORD**
> <field identifier 1> : <data type 1>;
> <field identifier 2> : <data type 2>;
> .
> .
> .
> <field identifier *n*> : <data type *n*>
> **END;** { of **RECORD** definition }

The syntax diagram for this is

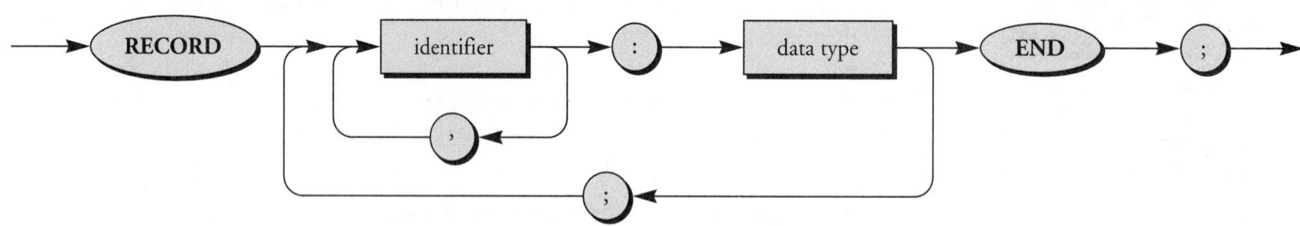

The following comments are in order concerning this form.

1. The type identifier can be any valid identifier. It should be descriptive to enhance program readability.
2. The reserved word **RECORD** must precede the field identifiers.
3. Each field identifier within a record must be unique. However, field identifiers in different records may use the same name. Thus,

```
FirstRecord = RECORD
                Name : PACKED ARRAY [1..30] OF char;
                Age : integer
              END;  {  of RECORD FirstRecord  }
```

and

```
SecondRecord = RECORD
                 Name : PACKED ARRAY [1..30] OF char;
                 Age : integer;
                 IQ : integer
               END;  {  of RECORD SecondRecord  }
```

can both be defined in the same program.

4. Data types for fields can be user defined. Thus, our earlier definitions could have been

```
TYPE
  NameString = PACKED ARRAY [1..30] OF char;
  CustomerInfo = RECORD
                   Name : NameString;
                   Age : integer;
                   AnnualIncome : real
                 END;  {  of RECORD CustomerInfo  }
VAR
  Customer : CustomerInfo;
```

5. **END** is required to signify the end of a **RECORD** definition. This is the second instance (remember **CASE**?) in which **END** is used without a **BEGIN.**
6. Fields of the same base type can be declared together. Thus,

```
Info = RECORD
         Name : NameString;
         Age, IQ : integer
       END;  {  of RECORD Info  }
```

is appropriate. However, it is good practice to list each field separately to enhance readability and to reinforce the concept of fields in a record.

The following example defines another record.

Example 12.1

Let's define a record for a student. The record is to contain a field for each of the following: student's name (Smith Jane), homeroom (127), class status (Fr, So, Jr, or Sr), previous credits earned (15), credits being taken (5), and grade point average (3.27). We can define a record and declare an appropriate variable as follows:

```
TYPE
  NameString = PACKED ARRAY [1..30] OF char;
  Class = (Fr, So, Jr, Sr);
  StudentInfo = RECORD
                  Name : NameString;
                  Homeroom : integer;
                  Status : Class;
```

```
                     CreditsEarned : 0..30;
                     CreditsTaking : 0..10;
                     GPA : real
                   END;  {  of RECORD StudentInfo  }
VAR
  Student : StudentInfo;
```

Fields in a Record

Now that we know how to define a record, we need to examine how to access fields in a record. For the purpose of our discussion, let's consider a record defined by

```
TYPE
  NameString = PACKED ARRAY [1..30] OF char;
  Employee = RECORD
               Name : NameString;
               Age : integer;
               MaritalStatus : char;
               Wage : real
             END;  {  of RECORD Employee  }
VAR
  Programmer : Employee;
```

Programmer can be visualized as pictured in Figure 12.2.

Each field within a record is a variable and can be uniquely identified by

<record name>.<field name>

A **field selector** is the period that separates the record name from the field name.

The period is a **field selector,** which separates the record name from the field name. Thus, the four field variables are

```
Programmer.Name
Programmer.Age
Programmer.MaritalStatus
Programmer.Wage
```

Each of these variables can be used in any manner consistent with the defined base type. To illustrate, if Programmer.Name and Programmer.Age have been assigned values and we wish to print the names of those employees under 30 years of age, we could use a fragment of code such as

◆ Figure 12.2

Defined fields in Programmer

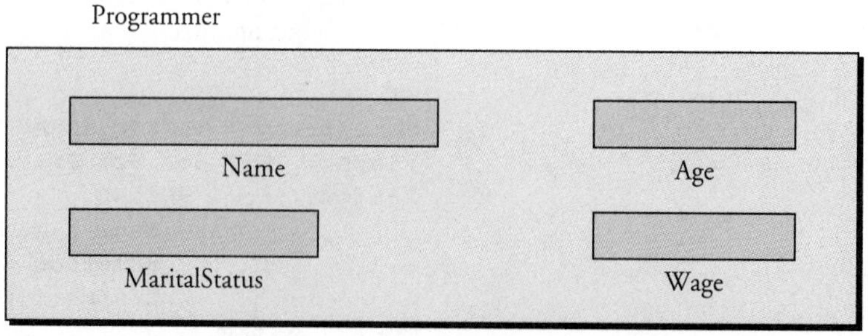

```
IF Programmer.Age < 30 THEN
  writeln (Programmer.Name:40);
```

If we wish to compute gross salary, we might have

```
read (Data, Hours);
GrossSalary := Hours * Programmer.Wage;
```

Other Fields

Thus far, our fields have been declared directly. Sometimes, when the structure of a record is being established, the data type of a field needs more development. For example, suppose we wish to declare a record for each student in a class and the record is to contain student name, class name, four test scores, 10 quiz scores, final average, and letter grade. This can be visualized as shown in Figure 12.3. In this case, Test and Quiz are both arrays. Thus, a subsequent development is shown in Figure 12.4.

◆ Figure 12.3

Fields in Student Record

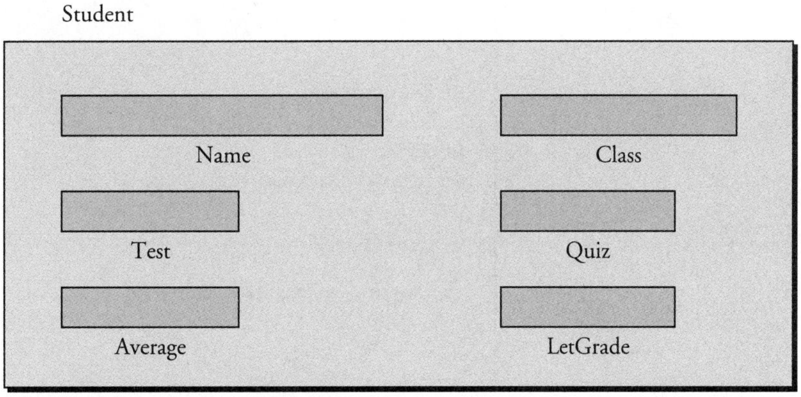

◆ Figure 12.4

Arrays as fields in a record

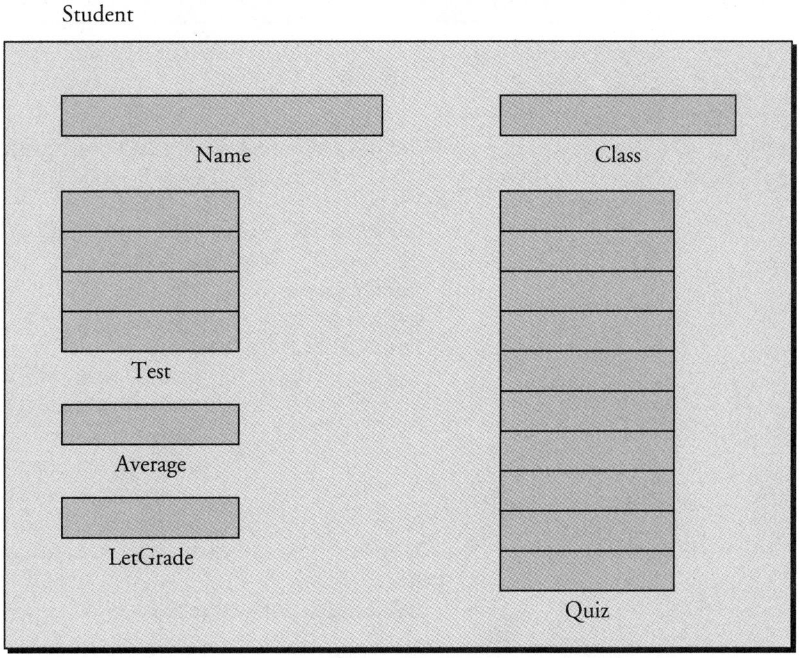

Communication and Style Tips

Use descriptive field names, appropriate subranges, and a descriptive variable name when defining records. For example, if you want a record to contain fields for a student's name, age, gender, and class status, you can use

```
TYPE
  NameString = PACKED ARRAY [1..20] OF char;
  StudentRecord = RECORD
                    Name : NameString;
                    Age : 0..99;
                    Gender : (Male, Female);
                    ClassStatus : (Fr, So, Jr, Sr)
                  END;  {  of RECORD StudentRecord  }
VAR
  Student : StudentRecord;
```

The fields would then be

```
Student.Name
Student.Age
Student.Gender
Student.ClassStatus
```

and you can use program statements such as

```
IF Student.Gender = Male THEN
```

or

```
IF Student.Age < 18 THEN
```

The record in Figure 12.4 can now be formally defined by

```
TYPE
  NameString = PACKED ARRAY [1..30] OF char;
  String10 = PACKED ARRAY [1..10] OF char;
  TestScores = ARRAY [1..4] OF integer;
  QuizScores = ARRAY [1..10] OF integer;
  StudentInfo = RECORD
                  Name: NameString;
                  Class : String10;
                  Test : TestScores;
                  Quiz : QuizScores;
                  Average : real;
                  LetGrade : char
                END;  {  of RECORD StudentInfo  }
VAR
  Student : StudentInfo;
```

If the student associated with this record earned an 89 on the first test and a 9 (out of 10) on the first quiz, this information could be entered by reading the values or by assigning them appropriately. Thus,

```
read (Data, Student.Test[1], Student.Quiz[1]);
```

or

```
Student.Test[1] := 89;
Student.Quiz[1] := 9;
```

will suffice.

Exercises 12.1

1. Explain why records are structured data types.
2. Write a test program to
   a. Define a **RECORD** type in which the record contains fields for your name and your age.
   b. Declare a record variable to be of this type.
   c. Read in your name and age from a data file.
   d. Print out your name and age.
3. Discuss the similarities and differences between arrays and records as structured data types.

Use the **TYPE** definition section to define a record for the part of Figure 12.5 indicated in Exercises 4–6. For each exercise, also declare a record variable to be of the defined type.

4. TeamMember, see Figure 12.5(a)

*5. Book, see Figure 12.5(b)

6. Student, see Figure 12.5(c)

For Exercises 7–9, draw a schematic representation of the record definition.

*7.
```
TYPE
  NameString = PACKED ARRAY [1..30] OF char;
  String11 = PACKED ARRAY [1..11] OF char;
  EmployeeInfo = RECORD
                   Name : NameString;
                   SSN : String11;
                   NumOfDep : integer;
                   HourlyWage : real
                 END;
VAR
  Employee : EmployeeInfo;
```

8.
```
TYPE
  HouseInfo = RECORD
                Location : PACKED ARRAY [1..20] OF char;
                Age: integer;
                NumRooms : integer;
                NumBaths : integer;
                BuildingType : (Brick, Frame);
```

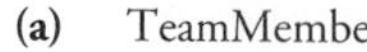

◆ Figure 12.5

Records with fields illustrated

(a) TeamMember

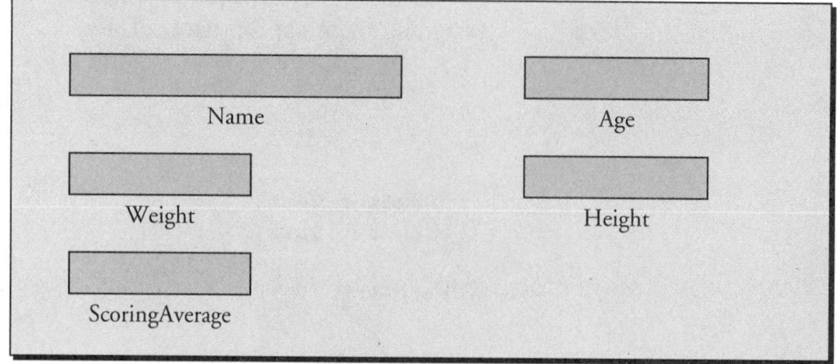

(b) Book

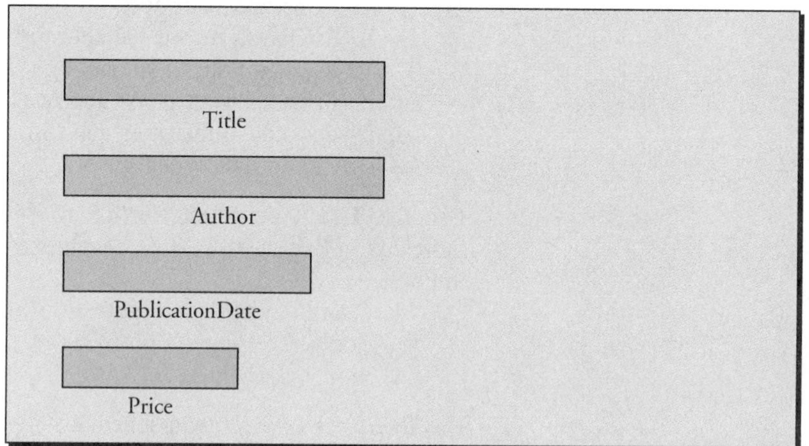

(c) Student

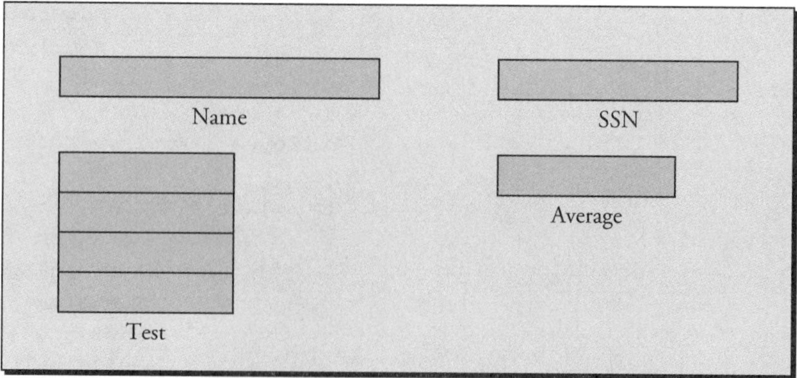

```
                    Taxes : real;
                    Price : real
                  END;
    VAR
      House : HouseInfo;
```

*9.
```
    TYPE
      NameString = PACKED ARRAY [1..30] OF char;
      String20 = PACKED ARRAY [1..20] OF char;
      String11 = PACKED ARRAY [1..11] OF char;
      PhoneBook = RECORD
                    Name : NameString;
                    Address : ARRAY [1..4] OF NameString;
                    PhoneNum : String11
                  END;
    VAR
      PhoneListing : PhoneBook;
```

For Exercises 10 and 11, use the **TYPE** definition section to define an appropriate **RECORD** type. Also declare an appropriate record variable.

10. Families in your school district; each record should contain the last name, parents' first and last names, address, number of children, and ages of children.

*11. Students in a school system; each record should contain the student's name, homeroom, classification (Fr, So, Jr, or Sr), courses being taken (at most six), and grade point average.

For Exercises 12–14, find all errors in the definitions or declarations.

12.
```
    TYPE
      Info : RECORD
               Name = PACKED ARRAY [1..30] OF char;
               Age : 0..100
             END;
```

*13.
```
    TYPE
      Member = RECORD
                 Age : integer;
                 IQ : integer
               END;
    VAR
      Member : Member;
```

14.
```
    VAR
      Member = RECORD
                 Name : PACKED ARRAY [1..30] OF char;
                 Age : 0..100;
                 IQ = 50..200
               END;
```

In Exercises 15–26, given the record defined by

```
TYPE
  NameString = PACKED ARRAY [1..30] OF char;
  Weekdays = (Mon, Tues, Wed, Thur, Fri);
  ListOfScores = ARRAY [1..5] OF integer;
```

```
  Info = RECORD
           Name : NameString;
           Day : Weekdays;
           Score : ListOfScores;
           Average : real
         END;
VAR
  Contestant : Info;
  Sum : integer;
```

assume values have been assigned as shown in Figure 12.6. Indicate if the exercise is valid. If it is invalid, explain why.

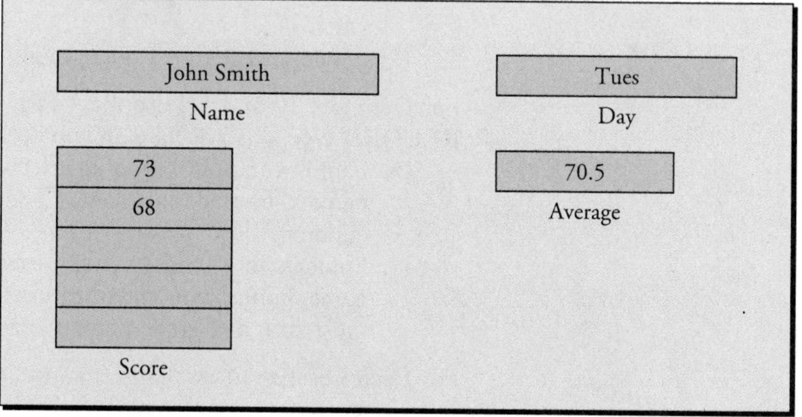

◆ Figure 12.6

Values in fields of Contestant

*15. `Day := Wed;`

16. `Contestant.Day := Wed;`

*17. `Score := 70;`

18. `Score[3] := 70;`

*19. `Contestant.Score[3] := 70;`

20. `Contestant[3].Score := 70;`

*21.
```
FOR J := 1 TO 5 DO
  Sum := Sum + Contestant.Score[J];
```

22. `Contestant.Score[3] := Score[2];`

*23. `Contestant.Score[3] := Contestant.Score[2] + 3;`

24. `Average := (Score[1] + Score[2] + Score[3]) / 3;`

*25.
```
IF Contestant.Day < Wed THEN
  Contestant.Average := Contestant.Score[1] +
                        Contestant.Score[2];
```

26. `writeln (Contestant.Name:40, Contestant.Average:10:2);`

12.2 Using Records

The previous section introduced the concept of **RECORD** as a structured data type. At this stage, you should be comfortable with this concept and be able to use the **TYPE** definition section to define such a data type. In this section, we will examine methods of working with records.

Objectives

- to be able to use **WITH . . . DO** when using records in a program
- to be able to copy complete records
- to be able to use a procedure to read data into a record
- to be able to use a procedure to print data from a record

WITH...DO Using Records

Let's consider a record that contains fields for a student's name, three test scores, and test average. This record can be defined by

```
CONST
  NameLength = 20;
  NumTests = 3;
TYPE
  NameString = PACKED ARRAY [1..NameLength] OF char;
  TestList = ARRAY [1..NumTests] OF integer;
  StudentRecord = RECORD
                    Name : NameString;
                    Score : TestList;
                    Average : real
                  END;  {  of RECORD StudentRecord   }
VAR
  Student : StudentRecord;
```

and envisioned as shown in Figure 12.7.

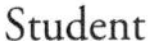

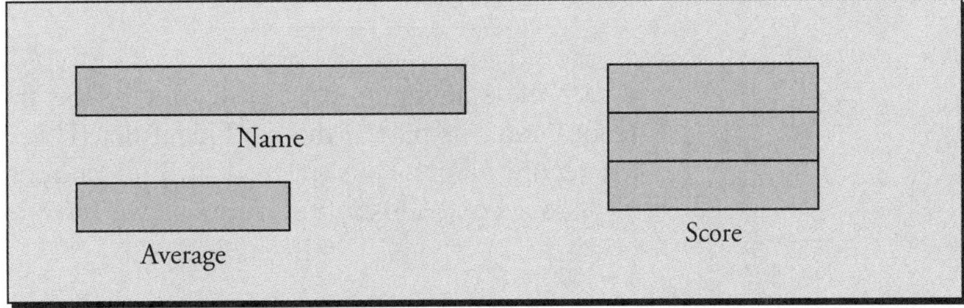

◆ Figure 12.7

Fields in Student

To use this record, we need to assign or read data into appropriate fields. Therefore, assume a line of data is

Washington Joe 79 83 94

T

These data can be read by the fragment of code

```
FOR J := 1 TO NameLength DO
  read (Data, Student.Name[J]);
FOR J := 1 TO NumTests DO
  read (Data, Student.Score[J]);
readln (Data);
```

The average can be computed by

```
Student.Average := (Student.Score[1] +
                    Student.Score[2] +
                    Student.Score[3]) / NumTests;
```

Notice each field identifier includes the record name. Fortunately, when working with fields of a record, Pascal provides a more convenient method of referring to these fields: a **WITH . . . DO** statement. Using this option, the previous fragment can be rewritten as

```
WITH Student DO
  BEGIN
    FOR J := 1 TO NameLength DO
      read (Data, Name[J]);
    FOR J := 1 TO NumTests DO
      read (Data, Score [J]);
    readln (Data);
    Average := (Score[1] + Score[2] + Score[3]) / NumTests
  END;  {  of WITH...DO  }
```

Formally, a **WITH . . . DO** statement has the form

> **WITH** <record name> **DO**
> **BEGIN**
> <statement 1>;
> <statement 2>;
> .
> .
> .
> <statement *n*>
> **END;**

where the statements used can refer to the field identifiers but do not include the record name as part of the field identifier. This eliminates use of the period following the record name. Thus, instead of Student.Score[J], we can use Score[J].

As a second illustration, suppose we have a record defined as

```
TYPE
  NameString = PACKED ARRAY [1..20] OF char;
  PatientInfo = RECORD
                  Name : NameString;
                  Age : integer;
                  Height : integer;
                  Weight : integer;
                  Gender : char
                END;  {  of RECORD PatientInfo  }
VAR
  Patient : PatientInfo;
```

Values can be assigned to the various fields specifically by

```
Patient.Name := 'Jones Connie        ';
Patient.Age := 17;
Patient.Height := 67;
Patient.Weight := 125;
Patient.Gender := 'F';
```

or by

```
WITH Patient DO
  BEGIN
    Name := 'Jones Connie        ';
    Age := 17;
```

```
    Height := 67;
    Weight := 125;
    Gender := 'F'
  END;  {  of WITH...DO  }
```

A single **WITH . . . DO** statement can be used with more than one record. For example, given the previous two record definitions, it is possible to write

```
WITH Student, Patient DO
  BEGIN
    Average := (Score[1] + Score[2] + Score[3]) / NumTests;
    Age := 17
  END;  {  of WITH...DO  }
```

This is equivalent to the nested use of **WITH . . . DO,** as follows:

```
WITH Student DO
  WITH Patient DO
    BEGIN
      Average := (Score[1] + Score[2] + Score[3]) / 3;
      Age := 19
    END;
```

In this nesting, the record identifier is associated with each field defined in that record. Thus

```
Age := 19
```

can be thought of as

```
Patient.Age := 19
```

Since Average is not a field in Patient, it will not be associated with the record identifier Patient. It will, however, be associated with the record identifier Student.

Unique field identifiers are not required when more than one record is used in a single **WITH . . . DO** statement. Instead, field identifiers are associated with the innermost record containing a field with that identifier. Innermost, in this sense, means the last listed record in the **WITH . . . DO** statement that contains the field in question. Thus

```
WITH Student, Patient DO
  writeln (Name);
```

causes Patient.Name to be printed.

In general, the use of multiple records in a single **WITH . . . DO** statement should be avoided when making a reference to a field identifier that is contained in more than one record. This reduces the possibility of misreading code and getting unexpected results.

Copying Records

How can information contained in one record be transferred to another record? This must be done, for example, when we want to sort an array of records. To illustrate how records can be copied, consider the following definitions and declarations:

```
TYPE
  InfoA = RECORD
            Field1 : integer;
            Field2 : real;
            Field3 : char
          END;  {  of RECORD InfoA  }
  InfoB = RECORD
            Field1 : integer;
            Field2 : real;
            Field3 : char
          END;  {  of RECORD InfoB  }
VAR
  Rec1, Rec2 : InfoA;
  Rec3 : InfoB;
```

The three records declared can be envisioned as shown in Figure 12.8. Now, suppose data have been assigned to Rec1 by

Copying records

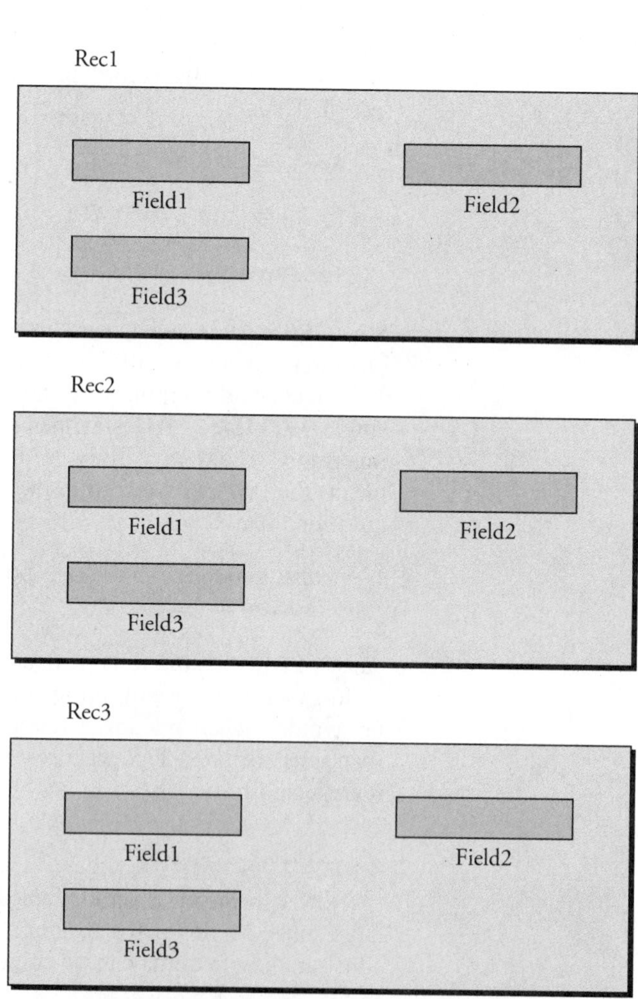

```
WITH Rec1 DO
  BEGIN
    Field1 := 25;
    Field2 := 89.5;
    Field3 := 'M'
  END;  {  of WITH...DO  }
```

These data can be copied to the corresponding fields of Rec2 by this statement:

```
Rec2 := Rec1;
```

This single assignment statement accomplishes all of the following:

```
Rec2.Field1 := Rec1.Field1;
Rec2.Field2 := Rec1.Field2;
Rec2.Field3 := Rec1.Field3;
```

Such an assignment can only be made when the records are of identical type. For example, notice InfoA and InfoB have the same structure but have been defined as different types. In this case, if you wish to assign the values in the fields of Rec1 to the corresponding fields of Rec3, the statement

```
Rec3 := Rec1;
```

produces a compilation error. Although Rec1 and Rec3 have the same structure, they are not of identical type. In this case, the information can be transferred by

```
WITH Rec3 DO
  BEGIN
    Field1 := Rec1.Field1;
    Field2 := Rec1.Field2;
    Field3 := Rec1.Field3
  END;  {  of WITH...DO  }
```

Reading Data into a Record

Once a record has been defined for a program, one task is to get data into the record. This is usually accomplished by reading from an input file. To illustrate, assume we have a record defined by

```
CONST
  NameLength = 20;
TYPE
  NameString = PACKED ARRAY [1..NameLength] OF char;
  PatientInfo = RECORD
                  Name : NameString;
                  Age : integer;
                  Height : integer;
                  Weight : integer;
                  Gender : char
                END;  {  of RECORD PatientInfo  }
VAR
  Patient : PatientInfo;
```

and a line of data is

```
Smith Mary          21 67 125F
```

These data could be read from the main program, but good program design would have us use a procedure for this task. The user-defined data type PatientInfo and a variable parameter must be used in the procedure heading. Thus, an appropriate procedure is

T

```
PROCEDURE GetData (VAR Patient : PatientInfo);
  VAR
    J : integer;
  BEGIN
    reset (Data);
    WITH Patient DO
      BEGIN
        FOR J := 1 TO NameLength DO
          read (Data, Name[J]);
        readln (Data, Age, Height, Weight, Gender)
      END  {  of WITH...DO  }
  END;  {  of PROCEDURE GetData  }
```

This procedure is called from the main program by

```
GetData (Patient);
```

As a second example of getting data for a record, let's write a program to be used to compute the grades of students in a class. As part of the program, a record type can be declared as

```
CONST
  NumQuizzes = 10;
  NumTests = 4;
  NameLength = 20;
TYPE
  NameString = PACKED ARRAY [1..NameLength] OF char;
  QuizList = ARRAY [1..NumQuizzes] OF integer;
  TestList = ARRAY [1..NumTests] OF integer;
  StudentRecord = RECORD
                    Name : NameString;
                    Quiz : QuizList;
                    Test : TestList;
                    QuizTotal : integer;
                    TestAverage : real;
                    LetterGrade : 'A'..'E'
                  END;  {  of RECORD StudentRecord  }
VAR
  Student : StudentRecord;
```

If each line of data contains a student's name, 10 quiz scores, and four test scores and looks like this:

```
Smith Mary J.          9 8 10 7 10 9 8 10 9 10 89 92 85 97 ■
```

Name — Quiz scores — Test scores

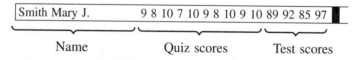

then a procedure to get these data is as follows:

```
PROCEDURE GetData (VAR Student : StudentRecord);
  VAR
    J : integer;
```

```
BEGIN
  reset (Data);
  WITH Student DO
    BEGIN
      FOR J := 1 TO NameLength DO
        read (Data, Name[J]);
      FOR J := 1 TO NumQuizzes DO
        read (Data, Quiz[J]);
      FOR J := 1 TO NumTests DO
        read (Data, Test[J])
    END;  {  of WITH...DO  }
  readln (Data)
END;  {  of PROCEDURE GetData  }
```

This procedure would be called from the main program by

```
GetData (Student);
```

Now let's continue this example by writing a function to compute the test average for a student. Since this average is found by using the four test scores in the record, such a function could be

```
FUNCTION TestAv (Test : TestList) : real;
  VAR
    J : integer;
    Sum : integer;
  BEGIN
    Sum := 0;
    FOR J := 1 TO NumTests DO
      Sum := Sum + Test[J];
    TestAv := Sum / NumTests
  END;  {  of FUNCTION TestAv  }
```

Since the array of test scores is the only parameter sent to the function and the average is normally stored in the field TestAverage, this function can be called by

```
Student.TestAverage := TestAv(Student.Test);
```

Printing Data from a Record

After information has been entered in fields of a record and appropriate calculations have been made, the next step is to print information from the record. Since this is frequently done in a procedure, let's assume the previous record for a student has the values illustrated in Figure 12.9.

If you want the output for a student to be

```
Name:          Smith Mary J.
Quiz Scores:   9  8 10  7 10  9  8 10  9 10
Quiz Total:    90
Test Scores:   89  92  85  97
Test Average:  90.75
Letter Grade:  A
```

a procedure that produces this output is

◆ Figure 12.9

Fields with values

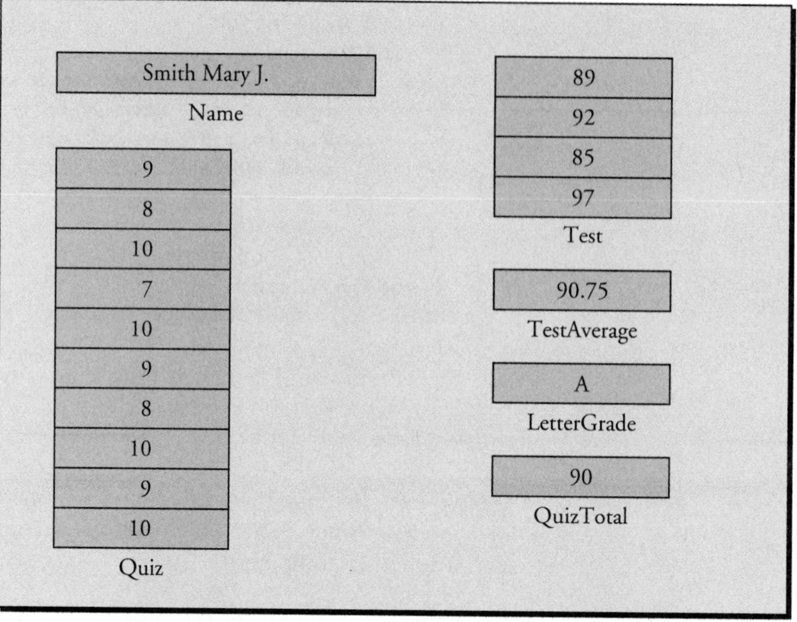


```
PROCEDURE PrintData (Student : StudentRecord);
  CONST
    Skip = ' ';
  VAR
    J : integer;
  BEGIN
    writeln;
    WITH Student DO
      BEGIN
        writeln ('Name:', Skip:9, Name);
        write ('Quiz Scores:');
        FOR J := 1 TO NumQuizzes DO
          write (Quiz[J]:3);
        writeln;
        writeln ('Quiz Total:', QuizTotal:5);
        write ('Test Scores:');
        FOR J := 1 TO NumTests DO
          write (Test[J]:4);
        writeln;
        writeln ('Test Average:', TestAverage:6:2);
        writeln ('Letter Grade:', LetterGrade:2)
      END  { of WITH...DO  }
  END;  {  of PROCEDURE PrintData  }
```

This procedure is called from the main program by

```
PrintData (Student);
```

Example 12.2

As a concluding example, let's consider a short interactive program that uses records and procedures to perform the arithmetic operation of multiplying two fractions. The program declares a record for each fraction and uses procedures to get the data, multiply

A Note of Interest

Using Key Fields in Records

The need to search records by certain key fields is a basic and very important process. To illustrate, consider how Ted Celentino, director of PARS applications for the on-line reservation system of TWA, responded to the question: "How are reservations indexed?" He said: "By the passenger's name, flight number, and departure date. All three are needed. If a passenger forgets his or her flight number, the agent can try to find a record of it by looking through all flights to the appropriate destination at that particular travel time. It's rare that a passenger doesn't know at least a couple of pieces of information that lead to his or her record."

the fractions, and print the results. Before writing this program, let's examine appropriate record definitions and a procedure for computing the product. A definition is

```
TYPE
  RationalNumber = RECORD
                     Numerator : integer;
                     Denominator : integer
                   END;  {  of RECORD RationalNumber  }
VAR
  X, Y, Product : RationalNumber;
```

A procedure for computing the product is

```
PROCEDURE ComputeProduct (X, Y : RationalNumber;
                          VAR Product : RationalNumber);
  BEGIN
    WITH Product DO
      BEGIN
        Numerator := X.Numerator * Y.Numerator;
        Denominator := X.Denominator * Y.Denominator
      END  {  of WITH...DO  }
  END;  {  of PROCEDURE ComputeProduct  }
```

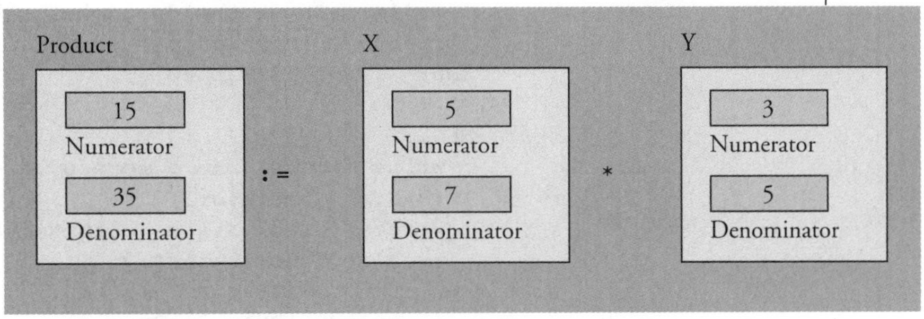

This procedure is called from the main program by

```
ComputeProduct (X, Y, Product);
```

A complete program for this problem follows:

```
PROGRAM Fractions (input, output);

{  This program illustrates the use of records with procedures. }
{  In particular, procedures are used to                         }
{                                                                }
{       1.  get the data                                         }
{       2.  perform computations                                 }
{       3.  print the results                                    }
{                                                                }
{  The specific task is to compute the product of two rational  }
{  numbers.                                                      }

TYPE
  RationalNumber = RECORD
                     Numerator : integer;
                     Denominator : integer
                   END;  {  of RECORD RationalNumber  }

VAR
  X, Y, Product : RationalNumber;
  MoreData : boolean;
  Response : char;

{****************************************************************}

PROCEDURE GetData (VAR X, Y : RationalNumber);

  {  Given:   Nothing                                            }
  {  Task:    Have entered from the keyboard the numerator and  }
  {               denominator of two fractions                   }
  {  Return:  Two records, each containing a field for the      }
  {               numerator and denominator of a fraction        }

  BEGIN
    WITH X DO
      BEGIN
        write ('Enter the numerator a of a/b.  ');
        readln (Numerator);
        write ('Enter the denominator b of a/b.  ');
        readln (Denominator)
      END;  {  of WITH X DO  }
    WITH Y DO
      BEGIN
        write ('Enter the numerator a of a/b.  ');
        readln (Numerator);
        write ('Enter the denominator b of a/b.  ');
        readln (Denominator)
      END  {  of WITH Y DO  }
  END;  {  of PROCEDURE GetData  }

{****************************************************************}

PROCEDURE ComputeProduct (X, Y : RationalNumber;
                          VAR Product : RationalNumber);

  {  Given:   Records for two fractions                          }
```

```
  {  Task:     Compute the product and store result                }
  {  Return:   Product of the fraction                             }
  BEGIN
    WITH Product DO
      BEGIN
        Numerator := X.Numerator * Y.Numerator;
        Denominator := X.Denominator * Y.Denominator
      END  {  of WITH...DO  }
  END;  {  of PROCEDURE ComputeProduct  }

{****************************************************************}

PROCEDURE PrintResults (X, Y, Product : RationalNumber);

  {  Given:    Records for each of two given fractions and their }
  {                product                                        }
  {  Task:     Print an equation stating the problem and answer; }
  {                standard fraction form should be used as       }
  {                output                                         }
  {  Return:   Nothing                                            }

  BEGIN
    writeln;
    writeln (X.Numerator:13, Y.Numerator:6, Product.Numerator:6);
    writeln ('--- * --- = ---':26);
    writeln (X.Denominator:13, Y.Denominator:6, Product.Denominator:6);
    writeln
  END;  {  of PROCEDURE PrintResults  }

{****************************************************************}

BEGIN  {  Main program  }
  MoreData := true;
  WHILE MoreData DO
    BEGIN
      GetData (X, Y);
      ComputeProduct (X, Y, Product);
      PrintResults (X, Y, Product);
      write ('Do you wish to see another problem?  <Y> or <N>  ');
      readln (Response);
      Moredata := (Response = 'Y') OR (Response = 'y');
      writeln
    END  {  of WHILE...DO  }
END.  {  of main program  }
```

A sample run of this program produces

```
Enter the numerator a of a/b.  3
Enter the denominator b of a/b.  4
Enter the numerator a of a/b.  1
Enter the denominator b of a/b.  2

            3     1     3
           --- * --- = ---
            4     2     8
```

```
Do you wish to see another problem?  <Y> or <N>  Y

Enter the numerator a of a/b.  3
Enter the denominator b of a/b.  2
Enter the numerator a of a/b.  7
Enter the denominator b of a/b.  10

            3     7     21
           --- * --- = ---
            2    10     20

Do you wish to see another problem?  <Y> or <N>  Y

Enter the numerator a of a/b.  2
Enter the denominator b of a/b.  3
Enter the numerator a of a/b.  4
Enter the denominator b of a/b.  5

            2     4      8
           --- * --- = ---
            3     5     15

Do you wish to see another problem?  <Y> or <N>  N
```

Exercises 12.2

For Exercises 1–5, assume a program contains the following **TYPE** definition and **VAR** declaration sections:

```
TYPE
  Info1 = RECORD
            Initial : char;
            Age : integer
          END;
  Info2 = RECORD
            Initial : char;
            Age : integer
          END;
VAR
  Cust1, Cust2 : Info1;
  Cust3, Cust4 : Info2;
```

Indicate if the statement is valid. Give an explanation for those that are invalid.

*1. `Cust1 := Cust2;`

2. `Cust2 := Cust3;`

*3. `Cust3 := Cust4;`

4.
```
WITH Cust1 DO
  BEGIN
    Initial := 'W';
    Age := 21
  END;
```

*5.
```
WITH Cust1, Cust2 DO
  BEGIN
    Initial := 'W';
```

```
    Age := 21
  END;
```

6. Write a test program to see what happens when two different records with the same field name are used in a single **WITH . . . DO** statement. Use the declarations and **TYPE** definitions in Exercises 1–5. For example,

```
WITH Student1, Student2 DO
  Age := 21;
writeln (Student1.Age);
writeln (Student2.Age);
```

*7. Assume the **TYPE** and **VAR** sections of a program include the following:

```
TYPE
  String11 = PACKED ARRAY [1..11] OF char;
  NameString = PACKED ARRAY [1..20] OF char;
  Info = RECORD
           Name : NameString;
           SSN : String11;
           Age : integer;
           HourlyWage : real;
           HoursWorked : real;
           Volunteer : boolean
         END;
VAR
  Employee1, Employee2 : Info;
```

a. Show three different methods of transferring all information from the record for Employee1 to the record for Employee2.
b. Suppose you wish to transfer all information from the record for Employee1 to the record for Employee2 except HoursWorked. Discuss different methods for doing this. Which do you feel is the most efficient?

8. Assume the **TYPE** and **VAR** sections of a program are the same as in Exercise 7. Write a procedure to be used to read information into such a record from a data file. A typical line of data is

```
Smith Jane M.          111-22-3333 25 10.50 41.5Y
```

where Y indicates the worker is a volunteer (**true**) and N indicates the worker is not a volunteer (**false**).

*9. Assume a record has been declared by

```
TYPE
  NameString = PACKED ARRAY [1..20] OF char;
  StudentInfo = RECORD
                  Name : NameString;
                  TotalPts : 0..500;
                  LetterGrade : char
                END;
VAR
  Student : StudentInfo;
```

Write a function to compute a student's letter grade based on cutoff levels of 90 percent, 80 percent, 70 percent, and 60 percent. Show how this function is used in a program to assign the appropriate letter grade to the appropriate field of a student's record.

10. Review Example 12.2, in which two fractions are multiplied. In a similar fashion, write procedures for
    a. Dividing two fractions (watch out for zero).
    b. Adding two fractions.
    c. Subtracting two fractions.
11. Some instructors throw out the lowest test score when computing the test average. Assume a record Student of type StudentRecord has been declared and data have been read into the appropriate fields.
    a. Write a function to compute the test average using the best three scores.
    b. Show how a constant in the **CONST** section can be used to generalize this to finding the best $n - 1$ of n scores.
    c. Rewrite the function using a sort to sort the array of scores from high to low and then add the first three from the array.
    d. Must the entire array be sorted in order to find the three highest scores? Explain.
12. Show how **PROGRAM** Fractions in Example 12.2 can be modified to check for nonzero denominators.

12.3 Data Structures with Records

Objectives

- to be able to declare a nested record
- to be able to use nested records in a program
- to be able to declare an array of records
- to be able to use an array of records in a program
- to be able to sort an array of records by a field
- to be able to use procedures for working with an array of records

Nested Records

The first concept to be examined in this section is that of a **nested record,** or a record that is a field in another record. For example, suppose you are working on a program to be used by a science department and part of your work is to declare a record for a teacher. This record is to contain fields for the person's name, room number, telephone number, and supply order. Let's assume that the supply order information is to contain the company name, a description of the item ordered, its price, and the quantity ordered. The record for each teacher, with SupplyOrder as a record within a record, can be visualized as shown in Figure 12.10.

Now let's look at how such a record can be declared. One possible method is

```
TYPE
  String20 = PACKED ARRAY [1..20] OF char;
  String12 = PACKED ARRAY [1..12] OF char;
  OrderInfo = RECORD
                CompanyName : String20;
                Item : String20;
                ItemPrice : real;
                Quantity : integer
              END;  {  of RECORD OrderInfo  }
  TeacherInfo = RECORD
                  Name : String20;
                  Room : integer;
                  Phone : String12;
                  SupplyOrder : OrderInfo
                END;  {  of RECORD TeacherInfo  }
VAR
  Teacher : TeacherInfo;
```

◆ Figure 12.10

An illustration of a nested record

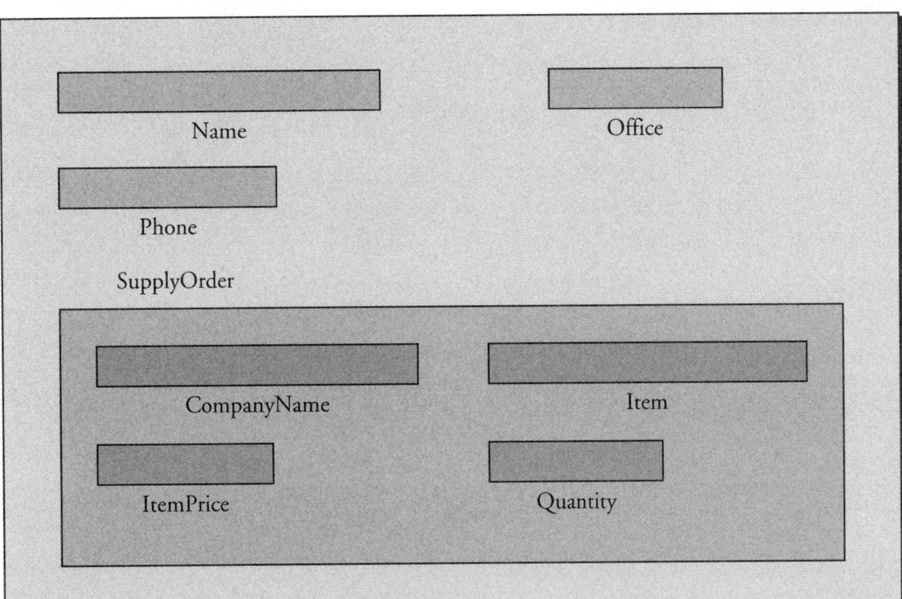

A **nested record** is a record that is a field in another record.

We must now consider how to access fields in the nested record. We do this by continuing our notation for field designators. Thus,

```
Teacher.Name
Teacher.Room
Teacher.Phone
```

refer to the first three fields of Teacher, and

```
Teacher.SupplyOrder.CompanyName
Teacher.SupplyOrder.Item
Teacher.SupplyOrder.ItemPrice
Teacher.SupplyOrder.Quantity
```

are used to access fields of the nested record

```
Teacher.SupplyOrder
```

Using WITH...DO

As expected, **WITH ... DO** can be used with nested records. Let's consider the problem of assigning data to the various fields of Teacher as previously declared. Assume we wish to have values assigned as shown in Figure 12.11. We can then use the following assignment statements:

```
WITH Teacher DO
  BEGIN
    Name := 'Bland Roy R.        ';
    Room := 327;
    Phone := '800-555-1212';
    SupplyOrder.CompanyName := 'BioSupplies        ';
```

◆ Figure 12.11

Values in fields of a nested record

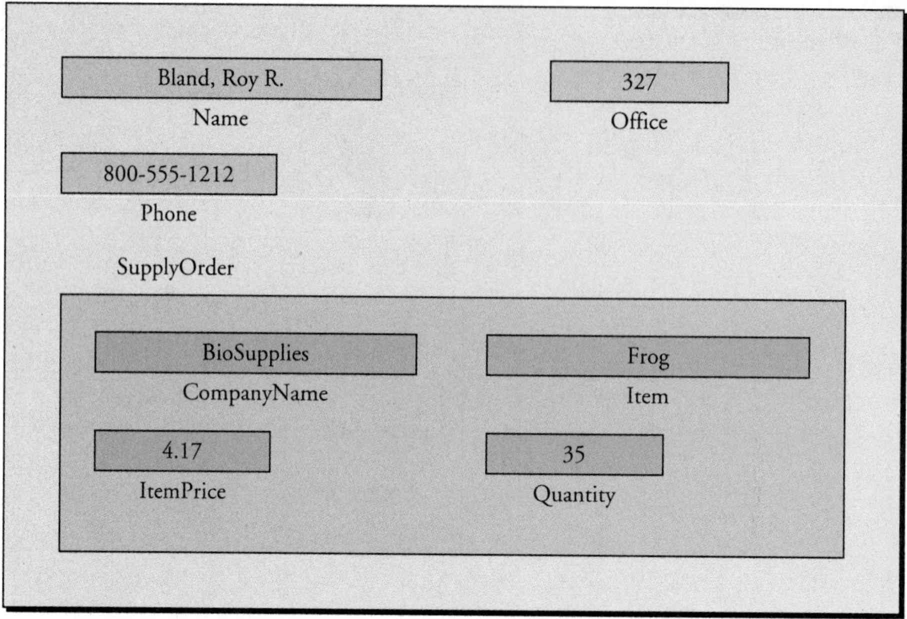


```
    SupplyOrder.Item := 'Frog                    ';
    SupplyOrder.ItemPrice := 4.17;
    SupplyOrder.Quantity := 35
  END;  {  of WITH Teacher DO  }
```

Note that the last four assignment statements all used fields in the record SupplyOrder. Thus, a **WITH . . . DO** statement can be used there as follows:

```
WITH Teacher DO
  BEGIN
    Name := 'Bland Roy R.          ';
    Room := 327;
    Phone := '800-555-1212';
    WITH SupplyOrder DO
      BEGIN
        CompanyName := 'BioSupplies        ';
        Item := 'Frog                ';
        ItemPrice := 4.17;
        Quantity := 35
      END  {  of WITH SupplyOrder DO  }
  END;  {  of WITH Teacher DO  }
```

A third way to accomplish our task is to use **WITH . . . DO** with both the main record name and the nested record name, as follows:

```
WITH Teacher, SupplyOrder DO
  BEGIN
    Name := 'Bland Roy R.          ';
    Room := 327;
    Phone := '800-555-1212';
    CompanyName := 'BioSupplies        ';
```

```
    Item := 'Frog                ';
    ItemPrice := 4.17;
    Quantity := 35
  END;  {  WITH...DO  }
```

Since SupplyOrder is nested within Teacher, each reference is distinctly identified and the fragment accomplishes our objective. When using nested records, it is important to identify fields distinctly. To illustrate, suppose Teacher1 and Teacher2 are of type TeacherInfo. Then each of the following is valid:

```
Teacher1.Name := Teacher2.Name;
Teacher1.SupplyOrder.Item := Teacher2.SupplyOrder.Item;
Teacher1.SupplyOrder := Teacher2.SupplyOrder;
```

Note that in the third statement, the contents of an entire record are being transferred. This statement is valid because both records are of type OrderInfo.

To illustrate some attempts to use inappropriate designators, let's assume Teacher, Teacher1, and Teacher2 are of type TeacherInfo and consider the following inappropriate references. In the designator

```
Teacher.Item := 'Frog                ';   (incorrect)
```

the intermediate descriptor is missing. Thus, something like

```
Teacher.SupplyOrder.Item
```

is needed. In

```
SupplyOrder.Quantity := 35;   (incorrect)
```

no reference is made to which record is being accessed. A record name must be stated, such as

```
Teacher1.SupplyOrder.Quantity
```

As our final example of working with nested records, let's write a procedure to get data from a data file for a record of type TeacherInfo with the following definitions and declarations:

```
TYPE
  String20 = PACKED ARRAY [1..20] OF char;
  String12 = PACKED ARRAY [1..12] OF char;
  OrderInfo = RECORD
                CompanyName : String20;
                Item : String20;
                ItemPrice : real;
                Quantity : integer
              END;  {  of RECORD OrderInfo  }
  TeacherInfo = RECORD
                  Name : String20;
                  Room : 100..399;
                  Phone : String12;
                  SupplyOrder : OrderInfo
                END;  {  of RECORD TeacherInfo  }
VAR
  Teacher : TeacherInfo;
```

If we assume the data for a teacher are on two lines of the data file and are of the form

(line 1) `Bland Roy R.             327 800-555-1212`

(line 2) `BioSupplies         Frog                        4.17 35`

a procedure to obtain these data is

```
PROCEDURE GetData (VAR Teacher : TeacherInfo);
  VAR
    J : integer;
    Blank : char;
  BEGIN
    reset (Data);
    WITH Teacher, SupplyOrder DO
      BEGIN
        FOR J := 1 TO 20 DO
          read (Data, Name[J]);
        read (Data, Room);
        read (Data, Blank);  {  Move the pointer  }
        FOR J := 1 TO 12 DO
          read (Data, Phone[J]);
        readln (Data);  {  Go to beginning of the next line  }

        {  Now read the second line  }
        FOR J := 1 TO 20 DO
          read (Data, CompanyName[J]);
        FOR J := 1 TO 20 DO
          read (Data, Item[J]);
        readln (Data, ItemPrice, Quantity)
      END  {  of WITH Teacher, SupplyOrder DO  }
  END;  [  of PROCEDURE GetData  }
```

This procedure is called from the main program by

```
GetData (Teacher);
```

Array of Records

An **array of records** is an array whose component type is a record.

Next, we use structured data types to look at an array of records. It is easy to imagine needing to make a list of information about several people, events, or items. Furthermore, it is not unusual for the information about a particular person, event, or item to consist of several different data items. When this situation occurs, a record can be defined for each person, event, or item and an array of these records can be used to achieve the desired result. In such situations, an **array of records** is frequently used instead of a parallel array.

For example, suppose the local high school sports boosters want a program to enable them to keep track of the names and donations of its members. Let's assume a maximum of 50 members are making a donation. This problem was solved in Chapter 11 using parallel arrays; it can now be solved by using an array of records. Each record will have two fields: the donor's name and the amount donated. The record can be visualized as shown in Figure 12.12.

We now declare an array of these records to produce the arrangement shown in Figure 12.13. The necessary definitions and declarations needed are

```
CONST
  ClubSize = 50;
TYPE
  NameString = PACKED ARRAY [1..20] OF char;
  MemberInfo = RECORD
                 Name : NameString;
                 Amount : real
               END;  {  of RECORD MemberInfo  }
  DonorList = ARRAY [1..ClubSize] OF MemberInfo;
VAR
  Donor : DonorList;
  TempDonor : MemberInfo;
  Count : integer;
```

◆ Figure 12.12

Fields in TempDonor

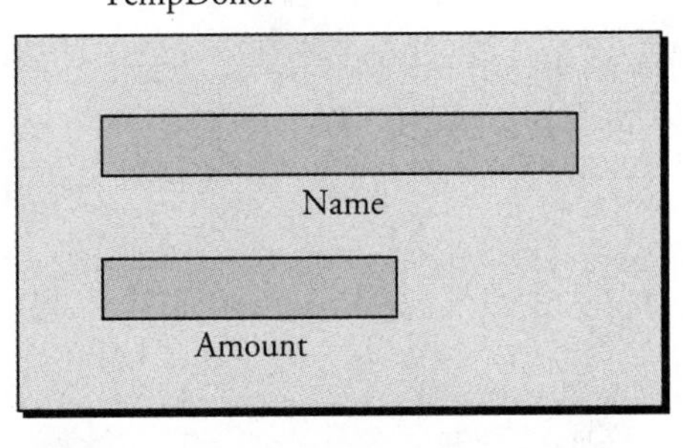

◆ Figure 12.13

An illustration of an array of records

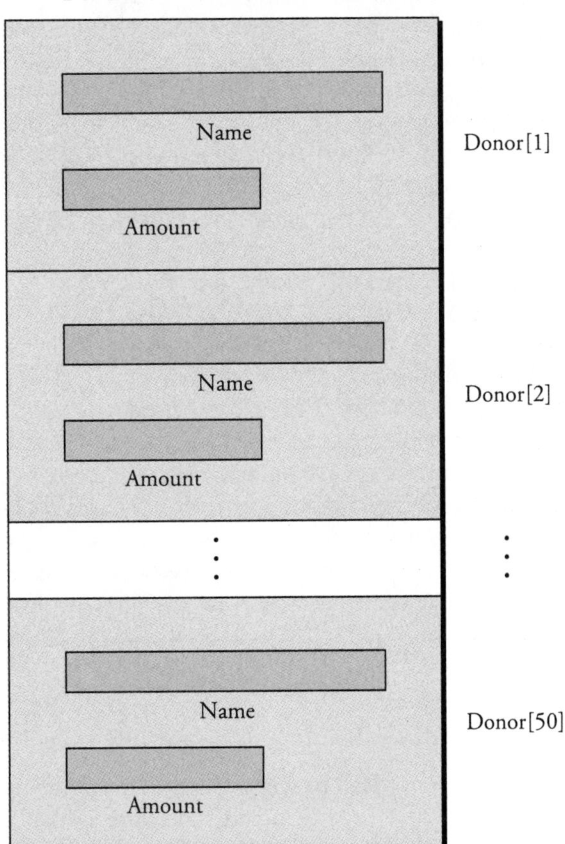

A Note of Interest

Computer Insecurity

In February 1994, college administrators across the country appealed to students and faculty members to change the way they log on to their computers after security experts announced that tens of thousands of passwords had been stolen by hackers on the Internet. The Computer Emergency Response Team Coordination Center—a federally financed unit responsible for security on the Internet—issued the alert after a rash of break-ins. The Internet, a worldwide web of computer networks, is used by millions of people.

Security experts said hundreds of Internet computers had been affected, including those at dozens of colleges, but declined to identify them. Institutions that fall victim to attacks often shun publicity because they want to avoid embarrassment and because they are afraid they may become targets for other hackers.

FBI Seeks Culprits

Some administrators, still unsure about whether their computers had been attacked, looked through their systems for evidence of intruders. The Federal Bureau of Investigation maintains on-going searches for the culprits.

Computer administrators in higher education had varying opinions about what the event would mean to the future of the Internet. Although none of them suggested that their institutions would permanently disconnect from the Internet, several said universities might need to rethink what kinds of data should be stored in computers connected to the network. Others, puzzled by all the hullabaloo, said that battles with "crackers"—a name given to mean-spirited hackers—were part of business as usual on the Internet. Computer-system administrators at some colleges and universities said they were forcing users to change passwords on systems under their control and encouraging users of other systems on their campuses to do likewise.

The following guidelines are helpful to anyone who uses on-line services.

Tips from Campus Computer Experts to Protect Passwords

- Change passwords as frequently as possible.
- Avoid writing down a password.
- Do not cooperate with anyone who orders you to use a specific password. Crackers occasionally call users at random and impersonate administrators of their local computer systems. Report such incidents in person to local system administrators.
- Never include your password in electronic mail unless you are using an encryption program to scramble your messages. Electronic mail can be read by others as it travels through the network.
- Passwords should never be actual words. Crackers can run dictionary programs that try every word in the language until the password is found. (Until recently, some security experts advised that selecting memorable foreign words was relatively safe, but the sophisticated cracker is now armed with dictionaries that cover a multitude of languages.)
- Do not choose passwords that consist of nicknames, birth dates, names of spouses or children, or other information that might be known to a cracker.
- The passwords that are hardest to crack consist of jumbles of letters, numbers, and punctuation marks. However, some punctuation marks should not be used on some systems. One useful strategy for creating memorable passwords involves using the first few letters of each word of a phrase or book title, much like military abbreviations. The password "AMHERDIC" could be made from The American Heritage Dictionary, for example. But don't build a password out of a phrase that you use to sign your electronic mail.
- Whenever possible, use a telephone and a modem to dial directly into a remote computer and avoid using the telnet command through the Internet. The telephone system is much more secure than the Internet.

Before we proceed, the following should be noted:

1. Structures are built in the **TYPE** definition section to facilitate later work with procedures and functions.

2. Each record is now an array element and can be accessed by a reference to the index. Thus, if the third member's name is Tom Jones and he donates $100.00, you can write

```
Donor[3].Name := 'Jones Tom             ';
Donor[3].Amount := 100.0;
```

Better still, you can use **WITH . . . DO** to get

```
WITH Donor[3] DO
  BEGIN
    Name := 'Jones Tom             ';
    Amount := 100.0
  END;  {  of WITH...DO  }
```

3. Since all records in an array are of identical type, the contents of two records can be interchanged by

```
TempDonor := Donor[J];
Donor[J] := Donor[K];
Donor[K] := TempDonor;
```

This is needed if records are to be sorted by one of their fields.

4. The distinction in syntax should be noted when using an array of records versus an array as a field within a record. For example, if an array of five scores has been defined as a field in an array of records, as shown in Figure 12.14, the following distinctions should be noted:
   a. `Student[2].Average` (Average for student 2)
   b. `Student[2].Score[4]` (Score on test 4 for student 2)
   c. `Student.Score[2]` (Not defined; Student is an array)

Now let's return to the problem posed by the sports boosters. A first-level pseudocode design is

1. Get the data
2. Sort alphabetically by name
3. Print the sorted list

If we assume each line of the data file is of the form

Jones Tom	100.0

a procedure to get the data is not difficult. We have to remember, however, to count the actual number of donors read. Such a procedure is

```
PROCEDURE GetData (VAR Donor : DonorList;
                   VAR Count : integer);
  VAR
    J : integer;
  BEGIN
    Count := 0;
    reset (Data);
    WHILE NOT eof(Data) AND (Count < ClubSize) DO
      BEGIN
        Count := Count + 1;
        WITH Donor[Count] DO
```

◆ Figure 12.14

Array of records

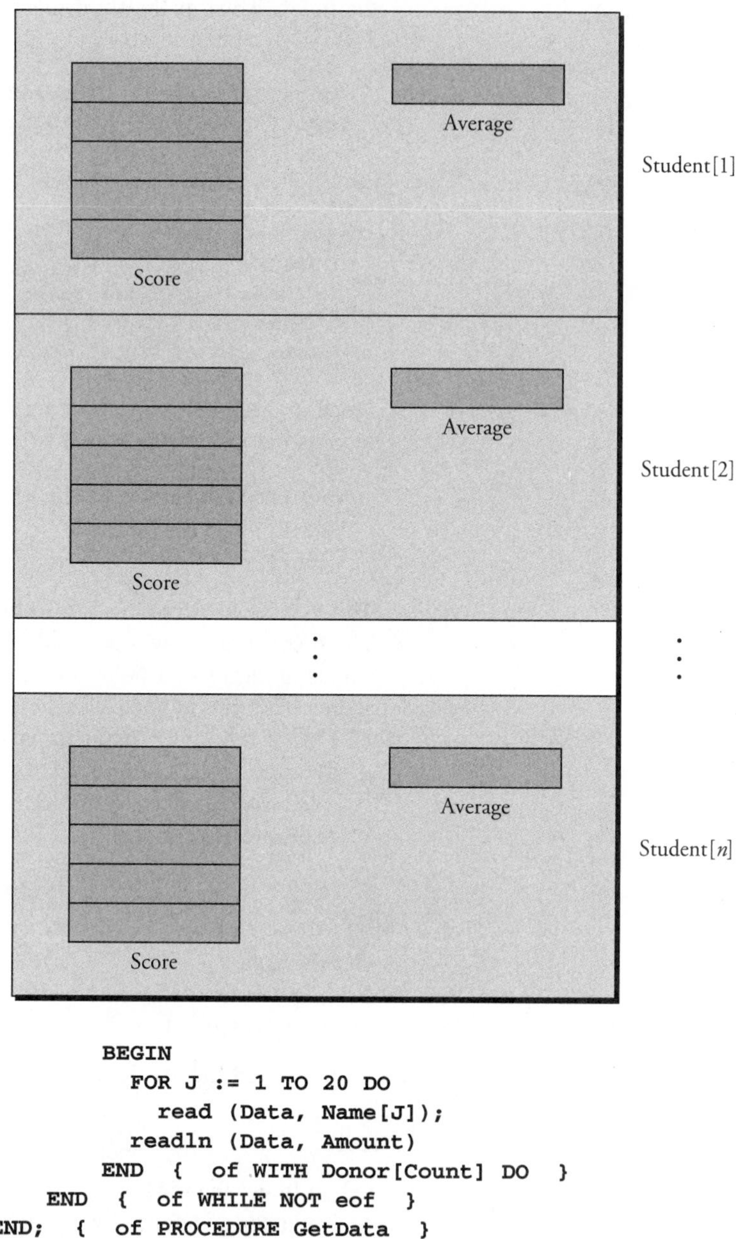


```
        BEGIN
          FOR J := 1 TO 20 DO
            read (Data, Name[J]);
          readln (Data, Amount)
        END  {  of WITH Donor[Count] DO  }
      END  {  of WHILE NOT eof  }
    END;  {  of PROCEDURE GetData  }
```

This procedure is called from the main program by

```
GetData (Donor, Count);
```

and Count will contain the actual number of donors after the procedure is called.

The next procedure in this problem will require a sort. A sort that actually exchanges entire records is not very efficient. When working with an array of records, it is more efficient to use an **index sort,** which essentially uses a separate array to reorder the indices in the desired order. However, the formal development of this sorting technique is deferred to a subsequent course. For now, recall the selection sort developed in Chapter 10, as follows:

An **index sort** is a sort that uses a separate array to sort the indices of an array of records.

```
FOR J := 1 TO N - 1 DO {  Find the minimum N - 1 times   }
  BEGIN
    Index := J;
    FOR K := J + 1 TO N DO
      IF A[K] < A[Index] THEN  {  Find smallest number   }
        Index := K;
    IF Index <> J THEN
      Swap (A[Index], A[J])
  END;  {  of one pass  }
```

With suitable changes, the array of records can be sorted alphabetically by

```
PROCEDURE Sort (VAR Donor : DonorList;
                Count : integer);

  VAR
    J, K, Index : integer;
    Temp : MemberInfo;
  BEGIN
    FOR J := 1 TO Count - 1 DO
      BEGIN
        Index := J;
        FOR K := J + 1 TO Count DO
          IF Donor[K].Name < Donor[Index].Name THEN
            Index := K;
        IF Index <> J THEN
          Swap (Donor[Index], Donor[J])
      END  {  of FOR loop  }
  END;  {  of PROCEDURE Sort  }
```

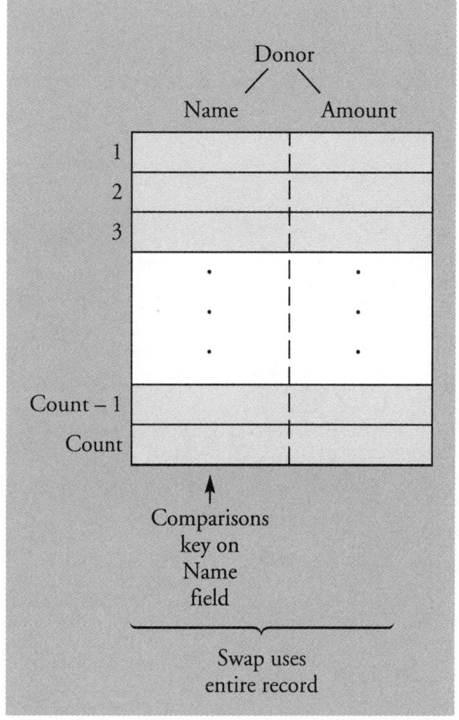

This procedure is called from the main program by

```
Sort (Donor, Count);
```

In this procedure, note that the sort is by only one field in the record—specifically, the donor's name:

```
IF Donor[K].Name < Donor[Index].Name THEN
```

However, when the names are to be exchanged, contents of the entire record are exchanged by

```
Temp := Donor[Index];
```

in **PROCEDURE** Swap.

We conclude this program by writing a procedure to print the results. If we want the output to be

```
                 Local Sports Boosters
                     Donation List
  ----------------------------------------

     Name                            Amount
     ----                            ------

  Alexander Candy                    300.00
  Born Patty                         100.00
  Generous George                    525.00
  Lasher John                        175.00
  Smith John                         100.00
       .                                .
       .                                .
       .                                .
```

a procedure to produce this is

```
PROCEDURE PrintList (VAR Donor : DonorList;
                     Count : integer);
  CONST
    Skip = ' ' ;
  VAR
    J : integer;
  BEGIN
    writeln;
    writeln (Skip:21, 'Local Sports Boosters');
    writeln (Skip:25, 'Donation List');
    writeln (Skip:10, '----------------------------------------');
    writeln;
    writeln (Skip:13, 'Name', Skip:27, 'Amount');
    writeln (Skip:13, '----', Skip:27, '------');
    writeln;

    {  Now print the list  }
    FOR J := 1 TO Count DO
      WITH Donor[J] DO
```

```
        writeln (Skip:10, Name, Amount:20:2);
    writeln
  END;  {  of PROCEDURE PrintList  }
```

With these three procedures available, the main program is then

```
BEGIN  {  Main program  }
  GetData (Donor, Count);
  Sort (Donor, Count);
  PrintList (Donor, Count)
END.  {  of main program  }
```

This example is less involved than many of your problems will be, but it does illustrate an array of records, appropriate notation for fields in an array of records, how to sort an array of records by using one field of the records, and the use of procedures with an array of records.

Exercises 12.3

*1. Consider the declaration

```
TYPE
  B = RECORD
        C : real;
        D : integer
      END;
  A = RECORD
        E : boolean;
        F : B
      END;
VAR
  G : A;
```

Give a schematic representation of the record G.

For Exercises 2–11, using the declaration from Exercise 1, indicate which are valid references.

2. `G.E`
*3. `G.C`
4. `G.F.D`
*5. `F.D`
6. `G.A`
*7. `A.F.C`
8. `A.E`
*9. `WITH G DO`
10. `WITH G, F DO`
*11. `G.F.C`

12. Using the declaration in Exercise 1, why would it be incorrect to define record A before record B?

*13. Give an appropriate definition and declaration for a record that is to contain fields for a person's name, address, social security number, annual income, and family information. Address is a record with fields for street address, city, state abbreviation, and zip code. Family information is a record with fields for marital status (S, M, W, or D) and number of children.

14. Write a test program that illustrates the difference between an array of records and a record with an array component.

*15. Declare an array of records to be used for 15 players on a basketball team. The following information is needed for each player: name, age, height, weight, scoring average, and rebounding average.

16. Consider the following definitions and subsequent declarations:

```
TYPE
  NameString = PACKED ARRAY [1..20] OF char;
  Mood = (Quiet, Bright, Surly);
  CurrentHealth = (Poor, Average, Good);
  PatientInfo = RECORD
                  Name : NameString;
                  Status = RECORD
                             Mental : Mood;
                             Physical : CurrentHealth
                           END;
                  PastDue : boolean
                END;
VAR
  Patient1, Patient2 : PatientInfo;
```

a. Give a schematic representation for Patient1.
b. Show how a single letter (Q, B, S) can be read from a data file and then have the appropriate value assigned to Patient1.Status.Mental.
c. Write a procedure to read a line of data and assign (if necessary) appropriate values to the various fields. A typical data line is

```
Smith Sue          BAF█
```

and indicates that Sue Smith's mood is bright, her health is average, and her account is not past due.

*17. Consider the following declaration of an array of records:

```
CONST
  ClassSize = 35;
TYPE
  NameString = PACKED ARRAY [1..20] OF char;
  Attendance = (Excellent, Average, Poor);
  TestList = ARRAY [1..4] OF integer;
  StudentInfo = RECORD
                  Name : NameString;
                  Atten : Attendance;
                  Test : TestList;
                  Aver : real
                END;
  StudentList = ARRAY [1..ClassSize] OF StudentInfo;
VAR
  Student : StudentList;
```

a. Give a schematic representation for Student.
b. Explain what the following function accomplishes:

```
FUNCTION GuessWhat (Test : TestList) : real;
  VAR
    K, Sum : integer;
  BEGIN
    Sum := 0;
    FOR K := 1 TO 4 DO
      Sum := Sum + Test[K];
```

```
    GuessWhat := Sum / 4
  END;
```

c. Write a procedure to print the information for one student. In this procedure, the entire word describing attendance is to be printed.

18. Declare an array of records to be used for students in a classroom (at most 40 students). Each record should contain fields for a student's name, social security number, 10 quiz scores, three test scores, overall average, and letter grade.

For Exercises 19–22, reconsider the problem in this section that kept a record of the name and amount donated for each member of the local high school boosters club. Expanding on that problem, write a procedure or function for each of the following.

*19. Find the maximum donation and print the amount together with the donor's name.

20. Find the sum of all donations.

*21. Find the average of all donations.

22. Sort the array according to size of the donation, largest first.

23. Consider the following definitions and declarations:

```
CONST
  NameString = PACKED ARRAY [1..70] OF char;
TYPE
  EmployeeInfo = RECORD
                   Name : NameString;
                   Classification : String2;
                   SSN : String11;
                   HourlyRate : real
                 END;
  EmployeeList = ARRAY [1..MaxLength] OF EmployeeInfo;
VAR
  Employee : EmployeeList;
```

All employees with a job classification of C4 are to receive a pay raise of 7.5 percent. Write a segment of code to search the array Employee and record the new hourly rate for employees as appropriate.

24. Suppose you are using a program that contains an array of records in which each record is defined by

```
CONST
  NameString = PACKED ARRAY [1..70] OF char;
TYPE
  .
  .
  .
  CustomerInfo = RECORD
                   Name : NameString;
                   AmountDue : real
                 END;
```

a. Use the selection sort to sort (and then print) the records alphabetically.

b. Re-sort the array by the field AmountDue. Print a list ordered by AmountDue where anyone with an amount due of more than $100 is designated with a triple asterisk (***).

12.4 Record Variants

Objectives

- to be able to define a record with a variant part
- to be able to use a record that contains a variant part

You should have noticed by now that when records are defined, each record has certain fixed fields. Since it is sometimes desirable to use a record structure in which the number and type of fields vary, Pascal allows records to be defined with a **variant part.** For example, a real estate company might want the records for their customers to contain different information depending on whether the property for sale is a house or a business. For houses, the number of bedrooms, bathrooms, and whether or not there is a fireplace could be indicated; for businesses, the number of offices and amount of possible rental income could be listed.

The **variant part** of a record structure is the part in which the number and type of fields can vary.

Defining a Variant Part

To define the variant part of a record, we use a form of the **CASE** statement to specify which fields should be included. Then, depending on the value of the identifier in the **CASE** part of the definition, the desired fields are listed. In the real estate example, we could have

```
TYPE
  PropertyType = (House, Business);
  Listing = RECORD
              CASE Kind : PropertyType OF
                House    : (NumBedrms : integer;
                            NumBaths : integer;
                            Fireplace : boolean);
                Business : (NumOffices : integer;
                            RentalIncome : integer)
            END;  {  of RECORD Listing  }
VAR
  Property : Listing;
```

Now Property is a record with a variant part. Kind is not a reserved word and is called the **tag field.** Depending on the value assigned to Kind, the appropriate fields are available. If the assignment

The **tag field** is a field used in defining variant records. Values of the tag field determine the variant record structure.

```
Property.Kind := House;
```

is made, the record can be envisioned as shown in Figure 12.15(a). If the assignment

```
Property.Kind := Business;
```

is made, we have the record illustrated in Figure 12.15(b).

In actual practice, records with variant parts usually have fixed parts also. Suppose the address and price of each property listed for sale should be included. Since fields for these would be defined for every record, these fields would be referred to as the **fixed part.** A complete definition is as follows:

Fixed parts are fields in a record that exist for all records of a particular type.

```
TYPE
  PropertyType = (House, Business);
  String30 = PACKED ARRAY [1..30] OF char;
  Listing = RECORD
              Address : String30;                          } fixed
              Price : integer;                             } part
              CASE Kind : PropertyType OF                  } tag field
                House    : (NumBedrms : integer;           }
                            NumBaths : integer;            }
                            Fireplace : boolean);          } variant
                Business : (NumOffices : integer;          } part
                            RentalIncome : integer)        }
            END;  {  of RECORD Listing  }
VAR
  Property : Listing;
```

◆ Figure 12.15

Fields in a variant record

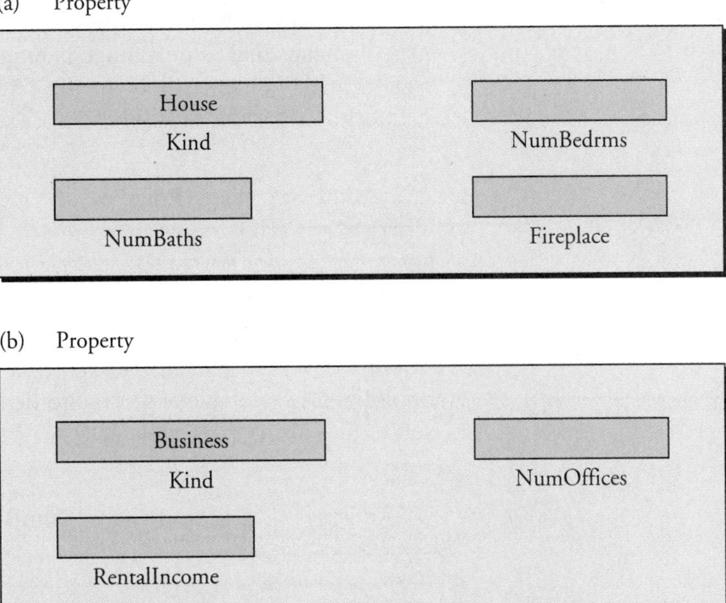

The following points concerning variant parts should now be made.

1. The variant part of a record must be listed after the fixed part.
2. Only one variant part can be defined in a record.
3. The data type for the tag field must be ordinal.
4. Only one **END** is used to terminate the definition. This terminates both **CASE** and **RECORD.**

Records with variant parts are defined by a form as follows:

```
<record name> =  RECORD
                   <field 1> : <type>;                  }
                   <field 2> : <type>;                  }
                       .                                }  fixed
                       .                                }  part
                       .                                }
                   <field n> : <type>;                  }
                   CASE <tag field> : <tag type> OF  }  tag field
                      <value 1> : (<field list>);       }
                      <value 2> : (<field list>);       }
                         .                              }  variant
                         .                              }  part
                         .                              }
                      <value m> : (<field list>)        }
                 END;
```

It is possible to completely avoid the use of variant parts of a record, listing all possible fields in the fixed part and then using them appropriately. However, this usually means that more storage is required. To illustrate, let's consider how memory is allocated. For each field in the fixed part of the previous example, an area in memory is reserved as follows:

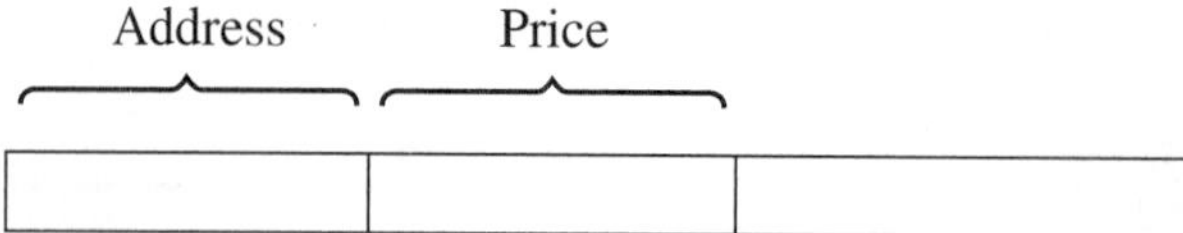

For the variant part of the record, a single area is reserved that will subsequently be utilized by whichever fields are determined by the value of the tag field. In this sense, they overlap as indicated.

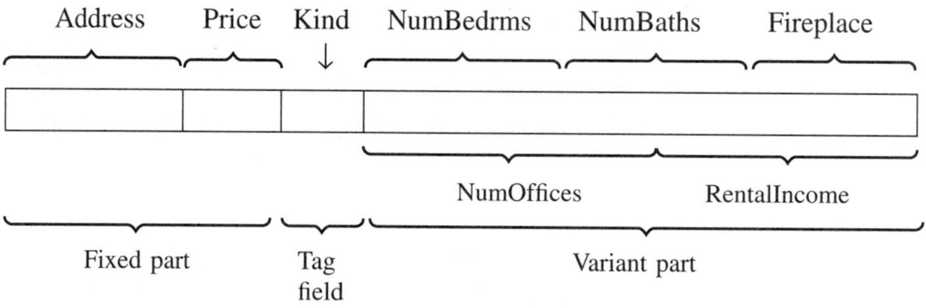

A note of caution is in order when variant records are included as part of programs. Careful programming is needed to initialize properly the variant part or unexpected results can be obtained. For example, using the previous illustration, suppose the initial value of Kind is House with values for NumBedrms, NumBaths, and Fireplace. If a subsequent value of Kind is Business and no new data are read or assigned, the value of NumOffices can in fact be NumBedrms.

We close this section with an example that illustrates a definition and subsequent use of a record with a variant part.

Example 12.3

Let's define a record to be used when working with plane geometric figures. The record should have fixed fields for the type of figure (a single character designator) and area. The variant part should have fields for information needed to compute the area. After the record is defined, we write a procedure to get data from a line of the data file. We then write a function that can be used to compute the area of the plane figure. To complete the definition of the record, let's assume we are working with at most the geometric figures circle, square, and triangle (C, S, and T, respectively). An appropriate definition is

```
TYPE
  FigureShape = (Circle, Square, Triangle);
  FigureInfo = RECORD
                 Object : char;
                 Area : real;
```

```
                  CASE Shape : FigureShape OF
                    Circle   : (Radius : real);
                    Square   : (Side : real);
                    Triangle : (Base, Height : real)
                  END;  {  of RECORD FigureInfo  }
VAR
  Figure : FigureInfo;
```

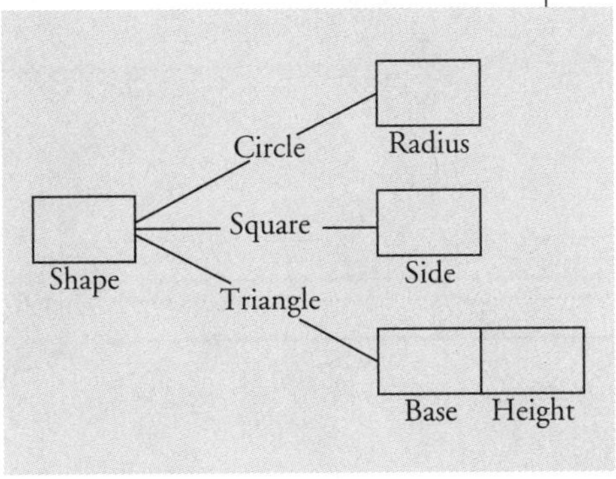

Each data line has a single character designating the kind of figure followed by appropriate information needed to compute the area. For example,

```
T 6.0 8.0■
```

represents a triangle with base 6.0 and height 8.0. A procedure to get a line of data is

```
PROCEDURE GetData (VAR Figure : FigureInfo);
  BEGIN
    reset (Data);
    WITH Figure DO
      BEGIN
        read (Data, Object);
        CASE Object OF
          'C' : BEGIN
                  Shape := Circle;
                  readln (Data, Radius)
                END;
          'S' : BEGIN
                  Shape := Square;
                  readln (Data, Side)
                END;
          'T' : BEGIN
                  Shape := Triangle;
                  readln (Data, Base, Height)
                END
        END  {  of CASE Object  }
      END  {  of WITH...DO  }
  END;  {  of PROCEDURE GetData  }
```

This is called from the main program by

```
GetData (Figure);
```

Finally, a function to compute the area is

```
FUNCTION Area (Figure : FigureInfo) : real;
  CONST
    Pi = 3.14159;
  BEGIN
    WITH Figure DO
      BEGIN
        CASE Shape OF
          Circle   : Area := Pi * Radius * Radius;
          Square   : Area := Side * Side;
          Triangle : Area := 0.5 * Base * Height
        END  {  of CASE Shape  }
      END  {  of WITH...DO  }
  END;  {  of FUNCTION Area  }
```

This function is called by

```
Figure.Area := Area(Figure);
```

Exercises 12.4

1. Explain how memory may be saved when records with variant parts are declared.
2. Assume a record is defined by

   ```
   TYPE
     TagType = (One, Two);
     Info = RECORD
              Fixed : integer;
              CASE Tag : TagType OF
                One : (A, B : integer);
                Two : (X : real;
                       Ch : char)
            END;
   ```

   and the variable declaration section of a program includes

   ```
   VAR
     RecordCheck : Info;
   ```

   What is the output from the following fragment of code?

   ```
   WITH RecordCheck DO
     BEGIN
       Fixed := 1000;
       Tag := One;
       A := 100;
       B := 500;
       writeln (Fixed:15, A:15, B:15);
       Tag := Two;
       X := 10.5;
       Ch := 'Y';
       writeln (Fixed:15, X:15:2, Ch:15);
       writeln (A:15, B:15, X:15:2, Ch:15)
     END;
   ```

In Exercises 3–6, find all errors in the definitions.

*3.
```
TYPE
  Info = RECORD
           A : real;
           CASE Tag : TagType OF
             B : (X, Y : real);
             C : (Z : boolean)
         END;
```

4.
```
TYPE
  TagType = (A, B, C);
  Info = RECORD
           D : integer;
           Flag : boolean;
           CASE Tag : TagType OF
             A : (X, Y : real);
             B : (Z : real)
         END;
```

*5.
```
TYPE
  TagType = (A, B, C);
  Info = RECORD
           D : integer;
           Flag : boolean
           CASE Tag OF
             A : (X : real);
             B : (Y : real);
             C : (Z : real)
         END;
```

6.
```
TYPE
  TagType = (A, B, C);
  Info = RECORD
           D : integer;
           CASE Tag1 : TagType OF
             A : (X : real);
             B : (Y : real);
             C : (Z : real)
             END;
           CASE Tag2 : TagType OF
             A : (X1 : real);
             B : (Y1 : real);
             C : (Z1 : real)
         END;
```

*7. Define a record with a variant part to be used for working with various publications. For each record, there should be fields for the author, title, and date. If the publication is a book, there should be fields for the publisher and city. If the publication is an article, there should be fields for the journal name and volume number.

8. Redefine the following record without using a variant part.

```
TYPE
  Shapes = (Circle, Square, Triangle);
  FigureInfo = RECORD
```

```
                    Object : char;
                    Area : real;
                    CASE Shape : Shapes OF
                      Circle   : (Radius : real);
                      Square   : (Side : real);
                      Triangle : (Base, Height : real)
                  END;
VAR
  Figure : FigureInfo;
```

*9. Using the record defined in Exercise 8, indicate the names of the fields available and provide an illustration of these fields after each of the following assignments is made:
   a. `Shape := Circle;`
   b. `Shape := Square;`
   c. `Shape := Triangle;`

10. Redefine the record defined in Exercise 8 to include rectangles and parallelograms.

Focus on Program Design: Case Study

Using an Array of Records

The sample program for this chapter features working with an array of records. The array is first sorted using the field containing a name. It is then sorted using the field containing a real.

Let's write a program to help your local high school sports boosters keep records of donors and amounts donated. The data file consists of a name (first 20 positions) and an amount donated (starting in position 21) on each line. For example,

```
Jones Jerry          250
```

Your program should get the data from the data file and read it into a record for each donor. Output should consist of two lists as follows:

1. an alphabetical listing together with the amount donated
2. a listing sorted according to the amount donated

A first-level pseudocode development for this problem is

1. Get the data
2. Sort by name
3. Print the first list
4. Sort by amount
5. Print the second list

A complete structure chart is given in Figure 12.16. Module specifications for the main modules are

1. GetData Module

   Data received: None
   Information returned: Array of records containing names, amounts, and array length
   Logic: Use a **WHILE NOT eof** loop with a counter to read the data file.

◆ Figure 12.16

Structure chart for **PROGRAM** Boosters

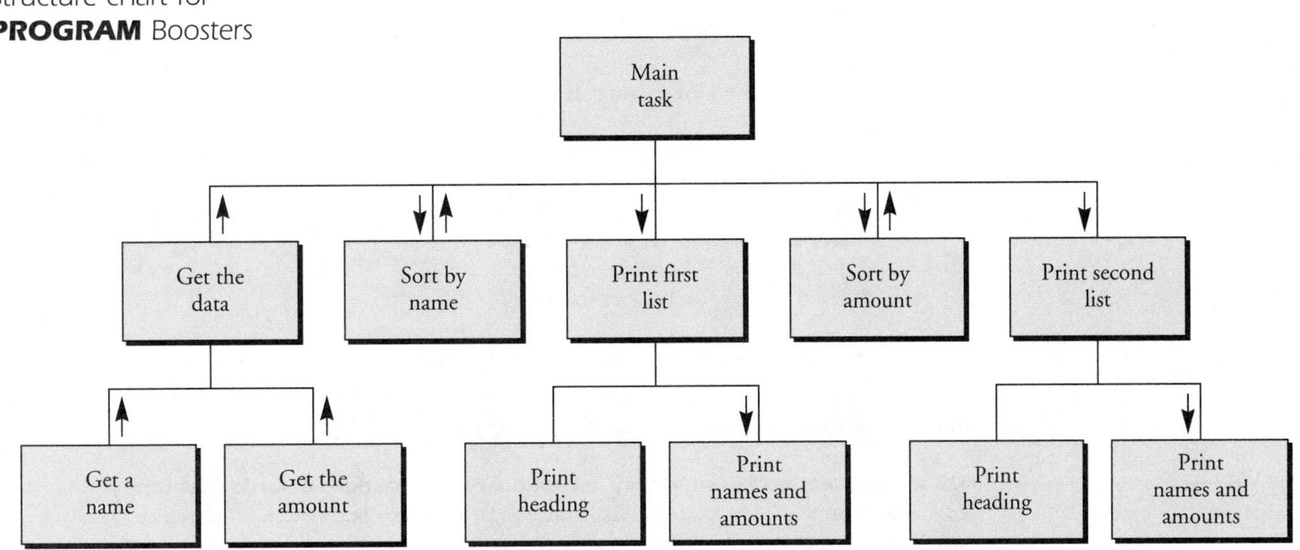

2. SortByName Module

   Data received: Unsorted array of records containing names and amounts with the list length

   Information returned: An alphabetized list of names with associated amounts

   Logic: Use a selection sort to sort the array of records.

3. PrintList Module

   Data received: Array of records
   Array length

   Information returned: None

   Logic: Call **PROCEDURE** PrintHeading.
   Use a loop to print the names and amounts.

4. SortByAmount Module

   Data received: Array of records sorted alphabetically
   List length

   Information returned: Array of records sorted by size of donation

   Logic: Use a selection sort to sort the list of donations.

A refinement of the pseudocode yields

1. Get the data
   WHILE NOT eof(Data) **DO**
   1.1 Get a name
   1.2 Get the amount
2. Sort by name (use selection sort)
3. Print the first list
   3.1 Print a heading
   3.2 Print the names and amounts
4. Sort by amount (use selection sort)

5. Print the second list
   5.1 Print a heading
   5.2 Print the names and amounts

The main driver for the program is

```
BEGIN  {  Main program  }
  reset (Data);
  GetData (Donor, Count);
  SortByName (Donor, Count);
  PrintList (Donor, Count);
  SortByAmount (Donor, Count);
  PrintList (Donor, Count)
END.  {  of main program  }
```

A complete program for this problem follows:

```
PROGRAM Boosters (input, output, Data);

{  This program uses an array of records to process information }
{  for donors to the local high school sports boosters.  Output }
{  includes two lists, one  sorted by  name and  one sorted  by }
{  amount donated. Information is stored in the text file Data. }

CONST
  ClubSize = 50;
  MaxLength = 20;

TYPE
  NameString = PACKED ARRAY [1..MaxLength] OF char;
  MemberInfo = RECORD
                 Name : NameString;
                 Amount : real
               END;  {  of RECORD MemberInfo  }
  DonorList = ARRAY [1..ClubSize] OF MemberInfo;

VAR
  Count : integer;       {  Counter for number of donors          }
  Donor : DonorList;     {  Array of records, one for each donor  }
  Data : text;           {  Data file of names and amounts        }

{*************************************************************}

PROCEDURE GetData (VAR Donor : DonorList;
                   VAR Count : integer);

  {  Given:   Nothing                                             }
  {  Task:    Read donor names and amounts from the text file,    }
  {                Data, into an array of records                 }
  {  Return:  An array of records and number of donors            }

  VAR
    J : integer;
  BEGIN
    Count := 0;
```

```
    WHILE NOT eof(Data) AND (Count < ClubSize) DO
      BEGIN
        Count := Count + 1;
        WITH Donor[Count] DO
          BEGIN
            FOR J := 1 TO MaxLength DO                         1
              read (Data, Name[J]);
            readln (Data, Amount)
          END  {  of WITH...DO  }
      END;  {  of WHILE NOT eof  }
    IF NOT eof(Data) THEN
      writeln ('Not all data read.')
  END;  {  of PROCEDURE GetData  }

{*****************************************************************}

PROCEDURE Swap (VAR Record1, Record2 : MemberInfo);

  {  Given:   Two records                                          }
  {  Task:    Interchange contents of records                      }
  {  Return:  Records with contents interchanged                   }

  VAR
    Temp : MemberInfo;
  BEGIN
    Temp := Record1;
    Record1 := Record2;
    Record2 := Temp
  END;  {  of PROCEDURE Swap  }

{*****************************************************************}

PROCEDURE SortByName (VAR Donor : DonorList;
                      Count : integer);
                                                                   2
  {  Given:   An array of records and number of records           }
  {  Task:    Sort alphabetically by the field Donor[J].Name      }
  {  Return:  An alphabetized array of records                    }

  VAR
    J, K, Index : integer;
    Temp : MemberInfo;
  BEGIN
    FOR J := 1 TO Count - 1 DO
      BEGIN
        Index := J;
        FOR K := J + 1 TO Count DO
          IF Donor[K].Name < Donor[Index].Name THEN
            Index := K;
        IF Index <> J THEN
          Swap (Donor[Index], Donor[J])
      END  {  of FOR J loop  }
  END;  {  of PROCEDURE SortByName  }

{*****************************************************************}
```

```
PROCEDURE SortByAmount (VAR Donor : DonorList;
                        Count : integer);

  { Given:   An array of records and number of records          }
  { Task:    Sort by amount donated, Donor[J].Amount            }
  { Return:  An array of records sorted by amount donated       }

  VAR
    J, K, Index : integer;
    Temp : MemberInfo;
  BEGIN                                                             4
    FOR J := 1 TO Count - 1 DO
      BEGIN
        Index := J;
        FOR K := J + 1 TO Count DO
          IF Donor[K].Amount > Donor[Index].Amount THEN
            Index := K;
        IF Index <> J THEN
          Swap (Donor[Index], Donor[J])
      END  { of FOR J loop }
  END;  { of PROCEDURE SortByAmount }

{**************************************************************}

PROCEDURE PrintHeading;

  { Given:   Nothing                                            }
  { Task:    Print a heading for the output                     }
  { Return:  Nothing                                            }

  CONST
    Skip = ' ';
  BEGIN
    writeln (Skip:7, 'Local Sports Boosters');
    writeln (Skip:11, 'Donation List');
    writeln ('---------------------------------');
    writeln;
    writeln (Skip:5, 'Name', Skip:19, 'Amount');
    writeln (Skip:5, '----', Skip:19, '------');
    writeln
  END;  { of PROCEDURE PrintHeading }                               3

{**************************************************************}

PROCEDURE PrintList (VAR Donor : DonorList;
                     Count : integer);

  { Given:   An array of records and number of records             }
  { Task:    Print a list containing one column for the name and   }
  {                one column for the amount donated; output       }
  {                directed to the printer                         }
  { Return:  Nothing                                               }

  CONST
    Skip = ' ';
```

```
  VAR
    J : integer;
  BEGIN
    PrintHeading;
    FOR J := 1 TO Count DO
      WITH Donor[J] DO
        writeln (Name, '$':7, Amount:7:2);
    writeln;
    writeln;
    writeln
  END;  {  of PROCEDURE PrintList  }

{***************************************************************}

BEGIN  {  Main program  }
  reset (Data);
  GetData (Donor, Count);
  SortByName (Donor, Count);
  PrintList (Donor, Count);
  SortByAmount (Donor, Count);
  PrintList (Donor, Count)
END.  {  of main program  }
```

The output from this program is

```
           Local Sports Boosters
               Donation List
 ----------------------------------

      Name                    Amount
      ----                    ------

 Alexander Candy            $ 300.00
 Anderson Tony              $ 375.00
 Banks Marj                 $ 375.00
 Born Patty                 $ 100.00
 Brown Ron                  $ 200.00
 Darnell Linda              $ 275.00
 Erickson Thomas            $ 100.00
 Fox William                $ 300.00
 Francis Denise             $ 350.00
 Generous George            $ 525.00
 Gillette Mike              $ 350.00
 Hancock Kirk               $ 500.00
 Higgins Sam                $ 300.00
 Janson Kevin               $ 200.00
 Johnson Ed                 $ 350.00
 Johnson Martha             $ 400.00
 Jones Jerry                $ 250.00
 Kelly Marvin               $ 475.00
 Kneff Susan                $ 300.00
 Lasher John                $ 175.00
```

```
Lyon Elizabeth              $ 425.00
Moore Robert                $ 100.00
Muller Marjorie             $ 250.00
Smith John                  $ 100.00
Trost Frostie               $  50.00
Trudo Rosemary              $ 200.00
Weber Sharon                $ 150.00
Williams Art                $ 350.00
Williams Jane               $ 175.00
Wilson Mary                 $ 275.00


       Local Sports Boosters
           Donation List
----------------------------------

     Name                   Amount
     ----                   ------

Generous George             $ 525.00
Hancock Kirk                $ 500.00
Kelly Marvin                $ 475.00
Lyon Elizabeth              $ 425.00
Johnson Martha              $ 400.00
Anderson Tony               $ 375.00
Banks Marj                  $ 375.00
Francis Denise              $ 350.00
Gillette Mike               $ 350.00
Johnson Ed                  $ 350.00
Williams Art                $ 350.00
Higgins Sam                 $ 300.00
Alexander Candy             $ 300.00
Kneff Susan                 $ 300.00
Fox William                 $ 300.00
Darnell Linda               $ 275.00
Wilson Mary                 $ 275.00
Muller Marjorie             $ 250.00
Jones Jerry                 $ 250.00
Trudo Rosemary              $ 200.00
Brown Ron                   $ 200.00
Janson Kevin                $ 200.00
Lasher John                 $ 175.00
Williams Jane               $ 175.00
Weber Sharon                $ 150.00
Erickson Thomas             $ 100.00
Born Patty                  $ 100.00
Smith John                  $ 100.00
Moore Robert                $ 100.00
Trost Frostie               $  50.00
```

Running and Debugging Hints

1. Be sure to use the full field name when working with fields in a record. You should leave off the record name only when using **WITH . . . DO.**
2. Terminate each record definition with an **END** statement. This is an instance when **END** is used without a **BEGIN.**
3. Although field names in different record types can be the same, you are encouraged to use distinct names. This enhances readability and reduces the chances of making errors.
4. Be careful to note the distinction in syntax when using an array of records versus an array as a field within a record. For example, be able to distinguish between Student[K].Average, Student.Score[J], and Student[K].Score[J].
5. When sorting records using a key field, be careful to compare the key field only; then exchange the entire record accordingly.

Summary

Key Terms

array of records
field
field selector
fixed parts
index sort
nested record
record
tag field
variant part

Keywords

RECORD
WITH

Key Concepts

- A **RECORD** is a structured data type that is a collection of fields; the fields may be treated as a whole or individually.
- Fields in a record can be of different data types.
- Records can be declared or defined by

```
<record name> =  RECORD
                    <field identifier 1> : <data type 1>;
                    <field identifier 2> : <data type 2>;
                         .
                         .
                         .
                    <field identifier n> : <data type n>
                 END;  {  of RECORD definition  }
```

- Fields can be accessed as variables by

<record name>.<field identifier>

- Records can be schematically represented as in Figure 12.17.

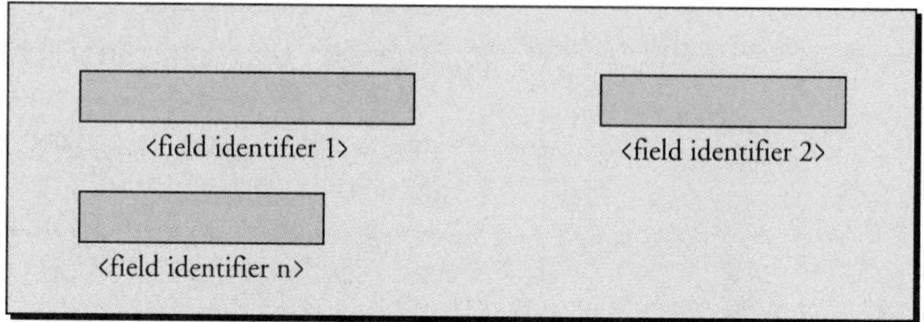

Figure 12.17
Fields in a record

- You can use **WITH** <record name> **DO** rather than make a specific reference to the record name with each field of a record; thus, you can use

```
WITH Student DO
  BEGIN
    Name := 'Smith John          ';
    Average := 93.4;
    Grade := 'A'
  END;
```

instead of

```
Student.Name := 'Smith John          ';
Student.Average := 93.4;
Student.Grade := 'A';
```

- If two records, A and B, are of identical type, contents of all fields of one may be assigned to corresponding fields of the other by a single assignment statement such as

```
A := B;
```

- Entire records or fields within a record can be passed to appropriate subprograms.
- A record can be used as a field in another record.
- A **WITH . . . DO** statement can be used to access fields of nested records.
- Records can be used as components of an array.
- An array of records can be sorted by one of the fields in each record.
- Linear and binary searches can be used with arrays of records. A key field is used for either search.
- Records with variant parts list all fixed fields (if any) first and then use a **CASE** statement to list the variant field; for example,

```
TYPE
  MaritalStatus = (Married, Single, Divorced);
  NameString = PACKED ARRAY [1..20] OF char;
  Info = RECORD
```

```
            Name : NameString;
            CASE Status : MaritalStatus OF
              Married  : (SpouseName : NameString;
                          NumKids : integer);
              Single   : (Gender : char;
                          Age : integer);
              Divorced : (NumKids : integer;
                          Age : integer;
                          Gender : char;
                          LivesAlone : boolean)
          END;  {  of RECORD Info  }
VAR
  Customer : Info;
```

- After a value has been assigned to a tag field, the remaining record fields are the ones listed in the **CASE** part of the definition; for example, if we use the previous definition and we have

```
Customer.Status := Divorced;
```

the record fields are as shown in Figure 12.18.

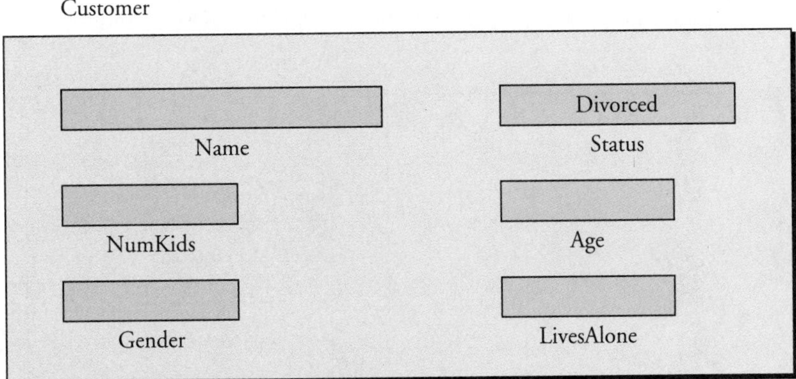

◆ Figure 12.18

Value of a tag field

Chapter Review Exercises

For Exercises 1–5, use a record containing the following information.

Student name (20 characters)
Homeroom number (**integer**)
Class (10 characters)
Lab fees paid (**boolean**)
GPA (**real**)

1. Write a type and variable definition for the record.
2. Draw a schematic representation of the record.
3. Write a procedure to read data for a student into the record.
4. Revise your definition to create an array of 50 of the record as you defined it.
5. Write a procedure to print a list of the names and homerooms of the students who have not paid their fees.

For Exercises 6–17, refer to the following record definition:

```
TYPE
  Rec1 = RECORD
           A : ARRAY [1..10] OF integer;
           B : real;
           C : PACKED ARRAY [1..3, 1..5] OF integer
         END;
  Arry = ARRAY [1..4] OF Rec1;
VAR
  X : Rec1;
  Y : Arry;
```

Which of the following references are appropriate?

6. `X.B`
7. `Y.B`
8. `X.A[1]`
9. `Y.A[1]`
10. `X[1].B`
11. `Y[1].B`
12. `Y[2].X[4]`
13. `Y[3]`
14. `X.C[3,4]`
15. `Y[5].B`
16. `Y.X.A`
17. `Y.B`

For Exercises 18 and 19, use a **TYPE** definition to declare the record illustrated. For each exercise, also declare a record variable to be of the illustrated type.

18. AmericanLeague

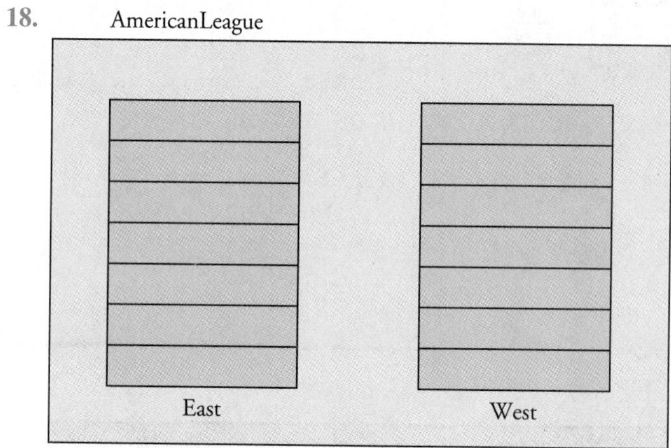

19. LanguagesLearned

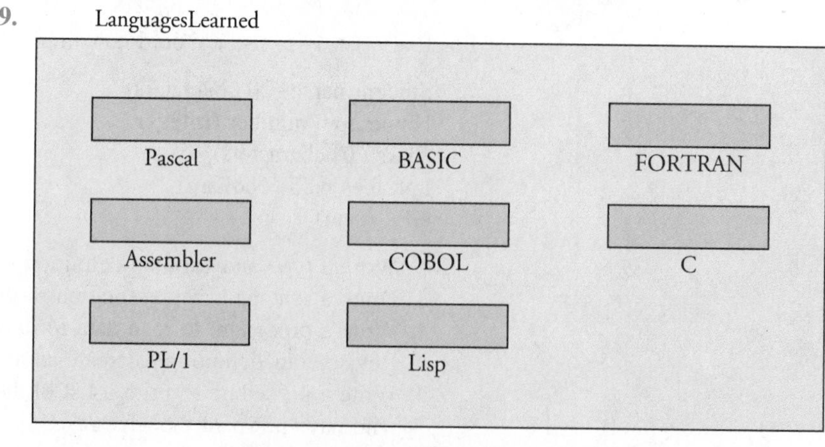

For Exercises 20–31, use the following record definitions:

```
TYPE
  A = RECORD
        B : ARRAY [1..5] OF integer;
        C : boolean;
        D : PACKED ARRAY [1..5, 1..10] OF char
      END;
  W = RECORD
        X : integer;
        Y : ARRAY [1..5] OF integer;
        Z : A
      END;
VAR
  G : A;
  H : W;
```

Which statements are appropriate?

20. `G.C := true;`
21. `G.B[3] := 2;`
22. `read (G.D[1];`
23. `H.Z.D[1,3] := 'A';`
24. `IF A.B[2] = 1 THEN`
    `write (A.B[2]);`
25. `H.X := H.Y[4] + H.Z.B[4];`
26. `writeln (H.A.D[5]);`
27. `IF G.D[4] = H.Z.D[4] THEN`
    `writeln;`
28. `H.B[1] := 3;`
29. `W.X := 3;`
30. `H.Z.C := true;`
31. `H.A.C := true;`
32. Write a record that can be used to keep track of the names of the nine starters on a baseball team, their positions, and their batting averages.
33. Include the record definition in Exercise 32 in another record to also keep the school names and nicknames of 10 high school baseball teams.
34. Write a procedure to check the record defined in Exercise 33 and print the name of the team having a shortstop named Mapes.

Note: Exercises 35–37 involve record variants and may be optional for you.

35. Define a record containing the names, heights, weights, and ages of baseball players. If the player is a pitcher, also include the innings pitched and earned run average. If the player is not a pitcher, include the number of home runs and batting average.
36. Write a procedure to read data into the record defined in Exercise 35.
37. List at least two advantages of using record variants.

Programming Problems

■ 1. Write a program to be used by the registrar of a university. The program should get information from a data file and the data for each student should include student name, student number, classification (1 for freshman, 2 for sophomore, 3 for junior, 4 for senior, or 7 for special student), hours completed, hours taking, and grade point average. Output should include an alphabetical list of all students, an alphabetical list of students in each class, and a list of all students ordered by grade point average.

2. Robert Day, basketball coach at Indiana College, wants you to write a program to help him analyze information about his basketball team. He wants a record for each player containing the player's name, position played, high school graduated from, height, scoring average, rebounding average, grade point average, and seasons of eligibility remaining.

   The program should read the information for each player from a data file. The output should include an alphabetized list of names together with other pertinent information, a list sorted according to scoring average, an alphabetized list of all players with a grade point average above 3.0, and an alphabetized list of high schools together with an alphabetized list of players who graduated from each school.

3. Final grades in Mr. Lae Z. Programmer's (Problems 5, 22, and 23, Chapter 5; Problem 13, Chapter 6; Problem 7, Chapter 7; Problem 5, Chapter 9; and Problem 3, Chapter 11) computer science class are to be computed using the following course requirements:

Requirement		Possible Points
1. Quiz scores (10 points each; count the best 10 out of 12)		100
2. Two hourly tests (100 points each)		200
3. Eight programming assignments (25 points each)		200
4. Two test program assignments (50 points each)		100
5. Final examination		100
	Total	700

   Cutoff percentages for the grades of A, B, C, D, and E are 90 percent, 80 percent, 70 percent, and 55 percent, respectively; grade E is <55 percent.

   Write a program to keep a record of each student's name, homeroom number, quiz scores (all 12), hourly examination scores, programming assignment scores, test program scores, and final examination score. Your program should read data from a data file, compute total points for each student, calculate the letter grade, and output results. The output should be sorted by total points from high to low and include all raw data, the 10 best quiz scores, total points and percentage score, and letter grade. Use procedures and functions where appropriate.

4. Write a program to input an unknown number of pairs of fractions with an operation (either +, −, *, or /) between the fractions. The program should perform the operation on the fractions or indicate that the operation is impossible. Answers should be reduced to lowest terms.

Sample Input	Sample Output

3/4 + 5/6	`3     5     19`
	`--- + --- = ---`
	`4     6     12`

4/9 - 1/6	`4     1     5`
	`--- - --- = ---`
	`9     6     18`

4/5 / 0/2	`4     0`
	`--- / --- = Impossible`
	`5     2`

4/3 + 7/0	`4     7`
	`--- + --- = Impossible`
	`3     0`

6/5 * 20/3	`6     20    8`
	`--- * --- = ---`
	`5     3     1`

5. Complex numbers are numbers of the form $a + bi$, where a and b are real and i represents $\sqrt{-1}$. Complex number arithmetic is defined by

Sum	$(a + bi) + (c + di) = (a + c) + (b + d)i$
Difference	$(a + bi) - (c + di) = (a - c) + (b - d)i$
Product	$(a + bi)(c + di) = (ac - bd) + (ad + bc)i$
Quotient	$(a + bi)/(c + di) = \dfrac{ac + bd}{c^2 + d^2} + \dfrac{bc - ad}{c^2 + d^2}i$

Write a program to be used to perform these calculations on two complex numbers. Each line of data consists of a single character designator (S, D, P, or Q) followed by four reals representing two complex numbers. For example, $(2 + 3i) + (5 - 2i)$ are represented by

```
S2 3 5 -2
```

A record should be used for each complex number. The output should be in the form $a + bi$.

6. The Readmore Public Library wants a program to keep track of the books checked out. Information for each book should be kept in a record and the fields should include the author's name, a nonfiction designator (**boolean**), the title, the library catalog number, and the copyright date. Each customer can check out at most 10 books.

Your program should read information from a data file and print two lists alphabetized by author name, one for nonfiction and the other for fiction. A typical data line is

Kidder Tracy	T Soul of a New Machine	81.6044 1982

↑ position 21 ↑ position 52

7. Modify Problem 6 so that a daily printout is available that contains a summary of the day's transactions at the Readmore Public Library. You will need a record for each customer containing the customer's name and library card number. Be sure to make provision for books that are returned.

8. Write a program to be used to keep track of bank accounts. Define a record that includes each customer's name, account number, starting balance, transaction record, and ending balance. The transaction record should list all deposits and withdrawals. A special message should be printed whenever there are insufficient funds for a withdrawal. When a name is read from the data file, all previous records should be searched to see if you are processing a new account. The final output for each customer should look like a typical bank statement.

9. Write a program that uses records to analyze poker hands. Each hand consists of five records (cards). Each record should have one field for the suit and one for the value. Rankings for the hands from high to low are

   Straight flush
   Four of a kind
   Full house
   Flush
   Straight
   Three of a kind
   Two pair
   One pair
   None of the above

   Your program should read data for five cards from a data file, evaluate the hand, and print the hand together with a message indicating its value.

10. Problem 9 can be modified in several ways. A first modification is to compare two different hands using only the ranking indicated. A second (more difficult) modification is to also compare hands that have the same ranking. For example, a pair of 8's is better than a pair of 7's. Extend Problem 9 to incorporate some of these modifications.

11. Divers at the Olympics are judged by seven judges. Points for each dive are awarded according to the following procedure:
    a. Each judge assigns a score between 0.0 and 10.0 inclusive.
    b. The high score and low score are eliminated.
    c. The five remaining scores are summed and this total is multiplied by 0.6. This result is then multiplied by the degree of difficulty of the dive (0.0 to 3.0).

    The first level of competition consists of 24 divers each making 10 dives. Divers with the 12 highest totals advance to the finals.

    Write a program to keep a record for each diver. Each record should contain information for all 10 dives, the diver's name, and the total score. One round of competition consists of each diver making one dive. A typical line of data consists of the diver's name, degree of difficulty for the dive, and seven judges' scores. Part of your output should include a list of divers who advance to the finals.

12. The University Biology Department has a Conservation Club that works with the state Department of Natural Resources. Their project for the semester is to help capture and tag migratory birds. You have been asked to write a computer program to help them store information. In general, the program must have information for each bird tagged entered interactively into an array of records and then stored in a text file for subsequent use. For each bird tagged, you need a field for the tag number, tagging site, sex, bird type, date, and name of the DNR officer doing the tagging. After all data have been entered, the program should print one list sorted by tag number and one sorted by bird type.

■ 13. Mrs. Crown, your computer science teacher, wishes to keep track of the maintenance record of her computers and has turned to you for help. She wants to keep track of the type of machine, its serial number (up to 10 characters), the year of purchase, and a **boolean** variable indicating whether the machine is under a service contract.

Write a program that permits the entry of records, then prints a list of the machines that are under warranty and a list of those not under warranty. Both lists should be arranged in order of serial number.

14. Most microcomputer owners soon develop a large, often unorganized, library of software on several floppy disks. This is your chance to help them. Define a record containing the disk number of each disk, and a list of up to 30 program titles on each disk. Write a program to read a text file containing the information for a disk and then print an alphabetized listing of the program titles on that disk.

15. Revise the program in Problem 14 to permit the user of the program to enter the program name desired, and have the program print the number of the disk(s) containing the program.

16. Write a program to read records containing the name, address, telephone number, and class of some of your friends. Print a list of the names of the students in the file who are in your class.

■ 17. The Falcon Manufacturing Company (Problem 23, Chapter 11) wishes to keep computerized records of its telephone-order customers. They want the name, street address, city, state, and zip code for each customer. They include either a "T" if the customer is a business, or an "F" if the customer is an individual. A 30-character description of each business is also included. An individual's credit limit is in the record.

Write a program to read the information for the customer from a text file and print a list of the information for businesses and a separate list of the information for individuals. There are no more than 50 records in the file.

18. Write a program that can be used to analyze quadrilaterals. Input consists of four pairs of integers, each of which represents a point in the plane. It is assumed the points represent the vertices of a quadrilateral given in counterclockwise order. Your program should indicate whether the quadrilateral is a square, a rectangle, a rhombus, or none of the above. All names that apply to the quadrilateral should be listed.

19. Standard Pascal does not support a string data type. However, strings may be simulated by using a record with two fields: one for the length, and one for the characters in the string. The field for length should be of type **integer,** and the field for the string should be a packed array of characters with 256 positions. Write a program that receives strings as input and creates an appropriate record

for each string. Your program should then be able to simulate the following string operations:

a. Determine the length of a string (the null string is of length zero). Do not count trailing blanks.
b. Make the string comparisons <, =, and >. The user should be able to compare strings of different lengths.
c. Concatenate strings. If String1 is "This is" and String2 is " one sentence.", the concatenation of String1 and String2 is "This is one sentence."

Output from your program should be any input string and sufficient displays to demonstrate your string operations.

Communication in Practice

1. Write a short paper that explains why the existence of the structured data type **RECORD** eliminates the need for working with parallel arrays. As part of your paper, show specifically how **PROGRAM** Donations in Section 12.3 can be rewritten using records.
2. Suppose you are part of a team that has been asked to develop a spreadsheet. Your specific task is to write all documentation for the sorting feature of the spreadsheet. The documentation is to include complete descriptions of forms of input and output, a logical development of the sorting process, and a description of the user interface message. Prepare a report that includes this documentation.
3. Visit your school office and discuss how records of students are processed. Discover what data are kept in each record, how the data are entered, and what the fields of each record are. Have someone explain what operations are used with a student's record. Specifically, how is information added to or deleted from a record? Discuss the issue of sorting records. What kinds of lists must be produced for those within the system who need information about students? Prepare a written report of your visit for the class. Be sure to include a graphic that shows how a student's record can be envisioned.
4. Select an unworked problem from the **Programming Problems** in this chapter. Construct a structure chart and write all documentary information necessary for this problem. Do not write code. When finished, have a classmate read your documentation to see if it is clear precisely what is to be done.
5. Modify one of the programs you developed in this chapter by deleting all documentation. Exchange your modified version with another student who has prepared a similar version. Write documentation for the exchanged program. Compare your results with the other student's original version.
6. Select an unworked problem from the **Programming Problems** in this chapter. For that problem, write documentation that includes a complete description of
   a. Required input
   b. Required output
   c. Required processing and computation.

   Exchange your documentation with another student who has the same assignment. Compare your results.

Chapter 13

More About Files

Chapter Outline

Chapter 9 introduced the concept of text files, which are used to provide data for a program and to store data between runs of a program. All data in a text file are stored as a sequence of characters of type **char.** We are now ready to examine files in more detail.

A note of caution is in order first. File manipulation is extremely system dependent. This is especially true with microcomputers. Since it is likely that your system differs from standard Pascal in some ways, you are encouraged to consult your system manual.

13.1 Binary Files

Objectives

- to understand the basic idea of a file in Pascal
- to be able to define a file type
- to understand the concept of a buffer
- to understand the differences between files and arrays as structured data types

Files that cannot be defined as text files are **binary files.** Information is stored in binary files by using the internal binary representation of each component. This method differs from data storage in a text file, where components are stored as lines of characters.

The advantage of using binary files is that they can be much more efficiently processed. Because the binary representation of data is already available, conversion between character representation and appropriate binary representation is not needed. A disadvantage of using binary files is that they cannot be created, examined, or modified by using a text editor. Binary files must be created by a program. Furthermore, all operations with binary files must be done within programs. In this section, we see how these operations are performed.

Basic Idea and Notation

Information can be saved between runs of a program by using secondary storage devices such as tapes or disks. (Personal computers use floppy or hard disks.) As a beginning programmer, you normally do not need to be concerned with the actual physical construct of these storage devices, but you do need to know how to work with them. To oversimplify, you need to be able to get data into a program,

A **binary file** is a file in which information is stored using binary representation for components.

A **file** is a data structure that consists of a sequence of components all of the same type.

A **component of a file** is one element of the file data type.

manipulate these data, and save the data (and results) for later use. If, for example, we write a program that computes grades for students in a class, we need to enter data periodically for processing. Pascal solves this problem with a structured data type **FILE.** A **file** is a data structure that consists of a sequence of components all of the same type. A **FILE** data type is defined by

```
TYPE
  <file identifier> = FILE OF <data type>;
VAR
  <file name> : <file identifier>;
```

Thus, if we wish to work with a file of integers, we define

```
TYPE
  FileOfInt = FILE OF integer;
VAR
  File1 : FileOfInt;
```

In this case, File1 is the desired file. Several comments are now in order.

1. Data entries in a file are called **components of the file.**
2. All components of a file must be of the same data type.
3. The only data type not permitted as a component of a file is another file type. This differs from arrays in that

   ```
   ARRAY [ ] OF ARRAY [ ] OF <data type>;
   ```

   is permitted, but

   ```
   FILE OF FILE OF <data type>;
   ```

   is not permitted.

Each of the following is a valid definition of a file type.

```
TYPE
  Identifier1 = FILE OF real;
  Identifier2 = FILE OF ARRAY [1..20] OF integer;
  Identifier3 = FILE OF boolean;
```

Files of records are frequently used in programs. Thus, to keep a record for each student in a class, you could have the definition

```
TYPE
  NameString = PACKED ARRAY [1..20] OF char;
  ExamScores = ARRAY [1..4] OF integer;
  QuizScores = ARRAY [1..10] OF integer;
  StudentInfo = RECORD
                  Name : NameString;
                  IDNumber : 0..999;
                  Exam : ExamScores;
                  Quiz : QuizScores;
```

```
                     Average : real;
                     Grade : char
                   END;  { of RECORD StudentInfo  }
  StudentFile = FILE OF StudentInfo;

VAR
  Student : StudentFile;
```

There is a difference between a text file and a file of characters. Although a text file consists of a sequence of characters, it also has "lines" separated by end-of-line markers. A file of characters, which is of the type **FILE OF char,** does not have line separators.

Comparison to Arrays

Binary files and one-dimensional arrays have some similarities. Both are structured data types, and components must be of the same type. There are, however, some important differences.

1. Files permit you to store and retrieve information between runs of a program.
2. Only one component of a file is available at a time.
3. Files must be sequentially accessed; that is, when working with files, the user starts at the beginning and processes the components in sequence. It is not possible (as it is with arrays) to access some component directly without first having somehow moved through the previous components.
4. Files do not have a defined length. Once a file has been defined, the number of components is limited only by the amount of storage available. However, this number is usually so large it can be considered unbounded.
5. Files are stored in secondary storage; arrays are stored only in memory.

T

File Window and Buffer Variables

Before we begin our specific work with files, we need to examine the concepts of a file window and a buffer variable. A file can be visualized as a sequence of components as follows:

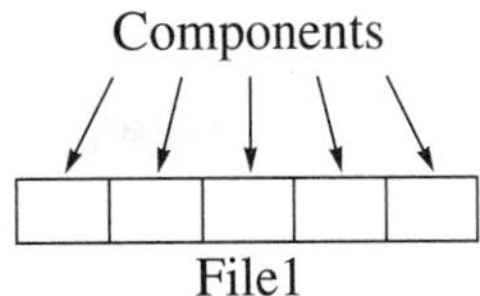

File window is a term used in this book, though not designated by Pascal, to indicate an imaginary window through which values of a file component can be transferred.

A **buffer variable** is the actual vehicle through which values are passed to or from a file component.

Only one of these components can be "seen" at a time. An imaginary window is associated with a file and values can be transferred to (or from) a component of the file only through this **file window.** Thus, the window must be properly positioned before the user attempts to transmit data to or from a component.

This imaginary window has no name in Pascal. However, a related concept, called a **buffer variable,** is the actual vehicle through which values are passed to or from the file component. When a file is declared in a program, a buffer variable is automatically declared and therefore available to the programmer. To illustrate, given the following declaration of FileA

```
TYPE
  FileInfo = FILE OF integer;
```

A Note of Interest

Relational Databases

One advance in data management that has gained tremendously in popularity and, in fact, is revolutionizing system development practices is the increased use of the database management system, known as DBMS. An especially important development in database technology is the relational database.

The relational DBMS is based on the concept of multiple "flat files" that are "related" via common fields. A flat file is essentially a two-dimensional matrix of columns and rows, where columns represent the fields contained in a record and rows contain different records. A simple example of the flat file concept is a spreadsheet, such as Lotus 1-2-3, although the analogy is somewhat misleading since spreadsheets are most commonly used for purposes other than database management.

In a relational database there are usually several flat files, each of which is used to store information about a different "entity" in the world. The objectives of relational technology are to insure that each file in the database contains information about only the entity with which it is associated and to provide links between files that represent the relationships between those entities that exist in the real world.

Let's look at a simple example of a relational database that is used to process customer orders. Such a relational database would contain at least two files: one for customer data and one for order data. The customer file would contain information (that is, fields) such as the customer's account number, name, address, and phone number; the order file would contain fields such as product number, product name, order quantity, unit cost, and total order cost. To enable the system to match an order to the customer who placed it, the customer's account number would also be contained in the order file. Thus, when the user needs to acquire combined order and customer information (for example, to prepare and mail an invoice), the two files can be temporarily "joined" based on common values in the respective customer account number fields in each file.

At the mainframe level of computing, the relational DBMS is one of several types of database management systems; other types are hierarchical and network systems. At the microcomputer level, however, DBMS software is almost exclusively relational. Such common packages as dBASE III, RBase System V, and SQLBase are all relational and provide essentially the same basic structures and capabilities, even though they require different syntax to accomplish similar activities.

```
VAR
  FileA : FileInfo;
```

the buffer variable (FileA^ or FileA↑) can be used in the program. The buffer variable is always the file name followed by a caret (^) or an up arrow (↑). Historically, the phrase "up arrow" has been used when referring to buffer variables. However, we will use the caret symbol when designating buffer variables because it is available on computer keyboards (above the 6). The buffer variable is not declared in the variable declaration section. In general, we have

Declaration	Buffer Variable
VAR <file name> : **FILE OF** <data type>;	<file name>^

The buffer variable is of the same data type as one component of the file. It allows the user to access data at the position of the file marker or pointer that is used when illustrating text files. Although it is intended to pass values to and from a file, a buffer variable can be used very much like a regularly declared variable of that type. From FileA (previously declared), FileA^ is a variable of type **integer** and statements such as

```
FileA^ := 21;
Age := FileA^;
GetData (FileA^);
```

where GetData is a procedure, are appropriate.

Exercises 13.1

1. Discuss the similarities between arrays and files.
2. Discuss the differences between arrays and files.

In Exercises 3–7, indicate which are valid declarations of files. Give an explanation for those that are invalid. State what the component type is for those that are valid.

*3.
```
TYPE
  FileOfAges = FILE OF 0..120;
VAR
  AgeFile : FileOfAges;
```
4.
```
TYPE
  NameString = PACKED ARRAY [1..20] OF char;
  FileOfNames = ARRAY [1..100] OF NameString;
VAR
  NameFile : FileOfNames;
```
*5.
```
TYPE
  FileA = FILE OF real;
  FileB = FILE OF FileA;
VAR
  RealFile : FileB;
```
6.
```
TYPE
  FileOfInt = FILE [1..100] OF integer;
VAR
  File1 : FileOfInt;
```
*7.
```
TYPE
  IntFile = FILE OF integer;
VAR
  OldFile, NewFile, TempFile : IntFile;
```
8. Assume a program contains the following definition and declaration sections. Which buffer variables are available? State the data type of each buffer variable.

```
TYPE
  FileOfAges = FILE OF 0..120;
  IntFile = FILE OF integer;
  RealFile = FILE OF real;
  TruthFile = FILE OF boolean;
  List20 = ARRAY [1..20] OF real;
```

```
    ListFile = FILE OF List20;
    StudentInfo = RECORD
                    Name : PACKED ARRAY [1..20] of char;
                    Age : 0..120
                  END;
    StudentFile = FILE OF StudentInfo;
  VAR
    File1, File2 : FileOfAges;
    OldFile : StudentFile;
    NewFile : ListFile;
    TempFile : RealFile;
    TransFile : TruthFile;
    A, B, C : IntFile;
```

*9. Define a file type and then declare a file to be used with records of patients for a physician. Information should include the name, address, height, weight, age, gender, and insurance company of each patient.

13.2 Working with Binary Files

Objectives

- to understand the concept of opening a file
- to be able to put data into a file using **write** or **put**
- to be able to retrieve data from a file using **read** or **get**
- to understand the difference between internal and external files
- to be able to use procedures when working with files

Now that we have examined the concepts of files, file windows, and buffer variables, we need to see how values are transmitted to and from file components. First, let's examine the process of putting data into a file.

Creating a File

Once a file has been declared in a program, entering data to the file is referred to as **writing to the file.** Before writing to a file, the file window must be positioned at the beginning of the file, by using the standard procedure **rewrite.** This is referred to as **opening a file.** Thus, if FileA is declared by

```
TYPE
  IntFile = FILE OF integer;
VAR
  FileA : IntFile;
```

then

```
rewrite (FileA);
```

opens FileA to receive values of type **integer.** At this stage, the window is positioned at the beginning of FileA and FileA is ready to receive the first component. Any components previously stored in FileA are no longer available. Successive components may be stored in FileA, and each new component is appended to the previous list of components.

Most versions of Pascal allow the user to transfer (write) values to a file by assigning the desired value to the buffer variable and using the standard procedure **put** with the buffer variable as an argument. We can, for instance, store the values 10, 20, and 30 in FileA by

Writing to a file is the process of entering data to a file.

Opening a file positions a pointer at the beginning of a file.

```
rewrite (FileA);   {  Open for writing  }
FileA^ := 10;
put (FileA);
FileA^ := 20;
```

```
put (FileA);
FileA^ := 30;
put (FileA);
```

The **put** procedure has the effect of transferring the value of the buffer variable to the component in the window and then advancing the window to the next component. After **put** is called, the buffer variable becomes unassigned; this sequence is illustrated in Table 13.1.

Table 13.1

Using **put** to write to a file

Pascal Statement	Buffer (FileA^)	Effect (FileA)
rewrite (FileA);		window at component 1; FileA: (empty)
FileA^ := 10;	10	window at component 1; FileA: (empty)
put (FileA);		FileA: 10; window at component 2
FileA^ := 20;	20	FileA: 10; window at component 2
put (FileA);		FileA: 10, 20; window at component 3
FileA^ := 30;	30	FileA: 10, 20; window at component 3
put (FileA);		FileA: 10, 20, 30; window at component 4

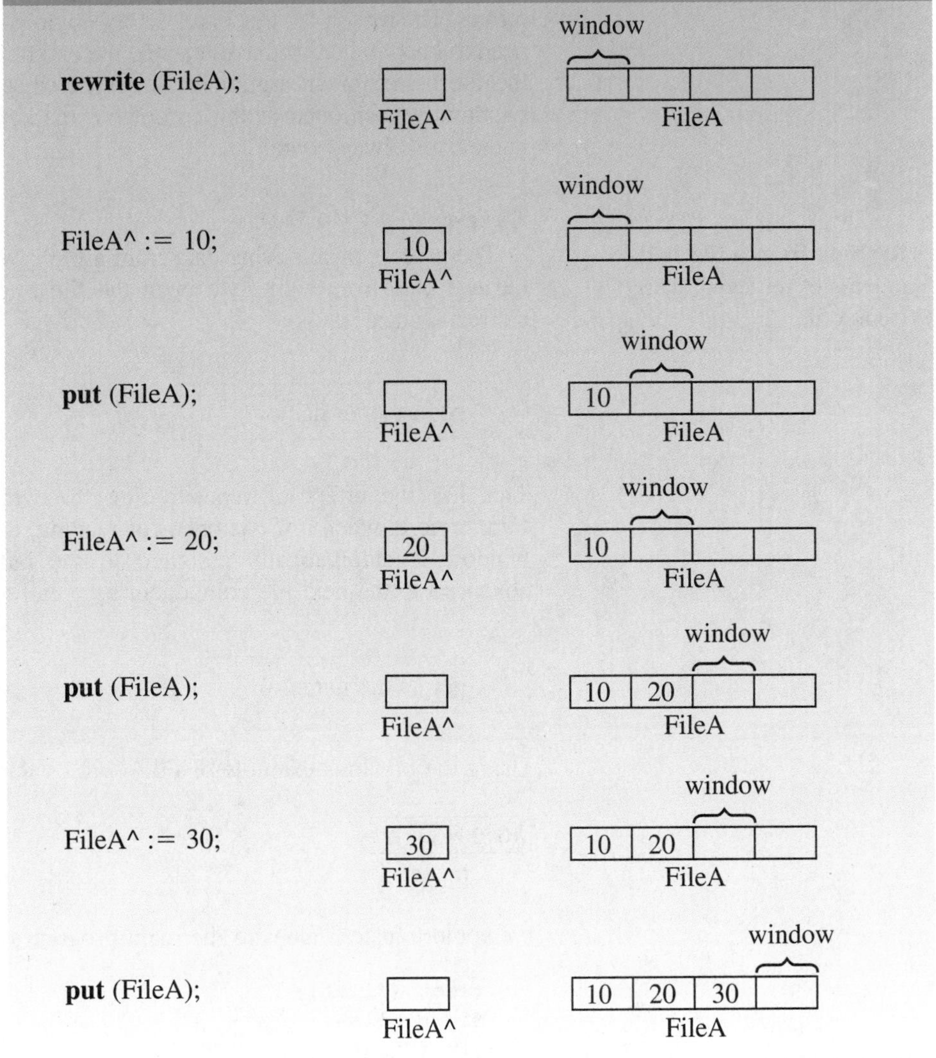

Standard Pascal also allows values to be written to a file using the procedure **write.** When this procedure is used, the argument for **write** is the file name followed by data items. Thus, the previous fragment could be

```
rewrite (FileA);  {  Open for writing  }
write (FileA, 10);
```

```
write (FileA, 20);
write (FileA, 30);
```

The procedure **writeln** can only be used with files of type **text.**

The Standard Function eof

The Boolean function **eof** can be used with binary files in much the same way it is used with text files. When a file is opened for writing, an end-of-file marker is placed at the beginning of the file. This can be thought of as the window being positioned at the end-of-file marker. When a value is transferred by **put** or **write,** the end-of-file marker is advanced to the same component position to which the window moves. The reason for this is relatively obvious. When retrieving data from a file, we need to know when we have reached the end of the file. The function **eof** is used with the file name for an argument. As expected, **eof** (<file name>) is **true** when the window is positioned at the end-of-file marker. When writing to a file, **eof** (<file name>) is always **true.**

Retrieving File Data

Reading from a file is the process of retrieving data from a file.

The process of retrieving data from a file is referred to as **reading from a file.** To retrieve data from a file, we open the file by using the standard procedure **reset.** Correct syntax is

reset (<file name>)

This has the effect of repositioning the window at the beginning of the file. Furthermore, when a file is open for reading, the value of the file component in the window is automatically assigned to the buffer variable. The window can be advanced to the next file component by a call to the following standard procedure:

get (<file name>)

Using the previous example of FileA with values as depicted

10	20	30	■

FileA

we could transfer values to the main program by

```
reset (FileA);
N1 := FileA^;
get (FileA);
N2 := FileA^;
get (FileA);
N3 := FileA^;
```

The position of the window and the transfer of values for this segment of code are illustrated in Table 13.2.

Table 13.2

Using **get** to read from a file

Pascal Statement	Buffer	Effect
reset (FileA);	FileA^ = 10	window on 10 in FileA: 10 20 30 ■; N1 = (empty), N2 = (empty), N3 = (empty)
N1 := FileA^;	FileA^ = 10	window on 10 in FileA: 10 20 30 ■; N1 = 10, N2 = (empty), N3 = (empty)
get (FileA);	FileA^ = 20	window on 20 in FileA: 10 20 30 ■; N1 = 10, N2 = (empty), N3 = (empty)
N2 := FileA^;	FileA^ = 20	window on 20 in FileA: 10 20 30 ■; N1 = 10, N2 = 20, N3 = (empty)
get (FileA);	FileA^ = 30	window on 30 in FileA: 10 20 30 ■; N1 = 10, N2 = 20, N3 = (empty)
N3 := FileA^;	FileA^ = 30	window on 30 in FileA: 10 20 30 ■; N1 = 10, N2 = 20, N3 = 30

This example of retrieving data is a bit contrived since we know there are exactly three components before the end-of-file marker. A more realistic retrieval would use the **eof** function; for example,

```
reset (FileA);
WHILE NOT eof(FileA) DO
```

```
BEGIN
  .
  .      (process FileA^)
  .
  get (FileA)
END;  {  of WHILE loop  }
```

The standard procedure **read** can also be used to transfer data from a file. After the file has been opened for reading, **read** can be used with the file name and variable names as arguments. Thus, the following code can replace the previous code fragment:

```
reset (FileA);
read (FileA, N1);
read (FileA, N2);
read (FileA, N3);
```

The previous code, using **get,** helps to make the function of a buffer understandable. However, many students find **read** easier to use.

Opening Files

Files cannot be opened for writing and reading at the same time. When a file is opened for writing, it remains open to receive values that are appended to the file until the window is repositioned by either the **rewrite** or **reset** statement, or until the program is terminated. Thus, we may create a file and then add to it later in the program without reopening it. Similarly, before we first read from a file, it must be opened by **reset** (<file name>). Values can then be transferred from the file using either **read** or **get.**

Now let's consider a short example in which we do something with each component of a file.

Example 13.1

Suppose we have a file of reals and we want to create another file by subtracting 5.0 from each component. Assume the following definitions and declarations:

```
TYPE
  RealFile = FILE OF real;
VAR
  OldFile : RealFile;
  NewFile : RealFile;
```

We can accomplish our objective by

```
reset (OldFile);  {  Open OldFile  }
rewrite (NewFile);  {  Open NewFile  }
WHILE NOT eof(OldFile) DO
  BEGIN
    NewFile^ := OldFile^ - 5.0;
    put (NewFile);
    get (OldFile)
  END;
```

Procedures and Files

Much of the work of processing files is accomplished by using procedures. Thus, we should continue to use the **TYPE** definition section to define file types. Files can be used as arguments in a procedure call; however, in the procedure heading, files must be listed as variable parameters. This requirement is implicit in the fact that a file variable cannot be assigned all at once (as a value parameter can be).

Example 13.2

Let's write a procedure to accomplish the task of Example 13.1.

```
PROCEDURE Subtract5 (VAR OldFile, NewFile : RealFile);
  BEGIN
    reset (OldFile);
    rewrite (NewFile);
    WHILE NOT eof(OldFile) DO
      BEGIN
        NewFile^ := OldFile^ - 5.0;
        put (NewFile);
        get (OldFile)
      END  {  of WHILE...DO  }
  END;  {  of PROCEDURE Subtract5  }
```

This procedure is called from the main program by

```
Subtract5 (OldFile, NewFile);
```

Even though no changes are made in OldFile, it is passed as a variable parameter.

Internal and External Files

Recall from Chapter 9 that files used to store data in secondary storage between runs of a program are called external files; files that are used for processing only and are not saved in secondary storage are called internal files. External files must be listed in the program heading in the following form:

PROGRAM <name> (**input, output,** <external file name>)

They are declared in the variable declaration section. Internal files are not listed in the program heading but are also declared in the variable declaration section.

In a typical programming problem, an external file in secondary storage is to be updated in some form. This requires some temporary internal files to be declared for use in the program. When the program is exited, all external files are saved in secondary storage and the internal files are no longer available.

Processing Files

Before looking at a specific problem for processing files, let's consider the general problem of updating an external file. Since we eventually will **rewrite** the external file, we must be careful not to erase the original contents before they have been saved and/or processed in some temporary internal file. We accomplish this by copying external files to temporary files and then working with the temporary files until the desired tasks are completed. At this point, we then copy the appropriate temporary file to the external file. In reality, this method may prove to be inefficient, but until you become more experienced in file manipulation, it is good practice to avoid working directly with external files.

Let's now consider a relatively short example of updating a file of test scores for students in a class. A detailed treatment of processing files is given in Section 13.3.

Example 13.3

Let's assume the external file TotalPts consists of total points for each student in a class. Further, let's assume the data file contains test scores that are to be added (in the same order) to the previous totals to obtain new totals. A first-level pseudocode solution to this problem is

1. Copy the totals to a temporary file from the external file
2. Process the temporary file
3. Copy the temporary file to the external file

Assume the program heading is

```
PROGRAM Grades (input, output, TotalPts);
```

and the definitions and declarations are

```
TYPE
  IntFile = FILE OF integer;
VAR
  TotalPts : IntFile;
  Temp1File : IntFile;
  Temp2File : IntFile;
```

A procedure to copy the contents from one file to another is

```
PROCEDURE Copy (VAR OldFile, NewFile : IntFile);
  BEGIN
    reset (OldFile);
    rewrite (NewFile);
    WHILE NOT eof(OldFile) DO
      BEGIN
        NewFile^ := OldFile^;
        put (NewFile);
        get (OldFile)
      END  {  of WHILE...DO  }
  END;  {  of PROCEDURE Copy  }
```

This is called from the main program by

```
Copy (TotalPts, Temp1File);
```

We can now process Temp1File by adding corresponding scores from the data file. A procedure for this is

```
PROCEDURE AddScores (VAR OldFile, NewFile : IntFile);
  VAR
    NewScore : integer;
  BEGIN
    reset (OldFile);
    rewrite (NewFile);
```

A Note of Interest

Backup and Recovery of Data

The need for organizational backup and recovery procedures to prevent loss of data is due to two types of events: in particular, natural disasters and simple human errors. Natural disasters, although infrequent, are typically large-scale emergencies that can completely shut down, if not ruin, an organization's computer facilities. Examples are such potentially catastrophic events as fires, floods, and earthquakes. Human errors, on the other hand, are the most frequent cause of computer problems (has anyone NEVER erased the wrong file by mistake?) but may not be as crippling as natural disasters. Although they may not result in catastrophic loss, human errors are, at the least, a nuisance to affected individuals.

Organizations have developed a variety of backup and recovery procedures to cope with system failures and to reduce resultant losses. To reduce losses from natural disasters, some organizations have prepared contingency plans to cover backup computer locations, off-site program and data storage, and emergency staffing requirements. These contingency plans can usually be put into effect quickly and with minimal disruption of computer services. To minimize human errors (accidents can never be eliminated), organizations typically try to provide sound user-training programs and user-based physical backup measures.

A more recent problem regarding backup and recovery of data has emerged. Specifically, as storage and retrieval technology changes, old data storage can become difficult to access. As an illustration, see the **Note of Interest** later in this chapter.

```
    WHILE NOT eof(OldFile) DO
      BEGIN
        read (NewScore);  {  Get score from data file  }
        NewFile^ := NewScore + OldFile^;
        put (NewFile);
        get (OldFile)
      END  {  of WHILE...DO  }
  END;  {  of PROCEDURE AddScores  }
```

This procedure could be called from the main program by

```
AddScores (Temp1File, Temp2File);
```

At this stage, the updated scores are in Temp2File and they need to be stored in the external file TotalPts before the program is exited. This is done by another call to Copy in the main program. Thus,

```
Copy (Temp2File, TotalPts);
```

achieves the desired results. The main program is then

```
BEGIN  {  Main program  }
  Copy (TotalPts, Temp1File);
  AddScores (Temp1File, Temp2File);
  Copy (Temp2File, TotalPts)
END.  {  of main program  }
```

Example 13.3 obviously overlooks some significant points. For example, how do we know that the scores match up or that each student's new score is added to that student's previous total? We will address these issues later in the chapter. Now let's see how one file can be appended to an existing file.

Example 13.4

Let's assume files are named OldFile and NewFile and our task is to append NewFile to OldFile. We will use the temporary file TempFile to complete this task. A first-level pseudocode development for this problem is

1. Reset OldFile and NewFile
2. Open TempFile for writing
3. **WHILE NOT eof**(OldFile) **DO**
   3.1 Write elements to TempFile
4. **WHILE NOT eof**(NewFile) **DO**
   4.1 Write elements to TempFile
5. Copy TempFile to OldFile

Step 3 can be refined to

3. **WHILE NOT eof**(OldFile) **DO**
   3.1 Write elements to TempFile
      3.1.1 Assign OldFile buffer value to TempFile buffer
      3.1.2 Write value to TempFile
      3.1.3 Advance window of OldFile

The code for this step is

```
WHILE NOT eof(OldFile) DO
  BEGIN
    TempFile^ := OldFile^;
    put (TempFile);
    get (OldFile)
  END;  {  of WHILE NOT eof  }
```

The complete code for this example is left as an exercise at the end of this section.

Exercises 13.2

1. Review the difference between internal files and external files.

In Exercises 2–4, write test programs that illustrate the question given.

2. What happens when you try to write to a file that has not been opened for writing?
3. What happens when you try to get data from a file that has not been reset?
4. What happens when a procedure uses a file as a value parameter?

*5. Declare an appropriate file and store the positive multiples of 7 that are less than 100.

6. Explain how the file of Exercise 5 can be saved for another program to use.

*7. Consider the file with integer components as shown.

0	5	10	15	■

FivesFile

Write a segment of code that would assign the values respectively to variables A, B, C, and D.

8. Consider the following file with component values as illustrated.

```
TYPE
  RealFile = FILE OF real;
VAR
  Prices : RealFile;
```

15.95	17.99	21.95	19.99	■	

Prices

a. Declare a new file and put values in the components that are 15 percent less than the values in components of Prices.
b. Update the values in Prices so that each value is increased by 10 percent.

*9. Discuss the difference between **reset** and **rewrite.**

10. You have been asked to write a program to examine a file of integers and replace every negative number with zero. Assume IntFile has been appropriately declared and contains five integer values. Why will the following segment of code not work?

```
rewrite (IntFile);
FOR J := 1 TO 5 DO
  BEGIN
    get (IntFile);
    IF IntFile^ < 0 THEN
      IntFile^ := 0;
    put (IntFile)
  END;
```

For Exercises 11–16, consider the files declared by

```
TYPE
  FileOfInt = FILE OF integer;
VAR
  File1, File2 : FileOfInt;
```

Find all errors in each exercise.

*11.
```
reset (File1);
FOR J := 1 TO 5 DO
  BEGIN
    File1^ := 10 * J;
    put (File1)
  END;
```

12.
```
rewrite (File1);
FOR J := 1 TO 5 DO
  BEGIN
    File1^ := 10 * J;
    put (File1)
  END;
```

*13.
```
rewrite (File1);
FOR J := 1 TO 5 DO
  BEGIN
    File1 := 10 * J;
    put (File1)
  END;
```

14.
```
rewrite (File1);
FOR J := 1 TO 5 DO
  File1^ := J * 10;
```

*15.
```
reset (File2);
WHILE NOT eof(File1) DO
  BEGIN
    File2^ := File1^;
    put (File2);
    get (File1)
  END;
```

16.
```
reset (File2);
rewrite (File1);
WHILE NOT eof(File2) DO
  BEGIN
    File1^ := File2^;
    put (File1);
    get (File2)
  END;
```

For Exercises 17–19, assume the files OldFile and NewFile are declared as

```
TYPE
  IntFile = FILE OF integer;
VAR
  OldFile, NewFile : IntFile;
```

Furthermore, assume OldFile has component values as illustrated.

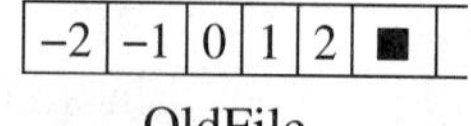

OldFile

Indicate the values in the components of both OldFile and NewFile after each segment of code.

*17.
```
reset (OldFile);
rewrite (NewFile);
WHILE NOT eof(OldFile) DO
  BEGIN
    IF OldFile^ > 0 THEN
      BEGIN
        NewFile1^ := OldFile^;
        put (NewFile)
      END;
    get (OldFile)
  END;
```

18.
```
rewrite (OldFile);
rewrite (NewFile);
WHILE NOT eof(OldFile) DO
  BEGIN
    IF OldFile^ > 0 THEN
      BEGIN
        NewFile^ := OldFile^;
        put (NewFile)
      END
  END;
```

*19.
```
reset (OldFile);
rewrite (NewFile);
WHILE NOT eof(OldFile) DO
  BEGIN
    NewFile^ := abs(OldFile^);
    put (NewFile);
    get (OldFile)
  END;
rewrite (OldFile);
reset (NewFile);
WHILE NOT eof(NewFile) DO
  BEGIN
    OldFile^ := NewFile^;
    put (OldFile);
    get (NewFile)
  END;
```

20. Assume OldFile and NewFile are as declared in Exercises 17–19. Furthermore, assume OldFile contains the values

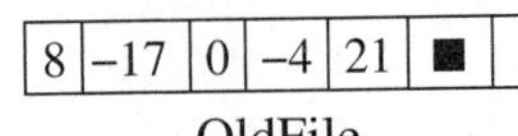

Indicate the output from the following segment of code and the values of the components in OldFile and NewFile.

```
reset (OldFile);
rewrite (NewFile);
WHILE NOT eof(OldFile) DO
  BEGIN
    NewFile^ := OldFile^;
    IF NewFile^ < 0 THEN
      writeln (NewFile^)
    ELSE
      put (NewFile);
    get (OldFile)
  END;
```

21. Assume you have declared three files (File1, File2, and File3) in a program such that the component type for each file is **real.** Furthermore, assume that both File1 and File2 contain an unknown number of values. Write a segment of code to transfer the corresponding sum of components from File1 and File2 into File3. Since File1 and File2 may have a different number of components, after one end-of-file is reached, you should add zeros until the next end-of-file is reached. Thus, your segment produces

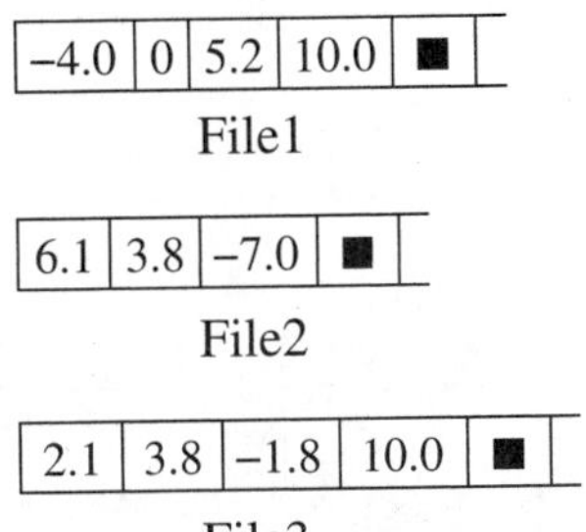

22. Write a complete program that finishes the work started in Example 13.4. Your program should print the contents of each file used and of the final file.

13.3 Files with Structured Components

In actual practice, components of files are frequently some structured data type. A program might use a file of arrays or a file of records. When such a file is desired, the user declares it as an external file and then creates components from a text file. Once the data have been thus converted, the user can access an entire array or record rather than individual fields or components. The data are also saved in structured form between runs of a program. When data have been stored in structured components, it is relatively easy to update and work with these files. For example, a doctor might

Objectives

- to be able to declare files that have records or arrays as components
- to understand why files with structured components are used
- to be able to create a file of records from a text file
- to be able to manipulate files with structured components

have a file of records for patients and wish to insert or delete records, choose to examine the individual fields of each record, print an alphabetical list of patients, or print a list of patients with unpaid bills.

Now let's examine a typical declaration. Suppose we are writing a program to use a file of records. Each record contains information about a student in a computer science class: the student's name, three test scores (in an array), identification number, and test average. A declaration for such a file could be

```
TYPE
  NameString = PACKED ARRAY [1..20] OF char;
  Scores = ARRAY [1..3] OF 0..100;
  StudentInfo = RECORD
                  Name : NameString;
                  Score : Scores;
                  IDNumber : 0..999;
                  Average : real
                END;   {  of RECORD StudentInfo  }
  StudentFile = FILE OF StudentInfo;
VAR
  Student : StudentFile;
```

Student is a file of records that can be illustrated as shown in Figure 13.1.

◆ Figure 13.1

File Student

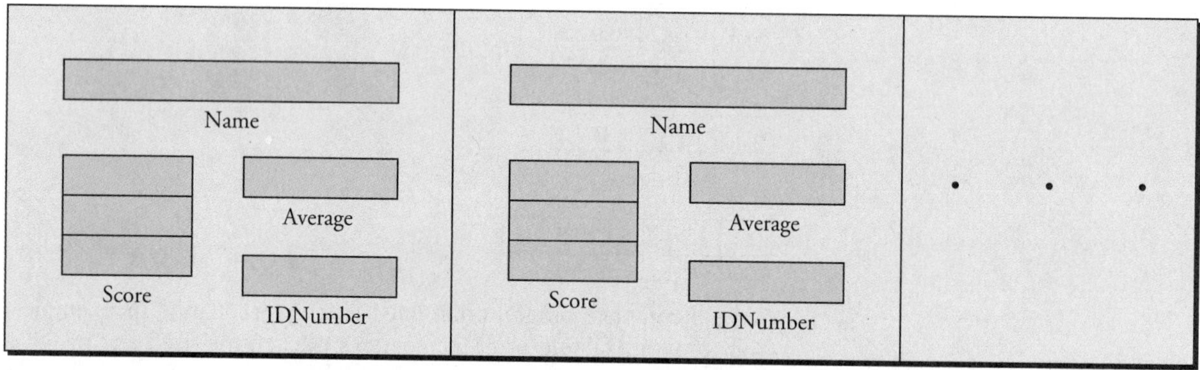

After Student has been properly opened for reading by **reset** (Student), the statement

```
get (Student);
```

causes the contents of a record to be transferred to Student^. The field identifiers are

```
Student^.Name
Student^.IDNumber
Student^.Score
Student^.Average
```

Student^.Score is an array. Components of this array are

```
Student^.Score[1]
Student^.Score[2]
Student^.Score[3]
```

If we wish to compute the average for a student whose record is in the buffer, we can write

```
Sum := 0;
WITH Student^ DO
  BEGIN
    FOR J := 1 TO 3 DO
      Sum := Sum + Score[J];
    Average := Sum / 3
  END;
```

At this stage, you may want to save this computed average for later use. Unfortunately, using **put** (Student) will not work because the file is open for reading rather than writing. We will solve this and other problems in the remainder of this section as we investigate methods of manipulating files.

Creating a File of Records

One of the first problems to be solved when working with files that contain structured variables is how to transfer data from some text file (usually **input**) into the appropriate file of structured components. Once the new file with structured components is created, it can be saved in secondary storage by declaring it as an external file. To illustrate the process of creating a file of records, let's continue the example of the file of records for students in a computer science class. Recall the earlier definitions and subsequent declaration:

```
TYPE
  NameString = PACKED ARRAY [1..20] OF char;
  Scores = ARRAY [1..3] OF 0..100;
  StudentInfo = RECORD
                  Name : NameString;
                  Score : Scores;
                  IDNumber : 0..999;
                  Average : real
                END;  {  of RECORD StudentInfo  }
  StudentFile = FILE OF StudentInfo;
VAR
  Student : StudentFile;
```

Before we can create the file of records, we need to know how data were entered in the text file named Data. For purposes of this example, assume data for each student are contained on a single line, 20 positions are used for the name, and an identification number is followed by three test scores. Thus, the data file could be

Smith John	065 89 92 76	▮	Jones Mary	021 93 97 85	▮	■

A procedure to create the file of records is

```
PROCEDURE CreateFile (VAR Student : StudentFile);
  VAR
    J : integer;
  BEGIN
    reset (Data);
    rewrite (Student);  {  Open for writing  }
    WHILE NOT eof(Data) DO
      BEGIN  {  Get data for one record  }
        WITH Student^ DO
          BEGIN
            FOR J := 1 TO 20 DO
              read (Data, Name[J]);
            read (Data, IDNumber);
            readln (Data, Score[1], Score[2], Score[3])
          END;
        put (Student)  {  Put buffer contents in file  }
      END
  END;  {  of PROCEDURE CreateFile  }
```

This procedure is called from the main program by

```
CreateFile (Student);
```

After it is executed, we have the records shown in Figure 13.2.

◆ Figure 13.2
File Student with values

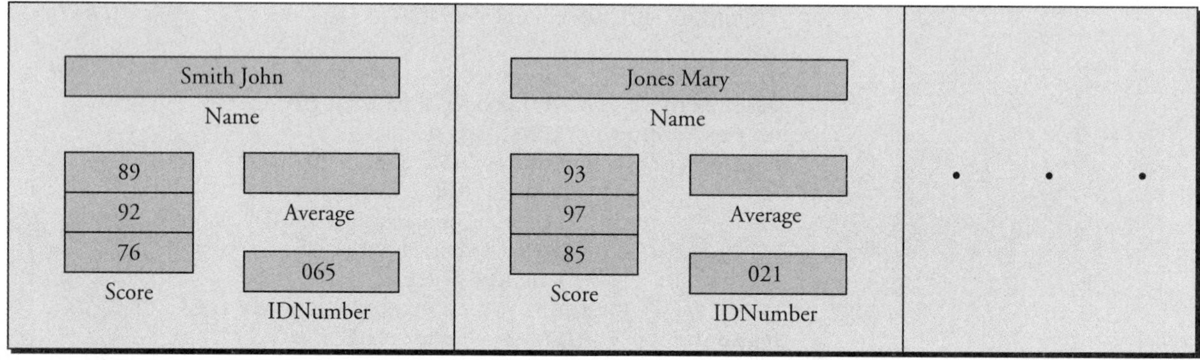

Storing Structured Files

Structured files may be stored in secondary memory for subsequent use. Files other than those of type **text** are stored as binary files. In this form, the data may be accessed by a program. However, an attempt to "look at" such a file by using a text editor or some other system command usually results in a display of gibberish characters.

Programmers need not worry about the form of data being stored. The change in representation is performed by the operating system. Even though you cannot "see" components of a file that has been saved in secondary memory, you should use files of structured components for the following reasons:

1. Values of structured file types can be read from or written to nontext files. For example, you can read or write an entire record.
2. The information in structured file types can be transferred more rapidly than it can in files of type **text** since the operating system does not do as much encoding and decoding.
3. Data are usually stored more compactly when saved as part of a structured file type.

A common error for beginning programmers is to create a text file that "looks like" a structured file and then attempt to use it as a structured file. For example, a text file of data may be arranged to look like a file of records by using a text editor. However, an attempt to read a record from this file results in an error. You must first create a file of records, as discussed previously.

File Manipulation

Several problems are typically involved with manipulating files and file components. Generally, a program starts with an existing file, revises it in some fashion, and then saves the revised file. Because files in standard Pascal must be accessed sequentially, this usually necessitates copying the existing external file to a temporary internal file, revising the temporary file, and copying the revised file to the external file. The existing external file is often referred to as the **master file.** The file containing changes to be made in the master file is called the **transaction file.**

A **master file** is an existing external file.

A **transaction file** is a file containing changes to be made in a master file.

To illustrate a simple update problem, let's consider again the problem using the file containing records for students in a computer science class. Assume that the external file has been named Student. Now suppose we wish to delete a record from Student (master file) because some student moved to Australia. This problem can be solved by searching Student sequentially for the record in question. The name in each record is examined. If the record is to be kept, it is put in a temporary file. The desired record is not transferred, thus accomplishing the update. Finally, Student is rewritten by copying the contents of the temporary file to Student.

A first-level pseudocode development is

1. Get the name to be deleted
2. Search Student for a match copying each nonmatch to TempFile
3. Copy the remainder of Student to TempFile
4. Copy TempFile to Student

Using the previous declarations and assuming that the name of the student whose record is to be deleted has been read into MovedAway, Step 2 can be solved by

```
reset (Student);  {  Open the files  }
rewrite (TempFile);
Found := false;
WHILE NOT eof(Student) AND NOT Found DO
  BEGIN
    IF Student^.Name = MovedAway THEN
      Found := true
    ELSE
      BEGIN
        TempFile^ := Student^;
        put (TempFile)
      END;
```

```
      get (Student)
    END;  {  of search for a student name  }

  {  Now copy the rest of student file  }
  WHILE NOT eof(Student) DO
    BEGIN
      TempFile^ := Student^;
      put (TempFile);
      get (Student)
    END;  {  of WHILE loop  }
```

We now need to copy TempFile to Student so that the revised master file is saved as an external file. A procedure for this was developed in Section 13.2; it is called from the main program by

```
Copy (TempFile, Student);
```

As a second illustration of file manipulation, let's consider the standard problem of merging two sorted files. For example, suppose the master file is a file of records and each record contains a field for the name of a customer. Furthermore, assume this file has been sorted alphabetically by name. Now suppose an alphabetical listing of new customers is to be merged with the old file to produce a current file containing records for all customers sorted alphabetically by name.

As before, we use a temporary file to hold the full sorted list and then copy the temporary file to the master file. This can be envisioned as illustrated in Figure 13.3. An algorithm for the merge is not too difficult. First, all files are opened. Then the initial records from MasterList and NewList are compared. The record containing the name that comes first alphabetically is transferred to TempFile. Then, as shown in the graphic documentation for the following program segment, the next record is obtained from the file containing the record that was transferred. This process continues until the end of one file is reached. At that time, the remainder of the other file is copied into TempFile.

◆ Figure 13.3

Merging files

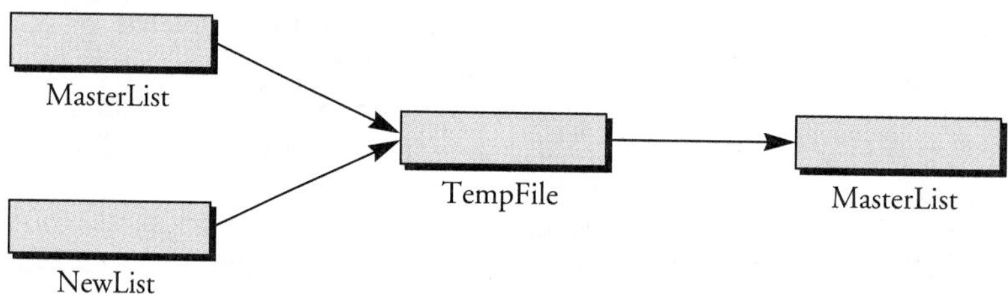

Assuming that each record has a field identified by Name, which is of type NameString, and that FileType has been defined as the type for files being used, a procedure for merging follows:

```
PROCEDURE Merge (VAR Master, NewFile : FileType);
  VAR
    TempFile : FileType;
  BEGIN
    reset (Master);
    reset (NewFile);
    rewrite (TempFile);
```

```
{ Compare top records until an eof of one of the
  input files is reached }
WHILE NOT eof(Master) AND NOT eof(NewFile) DO
  BEGIN
    IF Master^.Name < NewFile^.Name THEN
      BEGIN
        TempFile^ := Master^;
        get (Master)
      END
    ELSE
      BEGIN
        TempFile^ := NewFile^;
        get (NewFile)
      END;
    put (TempFile)
  END; { of WHILE NOT eof }
```

Current
last
record
Current
record
Master
Current
record
NewFile
TempFile
Transfer the smaller
of these two records
to the end of TempFile.
Then advance within
the file from which
that record was taken.

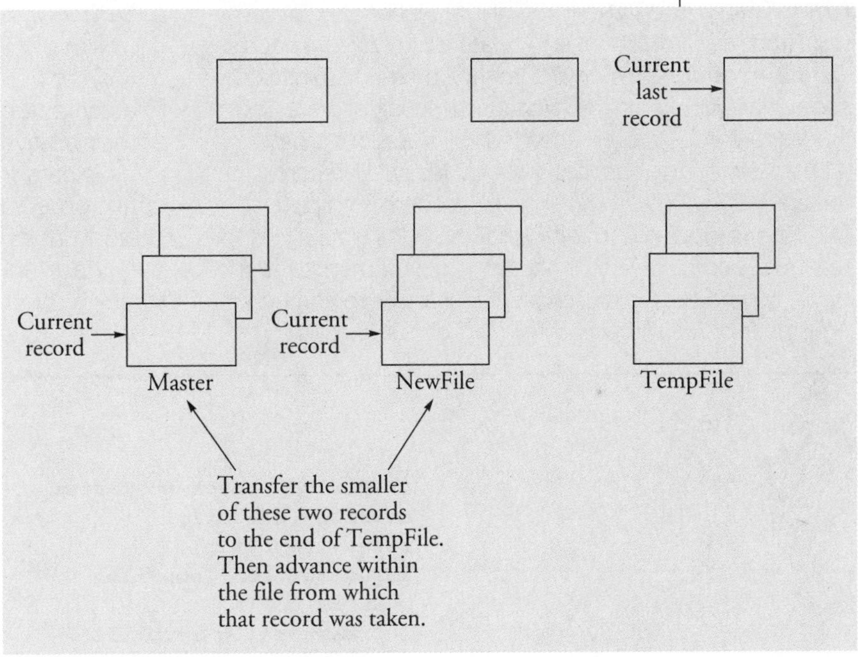

```
{ Now copy the remaining names }
WHILE NOT eof(Master) DO
  BEGIN
    TempFile^ := Master^;
    put (TempFile);
    get (Master)
  END;

WHILE NOT eof(NewFile) DO
  BEGIN
    TempFile^ := NewFile^;
    put (TempFile);
    get (NewFile)
  END;
```

A Note of Interest

History Stuck on Old Computer Tapes

A slice of recent U.S. history has become as unreadable as Egyptian hieroglyphics before the discovery of the Rosetta stone. And more historic, scientific, and business data are in danger of dissolving into a meaningless jumble of letters, numbers, and computer symbols.

Paying millions to preserve the information is part of the price for the country's embrace of more and more powerful computers. Much information from the past 30 years is stranded on computer tape from primitive or discarded systems—it's unintelligible, or soon to be so.

Hundreds of thousands of Americans researching family history (the largest use of the National Archives) will find records of their relatives beyond reach. Detection of diseases, environmental threats, or shifts in social class could be delayed because data were lost before researchers even knew which questions to ask.

"The ability to read our nation's historical records is threatened by the complexity of modern computers," said Representative Bob Wise, chairman of a House information subcommittee that wants the government to start buying computers to preserve data for future researchers. A number of records already are lost or out of reach:

- A total of 200 reels of 17-year-old Public Health Service computer tapes were destroyed because no one could find out what the names and numbers on them meant.
- The government's Agent Orange Task Force, asked to determine whether Vietnam soldiers were sickened by exposure to the herbicide, was unable to decode Pentagon computer tapes containing the date, site, and size of every U.S. herbicide bombing during the war.
- The most extensive record of Americans who served in World War II exists only on 1,600 reels of microfilm of computer punch cards. No staff, money, or machine is available to return the data to a computer so citizens can trace the war history of their relatives.
- Census data from the 1960s and NASA's early scientific observations of the earth and planets exist on thousands of reels of old tape. Some may have decomposed; others may fall apart if run through the balky equipment that survives from that era.

```
    {  Now copy back to Master  }
    rewrite (Master);
    reset (TempFile);
    WHILE NOT eof(TempFile) DO
      BEGIN
        Master^ := TempFile^;
        put (Master);
        get (TempFile)
      END
  END;  {  of PROCEDURE Merge  }
```

This procedure can be called from the main program by

```
Merge (Master, NewFile);
```

A final comment is in order. It is frequently necessary to work with files of records that have been sorted according to a field of the record. Since we might want to work with the records sorted by some other field, we must first be able to sort an unsorted file. In general, this is done by transferring the file components to array components, sorting the array, and transferring the sorted array components back to the file. This means that we must have some idea of how many components are in the file and declare the array length accordingly. The physical setting of a problem usually provides this information. For example, physicians will have some idea of how many patients (100, 200, or 1,000) they see.

Exercises 13.3

For Exercises 1–4, declare appropriate files. Fields for each record are indicated.

*1. Patient records for a physician; include name, age, height, weight, insurance carrier, and amount owed.
2. Flight information for an airplane; include flight number, airline, arrival time, arriving from, departure time, and destination.
*3. Bookstore inventory; include author, title, stock number, price, and quantity.
4. Records for a magazine subscription agency; include name and address, indicating street number, street name, city, state, and zip code.
*5. Suppose a text file contains information for students in a class. Information for each student will use three data lines as illustrated.

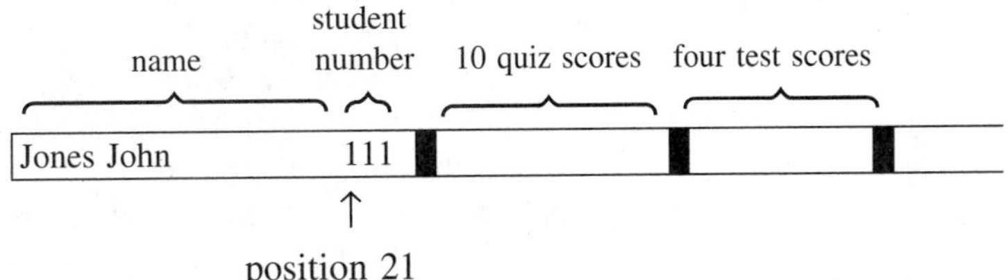

   a. Declare a file of records to be used to store these data.
   b. Write a procedure to create a file of records containing appropriate information from the text file.
   c. Write a procedure to sort the file alphabetically.
6. Write a test program that allows you to declare a file of records, read data into the file, and print information from selected records according to the value in some key field.
7. Illustrate the values of components and fields in Student and Student^ during the first pass through the loop in **PROCEDURE** CreateFile found under the earlier section "Creating a File of Records."
8. Consider the file Student declared by

```
TYPE
  NameString = PACKED ARRAY [1..20] OF char;
  Scores = ARRAY[1..3] OF 0..100;
  StudentInfo = RECORD
                  Name : NameString;
                  IDNumber : 0..999;
                  Score : Scores;
                  Average : real
                END;
  StudentFile = FILE OF StudentInfo;
VAR
  Student : StudentFile;
```

   Write a procedure for each of the following tasks. In each case, show how the procedure is called from the main program. (Assume the file has been alphabetized.)
   a. Add one record in alphabetical order.
   b. Add one record to the bottom of the file.

c. Update the record of 'Smith Jane ' by changing her score on the second test from an 82 to an 89.
d. The scores from test 3 are in a data file. Each line contains an identification number followed by three integer scores. Update Student to include these scores. (The first two scores have already been entered.)
e. Assume all test scores have been entered. Update Student by computing the test average for each student.
f. Print a list containing each student's name and test average; the list should be sorted by test average from high to low.

Focus on Program Design: Case Study

Using Files: Registrar Update

The case study for this chapter is an elementary version that could be expanded to a comprehensive programming project. Suppose the registrar of a local institution wants you to develop a program for updating a file of student records. A master file of student records currently exists; it is sorted alphabetically. Each record contains a field for the student's name, ID number, grade point average, and total hours completed. This file is to be updated by information contained in a transaction file. Each line in the transaction file contains a student number, letter grade for a course taken, and number of credit hours for the course. A typical data line is

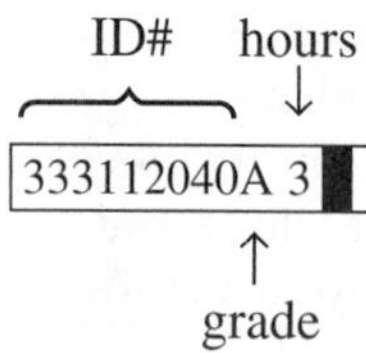

For each data line in the transaction file, your program should search the contents of the master file for a match. If a match is found, appropriate changes should be made in grade point average and total hours completed. If no match is found, the information should be printed in an Exception Report. After all transactions are completed, an alphabetized list should be printed and the master file should be updated.

A first-level pseudocode development for this is

1. Open the files
2. Copy contents of the master file to an array
3. Update the records
4. Print the list
5. Update the master file

A complete structure diagram for this program is given in Figure 13.4. Module specifications for the main modules are

1. PrepareFiles Module

   Data received: None
   Information returned: None
   Logic: Use **reset** to prepare files for reading.
2. LoadArray Module

   Data received: File of records

◆ Figure 13.4

Structure chart for the Case Study

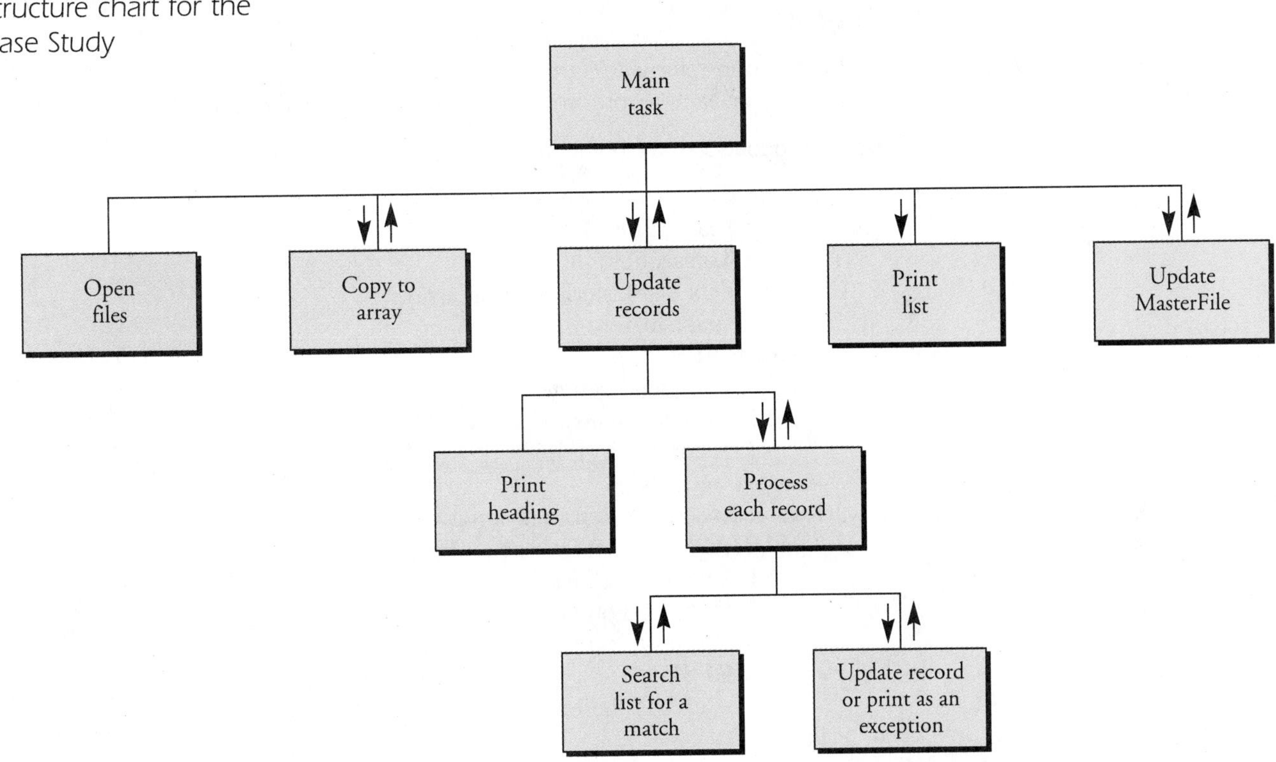

Information returned: Array of records
Number of records

Logic: Copy contents of each record in MasterFile to a record in Student.
Count the number of records in the array.

3. UpdateRecords Module

Data received: An array of records
Length of the array
A transaction file

Information returned: An updated array of records

Logic: For each data line in TransactionFile, search for a match in the array.
IF a match is found, **THEN**
update the record
ELSE
print out an Exception Report

4. PrintList Module

Data received: A sorted array of records
Length of the array

Information returned: None

Logic: Print a heading.
Print contents of each record.

5. UpdateMasterFile Module

   Data received: An array of records
   Length of the array
   MasterFile of records
   Information returned: An updated MasterFile
   Logic: For each record in Student, copy contents into a record in MasterFile

Further pseudocode development is

1. Open the files
   1.1 **reset** MasterFile
   1.2 **reset** TransactionFile
2. Copy contents of MasterFile to an array
   2.1 Set counter to zero
   2.2 **REPEAT**
      2.2.1 Increment counter
      2.2.2 Copy contents of one record
      UNTIL eof(MasterFile)
3. Update the records
   3.1 Print Exception Report heading
   3.2 **WHILE NOT eof**(TransactionFile) **DO**
      3.2.1 Search for a match
      3.2.2 **IF NOT** Found **THEN**
         print as part of Exception Report
         ELSE
         update the record
4. Print the list
   4.1 Print a heading
   4.2 Print an alphabetized list
5. Update the MasterFile
   5.1 **rewrite** MasterFile
   5.2 **FOR** each record in the array **DO**
      copy contents to a record in MasterFile

Step 3.2.1 is a sequential search of the array. If a match is found, the array position is returned. If not, a zero is returned. The portion of Step 3.2.2 designed to update the record consists of incrementing the grade point average. A **CASE** statement is used to direct action for grades of A, B, C, D, E, W, and I. This program assumes valid data are contained in TransactionFile. A complete program for this problem follows:

```
PROGRAM FileUpdate (input, output, MasterFile, TransactionFile);

{  This program updates a file of student records. Transactions }
{  are  stored in  the text  file  TransactionFile.  Each  line }
{  consists of a student number, grade for a course taken,  and }
{  credit hours for the course.  The file of records is  copied }
{  to  an array  of records  for processing.  This  facilitates }
{  searching for matches of student numbers.  It is assumed the }
{  master file is alphabetized.  If it is not, one could add  a }
{  procedure to sort the array before rewriting the master file.}

CONST
  MaxLength = 200;
  NameLength = 20;
  IDLength = 9;
```

```
TYPE
  NameString = PACKED ARRAY [1..NameLength] OF char;
  IDString = PACKED ARRAY [1..IDLength] OF char;
  StudentRecord = RECORD
                    Name : NameString;
                    IDNumber : IDString;
                    GPA : real;
                    Hours : integer
                  END;  {  of RECORD StudentRecord  }
  StudentList = ARRAY [1..MaxLength] OF StudentRecord;
  RecordsFile = FILE OF StudentRecord;

VAR
  NumberOfRecords : integer;    {  Number of records read          }
  Student : StudentList;        {  Array of student records        }
  MasterFile : RecordsFile;     {  Master file of student records  }
  TransactionFile : text;       {  Transaction file for updating   }

{*****************************************************************}

PROCEDURE PrepareFiles (VAR MasterFile : RecordsFile;
                        VAR TransactionFile : text);

  {  Given:   Nothing                                             }
  {  Task:    Open the files for reading                          }
  {  Return:  MasterFile and TransactionFile ready to be read     }   1

  BEGIN
    reset (MasterFile);
    reset (TransactionFile)
  END;  {  of PROCEDURE PrepareFiles  }

{*****************************************************************}

PROCEDURE LoadArray (VAR MasterFile : RecordsFile;
                     VAR Student : StudentList;
                     VAR NumberOfRecords : integer);

  {  Given:   Master file containing data for each student        }
  {  Task:    Create an array of student records from MasterFile  }
  {  Return:  Array of student records and number of records      }

  BEGIN
    NumberOfRecords := 0;
    get (MasterFile);                                                 2
    WHILE NOT eof(MasterFile) AND (NumberOfRecords < MaxLength) DO
      BEGIN
        NumberOfRecords := NumberOfRecords + 1;
        Student[NumberOfRecords] := MasterFile^;
        get (MasterFile)
      END;  {  of WHILE NOT eof  }
    IF NOT eof(MasterFile) THEN
      writeln ('There are more data.')
  END;  {  of PROCEDURE LoadArray  }

{*****************************************************************}
```

```
FUNCTION NewGPA (Hours, CourseHours : integer;
                 GPA, HonorPoints : real) : real;

  {  Given:   Total hours accumulated, credit hours for the       }
  {               course completed, current GPA, HonorPoints      }
  {               corresponding to the letter grade received      }
  {  Task:    Compute the new grade point average                 }
  {  Return:  New grade point average                             }

  VAR
    OldHours : integer;
  BEGIN
    OldHours := Hours;
    Hours := Hours + CourseHours;
    NewGPA := (OldHours * GPA + CourseHours * HonorPoints) / Hours
  END;  {  of FUNCTION NewGPA  }

{*****************************************************************}

FUNCTION SeqSearch (Student : StudentList;
                    IDNumber : IDString;
                    NumberOfRecords : integer) : integer;

  {  Given:   An array of student records, a student ID number,   }
  {               and the number of records                       }
  {  Task:    Sequentially search the array to find a match for   }
  {               the ID number                                   }
  {  Return:  The index of the record where a match was found;    }   3
  {               return 0 if not match                           }

  VAR
    Found : boolean;
    LCV : integer;
  BEGIN
    SeqSearch := 0;
    Found := false;
    LCV := 0;
    WHILE (LCV < NumberOfRecords) AND (NOT Found) DO
      BEGIN
        LCV := LCV + 1;
        IF Student[LCV].IDNumber = IDNumber THEN
          BEGIN
            SeqSearch := LCV;
            Found := true
          END  {  of IF...THEN  }
      END  {  of WHILE loop  }
  END;  {  of FUNCTION SeqSearch  }

{***************************************************************}

PROCEDURE UpdateRecords (VAR TransactionFile : text;
                         VAR Student : StudentList;
                         NumberOfRecords : integer);
```

```
{  Given:   A transaction file for updating records, an array   }
{               of student records, and the number of student   }
{               records                                         }
{  Task:    Read a line from the transaction file; search array }
{               Student for a match of IDNumber; IF match THEN  }
{               update hours and GPA; ELSE print as part of     }
{               Exception Report                                }
{  Return:  An updated array of student records                 }

CONST
  Skip = ' ';
VAR
  J, Index, CourseHours : integer;
  IDNumber : IDString;
  Grade : char;
  MatchFound : boolean;
BEGIN

  {  Print heading for the Exception Report  }
  writeln ('EXCEPTION REPORT':35);
  writeln ('ID NUMBER':20, 'GRADE':12, 'HOURS':10);
  writeln (Skip:10, '-------------------------------');
  writeln;

  {  Now read the transaction file  }
  WHILE NOT eof(TransactionFile) DO
    BEGIN
      FOR J := 1 TO IDLength DO                                          3
        read (TransactionFile, IDNumber[J]);
      readln (TransactionFile, Grade, CourseHours);
      Index := SeqSearch(Student, IDNumber, NumberOfRecords);
      MatchFound := Index <> 0;
      IF MatchFound THEN            {  Update student record  }
        WITH Student[Index] DO
          CASE Grade OF
            'A'  :  BEGIN
                      GPA := NewGPA(Hours, CourseHours, GPA, 4.0);
                      Hours := Hours + CourseHours
                    END;
            'B'  :  BEGIN
                      GPA := NewGPA(Hours, Coursehours, GPA, 3.0);
                      Hours := Hours + CourseHours
                    END;
            'C'  :  BEGIN
                      GPA := NewGPA(Hours, CourseHours, GPA, 2.0);
                      Hours := Hours + CourseHours
                    END;
            'D'  :  BEGIN
                      GPA := NewGPA(Hours, CourseHours, GPA, 1.0);
                      Hours := Hours + CourseHours
                    END;
            'E'  :  BEGIN
                      GPA := NewGPA(Hours, CourseHours, GPA, 0.0);
                      Hours := Hours + CourseHours
                    END;
```

```
          'W', 'I'  :                         {  do nothing  }
        END  {  of CASE Grade  }
      ELSE              {  Print as part of Exception Report  }
        writeln (IDNumber:20, Grade:10, CourseHours:10)
    END  {  of WHILE NOT eof(TransactionFile)  }
  END;  {  of PROCEDURE UpdateRecords  }

{*************************************************************}

PROCEDURE PrintList (VAR Student: StudentList;
                     NumberOfRecords : integer);

  {  Given:   An array of student records and number of records }
  {  Task:    Print a list of records with appropriate heading  }
  {  Return:  Nothing                                           }

  VAR
    J : integer;
  BEGIN

    {  Print a heading for the revised list  }
    writeln;                                                          4
    writeln ('UPDATED REPORT':30);
    writeln ('STUDENT FILE LISTING':34);
    writeln;
    writeln ('NAME':10, 'ID NUMBER':25, 'GPA':8, 'CREDITS':10);
    writeln ('-----------------------------------------------------');
    writeln;

    {  Now print the list  }
    FOR J := 1 TO NumberOfRecords DO
      WITH Student[J] DO
        writeln (Name:20, IDNumber:15, GPA:8:2, Hours:8)
  END;  {  of PROCEDURE PrintList  }

{*************************************************************}

PROCEDURE UpdateMasterFile (VAR MasterFile : RecordsFile;
                            VAR Student : StudentList;
                            NumberOfRecords : integer);

  {  Given:   An array of student records and the array length  }
  {  Task:    Copy the records into MasterFile for storage      }
  {  Return:  A file of student records                         }

  VAR
    J : integer;                                                      5
  BEGIN
    rewrite (MasterFile);
    FOR J := 1 TO NumberOfRecords DO
      BEGIN
        MasterFile^ := Student[J];
        put (MasterFile)
      END  {  of FOR loop  }
  END;  {  of PROCEDURE UpdateMasterFile  }

{*************************************************************}
```

```
BEGIN  {  Main program  }
  PrepareFiles (MasterFile, TransactionFile);
  LoadArray (MasterFile, Student, NumberOfRecords);
  UpdateRecords (TransactionFile, Student, NumberOfRecords);
  PrintList (Student, NumberOfRecords);
  UpdateMasterFile (MasterFile, Student, NumberOfRecords)
END.  {  of main program  }
```

If you use data in MasterFile as

```
BARRETT RODA         345678901 3.67 23
BORGNINE ERNEST      369325263 4.12 14
CADABRA ABRA         123450987 3.33 23
DJIKSTRA EDGAR       345998765 3.90 33
GARZELONI RANDY      444226666 2.20 18
GLUTZ AGATHA         320678230 3.00 22
HOLBRUCK HALL        321908765 3.50 29
HUNTER MICHAEL       234098112 2.50 22
JOHNSON ROSALYN      345123690 3.25 20
LOCKER HEATHER       369426163 4.00 30
MCMANN ABAGAIL       333112040 3.97 41
MILDEW MORRIS        234812057 3.67 34
MORSE SAMUEL         334558778 3.00 28
NOVAK JAMES          348524598 1.50 13
OHERLAHE TERRY       333662222 2.75 21
RACKHAM HORACE       345878643 4.00 30
SNYDER JUDITH        356913580 2.75 24
VANDERSYS RALPH      367120987 3.23 22
VAUGHN SARAH         238498765 3.00 24
WIDGET WENDELL       444113333 1.25 10
WILSON PHILIP        345719642 3.00 25
WITWERTH JANUARY     367138302 2.10 20
WORDEN JACK          359241234 3.33 25
WOURTHY CONSTANCE    342092834 3.50 32
```

and data in TransactionFile as

```
333112040A 3
333112040A 4
333112040A 4
444113333A 3
444113333A 4
444113333A 3
444113333A 2
238498765A 3
238498765A 3
238498765A 4
238498766A 4
369325263A 3
369325263A 3
369325263A 4
369325263C 4
320678230A 5
320678230A 3
320678230A 3
```

```
320678230A 4
444226666A 3
444226666A 4
444226666A 3
444226667A 4
367138302A 3
367138302A 3
367138302A 3
367138302B 3
367120987A 4
367120987A 4
367120987A 3
367120987I 3
367120987A 3
369426163A 4
369426163A 3
345678901A 3
345678901A 4
345678901A 3
345678900A 4
123450987A 3
123450987A 3
123450987A 4
123450987E 3
234098112A 3
234098112A 3
444226666D 3
367138302D 3
123450987C 4
123450987D 3
123450987A 2
333112040D 4
333112040A 3
444113333D 4
444113333A 3
369235263D 4
369235263A 3
320678230D 3
320678230D 4
320678230W 3
334229023D 4
```

output for this program is

```
              EXCEPTION REPORT
ID NUMBER          GRADE        HOURS
----------------------------------

238498766            A            4
444226667            A            4
345678900            A            4
369235263            D            4
369235263            A            3
334229023            D            4
```

```
                    UPDATED REPORT
                  STUDENT FILE LISTING

     NAME                 ID NUMBER     GPA   CREDITS
-----------------------------------------------------

BARRETT RODA              345678901     3.77     33
BORGNINE ERNEST           369325263     3.77     28
CADABRA ABRA              123450987     3.01     45
DJIKSTRA EDGAR            345998765     3.90     33
GARZELONI RANDY           444226666     2.66     31
GLUTZ AGATHA              320678230     3.02     44
HOLBRUCK HALL             321908765     3.50     29
HUNTER MICHAEL            234098112     2.82     28
JOHNSON ROSALYN           345123690     3.25     20
LOCKER HEATHER            369426163     4.00     37
MCMANN ABAGAIL            333112040     3.78     59
MILDEW MORRIS             234812057     3.67     34
MORSE SAMUEL              334558778     3.00     28
NOVAK JAMES               348524598     1.50     13
OHERLAHE TERRY            333662222     2.75     21
RACKHAM HORACE            345878643     4.00     30
SNYDER JUDITH             356913580     2.75     24
VANDERSYS RALPH           367120987     3.53     36
VAUGHN SARAH              238498765     3.29     34
WIDGET WENDELL            444113333     2.64     29
WILSON PHILIP             345719642     3.00     25
WITWERTH JANUARY          367138302     2.53     32
WORDEN JACK               359241234     3.33     25
WOURTHY CONSTANCE         342092834     3.50     32
```

Running and Debugging Hints

1. Be sure all files (except **input** and **output**) are properly opened for reading and writing. Remember, you must **reset** before reading from a file and **rewrite** before writing to a file.
2. Don't try to read past the end-of-file marker. This is a common error that occurs when trying to **read** without a sufficient check for **eof.**
3. Be careful to use file names as arguments correctly in **read, readln, write, writeln,** and **eof** statements.
4. List all external files in the program heading and then be sure to declare them in the variable declaration section.
5. Be sure all files listed in a procedure heading are variable parameters.
6. Protect against working with empty files or empty lines of a text file.
7. Remember, the file buffer is undefined when **eof** (<file name>) is **true.**

Summary

Key Terms

binary file
buffer variable
component of a file
file
file window
master file
opening a file
reading from a file
transaction file
writing to a file

Keywords

FILE
get
put

Key Concepts

- A file is a sequence of components all of the same data type; a typical declaration is

```
TYPE
  RealFile = FILE OF real;
VAR
  FileA : RealFile;
```

- Files that cannot be defined as text files are binary files.
- Information is stored in binary files by using the internal binary representation of each component.
- In standard implementations of Pascal, binary files must be accessed sequentially.
- File window is commonly used to describe the component of the file that is available for data to be passed to or from it.
- A buffer variable is an undeclared variable that is used to transfer data to or from a file component; if the file name is FileA, then the identifier for the buffer variable is FileA^.
- Before transferring values to a file (writing to a file), the file must be opened for writing by **rewrite** (<file name>). Values can then be transferred from the file buffer using **put** or **write** (<file name>, <value>); for example,

```
rewrite (NewFile);
NewFile^ := 10;
put (NewFile);
```

or

```
rewrite (NewFile);
write (NewFile, 10);
```

- Before transferring values from a file (reading from a file), the file must be opened for reading by **reset** (<file name>). Values can then be transferred from the file by assignments from the file buffer and by using **get** (<file name>) or **read** (<file name>, <variable name>); for example,

```
reset (NewFile);
A := NewFile^;
get (NewFile);
```

or

```
reset (NewFile);
read (NewFile, A);
```

- An end-of-file marker is automatically placed at the end of the file as **eof** (<file name>) when a file is created.
- A file cannot be opened for reading and writing at the same time.
- When a file is declared as a parameter in a procedure heading, it must be listed as a variable parameter; for example,

```
PROCEDURE Update (VAR OldFile, NewFile : <file type>);
```

- Components of a file can be arrays; the declaration

```
VAR
  F : FILE OF ARRAY [1..10] OF real;
```

can be depicted as shown in Figure 13.5, where F^ is an array and array components are denoted by F^[J].

◆ Figure 13.5

File of arrays

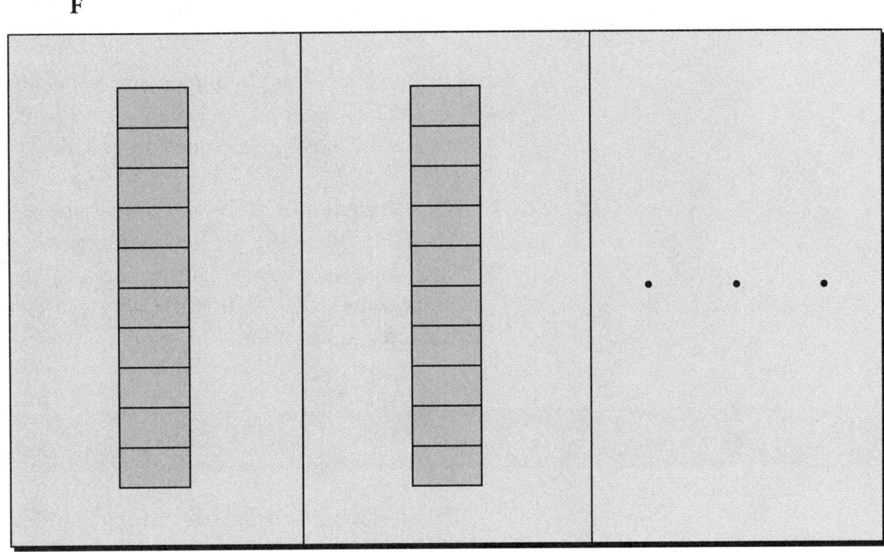

- File components can be records and can be declared by

```
TYPE
  RecType = RECORD
              Name : PACKED ARRAY [1..20] OF char;
              Age : 0..120;
              Gender : char
            END;  {  of RECORD RecType  }
VAR
  F : FILE OF RecType;
```

and depicted as shown in Figure 13.6. In this case, the buffer variable F^ is a record and fields can be denoted by

```
F^.Name
F^.Age
F^.Gender
```

◆ Figure 13.6

File of records

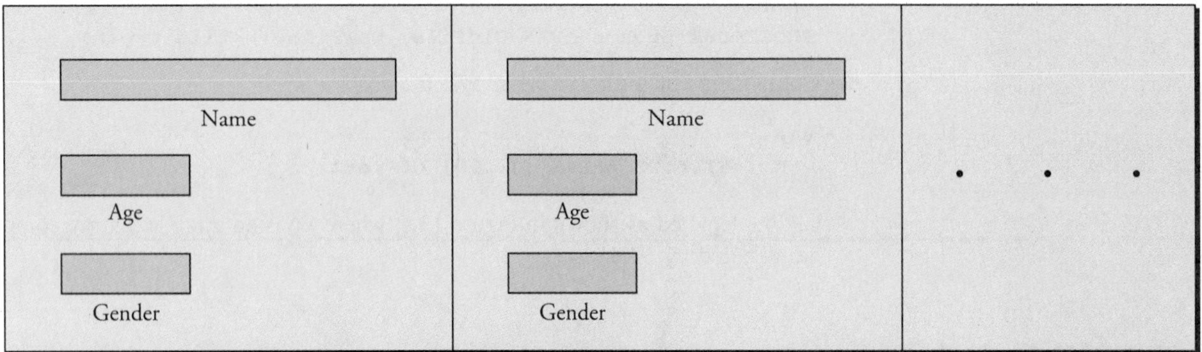

- Files with structured components frequently have to be processed and/or updated; for a file of records, you might insert or delete a record, sort the file by a field, merge two files, update each record, or produce a printed list according to some field.
- When updating or otherwise processing a file, changes are normally made in an internal (temporary) file and then copied back into the master (permanent) file.
- Since input data are generally in a text file, you need to create a file of structured components from the text file; you can then use **get** and **put** to transfer entire structures at one time.

Chapter Review Exercises

1. List three advantages of using data files in a program.
2. Explain how a sequential file is updated.
3. Explain the difference between the syntax and use of **write** and **put** statements.

For Exercises 4–8, indicate if the file definition is valid or invalid. If invalid, correct the definition or explain the error.

4.
```
TYPE
  ClassFile = FILE OF ClassName;
VAR
  File5 = ClassFile;
```
5.
```
TYPE
  QuizFile = FILE OF ARRAY [1..30] OF integer;
VAR
  QuizGrades : QuizFile;
```
6.
```
TYPE
  RealFile = FILE OF real;
  SecondFile = FILE OF RealFile;
VAR
  RealNumbers : SecondFile;
```

7.
```
TYPE
  String20 = PACKED ARRAY [1..20] OF char;
  RealArray = ARRAY [1..20] OF real;
  FileData = FILE OF String20, RealArray;
VAR
  X : FileData;
```
8.
```
TYPE
  FileData = PACKED ARRAY [1..30, 1..30] OF char;
  DataFile = FILE OF FileData;
VAR
  FileVariable : DataFile;
```
9. What are some of the differences between files and arrays?

For Exercises 10–14, indicate which are correct statements. Assume all variables are properly declared.

10. `write (FileA^);`
11. `put (FileA^);`
12. `ReadFile (VAR FileA^ : DataFile);`
13. `FileA^.B[7] = 4;`
14. `get (FileA);`
15. Declare a record, file, and variable declarations for a file to contain the names, addresses, and telephone numbers of your classmates.
16. Write a procedure to read in a record from the file declared in Exercise 15.
17. Explain the purpose of the **rewrite** statement.
18. Write a test program to determine if your implementation of Pascal permits the use of **write** statements on other than text files.
19. Under what conditions will **eof** be **true** when reading files? When writing files?
20. List the differences between internal and external files.
21. Write an appropriate file declaration for a file containing magazine subscription information. The file contains the subscribers' names, addresses, cities, states, zip codes, and subscription expiration dates (month and year).
22. Write a procedure for Exercise 21 to print the names of those subscribers whose subscription expires this month.
23. Write an appropriate file declaration for a file that contains 100 positive integers.
24. Write a procedure to read the file declared in Exercise 23 and print the sum of the integers in the file.
25. Write a procedure to sort the components of the file in Exercise 23 into ascending order.
26. Write appropriate file and variable declarations for a file containing the names and scoring average for the members of your school's basketball team.
27. Write a procedure to print the name of the player with the highest scoring average from the file in Exercise 26.

Programming Problems

1. The Pentagon is a mathematics magazine published by Kappa Mu Epsilon, a mathematics honorary society. Write a program to be used by the business manager for the purpose of generating mailing labels. The subscribers' information

should be read into a file of records. Each record should contain the subscriber's name; address, including street and street number, apartment number (if any), city, two-letter abbreviation for the state, and the zip code; and expiration information, including month and year.

Your program should create an alphabetically sorted master file, print an alphabetical list for the office, print a mailing list sorted by zip code for bulk mailing, and denote all last issues by a special symbol.

2. The relentless Mr. Lae Z. Programmer (Problems 5, 22, and 23, Chapter 5; Problem 13, Chapter 6; Problem 7, Chapter 7; Problem 5, Chapter 9; Problem 3, Chapter 11; and Problem 3, Chapter 12) now wants you to create a file of records for students in his computer science course. You should provide fields for the student's name, 10 quiz scores, six program scores, and three examination scores. Your program should
   a. Read in the names from a text file.
   b. Include procedures for updating quiz scores, program scores, and examination scores.
   c. Be able to update the file by adding or deleting a record.
   d. Print an alphabetized list of the database at any given time.

3. Write a program to do part of the work of a word processor. Your program should read a text file and print it in paragraph form. The left margin should be in column 10 and the right margin in column 72. In the data file, periods will designate the end of sentences and the asterisk (*) will denote a new paragraph. No word should be split between lines. Your program should save the edited file in a file of type **text.**

4. Slow-pitch softball is rapidly becoming a popular summer pastime. Assume your local community is to have a new women's league this year consisting of eight teams, with 15 players each. This league gets the field one night per week for four games. They will play a double round-robin (each team plays every other team twice, resulting in 14 games). Write a program to
   a. Create a file of records (one record for each team) in which the team name is included.
   b. Print a schedule.
   c. List the teams alphabetically by team name.
   d. Print a list of players for each team.

5. The registrar at State University (Problem 1, Chapter 12) wants you to write an interactive program to assist with record keeping. Your program should create a file of records. The record for each student should contain the student's name, identification number, credit hours completed, the number of credit hours in which currently enrolled, and grade point average. Your program should also contain a procedure for each of the following updates:
   a. List semester-end data of hours completed and grade point average for the semester.
   b. Insert a record.
   c. Delete a record.
   d. Print a list sorted alphabetically.
   e. Print a list sorted by grade point average.

6. The local high school sports boosters (Problems 1 and 2, Chapter 11) need more help. They want you to write a program to create a file of records in which each record contains the parents' names, the children's first names (at most 10 children), and the names of the sports in which the children participated.

A typical record is shown in Figure 13.7. Your program should create a data file and save it for later use, print an alphabetical list of parents' names, and print a list of the names of parents of football players.

Figure 13.7

Typical values for fields in a record

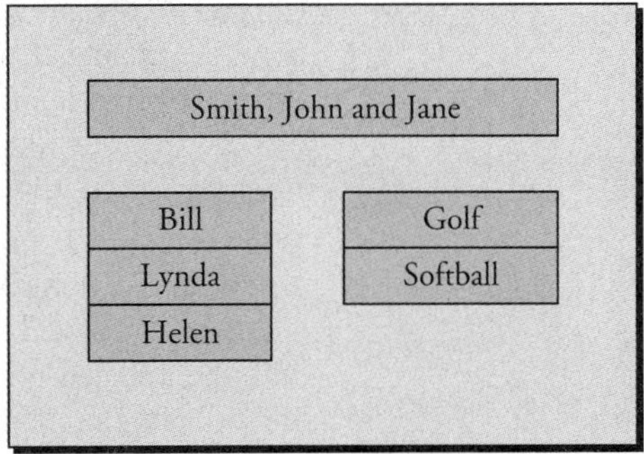

7. A popular use of text files is for teachers to create a bank of test items and then use them to generate quizzes using some form of random generation. Write a program to allow you to create files of type **text** that contain questions for each of three chapters. Second, generate two quizzes of three questions for each of the three chapters.
8. Public service departments must always be on the lookout for those who try to abuse the system by accepting assistance from similar agencies in different geographic areas. Write a program to compare names from one county with those from another county and print all names that are on both lists.
9. Write a program to be used by flight agents at an airport (see Exercise 2, Section 13.3). Your program should use a file of records in which the record for each flight contains flight number, airline, arrival time, arriving from, departure time, and destination. Your program should list incoming flights sorted by time, list departing flights sorted by time, add flights, and delete flights.
10. Congratulations! You have just been asked to write a program that will assign dates for the Valentine's Day dance. Each student record will contain the student's name, age, gender (M or F), and the names of three date preferences (ranked). Your program should
    a. Create a master file from the data file.
    b. Create and save alphabetically sorted files of males and females.
    c. Print a list of couples for the dance. The age difference may be no more than three years. Dating preferences should be in the following form.

	CAN'T MISS!	
First request	Matches	First request
	GOOD BET!	
First request	Matches	Second request
Second request	Matches	First request
	GOOD LUCK!	
	Any other matches	
	OUT OF LUCK!	
	You are not on any list	

It's obvious (isn't it?) that a person can have at most one date for the dance.

11. A data file consists of an unknown number of real numbers. Write a program to read the file and print the highest value, lowest value, and average of the numbers in the file.

■ 12. The Falcon Manufacturing Company (Problem 23, Chapter 11; and Problem 17, Chapter 12) wants you to write an inventory file program. The file should contain a 30-character part name, an integer part number, the quantity on hand, and the price of an item. The program should permit the entry of new items into the file and the deletion of existing items. The items to be changed will be entered from the keyboard.

■ 13. Write a program for the Falcon Manufacturing Company (Problem 12) to allow a secretary to enter an item number and a quantity, and whether it is to be added to or deleted from the stock. The program should prepare a new data file with the updated information. If the user requests to remove more items than are on hand, an appropriate warning message should be issued.

■ 14. Write a program to read the inventory file of the Falcon Manufacturing Company (Problems 12 and 13) and then print a listing of the inventory. The program should print an asterisk (*) next to the quantity of any item for which there are fewer than 50 on hand.

■ 15. Revise the program that you wrote in answer to Problem 23 in Chapter 11 to permit the sales figures of the Falcon Manufacturing Company to be read from a file. Also revise the program so that the information on the total dollar amount of sales for each product by each salesperson is written to a file for later use.

■ 16. Write a program to read the total dollars sales file from Problem 15 for last month and the corresponding file for this month and print a table showing the total sales by each salesperson for each product during the two-month period.

17. A data file contains an alphabetized list of the secondary students in your high school, and another contains an alphabetized list of the elementary students. Write a program to merge these two files and print an alphabetized list of all students in your school.

18. The Andover Telephone Company (whose motto is "We send your messages of Andover.") wants a computerized directory information system. The data file should contain the customer names and telephone numbers. Your program should permit:
    a. The entry of new customers' names and telephone numbers
    b. The deletion of existing customers' names and telephone numbers
    c. The printing of all customers' names and their telephone numbers
    d. The entry from the keyboard of a customer's name with the program then printing the telephone number (if found)

    Whenever customers' names and numbers are to be added or deleted, the file should be updated accordingly. You may assume there are no more than 50 customers.

19. Revise the program written to keep the grades of Mr. Laven's students (Problem 19, Chapter 11) to read the grades entered previously from a file and, when the program is complete, print the updated list of grades.

20. Recognizing your talents as a programmer, the principal of your high school wants you to write a program to work with a data file containing the names of the students who were absent at the start of the school day. These names are kept as 30-character packed arrays. The program should permit the principal to

enter the name of a student later in the day to check to see if the student was absent at the start of the day.

21. Revise Problem 13 from Chapter 12 to permit Ada Crown's computer maintenance records to be kept in a file. Your program should allow the data on a machine to be changed and new machines to be added.

Communication in Practice

1. Select a program from the **Programming Problems** section in this chapter that you have not yet worked. Construct a structure chart and write all documentary information for this program. Include variable definitions, subprogram definitions, required input, and required output. When you are finished, have a classmate read your documentation to see if precisely what is to be done is clear.
2. Remove all documentation from a program you have written for this chapter. Exchange this modified version with another student who has done the same thing. Write documentation for the exchanged program. Compare your documentation with that originally written for the program. Discuss the differences and similarities with the other students in the class.
3. Contact a programmer at some company or corporation to discuss data structures. Find out how much (if any) he or she uses arrays, records, and files. If the programmer does use arrays, records, or files, what kinds of programming problems require their use? Find out what kinds of operations are used with these data structures. What limitations do these structures possess for the problems that need to be solved? Write a complete report summarizing your discussion.
4. Problems involving data management are routinely addressed in nonprogramming courses taught in schools of business. These courses may be taught in departments such as Management Information Systems (MIS) or Business Information Systems (BIS). Contact an instructor of such a course and discuss the issue of using data structures to manage information. How are data structures presented to the classes? What are some typical real-world problems?

   Give an oral report of your discussion to your class. Compare and contrast the instructor's presentations with those provided in your own class. Use charts with transparencies as part of your presentation.
5. Select an unworked problem from the **Programming Problems** in this chapter. Construct a structure chart and write all necessary documentary information for this problem. Do not write code. Then have a classmate read your documentation to see if precisely what is to be done is clear.

Chapter 14

Sorting and Merging

Chapter Outline

The previous chapters have presented techniques for working with structured variables. In particular, we have seen how to sort lists in either ascending or descending order, search a list for some specific value, and merge lists that may or may not be sorted. We have also learned how to use recursion. In this chapter, we examine additional techniques for working with structured variables.

Unfortunately, this chapter cannot answer all of the questions associated with sorting and merging. This text and most beginning courses defer more extensive treatment and examination of other methods and their relative efficiency to later programming courses. A list of suggestions for further reading is included at the end of this chapter.

14.1 Sorting Algorithms

Objectives

- to understand the algorithm for an insertion sort
- to be able to use an insertion sort in a program
- to understand the algorithm for a bubble sort
- to be able to use a bubble sort in a program

Several algorithms can be used to sort elements in arrays and files. We have worked with the selection sort since Chapter 10. Three other commonly used sorting methods are the insertion sort, the bubble sort, and the quick sort. All of these sorts work relatively well for sorting small lists of elements.

However, when large databases are to be sorted, a direct application of an elementary sorting process usually requires a great deal of computer time. Thus, some other sorting method is needed—one that might involve using a different algorithm or dividing the lists into smaller parts, sorting these parts, and then merging the lists back together. In more advanced courses, you will examine the relative efficiency of sorts and methods for handling large databases. For now, let's consider these three sorting methods.

Insertion Sort

The purpose of a sort is to produce an array of elements sorted in either ascending or descending order. These elements are normally read from an input file into an array. Now let's see how an insertion sort arranges numbers in ascending order in an unsorted array.

Objectives

(continued)

- to understand the algorithm for a quick sort
- to be able to use a quick sort in a program

An **insertion sort** sorts an array of elements in either ascending or descending order. It starts with an empty array and inserts elements one at a time in their proper order.

The main principles of an **insertion sort** are:

1. Put the first K elements of an array in order.
2. Move the K + 1 element into Temp.
3. Move the sorted elements (1 to K) down, one at a time, until the value in Temp can be placed in order in the previously sorted portion of the array.

To illustrate how this works, consider the following array of integers:

A
4
2
0
15
8

The first step is to put the value from A[2] into Temp by using

```
Temp := A[2];
```

This produces

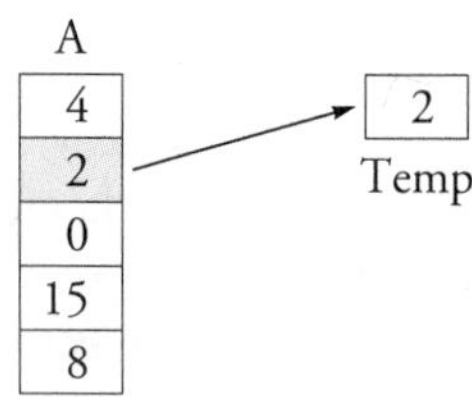

where the shaded cell can be thought of as waiting to receive a value. The value in Temp is then compared to values in the array before A[2]. Since A[1] > A[2], the value in A[1] is "moved down" to produce

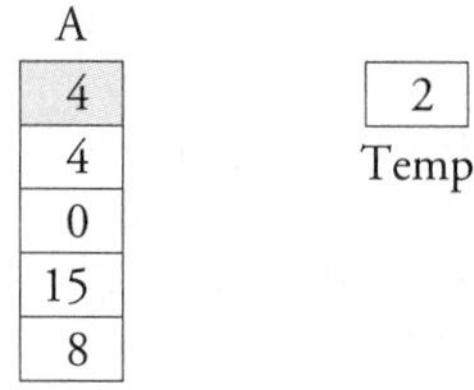

Since we are at the top of the array, the value in Temp is placed in A[1] to yield

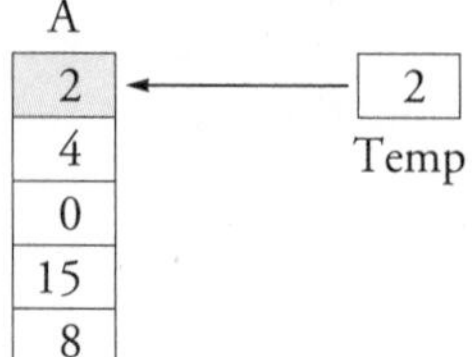

During the next pass, the value of A[3] is put into Temp and we have

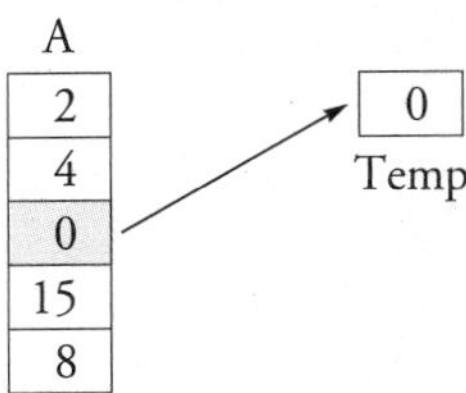

This value is compared to the values above it. As long as Temp is less than an array element, the array element is shifted down. This process produces

A
2
2
4
15
8
0
Temp

At this stage, the value in Temp is inserted into the array to produce the partially sorted array

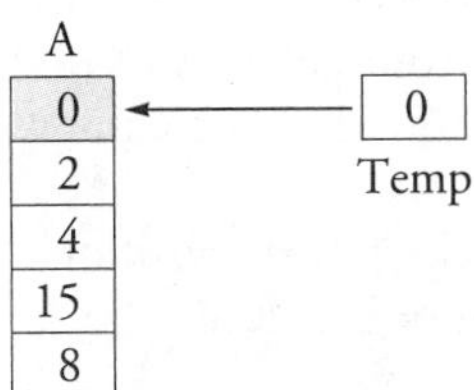

At the start of the next pass, Temp receives the value in A[4] to yield

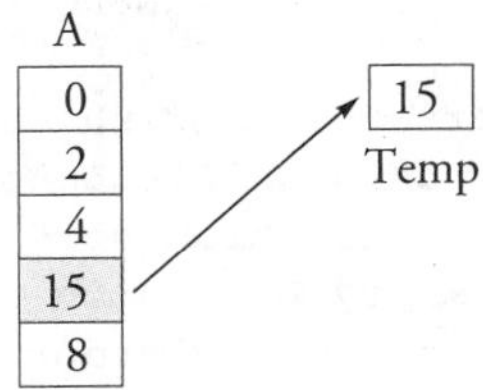

When the value in Temp is compared to A[3], the process terminates because Temp > A[3]. Thus, using the partially sorted array improves the efficiency of the sort.

On the last pass, Temp receives the value from A[5] and we have

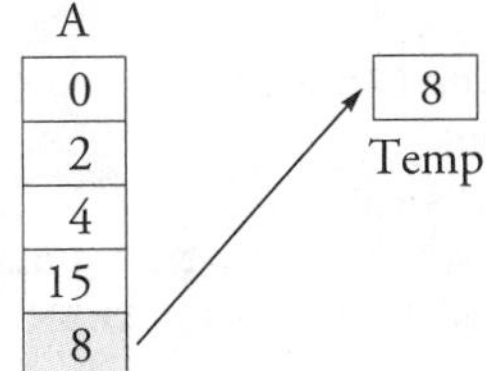

Since Temp < A[4], we obtain

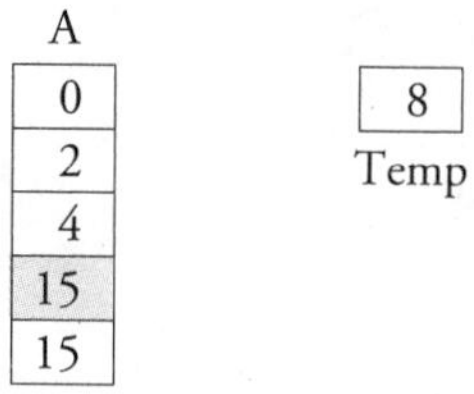

A	
0	8 (Temp)
2	
4	
15	
15	

At this stage, Temp > A[3], so we insert the value of Temp into A[4] to produce the following sorted array:

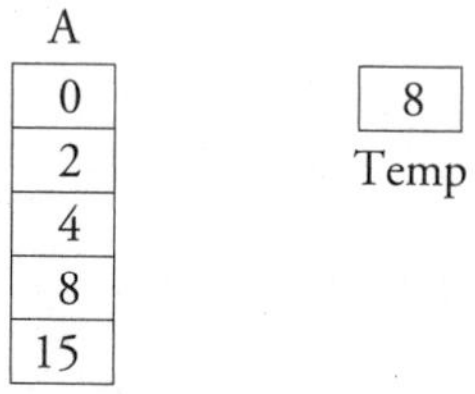

A	
0	8 (Temp)
2	
4	
8	
15	

In summary, the idea of an insertion sort is to do the following:

1. Remove an element from position (K + 1) in the array.
2. Slide the previously sorted elements down the array until a position is found for the new element.
3. Insert the element in its proper position.
4. Continue until the array is sorted.

A procedure for the insertion sort follows:

```
PROCEDURE InsertionSort (VAR List : SortArray;
                          ListLength : integer);

  {  Given:    An array List with entries in locations 1       }
  {                 through ListLength                          }
  {  Task:     Apply insertion sort logic to List               }
  {  Return:   The array List with entries sorted in            }
  {                 ascending order                             }

  VAR
    Index, K : integer;
    Temp : ElementType;
    Done : boolean;
  BEGIN
    FOR Index := 2 TO ListLength DO
      BEGIN
        Temp := List[Index];
        K := Index;
        Done := false;
        WHILE (K >= 2) AND (NOT Done) DO
          IF Temp < List[K-1] THEN
            BEGIN                          {  Move elements down  }
              List[K] := List[K-1];
```

```
                    K := K - 1
                  END
                ELSE
                  Done := true;  {  Found position for insertion  }
              List[K] := Temp                 {  Insert into array  }
            END  {  of FOR loop  }
        END;  {  of PROCEDURE InsertionSort  }
```

This procedure is called from the main program by

```
InsertionSort (UnsortedList, Length);
```

As expected, records can be sorted by examining some key field and then assigning the entire record accordingly. Thus, if an array type is

```
TYPE
  .
  .
  .
  StudentInfo = RECORD
                  Name : NameString;
                  Score : integer
                END;
  StudentList = ARRAY [1..ListLength] OF StudentInfo;
```

and the array is to be sorted according to student scores, the field comparison in **PROCEDURE** InsertionSort could be

```
IF Temp.Score < Student[K-1].Score
```

Bubble Sort

A **bubble sort** is a sort that rearranges elements of an array until they are in either ascending or descending order. Consecutive elements are compared, to move (bubble) the elements to the top or bottom accordingly during each pass.

The sorting algorithm commonly referred to as a bubble sort also rearranges the elements of an array until they are in either ascending or descending order. Like the selection sort, an extra array is not used. Basically, a **bubble sort** starts at the beginning of an array and compares two consecutive elements of the array. If they are in the correct order, the next pair is compared. If they are not in the correct order, they are switched and the next pair compared. When this has been done for the entire array, one pass has been made and the correct element is in the last position.

Starting at the top (the beginning of the array) each time, successive passes are made through the array until the array is sorted. Two items should be noted here:

1. A flag is needed to indicate whether or not an exchange was made during the pass through the array. If no exchange was made, the array is sorted.
2. Since each pass filters the largest (or smallest) element to the bottom, the length of what remains to be sorted can be decreased by 1 after each pass.

To illustrate how this algorithm works, assume the array is

A
12
0
3
2
8

The first pass through the array produces

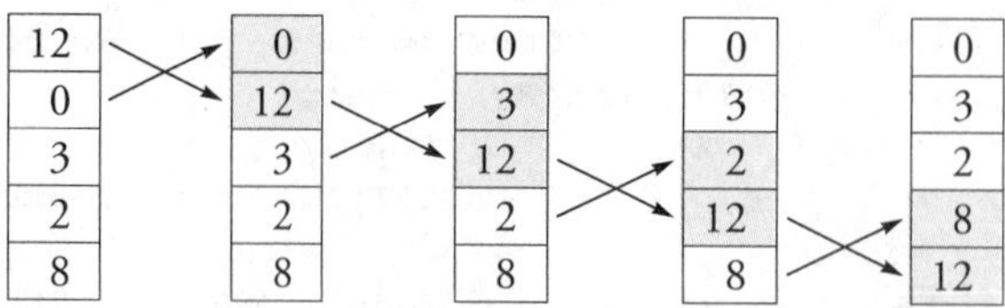

Since an exchange was made, we need to make at least one more pass through the array. However, the length is decreased by 1 because there is no need to compare the last two elements because the last element is in its correct position. A second pass through this array produces

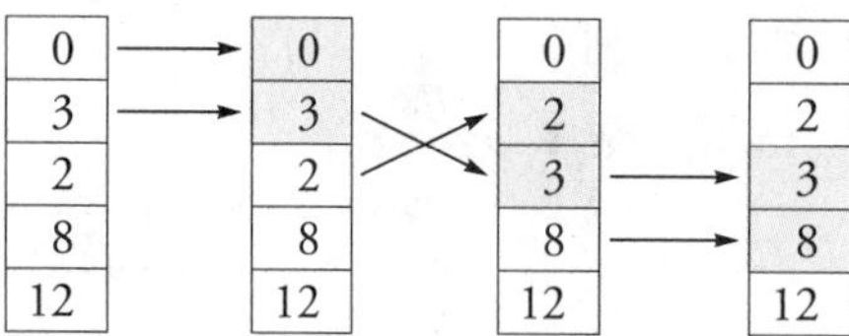

At this stage, the array is sorted, but because an exchange has been made, the length is decreased by 1 and another pass is made. Because no exchange is made during this third pass, the sorting process is terminated.

If we assume the variable declaration section includes

```
VAR
  ExchangeMade : boolean;
  J, Length, Last, Temp : integer;
```

the values to be sorted are in array A, and Length has been assigned a value, then an algorithm for a bubble sort could be

```
Last := Length - 1;
REPEAT
  ExchangeMade := false;
  FOR J := 1 TO Last DO
    IF A[J] > A[J+1] THEN
      BEGIN
        Swap (A[J], A[J+1]);
        ExchangeMade := true
      END;
  Last := Last - 1  {  Decrement length  }
UNTIL (NOT ExchangeMade) OR (Length = 1);
```

where Swap is the procedure used earlier to interchange the values of two variables. This procedure is called from the main program by

```
BubbleSort (ListName, Length);
```

where ListName is the name of the array to be sorted and Length is the number of elements in the array.

A Note of Interest

Gene Mapping: Computer Scientists Examine Problems of Genome Project

Deciphering the human genome is much like trying to read the instructions on a computer disk filled with programs written in the zeros and ones of electronic code—without knowing the programming language.

That was the message from molecular biologists to computer scientists at a meeting sponsored by the National Research Council. The biologists hope to involve the computer scientists in the U.S. Human Genome Project, a 15-year, $3-billion effort to identify and locate the information contained in human chromosomes.

Computer scientists, with their experience in managing information and using arcane programming languages to store data and convey instructions, could be particularly valuable in helping to read and organize the 3 billion "letters" that make up the human genetic code, the biologists said.

"The entire program for making 'me' is about 10 to the 10 bits" (about 10 trillion pieces of information), says Gerald J. Sussman, a professor of electrical engineering and computer science at the Massachusetts Institute of Technology. "It is no bigger than the U.S. tax code, or the design documents for the U.S. space shuttle." Figuring out what the program is, he said, is a computer science problem.

Biologists say they need computer scientists to

- Design easy-to-use databases that can handle the millions of pieces of information that need to be correlated to fully understand genetics—and life.
- Design computer networks that will allow biologists to share information conveniently.
- Create procedures that will allow biologists to analyze information pulled from laboratory experiments.
- Write programs that will let biologists simulate the formation and development of proteins.

Quick Sort

A **quick sort** is a relatively fast sorting technique that uses recursion.

One of the fastest sorting techniques available is the **quick sort.** It uses recursion and is based on the idea of separating a list of numbers into two parts. One part contains the numbers smaller than some number in the list and the other contains numbers larger than the number. Thus, if an unsorted array originally contains

14	3	2	11	5	8	0	2	9	4	20
A[1]	A[2]				A[6]					A[11]

we would select the element in the middle position, A[6], and then pivot on the value in A[6], which is 8 in our illustration. Our process would then put all values less than 8 on the left side and all values greater than 8 on the right side. This first subdividing produces

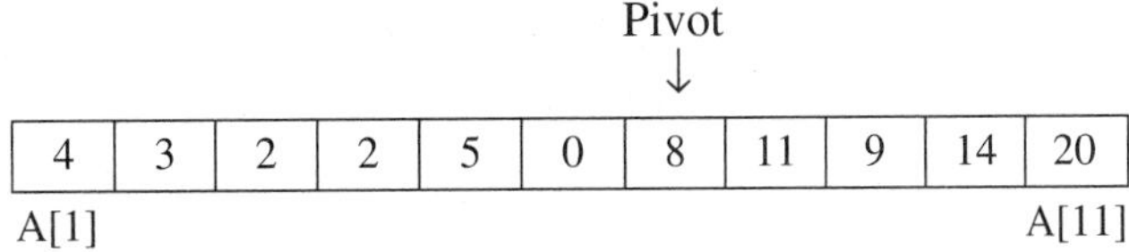

Now, each sublist is subdivided in the same manner. This process continues until all sublists are in order. The array is then sorted. This is a recursive process.

Before writing a procedure for this sort, let's examine how it works. First, why do we choose the value in the middle position? Ideally, we would like to pivot on the median of the list. However, it is not efficient to find this value first, so we choose the value in the middle as a compromise. The index of this value is found by (First + Last) **DIV** 2, where First and Last are the indices of the initial and final array elements. We then identify a LeftArrow and RightArrow on the far left and far right, respectively. This can be envisioned as

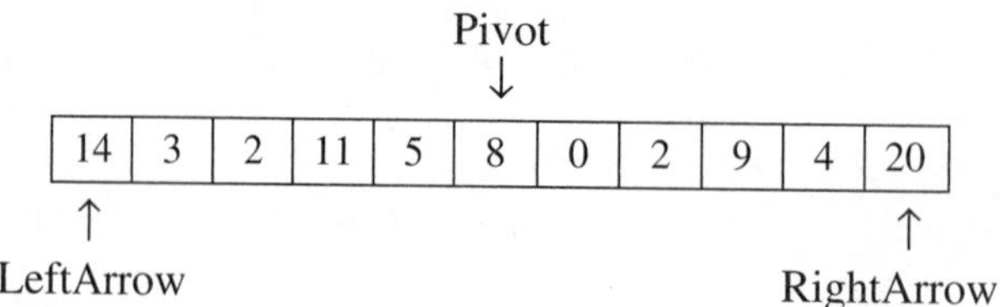

where LeftArrow and RightArrow represent the respective indices of the array components. Starting on the right, the RightArrow is moved left until a value less than or equal to the pivot is encountered. This produces

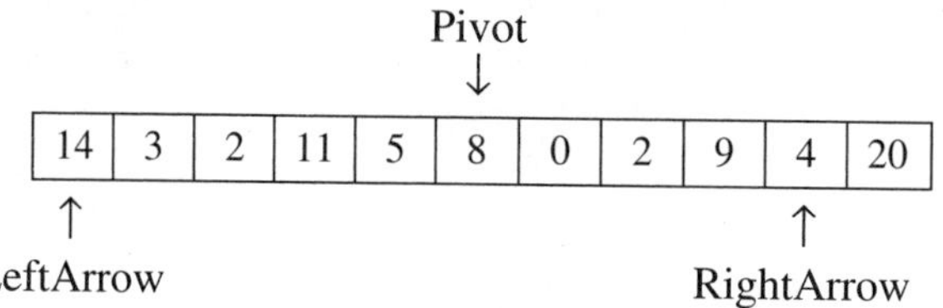

Since LeftArrow is already at a value greater than or equal to the pivot, it is not moved. The contents of the two array components are now switched to produce

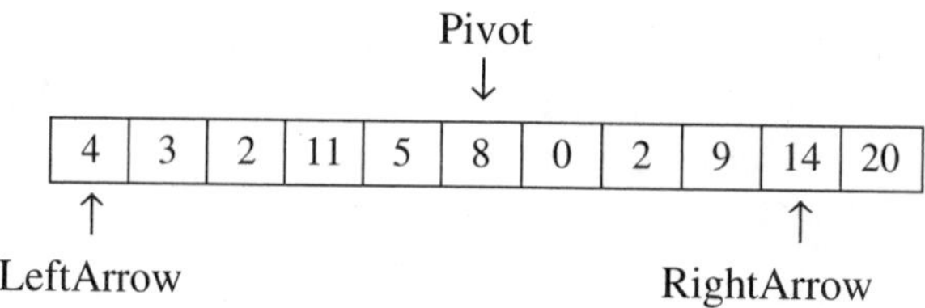

We continue by moving RightArrow left to produce

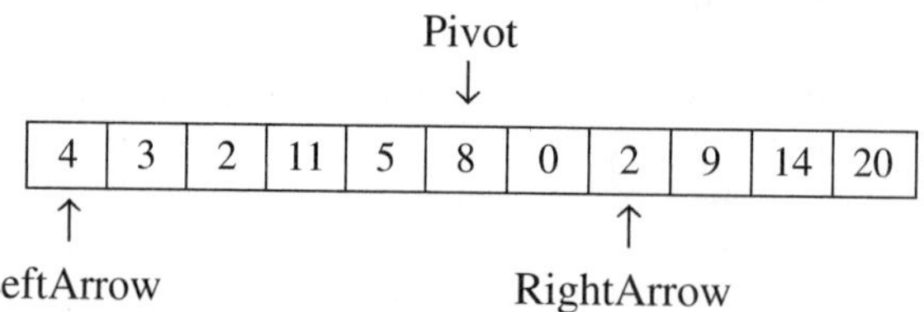

and by moving LeftArrow right to obtain

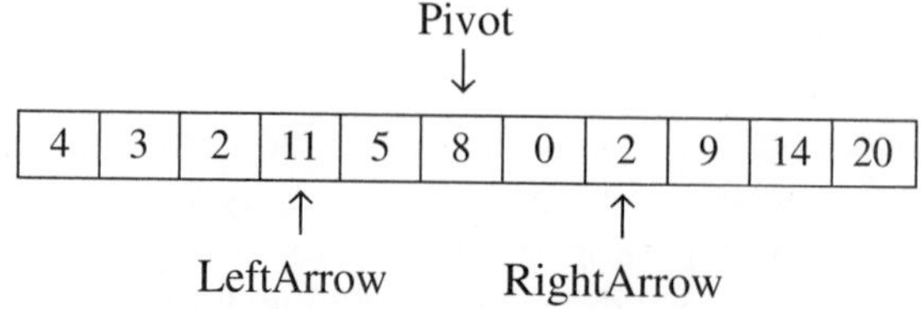

These values are exchanged to produce

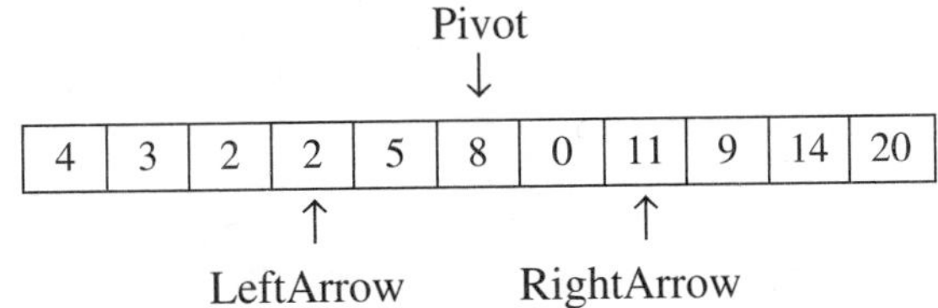

This process stops when LeftArrow > RightArrow is **true.** Since this is still **false** at this point, the next RightArrow move to the left produces

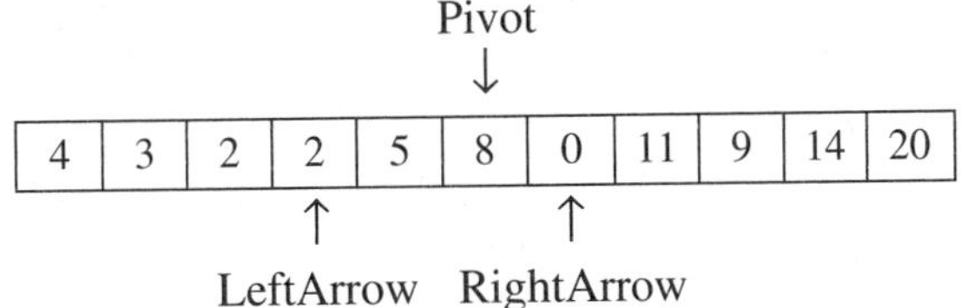

and the next LeftArrow move to the right yields

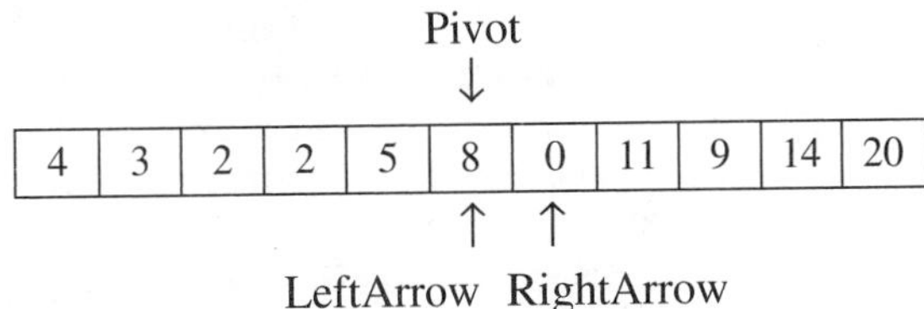

Since LeftArrow < Pivot is **false,** LeftArrow stops moving and an exchange is made to produce

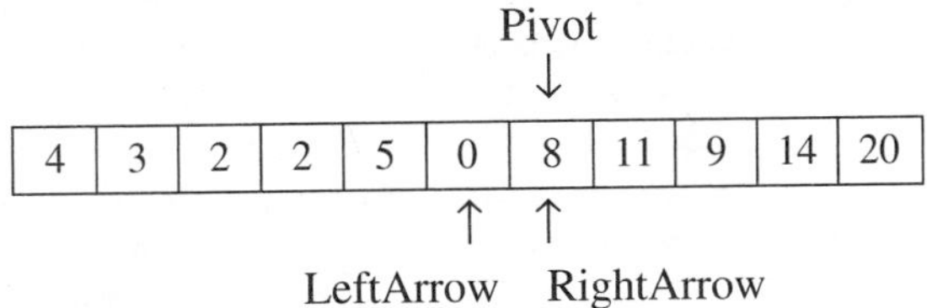

Notice that the pivot, 8, has been exchanged and now occupies a new position. This is acceptable because Pivot is the value of the component, not the index. As before, RightArrow is moved left and Left Arrow is moved right to produce

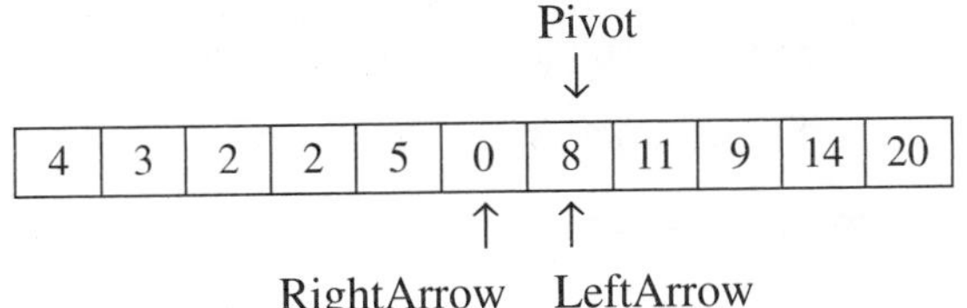

Since RightArrow < LeftArrow is **true,** the first subdivision is complete. At this stage, numbers smaller than Pivot are on the left side and numbers larger than Pivot are on the right side. This produces two sublists that can be envisioned as

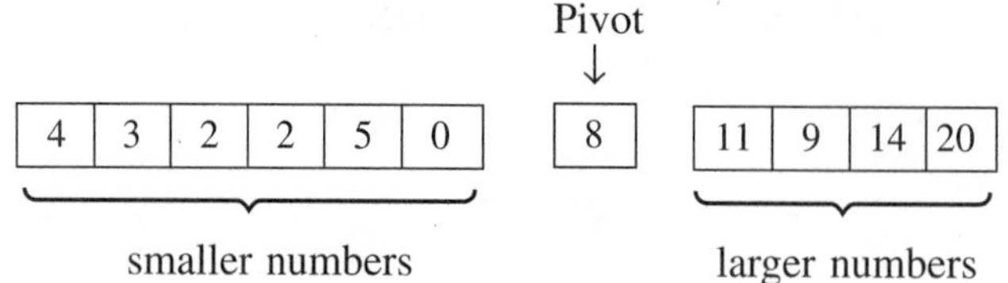

Each sublist can now be sorted by the same procedure. This requires a recursive call to the sorting procedure. In each case, the array is passed as a variable parameter together with the right and left indices for the appropriate sublist. A procedure for this sort is

```
PROCEDURE QuickSort (VAR Num : List;
                     Left, Right : integer);
  VAR
    Pivot, Temp, LeftArrow, RightArrow : integer;
  BEGIN
    LeftArrow := Left;
    RightArrow := Right;
    Pivot := Num[(Left + Right) DIV 2];
    REPEAT
      WHILE Num[RightArrow] > Pivot DO
        RightArrow := RightArrow - 1;
      WHILE Num[LeftArrow] < Pivot DO
        LeftArrow := LeftArrow + 1;
      IF LeftArrow <= RightArrow THEN
        BEGIN
          Temp := Num[LeftArrow];
          Num[LeftArrow] := Num[RightArrow];
          Num[RightArrow] := Temp;
          LeftArrow := LeftArrow + 1;
          RightArrow := RightArrow - 1
        END  {  of switching elements and then moving arrows  }
    UNTIL RightArrow < LeftArrow;
    IF Left < RightArrow THEN
      QuickSort (Num, Left, RightArrow);
    IF LeftArrow < Right THEN
      QuickSort (Num, LeftArrow, Right)
  END;  {  of PROCEDURE QuickSort  }
```

The pseudocode for a complete interactive program to illustrate the use of quick one is

1. Fill the array
2. Sort the numbers
3. Print the list

The complete program is

```
PROGRAM UseQuickSort (input, output);

{  This  program  illustrates  the  quick  sort  as  a sorting  }
{  algorithm.  The array elements are successively  subdivided  }
{  into "smaller" and "larger" elements in parts of the array.  }
{  Recursive calls are made to the PROCEDURE QuickSort.         }
```

```
CONST
  MaxLength = 30;

TYPE
  List = ARRAY [1..MaxLength] OF integer;

VAR
  Num : List;
  First, Last, Length : integer;

{*****************************************************************}

PROCEDURE FillArray (VAR Num : List;
                     VAR Length : integer);

  {  Given:   Nothing                                           }
  {  Task:    Read numbers entered from the keyboard into the   }
  {               array Num                                     }
  {  Return:  An array of numbers, Num, and number of elements  }
  {               in the array                                  }

  VAR
    Index : integer;
  BEGIN
    Index := 0;
    REPEAT
      Index := Index + 1;
      write ('Enter an integer, -999 to quit.  ');
      readln (Num[Index])
    UNTIL Num[Index] = -999;
    Length := Index - 1
  END;  {  of PROCEDURE FillArray  }

{*****************************************************************}

PROCEDURE QuickSort (VAR Num : List;
                     Left, Right : integer);

  {  Given:   An unsorted array of integers and array length    }
  {  Task:    Sort the array                                    }
  {  Return:  A sorted array of integers                        }

  VAR
    Pivot, Temp, LeftArrow, RightArrow : integer;
  BEGIN
    LeftArrow := Left;
    RightArrow := Right;
    Pivot := Num[(Left + Right) DIV 2];
    REPEAT
      WHILE Num[RightArrow] > Pivot DO
        RightArrow := RightArrow - 1;
      WHILE Num[LeftArrow] < Pivot DO
        LeftArrow := LeftArrow + 1;
      IF LeftArrow <= RightArrow THEN
```

```
        BEGIN
          Temp := Num[LeftArrow];
          Num[LeftArrow] := Num[RightArrow];
          Num[RightArrow] := Temp;
          LeftArrow := LeftArrow + 1;
          RightArrow := RightArrow - 1
        END  {  of IF...THEN  }
    UNTIL RightArrow < LeftArrow;
    IF Left < RightArrow THEN
      QuickSort (Num, Left, RightArrow);
    IF LeftArrow < Right THEN
      QuickSort (Num, LeftArrow, Right)
  END;  {  of PROCEDURE QuickSort  }

{****************************************************************}

PROCEDURE Printlist (VAR Num : List;
                     Length : integer);

  {  Given:   A sorted array of numbers and array length        }
  {  Task:    Print the numbers                                 }
  {  Return:  Nothing                                           }

  VAR
    Index : integer;
  BEGIN
    writeln;
    writeln ('The sorted list is:');
    writeln;
    FOR Index := 1 TO Length DO
      writeln (Num[Index])
  END;  {  of PROCEDURE PrintList  }

{****************************************************************}

BEGIN  {  Main program  }
  FillArray (Num, Length);
  QuickSort (Num, 1, Length);
  PrintList (Num, Length)
END.  {  of main program  }
```

A sample run of this program using the previous data produces

```
   Enter an integer, -999 to quit.  14
   Enter an integer, -999 to quit.  3
   Enter an integer, -999 to quit.  2
   Enter an integer, -999 to quit.  11
   Enter an integer, -999 to quit.  5
   Enter an integer, -999 to quit.  8
   Enter an integer, -999 to quit.  0
   Enter an integer, -999 to quit.  2
   Enter an integer, -999 to quit.  9
   Enter an integer, -999 to quit.  4
   Enter an integer, -999 to quit.  20
   Enter an integer, -999 to quit.  -999
```

```
The sorted list is:

0
2
2
3
4
5
8
9
11
14
20
```

Exercises 14.1

*1. Modify the insertion sort so that it sorts numbers from a data file rather than from an array. Explain why **PROCEDURE** InsertSort inserts the first element of the unsorted list into the first position of the sorted list.

2. The array

17
0
3
2
8

requires five exchanges of elements when sorted using a bubble sort. Since each exchange requires 3 assignment statements, there are 15 assignments for elements in the array. Sort the same array using the insertion sort and determine the number of assignments made.

*3. Modify the insertion sort by including a counter that counts the number of assignments of array elements made during a sort.

4. Using the modification in Exercise 3, sort lists of differing lengths that contain randomly generated numbers. Display the results of how many assignments were made for each sort on a graph similar to Figure 14.1. (Use lists whose lengths are multiples of 10.)

Figure 14.1
Array length

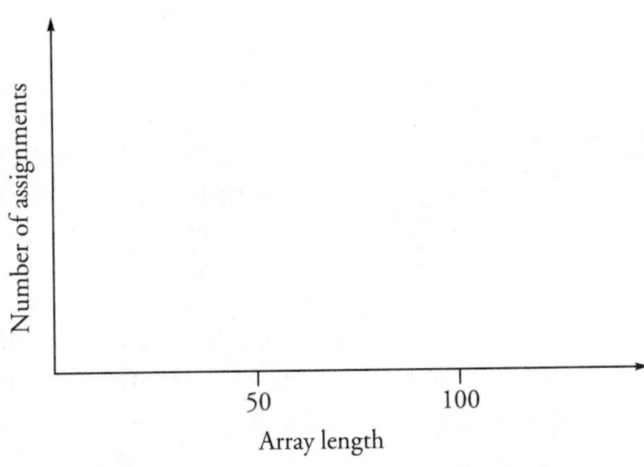

*5. Modify both the bubble sort and the selection sort (discussed in Chapter 10) to include counters for the number of assignments made during a sort.
6. Use the modified version of all three sorts to examine their relative efficiency; that is, run them on arrays of varying lengths and plot the results on a graph. What are your conclusions?
7. Write a short program to read numbers into an array, sort the array, print the sorted numbers, and save the sorted list for later use by some other program.
8. Modify all sorts to sort from high to low rather than low to high.
*9. Sorting parallel arrays is a common practice. An example of parallel arrays is an array of names and a corresponding array of scores on a test. Modify the insertion sort, bubble sort, and quick sort so that you can sort a list of names and test scores.
10. Write **PROCEDURE** Swap for the bubble sort to exchange the values of array components. Then rewrite the bubble sort using **PROCEDURE** Swap.
11. Suppose you are using a program that contains an array of records in which each record is defined by

```
TYPE
  .
  .
  .
 CustomerInfo = RECORD
                  Name : NameString;
                  AmountDue : real
                END;
```

   a. Use the bubble sort to sort and print the records alphabetically.
   b. Sort the array a second time by the field AmountDue. Anyone with an amount due of more than $100 will be designated with a triple asterisk (***).
12. Explain how an array of records with a key field Name can be sorted using a quick sort.
13. Modify **PROCEDURE** QuickSort to use the first element in an array as the pivot rather than the middle element.

14.2 Merging Algorithms

Two-Way Merge

It is often necessary to merge two sorted files or arrays to produce a single file or array. For example, you may wish to update a mailing list that has been sorted by customer name with names to be added to the list. If the names to be added are sorted alphabetically in a file, you need to merge two sorted files. One specific instance of using such a merge is given in Section 13.3, where a new file is merged with a master file to produce an updated master file. We now examine some more general versions of merging.

Objectives

- to be able to merge two sorted files
- to be able to merge two sorted arrays
- to be able to sort large files or arrays by a sort-merge
- to be able to update an existing sorted file by sorting a new file and then merging it with the existing file

A **two-way merge** is the process of merging two sorted lists.

The process of merging two sorted lists is referred to as a **two-way merge** and requires a third data structure (a file or an array). Assume we are to merge two files of integers—the previously sorted files File1 and File2—to produce the merged file FinalFile. The idea of this merge is not too difficult. Essentially, we compare elements at the top of each file and assign the higher (or the lower, if we are sorting from low to high) to FinalFile. We then compare the nonassigned element to the next element in the other file and repeat the process. We continue in this manner until the end of one file is reached and then sequentially assign all elements remaining in the other file to FinalFile.

A pseudocode development for this is

1. Open all files appropriately
2. **WHILE NOT** at end of either file **DO**
   2.1 **IF** File1 element > File2 element **THEN**
      2.1.1 Assign File1 element to FinalFile
      2.1.2 Move pointer to next element in File1
      ELSE
      2.1.3 Assign File2 element to FinalFile
      2.1.4 Move pointer to next element in File2
3. Assign remainder of File1
4. Assign remainder of File2

If we now assume File1, File2, and FinalFile are files of integers and File1 and File2 are sorted, the code for a two-way merge is

```
reset (File1);
reset (File2);
rewrite (FinalFile);
WHILE NOT eof(File1) AND NOT eof(File2) DO
  BEGIN
    IF File1^ > File2^ THEN
      BEGIN
        FinalFile^ := File1^;
        get (File1)
      END
    ELSE
      BEGIN
        FinalFile^ := File2^;
        get (File2)
      END;
    put (FinalFile)
  END;

{  Now assign the rest of the unused file. Only one
   of the following will actually be executed.  }

WHILE NOT eof(File1) DO
  BEGIN
    FinalFile^ := File1^;
    put (FinalFile);
    get (File1)
  END;
```

```
WHILE NOT eof(File2) DO
  BEGIN
    FinalFile^ := File2^;
    put (FinalFile);
    get (File2)
  END;
```

Sort-Merge

Large files or arrays present special problems when they need to be sorted. The algorithms we have studied thus far are relatively inefficient when it comes to sorting a long list. To illustrate how the inefficiency increases as lists get longer, consider a worst-case situation in which an array of components is to be sorted high to low using a bubble sort. This array is currently ordered from low to high, as illustrated:

A
1
2
3
4
5
6
7
8

This array will be sorted using (8 * 7) / 2, or 28, comparisons, which is the maximum required for an array of length 8. If the array to be sorted was of length 16, the maximum number of comparisons would be (16 * 15) / 2, or 120.

Since the number of comparisons increases so rapidly for progressively longer lists, a preferred method of sorting is to subdivide the list, sort the shorter lists, and then merge to get a single sorted list. To illustrate, let's continue the example of sorting an array with 16 elements. A bubble sort applied to the array requires at most 120 comparisons. Now, if we divide the array in half, sorting each half will require at most 28 comparisons. These two arrays can then be merged using at most 16 (8 + 8) comparisons. Thus, by subdividing, sorting, and then merging, an array of length 16 can be sorted using at most 72 comparisons rather than 120.

For longer arrays, the problem is even more critical. For example, using an array of length 1,000, a bubble sort requires (1,000 * 999) / 2, or 499,500, comparisons. If this is halved, each half sorted, and the sorted results merged, it requires at most (500 * 499) / 2 + (500 * 499) / 2 + 1,000, or 250,500, comparisons.

It is easy to see that this process of divide-and-conquer can be extended to each of the smaller arrays. To illustrate the efficiency of successively dividing lists to be sorted, suppose we originally have an array containing 1,024 items. If we subdivide until we get 128 lists of 8 items each, sort each list of 8 items, and then merge pairs of lists until we get a single sorted list, this process would require a maximum of 10,752 comparisons. A bubble sort on the original list would require a maximum of (1,024 * 1023) / 2, or 523,776, comparisons.

A **sort-merge** is the process of repeatedly subdividing a long list, sorting shorter lists, and then merging to obtain a single sorted list.

The process of repeatedly subdividing a long list, sorting shorter lists, and then merging to obtain a single sorted list is referred to as **sort-merge.** A sort-merge can be done by recursion. In this form, subdivisions are performed until each list contains one element. These single-element lists are then merged to achieve the desired result.

To illustrate this recursive sort-merge, let's write a procedure Merge to merge two parts of a global array A. The parts must be consecutive in the array and each part must already be sorted. This procedure is called by sending the index of the initial value and the index of the final value for each of the two portions that are to be merged. Our procedure merges them to form a single sorted portion of the array. Such a procedure follows:

```
PROCEDURE Merge (AInit, AFinal, BInit, BFinal : integer);
  VAR
    I, J, K, L : integer;
    NewList : ArrayType;
  BEGIN
    L := AInit;
    J := AInit;
    K := BInit;
    WHILE (J <= AFinal) AND (K <= BFinal) DO
      BEGIN
        IF A[J] < A[K] THEN
          BEGIN
            NewList[L] := A[J];
            J := J + 1
          END
        ELSE
          BEGIN
            NewList[L] := A[K];
            K := K + 1
          END;
        L := L + 1
      END;

    {  Now merge remainder of array  }
    FOR I := J TO AFinal DO
      BEGIN
        NewList[L] := A[I];
        L := L + 1
      END;
    FOR I := K TO BFinal DO
      BEGIN
        NewList[L] := A[I];
        L := L + 1
      END;
    FOR I := AInit TO BFinal DO
      A[I] := NewList[I];
```

Using this procedure, a recursive version of a sort-merge is

```
PROCEDURE SortMerge (First, Last : integer);
  VAR
    Mid : integer;
  BEGIN
    IF Last - First > 0 THEN
      BEGIN
        Mid := (First + Last) DIV 2;
        SortMerge (First, Mid);
        SortMerge (Mid + 1, Last);
        Merge (First, Mid, Mid + 1, Last)
      END
  END;  {  of PROCEDURE SortMerge  }
```

This is a relatively elegant version of a sort-merge. Unfortunately, it is not recommended for practical use. For long lists, several recursive calls to SortMerge are inefficient. A more practical method is to write a nonrecursive version and stop subdividing lists at some predetermined length. A specific example using a length of eight is left as an exercise.

Sort-Merge with Files

We close this section with a discussion of a problem encountered by programmers who work with files. Large databases (mailing lists, for example) are frequently stored in a file of records where the records are sorted according to some key field. As previously noted, this file is often referred to as the MasterFile or OldFile.

Periodically, this original file needs to be updated by adding more records. It is not unusual for these additional records to be entered into a new file (NewFile) in a random order. The problem of updating the master file is solved by sorting NewFile and merging it with the original to form a new MasterFile. This process is so standard that many programmers automatically think this is what is meant by the phrase "sort-merge." However, the phrase is not well defined and the process is also known by other names (for example, "sequential update").

Exercises 14.2

*1. Verify the worst-case possibility for sorting an array of 16 integers using a bubble sort. The array is in reverse order of the way it is to be sorted. Use a counter to count the number of comparisons.
2. Using the array in Exercise 1, sort each half with a bubble sort and then merge the two halves to get a sorted list. Use counters to count the number of comparisons made in both sorts and in the merge. Compare your results with the results from Exercise 1.
3. Write a test program to implement the two-way merge for two arrays.
4. Using **PROCEDURE** Merge in this section, write a program to implement the recursive procedure SortMerge.
5. Write a nonrecursive sort-merge to subdivide an array into subarrays of length eight, sort each subarray, and then merge the sorted subarrays to get a single sorted array.

Running and Debugging Hints

1. Sorting large files or long arrays can be very time consuming. Depending on the number of elements to be processed, use a divide-and-conquer approach; divide the list, sort the elements, and then merge them. Very large databases may require several subdivisions and subsequent merges.
2. When you use a key field to sort records, be careful to compare only the key field and then exchange the entire record accordingly.

Summary

Key Terms

bubble sort
insertion sort
quick sort
sort-merge
two-way merge

Key Concepts

- An insertion sort creates a sorted array from an unsorted array by inserting elements one at a time in their respective order.
- A bubble sort sorts an array by comparing consecutive element pairs in the array and exchanging them if they are out of order; several passes through the array are made until the list is sorted.
- A quick sort is one of the fastest sorting techniques available. It uses recursion and is based on the idea of separating a list into two parts.
- A two-way merge is used to merge two sorted lists to form a single sorted list.
- A sort-merge is a process whereby a long unsorted list is subdivided, the parts are sorted, and these are merged to form a sorted list.

Suggestions for Further Reading

Sorting and merging are subjects of numerous articles and books. This chapter provided some samples of each process. For variations and improvements on what is included here as well as other techniques, the interested reader is referred to the following books, which many consider to be classics in the field:

Baase, Sara. "Sorting." Chapter 2 in *Computer Algorithms: Introduction to Design and Analysis.* Reading, Mass.: Addison-Wesley Publishing Co., 1978.

Cormen, T. H., Leiserson, C. G., and Rivest, R. L. *Introduction to Algorithms.* New York, McGraw-Hill, 1990.

Gear, William. *Applications and Algorithms in Engineering and Science.* Chicago: Science Research Associates, 1978.

Horowitz, Ellis, and Sartaz Sahmi. "Divide and Conquer." Chapter 3 in *Fundamentals of Computer Algorithms.* Potomac, Md.: Computer Science Press, 1978.

Knuth, Donald. *The Art of Computer Programming.* Vol. 3, *Sorting and Searching.* Reading, Mass.: Addison-Wesley Publishing Co., 1975.

Sedgewick, Robert. *Algorithms.* Reading, Mass.: Addison-Wesley Publishing Co., 1988.

Chapter Review Exercises

1. Write a segment of code that performs an insertion sort to put an array of 20 real numbers into ascending order.
2. Rewrite Exercise 1 using a bubble sort.
3. Rewrite Exercise 1 using a quick sort.

For Exercises 4–6, make a data file with 1,000 unsorted integers (randomly generated would be best).

4. Read the integers into an array, sort them using a bubble sort, and print them. How long did this sort take?
5. Repeat Exercise 4 using an insertion sort.
6. Repeat Exercise 4 using a quick sort.

Programming Problems

■ 1. Write a program to update a mailing list. Assume you have a sorted master file of records where each record contains a customer's name, address, and expiration code. Your program should input a file of new customers, sort the file, and merge the file with the master file to produce a new master.

■ 2. Assume that Readmore Public Library (Problems 6 and 7, Chapter 12) has information about books on their shelves stored in a file of records named OldFile. Information about a new shipment of books is contained in the input file. Both files are sorted alphabetically by book title. Write a program to be used to update OldFile. For each book in the data file, your program should search the existing file to see if the additional book is a duplicate. If it is, change a field in the record to indicate that an additional copy has been obtained. If it is not a duplicate, insert the record in sequence in the file.

3. The Bakerville Manufacturing Company has to lay off all employees who started working after a certain date. Write a program that does the following:
   a. Inputs a termination date.
   b. Searches an alphabetical file of employee records to determine who will get a layoff notice.
   c. Creates a file of employee records for those who are being laid off.
   d. Updates the master file to contain only records of current employees.
   e. Produces two lists of those being laid off, one alphabetical and one by hiring date.

4. The Bakerville Manufacturing Company (Problem 3) has achieved new prosperity and can rehire 10 employees who were recently laid off. Write a program that does the following:
   a. Searches the file of previously terminated employees to find the 10 with the most seniority.
   b. Deletes those 10 records from the file of employees who were laid off.
   c. Inserts the 10 records alphabetically into the file of current employees.
   d. Prints an alphabetical list of current employees, a seniority list of current employees, an alphabetical list of employees who were laid off, and a seniority list of employees who were laid off.

5. The Shepherd Lions Club sponsors an annual cross-country race for area schools. Write a program that does the following:
   a. Creates an array of records for the runners; each record should contain the runner's name, school, identification number, and time (in a seven-character string, such as 15:17:3).
   b. Prints an alphabetical listing of all runners.
   c. Prints a list of schools entered in the race.
   d. Prints a list of runners in the race ordered by school name.
   e. Prints the final finish order by sorting the records according to the order of finish and printing a numbered list according to the order of finish.

Communication in Practice

1. Select a programming problem that you have not worked from the **Programming Problems** section of this chapter. Construct a structure chart and write all documentary information for this program. Include variable definition, subprogram definition, required input, and required output. When you are finished, have a classmate read your documentation to see if it is clear precisely what is to be done.
2. Remove all documentation from a program you have written for this chapter. Exchange this modified version with another student who has done the same thing. Write documentation for the exchanged program. Compare your documentation with the original program. Discuss the differences and similarities with the other students in your class.
3. Write a short paper containing descriptions of the bubble sort, the insertion sort, and the quick sort. In it, discuss the advantages and disadvantages of each sort.
4. Form a team of three or four students. The team should talk with the owner or manager of some local business that has not yet computerized its customer records to determine how the customer records are used. The team should then design an information processing system for the business. The system should include complete design specifications, with particular attention to searching and sorting. The team should then give an oral presentation to the class and use appropriate charts and diagrams to illustrate their design.

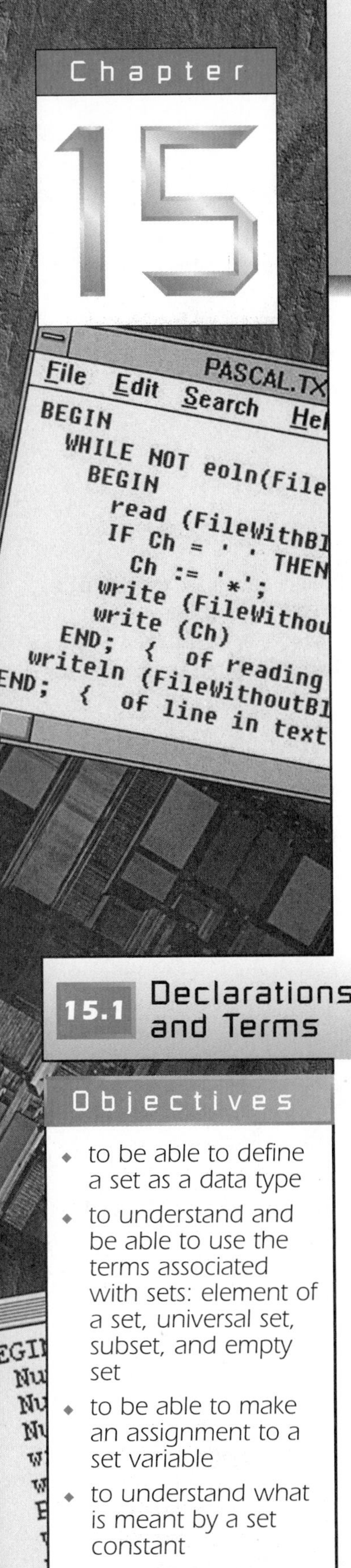
PASCAL.TX
File Edit Search He
BEGIN
WHILE NOT eoln(File
BEGIN
read (FileWithBl
IF Ch = ' ' THEN
Ch := '*';
write (FileWithou
write (Ch)
END; { of reading
writeln (FileWithoutBl
END; { of line in text
line 10

Chapter 15

Sets

Chapter Outline

Thus far we have investigated structured data types: arrays, records, and files. These data types are structured because, when each is declared, a certain structure is reserved to subsequently hold values. In an array, a predetermined number of elements that are all of the same type can be held. A record contains a predetermined number of fields that can hold elements of different types. A file is somewhat like an array but the length is not predetermined.

Another structured data type available in Pascal is a set. Since the implementation of sets varies greatly from system to system, you should check all of the statements and examples in this chapter on your system.

15.1 Declarations and Terms

Objectives

- to be able to define a set as a data type
- to understand and be able to use the terms associated with sets: element of a set, universal set, subset, and empty set
- to be able to make an assignment to a set variable
- to understand what is meant by a set constant

Basic Idea and Notation

A **set** in Pascal is a structured data type consisting of a collection of distinct elements from an indicated base type (which must be the ordinal data type). Sets in Pascal are defined and used in a manner consistent with the use of sets in mathematics. A set type is defined by

```
TYPE
  <type name> = SET OF <base type>
```

A set variable is then declared by

```
VAR
  <variable name> : <type name>
```

In a program working with characters of the alphabet, we might have

A **set** is a structured data type that consists of a collection of distinct elements from an indicated base type (which must be ordinal).

```
TYPE
  Alphabet = SET OF 'A'..'Z';
VAR
  Vowels, Consonants : Alphabet;
```

In a similar fashion, if our program analyzes digits and arithmetic symbols, we might have

```
TYPE
  Units = SET OF 0..9;
  Symbols = SET OF '*'..'/';   {  Arithmetic symbols  }
VAR
  Digits : Units;
  ArithSym : Symbols;
```

In these examples, Alphabet, Units, and Symbols are set types. Vowels, Consonants, Digits, and ArithSym are set variables.

T

A set can contain elements; these elements must be of the defined base type, which must be an ordinal data type. Most implementations of Pascal limit the maximum size of the base type of a set. This limit is such that a base type of **integer** is not allowed. Often the limit is at least 128 so base types of **char** and subranges of **integer** within 0..127 can usually be used.

Assignments to Sets

Once a set variable has been declared, it is undefined until an assignment of values is made. The syntax for assigning values is

<set name> := [<values>]

For example, we can have

```
Vowels := ['A', 'E', 'I', 'O', 'U'];
Consonants := ['B'..'D', 'F'..'H', 'J'..'N', 'P'..'T',
               'V'..'Z'];
Digits := [0..9];
ArithSym := ['+', '-', '*', '/'];
```

Notice that the assigned values must be included in brackets and must be of the defined base type. Appropriate values depend on the character set being used. Also, subranges of the base type can be used; thus,

```
Consonants := ['B'..'D'];
```

is the same as

```
Consonants := ['B', 'C', 'D'];
```

It is also possible to have set constants. Just as 4, 'H', and −56.20 are constants, [2, 4, 6] is a constant. In the previous example, this could have been caused by

```
Digits := [2, 4, 6];
```

A Note of Interest

Fractal Geometry and Benoit Mandelbrot

Fractal geometry as a serious mathematical endeavor began with the pioneering work of Benoit B. Mandelbrot, a fellow of the Thomas J. Watson Research Center, IBM Corporation. Fractal geometry is a theory of geometric forms so complex they defy analysis and classification by traditional Euclidean means. Yet fractal shapes occur universally in the natural world. Mandelbrot has recognized them not only in coastlines, landscapes, lungs, and turbulent water flow but also in the chaotic fluctuation of prices on the Chicago commodity exchange.

Although Mandelbrot's first comprehensive publication of fractal theory took place in 1975, mathematicians were aware of some of its basic elements during the period from 1875 to 1925. However, because mathematicians at that time thought such knowledge of "fractal dimension" deserved little attention, their discoveries were left as unrelated odds and ends. Also, the creation of fractal illustrations—a laborious and nearly impossible task at the turn of the twentieth century—can now be done quickly and precisely using computer graphics. (Even personal computers can now be used to generate fractal patterns with relative ease.)

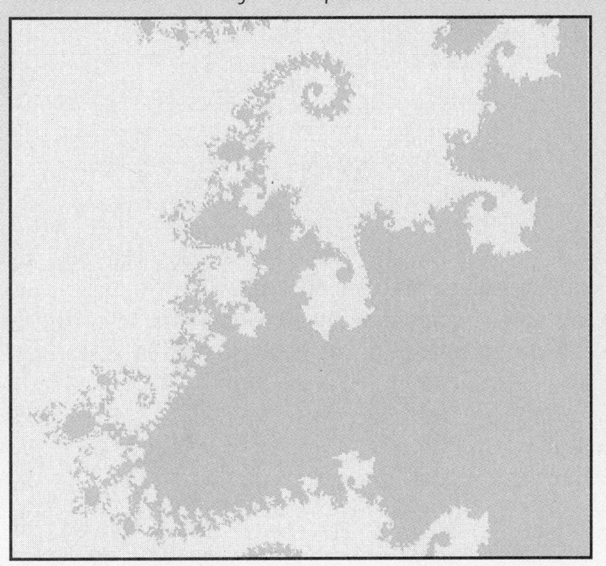

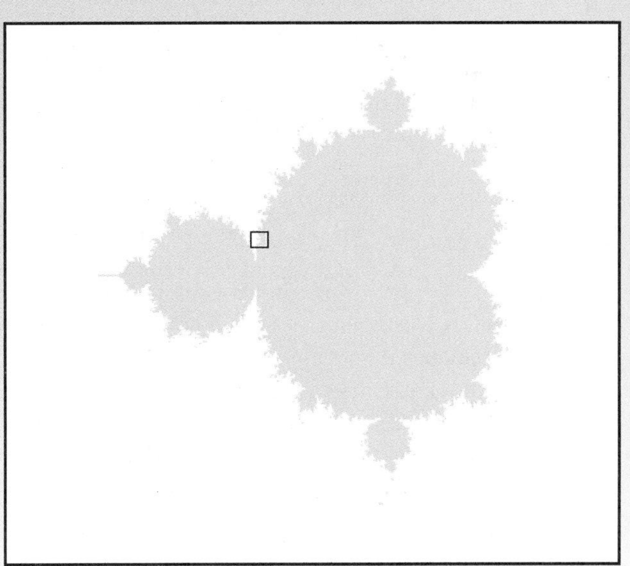

The figure on the left is an enlargement of the area of the Mandelbrot set defined by the square in the figure on the right.

Source: From For All Practical Purposes: Introduction to Contemporary Mathematics. By Consortium for Mathematics and Its Applications. Copyright © 1991 by COMAP, Inc. Reprinted by permission of W. H. Freeman and Company.

As mentioned, sets are structured data types because, in a sense, they can be thought of as containing a list of elements. However, in listing the elements, note that each element can be listed only once and order makes no difference; thus, [2, 4, 6] is the same as [4, 2, 6].

An **element of a set** is a value that has been assigned to a set.

Other Terminology

Once a value of the base type has been assigned to a set, it is an **element of the set.** Thus, if we have

```
Digits := [2, 4, 6];
```

2, 4, and 6 are elements of Digits.

A **universal set** is any set that contains all possible values of the base type.

As in mathematics, any set that contains all possible values of the base type is called the **universal set.** In

```
Digits := [0..9];
```

Digits is a universal set. It is also possible to consider a set constant as a universal set. Thus, ['A' .. 'Z'] is a universal set if the **TYPE** definition section contains

```
<type name> = SET OF 'A'..'Z';
```

Set A is a **subset** of set B if all the elements in A are also in B.

If A and B have been declared as sets of the same type and all of the elements of A are also contained in B, A is a **subset** of B. If we have

```
VAR
  A, B : Units;
```

and the assignments

```
A := [1, 2, 3, 4, 5];
B := [0..6];
```

have been made, A is a subset of B. Note, however, that B is not a subset of A since B contains two elements (0 and 6) that are not contained in A.

The **empty set** is a set that contains no elements. Also called a **null set.**

The **empty set,** or **null set,** is the set containing no elements. It is denoted by [ ].

These definitions permit set theory results of mathematics to hold in Pascal. Some of these follow:

1. The empty set is a subset of every set.
2. If A is a subset of B and B is a subset of C, then A is a subset of C.
3. Every set (of the base type) is a subset of the universal set.

Exercises 15.1

For Exercises 1–5, find all errors in the definitions and declarations. Explain your answers.

*1.
```
TYPE
  Numbers = SET OF real;
```

2.
```
TYPE
  Numbers = SET OF integer;
```

*3.
```
Type
  Alphabet : SET OF 'A'..'Z';
```

4.
```
TYPE
  Alphabet = SET OF ['A'..'Z'];
```

*5.
```
TYPE
  Conditions = (Sunny, Mild, Rainy, Windy);
  Weather = SET OF Conditions;
VAR
  TodaysWeather : Weather;
```

For Exercises 6 and 7, write test programs.

6. Discover if **char** is a permissible base type for a set.
7. Determine the limitation on the size of the base type for a set.
8. Suppose a set A is declared by

```
TYPE
  Letters = SET OF 'A'..'Z';
VAR
  A : Letters;
```

   a. Show how A can be made to contain the letters of your name.
   b. Assign the letters of the word *PASCAL* to A.
   c. Assuming the assignment

```
A := ['T', 'O', 'Y'];
```

   list all elements and subsets of A.

For Exercises 9–15, let the sets A, B, and U be declared by

```
TYPE
  Alphabet = SET OF 'A'..'Z';
VAR
  A, B, U : Alphabet;
```

and the assignments

```
A := ['B', 'F', 'J'..'T'];
B := ['O'..'S'];
U := ['A'..'Z'];
```

be made. Indicate if each statement is **true** or **false.**

*9. [ ] is a subset of B.
10. B is an element of A.
*11. B is a subset of A.
12. 'B' is an element of A.
*13. 'B' is a subset of A.
14. A is a subset of U.
*15. 'O' is an element of A.

For Exercises 16–21, assume A, B, and U are declared as in Exercises 9–15. Find and explain all errors in the assignment statement.

16. `A := 'J'..'O';`
*17. `U := [];`
18. `B := [A..Z];`
*19. `A := ['E', 'I', 'E', 'I', 'O'];`
20. `[] := ['D'];`
*21. `B := ['A'..'T', 'S'];`

For Exercises 22–25, let A be a set declared by

```
TYPE
  NumRange = 0..100;
VAR
  A : SET OF NumRange;
  M, N : integer;
```

Indicate if each statement is valid or invalid. If valid, list the elements of A. If invalid, explain why.

22. `A := [19];`

*23. `A := 19;`

24.
```
M := 80;
N := 40;
A := [M + N, M MOD N, M DIV N];
```

*25.
```
M := 10;
N := 2;
A := [M, M * N, M / N];
```

For Exercises 26–29, define a set type and declare a set variable to be used.

26. Set values consist of class in school (Freshman, Sophomore, Junior, or Senior).

*27. Set values consist of colors of the rainbow.

28. Set values consist of grades for a class.

*29. Set values consist of fruits.

30. Explain why **SET** is not an enumerated data type.

15.2 Set Operations and Relational Operators

Objectives

- to understand the set operations union, intersection, and difference
- to be able to use sets with relational operators

Set Operations

Pascal provides for the set operations union, intersection, and difference where, in each case, two sets are combined to produce a single set. If A and B are sets of the same type, these operations are defined as follows:

- The **union** of A and B is A + B, where A + B contains any element that is in A or that is in B.
- The **intersection** of A and B is A * B, where A * B contains the elements that are in both A and B.
- The **difference** of A and B is A – B, where A – B contains the elements that are in A but not in B.

The **union** of set A and set B is A + B, where A + B contains any element that is in A or that is in B.

The **intersection** of set A and set B is A * B, where A * B contains the elements that are in both A and B.

The **difference** of set A and set B is A – B, where A – B contains the elements that are in A but not in B.

To illustrate, suppose A and B are sets that contain integer values and the assignment statements

```
A := [1..5];
B := [3..9];
```

are made. The values produced by set operations follow:

Set Operation	Values
A + B	[1..9]
A * B	[3,4,5]
A - B	[1,2]

Multiple operations can be performed with sets. When such an expression is encountered, the same operator priority prevails that exists when arithmetic expressions are evaluated. Thus, if A and B contain the values indicated, then

```
A + B - A * B
```

produces

```
[1..5] + [3..9]   -   [1..5] * [3..9]
                             ↓
[1..5] + [3..9]   -      [3, 4, 5]
       ↓
    [1..9]        -      [3, 4, 5]
                  ↓
         [1, 2, 6..9]
```

Relational Operators

Relational operators can also be used with sets in Pascal. These operators correspond to the normal set operators equal, not equal, subset, and superset. In each case, a Boolean value is produced. If A and B are sets, these operators are defined as shown in Table 15.1.

Table 15.1

Set operations

Operator	Relational Expression	Definition
= (Equal)	**A = B**	A is equal to B; that is, every element in A is contained in B and every element in B is contained in A.
<> (Not equal)	**A <> B**	A does not equal B; that is, either A or B contains an element that is not contained in the other set.
<= (Subset)	**A <= B**	A is a subset of B; that is, every element of A is also contained in B.
>= (Superset)	**A >= B**	A is a superset of B (B is a subset of A); that is, every element of B is contained in A.

Boolean values associated with some set expressions follow:

Set Expression	Boolean Value
[1, 2, 3] <= [0..10]	**true**
[0..10] <= [1, 2, 3]	**false**
[0..10] = [0..5, 6..10]	**true**
[] = ([1, 2] - [0..10])	**true**
[1..5] <> [1..3, 4, 5]	**false**
[] <= [1, 2, 3]	**true**

Set Membership

Membership in a set is indicated in Pascal by the reserved word **IN.** The general form is

<element> **IN** <set>

where <element> and <set> are type compatible. This returns a value of **true** if the element is in the set and a value of **false** if it is not. To illustrate, suppose A and B are sets and the assignments

```
A := [0..20];
B := [5..10];
```

are made. The values of expressions using **IN** follow:

Expression	Boolean Value
`10 IN A`	**true**
`5 IN (A - B)`	**false**
`20 IN B`	**false**
`7 IN (A * B)`	**true**
`80 DIV 20 IN A * B`	**?**

Note that the last expression cannot be evaluated until priorities are assigned to the operators. Fortunately, these priorities are identical to those for arithmetic expressions; IN is on the same level as relational operators as shown in Table 15.2.

▼ Table 15.2

Operator priorities (including set operations)

Priority Level	Operators
1	()
2	**NOT**
3	*, /, **MOD, DIV, AND**
4	+, −, **OR**
5	<, >, <=, >=, =, <>, **IN**

Operations at each level are performed in order from left to right as they appear in an expression. Thus, the expression

```
80 DIV 20 IN A * B
```

produces

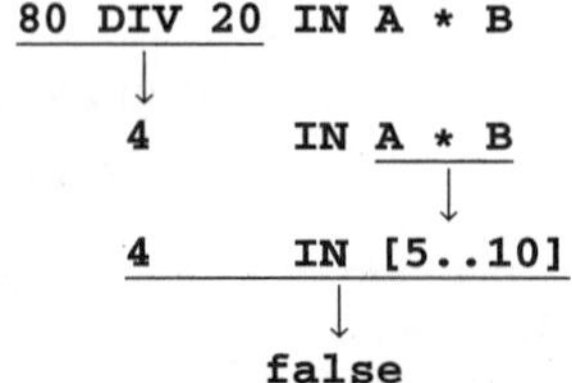

Exercises 15.2

*1. When using sets in Pascal, is >= the logical complement of <=? Give an example to illustrate your answer.

2. Let A and B be sets defined so that A := [0. .10] and B := [2, 4, 6, 8, 10] are valid. Write a test program to show that
   a. A + B = A
   b. A * B = B
   c. A – B = [0, 1, 3, 5, 7, 9]

In Exercises 3–6, find A + B, A * B, A – B, and B – A.

*3. `A := [-3..2, 8, 10], B := [0..4, 7..10];`
4. `A := [0, 1, 5..10, 20], B := [2, 4, 6, 7..11];`
*5. `A := [], B := [1..15];`
6. `A := [0..5, 10, 14..20], B := [3, 10, 15];`

For Exercises 7–14, given the following sets

```
A := [0, 2, 4, 6, 8, 10];
B := [1, 3, 5, 7, 9];
C := [0..5];
```

indicate the values in each set.

*7. `A * B - C`
8. `A * (B - C)`
*9. `A * (B + C)`
10. `A * B + A * C`
*11. `A - B * C`
12. `A - (B - (A - B))`
*13. `A * (B * C)`
14. `(A * B) * C`

For Exercises 15–20, using sets A, B, and C with values assigned as in Exercises 7–14, indicate whether the statement is **true** or **false.**

*15. `A * B = []`
16. `C <= A + B`
*17. `[5] <= B`
18. `A + B <> C`
*19. `A - B >= []`
20. `(A + B = C) OR ([] <= B - C)`

In mathematics, when X is an element of a set A, this is denoted by $X \in A$. If X is not in A, we write $X \notin A$. For Exercises 21–26, let B be a set declared by

```
VAR
  B : SET OF 0..10;
```

Examine the statements for validity and decide how Pascal handles the concept of not-an-element-of.

*21. `4 NOT IN B`
22. `4 NOT (IN B)`
*23. `NOT 4 IN B`
24. `NOT (4 IN B)`
*25. `4 IN NOT B`
26. `4 IN (NOT B)`

27. Write a short program to count the number of uppercase vowels in a text file. Your program should include the set type

```
TYPE
  AlphaUppercase = SET OF 'A'..'Z';
```

and set variable VowelsUppercase declared by

```
VAR
  VowelsUppercase : AlphaUppercase;
```

15.3 Using Sets

Objectives

- to understand how sets can be used in a program
- to be able to use sets in a program
- to understand the limitations of using sets with functions
- to be able to use sets with procedures

Uses of Sets

Now that we know how to declare sets, assign values to sets, and operate with sets, we need to examine some uses of sets in programs. First, however, we should note an important limitation of sets: As with other structured variables, sets cannot be read or written directly. However, the two processes—generating a set and printing the elements of a set—are not difficult to code. To illustrate how a set is generated, suppose we wish to create a set and have it contain all the characters in the alphabet in a line of text. (For this example we assume that the text file does not contain lowercase letters.) We can declare this set with

```
TYPE
  AlphaSymbols = 'A'..'Z';
  Symbols = SET OF AlphaSymbols;
VAR
  Alphabet : Symbols;
  SentenceChar : Symbols;
  Ch : char;
```

Code to generate the set SentenceChar is

```
Alphabet := ['A'..'Z'];
SentenceChar := [];
WHILE NOT eoln(Data) DO
  BEGIN
    read (Data, Ch);
    IF Ch IN Alphabet THEN
      SentenceChar := SentenceChar + [Ch]
  END;
```

In many examples, we assume the text file does not contain lowercase letters. As you will see in the **Focus on Program Design: Case Study,** a slight modification can be made to accommodate both uppercase and lowercase letters. For example, we could use both uppercase and lowercase letters by changing the set definitions to

```
TYPE
  Symbols = SET OF char;
VAR
  UppercaseAlphabet : Symbols;
  LowercaseAlphabet : Symbols;
  Alphabet: Symbols;
```

Alphabet could then be formed in the program by

```
UppercaseAlphabet := ['A'..'Z'];
LowercaseAlphabet := ['a'..'z'];
Alphabet := UppercaseAlphabet + LowercaseAlphabet;
```

or

```
Alphabet := ['A'..'Z', 'a'..'z']
```

The general procedure of getting values into a set is to initialize the set by assigning the empty set and use set union to add elements to the set.

The process of printing values of elements in a set is equally short. Assuming we know the data type of elements in the set, a loop can be used where the loop control

Communication and Style Tips

Sets with appropriate names are particularly useful for checking data. For example, a typical problem when working with dynamic variables (which are discussed in Chapter 17) is to examine an arithmetic expression for correct form. Thus, 3 + 4 is a valid expression but 3 + * 4 is not. As part of a program that analyzes such expressions, you might choose to define the following sets.

```
TYPE
  ValidDigits = SET OF '0'..'9';
  Symbols = SET OF char;
VAR
  Digits : ValidDigits;
  ValidOperator : Symbols;
  LeftSymbol, RightSymbol : Symbols;
```

These sets can now be assigned values such as

```
Digits := ['0'..'9'];
ValidOperator := ['+', '*', '-', '/'];
LeftSymbol := ['(', '[', '{'];
RightSymbol := [')', ']', '}'];
```

variable ranges over values of this data type. Whenever a value is in the set, it is printed. To illustrate, assume the set SentenceChar now contains some alphabetical characters we wish to print. Since we know the data type of the elements in SentenceChar is characters in 'A'..'Z', we can print the contained values by

```
FOR Ch := 'A' TO 'Z' DO
  IF Ch IN SentenceChar THEN
    write (Ch:2);
writeln;
```

This fragment of code produces the output

```
A B C D E H I K L M N O P S T U V Y
```

when the set SentenceChar is formed from the line of text

```
THIS LINE (OBVIOUSLY MADE UP!) DOESN'T MAKE MUCH SENSE.
```

Now that you are familiar with how to generate elements in a set and subsequently print contents of a set, let's examine some uses for sets in programs. Specifically, let's look at using sets to replace complex Boolean expressions, to protect a program against bad data, to protect against invalid **CASE** statements, and to aid in interactive programming.

Suppose we are writing a program to analyze responses to questions on a standard machine-scored form. If we want a certain action to take place for every response of A, B, or C, instead of

```
IF (Response='A') OR (Response='B') OR (Response='C') THEN
```

we can use

```
IF Response IN ['A', 'B', 'C'] THEN
      .
      .
      .
```

To demonstrate protecting a program against bad data, suppose we are writing a program to use a relatively large data file. Further, suppose the data are entered by operators in such a fashion that the first entry on the first line for each customer is a single-digit code followed by appropriate data for the customer. To make sure the code is entered properly, we can define a set ValidSym and assign it all appropriate symbols. Our program design can be

```
read (Data, Sym);
IF Sym IN ValidSym THEN
  BEGIN
    .
    .  (action here)
    .
  END
ELSE
  (error message here)
```

Specifically, a program for printing mailing labels might require a 3, 4, or 5 to indicate the number of lines for the name and address that follow. If we are writing a program that also partially edits the data file, we can have

```
read (Data, NumLines);
IF NumLines IN [3, 4, 5] THEN
  BEGIN
    .
    .  (process number of lines)
    .
  END
ELSE
  (error message here)
```

The third use of sets is to protect against invalid **CASE** statements. To illustrate, suppose we are working with a program that uses a **CASE** statement and the selector is a letter grade assigned to students. Without sets, the statement is

```
CASE LetGrade OF
  'A' : ...
  'B' : ...
  'C' : ...
  'D' : ...
  'F' : ...
END;  {  of CASE LetGrade  }
```

To protect against the possibility of assigning a value to LetGrade that is not in the **CASE** selector list, sets can be used as follows:

A Note of Interest

Object-Oriented Programming—Part 2

Object-oriented development is becoming increasingly important as a method to manage large and complex software systems. Object-oriented concepts are natural extensions of proper structured programming. If structured programming principles have been emphasized, the basic object-oriented idea of encapsulation logically follows.

Components of object-oriented programs are

"Object." The object in object-oriented programming includes the basic data or data structure and the related procedures and functions required to keep the object complete. This makes the object like an abstract data type.

"Method." A method is a procedure or function that becomes part of the object. It provides the abstraction to the object's data.

"Encapsulation." The combining of data structure and methods is called encapsulation. If encapsulation is performed correctly, the user of the object should never need to access the data of the object directly. Procedure and function headers are added to type definitions to describe encapsulation of the methods. The type definitions become the interface to the unit.

The idea of a data structure being linked to its procedures has been standard practice in creating abstract data types for years and is not a new concept created by object-oriented languages. What is new and exciting is what can now be done with the object. Other objects can inherit those same procedures and functions, and those same procedures and functions can easily be altered, if the need arises, without having to rewrite the whole unit. In fact, in order to create new objects, the programmer only needs to use the unit to create new methods and data items or to rename the existing methods.

```
IF LetGrade IN ['A'..'D,' 'F'] THEN
  CASE LetGrade OF
    'A' : ...
    'B' : ...
    'C' : ...
    'D' : ...
    'F' : ...
  END  {  of CASE LetGrade  }
ELSE
  (error message here)
```

A fourth use of sets is as an aid in writing interactive programs. Frequently a user will be asked to respond by pressing a certain key or keys. For example, a message such as the following may be given:

```
Do you wish to continue?
<Y> or <N> and press <Enter>.
```

In such cases, two problems can occur. First, the user might use uppercase or lowercase letters for a correct response. Second, the user might inadvertently strike the wrong key. To make this part of the program correct and guard against bad data, we can have a set declared and initialized as

```
GoodResponse := ['Y', 'y', 'N', 'n'];
```

and then use a **REPEAT . . . UNTIL** loop as follows:

```
REPEAT
  writeln ('Do you wish to continue?');
  writeln ('<Y> or <N> and press <Enter>.');
  readln (Response)
UNTIL Response IN GoodResponse;
```

We can then use a **boolean** variable Continue by first assigning it a value **false** and then follow the **REPEAT . . . UNTIL** loop with

```
Continue := Response IN ['Y', 'y'];
```

Sets with Functions

Sets can be used with subprograms. In general, set types can be used as parameters in much the same way that arrays, records, and files are used. However, when working with functions, sets cannot be returned as values of a function because functions cannot return structured types.

To illustrate using sets with functions, let's consider two examples.

Example 15.1

Let's write a function to determine the cardinality (size, or number of elements) of a set. Assuming appropriate **TYPE** definitions, such a function can be

```
FUNCTION Cardinality (S : <set type>) : integer;
  VAR
    Count : integer;
    X : <base type for set>;
  BEGIN
    Count := 0;
    FOR X := <initial value> TO <final value> DO
      IF X IN S THEN
        Count := Count + 1;
    Cardinality := Count
  END;
```

Initial value . . . Final value

If given X in set S, increase cardinality counter

S

This is called from the main program by

```
SetSize := Cardinality (<set name>);
```

Example 15.2

In our second example, let's consider a function to find the maximum (largest ordinal) element of a set. This function is typically applied to a set that contains elements in some subrange of the integers. If not, however, you can easily modify the function by considering the ordinals of set elements.

```
FUNCTION MaxElement (S : <set type>) : <base type>;
  VAR
    Temp : <base type>;
    X : <base type>;
  BEGIN
    IF S = [] THEN
      writeln ('You are working with an empty set!':40)
    ELSE
      BEGIN
        Temp := <initial value>;
        FOR X := <initial value> TO <final value> DO
          IF (X IN S) AND (X > Temp) THEN
            Temp := X;
          MaxElement := Temp
      END  {  of ELSE option  }
  END;  {  of FUNCTION MaxElement  }
```

Initial value
. . .
Final value
Any new value of X that is also in S causes Temp to be adjusted
S

This is called from the main program by

```
Largest := MaxElement (<set name>);
```

Sets with Procedures

Recall that sets cannot be returned as values of a function. However, when a program requires a set to be returned from a subprogram, the set can be used as a variable parameter with a procedure. In this manner, sets can be either generated or modified with subprograms. The **Focus on Program Design: Case Study** at the end of this chapter illustrates such a use.

Exercises 15.3

1. Modify the function MaxElement used in Example 15.2 to find the character in a line of text that is latest in the alphabet. Use this function with the **Focus on Program Design: Case Study** code presented at the end of this chapter.
2. Write a test program to create a set containing all the consonants from a line of text. Your program should also print all elements in the set.
*3. Write a short program to reproduce a text file where every vowel is replaced by an asterisk.
4. Modify the code used to find all the alphabet characters in a line of text so that a complete text file can be analyzed rather than just one line.
5. Write a program to simulate arithmetic indicated in a text file. The arithmetic expression should always be of the form digit-symbol-digit (9 + 8), where all digits and symbols are given as data of type **char.** Your program

should protect against bad operation symbols, bad digits (actually non-digits), and division by zero.

6. To illustrate how sets can be used to protect against invalid values for **CASE** selectors, write a short program that uses a **CASE** statement. Run it with an invalid **CASE** selector value. Change the program so the **CASE** statement is protected by using a set. Rerun the program with the same invalid selector.

*7. Write a Boolean function to analyze an integer between −9,999 and 9,999 and return the value **true** if the integer contains only odd digits (1,731) and **false** otherwise.

8. Write a function that returns the length of a string passed to the function as a packed array. Punctuation marks and internal blanks should add to the string length. Blanks at the beginning or end should not.

Focus on Program Design: Case Study

Text Analyzer

The sample program for this chapter illustrates a use of sets. In particular, a set is used as a variable parameter in a procedure. The specific problem is to write a program to determine the alphabetical characters used in a line of text. Output from the program is an echo print of the text line, a list of letters in the text, and the number of distinct letters used in the line.

A first-level pseudocode development for this problem is

1. Get the characters
2. Print the characters
3. Determine the cardinality of the set
4. Print a closing message

A structure chart for this program is given in Figure 15.1.

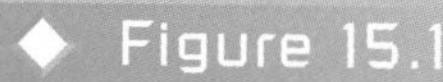

◆ Figure 15.1

Structure chart for **PROGRAM** SymbolCheck

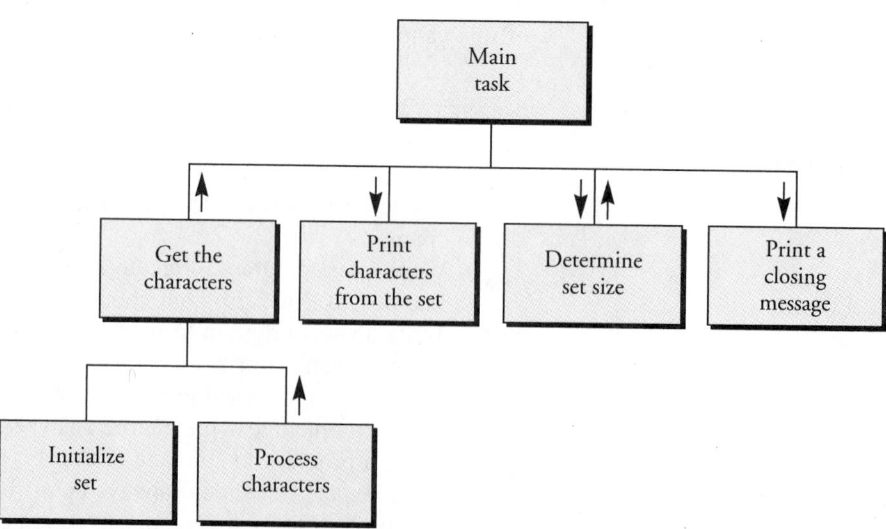

Module specifications for the main modules are

1. GetLetters Module
   Data received: None
   Information returned: A set of letters from a sentence
   Logic: Initialize the set.
   Add (union) distinct letters from a line of text.
2. PrintSet Module
   Data received: A set of letters
   Information returned: None
   Logic: Use a **FOR** loop to scan the alphabet and print the letters contained in the set.
3. Cardinality Module
   Data received: A set of letters
   Information returned: The cardinality of the set
   Logic: Use a function to count the number of distinct elements in a set.
4. PrintMessage Module
   Data received: Cardinality of the set
   Information returned: None
   Logic: Print a message indicating the set size.

A refinement of the pseudocode produces

1. Get the characters
   1.1 Initialize set
   1.2 **WHILE NOT eoln DO**
       1.2.1 Process a character
2. Print the characters
   2.1 **FOR** Ch := 'A' **TO** 'z' **DO**
       IF Ch is in the set **THEN**
           print Ch
3. Determine the cardinality of the set
   3.1 Initialize counter to 0
   3.2 **FOR** Ch := 'A' **TO** 'z' **DO**
       IF Ch is in the set **THEN**
           Increment counter
   3.3 Assign count to function name
4. Print a closing message

Step 1.2.1 could be refined to

1.2.1 Process a character
   1.2.1.1 Read a character
   1.2.1.2 Write a character (echo print)
   1.2.1.3 **IF** character is in the alphabet **THEN**
       Add it to the set of characters

The main program is

```
BEGIN  {  Main program  }
  reset (Data);
  GetLetters (SentenceChar);
  PrintSet (SentenceChar);
  SetSize := Cardinality(SentenceChar);
  PrintMessage (SetSize)
END.  {  of main program  }
```

A complete program for this is

```
PROGRAM SymbolCheck (input, output, Data);

{  This program illustrates working with sets.  It reads a line }
{  of  text and  determines the  number of  distinct letters in }
{  that line.  Output  includes  the  distinct letters  and the }
{  set cardinality.  Information for this program is stored in  }
{  the text file Data.                                          }

CONST
  Skip = ' ';

TYPE
  AlphaSymbols = SET OF 'A'..'z';

VAR
  SentenceChar : AlphaSymbols;       {  Set of possible letters  }
  SetSize : integer;                 {  Cardinality of the set   }
  Data : text;                       {  Data file                }

{*************************************************************}

PROCEDURE GetLetters (VAR SentenceChar : AlphaSymbols);

  {  Given:   Nothing                                          }
  {  Task:    Read characters from the text file Data; echo    }
  {               print them; store the alphabetical           }
  {               characters in a set                          }
  {  Return:  The set of letters contained in the line of      }
  {               text                                         }

  VAR
    Ch : char;
    Alphabet : AlphaSymbols;
  BEGIN
    reset (Data);                                              1
    SentenceChar := [];
    Alphabet := ['A'..'Z'] + ['a'..'z'];
    writeln (Skip:10, 'The line of text is below:');
    writeln; write (Skip:10);
    WHILE NOT eoln(Data) DO
      BEGIN
        read (Data, Ch);
        write (Ch);                               {  echo print  }
        IF Ch IN Alphabet THEN
          SentenceChar := SentenceChar + [Ch]
      END;  {  of WHILE NOT eoln(Data)  }       {  of one line  }
    writeln
  END;  {  of PROCEDURE GetLetters  }

{*************************************************************}
```

```
PROCEDURE PrintSet (SentenceChar : AlphaSymbols);

  {  Given:    A set of characters                                    }
  {  Task:     Print all characters in the set                        }
  {  Return:   Nothing                                                }

  VAR
    Ch : char;
  BEGIN                                                                  2
    writeln;
    writeln (Skip:10, 'The letters in this line are:');
    writeln; write (Skip:10);
    FOR Ch := 'A' TO 'z' DO
      IF Ch IN SentenceChar THEN
        write (Ch:2);
    writeln
  END;  {  of PROCEDURE PrintSet  }

{*************************************************************}

FUNCTION Cardinality (SentenceChar : AlphaSymbols) : integer;

  {  Given:    A set of characters                                    }
  {  Task:     Determine the number of characters in the set          }
  {  Return:   The set size (cardinality)                             }

  VAR
    Count : integer;
    X : char;                                                            3
  BEGIN
    Count := 0;
    FOR X := 'A' TO 'z' DO
      IF X IN SentenceChar THEN
        Count := Count + 1;
    Cardinality := Count
  END;  {  of FUNCTION Cardinality  }

{*************************************************************}

PROCEDURE PrintMessage (SetSize : integer);

  {  Given:    The cardinality of the set                             }
  {  Task:     Print a closing message                                }
  {  Return:   Nothing                                                }  4

  BEGIN
    writeln; write (Skip:10);
    writeln ('There are', SetSize:5, ' letters in this sentence.')
  END;  {  of PROCEDURE PrintMessage  }

{*************************************************************}

BEGIN  {  Main program  }
  reset (Data);
```

```
  GetLetters (SentenceChar);
  PrintSet (SentenceChar);
  SetSize := Cardinality(SentenceChar);
  PrintMessage (SetSize)
END.  {  of main program  }
```

When this program is run on the line of text

```
The numbers -2, 5, 20 and symbols '?', ':' should be ignored.
```

the output is

```
The line of text is below:

The numbers -2, 5, 20 and symbols '?', ':' should be ignored.

The letters in this line are:

 T a b d e g h i l m n o r s u y

There are   16 letters in this sentence.
```

Running and Debugging Hints

1. When defining a set type, do not use brackets in the definition; thus, the following is incorrect:

```
TYPE
  Alphabet = SET OF ['A'..'Z'];
```

   The correct form is

```
TYPE
  Alphabet = SET OF 'A'..'Z';
```

2. Remember to initialize a set before using it in the program. Declaring a set does not give it a value. If your declaration is

```
VAR
  Vowels : Alphabet;
```

   the program should contain

```
Vowels := ['A', 'E', 'I', 'O', 'U'];
```

3. Attempting to add an element to a set rather than a set to a set is a common error. If you wish to add 'D' to the set ['A', 'B', 'C'], you should write

(continued)

```
['A', 'B', 'C'] + ['D']
```

rather than

```
['A', 'B', 'C'] + 'D'
```

This is especially important when the value of a variable is to be added to a set.

```
['A', 'B', 'C'] + Ch;
```

should be

```
['A', 'B', 'C'] + [Ch];
```

4. Avoid confusing arrays and array notation with sets and set notation.
5. Remember certain operators (+, –, and *) have different meanings when used with sets.

Summary

Key Terms

difference
element of a set
empty (null) set
intersection
set
subset
union
universal set

Keywords

IN
SET

Key Concepts

- In Pascal, **SET** is a structured data type that consists of distinct elements from an indicated base type; sets can be declared by

```
TYPE
  Alphabet = SET OF char;
VAR
  Vowels : Alphabet;
  GoodResponse : Alphabet;
```

  In this definition and declaration, Alphabet is a **SET** type and Vowels and GoodResponse are set variables.

- Values must be assigned to a set; thus, we could have

```
Vowels := ['A', 'E', 'I', 'O', 'U'];
GoodResponse := ['Y', 'y', 'N', 'n'];
```

- When listing elements in a set, order makes no difference and each element may be listed only once.
- Standard set operations in Pascal are defined to be consistent with set operations of mathematics; to illustrate, if

```
A := [1, 2, 3, 4];
```

and

```
B := [3, 4, 5];
```

the union, intersection, and difference of these sets are as follows:

Term	Expression	Value
Union	`A + B`	`[1..5]`
Intersection	`A * B`	`[3, 4]`
Difference	`A - B`	`[1, 2]`
	`B - A`	`[5]`

- Set membership is denoted by using the reserved word **IN.** Such an expression returns a Boolean value; thus, if

```
A := [1, 2, 3, 4];
```

we have

Expression	Value
`2 IN A`	**true**
`6 IN A`	**false**

- The relational operators (<=, >=, <>, and =) can be used with sets forming Boolean expressions and returning values consistent with expected subset and set equality relationships; to illustrate, if

```
A := [1, 2, 3];
B := [0..5];
C := [2, 4];
```

we have

Expression	Value
`A <= B`	**true**
`B <= C`	**false**
`B >= C`	**true**
`A = B`	**false**
`B <> C`	**true**

- Priority levels for set operations are consistent with those used for arithmetic expressions; they are

Priority Level	Operation
1	()
2	**NOT**
3	*, /, **MOD, DIV, AND**
4	+, −, **OR**
5	<, >, <=, >=, <>, =, **IN**

- Sets cannot be used with **read** or **write;** however, you can generate a set by initializing the set, assigning the empty set, and using set union to add elements to the set. For example, a set of characters in a text line can be generated by

```
S := [];
WHILE NOT eoln(Data) DO
  BEGIN
    read (Data, Ch);
    S := S + [Ch]
  END;
```

  This set can be printed by this code:

```
FOR Ch := <initial value> TO <final value> DO
  IF Ch IN S THEN
    write (Ch:2);
```

- Four uses for sets in programs are to replace complex Boolean expressions, to protect a program (or segment) from bad data, to protect against invalid **CASE** statements, and to aid in interactive programming.
- Sets can be used as parameters with subprograms.
- Sets cannot be returned as the value of a function.
- Sets can be generated or modified through subprograms by using variable parameters with procedures.

Chapter Review Exercises

1. Define a set and set variable to contain the even numbers from 2 to 20.
2. Write a procedure to read in integers and print them if they are in the set defined in Exercise 1.

For Exercises 3–11, refer to the sets below.

```
A := [1..5, 9..20];
B := [4..12];
```

What are the elements of the following?

3. `A * B`
4. `A + B`
5. `A - B`
6. `B - A`
7. `A + B - A * B`
8. `A * B - A + B`
9. `A - B + B`
10. Define a set that is a subset of set A and contains four elements.
11. If set D contains [1..20] as elements, what is the relationship of set D to set A?

For Exercises 12–18, indicate if the declarations are correct. If not, explain why.

12.
```
TYPE
  TestAnswers = SET OF [1..20, 'A'..'F'];
```
13.
```
TYPE
  B = SET OF integer;
```
14.
```
TYPE
  C = SET OF [1.0..4.0];
```
15.
```
TYPE
  D = SET OF [2, 5, 7, 12, 18, 35, 98];
```
16.
```
TYPE
  LetterGrades = ['A', 'B', 'C', 'D', 'F'];
  Grades = SET OF LetterGrades;
```
17.
```
TYPE
  E = SET OF [1..4];
```
18.
```
TYPE
  F = SET OF 1..4;
```
19. List at least 10 subsets of the set defined in Exercise 18.
20. List a superset of the set defined in Exercise 18.
21. Write a fragment of code of a set to contain the letters in the name of your school.
22. How many subsets are there of the set [1, 2]?

For Exercises 23–25, consider the following definitions and declarations:

```
TYPE
  IntType = SET OF 1..10;
  LetType = SET OF 'A'..'M';
VAR
  X : IntType;
  Y : LetType;
```

23. What is the value of X + Y?
24. Is [ ] a subset of X?
25. Is [ ] a subset of Y?

For Exercises 26–31, using the sets from Exercises 23–25, and the following defined variables,

```
A : IntType;
B : LetType;
```

indicate if the statements are valid. If they are not, explain why.

26. `A := 1;`
27. `A := [1];`
28. `[] := A + B;`
29. `B := B + 'A';`
30. `A := A + [10];`
31. `A := A + [11];`

For Exercises 32–35, find A + B, A * B, and A – B for the sets given.

32. `A := [1, 3..6, 10];, B := [4, 5, 6, 7];`
33. `A := [1..5, 9..12];, B := [6..8];`
34. `A := ['A'..'H'];, B := ['E'];`
35. `A := [1..5], B := [];`

Programming Problems

Each of the following programming problems can be solved with a program using sets. Hints are provided to indicate some of the uses; you may, of course, find others.

1. Write a program to be used to simulate a medical diagnosis. Assume the symptoms are coded as follows:

Symptom	Code
Headache	1
Fever	2
Sore throat	3
Cough	4
Sneeze	5
Stomach pain	6
Heart pain	7
Muscle pain	8
Nausea	9
Back pain	10
Exhaustion	11
Jaundice	12
High blood pressure	13

Further, assume each of the following diseases is characterized by the symptoms indicated here:

Disease	Symptoms
Cold	1, 2, 3, 4, 5
Flu	1, 2, 6, 8, 9
Migraine	1, 9
Mononucleosis	2, 3, 11, 12
Ulcer	6, 9
Arteriosclerosis	7, 10, 11, 13
Appendicitis	2, 6

Your program should accept as input a person's name and symptoms (coded) and provide a preliminary diagnosis. Sets can be used for

a. Bad data check
b. Symptoms = 1 .. 13;
   Disease = **SET OF** Symptoms;
c. Cold, Flu, Migraine, Mononucleosis, Ulcer, Arteriosclerosis, Appendicitis: Disease;

2. Write a program to serve as a simple text analyzer. Input is any text file. Output should be three histograms: one each for vowel frequency, consonant frequency, and other symbol frequency. Your program should use a set for vowels, one for consonants, and a third for other symbols.
3. Write an interactive program that allows the user to enter a date in numeric form (4 14 76) and then writes out the corresponding month, date, and year. For example, the input of 4 14 76 would produce output of

```
April fourteen, nineteen seventy-six
```

The program should work for any date during the twentieth century. Error messages should be printed for incorrect input. Thus, 4 31 76 should generate an error message because April has only 30 days. Also, 2 29 93 should produce an error because 1993 was not a leap year.

4. Write a program to serve as a simple compiler for a Pascal program. Your compiler should work on a program that uses only single-letter identifiers. Your compiler should create a set of identifiers, make sure identifiers are not declared twice, make sure all identifiers on the left of an assignment are declared, and make sure there are no type mismatch errors. For purposes of your compiler program, assume the following:

a. Variables are declared between **VAR** and **BEGIN;** for example,

```
VAR
  X, Y : real;
  A, B, C : integer;
  M : char;
BEGIN
```

b. Each program line is a complete Pascal statement.
c. The only assignments are of the form X := Y;. Output should include the program line number and an appropriate error message for each error. Run your compiler with several short Pascal programs as text files.

5. A number in exponential notation preceded by a plus or minus sign may have the form

Sign	Positive integer	Decimal	Positive integer	E	Sign	Exponent (three digits)
⎿⏌	⎿____⏌	•	⎿____⏌		⎿⏌	⎿____⏌

For example, −45.302E + 002 is the number −4530.2. If the number is in standard form, it will have exactly one digit on the left side of the decimal (−4.5302E + 003).

Write a program to read numbers in exponential form from a text file, one number per line. Your program should check to see if each number is in proper form. For those that are, print the number as given and the number in standard form.

6. Write a program to analyze a text file for words of differing length. Your program should keep a list of all words of length 1, 2, . . . , 10. It should also count the number of words whose length exceeds 10.

   A word ends when one alphabetical character is followed by a character not in the alphabet or when an end-of-line is reached. All words start with letters (7UP is not a word). Your output should be an alphabetized list for each word length. It should also include the number of words whose length exceeds 10 characters. An apostrophe does not add to the length of a word.

7. The Falcon Manufacturing Company (Problem 23, Chapter 11; Problem 17, Chapter 12; and Problems 12, 13, 14, 15, and 16, Chapter 13) wants a computerized system to check if a customer is approved for credit. A customer number should be entered from the keyboard, with the program printing the credit limit for the customer if credit has been approved, and "No credit" if it has not. Each line of a text file contains a customer number and the credit limit. Valid customer numbers range from 100 to 999, and credit limits are $100, $300, $500, $1,000, and unlimited credit.

8. Write a program in which you read a text file and print the number of times a character in the file matches a character in your name.

9. The Court Survey Corporation wishes to conduct a poll by sending questionnaires to men and women between 25 and 30 years of age living in your state or any state adjacent to it. A text file containing names, street addresses, cities, states, zip codes, and ages is to be read. The program prints the names and addresses of those persons matching the criteria.

10. Write a program to test your ESP and that of a friend. Each of you should secretly enter 10 integers between 1 and 100. Have the program check each list and print the values that are in both lists and the number of values in both lists.

11. Modify the Wellsville Wholesale Company commission problem (Problem 22, Chapter 10) to define the sales ranges as sets. Use these sets to verify input and determine the proper commission rate.

12. The Ohio Programmers' Association offices are in a large building with five wings lettered A through E. The office numbers in the wings are as follows:

Wing	Rooms
A	100–150 and 281–300
B	151–190 and 205–220
C	10–50 and 191–204
D	1–9 and 51–99
E	221–280 and 301–319

    Write a program that enables the receptionist, Ms. Wallace, to enter an office number from the keyboard and then have the computer print the wing in which the office is located.

Communication in Practice

1. Select a program from the **Programming Problems** section in this chapter that you have not yet worked. Construct a structure chart and write all documentary information for this program. Include variable definition, subprogram definition, required input, and required output. When you are finished, have a classmate read your documentation to see if it is clear precisely what is to be done.
2. Remove all documentation from a program you have written for this chapter. Exchange this modified version with another student who has done the same thing. Write documentation for the exchanged program. Compare your documentation with that originally written for the program. Discuss the differences and similarities with the other students in your class.
3. Not all programming languages include sets as a data structure. Examine several other languages to determine what data structures they include. Prepare a chart that compares and contrasts the data structures of Pascal (arrays, records, files, and sets) with the data structures of other languages. Give an oral presentation of your results to the class.

Chapter 16

Graphics

Chapter Outline

In this chapter, we discover how to create graphics displays on the screen. All prior output to the screen has been text: letters, numbers, and a few special symbols. Now we will see how geometric designs, charts, and other graphic displays are produced.

A note of caution is in order. This chapter is written for users of Turbo Pascal who have common display systems. If you are not using Turbo Pascal or if your display system is not consistent with what is presented in this chapter, you will need to refer to some other source to see how your system handles graphics.

16.1 Fundamentals of Graphics

Objectives

- to understand how graphics work in Turbo Pascal
- to get into the graphics mode
- to get out of the graphics mode
- to set colors for graphics operations
- to plot points and draw lines

In this section, we examine the fundamental aspects necessary to produce graphics displays, beginning with how the screen is configured. Next we consider color options, getting into and out of the graphics mode, and various forms of initialization for graphics. Then, we learn how to enter and exit the graphics mode, after which we investigate the elementary properties of plotting points and drawing lines.

The Screen

The standard display screen for personal computers contains 25 lines, each capable of holding 80 text characters. This can be envisioned as shown in Figure 16.1. Because there are 80 characters in each of 25 lines, you may think there are 80 × 25 = 2,000 positions on the screen. Actually, there are many more than 2,000 positions on a display screen because the screen actually consists of **pixels,** which is short for **picture elements.** A pixel is the smallest picture element on the display. When we work in a graphics mode, we work with these pixels instead of the character positions we use with text characters.

Many graphics screens are 320 pixels across and 200 pixels down, as shown in Figure 16.2. Such a screen contains 64,000 (320 × 200) pixels. Graphics displays using

◆ Figure 16.1

Standard display screen for text characters

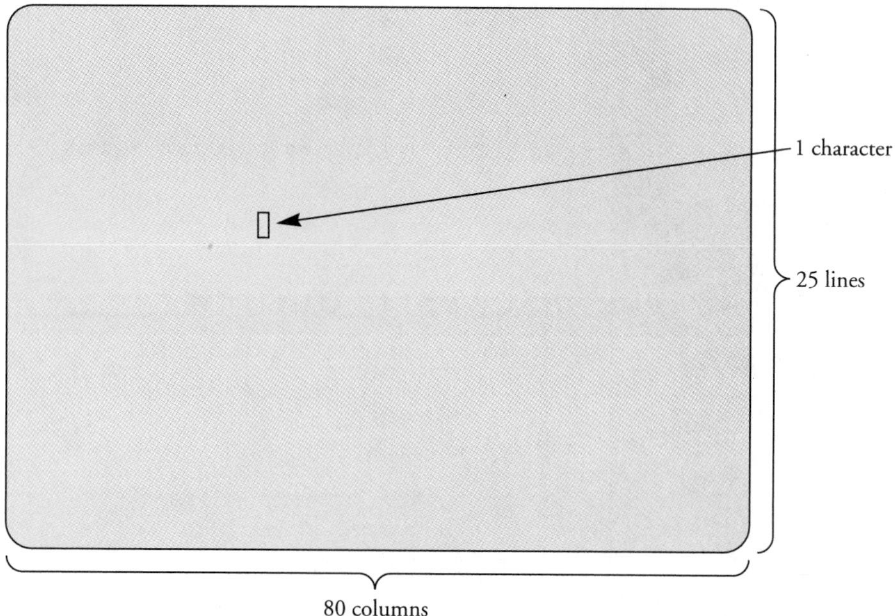

◆ Figure 16.2

Pixels on a screen

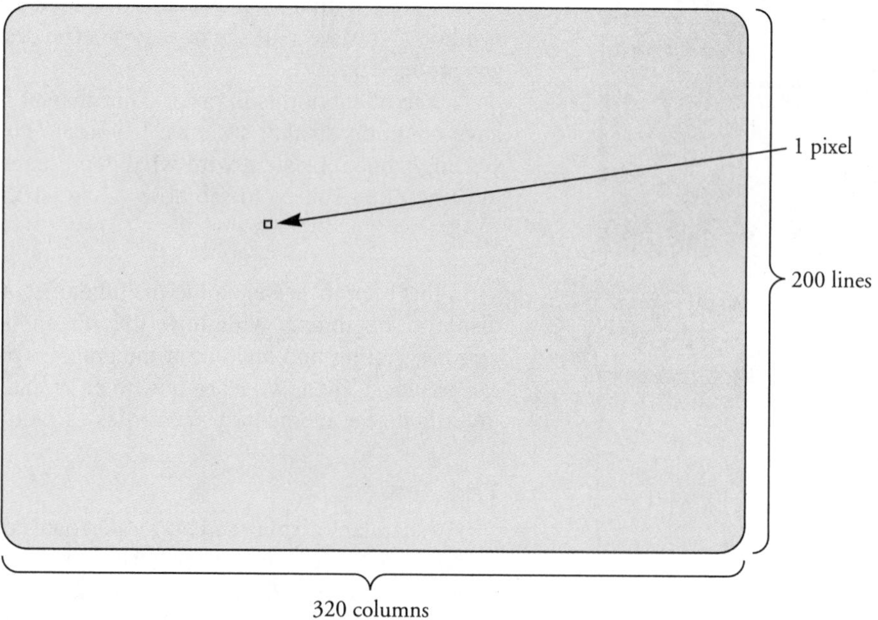

A **pixel** (short for **picture element**) is the smallest picture element on a display screen.

screens that are 320 × 200 pixels are said to be in a **medium-resolution mode.** If you have an option available that lets you use more pixels, you will be in **high-resolution mode.** (Systems that have 640 × 200 or 640 × 360 pixels are examples.) Although both of these options (and others) are available on some systems, the work in this chapter assumes a display that is 320 × 200 pixels.

Medium-resolution mode is a graphics display that uses a screen containing 320 × 200 pixels.

Color Options

Most personal computers have color graphics adapters that permit graphics to be displayed using a variety of colors. The number of colors available depends on the graphics mode available on your computer. A list of several graphics modes, together with resolutions and colors available, is given in Table 16.1.

Table 16.1

Graphics modes, resolution, and colors available

Mode			Number of Colors
Name	Code	Resolution	Available
CGAC0	0	320 × 200	4
CGAC1	1	320 × 200	4
CGAC2	2	320 × 200	4
CGAC3	3	320 × 200	4
VGALo	0	640 × 200	16
VGAMed	1	640 × 350	16
VGAHi	2	640 × 480	16
EGALo	0	640 × 200	16
EGAHi	1	640 × 350	16
HercMonoHi	0	720 × 348	Monochrome

High-resolution mode is a graphics display using a screen that contains more pixels than a screen in medium-resolution mode.

The examples in this chapter have been developed on the assumption that you are using a color monitor and working in one of the CGA modes. If you are working in some other mode, you will be in a high-resolution mode with 16 colors available instead of 4.

Turbo Pascal provides four palettes for the CGA modes. Each palette contains a background color and three other colors. The palettes are selected by specifying a graphics mode at the beginning of a program. The colors available in each mode are represented by integers 0, 1, 2, or 3 and are listed in Table 16.2

Table 16.2

Colors available in each mode

CGA	Color Number			
Mode	0	1	2	3
0	Background	LightGreen	LightRed	Yellow
1	Background	LightCyan	LightMagenta	White
2	Background	Green	Red	Brown
3	Background	Cyan	Magenta	LightGray

When we first enter graphics, we select the mode we want by using a program statement such as

```
GraphMode := CGAC1;
```

or the equivalent

```
GraphMode := 1;
```

We then have available the colors LightCyan, LightMagenta, White, and a background color of our choice. It is possible to change the mode later in the program.

After the mode is selected, any of the 16 colors can be specified as a background color by using the predefined procedure **SetBkColor.** The background colors are listed in Table 16.3.

▼ Table 16.3

Background colors

Number	Color	Number	Color
0	Black	8	DarkGray
1	Blue	9	LightBlue
2	Green	10	LightGreen
3	Cyan	11	LightCyan
4	Red	12	LightRed
5	Magenta	13	LightMagenta
6	Brown	14	Yellow
7	LightGray	15	White

SetBkColor requires a single argument, which can be any integer from 0 to 15, inclusive. Turbo Pascal also permits the use of predefined constants that describe the colors provided by each integer. Thus, if we wish the background color to be Green, we can use either

```
SetBkColor(2);
```

or

```
SetBkColor(Green);
```

During the running of a graphics program, we can control the colors we use by changing the mode and/or changing the color in each mode. Mode changes are accomplished by the predefined procedure

SetGraphMode (<argument>)

where the argument is an integer that specifies the mode. For the CGA medium-resolution mode, the argument will be one of the integers 0, 1, 2, or 3, as shown in Table 16.2.

We can then specify a foreground color by using the predefined procedure

SetColor (<argument>)

where the argument is an integer or a predefined constant. For the CGA medium-resolution mode, the argument will be 0, 1, 2, or 3. An argument of 0 will make the current drawing color the same as the background color (in effect, erasing it!). Arguments of 1, 2, or 3 will specify the respective colors listed in Table 16.2. Thus, if we are in CGA mode 1

```
SetColor(2);
```

will cause the current drawing color to be LightMagenta. Table 16.4 contains a summary list of the procedures to use in establishing the modes and colors when working with graphics.

Table 16.4

Procedures for selecting colors

Procedure	Purpose
`SetBkColor (<selection>)`	Establishes a background color.
`SetGraphMode (<selection>)`	Sets and/or changes modes for different color palettes.
`SetColor (<selection>)`	Specifies a foreground color.

Getting into Graphics Mode

Before we can do anything in graphics, we must get into the graphics mode. We will be using the units **Graph** and **Crt,** so our programs will begin with

```
PROGRAM GraphDemo;
USES
  Crt, Graph;
```

Before using any graphics in the main program, we must use the predefined procedure

InitGraph (<driver>, <mode>, <file path>)

where <driver> and <mode> are variable parameters of type **integer.** The parameter <driver> specifies which graph driver is to be used. Turbo Pascal internally associates each driver with a unique integer value. However, it is not necessary to know these values. Predefined constants CGA, VGA, EGA, and others can represent values of the parameter. Our examples use the CGA driver. Since this is a variable parameter, we use the variable GraphDriver to produce

```
GraphDriver := CGA;
InitGraph (GraphDriver, <mode>, <file path>);
```

The second parameter, <mode>, is also a variable parameter. Turbo Pascal supports any of the modes listed in conjunction with the names given in Table 16.1. Thus, if we want the mode CGAC1, we can use either

```
GraphMode := CGAC1;
```

or

```
GraphMode := 1;
```

where GraphMode is declared as a variable of type **integer.** Both the driver and the mode selection should be made before the call to **InitGraph.** Typically, a graphics program begins

```
PROGRAM GraphPrac;

USES
  Crt, Graph;

VAR
  GraphDriver, GraphMode : integer;

BEGIN
  GraphDriver := CGA;
  GraphMode := 1;
  InitGraph (GraphDriver, GraphMode, <file path>);
      .
      .
      .
```

The third parameter, <file path>, is the path required to locate the directory containing the BGI driver files (∗.BGI). If Turbo Pascal has been installed so that the user is already in that directory, the file path can just be the null string ' '. If Turbo Pascal is not in the same directory as the BGI driver, the file path must be specified. For example, the file path could be

```
'C:\TP\BGI'
```

In this case, the **InitGraph** procedure would be

```
InitGraph (GraphDriver, GraphMode, 'C:\TP\BGI');
```

Default Values

It is possible to enter the graphics mode with less fanfare. Turbo Pascal provides a method that automatically examines the hardware being used and determines which driver is needed. This mechanism uses the name **Detect** as follows:

```
GraphDriver := Detect;
```

One advantage of using **Detect** is that the user does not need to know which driver the hardware supports or what the code for the driver is. A second advantage of using **Detect** to specify the driver is that it also delivers the value of the mode when the **InitGraph** procedure is processed. A program using **Detect** begins

```
GraphDriver := Detect;
InitGraph (GraphDriver, GraphMode, '');
```

provided we are in the directory containing the driver specified in the first argument. If we do not want the default mode or if we want to change the mode at some point in the program, we merely assign a different mode by using

```
GraphMode := <value>;
```

For a more complete explanation of how the mode is specified when using **Detect,** see the Turbo Pascal Library Reference Manual.

Most examples in this chapter do not use default values provided by **Detect.** We assume a CGA driver and always specify a mode of 0, 1, 2, or 3. We also specify a file path for the BGI driver files. Therefore, a typical program begins

```
GraphDriver := CGA;
GraphMode := 1;
InitGraph (GraphDriver, GraphMode, 'C:\TP\BGI');
```

Getting Out of Graphics Mode

After we finish with graphics, we need to exit the graphics mode. This is accomplished by a call to the procedure **CloseGraph,** which requires no arguments and appears as a single line of code:

```
CloseGraph;
```

Calling this procedure has the effect of restoring the original screen mode before graphics was initialized. It also frees the memory allocated for graphics.

When it is necessary to move back and forth between graphics and text several times within a program, the procedure **RestoreCrtMode,** rather than **CloseGraph,** should be used. **RestoreCrtMode** returns the user to text mode but retains the current graphics settings. These settings can be reinstated by using the predefined procedure

```
SetGraphMode (GraphMode);
```

rather than going through **InitGraph** again. The procedure **SetGraphMode** can also be used to change the mode in a program by

```
GraphMode := 2;
SetGraphMode (GraphMode);
```

Modes can be changed as often as desired. When graphics is left for the final time, **CloseGraph** should be used.

Guarding against Initialization Errors

A call to **InitGraph** may not properly complete the initialization process. The predefined function **GraphResult** tests for proper initialization. If everything is correct, GraphResult is 0. Otherwise, **GraphResult** returns an integer from −1 to −14, inclusive. These numbers indicate different errors, which are listed in the Turbo Pascal Library Reference Manual.

GraphResult can be used in a fairly direct manner to guard against initialization errors. Since **GraphResult** must be zero to proceed in the graphics mode, an **IF . . . THEN . . . ELSE** statement of the form

```
IF GraphResult = 0 THEN
      .
      .  (program action here)
      .
ELSE
      .
      .  (error message here)
      .
```

can be used. Here, the error message could be

```
writeln ('Could not enter the graphics mode.');
```

A Note of Interest

An Artist of Interface

Millions of people encounter the graphic art of Susan Kare every day. Her carefully crafted images have won a place among the cultural symbols of our age, yet few people have any idea who she is or where her work can be seen.

Only a handful of industry insiders know that Kare is the artist responsible for the graphic appearance of some of the country's best-known computer software. Based in San Francisco, she designed most of the distinctive icons, typefaces and other graphic elements that gave the original Macintosh computer its characteristic—and widely emulated—appearance. Many consider her to be the mother of the famous Macintosh trash can.

Since then, Kare has parlayed her initial work for Apple Computer, Inc., into a full-time business, designing graphic user interfaces, or GUIs, for computer companies and software developers. The user interface is the software that allows an operator to control a personal computer and direct its functions. A decade ago, most interfaces forced the user to type cryptic commands in a blank space on the display.

With the introduction of the Macintosh in 1984, Apple pushed the world toward the graphic interface, which provides greater ease of use. A graphic interface allows an operator to control the computer by manipulating symbols displayed on its monitor, usually with a mouse or trackball.

The growing demand for graphic user interfaces has forced Kare to turn down work. She has rejected potential clients in part because she refuses to hire people to share the workload. "I do every job myself because I think of it as an art," she said. She works almost entirely on a computer, shunning traditional artist's tools for their electronic successors. "Anything that's bound for the screen, I do on the screen," she said. If there is a secret to her work, it is simplicity, restraint, and common sense.

It is possible to develop a more elaborate initialization process to be used with each graphics program. It is also possible to develop a procedure to find a specific error that prevents entry into the graphics mode. Let's look at the development of such a procedure.

GraphResult is reset to 0 after it is called, so we store the value it returns in the variable ErrorResult. We also declare the variable InitError to be of type **boolean** and assign it a value by using

```
InitError := (ErrorResult <> 0);
```

The predefined functions **GraphErrorMsg** and **Halt** are used during the termination process when initialization is not successful. **GraphErrorMsg** returns a specific error message; **Halt** causes a return to the operating system. Using these functions, the initialization procedure contains the code

```
ErrorResult := GraphResult;
InitError := (ErrorResult <> 0);
IF InitError THEN
  BEGIN
    writeln ('There is a graphics error.');
    writeln (GraphErrorMsg(ErrorResult));
    writeln ('Program aborted.');
    Halt
  END;
```

A complete initialization procedure is

```
PROCEDURE InitializeGraphics;

  {  Given:    Nothing                                      }
  {  Task:     Initialize graphics; provide error message   }
  {  Return:   Nothing                                      }

  VAR
    GraphDriver, GraphMode,
    ErrorResult : integer;
    InitError : boolean;
  BEGIN
    GraphDriver := CGA;
    GraphMode := 1;
    InitGraph (GraphDriver, GraphMode, 'C:\TP\BGI');
    ErrorResult := (GraphResult);
    InitError := (ErrorResult <> 0);
    IF InitError THEN
      BEGIN
        writeln ('There is a graphics error.');
        writeln (GraphErrorMsg(ErrorResult));
        writeln ('Program aborted.');
        Halt
      END
  END;  {  of PROCEDURE InitializeGraphics  }
```

This procedure is called from the main program by

```
InitializeGraphics;
```

If an error message is printed, it can be seen by opening the output window.

A Final Form

By now, you are probably becoming a little impatient with the process of getting into and out of graphics mode. That is only natural. However, once you master the entry and exit problems of graphics, you will be able to move on to creating graphic designs. We summarize the information presented thus far with two typical outlines for a graphics program.

Without using an initialization procedure, we have

```
PROGRAM Graphics;

USES
  Crt, Graph;

VAR
  GraphDriver,
  GraphMode : integer;

BEGIN
  GraphDriver := CGA;
  GraphMode := 1;
  InitGraph (GraphDriver, GraphMode, 'C:\TP\BGI');
```

```
    IF GraphResult = 0 THEN
              .
              .  (main part of graphics program here)
              .
    ELSE
              .
              .  (error message here)
              .
    CloseGraph
  END.
```

If we use the initialization procedure developed earlier, we have

```
PROGRAM Graphics;

USES
  Crt, Graph;

PROCEDURE InitializeGraphics;
    .
    .  (code for procedure here)
    .

BEGIN  {  Main program  }
  InitializeGraphics;
           .
           .  (main part of program here)
           .
  CloseGraph
END.  {  of main program  }
```

We use this form for our graphics programs in this chapter. Generally, we will only refer to **PROCEDURE** InitializeGraphics and not rewrite the procedure for each program.

Plotting Points

The most basic operation in graphics is plotting a point. For the sake of referencing coordinates, screens have the point with coordinates (0,0) in the upper left corner. The *x*-axis, or first coordinate, is numbered left to right, and the maximum coordinate value produces a point on the right side of the screen. Thus, if we are in medium resolution with 320 × 200 pixels, the upper right corner has coordinates (319, 0). Note, the pixel positions range from 0 to 319.

The vertical coordinates range from 0 to 199, with the numbers increasing as we move down the screen. Thus, (0, 50) is above (0, 100) on the screen. Coordinates of corners and a typical point are shown in Figure 16.3.

The predefined functions **GetMaxX** and **GetMaxY** return the maximum values of X and Y, respectively. These functions are used for centering, determining boundaries, and many other purposes when creating graphic designs.

Points are placed on the screen by the predefined procedure **PutPixel.** The general form of this procedure is

PutPixel (<X value>, <Y value>, <color>)

◆ Figure 16.3

Screen coordinates in medium resolution with 320 × 200 pixels

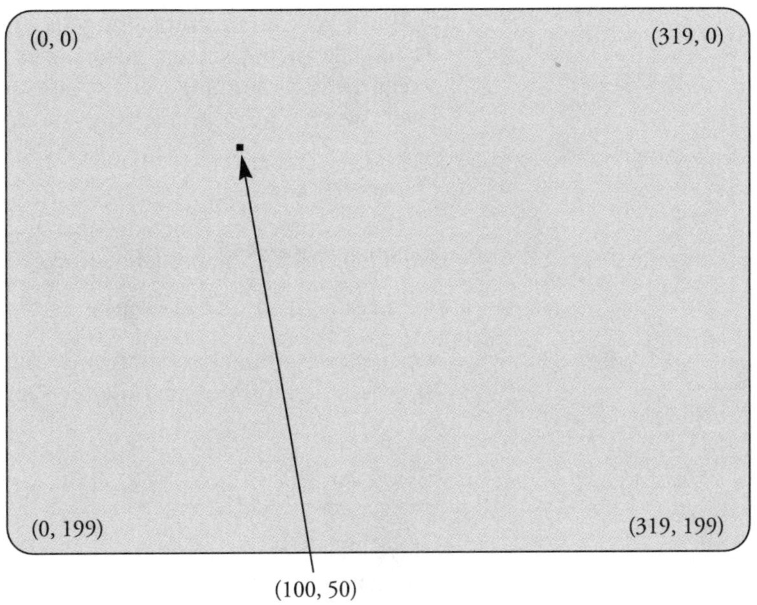

Thus, the line of code

```
PutPixel (100, 50, 3);
```

selects the pixel in position (100, 50) and colors it with color number 3 of whatever color mode is in effect when the procedure is called. Use of the functions **GetMaxX** and **GetMaxY** to determine screen boundaries is examined in the following example.

Example 16.1

Let's write a short program that plots a point in the middle of your graphics screen.

```
PROGRAM CenterPlot;

USES
  Crt, Graph;

VAR
  MidX, MidY : integer;

PROCEDURE InitializeGraphics;
  .
  .  (code for procedure here)
  .
BEGIN  {  Main program  }
  InitializeGraphics;
  SetBkColor (Green);
  MidX := GetMaxX DIV 2;
  MidY := GetMaxY DIV 2;
  PutPixel (MidX, MidY, 1);
  readln;
  CloseGraph
END.  {  of main program  }
```

When you run this program, you will need to look very closely to see the pixel in the middle of the screen. Also notice that a **readln** statement is used to hold the screen before returning you to text mode. You must press <Enter> to continue. Later, we will learn to make messages appear with graphics on the screen.

Drawing Lines

The second fundamental operation in graphics is drawing a line. This is accomplished by the predefined procedure **Line.** A typical call to this procedure is

```
Line (0, 0, 100, 100);
```

which causes a line to be drawn from the endpoint (0, 0) to the endpoint (100, 100). In general, the procedure **Line** requires four integer arguments of the form

Line (X1, Y1, X2, Y2)

where (X1, Y1) are coordinates of one endpoint and (X2, Y2) are coordinates of the other endpoint.

A **current pointer** keeps track of the current pixel position.

In graphics mode, an invisible **current pointer** keeps track of the current pixel position. This is analogous to the cursor visible on the screen in text mode. The current pointer can be moved in two different ways. If we know the specific location to which we want the current pointer to move, we can write

```
MoveTo (X, Y);
```

where (X, Y) is the desired location. We may also move the current pointer relative to its location. Thus, if we want to move it 10 positions to the right and 15 positions down, we write

```
MoveRel (10, 15);
```

In general, the predefined procedures for moving the current pointer are

MoveTo (X, Y)

and

MoveRel (DeltaX, DeltaY)

where X, Y, DeltaX, and DeltaY are integer variables. The variables X and Y range from 0 to **GetMaxX** and **GetMaxY,** respectively. Ranges for the arguments of **MoveRel** are

```
-GetMaxX < DeltaX < GetMaxX
-GetMaxY < DeltaY < GetMaxY
```

A negative argument for DeltaX moves the current pointer to the left from its current position; a positive argument moves it to the right. A negative argument for DeltaY moves the current pointer up from its current position; a positive argument moves it down. Moving the current pointer off the screen using **MoveRel** does not cause an error, but this possibility can be averted by using appropriate boundary values.

A second procedure for drawing lines is the predefined procedure **LineTo.** The general form of this procedure is

LineTo (X, Y)

where X and Y are integer variables. This causes a line to be drawn from the current pointer to the point with coordinates (X, Y). The uses of these procedures are shown in the following example.

Example 16.2

Let's see how a line with the endpoints (0, 30) and (100, 30) can be drawn using both the **Line** and **LineTo** procedures. Using the **Line** procedure, this can be accomplished with

```
Line (0, 30, 100, 30);
```

Using the **LineTo** procedure, we first position the current pointer at one end of the desired line using **MoveTo** and then finish the task using **LineTo** as follows:

```
MoveTo (0,30);
LineTo (100,30);
```

The **Line** procedure does not cause the current pointer to be moved. However, **LineTo** does cause the current pointer to be positioned at the point given by the coordinates that are arguments of the **LineTo** procedure. Thus, the previous call to

```
LineTo (100, 30)
```

will leave the current pointer at (100, 30).

A third predefined procedure can be used to draw a line segment. **LineRel** causes a line to be drawn from the current pointer to an endpoint with coordinates that are determined in relation to the current pointer. Thus, if we want a line to go from the current pointer to a point 20 pixels to the right and 30 pixels down, we write

```
LineRel (20, 30);
```

LineRel moves the current pointer to the position indicated by its arguments. The general form for **LineRel** is

LineRel (X, Y)

The advantage of this procedure is that we do not need to know the coordinates of the new endpoint. We only need to know where they are relative to the current pointer. **MoveRel** and **LineRel** are useful for drawing a shape with a starting point that can be changed, so the same shape can be drawn in different locations on the screen.

Variations of a Line

All lines drawn thus far have been drawn in a default mode. Turbo Pascal allows the user to specify three characteristics of a line—style, pattern, and thickness—which are specified by using the predefined procedure **SetLineStyle** of the form

SetLineStyle (<style>, <pattern>, <thickness>)

The line styles available for this procedure are illustrated in Table 16.5.

Table 16.5

Line styles

Style	Value	Result
SolidLn	0	______________________________
DottedLn	1	....
CenterLn	2	— – — – — – — – — – — – — – — –
DashedLn	3	--
UserBitLn	4	Result varies

All arguments of **SetLineStyle** are variables of type **word** (available in Turbo Pascal). If the variable declaration section includes

```
VAR
  Style : word;
```

we can use either

```
Style := DottedLn;
```

or

```
Style := 1;
```

to draw a dotted line.

The style **UserBitLn** allows the user to specify a particular 16-bit pattern. This option will not be developed here. The interested reader is directed to the Turbo Pascal Library Reference Manual.

A zero value is always used for the pattern argument. Nonzero values must be hexadecimal values, which specify the bit pattern when the first argument, <style>, is **UserBitLn.**

The third argument, <thickness>, can have a value of either 1 or 3. A value of 1 causes a line to be drawn that is one pixel wide. A value of 3 causes a line to be drawn that is three pixels wide. The predefined constants **NormWidth** and **ThickWidth** may also be used. The next example illustrates several methods of using **SetLineStyle.**

Example 16.3

Let's illustrate different ways to specify drawing a dotted line with extra thickness (three pixels). If we assume the variable declaration section includes

```
VAR
  Style, Pattern, Thickness : word;
```

then each of the following sections of code is appropriate:

1.
```
Style := DottedLn;
Pattern := 0;
Thickness := ThickWidth;
SetLineStyle (Style, Pattern, Thickness);
```

2.
```
Style := DottedLn;
Pattern := 0;
Thickness := 3;
SetLineStyle (Style, Pattern, Thickness);
```
3.
```
Style := 1;
Pattern := 0;
Thickness := 3;
SetLineStyle (Style, Pattern, Thickness);
```
4.
```
SetLineStyle (DottedLn, 0, ThickWidth);
```
5.
```
SetLineStyle (1, 0, 3);
```

As you can see, several variations for using **SetLineStyle** are available. In general, code is more readable when identifiers are used as shown in method 1. The line style you define remains in effect until you define a different setting or until you leave the graphics mode by using **CloseGraph.**

Clearing the Screen

Eventually, we will want to clear the screen while in graphics mode. This is accomplished by a call to the procedure **ClearDevice,** which uses no arguments and appears as a single line of code:

```
ClearDevice;
```

If we wish to clear the screen when not in graphics mode,

```
ClrScr;
```

will accomplish the task.

We conclude this section with a short graphics program that draws a border around the screen and then draws two diagonals in the rectangle that borders the screen. A variety of line styles and colors are used. Note, a **readln** statement is used to stop the program. When the program is run, <Enter> is pressed to continue. Later, we will examine different ways of stopping and slowing down the graphics display.

A first-level pseudocode development for this program is

1. Initialize graphics
2. Set colors
3. Determine screen size
4. Draw the diagonals
5. Draw the border

A second-level development is

1. Initialize graphics
2. Set colors
    2.1 Set background color
    2.2 Set current color
3. Determine screen size
    3.1 Get maximum width (X)
    3.2 Get maximum height (Y)
4. Draw the diagonals
    4.1 Draw first diagonal

   4.2 Position pointer
   4.3 Draw second diagonal
5. Draw the border
   5.1 Set style
   5.2 Draw side borders
   5.3 Change line style
   5.4 Draw top and bottom borders

A complete program for this problem follows:

```
PROGRAM LineExample;

{  This program uses the Line and LineTo procedures to draw   }
{  diagonals on the screen and then draw a border around the  }
{  screen. Different line styles and widths are used.         }

USES
  Crt, Graph;

VAR
  MaxX, MaxY : integer;

{*************************************************************}

PROCEDURE InitializeGraphics;

  {  Given:   Nothing                                          }
  {  Task:    Initialize graphics. Provide error message       }
  {                for unsuccessful initialization.            }
  {  Return:  Nothing                                          }

  VAR
    GraphDriver, GraphMode,
    ErrorResult : integer;
    InitError : boolean;
  BEGIN
    GraphDriver := CGA;
    GraphMode := 1;
    InitGraph (GraphDriver, GraphMode, 'C:\TP\BGI');
    ErrorResult := GraphResult;
    InitError := (ErrorResult <> 0);
    IF InitError THEN
      BEGIN
        writeln ('There is a graphics error.');
        writeln (GraphErrorMsg(ErrorResult));
        writeln ('Program aborted.');
        Halt
      END
  END;  {  of PROCEDURE InitializeGraphics  }

{*************************************************************}

PROCEDURE GetScreenSize (VAR MaxX, MaxY : integer);

  {  Given:   Nothing                                          }
```

```
  {  Task:     Get screen limits for X and Y.                    }
  {  Return:   Maximum values for X and Y                        }

  BEGIN
    MaxX := GetMaxX;
    MaxY := GetMaxY
  END;  {  of PROCEDURE GetScreenSize  }

{***************************************************************}

PROCEDURE DrawDiagonals (MaxX, MaxY : integer);

  {  Given:    Screen limits for X and Y                         }
  {  Task:     Draw both diagonals                               }
  {  Return:   Nothing                                           }

  BEGIN
    Line (0, 0, MaxX, MaxY);              {  Draw one diagonal  }
    readln;                                 {  Hold the screen  }
    MoveTo (0, MaxY);
    LineTo (MaxX, 0);               {  Draw the other diagonal  }
    readln                                  {  Hold the screen  }
  END;  {  of PROCEDURE DrawDiagonals  }

{***************************************************************}

PROCEDURE DrawBorder (MaxX, MaxY : integer);

  {  Given:    Screen limits for X and Y                         }
  {  Task:     Draw the screen border                            }
  {  Return:   Nothing                                           }

  VAR
    Style, Thickness : word;
  BEGIN

    {  Draw the right-side border  }
    Style := DottedLn;                      {  Change the style  }
    Thickness := NormWidth;
    SetLineStyle (Style, 0, Thickness);
    LineTo (MaxX, MaxY);              {  Draw the right border  }
    readln;                                 {  Hold the screen  }

    {  Draw the left-side border  }
    MoveTo (0, 0);                     {  Position the cursor  }
    LineTo (0, MaxY);                  {  Draw the left border  }
    readln;

    {  Draw the bottom border  }
    SetColor (2);    {  Switch from LightCyan to LightMagenta  }
    Thickness := ThickWidth;            {  Now use thick width  }
    Style := CenterLn;                {  Change the style again  }
    SetLineStyle (Style, 0, Thickness);
    LineTo (MaxX, MaxY);             {  Draw the bottom border  }
    readln;
```

```
    { Draw the top border }
    Style := DashedLn;                          { Try a new style }
    SetLineStyle (Style, 0, Thickness);
    Line (0, 0, MaxX, 0);                       { Draw the top border }
    readln
  END; { of PROCEDURE DrawBorder }

{****************************************************************}

BEGIN { Main program }
  InitializeGraphics;
  SetBkColor (Green);
  SetColor (1);
  GetScreenSize (MaxX, MaxY);
  DrawDiagonals (MaxX, MaxY);
  DrawBorder (MaxX, MaxY);
  CloseGraph
END. { of main program }
```

Output from this program (without color) is

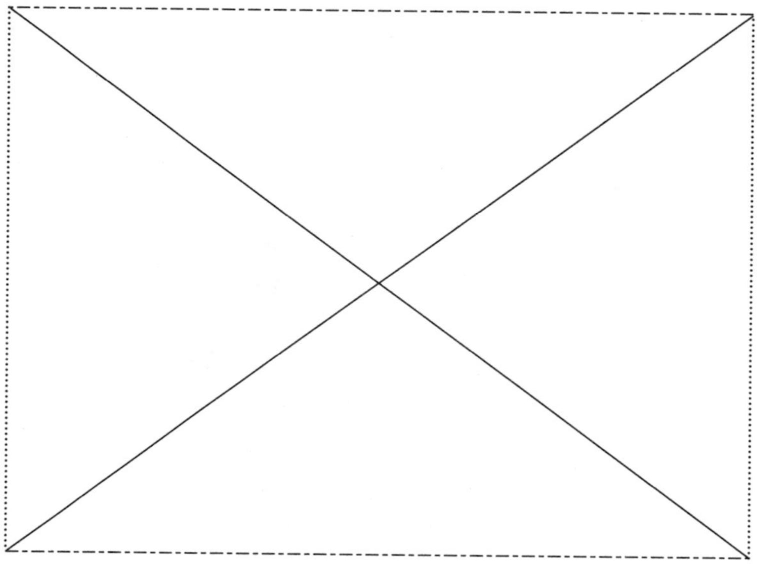

Exercises 16.1

*1. Explain why **InitGraph** (CGA, GraphMode) and **InitGraph** (GraphDriver, 2) are not valid calls to the procedure **InitGraph.**

2. Discuss the advantages and disadvantages of using background constants Black, Blue, and so forth, rather than their ordinals (0, 1, . . .), as arguments for **SetBkColor.**

*3. Write a "graphics shell" that can be used as the basis for all of your graphics programs. This shell should include the following:
   a. **USES**
      Crt, Graph;
   b. An initialization procedure that contains:
      i. The definition and initialization of GraphDriver and GraphMode
      ii. An **InitGraph** statement

iii. An **IF . . . THEN** statement for displaying an appropriate initialization error message

c. A **CloseGraph** statement

Save this shell, and make modifications to it when you want to write a graphics program.

4. Write a test program to determine what values are returned by **GetMaxX** and **GetMaxY** for the screen you are using.

*5. Use the functions **GetMaxX** and **GetMaxY** to locate the center of your screen. After finding the pixel that represents this center, do the following.
   a. Put a nine-pixel square in the center of the screen.
   b. Draw horizontal and vertical lines through this square.

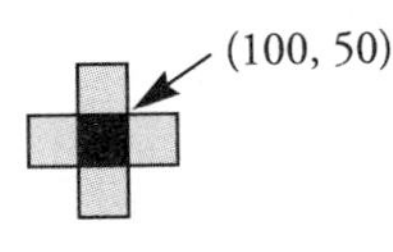

6. A single pixel is hard to see. Solve this problem by writing a procedure to plot a point that is actually five pixels with the indicated pixel in the middle. Thus, if you wish to see the point (100, 50), your procedure will actually display the five pixels shown in the margin.

7. Write a test program that shows the default colors available when you enter the graphics mode using

```
GraphDriver := Detect;
InitGraph (GraphDriver, GraphMode, 'C:\TP\BGI');
```

8. Use nested loops in a short program to display two thick lines of each color available on your screen.

9. Write a program that does the following:
   *a. Uses a loop and **LineRel** to fill your screen with horizontal lines that are 10 pixels apart.
   b. Uses a loop and **Line** to fill your screen with vertical lines that are 10 pixels apart.

10. Use **MoveTo** and **LineRel** to draw a 10-pixel × 10-pixel square with the upper left vertex at (100, 100).

*11. Write a program that displays 10-pixel × 10-pixel squares on a diagonal from the upper left corner of the screen to the bottom of the screen (probably at (199, 199).

12. Modify your program in Exercise 11 by changing the color of the squares on the diagonal.

13. Discuss the differences among the procedures **Line, LineTo,** and **LineRel.**

14. Write code segments that would produce images of the following types:
   a. A square
   b. A right triangle
   c. An isoceles triangle
   d. A pentagon

15. Write a code segment that would draw an image of a YIELD sign. The sign should look like this:

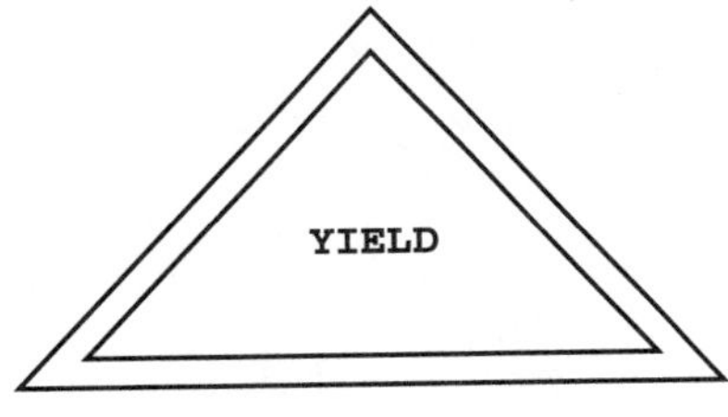

16. The Müller-Lyer illusion is caused by an image that consists of two parallel lines of equal length with different designs at the end of each line. One line looks like an arrow with two heads and the other line looks like an arrow with two tails.

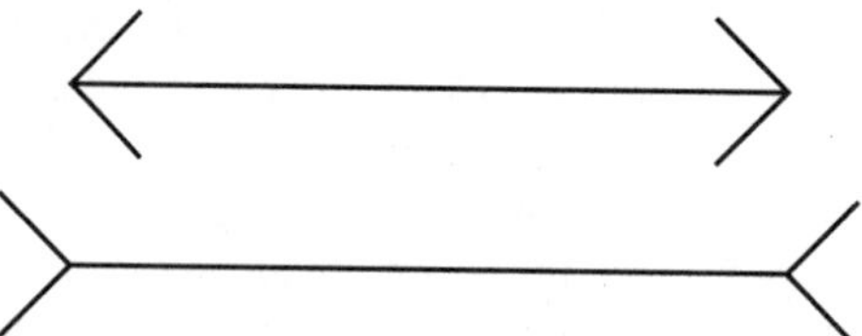

Write a program that displays the Müller-Lyer illusion.

17. Modify Exercise 9 so different line styles and widths are used to make the grid. Include examples of different styles and widths used in the same grid.

18. Use procedures to create a "house," as shown in the margin. Vary the colors for the roof, chimney, windows, and door.
19. Write a procedure that creates a design by using only the relative movements **LineRel** and **MoveRel.** Use this procedure in a program to show how the design can be moved around the screen by specifying different starting positions.
20. Use **GetMaxX** and **GetMaxY** in a program that allows you to normalize the screen in the following manner:
    a. The normalized origin is in the lower left corner of the screen.
    b. The screen range of the first coordinate of a point is from 0 to 1, moving left to right.
    c. The screen range of the second coordinate of a point is from 0 to 1, moving up the screen.

    The normalized corners of your screen are then

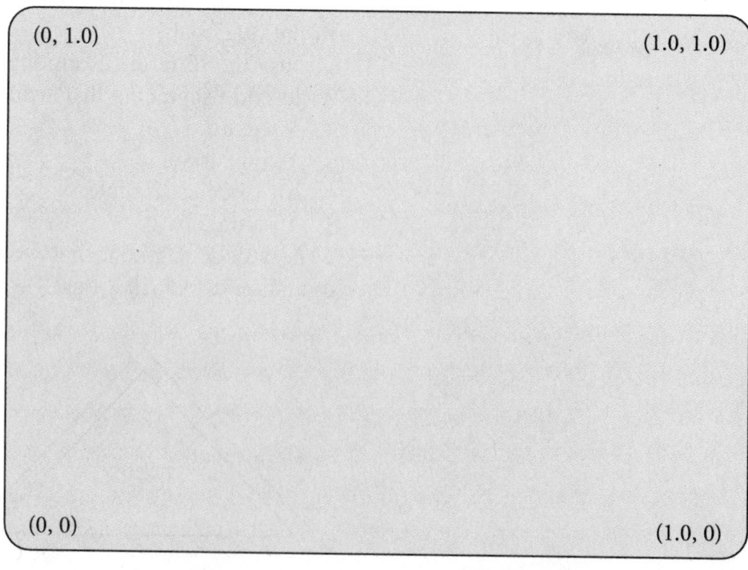

and the screen center is (0.5, 0.5). [*Hint:* If you use LargestX := **GetMaxX** and LargestY := **GetMaxY,** the normalized center is (round(0.5 * LargestX), round(0.5 * LargestY)].

16.2 Graphics Figures

Objectives

- to be able to construct geometric figures
- to be able to use the procedures **rectangle, circle, arc,** and **ellipse**
- to understand why an aspect ratio is needed

Several procedures in Turbo Pascal allow the user to construct geometric figures. In this section, we will see how to use a single procedure to display a rectangle, circle, arc, or ellipse.

Rectangles

A rectangle is determined by four vertices and can be displayed by using a sequence of **Line, LineRel,** or **LineTo** procedures. Thus, a rectangle with an upper left vertex of (10, 10) and dimensions of 100 × 50 can be shown by

```
ClearDevice;
MoveTo (10, 10);
LineTo (110, 10);
LineTo (110, 60);
LineTo (10, 60);
LineTo (10, 10);
```

When this segment of code is executed from graphics mode, the display shown in Figure 16.4 results.

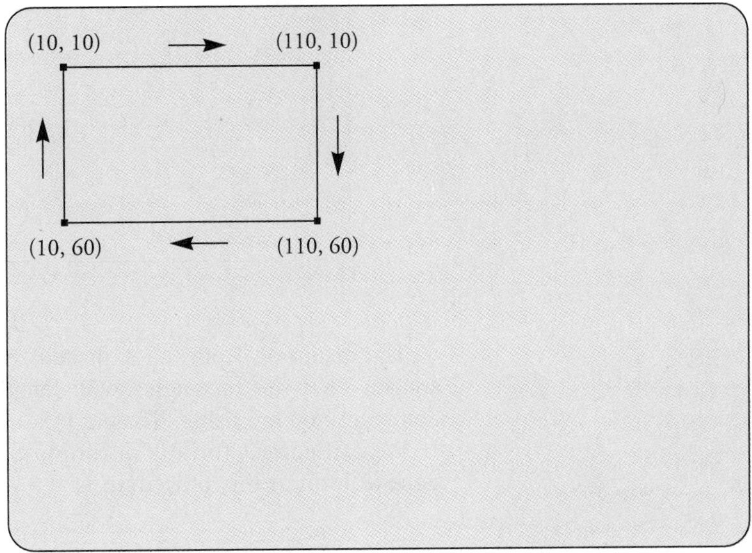

◆ Figure 16.4

A rectangle 100 × 50

Fortunately, the procedure **Rectangle** performs the same task. Using this procedure

```
Rectangle (10, 10, 110, 60);
```

causes the same figure to be displayed. The general form of procedure **Rectangle** is

Rectangle (X1, Y1, X2, Y2)

where (X1, Y1) is the upper left vertex and (X2, Y2) is the lower right vertex. Variables X1, Y1, X2, and Y2 are of type **integer** with the respective ranges

0 < X1 < X2 < **GetMaxX**
0 < Y1 < Y2 < **GetMaxY**

Aspect Ratio

Looking at your 100 × 50 rectangle, you probably notice the length (100) is less than twice the width (50). To see even more clearly that displays may be different from what you expect, draw a square of side length 150 by using

```
Rectangle (0, 0, 150, 150);
```

When this line of code is executed, the display shown in Figure 16.5 results.

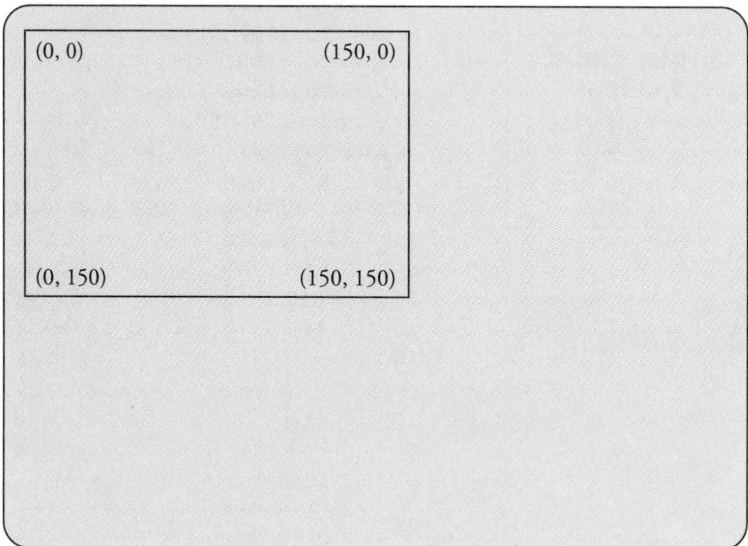

◆ Figure 16.5

A square of side length 150

The distortion from the expected results arises from the fact that pixels are not square. They are rectangles with lengths and widths that differ according to what computer you are using. Thus, a pixel can be envisioned as shown in Figure 16.6.

We can correct for this distortion by using the procedure **GetAspectRatio.** The general form of this procedure is

GetAspectRatio (Xasp, Yasp)

where Xasp and Yasp are variables of type **word.** The ratio of these variables can then be used to correct the distortion, so squares look square and rectangles are proportional. The segment of code

```
GetAspectRatio (Xasp, Yasp);
AspRatio := Xasp / Yasp;
```

◆ Figure 16.6

Shape of a pixel

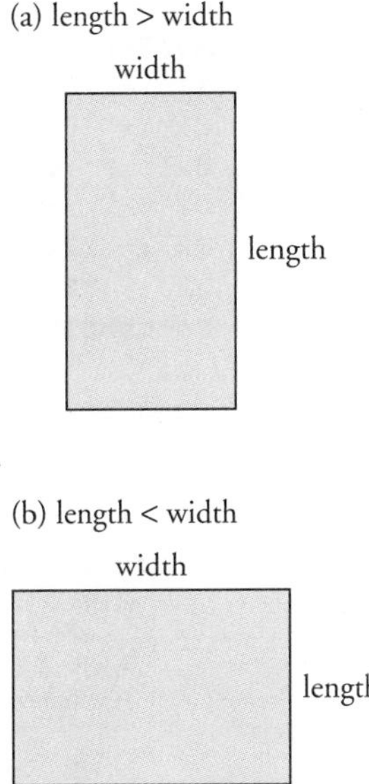

produces a value of approximately 6/5 (or 5/6), which can then be used to adjust one pair of sides of a rectangle to eliminate distortion. To illustrate, consider the following segment of code:

```
GetAspectRatio (Xasp, Yasp);
AspRatio := (Xasp / Yasp);
X1 := 10;
Y1 := 10;
DeltaX := 100;
DeltaY := round(100 * AspRatio);   {  AspRatio is a real  }
X2 := X1 + DeltaX;
Y2 := Y1 + DeltaY;
Rectangle (X1, Y1, X2, Y2);
```

When this code is run, a square of horizontal side length 100 is produced by starting at coordinates (10, 10) and going clockwise through (110, 10), (110, Y2), (10, Y2), and (10, 10). The square now looks like a square. [You may need to use AspRatio := Yasp/Xasp if your pixels appear as shown in Figure 16.6(b)].

An examination of the previous code reveals that the vertical (Y) coordinates have been adjusted so the change in Y looks the same as the change in X. The horizontal (X) values are absolute, and the vertical (Y) values are relative, as determined by the aspect ratio. This is illustrated in the following example.

Example 16.4

Let's construct a rectangle with a base that appears to be twice its height. Recall that our earlier attempt to display such a rectangle used the line of code

```
Rectangle (10, 10, 110, 60);
```

to draw a rectangle with a base of 100 and a height of 50. We can now make this rectangle appear to be twice as wide as it is high by using the aspect ratio to correct the vertical sides for distortion as follows:

```
GetAspectRatio (Xasp, Yasp);
AspRatio := (Xasp / Yasp);
X1 := 10;
Y1 := 10;
DeltaX := 100;
DeltaY := round(50 * AspRatio);   {  Correct distortion  }
X2 := X1 + DeltaX;
Y2 := Y1 + DeltaY;
Rectangle (X1, Y1, X2, Y2);
```

This segment of code produces the screen display shown in Figure 16.7.

◆ Figure 16.7

Rectangle using aspect ratio

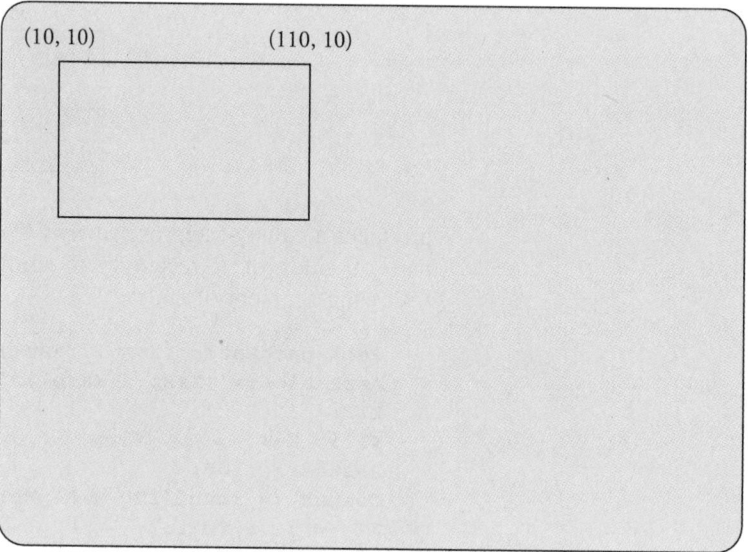

Using `Delay`

Some method is required to hold the graphics display on the screen long enough to enable the user to see what is being displayed. Thus far, we have been using the **readln** statement for this purpose. Since no message appears on the screen, we assume the user knows to press <Enter> to continue.

Another method for holding the screen display is the procedure **Delay.** This is a procedure in the **Crt** unit, not in the **Graph** unit. The form of the **Delay** procedure is

Delay (<LengthOfPause>)

where LengthOfPause is a variable of type **word.** The value of LengthOfPause is the approximate number of milliseconds the computer pauses before executing the subsequent line of code. Thus, if we want a display to appear for approximately one second, we use the code

```
LengthOfPause := 1000;
Delay (LengthOfPause);
```

The **Delay** feature allows the user to create animation. For example, we can make a square appear to move across the screen by the following process:

1. Select a color palette
2. Select a background color
3. Select a current color
4. Create a moving square by following these steps
   4.1 Set coordinates
   4.2 Display a square
   4.3 Pause
   4.4 Erase the square
   4.5 Repeat this process until the motion is to be terminated

The program in the next example creates animation.

Example 16.5

This example uses the **Delay** procedure to provide our first look at animation. Note that a constant is used to define LengthOfPause. Given this definition, we can easily change the rate at which the object moves. The following program moves a square of side length 20 across the top of the screen.

```
PROGRAM Animation;

{  This program demonstrates simple animation.  A square          }
{  appears to move horizontally by a sequence of drawing the      }
{  square, erasing the square, and then redrawing the square      }
{  to the right of the previous position.                         }

USES
  Crt, Graph;

CONST
  LengthOfPause = 100;
  SideLength = 10;

VAR
  X1, Y1, X2, Y2 : word;
  AspRatio : real;
  DeltaX, DeltaY : integer;

{****************************************************************}

PROCEDURE InitializeGraphics;

  {  Given:   Nothing                                            }
  {  Task:    Initialize graphics. Provide error message for     }
  {                unsuccessful initialization.                  }
  {  Return:  Nothing                                            }

  VAR
    GraphDriver, GraphMode,
    ErrorResult : integer;
    InitError : boolean;
```

```
  BEGIN
    GraphDriver := CGA;
    GraphMode := 1;
    InitGraph (GraphDriver, GraphMode, 'C:\TP\BGI');
    ErrorResult := GraphResult;
    InitError := (ErrorResult <> 0);
    IF InitError THEN
      BEGIN
        writeln ('There is a graphics error.');
        writeln (GraphErrorMsg(ErrorResult));
        writeln ('Program aborted.');
        Halt
      END
  END;  {  of PROCEDURE InitializeGraphics  }

{*****************************************************************}

PROCEDURE SetAspectRatio (VAR AspRatio : real);

  {  Given:   Nothing                                              }
  {  Task:    Set the aspect ratio                                 }
  {  Return:  The aspect ratio                                     }

  VAR
    Xasp, Yasp : word;
  BEGIN
    GetAspectRatio (Xasp, Yasp);
    AspRatio := Yasp / Xasp
  END;  {  of PROCEDURE SetAspectRatio  }

{*****************************************************************}

BEGIN  {  Main program  }
  InitializeGraphics;
  SetBkColor (0);
  SetAspectRatio (AspRatio);

  {  Initialize the first square  }
  X1 := 0;
  Y1 := 0;
  DeltaX := SideLength;
  DeltaY := round(SideLength * AspRatio);
  X2 := X1 + DeltaX;
  Y2 := Y1 + DeltaY;

  {  Display and erase squares across the screen  }
  REPEAT
    SetColor (1);
    Rectangle (X1, Y1, X2, Y2);
    Delay (LengthOfPause);
    SetColor (0);                               {  Erase the square  }
    Rectangle (X1, Y1, X2, Y2);
    X1 := X1 + DeltaX;
    X2 := X2 + DeltaX
  UNTIL X2 > GetMaxY;
```

```
  readln;
  CloseGraph
END.  {  of main program  }
```

Circles

The procedure **Circle** in Turbo Pascal allows the user to display a circle. The correct form of this procedure is

Circle (<Xcoor>, <Ycoor>, <Radius>)

where Xcoor and Ycoor are variables of type **integer** and represent the coordinates of the center of the circle. Radius is of type **word,** and its value is the number of pixels contained in the radius of the circle. To illustrate, a circle at the center of the screen with a radius of 50 can be displayed by using

```
Xcoor := GetMaxX DIV 2;
Ycoor := GetMaxY DIV 2;
Radius := 50;
Circle (Xcoor, Ycoor, Radius);
```

This segment of code produces the circle shown in Figure 16.8. The circle is drawn in the current color, and the interior of the circle is in the background color. Later, we will see how to vary the color of the interior of a circle.

Note that the circle displayed when **Circle** is called looks like a circle. No distortion is caused by the difference in the width and height of a pixel because the aspect ratio is automatically applied when **Circle** is called. The next example illustrates multiple uses of the **Circle** procedure.

◆ Figure 16.8

A circle with a radius of 50

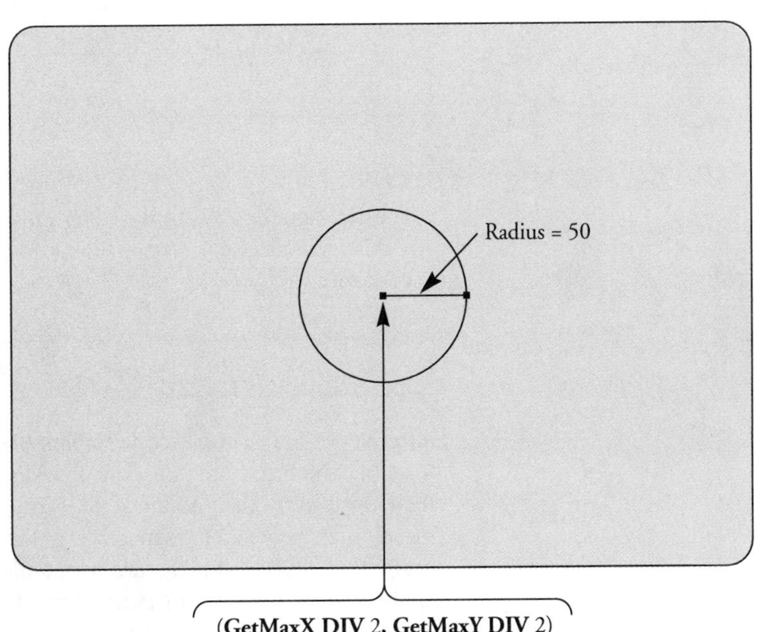

Example 16.6

In this example, we use the **Circle** procedure to display concentric circles, all of which are centered at the middle of the screen. We increase the radius by 20 pixels each time. The segment of code that accomplishes this task is

```
Xcoor := GetMaxX DIV 2;
Ycoor := GetMaxY DIV 2;
Radius := 20;
REPEAT
  Circle (Xcoor, Ycoor, Radius);
  Delay (100);
  Radius := Radius + 20
UNTIL Radius > GetMaxY DIV 2;
```

After running this segment of code, the screen display is

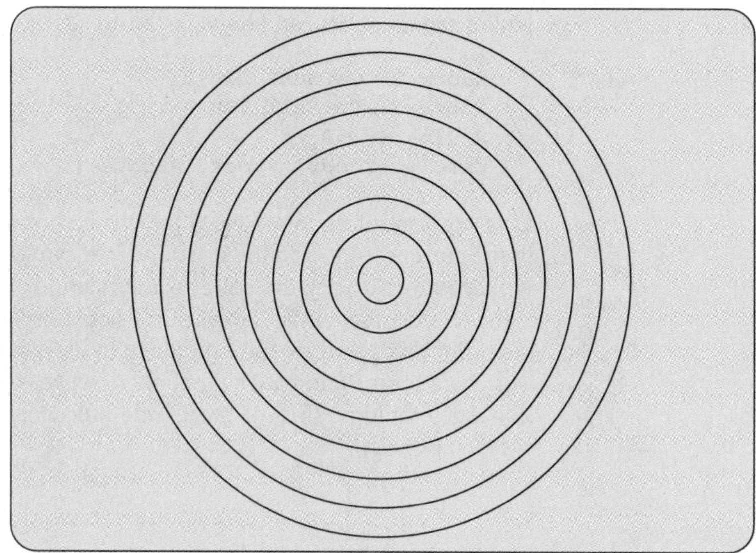

Arcs

The fundamental portion of any curve in two dimensions is an arc. Turbo Pascal provides the procedure **Arc,** which allows the user to draw arcs. The form of the **Arc** procedure is

> **Arc** (<Xcoor>, <Ycoor>, <AngleStart>, <AngleFinish>, <Radius>)

Here, Xcoor and Ycoor are variables of type **integer** and represent the center of the circle of which the arc is a portion. AngleStart, AngleFinish, and Radius are of type **word.** Radius is the radius of the circle of which arc is a portion. AngleStart and AngleFinish represent, respectively, the initial and terminal angles of the arc. An AngleStart of 0° means the arc begins horizontally to the right of the specified center (in the 3 o'clock position). An AngleFinish of 90° means the arc ends above the center and is formed in a counterclockwise manner. To illustrate

```
Arc (100, 100, 0, 90, 50);
```

produces the arc shown in Figure 16.9. As with circles, the arc is drawn in the current color. Also note that arcs do not need to be adjusted for distortion because the aspect ratio is automatically applied when **Arc** is called.

◆ Figure 16.9

Arc (100, 100, 0, 90, 50)

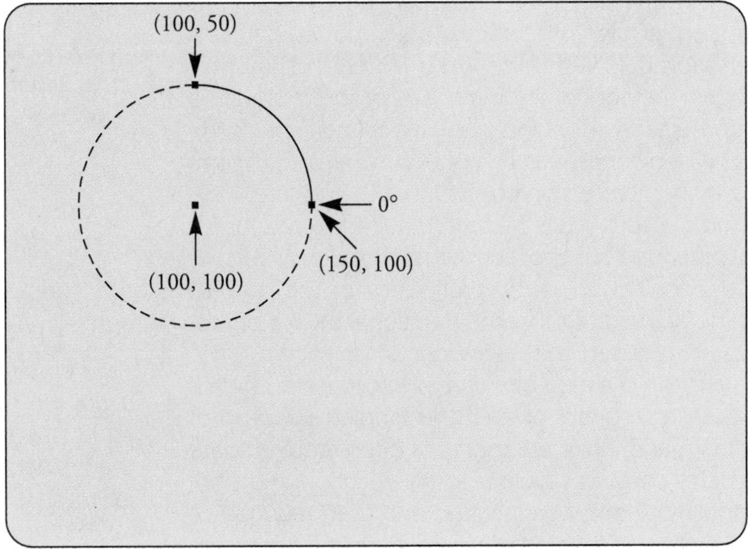

Elaborate curves can be displayed by joining the ends of arcs of differing radii. It may also be necessary to join the ends of an arc with a line segment. For these purposes, procedure **GetArcCoords** returns the coordinates of three points associated with an arc: the center (X, Y), the starting point (Xstart, Ystart), and the ending point (Xend, Yend). Turbo Pascal provides the predefined **ArcCoordsType** as the following **RECORD** type:

```
TYPE
  ArcCoordsType = RECORD
                    X, Y : integer;
                    Xstart, Ystart : integer;
                    Xend, Yend : integer
                  END;
```

If we wish to use the information provided by **GetArcCoords,** our declaration section should include

```
VAR
  ArcCoords : ArcCoordsType;
```

The program could then use the variable ArcCoords in a manner such as

```
GetArcCoords (ArcCoords);
WITH ArcCoords DO
  BEGIN
    .
    .  (Use coordinates here)
    .
  END;
```

A Note of Interest

The Impact of Computers on Art

Dana J. Lamb recently discussed the impact of computers on the arts in an article appearing in Academic Computing. Among other things, she reported part of a conversation held with Alice Jones, a freelance graphic designer, a member of a summer arts program studying developments in full-color graphics on personal computers. When Jones was asked about the use of computers in her professional pursuits, she indicated her study led her to believe the time required to produce a typical paste-up could be reduced by as much as 75 percent, depending upon the proficiency of the graphic artist. She pointed out that the traditional means of producing art required the teamwork of a graphic artist, typesetter, copy camera operator, photographer, and/or illustrator. The logistics of even the simplest paste-up of a few black-and-white photographs often required days in transit as copy was typeset at one location and photos and illustrations were created and then reduced or enlarged at two other locations—all traveling from each place of business to another while the graphic designer sits waiting. Jones observed that this dispersion of design components has been suddenly unified and put into the hands of the designer.

Later in the article, Lamb addressed the issue of how artists perceive the computer. According to Lamb, the opinions of those in the art world can be divided into three major groups:

1. Those who deny the computer has any legitimate place in the creation of art
2. Those who believe the computer should be included in the realm of traditional and/or nontraditional tools in the creation of art
3. Those who believe the computer, together with its fundamental structure, is an art medium unto itself.

Lamb concludes her article with the following paragraph:

> "It is easy to forget that we are witnessing the infancy of this medium in relationship to the arts because of its phenomenal growth in eight years. Artists have been using computers since the 1950s but up to the last decade were viewed as oddities with few arenas to exhibit or share their work. Those days are over, and as the image of these machines becomes less a philosophical issue and simply another tool in the creative process, we can move on to develop the 'clear path' between the visual concept and final product espoused."

For example, we can join the endpoints of an arc by using

```
GetArcCoords (ArcCoords);
WITH ArcCoords DO
  Line (Xend, Yend, Xstart, Ystart);
```

The following segment of code displays an arc that is one-quarter of a circle and then joins the endpoints after a slight delay:

```
SetColor (2);
SetBkColor (Green);
Arc (100, 100, 0, 90, 50);
Delay (1000);
GetArcCoords (ArcCoords);
WITH ArcCoords DO
  Line (Xend, Yend, Xstart, Ystart);
```

This code produces the screen display shown in Figure 16.10.

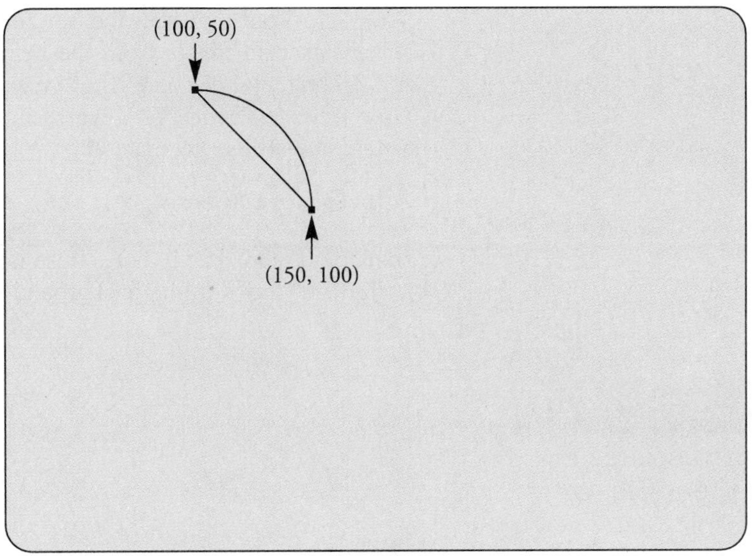

◆ Figure 16.10

Arc with chord drawn

Ellipses

The final geometric shape we consider is that of an ellipse. An ellipse differs from a circle in that it has a major axis and a minor axis, not just a radius. An example of an ellipse is shown in Figure 16.11.

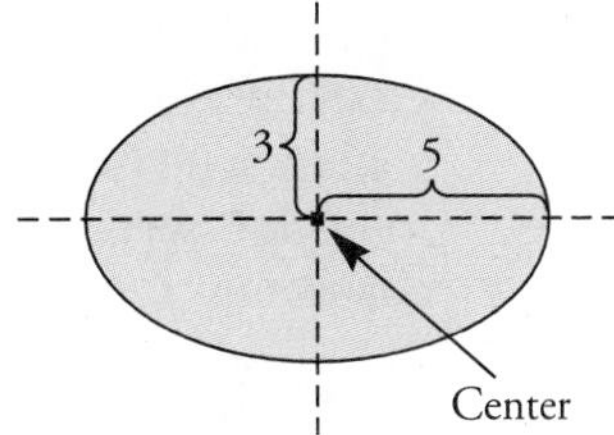

◆ Figure 16.11

An ellipse with a major axis of 10 and a minor axis of 6

The **Ellipse** procedure in Turbo Pascal is used to display an ellipse. The form of this procedure is

> **Ellipse** (<Xcoor>, <Ycoor>, <AngleStart>, <AngleFinish>, <Xrad>, <Yrad>)

Here, Xcoor and Ycoor are variables of type **integer** and represent the center of the ellipse; that is, they are coordinates of the point of intersection of the major and minor axes.

AngleStart and AngleFinish are variables of type **word** and represent the same functions they do for the **Arc** procedure. Thus, the portion of the ellipse that is displayed begins at AngleStart with a value of 0°, which is horizontally to the right of (Xcoor, Ycoor). The ellipse (or portion of it) is sketched in a counterclockwise manner until an angle of AngleFinish is reached. A complete ellipse is displayed anytime AngleFinish – AngleStart = 360°. Typically, the user begins at 0° and finishes at 360°.

Xrad and Yrad represent the horizontal axis and vertical axis, respectively. Xrad is the distance in pixels from the center of the ellipse to the point on the ellipse that is a horizontal distance Xrad pixels to the right of (Xcoor, Ycoor). This point is (Xcoor + Xrad, Ycoor). Yrad works in a similar manner in the vertical direction. To illustrate, the ellipse generated by

```
Ellipse (100, 100, 0, 360, 50, 25);
```

is shown in Figure 16.12. The ellipse is displayed in the current color. The interior of the ellipse is drawn in the background color.

◆ Figure 16.12

The ellipse displayed by **Ellipse** (100, 100, 0, 360, 50, 25)

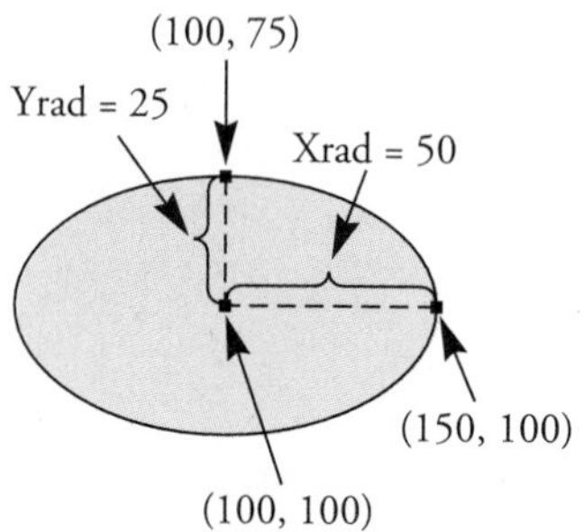

Using parts of ellipses allows us to work with arcs that are not parts of circles, which provides greater flexibility when creating designs. As with arcs, information about an ellipse or a portion of an ellipse can be retrieved by using the procedure **GetArcCoords,** which returns the center (X, Y), starting point (Xstart, Ystart), and ending point (Xend, Yend) of the portion of the ellipse last drawn. To illustrate, the following segment of code draws the top half of an ellipse and then draws a line connecting the endpoints:

```
Ellipse (100, 100, 0, 180, 50, 25);
GetArcCoords (ArcCoords);
WITH ArcCoords DO
  Line (Xend, Yend, Xstart, Ystart);
```

The display created by this code is shown in Figure 16.13.

◆ Figure 16.13

Display using **GetArcCoords**

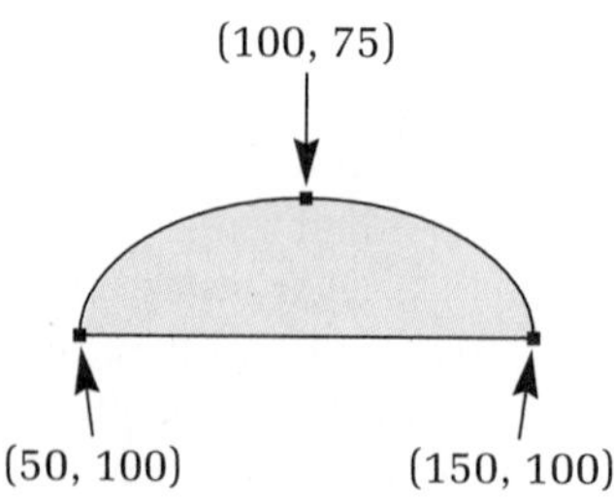

The procedures discussed in this section are summarized in Table 16.6.

Table 16.6

Procedures for geometric designs

Form and Parameters	Result of Call
`Rectangle (X1, Y1, X2, Y2);`	Displays a rectangle with upper left vertex (X1, Y1) and lower right vertex (X2, Y2).
`GetAspectRatio (Xasp, Yasp);`	Returns values that can be used to correct for distortion due to non-square pixels.
`Delay (LengthOfPause);`	Causes a display to remain on the screen for LengthOfPause milliseconds.
`Circle (Xcoor, Ycoor, Radius);`	Displays a circle with a center given by (Xcoor, Ycoor) and a radius of Radius.
`Arc (Xcoor, Ycoor, AngleStart, AngleFinish, Radius);`	Displays an arc as a portion of a circle with a center given by (Xcoor, Ycoor) and a radius of Radius. The arc begins at AngleStart and terminates at AngleFinish, moving counterclockwise. An AngleStart of 0° is horizontally to the right of (Xcoor, Ycoor) in the 3 o'clock position.
`GetArcCoords (ArcCoords);`	ArcCoords is of the predefined **RECORD** type **ArcCoordsType.** The procedure **GetArcCoords** returns the center (X, Y), starting point (Xstart, Ystart), and ending point (Xend, Yend) of an arc.
`Ellipse (Xcoor, Ycoor, AngleStart, AngleFinish, Xrad, Yrad);`	Displays all or a portion of an ellipse with a center given by (Xcoor, Ycoor). The ellipse begins at AngleStart and moves counterclockwise to AngleFinish. Xrad is the horizontal distance from the center of the ellipse to the point on the ellipse that is Xrad pixels to the right of (Xcoor, Ycoor); Yrad is the same in the vertical direction.

Exercises 16.2

*1. Recall how the procedure **LineTo** is used to display a rectangle with dimensions of 100 × 50 and an upper left vertex at (10, 10).
   a. Show how this rectangle can be produced using the **Line** procedure.
   b. Show how this rectangle can be produced using the **LineRel** procedure.

2. Write a test program to display the values of the arguments used in the procedure **GetAspectRatio** as well as the aspect ratio found when the quotient of these arguments is computed.

*3. Explain how a conversion can be made that allows you to think of the argument for **Delay** in terms of seconds rather than milliseconds. Thus, the form of the **Delay** procedure would become

```
Delay (NumSeconds);
```

4. Recall that a square moved across the top of the screen in Example 16.5.
   a. Write a program that causes a square to move down the diagonal from the upper left vertex to the lower right vertex.

b. Discuss why the animation does not appear to be "smooth." Make changes in the program to provide better animation.

5. Expand on Exercise 4 by moving a square across the top of the screen and then moving a circle across the bottom of the screen.
6. Use squares and circles to create a border for your screen. You can accomplish this by varying Exercises 4 and 5 so you do not erase the previous display.
*7. Use a loop and the erase technique of drawing in the background color to produce a dotted circle. Arcs on the circumference of the circle should alternate by an equal number of degrees from the background color to the current color. Use the **Arc** procedure.
8. Use the procedures discussed in this section to create a medium-sized face, complete with eyes, ears, nose, and mouth.
9. Write a program that causes the face you created in Exercise 8 to move across the screen.
10. Modify Exercise 8 so that a smile changes to a frown and one eye blinks.
11. Write a test program that demonstrates how the **Circle** procedure corrects for distortion. Your program should display a circle with a given radius and then plot two points on the circle. One point should be at angle 0°, the other, at angle 90°. Something like

```
Circle (100, 100, 50);
PutPixel (150, 100, 1);
PutPixel (100, 50, 1);
```

should suffice. Discuss the results of your test program.
12. Use the procedures discussed in this section to display the outline of an automobile.

16.3 Filling Patterns

Objectives

- to be able to select a pattern and color
- to be able to fill geometric figures with a pattern and color

There are many ways to change the color and design of the interior of closed regions. In this section, we look at some of the available methods.

Selecting a Pattern and a Color

The basic method for filling a region is a two-step process:

1. Select the pattern and the color of the interior.
2. Fill the region.

Turbo Pascal provides procedures to accomplish both of these tasks. The **SetFillStyle** procedure allows us to select a particular style and color for our filling pattern. The form of this procedure is

SetFillStyle (<pattern>, <color>)

where <pattern> is a variable (or predefined constant) of type **word** that can have any value listed in Table 16.7 and <color> is a variable of type **word** that specifies the color to be used to fill the region.

Table 16.7

Patterns for procedure **SetFillStyle**

Value	Predefined Constant	Pattern
0	**EmptyFill**	Background color
1	**SolidFill**	Solid fill with color
2	**LineFill**	
3	**LtSlashFill**	(light)
4	**SlashFill**	(thick)
5	**BkSlashFill**	(thick)
6	**LtBkSlashFill**	(light)
7	**HatchFill**	
8	**XHatchFill**	
9	**InterleaveFill**	
10	**WideDotFill**	
11	**CloseDotFill**	
12	**UserFill**	**SetFillPattern** defines pattern

The values 0 through 12 can be used for arguments of **SetFillStyle** if desired. However, the constant identifiers **EmptyFill** . . . **UserFill** are recommended because they are more descriptive.

The fill pattern **UserFill** requires special mention. You may use this to define your own filling pattern. It requires a call to **SetFillPattern** in which you define your own bit pattern. For further information, see the Turbo Pascal Library Reference Manual.

Filling Regions

Once a pattern and color have been selected, an enclosed region may be filled by using one of several available procedures. The first procedure we examine is **FloodFill.** The form of this procedure is

> **FloodFill** (<Xcoor>, <Ycoor>, <bordercolor>)

Here, Xcoor and Ycoor are variables of type **integer** and may be the coordinates of any point in the interior of the region to be filled. <bordercolor> is a variable of type **word** and represents the color of the border of the enclosed region.

When **FloodFill** is called, it fills the interior of the enclosed region with the current fill pattern and color established by **SetFillStyle.** The method used is to color pixels outward from the designated pixel until the border is reached. Thus, the coloring appears to spread from the selected pixel to the borders.

To see how **FloodFill** works, let's consider the rectangle defined by

```
Rectangle (0, 0, 100, 50);
```

If the border color is Red and we wish to fill this rectangle with a light backslash, we select **LtBkSlashFill** and a desired color with **SetFillStyle** before calling **FloodFill.** Thus, the segment of code

```
Rectangle (0, 0, 100, 50);
SetFillStyle (LtBkSlashFill, Green);
FloodFill (1, 1, Red);
```

causes the defined rectangle to be filled with the **LtBkSlashFill** pattern against the background color Green, as shown in Figure 16.14. If you run a short program containing these three lines of code, it appears the rectangle is being filled with the pattern and color when it is originally drawn. To get a better look at how **FloodFill** works, use **Delay** before **FloodFill** and increase the dimensions of your rectangle. For example

```
Rectangle (0, 0, 200, 150);
Delay (2000);
SetFillStyle (LtBkSlashFill, Green);
FloodFill (100, 75, Red);
```

allows you to see better how the rectangle gets filled.

It is important to remember that the point represented by (Xcoor, Ycoor) in

```
FloodFill (Xcoor, Ycoor, BorderColor);
```

must be located in the interior of the region to be filled. If it is located outside an enclosed region, the entire exterior will be filled. If it is located on the border of the region, nothing will happen.

Another filling procedure available is **FillEllipse.** The form of this procedure is

FillEllipse (<Xcoor>, <Ycoor>, <Xrad>, <Yrad>)

◆ **Figure 16.14**

A pattern-filled rectangle

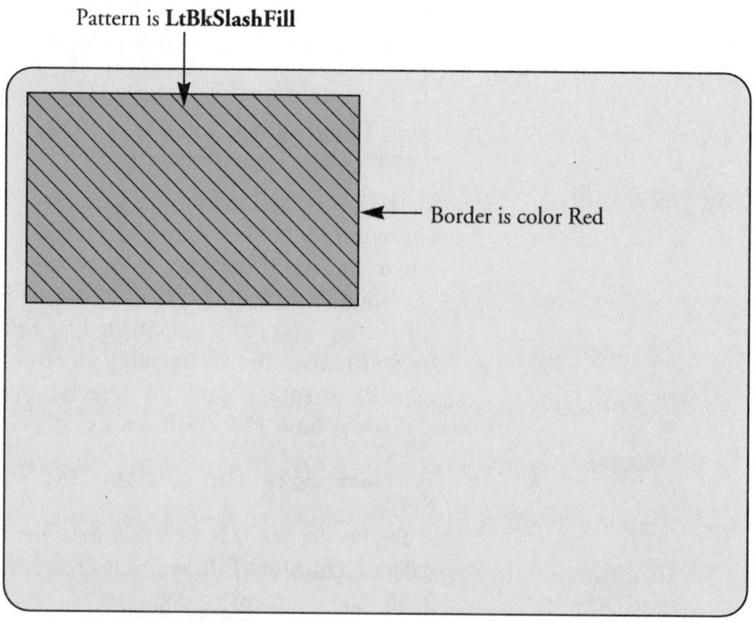

Here, Xcoor and Ycoor are variables of type **integer** and represent the center of the ellipse. Xrad and Yrad are variables of type **word** and represent the horizontal and vertical radii, respectively.

When **FillEllipse** is called, it causes the ellipse specified by (Xcoor, Ycoor, Xrad, Yrad) to be drawn and filled in with the current filling pattern. Note, there are no arguments for either a beginning angle or an ending angle, because **FillEllipse** can be used only with a complete ellipse. Hence, the default arguments are always from 0° to 360°.

A third, more general procedure for filling regions is also available. The procedure **FillPoly,** which allows the user to specify a polygonal region to be filled, is not developed here, however; refer to the Turbo Pascal Library Reference Manual for further information.

The following example illustrates the use of filling patterns with circles.

Example 16.7

This example creates a pattern of concentric circles in which each ring is filled with a different pattern. In Example 16.6 in Section 16.2, concentric circles are generated by the code

```
Xcoor := GetMaxX DIV 2;
Ycoor := GetMaxY DIV 2;
Radius := 20;
REPEAT
  Circle (Xcoor, Ycoor, Radius);
  Delay (100);
  Radius := Radius + 20
UNTIL Radius > GetMaxY DIV 2;
```

We now modify this code by changing the filling pattern after each circle is drawn and then filling the ring with the new pattern. Note that an appropriate pixel must be selected in each ring. The new segment of code is

```
SetBkColor (White);
SetColor (Blue);
Xcoor := GetMaxX DIV 2;
Ycoor := GetMaxY DIV 2;
Radius := 20;
Pattern := EmptyFill;
REPEAT
  Circle (Xcoor, Ycoor, Radius);
  SetFillStyle (Pattern, LightRed);
  FloodFill ((Xcoor + Radius - 5), Ycoor, Blue);
  Delay (100);
  Radius := Radius + 20;
  Pattern := succ(Pattern)
UNTIL Radius > GetMaxY DIV 2;
```

This segment of code produces the display shown in Figure 16.15.

◆ Figure 16.15

Concentric circles with various patterns

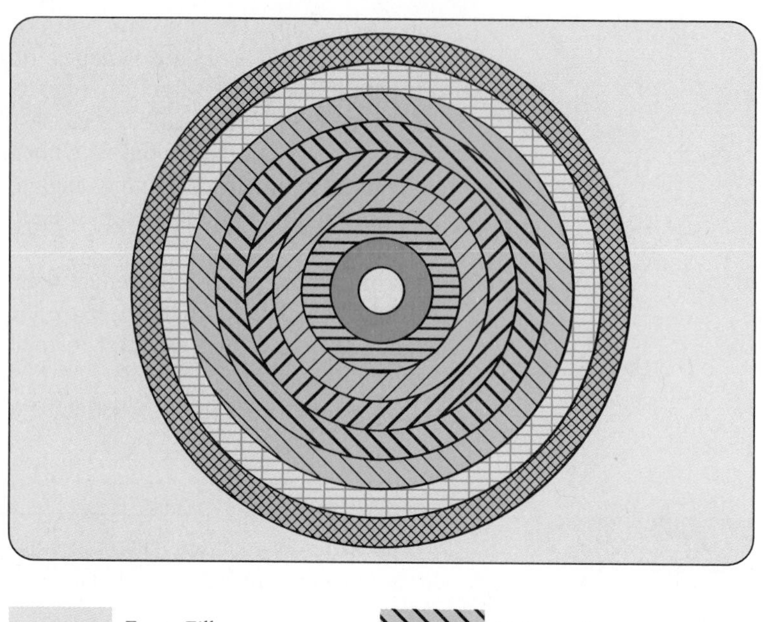

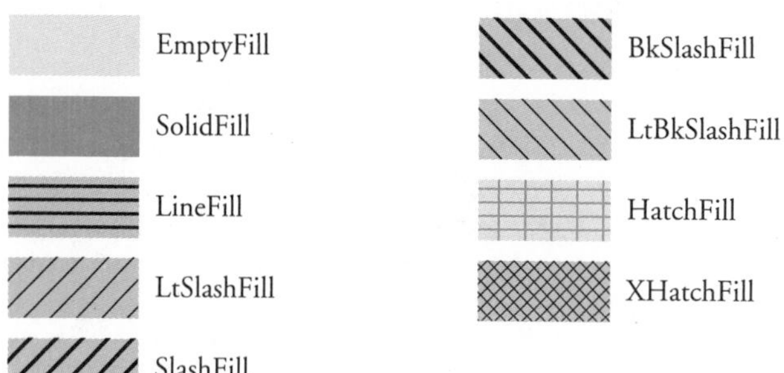

Exercises 16.3

*1. Write test programs to investigate what happens when procedure **FloodFill** is used with arguments that do not satisfy the conditions specified when **FloodFill** was defined. In particular, what happens when each of the following occurs?
   a. A color is used that is not the border color of the defined region.
   b. The point (Xcoor, Ycoor) is outside the defined region.
   c. The point (Xcoor, Ycoor) is on the border of the defined region.

2. Write a test program to see what happens when **FloodFill** is used when the region containing (Xcoor, Ycoor) is not an enclosed region. (Put a gap in the side of a rectangle.)

*3. Write a program that displays rectangles across the screen with different filling patterns.

4. Discuss how you could reverse the background color and the current drawing color of a graphics program.

*5. Write a program that adds animation to Exercise 3; that is, have the rectangles move as they change patterns across the screen.

6. Modify Exercise 5 by having ellipses with different patterns move down a diagonal, starting in the upper left corner.

7. Concentric circles containing different filling patterns are displayed in Example 16.7. The point in each region to be filled has the coordinates (Xcoor + Radius – 5, Ycoor).

a. Discuss other ways you could vary the X coordinate.
b. Would the same system work with the Y coordinate? Why or why not?

8. Create an outline of a house, and use different filling patterns for the door, windows, chimney, and siding.

16.4 Animation and Creating Designs

Objectives

- to produce horizontal motion
- to produce vertical motion
- to produce linear motion
- to understand how nonlinear motion can be produced
- to create figures
- to use procedures to produce figures with motion

Animation is the process of making a figure appear to be in motion.

In this section, we will see how to create figures and make them move on the screen. This process of having a figure appear to be in motion is called **animation,** as shown in Example 16.5.

Horizontal Motion

To cause animation horizontally, we will draw the figure, erase the figure, and then redraw the figure in a new position. For our example, let's consider a blinking square created by

```
FOR Index := 1 TO NumBlinks DO
  BEGIN
    SetColor (Red);                     {  Set the edge color  }
    Rectangle (100, 100, 200, 200); {  Draw the rectangle  }
    Delay (LengthOfPause);            {  Hold the display  }
    SetColor (Green);                 {  Prepare to erase  }
    Rectangle (100, 100, 200, 200);   {  Erase the square  }
    Delay (LengthOfPause)            {  Show a blank screen  }
  END;  {  of FOR loop  }
```

We let the X-coordinates of the vertices be variables X1 and X2 and the process of creating animation is

1. Set the color
2. Draw an initial square
3. Pause
4. Erase the square
5. Move horizontally (increment X1, X2)
6. Draw the square
7. Pause
8. Erase the square

.
.
.

This process is best completed by using repetition. However, first we need to answer several questions.

1. What is the best pause length?
2. How does one increment the X-coordinates of the vertices?
3. How does one ensure that motion stops at the screen boundary?

The first question can be answered by using the procedure **Delay** with a constant value for the display. This constant can then be modified to obtain reasonably smooth motion. In our example, we use

```
CONST
  Length = 10;
```

as an initial value. Our program then uses

```
Pause (Length);
```

when appropriate.

The second question is resolved by defining a constant DeltaX and then using the code

```
X1 := X1 + DeltaX;
X2 := X2 + DeltaX;
```

between displays of the figure. As before, you can then change the value of DeltaX to experiment with the speed and smoothness of motion. In our first example, we use

```
CONST
  DeltaX = 1;
```

Since we are considering only horizontal motion, it is not necessary to change the Y-coordinates. However, since we eventually will consider motion other than horizontal, we use variables Y1 and Y2 with assigned values.

The third question can be answered by the use of **GetMaxX** (or **GetMaxY** where appropriate). If X2 represents the X-coordinate of the vertices on the right side of the square, then a condition such as

```
WHILE X2 <= GetMaxX DO
  BEGIN
      .
      .   (move and display here)
      .
    <increment X2>
  END;
```

causes the animation to terminate when the right edge of the screen is reached. These ideas are all illustrated in the following example.

Example 16.8

Let's move a square from the left side of the screen to the right side. Note the use of the constant section. It is structured so that values can be changed to alter the animation.

```
PROGRAM HorizontalAnimation;

{  This program causes a square to move horizontally        }
{  across the screen.  Animation is achieved by redrawing   }
{  a square in the background color, incrementing the       }
{  coordinates, pausing, and then redrawing the figure.     }

USES
  Crt, Graph;

CONST
  FigureDisplay = 10;
  DeltaX = 1;

VAR
  X1, X2, Y1, Y2 : integer;

{***********************************************************}
```

```
PROCEDURE InitializeGraphics;
  VAR
    GraphDriver,
    GraphMode,
    ErrorResult : integer;
    InitError : boolean;
  BEGIN
    ClrScr;
    GraphDriver := Detect;
    GraphMode := 1;
    InitGraph (GraphDriver, GraphMode, 'C:\TP\BGI');
    ErrorResult := GraphResult;
    InitError := (ErrorResult <> 0);
    IF InitError THEN
      BEGIN
        writeln ('There is a graphics error.');
        writeln (GraphErrorMsg(ErrorResult));
        writeln ('Program aborted.');
        Halt
      END
  END;  {  of PROCEDURE InitializeGraphics  }

{************************************************************}

BEGIN  {  Main program  }
  InitializeGraphics;
  SetBkColor (Green);
  X1 := 0;                    {  Coordinates for first figure  }
  Y1 := 0;
  X2 := 100;
  Y2 := 100;
  SetColor (Red);                     {  Set the border color  }
  Rectangle (X1, Y1, X2, Y2);
  WHILE X2 <= GetMaxX DO           {  Stop at the screen edge  }
    BEGIN
      Delay (FigureDisplay);            {  Pause before moving  }
      SetColor (Green);      {  Prepare to erase the figure  }
      Rectangle (X1, Y1, X2, Y2);          {  Erase the figure  }
      X1 := X1 + DeltaX;         {  Move figure to the right  }
      X2 := X2 + DeltaX;
      SetColor (Red);
      Rectangle (X1, Y1, X2, Y2)     {  Draw the next figure  }
    END
END.  {  of main program  }
```

Vertical Motion

Causing figures to move vertically is similar to the process of moving horizontally; the difference is that we now define an increment in Y, DeltaY, rather than an increment in X. However, one additional problem needs to be resolved for vertical motion.

The screen orientation for the vertical (Y) axis is from zero at the top of the screen to **GetMaxY** at the bottom of the screen. Thus, to move a figure up the screen, we must decrease the value of the Y-coordinates that define the figure. This can be accomplished either by letting DeltaY be positive and subtracting it accordingly, or by letting DeltaY be negative and adding it accordingly.

We must also be aware of the screen boundary conditions for vertical motion. Since zero is at the top of the screen, when a figure moves down the screen, the control for keeping it on the screen could be

```
WHILE Y2 <= GetMaxY DO
```

If the figure moves up rather than down, we would use

```
WHILE Y2 >= 0 DO
```

The next example illustrates vertical motion.

Example 16.9

This example is a variation of Example 16.8. We start with a rectangle at the top of the screen and move it down until it reaches the bottom. In this case, we define DeltaY to be 1. A complete program for this follows:

```
PROGRAM VerticalAnimation;

{  This program causes a square to move down the screen.  }
{  The increment in Y is positive to move down.  The      }
{  boundary condition is determined by GetMaxY.           }

USES
  Crt, Graph;

CONST
  FigureDisplay = 10;
  DeltaY = 1;

VAR
  X1, X2, Y1, Y2 : integer;

{*************************************************************}

PROCEDURE InitializeGraphics;
  VAR
    GraphDriver, GraphMode,
    ErrorResult : integer;
    InitError : boolean;
  BEGIN
    ClrScr;
    GraphDriver := Detect;
    GraphMode := 1;
    InitGraph (GraphDriver, GraphMode, 'C:\TP\BGI');
    ErrorResult := GraphResult;
    InitError := (ErrorResult <> 0);
    IF InitError THEN
      BEGIN
        writeln ('There is a graphics error.');
        writeln (GraphErrorMsg(ErrorResult));
        writeln ('Program aborted.');
```

```
      Halt
    END
  END;  {  of PROCEDURE InitializeGraphics  }

{**********************************************************}

BEGIN  {  Main Program  }
  InitializeGraphics;
  SetBkColor (Green);
  X1 := 0;                        {  Coordinates for first figure  }
  Y1 := 0;
  X2 := 100;
  Y2 := 100;
  SetColor (Red);
  Rectangle (X1, Y1, X2, Y2);
  WHILE Y2 <= GetMaxY DO               {  Stop at the screen edge  }
    BEGIN
      Delay (FigureDisplay);              {  Pause before moving  }
      SetColor (Green);        {  Prepare to erase the figure  }
      Rectangle (X1, Y1, X2, Y2);             {  Erase the figure  }
      Y1 := Y1 + DeltaY;                {  Move the figure down  }
      Y2 := Y2 + DeltaY;
      SetColor (Red);
      Rectangle (X1, Y1, X2, Y2)          {  Draw the next figure  }
    END
END.  {  of main program  }
```

Linear Motion

After learning how to move figures horizontally and vertically, it is natural for students to want to examine other kinds of motion. The first kind we investigate is motion along a line.

Incrementing both X- and Y-coordinates before redrawing a figure causes the figure to move on a line. For example, if an initial square is drawn by

```
Rectangle (0, 0, 100, 100)
```

it can be moved down and to the right by using

```
X1 := X1 + DeltaX;
X2 := X2 + DeltaX;
Y1 := Y1 + DeltaY;
Y2 := Y2 + DeltaY;
```

before redrawing the figures.

When establishing the boundary conditions for motion that is both vertical and horizontal, we need to check all four screen edges. Our next example does this by introducing a Boolean variable, StillOnScreen, which assigns a value by

```
StillOnScreen := (X1 >= 0) AND (Y1 >= 0)
                 AND (X2 <= GetMaxX)
                 AND (Y2 <= GetMaxY);
```

The loop control then becomes

```
WHILE StillOnScreen DO
  BEGIN
    .
    .  (move the figure)
    .
  END;
```

The next example illustrates the use of such a variable in a program.

Example 16.10

The following program moves a figure from the upper left corner of the screen down and to the right simultaneously. Note the use of the Boolean variable StillOnScreen.

```
PROGRAM LinearMotion1;

{  This program causes a square to move along a line with    }
{  apparent slope M = -1.  This is caused by letting         }
{  DeltaX = 1 and DeltaY = 1.                                }

USES
  Crt, Graph;

CONST
  FigureDisplay = 10;
  DeltaX = 1;
  DeltaY = 1;

VAR
  X1, X2, Y1, Y2 : integer;
  StillOnScreen : boolean;

{*************************************************************}

PROCEDURE InitializeGraphics;

  (Code here is the same as before.)

{*************************************************************}

BEGIN  { Main program  }
  InitializeGraphics;
  SetBkColor (Green);
  X1 := 0;                      {  Coordinates for first figure  }
  Y1 := 0;
  X2 := 100;
  Y2 := 100;
  SetColor (Red);                       {  Set the border color  }
  Rectangle (X1, Y1, X2, Y2);
  StillOnScreen := (X1 >= 0) AND (Y1 >= 0)
                   AND (X2 <= GetMaxX)
                   AND (Y2 <= GetMaxY);
  WHILE StillOnScreen DO              {  Stop at the screen edge  }
    BEGIN
      Delay (FigureDisplay);            {  Pause before moving  }
```

```
          SetColor (Green);      { Prepare to erase the figure  }
          Rectangle (X1, Y1, X2, Y2);      { Erase the figure  }
          X1 := X1 + DeltaX;       { Move figure to the right  }
          X2 := X2 + DeltaX;
          Y1 := Y1 + DeltaY;            { Move the figure down  }
          Y2 := Y2 + DeltaY;
          SetColor (Red);
          Rectangle (X1, Y1, X2, Y2);  { Draw the next figure  }
          StillOnScreen :=
                 (X1 >= 0) AND (Y1 >= 0)      { Keep the figure }
                  AND (X2 <= GetMaxX)         { on the screen   }
                  AND (Y2 <= GetMaxY)
    END
END.  { of main program }
```

Several methods are available by which to get different forms of linear motion, the easiest of which is to vary DeltaX and DeltaY by changing their values. For example, you could try

```
DeltaX = 2;
DeltaY = 1;
```

if you want motion that moves horizontally more than vertically. Since this speeds up the motion, you might also want to display the figure longer before moving it.

A more elaborate method of varying linear motion is to let the Y-coordinates be functions of X. This takes advantage of the linear relationship between X and Y. If you use this method, you need to remember that the screen is a reflection (with respect to the *x*-axis) of the coordinate system with which students often work. Thus, if you want a figure to move down and to the right, you would use a line with positive slope rather than negative slope.

Now let's look at how we can use a linear function to get animation. Suppose we want to modify Example 16.10 so that the square moves along a line with apparent slope M = –1/2. This means that, on the screen, as X moves to the right by 2 pixels, Y moves down one pixel. Since moving Y down is achieved by increasing Y, we use the relationship Y = (1/2)X for incrementing Y. We must also remember that X- and Y-coordinates are of type **integer,** so we must round the values before trying to draw a figure. To illustrate, consider the rectangle whose coordinates are (0, 0, 100, 100). The change in X is still

```
X1 := X1 + DeltaX;
X2 := X2 + DeltaX;
```

However, Y changes as a function of the change in X. This can be defined by

```
Y1 := 0 + round(0.5 * (X1 - 0));
Y2 := 100 + round(0.5 * (X2 - 100));
```

Note that the original coordinates for Y1 and Y2 are used, with values being added to them as a result of the change in X from the original values of X1 and X2. Thus, the following code causes a square to move across the screen along a line with apparent slope of –1/2:

```
PROGRAM LinearMotion2;

{  This program is a variation of PROGRAM LinearMotion1.     }
{  The difference is that motion is along a line with        }
{  slope M = 0.5.  Note the use of round in determining Y-   }
{  coordinates.                                              }

USES
  Crt, Graph;

CONST
  FigureDisplay = 20;
  DeltaX = 1;
  DeltaY = 1;

VAR
  X1, X2, Y1, Y2 : integer;
  StillOnScreen : boolean;

{*************************************************************}

PROCEDURE InitializeGraphics;
```

(Code here is the same as before.)

```
{*************************************************************}

BEGIN  {  Main program  }
  InitializeGraphics;
  SetBkColor (Green);
  X1 := 0;                       {  Coordinates for first figure  }
  Y1 := 0;
  X2 := 100;
  Y2 := 100;
  SetColor (Red);                         {  Set the border color  }
  Rectangle (X1, Y1, X2, Y2);
  StillOnScreen := (X1 >= 0) AND (Y1 >= 0)
                   AND (X2 <= GetMaxX)
                   AND (Y2 <= GetMaxY);
  WHILE StillOnScreen DO              {  Stop at the screen edge  }
    BEGIN
      Delay (FigureDisplay);           {  Pause before moving  }
      SetColor (Green);        {  Prepare to erase the figure  }
      Rectangle (X1, Y1, X2, Y2);          {  Erase the figure  }
      X1 := X1 + DeltaX;           {  Move figure to the right  }
      X2 := X2 + DeltaX;
      Y1 := 0 + round(0.5 * (X1-0));{ Move the figure down  }
      Y2 := 100 + round (0.5 * (X2-100));
      SetColor (Red);
      Rectangle (X1, Y1, X2, Y2);  {  Draw the next figure  }
      StillOnScreen :=
             (X1 >= 0) AND (Y1 >= 0)     {  Keep the figure  }
              AND (X2 <= GetMaxX)        {  on the screen    }
              AND (Y2 <= GetMaxY)
    END
END.  {  of main program  }
```

Several methods exist by which to modify the process just developed for linear motion. First, the slope can be declared as an identifier and then appropriate values assigned for different slopes. Second, since the expressions X1 – 0 and X2 – 100 are always equal, they can be replaced by X1 – X0, where X0 is the initial value of X1. Third, both expressions can be algebraically simplified. However, leaving them in an unsimplified form may allow students to see more easily how linear motion is achieved.

Nonlinear Motion

A detailed development of nonlinear motion is not included in this work. However, we do look at some of the associated problems and include one example.

The major change for nonlinear motion is determining how Y varies as a function of X. For example, if you want motion along a parabola, Y varies as some function of X^2. When determining exactly what relationship to use, you must remember that a positive change in Y moves the figure down the screen, as illustrated in the next example.

Example 16.11

Let's have a square move from the lower left portion of the screen along a parabola. We decrease the size of the square used previously so that the parabolic nature of movement is more apparent. Note how the Y-coordinates are modified as a function of the square of the change in X. A factor of 0.01 is included to enhance the parabolic nature of the motion. The code that accomplishes this follows:

```
PROGRAM NonLinearMotion;

{  This program features nonlinear motion.  The increment    }
{  in Y is a function of X.  The square starts in the        }
{  lower left corner and moves up and to the right.          }

USES
  Crt, Graph;

CONST
  FigureDisplay = 50;
  DeltaX = 1;
  DeltaY = 1;

VAR
  X1, X2, Y1, Y2 : integer;
  StillOnScreen : boolean;

{*************************************************************}

PROCEDURE InitializeGraphics;

  (Code here is the same as before.)

{*************************************************************}

BEGIN  {  Main program  }
  InitializeGraphics;
  SetBkColor (Green);
```

```
X1 := 0;                      {  Coordinates for first figure  }
Y1 := GetMaxY - 20;
X2 := 20;
Y2 := GetMaxY;
SetColor (Red);                       {  Set the border color  }
Rectangle (X1, Y1, X2, Y2);
readln;
StillOnScreen := (X1 >= 0) AND (Y1 >= 0)
                 AND (X2 <= GetMaxX)
                 AND (Y2 <= GetMaxY);
WHILE StillOnScreen DO             {  Stop at the screen edge  }
  BEGIN
    Delay (FigureDisplay);            {  Pause before moving  }
    SetColor (Green);      {  Prepare to erase the figure  }
    Rectangle (X1, Y1, X2, Y2);        {  Erase the figure  }
    X1 := X1 + DeltaX;          {  Move figure to the right  }
    X2 := X2 + DeltaX;
    Y1 := (GetMaxY - 20) -
           round(0.01 * sqr(X1-0));             {  Move the  }
    Y2 := GetMaxY - round(0.01 * sqr(X2-20));{ figure up  }
    SetColor (Red);
    Rectangle (X1, Y1, X2, Y2);  {  Draw the next figure  }
    StillOnScreen :=
           (X1 >= 0) AND (Y1 >= 0)     {  Keep the figure  }
            AND (X2 <= GetMaxX)        {  on the screen    }
            AND (Y2 <= GetMaxY)
  END;
readln
END.  {  of main program  }
```

Perhaps the best way to achieve nonlinear motion is to normalize the screen so that it more closely resembles the Cartesian coordinate system. This can be done by defining the screen center to be (0, 0) and reversing the orientation for Y-coordinates. Although this has the effect of making curves look like what they are, it is a tedious, challenging process. It is recommended only for advanced students or for those who have the time to work on an extra project.

Creating Figures

Now we are ready to see how more elaborate figures can be created using graphics. Four levels of development are considered. First, we create a figure without using procedures; second, we create the same figure using procedures without parameters; third, we use parameters with the procedures; and finally, we add motion to the figure. Our model for this development is a fairly simple "smiley face," as shown in Figure 16.16. A first-level pseudocode development for creating this figure is

1. Outline the head
2. Draw the eyes
3. Draw the nose
4. Draw the mouth

We use a circle for the outline of the head whose center is (100, 100) with a radius of 75. Furthermore, let's use **SolidFill** as the fill pattern. Color choices are optional.

◆ Figure 16.16

A smiley face

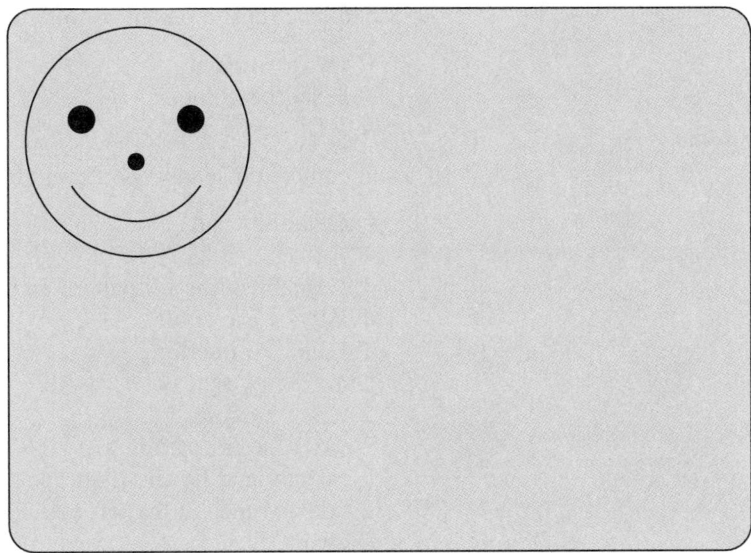

A second-level development is

1. Outline the head
   1.1 Set the color
   1.2 Establish the fill pattern and color
   1.3 Draw the circle
   1.4 Fill the interior

Circles also are used for making the eyes in Step 2 of our development. After some experimentation, let's let the eyes be centered at (140, 85) and (60, 85) with a radius of 8. A second-level development for drawing the eyes is then

2. Draw the eyes
   2.1 Set the color
   2.2 Set the fill pattern and color
   2.3 Draw and fill the right eye
   2.4 Draw and fill the left eye

Again, a circle is used to make the nose for our face. We use a center of (100, 110) and a radius of 5. The second-level development for making the nose is

3. Draw the nose
   3.1 Set the color
   3.2 Establish the fill pattern and color
   3.3 Draw the circle
   3.4 Fill the interior

Step 4 in our development uses an arc for creating the mouth. Again, after experimenting to find an arc to produce the desired smile, we use an arc with center (0, 0) ranging through the degree range 210° to 330° with a radius of 50. Specifically, the procedure call is

```
Arc (100, 100, 210, 330, 50);
```

A second-level development of this step is

4. Draw the mouth
   4.1 Set the color
   4.2 Draw the arc

Thus, a complete pseudocode development for making a smiley face is

1. Outline the head
   1.1 Set the color
   1.2 Establish the fill pattern and color
   1.3 Draw the circle
   1.4 Fill the interior
2. Draw the eyes
   2.1 Set the color
   2.2 Set the fill pattern and color
   2.3 Draw and fill the right eye
   2.4 Draw and fill the left eye
3. Draw the nose
   3.1 Set the color
   3.2 Establish the fill pattern and color
   3.3 Draw the circle
   3.4 Fill the interior
4. Draw the mouth
   4.1 Set the color
   4.2 Draw the arc

The complete program for making the smiley face follows, and when the program is run, a face (with appropriate colors) is produced as shown earlier in Figure 16.16.

```
PROGRAM Smiley1;

{  This program creates a smiley face.  No procedures are    }
{  used; instead, the main program is a linear development   }
{  of the face.                                              }

USES
  Crt, Graph;

CONST
  Pause = 500;

VAR
  GraphDriver, GraphMode,
  ErrorResult : integer;
  InitGraphicsOK : boolean;

BEGIN  {  Program  }
  ClrScr;
  GraphDriver := Detect;
  GraphMode := 1;
  InitGraph (GraphDriver, GraphMode, 'C:\TP\BGI');
  ErrorResult := GraphResult;
  InitGraphicsOK := (ErrorResult = 0);
  IF InitGraphicsOK THEN
```

```
      BEGIN
        SetBkColor (Green);

        {  Outline the head  }
        SetColor (LightRed);
        SetFillStyle (SolidFill, LightGray);
        Circle (100, 100, 75);
        FloodFill (100, 100, LightRed);
        Delay (Pause);

        {  Draw the eyes  }
        SetColor (Blue);
        SetFillStyle (SolidFill, Blue);
        Circle (140, 85, 8);
        FloodFill (140, 85, Blue);
        Circle (60, 85, 8);
        FloodFill (60, 85, Blue);
        Delay (Pause);

        {  Draw the nose  }
        SetColor (Red);
        SetFillStyle (SolidFill, Red);
        Circle (100, 110, 5);
        FloodFill (100, 110, Red);
        Delay (Pause);

        {  Draw the mouth  }
        SetColor (Red);
        Arc (100, 100, 210, 330, 50);
        readln
      END
    ELSE
      BEGIN
        writeln ('There is a graphics error.');
        writeln (GraphErrorMsg(ErrorResult));
        writeln ('Program aborted.');
        Halt
      END
  END.  {  of program  }
```

Using Procedures without Parameters

Our next example illustrates the use of procedures without parameters in making figures. We modify the previous example by creating a procedure for each step in the development.

Using procedures, the first-level pseudocode development previously shown for making a smiley face suggests a main program of

```
BEGIN
  InitializeGraphics;
  SetBkColor (Green);
  OutlineTheHead;
  DrawTheEyes;
  DrawTheNose;
  DrawTheMouth
END.
```

These procedures are developed by taking appropriate sections of code from **PROGRAM** Smiley1 and rewriting them as procedures. For example, **PROCEDURE** OutlineTheHead is

```
PROCEDURE OutlineTheHead;
  BEGIN
    SetColor (LightRed);
    SetFillStyle (SolidFill, LightGray);
    Circle (100, 100, 75);
    FloodFill (100, 100, LightRed);
    Delay (Pause)
  END;
```

After making similar changes for each of the remaining procedures, the complete program for **PROGRAM** Smiley2 using procedures is as follows:

```
PROGRAM Smiley2;

{  This program creates a smiley face by using procedures    }
{  without parameters.  Procedures for each component of     }
{  the face are called from the main program.                }

USES
  Crt, Graph;

CONST
  Pause = 500;

{************************************************************}

PROCEDURE InitializeGraphics;

  {  Given:    Nothing                                       }
  {  Task:     Initialize graphics; provide error message    }
  {  Return:   Nothing                                       }

  VAR
    GraphDriver, GraphMode,
    ErrorResult : integer;
    InitError : boolean;
  BEGIN
    GraphDriver := Detect;
    GraphMode := 1;
    InitGraph (GraphDriver, GraphMode, 'C:\TP\BGI');
    ErrorResult := GraphResult;
    InitError := (ErrorResult <> 0);
    IF InitError THEN
      BEGIN
        writeln ('There is a graphics error.');
        writeln (GraphErrorMsg(ErrorResult));
        writeln ('Program aborted.');
        Halt
      END
  END;  {  of PROCEDURE InitializeGraphics  }

{************************************************************}
```

```
PROCEDURE OutlineTheHead;

  {  Given:   Nothing                                          }
  {  Task:    Draw a circle for the head                       }
  {  Return:  Nothing                                          }

  BEGIN
    SetColor (LightRed);
    SetFillStyle (SolidFill, LightGray);
    Circle (100, 100, 75);
    FloodFill (100, 100, LightRed);
    Delay (Pause)
  END;  {  of PROCEDURE OutlineTheHead  }

{*********************************************************}

PROCEDURE DrawTheEyes;

  {  Given:   Nothing                                          }
  {  Task:    Use circles to draw the eyes                     }
  {  Return:  Nothing                                          }

  BEGIN
    SetColor (Blue);
    SetFillStyle (SolidFill, Blue);
    Circle (140, 85, 8);              {  Draw the right eye  }
    FloodFill (140, 85, Blue);
    Circle (60, 85, 8);               {  Draw the left eye   }
    FloodFill (60, 85, Blue);
    Delay (Pause)
  END;  {  of PROCEDURE DrawTheEyes  }

{*********************************************************}

PROCEDURE DrawTheNose;

  {  Given:   Nothing                                          }
  {  Task:    Use a circle to draw the nose                    }
  {  Return:  Nothing                                          }

  BEGIN
    SetColor (Red);
    SetFillStyle (SolidFill, Red);
    Circle (100, 110, 5);
    FloodFill (100, 110, Red);
    Delay (Pause)
  END;  {  of PROCEDURE DrawTheNose  }

{*********************************************************}

PROCEDURE DrawTheMouth;

  {  Given:   Nothing                                          }
  {  Task:    Use an arc to draw the mouth                     }
  {  Return:  Nothing                                          }
```

```
    BEGIN
      SetColor (Red);
      Arc (100, 100, 210, 330, 50)
    END;  {  of PROCEDURE DrawTheMouth  }

  {*************************************************************}

  BEGIN  {  Main program  }
    InitializeGraphics;
    SetBkColor (Green);
    OutlineTheHead;
    DrawTheEyes;
    DrawTheNose;
    DrawTheMouth;
    readln
  END.  {  of main program  }
```

Using Procedures with Parameters

Next we consider how to make the process of developing figures even more general. This is done by using variables rather than constant values in our procedures. Values are then passed to the procedures by appropriate calls from the calling program. To illustrate, again consider **PROCEDURE** OutlineTheHead, which contains the line of code

```
Circle (100, 100, 75);
```

If we want the outline to be elsewhere on the screen, we must change this line in the procedure. However, instead we write the procedure heading as

```
PROCEDURE OutlineTheHead (Xcoor, Ycoor, Rad);
```

and change the line of code to

```
Circle (Xcoor, Ycoor, Rad);
```

Now, if we want the center and radius to be (100, 100) and 75, respectively, we can accomplish this by a call from the main program of

```
OutlineTheHead (100, 100, 75);
```

PROCEDURE DrawTheEyes is somewhat more difficult to modify. Although circles are used for both eyes, the eyes have different centers. There are several ways to solve this problem. One method would be to write a separate procedure for each eye. In our next program, **PROGRAM** Smiley3, the eyes are set relative to the center of the face and, since they are 40 pixels right and left, respectively, and 15 pixels up from the center, they can be drawn by

```
Circle (Xcoor + 40, Ycoor - 15, Rad);  {  Right eye  }
Circle (Xcoor - 40, Ycoor - 15, Rad);  {  Left eye   }
```

where Xcoor and Ycoor are coordinates of the face center and Rad is the radius of each eye.

PROCEDURE DrawTheNose also uses the center of the head as reference coordinates for the center of the circle used for the nose. In this case, the nose is centered at (Xcoor, Ycoor + 10) with a radius of 5. The following program, **PROGRAM** Smiley3, draws a smiley face using procedures with parameters.

```
PROGRAM Smiley3;

{  This program produces a smiley face by using procedures  }
{  with parameters.  A reference point is established and   }
{  the face features are drawn with respect to the          }
{  reference point.                                         }

USES
  Crt, Graph;

CONST
  Pause = 500;

{***********************************************************}

PROCEDURE InitializeGraphics;

  {  Given:   Nothing                                        }
  {  Task:    Initialize graphics; provide error message     }
  {  Return:  Nothing                                        }

  VAR
    GraphDriver, GraphMode,
    ErrorResult : integer;
    InitError : boolean;
  BEGIN
    GraphDriver := Detect;
    GraphMode := 1;
    InitGraph (GraphDriver, GraphMode, 'C:\TP\BGI');
    ErrorResult := GraphResult;
    InitError := (ErrorResult <> 0);
    IF InitError THEN
      BEGIN
        writeln ('There is a graphics error.');
        writeln (GraphErrorMsg(ErrorResult));
        writeln ('Program aborted.');
        Halt
      END
  END;  {  of PROCEDURE InitializeGraphics  }

{***********************************************************}

PROCEDURE OutlineTheHead (Xcoor, Ycoor, Rad : integer);

  {  Given:   Nothing                                        }
  {  Task:    Draw a circle for the head                     }
  {  Return:  Nothing                                        }

  BEGIN
    SetColor (LightRed);
    SetFillStyle (SolidFill, LightGray);
    Circle (Xcoor, Ycoor, Rad);
```

```
    FloodFill (Xcoor, Ycoor, LightRed);
    Delay (Pause)
  END;  {  of PROCEDURE OutlineTheHead  }

{*************************************************************}

PROCEDURE DrawTheEyes (Xcoor, Ycoor, Rad : integer);

  {  Given:   Nothing                                         }
  {  Task:    Use circles to draw the eyes                    }
  {  Return:  Nothing                                         }

  BEGIN
    SetColor (Blue);
    SetFillStyle (SolidFill, Blue);
    Circle (Xcoor+40, Ycoor-15, Rad); { Draw the right eye  }
    FloodFill (Xcoor + 40, Ycoor - 15, Blue);
    Circle (Xcoor-40, Ycoor-15, Rad); {  Draw the left eye  }
    FloodFill (Xcoor - 40, Ycoor - 15, Blue);
    Delay (Pause)
  END;  {  of PROCEDURE DrawTheEyes  }

{*************************************************************}

PROCEDURE DrawTheNose (Xcoor, Ycoor, Rad : integer);

  {  Given:   Nothing                                         }
  {  Task:    Use a circle to draw the nose                   }
  {  Return:  Nothing                                         }

  BEGIN
    SetColor (Red);
    SetFillStyle (SolidFill, Red);
    Circle (Xcoor, Ycoor + 10, Rad);
    FloodFill (Xcoor, Ycoor + 10, Red);
    Delay (Pause)
  END;  {  of PROCEDURE DrawTheNose  }

{*************************************************************}

PROCEDURE DrawTheMouth (Xcoor, Ycoor, ArcStart,
                        ArcEnd, Rad : integer);

  {  Given:   Nothing                                         }
  {  Task:    Use an arc to draw the mouth                    }
  {  Return:  Nothing                                         }

  BEGIN
    SetColor (Red);
    Arc (Xcoor, Ycoor, ArcStart, ArcEnd, Rad)
  END;  {  of PROCEDURE DrawTheMouth  }

{*************************************************************}

BEGIN  {  Main program  }
  InitializeGraphics;
```

```
    SetBkColor (Green);
    OutlineTheHead (100, 100, 75);
    DrawTheEyes (100, 100, 8);
    DrawTheNose (100, 100, 5);
    DrawTheMouth (100, 100, 210, 330, 50);
    readln
  END.  {  of main program  }
```

Figures with Motion

Our final task for this section is to add motion to figures that are more elaborate than squares and rectangles; for example, we will move the smiley face across the screen using the principles of animation already developed. Our approach is to develop a figure using a reference point or points. We can move the figure by incrementing or decrementing the reference point or points. In moving the smiley face, the reference point is the center of the circle used to outline the head.

Using the reference point approach, all other parts of the figure need to be drawn in relation to the reference point. This allows us to achieve motion by using a loop whose body would include:

1. Draw the figure.
2. Delay.
3. Erase the figure.
4. Increment values.
5. Check to see if it is still on the screen.

To add motion to our programs for drawing the smiley face figure, we use a procedure that in turn calls procedures for various parts of the figure. Thus, the face is drawn by a call to

```
PROCEDURE DrawFace (X1, Y1 : integer);
  BEGIN
    OutlineTheHead (X1, Y1, 75, LightRed, LightGray);
    DrawTheEyes (X1, Y1, 8, Blue);
    DrawTheNose (X1, Y1, 5, Red);
    DrawTheMouth (X1, Y1, 210, 330, 50, Red)
  END;
```

Generally, erasing a figure is accomplished by redrawing the figure in the background color. This process can be shortened by using **FloodFill** on the part or parts of the figure that bound the region. For example, the smiley face is bounded by a circle. If this circle is filled with the background color, it is not necessary to redraw the eyes, nose, and mouth. Thus, the procedure for erasing our smiley face is

```
PROCEDURE EraseFace (X1, Y1 : integer;
                     BkColor : word);
  BEGIN
    OutlineTheHead (X1, Y1, 75, BkColor, BkColor)
  END;
```

Two parts of our design control how smoothly the animation appears: the length of **Delay** and the size of the increment. It is necessary to experiment with both of these, but be prepared for a motion that is not completely smooth. Our approach to animation does not take advantage of sophisticated techniques for achieving smooth motion. Also be aware that, as you make figures more complex, their motion will appear less smooth.

Finally, we must make sure our figure stays on the screen. This can be done by using a **FOR** loop and moving the figure a predetermined number of times. Another method to keep the figure on the screen is to determine a bounding value of the figure and then compare it with the screen boundaries before drawing the next figure. This is the method used for our animation of the smiley face.

The last program for our smiley face, **PROGRAM** Smiley4, incorporates most of the animation ideas discussed in this section. The main program shows the use of reference coordinates, along with procedures for drawing the smiley face, erasing it, and setting the boundaries for the animation.

The complete program is as follows:

```
PROGRAM Smiley4;

{  This program produces animation of a smiley face.  It     }
{  uses procedures with parameters to create the figure.     }
{  Animation is achieved by redrawing the figure in the      }
{  background color, moving the figure, and then redrawing   }
{  the figure.                                               }

USES
  Crt, Graph;

CONST
  Pause = 200;    {  Display time in milliseconds             }
  DeltaX = 15;    {  Horizontal movement of reference point   }

VAR
  X1, Y1 : integer;
  BkColor : word;
  StillOnScreen : boolean;

{************************************************************}

PROCEDURE InitializeGraphics;

  {  Given:   Nothing                                        }
  {  Task:    Initialize graphics; provide error message     }
  {  Return:  Nothing                                        }

  VAR
    GraphDriver, GraphMode,
    ErrorResult : integer;
    InitError : boolean;
  BEGIN
    GraphDriver := Detect;
    GraphMode := 1;
    InitGraph (GraphDriver, GraphMode, 'C:\TP\BGI');
    ErrorResult := GraphResult;
    InitError := (ErrorResult <> 0);
    IF InitError THEN
      BEGIN
        writeln ('There is a graphics error.');
        writeln (GraphErrorMsg(ErrorResult));
        writeln ('Program aborted.');
        Halt
```

```
      END
  END;  {  of PROCEDURE InitializeGraphics  }

{************************************************************}

PROCEDURE OutlineTheHead (Xcoor, Ycoor, Rad,
                          Color1, Color2 : integer);

  {  Given:   Nothing                                         }
  {  Task:    Draw a circle for the head                      }
  {  Return:  Nothing                                         }

  BEGIN
    SetColor (Color1);
    SetFillStyle (SolidFill, Color2);
    Circle (Xcoor, Ycoor, Rad);
    FloodFill (Xcoor, Ycoor, Color1)
  END;  {  of PROCEDURE OutlineTheHead  }

{************************************************************}

PROCEDURE DrawTheEyes (Xcoor, Ycoor, Rad, Color : integer);

  {  Given:   Nothing                                         }
  {  Task:    Use circles to draw the eyes                    }
  {  Return:  Nothing                                         }

  BEGIN
    SetColor (Color);
    SetFillStyle (SolidFill, Color);
    Circle (Xcoor+40, Ycoor-15, Rad); { Draw the right eye   }
    FloodFill (Xcoor + 40, Ycoor - 15, Color);
    Circle (Xcoor-40, Ycoor-15, Rad); {  Draw the left eye   }
    FloodFill (Xcoor - 40, Ycoor - 15, Color)
  END;  {  of PROCEDURE DrawTheEyes  }

{************************************************************}

PROCEDURE DrawTheNose (Xcoor, Ycoor, Rad, Color : integer);

  {  Given:   Nothing                                         }
  {  Task:    Use a circle to draw the nose                   }
  {  Return:  Nothing                                         }

  BEGIN
    SetColor (Color);
    SetFillStyle (SolidFill, Color);
    Circle (Xcoor, Ycoor + 10, Rad);
    FloodFill (Xcoor, Ycoor + 10, Color)
  END;  {  of PROCEDURE DrawTheNose  }

{************************************************************}

PROCEDURE DrawTheMouth (Xcoor, Ycoor, ArcStart,
                        ArcEnd, Rad, Color : integer);
```

```
  { Given:   Nothing                                              }
  { Task:    Use an arc to draw the mouth                         }
  { Return:  Nothing                                              }

  BEGIN
    SetColor (Color);
    Arc (Xcoor, Ycoor, ArcStart, ArcEnd, Rad)
  END;  {  of PROCEDURE DrawTheMouth  }

{*************************************************************}

PROCEDURE DrawFace (X1, Y1 : integer);

  { Given:   Reference coordinates for the figure             }
  { Task:    Using the given coordinates, call procedures     }
  {              to draw the figure                           }
  { Return:  Nothing                                          }

  BEGIN
    OutlineTheHead (X1, Y1, 75, LightRed, LightGray);
    DrawTheEyes (X1, Y1, 8, Blue);
    DrawTheNose (X1, Y1, 5, Red);
    DrawTheMouth (X1, Y1, 210, 330, 50, Red)
  END;  {  of PROCEDURE DrawFace  }

{*************************************************************}

PROCEDURE EraseFace (X1, Y1 : integer;
                     BkColor : word);

  { Given:   Reference coordinates and background color      }
  { Task:    Erase by redrawing in the background color      }
  { Return:  Nothing                                          }

  BEGIN
    OutlineTheHead (X1, Y1, 75, BkColor, BkColor)
  END;  {  of PROCEDURE EraseFace  }

{*************************************************************}

BEGIN  {  Main program  }
  InitializeGraphics;
  SetBkColor (Green);
  BkColor := Green;
  X1 := 100;                        {  Reference coordinates  }
  Y1 := 100;
  StillOnScreen := (X1 < GetMaxX - 85);
  DrawFace (X1, Y1);
  WHILE StillOnScreen DO
    BEGIN
      Delay (Pause);
      EraseFace (X1, Y1, BkColor);
      X1 := X1 + DeltaX;
      DrawFace (X1, Y1);
      StillOnScreen := (X1 < GetMaxX - 85)
```

```
    END;  {  of WHILE loop  }
  readln
END.   {  of main program  }
```

Exercises 16.4

1. There are many ways to modify **PROGRAM** Smiley1. Enhance this program in each of the following ways:
   *a. Make the right eye blink after the face has been drawn.
   *b. Have the mouth alternate between a smile and a frown.
   c. Add ears to the head.
   d. Allow the user to choose the color of the eyes.
2. Revise **PROGRAM** HorizontalMotion, which moves a square across the screen, so that a shadowing effect is shown by drawing the next figure before erasing the previous one.
*3. Write a program that incorporates the suggestions made for modifying the code for linear motion. Try several different values for the slope.
4. Write a program that has a square that bounces between the right side of the screen and the left side of the screen. Avoid creating an infinite loop in your program.
*5. Write a program that causes a square to bounce back and forth between the right edge and the left edge of the screen as it moves down the screen. Have the motion stop when the square hits the bottom of the screen. Vary the amount of vertical drop with different runs of the program.
6. Write a program that has a ball move diagonally around the screen. The ball should bounce off each screen edge. Control the length of motion or number of bounces to avoid an infinite loop.
7. Write an interactive graphics program that allows the user to select appropriate colors (background, for example). Use a **CASE** statement to convert the user's entry into the color(s) chosen.
8. Write a program that creates a snowman.
9. Write a program depicting a scene of mountains with snow on their peaks.
10. Write a program depicting a holiday scene. Include animation and blinking.

16.5 Bar Graphs and Charts

Objectives

- to construct a bar graph
- to construct a pie chart

There are several convenient ways to display bars, bar graphs, and charts. In this section, we examine the available procedures and how they can be used to create graphic displays.

Bars

The underlying requirement for constructing bar graphs is the ability to construct a single bar. This ability is provided by using the procedure **Bar.** The correct form of this procedure is

Bar (<UpLeftX>, <UpLeftY>, <LowRightX>, <LowRightY>)

where all variables are of type **integer.** As expected, (UpleftX, UpleftY) represents the coordinates of the upper left vertex of the bar and (LowRightX, LowRightY) represents the coordinates of the lower right vertex. We frequently use notation consistent with how rectangles are defined. Thus

```
Bar (X1, Y1, X2, Y2);
```

is the bar displayed in Figure 16.17. More specifically, Figure 16.18 contains a bar with an upper left vertex of (10, 10) and a lower right vertex of (40, 80).

The **Bar** procedure closely resembles the **Rectangle** procedure. The difference is that it automatically fills the interior with the border color. Thus

```
Bar (10, 10, 40, 80);
```

◆ Figure 16.17

The bar defined by **Bar** (X1, Y1, X2, Y2)

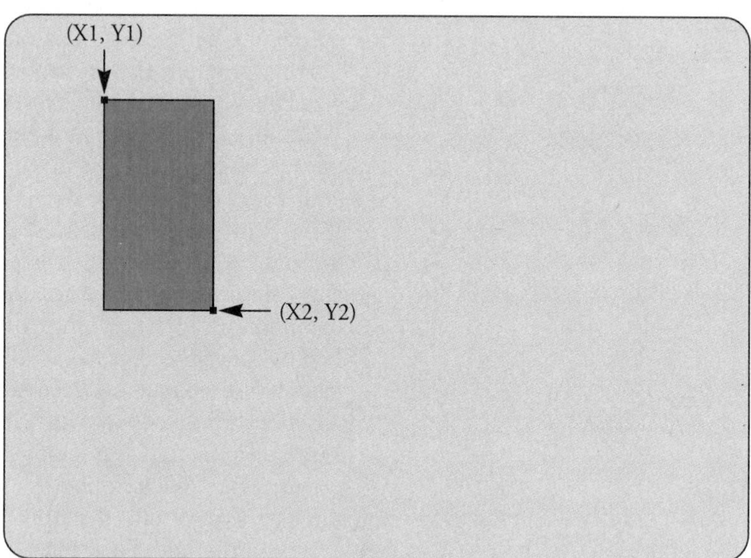

◆ Figure 16.18

The bar defined by **Bar** (10, 10, 40, 80)

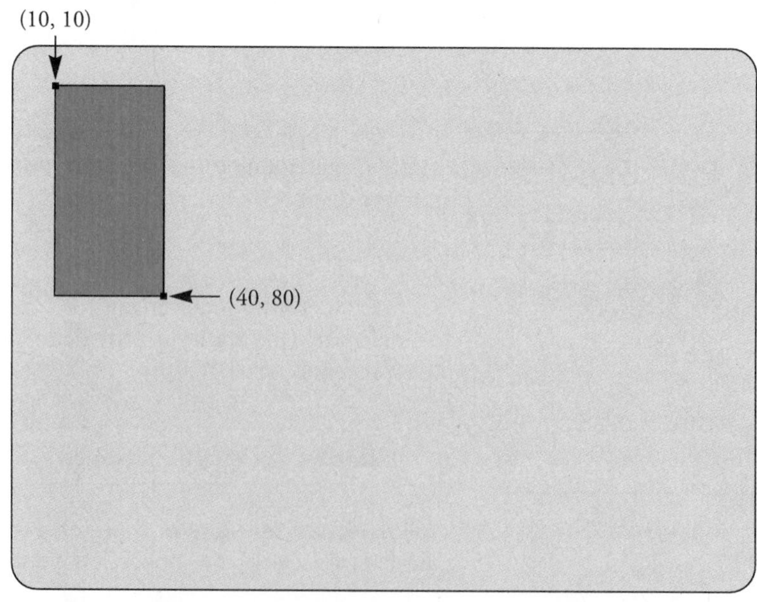

has the same effect as

```
Rectangle (10, 10, 40, 80);
FloodFill (11, 11, 3);
```

assuming color 3 is the border color for the rectangle.

It is possible to vary the color and pattern used to fill the interior of a bar by using the procedure **SetFillStyle.** Thus, if we want to fill a bar with the **SlashFill** pattern using color 2, we use the code

```
SetFillStyle (SlashFill, 2);
Bar (10, 10, 40, 80);
```

Bar Graphs

Bars can be used to create bar graphs. Suppose we want to display the grade distribution for some class. For sample data, let's assume the grades for 30 students are grouped as follows: A, 5; B, 7; C, 10; D, 6; E, 2.

Before we can create a bar graph to display these data, several issues must be considered. First, what are the relative heights of the bars? Given this particular range of numbers (2–10), an easy choice is to let each integer be represented by 10 pixels. Thus, the bar representing C's will be 100 pixels high and the one representing E's will be 20 pixels high.

Second, where do we want the bottom line of our graph to be located? If we want the graph to be centered vertically, we must determine how much of the vertical part of the screen is not being used by the bars. Since the tallest bar is 100 pixels, this leaves **GetMaxY** – 100 pixels not in use. We want one-half of these pixels to be above the graph and one-half to be below, so we define BottomEdge to be

```
BottomEdge := 100 + round((GetMaxY - 100) / 2);
```

which can be simplified to 50 + round(**GetMaxY** / 2). This is illustrated in Figure 16.19.

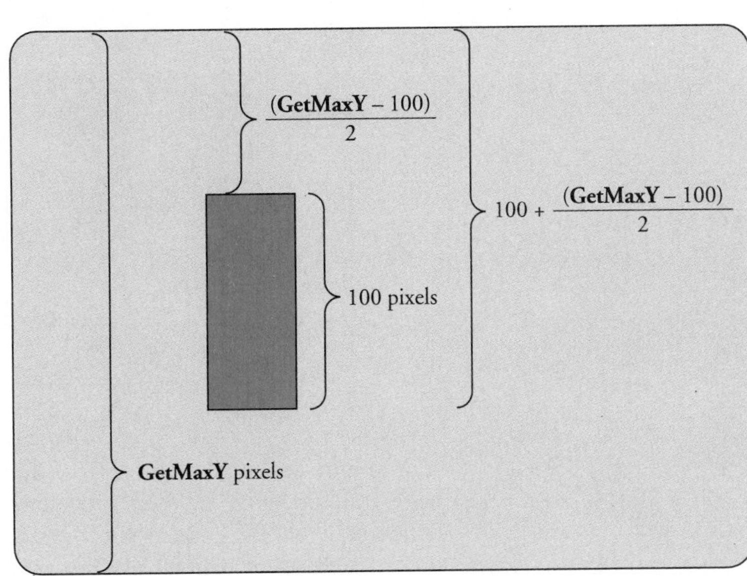

◆ Figure 16.19

Centering a bar of 100 pixels

With the bottom edge of the graph now defined, the Y-coordinates of the bar representing the number of C's will be Y1 = BottomEdge – 100 and Y2 = BottomEdge.

Third, how wide should our bars be? The width of the bars is a matter of choice. Our example uses a width of 10 pixels.

Fourth, how far apart should our bars be? Again, this is a matter of choice. Our example separates the bars by 10 pixels.

Finally, where should the bars start? We could center the chart horizontally in a similar manner to the way we centered it vertically. However, we choose to leave a left margin of 30 pixels.

Now that these decisions have been made, our first bar graph is created by the following code:

```
BottomEdge := 50 + round(GetMaxY / 2);
LeftEdge := 30;
Bar (LeftEdge, BottomEdge - 50,
     LeftEdge + 10, BottomEdge);      {  Bar for A's  }
Bar (LeftEdge + 20, BottomEdge - 70,
     LeftEdge + 30, BottomEdge);      {  Bar for B's  }
Bar (LeftEdge + 40, BottomEdge - 100,
     LeftEdge + 50, BottomEdge);      {  Bar for C's  }
Bar (LeftEdge + 60, BottomEdge - 60,
     LeftEdge + 70, BottomEdge);      {  Bar for D's  }
Bar (LeftEdge + 80, BottomEdge - 20,
     LeftEdge + 90, BottomEdge);      {  Bar for E's  }
```

When this segment of code is run, the display shown in Figure 16.20 results.

◆ Figure 16.20

A bar graph

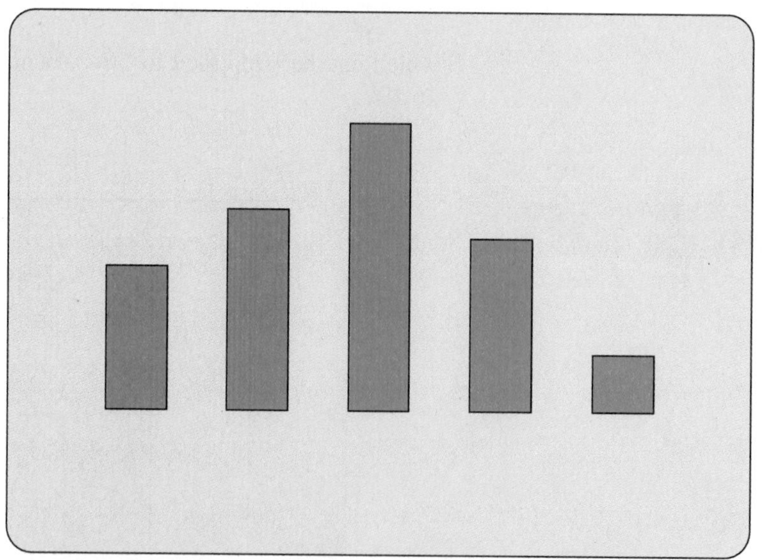

You may notice that the previous code is not very elegant. Since the intent was to help you see how the **Bar** procedure can be used to produce a bar graph, we deliberately left the code in this form. Several suggestions for modifications are made in the exercises at the end of this section.

When we constructed the bar graph in this example, we simplified an important consideration. We allowed our tallest bar to be 10 times the number of C's because the range of values was 2–10. In general, such easy choices are not usually available. A better method is to define the tallest bar to be a percentage (integer) of the vertical portion of the screen we want to use. We call this value MaxBarHeight. Then each remaining bar height can be determined relative to the tallest bar. For example, if the values range from 100 to 1,300 and one of the values is 685, the bar height for that bar will be 685 / 1,300 * MaxBarHeight. You will be asked to use this technique in an exercise at the end of this section.

Three-Dimensional Bars

A three-dimensional bar can also be used to construct bar graphs. Such a bar adds both depth and a top (optional) to a two-dimensional bar. The procedure for a three-dimensional bar is **Bar3D.** The correct form of this procedure is

Bar3D (X1, Y1, X2, Y2, <depth>, <top>)

Here, X1, Y1, X2, and Y2 are the same as the variables used in the **Bar** procedure. Depth is of type **word** and represents the depth desired for perspective; no standard exists for this, but the depth of most three-dimensional bars is 25 to 35 percent of the bar width. Top is a variable of type **boolean:** A value of **true** means a top is included; a value of **false** means a top is not included. We would exclude the top of a bar if we wanted to "stack" another bar on top of it. To illustrate, consider the three-dimensional bars displayed by

```
Bar3D (20, 20, 50, 70, 10, true);
Bar3D (100, 20, 130, 70, 10, false);
```

which are illustrated in Figure 16.21.

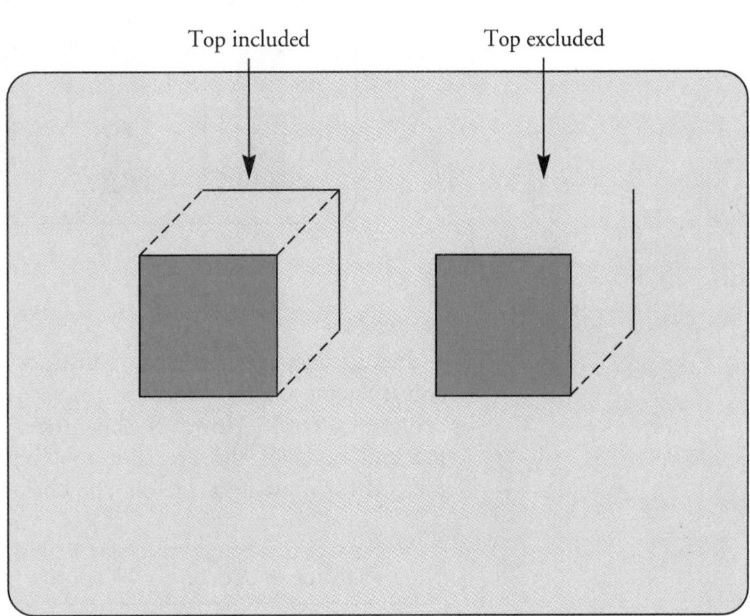

◆ Figure 16.21
Two three-dimensional bars

Default settings are used to fill in the "faces" of three-dimensional bars with the border color. We can change the filling pattern and color by using **SetFillStyle** before a call to **Bar3D.** The three-dimensional outline of the bar is drawn in the current line style, and color is determined by **SetLineStyle** and **SetColor.**

To illustrate the difference between a two-dimensional and a three-dimensional bar graph, let's reconsider the earlier example in which we displayed the results of a distribution of grades in a class in two dimensions, as shown in Figure 16.20 on page 826. Changing the **Bar** procedure

```
Bar (LeftEdge, BottomEdge - 50,
     LeftEdge + 10, BottomEdge);
```

to

```
Bar3D (LeftEdge, BottomEdge - 50,
       LeftEdge + 10, BottomEdge, 3, true);
```

yields a depth of 30 percent of the bar width (10 pixels) and puts a top on each bar. After similar changes are made in the remaining bars, the segment of code produces the display shown in Figure 16.22.

◆ Figure 16.22

A three-dimensional bar graph

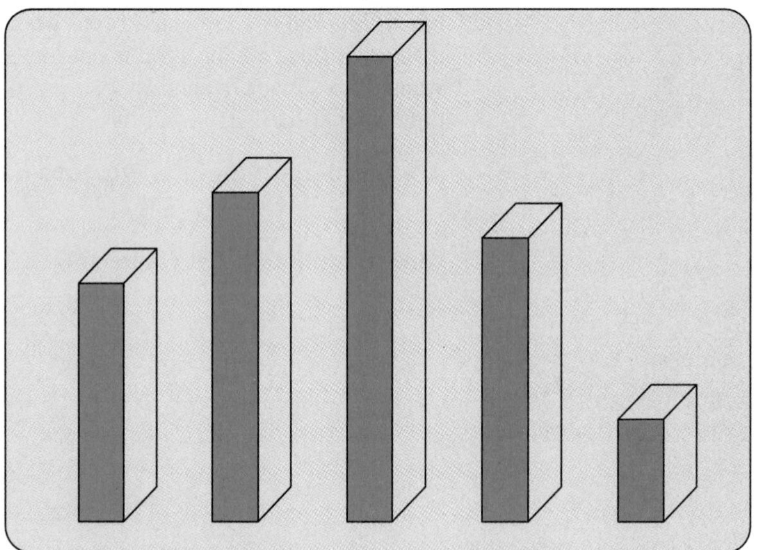

Sectors

Just as bars are needed to construct bar graphs, sectors of a circle are needed to construct pie charts. We create a sector by joining the endpoints of an arc to the center of a circle. However, this process requires that we identify the coordinates of the endpoints of the arc. Fortunately, the procedure **PieSlice** provides an easier method for drawing a sector. The correct form of this procedure is

PieSlice (<Xcoor>, <Ycoor>, <anglestart>, <anglefinish>, <radius>)

where the five arguments are of the same types and serve the same purposes as the respective arguments for **Arc.** The difference is that **PieSlice** causes the endpoints of the arc to be joined to the center of the circle of which the arc is a portion. To illustrate, let's consider

```
Arc (100, 100, 0, 45, 50);
```

and

```
PieSlice (100, 100, 0, 45, 50);
```

The results of these procedures are displayed in Figures 16.23(a) and (b), respectively. Note that the sector is filled with the border color by default.

◆ Figure 16.23

Arc and **PieSlice**

(a) **Arc** (100, 100, 0, 45, 50)

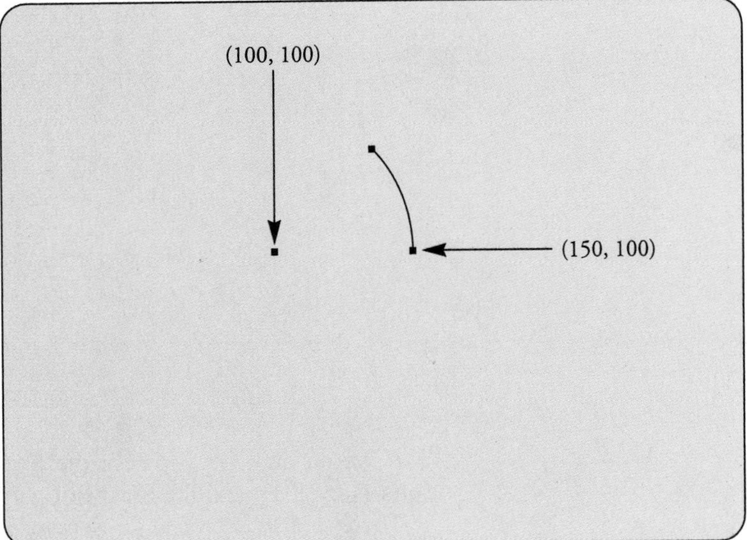

(b) **PieSlice** (100, 100, 0, 45, 50)

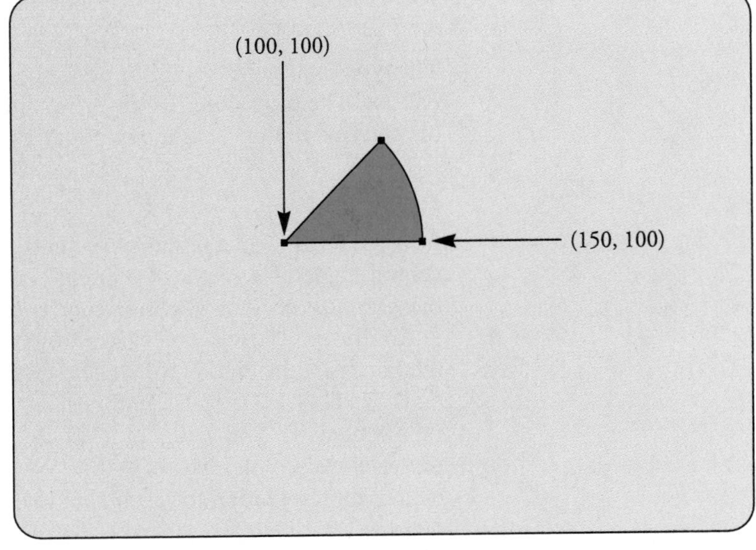

In general, the interior can be controlled by using **SetFillStyle** to specify a pattern and a color. To illustrate,

```
SetColor (1);
SetBkColor (4);
SetFillStyle (SlashFill, 2);
PieSlice (100, 100, 0, 90, 50);
```

produces the sector shown in Figure 16.24.

◆ Figure 16.24

Filling and coloring a sector

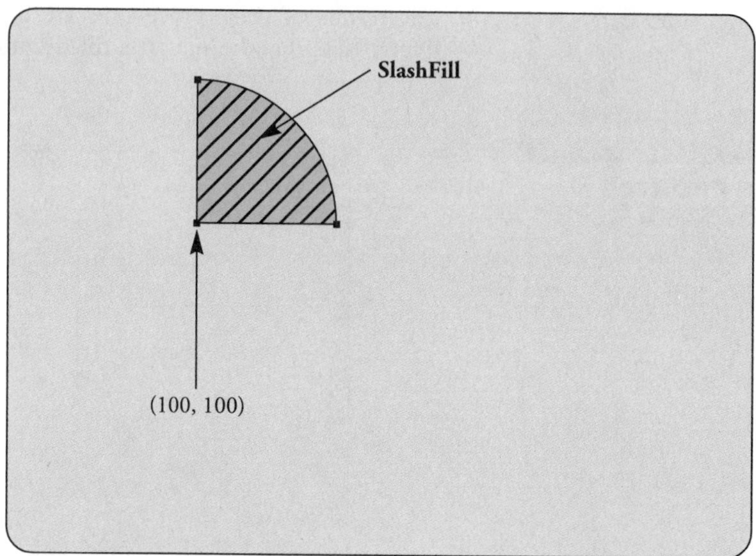

If we are in CGA mode 3, the background color is red(4), the current drawing color is cyan(1), and the **SlashFill** pattern is drawn with magenta(2).

There is also a procedure **Sector,** which can be used to display a portion of an ellipse. The correct form of this procedure is

Sector (<Xcoor>, <Ycoor>, <anglestart>, <anglefinish>, <Xrad>, <Yrad>)

The types and purposes of the arguments of **Sector** are identical to those in procedure **Ellipse**. The procedure **Sector** draws the indicated portion of the ellipse and then fills the interior in the same manner that **PieSlice** fills the interior of a sector.

Pie Charts

A pie chart is an alternative method for displaying data graphically. The size of the central angle of a sector of a circle corresponds to the height of a particular bar in a bar graph. Procedure **PieSlice** can be used to produce a pie chart.

To illustrate how a pie chart is formed, let's reconsider the data we used to produce the bar graph in Figure 16.20. The grade distribution for a class of 30 students is A, 5; B, 7; C, 10; D, 6; E, 2. Since the total number of grades is 30, each grade is represented by 360 / 30, or (12) degrees. Thus, the central angle for the sector representing the number of A's is $5 \times 12° = 60°$. In general, we can determine the degree representation for each data item by the quotient 360 / number of items. If we define

```
ItemAngleSize := 360 / TotalItems;
```

the central angle for each item is

```
ItemAngleSize * <number of items>
```

Using our grade distribution example, we have

```
ItemAngleSize := 360 / 30;
```

Central angles for data items A through E are indicated in Table 16.8. When we write code to produce a pie chart, the sector representing A's will have a central angle of 60°, the sector representing B's will have a central angle of 84°, and so on.

Table 16.8

Central angles for data items

Data Item	Number of Items	ItemAngle Size × Number of Items (slice size)
A	5	$\frac{360}{30} \times 5 = 60$
B	7	$\frac{360}{30} \times 7 = 84$
C	10	$\frac{360}{30} \times 10 = 120$
D	6	$\frac{360}{30} \times 6 = 72$
E	2	$\frac{360}{30} \times 2 = 24$

Next, we must determine how to start and end each sector. If we assume an angle start of 0°, the sector for A's will be generated by

```
AngleStart := 0;
AngleFinish := 60;
```

Several methods can be used to keep track of successive starting and finishing angles. In our example, we use the code

```
AngleStart := AngleFinish;  {  from previous slice  }
AngleFinish := AngleStart + SliceSize;
```

It is also customary to vary the filling pattern for each slice in a pie chart. This can be controlled by using **SetFillStyle** before each call to **PieSlice.** We use the technique of

```
Pattern := succ(pattern);
```

after suitable initialization of Pattern.

Based on the concepts developed in this section, the following program causes a pie chart to be displayed that represents the data used to produce the bar graph shown in Figure 16.20 on page 826.

```
PROGRAM PieChart;

{  This program uses the procedure PieSlice to produce     }
{  a pie chart.  Note how sectors are determined and       }
{  filled in PROCEDURE GraphSector.                        }
```

```
USES
  Crt, Graph;

CONST
  NumDataItems = 30;
  Radius = 50;
  Xcoor = 100;
  Ycoor = 100;

VAR
  AngleStart, AngleFinish : word;
  Pattern : word;
  SliceSize : word;
  ItemAngleSize : real;
  NumItems : integer;

{************************************************************}

PROCEDURE InitializeGraphics;

  {  Given:   Nothing                                          }
  {  Task:    Initialize graphics; provide error message       }
  {  Return:  Nothing                                          }

  VAR
    GraphDriver, GraphMode,
    ErrorResult : integer;
    InitError : boolean;
  BEGIN
    GraphDriver := CGA;
    GraphMode := 1;
    InitGraph (GraphDriver, GraphMode, 'C:\TP\BGI');
    ErrorResult := GraphResult;
    InitError := (ErrorResult <> 0);
    IF InitError THEN
      BEGIN
        writeln ('There is a graphics error.');
        writeln (GraphErrorMsg(ErrorResult));
        writeln ('Program aborted.');
        Halt
      END
  END;  {  of PROCEDURE InitializeGraphics  }

{************************************************************}

PROCEDURE GraphSector (NumItems : integer;
                       ItemAngleSize : real;
                       AngleStart : word;
                       VAR AngleFinish : word;
                       VAR Pattern : word);

  {  Given:   Number of items for the sector, angle size    }
  {                per item, angle start position, fill     }
  {                pattern for the last sector              }
  {  Task:    Create one sector of a pie chart              }
```

```
  {  Return:  Angle finish position and pattern used       }
  {                for the sector                          }

  VAR
    SliceSize : word;
  BEGIN
    SliceSize := round(NumItems * ItemAngleSize);
    AngleStart := AngleFinish;
    AngleFinish := AngleStart + SliceSize;
    SetFillStyle (Pattern, 2);
    PieSlice (Xcoor, Ycoor, AngleStart, AngleFinish, Radius);
    Pattern := succ(Pattern)
  END;  {  of PROCEDURE GraphSector  }

{*******************************************************}

BEGIN  {  Main program  }
  InitializeGraphics;

  {  Initialize  }
  SetBkColor (Green);
  AngleFinish := 0;
  Pattern := LineFill;
  ItemAngleSize := 360 / NumDataItems;

  {  Draw the pie sectors  }
  NumItems := 5;
  GraphSector (NumItems, ItemAngleSize, AngleStart,
               AngleFinish, Pattern);
  NumItems := 7;
  GraphSector (NumItems, ItemAngleSize, AngleStart,
               AngleFinish, Pattern);
  NumItems := 10;
  GraphSector (NumItems, ItemAngleSize, AngleStart,
               AngleFinish, Pattern);
  NumItems := 6;
  GraphSector (NumItems, ItemAngleSize, AngleStart,
               AngleFinish, Pattern);
  NumItems := 2;
  GraphSector (NumItems, ItemAngleSize, AngleStart,
               AngleFinish, Pattern);
  readln;
  CloseGraph
END.  {  of main program  }
```

When this program is run, the screen display shown in Figure 16.25 results.

Exercises 16.5

*1. Write a procedure to display vertical bars of width 10 and height 50 that are filled with different filling patterns. Have the base separated by a horizontal distance of five pixels.

2. Reconsider the bar graph example shown in Figure 16.20. Modify the segment of code in each of the following ways.
   a. Define and use a height for each bar, such as AHeight := 50.

◆ Figure 16.25

A pie chart

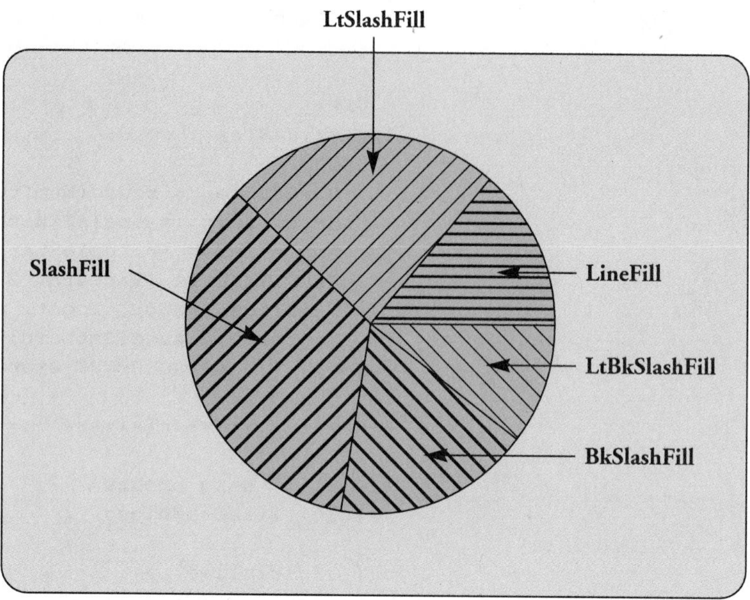

b. Define and use a bar width.
c. Define and use a distance between bars.
d. Revise the code to use a **FOR** loop to display the bars. A general form is

```
FOR Number := 1 TO 5 DO
  BEGIN
    .
    .  (set coordinates here)
    .
    Bar (X1, Y1, X2, Y2)
  END;
```

3. Reconsider the bar graph referred to in Exercise 2. Experiment with LeftEdge, bar width, and distance between bars to find the most appealing display.
4. Review the discussion in this section about using relative bar heights, where the tallest bar is defined to be of height MaxBarHeight. Use this technique to draw a bar graph of the values 120, 135, 180, 240, 290, and 345.
*5. Three-dimensional bars without tops are used when stacking bars. Write a short program to display five three-dimensional bars in a stack. Vary the patterns on the faces of the bars.
6. Find the average monthly rate of precipitation for the region in which your school is located. Display the results for one year in a two-dimensional bar graph.
7. Change your program so your display in Exercise 6 uses three-dimensional bars.
8. Write an interactive program that allows the user to experiment with different depths when displaying a three-dimensional bar. The user should be able to enter any depth between 0 and 100 percent of the bar width. Use **Delay** to create a significant pause to allow the user to view each display.

*9. Make a color wheel by using **PieSlice** and changing the color of the sector every 45°.
10. How can the colors and filling patterns be used to produce the outline of a sector? (Make the interior of the sector the same as the screen background.)
11. Use both **PieSlice** and **Sector** to fill a semicircle with a radius of 50. Compare the two displays. What are your conclusions?
12. Reconsider the pie chart developed in this section. Revise **PROGRAM** PieChart so the grades can be entered interactively.

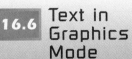

16.6 Text in Graphics Mode

Objectives

- to display text in graphics
- to select the style and font for text in graphics

As is true of most graphics packages, Turbo Pascal permits the combined display of graphics features and text on the same screen. In this section, we look at several procedures available in Turbo Pascal for printing characters while in a graphics setting. We will also see how the characters can vary in font, size, and orientation.

Graphics Characters

A standard-size character displayed while in the graphics mode occupies an 8 × 8 pixel square. Thus, when working with a 200 × 320 pixel screen, there are 25 lines of 40 characters each.

Displaying Characters with `OutText`

Two basic procedures are used for displaying characters in a graphics mode: **OutText** and **OutTextXY.** The correct form of procedure **OutText** is

OutText (<message>)

where <message> is a **string** or a variable of type **string.** If <message> is an actual string rather than a variable, it must be enclosed in quotes. Thus, we can print HI THERE by using either

```
OutText ('HI THERE');
```

or

```
Message := 'HI THERE';
OutText (Message);
```

When **OutText** is used to display characters, it starts printing at the current pointer position, which is the upper left corner of the 8 × 8 pixel square used to display the first character of the string. To illustrate, assume we have just entered the graphics mode and the default setting of the current pointer is at (0, 0). The segment of code

```
OutText ('HI THERE');
MoveTo (4, 9);
OutText ('HI THERE');
```

then produces the display shown in Figure 16.26.

◆ Figure 16.26

Display using **OutText**

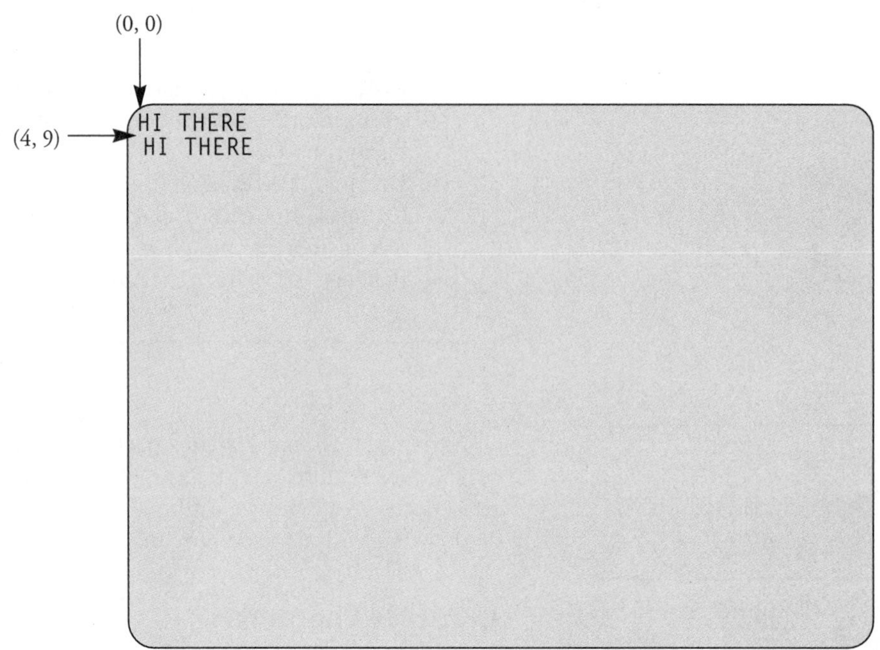

Use of **OutText** causes the current pointer to move. Its position becomes the upper left corner of the next available 8 × 8 pixel square after the last character in the string has been printed. Thus, if the current pointer is at (0, 0) and we print

```
OutText ('HI THERE');
```

the current pointer is then positioned as shown in Figure 16.27.

◆ Figure 16.27

Position of the current pointer after printing the first string

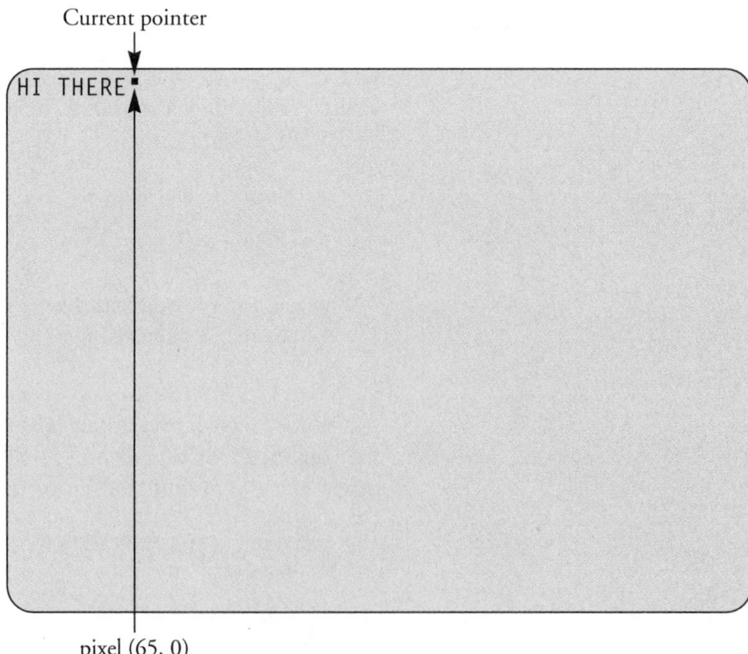

Text characters in graphics are not confined to the 25 lines of 40 characters on a 200 × 320 pixel screen. We can position a string to begin at any pixel on the screen by using **MoveTo.** After a call to **MoveTo,** the next character is displayed so its upper left corner is in the position designated by **MoveTo.** To illustrate, the segment of code

```
Message := 'HI THERE';
OutText (Message);
MoveTo (65, 4);
OutText (Message);
MoveTo (69, 12);
OutText (Message);
```

produces the display shown in Figure 16.28. If the message to be printed using **OutText** is too long for the screen, it is truncated at the viewpoint border.

◆ Figure 16.28

Display using **MoveTo**

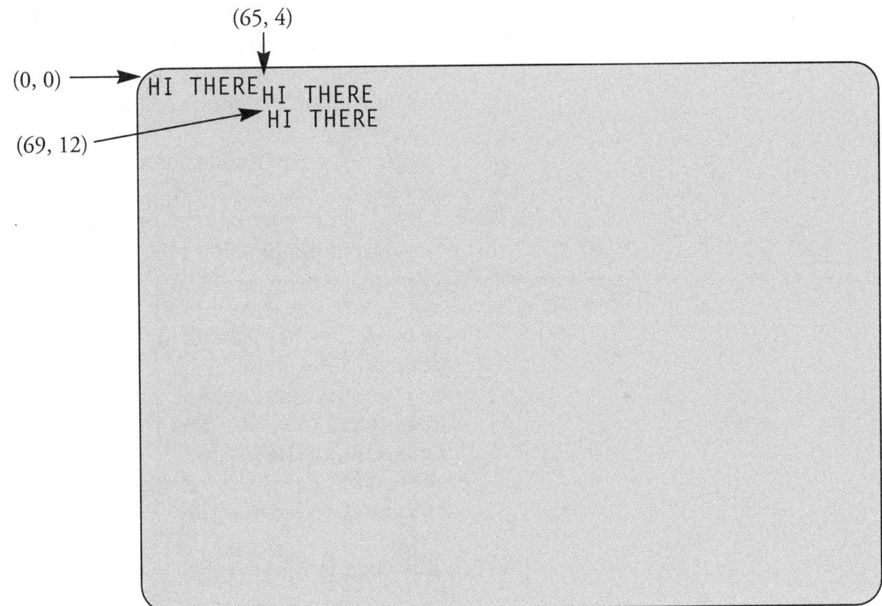

Displaying Characters with OutTextXY

The procedure **OutTextXY** can also be used to print messages while in a graphics mode. The correct form of this procedure is

OutTextXY (<Xcoor>, <Ycoor>, <message>)

where Xcoor and Ycoor are variables of type **integer** and message is of type **string.** Using **OutTextXY** causes the string to be printed with pixel position (Xcoor, Ycoor) being the upper left position of the first character. Thus, the display is the same as the two lines of code

```
MoveTo (Xcoor, Ycoor);
OutText (Message);
```

The difference between **OutText** and **OutTextXY** is that **OutTextXY** does not cause the current pointer to be moved. This means we can print a message anywhere we choose and the current pointer will remain where it was before **OutTextXY** was used. The next example illustrates how this feature can enhance your graphics work.

Example 16.12

This example uses **OutTextXY** to display a "continuation message" at the bottom of the graphics screen. Until now, we have been using a **readln** statement or the procedure **Delay** to hold the graphics screen and no message to press <Enter> to continue has been given. We can make our programs more user friendly by writing a procedure that displays a message directing the user appropriately. A typical procedure follows.

```
PROCEDURE ContinuationMessage;
  VAR
    Xcoor, Ycoor : integer;
  BEGIN
    Message := 'Press <Enter> to continue.';
    Xcoor := (GetMaxX - 8 * Length(Message)) DIV 2;
    Ycoor := GetMaxY - 8;
    OutTextXY (Xcoor, Ycoor, Message);
    readln
  END;  {  of PROCEDURE ContinuationMessage  }
```

Note that we have centered this message on the last line available for printing. If we use this procedure in conjunction with a modification of the earlier code used to display HI THERE on the screen, we have

```
Message := 'HI THERE';
OutText (Message);
ContinuationMessage;
OutTextXY (65, 4, Message);
ContinuationMessage;
OutTextXY (69, 12, Message)
ContinuationMessage;
```

When this code is run, the displays shown in Figures 16.29(a), (b), and (c) result.

Changing the Characters

While in a graphics mode, we can vary the characters used with a call to the procedure **SetTextStyle.** The correct form of this procedure is

> **SetTextStyle** (<font>, <direction>, <size>)

The font, **DefaultFont,** is a **bit-mapped font.** Characters appear in an 8 × 8 pixel square.

Stroked fonts are all fonts except **DefaultFont,** which is a bit-mapped font.

The first argument, <font>, is a variable of type **word** that allows the user to select from five available fonts. These predefined constants and how they look when displayed are shown in Table 16.9.

The constant **DefaultFont** has value zero. This font is referred to as a **bit-mapped font,** and characters appear in an 8 × 8 pixel square. The other fonts are **stroked fonts,** so called because of the manner in which the characters are constructed. These fonts do not appear in 8 × 8 pixel squares.

Figure 16.29

Display using a continuation message

(a)

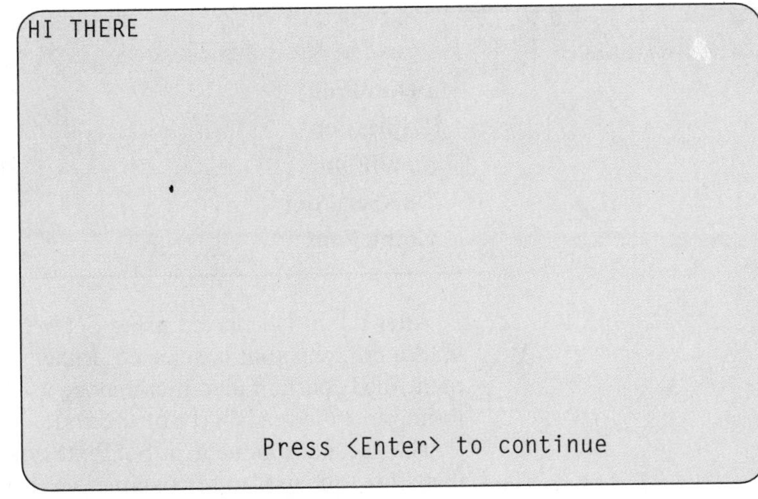

(b)

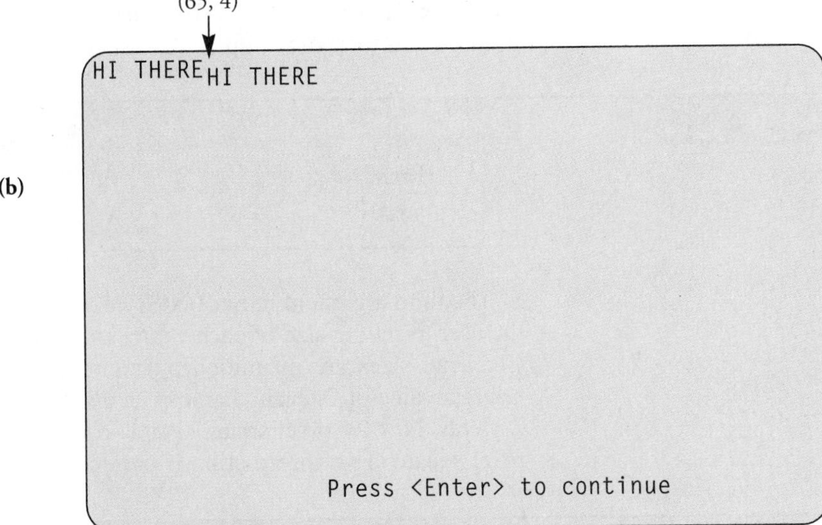

(c)

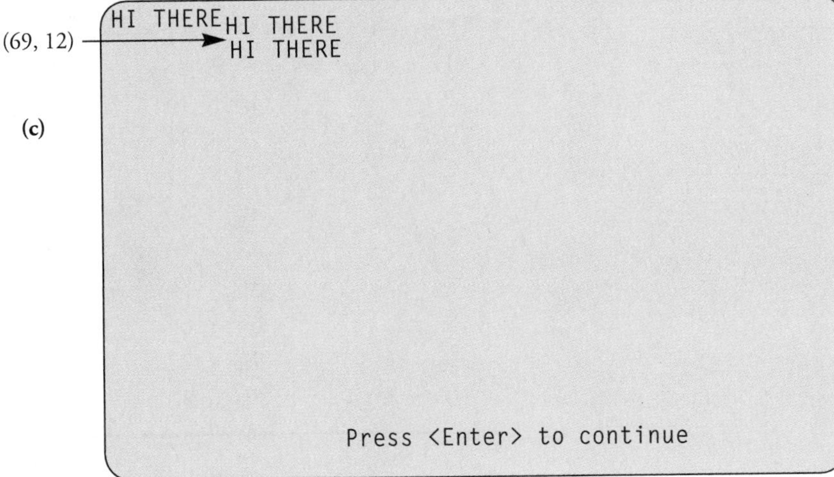

Table 16.9

Fonts

Font Name	Font Value	Font Style
DefaultFont	0	Default Font
TriplexFont	1	Triplex Font
SmallFont	2	Small Font
SansSeriFont	3	Sans Serif Font
GothicFont	4	Gothic Font

After a font is selected using **SetTextStyle,** all text displayed will be in that font until a different font is selected. Either the value (0, 1, 2, 3, or 4) of the font or the predefined constant identifier may be used. As usual, we recommend using identifiers to improve the readability of the code.

The second argument in **SetTextStyle,** <direction>, is a variable of type **word** that allows the user to select either vertical or horizontal display for the text. The two predefined constants and their values are listed in Table 16.10. The default setting is **HorizDir.** If we select **VertDir,** the text will begin to be printed at the indicated position and then move up (rather than down) the screen.

Table 16.10

Orientation

Orientation Name	Orientation Value
HorizDir	0
VertDir	1

The third argument in **SetTextStyle**, <size>, is a variable of type **word.** It allows the user to set the size of each character, with allowable values ranging from 1 to 10. Character sizes are magnified by multiples of the 8 × 8 pixel square. Thus, if we select a value of 2, each character is displayed in a 16 × 16 pixel square. A value of 3 yields 24 × 24 pixel squares, and so on, until a value of 10 produces an 80 × 80 pixel square. This information is summarized in Table 16.11.

Table 16.11

Character size

Size Value	Size of Character Display (in pixels)
1	8 × 8
2	16 × 16
3	24 × 24
4	32 × 32
5	40 × 40
6	48 × 48
7	56 × 56
8	64 × 64
9	72 × 72
10	80 × 80

The following example illustrates some displays that are available when **SetTextStyle** is used in a graphics mode.

Example 16.13

Let's write a segment of code to compare the five fonts available using **SetTextStyle.** Our segment uses the default values for orientation and size. The code is

```
Ycoor := 0;
FOR Font := DefaultFont TO GothicFont DO
  BEGIN
    SetTextStyle (Font, HorizDir, 1);
    OutTextXY (30, Ycoor, 'Can you read this?');
    Ycoor := Ycoor + 20
  END;
```

When this segment of code is run, the display shown in Figure 16.30 results.

◆ Figure 16.30

Comparing fonts

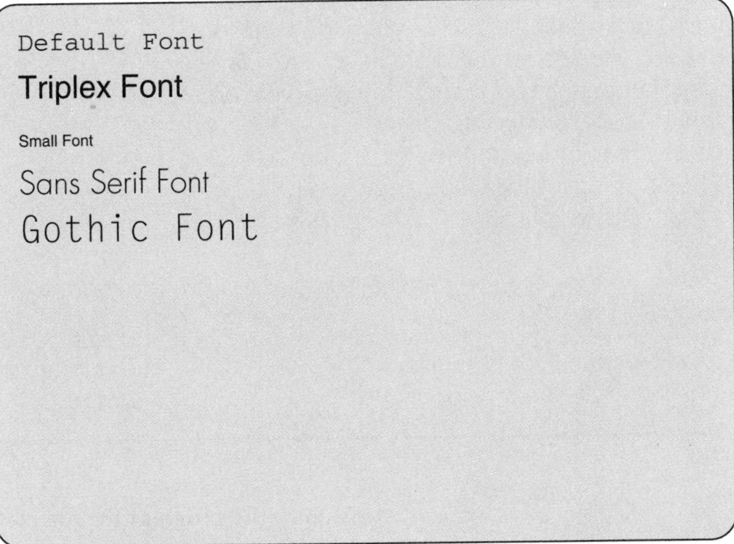

Several other text-related procedures are available, including **SetTextJustify, GetTextSettings, TextHeight,** and **TextWidth.** Detailed analyses of these procedures are beyond the scope of this text. The interested reader is referred to the Turbo Pascal Library Reference Manual.

The primary use of text in graphics is to generate more informative screen displays than those produced using graphics procedures without text. Graphs and charts require axes and labels. Headings can be produced for displayed text. Explanatory paragraphs can be put in rectangles using a combination of **Rectangle** and **OutTextXY.** These and many other capabilities should become a standard part of your program development when you are using graphics. The **Focus on Program Design: Case Study** for this chapter illustrates a combined use of graphics and text.

■ Exercises 16.6

1. Write a test program to see what happens in each of the following situations:
   a. **OutText** is used with a message that is too long for the viewing screen.
   *b. You try to print a character at the bottom of the screen when you do not have a complete 8 × 8 pixel square available.
2. Reconsider Example 16.12. In centering the message, why was the variable Xcoor defined as (**GetMaxX** – 8 * Length(Message)) **DIV** 2 rather than as (**GetMaxX** – Length(Message)) **DIV** 2?

A Note of Interest

Artificial Intelligence

Artificial intelligence (AI) research seeks to understand the principles of human intelligence and to apply those principles to the creation of smarter computer programs. The original goal of AI research was to create programs with human-like intelligence and capabilities, yet after many years of research, little progress has been made toward this goal.

In recent years, however, AI researchers have pursued much more modest goals with much greater success. Programs based on AI techniques are playing increasingly important roles in such down-to-earth areas as medicine, education, recreation, business, and industry. Such programs come nowhere near to achieving human levels of intelligence, but they often have capabilities that are not easily achieved with non-AI programs.

The main principles of AI can be summarized as follows:

Search: The computer solves a problem by searching through all logically possible solutions.

Rules: Knowledge about what actions to take in particular circumstances is stored as rules; each rule has the form.

IF <situation> **THEN** <action or conclusion>

Reasoning: Programs can use reasoning to draw conclusions from the facts and rules available to the program.

Planning: The control program plans the actions that must be taken to accomplish a particular goal, and then modifies the plan if unexpected obstacles are encountered; this is most widely used in robot control.

Pattern recognition: This is important for rule-based systems. The IF part of a rule specifies a particular pattern of facts; the rule is to be applied when that pattern is recognized in the facts known to the program.

Knowledge bases: Locations where the facts and rules that govern the operation of an AI program are stored.

*3. Modify the program that displays a bar graph of grades by pausing with a continuation message before each successive bar is displayed.

4. Modify **PROGRAM** PieChart by adding a legend that explains the filling pattern used in each sector. Your output should be

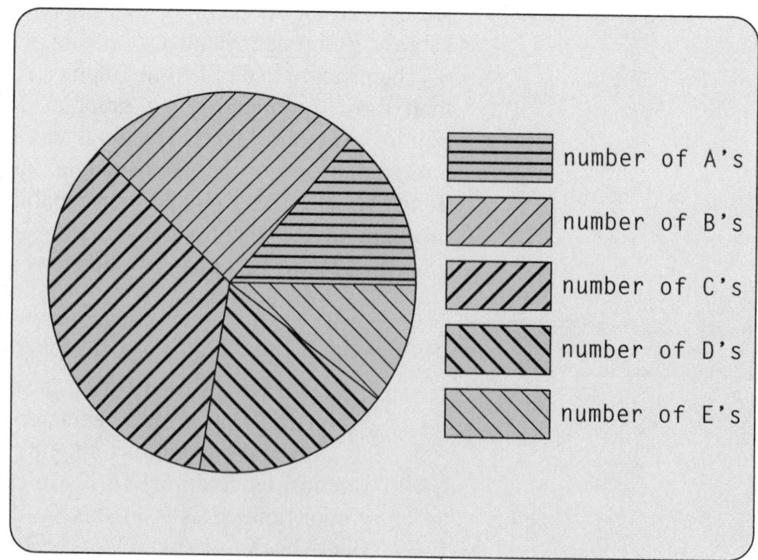

*5. Use the procedures **Rectangle** and **OutTextXY** to display a message in a box. Do this for both vertical and horizontal messages.
6. Reconsider the code in Example 16.13. Develop and run similar code segments that allow you to compare text direction and text size.
7. Combine Example 16.13 and Exercise 6 to produce a program that allows the user to compare text fonts, direction, and size with a continuation message at the bottom of each screen display.

Focus on Program Design: Case Study

Use of Text with Bar Graphs and Pie Charts

The summary program combines several of the concepts and program segments we have discussed thus far. In particular, this is an interactive program that allows the user to enter the grade distribution for a class and then elect to see these grades displayed in either a bar graph or a pie chart. A menu allows the user to choose the appropriate program action. This menu is

```
This program will graphically display the
distribution of grades for a class.  Please
choose one of the following and press <Enter>.

     <1> Enter grades

     <2> View bar graph

     <3> View pie chart

     <4> Quit
```

Both the bar graph and the pie chart combine graphics and text as part of the screen display. The bar graph display shows the letter grade below the appropriate bar. A title and continuation message appear as part of each display. A typical screen is

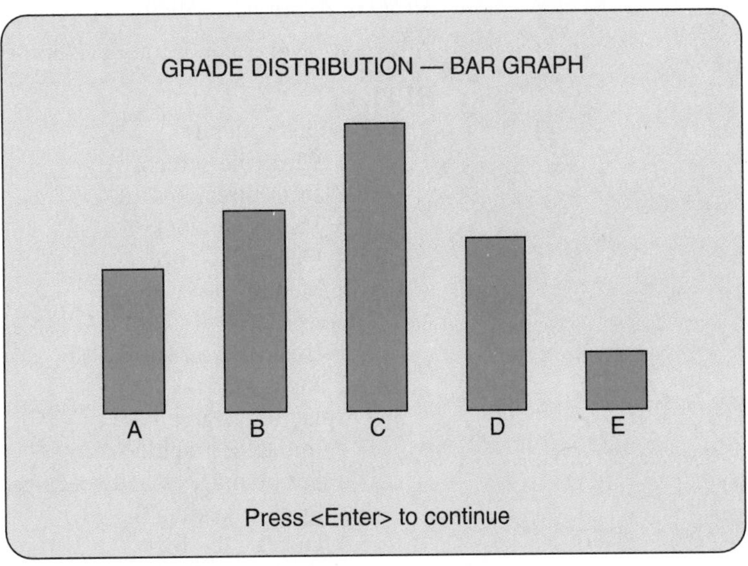

The pie chart display includes a legend that explains the various filling patterns in the sectors. A typical screen is

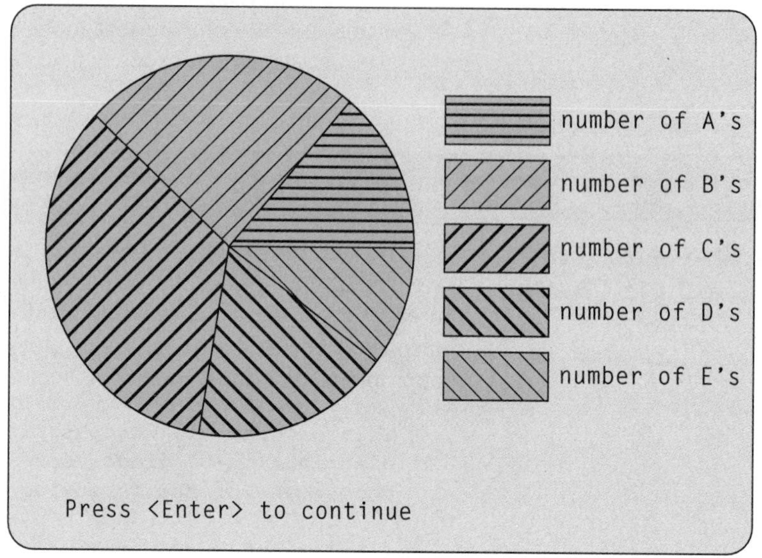

A first-level pseudocode development for this problem is

REPEAT
  1. Display a menu
  CASE MenuChoice **OF**
  2. Enter grades
  3. Display a bar graph
  4. Display a pie chart
  5. Exit the program
UNTIL program is exited

A second-level pseudocode development is

REPEAT
  1. Display a menu
    1.1 Clear the screen
    1.2 Print directions
    1.3 Print selections
    1.4 Get user choice
  CASE MenuChoice **OF**
  2. Enter grades
    2.1 Clear the screen
    2.2 Input grades
  3. Display a bar graph
    3.1 Initialize graphics
    3.2 Set boundaries and spacings for bars
    3.3 Print a heading
    3.4 Display the bars

3.5 Print a continuation message
3.6 Close graphics
4. Display a pie chart
4.1 Initialize graphics
4.2 Initialize angles and patterns
4.3 Print a heading
4.4 Display the sectors
4.5 Display the legends
4.6 Print a continuation message
4.7 Close graphics
5. Exit the program
UNTIL program is exited

In this second-level pseudocode stage, the following steps need additional development:

2.2 Input grades
3.4 Display the bars
4.4 Display the sectors
4.5 Display the legends

As part of entering grades, the program should have the user input how many of each grade were given, accumulate the total number of grades given, and determine the maximum number of any one grade. Thus, Step 2.2 is further developed as

2.2 Input grades
2.2.1 Get number for a grade
2.2.2 Accumulate total
2.2.3 Check for maximum

Further development of Steps 3.4, 4.4, and 4.5 is not included here because these subjects were discussed in detail earlier in this chapter. What was not shown earlier was the combining of text with graphics. You should look closely at how this capability is incorporated into the program. You should also pay particular attention to how the bar heights are scaled relative to the tallest bar.

A structure chart for **PROGRAM** GradeGraphs is shown in Figure 16.31. The module specifications for the main modules are

1. Menu Module
   Data received: None
   Information returned: Menu choice
   Logic: Display choices and request the user to enter choice from the keyboard.
2. EnterGrades Module
   Data received: None
   Information returned: Number for each grade (A, B, C, D, E)
   Total number of grades
   Maximum for any one grade
   Logic: Have the user enter the number for each grade.
   Accumulate a total.
   Find the maximum for any one grade.
3. MakeBarGraph Module
   Data received: Number for each grade
   Total number of grades
   Maximum for any one grade

◆ Figure 16.31

Structure chart for **PROGRAM** GradeGraphs

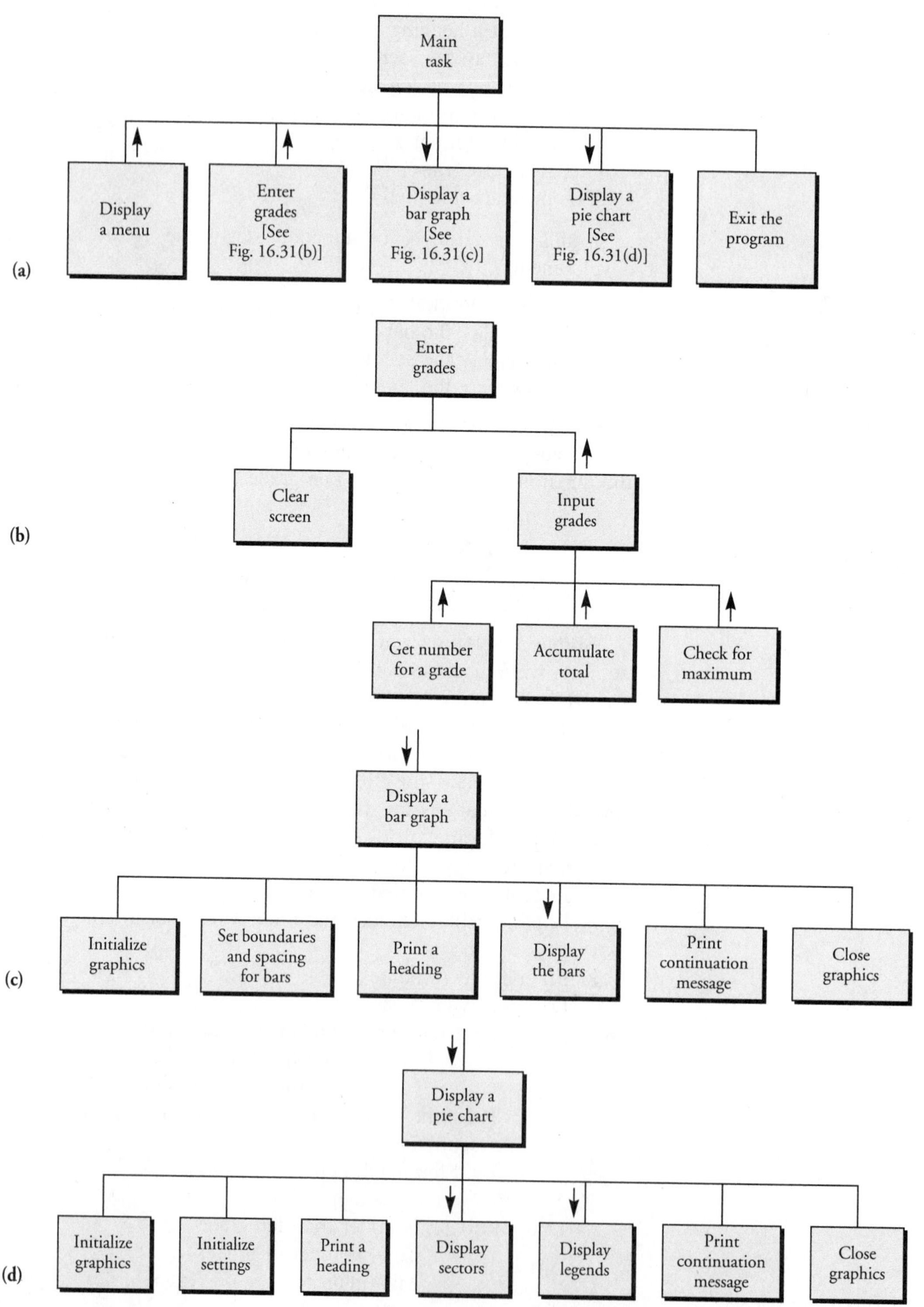

Information returned: None
Logic: Display a bar for each grade, using the maximum for scaling purposes. Include a heading, continuation message, and description of each bar.

4. MakePieChart Module
Data received: Total number of grades
Number for each grade
Information returned: None
Logic: Display a sector for each grade. Include a heading, continuation message, and legend for the sector patterns.

5. Exit Program Module
This option in the **CASE** statement consists of the null statement that permits an exit from the program.

The main program for this problem is

```
BEGIN  {  Main program  }
  InitializeGraphics;
  RestoreCrtMode;
  REPEAT
    Menu (Choice);
    CASE Choice OF
      1 : EnterGrades (NumGrades, MaxGrades, Total);
      2 : MakeBarGraph (NumGrades, MaxGrades, Total);
      3 : MakePieChart (NumGrades, Total);
      4 :   {  null statement - exit option  }
    END  {  of CASE Choice statement  }
  UNTIL Choice = 4
END.  {  of main program  }
```

A complete program for this problem follows:

```
PROGRAM GradeGraphs;

{  This program is a culmination of most of what has been   }
{  presented in this graphics chapter.  It features bar     }
{  graphs, pie charts, text in graphics, and user inter-    }
{  action.  The user is instructed to enter grades and      }
{  choose a display of a bar graph or a pie chart for       }
{  viewing the distribution of grades.                      }

USES
  Crt, Graph;

CONST
  Indent = ' ';

TYPE
  GradeList = ARRAY['A'..'E'] OF integer;

VAR
  MaxGrades,
  Total, Choice : integer;
  NumGrades : GradeList;

{***********************************************************}
```

```
PROCEDURE Menu (VAR Choice : integer);

  {  Given:   Nothing                                          }
  {  Task:    Have the user enter an option for further        }
  {                action                                      }
  {  Return:  Option for further action                        }

  BEGIN
    ClrScr;
    writeln ('This program will graphically display the');
    writeln ('distribution of grades for a class.  Please');
    writeln ('choose one of the following and press <Enter>.');
    writeln;
    writeln (Indent:4, '<1> Enter grades');
    writeln;
    writeln (Indent:4, '<2> View bar graph');
    writeln;
    writeln (Indent:4, '<3> View pie chart');
    writeln;
    writeln (Indent:4, '<4> Quit');
    readln (Choice)
  END;   {  of PROCEDURE Menu  }

{*************************************************************}

PROCEDURE InitializeGraphics;

  {  Given:   Nothing                                          }
  {  Task:    Initialize graphics. Provide error message       }
  {                for unsuccessful initialization.            }
  {  Return:  Nothing                                          }

  VAR
    GraphDriver,GraphMode,
    ErrorResult : integer;
    InitError : boolean;
  BEGIN
    GraphDriver := CGA;
    GraphMode := 1;
    InitGraph (GraphDriver, GraphMode, 'C:\TP\BGI');
    ErrorResult := GraphResult;
    InitError := (ErrorResult <> 0);
    IF InitError THEN
      BEGIN
        writeln ('There is a graphics error.');
        writeln (GraphErrorMsg(ErrorResult));
        writeln ('Program aborted.');
        readln;
        Halt
      END
  END;  {  of PROCEDURE InitializeGraphics  }

{*************************************************************}
```

```
PROCEDURE Continuation;
  BEGIN
    SetColor (2);
    OutTextXY (10, GetMaxY - 10, 'Press <Enter> to continue');
    readln
  END;  {  of PROCEDURE Continuation  }

{**********************************************************}

PROCEDURE EnterGrades (VAR NumGrades : GradeList;
                       VAR MaxGrades, Total : integer);

  {  Given:    Nothing                                      }
  {  Task:     Have the user enter the grade distribution   }
  {                 for a class                             }
  {  Return:   The grade distribution for a class,          }
  {                 the total number of grades, and         }
  {                 the maximum for any one grade           }

  VAR
    Grade : char;
  BEGIN
    ClrScr;

    {  Initialize variables  }
    MaxGrades := 0;
    Total := 0;

    {  Get input interactively  }
    FOR Grade := 'A' TO 'E' DO
      BEGIN
        write ('How many ',Grade,'''s?  ');
        readln (NumGrades[Grade]);
        Total := Total + NumGrades[Grade];
        IF NumGrades[Grade] > MaxGrades THEN
          MaxGrades := NumGrades[Grade]  { Find the maximum }
      END  {  of FOR loop  }
  END;  {  of PROCEDURE EnterGrades  }

{**********************************************************}

PROCEDURE MakeBarGraph (NumGrades : GradeList;
                        MaxGrades, Total : integer);

  {  Given:    The grade distribution for a class and       }
  {                 the total number of students in the     }
  {                 class                                   }
  {  Task:     Make and display a bar graph of the grades   }
  {  Return:   Nothing                                      }

  CONST
    LeftEdge = 50;
    BarWidth = 10;
    BarSeparation = 15;
```

```
VAR
  BottomEdge,
  MaxHeight,
  BarScale,
  X1, X2, Y1, Y2 : integer;
  Grade : char;

{==========================================================}

PROCEDURE DisplayBar (VAR X1, X2 : integer;
                      BottomEdge, BarScale : integer;
                      Num : integer);

  {  Given:   Ending position of the last bar (X2),         }
  {               distance between bars, bottom edge,       }
  {               scale for height and number of grades     }
  {  Task:    Display one bar                               }
  {  Return:  The new edges (X1, X2)                        }

  BEGIN
    X1 := X2 + BarSeparation;
    Y1 := BottomEdge - NumGrades[Grade] * BarScale;
    X2 := X1 + BarWidth;
    Bar (X1, Y1, X2, Y2)
  END;  {  of PROCEDURE DisplayBar  }

{==========================================================}

BEGIN  {  PROCEDURE MakeBarGraph  }
  SetGraphMode (1);
  SetBkColor (Green);

  {  Set the boundaries and spacings for the bars  }
  BottomEdge := GetMaxY - 50;
  X2 := LeftEdge - BarSeparation;
  Y2 := BottomEdge;
  MaxHeight := GetMaxY - 100; { Leave margins of 50 pixels }
  BarScale := round(MaxHeight/MaxGrades); {  Scale height }

  {  Print a heading  }
  OutTextXY (0, 10, 'GRADE DISTRIBUTION - BAR GRAPH');

  {  Display the bars  }
  FOR Grade := 'A' TO 'E' DO
    BEGIN
      DisplayBar (X1, X2, BottomEdge,
                  BarScale, NumGrades[Grade]);
      OutTextXY (X1, Y2 + 10, Grade)
    END;  {  of display for one bar  }
  Continuation;
  RestoreCrtMode
END;  {  of PROCEDURE MakeBarGraph  }

{************************************************************}
```

```
PROCEDURE MakePieChart (NumGrades : GradeList;
                        Total : integer);

  {  Given:   The grade distribution for a class and        }
  {                the total number of students in the      }
  {                class                                    }
  {  Task:    Make and display a pie chart of the grades    }
  {  Return:  Nothing                                       }

  CONST
    Radius = 50;
    Xcoor = 100;
    Ycoor = 100;
    Ystart = 45;
  VAR
    AngleStart, AngleFinish, SliceSize : integer;
    Pattern : word;
    ItemAngleSize : real;
    Grade : char;
    Y1 : integer;

  {==========================================================}

  PROCEDURE GraphSector (NumItems : integer;
                         ItemAngleSize : real;
                         AngleStart : integer;
                         VAR AngleFinish : integer;
                         VAR Pattern : word);

    {  Given:   Number of items for the sector, angle size  }
    {                per item, angle start position, fill   }
    {                pattern for the last sector            }
    {  Task:    Create one sector of a pie chart            }
    {  Return:  Angle finish position and pattern used      }
    {                for the sector                         }

    VAR
      SliceSize : word;
    BEGIN
      SliceSize := round(NumItems * ItemAngleSize);
      AngleStart := AngleFinish;
      AngleFinish := AngleStart + SliceSize;
      IF AngleFinish > 360 THEN
        AngleFinish := 360;
      Pattern := succ(Pattern);
      SetFillStyle (Pattern, 2);
      PieSlice (Xcoor, Ycoor, AngleStart, AngleFinish, Radius)
    END;  {  of PROCEDURE GraphSector  }

  {==========================================================}

  PROCEDURE DisplayLegend (VAR Y1 : integer;
                           VAR Pattern : word;
                           Grade : char);
```

```
  {  Given:     Initial Y, pattern for fill and Grade       }
  {  Task:      Draw a bar, pattern fill, show legend       }
  {  Return:    Ending Y and pattern used                   }

  CONST
    X1 = 175;
    X2 = 200;
    DeltaY = 15;
    BetweenBars = 10;
  VAR
    X, Y2 : integer;
  BEGIN
    Y2 := Y1 + DeltaY;
    Pattern := succ(Pattern);
    SetFillStyle (Pattern, 2);
    Bar (X1, Y1, X2, Y2);
    X := X2 + 10;
    OutTextXY (X, Y1, Grade);
    Y1 := Y2 + BetweenBars
  END;  {  of PROCEDURE DisplayLegend  }

{==========================================================}

BEGIN  { PROCEDURE MakePieChart  }

  {  Perform initialization  }
  SetGraphMode (1);
  SetBkColor (Blue);
  AngleFinish := 0;
  Pattern := SolidFill;
  ItemAngleSize := 360 / Total;

  {  Print a heading  }
  OutTextXY (0, 10, 'GRADE DISTRIBUTION - PIE CHART');

  {  Display sectors of the pie chart  }
  FOR Grade := 'A' TO 'E' DO
    GraphSector (NumGrades[Grade], ItemAngleSize,
                 AngleStart, AngleFinish, Pattern);

  {  Display legend for the sectors  }
  Y1 := Ystart;
  Pattern := SolidFill;
  FOR Grade := 'A' TO 'E' DO
    DisplayLegend (Y1, Pattern, Grade);
  Continuation;
  RestoreCrtMode
END;  {  of PROCEDURE MakePieChart  }

{**********************************************************}

BEGIN  {  Main program  }
  InitializeGraphics;
  RestoreCrtMode;
```

```
    REPEAT
      Menu (Choice);
      CASE Choice OF
        1 : EnterGrades  (NumGrades, MaxGrades, Total);
        2 : MakeBarGraph (NumGrades, MaxGrades, Total);
        3 : MakePieChart (NumGrades, Total);
        4 :   {  null statement - exit option  }
      END  {  of CASE statement  }
    UNTIL Choice = 4
  END.  {  of main program  }
```

A sample run of this program produces the following output:

```
This program will graphically display the
distribution of grades for a class.  Please
choose one of the following and press <Enter>.


     <1> Enter grades

     <2> View bar graph

     <3> View pie chart

     <4> Quit
1
```

Screen 1

```
How many A's?  4
How many B's?  7
How many C's?  10
How many D's?  5
How many E's?  3
```

Screen 2

```
This program  will graphically display the
distribution of grades for a class. Please
choose one of the following and press <Enter>.

        <1> Enter grades

        <2> View bar graph

        <3> View pie chart

        <4> Quit
2
```

Screen 3

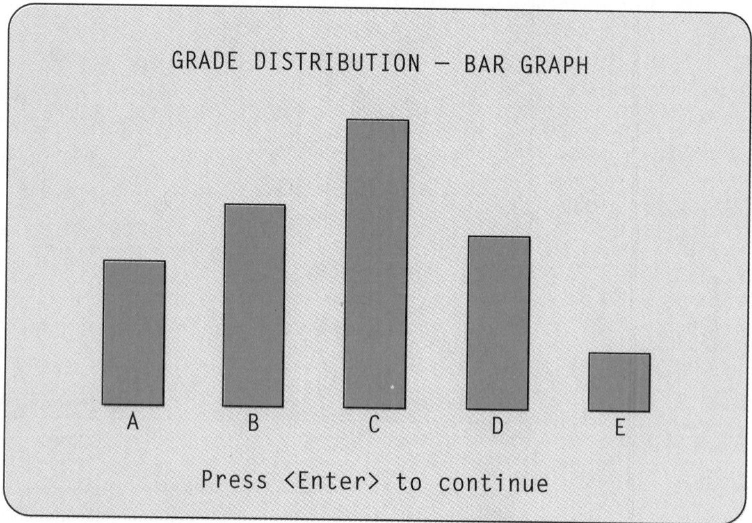

Screen 4

```
This program will graphically display the
distribution of grades for a class.  Please
choose one of the following and press <Enter>.

        <1> Enter grades

        <2> View bar graph

        <3> View pie chart

        <4> Quit
3
```

Screen 5

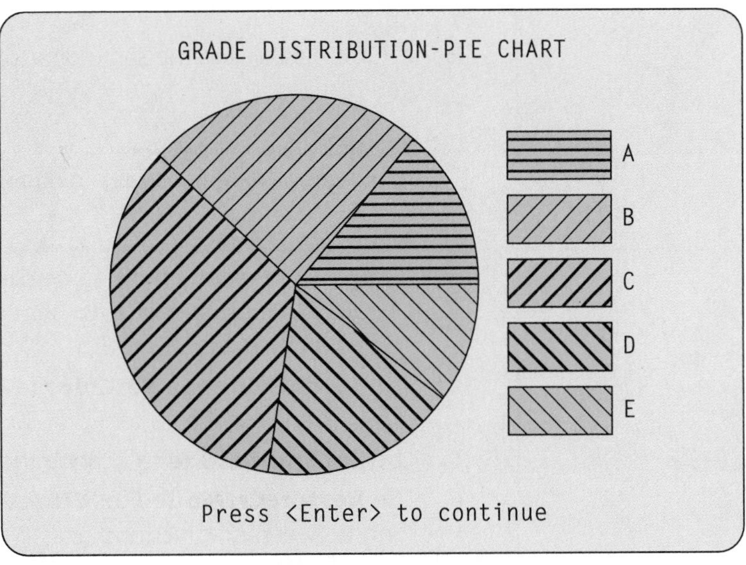

Screen 6

```
This program will graphically display the
distribution of grades for a class.  Please
choose one of the following and press <Enter>.

      <1> Enter grades

      <2> View bar graph

      <3> View pie chart

      <4> Quit
4
```

Screen 7

Running and Debugging Hints

1. Include both **Crt** and **Graph** in the **USES** section of your program when you plan to use graphics. A typical statement is

```
USES
  Crt, Graph;
```

(continued)

2. If Turbo Pascal is in the same directory as the BGI driver file (*.BGI), you can use

```
GraphDriver := Detect;
InitGraph (GraphDriver, GraphMode, '');
```

to initialize graphics.

3. If Turbo Pascal is not in the same directory as the BGI driver file (*.BGI), you must specify a file path in the **InitGraphics** procedure. The path could be C:\TP\BGI.
4. Use **SetBkColor** and **SetColor** to control screen colors for backgrounds and for the current drawing color.
5. Use **SetGraphMode** to change the available colors.
6. Use **RestoreCrtMode** (not **CloseGraph**) if you are going back and forth between graphics and text.
7. Use **GetAspectRatio** (Xasp,Yasp) to determine the relative width and height of a pixel. Then define an aspect ratio as AspectRatio := Xasp / Yasp. Use this ratio to produce proper perspectives for shapes.
8. Use **readln** to hold displays on the screen for an indefinite amount of time.
9. Use **Delay** to hold displays on the screen for a predetermined amount of time.
10. Achieve animation by using **Delay** and erasing the figure by drawing it in the background color.
11. Use a sequence of calls to **Bar** to produce a bar graph.
12. Determine bar heights for bar graphs as a function of the tallest bar.
13. Determine a bottom edge for bar graphs by using **GetMaxY.**
14. Use a sequence of calls to **PieSlice** to produce a pie chart.
15. Vary the patterns in a pie chart by using **succ**(Pattern) and **SetFill-Style** before calling **PieSlice.**
16. Display a legend for a pie chart to explain what the sectors represent.
17. Develop a continuation message by writing a procedure that uses **OutTextXY** to print a message at the bottom of a graphics display.
18. When making a pie chart, always make the last ending angle 360°.

Summary

Key Terms

animation
bit-mapped font
current pointer
high-resolution mode
medium-resolution mode
pixel (picture element)
stroked fonts

Keywords

Arc
ArcCoordsType
Bar
Bar3D
BkSlashFill
CenterLn
Circle
ClearDevice
CloseDotFill
CloseGraph
ClrScr
Crt
DashedLn
DefaultFont
Delay
Detect
DottedLn
Ellipse
EmptyFill
FillEllipse
FillPoly
FloodFill
GetArcCoords
GetAspectRatio
GetMaxX
GetMaxY
GetTextSettings
GothicFont
Graph
GraphErrorMsg
GraphResult
Halt
HatchFill
HorizDir
InterleaveFill
InitGraph
Line
LineFill
LineRel
LineTo
LtBkSlashFill
LtSlashFill
MoveRel
MoveTo
NormWidth
OutText
OutTextXY
PieSlice
PutPixel
Rectangle
RestoreCrtMode
SansSeriFont
Sector
SetBkColor
SetColor
SetFillPattern
SetFillStyle
SetGraphMode
SetLineStyle
SetTextJustify
SetTextStyle
SlashFill
SmallFont
SolidFill
SolidLn
TextHeight
TextWidth
ThickWidth
TriplexFont
UserBitLn
UserFill
VertDir
WideDotFill
word
XHatchFill

Key Concepts

- The predefined functions **GetMaxX** and **GetMaxY,** respectively, can be used to determine the number of pixels horizontally and vertically.
- Individual pixels can be plotted using **PutPixel** (X, Y, <color>).
- Lines can be drawn using **Line** (X1, Y1, X2, Y2) or **LineTo** (X, Y).
- The current pointer can be moved using **MoveTo** (X, Y).
- Four standardized styles of lines are available for **SetLineStyle.**
- Rectangles can be drawn using **Rectangle** (X1, Y1, X2, Y2).
- Circles can be drawn using **Circle** (Xcoor, Ycoor, Radius).
- **Delay** (LengthOfPause) can be used to hold a screen image a predetermined amount of time.
- Arcs can be drawn using **Arc** (Xcoor, Ycoor, AngleStart, AngleFinish, Radius).
- Ellipses can be drawn using **Ellipse** (Xcoor, Ycoor, AngleStart, AngleFinish, Xrad, Yrad).
- Several filling patterns are available; these patterns are set by a call to **SetFillStyle** (Pattern, Color).
- **FloodFill** (Xcoor, Ycoor, BorderColor) can be used to fill a closed region.
- **FillEllipse** (Xcoor, Ycoor, Xrad, Yrad) can be used to fill an ellipse.
- Animation is achieved by using **Delay** and then redrawing the figure in a new position.
- Figures can be moved by changing values in the X- and/or Y-coordinates of points.
- A bar can be drawn by using **Bar** (X1, Y1, X2, Y2).

- Sectors of a circle can be drawn by using **PieSlice** (Xcoor, Ycoor, AngleStart, AngleFinish, Radius).
- Either **OutText** or **OutTextXY** can be used to display text while in the graphics mode.
- Five predetermined fonts are available for text characters while in the graphics mode.
- The text font, direction, and size can be determined by a call to **SetTextStyle.**

Chapter Review Exercises

1. How is the procedure **InitGraph** used to get into the graphics mode?
2. What is a pixel?
3. Explain why background constants should be used rather than their ordinals.
4. How can you determine the center of your screen?
5. Write a program segment that will draw diagonals on your screen.
6. Explain the differences among the procedures **Line, LineTo,** and **LineRel.**
7. What does the statement PutPixel (50, 100, 2) cause to happen when it is executed?
8. Explain how you can make dots appear to be "bigger."
9. Use **MoveTo** and **LineRel** to draw a 20-pixel × 40-pixel rectangle with the upper left vertex at (50, 50).
10. Draw a 200-pixel × 200-pixel square using the procedure **Rectangle.** Does the figure drawn look square? Explain.
11. Explain why **GetAspectRatio** is necessary when creating graphics figures.

In Exercises 12–19, write a short program for each request.

12. Draw a circle of radius 100 whose center is at the middle of the screen.
13. Draw five concentric circles with their center at the middle of the screen.
14. Draw two circles that are tangent to each other at the screen center.
15. Draw one circle with radius 100 at the screen center. Draw four tangent circles with radius 25, as shown in the following figure:

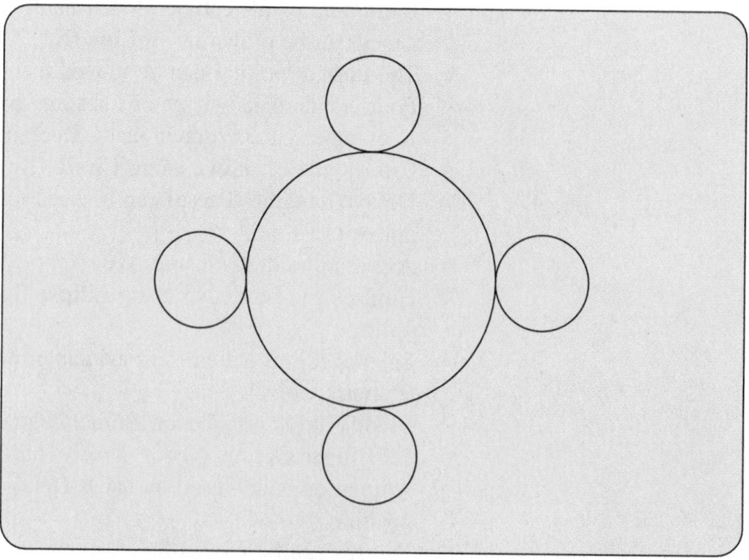

16. Draw an ellipse in the center of the screen with major axis 200 and minor axis 100.
17. Draw the largest possible ellipse that can be displayed on your screen.
18. Use the **Arc** procedure to write your name in cursive form.
19. Use lines to display your name in block form.

In Exercises 20–25, refer to Exercises 12–17.

20. Using **Delay,** fill the circle of Exercise 12 with five different patterns.
21. Fill the five circles of Exercise 13 with different colors, changing colors as you move from the smallest circle to the largest circle.
22. Fill the tangent circles of Exercise 14 with different colors and different patterns.
23. Fill the large circle of Exercise 15 with one pattern and color. Fill the other four circles with a different pattern and color.
24. Using **Delay,** fill the ellipse of Exercise 16 with five different patterns.
25. Using **Delay** and a loop, fill the ellipse of Exercise 17 with every combination of pattern and color available.

In Exercises 26–28, use bar graphs to display each of the grade distributions.

26. A – 5
    B – 10
    C – 15
    D – 10
    E – 5
27. A – 19
    B – 19
    C – 17
    D – 10
    E – 9
28. A – 2
    B – 4
    C – 30
    D – 1
    E – 0
29. Use a circle graph to display the data of Exercise 26.
30. Use a circle graph to display the data of Exercise 27.
31. Use a circle graph to display the data of Exercise 28.
32. What bar width do you prefer to use to display five data items in a bar graph? Why?
33. Use a **FOR** loop to draw a bar graph consisting of five bars such that
    a. the first bar is of height 2.
    b. each successive bar is twice the height of the previous bar.

In Exercises 34–37, write a short program for each request.

34. Use **Bar3D** to display the data of Exercise 26. Vary the color of each face.
35. Use **Bar3D** to display the data of Exercise 27. Vary the pattern of each face.
36. Use **Bar3D** to display the data of Exercise 28. Vary both the pattern and color of the face.
37. Explain the difference between procedure **PieSlice** and procedure **Sector.**

For Exercises 38–40, sketch what will be displayed when each of the procedure calls is executed.

38. `PieSlice (50, 50, 0, 90, 25);`
39. `Sector (50, 50, 0, 90, 25, 25);`
40. `Arc (50, 50, 0, 90, 25);`

For Exercises 41–79, indicate which are valid procedure calls. Explain the problem with those that are invalid.

41. `SetBkColor (2);`
42. `SetBkColor (Red);`
43. `SetBkColor (0 range);`
44. `SetBkColor (20);`
45. `SetColor (3);`
46. `SetColor (0);`
47. `SetColor (Green);`
48. `PutPixel (50, 50, 3);`
49. `PutPixel (0, 0, 0);`
50. `PutPixel (100, 100);`
51. `Line (10, 10, 50, 50);`
52. `Line (50, 50, 10, 10);`
53. `Line (-2, -2, 100, 100);`
54. `Line (20, 20, 20, 20);`
55. `MoveRel (10, 10);`
56. `LineTo (100, 100);`
57. `LineRel (100, 100);`
58. `SetLineStyle (1, 1, 2);`
59. `SetLineStyle (SolidLn, 0, NormWidth);`
60. `Delay (500);`
61. `Circle (200, 200);`
62. `Circle (50, 50, 100);`
63. `Arc (100, 100, 90, 270, 50);`
64. `Arc (50, 50, 0, 360, 2);`
65. `Ellipse (100, 100, 0, 180, 50);`
66. `Ellipse (100, 100, 90, 180, 50, 25);`
67. `FillEllipse (100, 100, 0, 90, 50, 25);`
68. `FillEllipse (100, 100, 50, 25, red);`
69. `Bar (10, 10, 30, 30);`
70. `Bar (30, 30, 10, 10);`
71. `Bar3D (10, 10, 30, 30, 5, true);`
72. `Bar3D (10, 10, 30, 30, 2, false);`
73. `Sector (100, 100, 0, 90, 50);`
74. `PieSlice (100, 100, 0, 90, 50);`
75. `OutText (100, 100, 'Hello');`
76. `OutText ('Press <Enter> to continue.');`
77. `SetTextStyle (SmallFont, VertDir, 3);`
78. `SetTextStyle (2, 1, 3);`
79. `SetTextStyle (5, 2, 4);`

For Exercises 80–84, write programs that cause the specified results.

80. A circle of radius 20 moves diagonally on the screen.
81. A square of size 10 × 10 moves from left to right at the top of the screen.
82. A square of size 10 × 10 moves from right to left at the bottom of the screen.
83. A smiley face that winks with the left eye.
84. A smiley face whose smile turns into a frown.

For Exercises 85–87, use **OutText** to modify the programs of Exercises 80–82 as indicated.

85. Modify Exercise 80 by displaying "Watch the circle move." in the upper right-hand corner.
86. Modify Exercise 81 by displaying "This square really moves!" at the bottom of the screen.
87. Modify Exercise 82 by displaying "Watch the square below." at the top of the screen.
88. Write a short program that displays the various fonts available.
89. Write a program that displays the fonts one at a time. Use a continuation message at the bottom of the screen for moving to the next font.

Programming Problems

1. Write a program that produces a kaleidoscope that fills your screen with varying patterns of different colors.
2. Write a program that produces a bouncing ball and moves it across the screen. Use **Delay** to achieve animation and to erase previous images. Use **Circle** in a procedure to display a single image.
3. Earlier in this chapter, you were asked to design a display of an automobile. Put this design in a procedure (if you haven't already done so), and then use the technique of animation to move the automobile around the screen.
4. Several modifications can be made in the **Focus on Program Design: Case Study** in this chapter. Write a complete program that includes the following enhancements.
   a. Enter the bar graph.
   b. Center and place the headings in a rectangle, such as

      GRADE DISTRIBUTION - BAR GRAPH

   c. Put a vertical scale on the graph to indicate the bar heights.
   d. Indicate the percent represented by each sector in the pie chart.
5. Write a program that displays closing prices on the New York Stock Exchange for several weeks. Your graph should have a horizontal axis and a vertical axis. Let the daily closing prices be plotted as nine pixel squares and connected by lines to the center of each square. Let the range for each day be shown by a vertical line. Typical output would be similar to the following graph:

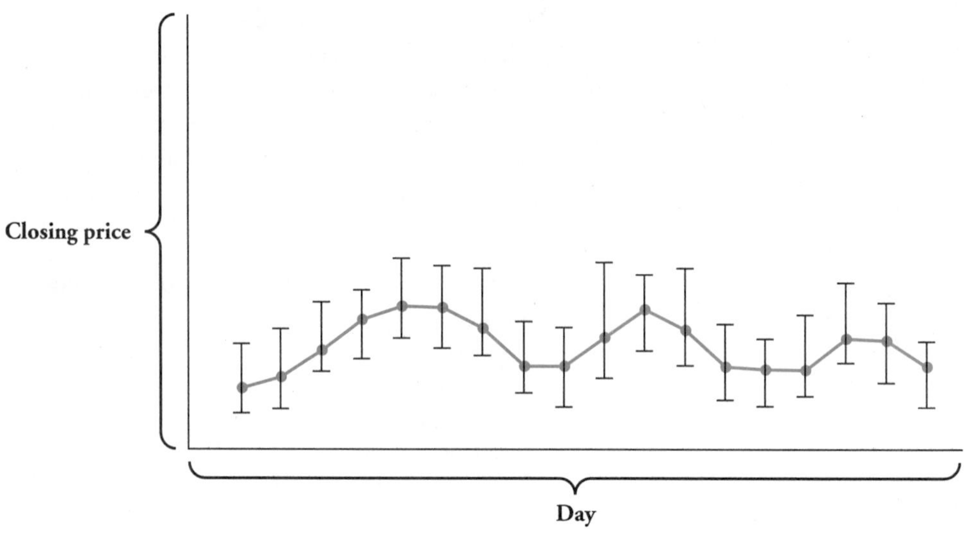

6. Examine the graphics features available in several spreadsheets. In particular, note how they can be used to display bar graphs, three-dimensional bar graphs, and pie charts. After running several sample graphs, compare your results with the results you obtain when you run the **Focus on Program Design: Case Study** in this chapter. Based on your findings, prepare a report for the class indicating what design specifications you believe the software engineers used to create the graphics part of the spreadsheets.
7. Develop a procedure that allows text display to be printed vertically "down" the screen, rather than "up" the screen as is the case when **SetTextStyle** has a second argument (direction) of 1. Use your procedure in a program that allows the user to select from the following menu of orientations:

   0—horizontal
   1—vertical (up)
   2—vertical (down)

8. Prepare an interactive program that allows the user to experiment with the background colors and the current drawing colors available. The user should be allowed to make the following choices:
   (1) Figure of a circle or square
   (2) Value of a radius or side length
   (3) Background color
   (4) Current drawing color
9. Modify the program you created in Problem 8 to allow the user additional choices of filling patterns and colors.
10. Develop a system for normalizing the screen coordinates in a graphics mode. In your normalized system, (0, 0) is in the lower left corner and (1, 1) is in the upper right corner. The x-axis extends from 0 to 1, left to right; the y-axis extends from 0 to 1, bottom to top. The center of this screen is (0.5, 0.5). Thus, your normalized screen would look like this:

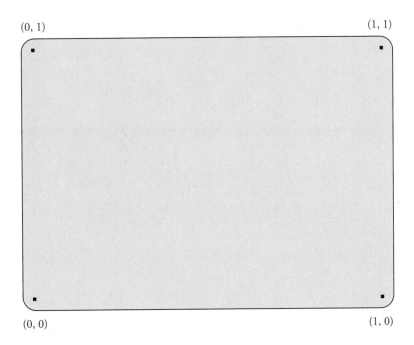

Give a report of your system to the students in your class. Show them how they can plot points and draw lines, rectangles, and other graphics figures using the normalized system.

11. Contact your local weather service bureau and determine the average precipitation in your region for each month of the year. Write a program that displays the distribution in a bar graph. Be sure to include suitable headings and messages as part of your output.

Communication in Practice

Select and run BGIDEMO.PAS. Obtain a hard copy of this program. Run the program again, and trace the code as you progress through the various screens. Discuss the documentation provided with the program. Make a list of the suggestions you have for modifying the documentation, and present these suggestions to the class.

Chapter 17

Dynamic Variables and Data Structures

Chapter Outline

Material in all previous chapters has focused almost exclusively on **static variables,** which have the following characteristics:

1. The size of a static variable (array length, for example) is fixed at compilation time.
2. A certain memory location is reserved for each static variable, and this memory location is retained for the declared variables as long as the program or subprogram in which the variable is defined is active.
3. Static variables are declared in a variable declaration section.
4. The structure or existence of a static variable cannot be changed during a run of the program. (Two exceptions are the length of a file and records with variant parts.)

A disadvantage of using only static variables and data structures is that the number of variables needed in a program must be predetermined. Thus, if we are working with an array and anticipate needing a thousand locations, we would define

```
<name> = ARRAY [1..1000] OF <base type>;
```

This creates two problems. We may overestimate the length of the array and use only part of it, thereby wasting memory. Or we may underestimate the necessary array length and be unable to process all the data until the program is modified.

Fortunately, Pascal solves these problems through the use of **dynamic variables.** Some of their characteristics follow:

1. Dynamic variable types are defined in the **TYPE** section.
2. Memory for dynamic variables is created as needed and returned when not needed during the execution of a program. Therefore, unneeded memory is not wasted and the programmer is limited only by the available memory.
3. A new (and significant) technique must be developed to form a list of dynamic variables; these lists are referred to as **dynamic structures.**
4. In some instances, working with dynamic structures can be slower than working with static structures; in particular, direct access of an array element has no analogue.

A **static variable** is a variable whose size (for example, array length) is fixed at compilation time.

A **dynamic variable** is a variable accessed by a pointer variable. Frequently designated as Ptr↑ or Ptr^.

A **dynamic structure** is a data structure that may expand or contract during execution of a program.

5. A significantly different method of accessing values stored in dynamic variables must be developed because memory locations are not predetermined.

Speed of execution also changes considerably when dynamic variables and data structures are used in a program. It takes much less time to manipulate dynamic variables than static variables. For long programs and large databases, this savings of time becomes a significant issue.

A complete development of dynamic variables and data structures is left to other courses in computer science. However, when you have finished this chapter, you should have a reasonable understanding of dynamic variables and data structures and be able to use them in a program. Here we carefully develop one type of dynamic data structure (linked list) and then introduce three others—the stack, the queue, and the binary tree.

You may find this material somewhat difficult. If so, do not get discouraged. Two reasons for the increased level of difficulty are that some of the work is not intuitive, and the level of abstraction is different from that of previous material. Therefore, as you work through this chapter, you are encouraged to draw several diagrams and write several short programs to help you understand concepts. You also may need to reread the chapter or particular sections to grasp the mechanics of working with dynamic variables.

17.1 Pointer Variables

Objectives

- to understand the difference between the address of a memory location and the value of a memory location
- to be able to define a pointer type
- to understand how a pointer variable is used to access a memory location
- to be able to use a pointer variable to manipulate data in a dynamic variable
- to be able to create and destroy dynamic variables during execution of a program

Computer Memory

Computer memory can be envisioned as a sequence of memory locations depicted as in Figure 17.1(a). Memory location is an area where a value can be stored. When a variable is declared in the variable declaration section of a program, a memory location is reserved during execution of that program block. This memory location can be accessed by a reference to the variable name and only data of the declared type can be stored there. Thus, if the declaration section is

```
VAR
  Sum : integer;
```

we can envision it as shown in Figure 17.1(b). If the assignment

```
Sum := 56;
```

is made, we have the arrangement shown in Figure 17.1(c).

Each memory location has an **address.** This is an integer value that the computer must use as a reference to the memory location. When static variables such as Sum are used, the address of a memory location is used indirectly by the underlying machine instruction. However, when dynamic variables are used, the address is used directly as a reference or pointer to the memory location.

The **value** that is the address of a memory location must be stored somewhere in memory. In Pascal, the value is stored in a **pointer variable** (frequently denoted as Ptr), which is a variable of a predefined type that is used to contain the address of a memory location. To illustrate, assume Ptr has been declared as a pointer variable. If 56 is stored in a memory location whose address is 11640, we can envision it as shown in Figure 17.1(d).

Objectives

(continued)

- to understand the difference between a pointer variable and the dynamic variable to which it refers
- to be able to use **NIL** with pointer variables

Working with Pointer and Dynamic Variables

Pointer variables are declared by using a caret (^) or an up arrow (↑) in front of the type name. Thus,

```
TYPE
  Ages = 0..120;
  PointerToAges = ^Ages;
VAR
  Ptr : PointerToAges;
```

declares Ptr as a pointer variable. Ptr cannot be assigned values of type Ages; Ptr can only contain addresses of locations whose values are of type Ages.

Once this declaration has been made, a dynamic variable can be created. A dynamic variable, designated as Ptr^, is a variable accessed by a pointer variable; a dynamic variable is not declared in the declaration section of a program. Using the standard procedure **new** with a pointer variable

```
new (Ptr);  {  This initializes a value for Ptr  }
```

creates the dynamic variable Ptr^. This can be illustrated by

Figure 17.1

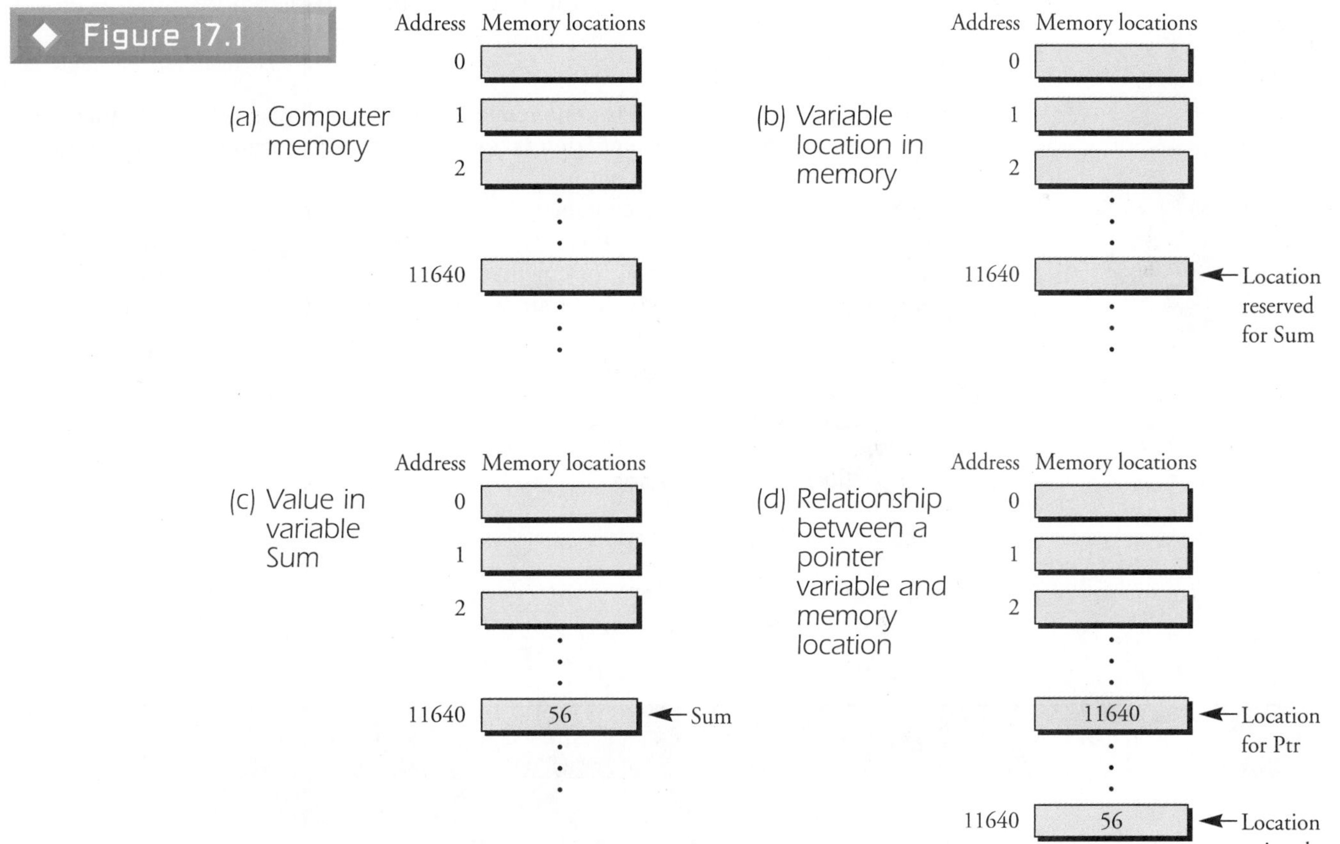

The **address** of a memory location is an integer value that the computer can use to reference a location.

The **value** of a memory location refers to the value of the contents of a memory location.

A **pointer variable** is a variable that contains the address of a memory location. Frequently designated as Ptr.

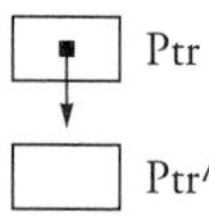

The pointer variable followed by a caret or an up arrow is always the identifier for a dynamic variable. We usually read Ptr^ as the object (variable) pointed to by Ptr.

To illustrate the relationship between pointer variables and dynamic variables, assume the previous declaration and the code

```
new (Ptr);
Ptr^ := 56;
```

This stage can be envisioned as

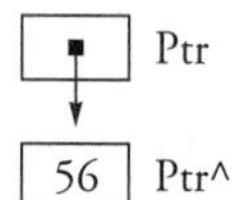

where Ptr contains the address of Ptr^.

Dynamic variables can be destroyed by using the standard procedure **dispose.** Thus, if we no longer need the value of a dynamic variable Ptr^,

```
dispose (Ptr);
```

causes the pointer variable Ptr to no longer contain the address for Ptr^. In this sense, Ptr^ does not exist, because nothing is pointing to it. This location has been returned to the computer for subsequent use.

Since pointer variables contain only addresses of memory locations, they have limited use in a program. Pointer variables of the same type can be used only for assignments and comparison for equality. They cannot be used with **read, write,** or any arithmetic operation. To illustrate, assume we have the following definition and declaration:

```
TYPE
  Ages = 0..120;
VAR
  Ptr1, Ptr2 : ^Ages;
```

Then

```
new (Ptr1);
new (Ptr2);
```

Communication and Style Tips

Ptr or some identifier containing Ptr (for example, DataPtr) is frequently used when declaring pointer variables. This reinforces the difference between working with a pointer variable (Ptr) and a dynamic variable (Ptr^).

creates the dynamic variables Ptr1^ and Ptr2^. If the assignments

```
Ptr1^ := 50;
Ptr2^ := 21;
```

are made, we can envision this as

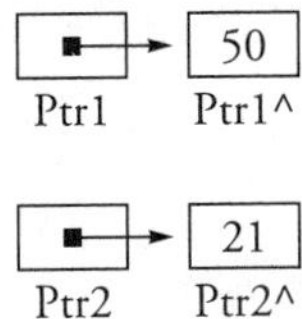

The expression Ptr1 = Ptr2 is then **false** and Ptr1 <> Ptr2 is **true.** If the assignment

```
Ptr1 := Ptr2;
```

is made, we can envision

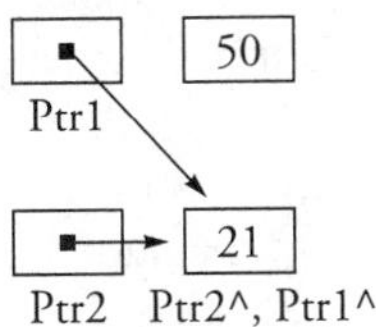

Then Ptr1 = Ptr2 is **true** and Ptr1 <> Ptr2 is **false.**

Note that in this last illustration, 50 no longer has anything pointing to it. Thus, there is now no way to access this value. Since we did not use **dispose,** the location has not been returned for subsequent reuse. Be careful to use **dispose** when necessary, or you could eventually run out of memory.

Dynamic variables can be used in any context used by static variables of the same type. To illustrate, assume the previous declarations for Ptr1 and Ptr2. If appropriate values (50 and 21) are in a data file, the segment

```
new (Ptr1);
new (Ptr2);
read (Data, Ptr1^, Ptr2^);
writeln ('The average of', Ptr1^:5, ' and', Ptr2^:5,
         ' is', (Ptr1^ + Ptr2^)/2:6:2);
```

produces

```
The average of   50 and   21 is 35.50
```

Defining and Declaring Pointer Variables

The previous definition and declarations of pointer types and pointer variables are relatively uncomplicated. However, in actual practice, pointer types and variables are a bit more complex. In the next section, for example, we will work with a dynamic variable as a record type where one of the fields in the record type is a pointer of the same type. Thus, we can have

A Note of Interest

When Will Object Technology Meet Its Potential?

Rebecca Wirfs-Brock, Director of Object Technology Services at Digitalk, addressed the issue of the potential of object technology in a guest editorial in a recent publication of the Journal of Object-Oriented Programming. A summary of her comments follows.

When will it be so easy to use objects that other competing technologies won't even be considered? Can we have a future in which objects nicely coexist with more traditional software? These questions are on the minds of industry watchers, application developers, and object technology suppliers alike. Sure, people really are starting to use objects. It isn't as controversial to start an object-oriented project as it used to be. Objects have come out of the research labs and are being used on management information systems (MIS) and engineering projects. For some, the rich development and prototyping environment alone is sufficient for them to switch. For others, touted benefits come with too high a risk factor and retraining cost. These people are waiting until enormous gains are well established and guaranteed.

I'm delighted that people are delivering software written in Smalltalk, C++, Eiffel, and CLOS. Proponents of object technology say it is easy to use. But developing applications with objects isn't a routine procedure just yet. It needs to get simpler.

Reusing software and constructing applications from standard components are great ideas. However, there are some fundamental hurdles that need to be cleared before we can efficiently build software this way.

Object-oriented application construction has many different dimensions that don't directly map to the ways engineers develop hardware. To achieve that next higher level of software productivity, we need to address the following needs.

- We need components that are easy to mix and match (for example, classes and subsystems of cooperating classes). These components should be supplied by different vendors and written in different languages with application-specific components.
- We must be able to use components in a variety of different contexts. Vendors need to supply us with components that work across different platforms.
- We need well-documented, standardized component libraries, subsystems, and architectural frameworks for building applications. We need to be able to construct simple applications largely by assembling them from components found in preexisting catalogs.
- For more complex applications, we need to construct applications out of subsystems, frameworks, and components organized and described in ways that are understandable without resorting to reading code. We need to be able to easily grasp accepted patterns for connecting these components.
- Finally, we need to enhance our ability to develop applications by refining existing components. Programming by refinement is an extremely powerful metaphor. It shouldn't be dropped when we adopt the mentality of construction from preexisting components. Refinement is what enables developers to add application-specific functionality while reusing most of an existing design.

```
TYPE
  NameString = PACKED ARRAY [1..20] OF char;
  DataPtr = ^StudentInfo;
  StudentInfo = RECORD
                  Name : NameString;
                  Next : DataPtr
                END;  {  of RECORD StudentInfo  }
VAR
  Student : DataPtr;
```

Notice that DataPtr makes a reference to StudentInfo before StudentInfo is defined. StudentInfo then contains a field of type DataPtr. This instance is an exception to the rule in Pascal that an identifier cannot be used before it is defined. Specifically, the following exception is permitted: Pointer type definitions can precede definitions of their reference types. The reverse is not true; a structure cannot contain a field or component of a pointer type that has not yet been defined. We will frequently want each record to point to another record. Using a record definition with one field for a pointer permits this.

Another note about working with pointers should be mentioned here. The reserved word **NIL** can be assigned to a pointer variable. Thus, you could have

```
new (Student);
Student^.Next := NIL;
```

This allows pointer variables to be used in Boolean expressions and is needed in later work. For example, if we are forming a list of dynamic variables where each dynamic variable contains a pointer variable for pointing to the next one, we can use **NIL** as a way to determine when we are at the end of a list. This idea and the concept of pointer type definitions are fully developed in the next section.

Exercises 17.1

*1. Discuss the difference between static and dynamic variables.

2. Write a test program to declare a single pointer variable whose associated dynamic variable can have values in the subrange 0 . . 50, and then do the following:
   a. Create a dynamic variable, assign the value 25 to it, and print the value.
   b. Create another dynamic variable, assign the value 40 to it, and print the value.

   At this stage of your program, where is the value 25 stored?

*3. Illustrate the relationship between pointer variables and dynamic variables produced by

```
TYPE
  Ptr = (Red, Yellow, Blue, Green);
VAR
  Ptr1, Ptr2 : ^Ptr;
BEGIN
  new (Ptr1);
  new (Ptr2);
  Ptr1^ := Blue;
  Ptr2^ := Red
END.
```

For Exercises 4–7, assume the **TYPE** and **VAR** sections are given as in Exercise 3. Find all errors.

4.
```
new (Ptr2);
Ptr2 := Yellow;
```

*5.
```
new (Ptr1);
new (Ptr2);
Ptr1^ := Red;
Ptr2^ := Ptr1^;
```

6.
```
new (Ptr1);
new (Ptr2);
Ptr1^ := Red;
Ptr1^ := Ptr2^;
```

*7.
```
new (Ptr1);
new (Ptr2);
Ptr1^ := Red;
Ptr2^ := Ptr1;
```

For Exercises 8–15, assume pointer variables are declared in the variable declaration section as

```
VAR
  RealPtr1, RealPtr2 : ^real;
  IntPtr1, IntPtr2 : ^integer;
  BoolPtr1, BoolPtr2 : ^boolean;
```

Indicate if the references are valid or invalid. Give an explanation for each invalid reference.

8. `IntPtr1 := IntPtr1 + 1;`

*9. `writeln (RealPtr2:30:2);`

10. `writeln (BoolPtr1^:15, IntPtr1^:15, RealPtr1^:15:2);`

*11.
```
IF IntPtr1 < IntPtr2 THEN
  writeln ('All done');
```

12.
```
IF BoolPtr NOT NIL THEN
  new (BoolPtr2);
```

*13.
```
IF RealPtr1 <> RealPtr2 THEN
  writeln (RealPtr1^:15:2, RealPtr2^:15:2);
```

14.
```
IF BoolPtr2 THEN
  new (BoolPtr1);
```

*15.
```
IF BoolPtr2^ THEN
  new (BoolPtr1);
```

16. Assume the declarations of Exercises 8–15. What is the output from the following fragment of code?

```
new (IntPtr1);
new (IntPtr2);
new (RealPtr1);
new (BoolPtr1);
IntPtr1^ := 95;
IntPtr2^ := 55;
RealPtr1^ := (IntPtr1^ + IntPtr2^) / 2;
BoolPtr1^ := true;
WHILE BoolPtr1^ DO
  BEGIN
    writeln (RealPtr1^:20:2);
    RealPtr1^ := RealPtr1^ - 5;
    IF RealPtr1^ < 0 THEN
      BoolPtr1^ := false
  END;
```

17.2 Linked Lists

Objectives

- to understand why a linked list is a dynamic data structure

A **linked list** can be implemented as a dynamic data structure and can be thought of as a list of data items in which each item is linked to the next one by means of a pointer. Such a list can be envisioned as

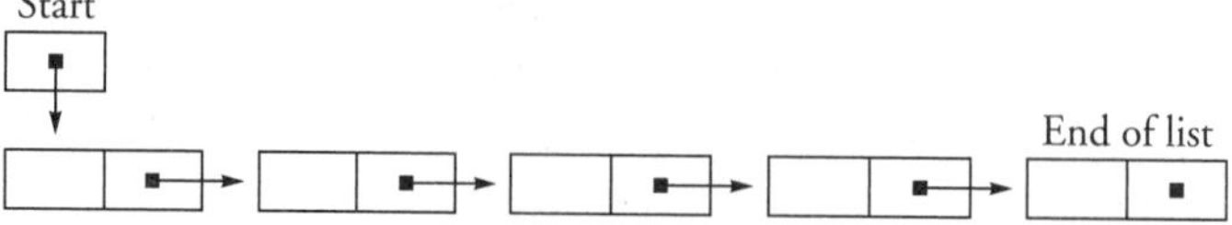

Objectives

(continued)

- to be able to create a linked list
- to understand how pointers are used to form a linked list
- to be able to print data from a linked list

Items in a linked list are called **components** or **nodes.** These lists are similar to arrays; data of the same type can be stored in each node. As shown in the previous illustration, each node of a linked list can store certain data as well as point to the next node. Consequently, a record is used for each node where one field of the record is reserved for the pointer. If names of students are to be stored in such a list, we can use the record definition from Section 17.1 as follows:

```
TYPE
  NameString = PACKED ARRAY [1..20] OF char;
  DataPtr = ^StudentInfo;
  StudentInfo = RECORD
                  Name : NameString;
                  Next : DataPtr
                END;  {  of RECORD StudentInfo  }
```

Thus, we can envision a list of names as

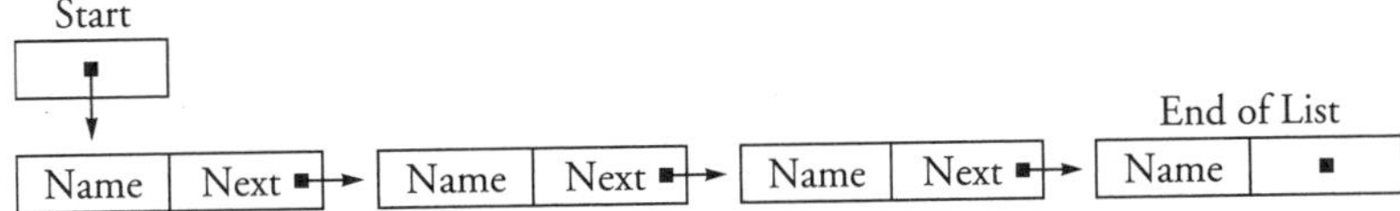

Communication and Style Tips

When working with linked lists, the identifier Next is frequently used as the name of the field in the record that is the pointer variable. This is to remind you that you are pointing to the next record. It makes code such as

```
P := P^.Next;
```

more meaningful.

A **linked list** is a list of data items in which each item is linked to the next one by means of a pointer.

A **component** of a linked list is one data item in the linked list. Also called a **node.**

Creating a Linked List

To create a linked list, we need to be able to identify the first node, the relationship (pointer) between successive nodes, and the last node. Pointers are used to point to both the first and last node. An auxiliary pointer is also used to point to the newest node. The pointer to the first node (Start) is not changed unless a new node is added to the beginning of the list. The other pointers change as the linked list grows. Once a linked list is created, the last node is usually designated by assigning **NIL** to the pointer. To illustrate, let's see how a linked list to hold five names can be formed. Using the **TYPE** definition section

```
TYPE
  NameString = PACKED ARRAY [1..20] OF char;
  DataPtr = ^StudentInfo;
  StudentInfo = RECORD
                  Name : NameString;
                  Next : DataPtr
                END;  {  of RECORD StudentInfo  }
```

and the variable declaration section

```
VAR
  Start, Last, Ptr : DataPtr;
```

we can generate the desired list with the following segment of code:

```
BEGIN
  new (Start);
  Ptr := Start;   {  Pointer to first node  }
  FOR J := 1 TO 4 DO
    BEGIN
      new (Last);
      Ptr^.Next := Last;
      Ptr := Last
    END;
  Ptr^.Next := NIL;
```

When this code is executed,

```
new (Start);
```

causes

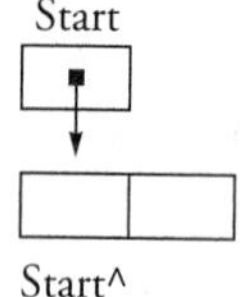

and

```
Ptr := Start;
```

produces

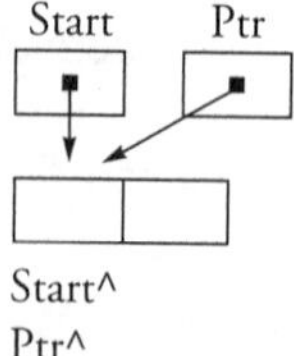

Now that we have started our list, the first pass through the **FOR** loop produces results as shown in Table 17.1.

Table 17.1 Adding a second node to a linked list

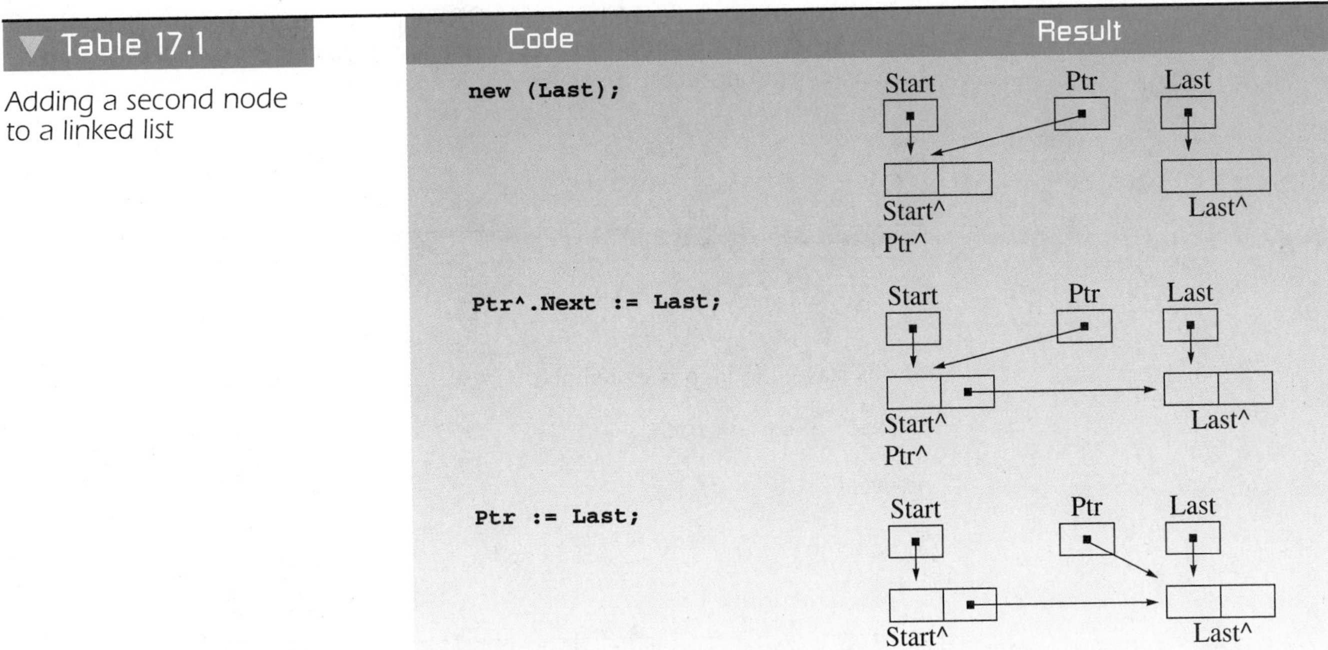

Similarly, the second time through the loop causes the list to grow as shown in Table 17.2.

Table 17.2 Adding a third node to a linked list

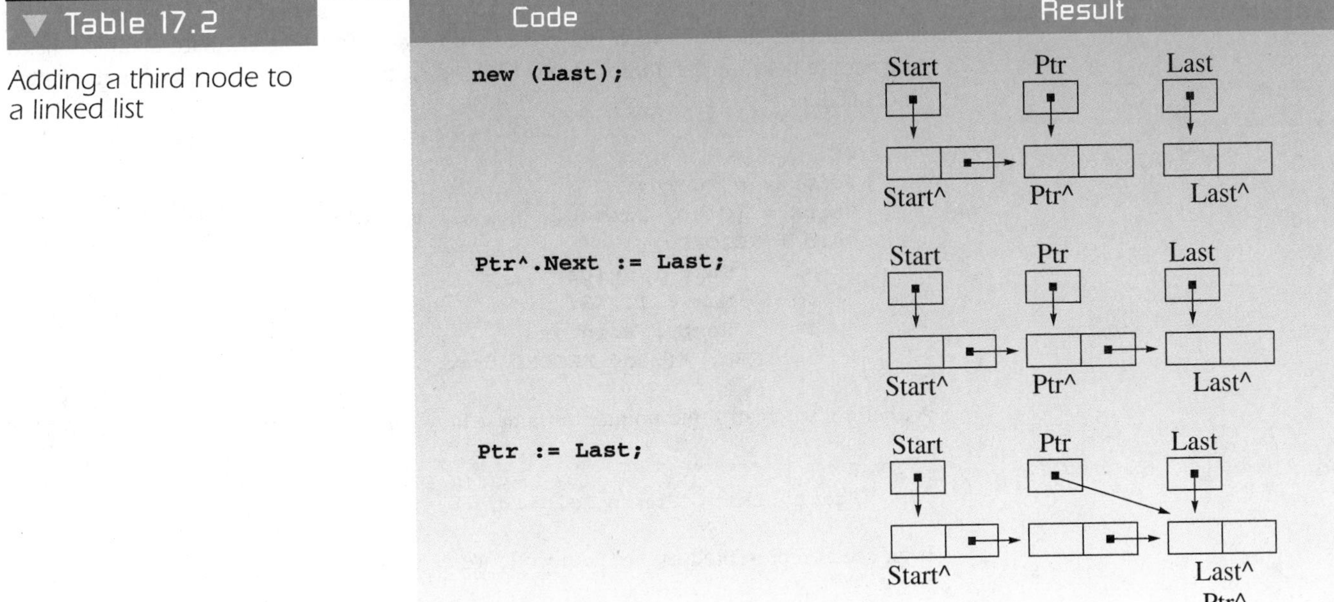

Each pass through the body of the **FOR** loop adds one element to the linked list and causes both Ptr and Last to point to the last node of the list. After the loop has been executed four times, we have

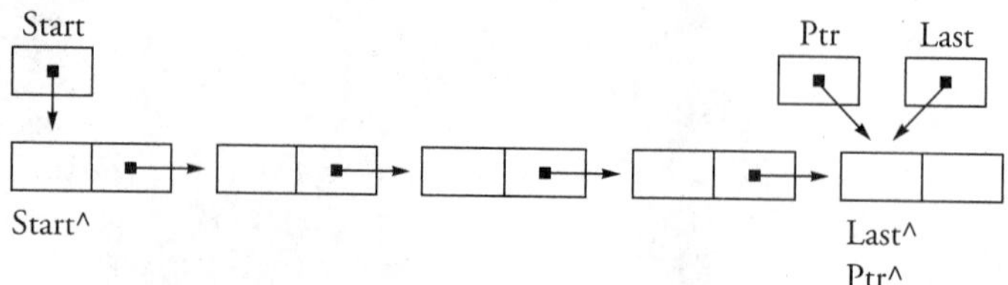

At this stage, the loop is exited and

```
Ptr^.Next := NIL;
```

produces

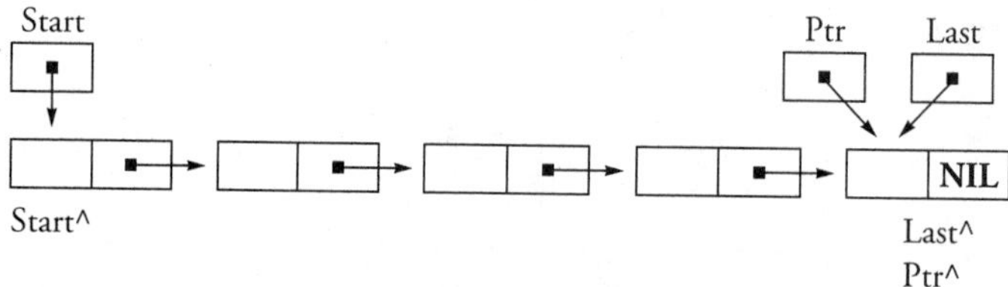

Now when we process the list, we can check the field name Next to determine when the end of the list has been reached. In this sense, **NIL** is used in a manner similar to the use of **eof** with files.

Example 17.1

Let's now create a linked list that can be used to simulate a deck of playing cards. We need 52 nodes, each of which is a record with a field for the suit (club, diamond, heart, or spade), a field for the number (1 to 13), and a field for the pointer. Such a record can be defined as

```
TYPE
  Pointer = ^Card;
  Suits = (Club, Diamond, Heart, Spade);
  Card = RECORD
           Suit : Suits;
           Num : 1..13;
           Next : Pointer
         END;  {  of RECORD Card  }
```

As before, we need three pointer variables; they can be declared as

```
VAR
  Start, Last, Ptr : Pointer;
```

If an ace is represented by the number 1, we can start our list by

```
BEGIN
  new (Start);
  Start^.Suit := Club;
```

```
Start^.Num := 1;
Ptr := Start;
Last := Start;
```

This beginning is illustrated by

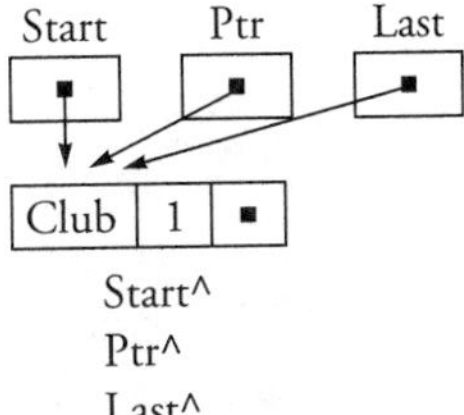

We can then generate the rest of the deck by

```
FOR J := 2 TO 52 DO
  BEGIN
    new (Last);
    IF Ptr^.Num = 13 THEN  {  Start a new suit  }
      BEGIN
        Last^.Suit := succ(Ptr^.Suit);
        Last^.Num := 1
      END  {  of IF...THEN option  }
    ELSE  {  Same suit, next number  }
      BEGIN
        Last^.Suit := Ptr^.Suit;
        Last^.Num := Ptr^.Num + 1
      END;  {  of ELSE option  }
    Ptr^.Next := Last;
    Ptr := Last
  END;  {  of FOR loop  }
Ptr^.Next := NIL;
```

The first time through this loop produces

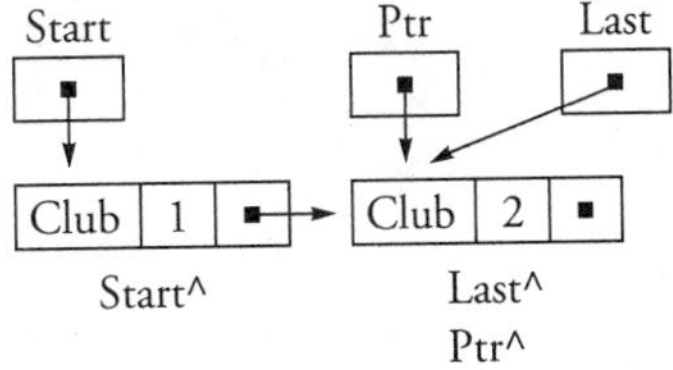

This loop is processed all 51 times and then exited, so when

```
Ptr^.Next := NIL;
```

is executed, we have the list shown in Figure 17.2.

Printing from a Linked List

Thus far, we have seen how to create a dynamic structure and assign data to components of such a structure. We conclude this section with a look at how to print data from a linked list.

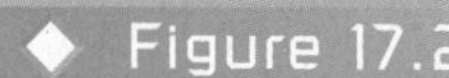
◆ Figure 17.2

A linked list simulating a deck of cards

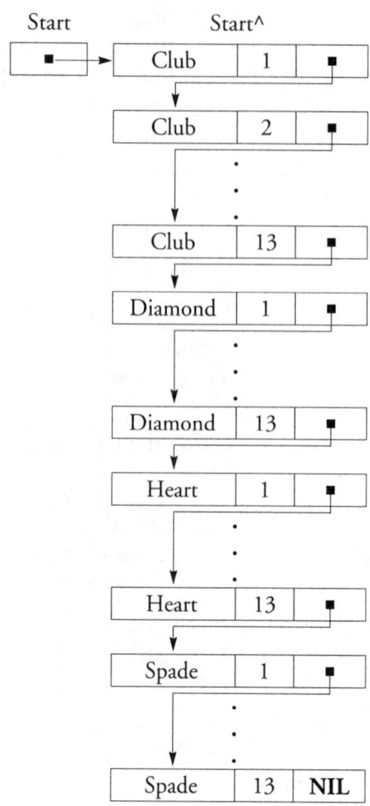

The general idea is to start with the first component in the list, print the desired information, and then move sequentially through the list until the last component (**NIL**) is reached. There are two aspects of this algorithm that need to be examined. First, the loop control depends on examining the current record for the value of **NIL** in the pointer field. If P is used to denote this field, we have

```
WHILE P <> NIL DO
  BEGIN
    .
    .
    .
  END;
```

Second, the loop increment is to assign the value of the Next field of the current record to the pointer (P) that is used as a loop control variable. To illustrate, assume the previous definitions and declarations are used to form a list of student names. If we declare the variable P by

```
VAR
  P : DataPtr;
```

we can then print the names by

```
BEGIN  {  Print names in list  }
  P := Start;
  WHILE P <> NIL DO
```

```
        BEGIN
          writeln (P^.Name:40);
          P := P^.Next
        END  {  of WHILE loop  }
    END;  {  of printing names  }
```

In general, printing from a linked list is done with a procedure. In this case, only the external pointer (Start, in our examples) needs to be used as a parameter. To illustrate, a procedure to print the previous list of names is

```
PROCEDURE PrintNames (Start : DataPtr);
  VAR
    P : DataPtr;
  BEGIN
    P := Start;
    WHILE P <> NIL DO
      BEGIN
        writeln (P^.Name:40);
        P := P^.Next
      END  {  of WHILE loop  }
  END;  {  of PROCEDURE PrintNames  }
```

This procedure is called from the main program by

```
PrintNames (Start);
```

Exercises 17.2

1. Discuss the differences and similarities between arrays and linked lists.
2. Write a test program to transfer an unknown number of integers from a data file into a linked list and then print the integers from the linked list.
*3. Write a procedure to be used with the test program in Exercise 2 to print the integers.
4. Explain why a linked list is preferable when you are getting an unknown number of data items from a data file.

For Exercises 5–7, suppose you are going to create a linked list of records where each record in the list should contain the following information about a student: name, four test scores, 10 quiz scores, average, and letter grade.

*5. Define a record to be used for this purpose.
6. What pointer type(s) and pointer variable(s) are needed?
*7. Assume the data for each student are on one line in the data file as

Smith Mary	97 98 85 90 9 8 7 10 6 9 10 8 9 7 ■

   a. Show how to get the data for the first student into the first component of a linked list.
   b. Show how to get the data for the second student into the second component.
8. Why are three pointers (Start, Last, Ptr) used when creating a linked list?

For Exercises 9–15, consider the following definitions and declarations:

```
TYPE
  P = ^Node;
```

```
       Node = RECORD
                Num : integer;
                Next : P
              END;
     VAR
       A, B, C : P;
```

Show how the schematic

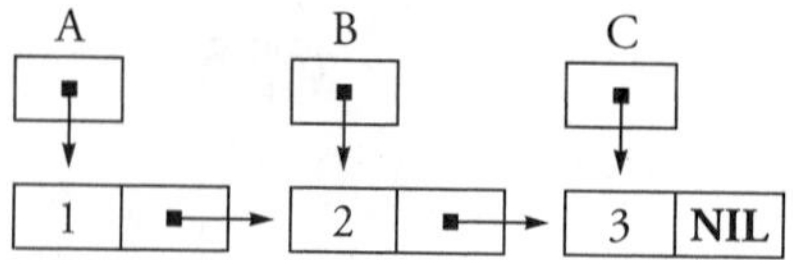

would be changed by each statement.

*9. `A := A^.Next;`
10. `B := A;`
*11. `C := A^.Next;`
12. `B^.Num := C^.Num;`
*13. `A^.Num := B^.Next^.Num;`
14. `C^.Next := A;`
*15. Write one statement to change

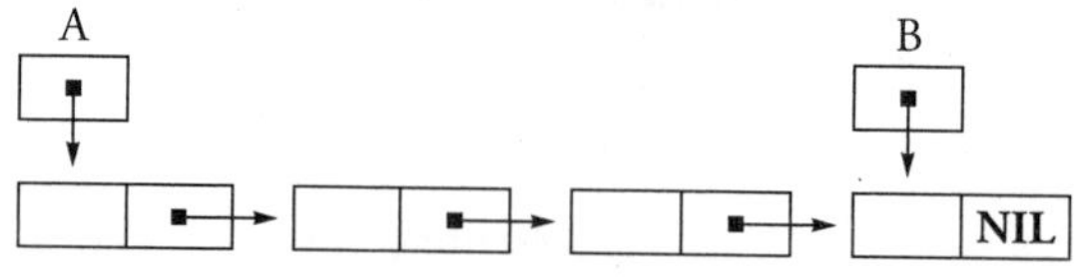

to

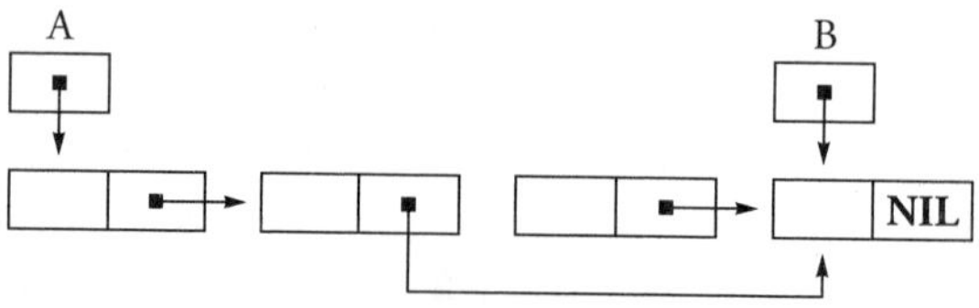

For Exercises 16–18, assume the definitions and declarations in Exercises 9–15. Indicate the output for each.

16.
```
new (A);
new (B);
A^.Num := 10;
B^.Num := 20;
B := A;
A^.Num := 5;
writeln (A^.Num, B^.Num);
```

*17.
```
new (C);
C^.Num := 100;
new (B);
B^.Num := C^.Num MOD 8;
new (A);
```

```
   A^.Num := B^.Num + C^.Num;
   writeln (A^.Num, B^.Num, C^.Num);
18. new (A);
   new (B);
   A^.Num := 10;
   A^.Next := B;
   A^.Next^.Num := 100;
   writeln (A^.Num, B^.Num);
```

*19. Write a function Sum to sum the integers in a linked list of integers. Show how it is called from the main program.

17.3 Working with Linked Lists

Objectives

- to be able to insert an element into a linked list
- to be able to delete an element from a linked list
- to be able to update an ordered linked list
- to be able to search a linked list for an element

In this section, we examine some of the basic operations required when working with linked lists. Working with a list of integers, we see how to create a sorted list. We then update a linked list by searching it for a certain value and deleting that element from the list.

The following **TYPE** definition is used for most of this section:

```
TYPE
  DataPtr = ^Node;
  Node = RECORD
           Num : integer;
           Next : DataPtr
         END;
```

Because most of the operations we examine will be used later, procedures are written for them.

Inserting an Element

The dynamic nature of a linked list implies that we are able to insert an element into a list. The three cases considered are inserting an element at the beginning, in the middle, and at the end of a list.

Push is a procedure for adding a node to the beginning of a linked list.

The procedure for inserting an element at the beginning of a list is commonly called **Push.** Before we write code for this procedure, let's examine what should be done with the nodes and pointers. If the list is illustrated by

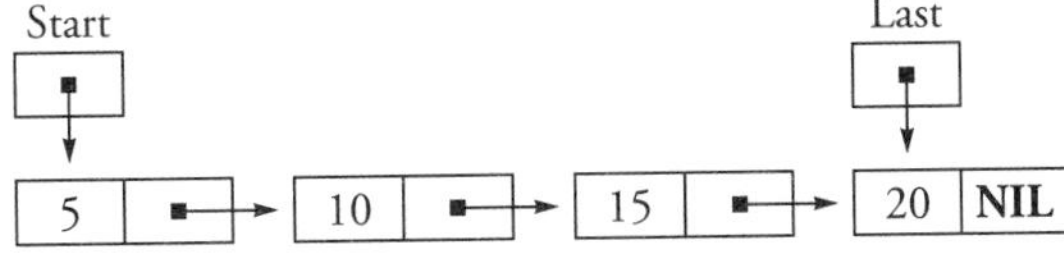

and we wish to insert

3

at the beginning, we need to get a new node by

```
new (P);
```

Communication and Style Tips

When working with linked lists of records, Node is frequently used as the record identifier. This facilitates the readability of program comments. Thus, comments such as "Get new node," "Insert a node," and "Delete a node" are meaningful.

assign the appropriate value to Num

```
P^.Num := 3;
```

and reassign the pointers to produce the desired result. After the first two steps, we have the following list:

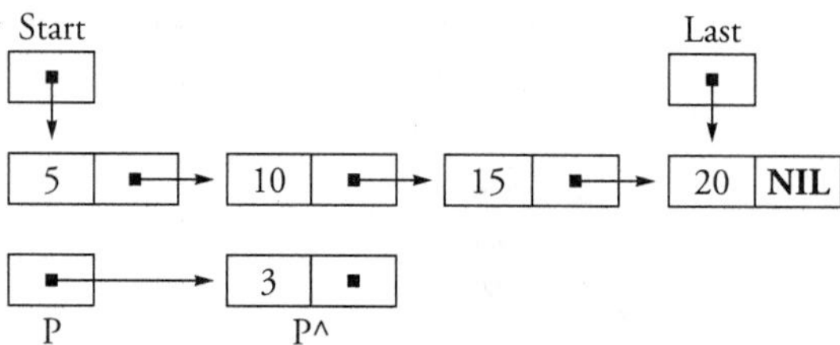

At this point

```
P^.Next := Start;
```

yields this list:

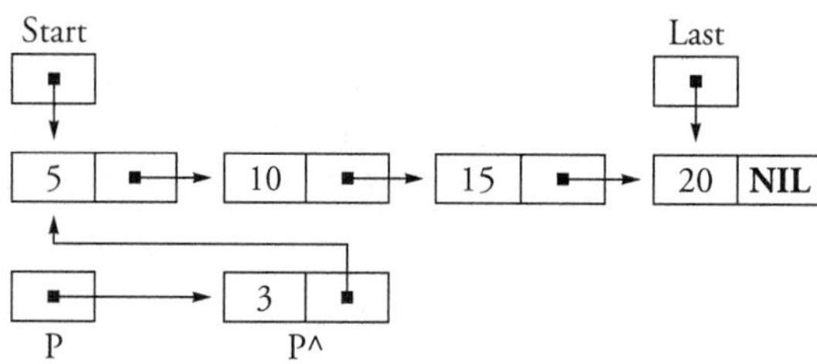

Then

```
Start := P;
```

yields the following list, in which **PROCEDURE** Push is now complete.

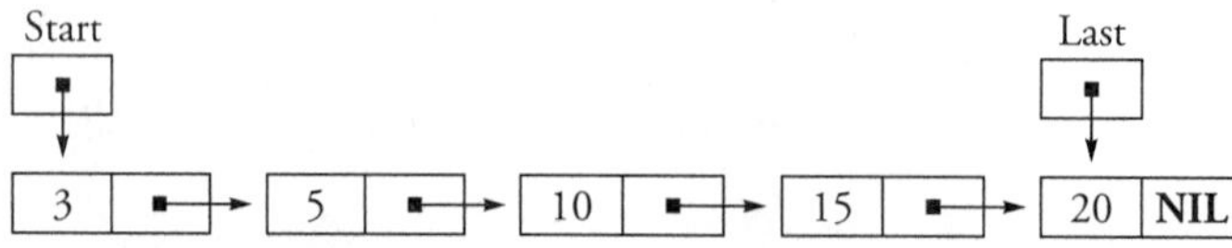

A procedure for this follows:

```
PROCEDURE Push (VAR Start : DataPtr;
                NewNum : integer);
  VAR
    P : DataPtr;
  BEGIN
    new (P);                    {  Get another node          }
    P^.Num := NewNum;           {  Assign the data value     }
    P^.Next := Start;           {  Point to the first node   }
    Start := P;                 {  Point to new first node   }
    IF Start^.Next = NIL THEN
      Last := Start     {  For a list with only one node     }
  END;  {  of PROCEDURE Push  }
```

This procedure can be called from the main program by

```
Push (Start, 3);
```

A note of caution is in order. This procedure is written assuming there is an existing list with **NIL** assigned to the pointer in the final node. If this is used as the first step in creating a new list, the assignment

```
Start := NIL;
```

must have been made previously.

The basic process for inserting a node somewhere in a linked list other than at the beginning or end is to get a new node, find where it belongs, and put it in the list. To do this, we must start at the beginning of a list and search it sequentially until we find where the new node belongs. When we next change pointers to include the new node, we must know between which pair of elements in the linked list the new node is to be inserted. Thus, if

12	■

is to be inserted in an ordered linked list such as

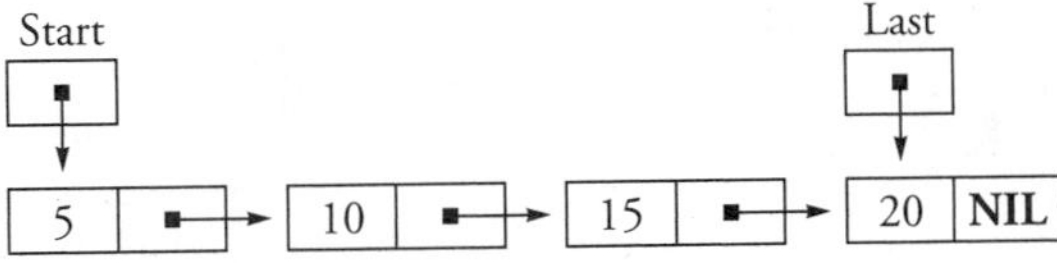

we need to know that the link

10	■	→	15	■	→

is in the list. Once this pair has been identified, the pointers will be changed to produce

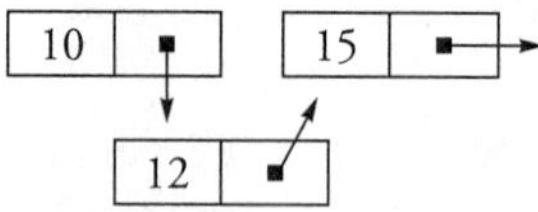

so that the new list with the new node inserted will be

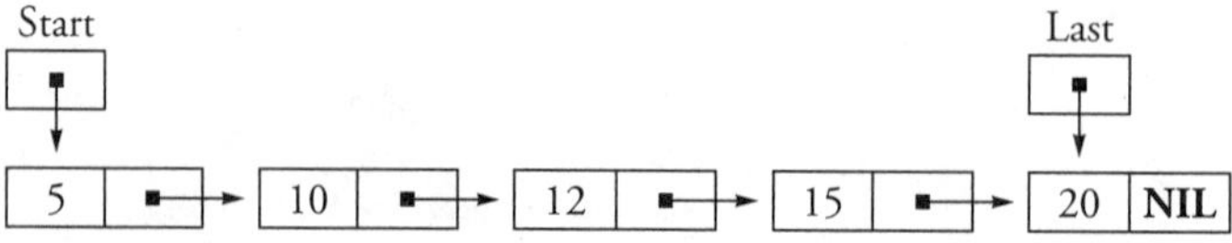

Now let's see how this can be done. We can get a new node by

```
new (P);
P^.Num := NewNum;  {  where NewNum has the value 12  }
```

To find where the new node belongs, we need two pointer variables to keep track of successive pairs of elements as we traverse the list. Assume Before and Ptr have been appropriately declared. Then

```
WHILE Ptr^.Num < NewNum DO
  BEGIN
    Before := Ptr;
    Ptr := Ptr^.Next
  END;
```

will search the list for the desired pair. (We assume that the node to be inserted is not at the beginning of the list.) Using the previous numbers, when this loop is completed we have the following arrangement:

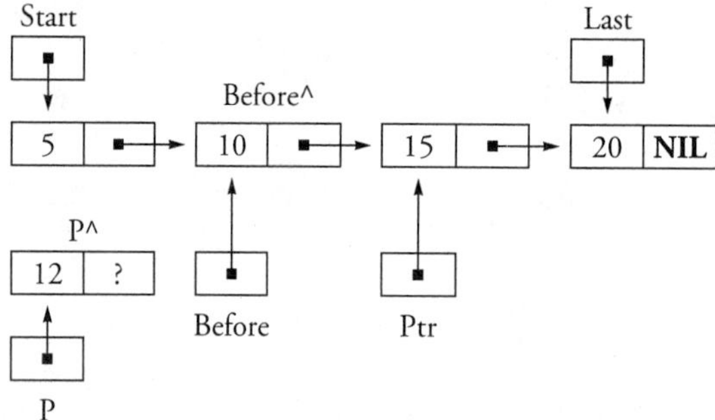

We can put the new node in the list by reassigning the pointers, using

```
P^.Next := Ptr;
Before^.Next := P;
```

The list can then be envisioned as follows:

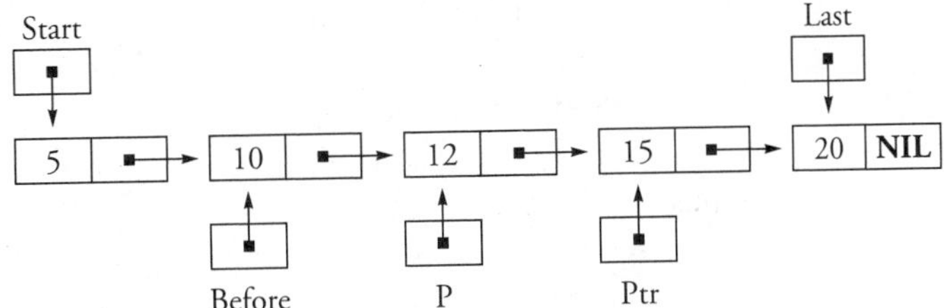

When this code is written together, we have

```
PROCEDURE InsertMiddle (Start : DataPtr;
                        NewNum : integer);
  VAR
    P, Ptr, Before : DataPtr;
  BEGIN

    {  Get a new node  }
    New (P);
    P^.Num := NewNum;

    {  Find where it belongs  }
    Ptr := Start;
    WHILE Ptr^.Num < NewNum DO
      BEGIN
        Before := Ptr;
        Ptr := Ptr^.Next
      END;

    {  Insert the new node  }
    P^.Next := Ptr;
    Before^.Next := P
  END;  {  of PROCEDURE InsertMiddle  }
```

It can be called from the main program by

```
InsertMiddle (Start, 12);
```

The next problem to consider when inserting a node is how to insert it at the end of the list. In the previous code, when Ptr is **NIL,** a reference to Ptr^ causes an error, so this cannot be used for inserting an element at the end of a list. This problem can be solved by using a Boolean variable called Looking, initializing it to **true,** and changing the loop control to

```
WHILE (Ptr <> NIL) AND Looking DO
```

The body of the loop then becomes the **IF . . . THEN . . . ELSE** statement

```
IF Ptr^.Num > NewNum THEN
  Looking := false
ELSE
  BEGIN
    Before := Ptr;
    Ptr := Ptr^.Next
  END;
```

The loop is followed by the statement

```
P^.Next := Ptr;
```

Thus, we have

```
new (P);
P^.Num := NewNum;
Ptr := Start;
Looking := true;
WHILE (Ptr <> NIL) AND Looking DO
  IF Ptr^.Num > NewNum THEN
    Looking := false
  ELSE
    BEGIN
      Before := Ptr;
      Ptr := Ptr^.Next
    END;
P^.Next := Ptr;
Before^.Next := P;
Last := P;
```

To see how this segment of code permits an element to be inserted at the end of a list, suppose NewNum is 30 and the list is

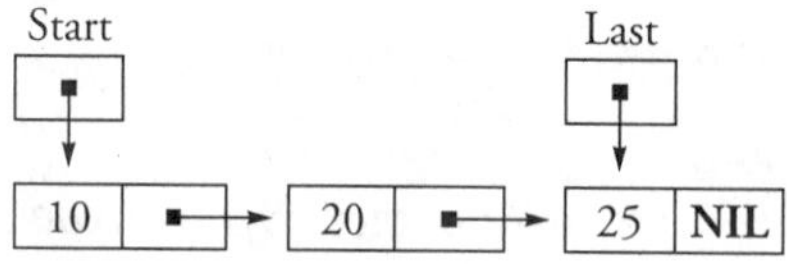

The initialization produces the list illustrated in Figure 17.3(a). Since Ptr <> **NIL** and Looking is **true,** the loop is entered. Ptr^.Num > NewNum (10 > 30) is **false,** so the **ELSE** option is exercised to produce the list shown in Figure 17.3(b). At this stage, Ptr <> **NIL** and Looking is still **true,** so the loop is entered again. Ptr^.Num > NewNum (20 > 30) is **false,** so the **ELSE** option produces the list illustrated in Figure 17.3(c). Since Ptr is not yet **NIL,** Ptr <> **NIL** and Looking is **true,** and the loop is entered. Ptr^.Num > NewNum is **false,** so the **ELSE** option produces the list shown in Figure 17.3(d). Now the condition Ptr <> **NIL** is **false,** so control is transferred to

```
P^.Next := Ptr;
```

When this and the two lines of code following it are executed, we get the arrangement shown in Figure 17.3(e).

One final comment is in order. A slight modification of this procedure accommodates an insertion at the beginning of a list. You may choose to reserve Push for this purpose. However, a single procedure that can insert an element anywhere in a linked list follows:

Figure 17.3

(a) Getting a new node for a linked list

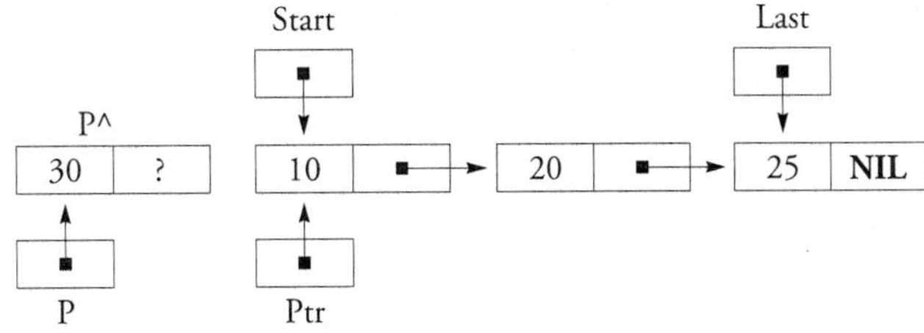

(b) Positioning Before and Ptr

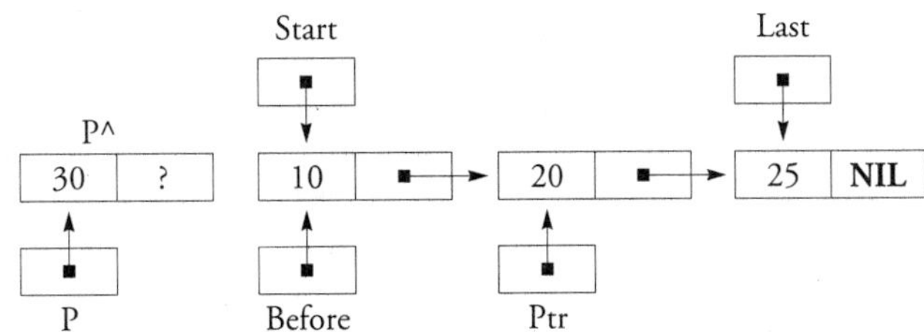

(c) Moving Before and Ptr

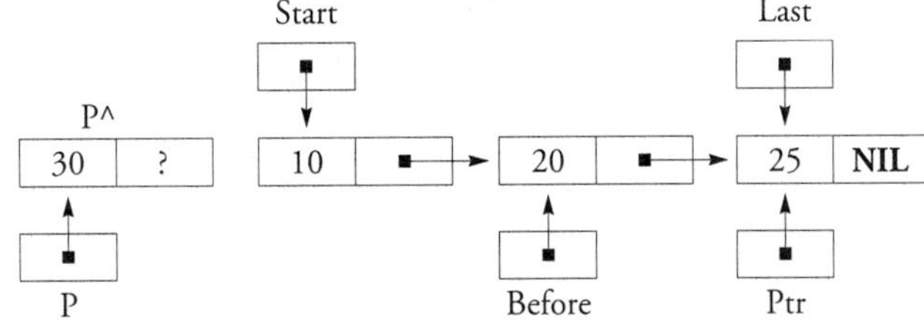

(d) Before and Ptr ready for insertion

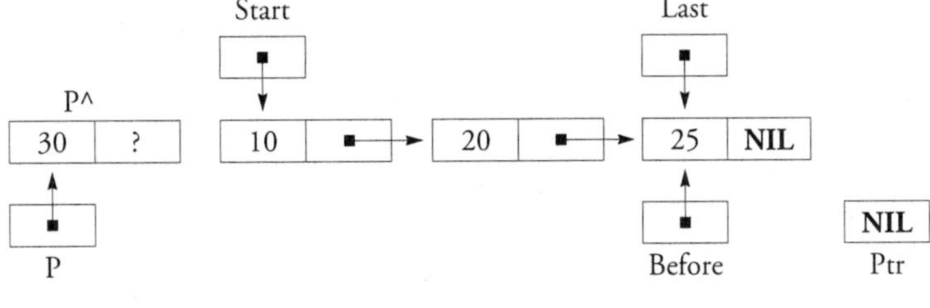

(e) Insertion at end of linked list is complete

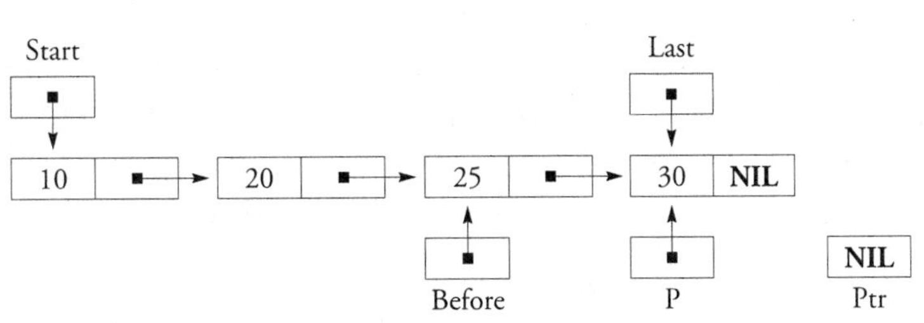


```
PROCEDURE Insert (VAR Start, Last : DataPtr;
                      NewNum : integer);
  VAR
    P, Ptr, Before : DataPtr;
    Looking : boolean;
  BEGIN

    { Initialize }
    new (P);
    P^.Num := NewNum;
```

```
Before := NIL;
Ptr := Start;
Looking := true;

{  Check for empty list  }
IF Start = NIL THEN
  BEGIN
    P^.Next := Start;
    Start := P
  END
ELSE
  BEGIN  {  insert new number in list  }
    WHILE (Ptr <> NIL) and Looking DO
      IF Ptr^.Num > NewNum THEN
        Looking := false
      ELSE
        BEGIN
          Before := Ptr;
          Ptr := Ptr^.Next
        END;  {  of ELSE option  }

    {  Now move the pointers  }
    IF Looking THEN
      Finish := Ptr;
    P^.Next := Ptr;

    {  Check for insert at beginning  }
    IF Before = NIL THEN
      Start := P
    ELSE
      Before^.Next := P
  END  {  of inserting new number  }
END;  {  of PROCEDURE Insert  }
```

Focus on Program Design: Case Study

Creating a Sorted Linked List

To illustrate how **PROCEDURE** Insert can be used to create a linked list of integers sorted from high to low, let's develop a short program to read integers from a data file, create a linked list sorted from high to low, and print contents of components in the linked list. A first-level pseudocode development of this is

1. Create the list
2. Print the list

Step 1 can be refined to

1. Create the list
   1.1 Create the first node
   1.2 **WHILE NOT eof**(Data) **DO**
       Insert in the list

A program that uses procedures for inserting an element and printing the list follows:

```
PROGRAM LinkListPrac (input, output, Data);

{  This program is an illustration of using linked lists.       }
{  It creates a sorted linked list from an unsorted data  file  }
{  and then prints the contents  of the  list.  Procedures are  }
{  used to                                                      }
{                                                               }
{        (1)  insert into the list                              }
{        (2)  print the list                                    }

TYPE
  DataPtr = ^Node;
  Node = RECORD
           Num : integer;
           Next : DataPtr
         END;  {  of RECORD Node  }

VAR
  Number : integer;    {  Number to be inserted                 }
  Start,               {  Pointer for the beginning of the list }
  Finish : DataPtr;    {  Pointer for the end of the list       }
  Data : text;         {  Data file                             }

{***************************************************************}

PROCEDURE Insert (VAR Start, Finish : DataPtr;
                  Number : integer);

  {  Given:   A linked list and number to be inserted in order  }
  {  Task:    Insert the number in numerical order in the       }
  {                linked list                                  }
  {  Return:  Nothing                                           }

  VAR
    P, Ptr, Before : DataPtr;
    Looking : boolean;
  BEGIN

    {  Initialize  }
    new (P);
    P^.Num := Number;
    Before := NIL;
    Ptr := Start;
    Looking := true;

    {  Now start the loop  }
    WHILE (Ptr <> NIL) AND Looking DO
      IF Ptr^.Num > Number THEN
        Looking := false
      ELSE
        BEGIN
          Before := Ptr;
          Ptr := Ptr^.Next
        END;  {  of ELSE option  }
```

```
      {  Now move the pointers  }
      IF Looking THEN
        Finish := Ptr;
      P^.Next := Ptr;

      {  Check for insert at beginning  }
      IF Before = NIL THEN
        Start:= P
      ELSE
        Before^.Next := P
    END;  {  of PROCEDURE Insert  }

{*****************************************************************}

PROCEDURE PrintList (Start : DataPtr);

  {  Given:   A pointer to the start of a linked list          }
  {  Task:    Print numbers from nodes of the linked list      }
  {  Return:  Nothing                                          }

  VAR
    P : DataPtr;
  BEGIN
    P := Start;
    WHILE P <> NIL DO
      BEGIN
        writeln (P^.Num);
        P := P^.Next
      END  {  of WHILE loop  }
  END;  {  of PROCEDURE PrintList  }

{*****************************************************************}

BEGIN  {  Main program  }

  {  Start the list  }
  reset (Data);
  new (Start);
  readln (Data, Number);
  Start^.Num := Number;
  Start^.Next := NIL;
  new (Finish);
  Finish := Start;  {  List has only one node  }

  {  Now create the remainder of the list  }
  WHILE NOT eof(Data) DO
    BEGIN
      readln (Data, Number);
      Insert (Start, Finish, Number)
    END;  {  of WHILE NOT eof  }
  PrintList (Start)
END.  {  of main program  }
```

When this program is run on the data file

42	2	-10	0	45	100	52	78	91	99	86	■

the output is

```
-10
0
2
42
45
52
78
86
91
99
100
```

Deleting a Node

Pop is a procedure to delete a node from a linked list.

A second standard operation when working with linked lists is that of deleting a node. First let's consider the problem of deleting the first node in a list. This process is commonly called **Pop.** Before we write code for this procedure, however, let's examine what should be done with the pointers.

Deleting the first node essentially requires a reversal of the steps used when inserting a node at the beginning of a list. If the list is

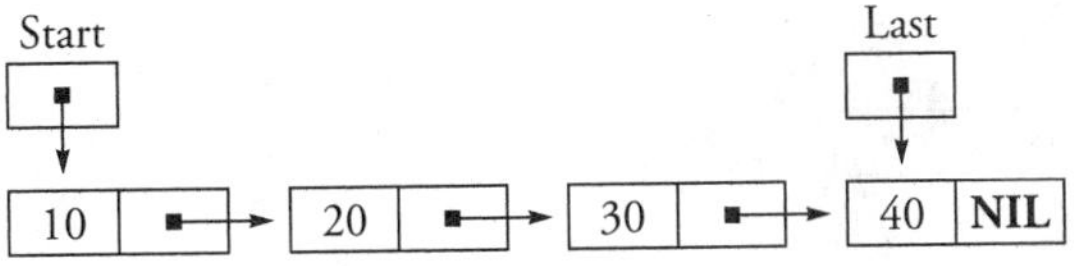

and we wish to produce a list as in

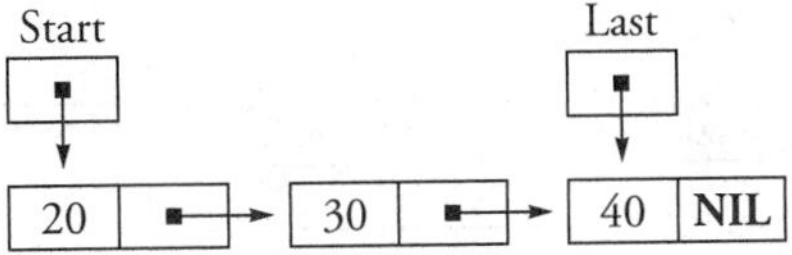

it might seem that

```
Start := Start^.Next;
```

can accomplish this. Not true. The use of this method poses two problems. First, you can (and probably will) want the value of some data fields returned to the main program. Thus, the values of the appropriate fields must be assigned to variable parameters. A second problem is that the first node has not been returned to the computer for subsequent reuse. Since one advantage of using dynamic variables is that unused storage is not wasted, the procedure **dispose** should be used with this node.

We can now write a procedure to delete the first node. Assuming the data value is to be returned to the main program, the procedure is

```
PROCEDURE Pop (VAR Start :DataPtr;
               VAR Number : integer);
  VAR
    P : DataPtr;
  BEGIN
    P := Start;              {  Use a temporary pointer       }
    Number := P^.Num;        {  Return value to main program  }
    Start := Start^.Next;    {  Move start to next node       }
    dispose (P)              {  Return P^ for later use       }
  END;  {  of PROCEDURE Pop  }
```

The next kind of deletion we examine is when the list is searched for a certain key value and the node containing this value is to be removed from the linked list. For example, if the list contains records for customers of a company, we might want to update the list when a former customer moves away. To illustrate the process, suppose the list is

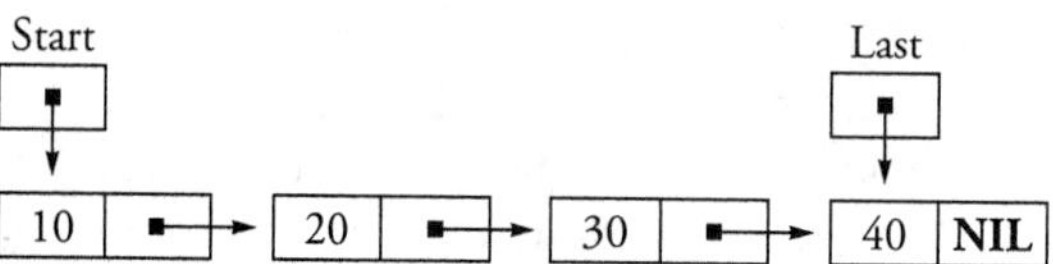

and we wish to delete

30 | ■

The new list is

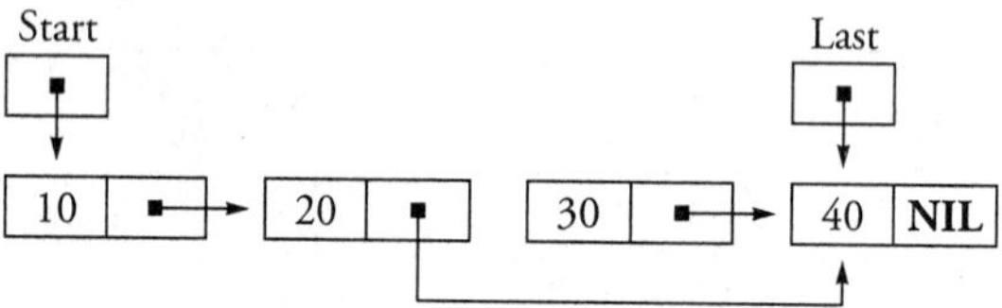

and the procedure **dispose** can be used to return the deleted node to the computer, producing

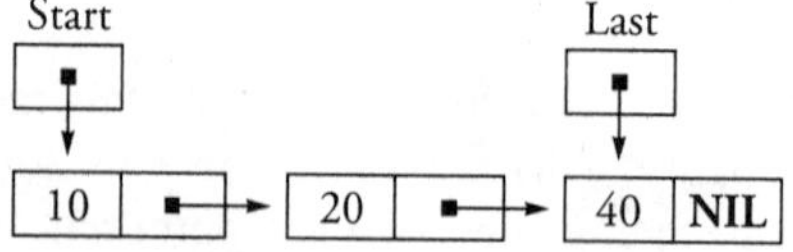

This method uses two temporary pointers. One pointer searches the list for the specified data value. Once it is located, the second pointer points to it so we can use **dispose** to return it for subsequent use. If Before and P are the temporary pointers, the code is

```
BEGIN
  Before := Start;
  WHILE Before^.Next^.Num <> NewNum DO
    Before := Before^.Next;
  P := Before^.Next;
  Before^.Next := P^.Next;
  dispose (P)
END;
```

Let's now see how this deletes

from the previous list.

```
Before := Start;
```

yields the following list:

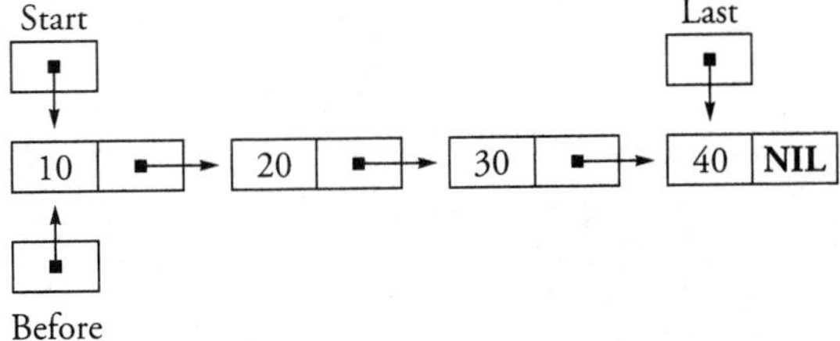

At this stage, NewNum is 30 and Before^.Next^.Num is 20. Since these are not equal, the pointer Before is moved by

```
Before := Before^.Next;
```

and we have this list:

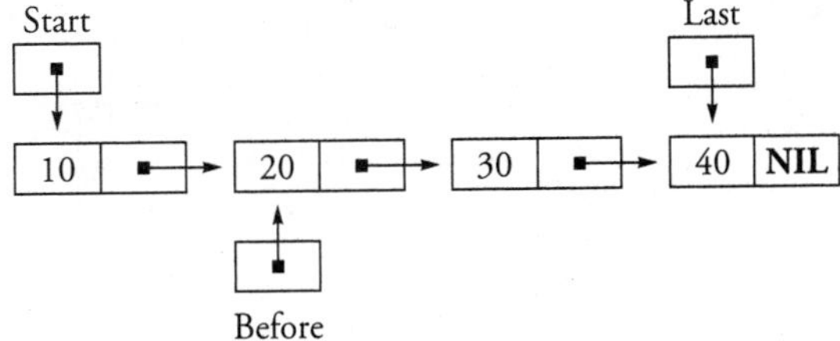

Now Before^.Next^.Num = NewNum (30); so the **WHILE** loop is exited.

```
P := Before^.Next;
```

produces this list:

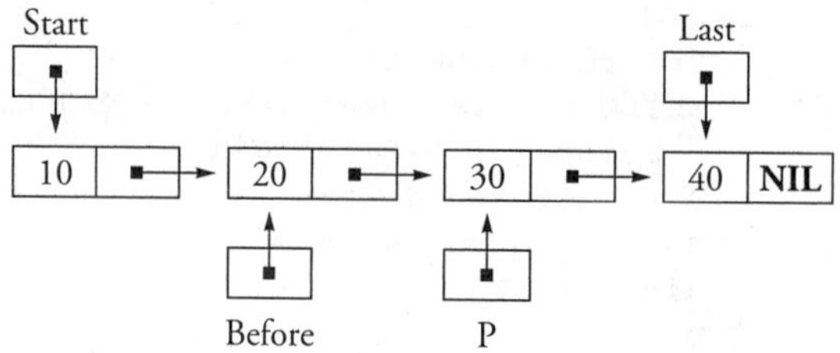

Now

```
Before^.Next := P^.Next;
```

yields the following list:

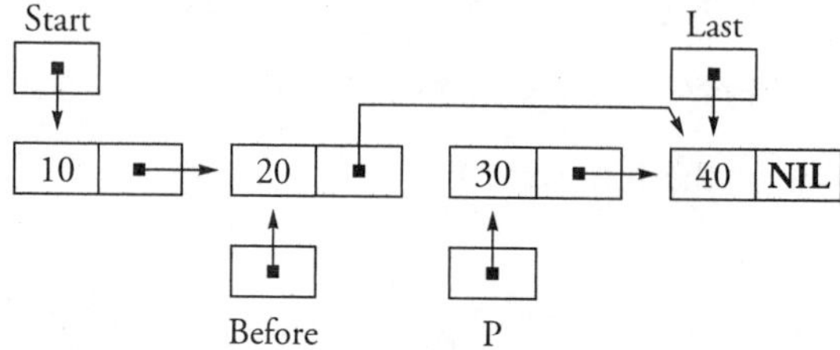

Finally, **dispose** (P); returns the node, so we have

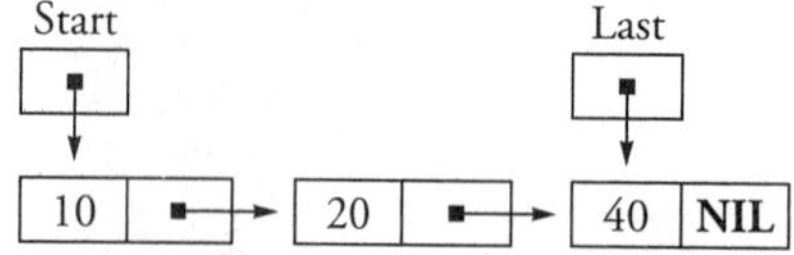

This process can be combined with deleting the first node to produce the following procedure:

```
PROCEDURE Delete (VAR Start : DataPtr;
                  Number : integer);
  VAR
    Before, P : DataPtr;
  BEGIN
    IF Number = Start^.Num THEN
      Pop (Start, Number)
    ELSE
      BEGIN
        Before := Start;
        WHILE Before^.Next^.Num <> Number DO
          Before := Before^.Next;
        P := Before^.Next;
        IF P^.Next = NIL THEN    {  Reset Last  }
          BEGIN
            Last := Before;
            Last^.Next := NIL
          END  {  of IF...THEN option  }
```

A Note of Interest

Using Pointers

Caution must be exercised when using pointers. Unless they are carefully described, it is easy to make a program hard to follow. Speaking to this point, Nazim H. Madhavji states: "It is often necessary to traverse deeply into the structure in order to access the required data, as can be seen in the following example, using pointers P1 and P2:

```
P1 := P2↑.IDType↑.ElementType↑.Fields ...
```

Such 'spaghetti-like' directions get more cumbersome as SomeType gets more complex. Often, access paths of this kind are diagrammatically represented with no absolute certainty of their correctness." He continues, saying: "By raising the level of description of dynamic data structures, the visibility of these structures in programmed text can be increased."

```
        ELSE
          Before^.Next := P^.Next;
        dispose (P)
      END  {  of ELSE option (not first node)  }
  END;  {  of PROCEDURE Delete  }
```

This procedure can now be used to delete any node from a linked list. However, it will produce an error if no match is found. A modification to protect against this possibility is left as an exercise.

Exercises 17.3

*1. Illustrate how **PROCEDURE** Insert works when inserting a node in the middle of a linked list.
2. Write a test program to see what happens when Ptr is **NIL** and a reference is made to Ptr^.
*3. Revise **PROCEDURE** Insert so that it calls **PROCEDURE** Push if a node is to be inserted at the beginning of a list.
4. Modify **PROCEDURE** Delete to protect against the possibility of not finding a match when the list is searched.
*5. Modify **PROCEDURE** Pop so that no data value is returned when Pop is called.
6. Write a complete program that allows the user to do the following:
   a. Create a linked list of records where each record contains a person's name and an amount of money donated to a local fund-raising group. The list should be sorted alphabetically.
   b. Use the linked list to print the donor names and amounts.
   c. Read a name that is to be deleted and then delete the appropriate record from the list.
   d. Print the revised list.
*7. Modify **PROCEDURE** Delete to delete the *n*th node rather than a node with a particular data value. For example, you might be asked to delete the fifth node.
8. Write a procedure to copy the integers in a linked list of integers into a file of integers.

9. Write a complete program that uses a linked list to sort a file of integers. Your program should create a sorted list, print the list, and save the sorted list for later use.
10. Write a procedure to delete duplicate records. Assume the list of records is ordered.

17.4 Other Dynamic Data Structures

Objectives

- to understand why a stack is a dynamic data structure
- to understand how to use a stack in a program
- to understand why a queue is a dynamic data structure
- to understand how to use a queue in a program
- to understand why a binary tree is a dynamic data structure
- to be able to create a binary search tree
- to be able to search a binary search tree

In this final section, we briefly examine some additional dynamic data structures: stacks, queues, and binary trees. All of these data structures have significant computer-oriented applications.

We used stacks in our earlier work with recursion in Section 8.4. Remember that each recursive call adds something to a stack until a stopping state is reached. Stacks are also used when evaluating arithmetic expressions that contain parentheses; partial computations are put "on hold" until needed later in the process.

Queues are used when data do not arrive in an orderly manner. A typical setting is the allocation of priorities to computer users in a time-sharing system. Another example of a queue is a single waiting line for multiple service windows, as might be found at an airport or a bank.

Binary trees are used in programs in which a series of yes/no questions relate to the data. Examples include sorting, computer games, and data that can be stored in the form of a matrix.

The concepts behind stacks, queues, and binary trees and their elementary use are emphasized in this section, which serves as an introduction to these dynamic data structures. A suggested reading list is included for students who desire a more detailed development of these concepts.

Stacks

A stack can be implemented as a dynamic data structure in which access can be made from only one end. Think of a stack as paper in a copying machine or trays in a cafeteria line. In both cases, the last one in will be the first one out; that is, items are put in, one at a time, at the top and removed, one at a time, from the top. This **last-in, first-out** order is referred to as **LIFO;** stacks are therefore often termed LIFO structures.

LIFO refers to a **last-in, first-out** dynamic data structure.

A stack can be envisioned as follows:

E
D
C
B
A

In this illustration, item E is considered the top element in the stack.

The two basic operations needed to work with stacks are the insertion of an element to create a new stack top (push) and the removal of an element from the top of the stack (pop). If a stack is represented by a linked list, push and pop are merely "insert at the beginning" and "delete from the beginning," as developed in Section 17.3.

To illustrate the use of a stack in a program, let's consider a program that will check an arithmetic expression to make sure that parentheses are correctly matched (nested). Our program considers

```
(3 + 4 * (5 MOD 3))
```

to make sure that the number of left parentheses matches the number of right parentheses. A first-level pseudocode for this problem is

1. Read a character
2. **IF** it is a "(" **THEN**
   Push it onto the stack
3. **IF** it is a ")" **THEN**
   Pop the previous "("
4. Check for an empty stack

The growing and shrinking of the stack can be illustrated as shown in Table 17.3.

Table 17.3

Using a stack

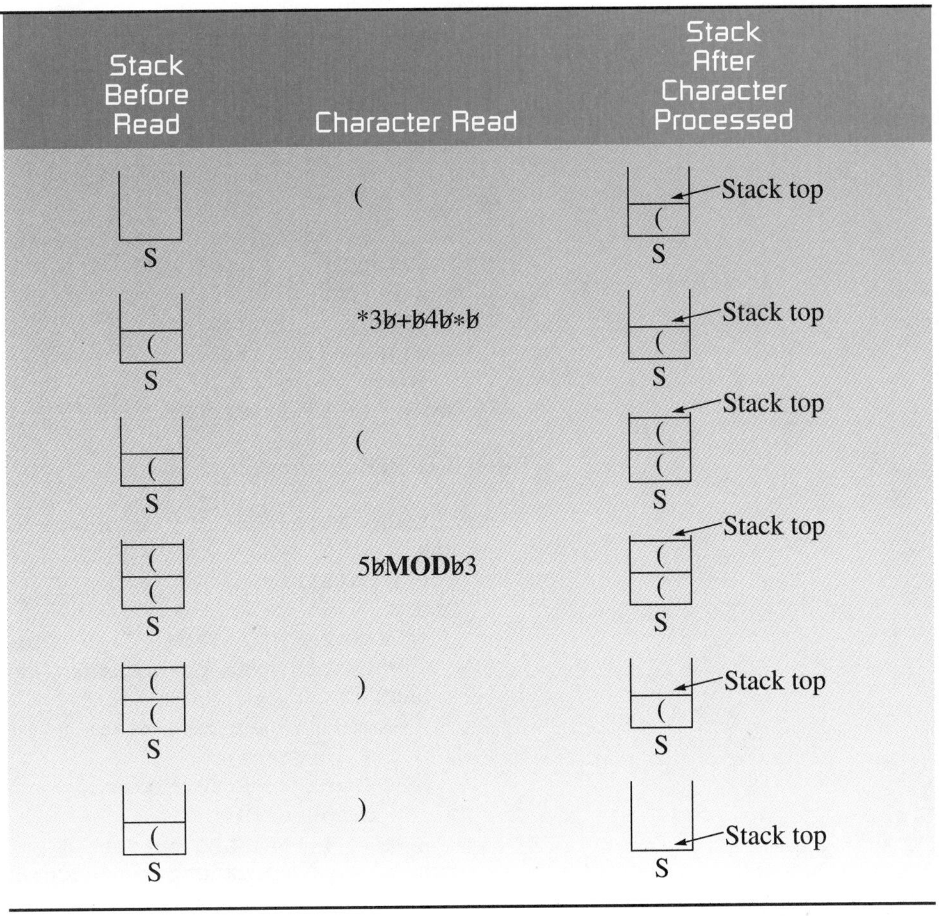

Stack Before Read	Character Read	Stack After Character Processed
S: (empty)	(	S: (← Stack top
S: (	*3b̸+b̸4b̸*b̸	S: (← Stack top
S: (	(	S: ((← Stack top
S: ((	5b̸**MOD**b̸3	S: ((← Stack top
S: ((	)	S: (← Stack top
S: (	)	S: (empty) ← Stack top

* b̸ represents a blank space.

Two points need to be made concerning this program. First, since the stack is represented by a linked list, the illustration could be

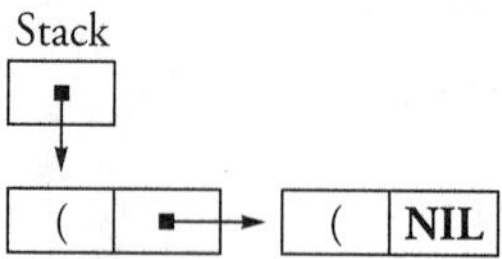

Second, before **PROCEDURE** Pop is used on a stack, a check must be made to make sure the stack is not already empty. Thus, **PROCEDURE** Pop is replaced by **PROCEDURE** PopAndCheck, in which a suitable error message will appear if we try to pop an empty stack.

Now let's prepare code for the previous problem. The following definitions are used:

```
TYPE
  DataPtr = ^Node;
  Node = RECORD
           Sym : char;
           Next : DataPtr
         END;
VAR
  Stack : DataPtr;
```

PROCEDURE Push is

```
PROCEDURE Push (VAR Stack : DataPtr;
                Symbol : char);
  VAR
    P : DataPtr;
  BEGIN
    new (P);
    P^.Sym := Symbol;
    P^.Next := Stack;
    Stack := P
  END;  {  of PROCEDURE Push  }
```

PROCEDURE PopAndCheck is

```
PROCEDURE PopAndCheck (VAR Stack : DataPtr);
  VAR
    P : DataPtr;
  BEGIN
    IF Stack = NIL THEN     {  Check for empty stack  }
      writeln ('The parentheses are not correct.')
    ELSE
      BEGIN  {  Pop the stack  }
        P := Stack;
        Stack := Stack^.Next;
        dispose (P)
      END  {  of ELSE option  }
  END;  {  of PROCEDURE PopAndCheck  }
```

Given these two procedures, the main body of a program that examines an expression for correct use of parentheses is

```
BEGIN  {  Main program  }
  reset (Data);
  Stack := NIL;
  WHILE NOT eoln(Data) DO
    BEGIN
      read (Data, Symbol);
      IF Symbol = '(' THEN
        Push (Stack, Symbol);
      IF Symbol = ')' THEN
        PopAndCheck (Stack)
    END;  {  of WHILE NOT eoln  }

  {  Now check for an empty stack  }
  IF Stack <> NIL THEN
    writeln ('The parentheses are not correct.')
END.  {  of main program  }
```

Several modifications of this short program are available and are suggested in the exercises at the end of this section.

Queues

A **queue** is a dynamic data structure where elements are entered from one end and removed from the other end.

FIFO refers to a **first-in, first-out** dynamic data structure.

A **queue** can be implemented as a dynamic data structure in which access can be made from both ends. Elements are entered from one end (the rear) and removed from the other end (the front). This **first-in, first-out** order is referred to as **FIFO;** queues are termed FIFO structures. A queue is like a waiting line. Think of people standing in line to purchase tickets: Each new customer enters at the rear of the line and exits from the front. A queue implemented as a linked list can be illustrated as

Front Rear NIL

Two basic operations needed to work with queues are the removal of an element from the front of the list and the insertion of an element at the rear of the list. If we use the definitions

```
TYPE
  DataPtr = ^Node;
  Node = RECORD
           Num : integer;
           Next : DataPtr
         END;
```

we can use variables declared by

```
VAR
  Front, Rear : DataPtr;
```

when working with such a structure.

Removing an element from the front of a queue is similar to the use of **PROCEDURE** PopAndCheck with a stack. The only difference is that after an element has been removed, if the queue is empty, Rear must be assigned the value **NIL.** A procedure for removing from the front of a queue follows. It is assumed that the value of the element removed is to be returned to the main program via a variable parameter.

```
PROCEDURE Remove (VAR Front, Rear : DataPtr;
                  VAR Number : integer);
  VAR
    P : DataPtr;
  BEGIN
    IF Front = NIL THEN   {  Check for empty queue  }
      writeln ('The queue is empty.')
    ELSE
      BEGIN   {  Pop the queue  }
        P := Front;
        Front := Front^.Next;
        Number := P^.Num;
        dispose (P)
      END;  {  of ELSE option  }
    IF Front = NIL THEN  {  Set pointers for empty queue  }
      Rear := NIL
  END;  {  of PROCEDURE Remove  }
```

This procedure is called from the main program by

```
Remove (Front, Rear, Number);
```

A procedure to insert an element at the rear of a queue (assuming there is at least one element in the queue) is similar to the procedure given in Section 17.3 for inserting an element at the end of a linked list. You are asked to write the code as an exercise at the end of this section.

A **tree** is a dynamic data structure consisting of a special node (a root) that points to zero or more other nodes, each of which points to zero or more other nodes, and so on.

Trees

A **tree** can be implemented as a dynamic data structure consisting of a special node called a root that points to zero or more other nodes, each of which points to zero or more other nodes, and so on. In general, a tree can be visualized as illustrated in Figure 17.4.

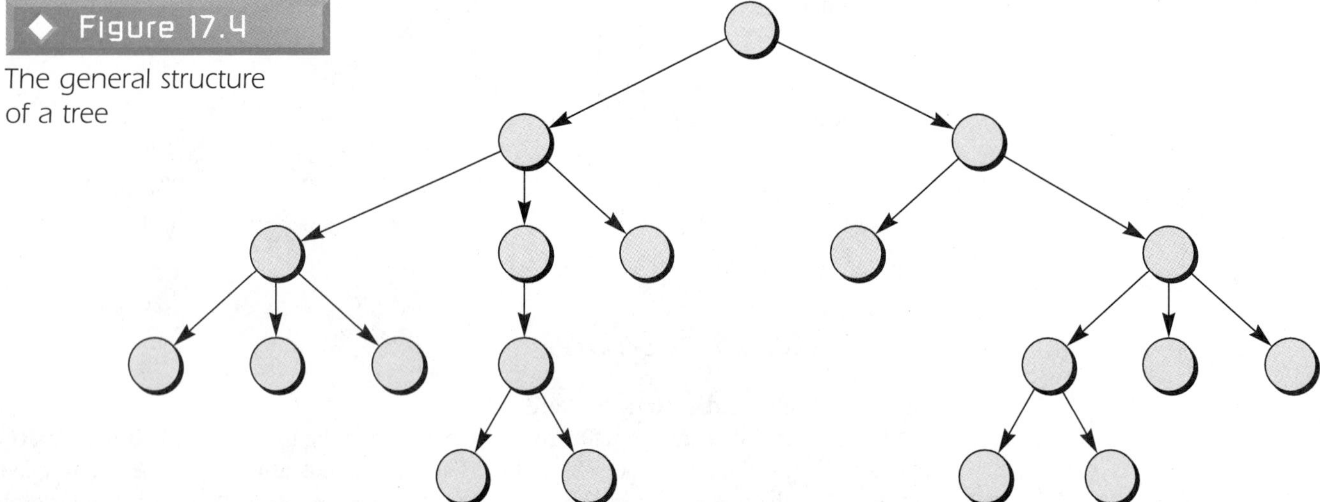

◆ Figure 17.4

The general structure of a tree

A **root** is the first, or top, node in a tree.

Children are nodes pointed to by an element in a tree.

A **parent** in a tree is a node that is pointing to its children.

A **leaf** in a tree is a node that has no children.

The **root** of a tree is its first, or top, node. **Children** are nodes that are pointed to by an element, a **parent** is the node that is pointing to its children, and a **leaf** is a node that has no children.

Applications for trees include compiler programs, artificial intelligence, and game-playing programs. In general, trees can be applied in programs that call for information to be stored so it can be retrieved rapidly. As illustrated in Figure 17.4, pointers are especially appropriate for implementing a tree as a dynamic data structure. An external pointer is used to point to the root and each parent uses pointers to point to its children. A more detailed tree is illustrated in Figure 17.5.

◆ Figure 17.5

Using pointers to create a tree

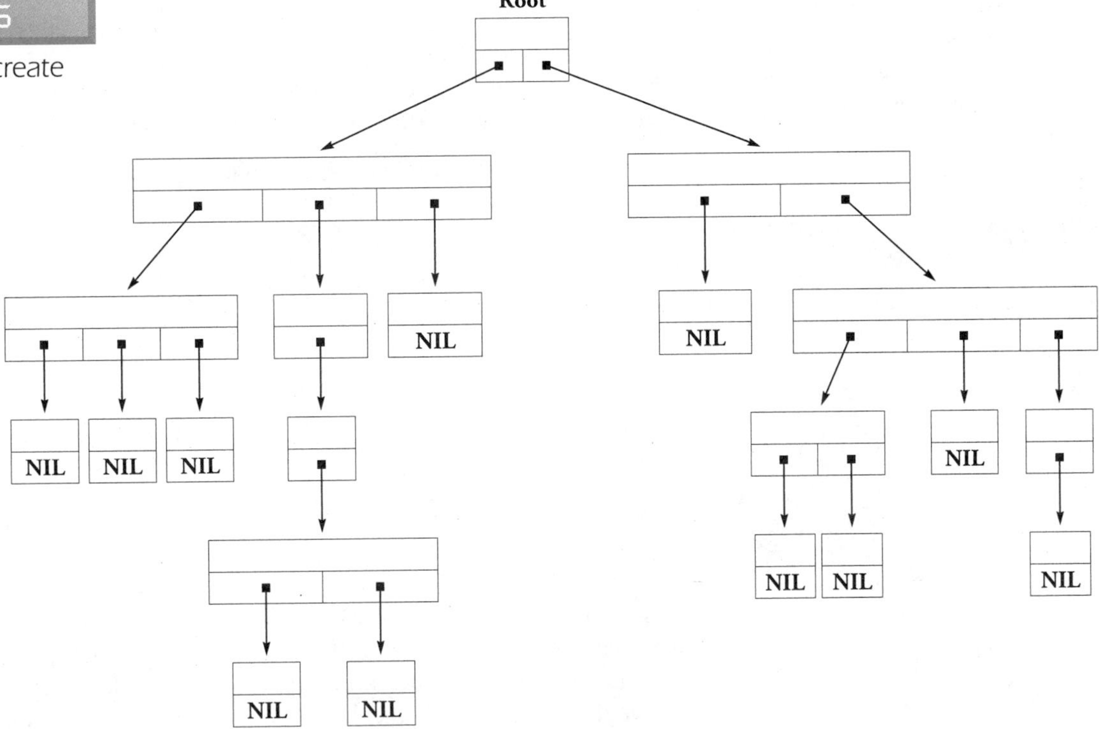

A **binary tree** is a tree such that each node can point to at most two children.

Binary Trees

From this point on, we restrict our discussion of trees to binary trees. In a **binary tree,** each node can point to at most two children. A binary tree is illustrated in Figure 17.6.

◆ Figure 17.6

A binary tree

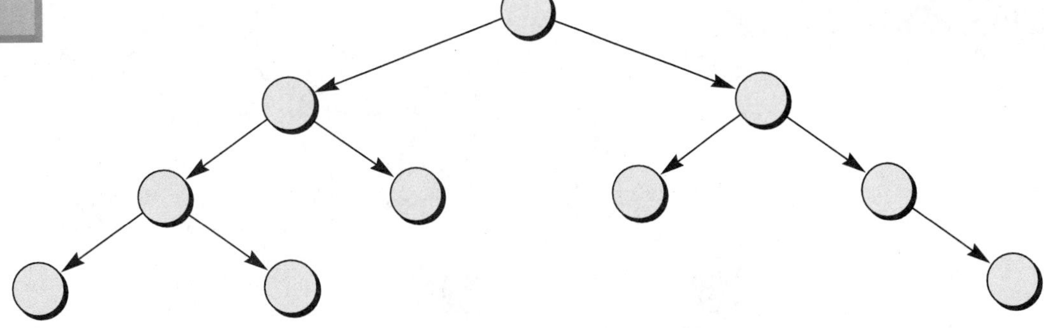

If a binary tree is used to store integer values, a reasonable definition for the pointer type is

```
TYPE
  Pointer = ^TreeNode;
  TreeNode = RECORD
               Info : integer;
               RightChild : Pointer;
               LeftChild : Pointer
             END;
```

A **binary search tree** is a binary tree such that (1) the information in the key field of any node is greater than the information in the key field of any node of its left child and any of its children and (2) the information in the key field of any node is less than the information in the key field of any node of its right child and any of its children.

A particularly important kind of binary tree is a **binary search tree,** which is a binary tree formed according to the following rules:

1. The information in the key field of any node is greater than the information in the key field of any node of its left child and any children of the left child.
2. The information in the key field of any node is less than the information in the key field of any node of its right child and any children of the right child.

Figure 17.7 illustrates a binary search tree.

◆ Figure 17.7

A binary search tree

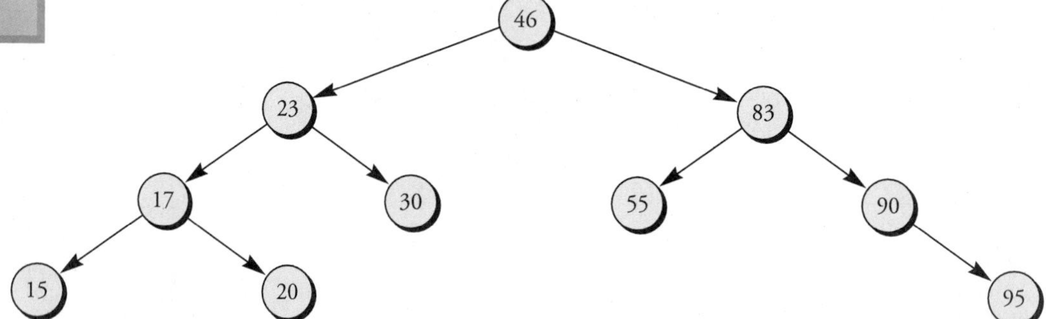

The reference to "search" is used because such trees are particularly efficient when searching for a value. To illustrate, suppose we wish to see whether or not 30 is in the tree. At each node, we check to see if the desired value has been found. If not, we determine on which side to continue looking until either a match is found or the value **NIL** is encountered. If a match is not found, we are at the appropriate node for adding the new value (creating a child). As we search for 30, we traverse the tree via the path indicated by the heavier arrows illustrated in Figure 17.8. Notice that after only two comparisons (<46, >23), the desired value has been located.

◆ Figure 17.8

Searching a tree for the value 30

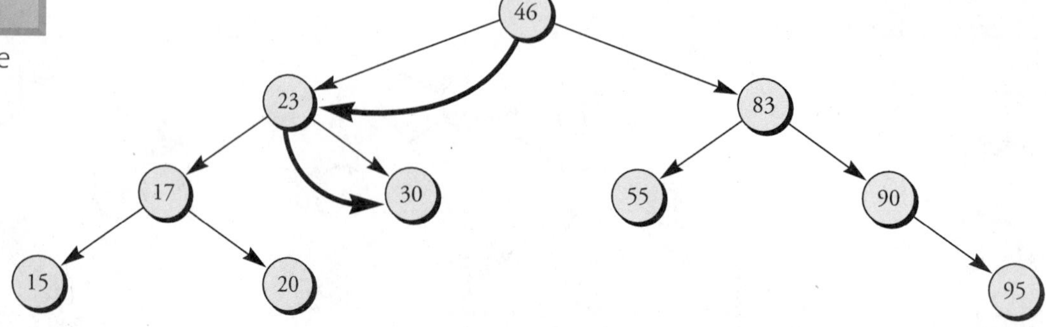

Now suppose we search the tree for the value 65. The path (again indicated by heavier arrows) is shown in Figure 17.9. At this stage, the right child is **NIL** and the value has not been located. It is now relatively easy to add the new value to the tree.

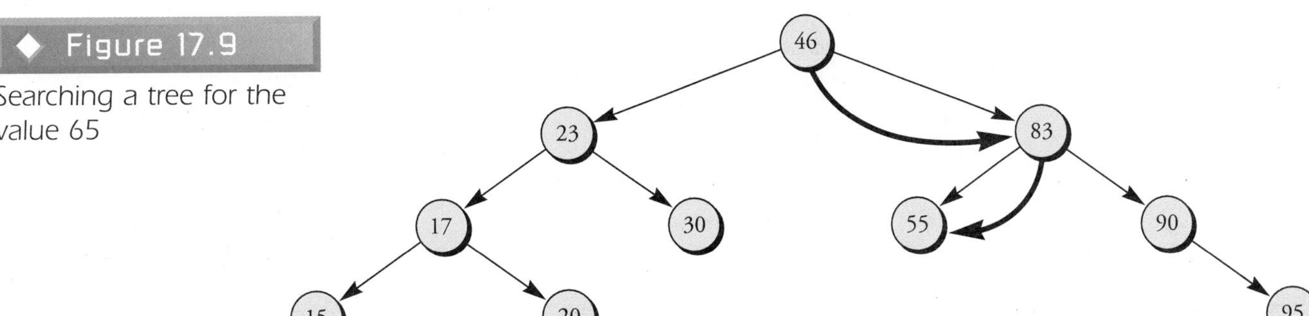

◆ Figure 17.9

Searching a tree for the value 65

Binary search trees can be used to store any data that can be ordered. For example, the registrar of a university might want to quickly access the record of a particular student. If the records are stored alphabetically by student name in a binary search tree, quick retrieval is possible.

Implementing Binary Trees

We conclude this chapter with a relatively basic implementation of binary search trees: a program to create a binary search tree from integers in a data file. We print the integers in order using a variation of the general procedure for searching a tree. The operations of inserting and deleting nodes are left as exercises at the end of this section.

Before we develop algorithms and write code for these implementations, we need to discuss the recursive nature of trees. (You may wish to reread Section 8.4 at this time.) When we move from one node to a right or left child, we are (in a sense) at the root of a subtree. Thus, the pseudocode process of traversing a tree is

1. **IF** LeftChild <> **NIL THEN**
   traverse left branch
2. Take desired action
3. **IF** RightChild <> **NIL THEN**
   traverse right branch

Steps 1 and 3 are recursive; each return to them saves values associated with the current stage together with any pending action. If the desired action is to print the values of nodes in a binary search tree, Step 2 is

2. Print the value

and when this procedure is called, the result is to print an ordered list of values contained in the tree. If we use the previous definitions,

```
TYPE
  Pointer = ^TreeNode;
  TreeNode = RECORD
               Info : integer;
```

```
                    RightChild : Pointer;
                    LeftChild : Pointer
                  END;
```

then a procedure for printing is

```
PROCEDURE PrintTree (T : Pointer);
  BEGIN
    IF T = NIL THEN
      {  do nothing  }
    ELSE
      BEGIN
        PrintTree (T^.LeftChild);
        writeln (T^.Info);
        PrintTree (T^.RightChild)
      END
  END;  {  of PROCEDURE PrintTree  }
```

This procedure is called from the main program by

```
PrintTree (Root);
```

Notice how the recursive nature of this procedure provides a simple, efficient way to inspect the nodes of a binary search tree.

The process of creating a binary search tree is only slightly longer than that for printing. A first-level pseudocode is

1. Initialize root to **NIL**
2. **WHILE NOT eof**(Data) **DO**
   2.1 Get a number
   2.2 Add a node

A recursive procedure can be used to add a node. An algorithm for this is

2.2 Add a node
   2.2.1 If the current node is **NIL,** store the value and stop
   2.2.2 If the new value is less than the current value, point to the left child and add the node to the left subtree
   2.2.3 If the new value is greater than the current value, point to the right child and add the node to the right subtree

Note that the recursive procedure to add a node adds only nodes containing distinct values. A slight modification (left as an exercise) allows duplicate values to be included.

A procedure for adding a node to a binary search tree is

```
PROCEDURE AddNode (VAR Node : Pointer;
                   Number : integer);
  BEGIN
    IF Node = NIL THEN  {  Add a new node  }
      BEGIN
        new (Node);
        Node^.Info := Number;
        Node^.LeftChild := NIL;
        Node^.RightChild := NIL
      END  {  of IF...THEN option  }
    ELSE IF Number < Node^.Info THEN
```

```
    AddNode (Node^.LeftChild, Number)    {  Move down left side    }
  ELSE
    AddNode (Node^.RightChild, Number)   {  Move down right side  }
END;  {  of PROCEDURE AddNode  }
```

A complete program to read unordered integers from a data file, create a binary search tree, and then print an ordered list follows:

```
PROGRAM TreePrac (input, output, Data);

{  This program illustrates working with a binary tree.  Note   }
{  the recursion used in AddNode and PrintTree.  Input is  an   }
{  unordered  list of  integers.  Output  is a sorted list of   }
{  integers that is printed from a binary search tree.          }

TYPE
  Pointer = ^TreeNode;
  TreeNode = RECORD
               Info : integer;
               RightChild : Pointer;
               LeftChild : Pointer
             END;  {  of RECORD TreeNode  }
VAR
  Root : Pointer;          {  Pointer to indicate the tree root  }
  Number : integer;        {  Integer read from the data file    }
  Data : text;             {  Data file                          }

{***************************************************************}

PROCEDURE AddNode (VAR Node : Pointer;
                   Number : integer);

  {  Given:   The root of a binary tree and a number            }
  {  Task:    Insert the number in the binary tree              }
  {  Return:  Nothing                                           }

  BEGIN
    IF Node = NIL THEN                          {  Add a new node  }
      BEGIN
        new (Node);
        Node^.Info := Number;
        Node^.LeftChild := NIL;
        Node^.RightChild := NIL
      END  {  of IF...THEN option  }
    ELSE IF Number < Node^.Info THEN      { Move down left side  }
      AddNode (Node^.LeftChild, Number)
    ELSE
      AddNode (Node^.RightChild, Number) { Move down right side }
  END;  {  of PROCEDURE AddNode  }

{***************************************************************}

PROCEDURE PrintTree (Node : Pointer);

  {  Given:   The root of a binary tree                         }
  {  Task:    Print numbers in order from nodes of the binary   }
```

```
  {                   tree                                         }
  {  Return:        Nothing                                        }

  BEGIN
    IF Node = NIL THEN
      {  Do nothing  }
    ELSE
      BEGIN
        PrintTree (Node^.LeftChild);
        writeln (Node^.Info);
        PrintTree (Node^.RightChild)
      END  {  of ELSE option  }
  END;  {  of PROCEDURE PrintTree  }

{*****************************************************************}

BEGIN  {  Main program  }
  reset (Data);
  new (Root);
  Root := NIL;
  WHILE NOT eof(Data) DO
    BEGIN
      readln (Data, Number);
      AddNode (Root, Number)
    END;  {  of WHILE NOT eof(Data)  }
  PrintTree (Root)
END.  {  of main program  }
```

When this is run on the data file

16	■	8	■	-5	■	20	■	30	■	101	■	0	■	10	■	18	■	■

the output is

```
-5
0
8
10
16
18
20
30
101
```

Exercises 17.4

*1. Use the program for checking parentheses (at the beginning of this section) to illustrate how the stack grows and shrinks when the following expression is examined:

```
(5 / (3 - 2 * (4 + 3) - (8 DIV 2)))
```

2. Write a test program to check an arithmetic expression for correct nesting of parentheses.

3. Modify the program in Exercise 2 so that several expressions can be examined; then give more descriptive error messages. Finally, include a **SET** for the parentheses symbols "(" and ")".
4. Write a program that utilizes a stack to print a line of text in reverse order.
*5. Stacks and queues can also be implemented using arrays rather than linked lists. With this in mind, do the following:
   a. Give appropriate definitions and declarations for using arrays for these data structures.
   b. Rewrite all procedures using array notation.
6. Write a procedure for inserting an element at the rear of a queue. Illustrate changes made in the linked list when such a procedure is executed.
7. Write a program that uses a stack to check an arithmetic expression for correct use of parentheses "( )," brackets "[ ]," and braces "{ }."

For Exercises 8–11, indicate which are binary search trees. Explain what is wrong with those that are not.

8.

*9.

10.

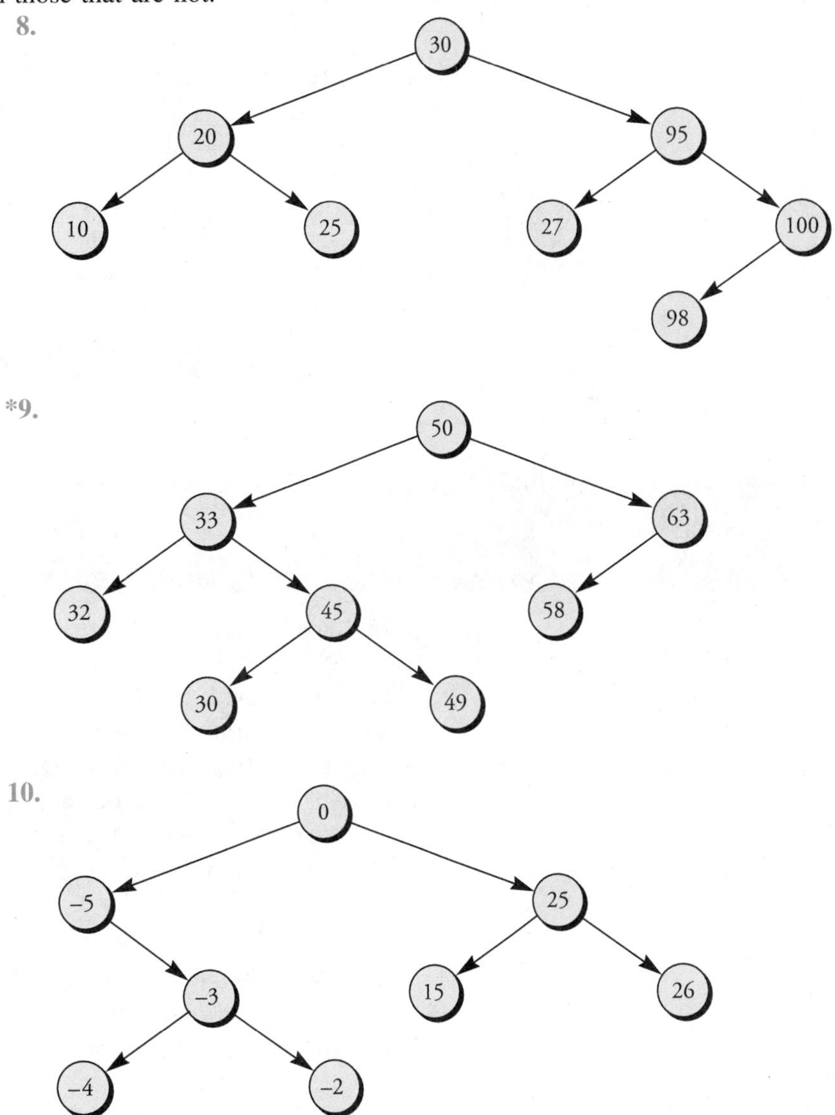

*11.

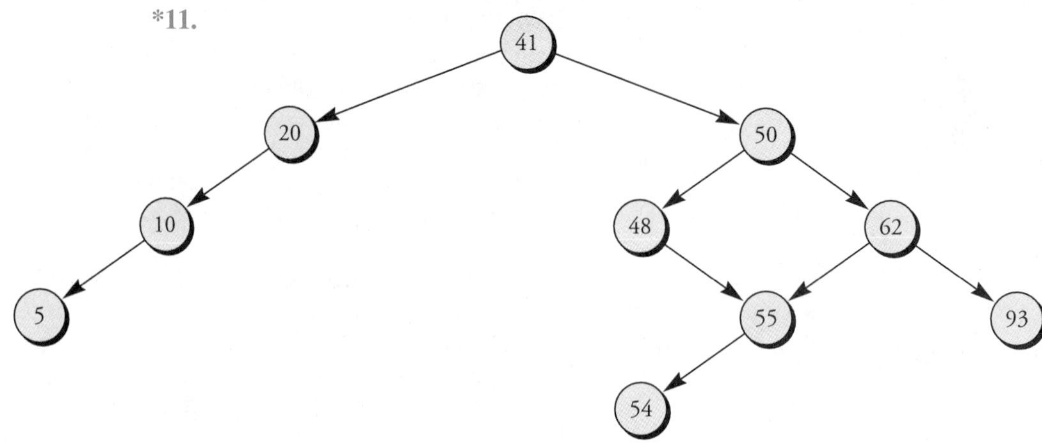

12. Write a procedure that allows the user to insert a node in a binary search tree.
*13. Modify **PROCEDURE** AddNode to include the possibility of having nodes equal in value.
14. Write a procedure that allows the user to delete a node from a binary search tree.
*15. Write a function to search a binary search tree for a given value. The function should return **true** if the value is found and **false** if it is not found.
16. Illustrate what binary search tree is created when **PROGRAM** TreePrac is run using the following data file:

Running and Debugging Hints

1. Be careful to distinguish between a pointer and its associated dynamic variable. Thus, if Ptr is a pointer, the variable is Ptr^.
2. When a dynamic variable is no longer needed in a program, use **dispose** so that the memory location can be reallocated.
3. After using **dispose** with a pointer, its referenced variable is no longer available. If you use **dispose** (Ptr), then Ptr^ does not exist.
4. Be careful not to access the referenced variable of a pointer that is **NIL.** Thus, if the assignment

```
Ptr := NIL;
```

is made, a reference to Ptr^.Info results in an error.
5. When using pointers with subprograms, be careful to pass the pointer (not the referenced variable) to the subprogram.

(continued)

6. When creating dynamic data structures, be careful to initialize properly by assigning **NIL** where appropriate and keep track of pointers as your structures grow and shrink.
7. Operations with pointers require that they be of the same type. Thus, exercise caution when comparing or assigning them.
8. Values may be lost when pointers are inadvertently or prematurely reassigned. To avoid this, use as many auxiliary pointers as you wish. This is better than trying to use one pointer for two purposes.

Summary

Key Terms

address (of a memory location)
binary search tree
binary tree
children
component (node) (of a linked list)
dynamic structure
dynamic variable
first-in, first-out (FIFO)
last-in, first-out (LIFO)
leaf
linked list
parent
pointer variable
Pop
Push
queue
root
stack
static variable
tree
value (of a memory location)

Keywords

dispose **new** **NIL**

Key Concepts

- Values are stored in memory locations; each memory location has an address.
- A pointer variable is one that contains the address of a memory location; pointer variables are declared by

```
TYPE
  AgeRange = 0..99;
VAR
  Ptr : ^AgeRange;
```

where the caret (^) or up arrow (↑) is used before the predefined data type.
- A dynamic variable is a variable that is referenced through a pointer variable; dynamic variables can be used in the same context as any other variable of that type. They are not declared in the variable declaration section. With the declaration

```
TYPE
  AgeRange = 0..99;
VAR
  Ptr : ^AgeRange;
```

the dynamic variable is Ptr^ and is available after **new** (Ptr) is executed.

- Dynamic variables are created by

```
new (Ptr);
```

and destroyed (memory area made available for subsequent reuse) by

```
dispose (Ptr);
```

- Assuming the definition

```
TYPE
  AgeRange = 0..99;
VAR
  Ptr : ^AgeRange;
```

the relationship between a pointer and its associated dynamic variable is illustrated by the code

```
new (Ptr);
Ptr^ := 21;
```

which can be envisioned as

21

Ptr Ptr^

- The only legal operations on pointer variables are assignments and comparison for equality.
- **NIL** can be assigned to a pointer variable; this is used in a Boolean expression to detect the end of a list.
- Dynamic data structures differ from static data structures in that they are modified during the execution of the program.
- A linked list is a dynamic data structure formed by having each component contain a pointer that points to the next component; generally, each component is a record with one field reserved for the pointer.
- A node is a component of a linked list.
- When creating a linked list, extra pointers are needed to keep track of the first, last, and newest component.
- When creating a linked list, the final component should have **NIL** assigned to its pointer field.
- Printing from a linked list is accomplished by starting with the first component in the list and proceeding sequentially through the list until the last component is reached; a typical procedure for printing from a linked list is

```
PROCEDURE Print (First : DataPtr);
  VAR
    P : DataPtr;
  BEGIN
    P := First;
    WHILE P <> NIL DO
      BEGIN
        writeln (P^.<field name>);
        P := P^.Next
      END
  END;  { of PROCEDURE Print }
```

- Inserting a node in a linked list should consider three cases: insert at the beginning, insert in the middle, and insert at the end.
- Inserting at the beginning of a linked list is a frequently used procedure and is referred to as Push; one version of this procedure is

```
PROCEDURE Push (VAR Start : DataPtr;
                NewNum : integer);
  VAR
    P : DataPtr;
  BEGIN
    new(P);
    P^.New := NewNum;
    P^.Next := Start;
    Start := P;
    IF Start^.Next = NIL THEN
      Last := Start
  END;  {  of PROCEDURE Push  }
```

- Searching an ordered linked list to see where a new node should be inserted is accomplished by

```
Ptr := Start;
WHILE (Ptr <> NIL) AND (Ptr^.Num < NewNum) DO
  BEGIN
    Before := Ptr;
    Ptr := Ptr^.Next
  END;
```

- When deleting a node from a linked list, we can delete the first node, or search for a particular node and then delete it.
- Deleting the first node is referred to as Pop; one version of this procedure is

```
PROCEDURE Pop (VAR Start : DataPtr;
               VAR NewNum : integer);
  VAR
    P : DataPtr;
  BEGIN
    P := Start;
    NewNum := P^.Num;
    Start := Start^.Next;
    dispose (P)
  END;  {  of PROCEDURE Pop  }
```

- When a node is deleted from a linked list, it should be returned for subsequent use by the computer; this is done by using the standard procedure **dispose.**
- A stack is a dynamic data structure where access can be made from only one end; stacks are referred to as last-in, first-out (LIFO) structures.
- A queue is a dynamic data structure where access can be made from both ends; queues are referred to as first-in, first-out (FIFO) structures.
- A tree is a dynamic data structure consisting of a special node (called a root) that points to zero or more other nodes, each of which points to zero or more other nodes, and so on. Trees are represented symbolically as

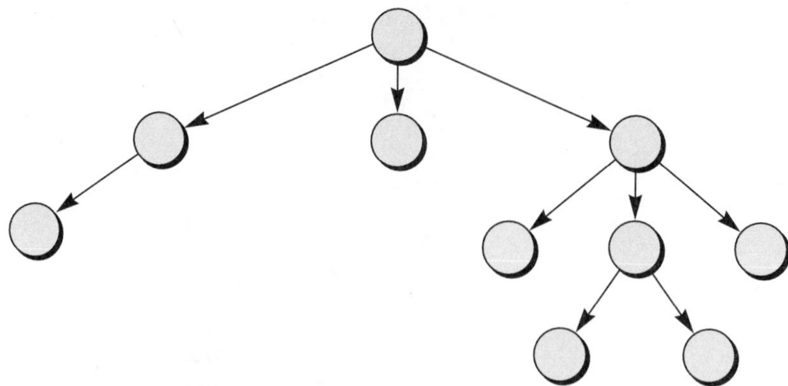

- A root is the first or top node of a tree.
- Trees are particularly useful in programs that use data that can be ordered and that need to be retrieved quickly.
- Binary trees are trees in which each node points to at most two other nodes; parent, right child, and left child are terms frequently used when working with binary trees. An illustration of a binary tree is

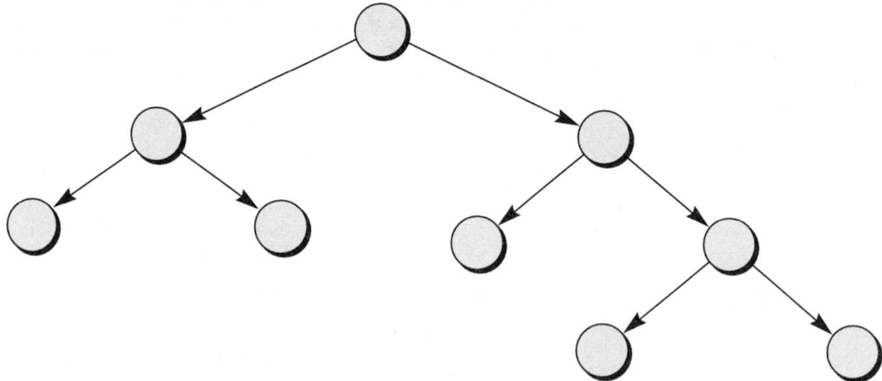

- Binary search trees are binary trees in which the information in any node is greater than the information in any node of its left child and any children of the left child and the information in any node is less than the information in any node of its right child and any children of the right child. An illustration of a typical binary search tree is

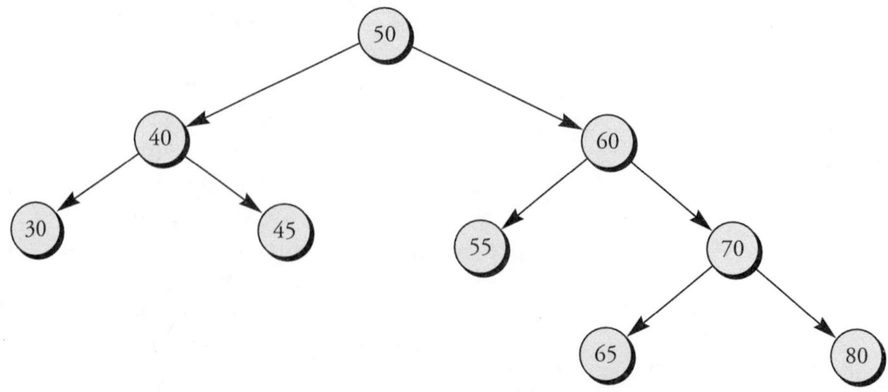

◆ Recursive procedures can be used when working with trees; to illustrate, the values in the nodes of a binary search tree can be printed (sequentially) with the following procedure:

```
PROCEDURE PrintTree (T : Pointer);
  BEGIN
    IF T = NIL THEN
      {  do nothing  }
    ELSE
      BEGIN
        PrintTree (T^.LeftChild);
        writeln (T^.Info);
        PrintTree (T^.RightChild)
      END  {  of ELSE option  }
  END;  {  of PROCEDURE PrintTree  }
```

Chapter Review Exercises

For Exercises 1–5, use the linked list

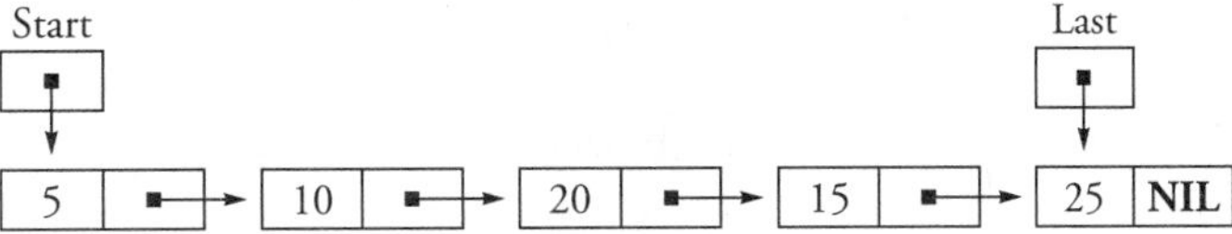

Write Pascal statements for each of the following:

1. Reorder the list so it is in an ordered sequence.
2. Have Last point to

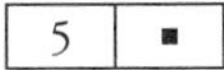

3. Print the first value.
4. Print the last value.
5. Replace **NIL** with a pointer to the following in order to create a circular list.

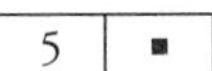

For Exercises 6–10, use the linked list

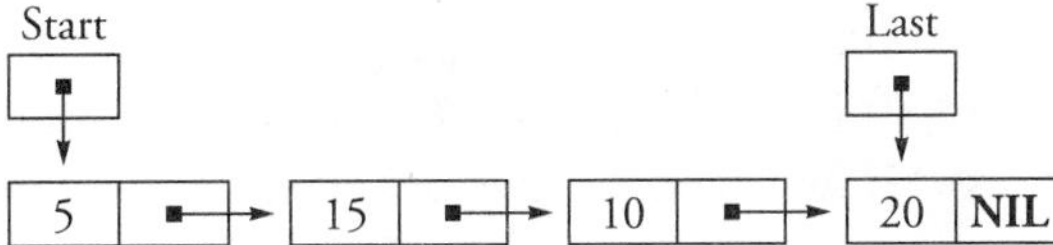

and the following segment of code:

```
Temp1 := Start^.Next;
Temp2 := Start^.Next^.Next^.Next;
Start^.Next := Start^.Next^.Next;
Start^.Next^.Next := Temp1;
Start^.Next^.Next^.Next := Temp2;
```

Illustrate what happens to the linked list as each statement is executed. Each statement presumes the previous code is executed.

6. `new (Temp1);`
   `Temp1 := Start^.Next;`
7. `new (Temp2);`
   `Temp2 := Start^.Next^.Next^.Next;`
8. `Start^.Next := Start^.Next^.Next;`
9. `Start^.Next^.Next := Temp1;`
10. `Start^.Next^.Next^.Next := Temp2;`
11. Assume a linked list has been formed where each node is a record defined by

    ```
    DataPtr := ^Info;
    Info = RECORD
             Num : integer;
             Next : DataPtr
           END;
    ```

    Write a procedure to sum the values contained in the field Num.

For Exercises 12–18, assume a binary search tree exists as illustrated here:

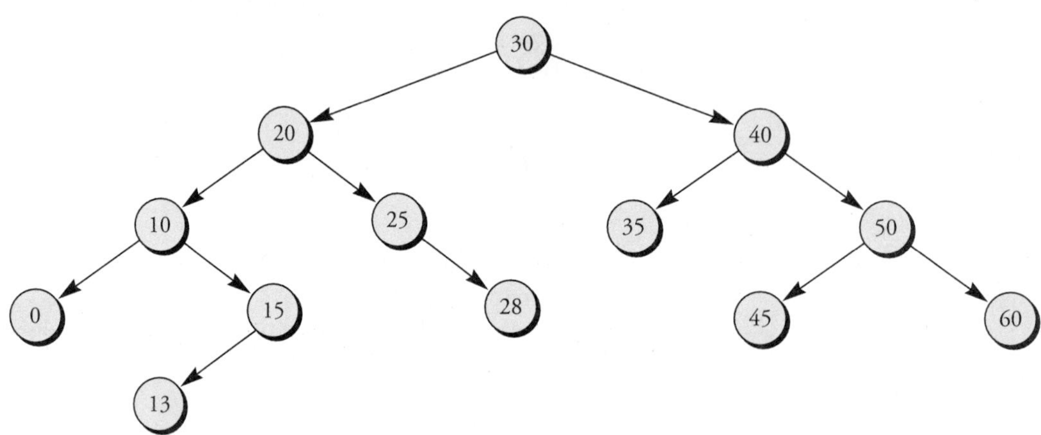

12. How would the tree be changed by inserting the node 12?
13. How would the tree be changed by inserting the node 17?
14. How would the tree be changed by inserting the node 61?
15. How would the tree be changed by inserting the node 52?
16. How would the tree look after deleting the node 15?
17. How would the tree look after deleting the node 10?
18. How would the tree look after deleting the node 45?

For Exercises 19–21, create a binary search tree assuming data are read in the indicated order.

19. 14, 20, 18, 30, 100, 3, 2, 10, 19
20. 5, 10, 15, 20, 25, 30
21. 30, 25, 20, 15, 10, 5
22. Assume each node of a binary search tree contains a three-letter word. Show how the tree looks if the following words are read (in order) as input.
    son, dad, dog, cat, ski, low, mom, mow, car, sob
23. Write a segment of code to return the number of elements in a linked list.
24. Write a **boolean** function that determines whether or not a linked list is in ascending order.

Suggestions for Further Reading

Nance, Douglas W., and Thomas L. Naps. *Introduction to Computer Science: Programming, Problem Solving, and Data Structures.* 3rd ed. St. Paul, Minn.: West Publishing Company, 1995.

Naps, Thomas L., and Bhagat Singh. *Program Design with Pascal: Principles, Algorithms, and Data Structures.* St. Paul, Minn.: West Publishing Company, 1988.

Naps, Thomas L., and Douglas W. Nance. *Introduction to Computer Science: Programming, Problem Solving, and Data Structures.* 3rd alternate ed. St. Paul, Minn.: West Publishing Company, 1995.

Naps, Thomas L., and George Pothering. *Introduction to Data Structures and Algorithm Analysis with Pascal.* St. Paul, Minn.: West Publishing Company, 1992.

Tenenbaum, Aaron M., and Moshe J. Augenstein. *Data Structures Using Pascal.* Englewood Cliffs, N.J.: Prentice Hall, 1981.

Programming Problems

1. Creating an index for a textbook can be accomplished by a Pascal program that uses dynamic data structures and works with a text file. Assume that data for a program is a list of words to be included in an index. Write a program that scans the text and produces a list of page numbers indicating where each word is used in the text.
2. One of the problems faced by businesses is how best to manage their lines of customers. One method is to have a separate line for each cashier or station. Another is to have one feeder line where all customers wait and the customer at the front of the line goes to the first open station. Write a program to help a manager decide which method to use by simulating both options. Your program should allow for customers arriving at various intervals. The manager wants to know the average wait in each system, average line length in each system (because of its psychological effect on customers), and the longest wait required.
3. Write a program to keep track of computer transactions on a mainframe computer. The computer can process only one job at a time. Each line of data contains a user's identification number, a starting time, and a sequence of integers

representing the duration of each job. Assume all jobs are run on a first-come, first-served basis. Your output should include a list of identification numbers, the starting and finishing times for each job, and the average waiting time for a transaction.

4. Several previous programming problems have involved keeping records and computing grades for students in some class. If linked lists are used for the students' records, such a program can be used for a class of 20 students or a class of 200 students. Write a record-keeping program that utilizes linked lists. Input is data from an unsorted file. Each student's information consists of the student's name, ten quiz scores, six program scores, and three examination scores. Output should include:
   a. A list, alphabetized by student name, incorporating each student's quiz, program, and examination totals; total points; percentage grade; and letter grade.
   b. Overall class average.
   c. A histogram depicting the class average.
5. Modify the program you developed for Readmore Public Library (Problems 6 and 7, Chapter 12; and Problem 2, Chapter 14) to incorporate a dynamic data structure. Use a linked list to solve the same problem.
6. Mailing lists are frequently kept in a data file sorted alphabetically by customer name. However, when they are used to generate mailing labels for a bulk mailing, they must be sorted by zip code. Write a program to input an alphabetically sorted file and produce a list of labels sorted by zip code. The following data are on file for each customer:

   a. Name
   b. Address, including street (plus number), city, two-letter abbreviation for the state, and zip code
   c. Expiration information, including the month and year

   Use a binary tree to sort by zip code. Your labels should include some special symbol for all expiring subscriptions. (See Problem 1, Chapter 14.)
7. It is possible for a program to contain many more operations with stacks than we developed in this chapter. Write a complete program that includes the following stack operations:

   a. Flush: empties a stack
   b. Copy: creates a duplicate stack
   c. StackLength: returns the number of elements in a stack
   d. DisplayStack: displays the contents of a stack
   e. DisplayReverseStack: displays the contents of a stack in reverse order
   f. CompareStacks: compares two stacks and returns the boolean value **true** if the stacks are identical and **false** if they are not identical

   Output from your program should demonstrate that all stack operations are functioning properly.
8. As a struggling professional football team, the Bay Area Brawlers have a highly volatile player roster. Write a program that allows the team to maintain its roster as a linked list alphabetically, ordered by player last name. Other data items stored for each player are

   a. Height
   b. Weight

c. Age
d. University affiliation

As an added option, have your program access players in descending order of weight and age.

9. Write a program that allows the input of an arbitrary number of polynomials as coefficient and exponent pairs. Store each polynomial as a linked list of coefficient–exponent pairs arranged in descending order by exponent. These pairs do not need to be entered in descending order; it is the responsibility of your program to arrange them that way. Your program should then be able to evaluate each of the polynomials for an arbitrary argument X and to display each of the polynomials in the appropriate descending exponent order. Make sure your program works for all "unusual" polynomials, such as the zero polynomial, polynomials of degree 1, and constant polynomials.

Communication in Practice

1. Select a program from the **Programming Problems** section of this chapter that you have not yet worked. Construct a structure chart and write all documentary information for this program. Include variable definition, subprogram definition, required input, and required output. When you are finished, have a classmate read your documentation to see if it is clear precisely what is to be done.
2. Remove all documentation from a program you have written for this chapter. Exchange this modified version with another student who has done the same thing. Write documentation for the exchanged program. Compare your documentation with that originally written for the program. Discuss the differences and similarities with the other students in your class.
3. Linked lists, stacks, and queues can be presented by using either dynamic variables or static variables (arrays). Talk with a computer science teacher who prefers the dynamic variable approach and with one who prefers the static variable approach. List the advantages and disadvantages of each method. Give an oral report to your class summarizing your conversations with the teachers. Create a chart to use as part of your presentation.

Glossary

abstract data type A class of objects, a defined set of properties of these objects, and a set of operations for processing the objects.

accumulator A variable that sums values.

actual parameter A variable or expression contained in a procedure or function call and passed to that procedure or function. *See also* **formal parameter.**

address Often called address of a memory location, this is an integer value that the computer can use to reference a location. *See also* **memory location** and **value.**

algorithm A finite sequence of effective statements that, when applied to the problem, will solve it.

animation The process of making a figure appear to be in motion.

application software Programs designed for a specific use.

argument A value or expression passed in a function or procedure call.

arithmetic/logic unit (ALU) The part of the central processing unit (CPU) that performs arithmetic operations and evaluates expressions.

array A structured variable designed to handle data of the same type.

array index The relative position of the components of an array.

array of records An array whose component type is a record.

ASCII collating sequence The American Standard Code for Information Interchange ordering for a character set.

assembly language A computer language that allows words and symbols to be used in an unsophisticated manner to accomplish simple tasks. Also referred to as a low-level language.

assertion Special comments used with selection and repetition that state what you expect to happen and when certain conditions will hold. *See also* **postcondition** and **precondition.**

assignment compatible Means an expression can be assigned to a variable.

assignment statement A method of putting values into memory locations.

auxiliary memory *See* **memory** and **secondary memory.**

batch input Input for a program being run in batch mode. Also referred to as stream input.

batch processing A technique of executing the program and data from a file that has been created. User interaction with the computer is not required during execution.

BEGIN . . . END block The segment of code between **BEGIN** and **END** that, when a compound statement is executed within a program, is treated as a single statement.

binary digit A digit, either 0 or 1, in the binary number system. Program instructions are stored in memory using a sequence of binary digits. Binary digits are called bits.

binary file A file in which information is stored using binary representation for components.

binary notation A method of representing integers using only 0's and 1's.

binary search The process of examining a middle value of a sorted array to see which half contains the value in question and halving until the value is located.

binary search tree A binary tree such that (1) the information in the key field of any node is greater than the information in the key field of any node of its left child and any of its children and (2) the information in the key field of any node is less than the information in the key field of any node of its right child and any of its children.

binary tree A tree such that each node can point to at most two children.

bit An abbreviation for binary digit.

bit-mapped font The default font for text display. Each character appears in an 8 × 8 pixel square. *See also* **stroked font.**

block A program in Pascal can be thought of as a heading and a block. The block contains an optional declaration part and a compound statement. The block structure for a subprogram is a subblock. *See also* **subblock.**

Boolean expression An expression whose value is either true or false. *See also* **compound Boolean expression** and **simple Boolean expression.**

bottom-up testing The method of independent testing of modules.

bubble sort A sort that rearranges elements of an array until they are in either ascending or descending order. Consecutive elements are compared to move (bubble) the elements to the top or bottom accordingly during each pass. *See also* **index sort, insertion sort, quick sort,** and **selection sort.**

buffer variable The actual vehicle through which values are passed to or from a file component.

built-in function *See* **standard function.**

bus A group of wires that enables communications between components of a computer.

byte A sequence of bits used to encode a character in memory. *See also* **word.**

call Any reference to a subprogram by an executable statement. Also referred to as invoke.

cancellation error Occurs when numbers of significantly different size are added or subtracted.

CASE statement A multiway selection statement. *See also* **IF . . . THEN** and **IF . . . THEN . . . ELSE.**

central processing unit (CPU) A major hardware component that consists of the arithmetic/logic unit (ALU) and the control unit.

character set The list of characters available for data and program statements. *See also* **collating sequence.**

children Nodes pointed to by an element in a tree.

code (writing) The process of writing executable statements that are part of a program to solve a problem.

cohesive subprogram A subprogram that has been developed to perform a single task.

collating sequence The particular order sequence for a character set used by a machine. *See also* **ASCII collating sequence** and **EBCDIC collating sequence.**

comment A nonexecutable statement used to make a program more readable.

compilation error An error detected when the program is being compiled. *See also* **design error, run-time error,** and **syntax error.**

compiler A computer program that automatically converts instructions in a high-level language to machine language.

component of a file One element of the file data type.

component of a linked list One data item in a linked list. Also referred to as a node.

component of an array One element of the array data type.

compound Boolean expression Refers to the complete expression when logical connectives and negation are used to generate Boolean values. *See also* **Boolean expression** and **simple Boolean expression.**

compound statement Uses the reserved words **BEGIN** and **END** to make several simple statements into a single compound statement.

constant The contents of a memory location whose contents cannot be changed.

constant definition section The section where program constants are defined for subsequent use.

control structure A structure that controls the flow of execution of program statements.

control unit The part of the central processing unit (CPU) that controls the operation of the rest of the computer.

counter A variable used to count the number of times some process is completed.

current pointer A pointer that keeps track of the current pixel position.

data The particular characters that are used to represent information in a form suitable for storage, processing, and communication.

data abstraction The separation between the conceptual definition of a data structure and its eventual implementation.

data type A formal description of the set of values that a variable can have.

data validation The process of examining data prior to their use in a program.

debugging The process of eliminating errors or "bugs" from a program.

declaration section The section used to declare (name) all symbolic constants, data types, variables, and subprograms that are necessary to the program.

declaration statement Defines types in the **TYPE** section, declares variables in the **VAR** section, and is used as the program heading.

decrement A decrease by 1 in a variable used as a loop index.

degenerate case *See* **stopping state.**

design error An error such that a program runs, but unexpected results are produced. Also referred to as a logic error. *See also* **compilation error, run-time error,** and **syntax error.**

difference The difference of set A and set B is A – B, where A – B contains the elements that are in A but not in B. *See also* **intersection, subset,** and **union.**

dynamic structure A data structure that may expand or contract during execution of a program.

dynamic variable Frequently designated as Ptr^ or Ptr↑, a dynamic variable is a variable accessed by a pointer variable. *See also* **static variable.**

EBCDIC collating sequence The Extended Binary Coded Decimal Interchange Code ordering for a character set.

echo checking A technique whereby the computer prints values of variables and data used in a program.

effective statement A clear, unambiguous instruction that can be carried out.

element of an array *See* **component of an array.**

element of a set A value that has been assigned to a set.

empty set A set containing no elements. Also called a null set.

empty statement A semicolon used to indicate that no action is to be taken. Also referred to as a null statement.

encapsulation The process of placing all implementation details in a distinct physical package.

end-of-file marker (eof) A special marker inserted by the machine to indicate the end of the data file. In this text it is represented by a black square (■).

end-of-line marker (eoln) A special marker inserted by the machine to indicate the end of a line in the data. In this text it is represented by a black column (▮).

entrance-controlled loop *See* **pretest loop.**

enumerated data type A user-defined data type.

error *See* **cancellation error, compilation error, design error, run-time error,** and **syntax error.**

executable section Contains the statements that cause the computer to do something. Starts with the reserved word **BEGIN** and concludes with the reserved word **END.**

executable statement The basic unit of grammar in Pascal consisting of valid identifiers, standard identifiers, reserved words, numbers, and/or characters, together with appropriate punctuation.

execute To perform a program by step.

exit-controlled loop *See* **posttest loop.**

exponential form *See* **floating point.**

expression The combination of two or more values to produce a single value.

extended IF statement Occurs when an **IF ... THEN ... ELSE** statement is used in the **ELSE** option of a selection statement.

external file A file used to store data in secondary storage between runs of a program. Also called a master file. *See also* **internal file.**

field A component of a record.

field selector The period that separates the record name from the field name.

field width The phrase used to describe the number of columns used for various output. *See also* **formatting.**

file A data structure that consists of a sequence of components all of the same type.

file window A term used in this book, though not designated by Pascal, to indicate an imaginary window through which values of a file component can be transferred.

first-in, first-out (FIFO) A dynamic data structure. *See also* **queue.**

fixed parts Fields in a record that exist for all records of a particular type. *See also* **variant part.**

fixed point A method of writing decimal numbers in which the decimal is placed where it belongs in the number. *See also* **floating point.**

fixed repetition loop A loop used if the number of times a segment of code needs to be repeated is known in advance. **FOR ... TO ... DO** is a fixed repetition loop. Also referred to as an iterated loop.

floating point A method for writing numbers in scientific notation to accommodate numbers that may have very large or very small values. Exactly one nonzero digit must appear on the left of the decimal. *See also* **fixed point.**

FOR loop A fixed repetition loop causing a fragment of code to be executed a predetermined number of times. **FOR ... TO ... DO** and **FOR ... DOWNTO ... DO** are **FOR** loops.

formal parameter A variable, declared and used in a procedure or function declaration, that is replaced by an actual parameter when the procedure or function is called. *See also* **actual parameter.**

formatting Designating the desired field width when printing integers, reals, Boolean values, and character strings. *See also* **field width.**

forward reference A method that allows a subprogram to call another subprogram that appears later in the declaration section.

function A subprogram whose purpose is to return a single value to the calling program. *See also* **standard function** and **user-defined function.**

global identifier An identifier that can be used by the main program and all subprograms in a program. Also referred to as a **global variable.**

global variable *See* **global indentifier.**

hardware The actual computing machine and its support devices.

higher-dimensional array An array of more than two dimensions.

high-level language Any programming language that uses words and symbols to make it relatively easy to read and write a program. *See also* **assembly language** and **machine language.**

high-resolution mode A graphics display that uses a screen containing more pixels than a screen in medium-resolution mode.

identifiers *See* **programmer-supplied identifiers.**

IF ... THEN statement A one-way selection statement. *See also* **CASE** and **IF ... THEN ... ELSE.**

IF ... THEN ... ELSE statement A two-way selection statement. *See also* **CASE** and **IF ... THEN.**

index *See* **loop index.**

index of an array component The relative position of the component in the array. Also called the subscript of an array component.

index sort A sort that uses a separate array to sort the indices of an array.

index type The data type used for specifying the range for the index of an array. The index type can be any ordinal data type that specifies an initial and final value.

infinite loop A loop in which the controlling condition is not changed in such a manner as to allow the loop to terminate.

input Data obtained by a program during its execution. *See also* **batch input** and **interactive input.**

input assertion A loop precondition.

input device A device that provides information to the computer. Typical devices are keyboards, disk drives, card readers, and tape drivers. *See also* **I/O device** and **output device.**

input statement An executable statement used to obtain input for a program.

insertion sort Sorts an array of elements in either ascending or descending order. Starts with an empty array and inserts elements one at a time in their proper order. *See also* **bubble sort, index sort, quick sort,** and **selection sort.**

integer arithmetic operations Operations allowed on data of type **integer.** This includes the operations of addition, subtraction, multiplication, **MOD,** and **DIV** to produce integer answers.

integer overflow Occurs when an attempt is made within a program to use an integer outside the range (**–maxint** –1, **maxint**).

interactive input A method of getting data into the program from the keyboard. User interaction is required during execution.

interface A formal statement of how communication occurs between a subprogram and the main program, and between the subprogram and other subprograms.

internal file A file used for processing only and not saved in secondary storage. Also called a temporary file. *See also* **external file.**

intersection The intersection of set A and set B is A * B, where A * B contains the elements that are in both A and B. *See also* **difference, subset,** and **union.**

invoke A reference to a subprogram by an executable statement. Also referred to as call.

I/O device Any device that allows information to be transmitted to or from a computer. *See also* **input device** and **output device.**

iterated loop *See* **fixed repetition loop.**

keywords Either reserved words or predefined identifiers.

last-in, first-out (LIFO) A dynamic data structure. *See* **stack.**

leaf In a tree, a node that has no children.

length of an array The number of components of an array.

linear search *See* **sequential search.**

linked list A list of data items where each item is linked to the next one by means of a pointer.

local identifier An identifier that is restricted to use within a subblock of a program. Also referred to as a local variable.

local variable *See* **local identifier.**

logic error An error in the design of the program. *See also* **design error.**

logical operator Either logical connective (**AND, OR**) or negation (**NOT**).

loop index Variable used for control values in a **FOR** loop.

loop invariant An assertion that expresses a relationship between variables that remains constant throughout all iterations of a loop.

loop variant An assertion that changes in terms of its truth between the first and final executions of a loop.

loop verification The process of documenting a loop to guarantee that the loop performs its intended task.

loops Program statements that cause a process to be repeated. *See also* **FOR loop, REPEAT . . . UNTIL loop,** and **WHILE . . . DO loop.**

low-level language What programmers call an assembly language.

machine language This language is used directly by the computer in all its calculations and processing.

main block The executable portion of a program. It often calls other parts of a program.

main (primary) memory Memory contained in the computer. *See also* **memory** and **secondary memory.**

main unit Consists of a central processing unit and main memory.

mainframe A large computer typically used by major companies and universities. *See also* **microcomputer, minicomputer, supercomputer,** and **workstation.**

master file An existing external file.

maxint The largest integer constant available to a particular system.

medium-resolution mode A graphics display that uses a screen containing 320 × 200 pixels.

memory The ordered sequence of storage cells that can be accessed by address. Instructions and variables of an executing program are temporarily held here. *See also* **main memory** and **secondary memory.**

memory location A storage cell that can be accessed by address. *See also* **memory.**

merge The process of combining lists. Typically refers to files or arrays.

microcomputer A personal computer with relatively limited memory. Generally used by one person at a time. *See also* **mainframe, minicomputer, supercomputer,** and **workstation.**

minicomputer A small version of a mainframe computer. It can be used by several people at once. *See also* **mainframe, microcomputer, supercomputer,** and **workstation.**

mixed-mode expressions Expressions containing data of both **integer** and **real** types; the value will be given as a real and not as an integer.

modem A device used to connect a computer to a telephone line.

modular development The process of developing an algorithm using modules. *See also* **module.**

modularity The property possessed by a program that is written using modules.

module An independent unit that is part of a larger development. Usually a procedure or function. *See also* **modular development.**

module specifications A description of data received, information returned, and logic used in the module.

negation The use of the logical operator **NOT** to negate the Boolean value of an expression.

nested IF statement A selection statement used within another selection statement.

nested loop A loop as one of the statements in the body of another loop.

nested record A record that is a field in another record.

nested selection Any combination of selection statements within selection statements. *See also* **selection statement.**

nested subprograms Functions or procedures within functions or procedures.

network A system that allows users of different computers to communicate and share resources.

node One data item in a linked list.

nonlocal identifiers Identifiers that are used in a block in which they are not defined.

null set *See* **empty set.**

null statement *See* **empty statement.**

object code *See* **object program.**

object program The machine code version of the source program. Also referred to as object code.

opened for reading Positions a pointer at the beginning of a file for the purpose of reading from the file.

opened for writing Positions a pointer at the beginning of a file for the purpose of writing to the file.

opening a file Positions a pointer at the beginning of a file. *See also* **opened for reading** and **opened for writing.**

operating system A large program that allows the user to communicate with the hardware.

ordinal data type A data type ordered in some association with the integers; each integer is the ordinal of its associated character.

output Information that is produced by a program.

output assertion A loop postcondition.

output device A device that allows you to see the results of a program. Typically it is a monitor or printer. *See* **input device** and **I/O device.**

overflow In arithmetic operations, a value may be too large for the computer's memory location. A meaningless value may be assigned or an error message may result. *See also* **underflow.**

packed array An array that has had data placed in consecutive bytes.

parallel arrays Arrays of the same length but with different component data types.

parameter *See* **actual parameter, argument, formal parameter, value parameter,** and **variable parameter.**

parameter list A list of parameters. An actual parameter list is contained in the procedure or function call. A formal parameter list is contained in the procedure or function heading.

parent In a tree, the node that is pointing to its children.

passed by reference When variable parameters are used in subprograms.

personal computer (PC) A self-contained computer with relatively limited memory; often called a microcomputer, it is generally used by one person at a time.

picture element A group of dots controlled by an electron beam.

pixel Short for picture element. The smallest picture element on a display screen.

pointer variable Frequently designated as Ptr, a pointer variable is a variable that contains the address of a memory location. *See also* **address** and **dynamic variable.**

pop A procedure to delete a node from a linked list.

postcondition An assertion written after a segment of code.

posttest loop A loop where the control condition is tested after the loop is executed. **REPEAT . . . UNTIL** is a post-test loop. Also referred to as an exit-controlled loop.

precedence rule The order of priority in which numeric operations are performed.

precondition An assertion written before a particular statement.

pretest condition A condition that controls whether the body of the loop is executed before going through the loop.

pretest loop A loop where the control condition is tested before the loop is executed. **WHILE . . . DO** is a pretest loop. Also referred to as an entrance-controlled loop.

primary memory *See* **main memory** and **memory.**

priming read A **read** statement performed before a loop is referenced.

procedural abstraction The process of considering only what a procedure is to do rather than details of the procedure.

procedure A subprogram designed to perform a specific task as part of a larger program. Procedures are not limited to returning a single value to the main program.

processing statement A statement that causes the computer to take action when a program is run.

program A set of instructions that tells the machine (the hardware) what to do.

program heading The first statement of any Pascal program; it must contain the reserved word **PROGRAM.**

program proof An analysis of a program that attempts to verify the correctness of program results.

program protection A method of using selection statements to guard against unexpected results.

program walk-through The process of carefully following (with pencil and paper) the steps the computer uses to solve the problem given in a program. Also referred to as trace.

programmer-supplied identifiers Identifiers provided by the person writing a program. *See also* **scope of identifier** and **standard identifier.**

programming language Formal language that computer scientists use to give instructions to the computer.

prompt A marker on the terminal screen that requests input data.

protection *See* **program protection.**

pseudocode A stylized half-English, half-code language written in English but suggesting Pascal code.

push A procedure for adding a node to the beginning of a linked list.

queue A dynamic data structure where elements are entered from one end and removed from the other end. Referred to as a FIFO (first-in, first-out) structure.

quick sort A relatively fast sorting technique that uses recursion. *See also* **bubble sort, index sort, insertion sort,** and **selection sort.**

reading from a file The process of retrieving data from a file.

real arithmetic operations Operations allowed on data of type **real.** This includes addition, subtraction, multiplication, and division.

real overflow Occurs when an attempt is made to store very large real numbers.

record A data structure that is a collection of fields that can be treated as a whole or that will allow you to work with individual fields.

recursion The process of a subprogram calling itself. A clearly defined stopping state must exist. Any recursive subprogram can be rewritten using iteration.

recursive step A well-defined step that leads to the stopping state in the recursive process.

recursive subprogram A subprogram that calls itself.

relational operator An operator used for comparison of data items of the same type.

REPEAT . . . UNTIL loop A post-test loop examining a Boolean expression after causing a fragment to be executed. *See also* **FOR loop, loops,** and **WHILE . . . DO loop.**

repetition *See* **loops.**

representational error An error caused by rounding and subsequent grouping of operands in arithmetic operations.

reserved words Words that have predefined meanings that cannot be changed. They are highlighted in text by capital boldface print; a list of Pascal reserved words is set forth in Appendix 1.

return type The data type for a function name.

robust The state in which a program is completely protected against all possible crashes from bad data and unexpected values.

root The first or top node in a tree.

round-off error An error that occurs when a decimal is either truncated or rounded off.

run-time error An error detected when, after compilation is completed, an error message results instead of the correct output. *See also* **compilation error, design error,** and **syntax error.**

scope of identifier The largest block in which the identifier is available.

scratch file *See* **temporary file.**

secondary (auxiliary) memory devices Peripheral devices for holding memory, usually disks or magnetic tape. *See also* **main memory** and **memory.**

selection sort A sorting algorithm that sorts the components of an array in either ascending or descending order. This process puts the smallest or largest element in the top position and repeats the process on the remaining array components. *See also* **bubble sort, index sort, insertion sort,** and **quick sort.**

selection statement The process of executing possible alternate segments of code. Pascal selection statements are **IF . . . THEN, IF . . . THEN . . . ELSE,** and **CASE.**

self-documenting code Code written with descriptive identifiers so that the purpose of the code is evident to those other than the original programmer.

sentinel value A special value that indicates the end of a set of data or of a process.

sequential algorithm *See* **straight-line algorithm.**

sequential (linear) search The process of examining the first element in a list and proceeding to examine the elements in order until a match is found.

set A structured data type that consists of a collection of distinct elements from an indicated base type (which must be ordinal).

side effect An unintentional change in a variable that is the result of some action taken in a program.

simple Boolean expression An expression where two numbers or variable values are compared using a single relational operator. *See also* **Boolean expression** and **compound Boolean expression.**

simple statement A single-action, executable statement.

software Programs that make the machine (the hardware) do something, such as word processing, database management, or games.

software engineering The process of developing and maintaining very large software systems.

software system life cycle The process of development, maintenance, and demise of a software system.

sort A method of arranging elements in an array. *See also* **bubble sort, index sort, insertion sort, quick sort,** and **selection sort.**

sort-merge The process of repeatedly subdividing a long list, sorting shorter lists, and then merging to obtain a single sorted list.

source program A program written by a programmer. *See also* **system program.**

stack A dynamic data structure where access can be made from only one end. Referred to as a LIFO (last-in, first-out) structure.

standard function A built-in function available in most versions of Pascal.

standard identifier Predefined word whose meaning can be changed if needed. Standard identifiers are highlighted in text by lowercase boldface print; a list of Pascal standard identifiers is set forth in Appendix 2.

standard simple type Any one of the predefined data types **integer, real, char,** or **boolean.**

statement The basic unit of expression in Pascal.

static variable A variable whose size (for example, array length) is fixed at compilation time. A certain memory area is reserved for each variable, and these locations are retained for the declared variables as long as the program or subprogram in which the variable is defined is active. *See also* **dynamic variable.**

stepwise refinement The process of repeatedly subdividing tasks into subtasks until each subtask is easily accomplished. *See also* **structured programming** and **top-down design.**

stopping state The well-defined termination of a recursive process. Also referred to as degenerate case.

straight-line algorithm Also called sequential algorithm, this algorithm consists of a sequence of simple tasks.

stream input *See* **batch input.**

string An abbreviated name for a string constant.

string constant One or more characters used as a constant in a program.

string data type A data type that permits a sequence of characters.

stroked font All fonts except default. Characters do not appear in 8 × 8 pixels. *See also* **bit-mapped fonts.**

structure chart A graphical representation of the relationship between modules.

structured programming Programming that parallels a solution to a problem achieved by top-down design. *See also* **stepwise refinement** and **top-down design.**

stub programming A no-frills, simple version of a final program.

subblock A block structure for a subprogram. *See also* **block.**

subprogram A program within a program. Procedures and functions are subprograms.

subrange The defined subset of values of an existing ordinal data type.

subscript of an array component *See* **index of an array component.**

subset Set A is a subset of set B if all the elements in A are also in B. *See also* **difference, intersection,** and **union.**

supercomputer A mainframe computer that is capable of amazing speed, often 50,000 times as fast as most microcomputers. *See also* **mainframe, microcomputer, minicomputer,** and **workstation.**

syntax The formal rules governing construction of valid statements.

syntax diagramming A method to describe formally the legal syntax of language structures; syntax diagrams are shown in Appendix 3.

syntax diagrams Diagrams that show the permissible alternatives for each part of each kind of sentence and where the parts may appear.

syntax error An error in spelling, punctuation, or placement of certain key symbols in a program. *See also* **compilation error, design error,** and **run-time error.**

system program A special program used by the computer to activate the compiler, run the machine code version, and cause output to be generated. *See also* **source program.**

system software Programs that allow users to write and execute other programs, including operating systems such as DOS.

tag field A field used in defining variant records. Values of the tag field determine the variant record structure.

temporary file An internal file that is used for processing only and is not saved in secondary storage. Also referred to as a scratch file. *See also* **internal file.**

test program A short program written to provide an answer to a specific question.

text file A file of characters that is divided into lines.

top-down design A design methodology for solving a problem whereby you first state the problem and then proceed to subdivide the main task into major subtasks. Each subtask is then subdivided into smaller subtasks. This process is repeated until each remaining subtask is easily solved. *See also* **stepwise refinement** and **structured programming.**

trace *See* **program walk-through.**

transaction file A file containing changes to be made in a master file.

tree A dynamic data structure consisting of a special node (a root) that points to zero or more other nodes, each of which points to zero or more other nodes, and so on.

two-dimensional array An array in which each element is accessed by a reference to a pair of indices.

two-way merge The process of merging two sorted lists.

type *See* **data type.**

type compatible When variables have the same base type. A value parameter and its argument must be type compatible. *See also* **type identical.**

type identical When variables are declared with the same type identifier. A variable parameter and its argument must be type identical. *See also* **type compatible.**

underflow If a value is too small to be represented by a computer, the value is automatically replaced by zero. *See also* **overflow.**

union The union of set A and set B is A + B, where A + B contains any element that is in A or that is in B. *See also* **difference, intersection,** and **subset.**

universal set Any set that contains all possible values of the base type.

unpacked array An array in which data are not in consecutive bytes.

user-defined data type A data type that is defined in the **TYPE** definition section by the programmer. Also referred to as enumerated data type.

user-defined function A subprogram (function) written by the programmer to perform a specific task. Functions return one value when called.

user-friendly A term used to describe an interactive program with clear, easy-to-follow messages for the user.

value Often called value of a memory location. Refers to the value of the contents of a memory location. *See also* **address** and **memory location.**

value parameter A formal parameter that is local to a subprogram. Values of these parameters are not returned to the calling program.

variable A memory location, referenced by an identifier, whose value can be changed during a program. *See also* **global identifier** and **local identifier.**

variable condition loop A loop in which conditions change within the body of the loop.

variable declaration section The section of the declaration section where program variables are declared for subsequent use.

variable dictionary A listing of the meaning of variables used in a program.

variable parameter A formal parameter that is not local to a subprogram. Values of these parameters are returned to the calling program.

variant part The part of a record structure in which the number and type of fields can vary. *See also* **fixed part.**

WHILE . . . DO loop A pretest loop examining a Boolean expression before causing a fragment to be executed. *See also* **FOR loop, loops,** and **REPEAT . . . UNTIL loop.**

word A unit of memory consisting of one or more bytes. Words can be addressed.

workstation Sits on a desktop but has a larger storage capacity and faster processing speeds than microcomputers.

writing to a file The process of entering data to a file.

Appendixes

Appendix 1

Reserved Words

The following words have predefined meanings in standard Pascal and cannot be changed. Each of these, except **GOTO** and **LABEL,** has been developed in the text. **GOTO** and **LABEL** are discussed in Appendix 7.

AND	**END**	**MOD**	**REPEAT**
ARRAY	**FILE**	**NIL**	**SET**
BEGIN	**FOR**	**NOT**	**THEN**
CASE	**FORWARD**	**OF**	**TO**
CONST	**FUNCTION**	**OR**	**TYPE**
DIV	**GOTO**	**PACKED**	**UNTIL**
DO	**IF**	**PROCEDURE**	**VAR**
DOWNTO	**IN**	**PROGRAM**	**WHILE**
ELSE	**LABEL**	**RECORD**	**WITH**

Appendix 2

Standard Identifiers

The standard identifiers for constants, types, files, functions, and procedures are given in this appendix. All have predefined meanings that could (but probably should not) be changed in a program. Summary descriptions are given for the functions and procedures.

Constants	*Types*	*Files*
false	**boolean**	**input**
maxint	**char**	**output**
true	**integer**	
	real	
	text	

Functions

Function	Parameter Type	Result Type	Value Returned
abs(*x*)	**integer**	**integer**	Absolute value of *x*
	real	**real**	
arctan(*x*)	**integer**	**real**	Arctangent of *x* (radians)
	real		
chr(*a*)	**integer**	**char**	Character with ordinal *a*
cos(*x*)	**integer**	**real**	Cosine of *x* (radians)
	real		
eof(F)	**file**	**boolean**	End-of-file test for F
eoln(F)	**file**	**boolean**	End-of-line test for F
exp(*x*)	**integer**	**real**	e^x
ln(*x*)	**integer (positive)**	**real**	Natural logarithm of *x*
	real (positive)		
odd(*a*)	**integer**	**boolean**	Tests for an odd integer *a*
ord(*x*)	nonreal scalar	**integer**	Ordinal number of *x*
pred(*x*)	nonreal scalar	same as *x*	Predecessor of *x*
round(*x*)	**real**	**integer**	Rounds off *x*
sin(*x*)	**integer**	**real**	Sine of *x*
	real		
sqr(*x*)	**integer**	**integer**	Square of *x*
	real	**real**	
sqrt(*x*)	***integer***	***real***	Square root of *x*
	real		
succ(*x*)	nonreal scalar	same as *x*	Successor of **x**
trunc(*x*)	real	integer	Truncated value of *x*

Procedures

Procedure Call	Purpose of Procedure
dispose (Ptr)	Returns variable referenced by Ptr to available space list.
get (F)	Advances the file pointer for the file F and assigns the new value to F^.
new (Ptr)	Creates a variable of the type referenced by Ptr and stores a pointer to the new variable in Ptr.
pack (U, J, P)	Copies unpacked array elements from U into the packed array P; copying starts with P[1] := U[J].
page (F)	Starts printing the next line of text F at the top of a new page.
put (F)	Appends the current value of F to the file F.
read (F, <variable list>)	Reads values from file F into indicated variables; if F is not specified, **input** is assumed.
readln (F, <variable list>)	Executes the same as **read** and then advances the file pointer to the first position following the next end-of-line marker.
reset (F)	Resets the pointer in file F to the beginning for the purpose of reading from F.
rewrite (F)	Resets the pointer in file F to the beginning for the purpose of writing to F.
unpack (P, U, J)	Copies packed array elements from P into the unpacked array U; copying starts with U[J] := P[1].
write (F, <parameter list>)	Writes values specified by parameter list to the text file F; if F is not specified, **output** is assumed.
writeln (F, <parameter list>)	Executes the same as **write** and then places an end-of-line marker in F.

Appendix 3

Syntax Diagrams

Syntax diagrams in this appendix are listed in the following order:

Program
- Identifier
- File List

Declarations and Definitions
- Label Declaration
- Constant Definition
- Type Definition
  - Type
    - Enumerated Type
    - Subrange Type
    - Pointer Type
    - Array Type
    - Record Type
      - Field List
        - Fixed Part
        - Variant Part
          - Variant Description
    - File Type
    - Set Type
- Variable Declaration
- Procedure and Function Declarations
  - Formal Parameter List

Body
- Compound Statement
  - Statement
    - Assignment Statement
      - Expression
        - Term
          - Factor
            - Variable
            - Set Value
      - Boolean Expression
- **read** or **readln** Statement
- **write** or **writeln** Statement

Procedure Statement
IF Statement
CASE Statement
- Case Label

WHILE Statement
REPEAT Statement
FOR Statement
WITH Statement
GOTO Statement
Empty Statement

Program

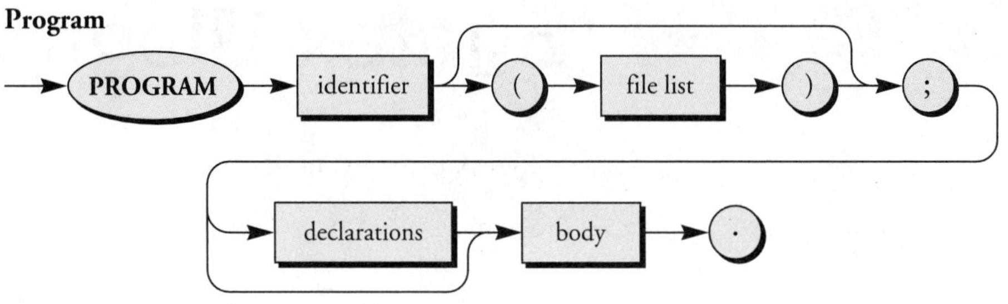

Identifier

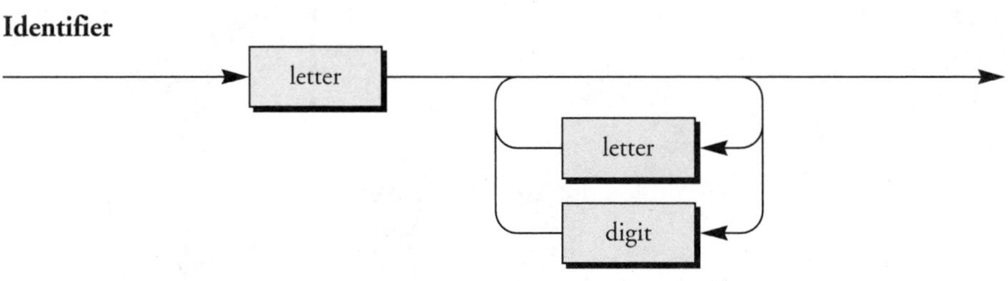

File List

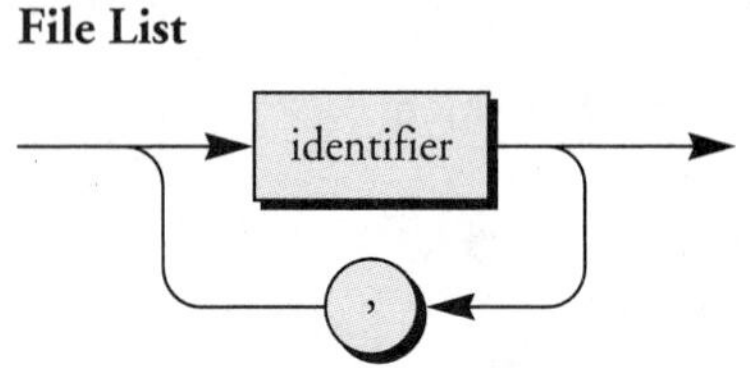

Declarations and Definitions

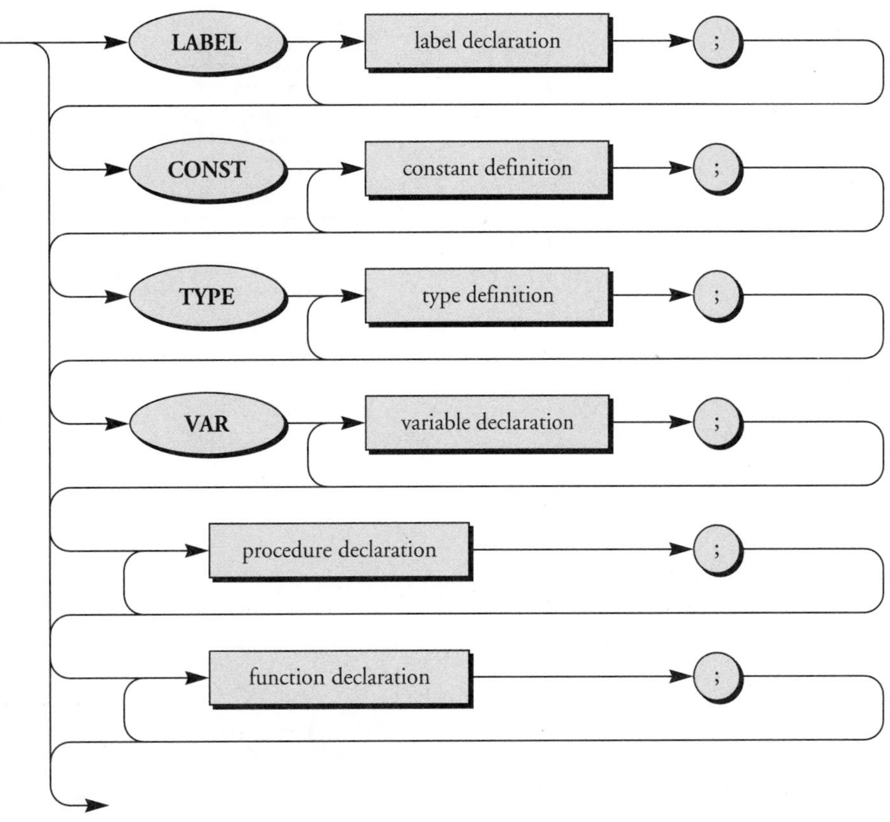

Label Declaration

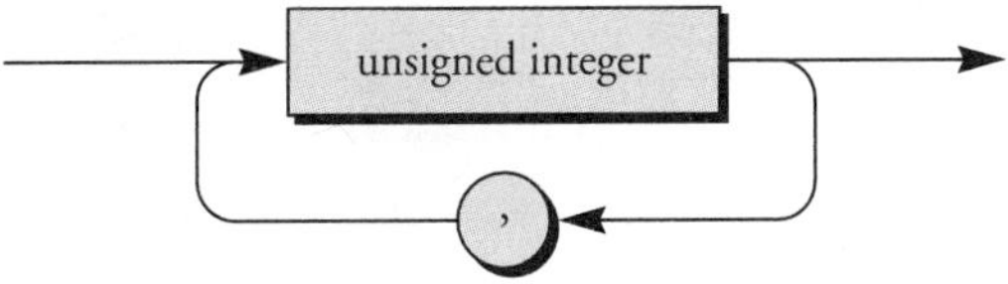

Constant Definition

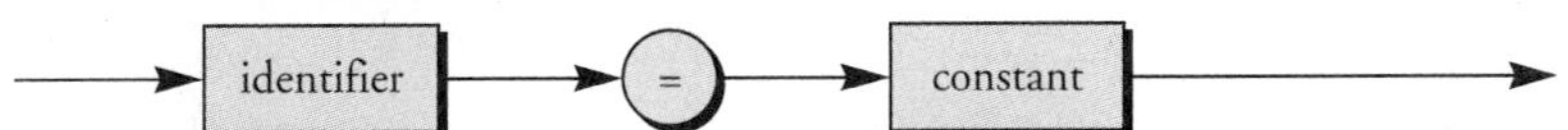

Type Definition

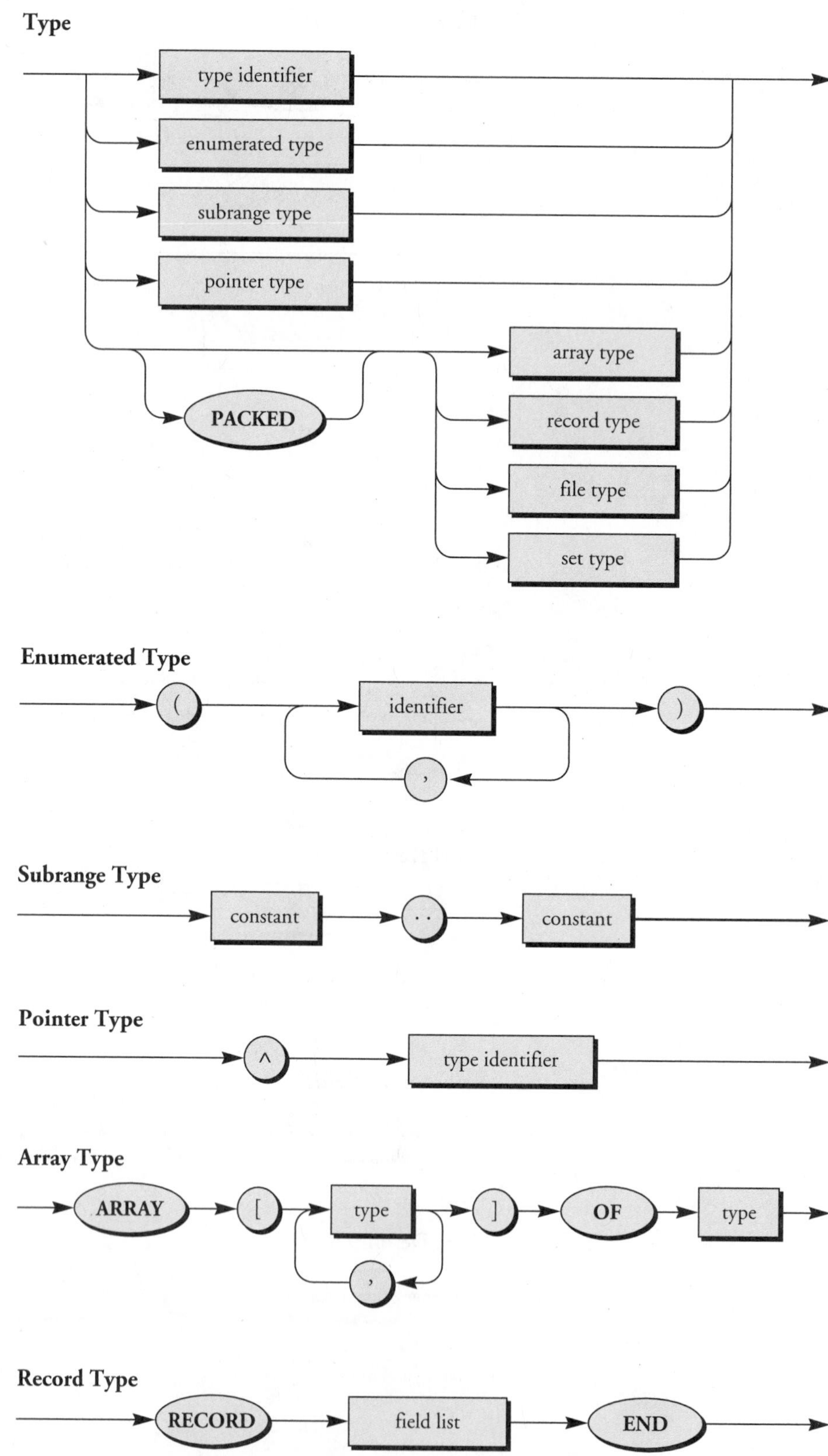
Type
type identifier
enumerated type
subrange type
pointer type
array type
PACKED
record type
file type
set type
Enumerated Type
(
identifier
)
,
Subrange Type
constant
..
constant
Pointer Type
^
type identifier
Array Type
ARRAY
[
type
]
OF
type
,
Record Type
RECORD
field list
END

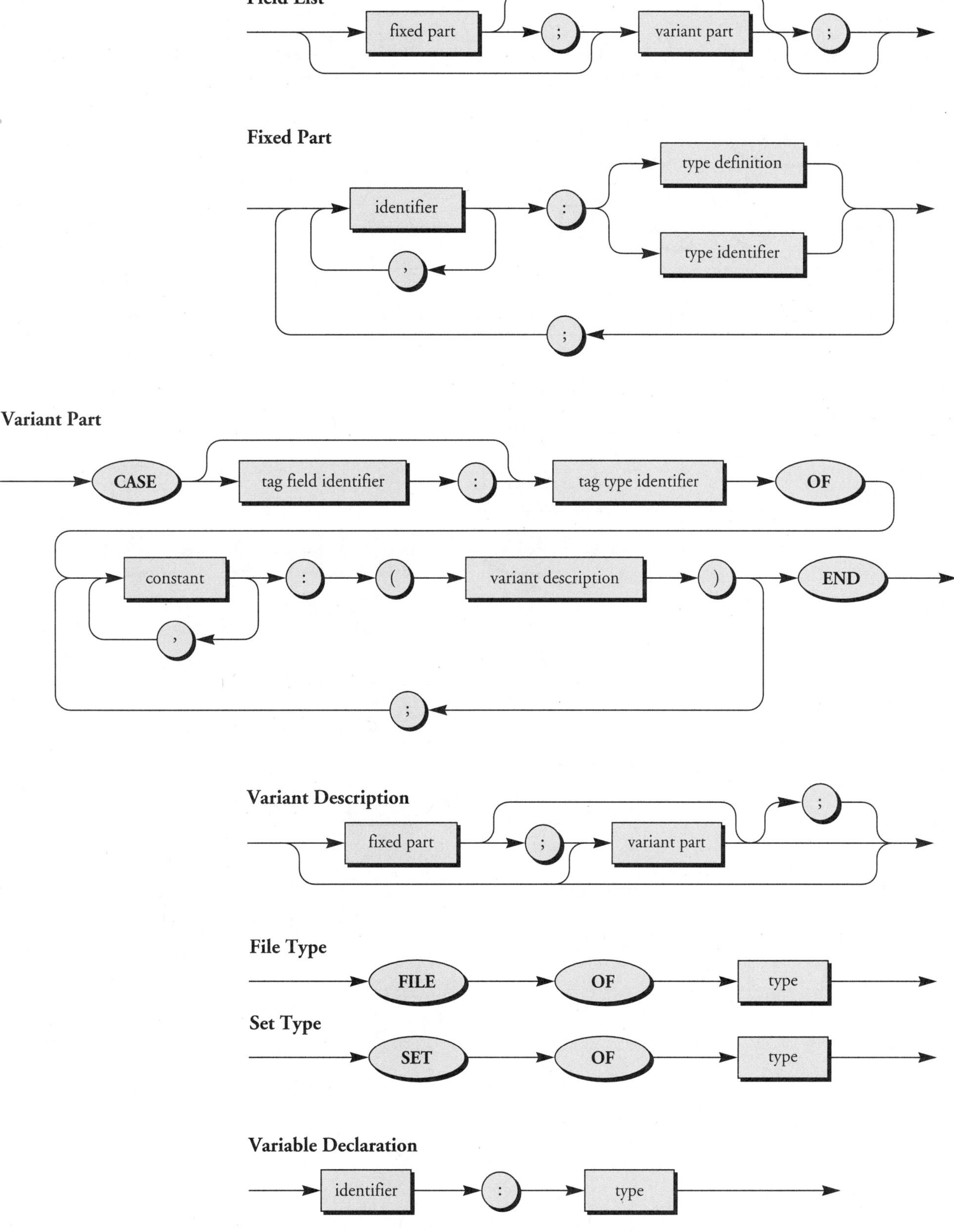
Field List
fixed part
;
variant part
;
Fixed Part
identifier
,
:
type definition
type identifier
;
Variant Part
CASE
tag field identifier
:
tag type identifier
OF
constant
,
:
(
variant description
)
END
;
Variant Description
fixed part
;
variant part
;
File Type
FILE
OF
type
Set Type
SET
OF
type
Variable Declaration
identifier
:
type

Procedure and Function Declarations

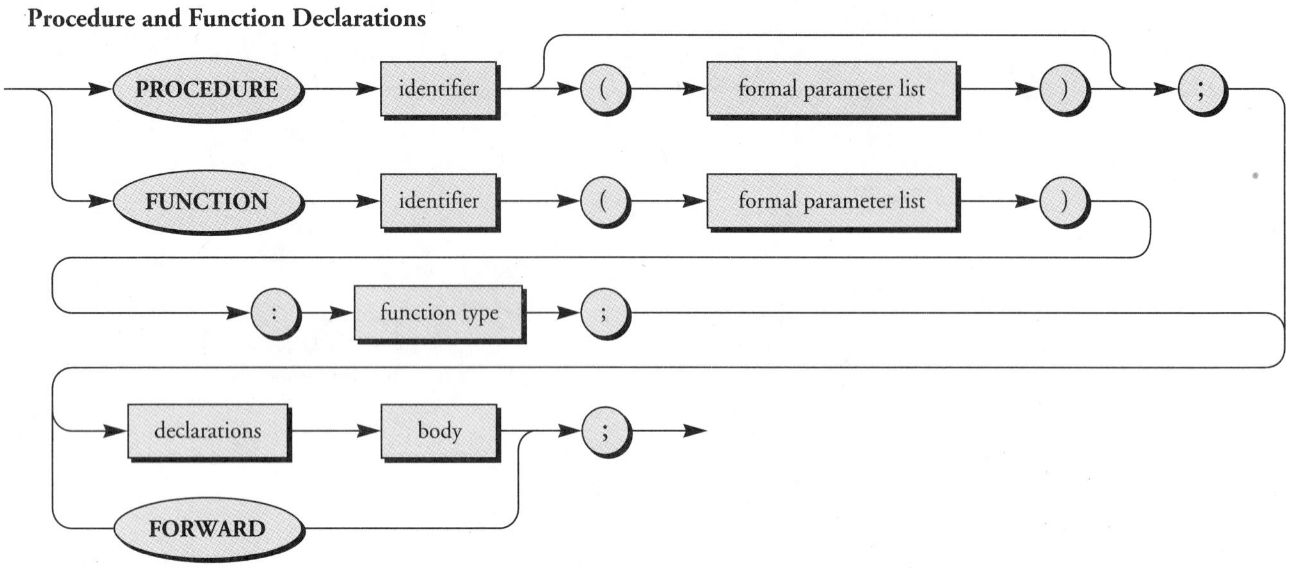

Formal Parameter List

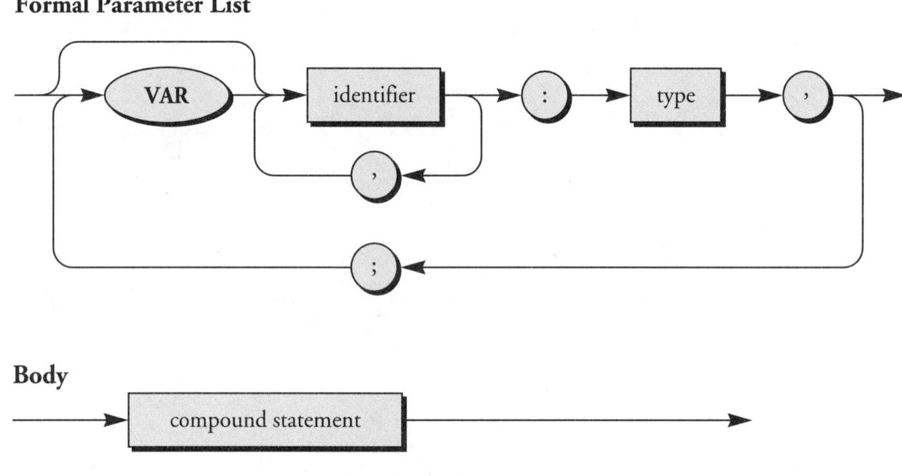

Body

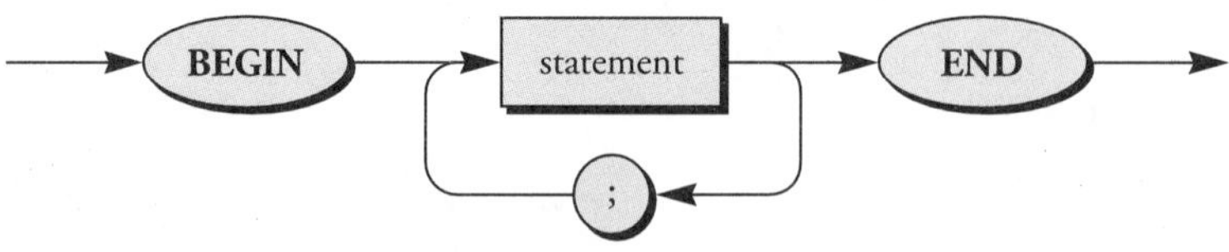

Compound Statement

BEGIN → statement → END (statements separated by ;)

Statement

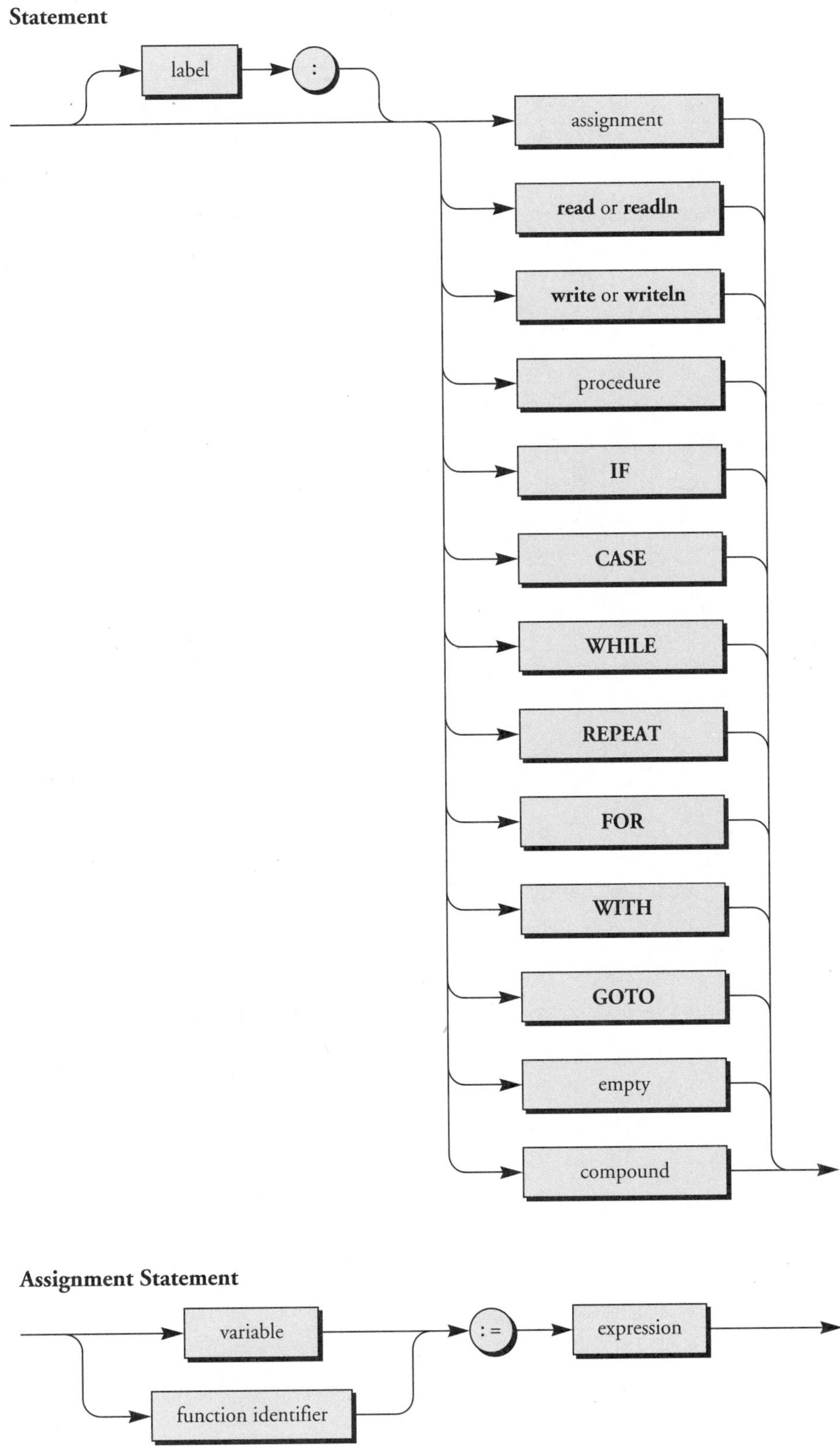
label
:
assignment
read or readln
write or writeln
procedure
IF
CASE
WHILE
REPEAT
FOR
WITH
GOTO
empty
compound
Assignment Statement
variable
function identifier
:=
expression

Expression

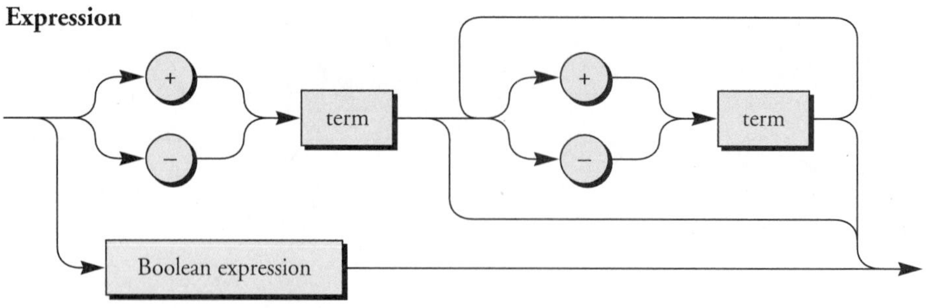

Term

factor
*
/
DIV
MOD
AND
factor

Factor

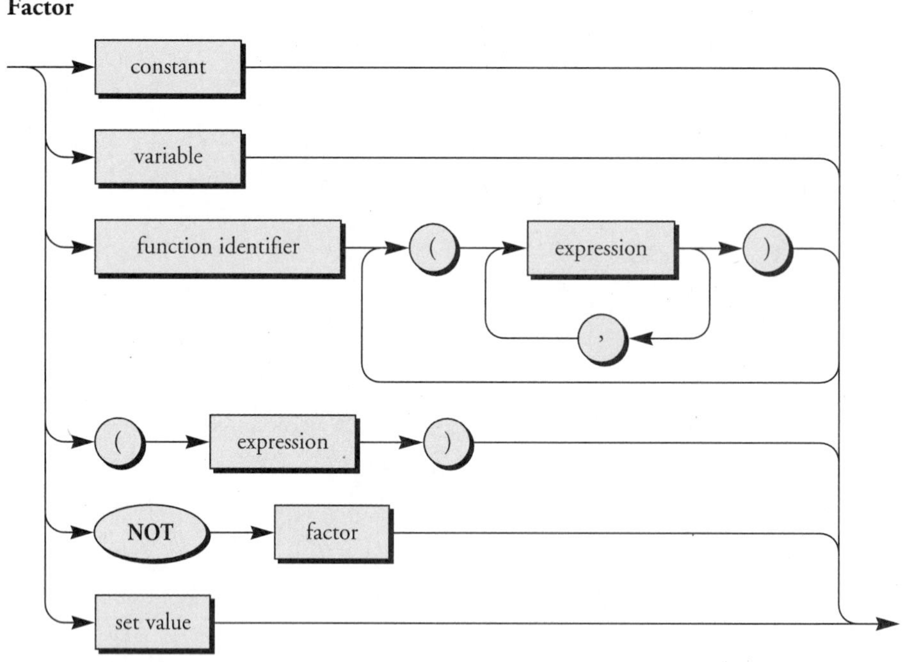

Variable

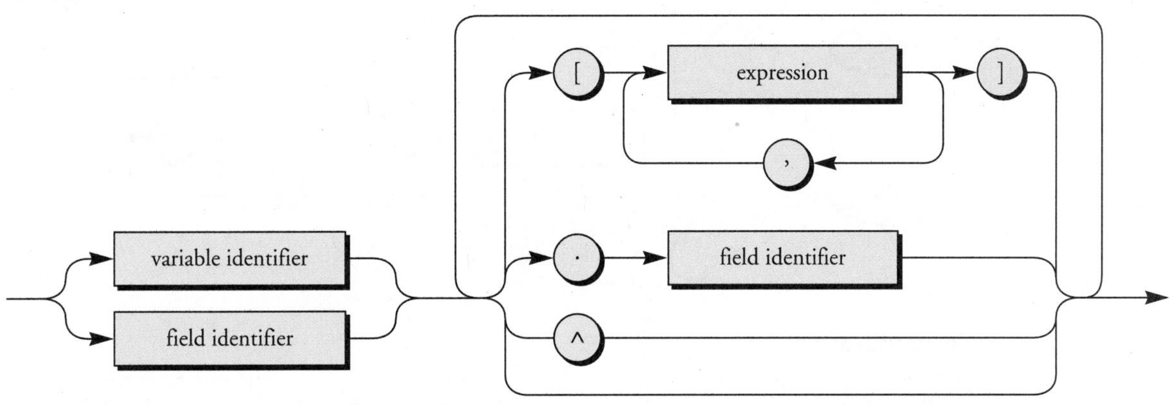

Set Value

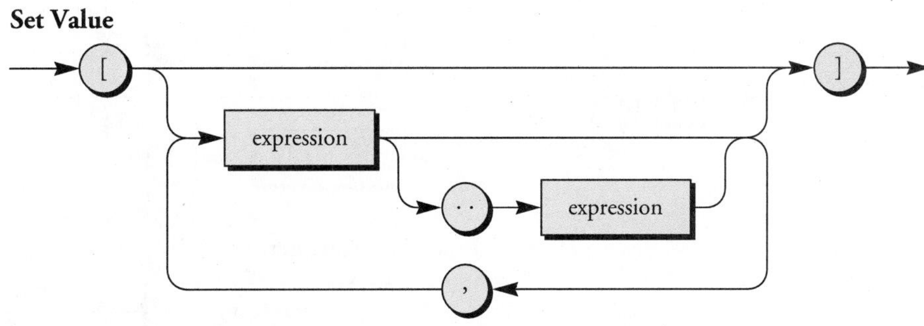

Boolean Expression

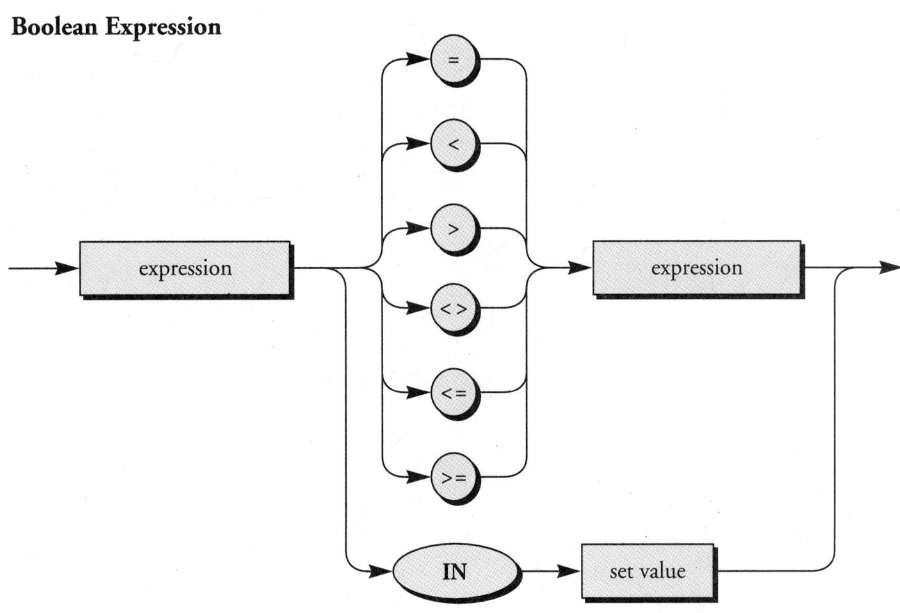

read or readln Statement

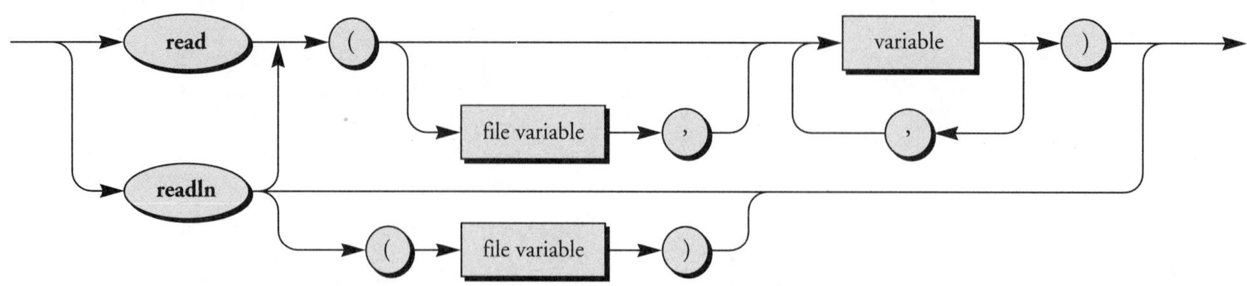

write or writeln Statement

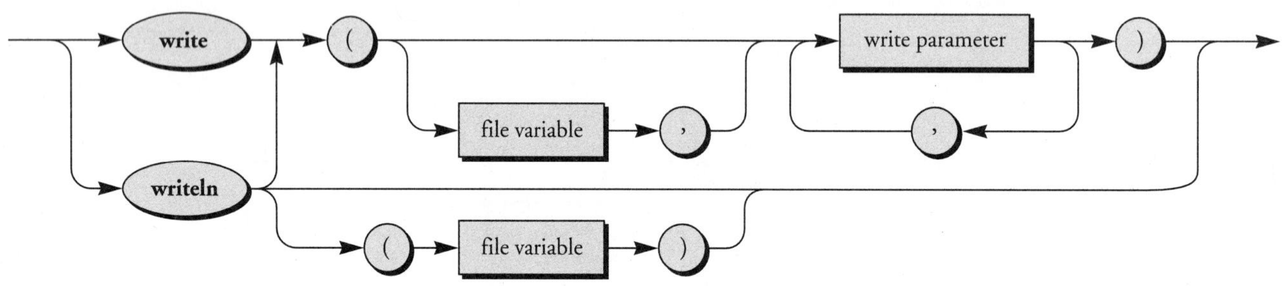

Procedure Statement

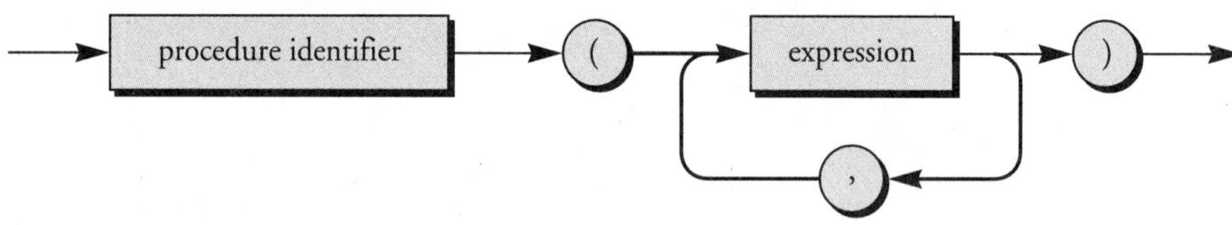

IF Statement

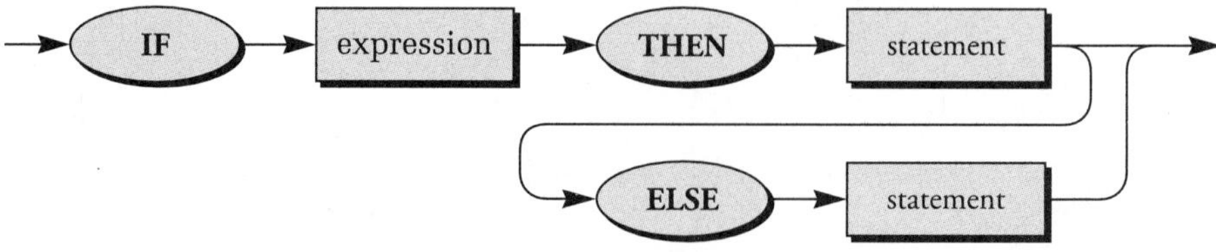

CASE Statement

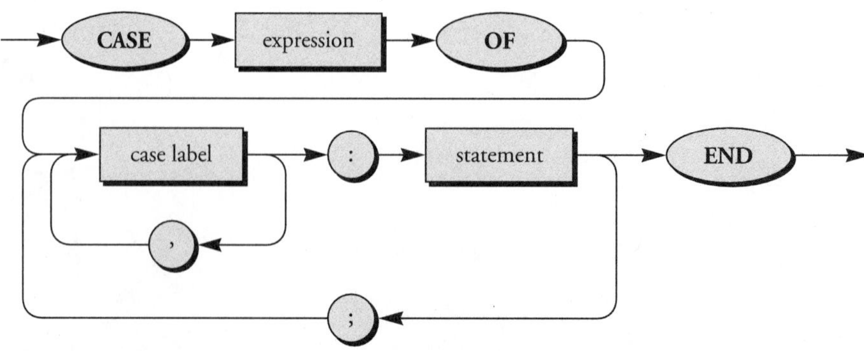

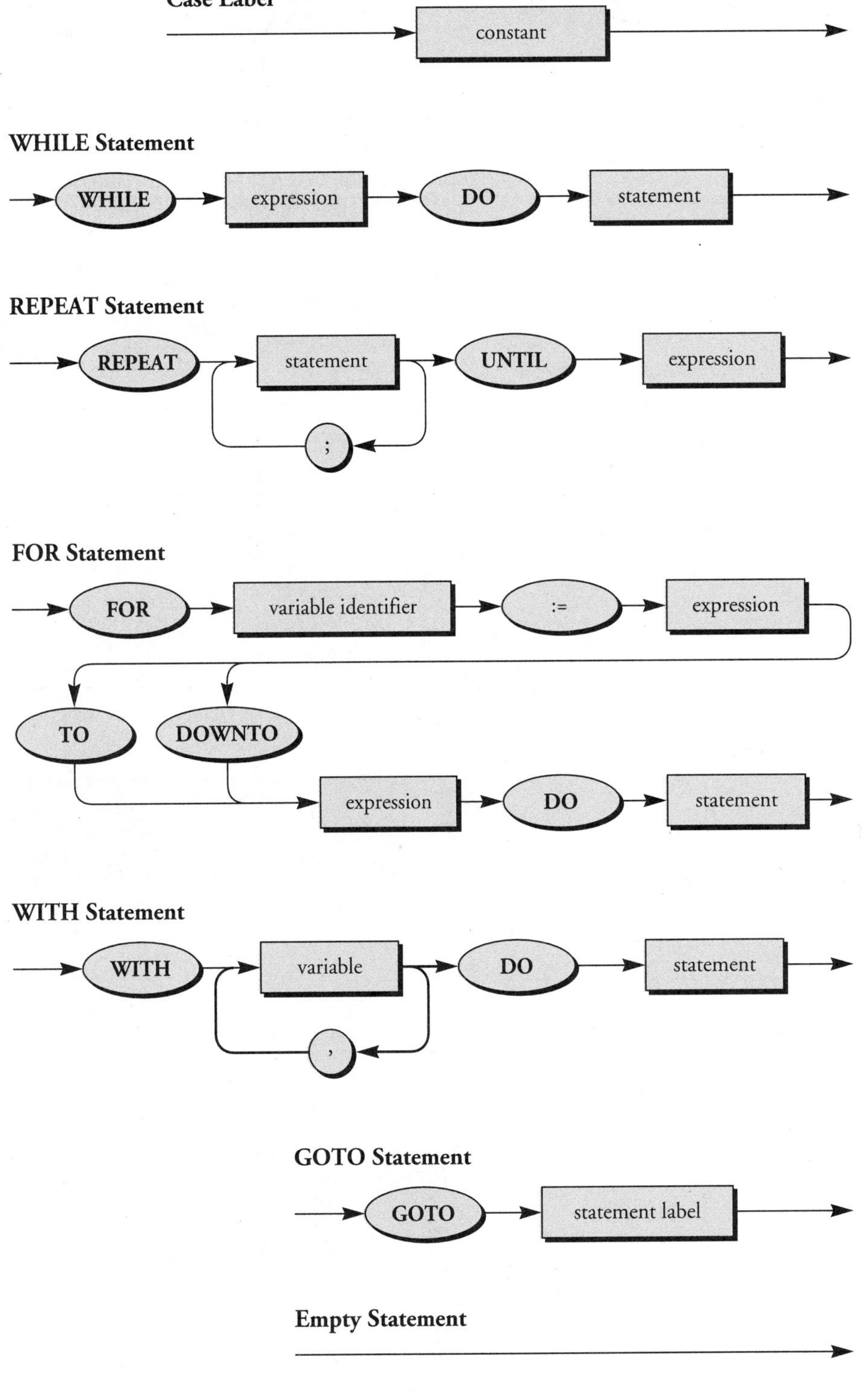
Case Label
constant
WHILE Statement
WHILE
expression
DO
statement
REPEAT Statement
REPEAT
statement
;
UNTIL
expression
FOR Statement
FOR
variable identifier
:=
expression
TO
DOWNTO
expression
DO
statement
WITH Statement
WITH
variable
,
DO
statement
GOTO Statement
GOTO
statement label
Empty Statement

Appendix 4 Character Sets

The two tables included here show the ordering of two common character sets. Note that only printable characters are shown for each set. Ordinals without character representations either do not have standard representation, or they are associated with unprintable control characters. In each list, the blank is denoted by "b̸".

The American Standard Code for Information Interchange (ASCII)

<table>
<tr><th rowspan="2">Left Digit(s)</th><th colspan="10">Right Digit</th></tr>
<tr><th>0</th><th>1</th><th>2</th><th>3</th><th>4</th><th>5</th><th>6</th><th>7</th><th>8</th><th>9</th></tr>
<tr><td>3</td><td></td><td></td><td>b̸</td><td>!</td><td>"</td><td>#</td><td>$</td><td>%</td><td>&</td><td>'</td></tr>
<tr><td>4</td><td>(</td><td>)</td><td>*</td><td>+</td><td>,</td><td>-</td><td>.</td><td>/</td><td>0</td><td>1</td></tr>
<tr><td>5</td><td>2</td><td>3</td><td>4</td><td>5</td><td>6</td><td>7</td><td>8</td><td>9</td><td>:</td><td>;</td></tr>
<tr><td>6</td><td><</td><td>=</td><td>></td><td>?</td><td>@</td><td>A</td><td>B</td><td>C</td><td>D</td><td>E</td></tr>
<tr><td>7</td><td>F</td><td>G</td><td>H</td><td>I</td><td>J</td><td>K</td><td>L</td><td>M</td><td>N</td><td>O</td></tr>
<tr><td>8</td><td>P</td><td>Q</td><td>R</td><td>S</td><td>T</td><td>U</td><td>V</td><td>W</td><td>X</td><td>Y</td></tr>
<tr><td>9</td><td>Z</td><td>[</td><td>\</td><td>]</td><td>↑</td><td>_</td><td>`</td><td>a</td><td>b</td><td>c</td></tr>
<tr><td>10</td><td>d</td><td>e</td><td>f</td><td>g</td><td>h</td><td>i</td><td>j</td><td>k</td><td>l</td><td>m</td></tr>
<tr><td>11</td><td>n</td><td>o</td><td>p</td><td>q</td><td>r</td><td>s</td><td>t</td><td>u</td><td>v</td><td>w</td></tr>
<tr><td>12</td><td>x</td><td>y</td><td>z</td><td>{</td><td>|</td><td>}</td><td>~</td><td></td><td></td><td></td></tr>
</table>

Codes less than 32 or greater than 126 are nonprintable.

The Extended Binary Coded Decimal Interchange Code (EBCDIC)

<table>
<tr><th rowspan="2">Left Digit(s)</th><th colspan="10">Right Digit</th></tr>
<tr><th>0</th><th>1</th><th>2</th><th>3</th><th>4</th><th>5</th><th>6</th><th>7</th><th>8</th><th>9</th></tr>
<tr><td>6</td><td></td><td></td><td></td><td></td><td>b̸</td><td></td><td></td><td></td><td></td><td></td></tr>
<tr><td>7</td><td></td><td></td><td></td><td></td><td>¢</td><td>.</td><td><</td><td>(</td><td>+</td><td>|</td></tr>
<tr><td>8</td><td>&</td><td></td><td></td><td></td><td></td><td></td><td></td><td></td><td></td><td></td></tr>
<tr><td>9</td><td>!</td><td>$</td><td>*</td><td>)</td><td>;</td><td></td><td>-</td><td>/</td><td></td><td></td></tr>
<tr><td>10</td><td></td><td></td><td></td><td></td><td></td><td></td><td>^</td><td>,</td><td>%</td><td>_</td></tr>
<tr><td>11</td><td>></td><td>?</td><td></td><td></td><td></td><td></td><td></td><td></td><td></td><td></td></tr>
<tr><td>12</td><td></td><td></td><td>:</td><td>#</td><td>@</td><td>'</td><td>=</td><td>"</td><td></td><td>a</td></tr>
<tr><td>13</td><td>b</td><td>c</td><td>d</td><td>e</td><td>f</td><td>g</td><td>h</td><td>i</td><td></td><td></td></tr>
<tr><td>14</td><td></td><td></td><td></td><td></td><td></td><td>j</td><td>k</td><td>l</td><td>m</td><td>n</td></tr>
<tr><td>15</td><td>o</td><td>p</td><td>q</td><td>r</td><td></td><td></td><td></td><td></td><td></td><td></td></tr>
<tr><td>16</td><td></td><td></td><td>s</td><td>t</td><td>u</td><td>v</td><td>w</td><td>x</td><td>y</td><td>z</td></tr>
<tr><td>17</td><td></td><td></td><td></td><td></td><td></td><td></td><td></td><td>\</td><td>{</td><td>}</td></tr>
<tr><td>18</td><td>[</td><td>]</td><td></td><td></td><td></td><td></td><td></td><td></td><td></td><td></td></tr>
<tr><td>19</td><td></td><td></td><td></td><td>A</td><td>B</td><td>C</td><td>D</td><td>E</td><td>F</td><td>G</td></tr>
<tr><td>20</td><td>H</td><td>I</td><td></td><td></td><td></td><td></td><td></td><td></td><td></td><td>J</td></tr>
<tr><td>21</td><td>K</td><td>L</td><td>M</td><td>N</td><td>O</td><td>P</td><td>Q</td><td>R</td><td></td><td></td></tr>
<tr><td>22</td><td></td><td></td><td></td><td></td><td></td><td></td><td>S</td><td>T</td><td>U</td><td>V</td></tr>
<tr><td>23</td><td>W</td><td>X</td><td>Y</td><td>Z</td><td></td><td></td><td></td><td></td><td></td><td></td></tr>
<tr><td>24</td><td>0</td><td>1</td><td>2</td><td>3</td><td>4</td><td>5</td><td>6</td><td>7</td><td>8</td><td>9</td></tr>
</table>

Codes not listed in this table are nonprintable.

Appendix 5

Compiler Error Messages

This list contains typical error messages used by a compiler to identify compilation errors. Such errors are identified by number with appropriate messages produced at the bottom of a compilation listing. Different compilers produce different error messages.

```
  1  ERROR IN SIMPLE TYPE.
  2  IDENTIFIER EXPECTED.
  3  'PROGRAM' EXPECTED.
  4  ')' EXPECTED.
  5  ' ' EXPECTED.
  6  UNEXPECTED SYMBOL.
  7  ERROR IN PARAMETER LIST.
  8  'OF' EXPECTED.
  9  '(' EXPECTED.
 10  ERROR IN TYPE.
 11  '[' EXPECTED.
 12   ']' EXPECTED.
 13  'END'EXPECTED.
 14  ';' EXPECTED.
 15  INTEGER CONSTANT EXPECTED.
 16  '=' EXPECTED.
 17  'BEGIN' EXPECTED.
 18  ERROR IN DECLARATION PART.
 19  ERROR IN FIELD-LIST.
 20  ',' EXPECTED.
 21  '..' EXPECTED.

 40  VALUE PART ALLOWED ONLY IN MAIN PROGRAM.
 41  TOO FEW VALUES SPECIFIED.
 42  TOO MANY VALUES SPECIFIED.
 43  VARIABLE INITIALIZED TWICE.
 44  TYPE IS NEITHER ARRAY NOR RECORD.
 45  REPETITION FACTOR MUST BE GREATER THAN ZERO.
 50  ERROR IN CONSTANT.
 51  ':=' EXPECTED.
 52  'THEN' EXPECTED.
 53  'UNTIL' EXPECTED.
 54  'DO' EXPECTED.
 55  'TO' OR 'DOWNTO' EXPECTED.

 57  'FILE' EXPECTED.
 58  ERROR IN FACTOR.
 59  ERROR IN VARIABLE.
 60  FILE TYPE IDENTIFIER EXPECTED.

101  IDENTIFIER DECLARED TWICE.
102  LOWBOUND EXCEEDS HIGHBOUND.
103  IDENTIFIER IS NOT OF APPROPRIATE CLASS.
104  IDENTIFIER NOT DECLARED.
105  SIGN NOT ALLOWED.
```

106 NUMBER EXPECTED.
107 INCOMPATIBLE SUBRANGE TYPES.
108 FILE NOT ALLOWED HERE.
109 TYPE MUST NOT BE REAL.
110 TAGFIELD TYPE MUST BE SCALAR OR SUBRANGE.
111 INCOMPATIBLE WITH TAGFIELD TYPE.
112 INDEX TYPE MUST NOT BE REAL.
113 INDEX TYPE MUST BE SCALAR OR SUBRANGE.
114 BASE TYPE MUST NOT BE REAL.
115 BASE TYPE MUST BE SCALAR OR SUBRANGE.
116 ERROR IN TYPE OF STANDARD PROCEDURE PARAMETER.
117 UNSATISFIED FORWARD REFERENCE.

119 FORWARD DECLARED; REPETITION OF PARAMETER LIST NOT ALLOWED.
120 FUNCTION RESULT TYPE MUST BE SCALAR, SUBRANGE, OR POINTER.
121 FILE VALUE PARAMETER NOT ALLOWED.
122 FORWARD DECLARED FUNCTION; REPETITION OF RESULT TYPE NOT ALLOWED.
123 MISSING RESULT TYPE IN FUNCTION DECLARATION.
124 FIXED-POINT FORMATTING ALLOWED FOR REALS ONLY.
125 ERROR IN TYPE OF STANDARD FUNCTION PARAMETER.
126 NUMBER OF PARAMETERS DOES NOT AGREE WITH DECLARATION.
127 INVALID PARAMETER SUBSTITUTION.
128 PARAMETER PROCEDURE/FUNCTION IS NOT COMPATIBLE WITH DECLARATION.
129 TYPE CONFLICT OF OPERANDS.
130 EXPRESSION IS NOT OF SET TYPE.
131 TESTS ON EQUALITY ALLOWED ONLY.
132 '<' AND '>' NOT ALLOWED FOR SET OPERANDS.
133 FILE COMPARISON NOT ALLOWED.
134 INVALID TYPE OF OPERAND(S).
135 TYPE OF OPERAND MUST BE BOOLEAN.
136 SET ELEMENT MUST BE SCALAR OR SUBRANGE.
137 SET ELEMENT TYPES NOT COMPATIBLE.
138 TYPE OF VARIABLE IS NOT ARRAY.
139 INDEX TYPE IS NOT COMPATIBLE WITH DECLARATION.
140 TYPE OF VARIABLE IS NOT RECORD.
141 TYPE OF VARIABLE MUST BE FILE OR POINTER.
142 INVALID PARAMETER SUBSTITUTION.
143 INVALID TYPE OF LOOP CONTROL VARIABLE.
144 INVALID TYPE OF EXPRESSION.
145 TYPE CONFLICT.
146 ASSIGNMENT OF FILES NOT ALLOWED.
147 LABEL TYPE INCOMPATIBLE WITH SELECTING EXPRESSION.
148 SUBRANGE BOUNDS MUST BE SCALAR.
149 INDEX TYPE MUST NOT BE INTEGER.
150 ASSIGNMENT TO THIS FUNCTION IS NOT ALLOWED.
151 ASSIGNMENT TO FORMAL FUNCTION IS NOT ALLOWED.
152 NO SUCH FIELD IN THIS RECORD.

155 CONTROL VARIABLE MUST NOT BE DECLARED ON AN INTERMEDIATE LEVEL.
156 MULTIDEFINED CASE LABEL.
157 RANGE OF CASE LABELS IS TOO LARGE.

158 MISSING CORRESPONDING VARIANT DECLARATION.
159 REAL OR STRING TAGFIELDS NOT ALLOWED.
160 PREVIOUS DECLARATION WAS NOT FORWARD.
161 MULTIPLE FORWARD DECLARATION.

164 SUBSTITUTION OF STANDARD PROCEDURE/FUNCTION NOT ALLOWED.
165 MULTIDEFINED LABEL.
166 MULTIDECLARED LABEL.
167 UNDECLARED LABEL.
168 UNDEFINED LABEL IN THE PREVIOUS BLOCK.
169 ERROR IN BASE SET.
170 VALUE PARAMETER EXPECTED.

172 UNDECLARED EXTERNAL FILE.
173 FORTRAN PROCEDURE OR FUNCTION EXPECTED.
174 PASCAL PROCEDURE OR FUNCTION EXPECTED.
175 MISSING FILE 'INPUT' IN PROGRAM HEADING.
176 MISSING FILE 'OUTPUT' IN PROGRAM HEADING.
177 ASSIGNMENT TO FUNCTION ALLOWED ONLY IN FUNCTION BODY.
178 MULTIDEFINED RECORD VARIANT.
179 X-OPTION OF ACTUAL PROCEDURE/FUNCTION DOES NOT MATCH FORMAL DECLARATION.
180 CONTROL VARIABLE MUST NOT BE FORMAL.
181 ARRAY SUBSCRIPT CALCULATION TOO COMPLICATED.
182 MAGNITUDE OF CASE LABEL IS TOO LARGE.
183 SUBRANGE OF TYPE REAL IS NOT ALLOWED.

198 ALTERNATE INPUT NOT FOUND.
199 ONLY ONE ALTERNATE INPUT MAY BE ACTIVE.

201 ERROR IN REAL CONSTANT DIGIT EXPECTED.
202 STRING CONSTANT MUST BE CONTAINED ON A SINGLE LINE.
203 INTEGER CONSTANT EXCEEDS RANGE.
204 8 OR 9 IN OCTAL NUMBER.
205 STRINGS OF LENGTH ZERO ARE NOT ALLOWED.
206 INTEGER PART OF REAL CONSTANT EXCEEDS RANGE.
207 REAL CONSTANT EXCEEDS RANGE.

250 TOO MANY NESTED SCOPES OF IDENTIFIERS.
251 TOO MANY NESTED PROCEDURES AND/OR FUNCTIONS.

255 TOO MANY ERRORS ON THIS SOURCE LINE.
256 TOO MANY EXTERNAL REFERENCES.

259 EXPRESSION TOO COMPLICATED.
260 TOO MANY EXIT LABELS.
261 TOO MANY LARGE VARIABLES.
262 NODE TO BE ALLOCATED IS TOO LARGE.
263 TOO MANY PROCEDURE/FUNCTION PARAMETERS.
264 TOO MANY PROCEDURES AND FUNCTIONS.

300 DIVISION BY ZERO.

302 INDEX EXPRESSION OUT OF BOUNDS.
303 VALUE TO BE ASSIGNED IS OUT OF BOUNDS.

304 ELEMENT EXPRESSION OUT OF RANGE.

350 ONLY THE LAST DIMENSION MAY BE PACKED.
351 ARRAY TYPE IDENTIFIER EXPECTED.
352 ARRAY VARIABLE EXPECTED.
353 POSITIVE INTEGER CONSTANT EXPECTED.

397 PACK AND UNPACK ARE NOT IMPLEMENTED FOR DYNAMIC ARRAYS.
398 IMPLEMENTATION RESTRICTION.

Appendix 6 Turbo Pascal Notes

This text is written using standard Pascal. The decision to use standard Pascal rather than some other version was made for three reasons:

1. Standard Pascal is still frequently used at many colleges and universities.
2. Although many different versions of Pascal are available, no single one is dominant.
3. Standard Pascal is the easiest version from which to adapt if some other version is being used.

Recently, however, Turbo Pascal has begun to grow rapidly in popularity. Turbo's popularity is a function of the increasing use of personal computers, good compiler programs, and Turbo's relatively low cost.

The third edition of this text has responded to the increasing use of Turbo Pascal by expanding this appendix. Here, reference is made to parts of the text where specific differences occur between standard and Turbo Pascal. These differences are explained in some detail with reference to specific page references. Page numbers are listed in bold type. Appropriate comments follow them. Turbo logos, shown to the left, are used throughout the text to indicate a reference to this appendix.

Turbo Pascal Notes

Page 29: Additional reserved words in Turbo Pascal are

CONSTRUCTOR	**INTERFACE**	**USES**
DESTRUCTOR	**OBJECT**	**VIRTUAL**
IMPLEMENTATION	**PRIVATE**	**XOR**

Page 30: Standard identifiers in Turbo Pascal are

Data Types	Constants	Functions	Procedures	Files
boolean	**false**	**abs**	**dispose**	**input**
byte	**maxint**	**arotan**	**get**	**lst**
char	**true**	**chr**	**new**	**output**
comp		**cos**	**pack**	
double		**eof**	**page**	
extended		**eoln**	**put**	
integer		**exp**	**read**	
longint		**ln**	**readln**	
real		**odd**	**reset**	
shortint		**ord**	**rewrite**	
single		**pred**	**unpack**	
string		**round**	**write**	
text		**sin**	**writeln**	
word		**sqr**		
		sqrt		
		succ		
		trunc		

Page 31: Use of the underscore is allowed in Turbo Pascal. Thus, NumberOfTests could appear as Number_Of_Tests.
Page 33: Turbo does not require a file list with the program heading.

```
PROGRAM <name>;
```

is sufficient.
Page 40: The constant **maxint** is 32767. Most versions of Turbo also include the integer data types **byte, word, shortint,** and **longint.** For those versions, the constant **longmaxint** is 2147483647.
Page 41: Most versions of Turbo also include the real data types **single, double, extended,** and **comp:** the data type **single** is a floating-point type with a range of $1.5 * 10^{-45}$ to $3.4 * 10^{38}$ (positive and negative); **double** is a floating-point type with a range of $5.0 * 10^{-324}$ to $1.7 * 10^{308}$ (positive and negative); **extended** is a floating-point type with a range of $3.4 * 10^{-4932}$ to $1.1 * 10^{4932}$ (positive and negative); and **comp** is an integral type with a range of $-9.2 * 10^{18}$ to $9.2 * 10^{18}$.
Page 42: string data types may be defined. For an explanation and illustration of declaring and using strings, see the note for page 518.
Page 43: Default output is to the monitor. Output can be directed to the printer by using lst (short for list) within a **writeln** statement. Thus

```
writeln ('Hello');
```

goes to the screen and

```
writeln (1st, 'Hello');
```

outputs to the printer.

In later versions of Turbo, the use of lst to send output to the printer is only available if you link a library procedure to your program. The standard file lst is defined in the unit Printer and is linked by

```
Uses Printer;
```

following the program header. Using lst, however, is not practical while debugging.

For ease in directing output between the CRT and the printer, Marilyn Jussel (Kearney State College) suggests a standard procedure that allows the user to select the output destination without changing code. While debugging, the output goes to the screen; otherwise, the output goes to the printer.

The version that requires the library unit CRT is

```
Uses CRT

PROCEDURE Output_To_Where;

  VAR
    OutFile : text;
    Choice : char;

  BEGIN
    writeln ('Do you want printer output?');
    write ('Please enter choice (Y or N) ');
    readln (Choice);
    IF (upcase(Choice) = 'Y') THEN
      assign (OutFile, 'prn')
    ELSE
      AssignCRT (OutFile);  {  Procedure defined in Unit CRT   }
    rewrite (OutFile)
  END;  {  of PROCEDURE Output_To_Where  }
```

The second version does not require a library unit. The only change to the preceding segment of code is to convert the line following **ELSE** to

```
assign (OutFile, 'con');
```

The distinction should be made that on the screen, the command

```
writeln;
```

produces a blank line; on the printer, the programmer must include the output file name:

```
writeln (OutFile);
```

Page 44: There is no default field width. Thus

```
writeln (100, 87, 95);
```

produces

```
1008795
```

Page 44: The last line of output for Example 2.1 is

```
Pittsburgh, PA15238
```

Page 48: The same table is produced using Turbo.
Page 60: The **MOD** operator returns the remainder obtained by dividing its two operands; that is

```
i MOD j = i - (i DIV j) * j
```

The sign of the result of **MOD** is the same as the sign of *i*. An error occurs if *j* is zero. To better illustrate the difference, consider the expression −17 **MOD** 3. In standard Pascal, the result is 1; in Turbo Pascal, the result is −2.
Page 62: Turbo Pascal displays the error message

```
ARITHMETIC OVERFLOW
```

and halts execution.
Page 65:

```
writeln (maxint + 1);
```

produces

```
-32768
```

Page 67: Numeric variables have a default setting of zero.
Page 76: The standard file **input** is not required as part of the heading. When omitted, the default input file is the keyboard.
Page 77: Interactive programs should use **readln** rather than **read.** In order for **read** to be used in an interactive program, a compiler directive ({$B−}) should be used. However, this directive restricts editing. For best results, use separate **readln**s for character data.
Page 83: Reading character data using **readln** presents no problems. However, if characters are mixed with numbers, each number must be followed by a blank, tab, or carriage return. Thus

```
23A
```

is not allowed. It should be entered as

```
23 A
```

If you wish to enter the fraction 2/3 symbolically, it would have to be 2 /3 or 2 / 3.
Page 84: Turbo Pascal does not read the end-of-line marker as a blank.
Page 136: The error message is

```
Run-time error 04, PC=2CEA
Program aborted
```

Page 138: The Turbo compiler is especially helpful when you are debugging. After listing an error message (see previous note), it continues with directions for subsequent action. For example, the full screen message for division by zero of the previous note is

```
Run-time error 04, PC=2CEA
Program aborted

Searching
7 lines

Run-time error position found. Press <Esc>
```

When the <Esc> key is pressed, the editor is automatically reentered and the cursor is located at the position at which execution was halted.

Page 139: No error message is produced. The default value for variables is zero. Thus, A + B has the value 10 + 0 and the Average is 5.0.

Page 167: The markers **eoln** and **eof** should be used only when reading from text files (see note for page 436). Both functions work if the file is a logical device: **eoln** is **true** if the character read is an <Enter> or if **eof** is **true; eof** is **true** if the character read is a Ctrl-Z. However, when getting input interactively, it is preferable to use Boolean flags other than **eoln** and **eof.**

Page 173: The logical operator **XOR** is available in Turbo Pascal. E1 **XOR** E2 is **true** whenever exactly one of E1 or E2 is **true.**

Page 212: Turbo Pascal does not include an **OTHERWISE** option for a **CASE** statement. However, an equivalent **ELSE** option is available. Syntax for the **ELSE** option is

```
CASE <selector> OF
   <label 1> : <statement 1>;
       .
       .
       .
   <label 2> : <statement n>
ELSE
  BEGIN
     <statement 1>;
         .
         .
         .
     <statement m>
  END { of ELSE option }
END { of CASE statement }
```

Page 241: All variables are initialized to zero as a default setting. When a loop has been exited, the loop index retains the last assigned value.

Page 258: See note for page 167.

Page 260: See note for page 167.

Page 436: Text files are written using the Turbo editor. You can create a data disk by using the Turbo editor in the same way you would write a program. However, instead of program lines, you enter appropriate lines of data. When finished, you exit the editor and save the file on the disk by entering 'S'.

When the file is saved on the disk, it is listed in the directory as DATA1.PAS (unless some other designator is specified). You can then use the data file by declaring a file of type **text** in the variable declaration section. The file name does not have to be listed in the program heading. Thus, you could have

```
PROGRAM UseData;
VAR
  DataFile : text;
```

Within the program, you must then assign the file name on the directory to the declared file. This can be accomplished by

```
assign (DataFile, 'DATA.PAS');
reset (DataFile);
```

Notice DataFile is **reset** to guarantee the pointer is at the beginning of the file. At this stage, you can use **read** or **readln** to get input from the text file DataFile. You can accomplish this by including the file name in the **read** or **readln** command. Thus, you might have

```
WHILE NOT eof(DataFile) DO
  BEGIN
    readln (DataFile, Num);
    writeln (Num)
  END;
```

When you finish reading from a text file, you should close it with a **close** command. In the previous example, this would be

```
close (DataFile);
```

The Boolean flags **eoln** and **eof** can be used with text files. The text file must be included as an argument. Thus, you might have such statements as

```
WHILE NOT eof(Data);
```

or

```
WHILE NOT eoln(Data);
```

When reading from a text file, you must include the file name as an argument. Typical statements are

> **read** (Data, <variables here>)
> or
> **readln** (Data, <variables here>)

Page 443: Turbo Pascal does not differentiate between internal and external files. In Turbo, all files are treated the same as external files in other versions of Pascal.
Page 518: A **string** data type is available in Turbo Pascal. Correct syntax is

```
VAR
  Name : string;
```

or

```
VAR
  Name : string[n];
```

for early versions of Turbo, where *n* specifies the string length (from 1 through 255). With this declaration, you can have a statement such as

```
readln (Data, Score, Name);
```

as part of a program. Several string functions and procedures are available in Turbo. They include **delete, insert, str, concat(+), copy, length, pos, val,** and **numstr.** Students working in a Turbo environment are encouraged to become familiar with each of these.

Page 519: All variables are automatically packed in Turbo. Thus, packed arrays need not be declared and procedures **pack** and **unpack** have no effect. (For a discussion of **pack** and **unpack,** see Appendix 8.)

Page 521: For the first reference, see the note for page 518. In Turbo, the length of a string variable is dynamic. The actual length is determined by the current string value assigned to that variable. Therefore, even though Name may be declared as string[20], if Name is assigned 'Sue', its length will be 3.

Page 521: See note for page 518.

Page 570: Since **string** is a data type available in Turbo Pascal, packed arrays of characters are not needed. An array of **strings** can be thought of as a one-dimensional array.

Page 619: Loops are not needed for reading names when using a **string** data type. The code on page 619 could be replaced by

```
WITH Student DO
  BEGIN
    read (Data, Name);
    FOR J := 1 TO 3 DO
      read (Data, Score[J];
  readln (Data);
  Average := (Score[1] + Score[2] + Score[3]) / 3
END;
```

Page 624: See note for page 619.

Page 669: File names are not required as part of a program heading. If information is stored in a binary file named DATA, it is listed in the directory as DATA.PAS. Assuming such a file of integers exists, the following program illustrates how the data can be accessed:

```
PROGRAM UseData;
VAR
  DataFile : FILE OF integer;
  Num : integer;
BEGIN
  assign (DataFile, 'DATA.PAS');
  reset (DataFile);
  WHILE NOT eof(DataFile) DO
    BEGIN
      read (DataFile, Num);
      writeln (Num)
```

```
    END;
  close (DataFile)
END.
```

The effect of this program is to print the integers in DATA.PAS to the screen.

Turbo Pascal permits random access of binary files. Using the procedure **seek,** a particular file component can be located by

```
seek (<file name>, <position -1>);
```

The component can then be obtained by

```
read (<file name>, <component>);
```

Random access files can be opened for reading (**read**) and writing (**write**) at the same time. Thus, if you are updating a file, you reposition the pointer by

```
seek (<file name>, <position -1>);
```

after processing a component, and then **write** the updated component to the file by

```
write (<file name>, <component>):
```

When you are finished, you should close the file by

```
close (<file name>);
```

Page 671: Random access of files is available in Turbo Pascal.
Page 674: Files in Turbo may be created in two ways. Files of type **text** are created by using the Turbo editor with an appropriately named data file. Both numeric and non-numeric data may be entered in a text file. Both **read** and **readln** may be used to retrieve data from a text file.

Binary files must be created from a program by writing to a defined file. A sample program that creates a binary file of integers from a text file follows:

```
PROGRAM FilePrac;

VAR
  Num : integer;                { Integers moved between files }
  NewFile : FILE OF integer;    { Binary file of integers      }
  OldFile : text;               { Existing text file           }
BEGIN
  assign (OldFile, 'INTDATA.PA S');
  assign (NewFile, 'NEWDATA.PA S');
  reset (OldFile);
  rewrite (NewFile);
  writeln ('OldFile', 'Values to NewFile':28);
  writeln ('-------', '-----------------':28);
  WHILE NOT eof(OldFile) DO
    BEGIN
      readln (OldFile, Num);    { Read from the text file      }
      write (Num:2);              { Display the number         }
      Num := Num * 10;
      writeln (Num:20);         { Display the new number       }
      write (NewFile, Num)      { Write to the binary file     }
```

```
    END;
  close (OldFile);
  close (NewFile);
  reset (NewFile);
  writeln;

  {  Now display contents of the binary file.            }
  writeln ('Values from NewFile');
  writeln ('-------------------');
  WHILE NOT eof(NewFile) DO
    BEGIN
      read (NewFile, Num);
      writeln (Num)
    END;
  close (NewFile)
END.  {  of main program  }
```

Output from this program is

```
OldFile            Values to NewFile
-------            -----------------
 2                   20
 4                   40
 6                   60
 8                   80
10                  100

Values from NewFile
-------------------
20
40
60
80
100
```

Page 674: get and **put** are not used in Turbo Pascal. All files are accessed using **read, readln, write,** or **writeln** statements. This simplifies working with files, since you no longer must work with file windows and buffer variables.
Page 679: There are no internal files in Turbo Pascal.
Page 688: The following program is a sample of creating a file of records in Turbo. Specifically, this program creates a file of records for Programming Problem 9 in Chapter 13.

```
PROGRAM CreateDataFile;

TYPE
  Flight = RECORD
             FlightNumber : integer;
             ETA : 0..2400;
             ETD : 0..2400;
             Orig, Dest : string[15]
           END;  { of RECORD }

VAR
  FlightFile : FILE OF Flight;
```

```
    FlightRec : Flight;
    MoreData : boolean;
    Continue : char;

  BEGIN
    assign (FlightFile, 'NewFile.pas');
    rewrite (FlightFile);
    MoreData := true;
    WHILE MoreData DO     { Get one flight record }
      BEGIN
        WITH FlightRec DO
          BEGIN
            ClrScr;
            writeln ('Enter a data line');
            writeln ('Origin        *Destination    *
                      ETA    ETD    Flight Num');
            readln (Orig, Dest, ETA, ETD, FlightNumber)
          END;
        write (FlightFile, FlightRec);    {  Write one record to
                                             the file }
        write ('Continue? y or n   ');
        readln (Continue);
        MoreData := (Continue = 'y') OR (Continue = 'Y')
      END;  {  of getting data  }
    close (FlightFile);
    reset (FlightFile);     { Print contents of the binary file }

    {  Display contents of the binary file  }
    WHILE NOT eof(FlightFile) DO
      BEGIN
        read (FlightFile, FlightRec);
        WITH FlightRec DO
          writeln (Orig:12, Dest:12, ETA:5, ETD:5,
  FlightNumber:5)
      END
  END.  {  of program  }
```

A sample run of this program produces the binary file

```
Detroit       Chicago        752  756  521
Chicago       Tampa         1157  857  911
```

Page 736: The maximum number of elements in a set is 256, and the ordinal values of the base type must be within the range of zero through 255.
Page 763: This chapter is specifically for users of Turbo Pascal. Graphics is not part of standard Pascal.
Page 867: Turbo Pascal uses a caret (^) rather than an up arrow (↑) to indicate pointer variables.

Appendix 7

GOTO Statement

In your work with computers, you may have heard of a **GOTO** statement. It is another statement in Pascal that allows a programmer to transfer control within a program. The **GOTO** statement has the effect of an immediate unconditional transfer to an indicated designation. You should not use **GOTO** statements in a Pascal program, but for the sake of completeness, you should be aware of their existence and how they work.

Early programming languages needed a branching statement; therefore, both FORTRAN and BASIC were designed using a **GOTO** statement for branching. Subsequent languages, particularly Pascal, included more sophisticated branching and looping statements. These statements led to an emphasis on structured programming, which is easier to design and read. If you are a beginning programmer and have not used the **GOTO** statement in another language, you should continue to develop your skills without including this statement. If you have already written programs in a language that uses **GOTO** statements, you should still attempt to write all Pascal programs without **GOTO** statements.

One instance in which **GOTO** statements might be appropriate is in making a quick exit from some part of the program. For example, if you are getting data from somewhere within a program and you have a check for valid data, your design could include a program segment such as

```
read (data);
IF (<bad data>) THEN
  BEGIN
    <Write error message>;
    GOTO <end of program>
  END
ELSE
  <Process data>
```

Keeping the previous admonitions against using **GOTO** statements in mind, we will now briefly examine the form, syntax, and flow of control for these statements.

GOTO statements require the use of numerically labeled statements. Thus, your program could contain

```
LABEL
  <label 1>,
  <label 2>;
     .
     .
     .
GOTO 100;
     .
     .
     .
100: <program statement>;
     .
     .
     .
```

All labels must be declared in a label declaration section that precedes the constant definition section in a program. Each label can only be used for a single program statement. The form for the label declaration section is

```
LABEL
    <label 1>,
    <label 2>,
        .
        .
        .
    <label n>;
```

Correct form for a **GOTO** statement is

```
GOTO <numerical label>
```

where <numerical label> is an integer from 1 to 9999 inclusive. Declared labels are then used with appropriate statements in a program. Proper syntax for labeling a statement is

```
<label>: <program statement>
```

Consider the fragment

```
BEGIN
  read (Num);
  IF Num < 0 THEN
    GOTO 100
  ELSE
    Sum := Sum + Num;
        .
        .
        .
  100: writeln ('Data include a negative number,':40)
END.
```

In this instance, when a negative number is encountered as a data item, an appropriate message is printed and the program is terminated.

GOTO statements permit you to immediately transfer out of any control structure. As stated, we recommend you avoid the use of this statement whenever possible. However, if you must use it, use it only for an immediate exit from some point in the program; never use it to construct a loop in Pascal.

Appendix 8

Packing and Unpacking

The basic trade-off between working with arrays and packed arrays is that packed arrays require less memory but more time to access individual components. It is possible to facilitate working with packed and unpacked arrays (arrays that are not packed) by using assignment loops. For example, consider the following declarations:

```
TYPE
  String10 = PACKED ARRAY [1..10] OF char;
  Array10 = ARRAY [1..10] OF char;
VAR
  PakName : String10;
  UnpakName : Array10;
```

We now have reserved memory for

PakName

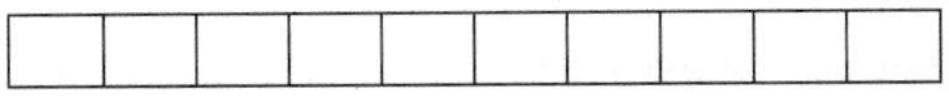

and

UnpakName

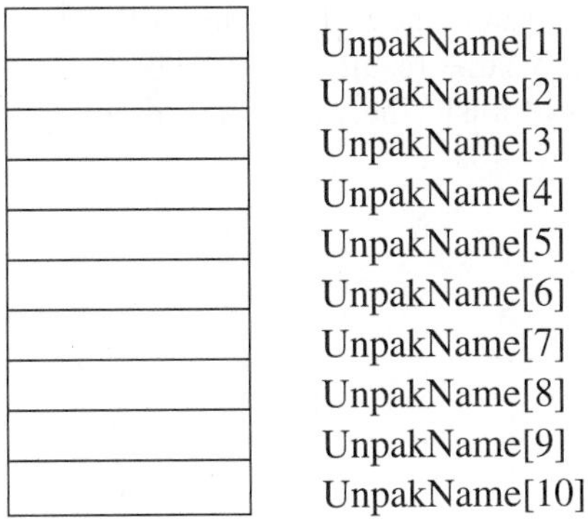

	UnpakName[1]
	UnpakName[2]
	UnpakName[3]
	UnpakName[4]
	UnpakName[5]
	UnpakName[6]
	UnpakName[7]
	UnpakName[8]
	UnpakName[9]
	UnpakName[10]

Now suppose UnpakName contains the name 'John Smith'.

UnpakName

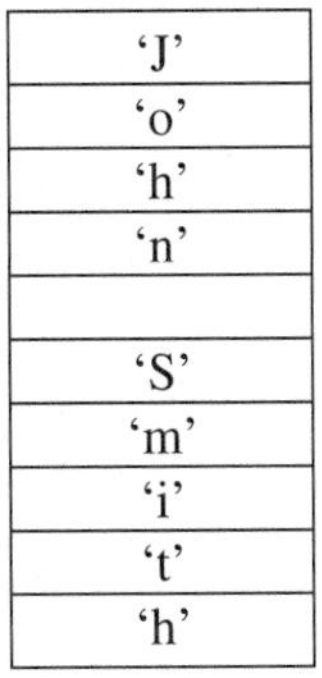

'J'
'o'
'h'
'n'
'S'
'm'
'i'
't'
'h'

and we wish to put the characters into a packed array for storage, sorting, or writing. This can be accomplished by

```
FOR J := 1 to 10 DO
  PakName[J] := UnpakName[J];
```

which produces

PakName

'J'	'o'	'h'	'n'	' '	'S'	'm'	'i'	't'	'h'

This string can still be accessed as one packed array variable.

A **FOR** loop can also be used to transfer elements from a packed array to an unpacked array, but Pascal does provide standard procedures for both of these processes. An array can be packed by

```
pack (UnpackedArray, J, PackedArray);
```

which fills all of PackedArray with elements of UnpackedArray, starting with Unpacked Array [J]. An array can be unpacked by

```
unpack (PackedArray, UnpackedArray, K);
```

which copies all elements of PackedArray into UnpackedArray, putting the first element in UnpackedArray [K]. For these procedures, PackedArray and Unpacked-Array do not have to be of the same length and K may be a constant or an expression. Unfortunately, **pack** and **unpack** are difficult to use. Therefore, since **FOR** loops can accomplish the same results and are about as efficient, you will do well to use them if you wish to transfer between packed and unpacked arrays.

Answers to Selected Exercises

This section contains answers to selected exercises (marked by asterisks in the text) from the exercise sets at the end of each section. In general, answers to odd-numbered problems are given.

CHAPTER 2

Section 2.1

1. Is an effective statement.
3. Is an effective statement.
5. Is not an effective statement because you cannot determine in advance which stocks will increase in value.
7. For this problem we need to know the number of names to be alphabetized, whether or not they are given in a last name–first name order, and whether the alphabetization is to be by last name.
9. 1. Select a topic
   2. Research the topic
   3. Outline the paper
   4. Refine the outline
   5. Write the rough draft
   6. Read and revise the rough draft
   7. Write the final paper
11. 1. Get a list of colleges
    2. Examine criteria (programs, distance, money, and so on)
    3. Screen to a manageable number
    4. Obtain further information
    5. Make a decision
13. 1. Get information
       1.1 Determine the number of grades to be averaged
       1.2 Get the grades
    2. Perform computations
       2.1 Add the grades together
       2.2 Divide the sum by the number of grades to get the average
    3. Print the results
       3.1 Print the grades
       3.2 Print the average
15. First-level development
    1. Get information for first employee
    2. Perform computations for first employee
    3. Print results for first employee
    4.
    5. } Repeat for second employee
    6.

    Second-level development
    1. Get information for first employee
       1.1 Get hourly wage
       1.2 Get number of hours worked
    2. Perform computations for first employee
       2.1 Compute gross pay
       2.2 Compute deductions
       2.3 Compute net pay
    3. Print results for first employee
       3.1 Print input data
       3.2 Print gross pay
       3.3 Print deductions
       3.4 Print net pay
    4.
    5. } Repeat for second employee
    6.

    Third-level development
    1. Get information for first employee
       1.1 Get hourly wage
       1.2 Get number of hours worked
    2. Perform computations for first employee
       2.1 Compute gross pay
       2.2 Compute deductions
          2.2.1 Federal withholding
          2.2.2 State withholding
          2.2.3 Social security
          2.2.4 Union dues
          2.2.5 Compute total deductions
       2.3 Compute net pay
          2.3.1 Subtract total deductions from gross
    3. Print results for first employee
       3.1 Print input data
          3.1.1 Print hours worked
          3.1.2 Print hourly wage
       3.2 Print gross pay
       3.3 Print deductions
          3.3.1 Print federal withholding
          3.3.2 Print state withholding
          3.3.3 Print social security
          3.3.4 Print union dues
          3.3.5 Print total deductions
       3.4 Print net pay
    4.
    5. } Repeat for second employee
    6.

Section 2.2

3. Valid. A good, descriptive identifier name.
5. Invalid. An identifier cannot contain a space.
7. Valid.
9. Invalid. & cannot be in an identifier name; only letters and numbers can be used.
11. Invalid. Identifiers cannot contain asterisks. This is an example of an arithmetic operation, not an identifier.
13. Invalid. An identifier cannot contain a comma.
15. Is valid.
17. Is missing an identifier for the program name.
19. Uses an improper identifier for the program name.

Typical constant definitions that might be used for Exercises 22–25 are

```
CONST
  Name = 'Julie Adams';
  Age = 18;
  BirthDate = 'November 10, 1980';
  Birthplace = 'Carson City, MI';
```

27. A variable declaration can only specify a type of variable, not a value. This should be a constant definition such as:

```
CONST
  Age = 18;
```

29. The constant name and value must be separated by an equal sign, such as:

```
Car = 'Cadillac';
```

31. This is valid, although you should be consistent with the spacing of your entries. If all reals are listed on the same line, then all integers should be also. It could be revised to read:

```
VAR
  Num1, Num2, Num3 : real;
  Score, Num : integer;
```

or

```
VAR
  Num1
  Num2
  Num3 : real;
  Score,
  Num : integer;
```

Section 2.3

1. Is a valid **integer.**
3. Is invalid, it has a comma.
5. Is a valid **integer.**
7. Is a valid **integer.**
9. Valid. The positive sign is ignored.
11. Invalid. All reals must have at least one digit to the right of the decimal. This should be expressed as 492.0.
13. Valid. A decimal point is not required in floating-point form.
15. Invalid. Real numbers cannot contain commas. Also, floating-point notation normally uses only one digit before the decimal, although this is not required. Therefore, this could be correctly written as 43162.3E5 or as 4.31625E9.
17. Valid. Trailing zeros after the decimal are ignored, along with the positive sign. This has the same value as 1.43E2.
19. 7.43927E11
21. 1.4768E1
23. −1004.6
25. 90200000000.0
27. −0.00802
29. Is a **real.**
31. Is an **integer.**
33. Is a string constant.
37.

```
writeln ('Score':14);
writeln ('-----':14);
writeln (86:13);
writeln (82:13);
writeln (79:13);
```

41.

```
PROGRAM Exercise41 (output);

BEGIN
  writeln ('Student Name':31, 'Test Score':18);
  writeln;
  writeln ('Adams, Mike':30, 73:16);
  writeln ('Conley, Theresa':34, 86:12);
  writeln ('Samson, Ron':30, 92:16);
  writeln ('O''Malley, Colleen':36, 81:10)
END.
```

47. 2.13 (The 2 is in column 12.)
49. −42.100
51. 1.0250000000E+01 (Note the conversion to floating point)
53.

```
PROGRAM Exercise53 (output);

BEGIN
  writeln ('Hourly Wage', 'Hours Worked':22,
           'Total':14);
  writeln;
  writeln (5.0:8:1, 20.0:22:1, 100.0:18:2);
  writeln (7.5:9:2, 15.25:22:2, 114.375:18:3)
END.
```

CHAPTER 3

Section 3.1

1. 11
3. 3
5. 126
7. 48
9. 1
11. 2.13
13. 1.2 Do the addition first, since it is in parentheses.
15. −40.0

−2.0 * ((56.8 / 4.0 + 0.8) + 5.0)
Division in the parentheses first
−2.0 * ((14.2 + 0.8) + 5.0)
Addition next
−2.0 * (15.0 + 5.0)
Complete the parentheses
−2.0 * 20
All that's left is to multiply
−40.0

17. 17.3 800.0E−2 is equal to 8.0, so the problem is really 8.0 / 4.0 + 15.3
19. Is valid, type **integer;** its value is 26.
21. Is invalid.
23. Is valid, type **real;** its value is 4.0.
25. Is valid, type **real;** its value is 10.79.
27. Is invalid.
29. Invalid. **DIV** with 4.0 is not permitted.
31. Valid. This gives an **integer** answer with an **integer** format.
33. Valid. The **DIV** operation is done before the /, and is valid at that point. The final answer is **real.**

Section 3.2

1. Is a valid assignment statement.
3. Is invalid. A real cannot be assigned to an integer variable.
5. Is a valid assignment statement.
7. Is invalid. IQ/3 is a real.
11. 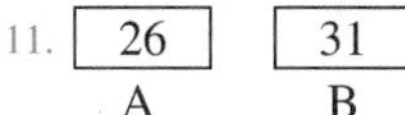

13. A = 9, B = 9, Temp = 13
15. d := r * t;
17. S := n * (n − 1) / 2;
19. 3
21. 8
23.
```
Gender      M
Age        18
Height     73 inches
Weight     186.5 lbs
```
25.
```
******************************
*                            *
*   Name      Age   Gender   *
*   ----      ---   ------   *
*                            *
*   Jones      21        M   *
*                            *
******************************
```

Section 3.3

Answers for Exercises 2–13 may vary according to the compiler used.

3. An error occurs. Since Num2 is an integer, it only reads 65 from 65.3.
5. [−20] [65.3] [b̸] — Num2, Num3, Ch
7. [65] [15.0] — Num2, Num3
9. [15] [b̸] [65.3] — Num1, Ch, Num3
11. [15] [65.3] [b̸ | −20] — Num1, Num3, Ch, Num2
13. [1̸5̸ 3] [65] ['.'] — Num2, Num2, Ch
15. 18 19 M
17. Output depends on how unformatted reals are displayed.
19. ['1'] [8] — Ch, A; [18 ■ 19M ■ −14.3 ■ JO ■ 142.1F ■] ↑
21. All variables unassigned

[18 ■ 19M ■ −14.3 ■ JO ■ 142.1F ■] ↑

23. 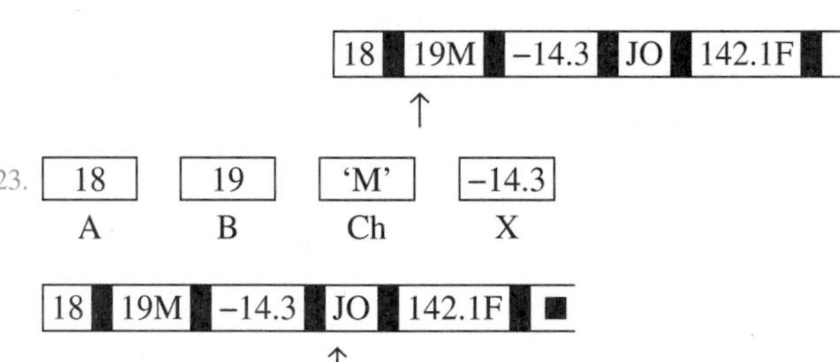

25. [18] [4] ['1'] — A, B, Ch

[18 ■ 19M ■ −14.3 ■ JO ■ 142.1F ■ ■] ↑

27. Is valid, but stored as **reals.**
29. Is valid.
31. Is not valid.
33.
```
write ('Enter the number of hours
       worked.  ');
readln (HoursWorked);
write ('What was the rate of pay?  ');
readln (RateOfPay);
```
35.
```
write ('Enter the vehicle price.  ');
readln (VehiclePrice);
write ('Enter the sales tax rate.  ');
readln (SalesTaxRate);
```

To determine the answers to Exercises 37–44, run the following short program on your computer and examine the output.

```
PROGRAM InputPrac (input, output);
VAR
  Num1, Num2 : integer;
  Num3 : real;
  Ch : char;
BEGIN
  readln (Num1, Num2, Ch, Num3);
  writeln (Num1:5, Num2:5, Ch:5,
Num3:10:2)
END.
```

Section 3.4

3.
```
Computer Science          Test #2
---------------------------------

Total points                  100
My score                       93
Class average                82.3
```

Section 3.5

1. 15.2
3. 0
5. −4.5
7.
```
PROGRAM FunctionError (output);

VAR
  A : integer;
  B : real;
  C : char;
BEGIN
  A := chr(64);
  B := succ(B);
  A := sqrt(B);
  B := sqrt(C);
  A := ord(1.23);
  C := abs(A);
  C := round (C)
END.
```

9. Invalid. **sqrt** produces a real answer, and **MOD** works only with integers.
11. Valid. The value is 1.0.
13. Invalid. 16 **DIV**(−3) = −5, and **sqrt** does not work with negative numbers.
15. Valid. The answer is 14.4.
25. 4
(depends on character set—65 in ASCII)
29. `IntValue := ord(Digit) - ord('0');`
31. `Volume := 4 / 3 * 3.14 * r * r * r;`

CHAPTER 4

Section 4.1

1. `Total := Test1 + Test2 + Test3 + Test4;`
3. `TotalIncome := Salary + Tips;`
5. `Grade := TotalPoints / 6;`
7.
```
writeln (NumberAttending:5,
         TicketPrice:10:2,
         TotalReceipts:10:2);
```
9.
```
PROGRAM BoxVolume (output);
CONST
  Skip = ' ';
VAR
  Length, Width, Height, Volume : integer;
BEGIN
  Length := 8;
  Width := 3;
  Height := 2;
  Volume := Length * Width * Height;
  writeln (Skip:10, 'Length =', Length:10);
  writeln (Skip:10, 'Width =', Width:10);
  writeln (Skip:10, 'Height =', Height:10);
  writeln;
  writeln (Skip:10, 'Volume =', Volume:10)
END.
```
13. Is acceptable.
15. Is acceptable.
17. Is acceptable.
19. Should have consistent comment starts.

Section 4.2

1. There should be a semicolon after Y in the first line. In the second line, '=' should be replaced by ':='. The correct code is

```
X := 3 * Y;
Y := 4 - 2 * Z;
writeln (X, Y);
```
3. The added semicolons are circled for your convenience.

```
PROGRAM ExerciseThree (output)(;)

CONST
  Name = 'Jim Jones'(;)
  Age = 18(;)

VAR
  Score : integer(;)

BEGIN
  Score := 93(;)
  writeln ('Name':13, Name:15)(;)
  writeln ('Age':12, Age:16)(;)
  writeln ('Score':14, Score:14)
END.
```

5. The misspelled keywords (with the correct spelling) follow.

PROGRRAM	(should be **PROGRAM**)
reals	(should be **real**)
chr	(should be **char**)
interger	(should be **integer**)
writln	(should be **writeln**)

7. Invalid. A real cannot be assigned to an integer.
9. Valid. But the assignment statement should be

```
X := Score / 6.0;
```

11. Invalid. A real cannot be assigned to an integer.
13. Invalid. If the letter A is desired, it must be in single quotations. It is not legal to assign an integer to a character variable.
15. Invalid—a character cannot be assigned to a real variable.
17. Is invalid. The operand (+) is on the left of an assignment statement.
19. Is invalid. Wage should be spelled Wages.
21. Is invalid. Hours has not been declared.
23. Is invalid. A value cannot be assigned to a constant.
25. Valid.
27. Valid. But it prints the word Name, not the value of the constant, since Name is in single quotations.
29. Valid. But it prints the letters A and B, not the values of the variables.
31. Invalid. The prompt (B =) must be in single quotations. It should be

```
writeln ('A = ':10, A:3, 'B = ':10, B:3);
```

33. Valid. But it prints the value of Wages in exponential form since no formatting is used. It would be better to use

```
writeln (Wages:10:2, ' are wages');
```

35. Errors are circled.

```
PROGRAM Errors (output();                          should be)

(*****************************************)
(*                                       *)
(*  There are thirteen errors.           $)        should be *
(*                                       *)
(****************************************          ) missing

VAR
  Day : char;
  Percent:real                                     ; missing
  A, B ; int;                                      ; should be : and int should be integer

BEGIN ( Main program )                             ( ) should be { } or (* *)
  Day = 'M';                                       should be :=
  Percentage := 72 / 10;                           should be Percent
  A := 5;
  B := A * 3.2;                                    B is of type integer
  writln(A, B:20);                                 should be writeln
  writeln (Day:10:2);                              incorrect formatting
  writeln (A+B:8, Percent:18)
END                                                . missing
```

Section 4.3

1.

Value of Num1	Value of Num2	Value of Num3
33	Undefined	Undefined
33	−2	Undefined
28	−2	Undefined
28	28	Undefined
28	28	30
28	28	30
28	28	1
29	28	1

3.

Code with Errors	Corrected Code
`Max = 100.0 : real;`	`Max = 100.0;`
`Score, Sum : integer`	`Score, Sum : integer;`
`Score := 86.0;`	`Score := 86;`
`Score + Sum := Sum`	`Sum := Score + Sum;`
`writeln (Sum:15:2)`	`writeln (Sum:15)`

5. Your answer to this exercise will depend on the type of output that you choose. It is suggested that the output be better formatted to achieve a neater spacing, better use of underlines, and logical output. All of these changes can be made through better use of formatting in **write** and **writeln** statements.

As presented in the text, the output is extremely difficult to read. A little time spent in planning neat output (just like the time spent in planning programs) will pay dividends.

7. The run-time errors are
   a. A division by zero error occurs at

```
X := X / (4 MOD 2);
```

since 4 **MOD** 2 is equal to zero.

b. Once the error in **a** occurs, further calculations involving the variable used are invalid, so

```
X := 3 * X;
```

causes an error.

c. Since it no longer has a valid value, X cannot be printed.

CHAPTER 5

Section 5.1

1. **true true false**
   false
3. Is invalid.
5. Is valid.
7. Is invalid.
9. Invalid. The correct expression is (3 < 4) **OR** (5 <> 6).
11. Valid. Answer is **false.**
13. Valid. Answer is **true.**
15. Valid. Answer is **true.**
17. Is **true.**
19. Is **true.**
21. Is **false.**
23. Is **true.**
25. Is **false.**
27. Is **false.**
29. Is **true.**
31. Is **false.**

Section 5.2

```
 1. 10       5
 3. 5        B has no value.
 5. 15       4
    15       4
```

9. `3 < X < 10`

   cannot be evaluated. This should be

   `(3 < X) AND (X < 10)`
11. `IF Ch = 'A' OR 'B' THEN`

    should be

    `IF (Ch = 'A') OR (Ch = 'B') THEN`
13. **5 150**
15. The first program always prints the number entered, its square, and its cube, regardless of the value entered. If the decision is **true,** the first **writeln** after the decision is executed. If the decision is **false,** the **writeln** is not executed. The only difference in the output is whether there is no blank line (when Num <= 0) or one blank line (if Num > 0) after the input.

    In the second program, the number, square, and cube are printed only when a positive number is entered. This is due to the use of the **BEGIN. . .END** block in the decision statement, which ties all the subsequent statements to the outcome of the decision.
17. A semicolon is needed after **read** (A).
19. Correct, assuming that this is the end of the entire program.
21.
```
BEGIN
  readln (Num1, Num2, Num3);
  Total := Total + Num1 + Num2 + Num3;
  writeln (Num1, Num2, Num3);
  writeln;
  writeln (Total)
END;
```
23.
```
read (Ch1, Ch2, Ch3);
IF (Ch1 <= Ch2) AND (Ch2 <= Ch3) THEN
  writeln (Ch1, Ch2, Ch3);
```
This can also be written as
```
read (Ch1, Ch2, Ch3);
IF Ch1 <= Ch2 THEN
  IF Ch2 <= Ch3 THEN
    writeln (Ch1, Ch2, Ch3);
```

Section 5.3

```
1. -14       14
3. 10         5
    5         0
```

5. Since the intent appears to be a statement that counts characters other than periods, a **BEGIN . . . END** block should be included in the **IF . . . THEN** option.

```
IF Ch <> '.' THEN
  BEGIN
    CharCount := CharCount + 1;
    writeln (Ch)
  END
ELSE
  PeriodCount := PeriodCount + 1;
```
7. Technically this fragment will run. However, since it appears that OldAge := OldAge + Age is to be included in the **ELSE** option, the programmer probably meant

```
ELSE
  BEGIN
    OldCount := OldCount + 1;
    OldAge := OldAge + Age
  END;
```

Section 5.4

1. X = 38.15, Y = 763.0.
3. X = 600.0, Y = 1200.0.
7.
```
read (Num);
  IF Num > 0 THEN
    IF Num <= 10000 THEN
      BEGIN
        Count := Count + 1;
        Sum := Sum + Num
      END
    ELSE
      writeln ('Value out of range':27)
  ELSE
    writeln ('Value out of range':27);
```

9.
```
IF C <= 0 THEN
  IF A > 0 THEN
    IF B > 0 THEN
      writeln ('Option one':19)
    ELSE
      writeln ('Option two':19)
  ELSE
    writeln ('Option two':19)
ELSE
  writeln ('Option one':19);
```

11. a. -5 5
b. -3 -3
c. 18 8
d. 6 -4

13. a. -5 5
b. -3 -3
c. 18 8
d. -4 -4

15.
```
PROGRAM Exercise15 (input, output);

  VAR
    Score = integer;

  BEGIN
    readln (Score);
    writeln;
    IF Score > 24 THEN
      IF Score > 49 THEN
        IF Score > 74 THEN
          writeln ('Score is in quartile 1')
        ELSE
          writeln ('Score is in quartile 2')
      ELSE
        writeln ('Score is in quartile
  3')
    ELSE
      writeln ('Score is in quartile 4')
  END.
```

Section 5.5

3.
```
IF ((Age DIV 10) > 10) OR
   ((Age DIV 10) < 1) THEN
  writeln ('Value of age is', Age)
ELSE
  .
  .     (CASE statement here)
  .
```

5. The second part of the **CASE** should be:

```
6, 7 : Num := Num + 6;
```

A colon, not a semicolon, is used to separate the label from the statement. Also, the value 7 is repeated in two parts of the **CASE.** This cannot be done.

7. Quotation marks are needed around the values of Ch, such as

```
'A' : Points := 4.0;
'B' : Points := 3.0;
  .
  .
  .
```

9. The value of Num/10 is a real number. Reals are not permitted as selectors in a **CASE** statement.

11. **You have purchased Super Unleaded gasoline**

13. **5 10 -5**

15.
```
CASE Score OF
  1, 2, 3, 4 : Grade := 'E';
  5, 6       : Grade := 'D';
  7          : Grade := 'C';
  8          : Grade := 'B';
  9          : Grade := 'A'
END;
```

17. Assume there is a variable ClassType. The design of the fragment to compute fees is

```
readln (ClassType);
CASE ClassType OF
  'U' :
  'G' :     (list options here)
  'F' :
  'S' :
END;  {  OF CASE  }
```

CHAPTER 6

Section 6.2

1.
```
*
 *
  *
   *
    *
     *
```

3.
```
**   2
**   3
**   4
**   5
**   6
**   7
**   8
**   9
**  10
**  11
**  12
**  13
**  14
**  15
**  16
**  17
**  18
**  19
**  20
```

5.
```
PROGRAM LCVCheck (input, output);
VAR
  LCV : integer;
BEGIN
  FOR LCV := 1 TO 10 DO
    BEGIN
      LCV := 2 * LCV;
      writeln (LCV)
    END
END.
```

7.
```
FOR Index := 1 TO 4 DO
  writeln ('*':10);
```

9.
```
writeln ('*':10);
FOR Index := 1 TO 3 DO
  writeln ('*':10-Index, '*':2*Index);
writeln ('**** ****':14);
FOR Index := 1 TO 2 DO
  writeln ('* *':11);
writeln ('***':11);
```

11. The semicolon following **DO** should be omitted. This is a very common error, and will not cause the compiler to give an error message. The **writeln** statement is *not* a part of the loop if the semicolon is there, since the semicolon closes the loop.

13. The equal sign in the **FOR** statement should be replaced with an assignment sign.

```
FOR Index := -3 TO 3 DO
```

15.
```
FOR Index := 1 TO 5 DO
  write (Index:3);
FOR Index := 5 DOWNTO 1 DO
  write (6-Index:3);
```

17.
```
Sum := 0;
FOR Index := 4 DOWNTO 1 DO
  BEGIN
    writeln ('*':26-Index);
    Sum := Sum + Index
  END;
```

19.
```
PROGRAM Exercise19 (output);

VAR
  Fahrenheit, Starting, Ending : integer;
  Celsius  :  real;

BEGIN
  writeln;
  write ('Enter the starting and ending
         Fahrenheit values. ');
  readln (Starting, Ending);
  writeln; writeln;
  writeln ('Temperature':16);
  writeln ('Fahrenheit', 'Celsius':10);
  writeln ('----------', '-------':10);

  FOR Fahrenheit := Starting TO Ending DO
    BEGIN    { Loop for the Fahr. temp. }
      Celsius := (5 / 9) * (Fahrenheit - 32);
      writeln (Fahrenheit:6, Celsius:14:2)
    END    { of FOR loop }
END.  {  of program  }
```

Section 6.3

3.
```
 1
 2
 3
 4
 5
 6
 7
 8
 9
10
```

5.
```
54        50
```

7.
```
      96.00        2.00
```

9. This is not an infinite loop. The output of the program will be:

```
 2
 4
 8
16
```

11. This is not an infinite loop. It will run one time through, and produce the output

```
15       3
```

In the first time through, the value of B becomes 14, and 14 **DIV** 3 is not equal to 5.

13. **A 18 - 14.3B C 21 10.00D E 19 - 11.5F**

15. **A 18 - 14.3B**

17. This code works, but since we are reading an entire line of data with **readln,** the **eoln** is not **true** until we reach **eof.** Thus, the entire data file is printed.

21.
```
Count := 0;
Positive := true;
WHILE Count < 3 DO
  BEGIN
    Count := Count + 1;
    write ('Enter a number. ');
    readln (Num);
    IF Num < 0 THEN
      Positive := false;
    Sum := Sum + Num
  END;
IF Positive THEN
  writeln ('Their sum is ', Sum);
```

23.
```
Current := 1;
Square := 1;
WHILE (sqr(Current) - Square ) <= 25 DO
  BEGIN
    Square := sqr(Current);
    writeln (Current:10, Square:10);
    Current := Current + 1
  END;
```

25.
```
write ('What integer do you want to use? ');
readln (Num);
IF Num < 10000 THEN
  BEGIN
    PowerOfNum := Num;
    WHILE PowerOfNum < 10000 DO
      BEGIN
        writeln (PowerOfNum);
        PowerOfNum := PowerOfNum * Num
      END;
```

Section 6.4

1. A **REPEAT . . . UNTIL** loop tests the Boolean expression after the loop has been executed. A **WHILE . . . DO** loop tests the Boolean expression before the loop is executed. This means the loop would not be executed if an attempt was made to read from an empty file.

3.
```
1  9
2  8
3  7
4  6
5  5
6  4
```

5.
```
 1
 2
 3
 4
 5
 6
 7
 8
 9
10
```

7. This is an infinite loop. There is no provision to change the value of J inside the loop, so the condition can never be met.

9. This is an infinite loop. Although A is changed within the loop, it can never equal 20. The condition is never met, so execution continues.

11. `A 18 -1.3B`

13. Same as Exercise 11.

15.
```
A 18 -1.3 B
C 21 10.0 D
E 19-11.5 F
```

17.
```
Current := 1;
Square := 1;
REPEAT
  Square := sqr(Current);
  writeln (Current:10, Square:10);
  Current := Current + 1
UNTIL sqr(Current) - Square > 25;
```

19.
```
Count := 0;
Positive := false;
REPEAT
  Count := Count + 1;
  write ('Enter a number. ');
  readln (Num);
  IF Num > 0 THEN
    Positive := true;
  Sum := Sum + Num
UNTIL Count = 3;
IF Positive THEN
  writeln ('Their sum is ', Sum);
```

21.
```
PROGRAM Exercise21 (input, output);

VAR
  Sum, I, Max : integer;

BEGIN
  Sum := 0;
  I := 0;
  writeln ('What is the maximum sum desired? ');
  readln (Max);
  REPEAT
    I := I + 1;
    Sum := Sum + I
  UNTIL Sum > Max;
  writeln ('Sum exceeds ', Max, ' for N = ', I)
END.
```

23.
```
readln (Num);
IF Num < 10000 THEN
  BEGIN
    PowerOfNum := Num;
    REPEAT
      writeln (PowerOfNum);
      PowerOfNum := PowerOfNum * Num
    UNTIL PowerOfNum > 10000
  END;
```

Section 6.5

3. This can only be converted to a **REPEAT . . . UNTIL** loop. It cannot be converted to a **FOR** loop of either type since this loop must run a variable number of times.

5. The loop in Exercise **4** can be rewritten in each of the following ways.

a.
```
WHILE X < 4.0 DO
  BEGIN
    writeln (X:20:2);
    X := X + 0.5
  END;
```

b.
```
FOR J := 1 TO 8 DO
  BEGIN
    writeln (X:20:2);
    X := X + 0.5
  END;
```

c.
```
FOR J := 8 DOWNTO 1 DO
  BEGIN
    writeln (X:20:2);
    X := X + 0.5
  END;
```

7. Since the condition 6 < 5 is **false,** the loop will not be entered. In a **REPEAT . . . UNTIL** loop, the loop body is always executed at least once before the Boolean expression controlling the loop is evaluated.

Section 6.7

1.
```
PROGRAM Exercise1 (input, output);

VAR
  I, J, Ending1, Ending2 : integer;
```

```
BEGIN
  write ('What are the two maximum values
          desired? ');
  readln (Ending1, Ending2);
  FOR I := 1 TO Ending1 DO
    FOR J := 1 TO Ending2 DO
      writeln (I, ' * ', J, ' = ', I * J)
END.
```

This reads the two ending values desired, then uses nested loops to control the execution through values up to those specified by the user of the program.

7.
```
10  12  14  16  18  20
15  18  21  24  27  30
20  24  28  32  36  40
25  30  35  40  45  50
30  36  42  48  54  60
```

9. When K is 1, the inner loop runs from 1 to 10, summing these values. When K = 2, the inner loop takes on the values 11 to 20. This continues in this manner until the last pass through the program, when K = 10 and the inner loop runs from 91 to 100. This program finds the sum of 1 + 2 + 3 + 4 + · · · + 100, which is 5050.

11.
```
FOR K := 1 TO 5 DO
  BEGIN
    write (' ':K);
    FOR J := K TO 5 DO
      write ('*');
    writeln
  END;
```

13.
```
FOR K := 1 TO 7 DO
  IF K < 5 THEN
    BEGIN
      FOR J := 1 TO 3 DO
        write ('*');
      writeln
    END
  ELSE
    BEGIN
      FOR J := 1 TO 5 DO
        write ('*');
      writeln
    END;
```

15. The fragment for this is:

```
FOR J := 2 TO 5 DO                                          {  Print 4 rows  }
  BEGIN
    FOR K := 1 TO 5 DO                                   {  5 terms per row  }
      write (J * K:4);                     {  Print the product of K and J  }
    writeln                   {  Skip to next line before incrementing K  }
  END;
```

Section 6.8

1. This is an infinite loop.
3. This **IF . . . THEN** statement is **true** only for multiples of 5. It prints a list of multiples of 5, starting with 5 and ending with 100.
5. 5   –5

7.
```
5
4
3
2
```
9.
```
Count := 0;
Sum := 0.0;
WHILE NOT eof DO
  BEGIN
    readln (Num);
    IF Num > 0.0 THEN
      BEGIN
        Count := Count + 1;
        Sum := Sum + Num
      END
  END;  {  of WHILE loop  }
```
11.
```
WHILE NOT eof DO  {  Process one line  }
  BEGIN
    write (' ':10);
    WHILE NOT eoln DO  {  Process one char-
acter  }
      BEGIN
        read (ch);
        IF Ch <> '' THEN
          write (Ch)
      END;  {  of inner WHILE loop  }
    readln;  {  Advance the pointer  }
    writeln
  END; { of outer WHILE loop  }
```

CHAPTER 7

Section 7.2

1. A procedure is a subprogram. As such it is contained within a complete program. It is headed by the reserved word **PROCEDURE** and has a semicolon after the last **END**, whereas a program is headed by the reserved word **PROGRAM** and has a period after the last **END.**
3.
```
PROCEDURE PrintHeading;
  CONST
    Splats = '******************************';
    Edge = '*                            *';
    Name = 'John J. Smith';
    Date = 'September 15, 1998';
  BEGIN
    writeln (Skip:20, Splats);
    writeln (Skip:20, Edge);
    writeln (Skip:20 '*', Skip:5, Name, Skip:10, '*');
    writeln (Skip:20 '*', Skip:5, Date, Skip:5, '*');
    writeln (Skip:20, Edge);
    writeln (Skip:20, Splats)
  END;  {  of PROCEDURE PrintHeading  }
```
5. Suppose you want the heading to be

```
                    R & R Produce Company
                    ---------------------

Items Purchased     Price per Item     Total per Item
---------------     --------------     --------------
```

A procedure to produce the output is

```
PROCEDURE PrintHeading;
  CONST
    Skip = ' ';
```

```
BEGIN
  writeln; writeln;
  writeln (Skip:20, 'R & R Produce Company');
  writeln (Skip:20, '--------------------');
  writeln;
  write (Skip:5, 'Items Purchased');
  write (Skip:5, 'Price per Item');
  writeln (Skip:5, 'Total per Item');
  write (Skip:5, '---------------');
  write (Skip:5, '--------------');
  writeln (Skip:5, '--------------');
  writeln
END;
```

7.
```
PROCEDURE MotelHeading;
  BEGIN
    writeln ('////////////////////////////////////');
    writeln;
    writeln ('     Sleep E-Z-E Motel');
    writeln ('     5975 N. Memorial Drive');
    writeln ('     Lancaster, Ohio 43130')'
    writeln;
    writeln ('------------------------------------');
    writeln
  END;
```

9. This exercise demonstrates one advantage of output procedures, and the potential they have to shorten and simplify your code.

a.
```
PROGRAM Exercise9A (output);
BEGIN
  writeln ('/////////////////////////////////':45);
  writeln ('/                               /':45);
  writeln ('/      Special Olympics         /':45);
  writeln ('/      ------- --------         /':45);
  writeln ('/////////////////////////////////':45);
  writeln;
  writeln ('/////////////////////////////////':45);
  writeln ('/                               /':45);
  writeln ('/      Special Olympics         /':45);
  writeln ('/      ------- --------         /':45);
  writeln ('/////////////////////////////////':45);
  writeln;
  writeln ('/////////////////////////////////':45);
  writeln ('/                               /':45);
  writeln ('/      Special Olympics         /':45);
  writeln ('/      ------- --------         /':45);
  writeln ('/////////////////////////////////':45);
  writeln
END.
```

b.
```
PROGRAM Exercise9B (output);

PROCEDURE PrintHeading;
  BEGIN
    writeln ('/////////////////////////////////':45);
    writeln ('/                               /':45);
    writeln ('/      Special Olympics         /':45);
    writeln ('/      ------- ---------        /':45);
    writeln ('/////////////////////////////////':45);
    writeln
END;
```

```
BEGIN  {  Main program  }
  PrintHeading;
  PrintHeading;
  PrintHeading
END.   {  of main program  }
```

11.
```
She loves me.
She loves me not.
She loves me.
She loves me not.
She loves me.
```

Section 7.3

3. A and B are variable parameters. X is a value parameter.
5. X, Y, and Z are variable parameters. A, B, and Ch are value parameters.
7. Invalid. A question mark cannot be used in a procedure name. All procedure names must be valid identifiers.
9. Invalid. Semicolons must be used to separate parameter types in the list.
11. **Prob11 (Num1, Num2, Letter);**
13. **FindMax (Num1, Num2, Max);**
15. **SwitchAndTest (Num1, Num2, Flag);**
17. **-3 2**
19. **10 0**
21.
```
PROCEDURE MaxAndAver (X, Y, Z : real;
                      VAR Max, Aver : real);
  BEGIN
    Max := X;
    IF Y > Max THEN
      Max := Y;
    IF Z > Max THEN
      Max := Z;
    Aver := (X + Y + Z) / 3.0
  END;
```
23.
```
PROCEDURE TempConv (Fahr : real;
                    VAR Celsius : real);
  BEGIN
    Celsius := (5 / 9) * (Fahr - 32.0)
  END;
```
25. Inappropriate. The number of parameters does not match.
27. Appropriate.
29. Inappropriate. The order of parameter types does not match.
31. Inappropriate. The number of parameters does not match.

Section 7.4

3. Is invalid. The data type for what will be returned to the calling program must be listed.

```
FUNCTION RoundTenth (X : real) : real;
```

5. Is valid.
7. Is invalid. The comma following **char** should be a semicolon.
9. There is a type mismatch in this function. The function header calls for an integer to be returned, but the assignment statement in the function gives a real value. The function header can be changed to

```
FUNCTION AvOf2 (N1, N2 : integer) : real;
```

11.
```
FUNCTION MaxOfTwo (X, Y : real) : real;
  BEGIN
    IF X > Y THEN
      MaxOfTwo := X
    ELSE
      MaxOfTwo := Y
  END;
```
13.
```
FUNCTION RoundTenth (X : real) : real;
  BEGIN
    RoundTenth := (round(X * 10)) / 10
  END;
```
15.
```
FUNCTION SignOfReal (X : real) : char;
  BEGIN
    IF X >= 0 THEN
      SignOfReal := '+'
    ELSE
      SignOfReal := '-'
  END;
```
17.
```
FUNCTION Parking (Time : integer) : real;
  VAR
    Hours : integer;
  BEGIN
    IF Time MOD 60 = 0 THEN
      Hours := Time DIV 60
    ELSE
      Hours := Time DIV 60 + 1;
    Parking := Hours * 0.75
  END;
```

This assumes the time is entered in minutes.

19.
```
FUNCTION Factorial (N : integer) : integer;
  VAR
    Fact, J : integer;
  BEGIN
    Fact := 1;
    FOR J := 1 TO N DO
      Fact := Fact * J;
    Factorial := Fact
  END;
```
21. There are several reasonably short methods of writing such a function. If we assume the main program checks for a valid symbol, one such function is

```
FUNCTION Arithmetic (Operand : char;
                     N1, N2 : integer)
                     : integer;
  BEGIN
    IF Operand = '+' THEN
      Arithmetic := N1 + N2
    ELSE
      Arithmetic := N1 * N2
  END;  {  of FUNCTION Arithmetic  }
```

Section 8.1

7. Identifiers for this program are represented schematically by the figure at right.

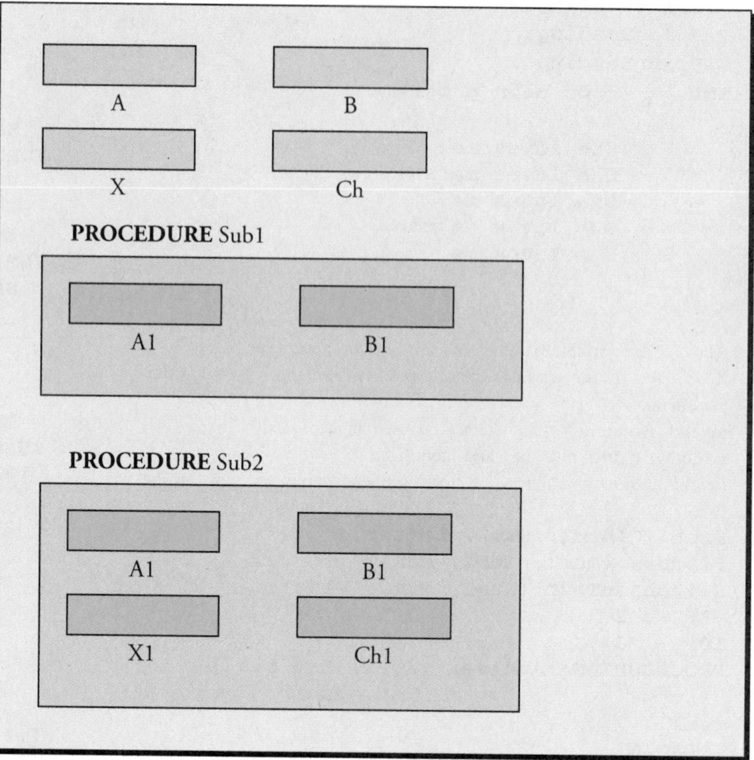

9. **10**
   20
   10
   30
   30
11. **17 7**
13. **17 17**
15. No errors. The variables defined in the procedure heading will be local to it.
17. The disadvantages of using the same variable names in both the main program and subprogram include the following:

   - There will be confusing references to variables.
   - There will be additional problems in debugging.
   - Determining the scope of a statement will be difficult.
   - It will be easy to forget where values are changed and the scope of those new values.

   It is sometimes easier to match parameters using the same name. This, however, does not offset the disadvantages.
19. The main program is trying to access an identifier that is not available. The line

```
writeln (X1:20:2);
```

   in the main program is inappropriate because the scope of X1 is **PROCEDURE** Sub1.

Section 8.2

1. a. variable parameters
   b. variable parameters
   c. value parameters
3. The pseudocode design indicates procedures could be written for

1. Initialize variables	**Initialize (<parameter list>);**
2. Print a heading	**PrintHeading;**
3.1 Get new data	**GetData (<parameter list>)**
4. Print results	**PrintResults (<parameter list>);**

   Until more is known about the problem, Step 3.2 (perform computations) cannot be determined. However, if we assume a function (Compute) is written for this, a main program could be

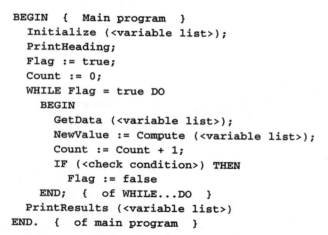

```
BEGIN  {  Main program  }
  Initialize (<variable list>);
  PrintHeading;
  Flag := true;
  Count := 0;
  WHILE Flag = true DO
    BEGIN
      GetData (<variable list>);
      NewValue := Compute (<variable list>);
      Count := Count + 1;
      IF (<check condition>) THEN
        Flag := false
    END;  {  of WHILE...DO  }
  PrintResults (<variable list>)
END.  {  of main program  }
```

5.
```
FUNCTION Discriminant (A, B, C : real) : real;
  BEGIN
    Discriminant := B * B - 4 * A * C
  END;
```

Section 8.3

1. a. In a nested subprogram, a local variable may be used within the subprogram in which it is declared, and subprograms declared within that subprogram, or any subprograms called by that subprogram. Its scope is that subprogram and all others contained in or called by it.
3. This results in an error because AddTwo calls AddOne, and AddOne has not yet been declared. It can be corrected by placing AddOne before **PROCEDURE** AddTwo.
5. The parameters for AddOne are declared twice. Once the parameters are declared along with the forward reference, they must not be repeated during the function definition. A comment could be used instead, such as:

```
FUNCTION AddOne;  { (A:integer) : integer  }
```

7. No errors.

9. A schematic representation is shown at right. X, Y, and Ch can be used in all subblocks of Exercise Nine. X1, Ch1, and J declared in **PROCEDURE** A can be used in all subblocks of **PROCEDURE** A but cannot be used in **PROCEDURE** B or ExerciseNine. M and Y1 can be used only in **FUNCTION** Inner. X1 and Ch2, declared in **PROCEDURE** B, can be used only in **PROCEDURE** B.

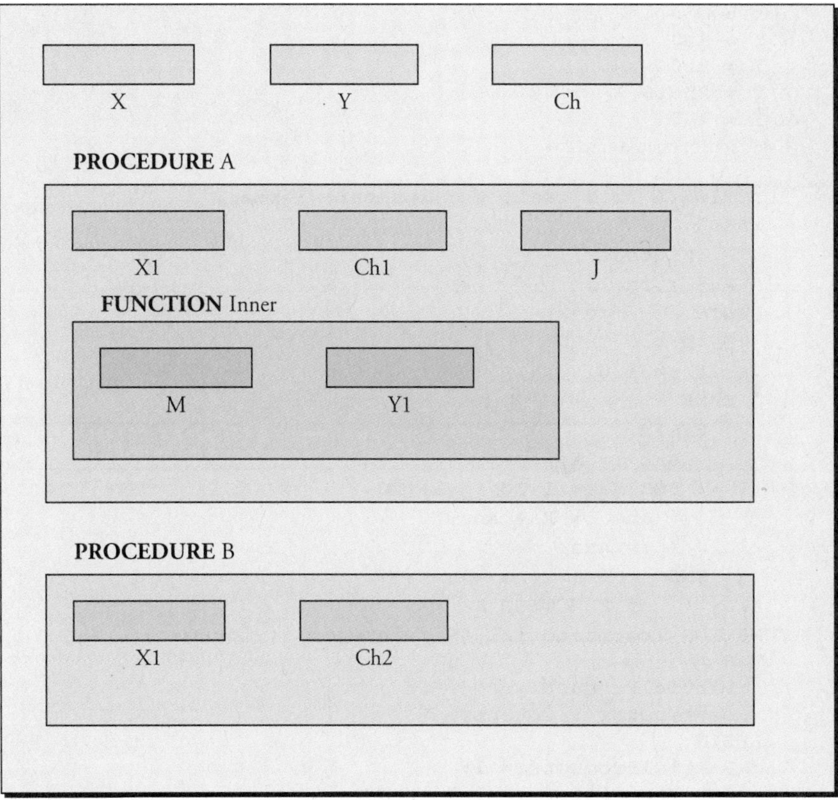

11. a. A schematic representation is shown at right. A, B, and Num are available to all blocks. A1, B1, Prod, and K are available to **FUNCTION** MaxPower and **PROCEDURE** Sort. A2, B2, and Temp are available only to **PROCEDURE** Sort.
 b. 243
 c. This function performs the task of computing *A* to the power of *B* (A^B), where *A* is the smaller of the two positive integers *A* and *B*.

PROGRAM ExerciseEleven

A B Num

FUNCTION MaxPower

A1 B1 Prod K

PROCEDURE Sort

A2 B2 Temp

Section 8.4

1. There is no stopping state.
3. a. **Y = 9.0**
   b. **Y = 8.0**
   c. **Y = 256.0**
   d. **Y = 1.0**
5. Using repetition, the function is:

```
FUNCTION A (X : real; N : integer) : real;
  VAR
    J : integer;
    Ans : real;
  BEGIN
    IF N = 0 THEN
      A := 1.0
    ELSE
      BEGIN
        Ans := X;
        FOR J := 1 TO (N-1) DO
          Ans := X * Ans;
        A := Ans
      END
  END; {  of FUNCTION A  }
```

7.
```
FUNCTION IterFactorial (N : integer) : integer;
  VAR
    PartialProduct,
    NextFactor : integer;
  BEGIN
    PartialProduct := 1;
    FOR NextFactor := 2 TO N DO
      PartialProduct := PartialProduct * NextFactor;
    IterFactorial := PartialProduct
  END;  {  of FUNCTION IterFactorial  }
```

CHAPTER 9

Section 9.1

3. The variables should be formatted so the integers will be separated by blanks.

You should check your answers to Exercises 5–21 on your computer due to possible differences in reading text files. Your answers might be as shown here.

5. **18 19 M**
7. **18   19M-1.4300000000E+01**
   18 19   M   -14.30 (Ch = ' ', since it read the end-of-line marker following –14.3.)
9. Ch = '1', A = 8, the pointer is at the end-of-line marker.
11. No values assigned, the pointer is at the 1 of 19M.
13. A = 18, B = 19, Ch = 'M', X = –14.3, the pointer is at J.
15. A = 18, Ch = '1', B = 4, the pointer is at the end-of-line marker. The **readln** (A, Ch) reads in the '1' from 19M. It moves the pointer to the next item, –14.3. The **readln** (Ch, Ch, B) reads into Ch first the '–' and then the '1'. The integer portion of the number 4.3 is then read into B.
17. Valid, but stored as reals.
19. Valid.
21. An error results. **readln** moves the pointer to 19M. The next **read** first reads the 1 and then the 9 into Ch. It then attempts to read the letter M into A. Since an integer is expected, this causes a type mismatch error.
25.
```
PROGRAM DeleteBlanks (input, output, NoBlank);
VAR
  NoBlank : text;
  Ch : char;
BEGIN
  rewrite (NoBlank);  {  Open for writing  }
  WHILE NOT eof DO
    BEGIN
      WHILE NOT eoln DO
        BEGIN
          read (Ch);
          IF Ch <> ' ' THEN
            write (NoBlank, Ch)
        END;  {  of WHILE NOT eoln  }
      readln;
      writeln (NoBlank)
    END  {  of WHILE NOT eof  }
END.  {  of main program  }
```

Section 9.2

3. Jane is listed in both types Names and People.
5. Parentheses are needed around the values. Thus, it should be

```
TYPE
  Letters = (A, C, E);
```

7. Is valid.
9. Is valid (but a poor choice).
11. Is valid.
13. Is invalid; you cannot **read** user-defined ordinals.

Section 9.3

1. The definition is invalid; 10 . . 1 is not a subrange of an existing ordinal data type.
3. All definitions and declarations are valid. However,

   ```
   Hue := Blue
   ```

   is an invalid use because Blue is not in the subrange defined for Stripes.
5. All definitions and declarations are valid, but

   ```
   Score2 := Score1 + 70
   ```

   will produce a run-time error because the intended value is not in the defined subrange.
7. Dependents usually refers to the number of single-family dependents for tax purposes. Twenty is a reasonable maximum.
9. The subrange was chosen for a maximum score of 10. This would vary for other maximum scores.

Subranges for Exercises 11–15 will vary. Possible subranges are shown here.

11. `TwentiethCentury = 1901..1999;`
13. `JuneTemp = 40..85;`
15. `LightColors = Pink..White;`
17. The pairs are compatible. The base type is ChessPieces.
19. The pairs are compatible. The base type is **integer.**
21. The pairs are incompatible.
23. Invalid. The variable parameters are not of identical type.
25. Valid. Total and B are compatible since their base type is **integer.**

Section 9.4

1. Oak
3. 2
5. 3
7. 0
9. 'D'
11. 'H'
13. Invalid; **pred**('K') is a character; thus, the operation, '+', is not defined.
15.

```
PROGRAM ExerciseFifteen (output);

VAR
  Ch : char,

BEGIN
  FOR Ch := 'A' TO 'z' DO
    writeln (ord(Ch):5, Ch:4)  {Print the ordinal value}
END.
```

17. For a **WHILE** loop, you could use the Boolean expression **WHILE** Day < Sat **DO.**

```
Day := Sun;
WHILE Day < Sat DO
  BEGIN
      .
      .   (body of loop here)
      .
  END;
```

A **FOR** loop could be controlled by the Boolean expression

```
FOR Day := Sun TO Fri DO
  BEGIN
      .
      .   (body of loop here)
      .
  END;
```

19. The last value (Sat) is not being considered. This could be altered by using a **FOR** loop and including Sat or using a variable control loop and adding a **writeln** statement such as

```
writeln ('Weekend':20);
```

outside the loop.

21.

```
FUNCTION ConvertTwo (Ch1, Ch2 : char):integer;
  VAR
    TensDigit, UnitsDigit : integer;
  BEGIN
    TensDigit := Convert(Ch1);
    UnitsDigit := Convert(Ch2);
    ConvertTwo := 10 * TensDigit + UnitsDigit
  END;
```

This function uses **FUNCTION** Convert from Exercise 20.

CHAPTER 10

Section 10.1

1.
```
TYPE
  ScoreList = ARRAY [1..35] OF integer;
VAR
  Score : ScoreList;
```

3.
```
CONST
  NumQuestions = 50;
TYPE
  AnswerList = ARRAY [1..NumQuestions] OF char;
VAR
  Answer : AnswerList;
```

Note: It is possible to use an array of element type **boolean** here.

5. A sample for this is

```
PROGRAM ExerciseFive (input, output);

TYPE
  Entries = ARRAY [1..3] OF integer;              {  A type for array  }

VAR
  Sum, Index : integer;
  Number : Entries;                    {  Part A -- array is declared  }

BEGIN
  Sum : 0;
  FOR Index := 1 TO 3 DO
    BEGIN
      read (Number [Index]);             {  Part B -- read values in  }
      Sum := Sum + Number[Index]         {  Part C -- sum components  }
    END;
  writeln ('The sum of the components is', Sum:5);
  writeln;
  write ('and the values entered are ');
  FOR Index := 1 TO 3 DO                        {  Part D -- output  }
    write (Number[Index])
END.
```

Notice the use of a **FOR** loop to easily permit the use of all three subscripts of the array during input and output.

7. No error.
9. The index range should be [1 . . 10] rather than [1 **TO** 10].
11. [1 . . . 5] should be [1 . . 5]
13. Valid.
15. Invalid. List components are of type **integer** and cannot be assigned a real value.
17. Valid.
19. Valid.
21. Invalid. The index 102 is outside of the range.
23. Invalid. The operator **DIV** should be used for integer division. It should read:

```
List[40] := List[41] DIV 2;
```

25.
```
TYPE
  Name = ARRAY [1..30] OF char;
VAR
  CompanyName : Name;
```

27. a. The array looks like

WaistSize

	WaistSize[1]
	WaistSize[2]
	WaistSize[3]
	WaistSize[4]
	WaistSize[5]

b. After the assignments, the values are

WaistSize

34	WaistSize[1]
30	WaistSize[2]
36	WaistSize[3]
35	WaistSize[4]
32	WaistSize[5]

29. Money

10.04	Money[1]
19.26	Money[2]
17.32	Money[3]

Section 10.2

1. List

0	List[1]
0	List[2]
1	List[3]
1	List[4]
1	List[5]

3. Answer

false	Answer[1]
true	Answer[2]
false	Answer[3]
true	Answer[4]
false	Answer[5]
true	Answer[6]
false	Answer[7]
true	Answer[8]
false	Answer[9]
true	Answer[10]

7. A program for this is

```
PROGRAM ExerciseSeven (input, output);

TYPE
  List = ARRAY [1..20] OF integer;

VAR
  Count, Index : integer;
  Values : List;

BEGIN
  Count := 0;
  FOR Index := 1 TO 20 DO
    BEGIN
      read (Values[Index]);
      IF Values [Index] >= 55 THEN
        Count := Count + 1
    END;
  writeln ('There are ', Count:2,
           'values.')
END.
```

9. The final values are

List

0	List[11]
3	List[12]
0	List[13]
0	List[14]
20	List[15]
14	List[16]
0	List[17]

This code converts any negative numbers to zero.

11. **JOHN SMITH**
13. **HTIMS NHOJ**
15. Valid.
17. Valid.
19.
```
writeln ('Test Number', 'Score':10);
writeln ('-----------', '-----':10);
writeln;
FOR Index := 1 TO 50 DO
  writeln ('<':4, Index:2, '>',
           TestScore[Index]:11);
```

Section 10.3

1. a. after one pass / after two passes

after one pass	after two passes
−20	−20
10	−2
0	0
10	10
8	8
30	30
−2	10

b. Three exchanges are made.

3. A high-to-low sort is achieved by changing

```
IF A[K] < A[Index] THEN
```

to

```
IF A[K] > A[Index] THEN
```

Section 10.4

1. Is valid; it can be called by

```
NewList (List1, Aray);
```

3. Is invalid; array declaration cannot be included in the heading.
5. Is invalid; Column cannot be used as a variable name.
7. Is invalid; Name is not a data type.
9. Is invalid; Name is not a data type.
13.
```
PROCEDURE ChangeList (X : Row;
                      N : String20;
                      D : Week);
```
15. This call is inappropriate because the argument, String20, is a data type rather than a variable.
17.
```
PROCEDURE CountA (L : List20;
                  VAR Ct : integer);
```
could be called by

```
CountA (List, Count);
```

A variable parameter is needed to return the count to the main program.

19.
```
PROCEDURE ReadAndCheck (VAR A : List50;
                        VAR Ct1, Ct2 : integer);
```
could be called by

```
ReadAndCheck (List, Count1, Count2);
```

Variable parameters are needed to save the counts for later use.

21. The arrays now contain

List1	Subscript	List2
0	1	1
0	2	4
0	3	9
0	4	16
0	5	25
0	6	36
0	7	49
0	8	64
0	9	81
0	10	100

Section 10.5

1. Is valid and **true.**
3. Is valid and **true.**
5. Is invalid.
7. A test program to evaluate this is

```
PROGRAM ExerciseSeven (input, output);

VAR
  Test : boolean;

BEGIN
  IF 'William Joe' < 'Williams Bo' THEN
    Test := true
  ELSE
    Test := false;
  writeln;
  writeln ('This result is ', Test)
END.
```

This program should compile and run without error. If you are using ASCII or EBCDIC on your computer, the answer will be **true.** If you are using CDC ASCII, it will be **false.** If your machine uses another character set, notice carefully the output.

9.
```
To err is human. Computers do not forgive.
There are 15 blanks.
```

11.
```
To err is human. Computers do not forgive.
        .evigrof ton od sretupmoC .namuh si rre oT
```
(8 blanks)

13. Invalid. The process of addition does not apply to strings.
15. Valid. Single characters can be assigned with this type of statement.
17.
```
MCount := 0;
FOR J := 1 TO 100 DO
  IF Message[J] = 'M' THEN
    MCount := MCount + 1;
```

Section 10.6

1.
```
FOR Index := 1 TO Length DO
  IF Num = A[Index] THEN
    writeln (Num, ' is in position', Index:5);
```
3. The value of Index in the loop can be used as a counter.

5. a. **Num = 18**

	First	Last	Mid	A[Mid]	Found
Before loop	1	5	Undefined	Undefined	**false**
After first pass	1	2	3	37	**false**
After second pass	1	2	1	18	**true**

c. **Num = 76**

	First	Last	Mid	A[Mid]	Found
Before loop	1	5	Undefined	Undefined	**false**
After first pass	4	5	3	37	**false**
After second pass	4	3	4	92	**false**

Since First > Last, the loop will be exited and an appropriate message should be printed.

9.
```
PROCEDURE Delete (VAR Student : FileType;
                  SSN : String11);

VAR
  First, Last, Mid : integer;
  Found : boolean;
  S : ARRAY [1..MaxStudent] OF String11;

BEGIN
  First := 1;
  Last := 0;
  reset (Student);
  WHILE NOT eof(Student) DO
    BEGIN
      Last := Last + 1;
      GetData (Student, S[Last])
    END;
    Found := false;
    Count := 0;
    WHILE NOT Found AND (First <= Last) DO
      BEGIN
        Count := Count + 1;                    {  Increment the counter  }
        Mid := (First + Last) DIV 2;
        IF SSN < S[Mid] THEN
          Last := Mid - 1
        ELSE IF SSN > S [MID] THEN
          First := Mid + 1
        ELSE
          Found := true
      END;  {  of WHILE...DO  }
{  The search has returned the position in MID. Now,                  }
{  we delete the value by pushing all the remaining                   }
{  components up one position in the array.                           }
  IF NOT Found THEN
    writeln ('That number is not in the list!')
  ELSE
```

```
    BEGIN
      FOR J := MID TO Length - 1 DO
        S[J] := S[J + 1];
      Length := Length - 1
    END;
{ To complete the routine, we rewrite the file                    }
  rewrite (Student);
  FOR J := 1 TO Length DO
    write (Student, S[J])
END;  {  of PROCEDURE Delete  }
```

CHAPTER 11

Section 11.1

1. `DrugPrice : ARRAY [1..4, 1..5] OF real;`
   `DrugPrice : ARRAY [1..4] OF ARRAY [1..5] OF real;`
3. `QuizScore : ARRAY [1..30, 1..12] OF integer;`
   `QuizScore : ARRAY [1..30] OF ARRAY [1..12] OF integer;`
5. ShippingCost

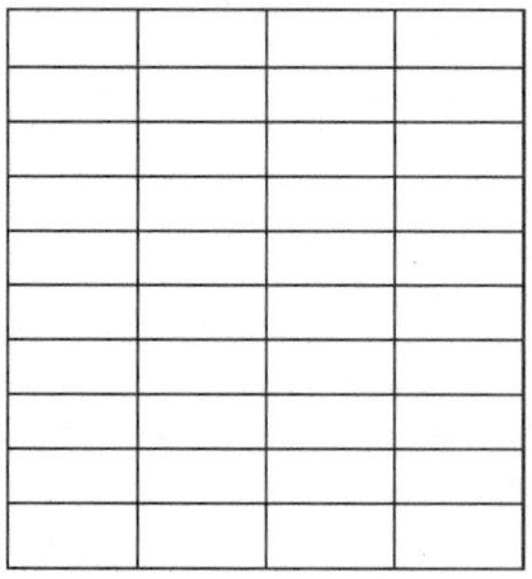

   40 locations available

   GradeBook

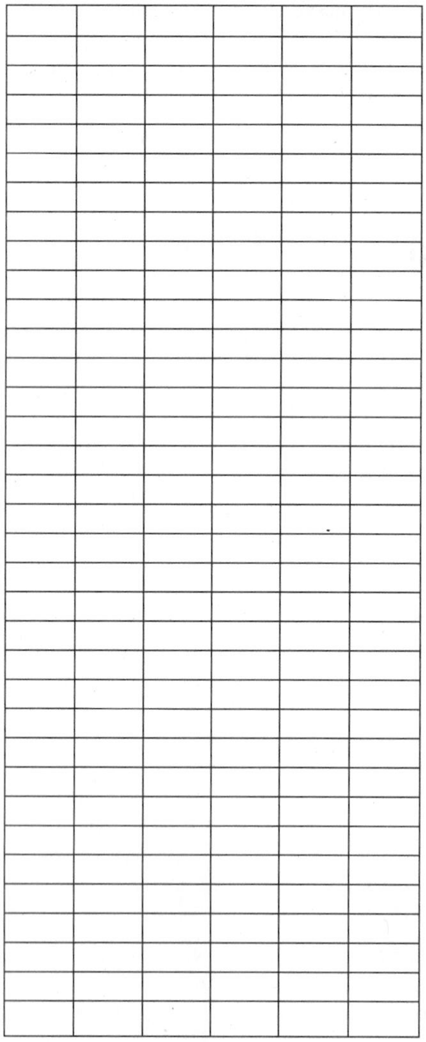

   210 locations available

7. Schedule

25 locations available

9.

0	−1	−2	−3	−4	(When J = 2)
1	0	−1	−2	−3	(When J = 2)
2	1	0	−1	−2	(When J = 3)

11.

1	1	1	1	1
2	2	2	2	2
3	3	3	3	3

13.
```
FOR J := 1 TO 3 DO
  FOR K := 1 TO 6 DO
    A[J,K] := 2 * J + K;
```
15.
```
FOR J := 1 TO 3 DO
  FOR K := 1 TO 6 DO
    A[J,K] := 2 * J;
```
17.
```
TYPE
  String20 = PACKED ARRAY [1..20] OF char;
  NameList = ARRAY [1..50] OF String20;
VAR
  Name : NameList;

FOR J := 1 TO 50 DO            {  Loop to get data  }
  BEGIN
    FOR K := 1 TO 20 DO        {  Read one line  }
      read (Name[J,K]);
    readln
  END;
```
19.

−2.0	−1.5	0.0	−4.0	−5.0
0.0	−4.0	3.0	1.0	2.0
1.0	2.0	3.0	8.0	−6.0
−4.0	−0.25	−1.0	−1.50	−20.50

21. a.
```
FOR J := 1 TO 4 DO
  BEGIN
    MinRow[J] := Table[J,1];
    FOR K := 2 TO 5 DO
      IF Table[J,K] < MinRow[J] THEN
        MinRow[J] := Table [J,K]
  END;
```
23. a.
```
TYPE
  Table = ARRAY [1..3, 1..8] OF integer;
```
b.
```
PROCEDURE Replace (VAR A : Table);
  VAR
    J, K : integer;
  BEGIN
    FOR J := 1 TO 3 DO
      FOR K := 1 TO 8 DO
        IF A[J,K] < 0 THEN
          A[J,K] := 0
END;  {  of PROCEDURE Replace  }
```
c. **PROCEDURE** Replace of **b** could be called by

```
Replace(Table3X5);
```

25. a. Reading values into A and B depends on how data are arranged in the data file.
    b.
```
FOR Row := 1 TO M DO
  FOR Column := 1 TO P DO
    BEGIN
      {  Compute partial products down a column  }
      Sum := 0;
      FOR InnerDimension := 1 TO N DO
        Sum := Sum + A[Row, InnerDimension] *
                 B[InnerDimension, Column] ;
      C[Row, Column] := Sum
    END;  {  of summing down one column  }
```

Section 11.2

1. This prints an alphabetical listing of the states whose first letter is *O*.
3. This lists the first two letters of each state.
5.
```
FOR J := 1 TO ListLength DO
  BEGIN
    FOR K := 1 TO 6 DO                    {  Get the six characters  }
      Surname[K] = Name[J,K];
    IF Surname = 'Smith,' THEN
      writeln (Name)
  END;
```
7. The number of data lines will be saved as NumLines.

```
J := 0;
WHILE NOT eof(Data) DO
  BEGIN
    J := J + 1;                      {  J will be the number of lines  }
    read (Data, Name[J,1]);                  {  Get the first letter  }
    K := 1;                                          {  Initialize K  }
    WHILE Name[J,K] <> '*' DO              {  Read until we find '*'  }
      BEGIN
        K := K + 1;                     {  Increment the value of K  }
        read (Data, Name[J,K])            {  Get the next character  }
      END;
    Length := K;                  {  Get actual number of characters  }
    FOR K := Length TO 20 DO                {  Fill rest of the string  }
      Name[J,K] := ' ';                                {  with blanks  }
    readln (Data)              {  Advance the pointer to the next line  }
  END;
NumLines := J;
```

Section 11.3

1. a. These declarations are not appropriate because Names is an array of 10 elements while Amounts is an array of 15 elements.
   b. These are appropriate because both Table and Names represent an array of size 12 × 10.
5. We can employ the same declarations as in Exercise 3, and make a slight modification in the procedure itself. We will use a **readln** when reading the age in order to advance the pointer to the next line of the file. We also use a **readln** when getting the marital status and the income to position the pointer at the start of the next line. The new procedure is

```
PROCEDURE GetLists (VAR Nm : NameArray;
                    VAR Ag : AgeArray;
                    VAR Marital : MaritalArray;
                    VAR Inc : IncomeArray);
  VAR
    J, K : integer;
```

```
  BEGIN
    J := 1;
    WHILE NOT eof(Data) AND (J <= 100) DO
      BEGIN
        FOR K := 1 TO NameLength DO
          read (Data, Nm[J,K]);
        readln (Data, Ag[J]);              {  Advance to the next line  }
        readln (Data, Marital[J], Inc[J]);     {  Advance line pointer   }
        J := J + 1
      END
  END;  {  of PROCEDURE GetLists  }
```

Section 11.4

1. 2 * 3 * 10 = 60
3. 3 * 2 * 11 = 66
5. The program uses nested loops to control the changing of rows, columns, and pages of the table.

```
PROGRAM ExerciseFive (input, output);

TYPE
  TableArray = ARRAY [1..3, 1..4, 1..5] OF integer;

VAR
  Table : TableArray;

PROCEDURE GetTable (VAR A : TableArray);
  VAR
    I, J, K : integer;
  BEGIN
    FOR I := 1 TO 3 DO
      FOR J := 1 TO 4 DO
        FOR K := 1 TO 5 DO
          read (A[I, J, K])
  END;  {  of PROCEDURE GetTable  }

PROCEDURE PrintTable (VAR A : TableArray);
  VAR
    I, J, K : integer;
  BEGIN
    FOR I := 1 TO 3 DO
      BEGIN
        writeln ('Table values         page ', I);
        writeln;            { Print page number and skip a line  }
        FOR J := 1 TO 4 DO
          BEGIN
            FOR K := 1 TO 5 DO
              write (A[I, J, K]:5);
            writeln     {  Drop to next line and print next row  }
          END;
        writeln; writeln
      END
  END;   {  of PROCEDURE PrintTable  }

BEGIN {  Main Program  }
  GetTable (Table);
  PrintTable (Table)
END. {  of main Program  }
```

CHAPTER 12

Section 12.1

5.
```
TYPE
  Book = RECORD
           Title : PACKED ARRAY [1..30] OF char;
           Author : PACKED ARRAY [1..20] OF char;
           Publication Date : integer;
           Price : real
         END; {  of RECORD Book  }
VAR
  LibraryHolding : Book;
```

7. Employee

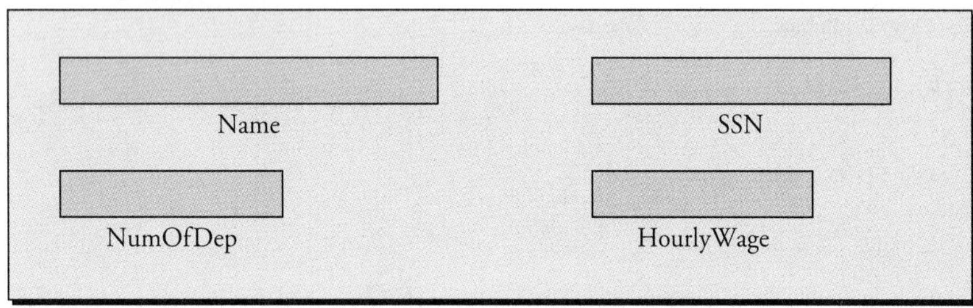

9. PhoneListing

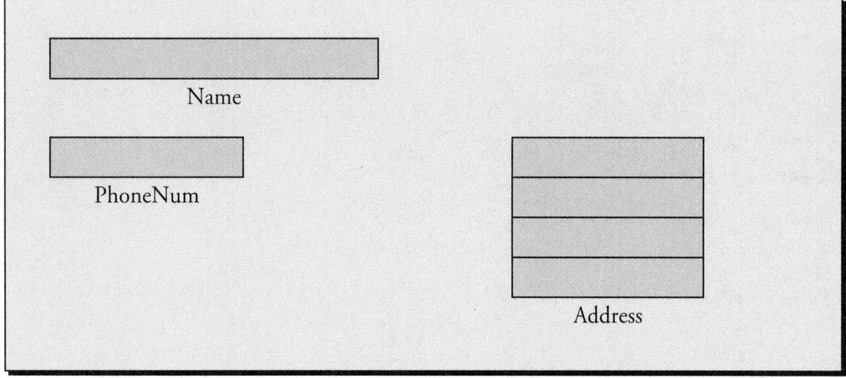

11.
```
Students = RECORD
             StudentName : PACKED ARRAY [1..30] OF char;
             HomeRoom : integer;
             Classification : PACKED ARRAY [1..2] OF char;
             Courses : PACKED ARRAY [1..6, 1..10] OF char;
             GPA : real
           END; {  of RECORD Students  }
VAR
  Pupil : Students;
```

This permits up to six courses, with up to 10 characters in each course name.

13. Member is used as both a variable and a data type.
15. Invalid. The record name must be specified. It should be:

```
Contestant.Day := Wed;
```

17. Invalid. Score must have the record name indicated, and it must be subscripted. The correct form is shown in question 19.
19. Valid.
21. Valid.
23. Valid.
25. Valid. However, this will not correctly find the average of the two values.

Section 12.2

1. Is valid.
3. Is valid.
5. Is valid but demonstrates a poor practice. For better readability, you should always determine precisely which fields are being used.
7. a. The three different methods you could use are

(1)
```
Employee2 := Employee1;
```
(2)
```
WITH Employee2 DO
  BEGIN
    Name := Employee1.Name;
    SSN := Employee1.SSN;
    Age := Employee1.Age;
    HourlyWage := Employee1.HourlyWage;
    HoursWorked := Employee1.HoursWorked;
    Volunteer := Employee1.Volunteer
  END;  {  of WITH...DO  }
```
(3)
```
WITH Employee1 DO
  BEGIN
    Employee2.Name := Name;
    Employee2.SSN := SSN;
    Employee2.Age := Age;
    Employee2.HourlyWage := HourlyWage;
    Employee2.HoursWorked := HoursWorked;
    Employee2.Volunteer := Volunteer
  END;  {  of WITH...DO  }
```
b. Did you consider the following?

```
WITH Employee2 DO
  BEGIN
    Temp := HoursWorked;
    Employee2 := Employee1;
    HoursWorked := Temp
  END;
```

9.
```
FUNCTION ComputeGrade (Pts : integer) : char;
  VAR
    Percent : real;
  BEGIN
    Percent := Pts / 5;  {  Compute percent  }
    IF Percent < 60 THEN
      ComputeGrade := 'E'
    ELSE IF Percent < 70 THEN
      ComputeGrade := 'D'
    ELSE IF Percent < 80 THEN
      ComputeGrade := 'C'
    ELSE IF Percent < 90 THEN
      ComputeGrade := 'B'
    ELSE
      ComputeGrade := 'A'
  END;  {  of FUNCTION ComputeGrade  }
```

This can be called by

```
With Student DO
  LetterGrade := ComputeGrade(TotalPts);
```

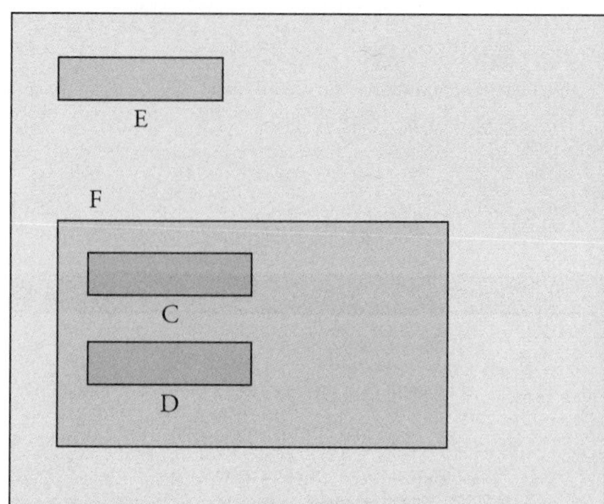

Section 12.3

1. See figure at right.
3. Is an invalid reference.
5. Is a valid reference.
7. Is an invalid reference.
9. Is a valid reference.
11. Is a valid reference.
13.
```
TYPE
  String20 = PACKED ARRAY [1..20] OF char;
  Status = ('S', 'M', 'W', 'D');
  NumKids = 0..15;
  FamilyRec = RECORD
                MaritalStatus : Status;
                Children : NumKids
              END;  {  of FamilyRec  }
  AddressRec = RECORD
                 Street : String20;
                 City : String20;
                 State : PACKED ARRAY [1..2] OF char;
                 ZipCode : integer
               END;  {  of AddressRec  }
  CustomerInfo = RECORD
                   Name : String20;
                   Address : AddressRec;
                   SSN : PACKED ARRAY [1..11] OF char;
                   AnnualIncome : real;
                   FamilyInfo : FamilyRec
                 END;  {  of CustomerInfo  }
VAR
  Customer : CustomerInfo;
```
15.
```
CONST
  SquadSize = 15;
TYPE
  String20 = PACKED ARRAY[1..20] OF char;
  AgeRange = 15..25;
  HeightRange = 70..100;
  WeightRange = 100..300;
  PlayerInfo = RECORD
                 Name : String20;
                 Age : AgeRange;
                 Height : HeightRange;
                 Weight : WeightRange;
                 ScoringAv : real;
                 ReboundAv : real
               END;  {  of PlayerInfo  }
  PlayerList = ARRAY [1..SquadSize] OF PlayerInfo;
VAR
  Player : PlayerList;
```

17. a. Student

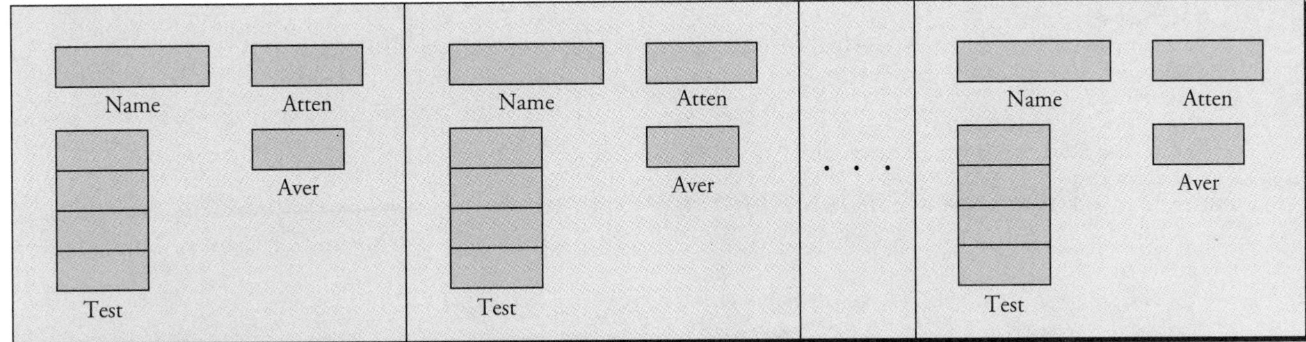

b. This function computes the test average for one student. It could be called by

```
WITH Student[K] DO
  Aver := GuessWhat(Test);
```

c. Format and headings will vary according to personal preference. However, your procedure should include

```
WITH St DO  {  Printout for St  }
  BEGIN
    .
    .
    .
    write ('Your attendance was ');
    CASE Atten OF
      Excellent : writeln ('excellent.');
      Average   : writeln ('average.');
      Poor      : writeln ('poor.')
    END;  {  of CASE  }
    .
    .
    .
  END;  {  of WITH...DO  }
```

19.
```
PROCEDURE FindMax (Giver : DonorList;
                   Temp : MemberInfo;
                   Ct: integer);
  VAR
    J : integer;
  BEGIN
    Temp := Giver[1];                       {  Hold the first entry  }
    FOR J := 2 TO Ct DO
      IF Giver[J].Amount > Temp.Amount THEN
        Temp := Giver[J];
    write ('The maximum donation was $', Temp.Amount:6:2);
    writeln (' given by ', Temp.Name)
  END;   {  of PROCEDURE FindMax  }
```

21.
```
FUNCTION FindAverage (Giver : DonorList; Ct : integer) : real;
  VAR
    J : integer;
    Sum : real;
  BEGIN
    SUM := 0;
    FOR J := 1 TO Ct DO
      Sum := Sum + Giver[J].Amount;
    FindAverage := Sum / Ct
  END;   {  of FUNCTION FindAverage  }
```

Section 12.4

3. The type TagType for the tag field Tag has not been defined.
5. There is a syntax error. A semicolon is needed between **boolean** and **CASE.** Also, a type has not been given for the tag field. It should be

```
CASE Tag : TagType OF
```

7.
```
PubType = (Book, Article);
DataRange = 1600..2000;
PublicationInfo = RECORD
                    Author : String30;
                    Title : String30;
                    Date : DataRange;
                    CASE Pub : PubType OF
                      Book    : (Publisher : String30;
                                 City : String30);
                      Article : (JournalName : String30;
                                 VolumeNumber : integer)
                    END;
```

9. a. Figure

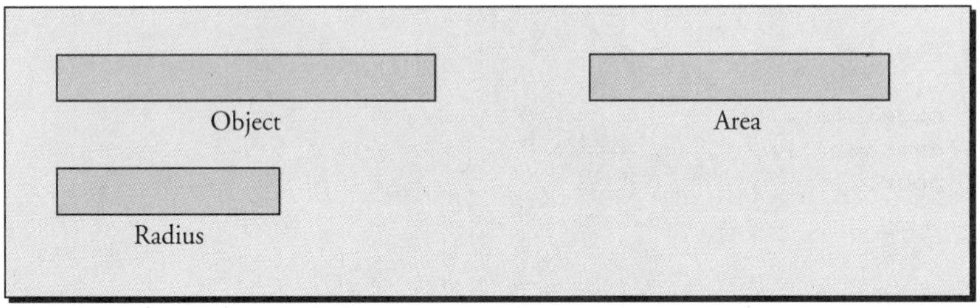

Object	Area
Radius	

b. Figure

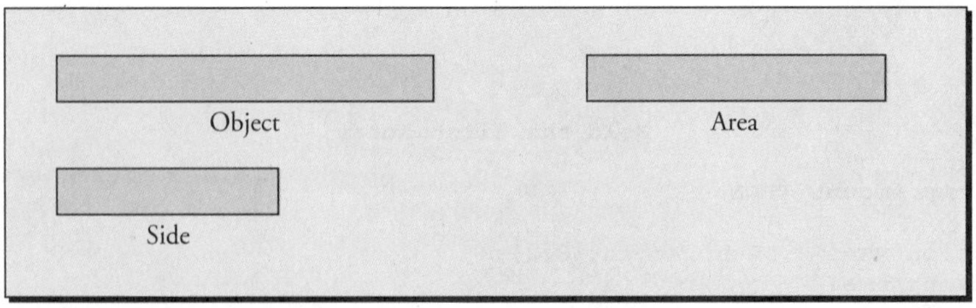

Object	Area
Side	

c. Figure

Object	Area
Base	Height

CHAPTER 13

Section 13.1

3. Is valid; the component type is an integer in the subrange 0 . . 120
5. Is invalid; component type for a file cannot be another file.
7. Is valid; the component type is **integer.**
9.
```
TYPE
  String20 = PACKED ARRAY [1..20] OF char;
  AddressType = ARRAY [1..3] OF String20;
  SexType = (M, F);
  PatientInfo = RECORD
                  Name : String20;
                  Address : AddressType;
                  Height : 0..200;
                  Weight : 0..300;
                  Age : 0..120;
                  Sex : SexType;
                  InsuranceCo : String20
                END;  {  of PatientInfo  }
  PatientFile = FILE OF PatientInfo;
VAR
  Patient : PatientFile;
```

Section 13.2

5.
```
TYPE
  FileType = FILE OF 0..100;
VAR
  SevenMult : FileType;
```

A fragment of code for this problem is

```
rewrite (SevenMult);  {  Open the file  }
Num := 1;
Sevens := 7;
WHILE Sevens < 100 DO
  BEGIN
    SevenMult^ := Sevens;
    put (SevenMult);
    Num := Num + 1;
    Sevens := 7 * Num
  END;  {  of WHILE...DO  }
```

7.
```
reset (FivesFile);
A := FivesFile^;
get (FivesFile);
B := FivesFile^;
get (FivesFile);
C := FivesFile^;
get (FivesFile);
D := FivesFile^;
```

9. The **reset** procedure opens a file so that values may be read from the file. Contents of the file are not altered by this command. When **reset** (<file name>) is executed, the value of the first component is copied into the buffer variable. The **rewrite** procedure opens a file so that values may be written to the file. When **rewrite**(<file name>) is executed, any previous contents are lost.

11. The **reset** procedure opens the file for reading from the file, and **put** is used to write to the file. It appears that

```
reset(File1);
```

should have been

```
rewrite(File1);
```

13. The buffer variable is not properly written.

```
File1 := 10 * J;
```

should be

```
File1^ := 10 * J;
```

15. The files are mixed up. It appears that the intent is to copy the contents of File1 into File2.

17. This code writes the positive numbers in OldFile into NewFile. The contents of OldFile are unchanged. NewFile contains

1	2	■

19. The first part of the code creates NewFile with its elements being the absolute value of the elements in OldFile. The second part of the code copies NewFile back to OldFile. The outcome is two identical files containing

2	1	0	1	2	■

Section 13.3

1.
```
TYPE
  String20 = PACKED ARRAY [1..20] OF char;
  PatientInfo = RECORD
                  Name : String20;
                  Age : 0..120;
                  Height : 0..100;
                  Weight : 0..350;
                  InsCompany : String20;
                  AmtDue : real
                END;  {  of RECORD PatientInfo  }
  PatientFile = FILE OF PatientInfo;
VAR
  Patient : PatientFile;
```

3.
```
TYPE
  String20 = PACKED ARRAY [1..20] OF char;
  BookInfo = RECORD
               Author : String20;
               Title : String20;
               StockNumber : integer;
               Price : real;
               Quantity : 0..500
             END;  {  of RECORD BookInfo  }
  BookFile = FILE OF BookInfo;
VAR
  Book : BookFile;
```

5. a.
```
TYPE
  String20 = PACKED ARRAY [1..20] OF char;
  QuizList = ARRAY [1..10] OF 0..10;
  TestList = ARRAY [1..4] OF 0..100;
  StudentRec = RECORD
                 Name : String20;
                 Number : integer;
                 Quiz : QuizList;
                 Test : TestList
               END;  {  of RECORD StudentREC  }
  StudentFile = FILE OF StudentRec;
VAR
  Student : StudentFile;
```

b.
```
PROCEDURE GetData (VAR St : StudentFile);
  VAR
    J : integer;
  BEGIN
    rewrite (St);      {  Open St for writing  }
    WHILE NOT eof(input) DO
      BEGIN
        WITH St^ DO   {  Get data for one student  }
          BEGIN
            FOR J := 1 TO 20 DO
              read (Name[J]);  {  Get a name  }
            read (Number);      {  Get student ID  }
            FOR J := 1 TO 10 DO
              read (Quiz[J]);  {  Get quiz scores  }
            FOR J := 1 TO 4 DO
              read (Test[J])  {  Get test scores  }
          END;  {  of WITH...DO  }
        readln;
        put (St)  {  Move data to file  }
      END  {  of WHILE NOT eof  }
  END;  {  of PROCEDURE GetData  }
```

c. The basic design for this task is to
1. Transfer records to an array
2. Sort the array
3. Transfer records from the array back to the file

Assuming suitable definitions and declarations have been made, a procedure for this is

```
PROCEDURE SortFile (VAR St : StudentFile);
  VAR
    Temp : StudentRec;
    J, K, Length, Index : integer;
    TempList : ARRAY [1..MaxSize] OF StudentRec;
  BEGIN
    reset (St);
    J := 0;
    WHILE NOT eof(St) DO  {  Copy to array  }
      BEGIN
        J := J + 1;
        TempList[J] := St^;
        get (St)
      END;
    Length := J;

  {  Now sort the array  }
    FOR J := 1 TO Length-1 DO
      BEGIN
        Index := J;
        FOR K := J + 1 TO Length DO
          IF TempList[K].Name < TempList[Index].Name THEN
            Index := K;
        IF Index <> J THEN
          Swap (TempList[Index], TempList[J])
        END;  {  of one pass  }

  {  Now copy back to the file  }
      rewrite (St);
      FOR J := 1 TO Length DO
        BEGIN
          St^ := TempList[J];
          put (St)
        END
      END;  {  of PROCEDURE SortFile  }
```

CHAPTER 14

Section 14.1

1.
```
PROCEDURE InsertionSort (VAR NumList : List;
                         VAR NewLength : integer);
  VAR
    Num, Temp, K : integer;
    Done : boolean;
```

```
  BEGIN
    readln (Num);
    List[1] := Num;
    NewLength := 1;
    WHILE NOT eof DO
      BEGIN
        NewLength := NewLength + 1;
        readln (Num);
        Temp := Num;
        K := NewLength;
        Done := false;
        WHILE K >= 2 AND NOT Done DO
          IF Temp < List[K - 1] THEN
            BEGIN
              List[K] := List[K - 1];
              K := K - 1
            END  {  of IF...THEN option  }
          ELSE  {  Temp >= List value  }
            Done := true;
        List[K] := Temp
      END  {  of WHILE NOT eof  }
 END;  {  of PROCEDURE InsertionSort  }
```

3. Rewrite the sort as

```
BEGIN
  Count := 0;
  FOR Index := 2 TO ListLength DO
    BEGIN
      Temp := List[Index];
      Count := Count + 1;      {  Increment counter  }
      Done := false;
      WHILE (K >= 2) AND (NOT Done) DO
        IF Temp < List[K - 1] THEN
          BEGIN
            List[K] := List[K - 1];
            Count := Count + 1;   {  Increment counter  }
            K := K - 1
          END  {  of IF...THEN option  }
```

5. The bubble sort modification is

```
BEGIN  {  Exchange values  }
  Temp := A[J];
  A[J] := A[J+1];
  A[J+1] := Temp;
  ExchangeMade := true;
  Count := Count + 3  {  Counter here  }
END;  {  of exchanging values  }
```

9. Assume the arrays are A and B. The bubble sort change is then

```
BEGIN  {  Exchange values  }
  TempA := A[J];
  TempB := B[J];
  A[J] := A[J+1];
  B[J] := B[J+1];
  A[J+1] := TempA;
  B[J+1] := TempB;
  ExchangeMade := true
END;  {  of exchanging values  }
```

Section 14.2

1. Modify the code for a bubble sort by

```
FOR J := 1 TO Length DO
  BEGIN
    Count := Count + 1;  {  Counter here  }
    IF A[J] > A[J+1] THEN
      BEGIN
        .
        .
        .
      END;
```

CHAPTER 15

Section 15.1

1. **real** is not an ordinal data type.
3. : should be =.

5. No errors.
9. **true.** The null set is a subset of any set.
11. **true.** All of the elements of B are also contained in A.
13. **false.** An element is not a set, so it cannot be a subset. It would be correct to say that ['B'] is a subset of A.
15. **true.** 'O' is contained within the range 'J' . . 'T' in A.
17. No errors.
19. 'E' and 'I' are listed more than once.
21. Since 'S' is in the subrange 'A' . . 'T', it is listed more than once.
23. Invalid. Elements assigned to a set must be in brackets.
25. Invalid. The operation M/N produces a real number, and reals cannot be included in sets.
27.
```
TYPE
  Hues = (Red, Orange, Yellow, Green,
          Blue, Indigo, Violet);
  RainbowSet = SET OF Hues;
VAR
  Rainbow : RainbowSet;
```
29.
```
TYPE
  SomeFruits = (Apple, Orange, Banana,
                Grape, Pear, Peach,
                Strawberry);
  FruitSet = SET OF SomeFruits;
VAR
  Fruit : FruitSet;
```

Section 15.2

1. No. When A = B, both A >= B and A <= B are **true.**
3. A + B = [−3 . . 4, 7 . . 10]
A ∗ B = [0, 1, 2, 8, 10]
A − B = [−3, −2, −1]
B − A = [3, 4, 7, 9]
5. A + B = B
A ∗ B = A
A − B = A
B − A = B
7. A ∗ B − C = [ ]
[0, 2, 4, 6, 8, 10] ∗ [1, 3, 5, 7, 9] − [0 . . 5]
First intersection
[ ] − [0 . . 5]
Next, subtract
[ ]
9. A ∗ (B + C) = [0, 2, 4]
[0, 2, 4, 6, 8, 10] ∗ ([1, 3, 5, 7, 9] + [0 . . 5])
Start in parentheses
[0, 2, 4, 6, 8, 10] ∗ ([0 . . 5, 7, 9])
Then intersection
[0, 2, 4]
11. A − B ∗ C = [0, 2, 4, 6, 8, 10]
[0, 2, 4, 6, 8, 10] − [1, 3, 5, 7, 9] ∗ [0 . . 5]
Intersection first
[0, 2, 4, 6, 8, 10] − ([1, 3, 5])
Then the difference
[0, 2, 4, 6, 8, 10]
13. A ∗ (B ∗ C) = [ ]
[0, 2, 4, 6, 8, 10] ∗ ([1, 3, 5, 7, 9] ∗ [0 . . 5])
Start in parentheses
[0, 2, 4, 6, 8, 10] ∗ ([1, 3, 5])
[ ]

15. Is **true.**
17. Is **true.**
19. Is **true.**
21. Invalid. **NOT** is evaluated first, but there is not a logical expression for it.
23. Invalid. **NOT** is evaluated first, and **NOT** 4 is meaningless.
25. Invalid. **NOT** B is meaningless.

Section 15.3

3. Modify **PROGRAM** DeleteBlanks presented in Section 9.1 by changing

```
IF Ch = ' ' THEN
  Ch := '*';
```

to

```
IF Ch IN Vowels THEN
  write '*'
ELSE
  write (Ch);
```

7.
```
FUNCTION AllOddDigits (Num : integer) :
boolean;
  TYPE
    Digits = SET of 0..9;
  VAR
    EvenDigits : Digits;
    NumDigits, J, Digit : integer;
  BEGIN
    EvenDigits := [0,2,4,6,8];
    IF Num DIV 1000 = 0 THEN
      IF Num DIV 100 = 0 THEN
        IF Num DIV 10 = 0 THEN
          NumDigits := 1
        ELSE NumDigits := 2
      ELSE NumDigits := 3
    ELSE NumDigits := 4;
    AllOddDigits := true;
    FOR J := 1 TO NumDigits DO
      BEGIN
        Digit := abs(Num MOD 10);
        IF Digit IN EvenDigits THEN
          AllOddDigits := false;
        Num := Num DIV 10
      END  {  of FOR loop  }
  END;  {  of FUNCTION AllOddDigits  }
```

CHAPTER 16

Section 16.1

1. The driver and the mode are both variable parameters. Thus, constants CGA and 2 cannot be used.

3. Combining **PROCEDURE** InitializeGraphics with **PROGRAM** Graphics in this section produces

```
PROGRAM Graphics;
USES
  Crt, Graph;
VAR
  .
  .
  .
PROCEDURE InitializeGraphics;
  VAR
    GraphDriver, GraphMode,
    ErrorResult : integer;
    InitError : boolean;
  BEGIN
    GraphDriver := detect;
    GraphMode := 1;
    InitGraph (GraphDriver, GraphMode, ' ');
    ErrorResult := GraphResult;
    InitError := (ErrorResult < > 0);
    IF InitError THEN
      BEGIN
        writeln ('There is a graphics error.');
        writeln (GraphErrorMsg(ErrorResult));
        writeln ('Program aborted.');
        Halt
      END
  END;  {  of PROCEDURE InitializeGraphics  }

BEGIN  {  Main program  }
  InitializeGraphics;
          .
          .  (main part of program here)
          .
  CloseGraph
END.  {  of  PROGRAM  Graphics  }
```

5. a. Find the coordinates of the center by using

```
Xvalue := GetMaxX DIV 2;
Yvalue := GetMaxY DIV 2;
```

One way to create a nine-pixel square with center (Xvalue, Yvalue) is to use

```
FOR Y := Yvalue - 1 TO Yvalue + 1 DO
  Line (Xvalue - 1, Y, Xvalue + 1, Y);
```

9. a. Consider the fragment of code

```
FOR Y := 0 TO GetMaxY DIV 10 DO
  BEGIN
    MoveTo (0,10 * Y);  {  Start at the left edge.  }
    LineRel (GetMaxX,0)  {  Draw the horizontal line.  }
  END;
```

11. One method of accomplishing this is to use

```
NumSquares := GetMaxY DIV 10;
MoveTo (0, 0);
FOR J := 1 TO NumSquares DO
  BEGIN
    MoveRel (10, 10);  {  Start at the lower right corner.  }
    LineRel (0, -10);
    LineRel (-10, 0);
    LineRel (0, 10);
    LineRel (10, 0)
  END;
```

Section 16.2

1. a. The following code produces the same rectangle.

```
ClearDevice;
Line (10, 10, 110, 10);
Line (110, 10, 110, 60);
Line (110, 60, 10, 60);
Line (10, 60, 10, 10);
```

3. The default unit for **Delay is** approximately one millisecond. Thus, the pause length in seconds should be multiplied by 1000 before making a call to **Delay.**
7. Consider the code

```
SetBkColor (Green);
SetColor (Blue);
Circle (100, 100, 50);  {  Draw the circle.  }
SetColor (Green);
FOR Theta := 0 TO 180 DO  {  Erase alternate degree arcs.  }
  arc (100, 100, 2 * Theta, 2 * Theta + 1, 50);
```

Section 16.3

1. a. Try something like

```
SetColor (2);
Rectangle (10, 10, 100, 100);
FloodFill (15, 15, 3);
```

3. One method of accomplishing the task is to use the code

```
Pattern := LkBkSlashFill;
FOR J := 1 TO 5 DO  {  Draw five rectangles.  }
  BEGIN
    X1 := 50 * J;
    X2 := X1 + 40;
    Y1 := 20;
    Y2 := 100;
    Rectangle (X1, Y1, X2, Y2);     {  Draw the rectangle.  }
    Pattern := succ(Pattern);       {  Change the pattern.  }
    SetFillStyle (Pattern, 2);
    FloodFill (X1 + 1, Y1 + 1, 3)   {  Fill the rectangle.  }
  END;
```

5. Use a combination of **Delay** and **ClearDevice** for animation.

Section 16.4

1. a. At the end of the program, alternate the right eye in the program with the segment of code

```
SetColor (<color>);
SetFillStyle (SolidFill, <color>);
Circle (140, 85, 8);
FloodFill (140, 85, <color>);
```

   b. Modify the line

```
Arc (100, 100, 210, 330, 50);
```

   Experiment with values to achieve the desired effect.

3. Consider the lines of code

```
Y1 := 0+ round (0.5 * (X1 - 0));
Y2 := 100 + round (0.5 * (X2 - 100));
```

   Replace the value 0.5 with different values and examine the results.

5. Combine segments of code from the programs HorizontalAnimation and VerticalAnimation. When the screen edge is reached (X2 = GetMaxX or X1 = 0), increment Y1 and Y2. At that point, move the square in the opposite horizontal direction by changing the sign of DeltaX.

Section 16.5

1.
```
PROCEDURE DrawPatternBars (NumBars : integer);
  VAR
    Pattern : word;
    X1, X2, Y1, Y2, J : integer;
  BEGIN
    Pattern := 0;  {  Select lowest ordinal.  }
    X1 := 20;      {  Initialize coordinates  }
    Y1 := 20;      {  for the first bar.      }
    X2 := X1 + 10;
    Y2 := 70;
    FOR J := 1 TO NumBars DO
      BEGIN
        SetFillStyle (Pattern, 2);
        Bar (X1, Y1, X2, Y2);
        Pattern := succ(Pattern);  {  Change the pattern.  }
        X1 := X1 + 15;
        X2 := X1 + 10
      END  {  of FOR loop  }
  END;  {  of PROCEDURE DrawPatternBars  }
```

5. One way to accomplish the task is with the following code:

```
{  Initialize for the first bar.  }
Pattern := 0;
SetFillStyle (Pattern, 2);
X1 := 100;
DeltaX := 40;
X2 := X1 + DeltaX;
Y1 := GetMaxY - 30;                     {  Start at the screen bottom.  }
Y2 := Y1 + 30;
Depth := DeltaX DIV 4;                  {  Use 25% depth.               }
Bar3D (X1, Y1, X2, Y2, Depth, false);   {  Draw the first bar.          }

{  Draw the remaining bars.  }
FOR index := 2 TO 5 DO             {  Draw successive bars.    }
```

```
    BEGIN
      Delay (500);              {  Slow down the display.   }
      Y2 := Y1;                 {  Coordinates for new bar  }
      Y1 := Y1 - 30;
      Pattern := succ(Pattern); {  Change the pattern.      }
      SetFillStyle (Pattern, 2);
      Bar3D (X1, Y1, X2, Y2, Depth, false)
    END;  {  of FOR loop for drawing bars  }
```

9. Alternating colors in sectors of 45° can be generated by the code

```
{  Initialize the settings.  }
SetGraphMode (1);
X := 100;  {  Coordinates for center.  }
Y := 100;
Rad := 50;
AngleSize := 45;

FOR Quadrant := 1 TO 4 DO
  BEGIN

    {  Color one sector.  }
    SetColor (1);  {  Select a color.  }
    AngleStart := 90 * Quadrant - 2 * AngleSize;
    AngleFinish := AngleStart + AngleSize;
    PieSlice (X, Y, AngleStart, AngleFinish, Rad);
    Delay (200);

    {  Color the next sector in Quadrant.  }
    SetColor (2);  {  Change the color.  }
    AngleStart := AngleFinish;
    AngleFinish := 90 * Quadrant;
    PieSlice (X, Y, AngleStart, AngleFinish, Rad);
    Delay (500)
  END;
```

Section 16.6

1. b. Try something like

```
MoveTo (GetMaxY - 4);
OutText ('What happens?');
```

3. Use **PROCEDURE** ContinuationMessage in this section, and call it from **PROCEDURE** GraphSector:

```
PROCEDURE GraphSector (<parameter list>);
  VAR
    .
    .
    .
  BEGIN
    .
    .
    .
  PieSlice (<arguments>);
  ContinuationMessage
  END;
```

5. To illustrate a horizontal message, modify **PROCEDURE** ContinuationMessage to be

```
PROCEDURE ContinuationMessage;
  VAR
    .
    .
    .
  BEGIN
    Message := ('Press <Enter> to continue.');

    {  Set coordinates for message.  }
    Xcoor := (GetMaxX - 8 * Length(Message)) DIV 2;
    Ycoor := GetMaxY - 10;

    {  Set coordinates for rectangle.  }
    X1 := Xcoor - 2;
    Y1 := Ycoor - 2;
    X2 := X1 + 8 * Length(Message) + 2;
    Y2 := Y1 + 10;
    Rectangle (X1, Y1, X2, Y2);  {  Draw the rectangle.  }
    OutTextXY (Xcoor, Ycoor, Message)  {  Print the message.  }
  END;
```

The same principle is used when displaying vertical messages. In this case, however, use

```
SetTextStyle (<font>, 1, <size>);
```

to produce the vertical display.

CHAPTER 17

Section 17.1

1. When using static variables, memory is allocated for each new variable or array element that is declared during compilation. That memory usage is fixed at this time and cannot be returned. When using dynamic variables, memory is allocated only as a variable is created for use and can be returned for reuse when the variable is no longer needed.

3. 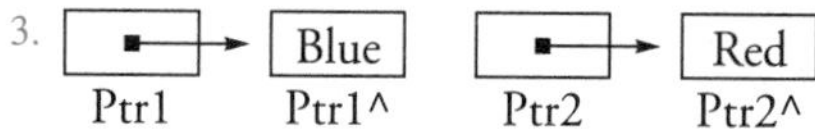

5. Valid.
7. Invalid. The pointer Ptr1 cannot be assigned to the dynamic variable Ptr2^. This is a common type of error—do not confuse the pointer and the associated dynamic variable.
9. Is invalid; pointers cannot be used with **writeln.**
11. Is invalid; $<$ is not a valid comparison for pointers.
13. Is valid.
15. Is valid.

Section 17.2

3. Assume the file name is Num. A procedure is then

```
PROCEDURE PrintNumbers (First : DataPtr);
  VAR
    P : DataPtr;
  BEGIN
    P := First;
    WHILE P <> NIL DO
      BEGIN
        writeln (P^.Num);
        P := P^.Next
      END
  END;  {  of PROCEDURE PrintNumbers  }
```

and is called by

```
PrintNumbers (Start);
```

5.
```
TYPE
  String20 = PACKED ARRAY [1..20] OF char;
  TestList = ARRAY [1..4] OF 0..100;
  QuizList = ARRAY [1..10] OF 0..10;
  DataPtr = ^StudentInfo;
  StudentInfo = RECORD
                  Name : String20;
                  Test : TestList;
                  Quiz : QuizList;
                  Average : real;
                  Grade : char;
                  Next : DataPtr
                END;  {  of RECORD StudentInfo  }
VAR
  Student : DataPtr;
```

7. a. Assume Start, Ptr, and Last have been declared to be of type DataPtr. Data for the first student can then be obtained by

```
new (Start);
Ptr := Start;
Last := Start;
WITH Start^ DO
  BEGIN
    FOR J := 1 TO 20 DO
      read (Name[J]);
    FOR J := 1 TO 4 DO
      read (Test[J]);
    FOR J := 1 TO 10 DO
      read (Quiz[J]);
    Next := NIL
  END;  {  of WITH...DO  }
readln;
```

b. Data for the second student can be obtained by

```
new (Last);
Ptr^.Next := Last;
Ptr := Last;
WITH Last^ DO
  BEGIN
    FOR J := 1 TO 20 DO
      read (Name[J]);
    FOR J := 1 TO 4 DO
      read (Test[J]);
    FOR J := 1 TO 10 DO
      read (Quiz[J])
  END;
readln;
Ptr^.Next := NIL;
```

For Exercises 9, 11, and 13, working from the original each time, we get

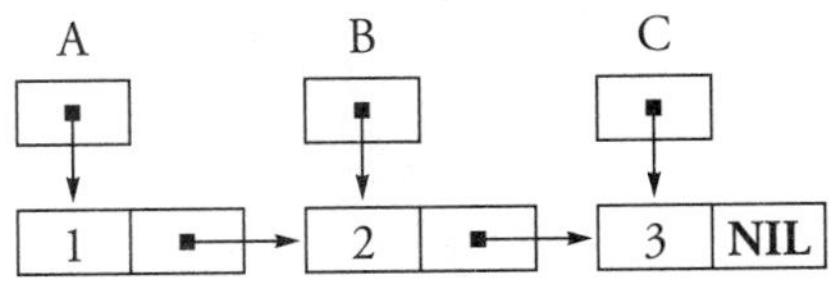

9. 11. 13.

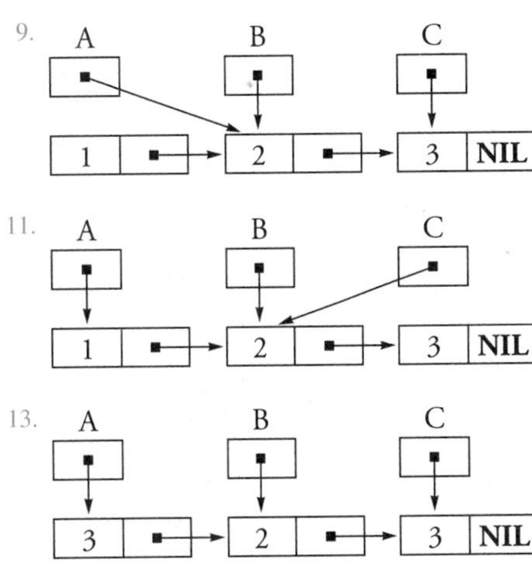

15. **A^.Next^.Next := B;**

17. This example is fairly straightforward. The values assigned to each of these is set by the assignment statements. B^. Num is the result of 100 **MOD** 8, which is 4. A^.Num is assigned to the sum of 100 and 4. The output is:

```
104   4 100
```

19. Assume the linked list has been declared and values read into the field Num for each component of the list. Furthermore, assume Start is the pointer to the first node. A function for summing is then

```
FUNCTION Sum (First : DataPtr) : integer;
  VAR
    Total : integer;
    P : DataPtr;
  BEGIN
    Total := 0;
    P := First;
    WHILE P <> NIL DO
      BEGIN
        Total := Total + P^.Num;
        P := P^.Next
      END;
    Sum := Total
  END;  {  of FUNCTION Sum  }
```

Section 17.3

1. Assume the original list can be envisioned as

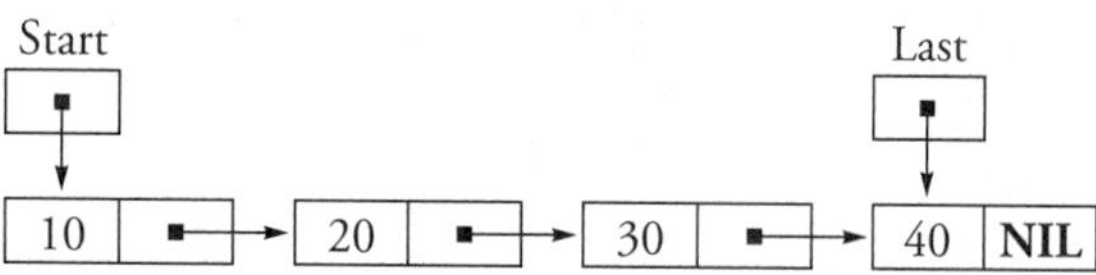

and you wish to insert 25 into the list. The initialization produces

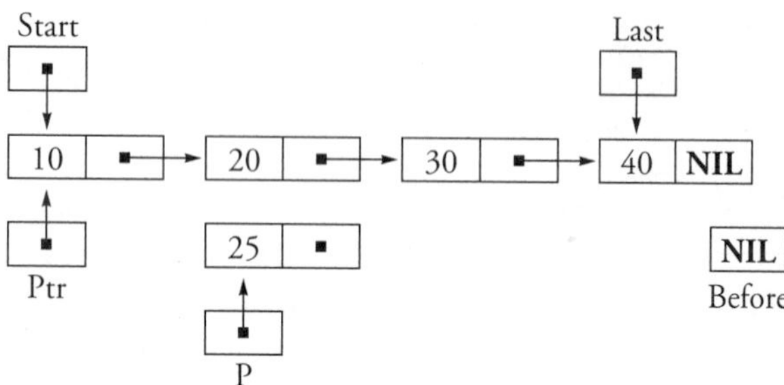

Since the list is not empty, the **WHILE . . . DO** loop will be executed until we have

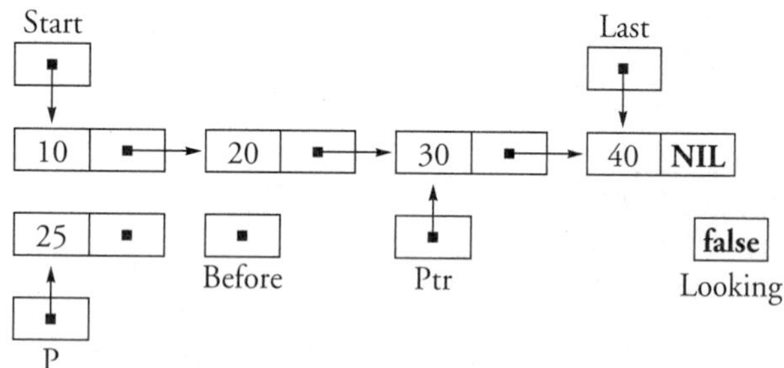

The pointers are then moved to obtain

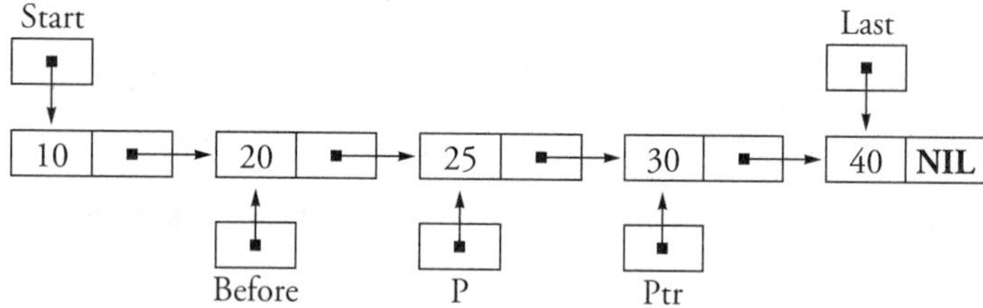

3. The new code is

```
IF Before = NIL THEN
  Push (Start, NewNum)     {  Call to Push  }
ELSE
  Before^.Next := P;
```

5. The heading becomes

```
PROCEDURE Pop (VAR Start : DataPtr);
```

and the line

```
NewNum := P^.Num
```

should be deleted.

7.
```
PROCEDURE Delete (VAR Start : DataPtr;
                  Position : integer);
  VAR
    Before, P : DataPtr;
  BEGIN
    IF Position = 1 THEN
      Pop (Start, Start^.Num)
    ELSE
      BEGIN
        Before := Start;
        FOR J := 1 TO (Position - 2) DO
          Before := Before^.Next;
        P := Before^.Next;
        Before^.Next := P^.Next;
        dispose (P)
      END   {  of ELSE option  }
  END;  {  of modified PROCEDURE Delete  }
```

Section 17.4

1. Illustrating only the parentheses, the stack changes as shown at the right

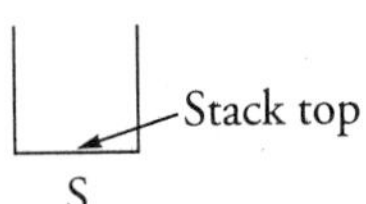

Character Read	New Stack
"("	(
"("	((
"("	(((
")"	((
"("	(((
")"	((
")"	(
")"	

5. a.
```
CONST
  MaxStack = <value>;
TYPE
  Stack = RECORD
            Item : ARRAY [1..MaxStack] OF <data type>;
            Top : 0..MaxStack
          END;
VAR
  S : Stack;
```
b. Push becomes

```
PROCEDURE Push (VAR S : Stack;
                X : integer);
```

```
  BEGIN
    IF S.Top = MaxStack THEN
      writeln ('Stack overflow')
    ELSE
      BEGIN
        S.Top := S.Top + 1;
        S.Item[S.Top] := X
      END
  END;  {  of PROCEDURE Push  }
```

PopAndCheck becomes

```
PROCEDURE PopAndCheck (VAR S : Stack;
                       VAR X : integer;
                       VAR Underflow : boolean);
  BEGIN
    IF Empty(S) THEN  {  Check for empty stack  }
      Underflow := true
    ELSE
      BEGIN
        Underflow := false;
        X := S.Item[S.Top];
        S.Top := S.Top - 1
      END  {  of ELSE option  }
  END;  {  of PROCEDURE PopAndCheck  }
```

9. The node for 30 would not appear to the left of 45. It should be a left child of 33, not on its right side. Assuming that the 30 was entered after the 32, the correct tree in this area is

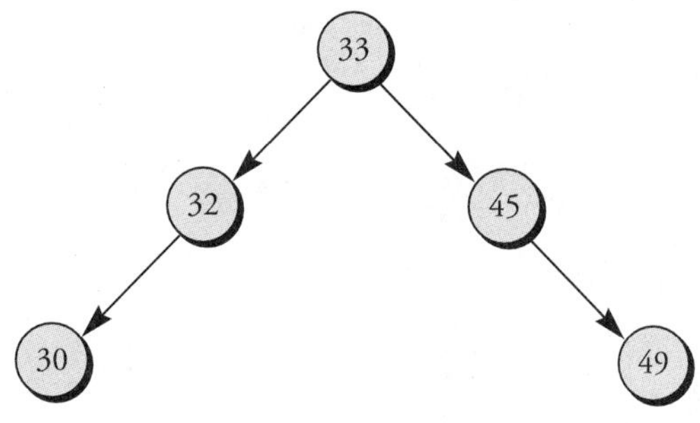

11. The element 55 cannot be linked to two nodes. In a binary search tree, any node can be a child of only one node.
13. Change the **ELSE** option to

```
ELSE IF Num = Node^.Info THEN
  writeln (Num, 'is a duplicate value.')
ELSE IF Num < Node^.Info THEN
  AddNode (Node^.LeftChild, Num)
ELSE
  AddNode (Node^.RightChild, Num)
```

15.
```
FUNCTION Search (Node : Pointer;
                 NewNum : integer) : boolean;
  VAR
    Found : boolean;
    Current : Pointer;
  BEGIN
    Current := Node;
    Found := false;
    WHILE (Current <> NIL) AND NOT Found DO
      IF Current^.Num = NewNum THEN
        Found := true
      ELSE IF Current^.Num < NewNum THEN
        Current := Current^.RightChild
      ELSE
        Current := Current^.LeftChild;
    Search := Found
  END;  {  of FUNCTION Search  }
```

Index

B

C

D

E

Credits

PHOTOS

Figures 1.4, 1.5a, 1.5b, 1.5c, 1.6a and 1.6b: Courtesy of IBM Corporation.

Figure 1.5d: Courtesy of Apple Computer, Inc.

Figure 1.8: Robert Barclay.

NOTES OF INTEREST

Page 13: Advances in Computing Technology

Page 15: Why Learn Pascal?
Reprinted with permission from "Pascal," by T. Woteki and A. Freiden, published in the September 1983 issue of *Popular Computing* magazine. © McGraw-Hill, Inc., New York. All rights reserved.

Page 22: Object-Oriented Programming (OOP)—Part 1

Page 27: Software Verification
From Ivars Peterson, "Finding Fault: The Formidable Task of Eradicating Software Bugs," *SCIENCE NEWS*, February 16, 1991, Vol. 139. Reprinted with permission from *SCIENCE NEWS*, the weekly newsmagazine of science. Copyright © 1991 by Science Services, Inc. Photo courtesy of Ontario Hydro.

Page 38: Blaise Pascal
Adapted from William Dunham, *Journey Through Genius: The Great Theorems of Mathematics,* John Wiley & Sons, 1990. Photos: Courtesy of IBM Corporation.

Page 50: Computer Ethics: The ACM Code of Ethics.

Page 71: Ethics and Computer Science
From the *Minneapolis Star/Tribune,* October 14, 1990, The Washington Post reprinted with permission.

Page 89: Defined Constants and Space Shuttle Computing, *Communications of the ACM* 27, No. 9 (September 1984):/880. Copyright 1984, Association for Computing Machinery, Inc. Reprinted by permission of Association for Computing Machinery, Inc.

Page 97: Herman Hollerith
Reprinted by permission for *Introduction to Computers with BASIC,* pp. 27–28, by Fred G. Harold. Copyright © 1984 by West Publishing Company. All rights reserved. Photos courtesy of IBM Corporation.

Page 118: Program Documentation—EDS Style

Page 125: Communication Skills Needed
From P. Jackowitz, R. Plishka, J. Sidbury, J. Hartman, and C. White, ACM Press *SIGCSE Bulletin* 22, No. 1 (February, 1990). Copyright 1991, Association for Computing Machinery, Inc. Reprinted by permission of Association for Computing Machinery, Inc.

Page 133: Computer Ethics: Copyright, Intellectual Property, and Digital Information

Page 140: A Software Glitch
From Ivars Peterson, "Finding Fault: The Formidable Task of Eradicating Software Bugs," *SCIENCE NEWS*, February 16, 1991, Vol. 139. Reprinted with permission from *SCIENCE NEWS*, the weekly newsmagazine of science. Copyright 1991 by Science Services, Inc.

Pages 152 and 154: Debugging or Sleuthing
From J. Bentley, *Communications of the ACM* 28, No. 2 (February 1985): 139. Copyright 1985, Association for Computing Machinery, Inc. Reprinted by permission of Association for Computing Machinery, Inc.

Page 174: George Boole
Adapted from William Dunham, *Journey Through Genius: The Great Theorems of Mathematics,* John Wiley & Sons, 1990. Photo: The Bettmann Archive.

Page 185: New Legal Research Uses Plain English

Page 25: Charles Babbage
Reprinted by permission from *Introduction to Computers with BASIC,* pp. 24–26, by Fred G. Harold. Copyright © 1984 by West Publishing Company. All rights reserved. Photos courtesy of IBM Corporation.

Page 261: Ada Augusta Byron
Reprinted by permission from *Introduction to Computers with BASIC,* pp. 26–27, by Fred G. Harold. Copyright © 1984 by West Publishing Company. All rights reserved. Photo: The Bettmann Archive.

Page 321: Structured Programming

Page 347: Computer Ethics: Hacking and Other Intrusions
Reprinted by permission from *Computers Under Attack: Intruders, Worms, and Viruses,* pp. 150–155, edited by Peter J. Denning, Article 7, "The West German Hacker Incident and Other Intrusions," by Mel Mandell. Copyright 1990, Association for Computing Machinery, Inc.

Page 382: Inspections: Debugging in the 1990s

Page 390: Niklaus Wirth
Adapted from Nicklaus Wirth, Programming Language Design to Computer Construction, 1984 Turing Award Lecture, *Communications of the ACM* 28, No. 2 (February 1985).

Page 453: Career Opportunities in Computer Science
From Carol Wilson, Western Kentucky University, Bowling Green, Kentucky, 1991.

Page 459: Keeping Pace with Changing Technology
Condensed from Information Superhighway, How the Technology Is Changing, *The Globe and Mail,* August 16, 1996, Toronto.

Page 464: Computer Ethics: Viruses
From Philip J. Hilts, Science Lab, in *The Washington Post National Weekly Edition,* May 23–29, 1988. Reprinted by permission of The Washington Post.

Page 488: Monolithic Idea—Invention of the Integrated Circuit
Adapted from T. R. Reid, "The Chip," *Science,* February 1985, pp. 32–41.

Page 501: Computer Science and Women in Business
From Carol Wilson, Western Kentucky University, Bowling Green, Kentucky, 1991.

Page 586: Computer Ethics: Worms
Reprinted by permission from *Computers Under Attack: Intruders, Worms, and Viruses,* pp. 191 and 265, edited by Peter J. Denning, Article 9,

"Computer Security in the Business World," by Maurice V. Wilkes; and Article 16, "The 'Worm' Programs—Early Experience with a Distributed Computation," by John F. Shoch and Jon A. Hupp. Copyright 1990, Association for Computing Machinery, Inc.

Page 627: Using Key Fields in Records
From David Gifford and Alfred Spector: "The TWA Reservations System: An Interview with Carol Flood and Ted Celentio," *Communications of the ACM* 17, No. 7 (July 1984): 650–657, Copyright 1984, Association for Computing Machinery, Inc. Reprinted by permission of Association for Computing Machinery, Inc.

Page 637: Computer Insecurity
From *The Chronicle of Higher Education,* by David L. Wilson, February 16, 1994. Reprinted by permission.

Page 672: Relational Databases
From William D. Nance, Management Information Systems, San Jose State University, San Jose, California, 1991.

Page 681: Backup and Recovery of Data
From William D. Nance, Management Information Systems, San Jose State University, San Jose, California, 1991.

Page 692: History Stuck on Old Computer Tapes
From the *Minneapolis Star/Tribune,* "30 Years of History Stuck on Old Computer Tapes," January 2, 1991. Reprinted by permission of the Associated Press.

Page 719: Gene Mapping Computer Scientists Examine Problems of Genome Project
From *The Chronicle of Higher Education,* May 9, 1990. Reprinted by permission of The Chronicle of Higher Education.

Page 737: Fractal Geometry and Benoit Mandlebrot
Figure from *Integrated Computer Graphics,* p. 128, by Bruce Mielke. Copyright © 1991 by West Publishing Company.

Page 747: Object-Oriented Programming—Part 2
Adapted from "Starting with the Basics of Object-Oriented Programming Using Turbo Pascal 5.5," by Captain Byron B. Thatcher, in *Interface: The Computer Education Quarterly* 12, Issue 4 (1990): 15–18.

Page 770: An Artist of Interface
From Ron Wolf, "Artist a Go-Between for Users, Computers," *The Chicago Tribune,* June 10, 1990. Reprinted by permission from Knight-Ridder Tribune News.

Page 792: Impact of Computers on Art
From Dana J. Lamb, "The Impact of the Computer on the Arts," *Academic Computing,* April, 1989, pp. 22–24. Reprinted by permission from Academic Computing.

Page 842: Artificial Intelligence
Reprinted by permission from *The Mind Tool,* Fifth Ed., pp. 394–398, by Neill Graham. Copyright © 1989 by West Publishing Company. All rights reserved.

Page 870: When Will Object Technology Meet Its Potential?
Reprinted by permission of Sigs Publications, Inc. Copyright © 1992.

Page 895: Using Pointers
From Nazim H. Madhavji, "Visibility Aspects of Programmed Dynamic Data Structures," *Communications of the ACM* 27, No. 8 (August 1984): 766. Copyright 1984, Association for Computing Machinery, Inc. Reprinted by permission of Association for Computing Machinery, Inc.